BRANSON'S

NORTH CAROLINA

BUSINESS DIRECTORY,

1896.

VOLUME VIII.
(Thirtieth Year of Publication.)

EDITED BY

LEVI BRANSON, A. M.

"Ho! for Carolina! that's the land for me;
In her happy borders roam the brave and free."

"Oh! there is no land on earth like this fair land of ours."

[☞ LOOK ALSO IN THE ADDENDA.]

PRICE, $5.00.

RALEIGH, N. C.:
LEVI BRANSON, OFFICE PUBLISHER,
OFFICE: ROOM NO. 31, BRANSON HOUSE.
1896.

See preceding page; also College Circular, page 666.

THE NORTH CAROLINA COLLEGE OF AGRICULTURE AND MECHANIC ARTS, Raleigh, N. C.

Apply for Catalogue to ALEX. Q. HOLLADAY, President.

CITIES, TOWNS, POST-OFFICES.

Post-Office.	County.	Post-Office.	County.
Aaron	Wayne	Amity	Iredell
Abbottsburg	Bladen	Ammon	Bladen
Abbott's Creek	Davidson	Anderson	Caswell
Abell's	Johnston	Andrews	Cherokee
Aberdeen	Moore	Angeline	Henderson
Abernethy	Iredell	Angle	Wayne
Abi	Stanly	Angola	Onslow
Abshers	Wilkes	Anna	Alleghany
Aconite	Randolph	Auneta	Hertford
Acresville	Beaufort	Ansonville	Anson
Acton	Buncombe	Antioch	Robeson
Adams	Iredell	Antler	Moore
Addie	Jackson	Antonia	Cumberland
Adelaide	Rockingham	Apex	Wake
Adley	Wilkes	Applegrove	Ashe
Adair	Gates	Appletree	Greene
Adoniram	Granville	Applewhite	Columbus
Advance	Davie	Aquone	Macon
Affinity	Robeson	Arapahoe	Pamlico
Afton	Warren	Arcadia	Davidson
Agate	Hertford	Archdale	Randolph
Aho	Watauga	Archer	Johnston
Ahoskie	Hertford	Arcola	Warren
Ai	Person	Arcot	Sampson
Airbellows	Alleghany	Arden	Buncombe
Airlie	Halifax	Argo	Nash
Albans	Union	Argyle	Cumberland
Albemarle (c. h.)	Stanly	Arlington	Mecklenburg
Albertson	Duplin	Armfield	Iredell
Alberty	Surry	Armour	Columbus
Albright	Alamance	Armstrong	McDowell
Alco	Montgomery	Arnold	Davidson
Alderman	Cumberland	Arnt	Catawba
Alexander	Buncombe	Arolina	Richmond
Alexis	Gaston	Asbury	Montgomery
Alfordsville	Robeson	Ascend	Chatham
Algiers	Ashe	Ash	Brunswick
Allgood	Yadkin	Ashboro (c. h.)	Randolph
Alleghany	Madison	Asheville (c. h.)	Buncombe
Allemance	Guilford	Ashford	McDowell
Allensville	Person	Ashhill	Surry
Allenton	Robeson	Ashland	Caswell
Allenton Ferry	Montgomery	Ashley	Ashe
Allhealing	Gaston	Ashpole	Robeson
Alliance	Pamlico	Ashton	Pender
Allison	Caswell	Askewville	Bertie
Allreds	Montgomery	Askin	Craven
Alma	Robeson	Aspengrove	Rockingham
Almond	Swain	Atia	Johnston
Alpha	Rowan	Athens	Robeson
Alpine	Sampson	Athlone	Yancey
Alspaugh	Forsyth	Atkinson	Pender
Altamahaw	Alamance	Atlantic	Carteret
Altamont	Mitchell	Atlee	Rockingham
Altan	Union	Auburn	Wake
Alto	Buncombe	Augusta	Davie
Amantha	Watauga	Aulander	Bertie
Amboy	Chowan	Aurelian Springs	Halifax
Amelia	Alleghany	Aurora	Beaufort
Ames	Union	Austin	Wilkes
Amherst	Martin	Autryville	Sampson

Post-Office.	County.
Camp Creek	Burke
Cana	Bavie
Candler	Buncombe
Candor	Montgomery
Cane Creek	Alamance
Cane River	Yancey
Canto	Buncombe
Canton	Haywood
Cape	Randolph
Capel's Mills	Richmond
Caraway	Randolph
Carbonton	Moore
Carl	Montgomery
Carlisle	Davidson
Carlos	Cumberland
Carlton	Vance
Carmel	Montgomery
Carpenter	Gaston
Carr	Orange
Carriers's Springs	Buncombe
Carson	Catawba
Carson's Creek	Transylvania
Carter's Mills	Moore
Carthage (c. h.)	Moore
Cary	Wake
Casar	Cleveland
Cascade	Guilford
Case's	Rockingham
Cashiers	Jackson
Castalia	Nash
Castle	New Hanover
Castoria	Greene
Cataloochee	Haywood
Catawba	Catawba
Cates	Person
Catfish	Catawba
Catharine Lake	Onslow
Cathey	Jackson
Caudill's	Johnston
Cavenaugh	Duplin
Cedar	Bladen
Cedarcliff	Alamance
Oedarcreek	Cumberland
Cedarfalls	Randolph
Cedargrove	Orange
Cedarhill	Anson
Cedarmountain	Transylvania
Cedarpoint	Carteret
Cedarrock	Franklin
Cedarrun	Alexander
Cedarvalley	Caldwell
Ceffo	Person
Celo	Yancey
Center	Guilford
Center Grove	Person
Centerville	Franklin
Central Falls	Randolph
Cerro Gordo	Columbus
Chadbourn	Columbus
Chafin	Harnett
Chalk Level	Harnett
Chambers	Burke
Chance	Sampson
Chandler	Montgomery
Chapanoke	Perquimans
Chapel Hill	Orange
Charity	Yadkin

Post-Office.	County.
Charlotte (c. h.)	Mecklenburg
Charm	Robeson
Chatham	Surry
Cheeks	Randolph
Cheoah	Graham
Cherokee	Swain
Cherryfield	Transylvania
Cherrygrove	Caswell
Cherrylane	Alleghany
Cherrypoint	Craven
Cherryville	Gaston
Chesterfield	Burke
Chestnut	Catawba
Chestnut Ridge	Yadkin
Chiloe	Moore
Chimney Rock	Rutherford
Chinagrove	Rowan
Chinquapin	Duplin
Chockoyotte	Halifax
Chocowinity	Beaufort
Chronicle	Catawba
Chublake	Person
Churchill	Warren
Churchland	Davidson
Cid	Davidson
Cisco	Chowan
City	Alleghany
Clara	Stokes
Claremont	Catawba
Clarendon	Columbus
Clark	Craven
Clark's Mills	Moore
Clarkton	Bladen
Clay	Granville
Clayfork	Cumberland
Clayroot	Pitt
Clayton	Johnston
Clearcreek	Cabarrus
Clearrun	Sampson
Clement	Sampson
Clemmonsville	Forsyth
Cleone	Union
Cleveland	Rowan
Cleveland Mills	Cleveland
Cliffdale	Rutherford
Clifford	Rutherford
Clifton	Ashe
Cliftonville	Wilson
Climax	Guilford
Clingman	Wilkes
Clinton (c. h.)	Sampson
Clio	Iredell
Closs	Lenoir
Clotho	Transylvania
Cloudland	Mitchell
Cluster	Mecklenburg
Clover	Polk
Clover Orchard	Alamance
Clyde	Haywood
Coahoma	Lenoir
Coakley	Edgecombe
Coalville	Cherokee
Cobb's	Cherokee
Coburn's Store	Union
Cochrum	Yadkin
Coddle	Cabarrus
Cody	Surry

Post-Office.	County.	Post-Office.	County.
Coffer	Moore	Creeksville	Northampton
Cogdell	Wayne	Creston	Ashe
Coharie	Sampson	Creswell	Washington
Cohooque	Craven	Cricket	Wilkes
Coinjock	Currituck	Crimsic	Lincoln
Cokes	Vance	Crisp	Edgecombe
Coleman	Columbus	Croatan	Craven
Coleraine	Bertie	Cracker	Cleveland
Coleridge	Randolph	Croft	Mecklenburg
Cole's Store	Randolph	Cromartie	Robeson
Colfax	Guilford	Cronly	Columbus
Colington	Dare	Crossnore	Mitchell
Collettsville	Caldwell	Crossroads Church	Yadkin
Collinsville	Polk	Crossrock	Madison
Colly	Bladen	Crouse	Lincoln
Colon	Chatham	Crow	Ashe
Columbia (c. h.)	Tyrrell	Crowder's Creek	Gaston
Columbus (c. h.)	Polk	Crowell's	Halifax
Comet	Ashe	Crumpler	Ashe
Comfort	Jones	Cruso	Haywood
Como	Hertford	Crutchfield	Surry
Company Mills	Guilford	Crystal	Guilford
Concert	Ashe	Cuba	Rutherford
Conclave	Richmond	Culberson	Cherokee
Concord (c. h,)	Cabarrus	Culbreth	Granville
Conetoe	Edgecombe	Cullasaja	Macon
Connelly's Springs	Burke	Culler	Stokes
Connor	Wilson	Cullowhee	Jackson
Conoho	Martin	Cumberland	Cumberland
Conover	Catawba	Cumnock	Chatham
Conrads	Yadkin	Cunningham	Person
Contentnea	Greene	Currie	Pender
Conway	Northampton	Curriersville	Moore
Cook	Catawba	Currituck (c h)	Currituck
Cool Spring	Iredell	Curtis	Alamance
Cooper	Cumberland	Cypresscreek	Bladen
Copal Grove	Stanly	Cyrus	Onslow
Copeland	Surry	Dabney	Vance
Cora	Caldwell	Daisy	Forsyth
Corapeake	Gates	Dale	Surry
Corbett	Caswell	Dalila	Sampson
Corine	Duplin	Dallas (c h)	Gaston
Corinth	Chatham	Dalton	Stokes
Cornatzer	Davie	Dana	Henderson
Cornelia	Cumberland	Danamora	Guilford
Cornwall	Granville	Danbury (c h)	Stokes
Corolla	Currituck	Danriver	Stokes
Costner	Gaston	Danville	Guilford
Cottonville	Stanly	Darby	Wilkes
Cottonwood	Mecklenburg	Dardens	Martin
Council's Station	Bladen	Darfer	Cleveland
County Line	Davie	Darkridge	Watauga
Cove	Craven	Darlington	Rutherford
Cove Creek	Haywood	Daughton	Pender
Covington	Richmond	Davenport	Mecklenburg
Cowan's Ford	Mecklenburg	Davidson	Mecklenburg
Cowart's	Jackson	Davidson's River	Transylvania
Coxville	Pitt	Davis	Carteret
Cozart	Granville	Dawson	Halifax
Crabtree	Haywood	Dawson's Landing	Bladen
Craig	McDowell	Daybook	Yancey
Cranberry	Mitchell	Dayton	Durham
Craters	Forsyth	Dealville	Alexander
Craven	Rowan	Debruhls	Craven
Crawford	Macon	Decatur	Polk
Creedmoor	Granville	Deckhill	Watauga
Creek	Warren	Deepcreek	Anson

Post-Office.	County.	Post-Office.	County.
Flora	Randolph	Gatewood	Caswell
Floral College	Robeson	Gath	Orange
Florence	Pamlico	Gaylord	Beaufort
Florian	Anson	Gem	Buncombe
Flowerhill	Randolph	Geneva	Rockingham
Flows	Cabarrus	Genoa	Wayne
Flox	Onslow	Gentry	Rockingham
Floyd	Cumberland	Georgetown	Jackson
Fly	Montgomery	Georgeville	Cabarrus
Flynn	Moore	Germanton	Stokes
Folsom	Bladen	Gethsemane	Edgecombe
Fonta Flora	Burke	Ghio	Richmond
Fontcol	Richmond	Gibbs	Burke
Footville	Yadkin	Gibraltar	Union
Forbush	Yadkin	Gibson's Mills	Richmond
Ford	Stanly	Gibson's Station	Richmond
Forest City	Rutherford	Gibsonville	Guilford
Forestville	Wake	Gift	Johnston
Forge	Surry	Gilbert	Moore
Forkade	Moore	Gilead	Beaufort
Forkchurch	Davie	Giles' Mills	Sampson
Forkcreek	Randolph	Gilkey	Rutherford
Forks of Pigeon	Haywood	Gillburg	Vance
Forney's Creek	Swain	Gillisville	Cumberland
Fort Barnwell	Craven	Gilmer's Store	Guilford
Fort Landing	Tyrrell	Gilreath	Wilkes
Foscue	Watauga	Gladecreek	Alleghany
Foster	Person	Gladesboro	Randolph
Fountain Hill	Greene	Gladstone	Stanly
Fouroaks	Johnston	Glady	Buncombe
Foust's Mills	Randolph	Glenaloon	Chatham
Fowle	Jones	Glen Alpine	Burke
Foxville	Buncombe	Glen Ayre	Mitchell
Francisco	Stokes	Glenbrook	Montgomery
Frank	Mitchell	Glenburnie	Caldwell
Franklin (c h)	Macon	Glendale	Alamance
Franklinton	Franklin	Glendon	Moore
Franklinville	Randolph	Glenfield	Greene
Freeman's Mills	Guilford	Glenmore	Johnston
Fremont	Wayne	Glenola	Randolph
Friedberg	Davidson	Glenview	Halifax
Friendship	Guilford	Glenville	Jackson
Friezeland	Madison	Glenwood	Johnston
Fruitland	Henderson	Gliden	Chowan
Fry	Anson	Globe	Caldwell
Fuller's	Randolph	Glover	Nash
Fullmore	Robeson	Godwin	Cumberland
Fulp	Stokes	Goff	Chatham
Furches	Ashe	Golden	Rutherford
Furrs	Cabarrus	Goldhill	Rowan
Gaddysville	Robeson	Goldknob	Rowan
Galloway	Transylvania	Goldpoint	Martin
Galveston	Durham	Goldrock	Nash
Gamble's Store	Rutherford	Goldsboro (c h)	Wayne
Gamewell	Caldwell	Goldston	Chatham
Gannaway	Caswell	Good	Chatham
Gapcreek	Ashe	Goodman	Anson
Garden City	McDowell	Good Spring	Surry
Gardencreek	Haywood	Goodwill	Forsyth
Gardnerville	Pitt	Gordonton	Person
Garfield	Rowan	Gorman	Durham
Garland	Sampson	Goshen	Wilkes
Garmond	Cabarrus	Gould	Gaston
Garner	Wake	Govern	Cabarrus
Garysburg	Northampton	Governor Island	Swain
Gastonia	Gaston	Grace	Buncombe
Gatesville (c h)	Gates	Grade	Alexander

Post-Office.	County.
Grady	Robeson
Gragg	Caldwell
Graham (c h)	Alamance
Graingers	Lenoir
Grandfather	Watauga
Grange	Transylvania
Granite Falls	Caldwell
Granite Hill	Iredell
Grantham	Wayne
Grantsboro	Pamlico
Grantville	Buncombe
Grapecreek	Cherokee
Grapevine	Madison
Grassycreek	Ashe
Grassyknob	Rutherford
Gravelhill	Bladen
Gravelspring	Chatham
Gray	Alleghany
Graybeal	Ashe
Graychapel	Randolph
Graycreek	Cumberland
Grayson	Ashe
Greenback	Warren
Greenhill	Rutherford
Greenleaf	Wayne
Greenless	McDowell
Green Mountain	Yancey
Greenpark	Watauga
Greenriver	Polk
Greensboro (c h)	Guilford
Greenville (c h)	Pitt
Greenwood	Moore
Greer	Watauga
Gregory	Currituck
Greystone	Vance
Griffith	Mecklenburg
Grifton	Pitt
Grigsby	Ashe
Grimesland	Pitt
Grimsley	Ashe
Grindool	Pitt
Grissom	Granville
Grists	Columbus
Grit	Pender
Grogansville	Rockingham
Grotto	Moore
Grove	Chatham
Grovehill	Warren
Grover	Cleveland
Gudger	Tyrrell
Gudger's Mills	Buncombe
Guilford College	Guilford
Gulf	Chatham
Gulley's Mill	Wake
Gumberry	Northampton
Gumbranch	Onslow
Gumneck	Tyrrell
Gunpowder	Caldwell
Guy	Cherokee
Guyton	Bladen
Gypsy	Henderson
Hackney	Chatham
Haddock	Columbus
Hadley	Chatham
Hagers	Lincoln
Hale	Mitchell
Halewood	Madison

Post-Office.	County.
Halifax (c h)	Halifax
Hallsboro	Columbus
Hall's Ferry	Davie
Hall's Mills	Wilkes
Hallsville	Duplin
Ham	Bladen
Hamer	Caswell
Hamilton	Martin
Hamlet	Richmond
Hampton	Granville
Hamptonville	Yadkin
Hamrick	Rutherford
Handy	Davidson
Hames	Davidson
Hanging Dog	Cherokee
Hannersville	Davidson
Harbinger	Currituck
Hardbank	Stokes
Hardeesville	Greene
Harden	Gaston
Hargrove	Granville
Harley	Wilkes
Harlowe	Carteret
Harman	Watauga
Harmony	Iredell
Harper	Johnston
Harper's Crossroads	Chatham
Harrell's Store	Sampson
Harrellsville	Hertford
Harrington	Harnett
Harrisburg	Cabarrus
Harris	Jackson
Harrison	Mecklenburg
Harrison Creek	Pender
Harrisville	Montgomery
Hartland	Caldwell
Harts	Rowan
Hartshorn	Alamance
Hartsville	Wake
Harvey	Lincoln
Haslin	Beaufort
Hassell	Martin
Hasty	Richmond
Hatteras	Dare
Hattie	Watauga
Havelock	Craven
Hawley's Store	Sampson
Hawriver	Alamance
Hayesville (c h)	Clay
Hay Meadow	Wilkes
Hayne	Sampson
Hayseed	Catawba
Haystack	Surry
Haywood	Chatham
Healing Springs	Davidson
Heath	Union
Heathsville	Halifax
Hebron	Mecklenburg
Hedrick	Alexander
Heflin	Nash
Heilig	Rowan
Helton	Ashe
Henderson (c h)	Vance
Hendersonville (c h)	Henderson
Hendrix	Wilkes
Henrietta	Rutherford
Herry	Lincoln

Post-Office.	County.	Post-Office.	County.
Hensley	Yancey	Hot Springs	Madison
Hera	Transylvania	Huck	Caldwell
Hermitage	Ashe	House	Pitt
Herrell	Mitchell	Houstonville	Iredell
Herring	Sampson	Howard	Bertie
Hertford (c h)	Perquimans	Howellsville	Bladen
Hester	Granville	Hoyle	Randolph
Hester's Store	Person	Hub	Columbus
Hewitt's	Swain	Hubert	Onslow
Hexlena	Bertie	Hudson	Caldwell
Hibriten	Caldwell	Hughes	Mitchell
Hickory	Catawba	Hugo	Lenoir
Hickory Grove	Wake	Hull's Cross Roads	Lincoln
Hicksville	Rutherford	Hulon	Forsyth
Hiddenite	Alexander	Humphrey	Duplin
Higdonville	Macon	Hunter's Bridge	Beaufort
Higgins	Yancey	Huntersville	Mecklenburg
Highgate	Alleghany	Huntingcreek	Wilkes
Highlands	Macon	Huntley	Sampson
Highpoint	Guilford	Hunts	Nash
Hightowers	Caswell	Huntsville	Yadkin
Highview	Person	Hurdles Mills	Person
Hill	Pitt	Husk	Ashe
Hillgirt	Henderson	Hyatt	Anson
Hilliardston	Nash	Hycote	Caswell
Hillsboro (c. h.)	Orange	Idaho	Cumberland
Hillsdale	Guilford	Idalia	Beaufort
Hill's Store	Randolph	Idlewild	Ashe
Hiltop	Stokes	Idol	Ashe
Hinton	Guilford	Ilex	Davidson
Hives	Sampson	Inanda	Buncombe
Hiawassee	Cherokee	Indiantown	Camden
Hobbsville	Gates	Indiantrail	Union
Hobgood	Halifax	Inex	Warren
Hobton	Sampson	Ingalls	Mitchell
Hobucken	Pamlico	Ingleside	Franklin
Hocut	Bladen	Ingold	Sampson
Hodge	Cleveland	Ingram	Northampton
Hoffman	Richmond	Ink	Wilkes
Hogan	Rockingham	Inland	Moore
Hogback Valley	Transylvania	Inman	Robeson
Hollands	Pitt	Institute	Lenoir
Hollis	Rutherford	Inverness	Cumberland
Holloway	Person	Ira	Wilkes
Hollybush	Cleveland	Iredell	Brunswick
Hollyridge	Onslow	Ironduff	Haywood
Holly Springs	Wake	Ironhill	Columbus
Hollywood	Carteret	Iron Station	Lincoln
Holman	Davie	Irvin	Transylvania
Holman's Mills	Alamance	Island Ford	Rutherford
Holsclaw	Alexander	Ita	Halifax
Holt	Guilford	Itimer	Johnston
Homestead	Graham	Itom	Rutherford
Hominy Creek	Buncombe	Invanhoe	Sampson
Honey	Union	Ivy	Madison
Hoods	Mecklenburg	Jackdaw	Stanly
Hooker	Alleghany	Jackson (c. h.)	Northampton
Hookerton	Greene	Jackson Hill	Davidson
Hooverhill	Randolph	Jackson's Creek	Randolph
Hope	Union	Jackson Springs	Moore
Hope Mills	Cumberland	Jacksonville (c. h.)	Onslow
Hopewell	Mecklenburg	Jacob's Fork	Catawba
Hopper	Rockingham	James City	Craven
Horners	Moore	Jamestown	Guilford
Hornet	Mecklenburg	Jamesville	Martin
Horseshoe	Rutherford	Jarretts	Swain
Hothouse	Cherokee	Jarvisburg	Currituck

Post-Office.	County.	Post-Office.	County.
Jason	Greene	King's Mountain	Cleveland
Jasper	Craven	Kingville	Columbus
Jefferson (c. h.)	Ashe	Kingwood	Mecklenburg
Jennings	Iredell	Kinnon	Cumberland
Jeptha	Transylvania	Kinsey	Cherokee
Jerome	Bladen	Kinston (c. h.)	Lenoir
Jerusalem	Davie	Kitchin	Halifax
Jessamine	Beaufort	Kittrell	Vance
Jesup	Moore	Kitty Hawk	Currituck
Jewel	Stokes	Kluttz	Cabarrus
Jimes	Davidson	Knap of Reeds	Granville
Joe	Madison	Knobcreek	Cleveland
Joford	Duplin	Knoll	Macon
Johnson	Graham	Knot's Island	Currituck
Johnson's Mills	Pitt	Knott's Store	Anson
John Station	Richmond	Knottville	Wilkes
Johnstown	Lincoln	Kyles Landing	Cumberland
Jolliet	Forsyth	Lacey	Alamance
Jonasridge	Burke	Luckey	Alexander
Jonathan	Haywood	LaCrosse	Guilford
Jonesboro	Moore	Ladonia	Surry
Jonescreek	Anson	LaGrange	Lenoir
Jonesmine	Davidson	Lake Comfort	Hyde
Jonesville	Yadkin	Lake Landing	Hyde
Joppa	Orange	Lake Waccamaw	Columbus
Joy	Burke	Lamar	Ashe
Joynes	Wilkes	Lambsville	Chatham
Jubilee	Davidson	Lamm	Wilson
Judith	Union	Lamont	Guilford
Judson	Swain	Lancaster	Edgecombe
Jugtown	Catawba	Lane's Creek	Union
Julian	Guilford	Langdon	Rockingham
Jumbo	Caldwell	Langley	Pitt
Juno	Buncombe	Lanier	Onslow
Jupiter	Buncombe	Lansing	Ashe
Justice	Franklin	Lark	Cleveland
Kadar	Wake	Lasker	Northampton
Kappa	Davie	Lassiter	Randolph
Kapp's Mill	Surry	Latham	Beaufort
Katesville	Franklin	Lattimore	Cleveland
Kawana	Mitchell	Laurel	Franklin
Keener	Sampson	Laurel Bluff	Surry
Kehukee	Pasquotank	Laurel Branch	Alleghany
Keith	Pender	Laurel Hill	Richmond
Kelford	Bertie	Laurel Springs	Alleghany
Kelly	Bladen	Laurelton	Madison
Kelsy	Watauga	Laurinburg	Richmond
Kelvingrove	Wake	Lavinia	Haywood
Kemp's Mills	Randolph	Lawhorn	Moore
Kenansville (c. h.)	Duplin	Lawndale	Cleveland
Kendall	Wilkes	Lawrence	Edgecombe
Kenly	Johnston	Laws	Orange
Kernersville	Forsyth	Lawsnville	Rockingham
Kerr	Sampson	Layton	Rockingham
Kershaw	Pamlico	Leachburg	Johnston
Key	Harnett	Lead	Henderson
Keyser	Moore	Leading	Cabarrus
Kidsville	Lincoln	Leavitt	Harnett
Kiger	Stokes	Leaksville	Rockingham
Kirkey	McDowell	Leander	Watauga
Kilby	Alexander	Leasburg	Caswell
Kildee	Randolph	Leatherman	Macon
Kimbolton	Chatham	Leavitt	Cumberland
Kimesville	Guilford	Lebanon	Columbus
Kind	Madison	Ledford	Clay
King	Stokes	Ledger	Mitchell
Kingcreek	Caldwell	Lee	Madison

Post-Office.	County.	Post-Office.	County.
Leechville	Beaufort	Lonely	Moore
Leesville	Robeson	**Longcreek**	Pender
Leewood	Chatham	Longford	Iredell
Legal	Harnett	Long Island	Catawba
Leggett	Edgecombe	Longleaf	Moore
Lego	Guilford	Longpine	Anson
Leicester	Buncombe	Longshoals	Lincoln
Lemay	Wake	Long's Store	Union
Lemon Springs	Moore	Longtown	Yadkin
Lenoir (c. h.)	Caldwell	Longview	Guilford
Lenox Castle	Rockingham	Loretta	Catawba
Lentz	Rowan	Lotta	Hertford
Leo	Stanly	**Louisburg** (c. h.)	Franklin
Leon	Duplin	Louise	Catawba
Leonard	Madison	Lovelace	Wilkes
Leota	Alamance	Lovelady	Mecklenburg
Leroy	Columbus	Lovelevel	Union
Letha	Franklin	Lowder	Stanly
Letitia	Cherokee	Lowe	Robeson
Levelcross	Randolph	**Lowell**	Gaston
Levelplains	Randolph	Lowesville	Lincoln
Levi	Davidson	Lowgap	Surry
Lewisfork	Wilkes	Lowland	Pamlico
Lewiston	Bertie	Loy	Alamance
Lewisville	Forsyth	Loyd	Lincoln
Lexington (c. h.)	Davidson	Lucama	Wilson
Liberty	Randolph	Lucia	Gaston
Liberty Store	Guilford	Lucile	Wilkes
Light	Davidson	Luck	Madison
Lilac	Davidson	Lufty	Gaston
Lilesville	Anson	Lul	Wake
Lillington (c. h.)	Harnett	**Lumber Bridge**	Robeson
Lilly	Camden	**Lumberton** (c. h.)	Robeson
Lima	Craven	Lupton	Carteret
Limerock	Stokes	Luster	Durham
Limestone	Buncombe	Luther	Buncombe
Lincolnton (c. h.)	Lincoln	Lutterloh	Chatham
Linden	Harnett	Lydia	Sampson
Lindhurst	Chatham	Lyman	Duplin
Lindsay	Orange	Lynch	Madison
Line	Rutherford	Lyndover	Durham
Linney	Ashe	Lynn	Polk
Linville	Mitchell	Lyons	Granville
Linville's Store	Burke	Lyon's Landing	Bladen
Linwood	Davidson	Lytch	Richmond
Lipe	Rowan	Lytton	Randolph
Lisbon	Sampson	**McAdenville**	Gaston
Lisk	Rowan	McArthurs	Robeson
Lissa	Sampson	McCains	Union
Littlecreek	Madison	McCall	Caldwell
Littlefield	Pitt	McClammy	Wayne
Little Pine Creek	Madison	McCray	Alamance
Little River	Alexander	McCurdy	Iredell
Little River Academy	Cumberland	McFarlan	Anson
Little Rock Creek	Mitchell	McGowen	Duplin
Little's Mills	Richmond	McKee	Davidson
Little Sugarloaf	Bladen	McKoy	Sampson
Littleton	Halifax	McLeansville	Guilford
Lizzie	Greene	McNair	Richmond
Lockville	Chatham	McNatt	Robeson
Loco	Onslow	McNeely	Rockingham
Locusthill	Caswell	Mabel	Watauga
Locust	Stanly	Mabry	Stanly
Lodo	Mecklenburg	Macedonia	Montgomery
Loftis	Transylvania	Machpelah	Lincoln
Logan's Store	Rutherford	Mack	Rutherford
Lomax	Wilkes	**Mackey's Ferry**	Washington

Post-Office.	County.	Post-Office.	County.
Macon	Warren	Medoc	Halifax
Madge	Mecklenburg	Meeksville	Wilson
Madison	Rockingham	Meganna	Buncombe
Magnestic City	Mitchell	**Newbern** (c. h.)	Craven
Magnolia	Duplin	Meherrin	Northampton
Maiden	Catawba	Meiggs	Surry
Maitland	Sampson	Melanchthon	Randolph
Makatoka	Brunswick	Melrose	Robeson
Makelyville	Hyde	Melville	Alamance
Malee	Richmond	Melvin Hill	Polk
Malmo	Brunswick	Memory	Rutherford
Mana	Yadkin	Menola	Hertford
Manchester	Cumberland	Merchant Mills	Gates
Mangum	Richmond	Meredith	Orange
Manly	Moore	Merrimon	Carteret
Manndale	Alamance	Merritt	Pamlico
Manning	Rowan	Merryhill	Bertie
Mann's Harbor	Dare	Merrymount	Warren
Manson	Warren	Merryoaks	Chatham
Manteo (c. h.)	Dare	Mesic	Pamlico
Maple Cypress	Craven	Metal	Cleveland
Maplehill	Pender	Method	Wake
Maplesprings	Wilkes	Mica	Mitchell
Mapleton	Hertford	Micaville	Yancey
Mapleville	Franklin	Michael	Davidson
Marble	Cherokee	Micro	Johnston
Marengo	Anson	**Middleburg**	Vance
Margettsville	Northampton	Middlecane	Watauga
Maribel	Pamlico	Middletown	Hyde
Marines	Onslow	Midway	Davidson
Marion (c. h.)	McDowell	Mildred	Edgecombe
Mariposa	Lincoln	Milesville	Caswell
Marler	Yadkin	Millboro	Randolph
Marley's Mills	Randolph	Millbridge	Rowan
Marlville	Bladen	Millbrook	Wake
Marmaduke	Warren	Millcreek	Person
Marsh	Davidson	Milledgville	Montgomery
Marshall (c. h.)	Madison	Miller	Iredell
Marshallburg	Carteret	Miller's Creek	Wilkes
Mars Hill	Madison	Millertown	Rowan
Marshville	Union	Millhill	Cabarrus
Martha	Randolph	Milligan	Cleveland
Martin	Yadkin	Millingport	Stanly
Martindale	Mecklenburg	Millprong	Robeson
Martin's Mill	Montgomery	Millshoal	Macon
Mascot	Buncombe	Millspring	Polk
Mashoes	Dare	Mills River	Henderson
Massey	Wake	Millstone	Catawba
Mast	Watauga	Millwood	Chatham
Matthews	Mecklenburg	**Milton**	Caswell
Maud	Randolph	Milwaukee	Northampton
Maximo	Cabarrus	Mineola	Beaufort
Maxton	Robeson	Mingo	Sampson
Maxwell	Henderson	Minneapolis	Mitchell
May	Harnett	Minthill	Mecklenburg
Mayodan	Rockingham	Miranda	Rowan
Mayfield	Rockingham	Mission	Stanly
Mayhew	Iredell	Mitchiner	Franklin
Mayo	Rockingham	Mitford	Rowan
Mayoville	Jones	Mix	Sampson
Maywood	Alamance	Mizpah	Stokes
Meadowhill	Caldwell	**Mocksville** (c. h.)	Davie
Meadows	Stokes	Moffitt	Randolph
Meatcamp	Watauga	Mohawk	Harnett
Mebane	Alamance	Mollie	Columbus
Mechanic	Randolph	Monbo	Catawba
Medlin	Swain	**Moncure**	Chatham

Post-Office.	County.
Money	Henderson
Monroe (c. h.)	Union
Monroeton	Rockingham
Montague	Pender
Monteith	Mecklenburg
Montezuma	Mitchell
Montford	McDowell
Montgomery	Montgomery
Monticello	Washington
Montland	Alleghany
Montrose	Cumberland
Montvale	Transylvania
Mooresboro	Cleveland
Moores Creek	Pender
Mooresville	Iredell
Mooshaunee	Moore
Moravian Falls	Wilkes
Morehead City	Carteret
Moretz	Watauga
Morganhill	Buncombe
Morgan's Mill	Union
Morganton (c. h.)	Burke
Moirah	Person
Morrisville	Wake
Moorosenean	Robeson
Morton's Store	Alamance
Morven	Anson
Moscow	Bladen
Moser	Surry
Mossneck	Robeson
Moulton	Franklin
Mountain Creek	Catawba
Mountain Island	Gaston
Mountainview	Warren
Mount Airy	Surry
Mount Bethel	Alexander
Mount Carmel	Moore
Mount Energy	Granville
Mount Gilead	Montgomery
Mount Gould	Bertie
Mount Holly	Gaston
Mount Mitchell	Buncombe
Mount Mourne	Iredell
Mount Nebo	Yadkin
Mount Olive	Wayne
Mount Pisgah	Alexander
Mount Pleasant	Cabarrus
Mount Sterling	Haywood
Mount Tirzah	Person
Mountulla	Rowan
Mount Vernon	Rowan
Mount Vernon Springs	Chatham
Mount Zion	Wilkes
Moyock	Currituck
Moyton	Wilson
Mullick	Chatham
Mulberry	Wilkes
Mullen	Randolph
Mullgrove	Catawba
Mumford	Pasquotank
Murfreesboro	Hertford
Murphy (c. h.)	Cherokee
Mutienz	Caldwell
Myatt Mills	Wake
Myrtle	Rutherford
Myrts	Duplin
Naghead	Dare

Post-Office.	County.
Nalis	Montgomery
Nance	Rockingham
Nashville (c. h.)	Nash
Nathans Creek	Ashe
Nat Moore	Bladen
Natural Wells	Duplin
Neal	Halifax
Nealsville	McDowell
Neatman	Stokes
Nebo	McDowell
Needmore	Swain
Negrohead	Union
Nelson	Durham
Nestor	Davie
Net	Iredell
Nettieknob	Ashe
Neuse	Wake
Nevin	Mecklenburg
Newbern	Craven
Newcastle	Wilkes
Newell	Mecklenburg
Newfound	Buncombe
Newhill	Wake
Newhope	Iredell
Newhope Academy	Randolph
Newhouse	Cleveland
Newlight	Wake
New London	Stanly
Newman	Warren
Newmarket	Randolph
Newport	Carteret
New River	Alleghany
New Salem	Randolph
Nesom	Halifax
New Stirling	Iredell
Newton (c. h.)	Catawba
Newton Grove	Sampson
Nicanor	Perquimans
Nicholson	Alamance
Nicholson's Mills	Iredell
Nicholsonville	Cleveland
Nimrod	Mecklenburg
Nina	Cherokee
Nixonton	Pasquotank
Noblin	Granville
Noise	Moore
Nunah	Macon
Norfleet	Halifax
Norris	Watauga
Northbrook	Lincoln
Northcove	McDowell
North Harlowe	Craven
Northside	Granville
North Wilkesboro	Wilkes
Norton	Jackson
Norval	Harnett
Norwood	Stanly
Nottla	Cherokee
Nulin	Alleghany
Nussman	Cabarrus
Nutbush	Carteret
Nye	Robeson
Oakdale	Alamance
Oakforest	Iredell
Oakgrove	Union
Oakhill	Granville
Oakland	Nash

Post-Office.	County.	Post-Office.	County.
Ranger	Cherokee	Riverside	Ashe
Rankin	Mecklenburg	Riverton	Richmond
Ransom's Bridge	Franklin	Riverview	Mecklenburg
Ransomville	Beaufort	Rives' Chapel	Chatham
Rathbone	Guilford	Roane's Mill	Macon
Ravens	Swain	Roanoke	Rockingham
Ray	Madison	Roanoke Rapids	Halifax
Raywood	Union	Roaringgap	Wilkes
Readybranch	Wilkes	Roaring River	Wilkes
Record	Columbus	**Robbinsville** (c. h.)	Graham
Redalia	Pitt	Roberdell	Richmond
Redbanks	Robeson	**Robersonville**	Martin
Reddies' River	Wilkes	Roberts	Ashe
Redhill	Mitchell	Robeson	Columbus
Redland	Davie	Robin	Cumberland
Redmountain	Durham	Rochdale	Pitt
Redoak	Nash	Rochester	Robeson
Redshoals'	Stokes	Rock	Rowan
Red Springs	Robeson	Rockcreek	Alamance
Reedy	Davidson	Rockcut	Iredell
Reelsboro	Pamlico	Rockett	Catawba
Reepsville	Lincoln	Rockford	Surry
Reese	Watauga	**Rockingham** (c. h.)	Richmond
Refuge	Robeson	Rocklevel	Rockingham
Register	Bladen	Rockrest	Union
Rehoboth	Northampton	Rockspring	Orange
Reidsville	Rockingham	Rockview	Buncombe
Reinhardt	Lincoln	Rockwell	Rowan
Reitzel	Randolph	Rockyhock	Chowan
Relief	Mitchell	**Rocky Mount**	Edgecombe
Rella	Stokes	Rockypass	McDowell
Rennert	Robeson	Rockypoint	Pender
Renston	Pitt	Rocky Springs	Rockingham
Repose	Lenoir	Rodanthe	Dare
Republic	Yadkin	Roe	Carteret
Resaca	Duplin	Rogers' Store	Wake
Rest	Stanly	Rolesville	Wake
Resthaven	Buncombe	Rollins	Burke
Retreat	Haywood	Rome	Johnston
Reuben	Union	Romolo	Halifax
Rex	Robeson	Ronda	Wilkes
Reynoldson	Gates	**Roper**	Washington
Rhodes	Cumberland	Roscoe	Chatham
Rialto	Chatham	Rose	Alamance
Riceville	Buncombe	Roseboro	Sampson
Richardson	Bladen	Rosedale	Pasquotank
Richardson's Creek	Union	Rosehill	Duplin
Richfield	Stanly	Rosemead	Bertie
Richlands	Onslow	Roseville	Person
Richmond	Chatham	Rosewood	Chatham
Richmond Hill	Yadkin	Rosinburg	Wake
Rich Square	Northampton	Rosindale	Bladen
Riddicksville	Hertford	Roslin	Cumberland
Riddle	Camden	Rougemons	Durham
Ridgespring	Greene	Round Mountain	Wilkes
Ridgeville	Caswell	Roundpeak	Surry
Ridgeway	Warren	Rountree	Pitt
Riggsbee	Chatham	Rowan	Rowan
Riley's Crossroads	Franklin	Rowell	Davidson
Riley's Store	Randolph	Rowland	Robeson
Rimer	Cabarrus	**Roxboro** (c. h.)	Person
Ringwood	Halifax	**Roxobel**	Bertie
Rippetoe	Caldwell	Royal	Franklin
Risden	Caldwell	Rozier	Robeson
Ritchie	Stanly	Rubicon	Moore
Riverdale	Craven	Rudisill	Catawba
Riverhill	Iredell	**Ruffin**	Rockingham

Post-Office.	County.	Post-Office.	County.
Rugby	Henderson	Senia	Mitchell
Ruralhall	Forsyth	Sessom	Robeson
Rushing	Union	Settle	Iredell
Rusk	Surry	Sevensprings	Wayne
Russell	Rowan	Severn	Northampton
Ruth	Forsyth	Seward	Forsyth
Rutherford College	Burke	Sexton	Madison
Rutherfordton (c. h.)	Rutherford	Shallotte	Brunswick
Rutherwood	Watauga	Shallowford	Alamance
Ryan	Robeson	Shamrock	Mecklenburg
Ryland	Chowan	Shankle	Stanly
Saddletree	Robeson	Shannon	Robeson
Safe	Duplin	Sharon	Cleveland
Sago	Mecklenburg	Sharp	Rockingham
Sains	Lincoln	Sharpsburg	Nash
Saint John	Hertford	Shawboro	Currituck
Saint Jude	Watauga	Shawnee	Catawba
Saint Lawrence	Chatham	Shaw's Mills	Guilford
Saint Lewis	Edgecombe	Sheffield	Davie
Saint Paul	Robeson	Shelby (c. h.)	Cleveland
Saint Phillip	Brunswick	Shelton	Surry
Salem	Forsyth	Sherrill's Ford	Catawba
Salem Chapel	Forsyth	Sherwood	Cumberland
Salem Church	Randolph	Sheva	Mecklenburg
Salisbury (c. h.)	Rowan	Shiloh	Camden
Saluda	Polk	Shine	Greene
Samuel	Surry	Shinsville	Iredell
Sandbluff	Bladen	Shoals	Surry
Sandifer	Mecklenburg	Shocco	Warren
Sards	Watauga	Shooting Creek	Clay
Sandy	Madison	Shope	Buncombe
Sandycross	Gates	Shopton	Mecklenburg
Sandygrove	Alamance	Shore	Yadkin
Sandymush	Buncombe	Shortoff	Macon
Sandyridge	Stokes	Shotwell	Wake
Sandysprings	Polk	Shoup's Ford	Burke
Sanford	Moore	Shull's Mills	Watauga
Sans Souci	Bertie	Sidney	Beaufort
Sapona	Davidson	Sigma	Iredell
Sapphire	Jackson	Silascreek	Ashe
Saratoga	Wilson	Siler City	Chatham
Sardis	Mecklenburg	Silkhope	Chatham
Sarecta	Duplin	Siloam	Surry
Sarem	Gates	Silver	Stanly
Satterwhite	Granville	Silverdale	Onslow
Saulston	Wayne	Silverhill	Davidson
Saunders	Cabarrus	Silverstone	Watauga
Saw	Rowan	Sim	Robeson
Sawmill	Caldwell	Simmongrove	Chatham
Sawyersville	Randolph	Simpson's Store	Rockingham
Saxapahaw	Alamance	Sincerity	Union
Saxon	Stokes	Sioux	Yancey
Scalesville	Guilford	Sitton	Henderson
Scaly	Macon	Sixforks	Wake
Scarboro	Montgomery	Sixruns	Sampson
Science	Randolph	Skinnersville	Washington
Scotland Neck	Halifax	Skyco	Dare
Scotts	Iredell	Skyland	Buncombe
Scotts Creek	Jackson	Skyuka	Polk
Scotts Hill	Pender	Sladesville	Hyde
Scottsville	Ashe	Slate	Stokes
Scranton	Hyde	Sligo	Currituck
Scuppernong	Washington	Sloan	Duplin
Seaboard	Northampton	Sloop Point	Pender
Sedge's Garden	Forsyth	Smith	Stokes
Selma	Johnston	Smithfield (c. h.)	Johnston
Semora	Caswell	Smithgrove	Davie

Post-Office.	County.	Post-Office.	County.
Smith's Ford	Cabarrus	Stephenson	Johnston
Smyrna	Carteret	Sterling	Robeson
Snapp	Gaston	Stevens	Union
Snead's Ferry	Onslow	Stewart	Richmond
Snow Camp	Alamance	Stice	Cleveland
Snowcreek	Iredell	Stockville	Buncombe
Snowden	Currituck	Stokes	Pitt
Snowhill (c. h.)	Greene	Stokesdale	Guilford
Soapstone Mount	Randolph	Stone Mountain	McDowell
Sodahill	Watauga	Stoneville	Rockingham
Solitude	Ashe	Stonewall	Pamlico
Somerset	Chowan	Stonycreek	Caswell
Sonoma	Haywood	Stonyfork	Watauga
Sophia	Randolph	Stonyknoll	Surry
Southcreek	Beaufort	Stonypoint	Alexander
Southern Pines	Moore	Stonyridge	Surry
South Gaston	Halifax	Stophel	Iredell
South Lowell	Durham	Stork	Chatham
South Mills	Camden	Stovall	Granville
Southpoint	Gaston	Strabane	Lenoir
Southport (c. h.)	Brunswick	Straits	Carteret
South River	Rowan	Straw	Wilkes
Southtoe	Yancey	Strieby	Randolph
South Washington	Pender	Stubbs	Cleveland
Sparkling Catawba Springs	Catawba	Stumpsound	Onslow
Sparkman	Onslow	Stumpypoint	Dare
Sparta (c h)	Alleghany	Sturgill	Ashe
Spear	Mitchell	Success	Buncombe
Speed	Edgecombe	Sue	Columbus
Speedwell	Jackson	Sugargrove	Watauga
Speight's Bridge	Greene	Sugarhill	McDowell
Spencer	Moore	Suit	Cherokee
Spero	Randolph	Sulphur Springs	Montgomery
Spillman	Yadkin	Summerfield	Guilford
Spilona	Johnston	Summerville	Harnett
Splendor	Henderson	Summit	Wilkes
Split Mountain	Haywood	Sumner	Guilford
Spout Springs	Harnett	Sunbury	Gates
Spray	Rockingham	Sunnyside	Rowan
Spring Creek	Madison	Sunset	Granville
Springdale	Haywood	Sunshine	Rutherford
Springer	Onslow	Supply	Brunswick
Springfield	Wilkes	Surl	Person
Springhill	Halifax	Sussex	Ashe
Springhope	Nash	Sutherlands	Ashe
Springle	Carteret	Sutphin	Alamance
Sprucepine	Mitchell	Sutton	Franklin
Spurrier	Mecklenburg	Swain	Swain
Stackhouse	Madison	Swancreek	Yadkin
Stagville	Durham	Swannanoa	Buncombe
Stanback	Alamance	Swanner	Alexander
Staley	Randolph	Swann Station	Moore
Stallings	Franklin	Swanquarter (c h)	Hyde
Stanhope	Nash	Swansboro	Onslow
Stanley	Gaston	Sweet Home	Iredell
Stantonsburg	Wilson	Sweetwater	Watauga
Star	Montgomery	Sweepsonville	Alamance
Starlight	Wayne	Swift Island	Montgomery
Starsburg	Cumberland	Swinton	Moore
Startown	Catawba	Sylva	Jackson
Stateroad	Surry	Sylvester	Alamance
Statesville (c h)	Iredell	Tabernacle	Guilford
Stedman	Cumberland	Tablerock	Burke
Steele Creek	Mecklenburg	Tabor	Columbus
Stekoah	Graham	Talbot	Wilson
Stella	Carteret	Tampa	Mecklenburg
Stem	Granville	Tarboro (c h)	Edgecombe

Post-Office.	County.
Tarheel	Bladen
Tariff	Columbus
Tar Landing	Onslow
Tar River	Granville
Taylor	Wilson
Taylor's Bridge	Sampson
Taylorsville (c h)	Alexander
Teachey's	Duplin
Teague	Haywood
Teer	Orange
Telephone	Person
Tempting	Moore
Tennyson	Davie
Terrapin	Halifax
Terrell	Catawba
Thagardville	Moore
Thaxton	Ashe
Thelma	Halifax
Theodore	Buncombe
Thermal City	Rutherford
Theta	Madison
Thomasville	Davidson
Thompsonville	Rockingham
Threeforks	Yancey
Thurman	Craven
Thurston	Alexander
Tiger	Rutherford
Tilden	Yadkin
Tillery	Halifax
Tillman	Chatham
Timberlake	Person
Timothy	Sampson
Tippecanoe	Sampson
Tiptop	Transylvania
Tobaccoville	Forsyth
Todd	Ashe
Tolarsville	Robeson
Tolers	Orange
Toluca	Cleveland
Tomahawk	Sampson
Tomotla	Cherokee
Tomcreek	McDowell
Tony	Caswell
Topia	Alleghany
Topsail Sound	Pender
Towncreek	Brunswick
Townsville	Vance
Tracadia	Yadkin
Tracy	Watauga
Tradingford	Rowan
Trailbranch	Madison
Transon	Ashe
Traphill	Wilkes
Treetop	Ashe
Trenton (c h)	Jones
Triangle	Lincoln
Trinity	Randolph
Trio	Rutherford
Triplett	Watauga
Trotville	Gates
Trout	Ashe
Troutmans	Iredell
Troy (c h)	Montgomery
Troyville	Harnett
Truth	Chatham
Tryon	Polk
Tuckahoe	Jones

Post-Office.	County.
Tuckaseegee	Jackson
Tulin	Cabarrus
Tulip	Stokes
Tulls	Currituck
Tulula	Graham
Tunis	Hertford
Turkey	Sampson
Turlington	Harnett
Turnage	Edgecombe
Turners	Polk
Turnerburg	Iredell
Turner's Mountain	Surry
Turnpike	Buncombe
Turtletown	Cherokee
Tuscarora	Craven
Tuscola	Haywood
Tusquitee	Clay
Tweed	Buncombe
Twine	Clay
Twitty	Rutherford
Tyner	Chowan
Tyra	Moore
Tryo Shops	Davidson
Tysor Mills	Chatham
Ulah	Randolph
Umbra	Durham
Unaka	Cherokee
Uncas	Mecklenburg
Union	Hertford
Unionhope	Nash
Union Mills	Rutherford
Unionridge	Alamance
Unionville	Union
Unity	Mecklenburg
University Station	Orange
Upton	Caldwell
Upward	Henderson
Uree	Rutherford
Valdese	Burke
Valle Cruces	Watauga
Valley	Mitchell
Vance	Iredell
Vanceboro	Craven
Vanceville	Buncombe
Vandalia	Guilford
Vandemere	Pamlico
Vander	Cumberland
Vann	Union
Vannoy	Wilkes
Vanteen	Wake
Variety Grove	Harnett
Varina	Wake
Vashti	Alexander
Vass	Moore
Vaughan	Warren
Vega	Sampson
Velna	Randolph
Venable	Surry
Veni	Halifax
Verble	Rowan
Vernon	Ashe
Verona	Onslow
Vests	Cherokee
Veto	Wake
Viands	Wilkes
Vicksboro	Warren
Victor	Moore

Post-Office.	County.	Post-Office.	County.
Vienna	Forsyth	West Asheville	Buncombe
Vilas	Watauga	Westbrook	Bladen
Villanow	Moore	West Durham	Durham
Vincent	Alamance	**Westend**	Moore
Vineland	Columbus	Western	Haywood
Viola	Pender	Westfield	Surry
Virgil	Watauga	Westminster	Guilford
Vivian	Gates	West Raleigh	Wake
Voline	Robeson	West's Mill	Macon
Vollers	Robeson	Westville	Harnett
Vultare	Northampton	Wharf	Anson
Waco	Cleveland	Wharton	Beaufort
Waddells	Rockingham	Wheatmore	Randolph
Wade	Cumberland	Wheeler	Ashe
Wadesboro (c h)	Anson	Whetstone	Granville
Wadeville	Montgomery	Whichard	Pitt
Wagoner	Ashe	**Whitakers**	Edgecombe
Wailes	Mecklenburg	Whitehall	Bladen
Wakefield	Wake	Whitehead	Alleghany
Wake Forest	Wake	Whitehouse	Randolph
Wakulla	Robeson	Whitener	Catawba
Waldo	Chatham	Whiteplains	Surry
Walker	Polk	Whiteroad	Forsyth
Walkersville	Union	Whiterock	Madison
Walkertown	Forsyth	Whiteside Cove	Jackson
Walkup	Union	White Store	Anson
Wallace	Duplin	**Whiteville** (c h)	Columbus
Wallburg	Davidson	Whitford	Jones
Walnutcove	Stokes	Whitley	Stanly
Walnutrun	Madison	Whitsett	Guilford
Walter	Wayne	**Whittier**	Swain
Wanchese	Dare	Whittington	Wilkes
Wardlaw	Union	Whynot	Randolph
Ward's Mill	Onslow	Wicker	Cumberland
Warlick	Burke	Wiggins Cross-roads	Gates
Warne	Clay	Wikles Store	Macon
Warren Plains	Warren	Wilbanks	Wilson
Warrenton (c h)	Warren	Wilbar	Wilkes
Warsaw	Duplin	Wildcat	Northampton
Washburn	Rutherford	Wildwood	Carteret
Washington (c h)	Beaufort	Wiles	Wilkes
Watauga Falls	Watauga	White	Yancey
Waterlily	Currituck	**Wilkesboro** (c h)	Wilkes
Waterloo	Union	Wilkins	Granville
Watkins	Vance	Wilkesville	Robeson
Watkinsville	Stokes	Willard	Pender
Watsonville	Rowan	Willardville	Durham
Watts	Iredell	Willeyton	Gates
Waugh	Iredell	Williams	Yadkin
Waverly	Cleveland	Williamsboro	Vance
Waxhaw	Union	Williamsburg	Iredell
Way	Union	Williams' Mills	Chatham
Waycross	Sampson	**Williamston** (c h)	Martin
Waynesville (c h)	Haywood	Willis' Creek	Bladen
Wayside	Swain	Willow	Gates
Weasel	Ashe	Willowgreen	Greene
Weaversford	Ashe	**Wilmington** (c h)	New Hanover
Weaverville	Buncombe	Wilmot	Jackson
Webster (c h)	Jackson	**Wilson** (c h)	Wilson
Weeksville	Pasquotank	Wilson's Mills	Johnston
Wehutt	Cherokee	Wilson's Store	Stokes
Weisner	Iredell	Wilton	Granville
Welcome	Davidson	Winchester	Union
Weldon	Halifax	**Windsor** (c h)	Bertie
Wentworth (c h)	Rockingham	Winfall	Perquimans
Wesley	Surry	Winnie	Bladen
West	Columbus	Winslow	Harnett

Post-Office.	County.	Post-Office.	County.
Winstead	Person	Wyatt	Wake
Winsteadville	Beaufort	Wyo	Yadkin
Winston (c h)	Forsyth	Wythe	Harnett
Winterville	Pitt	Xenia	Duplin
Winthrop	Carteret	**Yadkin College**	Davidson
Winton (c h)	Hertford	Yadkin Falls	Stanly
Wise	Warren	Yadkin Valley	Caldwell
Wit	Carteret	Yadkinville (c h)	Yadkin
Withers	Stokes	Yale	Henderson
Wittenberg	Alexander	**Yanceyville** (c h)	Caswell
Wolfcreek	Cherokee	Yancy	Person
Wolf Mountain	Jackson	Yarbro	Caswell
Wolfsville	Union	**Yeatesville**	Beaufort
Woodard	Bertie	Yellowcreek	Graham
Woodburn	Person	Yerger	Watauga
Woodland	Northampton	Yoder	Catawba
Woodlington	Lenoir	Yokley	Davidson
Woodleaf	Rowan	York Collegiate Institute	Alexander
Woodley	Chown	Yost	Rowan
Woodsdale	Person	**Youngsville**	Franklin
Woodside	Rowan	Yuma	Watauga
Woodville	Perquimans	Zacho	Granville
Woodworth	Vance	Zeb	Rowan
Worry	Burke	Zionville	Watauga
Worthville	Randolph	Zirconia	Henderson
Wrendale	Edgecombe	Zoar	Union
Wrightsville	New Hanover	Zorah	Craven

RAILROADS OF NORTH CAROLINA.

OFFICERS, STATIONS, ETC.

ATLANTIC COAST LINE SYSTEM.

Officers.—W. G. Elliott, President; H. Walters, Vice-President; J. F. Post, Jr., Secretary and Treasurer; J. R. Kelly, Manager; J. F. Divine, General Superintendent; T. M. Emerson, Traffic Manager; F. Gardner, Chief Engineer. Principal offices at Wilmington. Total mileage of system in North Carolina, 700.22 miles.

WILMINGTON & WELDON R. R.

Station.	Dist.	Station.	Dist.
Wilmington	0	Pikeville	92.0
Union Depot	1.2	Fremont	95.2
Wrightsboro	4.2	Black Creek	101.9
Castle Hayne	8.7	Contentnea	104.9
Rocky Point	14.2	Wilson	108.1
Burgaw	22.4	Elm City	114.6
South Wash'g'n	29.4	Sharpsburg	119.1
Wallace	35.8	Rocky Mount	124.5
Teachey's	38.1	Battleboro	132.6
Rose Hill	42.2	Whitaker's	136.8
Magnolia	47.4	Enfield	142.9
Warsaw	54.8	Ruggles	150.3
Faison's	63.3	Scotl'd N'ck "Y"	152.8
Mount Olive	69.9	Halifax	153.8
Dudley	75.3	Weldon	161.4
Goldsboro	84.3		

CLINTON BRANCH.

Station.	Dist.	Station.	Dist.
Warsaw	0	Clinton	13.40
Elliott	7		

NASHVILLE BRANCH.

Station.	Dist.	Station.	Dist.
Rocky Mount	0	Spring Hope	19.2
Nashville	10.2		

WILSON AND FAYETTEVILLE BRANCH.

Station.	Dist.	Station.	Dist.
South Rocky Mt	0	Godwin	73.1
Sharpsburg	4.4	Wade	77.9
Elm City	8.9	Luray	83.6
Wilson	15.4	Fayetteville	89.3
Contentnea	18.6	Hope Mills	96.0
Lucama	23.6	Parkton	102.5
Penly	30.8	Rennert	109.8
Jerome	36.0	Bules	116.2
Selma	40.6	Pembroke	121.0
Smithfield	44.4	Elrod	126.3
Four Oaks	51.3	Rowland	132.4
Benson	59.5	Hamer, S. C	136.3
Dunn	65.6	Florence, S. C	172.3

SCOTLAND NECK AND KINSTON BRANCH.

Station.	Dist.	Station.	Dist.
Peuder	0	Parmele	42.80
Scotl'd N'ck "Y"	1	Grindool	46.30
Tillery	7.6	House	54.30
Spring Hill	11.6	Greenville	57.70
Scotland Neck	17.9	Ayden	67.20
Hobgood	24.60	Griffton	74.30
Goose Nest	31.50	Grainger's	79.90
Hassel	36.30	Kinston	85.90

TARBORO BRANCH.

Station.	Dist.	Station.	Dist.
Rocky Mount	0.0	Parmele	32.0
Rocky Mt "Y"	0.6	Robertsonville	35.2
Kingsboro	8.0	Everett	39.9
Hartsboro	9.4	Williamston	46.6
Tarboro	15.5	Johnson's	49.6
Mildred	20.2	Jamesville	57.0
Conetoe	23.2	Plymouth	68.1
Bethel	28.4		

WASHINGTON BRANCH.

Station.	Dist.	Station.	Dist.
Washington	0.0	Wichards	16.0
Wharton	5.1	Parmele	25.0
Pactolus	9.0		

CHERAW & DARLINGTON.

Station.	Dist.	Station.	Dist.
Wadesboro	0	Cash	31
Bennett	7	Darlington, S. C.	55
Morven	10	Florence, S. C.	65
McFarlan	14	15 miles in N. C.	
Cheraw, S. C	25		

MIDLAND NORTH CAROLINA.

Station.	Dist.	Station.	Dist.
Goldsboro	0.0	Holt's Mill	12.0
Copeland	4.8	Plius	17.5
Joyner	10.9	Smithfield	18.0

WILMINGTON, COLUMBIA AND AUGUSTA.

Station.	Dist.	Station.	Dist.
Wilmington	0	Waccamaw	35.9
Union Depot	1.0	Bogue	40.3
Hilton	1.7	Whiteville	46.3
Navassa	4.8	Chadbourn	53
Malmo	10.9	Cerro Gordo	59.4
Farmer	13.5	Fair Bluff	65.2
Brinkley	18.7	Pee Dee, S. C	87
Freeman	22.3	Florence, S. C.	110
Maxwell	28.6	68 miles in N. C.	
Springer's	33.7		

PETERSBURG.

Station.	Dist.	Station.	Dist.
Weldon	0	Pleasant Hill	8.2
S. & R. Junction	20	Petersburg, Va.	61.0
Gary's	27	Richmond, Va.	84.0

WILMINGTON, CHADBOURN AND CONWAY.

Station.	Dist.	Station.	Dist.
Hub	.00	Mount Tabor	24.00
Ilion	3.00	Conway, S. C	50.00
Chadbourn	11.00	26 miles in N. C.	
Clarendon	19 20		

NORFOLK AND CAROLINA.

Station.	Dist.	Station.	Dist.
Tarboro	0	Ahoskie	43
Hobgood	13	Tunis	52
Palmyra	17	Eure	56
Neal's	22	Gates	63
Kelford	27	Drum Hill	68
Aulander	34	Norfolk, Va	101
Early's	40		

SEABOARD AIR-LINE SYSTEM.

Officers.—R. C. Hoffman, President, Baltimore, Md.; E. St. John, Vice-President and General Manager, Portsmouth, Va.; John H. Sharp, Treasurer; V. E. McBee, Supt. and General Agent, Atlanta, Ga.; H. W. B. Glover, Traffic Manager; T. G. Anderson, General Passenger Agent, Portsmouth, Va. Total mileage in North Carolina, 607.79 miles.

SEABOARD AND ROANOKE.

Station.	Dist.	Station.	Dist.
Portsmouth, Va.	0	Gumberry	74
Roger's T. O., N.C	62	Gary's	78
Margarettsville	64	Weldon	80
Sanford	67	20 miles in N. C.	
Seaboard	70		

RALEIGH & GASTON.

Station.	Dist.	Station.	Dist.
Weldon	0	Henderson	55
Boling	7	Kittrell	63
Gaston	12	Franklinton	72
Summit	15	Youngsville	78
Littleton	21	Wake	83
Vaughn	27	Forestville	84
Macon	32	Wyatt	86
Warren Plains	37	Neuse	90
Ridgeway	42	Millbrook	94
Manson's	45	Raleigh	100
Middleburg	50	Louisburg (L. R.	
Greystone	52	R.)	82

MURFREESBORO.

Station.	Dist.	Station.	Dist.
Pendleton	0	Murfreesboro	6
Watson	3		

ROANOKE AND TAR RIVER.

Station.	Dist.	Station.	Dist.
Boykins, Va.	0	Woodland	19
Severn, N. C	5	McDonnell's Sid	21
Steamer's Siding	7	Rich Square	23
Pendleton	8	Taylor's Siding	25
Conway	11	Jenkln's Siding	26
White's Siding	12	Roxobel	28
Bridger's Siding	13	Kelford	30
Gravel Pit	15	Beverly	31
Potecasi	16	Turner's Siding	32
Truitt's	17	Lewiston	36
Lassiter's Siding	17		

RALEIGH & AUGUSTA AIR-LINE.

Station.	Dist.	Station.	Dist.
Raleigh	0	Manly	69
Cary	8	Southern Pines	70
Apex	14	Aberdeen	75
New Hill	21	Pine Bluff	76
Merry Oaks	26	Keyser	80
Moncure	31	Hoffman	87
Osgood	38	Hamlet	100
Colon	39	Ghio	105
Sanford	44	Gibson	110
Lemon Springs	51	Pittsboro (P.R.R)	43
Cameron	57	Carthage (C.R.R)	67
Vass	62		

DURHAM AND NORTHERN.

Station.	Dist.	Station.	Dist.
Henderson	0	Hester	20
Watkins	7	Creedmore	24
Dickerson's	10	Dutchville	28
Clay	13	Bennehan	29
Tar River	17	Durham	41

CAROLINA CENTRAL.

Station.	Dist.	Station.	Dist.
Wilmington	0	Edward's Mill	51
Meares	4	Bladenboro	53
Phenix	7	Yorkville	56
Northwest	14	Big Swamp	57
Crouly	17	Branch's X R'ds.	60
Armour	21	Allenton	62
Marlville	25	Lumberton	67
Council's	33	Barker's Cut	71
Jarvis	35	Pine Log	73
Rosindale	37	Moss Neck	76
Elkton	42	Pembroke	79
Clarkton	45	Pate's	80
Thompson's Mill	48	Red Banks	82
Abbottsburg	49	Alma	86

CAROLINA CENTRAL—Continued.

Station.	Dist.	Station.	Dist.
Maxton	88	Mathews	176
Southerland's	92	Wolf's	183
Laurinburg	95	Charlotte	187
Elmore	98	Paw Creek	194
Laurel Hill	100	Mt. Holly	198
Old Hundred	103	Stanley Creek	205
Powhatan	107	Iron	212
Beaman's Mill	108	Lincolnton	219
Hamlet	110	Crouse's	224
Rockingham	116	Cherryville	229
Midway	116	Waco	232
Pee Dee	124	Buffalo	236
Lilesville	130	Cleveland	237
Wadesboro	135	Shelby	241
Rackles	136	Lattimore	247
Polkton	143	Mooresboro	251
Peachland	147	Ellenboro	254
Beaver Dam	153	Allen's	255
Ames	157	Harrell's	258
Monroe	163	Bostic	261
Secrest's Mill	166	Forest City	263
Stout's	170	Roger's T. O	266
Indian Trail	173	Rutherfordton	267

GEORGIA, CAROLINA & NORTHERN.

Station.	Dist.	Station.	Dtsi.
Monroe	0	Osceola, S. C	17
Potter	8	Atlanta, Ga	268
Waxhaw	12	15 miles in N. C.	

PALMETTO.

Station.	Dist.	Station.	Dist.
Cheraw	0	Hamlet	18.2
Koilock	2.4	7.33 miles in N. C.	
Osborne	11.2		

SOUTHERN RAILWAY COMPANY.

Officers.—Samuel Spencer, President, New York; A. B. Andrews, 1st Vice-President, Raleigh, N. C.; W. H. Baldwin, 2d Vice-President; J. F. Hill, Secretary; H. C. Ansley, Treasurer; C. H. Hudson, Chief Engineer; W. H. Green, General Superintendent; J. M. Culp, Traffic Manager; W. A. Turk, General Passenger Agent; H. F. Smith, General Freight Agent, Washington, D. C. Total mileage in North Carolina, 1000.98.

ATLANTA & CHARLOTTE AIR-LINE.

Station.	Dist.	Station.	Dist.
Charlotte	0	Bessemer City	28.3
Lodo	4.9	Kings Mountain	33.4
Bellemont	11.4	Grove	41.4
Lowell	16.1	Atlanta	267.40
Gastonia	21.7	48 miles in N. C.	

ATLANTIC, TENNESSEE AND OHIO.

Station.	Dist.	Station.	Dist.
Charlotte	0	Mount Mourne	24.60
Derita	5.40	Mooresville	28.30
Croft	9.80	Shepherd's	32.20
Huntersville	14.90	Troutman's	38.30
Caldwell's	17.60	Statesville	44.00
Davidson	21.70		

ASHEVILLE & SPARTANBURG.

Station.	Dist.	Station.	Dist.
Spartanburg	0	Rutledge	57.3
Landrum, S. C	23.0	Arden	58.7
Tryon	26.6	Skyland	60.2
Melrose	32.4	Busbee	16.3
Saluda	35.3	Buena Vista	61.2
Flat Rock	41.1	Biltmore	67.4
Hendersonville	47.6	Asheville	69.4
Hillgirt	51.3	41 miles in N. C.	
Fletcher's	55.9		

CHARLOTTE, COLUMBIA & AUGUSTA.

Station.	Dist.	Station.	Dist.
Charlotte (Trade Street)	0	Catawba Riv. S.C	20.5
		Rock Hill, S. C.	25.00
Charlotte (South Switch)	0.6	Columbia (Union Depot)	109.3
Five-mile Siding	5.0	Keisler's	129.8
Pineville	10.4	10 miles in N. C.	
Fort Mill, S. C.	17.00		

HIGH POINT, RANDLEMAN, ASHBORO & SOUTHERN.

Station.	Eist.	Station.	Dist.
High Point	0	Randleman	18.9
Trinity	4.5	Spero	23.90
Glenola	9.4	Ashboro	27.7
Sophia	14.6		

NORTH CAROLINA.

Station.	Dist.	Station.	Dist.
Goldsboro	0	Haw River	103.9
Grant's	1.9	Graham	106.6
Asylum	3.1	Burlington	108.3
Rose	6.0	Elon College	113.0
Jones	9.9	Gibsonville	115.0
Princeton	12.0	McLeansville	121.7
Pine Level	17.8	Greensboro	129.7
Selma	20.5	Pomona	132.80
Wilson's Mills	26.0	Jamestown	139.90
Clayton	33.6	High Point	144.90
Auburn	39.6	Thomasville	151.50
Garner	42.8	Conrad's	157.20
Raleigh	48.5	Lexington	162.30
Method	51.8	Linwood	168.50
Asbury	54.8	Holtsburg	172.00
Cary	56.9	Salisbury	179.10
Morrisville	61.0	Sumner	183.70
Nelson's	65.7	China Grove	188.50
Brassfield	69.0	Glass	195.70
East Durham	73.0	Concord	201.50
Durham	74.7	Harrisburg	209.30
University	83.3	Newell's	214.70
Hillsboro	88.8	Air Line Junc.	221.20
Efland	92.7	C. C. Crossing	222.30
Mebane	98.0	Charlotte	222.70

NORTH CAROLINA MIDLAND.

Station.	Dist.	Station.	Dist.
Winston-Salem	0	Idols	13.7
Davis' School	2.2	Advance	16.6
Atwood	7.4	Cornatzer	21.1
Muddy Creek	10.0	Dutchman's Cr'k	22.8
Clemmonsville	12.4	Mocksville	26.7

NORTH-WESTERN NORTH CAROLINA.

Station.	Dist.	Station.	Dist.
Greensboro	0	Tobaccoville	45.9
Pomona	3.0	Donnaha	50.5
Terra Cotta	4.2	Teagues	54.1
Guilford College	6.5	Shoals	56.7
Friendship	9.9	Siloam	60.8
Kernersville	17.4	Rockford	67.4
Winston-Salem	28.7	Crutchfield	73.3
Tice's	30.3	Birch	77.5
Alspaugh	32.6	Elkin	83.7
Hanes' Rock Sid	34.0	Ronda	89.6
Old Town Siding	35.0	Roaring River	94.0
Miller's Siding	35.5	Pioche	96.6
Brickyard Sidl'g	35.8	Quarry	97.8
Bethania	36.1	Smith's Siding	98.6
Rural Hall	41.3	Wilkesboro	103.2

OXFORD & CLARKSVILLE.

Station.	Dist.	Station.	Dist.
Keysville, Va	0	Oxford	55.3
Clarksville, Va	31.3	Providence	61.1
Soudan, Va	36.4	Stem's	66.8
Bullock's, N. C.	42.1	Lyon's	70.2
Stovall	45.4	Wilkins	72.4
48-Mile Siding	48.0	Green's	75.3
Gregory's	48.7	Elerbee	78.0
Lewis	50.6	Holloway	80.3
Rock Siding	53.0	Durham	87.8
O. & H. Junction	54.5	49 miles in N. C.	

PIEDMONT.

Station.	Dist.	Station.	Dist.
Richmond, Va	0	Yates	162
North Danville	140	Reidsville	164.7
Junction	140.2	Mizpah	168
Danville	140.6	Benaja	173.6
Stokesland	145.7	Brown's Sum'lt	177.1
Pelham, N. C.	149.3	Morehead	180.8
Ruffin	155.6	Greensboro	189
Stacy	158	43 miles in N. C.	

STATESVILLE & WESTERN.

Station.	Dist.	Station.	Dist.
Statesville	0	Sloan	11
Iredell	6	Hiddenite	15
Scott's	9	Taylorsville	20

STATE UNIVERSITY.

Station.	Dist.	Station.	Dist.
Chapel Hill	0	Duke's Siding	9
Robson	6.2	University Sta	10.2

OXFORD & HENDERSON.

Station.	Dist.	Station.	Dist.
Oxford	0	Dabney	7.7
Horner's	3.2	Henderson	13
Huntsboro	5		

WESTERN NORTH CAROLINA.

Station.	Dist.	Station.	Dist.
Salisbury	0	Dendron	114.50
Majolica	5	Round Knob	115.30
Kincaid	8	Childs	117.50
Cleveland	13.4	Mud Cut	118.70
Elmwood	18.4	Swan Tunnel	122
Gilbert's	18.90	Terrell	122.70
Statesvile	25.6	Black Mount'n	124.60
Plott's	32.8	Cooper's	129.30
Erminie	37	Azalea	130.80
Catawba	38.4	Biltmore	135.50
Claremont	42.5	Asheville	140.50
Newton	47.7	Murphy Junc.	141.70
Conover	49.40	Montford	143
Hickory	57.10	Olivette	147.60
Hildebran	61.50	Alexander	152
Connelly's Sp'gs	67.40	Rollins	161.60
Drexel	73.50	Marshall	162.80
Morganton	78	Barnard	170.40
Calvin	81.50	Stewart's	172.30
Glen Alpine	84	Sandy Bottom	172.60
Bridgewater	88.90	Stackhouse	174.80
Nebo	93.80	Hot Springs	178.70
Marion	99.20	Limebrook	181.70
Greenlee	104.90	Paint Rock	184.90
Old Fort	110.00		

WESTERN NORTH CAROLINA—MURPHY DIVISION.

Station.	Dist.	Station.	Dist.
Asheville	0	Wilmot	54.7
Murphy Jun	1.2	Whittier	58.6
Emma	2.2	Bryson City	65.1
Sulphur Springs	4.8	Epps' Spring	69.7
Hominy	8.7	Bushnell	77.6
Luther's	12.2	Welch	81.2
Turnpike	14	Almond	84.10
Carmen	18	Wesser Creek	89.3
Canton	18.7	Hewitt	93.7
Clyde	22.5	Nantahala	95.80
Waynesville	28.4	Jarrett's	95.8
Moody's	28 9	Topton	99.7
Cole's	29.50	Rhodo	103.1
Balsam	36.3	Andrews	108 2
Hall	40.7	Hiwassee	114
Addie	43	Talc Mills	117
Sylva	47.4	Tomotla	117.8
Dillsboro	48.9	Murphy	123.6
Barker's Creek	49.4		

YADKIN.

Station.	Dist.	Station.	Dist.
Salisbury	0	Richfield	21
Granite Quarry	5	New London	24
Rockwell	10.3	Albemarle	30.9
Gold Hill	15.0	Norwood	41
Misenheimer Springs	19		

MISCELLANEOUS ROADS.

ATLANTIC AND NORTH CAROLINA RAILROAD COMPANY.

Officers.—W. S. Chadwick, President; F. C. Roberts, Secretary and Treasurer; S. L. Dill, Auditor, G. F. and P. A. and Superintendent; W. K. Styron, Assistant Auditor, Newbern, N. C.

Station.	Dist.	Station.	Dist.
Goldsboro	0	Newbern	59
Best's	9	Riverdale	68
LaGrange	14	Croatan	70
Falling Creek	20	Havelock	76
Kinston	26	Newport	84
Caswell	30	Wildwood	87
Dover	35	Atlantic	89
Core Creek	42	Morehead City	93¾
Tuscarora	48	Atlantic Hotel	94
Clark's	51	Morehead Depot	95

ATLANTIC AND DANVILLE RAILROAD COMPANY.

Officers.—B. Newgass, President; Adam Tredwell, Secretary and Treasurer; Charles O. Haines, Superintendent, etc., Norfolk, Va.

Station.	Dist.	Station.	Dist.
Alton	0	Milton	17
Cuningham	6	Blanche	23
Semora	11		

ABERDEEN AND ROCKFISH RAILROAD COMPANY.

Officers.—John Blue, President; N. S. Blue, Secretary, Aberdeen; John Blue, General Manager, etc.

Station.	Dist.	Station.	Dist.
Aberdeen	0	Buffalo	
Leavitt's		Endor	12.75
Hilton			

CAPE FEAR AND YADKIN VALLEY RAILWAY COMPANY.

Officers.—John Gill, Receiver, Baltimore, Md.; W. A. Lash, President; J. W. Fry, General Manager, Greensboro, N. C.

Station.	Dist.	Station.	Dist.
Mount Airy	0	Goldston	117
Ararat	9	Gulf	121
Pilot Mountain	15	Egypt	124
Pinnacle	20	Sanford	130
Dalton	22	Jonesboro	133
Rural Hall	30	Swann's	138
Germanton	35	Spout Spring	147
Walnut Cove	40	Manchester	154
Belew's Creek	46	Fayetteville	176
Stokesdale	52	Stedman	177
Summerfield	58	Autryville	180
Battle Ground	64	Roseboro	188
Greensboro	70	Parkersburg	197
Pleasant Garden	78	Garland	202
Climax	83	Tomahawk	208
Julian	86	Kerr	212
Liberty	93	Granhoe	217
Staley	98	Atkinson	224
Siler City	105	Currie	230
Ore Hill	109	Wilmington	248
Richmond	114		

MADISON BRANCH.

Station.	Dist.
Madison	63
Ellisboro	59

FACTORY BRANCH.

Station.	Dist.	Station.	Dist.
Ramseur	101	Cedar Falls	97
Franklinsville	98	Millboro	93

SOUTH CAROLINA BRANCH.

Station.	Dist.	Station.	Dist.
Bennettsville	223	Floral College	199
Tatum	217	Wakulla	195
McCall	214	Red Springs	190
Hasty	210	Shandon	187
John's	208	Lumber Bridge	182
Stuart	206	McNatt's	179
Maxton	202	Hope Mills	173

ABERDEEN AND WEST END RAILROAD COMPANY.

Officers.—A. F. Page, President; Robert N. Page, Secretary and Treasurer; Junius R. Page, General Superintendent; Henry A. Page, G. F. and T. Agent, Aberdeen.

Station.	Dist.	Station.	Dist.
Aberdeen	0	Candor	25
Linden	7	Troy	38
West End	13	Star	33
Eagle Springs	20	Asheboro	56

CARTHAGE RAILROAD.

Officers.—J. C. Black, President; W. J. Adams, Secretary; W. C. Petty, General Manager, Carthage.

Station.	Dist.	Station.	Dist.
Cameron	0	Hannon	17.10
Kelly	6.30	Curriesville	21.00
Carthage	10.00		

CALDWELL AND NORTHERN.

Officers.—Wm. Harvey, President; Geo. W. Lex, Secretary, Philadelphia, Pa.; John M. Bernhardt, Superintendent, Lenoir, N. C.

Station.	Dist.
Lenoir	0
Collettsville	10.66

CHESTER AND LENOIR RAILROAD COMPANY.

Officers.—G. W. F. Harper, President, Lenoir, N. C.; J. J. McLure, Secretary, Chester, S. C.

Station.	Dist.	Station.	Dist.
Chester, S. C.	0	Newton	80
Crowder Creek	39	Hickory	90
Gastonia	45	Granite Falls	98
Dallas	50	Saw Mills	101
Hardin's	56	Hudson	103
Lincolnton	64	Lenoir	110
Maiden	72	62 miles in N. C.	

JAMESVILLE AND WASHINGTON.

Station.	Dist.
Washington	0
Cherry's	6

EAST TENNESSEE AND WESTERN NORTH CAROLINA RAILROAD COMPANY.

Frank Firmstone, President, Philadelphia, Pennsylvania.

Station.	Dist.
Cranberry	0
State Line	3
Johnson City, Tenn	34

EGYPT RAILWAY COMPANY.

Samuel A. Henszey, Pres., Cumnock, N. C.

Station.	Dist.	Station.	Dist.
Egypt Junction	0	Endor	5.5
Lobdell	1.3	Oakdale	6.0
Millport	2.2	River Point	6.5
Clarendon	3.0	Egypt, Fourth St.	7.0
Boudinot	4.5	Egypt, Myrtle St.	8.0

GLENDON AND GULF RAILROAD COMPANY.

John B. Leming, Pres., Bridesbury, Pa.

Station.	Dist.	Station.	Dist.
Gulf	0	Haw Branch	7
Palmer	3	Riverside	8
Carbonton	5	Glendon	10

HENDERSONVILLE AND BREVARD RAILWAY T. & T. COMPANY.

A. E. Boardman, Presid't, Brevard, N. C.

Station.	Dist.	Station.	Dist.
Hendersonville	0	Penrose	8.2
Horse Shoe	1.1	Davidson River	0
Cannon	1.7	Brevard	3.5
Morey	4.8		

NORFOLK AND WESTERN RAILROAD COMPANY.

F. J. Kimball, Receiver, Philadelphia, Pa.

LYNCHBURG AND DURHAM DIVISION.

Station.	Dist.	Station.	Dist.
Durham	0	Woodsdale	39
Fairntosh	10	Denniston Junc-	
Willardsville	12	tion, Va	44
Ballton	14	Black Walnut	48
Lyndour	20	South Boston	55
Helena	24	Lynchburg	115
Roxboro	32	43.40 miles in N. C.	

ROANOKE AND SOUTHERN DIVISION.

Station.	Dist.	Station.	Dist.
Winston-Salem	0	Madison	32
Ogburn	4	Stoneville	40
Walkertown	9	Price-State Line.	46
Dennis	12	Ridgeway, Va.	50
Fulp	15	Martinsville	60
Walnut Cove	18	Roanoke	122
Ladford	24		

MOORE COUNTY RAILROAD COMPANY.

W. B. Eckhout, Gen. Manager and Treas.

Station.	Dist.	Station.	Dist.
Aberdeen	0	Craigrownie	12.50
Flynn	9		

MARIETTA AND NORTH GEORGIA RAILROAD COMPANY.

J. B. Glover, Receiver and General Manager, Marietta, Ga.

Station.	Dist.	Station.	Dist.
Marietta, Ga	0	Kinsey's	102
State Line, N. C.	94	Murphy	108
Culberson	97	13.25 miles in N. C.	
Notla	100		

NORTHAMPTON AND HERTFORD RAILWAY COMPANY.

J. S. Clark, President, 18 Broadway, N. Y.

Station.	Dist.
Gumberry	0
Jackson	9

NORFOLK AND SOUTHERN RAILWAY COMPANY.

Officers.—W. B. Dickerman, President, New York City; H. C. Hudgins, G. F. and P. Agent, Norfolk, Va.

Station.	Dist.	Station.	Dist.
Norfolk, Va	0	Gregory's	37
Moyock, N. C	25	Belcross	40
Snowden	31	Camden	42
Shawboro	35	Elizabeth City	45

NORFOLK & SOUTHERN—Continued.

Station.	Dist.	Station.	Dist.
Pasquotank	52	Mackey's Ferry	83
Okisko	53	Chesson	85
Chapanoke	55	Roper	88
Winfall	60	Turnpike	99
Perquimans	61	Bishop Cross	100
Hertford	62	Pantego	103
Yeopim	66	Belhaven	106
Edenton	74	83 miles in N. C.	

OHIO RIVER AND CHARLESTON RAILWAY COMPANY.

Sam. J. Hunt, President, Cincinnati, Ohio.

Station.	Dist.	Station.	Dist.
Marion	0	Forest City	31.2
Gardner's	5	Henrietta	39
Glenwood	7	Mooresboro	43
Weaver's	14	Shelby	55
Golden Valley	15	Blacksburg	68
Millwood	20	64.50 miles in N. C.	
Rutherfordton	25		

WARRENTON RAILROAD COMPANY.

W. J. White, Pres., Warrenton, N. C.

Station.	Dist.
Plains	0
Warrenton	8

NEW HANOVER TRANSIT COMPANY.

Station.	Dist.
Wilmington	0
Carolina Beach	8

SUFFOLK AND CAROLINA RAILWAY COMPANY.

Wm. H. Bosley, Pres., Baltimore, Md.

Station.	Dist.	Station.	Dist.
Suffolk	0	Hobbs	32
Corapeake — State		Gliden	34
Line	15	Ryland	37
Dennis	19	Chowan	69
Sunberry	22	Montrose Landing	40
Cross	23	25 miles in N. C.	
Bosley	26		

WILMINGTON, NEWBERN AND NORFOLK RAILWAY COMPANY.

Officers.—Thos. A. McIntyre, Pres., New York City; J. W. Martenis, Manager.

Station.	Dist.	Station.	Dist.
Wilmington	0	Edgecombe	27.21
Coast Railroad		Mineral Springs	31.36
Crossing	2.18	Folkstone	34.66
Baymead	8.29	Cedarhurst	40.37
Kirkland	11.36	Winona	44.17
Scott's Hill	15.42	Jacksonville	50.15
Ocean View	14.28	Northeast	56.15
Hampstead	16.50	White Oak	61.85
Cypress Lake	18.84	Maysville	66.15
Armandale	20.66	Ravenswood	71.41
Big Sandy Run	22.29	Pollocksville	78.59
Glenoe	23.51	Newbern	87.25

WILMINGTON SEACOAST RAILROAD COMPANY.

Geo. R. French, Pres., Wilmington, N. C.

Station.	Dist.
Wilmington	0
Hammocks	10.21
Atlantic	11.82

WINTON RAILROAD COMPANY.

P. D. Camp, Pres., Franklin, Va.

Station.	Dist.
St. John's	0
Winton	15

CASHIE AND CHOWAN RAILROAD.

Greenleaf Johnson, Pres., Norfolk, Va.

DANVILLE, MOCKSVILLE & SOUTHEASTERN RAILROAD COMPANY.

Thomas R. Sharp, President, Sharp, N. C.

LAUREL RIVER AND HOT SPRINGS RAILROAD COMPANY.

J. Wyman, President, Lynn, Mass.

WELLINGTON AND POWELLSVILLE RAILROAD COMPANY.

J. W. Branning, President, Edenton, N. C.

FORSYTH COUNTY'S NEW COURT-HOUSE.

INDEX TO ADVERTISEMENTS

OF PROMINENT FIRMS.

Branson

Branson, North Carolina

Business Directory

Business Directory of North Carolina

Business Advertisements

THE BUSINESS MAN

Will find the most progressive towns and cities in which to locate, on the line of THE SOUTHERN RAILWAY.

Investor and Speculator

Will find the best opportunities along the line of THE SOUTHERN RAILWAY

The Agriculturist and Horticulturist

Will find the best and cheapest lands along the line of THE SOUTHERN RAILWAY.

The Manufacturer

Will find the most desirable sites for his factory in the territories reached by THE SOUTHERN RAILWAY.

The Health and Home Seeker

Will find that THE SOUTHERN RAILWAY reaches the most healthful and inviting sections of the South.

The Best Openings

For all are found along the line of THE SOUTHERN RAILWAY.

Information (how to get it).

Call upon any agent of THE SOUTHERN RAILWAY, or the leading citizens of any city or town on THE SOUTHERN.

If you are not satisfied, and desire detailed information and facts about the South, call on or address M. V. RICHARDS, Land and Industrial Agent THE SOUTHERN RAILWAY, Washington, D. C.

ROUND KNOB (WESTERN NORTH CAROLINA) ON THE SOUTHERN RAILWAY.

SOUTHERN
RAILWAY.

The National Highway between the North and the South, and offering magnificent Passenger Train Service. . . . .

Operating the Famous——

"Washington and Southwestern Limited,"
"United States Fast Mail,"
"Washington and Chattanooga Limited,"
and "Norfolk and Chattanooga Limited."

The Scenic Route of the World—through Western North Carolina—the glorious "Land of the Sky."

THE SHORT LINE TO FLORIDA.

Pullman Palace Cars between all Principal Points.

Apply to any ticket agent or representative of the Passenger Department for full information relative to tickets, schedules, etc., or address the General Passenger Agent.

W. H. GREEN,	J. M. CULP,	W. A. TURK,
General Superintendent.	Traffic Manager.	General Passenger Agent.

General Offices: 1300 PENNSYLVANIA AVENUE, WASHINGTON, D. C.

WHY NOT BE UP-TO-DATE?

S. A. L.

THE SEABOARD AIR LINE

Traverses the Beautiful Piedmont Country of the Carolinas and Georgia, and offers the Best Facilities of Transit between the Atlantic Ports and the South, West, Pacific Coast and Mexico.

Pursuing a Wise and Liberal Policy, its Management Seeks the Larger Development of the Territory on its Lines, which means the addition of Incalculable Wealth to the South.

Practical Farmers are Especially Invited to settle along its Lines. Lands here combine with Cheapness, Extraordinary Advantages of Soil, Climate, Water, Timber, Stone and Convenient Markets.

Superadded to the excellent service on its own railway, the SEABOARD AIR LINE commands the superior advantages afforded by a splendid and perfect system of water communications extending in close connection with its trains to and from the principal northern cities. The magnificent harbor of Norfolk-Portsmouth is the converging and departing point for scores of the finest steamers in the world. The vessels of the larger companies are splendid sea-going steamships elegantly furnished for the conveyance of passengers, with superior accommodations for the transfer of large cargoes and consignments. Daily these vessels are moored alongside the numerous wharves of the SEA-BOARD.

The advantages of such a complete and comprehensive water system working in harmony with so prompt and reliable a land carrier as the SEABOARD AIR LINE, are obvious. Fruits, berries, melons, garden truck and perishable stuff reach their destination in better condition, and will command better prices than if jolted and pounded by railway transport over the same distance.

The Seaboard Air Line Territory.

Dense groves of pine and hardwood trees, heavily clothed with verdure and clinging vines, alternate with fields of tobacco, cotton, corn, peas and oats. The soil, no matter how light or sandy, is notably rich in the elements of luxuriant vegetation, and two-thirds of it still open to cultivation.

The Piedmont section, that high, undulating plateau which separates the lowlands of the coast from the western or mountain section, shares with Italy its characteristic sunny skies and delightful climate. It is watered by several large rivers, many creeks and innumerable living springs, while the average rain-fall (from forty to fifty-two inches) is so seasonable and equally distributed that droughts of serious detriment are unknown.

Cotton, corn, tobacco, fruits and vegetables yield abundant crops in this territory, but certain portions of it are peculiarly adopted to special forms of plant life. The trucking lands around Portsmouth for ten miles out (and it might be made fifty miles) constitute a series of rich vegetable gardens, the sales from which approximate $8,000,000 annually. The same field here will produce five crops in one season. After kale is shipped, cucumbers and peas are planted in alternate rows. When they are marketed and the vines plowed under, grass springs up and a crop of hay is gathered, after which fall potatoes are dropped. The strawberry crop is also early and profitable.

For sixty miles along the road from Wilmington, truck farmers make two crops of Irish and sweet potatoes, peas, beans, cabbage, tomatoes and peanuts per year from the same land, the season coming in between that of Florida and Norfolk. In the vicinity of Raleigh and Charlotte and other cities, as well as in many flourishing smaller towns, trucking in connection with poultry raising is very profitable, with future possibilities practically unlimited.

Tobacco and Hop Lands.

The SEABOARD AIR LINE passes through the finest tobacco lands in the South, on which the most wonderful results have been attained. The heart of this paradise, producing the famous "golden leaf" (the best and highest priced grade in the world is penetrated by the railway lines from Weldon to Raleigh, with the forty-two mile branch from Henderson to Durham and by the branch lines to Warrenton and Louisburg.

The yield of the "golden leaf" and the prices it commands are remarkable. From $300 to $450 an acre is an average profit. Improved farms have reimbursed purchasers their entire cost from the profits of the first season's crop.

Hop growing, a new and important industry in North Carolina, has proved a success, and is destined to fill a formost place among useful products. Subjected to every known test by experienced hop growers, it has been found that in certain Carolina fields adjacent to the SEABOARD AIR LINE the yield is equal to that in the west, while it is richer in lupuline and possesses a much finer aroma than any other American hop. The cost of production is less than one-half that of New York, and not more than half the cost in the most favored localities on the Pacific coast. Hop culture has come south to stay.

This middle section blends the soils of both the eastern and western divisions, and is so diversified that, with its favorable climatic conditions, it offers the widest range of agricultural possibilities. It is here that the culture of cotton is largely extended, and coal, building-stone and minerals are found. Coal abounds, but its mining on a commercial scale has been limited to Egypt, in Chatham county, where the annual output is 350,000 tons of a quality superior to the Pocahontas and many other coals.

Cotton Manufacturing.

In North Carolina 149 cotton mills are now in operation, representing 19,000 looms and 756,000 spindles. But these cotton and wool mills, successful as they have proved, are but the vanguard of what is to follow. The *Manufacturers' Record* (which is good authority on all southern interests) declares that "the largest future possibilities for the profitable development of cotton industries are located in the Piedmont section in the Carolinas and Georgia, which is tributary to the SEABOARD AIR LINE SYSTEM." The territory thus outlined is about 500 miles long by 100 to 150 miles wide, covering an area of 50,000 to 60,000 square miles. Within this circumscribed limit, the *Record* locates the "future situs of the cotton manufacturing of the south, and 'that mean' [it adds] so far as human foresight can predict, the future situs of the cotton manufacturing of the world." Among the reasons adduced in support of this prediction and belief are: Elevation above sea level; abundant and cheap water power and coal; a plentiful supply of native American operatives; cost of labor, because of low cost of living; unsurpassed healthfulness; cotton supply at hand, and cheap and abundant transportation to the markets of the world."

Fruits and Fruit Lands.

Peaches, pears, plums, apricots, figs, apples, grapes and berries grow profusely all over the Carolinas and Georgia. It has been found, by practical experience, that the elevated sand-hill region in the long-leaf pine belt between Sanford and Hamlet, on the SEABOARD AIR LINE, is a most prolific producer of fruits of various kinds. The peaches, pears, plums and grapes of the Niagara and Deleware variety, and blackberries, make large yields, which are distinguished alike for their size, firm texture and delicious flavor. Orchards and vineyards have been planted at Southern Pines, Manly and Pine Bluff, and the fruitage has brought the highest prices from Northern dealers. One farm of 360 acres, within three miles of Southern Pines, mostly planted in peaches, has returned its owner this season a profit of $8,063.51 over all expenses. Orchards of less size have done as well in proportion. The net profits of the grape yield were also more than satisfactory. The first Delaware shipments this season sold in New York at twenty cents a pound. Black berries produced 3,000 to 5,000 quarts per acre, on which the profit was four to six cents a quart. The net profit on grapes was five cents per pound. The "scuppernong" grape is indigenous, and, like a banyan, spreads over an immense area. It is not a table grape, but the wine from it can hardly be excelled for body and flavor.

Cereals and Grasses, Sanitary Resorts, Etc.

Though cotton, tobacco, garden truck, and (latterly) fruits are the leading money crops, North Carolina, in proportion to her population, has not lagged in the production of cereals and grasses. In 1894 the harvest of rye from 13,110 acres was 478,017 bushels; of hay, 164,525 acres, 228,561 tons; of potatoes, 17,955 acres, 1,113,210 bushels; of wheat, 695,147 acres, 3,475,725 bushels; of corn, 2,259,663 acres, 22,939,484 bushels, and of oats from 527,892 acres, 5,754,024 bushels. This total will be largely exceeded, in some instances doubled, in the summarized reports for 1895.

Almost the entire State of North Carolina is one vast sanitarium. Scores of places on the SEABOARD AIR LINE are welcome resorts to those in search of rest and recreation. The odors of the pine forests are balsam for sore lungs. Wild game and fish in most localities tempt the sportsman. The summer temperature cooled by ocean breezes blowing inland, is never excessively hot, and the nights are refreshingly cool. Any tendency to extreme cold in the winter season is sensibly modified by the Gulf Stream. The climate is at all seasons exhilarating and soothing, invigorating and mild; a happy medium between the rigorous Northern winters and the enervating summers of the far South. Other sanitary accessories are numerous. Mineral springs abound everywhere, many of them noted far and near for their medicinal efficacy. Southern Pines, by reason of its altitude, perfect drainage, sandy soil, pure water and curative ozone, exhaled from long leaf pines, is especially favored, both as a resort and permanent abiding place. Numerous summer visitors go to localities in the western section and find health in its mountain air, forests and streams.

All communications in regard to lands, or the investment of capital in the South should be addressed to

GEO. L. RHODES, General Agent, Portsmouth, Va.

SOME OF THE PEOPLE WHO WORKED ON THE NORTH CAROLINA BUSINESS DIRECTORY FOR 1896.

LEVI BRANSON, A. M......................Compiler and Publisher.
MRS. EDITH C. BRANSON.....................Copyist and Assistant Editor
MISS DAISY BRANSON........................Copyist and Assistant.
EDWARDS & BROUGHTON.....................Job Printers and Binders.
T. J. BASHFORD ....Bookkeeper.
CHAS. C. HERVEY ....Clerk.
EDGAR E. BROUGHTON......................Clerk.
E. S. CHEEK ....Foreman.
MAXWELL J. GORMAN.......................Proof Reader.
MISS MAMIE EDWARDS......................Assistant Proof Reader.
JAS. C. BIRDSONG..........................Make-up.
R. E. LEE................................Make-up.
CHAS. D. CHRISTOPHERS ....Compositor.
S. L. NICHOLS............................Compositor.
C. J. BETTS ....Compositor.
L. W. SMITH.............................Compositor.
W. C. UZZLE ....Compositor.
CHARLES H. JONES ....Compositor.
PAL. VAUGHAN............................Compositor.
JOHN W. CHEEK..........................Foreman Job Department
ED. C. OWEN............................Compositor.
THOS. W. ADAMS.........................Compositor.
C. R. THOMAS...........................Apprentice.
H. E. UPCHURCH ....Pressman.
EUGENE ROGERS.........................Pressman.
GEORGE C. DICKINSON...................Pressman.
SIMEON SMITH ....Pressman.
JOHN H. RHODES (col.)..................Pressman.
MRS. C. H. LEWELLYN....................Forewoman of Folding Room
MISS BARBARA ADAMS....................Book Folder.
MISS MINNIE WARREN....................Book Folder.
MISS ALICE TANT.......................Book Folder.
MISS IDA BROUGHTON....................Book Folder.
MISS NANNIE EDWARDS..................Book Folder.
MISS BEULAH THOMPSON................Book Folder.
W. H. MILLER ....Foreman of Bindery
W. E. BAILEY.........................Journeyman Binder.
JAMES M. WARREN ....Journeyman Binder.
E. WALTER EDWARDS..................Journeyman Binder.
ALEX. ELLERBEE.....................Apprentice Binder.
ARTHUR BASHFORD...................Apprentice Binder.
J. P. MEDLIN.......................Ruler.
MISS ROSA FERRELL.................Feeder of Ruling Machine
LEWIS BASHFORD..................Assistant.

ALSO MORE THAN ONE HUNDRED CORRESPONDENTS.

TESTIMONIALS

ABOUT

Branson's North Carolina Business Directory.

I find Branson's Directory very valuable as a book of reference in this office, in fact almost indispensible, and am pleased to know a revised and enlarged edition will soon be issued.
April 1, 1895. ELIAS CARR, *Governor.*

I have found Branson's Directory a very useful book to me as a public officer. My opinion is that it is a good book for any family or for any business man, in many directions. JOHN C. SCARBOROUGH,
Raleigh, N. C., April 6, 1895. *State Supt. Public Instruction.*

MR. LEVI BRANSON.
Dear Sir:—It gives me great pleasure to say that I consider your Directory as almost indispensable to a public officer of this State.
Raleigh, April 6, 1895. F. I. OSBORNE, *Attorney General.*

I am pleased to say I consider Mr. Levi Branson's Directory a splendid reference book for all public officers. W. H. WORTH.
Raleigh, N. C., April 6, 1895. *State Treasurer.*

I have always found Branson's N. C. Directory an exceedingly accurate and useful reference book—a necessity in my office. C. M. BUSBEE,
Raleigh, N. C., April 8, 1895. *Postmaster.*

I know, from experience, that Branson's Directory of North Carolina is of great benefit to any man in official position, or conducting any business in which general correspondence is required. For newspapers it is an indispensable publication in this State. H. W. AYER,
Raleigh, N. C., April 8, 1895. *Sec. Raleigh Cham. of Commerce.*

LEVI BRANSON.
Dear Sir:—It gives me great pleasure to say that I consider your Directory almost indispensable to me as Sheriff, and cannot see how any public officer can do without one of them. M. W. PAGE,
Raleigh, N. C., April 8, 1895. *Sheriff.*

DR. LEVI BRANSON.
Dear Sir:—Permit me to say that we have used your Directory for years, and cannot get along without it. I cannot see how any public officer or business man can do without one. THOMAS BADGER,
April 9, 1895. *Mayor of City of Raleigh.*

DR. BRANSON:—I am glad to learn that it is your intention to issue a revised edition of your N. C. Business Directory, as I have found it of great use in this office. C. D. HEARTT,
Raleigh, N. C., April 9, 1895. *Chief of Police.*

Dear Sir:—Branson's Directory has been of much use to me in the past, and I am glad to know you are to issue a revised edition of it.
April 9, 1895. Very truly, S. A. ASHE,
Attorney at Law.

We have subscribed in the past to Branson's Directories and have considered them valuable for purposes of reference. W. S. PRIMROSE.
Raleigh, N. C., April 11, 1895. *President N. C. Home Ins. Co.*

We have, for many years, considered Branson's Directory an indispensable aid in conducting our business. N. C. BOOK CO.,
Raleigh, N. C., April 11, 1895. E. G. HARRELL, *Manager.*

We have used Branson's N. C. Business Directory since it was first published, and found it of much practical use, as it contains much condensed information.
Raleigh, N. C., April 15, 1895. JONES & POWELL.

I am pleased to say that, for a number of years, I used Branson's Directory of North Carolina to great advantage, and have subscribed for a copy of the eighth edition. GEORGE ALLEN,
Raleigh, N. C., April 15, 1895. Real Estate Dealer.

The work of Dr. Branson in exhibiting the department of labor in towns, as well as in the State, has been well done for a number of years. His late work is equally meritorious as any preceding one, if not better. The State cannot afford to lose any opportunity to recognize that which advertises its attractions. I so recognize the work of Dr. Branson. ROBT. M. FURMAN,
Raleigh, N. C., April 5, 1895. State Auditor,

I have known and used Branson's N. C. Business Directory for years, and do not know anything equal to it for office use in this State. I am glad to know Mr. Branson will soon issue a revised and enlarged edition. It is one of the very best books of its kind. D. H. YOUNG,
April 6, 1895. Clerk Superior Court of Wake County.

The Yarboro House has used Mr. Branson's Directories for many years, and considers them very valuable to any business man. L. T. BROWN,
Raleigh, N. C., April 8, 1895. Proprietor Yarboro House.

I feel the need every day of a first class, reliable, new directory of North Carolina, and am glad to know that Rev. L. Branson, D. D., is going to issue such a Directory soon. Every citizen ought to give assistance in order to make it represent the growth and progress of the State. JOSEPHUS DANIELS,
Raleigh, N. C., April 15, 1895. Editor News and Observer.

Branson's Directory fills a place that no other publication in North Carolina attempts, and the information given in the Directory is of great value to our professional and business men, and to public officers. We shall be glad to receive the coming edition. EDWARDS & BROUGHTON,
Raleigh, N. C., April 16, 1895. Publishers and Printers.

I believe this Directory will prove a very useful book, and have subscribed for same. JNO. T. PULLEN,
April 16, 1895. Cashier Raleigh Savings Bank.

We have used Branson's Business Directory continuously since its first publication, and find it of great value and use in our business. We are very glad to know it is to be revised and enlarged.
April 16, 1895. W. H. & R. S. TUCKER & Co.

I believe Branson's Directory will be very useful to any man in official or business position, where his duties require of him a knowledge of persons in the various businesses, professions and callings throughout the State of North Carolina. W. L. CUNINGGIM,
Wilmington, N. C., April 19, 1895. Pastor 5th St. Meth. E. Ch., South.

We have found Branson's Directory reliable as a reference book and useful as such. It contains much important information connected with the business interests of North Carolina. WORTH & WORTH,
Wilmington, N. C., April 22, 1895. Commission Merchants.

Often in my correspondence has Branson's State Directory been a friend indeed in time of need, giving me the names or post-offices or location of some man in business. I really appreciate it as a reference book.
April 29, 1895. D. H. TUTTLE,
Pastor Central M. E. Church, Raleigh, N. C.

We consider Branson's Directory a fine advertising medium, and a book of useful reference. WHITING BROS.,
Raleigh, N. C., April 29, 1895. Clothing Merchants.

I have used the Directories gotten up by Dr. Branson for years past; am glad to hear that he is going to get out a new edition. It is a work almost indispensable to every business man. J. J. THOMAS,
April 30, 1895. Pres. Com. and Farmers' Bank, Raleigh, N. C.

I have known Branson's Directory of North Carolina for many years, and have always found it trustworthy and useful to all classes of business men. It gives me pleasure to recommend it. ALEX. Q. HOLLADAY,
April 30, 1895. *Pres. of N. C. A. and M. College, West Raleigh, N. C.*

I feel that Branson's Directory can be made very useful in the life insurance business, and therefore ordered the forthcoming edition.
J. D. BOUSHALL, *Gen. Agt. Ætna Life, Raleigh, N. C.*

I consider Branson's Directory almost indispensable to a business man doing a general business. It contains a great deal of valuable information well condensed. JOHN C. DREWRY.
May 14, 1895. *State Agent for Mutual Benefit Life Ins. Co.*

I have been using Branson's State Directory for twenty years or more, and find it of great value for office reference in my office.
Pomona, N. C., May 14, 1895. J. VAN LINDLEY.

Dr. Branson's large experience in preparing directories enables him to furnish a very comprehensive and useful book, which is of great service and is trustworthy as a book of reference. JOS. G. BROWN,
May 27, 1895. *President Citizens National Bank.*

I have used Branson's North Carolina Business Directory for the last eight or ten years and find it very useful in my practice. I have this day renewed my subscription. B. C. BECKWITH,
Raleigh, N. C., May 29, 1895. *Attorney at Law.*

I do not hesitate to give Branson's North Carolina Business Directory my unqualified recommendation. JOHN W. HINSDALE,
Raleigh, N. C., June 10, 1895. *Attorney at Law.*

I have used Dr. Branson's Directory for many years, and have found it a very accurate and useful book. W. J. YOUNG,
Raleigh, N. C., June 10, 1895. *Principal of Inst. for D. D. and Blind.*

I have used two editions of Dr. Branson's North Carolina Directory, and I have found it so useful and convenient that I would not be without it. I am glad he is revising and will soon publish a new edition. I regard it as a valuable book for anyone who cares to keep posted on the interests of the State.
June 29, 1895. E. E. HILLIARD, *Ed. Scotland Neck Commonwealth.*

Dr. Branson's North Carolina Directory has become a necessity to business men. It is accurate and valuable. I am glad that a new edition is soon to be published. JAS. C. MACRAE,
July 27, 1895. *Ex-Justice Supreme Court.*

A business directory of the State is useful in various ways to physicians as to others, and I am glad to know that a new edition of "Branson's" is to appear.
Raleigh, August 8, 1895. K. P. BATTLE, JR., M. D.

Every business man, every professional man, and every one who is interested in the history and progress of North Carolina, ought to have Branson's Directory. I am satisfied that great pains will be taken to make the next edition accurate and interesting. A. C. AVERY,
Morganton, N. C., August 21, 1895. *Justice Supreme Court.*

I take great pleasure in recommending Dr. Branson's North Carolina Business Directory. It has been a great aid to me in my editorial work.
Elizabeth City, December 17, 1895. R. B. CREECY, *Ed. Economist.*

I take pleasure in recommending Branson's Directory to the public as a most useful book of reference, and I think business men will find it very convenient to have a copy at hand in their office. THOS. J. JARVIS,
Greenville, N. C., January 20, 1896. *Ex-Gov. of North Carolina.*

I have found Branson's Directory an exceedingly useful book and very serviceable to me in the practice of my profession. CHAS. W. TILLETT,
Charlotte, N. C., February 2, 1896. *Attorney at Law.*

To Physicians.....

Arrangements were made to carry a Committee of Medical Experts through the South to report on the healthfulness of its climate. The Committee was composed of Dr. W. C. Wile, A. M., M. D., LL. D., Editor *New England Medical Monthly*, Danbury, Conn., Chairman of the delegation; Dr. Ferdinand King, Editor of the *New York Polyclinic*, Secretary; Dr. E. C. Angell, representing *The Sanitarian*, of Brooklyn, N. Y.; Hon. Clark Bell, Editor *New York Medico-Legal Journal;* Dr. Howard Van Rensselear, A. M., M. D., Ph. D., Editor *Medical*

NEAR SOUTHERN PINES, N. C.

Annals, Albany, N. Y.; Dr. W. Blair Stewart, A. M., M. D., Professor in the Philadelphia Medico-Chirurgical College; Dr. Geo. Taylor Stewart, of the *New York Medical Times*, and Superintendent of Ward's Island Hospital.

Their report as to health resorts gives Southern Pines, N. C., the lead. Following is an extract from their report:

"For persons whose health requires a mild winter climate, Southern Pines, because of the dryness of its soil, its elevation above sea-level, the invigorating quality of its atmosphere and its accessibility, presents natural advantages that highly commend it to the favorable attention of the medical profession."

Prominent Medical Journals Commend
Southern Pines.

Homeopathic Physician, of Philadelphia, Pa.—"Prominent physicians have visited the place for investigation, and without a single exception say it is the best."

Cincinnati Medical Journal, April, 1894.—"Thousands of Northern invalids have visited the place, and many remarkable cures have been effected."

The Prescription, April, 1894.—"Its bound to prove a Mecca for people suffering from pulmonary complaints."

Southern Medical World, November, 1893.—"A new winter health resort, * * * the best in the United States."

The Sanitarian, March, 1894.—"In soil and climate, Nature seems to have made it an ideal place. The air is dry, balmy, balsamic and ozonic."

SOUTHERN PINES—HOME PARLOR.

The Medical Times and Register, March, 1894—"As soon as the place becomes better known, it will prove the most popular health resort in the country."

New York Polyclinic, March, 1894.—"Situated in the centre of the renowed long-leaf pine belt, famous alike for its elevation, its health-giving balsamic odors, and its absolute freedom from malaria. There is absolutely no moisture in the atmosphere. The hotels are first-class and reasonable in their charges."

Philadelphia Times and Register, September, 1892.—"Whatever may be the dangers of infection in the older resorts, there is none at Southern Pines."

New England Medical Monthly.—"One point impressed me at once—the desire to sleep. It was said by the people who were there for their health, that the desire for sleep for the first two or three weeks is almost irresistable. Rest, blessed rest, gives Nature a chance to get in her fine work."

BRANSON'S
North Carolina Business Directory.

Abbreviations.—Agt, for Agent ; Ast, Assistant ; bet, between ; bkpr, bookkeeper ; (col), colored ; clk, clerk ; Co, Company or county ; mfg, manufacturing ; N, north ; E, east ; S, south ; W, west ; mgr, Manager ; pres, President ; priu, Principal ; sec, Secretary ; treas, Treasurer ; sup, Superintendent ; bap, Baptist ; meth, Methodist ; chris, Christian ; presb, Presbyterian ; com mcht, Commission Merchant ; luth, Lutheran. The others are so palpable as not to need explanation.

ALAMANCE COUNTY.

AREA, 430 SQUARE MILES.

POPULATION, 18,271; White 12,688, Colored 5,583.

ALAMANCE was formed in 1848, from Orange county. It is named after Alamance creek, on the banks of which the battle of Alamance was fought between the Royalists under William Tryon and the Regulators under Herman Husbands and others.

GRAHAM is the county-seat. It is on the North Carolina Railroad, 54 miles west of Raleigh. Population 1,500.

Surface—Moderately uneven; water-power good and abundant; soil generally good.

Staples—Wheat, corn and tobacco.

Fruits—Apples, peaches, pears, cherries, grapes, apricots, etc.

Timbers—Hickory, poplar and the general varieties of oak.

Factories—This claims to be the banner county for cotton factories.

TOWNS AND POST OFFICES.

	POP.		POP.
Albright,	100	Mebane,	300
Altamhaw,	200	Melville,	25
Burlington,	3,500	Morton's Store,	35
Cane Creek,	25	Nicholson,	10
Carney,	25	Oak Dale,	40
Cedar Cliff,	20	Osceola,	350
Clover Orchard,	50	Pleasant Gr've,	25
Curtis,	25	Pleasant L'dge,	10
Elon College,	500	Rock Creek,	25
Glendale,	25	Rose,	25
Graham		Sandy Grove,	25
(C.H.),	1,500	Saxapahaw,	200
Hartshorn,	20	Shallow Ford,	10
Haw River,	1,600	Snow Camp,	65
Holman's Mills,	150	Stainback,	25
Lacey,	20	Sutphin,	25
Loy,	25	Swepsonville,	500
Leota,	25	Sylvester,	25
Manndale,	25	Union Ridge,	100
Maywood,	20	Vincent,	25
McCray,	50		

COUNTY OFFICERS.

Clerk Superior Court—G. D. Vincent.
Commissioners—S. H. Webb, chairman; C. H. Roney, A. J. Albright, W. K. Holt, Peter Michael.
Coroner—J. T. F. Cummings.
Register of Deeds—P. A. Mitchell.
Sheriff—R. T. Kernodle.
Solicitor (5th Dis.)—W. P. Bynum.
Surveyor—W. A. Patterson.
Treasurer—R. C. Dickey.
Co. Examiner—Rev. P. H. Fleming.
Co. Physician—Dr. R. A. Freeman.

COURTS.

First Monday after first Monday in March; tenth Monday after first Monday in September.

TOWN OFFICERS.

BURLINGTON—*Mayor*, Chas. E. McLean. *Commissioners*—B. R. Sellars. John C. Staley, Geo. W. Picket, H. K. Hall, J. H. Heritage, R. L. Sutphin, J. C. Hall, S. Hughes. *Secretary and Treasurer*—J. C. Staley.

GRAHAM — *Mayor,* H. W. Scott. *Commissioners*—W. S. Vestal, W. H. Holt, A. S. Bain, McBride Holt. *Chief of Police*—W. H. Forshee. *Sec'y and Treas.*—J. D. Kernodle.

SWEPSONVILLE—*Mayor,* —— ——.
MEBANE— ——.
ELON COLLEGE— ——.

TOWNSHIPS AND MAGISTRATES.

Albright's—J. R. Stockard. Lewis H. Holt, S. P. Holt, J. N. Wood, Alson B. Nicholson, Alson Sharp, G. S. Coble (Nicholson), W. H. Loy (Loy's Creek).

ALAMANCE COUNTY.

Boon Station—J. B. Summers (Altamahaw), J. M. Jobe (Burlington), J. P. Albright, J. C. Whitsell, Peter Hughes, Riley Ingle, Jos. McCadams (Elon).

Burlington—J. C. Robertson, Z. M. Foust, W. A. Hall, John R. Ireland, John G. Fowler, Isaac N. Walker, W. C. Isley, Thomas R. Simpson, Daniel Humble, J. C. F. Griffin (Burlington).

Coble's—J. R. Garrett (Carney), J. A. Fogalman, P. S. Page, W. R. Garrett, W. A. Patterson, A. L. Coble (Rock Creek), George W. Vestal, John Dixon (Oakdale).

Faucett's—F. U. Blanchard, E. Long, Jonathan Brooks, J. A. Lineberry (McCray), E. W. Wilkins, Robt. Fitch (Union Ridge), John G. Fowler (Big Falls).

Graham—W. P. White, George S. Rogers, J. L. Scott, J. W. Harden, W. H. Holt, H. M. Ray (Graham), J. H. Cox (Haw River).

Melville—J. H. Blackman, C. Sellars, J. W. B. Bason, Geo. W. P. Cates (Haw River), R. W. Scott (Melville), W. H. Lashley, J. F. Jobe (Mebane).

Morton's—W. F. Ireland (Burlington), P. Y. Bowles. Jos. W. Gilliam, J. H. Rose, Jas. W. Summers(Maywood), L. D. Rippy, A. T. Gilliam (Altamahaw), A. Isley (Shallow Ford), T. B. Booker (Maywood).

Newlin's—W. J. Stockard, David M. Moore, A. N. Robertson (Saxapahaw), H. D. Stagg (Cane Creek).

Thompson—G. T. Morrow, Jacob S. Long, Jas. T. Bradshaw, Benj. J. Williamson, H. M. Cates (Saxapahaw).

Patterson's—Sylvester Spoon, Robt. Thompson (Rock Creek), H. M. C. Stroud, W. A. Tinnin, O. N. Hornaday (Oakdale).

Pleasant Grove—Levi Whited, W. B. Sellars (Stainback), W. J. Fitch (McCray), Thomas W. Vincent, W. A. Browning (Pleasant Grove), B. F. White, J. P. Borland (Mebane).

CHURCHES.

Names, Post Offices, Pastors and Denom.

METHODIST.

Bethel—Burlington.
Chapel—Burlington, L. E. Thompson.
Church—Burlington, L. E. Thompson.
Church (col.)—Burlington.
Church—Swepsonville.
Church—Union Ridge.
Holt's Chapel—Haw River.
Macedonia—Curtis.
Phillips' Chapel—Saxapahaw.
Salem—Saxapahaw.

ALAMANCE COUNTY.

Shiloh—Morton's Store.
Wood Chapel (col.)—Curtis, W. F. Sewell.
Wyman's Chapel (col.)—Graham, W. F. Sewell.

METHODIST PROTESTANT.

Belmont—Graham.
Bethel—Clover Orchard, W. W. Amick.
Carolina—Big Falls.
Church—Burlington, J. G. Holloway.
Church—Haw River.
Church—Rock Creek, W. W. Amick.
Concord—Saxapahaw, W. W. Amick.
Friendship—Curtis, W. W. Amick.
Hebron—Mt. Willing, W. W. Amick.
Mt. Hermon—Curtis, W. W. Amick.
Mt. Pleasant—Curtis.
Salem—Saxapahaw, W. W. Amick.

CHRISTIAN.

Archie's Grove (col.)—Burlington.
Bethlehem—Altamahaw, C. C. Peel.
Church—Shallow Ford, P. T. Clapp.
Church (col.)—Graham, G. W. Dunn.
Church—Haw River, C. C. Peel.
Church—Burlington, P. H. Fleming.
Church (col.)—Burlington, T. J. Levister.
Church—Elon College, Prof. J. O. Atkinson.
Church (col.)—Mebane, C. W. Ray.
Green Level (col.)—Haw River, G. W. Dunn.
Long's Chapel—Haw River, P. T. Clapp.
Main St.—Graham, P. H. Fleming.
McBroom's (col.)—Haw River, Wm. McBroom.
Melvin (col.)—Swepsonville, C. W. Ray.
Mt. Zion—Mebane, W. D. Harward.
Providence—Graham, P. H. Fleming.
Union (col.)—Union Ridge, C. W. Ray.
Union—McCrary's Store, C. C. Peel.

BAPTIST.

Church (col.)—Haw River.
Church—Graham, John C. Hocutt.
Church (col)—Graham, —— Long.
Church—Swepsonville, John C. Hocutt.
Church—Haw River, John C. Hocutt.
Church—Burlington, Robert Van Deventer.
Glencoe—Burlington, Alvis Andrews.
Moore's Chapel—Saxapahaw, J. W. Watson.

PRIMITIVE BAPTIST.

Deep Creek—McCray's Store.
Gilliam—Morton's Store.

PRESBYTERIAN.

Church—Burlington, M. McG. Shedds.
Church—Mebane, H. C. Kegley.

ALAMANCE COUNTY.

Church (col.)—Burlington.
Cross Roads—Mebane, R. W. Cuthbertson.
Church—Graham, W. P. McCorkle.
Hawfield's—Mebane, R. W. Cuthberson.
Moore's Chapel (col.)—Mebane.
Stony Creek—McCray's Store, N. B. Campbell.

LUTHERAN.

Law's—Brick Church, H. M. Brown.
Macedonia—Burlington, V. Y. Boozer.
Mt. Pleasant—Haw River, D. I. Offman.
Richland——, H. M. Brown.
Sharon—Gibsonville, E. P. Parker.
St. Paul's—Holt's Store, H. M. Brown.

REFORMED.

Stiners—Graham.
St. Mark's—Gibsonville.
Barker's—Liberty.

FRIENDS.

Cane Creek—Clover Orchard.
Spring Meeting House—Clover Orchard.

FREE CHURCH.

Union Church—Burlington.

EPISCOPAL.

Church—Burlington, — Barber.

MINISTERS RESIDENT.

Names, Post Offices and Denominations.

CHRISTIAN.

Atkinson, Prof. J. O., Elon College.
Boon, C. A., Elon College.
Dunn, G. W. (col.), Graham.
Fleming, P. H., Graham.
Harden, M. D., (col.), Graham.
Herndon, Dr. W. T., Elon College.
Holt, J. W., Burlington.
Hurley, M. L., Elon College.
Iseley, A. F., Shallow Ford.
Klapp, P. T., Elon College.
Levister, T. J., (col.), Burlington.
McBroom, William (col.), Haw River.
McBroom, Henry (col.), Haw River.
Newman, J. U., Elon College.
Peel, C. C., Haw River.
Ray, C. W. (col.), Haw River.
Stroud, T. M., Union Ridge.
Trolinger, James (col.), Haw River.
Williams, D. W. (col.) Burlington.

BAPTIST.

Andrews, Alvis, Burlington.
Hocutt, John C., Graham.
Van Deventer, Robert, Burlington.

PRIMITIVE BAPTIST.

Bunch, J. A., Burlington.
Faucette, Ellis (col.), Burlington.

ALAMANCE COUNTY.

PRESBYTERIAN.

Culbertson, W. W., Mebane.
Kegley, H. C., Mebane.
McCorkle, W. P., Graham.
McShedds, M. McG., Burlington.

METHODIST.

Dailey, J. A., Burlington.
Hunt, Moses J., Burlington.
Thompson, L. E., Burlington.

LUTHERAN.

Boozer, V. Y., Burlington.

HOTELS AND BOARDING HOUSES.

Names, Post Offices and Proprietors.

Boarding, Burlington, T. J. Hall.
Boarding, Burlington, Dr. R. A. Freeman.
Boarding, Haw River, J. H. Blackman.
Burlington Inn, Burlington, Ward Bros.
College Hotel, Elon College, Buck Smith.
Eagle House, Burlington, J. P. Albright.
Harden House, Graham, Mrs. S. E. Harden.
Henley House, Burlington, —Henley.
Hotel, Mebane, E. A. White.
Hotel, Graham, W. H. Forshee.
Hotel, Elon College, W. L. Smith.
Hunter House, Graham, Mrs. Corinna Hunter.
Turrentine House, Burlington, J. A. Turrentine.
Wilson House, Burlington, J. L. Wilson.

LAWYERS.

Names and Post Offices.

Carroll, W. H., Burlington.
Hughs, Henan, Graham.
Kernodle, J. D. Graham.
Long, Jacob A., Burlington.
McLean, C. E., Burlington.
Parker, E. S., Jr., Graham.
Parker, E. S., Graham.
Webb, Sam. H., Saxapahaw.

MANUFACTORIES.

Kinds, Post Offices and Proprietors.

Alamance Mills, Burlington, E. M. Holt & Sons; spindles, 1,000; looms, 94.
Alamance Cotton Mills, Burlington, 7 miles south; E. M. Holt's Sons, successors to E. M. Holt; established in 1837; cap. stock, $50,000; spindles, 1,200; looms, 92; daily consumption, 750 pounds; hands, 85.

| ALAMANCE COUNTY. | ALAMANCE COUNTY. |

Altamahaw Cotton Mills, Elon College; Holt, Gant & Holt, prop'rs; established in 1880; spindles, 6,500; looms, 800.

Aurora Cotton Mills, Burlington; Lawrence S. Holt; estab. 1885; spindles, 4,620; looms, 500; hands, 175.

Belmont Cotton Mills, Graham; L. B. & L. S. Holt; estab. 1879; spindles, 3,592; looms, 126.

Buggies, etc., Burlington. L. J. Fonville.

Buggies. Graham. J. H. Loy.

Canning. Graham, G. A. & W. C. Curtis.

Canning, Graham, Dr. G. R. Foust.

Carolina Cotton Mills. Burlington, J. H. & W. E. Holt & Co.; estab. 1869; spindles, 3,073; looms, 58.

Carriages, etc., Graham. W. F. Jones.

Coffins (wholesale). Burlington, J. L. Erwin. sec. and treas., and mgr.

Dixon Mfg Co., Snow Camp. T. F. McIver, sec. and treas; spindles, 476; looms, 13.

Doors. Sash and Blinds. Burlington, George W. Anthony.

Elmira Cotton Mills Co., Burlington. W. L. & E. C. Holt; estab. in 1886; spindles, 3,750; looms. 256; hands, 185.

E. M. Holt Plaid Mill. Burlington, L. Banks Holt, pres.; J. H. Erwin, sec. and treas.; capital, $40,000; looms, 140; hands, 80.

Foundry, Burlington, H. L. Holt.

Foundry, Cane Creek. S. Dixon & Co.

Glencoe Cotton Mills, Burlington, W. E. & J. H. Holt, Props. Spindles, 3,600; looms, 186.

Granite Cotton Mills. Haw River. B. S. Roberson. sec'y and treas.; established in 1845. Spindles, 8,500; looms, 434.

Juanita Cotton Mills, Burlington, G. Rosenthal. Spindles, 6,172.

Lakeside Cotton Mill. Burlington, S. M. Holt, Manager. Looms, 150; spindles, 3,300. Capital, $80,000.

Oneida Cotton Mills (No. 1). Graham. L. Banks Holt; established in 1886. Spindles, 4,424; looms, 385; hands, 315.

Oneida Mills (No. 2). Graham. L. Banks Holt. Spindles. 4,400; looms, 277.

Oneida Mills (No. 3), Graham. L. Banks Holt. Hands. 25; spindles, 4,400; looms, 383.

Ossipee Cotton Mills. Elon College; established in 1882; Jas. N. Williamson, & Sons, props. Hands. 175; spindles, 4,600; looms, 200.

Railroad Repair Shops, Burlington. N. C. R. R. Co.

Railroad Shops. Burlington, — Inge, Master Mechanic.

Repair Shops, Burlington, R. W. Tate & Bro.

Saxapahaw Cotton Mills, Graham, White, Williamson & Co. Props. Spindles. 4,704; looms, 71; hands, 110.

Shoes, Graham, J. D. Vaughn.

Shoes, Graham, W. N. Murray.

Shoes, Burlington, J. H. Sullivan & Co.

Shoes, Burlington. Geo. Hunter.

Sidney Cotton Mills. Graham; established in 1886; Scott. Donnell & Scott (steam). Capital, $40,000; No. looms, 101; spindles, 1,000; hands, 56.

Tannery, Burlington. Ellis Faucett.

The Cora Manufacturing Co., Haw River. Thomas M. Holt. president; spindles, 7,000; looms. 250.

Thos. M. Holt Manufacturing Co., Haw River, B. S. Robertson; capital, $200,000; spindles. 7,168; looms, 252; hands, 360.

Virginia Mills, Swepsonville, E. M. Cooke, secretary; capital, $100,000; looms, 150.

Windsor Cotton Mills, Burlington, R. L. & J. H. Holt, Jr.; capital, $40,000; spindles. 3,120; looms, 160.

MERCHANTS AND TRADESMEN.

Name, Post-office, and Line of Business

ALTAMAHAW.

Holt. Gant & Holt,	G S
Markel. A.,	G S
Paris. W. H. & Bro.,	G S

BIG FALLS.

Juanito General Store,	G S

BURLINGTON.

Allen, T. E. & Co.,	G S
Barnwell. J. C.,	G S
Burlington Furniture Co., C. B. Ellis, manager,	Furniture
Carroll, W. H.,	Gen. Ins. Agent
Cates & Co.,	Drugs
Clapp. Wilborn,	G S
Coble, Joe V.,	Livery
Fitzgerald, ——,	Barber
Fix, Joseph,	Postmaster
Fogleman, G. W.,	D G and Shoes
Foster, H. C.,	G S
Foster, John R.,	G S
Fowler, J. J.,	G S
Freeman & Page,	Drugs
Furgeson, J. E.,	G S
Hay, W. E.,	G S
Hay. Frank,	G S
Hessee, J. A. & M. A.,	G S
Holt. E. M., Sons.	G S
Holt, W. E. & J. H. (Glenco Mills)	G S

ALAMANCE COUNTY.

Holt, J. H. & W. E. & Co. (Carolina Mills), G S
Holt & May, G S and Hardware
Hughes & Ellis, Furniture
Ingle & Jobe, Undertakers
Ingle, W. T. & J. W., G S
Iseley, J. A., & Bro.,Who and Ret G S
Iseley, W. C.,
Buggies, Wagons, Guano, &c
Kivett, T. H., G S
Lasley, J. W. & W. W., G S
Lambe, T. J., Clothier
Matthews. J. J., Ice
Mebane, W. G. & Co., Insurance
Mebane, W. G. & Co., Who Grocers
Moore & Moore, Livery
Moore, White & Co., G S
Neese, C. F., Jeweler
Neese, C. F., Bookstore
Rowhut, C. F., G S
Sellars, B. A. & Son, G S
Sharp, S. M. & Co., G S
Simpson, W. E., G S
Smith, G. D., G S
Spoon, J. M. & R. L., G S
Stafford & Stroud Drug Co., Drugs
Stewart, J., Jeweler
Tate & Albright, General Ins Agts
Thomas, S. (col.), Tinner
Thompson, Mrs. K. T., Millinery
Thompson, R. N. & J. N., G S
Townsend, C. C. & Co.,
Harness and Buggies
Tisdale, J. M., G S
Townsend, C. C. & Co., Buggies, &c
Walker, Mrs. M. A. & Co., Millinery
White, Pickad & White, G S
and Livery
White & Co., G S
Williams & Lindsay, Barbers
Wilson, S. P., G S
Winningham, A., G S
Zachary, H. C., Contractor

CANE CREEK.
Braxton, R. G., G S
Teague, D. F., G S

CLOVER ORCHARD.
Cooper, J. D., G S

CURTIS.
Iseley, Robert T., G S

ELON COLLEGE.
Hines, H. L., G S
Kernodle, Swain & Kernodle, G S
Kernodle, Dr. G. W., Drugs
Low, T. G., G S
Mebane, J. R., G S
Porter & Co., G S
Williamson, J. N. & Son, G S
York, Edwards & Co., G S

GRAHAM.
Albright, T. A. & Co., Drugs
Allen, J. W. (col.), Barber

ALAMANCE COUNTY.

Bain & Thompson, G S
Bell, A. L., G S
Cole & Flinton, G S
Farrell, J. B., Grocer
Freeland, Misses, Milliners
Graham Produce Co., T. M. Duck,
Manager, Grocers
Hargrove, Ellis (col.), Barber
Holt, L. B. & Co.,
Wholesale and Retail G S
Holt, W. H., G S
Holt, C. M. Sons, G S
Hornaday, W. C., Livery
Jones, W. F., Undertaker
Loy, O. C., Jeweler
McLean, S. G., Postmaster
Montgomery, T. C., Depot Agent
Moore, W. C., Livery
Moore, W. A., Ice
Murray, W. N., Shoemaker
Nicks, W. J., G S
Scott, Dennell & Scott, Grocers
Scott & Co., G S
Simmons, J. C., Drugs
Tate, A. B., G S
Van Buren, Martin, Livery
Watson & White, G S

HARTSHORN.
Garrett, W. R., G S

HAW RIVER.
Albright, C. P. & Co., Drugs
Dickey, A. S., G S
Goodman, B. & Co., G S
Granite M'fg Co., G S
Hughes, B. N., G S
Keck, L. J., G S
King & Johnson, G S
McAdams, J. S., G S
Thompson, C. Kerr, Postmaster

HOLMAN'S MILL.
Hollman, W. C., G S

LEOTA.
McBane, J. S., G S
McBane, D. E., G S

LOY.
Councilman, H. C., G S

MANNDALE.
McBane, M. C., G S

MAYWOOD.
Barnett Bros., G S
Foster, Zeb. V., G S

M'CRAY.
Long, E., G S

MEBANE.
Dick, James T., Livery
Dick, James T., G S
Jones, W. F., G S
Lashley, J. H., G S
Scott, S. K., G S
White & Thompson, G S
York, Dr. N. D., Drugs

ALAMANCE COUNTY.

MELVILLE.
Walker, R. L.,   Drugs
NICHOLSON'S.
Clandenen, J. E.,   Coachmaker
Cook, Geo. H.,   G S
OAK DALE.
Foster, J. R. & Bro.,   G S
Hallman, W. C. & Co.,   G S
Kimory, S. S.,   G S
OSCEOLA.
Holt, L. B. & L. S. (Bellmont
  Mills),   G S
PLEASANT GROVE.
Crawford & Dailey,   G S
Hesse, J. A. & M. A.,   G S
SAXAPAHAW.
White, Williamson & Co.,   G S
SNOW CAMP.
Coble, J. R. & Co.,   G S
Dixon, J. M.,   G S
STAINBACK.
Stainback & Co.,   G S
SWEPSONVILLE.
Payne, W. T.,   G S
Virginia Cotton Mills,   G S
UNION RIDGE.
Aldridge, W. H. & Sons,   G S
McAuley, L. H.,   G S
Maynard, G. R.,   G S
VINCENT.
Maynard, G. R.,   G S

MINES.

Kinds, Post Office and Proprietors.

Copper, Clover Orchard (not in opera-
  tion), Peter Adam's heirs.
Gold, Clover Orchard (not in opera-
  tion), Foust & Newlin.
Gold, Graham (not in operation), M.
  J. Anthony.
Gold, Haw River (not in operation),
  Thos. Dixon's heirs.
Gold, Haw River (not in operation),
  Pleasant Dixon.
Gold, Graham (not in operation),
  Peter F. Holt's heirs.
Whetstone Quarry, Holman's Mills,
  W. G. Moser.

MILLS.

Kinds, Post Offices and Proprietors.

Corn and saw, Snow Camp, Calvin
  Thompson.
Corn, Morton's Store, J. N. William-
  son.
Corn, Graham, J. W. Harden.

ALAMANCE COUNTY.

Corn, flour and saw, Clover Orchard,
  Wm. G. Moser.
Corn, Clover Orchard, Thomas Staf-
  ford's heirs.
Corn, Clover Orchard, Clayborn Guth-
  rie.
Flour and corn, Rock Creek, Milton
  Coble.
Flour and corn, Rock Creek, G. M.
  Albright.
Flour and corn, Saxapahaw, White,
  Williamston & Co.
Flour and corn, Pleasant Grove, T. W.
  & W. E. Vincent.
Flour and corn, Pleasant Grove, Sam.
  J. Crawford.
Flour and corn, Mebane, L. Banks
  Holt.
Flour and corn, Patterson's Store,
  Hanner & Kime.
Flour and corn (steam), Clover Or-
  chard, W. C. Holman.
Flour, corn and saw, Cedar Cliff, Jas.
  Newlin.
Flour and corn, Holman's Mills, Allen
  & Stuart.
Flour and corn, Long Branch, James
  Thompson.
Flour and corn, Hartshorn, W. A.
  Patterson & Sons.
Flour and corn, Hartshorn, Hanner
  Bros.
Flour, corn and saw, Haw River, C. J.
  Kerr.
Flour and corn, Clover Orchard, John
  Dixon & Co.
Flour and corn, Curtis, Coble Dixon's
  Sons.
Flour and corn, Altamahaw, Holt,
  Grant & Holt.
Flour and corn, Clover Orchard, J. &
  David Nixon.
Flour, corn and saw, Cedar Cliff, Jas.
  Newlin.
Flour and corn, Burlington, E. M.
  Holt's sons.
Flour and corn, Big Falls, Juanito Co.
Merchant flour and corn (roller), Haw
  River, Granite Mfg Co.
Merchant flour (roller), Burlington, S.
  Ireland & Sons.
Saw and gin, Clover Orchard, Clay-
  born Guthrie.
Steam saw, Rock Creek, Kinnery &
  Hornaday.
Steam saw, Patterson's Store, W. A.
  & J. M. Tinnin.

PHYSICIANS.

Names and Post Offices.

Anderson, C. A., Burlington.
Brooks, J. H. (dentist), Union Ridge.
Clendenin, Wm., Haw River.

ALAMANCE COUNTY.

Cummings. J. T. F., Gibsonville.
Fancett,——. Burlington.
Fancett, T. S. Burlington.
Freeman, Rich. Burlington.
Goley, W. R., Graham.
Kernodle, Geo. W., Morton's Store.
Kernodle, Loftin. Osceola.
Laird, E. C., Haw River.
Lasley, J. W., Burlington.
Long, Geo. W., Graham.
Mann, E. D., Saxapahaw.
McCauley, J. W., Pleasant Grove.
Montgomery, D. A., Burlington.
Murphy, J. S., Burlington.
Nuse, Alfred, Saxapahaw.
Nuse, Pat., Burlington.
Page, J. W., Burlington.
Patterson, T. W., Haw River.
Pickett, Jno. A., Osceola.
Stafford, W. G., Burlington.
Stockard, Dick (dentist), Burlington.
Tate, W. N., Mebane.
Thompson, W. H. (dentist), Melville.
Thompson, J. B., Graham.
Watson, G. S., Union Ridge.
Watson, E. F., Iola.
Williams, T. R., Swepsonville.
Williamson, J. L., Graham.
York, N. D., Mebane.

SCHOOLS.

Names, Post-offices and Principles.

Academy, Haw River, Prof. J. W. Johnston.
Academy, Oak Dale, G. H. Ross.
Bethel Academy, Clover Orchard.
Cross Roads, Stainback, Miss Annie Winston.
Elon College, Elon College, Rev. W. W. Staley, D. D.
Eureka, Nicholson's, Prof. Jennings.
Female School, Mebane, Miss Zella McCulloch.
Friendship, Curtis, Prof. Stone.
Gilliam's Academy, Morton's Store, J. W. Gilliam.
Graham School, Graham. Prof. T. R. Foust.
Hawfield's, Mebane. Miss Annie Winston.
High School, Burlington, Prof. Fonville.
Methodist Academy (Trinity College Annex), Burlington. Prof. Hoyle.
Pleasant Lodge, Pleasant Lodge.
Public School, Burlington, Prof. T. E. McKeel.
Public School, Graham, W. P. White.
Salem Academy, Cedar Cliff.
Sylvan, Snow Camp.
Union Academy, Union Ridge, Rev. L. W. Stroud.
Public Schools—White, 52; Colored, 21.

ALAMANCE COUNTY.

TEACHERS.

Names and Post-offices,

WHITE.

Albright, Sallie, Burlington.
Albright, Zora, Burlington.
Albright, Flora, Graham,
Anderson, J. M., Stainback,
Barnwell, Dora, Pleasant Grove.
Barnwell, Cora, Pleasant Grove.
Braxton, J. G., Cane Creek.
Browning, Sallie, Pleasant Grove.
Cobb, Jno. T., Elon College.
Compton, Lela, Burlington.
Crutchfield, J. E., Mebane.
Foust, Lizzie, Melville.
Foust, Lettie, Graham.
Garrett, Sallie, Curtis.
Garrett, J. C., Curtis.
Hall, Annie, Burlington.
Hurdle, Sallie, Union Ridge.
Iseley, J. A., Mebane.
Iseley, Rev. A. F., Shallow Ford.
Johnston, J. W., Haw River.
Johnston, C. D., Haw River.
Johnson, R. W., Oakdale.
Jones, M. Dora, Graham.
Kirkpatrick, Lula, Mebane.
Lewis, J. W., Altamahaw.
Long, Annie, Graham.
Matleck, Mamie, Maywood.
May, J. M., Brick Church.
McAdams, J. C., Burlington.
McCauley, Della, Union Ridge.
McCulloch, Jr., R. W., Maywood.
McKeel, T. E., Burlington.
Montgomery, H. M., Burlington.
Moore, J. E., Saxapahaw.
Moore, A. M., Cedar Cliff.
Newlin, Annie J., Swepsonville.
Paris, H. G., Saxapahaw.
Plates, G. W., Haw River.
Ratliffe, Jennie, Elon College.
Reitzel, Fannie, Hartshorn.
Robertson, J. B., Hartshorn.
Ross, G. H., Oakdale.
Spoon, Fannie C., Rock Creek.
Stewart, Emma C. Burlington.
Stone, J. A., Curtis.
Stroud, Rev. F. W., Union Ridge.
Summers, J. F., Morton's Store.
Thompson, D. H., Holman's Mills.
Thompson, W. J., Snow Camp.
Thompson, C. C., Nicholson.
Thompson, A. A., Mebane.
Thompson, W. J., Holman's Mills.
Walters, W. T., Burlington.
Watson, Lesta, Maywood.
Webster, Annie, Swepsonville.
White, Mrs. W. P., Graham.
White, W. P., Graham.
Whitesell, Mintie A., Elon College.
Woody, Mattie, Saxapahaw.
Wood, Inez E., Swepsonville.
Wood, Ora, Graham.

ALAMANCE COUNTY.

COLORED.

Clark, W. A., Mebane.
Dunn, Rev. G. W., Graham.
Foust, Fannie J., Swepsonville.
Freeland, Alice, Graham.
Freeland, N. A., Mebane.
Hall, W. R., Nicholson.
Harbor, Mary E., Haw River.
Hoskins, H. L., Mebane.
Hoskins, Rev. M. G., Mebane.
Hunter, John, Graham.
Jones, W. H., Mebane.
Iseley, H. A., Nicholson.
Lee, Matilda C., Mebane.
Mabry, G. S., Graham.
Mabry, Emma J., Graham.
McBrown, J. H., Haw River.
Moore, Mary E., Mebane.
Murray, David A., Mebane.
Murray, Alice J., Mebane.
Murray, Viney M., Mebane.
Murray, Ora V., Mebane.
Ochiltree, R. M., Graham.
Ochiltree, Cora V., Graham.
Patterson, Annie, Rock Creek.
Robeson, J. B., Sutphin.
Rodgers, J. S., Graham.
Siler, C. D., Burlington.
Trolinger, J. M., Haw River.
Williamson, Mack C., Mebane.
Wood, W. H., Mebane.
Wood, Cynthia, Mebane.
Yancey, Rosa B., Altamahaw.

LOCAL CORPORATIONS.

Alamance Farm (Stock and Poultry), Graham; L. Banks Holt, Prop.
Burlington Banking Co., Burlington (State Bank); Jos. Davidson, Pres.; Dr. J. W. Page, Vice-Pres.; I. C. Staley, Cash. Subscribed capital, $10,000.
Maplewood Poultry Yard, Graham; Mitchell Bros.
Poultry farm, Graham, W. Cooper.
Poultry farm, Graham, B. N. Turner.

NEWSPAPERS.

Alamance Gleaner, Graham, dem. weekly; J. D. Kernodle, editor and prop.
Burlington News, Burlington, dem., weekly and daily; C. W. Hunt, editor and prop.
Elon College Monthly, Elon College, Students editors and pubrs.

FARMERS.

Names and Post Offices.

Albright's—A G Albright, J T Albright, F Clendenin, Wm Clendenin, Jas C Covington, Wm F Covington, T M Robertson, David Turner.

ALAMANCE COUNTY.

Altamahaw—T B Barber, G N Barber, D M Barber, W T Bowles, P T Bowles, Thomas Bowles, Leath Freeman, W H Horton, U W Horton, O H Beck, Wesley Beck, R A Matlock, Seymore McIntyre, J C McCulloch, David Michael, W F Morton, John S Morton, Walter Price, L D Ripley, C N Roney, Jas M Ross, T M Ross, J Hawkins Simpson, Jefferson Simpson, J H Ross, O P Shelton, J N Simpson, B L Simpson, Monroe Simpson, J M Stacey, George Stubblefield, Fin Stubblefield, G F Summers, Riley Sutton, Geo T Sutton, Peter Sutton, W T Sutton, Dan'l Tickle, Riley Tickle, L C Tickle, Henry Troxler, P P Troxler, D. W Waymick.

Burlington—Ruffin Andrews, J D Bason, G F Blackman, W J Boon, W A Boon, Jno A Bryan, Jr, Jno A Bryan, Sr, J A Bunch, H M Boon, Wm Boon, H A Cheek, G N Cheek, A J Capps, William Capps, G N Davenport, R C Dickey, B T Elden, C M Enliss, John D Faucette, Jos Fix, L J Fonville, W H Fogleman, J H Foster, J E Forshee, John Q Grant, H E Garrison, Geo A Garrison, B F Garrison, W A Godfrey, Mrs M J Greeson, C J Greeson, L L Hall, E B Hall, J H Harden, H J Hawk, G N Holt, Rev J W Holt, L W Holt, J G Holt, J A Holt, Thos Holt, W H Holt, J H Hall, R W Ingle, Christian Iseley, S E Jeffries, J M Jobe, G A Keck, J E Kirkpatrick, J N Kirkpatrick, W G Kirkpatrick, Long & Anderson, J S Long, H R May, H P May, Jos McAdams, John M McCauley, L J Michael, W O Montgomery, D A Montgomery, W V Montgomery, E G Morton, J T C Moore, J S Murphey, T W Nance, G M Noah, John H Perry, S R Pickett, R M Pyle, P L Ray, J M Sellars, L P Shepherd, T R Simpson, S R Story, R M Stockard, Geo Sykes, Jno A Sykes, J W Teagen, Ed Teagen, H J Tickle, R N Thompson, W C Thurston, H W Trolinger, Geo Troxler, J M Turner, J A Turrentine, W H Turrentine, I N Walker, J M Williams, H & L D Whitsett, D Worth.

Carney—A J Albright, J M Albright, G M Albright, H C Barnhardt, H M Bryan, Lewis Clopp, J N Clopp, A L Coble, J F Coble, J W Coble, W L Coble, C C Curtis, E R Enless, Jno T Fogleman, J M Fogleman, G B Johnson, Dan Keck, Wm D Liner, T L Moser, C F Moser, J A Moser, G A Murray, Duncan Sharp, L P Sharp, A A Sharp, Wm L Spoon, H M Spoon, Jno M Spotlesly, Jacob R Shepherd, Jno M Tinnin, Wm A Tinnin, S F Vestal, Geo W Vestal

ALAMANCE COUNTY.

Cedar Cliff—John S Albright, S P Holt, W H Holt, Patterson Payne, J C Payne, Loton Payne, A M Payne, G W Rich, N Robertson, W M Robertson, W M Williams.

Curtis—W G Albright, N Albright, W R Garrett, Jer Garrett, G W Garrett, Henry N Garrett, H W Graves, N W Graves, S J Hoffman, W L Holt, LaFayette Holt, Jos C Iseley, A M Iseley, W L Iseley, J S Iseley, J R Iseley, J Iseley, M V Iseley, Henry Iseley, A L Iseley, J R Iseley, Haywood Iseley, Wesley Iseley, W A Patterson, L L Patterson, E Patterson, G W Patterson, C F Robertson, Jas P Sharp, Wm B Sharp, Alfred Sharp, Wm A J Sharp, T C Sharp, J J Sharp, J C Sharp, Jer Sharp, L P Sharp, Wm Shoffner, D G Shoffner, M D Shoffner, Jack Shoffner.

Elon College—J P Albright, H N Albright, Henry Baldwin, A C Baldwin, W T Barham, D R Barber, J D Barber, P L Barnhardt, C A Boon, M V Boon, W A Burke, W J Cates, S M Chimes, J R Christman, H G Christman, D L Christman, J H Clapp, D M Clapp, P M Clapp, John T Cobb, P M Coble, J O Coble, Wilkins Coble, M R Cook, J D Cook, Scott Crawford (col.), John Crawford (col.), Samuel Crawford, J A Crouse, J T F Cummings, Carmp Cummings (col.), W J Diamond, P P Dick, Alfonza Gerringer, Joshua Gerringer, J B Gerringer, Peter Gerringer, Jac N Gerringer, John H Gerringer, Sidney Gerringer, Stout Griffith (col.), James Haithcox (col.), W T Herndon, Geo H Huffman, George W Huffman, P P Huffman, R L Huffman, Dan. Huffman, Geo W Huffman, Jac M Huffman, John Huffman, Jac A Huffines, D R Huffines, Wm P Huffines, M A Huffines, Peter Hughes, Josesph H Hughes, W R Ingle, W G Ingle, Jos Jones, George Kernodle, J T Kernodle, R A C Kernodle, P T Klapp, John J Lambeth, Daniel Low, Yancey Low, John C Low, J H Loy, Rankin Loy, Daniel Loy, Jos G May, H P May, T A May, Montgomery May, Jos McAdams, R J Mebane, Peter Michael, W C Mills (col.), Jackson Murray, J N Newman, Geo M Patton, John R Petigrew, Sidney Petigrew, Levi Pinnix (col.), Jos Rumbly, Dan'l Rumbly, John W Sharp, Geo Shepard, W L Smith, J J Snipes (col.), Chas Sumner, Geo Summers, Abe Summers, J B Summers, Andrew Summers, P Summers, Jno M Sutton, J M Sutton, Joel W Swing, W S Tate, T M Thompson, Yancey Tickle, Caleb Tickle, Jules C

ALAMANCE COUNTY.

Tickle, Levi R Tickle, Cad Troller, Linton Wagoner, John Wagoner, Jno Westmoreland, Luther Whitesell, T C Whitesell, J A Whitesell, Jno Whitesell, J C Whitesell, P H Williams, N A Williams, P J Wyrick, Jas Younger.

Graham—Alamance Farm, L Banks Holt, prop; Alamance Stock Farm, L Banks Holt, prop; Alamance Pet Stock and Poultry Farm, L Banks Holt, prop; Henry Albright, L A and J D Albright, Alex Albright, Abram Browdie, J N H Clendenin, Pinkney Capps, W L Cooper, G A Curtis, W C Curtis, T C Foust, G E Freeland, J W Freeland, D K Gant, T J Griffin, J W Harden, Jos P Harden, H M Holt, McBride Holt, Mrs Pauline Holt, N C Horneday, J B Jones, W F Jones, Jos T Long, J A Long, Oliver Newlin, W H Parris, Lem Rippey, R P D Roy, H M Roy, G S Rogers, A B Lots, Wm M Walters, R L Walker, W G Wilson, S H Webb & Co, Mrs M Whitsell

Haw River—J H Anderson, N H Anderson, Jos Baker, Audrey Barker, J F Barker, J W Bason, Wm M Benson, L Brown, Madison Crawford, Pleas Dixon, J T Dixon, Hugh Dixon, David Dixon, Abel Horn, J F Job, Wm A Keck, Chas J Kerr, J P Kerr, H C King, J G Lashley, C Sellars, Mrs V B Swepson, M E Terrell, Jno A Trolinger, Wm H Trolinger.

Loy—Alfred Iseley, G M Keck, J H Loy, W H Loy, A M Ricard, John Roney, Geo Rumbley.

Maywood—G D Barnett, Y A Barnett, G L Barnett, J J Barnett, P H Boon, J G Boon, J R Branock, W S Coffey, J C Cox, H H Dailey, G H Dailey, J M Evans.

McCray—Wm A Blanchard, F U Blanchard, Jonathan Brooks, Geo W Faucette, Wm F Faucette, G E Faucette, B F Fonvell, Carl Fonvell, B B Fonvell, F W Fonvell, Eli Graham, J P Graham, Jno A Graham, Henry Hall, A O Huffman, G Z Hurdle, Jno G Jeffreys, Jno W King, L H Lee, Elija Long, Thos Linebery, Job A Linebery, Geo R Maynard, Benj McAdams, Jno W McAdams, Willy C Murray, C H Roney, Geo W Webb (col).

Mebane—S L Bunch, A V Craig, S L Crutchfield, R W Culbertson, Jos T Dick, Samuel Faucette, G C Faucette, Thos F Foster, Wm M Fowler, Jno H Fowler, W O Fowler, Thaddius Freshwater, Henry Freshwater, Jos C Freshwater, Calvin Gibson, James Gibson, James Gill, Robt Q Hailey, Chas F Harris, J T Holt, Jno W Johnston, T

ALAMANCE COUNTY.

C Johnston, W A Kirkpatrick. Peter H Long. O M Martindale. J R McAdams. W G McAdams. Joe T McAdams, B F Mebane. Elijah Miles. E S Parker, J A Patton, Alex Patton, Wm Patton. Nat C Rogers. S K Scott. R W Scott. T B Thompson, S J Thompson. J W Thompson, Chas A Thompson. T B Thompson, Jr, Dan'l Thompson, Henry R Thompson, J J Thompson. A A Thompson. E S Loto, W N Loto. R E Loto, Geo W Loto. Calvin Loto, J A Loto, G D Vincent. Jas M Walker, C F Webster, A T Webster, R F White, R D White. White Bros. S A White, J I White, Wm A Woods.

Morton's Store—M G Faucette, Rob't H Faucette, Geo W Foster, G N W Garrison. G Mc Garrison, G A Garrison, Lewis Gellinger. Jas W Gilliam. John W Gilliam.

Nicholson's—David Bivens. Daniel Bivens. W F R Clapp. J E Clendenin, W N Coble. Willis Coble, G S Coble, W N Coble, G H Cook. T H Cooper. A G Cooper, Sam Cooper. D Cooper. Isaac Crabtree, A M Crabtree, G K Faust. Thos Gibson. E R Graves, R O Hargis, G M Holt. L H Holt, J L Holt. Isaac Holt, A L Holt. J W Holmes. G W Holmes. H M Isley, W M Isley. Phillip Isley, W H Moser, J L Neese, A B Nicholson. H G Nicholson, Jno Payne, A Sharp, H G Sharp. John Sharp, Jerry Sharp, W A J Sharp, W G Sharp. W M Steel. Geo Steel, J R Stockard. W P Thompson, C H Thompson. R T Thompson, G W Thompson, G F Thompson, J N Wood.

Oakdale—John R Adams. John P Albright. John N Alexander, Dan M Alexander. Ed M Alexander, S A Alexander, Eli M Alexander, O N Allen, John R Anderson, Wm W Atkinson, J M Bunton, M Bunton, Sam A Clapp. G A Clendenin, Henry Coble, Wm R Coble, Stanley Coble, Geo W Coble, Milton Coble, John R. Enliss. Jos M Enliss. George A Foster, J W Fowler, Jacob Garrett. O D Holt, O N Horneday, M F Horneday, R G Horneday, Wm H Ingold, A K Johnson, S S Kinney, Ed Kinney, Wm H Kinney, Geo W Patterson. J S Patterson, J P Pike. Wm A Rich, John Spoon. A T Spoon. S F Spoon, S Spoon, H M C Stroud, Hiram Wells, Joel Wells.

Osceola—J A Coble, L B & L S Holt, W E Holt. Holt & Housewood, H G Nicholson, P S Page, G E Watkins. H L Watkins.

Pleasant Grove—A C Barnwell, Eli Barton, William Barton, B S Benson, W A Bird, John A Bird, A G Boland, A L Boland, S T Boynes, L O

Boynes, J M Bradley, W P Browning, Wm H Browning. S J Cranford, W R Delubar. Jas A Dickey. Allen Dickey, L R Dixon, W R Edgeworth. John N Evans, Wm J Fitch, Gabe Fonville, Geo W Graham, J F Garrison, R Garrison. Bynum Jeffries. L M Johnston, Chas D Johnston. John Horn. Jos E Horn, W A Hughes. M H Hessee, Jno A Hessee. J F King, J H King, J B King, G T King, John W King, Thos L Lashley, Jas W Lea. Wm C Lineberry, Egbert Malone. Jos N Malone, W F Mayhan, J M Mayhan. C G Maynard, J W McCauley, Jas McAdams, L B McAdams, G A Mitchell. Joseph Mitchell. E C Murray. Eli Murray. L C Murray. Josiah Pace, John Parker, George Patton, J W Pettigrew. W J Pettigrew, H J Pritchett, Walter Pritchett. Lewis B Ray, Geo T Richmond, J M Roney. T P Rogers, W B Sellers, W H Smith, L M Squires, J J Squires. J W Stainback, J M Teer, Robt F Terry, B F Trolinger, Ed Truit, J H Tarpley. L E Tate, J G Tate. J L Tate. J H Turner, W J Turner. L J Walker, J C Walker, B F Walker, L B Ward. Z B Ward, J H Warren, Levi Whitted, B F White. H P White. Alfred Wyatt, J M E Wyatt. Thomas W Vincent, W E Vincent.

Sandy Grove—D H Albright, T F Albright, D F Carter. S H Carter, M F Collier. Wm Cottener, D Cox, H W Dixon, T C Dixon, T J Dixon. Peter Dixon. A E Fox, J Hinshaw, Jno Hinshaw, J T Johnson, M A Lineberry, W A Lamb, J W Overman, Wm Teague, C Thompson. A G Wright.

Saxapahaw—Jno H Braxton. Jonathan Braxton, Jos T Coggins, A G Cooper, Wm. P Durham, W H Gilliam. Geo Guthrie, Thos N Guthrie, J H Moore. Chesley Moore. David M Moore, Wm Morlett. Robt G Morlett, Jno F Morlett. Jno H Morgan, B F Morgan, Jos P Neese, J R Newlin, Geo Pendleton.

Shallow Ford—D M Ireland, Asa Iseley. A F Iseley. D W Kernodle, J M Kernodle.

Snow Camp—J R Coble, Stanley Coble. Robt Dark. Malon Dixon. David Dixon. Jno M Foust. Geo Foust, Jno A Foust. Elbridge Foust. Wm A Foust, Jacob Foust. Levi Herring, H Herring, O N Horneday. W C Holman. G P Johnson, Oliver McPherson, Gray McPherson, Thos N McPherson. C A McPherson. W K McPherson, J I McPherson.

Stainback—L W Allen. Wm J Allen, J A Allen, Jno P Allison, R L Aldridge, W J Anderson.

Union Ridge—William H Aldridge, Lewis H Aldridge, Jno N Aldridge, Jno A Bosnell, W G Coutrell, Alexander Coutrell, Jas A Ector Jno B Ector, Wm H Evans, Robt W Fitch, Sterlin Foster, Jas S Foster, J H Foster, J M Garrison, Nathan C Garrison, Gus A Garrison, Wm F Graham, Albert Graham, Jas H Graham, J Wm Hughes, Jno H Hughes, Thos R Hughes, B F Hurdle, Jno A Hurdle, Jas L Hurdle, James M Hurdle, R T Kernodle, Jno D Kernodle, W A McCauley, A J McCauley. H W McCauley, Levi H McCauley, M R Sartin, D P Sartin, Jos M Tapscott, Thos J Tapscott, Job H Walker, Jno M Wallace, Geo S Watson, Y B Warrey, Jno H Wilkins, E W Wilkins.

ALEXANDER COUNTY.

AREA, 300 SQUARE MILES.
POPULATION, 9,430; White 8,588, Colored 842.

ALEXANDER COUNTY was formed in 1846 from Iredell, Caldwell and Wilkes, and was named after the Alexander family, so noted in Revolutionary times.

TAYLORSVILLE is the county-seat, and is about 150 miles west of Raleigh. Population 500.

Surface—Hilly, and in places mountainous; soil productive; water-power abundant.

Fruits—Apples, peaches and nearly all the ordinary products.

Timber—Plentiful, especially oak and hickory; some white pine; mahogany and poplar, persimmon, dog-wood, wahoo, birch, wild locust, etc.

POST OFFICES.

	POP.		POP.
Avilla,	25	Mount Bethel,	20
Bently,	20	Mount Pisgah,	20
Broad Shoals,	20	Partee,	22
Cedar Run,	40	Polycarp,	20
Dealville,	15	Stony Point,	26
Elk Shoals,	40	Swanner,	50
Ellendale,	25	Taylors-	
Grade,	20	ville (C. H.)	500
Hedrick,	20	Thurston,	10
Hiddenite,	100	Vashti,	15
Kilby,	25	Wittenberg,	50
Holsclaw,	7	York Collegi-	
Lackey,	10	ate Institute,	76
Little River,	30		

COUNTY OFFICERS.

Clerk Superior Court—R. B. Tool.
Commissioners—A. A. Hill, chairman; E. C. Sloan, J. M. Deal.
Register of Deeds—T. A. Hudson.
Sheriff—J. W. Watts.
Solicitor 9th District—M. L. Mott.
Coroner—W. F. Heflin.
Standard Keeper—W. M. Smith.
County Examiner—W. M. Smith.

COURTS.

First Monday before the first Monday in March, and sixth Monday before the first Monday in September.

TOWNSHIPS AND MAGISTRATES.

Ellendale—J. B. Echird, G. C. Teague (Ellendale), G. A. Cline (Dealsville), R. S. Austin (Holsclaw), M. Pernell (Holsclaw), John M. Natts (Partee), Ed. W. Moore (Taylorsville), A. W. White (Avilla).

Gwaltney's—A. A. Martin, A. Mayberry, J. L. Bruner (Grade), W. H. Woodfin, J. Marshall Adams (Vashti), Wm. F. Patterson (York Institute).

Little River—J. C. Pearson, A. M. Bumgarner (Swanner), Arthur L. Watts (Taylorsville), W. N. Barnes (Partee), Lee St. Clair (Swanner), G. C. Chapman (Partee).

Miller's—B. S. Harris (Stony Point), W. G. Gryder, Jere. W. Brice (Thurston), G. Hoyle Martin, G. T. Hedrick, E. L. Alexander Hedrick).

Sharpe's—A. C. Shoemaker (Stony Point), T. F. Murdoch, R. M. Sharpe, Geo. Walden (York Institute), Frank Hines, N. C. Beckham (Stony Point), P. P. Matheson, T. J. Sharp (Hiddenite).

Sugar Loaf—F. C. Gwaltney, J. P. Stephenson (Vashti), Romulus R. Kirby, Thomas H. Crouch, W. Loyd Kerby (Kirby).

Taylorsville—J. N. Smith, J. E. Cheatham, J. G. Harrington, J. P. Matheson, B. F. F. Pool, J. L. Lefler, J. Lee Icenhour (Taylorsville), Thos. Little (Broad Shoal), Hosea Christopher (Thurston).

Wittenberg—A. A. Deal (Polycarp), G. F. Downs, Lawson Lael, A. C. Flowers (Mount Bethel), M. P. Johnson, W. W. Teague (Bently).

CHURCHES.

Names, Post Offices, Pastors and Denom.

METHODIST.

Carson's Chapel, Taylorsville.
Church, Taylorsville.
Hopewell, York Institute.
Liberty, Taylorsville.
Pisgah, Mt Pisgah.
Rocky Spring, York Institute.
Stony Point, Stony Point.
Union (southeast corner of county).

BAPTIST.

Antioch, Little River, L P Gwaltney.
Bethel, Cedar Run, L P Gwaltney.
Concord, Swanner, W J Bumgarner.
Charity, Macedonia, J A White.
Church, Taylorsville, J A White.
Dover, Partee, J B Pool.
Mount Olive, Taylorsville, W J Bumgarner.

ALEXANDER COUNTY.

Pilgrim, York Institute, L P Gwaltney.
Sulphur Springs, Taylorsville, L P Gwaltney.
Three Forks, Taylorsville, L P Gwaltney.

PRESBYTERIAN.

Church, Taylorsville, —— Crawford.
Salem, Taylorsville, W A White.

LUTHERAN.

Church, Taylorsville, J C Lang.
Friendship, Wittenberg, J C Lang.
Salem, Taylorsville, J C Lang.

MINISTERS RESIDENT.

Names, Post Offices and Denom.

METHODIST.

Barker, John, Sweet Home.

BAPTIST.

Bumgarner, W J, Clendall.
Gwaltney, J P, York Collegiate Institute.
Gwaltney, L P, Vashti.
Pool, Jones B, Taylorsville.
Pool, C C, Partee.

HOTELS.

Names and Post Offices

Hotel (All Healing Springs) Ellendale. R F Cobb.
Hotel (Springs) Ellendale, Lawson Teague.
Piedmont, Taylorsville, E Hedrick.

LAWYERS.

Names and Post Offices.

Burke, J H, Taylorsville.
Burke, B, Taylorsville.
Linney, R Z, Taylorsville.
McIntosh, A C, Jr, Taylorsville.
Smith, W M, Taylorsville.

MANUFACTORIES.

Kinds, Post Offices and Proprietors.

Millwrighting, Stony Point.
Millwrighting, Hedrick, W A Dunn.
Sash, Doors and Blinds, Taylorsville. Ingram & Allen Co.
Spokes and Handles, Vashti, Vashti Spoke and Handle Co.
Tannery, Hedrick, J P White & Son.
Plug and Smoking Tobacco, Taylorsville. R P Matheson.
Tannery, Wittenberg, W W Smith.
Tannery, York Institute, W C Linney.
Tannery, Little River, Deal & Johnson.

ALEXANDER COUNTY.

Tannery, Hiddenite, J L Davis.
Tannery, Taylorsville, J M Matheson.
Tannery, Ellendale, J M Deal & Sons.
Saddles and Harness, Dealsville, J M Deal.
Saddles and Harness, Taylorsville, J P Thompson and Sam Elliott.
Saddles and Harness, Taylorsville, Bruce & Elliott.

MERCHANTS AND TRADESMEN.

Name, Post-office, and Line of Business.

CEDAR RUN.

Campbell, Thaddeus	G S

DEALVILLE.

Deal, J M	G S
Deal, W D	G S

ELK SHOALS.

Payne, O C	G S

ELLENDALE.

Flemming, A J	G S
Tuttle, R F	G S

GRADE.

Godfrey, S	G S
Mayberry, Abel	G S

HEDRICK.

Hedrick, J T	G S
Moore, G D	G S
Moose, J A	G S
Smith & Paine.	G S

HIDDENITE.

Smith & Beckham.	G S
Thomas Bros & Co.	G S
Warren, Mrs L C	Millinery

KIRBY.

Russell, J P	G S

LITTLE RIVER.

Tuttle, R F	G S

MOUNT BETHEL.

Downs, J F	G S
Tuttle, W T	G S

MOUNT PISGAH.

Tuttle, L A	G S

PARTEE.

Coob, R F	G S

POLYCARP.

Bowman, E	G S

STONY POINT.

Moore, J A & Co.	G S
Shoemaker, A C	G S

SWANNER.

Barnes, J C	G S

TAYLORSVILLE.

Alspaugh, U L	G S
Chapman, E E	Shoemaker

ALEXANDER COUNTY.

Feemster Bros & Co,	G S
Flowers, G W & Son	G S
Murphy & Summers,	G S
Matheson, W P	Fertilizers
Matheson, R P	Fertilizers
Norton, Lula	Millinery
Nelson, W B & Co	Grocers
Robinett & Co,	Livery Stables
Taylorsville Drug Co,	Drugs
Thomas, G W & Son	G S
Sloan, E C	G S
Warren, W M,	G S

VASHTI.

Campbell & Williams,	G S

MINES AND MINERAL SPRINGS.

Kinds, Post Offices and Proprietors.

All Healing Springs (6 miles west of Taylorsville), ——, Ellendale.
Ellendale Chalyleate Springs (10 miles west of Taylorsville), Phill Tuttle.
Londermilk's Sulphur (3 miles west of Taylorsville), M. Swain, Taylorsville.
Sulphur Springs (6 miles east of Taylorsville), J. L. Davis, Stony Point.
These springs have been proven to possess the very best medical qualities.
Hiddenite, Hiddenite, W. E. Hidden.

MILLS.

Kinds, Post Offices and Proprietors.

Flour and grist, Taylorsville, W B Matheson.
Flour and grist, Taylorsville, F J Carrell.
Flour and grist, Taylorsville, Thomas Little.
Flour, grist and saw, Taylorsville, J C Bell & Co.
Flour, grist and saw, Taylorsville, R Watts.
Flour and grist, Taylorsville, Thomas Webster.
Flour and grist, Grade, Jones & Co.
Flour, grist and corn, Partee, A C Watts.
Flour and grist, Little River, Lawrance & Bowman.
Roller flour mills, Taylorsville, U S Alspaugh.
Saw, Ellendale, Wm Watts.
Saw and grist, Hiddenite, J L Davis.

PHYSICIANS.

Names and Post Offices.

Carson, C J, Taylorsville.
Little, H McD, Taylorsville.
Oxford, J M, Taylorsville.
Killian, R B, Taylorsville.
Kirley, T A, Taylorsville (dentist).

ALEXANDER COUNTY.

SCHOOLS.

Names, Post Offices and Principals.

Academy, Taylorsville, J S White.
Academy, Ellendale, James B Pool.
Sulphur Springs Academy.
Public schools, white, 48; colored, 7.

TEACHERS.

Names and Post Offices.

Bowles, J W, Taylorsville.
Baker, D M, Cedar Run.
Crouch, H M, Swanner.
Cobb, —, Glendale.
Cline, J A, Taylorsville.
Campbell, Frank, Cedar Run.
Carson, W P, Cedar Run.
Drum, C A, Hedrick.
Davis, R L, Hiddenite.
Echard, J B. Ellendale.
Gwaltney, Rev J P, York Institute.
Gwaltney, J L, Taylorsville.
Hendren, J J, Vashti.
Hendren, J W, Vashti.
Heffner, C N P, Taylorsville.
Hedrick, J F, Hedrick.
Johnson, A F, Vashti.
Kirkpatrick, Miss Lula, Taylorsville.
Linney, J C, Vashti.
Linney, Miss M M, Vashti.
Linney, Miss Pearlie, Vashti.
Linney, Miss F C, Taylorsville.
Martin, A B, Clio.
Mayberry, S A, Vashti.
Matheson, D Mc, Taylorsville.
McAlpine, E C, Partee.
Millsaps, E S, Clio.
Millsaps, J W, Grade.
Moore, T B, Taylorsville.
Oxford, J A, Ellendale.
Pool, Rev C C, Partee.
Pool, O F F, Vashti.
Pool, Rev J B, Taylorsville.
Pool, J J H, Taylorsville.
Pool, Rev D W, Vashti.
Price, J W, Thurston.
Rivers, Mrs Iona, Taylorsville.
Reese, W J, Ellendale.
Sharpe, Miss Nannie, Taylorsville.
Sharpe, Miss Emma, Taylorsville.
Stevenson, Miss Emma, Taylorsville.
Smith, Miss C J, Taylorsville.
Smith, G T, Vashti.
Smith, H L, York Institute.
Smith, J N, Taylorsville.
Teague, G C, Vashti.
Teague, V W, Taylorsville.
Teague, J R, Ellendale.
Thompson, Miss Maggie, Taylorsville.
Turner, J E C, Taylorsville.
Walden, Miss Addie, York Institute.
Watts, Butler, Taylorsville.

ALEXANDER COUNTY.	ALEXANDER COUNTY.
LOCAL CORPORATIONS.	**FARMERS.**
Lee Lodge, No 253, Masonic. Taylorsville: meets first Saturday, Tuesday of Court, June 24 and December 27.	Post Offices and Names. *Hiddenite*—W C Beekham, E H Crouch, T J Sharp. *Elk Shoals*—J D Moore, J H O Newton, C C Payne, P. T. Prichard.

ALLEGHANY COUNTY.

AREA, 300 SQUARE MILES.
POPULATION, 6,523; White 6,061, Colored 460.

This county was formed in 1859 from a portion of Ashe county, and derives its name from the mountains in which it is situated. It borders on the State of Virginia.

SPARTA, the county-seat, is about 180 miles north-west of Raleigh. Population, 148.

Surface—Hilly, and in places mountainous.

Staples—Corn, wheat, oats and live stock.

Fruits—Apples,peaches, pears, cherries, etc.

Timbers—Oak, chesnut, walnut, poplar, white pine, maple, etc.

TOWNS AND POST OFFICES.

	POP.		POP.
Amelia,	25	Hooker,	10
Anna.	20	Laurelbranch,	10
Boyer,	23	Laurel Spri'gs,	15
Brooks,	25	Montland,	25
Cherry Lane,	20	New River,	40
City,	20	Nulin,	25
Edmonds.	20	Olney,	15
Edwards X-ro'ds	10	Peden,	20
Elk Creek,	50	Piney Creek,	75
Eunice,	20	Prather'sCr'k,	25
Glade Creek,	25	Sparta (C. H.),	148
Gray,	55	Topia,	25
Highgate,	100	Whitehead,	25

COUNTY OFFICERS.

Clerk Superior Court—M E Cox.
Commissioners—Allen Jones, chairman: B J Carson, Jr, J W Bellows.
Coroner—Thos Edwards.
Register of Deeds—J N Edwards.
Sheriff—W F Thompson.
Solicitor 7th District—M L Mott.
Surveyor—J L Joins.
Treasurer—L J Jones.
Standard Keeper—
County Examiner—T J Fender.

COURTS.

Superior Court—First Monday after third Monday in March and September.

TOWNSHIPS AND MAGISTRATES.

Cherry Lane—A A Woodruff, G W Miles, A M Smith, John A Woodruff, Chas Crouse, R H Gentry, W Smith, J F Roberts (Cherry Lane).

Cranberry—J H Doughton, Terrill Candill, Tobias Blevin, Jesse Atwood (Sparta).

Gap Civil—H M Crouse, C J Edwards, J M Gambill, George McReaves, J E Moxley, J P Moxley, W L Hoppers, J C Roup (Sparta).

Glade Creek—J M Wagoner, Morgan Edwards, R A Choate, T C Higgins, Nathan Davis, Wm Evens, P C Higgins.

Piney Creek—C Parsons, Wm Halsey, J S Parsons, J C Field, W W Nash.

Prather's—Haywood Estep, Julius L Smith, A W Long, M F Jones, A C Black, F B Warren, J S Owens (Prather's Creek).

CHURCHES.

Names, Post Offices, Pastors and Denom.

METHODIST.

Shiloh, Sparta.
Selma, Cherry Lane.
Mt. Pleasant, Mouth of Wilson, Va.
Mt Zion, Scottsville, J H Perry.

PRIMITIVE BAPTIST.

Antioch, Elk Creek, J E Scott.
Piney Creek, Piney Creek.
Zion, Sparta, Com Collins.
Elk Creek, J E Croft.
Little River, Eunice, C H Collins.

UNION BAPTIST.

New Salem, Sparta, C Blevins.
Shelter, New Resen, J W Dendreth.
Mt Carmel, Piney Creek, —— Baldwin.

BAPTIST.

Sparta, Jas Shumate.
Union, Sparta, A J Taylor.

MINISTERS RESIDENT.

Names, Post Offices and Denom.

METHODIST.

Boyer, H K, Sparta.
Doughton, J B, Sparta.
Hines, Richard, Elk Creek.
Pugh, John L, Mouth of Wilson, Va.
Roberts, J F, Cherry Lane.

UNION BAPTIST.

Blevens, Calaway, Sparta.
Edwards, I, Eunice.
McBright, A, Cherry Lane.
Landreth, I W, Elk Creek.
Wagoner, A J, Prather's Creek.

ALLEGHANY COUNTY.

PRIMITIVE BAPTIST.

Craft, Joseph, Anna.
Craft, W R, Anna.
Couse, J M, Brooks.
Collins, C H, Eunice.
Sanders, Riley, Sparta.
Taylor, A J, Sparta.
Wyatt, E. Rainy Creek.
Wyatt, J M, New River.

BAPTIST.

Cheek, F B, Whitehead.
Shumate, James, Sparta.

GERMAN BAPTIST.

Reid, A J, Scottville.
Woodie, John C, Scottville.

HOTELS.

Names, Post Offices and Proprietors,

Jones House, Sparta, H F Jones.
Carson House, Sparta, A J Carson.
Hackler House, Sparta, R H Hackler.
Williams House, Sparta, L Williams.

LAWYERS.

Names and Post Offices.

Doughton, R A, Sparta.
Fields, W C, Sparta.

MANUFACTORIES.

Kinds, Post Offices and Proprietors.

Brooms, Edmonds, A G Carico.
Brooms, Edmonds, A O Carico.
Cabinet, Sparta, L Williams.
Carriages, Sparta, W M Burkett & Bro.
Coopering, Edmonds, Isaac Holt.
Saddles and Harness, Sparta, W K
  Holbrook.
Tannery, Sparta, Wesley Gilham.
Blacksmith, Eunice, E Spurlin.

MERCHANTS AND TRADESMEN.

Names, Post Offices and Line of Business.

CHERRY LANE.

Hutchinson, J C,	G S
McCann, W L.	G S

EDWARDS' X ROADS.

Gentry, W R,	G S
Collins, M L,	G S

EDMONDS.

Carico, A O.	Live Stock and G S
Carico, F H,	Live Stock
Higgins, Martin,	Live Stock
Higgins, P C.	Live Stock

ALLEGHANY COUNTY.

ELK CREEK.

Cheek, W B & Co,	G S
Feilds, Hackler & Co,	G S

EUNICE.

Higgins & Hale,	G S

LAUREL BRANCH.

McCann, J P.	G S

HOOKER.

Gentry, R H & Son,	G S
Kennedy, W B & Co,	G S

LAUREL SPRINGS.

Doughton, R L,	Live Stock
Doughton, J H,	Live Stock
Gentry, W R.	G S
Miller, John S,	Live Stock
Reeves, John.	Live Stock

MOUTH OF WILSON, VA.

McMillan, F J & Son,	Live Stock and G S

NEW RIVER.

Pierce, R K.	G S

NULIN.

Parsons, T F,	G S

PINEY CREEK.

Edward, A M,	G S
Billings, W H,	G S

PRATHER'S CREEK.

Jones, J C.	G S

SCOTTSVILLE.

Jones, L A,	G S
Abshere & Dancy.	G S

SPARTA.

Carson, A S & J M.	Editor Newspaper
Ednards, Haywood,	G S
Fields, Carson & Bro,	G S
Fields & Hackler,	G S
Jones, H F,	G S
Ednards, W S.	G S
Choat, S A & John.	Cattle Dealers
Thompson, William.	Live Stock
Roger, H K.	G S

TOPIA.

Waddell, Lee A,	G S
Warden, F R,	G S

WHITEHEAD.

Hooper, W L,	G S
Joines & Nooner.	G S
Carson & Doughton,	G S

MINES.

Kinds, Post Offices and Proprietors.

Copper, Sparta, Noah Long.
Iron, Edmonds, Hester Collins.
Iron, Edmonds, James Galion.

5

ALLEGHANY COUNTY.

MILLS.

Kinds, Post Offices and Proprietors.

Flour, corn and saw, Cherry Lane, M Woodruff.
Corn and saw, Cherry Lane, S Bryan.
Corn, Gap Civil, L J Joines.
Corn, Gap Civil, H S & C J Edwards.
Flour and corn, Gap Civil, Duncan & Woodruff.
Flour, corn and saw, Crab Creek, P C Higgins.
Flour and corn, Glade Creek, Edwards Creed.
Corn and flour, Piney Creek, W W Hash.
Corn and saw, Prather's Creek, John Grubb.
Flour, corn and saw, Scottsville, N H Vanhoy.
Flour and corn, Scottsville, John H Jones.
Corn and saw, Sparta, H. F Jones.
Flour, corn and saw, Cherry Lane, Woodruff & Smith.

PHYSICIANS.

Names and Post Offices.

Daughton, J L, Sparta.
Hanks, H, Sparta.
Higgins, Abner, Eunice.
Jones, Ebenon, Prather Creek.
Landreth, Stephen, Sparta.
Beeves, B E, Laurel Springs.
Smith, John L, Sparta.
Thompson, Robert, Sparta.
Waddell. B C, Topia.

SCHOOLS.

Names, Post Offices and Principals.

Collegiate Institute, Sparta.
Brown, S W, Sparta.
Public schools—35 for whites; 4 for colored.

TEACHERS.

Names and Post Offices.

WHITE.

Black, Lee, Topia.
Brown, Rev S W, Sparta.
Cheek, George, Whitehead.
Connett, E C. Laurel Springs.
Cheek, J M, Whitehead.
Duncan, Chrochett, Hooker.
Doughton, W F, Laurel Springs.
Evans, J T, Piney Creek.
Edwards, E H, Eunice.
Fowler, R J, Sparta.
Gentry, A M, Piney Creek.
Hardin, W R, Sparta.
Joines, J L, Edwards' X Roads.

ALLEGHANY COUNTY.

Kirk, W M, Laurel Springs.
Long, Matthew, Laurel Springs.
Long, Miss Bettie, Laurel Springs.
Reeves, Everett, Laurel Springs.
Tender, T J, Whitehead.
Whittington, Miss Nora, Scottsville.

FARMERS.

Names and Post Offices.

Cherry Lane—Frank Bryan, A J Bryan, F Bryan. William Kenaday, Thompson Kenaday, M Jennings, Jack Woodruff, A A Woodruff.
Edwards' X Roads—James Adres, Reeves Cox. J R Cox, M L Collins, M Edwards. Eli Hudson, William Jennings, M T Norman.
Edmonds—F H Carico, A G Carico. A Q Carico. S Rolarbs.
Elk Creek—J Atwood, D Black, Wm Black, Alex Black, Allie Black, Thos Carson, A J Carson, J Crowse, W B Cheek, C Cox, W E Cox, Floyd Cox, S O Edwards. F C Edwards, O Edwards. Lige Erwin, S G Erwin, H D Estep, Huram Estep, R Gambrill, A Hampton, H Hill, M F Jones. D C Jones, Wm Jones. Allen Jones. D T Jones, Millard Jones, W D Maxwell, A M McMillan, Alex McMillan, Frank McMillan, Norman Jones. F M & Y L Osborn, Wiley Reeves. A D Reeves. G T Reeves, H S Reeves, A Richardson, J Roup, Richard Sanders, J F South.
Eunice—M Cheek, Morgan Edwards, E H Edwards, D R Edwards, Mart Higgins, P C Higgins, Martin Wilson.
Laurel Branch—W P Candill, C Crouse. M V P Harris. Wm Harris, J G Harris. H Harris, T L Harris J F Roberts. D F Roberts, A M Smith, E Simmons, M Woodruff.
Laurel Springs — Tobias Blevins, Josiah Blevins. R L Doughton, J H Doughton, Calvin Long, John S Miller, C Osborne, J A Osborne, Joseph Phillips. W B Reeves, J H Stamper, Ben Taylor, A J Taylor. C J Taylor, Dock Taylor.
New River—L J Candill, S F Halsey, M F Osborn, L Parsons, Freeling Parsons, Floyd Parsons. J M Parsons. S Parsons. Joshua Pritchett, F N Roup, D Sturgill.
Piney Creek—John S Parsons, C Parsons, John Weaver, J R Wyatt.
Sparta—T J Carson, R S Carson, A J Carson, A Carson, J F Candill, Henderson Crouse. Henderson Cheek, F B Cheek. S A Choat, John Choat, C J Edwards, Thomas Edwards, Richard Edwards, Jr, H S Edwards, C W Edwards. C F Edwards, Rufus Edwards,

ALLEGHANY COUNTY.

H J Estep, David Evans, Wm Evans, J B Doughton, R A Doughton, C H Doughton, H A Duncan, F B Fields, J Fender, W C Fields, John Truit, James Gambill, William Gambill, John Gambill, Robert Gambill, John Gambill, Jr, Thompson Gambill, R C Gentry, Wesley Gilham, Alex Hampton, W E Hardin, W K Holbrook, William Hoppers, Thomas Jarvis, H F Jones, Thomas Maxley, Alex Maxley, Sr, Mrs C A Parks, M B Reeves, George Mc Reeves, Warren Rector, H K Boyer, Richard Sanders, G W Sexton, J L Smith, J H Smith, Silas Teder, John Teder, Wm F Thompson, Robert Thompson, J T Thompson, S H Thompson, A H Toliver, Jesse Toliver, M B Toliver, A J Wagoner, J Wagoner, J D Wagoner, John Whited, Wm Whited, A J Willey, W A Woodruff.

The Centennial Cotton Press, Hall Self-Feeding Gin and Erie City Engines make up the Farmer's Outfit.

ANSON COUNTY.

AREA, 500 SQUARE MILES.

POPULATION, 20,026; White, 10,237, Colored 9,789.

ANSON COUNTY was formed in 1749, from Bladen county, and derives its name from Admiral Anson, the celebrated circumnavigator. It comprised at that time all that portion of the State west of New Hanover and Bladen.

WADESBORO, the county-seat, is 143 miles south of Raleigh. Population 1,500.

Surface—Undulating, soil good, water plentiful.

Staples—Cotton, corn, oats, tobacco and wheat.

Fruits — Apples, peaches, plums, pears, cherries, grapes, strawberries and melons.

Timbers—Pine, oak, hickory, poplar, gum, beech, birch, maple, etc.

TOWNS AND POST OFFICES.

	POP.		POP.
Ansonville,	300	Lilesville,	280
Bennett,	25	Long Pine,	25
Beverly,	25	McFarlan,	100
Cairo,	40	Marengo,	50
Cedar Hill,	75	Morven,	300
Deep Creek,	10	Paris,	30
Diamond Hill,	45	Peachland,	150
Eggtown,	20	Pee Dee,	40
Florian,	75	Polkton,	200
Fray,	35	Poplar Hill,	50
Goodman,	50	Wadesboro	
Hyatt,	25	(C H),	1,500
Jones' Creek,	70	Wharf,	25
Knott's Store,	10	White's Store,	75

COUNTY OFFICERS.

Clerk Superior Court—J C McLauchlin.

Commissioners—H W Ledbetter (ch), E J Lilly, W D Webb, A S Morrison, I W Thomas.

Coroner—E F Fenton.

Register of Deeds—S A Benton.

Sheriff—B L Wall.

Solicitor 7th District—A J Seawell.

Surveyor—R J Flake.

Standard Keeper—D L Saylor.

Treasurer—J O Craig.

County Examiner—W D Redfearn.

COURTS.

Eighth Monday before the first Monday in March; eighth Monday after first Monday in March; first Monday in September; twelfth Monday after first Monday in September.

TOWN OFFICERS.

WADESBORO—*Mayor*, J T. Bennett. *Commissioners*, J A Leak, J A Hardison, J J Little. *Clerk*, D A McGregor, P R Bennett. *Constables*, S S Shepard, C B Luther.

POLKTON—*Mayor*, R J Austin. *Commissioners*, W F Crump, Dr L C Smith, J T Beacham, J P Billingsley.

McFARLAN—*Mayor*, W E Pennington. *Commissioners*, C E Braswell, R J Northcutt, Jas T Moore.

MORVEN—*Mayor*, C C Moore. *Clerk*, E R Little. *Constable*, H E Teal.

LILESVILLE—*Constable*, W S Leithen.

PEACHLAND—*Mayor*, Vernon Allen. *Clerk*, C B Moore.

TOWNSHIPS AND MAGISTRATES.

No. 1, Wadesboro—W J Ashcraft, J C Parsons, Geo K Little, Isaac H Horton, W W Henley, C W Covington (Wadesboro), J T Martin (Florian).

No. 2, Morven—J A Nivens, C C Moore, R J Baucom, D M Johnson, Hugh Johnson, E A Parsons (Morven), J S Jones, W E Pennington (McFarlan), W A Pratt (Cairo), A D Liles (Pee Dee).

No. 3, Gulledge's—C S Myers, E D Myers, T V Hardison, J T Phillips, G C Ratliff (Jones' Creek), J T Capel (Wadesboro), S T Flake (Wadesboro).

No. 4, White's Store—Addison Lowry, Z T Redfearn (Long Pine), J W Jones, E E Barrett, J T Collins, David Huntley, F C Broadaway (White's Store).

No. 5, Lanesboro—George W Allen (Knott's Store), Isaac M Williams, Eli Pope, J C Carpenter (Polkton), T V Howell, C S Redfearn, Marcus L Horne, B H Griffin (Peachland).

No. 6, Burnsville—J D Hyatt (Hyatt's), H P Meggs, H H Hays, W P Davis, J P Hill (Kendall's), I F Thomas, J C Caudle (Diamond Hill).

No. 7, Ansonville - Jas W Henley, J E McSwain, D R Dunlap (Cedar Hill), J A Colson, B K Threadgill, B B Staten (Ansonville), W R Hough (Wadesboro).

No. 8, Lilesville—James B Lindsey, Chas N Ingram, Jas T Porter, J J Colson, W B Ingram, W H Clark, W M Thompson (Lilesville), Thos D Richardson, Clarence S Ratliff (Pee Dee),

BUSINESS DIRECTORY.

ANSON COUNTY.

CHURCHES.

Names, Post Offices, Pastors and Denom.

METHODIST.

Bethel—Wadesboro. S S Gasque.
Chuch—Wadesboro. T P Bonner.
Concord—Ansonville, J H Moore.
Church—Long Pine. S S Gasque.
Church—Lilesville. B A York.
New Forestville—Lilesville. B A York.
Olivet—Lilesville. B A York.
Pleasant Hill—S S Gasque.
Poplar Hill—Knott's Store. SS Gasque
Sandy Plains—S S Gasque.
Savannah Creek—Lilesville, B A York.
Shiloh—Cairo. B A York.
Shady Grove—Lilesville. B A York.
Salem—Beverly. B A York.
Union—White's Store. S S Gasque.

BAPTIST.

Ansonville —Red Hill.
Brown's Creek—Wadesboro.
Church—Ansonville.
Church—Polkton.
Cool Spring—Morven. J W Hartsell.
Church—Wadesboro. N R Pittman.
Church—Deep Creek. J A Bivens.
Church—Red Hill. J Q Adams.
Deep Springs—Polkton.
Flat Fork—Wadesboro. G O Wilhoit.
Gum Springs—Lilesville, C H Martin.
Milton's—White's Store. J A Bivens.
Mount Olive—C H Martin.
Pee Dee—Lilesville.
Pleasant Grove—Lanesboro, G W Rollins.
Pleasant Grove—Wadesboro.
Piney Grove—Lanesboro, G W Rollins.
Rocky River—Ansonville. G O Wilhoit.

PRESBYTERIAN.

Church—Morven, E L Siler.
Church—Wadesboro, E L Siler.
Church—Morven. P G Lowry (col).
Church—Wadesboro, P G Lowry (col).
Church—Polkton, M C Arrowwood.

EPISCOPAL.

Calvary—Wadesboro.
Church—Ansonville.

PRIMITIVE BAPTIST.

Lawyer Springs—E L Siler.
Mineral Springs—Knott's Store, —— Snider.

MINISTERS RESIDENT.

Names, Post Offices and Denominations.

METHODIST.

Bonner, T P, Wadesboro.
Gasque, S S, Morven.
Merritt, ——. Peachland.

ANSON COUNTY.

Moore, J H, Ansonville.
Stubbs, W J F, Morven.
York, B A, Lilesville.

BAPTIST.

Adams, J Q. Wadesboro.
Boyd, J P, Polkton.
Hartsell, J W. Morven.
Martin, C H. Polkton.
Seago, P H, Lilesville.
Wilhoit. G O, Ansonville.

PRESBYTERIAN.

Lowry. P G (col.), Wadesboro.
Siler, E L, Wadesboro.

A. M. E. ZION.

Settle. J S, Polkton.

HOTELS.

Names, Post Offices and Proprietors.

Burns. Wadesboro, Mrs. Malloy.
Central, Wadesboro, Dr M C Gill and and C H Burge.
Hotel. Lilesville, Col — Frederick.
Hotel. Peachland. Mr — Bidell.
Hotel. Ansonville.
Hotel. Morven. Mrs Lowry.
National Hotel. Wadesboro. R A Smith.
Polkton, Polkton, J C Caraway.

LAWYERS.

Names and Post Offices.

Bennett. R S. Wadesboro.
Bennett, J T and Bennett, C D. Wadesboro
Little. R E. Wadesboro.
Lockhart, J A. Wadesboro.
Robinson, L D, Wadesboro.

MANUFACTORIES.

Kinds, Post Offices and Proprietors.

Boots and shoes, Wadesboro, Joel Horne.
Brown stone quarry. Wadesboro, Wadesboro Brown Stone Co.
Coffins, Morven, J M Brasing & Co.
Cotton Mill Co, Wadesboro, W J McLendon, pres: W L Steel. sec'y and treas. Investment, $115,000.
Harness and saddles, Wadesboro, C S Wheeler.
Merchant mills. Wadesboro, Thomas Salton.
Saddles, collars and harness, Wadesboro, C S Wheeler.
Shoes and boots. Wadesboro, V Wilson and Austin Ramsay (col.).
Shoe factory. Ansonville. Jas Hair.
Silk mill. Wadesboro, Murray, Singleton & Co (New York), Rob't Singleton. manager.

ANSON COUNTY.

Tannery (Kendall's Tanyard), Goodman, J C Goodman.
Wagon, Lilesville, J A McAlister.
Wagons, Wadesboro, Springer & Green.
Wagons, Wadesboro, H D Pinkston.
Wagons, Wadesboro, D L Saylor & Son.

MERCHANTS AND TRADESMEN.

Name, Post Office, and Line of Business.

ANSONVILLE.

Richardson, J R,   G S
Ross, J F,   G S
Wilhoit, W H,   G S

BEVERLY.

Flake, W T,   G S

DIAMOND HILL.

Dunn, B D,   G S

EGGTOWN.

Threadgill, B F,   G S

GOODMAN.

Waddell, W A,   G S

LILESVILLE.

Birmingham, J C,   G S
Frederick, C L,   G S
Horne, T A,   G S
Lilly & Williams,   G S
Liles & Ingram,   G S

MCFARLAND.

Odom, J W,   G S

MORVEN.

Carrington, C B,   G S
Dunn, Mrs Nellie,   Millinery
Grigg, J W & Co,   Dry Goods
Hardison, J M,   G S
Hines, J C,   Drugs
Little Bros.   G S
Martin, G A,   G S
Moore, J E,   G S

PEACHLAND.

Griffin, W H,   G S

PEE DEE.

Richardson, T P,   G S

POLKTON.

Austin, R J,   Grocer
Beacham, J T,   G S
Caraway, J C,   G S
Caudle, A L,   Grocer
Gulledge, R H,   Grocer
Ledbetter, C B,   G S
O'Neal, T R,   G S

WADESBORO.

Allen, F C,   G S
Adams, T W & Co,   Job Printers
Ashcraft, R W,   Grocer
Alexander & Coppedge,   Grocers

ANSON COUNTY.

Brasington, C S,   Dry Goods
Biglow & Flake,   Grocers
Bailey, B R,   Saloon
Bennett Bros,   Dry Goods
Burns & Marshall,   G S
Burns & Crowder,   G S
Covington Bros,   G S
Covington, E A & B G,   Hardware
Crowder, B H, Jewelry and Novelties
Crowder, B H & Co,   Gro and Conf
Crowson, T S,   Dry Goods
Henry, T B,   Furniture
Hargrove & Co,   Clothiers
Huntley, W J,   G S
Horton, I H,   Dry Goods and Shoes
Hardison, W C,   G S
Hammonds & Alexander,   Grocers
Huntley, L J & Co,   G S
Little, Julius A,   Postmaster
Lowe, John,   Confectioner
Little, H W,   G S
McKeithan, H H, F'ght and Tic. Agt and Tel. Op. C. C. R. R
Marshall, J C & Little, J M,   General Ins Agts
Miller & Hasty,   Meat and Vegetable Market
Plankett, James,   Gro and Confec
Crowder, B H,   Jewelry and Book
Parsons & Hardison,   Drugs
Rose, W A, F'ght and Ticket Agt, Cheraw & Wadesboro R R
Rose, Walter,   Western Union Tel Operator
Redfearn, J T,   Grocer
Redfearn, R J W,   Gro and Conf
Rose, W A,   Fire Ins Agt
Tarlton, Virgil,   Grocer
Tomlinson, A B,   Gro and Hardware
Tice, T J,   Grocer
Williams, Henry,   Grocer
Wheeler, C S,   Harness and Saddles

MINES.

Kinds, Post Office and Proprietors.

Brownstone Quarry, Wadesboro, D B Groff, Washington, D C, owner; W A Polk, mgr.

MILLS.

Kinds, Post Offices and Proprietors.

Corn and floor, Jones' Creek, J P Ratliff.
Corn and flour, Deep Creek, Nat Ratliff.
Corn and flour, Deep Creek, Wm Gulledge.
Corn and flour, White's Store, K W Kendall.
Corn and flour, Long Pine, Addison Lowry.

ANSON COUNTY.

Corn and flour, White's Store, Nat Chambers.

Corn and floor, Polkton, Ashford & Williams.

Corn and floor, Madra, H Haney.

Corn and flour, Madra, G S Little.

Corn and flour, Cairo, E M Diggs.

Corn and flour, Cairo. E Y DeBerry.

Corn and flour, Lilesville, W E Williams.

Corn and flour, Lilesville, B V Henry.

Corn and flour, Lilesville, John Watt.

Corn and flour, Lilesville, R R Liles.

Corn and flour, Lilesville. J W McGregor.

Corn and flour, Diamond Hill. — Sipe.

Corn. flour and saw, Lanesboro, Williams & Co,

Corn, flour and saw, Ansonville, D. Hancock.

Corn. flour and saw, Ansonville, J. Medley's estate.

Wheat, corn and saw, Lanesboro, L Caudle.

Corn and wheat, Beverly, Threadgill estate.

Corn and flour, White's Store, A W L Falkner.

Corn (steam). White's Store, John Poplin's estate.

Corn, wheat and gin, Cedar Hill, G B Dunlap.

Corn and cotton gin, Bennett's Station, Bennett & Dunlap.

Corn and cotton gin, Morven. C Jarman.

Saw and planing. Wadesboro, J M Brasington & Co.

Saw and planing. Wadesboro, S V Hardison.

Saw and Planing. Wadesboro. Geo S Little.

Saw and planing. Ansonville, S H Hyatt.

Steam saw and gin. McFarlan. McFarlan Mill, Gin and Mfg. Co.. Dr W J McLendon. Pres.

Steam saw. Morven. Henry Teal.

Steam saw, Lilesville. J B Ingram.

Steam saw, Polkton. J M Williams & Co.

Steam saw. Diamond Hill, William Tucker.

Steam saw, Red Hill, D Hancock.

Steam saw, Ansonville. R A Carter.

Steam saw. Cedar Hill. D R Dunlap.

Steam saw. Wadesboro, I H Holder.

Steam saw. Morven. John Gardner.

Steam brickmaking. Wadesboro, W T Brasington.

Wheat and corn (two mills), J M Williams.

Wheat and corn (Grassy Island), Ansonville. W A Smith.

ANSON COUNTY.

Wheat and corn, Wadesboro, A B Huntley,

Wheat and corn, Wadesboro, Thos Salton.

Wheat and corn, Diamond Hill, J W Thomas,

Wheat and corn. Lilesville, Ingram Bros.

Wheat and corn, Lilesville, Y A Allen

Wheat, corn and cotton gin, Morven, Y C Allen.

PHYSICIANS.

Names and Post Offices.

Ashe, E S. Wadesboro,

Battle. J T J. Wadesboro.

Battle, A J, Wadesboro.

Barrett. W W, Peachland,

Beckwith, R B, Lilesville.

Beeman, P T, Lanesboro.

Bennett, J H, Wadesboro.

Bennett, J W. Wadesboro.

Carpenter, S B. Cedar Hill.

Dunlap, J M. Cedar Hill,

Gaither, W W. Lilesville.

Ingram. W A, Wadesboro.

Maynard, A A, Cairo.

McRae, J A, White's Store.

Misenheimer, S F. Morven.

Ross. R D. Morven.

Smith, L C, Polkton.

SCHOOLS.

Names, Post Offices and Principals.

Anson Institute, ——. Daniel A McGregor.

Academy, Polkton, W F Hambert.

Cedar Hill Academy. ——. Stokes Clark.

Carolina College. Ansonville. W D Redfearn and J C Hines.

Graded Institute, Wadesboro, J A McLauchlin.

High School. Morven, G Pitcher.

Red Hill Academy. ——

White, 44 ; Colored, 33.

TEACHERS.

Names and Post Offices.

Allen, Miss Annie, Wadesboro.

Baldwin, Prof. Morven.

Baucom, H M. Peachland.

Boyal. Rev John Polkton.

Carpenter, J A, Deep Creek.

Clark, Stokes, Cedar Hill.

Clark, Walter, Cedar Hill.

Clark, R A, Ansonville.

Colson, John, Beverly.

Crowder, Miss Mary, Wadesboro.

Dunlap, W F, Cedar Hill.

ANSON COUNTY.

Eason, E A, Long Pine.
Effird. Hugh M, Goodman.
Fenton, E F, Wadesboro.
Ferrill, Alice, Lilesville.
Flake, Miss Annie, Beverly.
Gaddy, Mary, Cedar Hill.
Gaddy, E W, Florian.
Gaddy, Ida, Deep Creek.
George, Cora, Cedar Hill.
Goodman, Walter, Goodman.
Hambert, W F, Polkton.
Hambert, Prof. Polkton.
Harlee, Capt W F, Florian.
Hines, J C, Ansonville.
Hines, J C, Morven.
Howell, T B, Peachland.
Hundley, A E. Cedar Hill.
Knott, Effie, Lilesville.
Lilly, Miss Virginia, Wadesboro.
Miggs, H P, Olive Branch.
McGregor, D A, Wadesboro.
McLauchlin, J A, Wadesboro.
McLendon, John C, Peachland.
McLauchlin, James, Wadesboro.
Nance, Davidson, Ansonville.
Pitcher, G, Morven.
Ratliff, J T, Jones' Creek.
Redfearn, Rev W D, Ansonville.
Robinson, J W, Ansonville.
Smith, Miss Florence, Lilesville.
Tilman, E E, Deep Creek.
Wilhoit, Miss Minnie, Ansonville.
Wallen, R W, Polkton.

LOCAL CORPORATIONS.

Brown Stone Co, Wadesboro; capital $150,000.
First National Bank, Wadesboro: $50,-000 capital; Jas A Leak, pres: J D Leak, cashier; W L Marshall, assistant cashier.
Knights of Pythias, Wadesboro.
Knights of Honor, Wadesboro.
Wadesboro Silk Factory, Wadesboro.
Woodmen of the World, Wadesboro.

NEWSPAPERS.

Messenger and Intelligencer (weekly, democratic), J G Boylin, editor and proprietor.
The Telephone, Morven (weekly, democratic), John H Walsh, editor and proprietor.
Westminister Tidings, Wadesboro; E L Siler, editor and proprietor.
The Plowboy, Wadesboro, E W Flake, editor and proprietor.
The Pee Dee Baptist (Baptist monthly), Wadesboro, J Q Adams, editor; M L Kelser and J P Boyd, associates.

FARMERS.

Names and Post Offices.

Ansonville—G T Dular, S R Hyatt, J R Little, T C Robinson, W A Smith.

ANSON COUNTY.

Bennett — James E Jones, Peter Jones, E C Jones.
Beverly—C W Beverly, W P Beverly.
Cairo—Adam Bennett, T E Diggs, W R Diggs, J L Diggs, P H Diggs, Abner Flowers, W S Flowers, S C Liles, A A Maynard, Jno O Nevin, H J Pratt, B J Pratt, W A Pratt, C H Ratliff, Geo W Ratliff, T J Ratliff, J B Ratliff, J M Ratliff, W P Smith, W B Streater, J C Streater, W F Williams.
Cedar Hill—R A Biler, S M Clark, J A Dunlap, G B Dunlap, D R Dunlap, J Q Mills, J B Parker.
Deep Creek—R J Beverly, J T Gaddy, J M Gaddy, Wm Gaddy, E L Griggs, Peter Griggs, J T Gulledge, S T Gulledge, W L Little, W B Little, G T Little, A McGregor, E D Myers, J T Poster, G C Ratliff, B L Robinson, T L Robinson, C P Robinson, A D Tailton, F S Tillman.
Diamond Hill—C J Blalock, Ben Blalock, J W Burns, J A Burns, Monroe Burns, Mark Burns, W H Bivens
Goodman—W A Allen, J M Broadway, W M Broadway, Willey Bowers, J E Effird, J C Goodman, T B Goodman.
Hyatt—H M Baker, H A Clark, M T Curler, H H Curler, D Hancock, Geo P Hendley, J D Hyatt, W W Hyatt, S C Lee, G T Lee.
Jones' Creek—J W Brasington, C C Bowman, J T Capel, Henry Hamie, R B Huntley, N G Jones, C W Morgan, J P Ratliff, A D Sinclair, Jas T Webb.
Lilesville—J R Allen, Bob Allen, Jas Allen, Sherwood Bailey, Y C Allen, Joseph W Allen, W M Ballard, Frank Ballard, D W Bailey, Alf Bailey, W T Bailey, Stephen Bennett, Charles Bennett, Shade Bennett, Isaac Bennett, Lee Bennett, P L Bennett, Henry Bennett, Abram Bennett, James Bennett, Wash Bennett, Dr R R Beckwith, Amos Best, J C Birmingham, G B Birmingham, John Blackman, B Blackman, Moses Blackman, Dock Blackman, A M Boggan, S V Boone, W T Brooks, John Brooks, Oliver Boggan, John Bowman, W B Bryant, W H Bryant, Harry Byrd, Lewis Byrd, W H Byrd, C M Byrd, J E Capel, Dock Capel, L T Carter, Adam Clark, T S Clark, Dick Cox, W R Cox, P F Cox, W J Cox, W S Cox, H H Cox, Harrison Cole, J D Cowick, J B Coppedge, J H Coppedge, J W Currie, Daniel L Currie, L P Crump, Hampton Crump, J A Dobbs, E V Dobbs, A Dawkins, W T Dawkins, S S Dawkins, Jack Dickson, John Diggs, Joe Diggs, Solomon Dockery, R F Donner, W H

ANSON COUNTY. ANSON COUNTY.

Donner, F E Donner, Geo R Donner, Albert B Dunlap, Ed A Eason, J S Eason, Pleasant Eddings, John Eddings, Will Freeman, S T Flake, Jos Fladger, H J Goodwin, Jas Goodwin, Chas F Goodwin, W J Gulledge, J W Gaines, Sim Gatewood, Wm Gilmore, Sandy Hare, Riley Harris, W J Harris, F P Harris, B T Harris, Bradley B Harris, J T Harris, George Harris, S E Hatcher, W R Hatcher, Geo Harris, H H Hays, William Hatchcock, Jas Hatchcock, R L Henry, B V Henry, G J Henry, T F Henry, Wilson Henry, Jas P Henry, B L Henry, W F Henry, E M Henry, C L Henry, L G Henry, John Hinson, W C Hildreth, George Hinson, J E Hill, Henry P Hill, John Horn, Ed Horn, T A Horn, W L Horn, S Z Holder, Hugh Howell, E J Hutchinson, Noah Huntley, D D Hudson, J T Hudson, Levi Ingram, Wat Ingram, J B Ingram, T J Ingram, C N Ingram, Geo A Ingram, N D Ingram, W E T Ingram, W B Ingram, Charles Nixon Ingram, Wash Ingram, Jacob Ingram, Geo D Ingram, Press Ingram, Will Ingram, Jeff Ingram, Adam Ingram, Dave Ingram, Jno Ingram, Jr, Walter Ingram, Rich Ingram, Jr, Thos M Ingram, Fletcher Ingram, Allen Ingram, J H Ingram, Samuel Ingram, Wade Ingram, Richmond Ingram, Charles E Ingram, Ellis Ingram, C M Ingram, Edmond Ingram, Dargan Ingram, W T Jeanes, Alex Jones, L N Jones, B K Jones, Rowland F Kelley, B E Kelly, Calvin Kirby, Jas W King, Ben King, Ferry Knotts, Hamilton Knotts, Sam Knotts, Joseph Knotts, James F Knotts, John T Knotts, W E Knotts, W T Knotts, A S Knotts, Charlie Lear, Boston Leak, Jim Lindsay, Arch Lindsay, Madison Lintow, E J Lilly, Jim Liles, Washington Liles, W T Liles, A P Liles, B R Liles, L F Liles, Wash Lindsay, Willis Lindsay, Chas Lindsay, Fenelly Lindsay, C B Lindsay, J J Lindsay, S L Lindsay, Jesse I Lindsay, S S Lindsay, L L Little, Jessie Lee Lee, B J Lee, Dan'l Livingston, George Livingston, John Livingston, W H Livingston, H A Livingston, F A Livingston, W A Livingston, H E Livingston: John T Livingston, Daniel Lowe, J G Lowe, Joe A Lowe, J C Long, G E Long, Geo Long, J M Long, Frank Loving, Jerry Lucas, Dick Love, W S Luther, Sidney Luther, A W Maness, J F Maness, A D Maness, M C Maness, G W Maness, Henry Marks, J R Martin, Norman Matheson, J L Matheson, Charles A Meacham, J J Meacham, Henry Mills, Andrew Mills, T B Mills, P F Morton.

W T Meek, Frank Melton, W J McKaskel, John W McQuag, J A McAlister, Daniel McLaurin, W S McGregor, J D McGregor, J W McGregor, P M Moore, John Moore, Albert Moose, G W Moss, R S Morten, W M Morten, J A Morten, Joel Newton, Wm Parsons, Frank Parsons, Henry Price, Ed Price, Thomas P Price, W M Pickett, Peter Pickett, James T Poplin, J T Poplin, J A Poplin, J H Poplin, Pink Ramsey, Hamp Randall, Ned Reid, W T Ricketts, Alonzo Rosie, Ransom Rosie, J P Rosie, J B Saunders, Rev B Saunders, P Z Seago, P H Seago, J Thos Seago, E T Seago, P A Sellars, Gideon Sinclair, J A Smart, Wm Spencer, Jack Smith, Jess Smith, George Smith, Jim Smith, Gaston Smith, Sandy Smith, Atlas Smith, Sol Smith, Wash Smith, Clark Smith, Wiley Smith, Chas Smith, Jerry Smith, Burwell Smith, W S Swink, Jas Swink, Sam Sturdivent, Wash Steele, Smith Streater, R H Teal, J M Thomas, H M Thomas, J J Tyson, J A Tysen, W M Thompson, James D Ussery, W M Waddell, John Watson, Peter W Watson, Monroe Watkins, J D Watkins, B J Webb, G W Wilson, J W Williams, W E Williams, L M Williams, Z T Williams.

Marengo—W H Clark, J A Clark, John Clark, Rev J C Cox, J M McDuffie, E N Goodwin, Frank Hinson, Berry Hinson, H R Helms, Jas Hough, T J Hicks, J E Hicks, J Manus Liles, Julius Lindsay, G W McDuffie, Alex Richardson, Edmond Spencer, Lee Spencer, Frank Spencer, Eli Spencer, Oudy Spencer, Scipio Spencer, E M Spencer, H T Spencer, J F Spencer, W S Spencer, John Spencer, Alexander Spencer, J C Wall, H J Wall, S G Wall, Mial Wall, J T Wall.

McFarlan—J A Brooks, J S Cruch, J B Cottingham, E B Curtis, B F Holt, W T Hendricks, P J Jones, J S Jones, H D Johnson, Hugh Johnson, R W Johnson, George Kendall, Wm Kelly, Neill McLaurin, J T Moore, L T Morgan, C T Northcut, J W Odom, C D Thomas.

Morven—J C Ballard, Frank Boggan, Henry Capel, C B Covington, H T Covington, T C Cox, J C Cox, J R Dunn, C H Dunn, J B Gaddy, Joseph Gennesett, J T Gatling, R H Gatling, C H German, Joel Gulledge, T V Hardison, J T Henry, J T Little, C H May, C C Moore, M W Mowery, J W Pratt, J L Pratt, S M Pratt, Sam Robinson, D W Robinson, W B Sellers, W J F Stubbs, W F Stubbs, M O Strickland, N J Thompson.

ANSON COUNTY.

ANSON COUNTY.

Paris—Frank Bennett. J J Dunlap, Filmore Carpenter, Edwin Wall.

Peachland—Vernon Allen, H R Beaman, L L Beaman, Wiley Bowers, C C Davis. Staley Edwards, C P Griffin, H A Horn, W L Horn. A D Howell.

Pee Dee—J W Adcock. J D Adcock, John W Atkinson, J R Atkinson, H M Boggan, J S Boggan, J W Boggan, A A Cox. E J DeBerry, H P DeBerry, Ben Diggs, Alex Diggs, Wm Diggs, R E Diggs, Geo Dunlap, Moses Dunlap, Herbert Donner, J B Fincher, B F Gatlings, Chas Howard, Jacob Hatley, J T High, J C Hudson, J J Hudson, W B Hinson, T B Hinson. H R Hinson, T G Liles, A D Liles, M D Liles, D S Liles, J C Liles. Needham Liles, S F Liles, Wm R McQuay, W J Martin, A N McLaurin, Watt Ratliff, Wiley Ratliff, Frank Ratliff, G G Ratliff, James Ratliff, C S Ratliff, Jack Richardson, T P Richardson. Eben Robinson. Tyre Robinson, Henry C Robinson, A B Robinson, D C Robinson, Wm Robinson. Jim Robinson, Sam Wall, Simon Wall. Perry Wall, T G Wall, A G Wall, J A Wall, J R Webb, W C Webb.

Polkton—T W Allen, J F Allen. G W Allen, J L Allen, J W Beachim. N J Bennett, S W Birmingham. J P Billingley, J C Caraway. Stephen Crump, Jno T Edwards, R B Gaddy, W A Hulbert, C B Ledbetter, J F McCallum. D M Smith, I M Williams, J A Williams.

Smith—Wiley ———

Wadesboro—M H Allen. Jos Allen, J T Allen, R T Bennett, Dr J T J Battle, F S Bailey, Alex Biles, J T Billingsbly. J W Billingsbly, J A Boggan, W N Bennett, R A Biles, Sidney Broadway, W E Birmingham, W O Bennett, R R Bennett. Dr E A Covington, C W Covington, T T Caraway, C T Coppedge, W G Carpenter, J I Dunlap, Jesse Edwards, J L Edwards, J M Flake, C C Farrelly. Gaston P Forte, S E Forte, S T Flake, Jos Gaddy, W F Ganes. T A Gatewood, S Gatewood, J M Gray, Flor Gilmore, Joe Goodwin, E E Garris, J A Garris, W B Gray. Alex Howze, W W Hendley, B R Hill, Jno E Hill, J T Hendley, T S Henry, S J Harie. W H Hildreth, W G Huntley, W H Huntley.

Alex Hanna, Jno Hanna, Jas Hanna, W M Hane, G M Hunsucker, Eli Hildreth, R F Henley, C R Hinson, C F Henry, James Henry, J T Horne, G W Huntley, Brooks Hailey, T C Hill, J T Horn. Peter Jones, J J Jowers, B F Knotts. W A Liles, A L Leggette, E F Leggette, W J McLendon, C M Little, J A Leak, W R Lockhart, N P Liles, G R Little, Carl Lawson, John Lefler, C A Lawson, Robert Lampley, J J Little, Major Little. Wm Little, G K Little, H W Ledbetter, W P Ledbetter, T M Lilley, J A Livingston. W B Lockhart, R A Lindsay, P G Lowry, E S Marsh, J T Martin, J D Mills, J Ed Morten. J M Murry, S P Martin, James McQuaiz, B T Mills, John W Mills, J J Medley, J F Medley, Wat Moore, M A Polk. J T Pinkston, W A Polk. W F Pinkston, H C Parsons, L J Pinkston. R J W Redfearn, J S Richardson, T D Smith. W C Staten. P A Sellers, James Sinclair, Burrel Studivant. D D Short, John- Short, Sill Short. J W Sullervan, J A Sullervan, Walter Sykes. Eli Simons, S S Shepherd. D L Smith, Richmond Sturdivant, Richard Talton, T T Talton. Sam Tysen, W M Tyson. J S Teal, A C Teal. W D Teal. T R Tomlinson, J C Trexler. W G Tice, T J Tice, J W Thomas, W L Tillman. S H Threadgill, Daniel Tillman, J K Tyson, R T Sturdivant. J C Sykes. W A Winfill, R R Winfill, J A Winfill, Eben Winfill, C A Winfill, W L Winfill, W D Webb. J M Wall. Bill Wall, A R White, J W Williams, Jno Willoughby, W S Watkins, J W Watkins, T T Watkins. Jno S Watkins. T J Watkins, G D Watkins, Cab Watkins, R T Watkins, Jeff Watkins, R J Winfield, Thomas Winfield.

White's Store—B T Barrett, E E Barrett. F C Broadway, J B Burch, W M Gaddy, E D Gaddy, Jackson Hubbert. John W Huntley, John C Huntley, J W Jones, Addison Laury, J T Lowry. Adam Lockhart, E E McRae, Dr J A McRae, J E Marsh, H G Marsh, G F Myers, H A Redfearn, A S Redfearn, B B Redfearn, John Richardson, C H Rivers. M K Watson, J M Watson, A K Watts.

ASHE COUNTY.

AREA, 450 SQUARE MILES.

POPULATION, 15,628; White 15,033, Colored 595.

ASHE COUNTY was formed in 1799 from a portion of Wilkes. It is the extreme northwest corner of the State. It was named in honor of Governor Samuel Ashe.

JEFFERSON is the county-seat, and is situated 202 miles northwest of Raleigh. It has a population of about 350.

Surface—It lies on the north and west of New river. The western part of the county is mountainous; the eastern and middle portions are more level and quite fertile.

Staple Products—Wheat, corn, butter, grass and live stock.

Fruits—Apples, peaches, cherries, grapes and berries.

Timbers — Walnut, oak, hickory, sugar maple, poplar, cucumber, etc.

TOWNS AND POST OFFICES.

	POP.		POP.
Algiers,	25	Idlewild,	15
Apple Grove,	35	Idol,	25
Asheley,	25	Jefferson(C H)	600
Baldwin,	10	Lamar,	65
Beaver Creek,	50	Lansing,	40
Berlin,	25	Linney,	35
Bernice,	20	Laurel Spri'gs,	80
Blevens,	35	Nathan's Cr'k,	25
Bly,	25	Nettle Knob,	25
Bud,	20	Obids,	20
Clifton,	40	Ore Knob,	272
Comet,	20	Pinckton,	50
Concert,	50	Riverside,	25
Creston,	60	Roberts,	50
Crow,	40	Roten,	10
Crumpler,	50	Scottsville,	130
Dresden,	25	Silas Creek,	20
Dyson,	60	Solitude,	40
Elk X-Roads,	25	South Fork,	25
Eugene,	10	Sturgills,	20
Eye,	20	Sutherland's,	25
Fig,	23	Sussex,	25
Furches,	25	Transon,	50
Gap Creek,	25	Thaxton,	35
Grassy Creek,	50	Todd,	15
Graybeal,	20	Treetop,	30
Grayson,	40	Trout,	50
Gregsby,	50	Vernon,	25
Grimsley,	30	Wagoner,	60
Hastings,	50	Walnut Hill,	25
Helton,	100	Weasel,	25
Hermitage,	43	Weaversford,	40
Husk,	25	Wheeler,	35

COUNTY OFFICERS.

Clerk Superior Court—P Blevin,

Commissioners—E E Phillips, chairman.

Register of Deeds—M L Smith.

Sheriff—Byron Sturgill.

Solicitor 6th District—J F Spainhour.

Treasurer—B Sturgill.

County Examiner—J W Jones.

COURTS.

Sixth Monday after first Monday in March, and third Monday after the first Monday in September.

TOWNSHIPS AND MAGISTRATES.

Chestnut Hill—John Gentry, Emory Gambill, M M Blevins, Robert Phipps, Frank Jones, Smith Carson, J A Dixon, Jas McMillan (Jefferson).

Creston—Wm A McMillan, Alex Oliver, Claude Foster, Joseph Maxwell, Marion Goss, Jonathan Osborn, Robert Parsons (Creston).

Grassy Creek—F F Smith, John A Pierce, M C Hash, Jas Stump, Emery Waddell, Wilson Hudler, Emmett Stump, F C Deloard, Marcus Blevin (Grassy Creek).

Helton—G J Baldwin, M S May, Millard Kirby, W W Testerman, David Pennington, J E Phipp, W S Jones (Helton).

Horse Creek—F S Hampton, John Ham, G W Davis, James Greer, Sr., Ambrose Clark, John Welch, S M Brooks, W R Miller (Jefferson.)

Jefferson—W H Gentry, S T Sandifer, F L Colvert, C W Ray, E J Johnson, R V Idol, Peter Caldison, D J Perkinson, David Hodgson, W C Brannoch (Jefferson).

Laurel—Newell Stewart, Jas Martin, David May, R A Jones, Elihu Graybeal, Robert Thompson, Rufus Graybeal, John Pennington (Jefferson).

North Fork—Calvin Maxwell, Jack Sturgill, John Wilson, Alvin Cole, J H Hardin, Calvin Maxwell, Thos D Arnold, Milton Roark, E J Roark, Jos Brown, W B Graybeal, A W Osborn (Jefferson).

Obids—Mac Absher, E C Sweet, H L Burgess, Joseph Galloway, John Miller, Nelson Walters, H B Miller, Jacob Blackburn (Obids).

Old Field—John Hardin, Thos Greer, Jas Bledsoe, Jacob Houck, Green McGuire, H G Phipps, David Lawrence, F P McGuire, J H Worley (Jefferson).

Peak Creek—Wash Woody, W R Pennington, J F Reeves, John F Phipps, Jas B Woodie, David A Osborne, W B Carson, M Richardson (Jefferson).

Piney Creek—J M Grimsley, W H Graybeal, Wm Roberts, Wm Miller, Drury Hart, M W Thompson, Harvey Ashley (Jefferson).

Pine Swamp — Pressley Shepard, John V Hartzog, Felix Howell, N H Waugh, J F Hartzog, J F Taylor, Jonathan Taylor, Arthur Phillips, Geo W Brown, A S Cooper (Jefferson).

MANUFACTORIES.

Kinds, Post Offices and Proprietors.

Creston Wagon Works, Creston, N J Lillard.

Grassy Creek Tanning Co, Grassy Creek, Geo Collier.

Grassy Creek Furniture Co, Grassy Creek, F H Hatch.

Helton Roller Mills, Helton, W E Perkins & Bro.

Jefferson Tannery, Jefferson, Foster Bros.

Sussex Wagon Co, Sussex, R L Pierce.

Transon Tannery, Transon, S M Transon.

Treetop Tannery, Treetop, G W Ray & Son.

MERCHANTS AND TRADESMEN.

Names, Post Offices, Lines of Business.

ASHLEY.

Grop, Isham S,	G S
Standberry, W J,	G S

BALDWIN.

Hardin & Phipps,	G S

BEAVER CREEK.

Hamilton, R A,	Mill
Hamilton, W H,	G S
Walters, J C,	G S

BERLIN.

Eller, E C & Co,	G S

CLIFTON.

Jones, R W & Co.	G S

CRESTON.

Foster, C B,	G S
Lillard, N J,	G S and Carriages
Thomas, J D,	G S

CRUMPLER.

Ballon, J U,	G S
Baylor, Wylie & Co.	G S
Palmer's Bromide Arsenic Springs Co	
Pasley, J L,	G S
Robinson, J H,	G S

ASHE COUNTY.

DRESDEN.

Wilcox Bros.	G S

EYE.

Miller, Wm & Bros,	G S

GAP CREEK.

Spoon & Hedrick.	G S

HELTON.

Perkins, W E.	G S
Perkins, W E & Bro.	Millers

GRASSY CREEK.

Eller, Rollins & Co.	G S
Greer, P J.	G S

GREGSBY.

Miller, J S & Son.	G S

HUSK.

Banguess, T J & R.	Millers

IDLEWILD.

Hartzog, John N.	G S

JEFFERSON.

Carson, J M.	G S
Foster, J E & N A.	G S
McNeill Bros.	G S

LANSING.

Perkins, W H.	G S

NATHAN'S CREEK.

Cox, S V,	G S
McMillan, J B & Son.	G S

NETTLE KNOB.

Goodman, F V.	G S
Good, P C & Son.	G S
Wilcon, G G.	G S

OBID.

Long & Lyon,	G S
Miller, A L	G S

PINCKTON.

Miller, F M	G S

RIVERSIDE.

McGuire Bros,	G S

SCOTTSVILLE.

Marsh Bros & Co.	G S
Shepherd & Fender.	G S

SILAS CREEK.

Baker, M F & Co,	G S
Dickson & Eller,	G S
Jones, W S & Co,	G S

SOLITUDE.

Graybeal, Wm M	G S
Jones, Riley A	G S
Maxwell L & C	G S
Mercer & Lewis	G S

STURGILL.

Sturgill, B	G S

SUSSEX.

Hadler, Porter & Co,	G S

ASHE COUNTY.		ASHE COUNTY.

SUTHERLAND.

Donnelly, G M	G S
Shell, W G & Son,	G S
Spainhour, W R	G S

THAXTON.

Martin, B Y & Son,	G S

VERNON.

Spicer & Seagraves.	G S

WAGONER.

Bare, J D	G S
Long, M & Son,	G S
Walsh, A F	G S

WEAVER'S FORD.

Dickson, J A (near)	Miller.
Pierce, Rufus R	G S
Tucker, J W & Son,	G S
Tucker, Sidney	G S

WHEELER.

Powell, L C	G S

TEACHERS.

Names and Post Offices.

Baker, G W, Jefferson.
Barlow, A W, Bly.
Blankenbecker, J W, Sussex.
Blevin, A B, Blevin.
Badger, Miss Elsie, Berlin.
Carson, Testerman, Silas Creek.
Clark, John, Seminary.
Dixon, C M, Silas Creek.
Duncan, J E, Jefferson.

Eller, E E, Pinckton.
Eller, A S J, Berlin.
Eldreth, J L, Ashby.
Francis, Eli, Eugene.
Francis, W S, Berlin.
Gass, Phos, J, Creston.
Graybeal, J W, Seminary.
Graybeal, D M, Graybeal.
Graybeal, Sherman, Lansing.
Graybeal, W H, Lansing.
Goodman, W A, Trap Hill.
Goodman, G B, Beaver Creek.
Haynes, B D, Laurel Springs.
Hodgson, T A, Treetop.
Johnson, W E, Clifton.
Jones, J W, Clifton.
Johnson, E J, Jefferson.
Johnson, Ed, Jefferson.
Johnson, Wm, Seminary.
Jones, A L, Silas Creek.
Lyon, D M, Dobson.
Morton, Ella, Transon.
Maxwell, Laura, Creston.
McEwin, Miss Sallie, Jefferson.
Miller, J A, Bly.
Porter, W M, Shoals.
Porter, John, Linney.
Porter, John, Seminary.
Pennington, E R, Sturgill.
Pennington, H K, Graybeal.
Phipps, Wm, Graybeal.
Sawyer, G W, Crumpler.
Shepherd, Fieldon, Pinckton.
Stuart, J H, Silas Creek.
Tucker, E T, Furches.
Thompson, Mc———, Tusk.
Wakefield, E F, Jefferson.

OLD DOMINION STEAMSHIP CO.,

WASHINGTON, N. C.

Steamers of the Old Dominion Steamship Company between Washington, N. C., and Norfolk, connect at Norfolk with steamers for New York, Baltimore, Philadelphia, Boston and Providence, and with all Railroads for East, West, North and South.

At Washington with Steamers for South Creek, Aurora, Makeleysville, Scranton and Bell Hann; also with Norfolk and Southern Railroad and Bell Hann, for all points between Bell Hann and Norfolk; also with Steamers on Tar River for Boyd's Ferry, Pactolus, Saft's Landing, Greenville, Center Bluff, Falkland, Hill, Sparta and Tarboro.

Passenger accommodations on all Steamers. Freight delivered with dispatch, and as low as by any other Line.

JOHN MYERS SONS, Agents.

BEAUFORT COUNTY.

AREA, 720 SQUARE MILES.

POPULATION, 2,892; White 11,689, Colored 9,203.

BEAUFORT COUNTY was formed in 1741 from Bath county, and takes its name from Henry, Duke of Beaufort, one of the Lords Proprietors, who surrendered their rights to the English Crown in 1729.

WASHINGTON, the county-seat, on Pamlico river, is situated 127 miles east of Raleigh, and has a population of 5,300.

Surface—Much of the land in this county is low and swampy, but generally rich and very productive when well drained. The Pamlico river runs directly through the county. Navigation good.

Staples—Cotton, corn, rice, trucking, fish, naval stores, shingles and lumber. Large quantities of corn and cotton are produced on the South creek and other swamp lands along the Pamlico river.

Fruits — Apples, peaches, grapes, melons, etc.

Timber—Cypress, pine, oak, gum, juniper, etc.

TOWNS AND POST OFFICES.

	POP.		POP.
Acresville,	25	Jessamine,	
Aurora,	400	Latham's,	40
Bath,	500	Leechville,	150
Beckwith,	30	Mineola,	
Belle Forte,	20	Pantego,	250
Bishop,	25	Pungo,	50
Blount's Creek,	20	Pentown,	
Bunyon,	20	Ransomville,	20
Chocowinity,	100	Sidney,	
Durham's Cr'k,	75	South Creek,	150
Edwards' Mill,	250	Washington	
Gaylord,		(C H),	5,300
Gilead,	10	Winsteadville,	25
Haslin,	75	Wharton,	
Hunter's B'dge,	50	Yeatesville,	100
Idalia,	100		

COUNTY OFFICERS.

Clerk Superior Court—G W Guilford.
Commissioners—Dr W J Bullock, ch: C M Brown, Henry Bonner, D W Gaskill, W B Campbell.
Coroner—D J Tayloe.
Register of Deeds—O B Stilley.
Sheriff—R T Hodges.
Solicitor 1st District—W J Leary.
Surveyor—M L Waters.
Standard Keeper—O H P Tankard.
Treasurer—R T Hodges.
Attorney for County Commissioners— George H Brown, Jr.

Superintendent of Health—Dr Joshua Tayloe.
County Examiner—Dr B Stilley, Edards post office.

COURTS.

Second Monday before first Monday in March; first Monday after first Monday in March and September.

TOWN OFFICERS.

AURORA—*Mayor*, L T Thompson; *Commissioners*, J B Whitehurst, Alex Hendnell, W H Gaskins; *Clerk*, C C Bryan; *Treasurer*, B F Mayo; *Chief of Police*, G A Litchfield.
U. S. Collector of Customs, A Mayo.
U. S. Commissioner, E S Simmons.
BATH—*Mayor*, Jas S Marsh; *Commissioners*, J W Smith, T A Brock, Jno R Beasley.
EDWARDS' MILL—*Mayor*, T R Boyd; *Commissioners*, E J Edwards, A O Warren, W B Redditt, S F Cratch.
PANTEGO—*Mayor*, P P Williamson; *Commissioners*, W F Frisbee, C P Aycock; *Town Clerk*, Geo E Hicks; *Treasurer*, J W Topping; *Constable*, A B Jones.
WASHINGTON—*Mayor*, J Havens; *Commissioners*, J Havens, S R Fowle, W H Howard (col.), A D Peyton (col.), J G Chauney, N E Mitchell; *Town Clerk and Tax Collector*, Jno B Ross; *Treasurer*, Jno B Sparrow; *Sergeant*, M J Fowler; *Assistant Sergeant and Engineer of Fire Department*, E T Stuart.

TOWNSHIPS AND MAGISTRATES.

Bath—J T Linton (Sidney), J T Jackson, W R Brinn (Yeatesville), Ira T Bishop, G C Respess (Ransomville), G M D Whitley, H H Oden (Hunter's Bridge), T B Clayton, J S Marsh, Jno F Harding, S A Cutler (Bath).

Chocowinity—W H Patrick, H E Harding, W O Ellis, John A Buck, F H Von Eberstein, B E Downs (Chocowinity), C C Jones, J B Hill (Blount's Creek).

Longacre—M Jordan, J T Windley, Henry S Latham, J W Bowen, T I Waters (Pinetown), T H Harvey, H A Cutler, John Sparrow (Bunyon).

Pantego—P P Wilkinson, W L Judkins, J F Latham, John L Ratliff

BEAUFORT COUNTY.

(Pantego), W D Sadler (Leechville), H L Davis (Pungo).

Richland—L R Mayo, H G Sawyer (South Creek), J M Litchfield, J E Hadnell, J W Chapin (Aurora), C C Adams, C E Tutin, Burton Stilley, J L Butt (Edwards'), M B Wilkinson (Idalia).

Washington—E S Simmons, W A Potts, J H Blount, T E Cutler, R W Minor, W A Alligood (Washington), H E Hodges, Thomas Whichard, H B Cherry, John G Hodges, T R Hodges, N T Woolard (Mineola), J W Leggett (Latham).

CHURCHES.

Names, Post Offices, Pastors and Denom.

FREE-WILL BAPTIST.

Angel's Visit (colored)—Jack Creek. Frank Rodman.

Bearer's (col.) — Washington, Louis Bearer.

Beech Grove (col.)—Chocowinity, A Rodman.

Church—Pantego, Malachi Linton.

Dudley Chapel (col.)—Washington, D D Dudley.

Free Mount (col.)—Washington, Alfred Carmer.

Hebron (col.)—Pantego, John Windley.

Maple Chapel (col.)—Longacre, Frank Rodman.

Oak Grove (col.)—Yeatesville, A Rodman.

Reed Chapel (col.)—Aurora, Elder Harding.

Reidsville (colored) — Bath, Alfred Carmer.

Rice Patch (colored) — Chocowinity, Elder Whitfield.

Rodman's (col.)—Bath, Frank Rodman.

St. Matthew's (col.)—Durham's Cre'k, John Windley.

Spring Green (col.)—North Creek, M Hardy.

Weeping Rachel (col.)—Aurora, Elder Harding.

Woodstock Chapel (col.)—Jack Creek. Manders Hardy.

Church (colored)—Pantego, Anthony Jones.

BAPTIST.

Christian's Delight—Yeatesville, Malachi Linton.

Church—Washington.

Church—Pantego.

Mount Zion (col.)—Yeatesville, John Windley.

Spring Garden (col.)—Washington.

BEAUFORT COUNTY.

Zion Temple (col.)—Pantego, John Windley.

PRIMITIVE BAPTIST.

North Creek—Bath, D W Toppings.

METHODIST.

Asbury—Washington, J W Martin.

Aurora—Aurora, W C Merritt.

Bethany—Winsteadville, Y E Wright.

Campbell's Creek—Aurora, W C Merritt.

Church—Leechville, Y E Wright.

Church—Pantego, Y E Wright.

Church—Pinetown, J W Martin.

Church—Blount's Creek, N L Seabolt.

Church—Washington, R J Moorman.

Church—Bath, Y E Wright.

Durham's Creek—Aurora, W C Merritt.

Oregon (col.)—Oregon Mills.

Providence—Chocowinity,NLSeabolt.

Ware's Chapel — Washington, J W Martin.

White Marsh—Bath, N L Seabolt.

DISCIPLES OF CHRIST.

Athens' Chapel—Bath, W O Winfield.

Beaver Dam—Bunyon, John R Winfield.

Church—Pantego, Prof Tingle.

Church (col.)—Pantego, Jno Windley.

Haw Branch—Chocowinity.

Head of Pungo—Pungo, D H Adams.

Old Ford—Washington, J L Windfield.

Pantego—Pantego, John R Winfield.

Pungo Chapel—Leechville, John R Winfield.

EPISCOPAL.

Chapel of the Cross—Aurora, N C Hughes.

St. Peter's—Washington, Nathaniel Harding.

St. Luke—Pantego.

St. Thomas—Bath, Francis Joyner.

St. James—Pantego, Francis Joyner.

Trinity—Chocowinity, N C Hughes.

Zion—Bunyon, Francis Joyner.

PRESBYTERIAN,

Church—Washington, C M Payne.

Church—Aurora, Dr F H Johnson.

C. M. E. C. A.

Church—Washington.

AFRICAN METHODIST EPIS. ZION.

Church (col.)—Aurora, R D McIver.

MINISTERS RESIDENT.

Names, Post Offices and Denominations.

METHODIST.

Martin, J W, Bunyon.

Merritt, W C, Aurora.

Moorman, R J, Washington.

BEAUFORT COUNTY.

Seabolt. N L. White Marsh.
Vines. Augustus. Washington.
Vines, F. Washington.
Woolard. W M. Bunyon.
Wright, Y E. Pantego.

FREE WILL BAPTIST.

Linton. J W. Yatesville.
Linton. M. Yatesville.
Windley, John. Pantego.

PRIMITIVE BAPTIST.

Topping, Dan. Pantego.

DIS. CHRIST.

Adams. David H. Pungo.
Girganus, J M. Monticello (Washington co).
Latham. Aug. Washington.
Warren. Ed. Pantego.
Winfield. John R. Pantego.

PRESBYTERIAN.

Payne. C M. Washington.
Smith, Samuel M. Washington.

EPISCOPAL.

Harding, Nathaniel, Washington.
Hughes, N C, Chocowinity.

COL. M. E. C. A.

Beebee. Joseph A (Bishop). Washington.
Dibble, Sylvester. Washington.

HOTELS AND BOARDING HOUSES.

Names, Post Offices and Proprietors.

Clark Hotel. Pantego, Walter Clark.
Hotel. Aurora, Mrs W A Thompson.
Hotel Nicholson, Washington. John Burgess.
Washington Hotel. Washington. N C Hughes.

LAWYERS.

Names and Post Offices.

Beckwith, Sidney. Washington.
Bragaw. S C. Washington.
Brown, G H, Jr (Judge Superior Ct), Washington.
Nicholson, B B. Washington.
Rodman, Wm B. Washington.
Simmons. E S. Washington.
Small. John H. Washington.
Warren, C F. Washington.

MANUFACTORIES.

Kinds, Post Offices and Proprietors.

Barrels, Aurora, J B Whitehurst.
Boots and Shoes. Washington, S S Price (col).
Boots and Shoes, Washington, J Habourn.

BEAUFORT COUNTY.

Builder and contractor, Chocowinity, John Edwards.
Builder and contractor, Chocowinity, Lacy Edwards.
Builder and contractor, Pantego, J E Gerkin.
Builder and contractor, Leechville, McKinsey Smithwick.
Builder and contractor. South Creek, Jonah Hurse.
Builder and contractor, Chocowinity, Lewis Grist.
Builder and contractor, Washington, John Gardner.
Builder and contractor, Aurora, R T Pickering.
Buggies and carts, Aurora. J H Jarvis.
Blacksmith, Washington, Jno Lanier.
Blacksmith, Washington, Smith & Son.
Blacksmith and wheelwright, South Creek, Langley Hawkins. .
Blacksmith and wheelwright, Washington. Benj Hodge.
Blacksmithing, Aurora, F C Burch,
Blacksmith and wheelwright, Chocowinity, W H Burk.
Blacksmith and wheelwright, Washington. Abner Alligood.
Blacksmith and wheelwright, South Creek, Noah W Moore.
Block and pump maker, Washington, W M Chauncey.
Candy. Washington, E R Mixon.
Coach factory, Washington, Ed Long.
Cultivators and planters, Aurora, T L Cherry.
Gun and locksmith. Washington, F J Haltzscheiter.
Hardwood and lumber, Washington, Bruce Walling.
Ironwork and wheelwright. Pantego, J O Neal.
Lumber and mouldings. Washington, Fulford Planing Mills Co.
Shipbuilding. Washington, John Myers & Son.
Ship building. Washington, Joseph A Farrow.
Tinware. Washington. W C Mallison.
Turpentine. Washington, S R Fowle & Son.
Undertaking and cabinet, Washington. W F Farrar.
Wheelwright. Washington, S S Latham.
Wheelwrighting. Washington. S C Roberson.

MERCHANTS AND TRADESMEN.

Names, Post Offices, Line of Business.

AURORA.

Bryan. J B & Son,   G S
Cherry, F F. agt.   G S

BEAUFORT COUNTY.		BEAUFORT COUNTY.	
Gaskins, W H,	G S	Butler, E S	Section Master
Hudneck, Alex,	G S	Bishop, J R, jr	G S
Jones, R L,	Horseshoer	Bishop, J R, sr	G S
Mayo, B F,	Postmaster	Clark, Walter	R R and Ex Agt
Lichfield, John	Carpenter	Clark, W F	Tel Op
Pickering, Richard,	Carpenter	Clark, S A	G S
Smithwick, J W P,	Drugs	Clark, Mrs A E	G S and Drugs
Snell, Mrs Mary B,	Milliner	Creedle, E S	
Thompson, L T,	G S	Frisbee, W F	Livery
Thompson, W R,	G S	Ratliff, C H	G S
Watson, Mrs M E,	Milliner	Ricks, J H	G S
Whitehurst & Hudnell,	G S	Shavender, J B	G S
		Smith, Mrs C C	Millinery
BATH.		Topping, Mrs B M	G S
Brooks, C K,	G S	Topping, B M	G S
Brown, Dr W D,	Drugs	Whitley, Thos H	G S
Davis, J W,	G S		
Roanoke R R & L Co,	Lumber	**PINETOWN.**	
Smith, J W & Co,	G S	Parker, Surrey	—
Whitley, T W,	G S		
BELLE FORTE.		**RANSOMVILLE.**	
Tooley, W B,	G S	Bishop, Ira P	G S
BUNYON.		**ROPER.**	
Elorn, W S D,	G S	Blount, F W	G S
Woolard, F A,	G S	**SOUTH CREEK.**	
Woolard, Eliza,	G S	Brothers, Joseph	G S
CHOCOWINITY.		Flowers, M R	G S
Hill, M M,	Gro	Springer's Lumber Co,	Lumber
DURHAM CREEK.		**WASHINGTON.**	
Bonner, L D,	G S	Archbell, M T	G S
Bonner, C W, jr,	G S	Ayers, E W	Life Insurance
Tripp, Edward,	Notary Pub	Ayers, E W	G S
EDWARDS' MILLS.		Bath, B	G S
Jones, Jesse R	G S	Bell, Mrs A E	Millinery
		Bell, J N, jr	Jeweler
HASLIN.		Bogart, M C	Drugs
Hope, John N	G S	Bragaw, S C	Notary Public
Hensey, S G	G S	Bragaw, Wm & Bro,	
Way, D C	G S		Gen Life and Fire Ins
Way, P C & Co,	Lumber	Brown, Thos F	Notary Public
Wilkinson, W H	G S	Brown, B T	G S
HUNTER'S BRIDGE.		Buckman, C F	G S
Buynoc, G S	—	Buckman, J E	G S
		Buckman, A M	G S
IDALIA.		Buckman, L D	Gro
Cuthrill, R S	G S	Buckman, J F	G S
		Call, W H	Gro
LEECHVILLE.		Campbell, J W & Co	G S
Bishop, S C	G S	Carmatt, L J	Notary Public
Clark, G D	Gro. and Drugs	Carter & Taylor,	G S
Freeman, M E	Gro. and Millinery	Catron, W Z	G S
Harris, W J	G S	Cherry, M L	—
Kramer, M	G S	Conkling, ——	—
Wilkinson, W H	G S	Creage, N E	—
MACKEY'S FERRY.		Crumpler & Brannan,	
Chesson, A L & Co,	G S	Fire, Indemnity and Accident Ins	
Davenport, W S	G S	Daniels & Co,	G S
OREGON.		Dixon, Maggie	—
Brothers, James	G S	Elam, Z B F	G S
		Evans, DeLancy	Fire Ins
PANTEGO.		Everette, L E	Notary Public
Aycock, C P	Gen Mdse	Fortescue, D F	—
Aycock, C P	Postmaster	Fowle, S R & Son,	
Aycock, C P	G S	Who and Ret Gro & G S	

7

BEAUFORT COUNTY.

Frizzle, W S & Son,   Gro
Fulford, N S & Co,   Hardware
Fulford Hardware Co,   Hardware
Gallagher. J M   Drugs
Havourn, Z   G S
Hanbo, Geo   ———
Harriss & Abell   D G and Clothing
Havens, J   ———
Howard. T P   ———
Hoyt, E G   Hardware and Ag Imp
Hoyt, E S   Hardware
Hoyt, J K.   Clo and Dry Goods
Kuch, Jno B   ———
Kelly, A S & Co   G S
Lane, A J   ———
Latham, Thos J   Notary Pub
Lupton, J T   ———
Lupton, G A   G S
Mallison. W C   Hardware and Gro
McCafferty, S D (col)   ———
McKeel, C B   G S
Mitchell, N E   G S
Mixon, E R   Who Gro and Candy
Morton, W B & Co   Gro
Meyers, J & P B   Millinery
Nicholson, B B   Notary Pub
Nobles, J L   ———
Paul Bros   G S
Paul, W S   ———
Peterson, Ed   G S
Phillips, Geo A   Mutual Ins
Phillips, Mrs A   G S
Phillips, Jno L   G S
Potts, W A   Life and Fire Ins
Reid, R J   G S
Rowe, L V   G S
Rowe, F V   Who and Ret Clothing
Shaw, R B
        Agt Ludden & Bates Pianos
Spencer Bros & Co,   G S and Lumber
Stilley, H E
Studdart, Geo J   Life Ins
Suskins, L B   G S
Vines, M A   ———
Whitley, A B   ———
Willis E K   G S
Willis, D R   G S
Wright, M J   Gro
Wright. M F   ———

WHARTON.

Johnson, R G   ———

WINSTEADVILLE.

Winstead, W F, agt   ———
Woolard, C W   G S

MILLS.

Kinds, Post Offices and Proprietors.

Corn and saw, Beaver Dam, J R Eborne
Corn, Chocowinity, State National
  Bank.
Corn, Longacre, George Boyd.

BEAUFORT COUNTY.

Corn and saw, Latham's, W S Hardi-
  son.
Corn, Washington, J Havens.
Flour, corn and saw, Blount's Creek,
  Johna Cox.
Flour, corn and saw, Durham's Creek,
  Joe Edwards.
Flour and corn, Pantego, C Russ.
Flour. corn and saw (steam), South
  Creek, Springer Lumber Co.
Flour, corn and saw, Washington, E
  P Hodge's estate.
Planing mill, Aurora, J B Whitehurst.
Planing mill, Washington, E M Short's
  Son.
Steam band-saw, Washington, S R
  Fowle & Son.
Steam gin and grist mill, Pantego, E
  S Waters.
Steam saw and gin. Pantego, R H
  Shavender.
Rice mill, Washington. Norwood,
  Giles & Co.
Saw, Leechville. D C Way & Co.
Saw and shingles, Leechville, W H
  Wilkerson.
Saw (steam), Aurora, J B White.
Steam saw and gin, Aurora, J B White-
  hurst.
Steam saw, Chocowinity, W H Bach.
Steam gin, Edwards' Mill, Thos Boyd.
Steam gin. Latham's. Jas W Hodges.
Steam saw and gin, Washington, Wool-
  ard Bros.
Steam saw, Washington, G W Kingler
  & Son.
Steam saw and planing, Washington.
  E M Short's estate.
Steam saw and gin, Washington, J
  W Hodges.
Steam gin, Washington, Sylvester
  Fleming.
Steam gin. Washington, J W Small-
  wood.
Steam gin, Washington, John Myer's
  Son.
Steam corn and gin, Yeatesville, J A
  H Tankard.
Steam saw and planing, Washington.
  Eureka Mills Co.
Steam saw, Yeatesville, Beaufort Co.
  Lumber Co., A B Covington, supt.
Steam saw and grist, Yeatesville.
  Brown & Rumley.

PHYSICIANS.

Names and Post Offices.

Blount, J G, Washington.
Blount, W A, Washington.
Bonner, T P, Aurora.
Bonner, Wm V, Aurora.
Bowen. W P, Bath.
Bullock, W J, Pantego.

Credle, E S, Druggist and Physician, Pantego.
Creddle, E S, Pantego.
Gallagher, J M, Washington.
Masters, Samuel, Blount's Creek.
Nicholson S T & Nicholson P A, Washington.
Nicholson, John, Bath.
Rodman, John C, Washington.
Smithwick, J W P, Aurora.
Stilley, Burton, Edwardsville.
Tayloe, Joshua, Washington.
Tayloe, D T, Washington.

SCHOOLS.

Names, Post Offices and Principals.

Academy, Chocowinity, Rev N C Hughes.
Academy, Pantego, T Lewis.
Academy (col.), Washington, L R Randolph.
Academy, Aurora, Robert Bonner.
Graded School, Worthington.
Primary, Washington, Mrs W H Call.
Primary, Washington, Miss H Griffin.
Griffin.
School, Washington, Mrs. —— Ward.
No. Public Schools, white, 68; colored, 30.

TEACHERS.

Names and Post Offices.

Beckwith, Mrs S T, Washington.
Bonner, Prof R, Aurora.
Bowman, Prof J E, Washington
Burgess, Miss Bethel, Washington.
Downs, Miss Laura E, Chocowinity.
Ellis, Wm O, Chocowinity.
Foreman, Mrs A B, Washington.
Hicks, Miss Winnie, Bath.
Hodgers, Miss Bertha, Minneola.
Hughes, Rev N Collin, Chocowinity
Joyner, Rev Francis, Bunyon.
Lewis, G E, Chocowinity.
Myers, Mrs W R, Washington.
Rodman, Mrs Lydia, Washington.
Russell, Mrs Sarah, Washington.
Satterthwaite, Miss Ann, Washington.
Scott, Lawrence, Blount's Creek.
Simmons, Miss Jennie, Pantego.
Warren, Miss Lucy, Chocowinity.
Winfield, Miss Mattie, Chocowinity.
Winfield, Miss Hattie, Yeatesville.
Windley, J T, Airesville.

LOCAL CORPORATIONS.

American Legion of Honor, Washington, Chicora Council, No 350; W B Matton, Com.
Bank of Washington, capital stock, $50,000; Seth Bridgman, Pres; Thos J Latham, Cash.

Board of Navigation, Washington, J L Fowle, S Bridgeman, W J Morton.
First National Bank, Washington, Jas L Ford, Pres; A M Dumay, Cash; capital stock, $50,000.
I O O F Lodge, Aurora, L T Thompson, N G.
Knights of Pythias, No ——.
Knights of Honor, Oregon Lodge, Aurora, J H Jarvis, Dictator.
Knights of Honor, Washington Lodge, No 1490; E S Hoyt, Dictator.
Ladies Southern Memorial Association, Washington; Mrs J G Bragass, Pres; Miss E M B Hoyt, Treas; M J Sparrow, Sec. A monument has been erected, costing $950.
Ocean Fire Co, No 2: one steamer and one emergency engine.
Orr Lodge, No 104, A F & A M, Washington; E S Hoyt, W M; Robert Hodges, Sec.
Pamlico Lodge, No 300, A F & A M, Aurora; W H Whitley, W M.
Phoenix Hook and Ladder Truck Co.
Royal Arcanum, No —.
Salamander Fire Co, No 1 (col.), Wm Nash, Capt. One engine and one emergency engine.
Vol'teer Fire Co, W D Buckman, Capt.
Washington Light Infantry, 165 men, organized 1883; G H Hill, Capt; W H McDuett, 1st Lieut; B C Mallison, 2d Lieut.

NEWSPAPERS.

Evening Messenger, daily, Dem, Washington, J A Arthur, editor an prop.
Washington Progress (ind, weekly), W L Jacobson, editor and prop.
Washington Gazette (Dem, weekly), $1.50; H A Latham, editor and prop.
Watch Tower (semi-monthly), Washington; J L Windfield, editor and prop.

FARMERS.

Names and Post Offices.

Acresville—S G Alligood, Absalom Alligood, jr, David Baynor, David Boyd, T W Boyd, Jno W Boyd, Jas D Boyd, Richard W Boyd, G Boyd, W T Boyd, I T Boyd, J F Boyd, S B Boyd, R J Boyd, Evan Boyd, G H Braddy, Daniel Braddy, M A Braddy, W H Braddy, Benj Brady, John L Gurganus, R P Gurganus, Geo Gurganus, E R Gurganus, H O Gurkin, J G Habourn, J W Harris, Geo W Harris, A C Harris, John A Harris, J H Latham, Geo Latham, H S Latham, W T Latham, Noah Lee, S F Osborn, John L Peele, B F Pinkham, Nelson Sheppard, Jesse B Stubbs, Levi Stubbs, G N Wallace

Levin Wallace, Artillery Wallace, Leb Wallace, Thomas J Waters, Isaiah Woolard, Absalom Woolard, S Ralh Woolard, A S Woolard Isaac Woolard, W M Woolard, Elija Woolard.

Aurora—C C Archtell, G R Bateman, R T Bonner, Henry Bonner, Chas W Bonner, C W Bonner, jr, L D Bonner, A B Chapin, J W Chapin, F F Cherry, Geo B Colbert, C S Dixon, John M Flowers, F B Guilford, B F Hollowell, C A Hollowell, J D Hudnell, Jerry B Hudnell, Robt Hudnell, sr, J M Litchfield, G R Mallison, Jesse W Mayo, L R Mayo, Tilman Mayo, John Pate, John T Rowe, J W Selby, B H Thompson, W G Watson, S M Watson, R F Weatherington, J B Whitehurst, Simon Whitehurst, C A Wilkinson, M B Wilkinson, M F Williamson.

Bath—J F Adams, Thos Alligood, J R Beasley, W H Beasley, J J Bonner, F P Brooks, C H Brooks, W W Campbell, J H Cox, B W Cuthrell, S A Cutler, Jesse W Cutler, Henry Cutler, J W Davis, T F Davenport, B J Draper, J D Elam, Mrs Laura M Gibbs, J F Harding, agt, A E Huurington, S S Lassiter, J W Latham, J S Marsh, W M Marsh, T M Midgett, J T Nicholson, C F Oden, J A Oden, A S Pilley, S H Sanderson, J B Skittlethorp, Howell C Swindell, W H Whitley, F P Whitley, G B Williams, W W Winfred, M W Woolard, A B Woolard.

Beckwith—J B Bellingsworth, J T Campbell, J P Campbell, J R Davis, J R Harrison, W S Paul.

Belle Porte—J L Bray, Jones Auidley, Geo L Swindell, W B Tooley, S J Topping.

Bishop—J R Bishop, Sr, Isaiah R Bishop, W E Campbell, George W Crumpler, J C Duke, G W Gaylord, Wm Gradeless, Hugh Jones, Herbert Jones, Jas M Ratiff, F R Swindell, jr, Ed S Waters, Jacob A Wilkinson.

Blount's Creek—Solomon Clayton, J R Cooper, John Cox, W H Cox, J B Cox, W B Cox, H M Cox, J C Gaskill, D W Gaskill, H W Jewel, J E Jones, Aravial Jones, John F Jones, C C Jones, B B Latham, J G Latham, C H Latham, W N Long, Nathan S Long, Adam McKoy, H R Mills, W H Moreslender, J A Pollard, W J Potter, E H Rowe, H D Stilley, F V Stilley, S W Stilley, W E Swindell, A S Warren, Elias Warren, Jesse J Warren, J W Weston, Caleb Williams, H B Williams.

Bunyon—J L Alligood, Guy Alligood, C W Allison, F G Alligood, John W Alligood, Jr, N C Alligood, J H Alligood, Chas Alligood, L Alligood, Sr, Wm H Allgood, Jarvis B Alligood, W J Alligood, S T Boyd, Jas T Boyd, R Candy, Cicero Candy, W A Cox, Danl Cutler, r, E M Cutler, C C N Cutler, J J Cutler, r, J S Cutler, Giles Cutler, A N Cutler, N S D Eloin, D D Everitt, W A Foreman, Thos H Harvey, F W Harvey, John Hawkins, Isaiah D Jackson, J McG Jefferson, D A Jefferson, Richard Johnson, Marcellus Jordan, Sally A Mish, Jas R Mitchell, R J Respess, John B Respess, J B Respess, Jr, James E Robinson, C E Tankard, G E Tankard, G L Wilkinson, John T Windley.

Chocowinity—L H Adams, Eph Adams, W J Archbell, S B Archbell, Eason Arnold, W A Blount, jr, W A B Branch, H J Bright, W A Brount, sr, R T Buck, J A Buck, Ransom Buck, J H Buck, J H Butler, S D Callis, W H Call, J M Curran, H D Clark, R B Clark, S J Dixon, F H Ebestein, Josephus Eckin, W D Ecklin, Lacy Edwards, Robert L Edwards, J W Elko, R L Forest, Jos F Golley, B F Godley, S L Grist, J B Grimes, H E Harding, Jos F Harding, Jas S Hill, J G Hill, H H Hill, sr, J H Hill, S V Hodges, N C Hughes, W M Lewis, Guilford Lewis, Thos M Moore, J F Moore, Geo B Nelson, D W Nobles, W H Patrick, J B Price, J J Roberts, W H Spear, Seth Sutton, Geo R Taylor, Isaac Taylor, J G Taylor, John Taylor, E A Taylor, Asa Turnage, J J Turnage, A J Tunstal, W B Warren, Thomas Wetherly, J T Winfield, E B Winfield, R L Winfield, S F Woolard, Fred Wolfenden.

Durham's Creek—D A Douty, J F Douty, J G Lewis, B B Ross, Absalom Tutin, A H C Winter.

Edwards' Mills—C C Adams, R T Adams, Alonzell D Bennell, Geo W Bennell, T R Boyd, W H Boyd, T R Crawford, Sam'l F Cratch, Joseph Edwards, W H Edwards, W B Reddick, L B Ross, W R Ross, Isaiah Rowe, Burton Stilley, Alonzo Stilley.

Gaylord—J H Bailey, Lenard Brinn, J B Brinn, A B Campbell, Jerry Gaylord, J T Gaylord, O F Mason, R L Paul.

Haslin—R D Adams, John N Hope, D H Jarvis, F S Jarvis, F P Latham, Thos W J Lewellyn, D C Way, Mrs S A Wilkinson.

Hunter's Bridge—R C Boyd, J W Cutler, D W Edmonson, J B Everitt, W A Everitt, J D Elliott, J W Letterton, W R Letterton, H H Oden, J C Oden, J P Wallace, N D Wallace.

Idalia—H P Alexander, V D Allen, Thos Allen, R T Bonner, L M Broom.

BEAUFORT COUNTY.

H H Broom, F C Buck, J R Calloway, W S Caton, C C Caton, B D Caton, Alex Cuthell, J E Deal, J G Deal, F B Hooker, G J Hooker, W D Hemming, Jonas Lamm, Josephus Peed, J B Prescott, A G Rives, H H Ross, Mrs S M Sparrow, D C Styron, W J Walker, A C Walker, M W Walker.

Leechville—S C Bishop, Robt Brummage, J D Clark, Laurence Clark, J A Dunbar, Mrs M J Edniston, Geo W Harris, Corbin Jones, M T Manning, E S Marsh, Jas W Paul, W H Wilkinson.

Pantego—C P Aycock, W J Bowen, W J Bullock, M Chambers, W Clark, E S Credle, Wm Credle, Frank Credle, W H Davis, W S Davis, T M Daw, F M Duke, M L Flynn, E W Gaylord, R W Gurganus, J E Gurkin, E H Gurkin, Mrs B B Houston, Mrs Sigourney Johnson, E H Jones, Albin Jones, W S Judkins, Lewis Latham, Jas F Latham, W H Pilley, Geo L Pilley, C H Ratliff, John L Ratliff, Jas H Ricks, Geo E Ricks, J C Ricks, J T Ricks, C C Russ, G S Russ, R H Shavender, Sam'l C Shavender, Aaron G Shavender, W T Spence, Jno W Topping, D J Topping, M J Whitley, S W Wilkinson, P P Wilkinson, D M Windley, Sam'l Windley, J D Windley.

Pungo—J S Adams, D H Adams, sr. B B Allen, T F Allen, Reuben Allen, Geo T Allen, N H Allen, J E Allen, Stephen Carter, J L Carter, David Carter, W S Davis, Geo Manning, Dan'l Paul, N W Paul, N B Paul, Ira Rose.

Ransomville—J W Aldred, John R Asben, G T Bishop, John H Credle, A B Harris, Wm Jarvis, G M Jordan, Geo C Respess, J G W Ross, J W Ross, J J Smith, J W Smith, J J Surmons, W H White, T Wilkins, Howard Wisnall.

Sidney—J P Archbell, B F Archbell, W N Archbell, J M Burbage, J B Burlage, Jerry Burlage, T G Jordan, C B Latham, agt, J W Linton, J E Norfleet, H D Satterthwaite.

South Creek—C B Austin, T R Beacham, Jos Brothers, J W Brothers, J G Burnett, M R Flowers, Jno W Herring, Jonah Hulse, R P Johnson, C D Jones, H A Kermon, Daniel Lewis, B H Mixon, G E Potter, H H G Sawyer, J F Smithwick, E D Springer, E Tuthill, B J West.

Washington—Ashly Ball, J R Ball,

BEAUFORT COUNTY.

Fleming Baugham, Thos H Blount, W R S Burbank, McG Button, J A Button, R G Chauncey, R C Cherry, R W Cherry, W S Cherry, C E Cherry, W G Cherry, R A Cooper, Harmon Corey, J L Corey, Mrs M Elon, Sylvester Fleming, S F Freeman, Mrs A B Garham, J B Grimes, J B Hardison, C T Hardison, Joshua Hardison, J W S Hardison, J R Hardison, T R Hodges, J H Hodges, R T Hodges, Jas W Hodges, H L Hodges, B R Hodges, B F Hodges, J J Hodges, J G Hodges, Mrs Elizabeth Hodges, W L Hodges, J A Hodges, J D Holland, Thos L Howard, J F Jackson, L H Jackson, Asa Jackson, Jos A Jackson, J T Jackson, Thomas Jenkins, J H Jolly, J W Lanier, J C Latham, J G Latham, E L Latham, W L Laughinghouse, J J Laughinghouse, J D Leggett, W S Leggett, Leggett Bros, J Leggett, N Leggett, J G Leggett, F Leggett, W W Leggett, J H Leggett, J R Lipscomb, A R Mitchell, J B Mixon, W E Perry, L H Perry, J R Perry, Eugene Perkins, G A Phillips, Nicholas Rawles, Mc G Rawles, J A Roberson, J H Roberson, Jos Roberson, J T Rogerson, O Rumley, W C Russ, B B Satterthwaite, E S Simmons, W D Singleton, M H Singleton, Emily B Smallwood, Thos E Smaw, Robt L Stalling, W H Stancel, Everits Swanner, Joshua Swanner, W H Swanner, D T Taylor, Kinchen S Taylor, W B Tellerton, R D Wall, Eugene Walker, R R Warren, H N Waters, H L Waters, R C Waters, C C Waters, F H Waters, Bartemus Waters, P S Waters, R W Waters, T H Whichard, J H Whitaker, S C Williams, J B Woolard, Jordan Woolard, H R Woolard, J R Woolard, Alex Woolard, S W Woolard, M T Woolard, J Wiley Woolard, H J Woolard, Mrs Lydia Woolard, R S Woolard.

Winsteadville—C A Campbell, C W Ellis, Mrs Martha Eborn, S B Fisher, W H Foreman, Levi Foster, B H Hardison, G W Hendnell, Mrs O A Winstead.

Yeatesville—W J Archbell, sr, W J Archbell, jr, W R Brimm, N A Eborn, Wm Edwards, J F Fortescue, B F Godley, Mrs. Emily Jones, T H Keep, J F Keep, Levi S Keep, J T Kellingsworth, M Linton, A L Satterthwaite, W M Shavender, Richard Tarkinton, W R Wilkinson, W B Windley, C A Windley, T A Windley, Asa B Windley, S B Windley.

BERTIE COUNTY.

AREA, 720 SQUARE MILES.

POPULATION, 19,176; White 7,885, Colored 11,291.

BERTIE COUNTY was formed in 1722, from Albemarle county (since abolished), and derives its name from James and John Bertie, who surrendered their proprietary rights to the English in 1729. The county is situated at the head of Albemarle Sound, and on the north of Roanoke river.

WINDSOR is the county-seat. It is 100 miles east of Raleigh, and has a population of 805.

Surface—Low and level; the soil is generally good, and quite productive when well drained.

Staples—Bertie is eminently adapted to the growth of cotton and corn—the great staples of the county. Sweet potatoes are also profitable. Shingles and staves are also exported in quantities.

Fruits — Apples, peaches, grapes, melons, etc.

Timbers—Pine, cypress, oak, juniper, gum, etc.

TOWNS AND POST OFFICES.

Askewville,	50	Lewiston,	525
Aulander,	250	Merry Hill	25
Avoca,	210	Mount Gould,	35
Branning,	300	Powellsville,	100
Coleraine,	325	Quitsna,	25
Drew,	30	Rosemead,	25
Evansville,	50	Roxobel,	200
Exeter,	25	Sans Souci,	75
Hexlena,	26	Windsor,	805
Howard,	40	Woodward,	25
Kelford,	25		

COUNTY OFFICERS.

Clerk Superior Court—W L Lyon.
Commissioners—J B Stokes (ch), E E Etheridge, T S Norfleet, Wm Pritchard, T J Webb.
Coroner—H J Slade.
Register of Deeds—Sol Cherry.
Sheriff—T C Bond.
Solicitor 2d District—Walter Daniel.
Surveyor—W H Smithwick.
Standard Keeper—Jas E Mitchell.
Treasurer—T C Bond.
County Examiner—R N Askew.

COURTS.

Second Monday before the first Monday in March, and first Monday after first Monday in September.

TOWN OFFICERS.

WINDSOR—*Mayor*, Dr H V Dunston. *Commissioners*, A S Rascoe, W S Gurey, P C Cooper, W H Pugh, Rhodes Tayloe.

TOWNSHIPS AND MAGISTRATES.

Coleraine—William S Tayloe, G N Green, John H White, Josiah Brown, C J Morris (Coleraine).

Indian Woods—David Outlaw, Chas Bond, Lee Bond, Jas T Morris, Lewis Bond, E B Outlaw (Windsor).

Merry Hill—R J Shields, E H Walke, G A Hardin, B W Hathaway, Joseph E Nichols, N T Phelps (Walke).

Mitchell's—W W Askew, John H Mitchell, B B Lassiter, Wm M Mitchell, John H Bowen, John L Harrington (Aulander).

Roxobel—Dr P E Jenkins, W J Watson, S A Norfleet, W P Harrell, I H Simmons (Roxobel).

Snake Bite—H K Parker, J R Cherry, Charles Tayloe, J S Drew, N Bunch (Windsor).

White—George W Cobb, J H Lawrence, W F McGlonhorn, W S Adams (Windsor).

Windsor—C T Harden, T Q Castellow, A J Pritchard, W D White, Stark Shiler, Thomas Gilliam, A S Barbee (Windsor).

Woodville—J W Spivey, J R Bazemore, E E Pittman, J A Medlin (Lewiston).

CHURCHES.

Names, Post Offices, Pastors and Denom.

BAPTIST.

Conarity—Aulander, —— Bristoe.
Cashie—Windsor, J B Boone.
Church—Coleraine, ——
Church—Aulander, M L Curtis.
Green's X Roads—Windsor, L F Burke.
Holly Grove—Windsor, C B Williams.
Mars Hill—Coleraine, M L Curtis.
Rocquist Chapel—Windsor, J R Matthews.
Sandy Run—Roxobel, W B Wingate.

METHODIST.

Church—Coleraine, Wm Grant.
Church—Powellsville, Wm Grant.
Church—Windsor, J D Goodchild.
St Mary's—Lewiston, J D Goodchild.
St Francis—Lewiston, J D Goodchild.
White Oak—Windsor, J D Goodchild.

EPISCOPAL.

Church—Windsor, E P Green.
Grace—Lewiston, ——.

MINISTERS RESIDENT.

Names, Post Offices and Denom.

BAPTIST.

Boone, J B, Windsor.
Bunch, Jeremiah, Windsor.
Gordan, W P, Coleraine.
Leggett, Bythel, Windsor.
White, Joseph, Walke.
Williams, B B, Coleraine.

METHODIST.

Goodchild, A R, Windsor.

HOTELS AND BOARDING HOUSES.

Names, Post Offices and Proprietors.

American House, Windsor, J R Moody.
Dunning House, Aulander, H J Dunning.
Freeman House, Windsor, Freeman & Mizell.
Hancock House, Lewiston, A F Hancock.
Hotel, Lewiston, Mrs. Aurelia Williams.

LAWYERS.

Names and Post Offices.

Harrell, H P, Lewiston.
Lewis, H W, Lewiston.
Martin, J B, Windsor,
Pugh, H P, Windsor.
Scull, St Leon, Windsor.
Winston, F D, Windsor.

MANUFACTORIES.

Kinds, Post Offices and Proprietors.

Blacksmith, Windsor, W A Brantly.
Blacksmith and wheelwright, Windsor, E S Dail.
Blacksmith and wheelwright, Lewiston, Samuel Whitley & Co.
Blacksmith and wheelwright, Windsor, Lewis Floyd.
Carriages, Powellsville, Raynor Bros.
Coaches, Kelford, Parker & Brown.
Coach and Buggy, Windsor, E S Dail.
Coaches, Aulander, W D Hoggard.
Lime, Windsor, R W Askew.
Millwright, Aulander, J B Cox.
Millwright, Aulander, W J Early.
Millwright, Windsor, W G Gurkin.
Millwright, Aulander, H J Slade.
Shingles and lumber, Lewiston, S H McRae.

Spoke and hub factory, Windsor, Peter Rascoe.

MERCHANTS AND TRADESMEN.

Name, Post-office and Line of Business.

AULANDER.

Name	Line
Benthal, W T,	G S
Butler, C,	G S
Burden, W G & Bro,	G S
Burden, J A & Co,	G S
Burden & Chamblee,	G S
Dunning, W J & Son,	G S
Early, J J & Co,	G S
Hale, W H, Jr.	G S
Hall, T C,	G S
Harmon & Bro,	G S
Hoggard, S N,	G S
Johnson, G F,	Lumber
Miller, H D,	G S
Minton, W T,	G S
Powell, D C,	G S
Powell, W C,	G S
Pritchard, Wm,	G S
Rice, E L & Bros,	G S
White, T J,	G S
White, W J,	G S

AVOCA.

Capehart, Dr W R.	Fishery and G S

COLERAINE.

Beasley, W H,	G S
Britton, D W,	G S
Dickerson, A C,	G S
Griffith & Garrett,	G S
Holley, Thomas D,	Fishery
Gerrigan, R B,	G S
McLaughlin, D L,	G S
Mizell, C E,	G S
Nowell, A,	G S
Newberne, D T,	G S
Parker, J B,	G S
Ward, V L,	G S
White, A D,	G S
Wilson, J F,	G S
Wynns, A S,	G S

DREW.

Name	Line
Bazemore, J G,	G S
Drew, J S,	G S

HOWARD.

Baker Bros,	G S
Miller, H D,	G S

KELFORD.

Name	Line
Baker & Brown,	G S
Clark, W W,	G S
Davis, H C,	Groceries
Duke & Brown,	G S
Pritchard, A H,	G S

LEWISTON.

Baker, G W,	G S
Balance, J H & H E,	G S
Bazemore, W S,	G S
Bazemore, H W,	G S

BERTIE COUNTY.

Bidger, J,   G S
Britt, J S,   G S
Eason, A T & Co,   G S
Hancock, A F,   Gro
Harrel, Brown & Co,   G S
Hoggard & Harrell,   G S
Hoggard, R H.   Gro
Meakin, J,   Lumber
Parrish, G W,   G S
Spivey, Mrs M B (near).   G S
White, D,   G S

MT. GOULD.

Jernigan, J H.   Fishery
Womble, G,   Fishery

POWELLSVILLE.

Alston, J J,   G S
Britton, J C,   G S

ROXOBEL.

Bell, Mrs E,   G S
Hardy, E R,   G S
Hedgepeth, L C,   G S
Jenkins, Dr P C,   G S
Liverman, A T,   G S

SANS SOUCI.

Freeman, J C,   Lumber
Leicester, A E,   G S
Sallinger, Mrs B & Co,   G S

WALKE.

Capehart, W R,   G S
Gill, H H & Co,   Lumber
Nichols, J B,   G S
Outlaw, B J (col.),   Gro
Smallwood, Mrs M E,   G S

WINDSOR.

Askew & Collins (col.),   Gro
Barrett, Mrs S C, Agent,   Millinery
Bazemore, R C,   G S
Collins, C E,   G S
Collins, A S,   G S
Davis, W M,   G S
Garley, Dr W S,   Drugs
Gurley, T P,   G S
Gurley, T & F,   G S
Hardin, C T,   Jeweler
Jacocks, C W,   Hardware
Lipittz, Mrs Lewis,   G S
McDonald & Allen (col.),   G S
Miller, H D,   G S
Myers, T E,   G S
Nichols, J B & Bro,   G S
Pugh Drug Co, Dr E W Pugh, Prop'r
Rascoe, A S,   D G and Furn
Sanders & Sutton,   G S
Sanderlin & Rone,   G S
Speller, J B & Co,   Gro
Spivey, J B & Son,   G S
Spruill, C W,   G S
Summs, J W,   G S
Tayloe, C & R,   G S

MILLS.

Kinds, Post Offices and Proprietors.

Corn, Aulander, C W Mitchell.

BERTIE COUNTY.

Corn, Coleraine, Thos D Holley.
Corn, Windsor, Geo A Hardin.
Lumber, Howard, Greenleaf, Johnson & Co.
Lumber and grist, Windsor, J R Jernigan.
Saw, Windsor, J R Jernigan.
Saw and corn (Mill Landing), Avoca, James Raynor.
Saw, Windsor, J W Drew.
Saw, Windsor, H H Gill & Co.
Saw, Lewiston, S J Meakin.
Saw, Lewiston, J W Spivey & Co.
Saw, Lewiston, W B Hearn.

PHYSICIANS.

Names and Post Offices.

Capehart, W R, Avoca.
Capehart, A, Lewiston.
Dunston, H V, Windsor.
Gurley, Whitmel S, Windsor.
Harrell, W J, Aulander.
Hathaway, B H, Walke.
Jenkins, P C, Roxobel.
Nowell, ——, Powellsville.
Pugh, E W, Windsor.
Sessoms, James H, Powellsville.
Smallwood & Griffin, Lewiston.
Stevens D (Dentist), Coleraine.
Watford, W R, Coleraine.

SCHOOLS.

Names, Post Offices and Principals.

Lewiston Male Academy,
Windsor Academy, Windsor, F G Tayloe.
No. of Public Schools, white, 60; colored, 50.

TEACHERS.

Names and Post Offices.

Askew, Mrs Rosa, near Windsor.
Berry, W W, Coleraine.
Gilliam, Mrs Mary E, Windsor.
Gray, Miss Minnie, Windsor.
Mitchell, Mrs Sarah E, Coleraine.
Moxley, W R, Lewiston.
Norman, Miss Lee A, Indian Woods.
Perry, A J M, Coleraine.
Selrel, Mrs Maude, Roxobel.
Tayloe, Miss Olivia, Holly Grove.
White, Wm D, near Windsor.

LOCAL CORPORATIONS.

Cashie and Chowan Railroad and Lumber Co.
Gilliam, G, Jr, & Lyon, Bankers and Brokers.

BERTIE COUNTY.

FARMERS.

Names and Post Offices.

Aulander—Jos Conner, A J Dunning, W J Dunning, Jas M Early, A W Early, John R Early, Miles Eure, J H Hall, A T Harman, W M Marsh, C W Mitchell, W H Mitchell, Joseph Powell, J H Rawls, Abner Rawls, Jno Ried, Asa Saunders, M L Taylor, J G Willoughby, G Williford, J J Williford.

Avoca—D Bell, D W R Capehart, J D Gaskins, W H Gill, W F McGlawhon, John Newberne.

Coleraine—W E Baker, Thos Beasley, J W Beasley, Dan Britton, E E Etheridge, J H Etheridge, jr., James Freeman, L P Freeman, Norman T Freeman, Thos D Holly, J W Mitchell, J Mizzle, E J Morris, A Nowell, W J Outlaw, Shade T Perry, G J Perry, J W Perry, E P Simmons, Jno H White, John Wilson, E Wilson.

Lewiston—A J Askew, J W Ballance, Edward Bazemore, K Bazemore, J H Britte, Wiley Carter, W D Garris,

BERTIE COUNTY.

J S Griffin, G P Hall, H P Harrell, J P Harrell, J P Johnson, D P Lewis, S H McRae, W D Miz-ll, J W Spivey, W H Spivey, Burgess Urquhart, W J Veale, J T Veale, J B Williford, J G Williams, M L Wood.

Powellsville—John C Britton, W B Cleaton, J W Mitchell, D V Sessoms, W H Tayloe.

Roxobel—J H Brown, W J Capehart, J H Hardy, J H Liverman, A T & G W Liverman, W C Liverman, S H Norfleet.

Windsor—Reuben Allen, W L Askew, W G Askew, James N Bazemore, N Bunch, Abram Burden, W G Burden, Sol Cherry, jr, George B Cooper, J W Cooper, G W Cobb, A J Cobb, A Craige, Wm M Davis, H V Dunston, Thos Eason, S Evans, Thos W Gilliam, jr, John A Grant, J B Gray, George Gray, Abram Jenkins, C T Keeter, J J & G L Mardre, P Q Matthews, W W Miller, J G Mitchell, John Mitchell, Henry Mizell, W E Mountain, E R Outlaw, Mrs. H. Ponnett.

BLADEN COUNTY.

AREA 900 SQUARE MILES.

POPULATION, 16,763; White 8,646, Colored 8,117.

BLADEN COUNTY was formed in 1734, from New Hanover county, and comprised at that time the whole western portion of the State. It was named in honor of Martin Bladen, one of the Lords Commissioners of Trade and Plantations.

ELIZABETHTOWN is the county-seat. and is situated on Cape Fear river, about 100 miles south of Raleigh. Population 576.

Surface—The land is level. The Cape Fear river runs directly through the county. Much of the land is marshy. The piney ridges are poor, but valuable for naval stores. The swamps are rich, when well drained. Navigation is convenient.

Staples—Cotton and naval stores are the leading staples. Sweet potatoes are cultivated to advantage. Corn grows well on drained lands. Lumber is an item of considerable importance.

Fruits — Apples, peaches, melons, grapes, etc.

Timbers—Long-leaf pine, oak, ash, cypress, gum, etc.

TOWNS AND POST OFFICES.

Abbottsburg.	210	Ham,	10
Ammon,	12	Hucut,	15
Bladenboro,	120	Jerome,	25
Brinkland,	30	Kelly,	25
Brompton,	15	Little Sugar	
Cedar,	20	Loaf,	25
Clarkton,	350	Lyon's Land-	
Colly,	20	ing,	25
Council's		Marlville,	20
Station,	25	Moscow,	20
Cypress Creek,	25	Nat Moore,	20
Dawson's		Perryville,	25
Landing,	100	Populi,	25
Downingville,	15	Register,	10
Dublin,	10	Richardson,	15
Edge,	—	Rosindale,	40
Elizabethtown,	576	Sandbluff,	25
Elkton,	25	Tarheel,	90
Ellis,	25	Westbrook,	20
Emerson,	20	Whitehall,	60
Folsom,	25	Willis Creek,	125
Gravel Hill,	38	Winnie,	25
Guyton,	30		

COUNTY OFFICERS.

Clerk Superior Court—W J Sutton.
Commissioners—C P Parham (ch), Cash Lyon, I H Smith, C K Council, Alex Council,

Coroner—J A Register.
Register of Deeds—J R Mulford.
Sheriff—S G Wooten.
Solicitor 7th District—H F Sewell.
Surveyor—
Standard Keeper—J N Singletary.
County Examiner—R J Dunham.
Treasurer—R R Bridgers.

COURTS.

Second Monday after the first Monday in March and seventh after first Monday in September.

TOWNSHIPS AND MAGISTRATES.

Abbott's—J H Thompson, S F Averett, R J McEwin, Z G Thompson, Jno S Cain, Alex Pone, Shade B Thompson, Milton B Singletary (Abbottsburg).

Bethel—Marshall Part, Forney Willis, D J Hester, Neill G Brisson, Rich W Cain, B M Roberts, J M Thomas, W H Bryan (Elizabethtown).

Bladenboro — Nathan Jones, C W Williams, Jos Hester, Monroe Hester, Amsey A. Hilburn, Owen Jones, T J Freeman, Ed Singletary (Bladenboro).

Brown Marsh—J M Pierce, J N Kelly, A K Cromartie, Jos W Hester, D D McKeithan, A M Johnson, Wm A McKeithan, David G McGee (Bladenboro).

Carver's Creek—A H Perry, J C Daniel, J P Council, Jr, D S Bright, W Benson, L W Russ, J J C Lucas, Braxton Bright (Elizabethtown).

Colly—J M Bell, George W Atkinson, H L Peterson, W M Lewis, J R Mulford, R M Currie, R H Mashburn (Colly).

Cypress Creek- J F Parker, W D Cromartie, Albert B Rives, G P Sutton, Lyon Robinson, Montgomery Long, Erastus Peterson, John L Long (Cypress Creek).

Elizabethtown—W B Hester, J W Cromartie, R C Cromatie, J M Bryan, H H Barnhill, W M Martin, John Mears, B G McGill (Elizabethtown).

French Creek—Calhoun Fredere, E L Henry, J F Croom, W H G Lucas, W L Bridgen, J H Squires, Sam M King, Branson Royals, A B Brooks (Elizabethtown).

Hollow—Daniel Patterson, Frank Davis, W B Singletary, E N Roberson, Peter Dunham, E J Smith, Dr Wm Willis, Thos Scriven (Elizabethtown).

BLADEN COUNTY.

Lake Creek—W C Johnson, W J Shaw, J N Corbett, Fred Dyson, John Ennis, Isaac Beattly, W R Dyson, W C Johnson (Elizabethtown).

Turnbull—M O Edge, R W Tatom, O J Gardiner, F P Smith, W J Register, Atlas Smith, Moses Edge, J M Melvin (Elizabethtown).

White's Creek—Dan J Clark, J A Wooten, N G Clark, W G Hall, Rufus Register, S H Wilburn, Nelson McCall, W J Register (Elizabethtown).

White Oak—C F Davis, I J Cain, Owen Register, R L Bryan, James A Dunham, McK Culbreth, J B Young, J B Rice (Elizabethtown).

CHURCHES.

Names, Post Offices, Pastors and Denom.

METHODIST.

Abbottsburg—Abbottsburg, G W Starling.
Antioch—Cypress Creek.
Bethel—Bladenboro.
Bethlehem—Dawson's Landing.
Bladen Springs—White Hall.
Blue Fields—Elizabethtown.
Carver's Creek—Panther's Creek.
Center—White Oak.
Church—Elizabethtown.
Deems' Chapel—Elizabethtown.
Purdie's—Elizabethtown.
Soul Chapel—White Hall.
Singletary's—Elizabethtown.
Shaw's—Elizabethtown,
Union—Clarkton.
Wayman—Panther's Creek.
Windsor—Cypress Creek.

ZION METHODIST.

Savannah Temple (colored)—Clarkton, Wm Sutton.
Piney Grove (col.)—Clarkton, Thomas Mitchell.

BAPTIST.

Brown's Creek— ——, A T Howell.
Brier Branch— ——, A T Howell
Church—Clarkton, Haynes Lennon.
Church—Abbottsburg. Ed Wooten.
Cypress Creek— ——, A T Howell.
French's Creek— ——, A T Howell.
Gilead—Bladenboro, A T Howell.
Hickory Grove—Bladenboro,E D Johnson.
Haw Bluff—Bladenboro, C E Newton.
Kate's Chapel— ——, A T Howell.
Mt Zion—Bladenboro, C E Newton.
New Hope—Register, Daniel Moore.
Pilgrim's Hill (col.)—Clarkton, Joseph McKay.
Sandy Grove—Bladenboro, John Prevatt.
Sand Hill (col.)—Clarkton, Jos McKay.

BLADEN COUNTY.

Shady Grove—Clarkton, Ed Wooten.
Pleasant Hill (col.)—Clarkton, A H Cromartie.
White Lake— ——, A T Howell.
White's Creek Chapel (col.)—Clarkton, H S McNeill.
Zion's Hill—Bladenboro, Rufus Hilburn.

PRIMITIVE BAPTIST.

Oak Grove—Bladenboro, —— Gore.

PRESBYTERIAN.

Beth Car—Tar Heel, Archibald McFadyen.
Church—Clarkton, Archibald McFadyen.
Church—Bladenboro, A McFadyen.
Church—Elizabethtown.
Mt Horeb—White Hall, T H Newkirk.
South River—Cypress Creek, J D Stanford.
White Plains—White Hall, T H Newkirk.

MINISTERS RESIDENT.

Names, Post Offices and Denominations.

BAPTIST.

Beard, Council, White Oak.
Clark, G L, Clarkton.
Cromartie, A H (col.), Register.
Johnson, E D, Tar Heel.
McKoy, Jos (col.), Register.
McNeill, H S (col.), Clarkton.
Melvin, W S, White Oak.
Moore, Daniel (col.), Elkinsville.

PRESBYTERIAN.

Kelly, James, Clarkton.
McFadyen, Archibald, Clarkton.

METHODIST.

Starling, ——, Elizabethtown.

ZION METHODIST.

Sutton, Wm (col.), Elizabethtown.

HOTELS AND BOARDING HOUSES.

Names, Post Offices and Proprietors.

Clark Hotel, Clarkton, Jno H Clark. jr.
Bizzell House, Elizabethtown, Mrs W J Bizzell.
Boarding House, Elizabethtown, Mrs Tredwell.
Hotel, Abbottsburg, D Thompson.
McGill House, Elizabethtown, Mrs Emma McGill.

LAWYERS.

Names and Post Offices.

Balentine, J H, Abbottsburg.
Buie, W D, Clarkton.
Lyon, C C, Elizabethtown.

BLADEN COUNTY.

McLean, C M. Elizabethtown
White, R S, Elizabethtown.

MANUFACTORIES.

Kinds, Proprietors and Post Offices.

Council Tool Co., Council's Station, J P Council.
Gem Canning Co, Bladenboro, W R Davis.

MERCHANTS AND TRADESMEN.

Names, Post Offices, Lines of Business.

ABBOTTSBURG.
Cain, John S.   Gro
Russ, R A,   G S
Smith, Isaac H,   G S
BLADENBORO.
Bridger, R L & Bro,   G S
Davis, J C.   Distillery
Furguson, S N,   G S
Singletary, J W,   G S
BRINKLAND.
Daniel, J C,   G S
CEDAR.
Dunham, P H (col),   G S
CLARKTON
Clark, J H,   G S
Clark, O L,   G S
Currie, N A & Co,   G S
Clark, J H,   Postmaster
Carter, W L,   Chief Asst Tel Op
Swindell, Hays (col),   G S
COUNCIL STATION.
Clark, J P,   G S
Council, J P, jr.   G S
Council, J S   G S
Holmes, A G,   G S
DAWSON'S LANDING.
Thompson, D C,   G S
DUBLIN.
Melvin Bros,   G S
Thomas, J M,   G S
ELIZABETHTOWN.
Barnhill, M E,   G S
Hales, T H,   G S
Hall, J W,   G S
Hester, R J & Co,   G S
Robinson. N,   G S
Shepheard, Mrs J R,   G S
Smith, D L,   G S
Smith, L M,   G S
ELKTON.
Hall, W E & Co,   G S
Lenron, D S,   G S
Melvin, W F   G S
Moore, Lewis (col),   G S
Spaulding, J A (col),   G S

BLADEN COUNTY.

GRAVEL HILL.
Anders, E C,   G S
HAM.
Munn, John A,   G S
HOCUT.
Hocut, A,   G S
JARVIS.
Perry, Meares & Co,   G S
KELLY'S.
Allen, R P   G S
Henry, Ed,   G S
LAKE CREEK.
Sessoms, Kelly & Sons,   G S
LITTLE SUGAR LOAF.
Bell, J N,   G S
Currie, D M,   G S
LYON'S LANDING.
Lyon, H J,   G S
MAGRUDER.
Corbett, W M,   G S
MARLVILLE.
Stanley, J C,   G S
NAT MOORE.
Corbett, D J,   G S
Squires, W H,   Gro
REGISTER.
Register, W J,   G S
RICHARDSON.
Jones, B L,   G S
ROSINDALE.
Clark, A A & Co,   Gro
McDougal, Geo C,   G S
Porter, Y R,   G S
TAR HEEL.
Robeson, Jas.   G S
Singletary, W B,   G S
WESTBROOK.
DeVane, R M,   G S
WHITE HALL
Green, Thos J,   G S
WHITE OAK.
Williamson, J S   G S
WILLIS' CREEK.
Jones. H,   G S
WINNIE.
Martin, A E,   G S
Thompson, D C,   G S
YORKVILLE.
Hester, Jos,   G S

MILLS.

Kinds, Post Offices and Proprietors.

Saw, Winnie, Owen J Tatum.
Saw, White Hall, Thos J Green.

BLADEN COUNTY.

PHYSICIANS.

Names and Post Offices.

Andrews, W K, Cypress Creek.
Clark, G L, Clarkton.
DeVane, J S, Brinkland.
Gillespie, D B, Brinkland.
Graham, Geo A, White Hall.
Lucas, Gaston, White Hall.
Monroe, W J, Council Bluff.
Robinson, Newton, Elizabethtown.
Sloan, Henry, Cypress Creek.
Tatum, M McI, White Oak.
Willis, Wm, Council Bluff.

SCHOOLS.

Names, Post Offices and Principals.

Academy, Elizabethtown, Miss Robinson.
Clarkton High School, M L Blue.
Maysville Academy, Tar Heel.
White Oak Academy, White Oak, Wm Brunt.

TEACHERS.

Names and Post Offices.

Anders, Mrs Low, Kelly.
Ash, S A, Bladenboro.
Bland, Miss Hattie E, Colly.
Blue, Miss Emma J, Clarkton.
Buie, D M, Clarkton.
Burney, Miss Lizzie, Winnie.
Burney, Miss Kelsey, Clarkton.

BLADEN COUNTY.

Burney, G W, Clarkton.
Casur, Peter (col), Westbrook.
Cashnell, Mrs H M, Abbottsburg.
Cromartie, Miss Nannie, Elizabethtown.
Cromartie, Miss Annie, Cypress Creek.
DeVane, Miss M S, Westbrook.
Edge, Mrs M J, Gerome.
Ferguson, Wm A, Bladenboro.
Gardner, Miss Ida M, Edge.
Hall, Miss M L, Elizabethtown.
Haines, C V, Westbrook.
Johnston, J M, Clarkton.
Kelly, Rev Jas, Clarkton.
Lee, Mrs, Francania, Little Sugar Loaf.
Love, Miss Hattie S, Marlville.
Loyd, S M (col), Elizabethtown.
McAlister, J C (col), Nat Moore.
McDougald, Miss Florence, Elkton.
McFadyen, Miss Alice, Clarkton.
McKay, C E (col), Elizabethtown.
Melvin, Miss Eliza C, Winnie.
Moore, Mrs T C, Ham.
Monroe, Miss Janie W, White Hall.
Munn, Angus, Tar Heel.
Peterson, Miss Rena, Hocut.
Perry, D T, Rosindale.
Rooks, J B, Colly.
Robeson, Mrs Minnie, Tar Heel.
Russ, Jas W. Ham.
Shaw, W I, Keer.
Smith, Miss Sallie L, Abbottsburg.
Smith, Addie M, Abbottsburg.
Smith, Miss Rebecca, White Hall.
Vickers, Miss Georgia, Dawson's Landing.
Williams, Geo (col), Register.

BRUNSWICK COUNTY.

AREA, 950 SQUARE MILES.

POPULATION, 10,900; White 6,139, Colored 4,761.

BRUNSWICK COUNTY was formed in 1764, from the counties of Bladen and New Hanover. It derives its name from the Prince of Brunswick, who, the same year, married the King's oldest sister. The county is situated on the west side of Cape Fear river, and is the extreme southern point of the State.

SOUTHPORT is the county-seat, and is situated at the mouth of the Cape Fear, 173 miles south of Raleigh. Population 1,600, white 1,000, colored 600.

Surface — Brunswick is generally level and sandy, much of the land is in swamps, and requires draining before cultivation.

Staples—Cotton, corn, ground peas, sweet potatoes, rice, turpentine and lumber. The soil next to the sound produces abundant crops of peanuts. Some farmers are growing grapes successfully.

Fruits — Apples, peaches, grapes, pears, melons, etc.

Timbers—Long-leaf pine, juniper, live oak, cypress, ash, etc.

U. S. FORTIFICATIONS.

Fort Caswell is 2 ms. below Southport.
Fort Johnston, at Southport, is not garrisoned.
Fort Anderson is 10 miles north of Southport.
Fort Fisher is near Southport, but is in New Hanover county, and is celebrated for the battles of 1864–'65.

TOWNS AND POST OFFICES.

	POP.		POP.
Ash,	25	Onion,	50
Bolivia	20	Phœnix,	60
Calabash,	100	Saint Phillip,	25
Elsaso,	25	Shallotte,	350
Excelsior,	100	Southport	
Exum,	15	(C H),	1,600
Iredell,	25	Supply,	17
Makatoka,	30	Town Creek,	40
Malmo,	26	Winnabow,	30

COUNTY OFFICERS.

Superior Court Clerk-Sam'l P Thorpe.
Commissioners—S J Stanly (ch.), S L Chumes, A V Goodman.
Coroner—George W Sellers.
Register of Deeds—J W Brooks.
Sheriff—D R Walker.

Solicitor 7th District—H F Sewell.
Standard Keeper—Theo McKeithan.
Treasurer—S M Robbins.
County Examiner—Geo Leonard.

COURTS,

Fifth Monday after the first Monday in March and first Monday after first Monday in September.

TOWN OFFICERS.

SOUTHPORT—*Mayor*, E H Crammer; *Aldermen*, J A Williams, J F Arnold, S W Lofew, E F Gordon, L A Galloway.

TOWNSHIPS AND MAGISTRATES.

Lockwood's Folly—Geo W Kirby, C D Robinson, Jesse Long (Supply), J H White, George Leonard, R V Leonard, Jackson Stanaland (Shallotte), S W Maultsby (Bolivia).

North West—J D Robbins, F M Moore (Phœnix), Benj J Walters, William L Hall, C C Potter, T B Jacobs, Everitt M Skipper (Farmer's), J C Rowell (Onion),

Shallotte—Thos H Patterson (Little River, S C), John F Norris (Iredell), Forney Gore (Little River, S C), Sam'l Bell, Isaac Milliken, E M Parker, Benj E Hewitt, E L Stanly (Shallotte).

Southport — Richard Dozier, T M Williams, S W Lehew, W T Pinner, John Wescott, B D Wescott, David Ward (Southport), F P Lennor (Supply),

Town Creek—J D McRae (Phœnix), Rufus Galloway (Winnabow), Sam'l D Swindell, J W Gay, Isham W Harrelson, M P White, Geo H Cannon, John P Cox, M A Maultsby (Town Creek).

Waccamaw—G B Ward, J A Phelps, John B Gause (Ash), C C Little, Ezekiel Little, A Milliken (Excelsior), Geo K Andrews (Shallotte), J W Brady (Exum).

CHURCHES.

Names, Post Offices, Pastors and Denom.

METHODIST.

Andrew's Chapel—Iredell, T J Browning.
Bethel—Bolivia, R F Taylor.
Church—Town Creek, Oliver Rider.
Concord—Supply, R F Taylor.

BRUNSWICK COUNTY.

Macedonia—Southport, R F Taylor.
New Hope—Shallotte, R F Taylor.
Piney Grove—Winnabow, R F Taylor.
Shallotte Village—Shallotte, R F Taylor.
Sharon—Supply, R F Taylor.
Shallotte Camp—Shallotte. R F Taylor.
Trinity—Snallotte, Oliver Rider.
Town Creek—El Paso, R F Taylor.
Zion—Town Creek, James Mitchell.

BAPTIST.

Antioch—Bolivia, W S Ballard.
Bethel—Southport, W S Ballard.
Beula—Little Rock, S C, W Carter.
Chapel—Shallotte, James A Mintz.
Friendship—Shallotte, J W Thorp.
Lebanon—Winnabow, — Hillreath.
Lovely Spring—Bolivia, D Hewitt.
Long Branch—Iredell, Jas A Mintz.
Mill Creek—Bolivia, Dempsey Hewitt.
New Britton—Excelsior, N Milliken.
Prospect—Supply. W Carter.
Union Chapel—Ash, C D Milliken.
Smithville—Southport, W S Ballard.
Silent Grove—Supply, J P Lennon.
Shilob—Supply, Demisey Hewitt.
Soldier Bay—Ash, C D Milliken.

EPISCOPAL.

St Philip's—Southport, — Wooten.
St. Philip's, Old Brunswick, 10 miles
above Southport, oldest church in
the State, now in ruins.

PRESBYTERIAN.

New Hope—Winnabow.

A. M. E.

Mt. Carmel (col.)—Southport, George
Washington.

MINISTERS RESIDENT.

Names, Post Offices and Denominations.

BAPTIST.

Ballard, W S. Southport.
Bennett, D R. Little River, S C.
Edwards, A A, Supply.
Hewitt, D L, Schallotte.
Milliken, Eli, Ash.
Milliken, C, Ash.
Mintz, J A. Shallotte.
Swain, E. Shallotte.
Whitt, M P, Phoenix.

METHODIST.

Andrews, G K, Ash.
Ferguson, W R, Southport.
Milliken, Irwin. Ash.
Rider, Oliver, Southport.
Swain, Jas, Shallotte.
Taylor, R F. Shallotte.
Williams, Benj, Supply.

BRUNSWICK COUNTY.

HOTELS AND BOARDING HOUSES.

Names, Post Offices and Proprietors.

Davis House, Southport, Capt Simon
Davis.
Fullwood House, Southport, Mrs Carrie Fullwood.
Hotel Brunswick, Southport, Chas Bennett.
Stuart House, Southport, Miss Kate
Stuart.

MANUFACTORIES.

Kinds, Post Offices and Proprietors.

Blacksmithing and wheelwrighting,
Excelsior, L F Coleman.
Blacksmithing and wheelwrighting.
Excelsior, Samuel Evans.
Blacksmithing and wheelwrighting,
Supply. ——
Blacksmithing and wheelwrighting,
Excelsior. John Russ.
Blacksmithing and wheelwrighting,
Shallotte, A S White.
Boatbuilding, Southport, T J Piver.
Building and contracting, Supply, W
T White.
Building and contracting, Southport,
Henry Daniel.
Coopering, Supply, Elkin Richards.
Turpentine, Shallotte, W A Rourk.
Turpentine, Shallotte, G E Brooks.
Turpentine, Shallotte, Jackson Stanland.
Turpentine distillery, Excelsior, Hall
& Flinn.
Turpentine distillery, Supply, R W
McKeithen.
Turpentine distillery, Shallotte, Thos
Lewis.
Turpentine distillery, Shallotte, Moore
& Leonard.
Turpentine distillery, Shallotte, C
Thomas.

MERCHANTS AND TRADESMEN.

Names, Post Offices and Lines of Business.

ASH.

Mintz & Mintz,	G S
Smith Valentine,	G S

CALABASH.

Justice, B H,	G S
Long, R H,	G S
Long, W H,	G S
Thomas, C,	G S
Wilson, Jesse,	G S

EXCELSIOR.

Flynn, J A,	G S

EXUM.

Bennett, J W,	G S

BEAUFORT COUNTY.		BEAUFORT COUNTY.	

IREDELL.

Brooks, J W,	G S
Standley, T B,	G S

MEARE'S BLUFF.

Robins, G M,	G S

PHŒNIX.

Chimus, A M,	G S
Hawes, J J,	G S
Moore, F M,	G S
Robbins, M S,	G S
Williams, A M,	G S

SHALLOTTE.

Brooks, G E & Co,	G S
Cannon, J W,	G S
Fink & Co,	G S
Holmes, James,	G S
Mintz & Mintz,	G S
Moore & Leonard,	G S
Robinson, J D,	G S
Rourk, C A,	G S
Stanland, P T,	G S
Stone, W H, jr,	G S
Stone, B F,	G S
Todd, M D,	G S
Tripp, L C,	G S
Tripp, J F,	G S
White, F P,	G S
White, J H,	G S

SOUTHPORT.

Bell, S F,	G S
Doshsher, St George & Co,	G S
Drew & Davis,	G S
Gordon, E F,	Jeweler
Guthrie & Ruark,	G S
Harper, J T,	G S
Watson, D I & Co,	Druggist
Weeks, Wm.	G S
Wescott, J T & Co,	G S

ST. PHILIP'S.

Brown, Fannie,	G S
Gore, C B,	G S
Maides, James,	G S
Murry, Archie,	G S
Murchison, J W,	G S

SUPPLY.

Burney, S S (col),	G S
Dixon, Sylvester,	G S
Fullwood, Aaron,	G S
Holden, John,	G S
Kirby, G W,	G S
McKeithan, R W,	G S
Phelps, J S,	G S
Robinson, J D,	G S
Robinson, J P,	G S

TOWN CREEK.

Cannon & Walker,	G S
Evans, A H,	G S
Johnson, J J,	G S
Gay, J W,	G S
Rabon, J W,	G S
Skipper, D R,	G S
Ward, J R,	G S

8

TURNOUT.

Medlin, W T,	G S
Murrell, W W,	G S
Reilly, Martha E.	G S

WINNABOW.

Gore, C B,	G S and Turp
Johnson, Mrs A J,	G S
Rabon, J W,	G S
Ward, J R,	G S

MILLS.

nds, Post Offices and Proprietors.

Corn, Shallotte, J H Mintz.
Corn, Southport, W Taylor.
Corn, Supply, R W McKeathan.
Steam saw, Ash, Valentine Smith.
Steam saw, Calabash, D B Stanley.
Steam saw, Shallotte, W H Stone.

PHYSICIANS.

Names and Post Offices.

Curtis, W G, Southport.
Goodman, E Y, Town Creek.
Henry, ——, Town Creek.
McNeil, D B, Supply.
McNeill, John, Shallotte.
Robbins, ——, Phœnix.
Watson, D I, Southport.

SCHOOLS.

Names, Post Offices and Principals.

High School, Southport, Miss Webb.
Institute, Southport, Prof Crichet.
Preparatory school, Shallotte, George
  Leonard.
Public schools, white, 40; colored, 21.

TEACHERS.

Names and Post Offices.

Bennett, J N, Winnabow.
Drew, A B, Southport.
Fountain, Miss Lydia, Southport.
Galloway, E B, Supply.
Gore, Forney, Calabash.
Gore, B F, Calabash.
Grimes, G C, Winnabow.
Hewett, Beaty, Calabash.
Jenrett, Mrs Ida, Calabash.
Jenrett, Isaac, Calabash.
Jenrett, John, Calabash.
Kirby, Lee, Supply.
Kirby, Willie, Supply.
Leonard, C N, Shallotte.
Lewis, R F, Shallotte.
McKeithan, W O, Supply.
Mintz, J C, Shallotte.
Moore, Miss Bettie, Shallotte.
Moore, Miss Ada, Shallotte.
Parker, E M, Shallotte.
Rourk, Peter, Shallotte.

BEAUFORT COUNTY.

Ruark, Miss Gussie, Southport.
Sellers, Miss A F, Supply.
Stanly, J A, Shallotte.
Stone, Miss Ellneda, Calabash.
Swain, Miss Amanda, Shallotte.
Swain, R N, Shallotte.
Turner, Miss Adda, Shallotte.
Vines, T L, Winnabow.
Weeks, Miss Sudie, Southport.
Willetts. Mrs Mary, Winnabow.
Wilson, Miss Carrie, Calabash.
Worthington, John, Shallotte.

LOCAL CORPORATIONS.

Atlanta Lodge, No. 43, Odd Fellows, Southport, R S Newton, N G; O Rider, vice-grand; Price Turpless, sec'y.
Cape Fear Life Saving Station, Southport (5 miles south), John L Watts, captain; John Price, 1st man.
Cape Fear Towing and Transportation Co, Southport, Wm St George, pres; S F Craig, sec and treas. Capital stock, $15.000.
Fort Caswell, Southport (two miles south), Capt Berhime, sergeant.
Fort Anderson, 5 miles south, Southport. Now abandoned.
Knights of Honor, Southport.
Oak Island Life Saving Station, two miles south of Southport, Dunbar Davis, captain; Samuel Bruckman, 1st man.
Pythagoras Lodge, No. --, A F & A M, Southport, D I Watson, W M.
Southport Lumber Co, Southport.
Southport Coaling Station, Southport.
Smith Island Light House, Southport, three miles south, James Dosher, keeper.

NEWSPAPERS.

Southport Leader, Southport, Ches Stevens, editor; C L Stephens and Percy J Farrell, props.

BEAUFORT COUNTY.

FARMERS.

Names and Post Offices.

Ash—E D Carliles, J B Gause, John H Long, Jos P Long, Rev C B Milliken, Rev Irwin Milliken, J W Mints, John N Mints, Wm Mints, S K Mints, J B Simmons, Jesse A Smith, A J Smith, V Smith, G B Ward.

Bolivia—J P Cox, J W Danford, A A Edwards, J M Harvell, G W Howard, J H Knox, Samuel W Maultsby, I McKeithan, F P McKeithan, W H Mercer, Fletcher Mercer, N T Mercer, A Robinson.

Excelsior—D D Butler, B L Butler, John Inman, Isaac Jernette, John W King, J F King, J W King, C C Little, D B McKeithan, V Smith.

Phœnix—Jack Hawes, B J Watters, A M Williams, F M Williams, J S Williams.

Shallotte—Samuel Frink, Thomas Lewis, J H Mints, W A Ruark, Peter Stanley, W H Stone, F P White, J H White.

Southport—Wm Brown, Chas Drew, W H Drew, Marion Galloway, George Greer, W T Jones, Jerritt Matthews, W A Moore, F D Price, W C Price, A J Robbins, G W Smith, S P Swain, B F Swain, C C Swain, David Ward, T J Wescott, John Wescott, B D Wescott.

Supply—A B Clemmons, sr, Badge-Clemmons, B Clemmons, W H Clemmons, F M Galloway, W T Gilbert, G W Kirby, J Lancaster, W A Lancaster, F P Lannon, R W McKeithen, J J Pigott, Joe Ruark, J Stanalan, Elisha Sellers, Guilford Sellers, B Sellers, Asbury Simmons, A Simmons, J W Woodsides.

Town Creek—G H Cannon, W W Drew, J B Evans, D L Russell, Edw W Taylor, D R Walker, Lindsey Walker.

BUNCOMBE COUNTY.

AREA, 520 SQUARE MILES.

POPULATION, 25,048, WHITE, 18,422; COLORED, 6,626.

BUNCOMBE COUNTY was formed in 1791, from Burke and Rutherford counties, and derives its name from Col. Edward Buncombe, of Tyrrell county, who was Colonel of the Fifth North Carolina Regiment in the Continental Army.

Colonel Buncombe raised a regiment, fed, clothed and drilled them at his own expense. He was killed in the first battle in which he was engaged. He nor his heirs ever received any pay. Gen. Vance offered a bill in Congress to appropriate $2,500 for a monument, which was refused.

It lies immediately west of the Blue Ridge, and is the centre of the Transmontane section.

ASHEVILLE, the county seat, is on the French Broad river. It was named in honor of Gov. Samuel Ashe, of New Hanover, and was originally called Morristown. Its elevation is 2,250 feet above sea level.

The population is about 13,000, including suburbs, and it is one of the most noted summer and winter resorts in the South.

Asheville is the metropolis of "The Land of the Sky."

Surface—Buncombe county is situated on the west side of the Blue Ridge, and occupies a beautiful rolling country down the Swannanoa and French Broad rivers, which streams water it finely, and along the valleys of which are found thousands of acres of very rich lands. Nearly all the land in this county is susceptible of cultivation, as the fine growth of timber, even on the sides of the mountains, indicates. The scenery is enchanting—the air invigorating.

Staples—Corn, wheat, rye, oats and live stock. Tobacco is now being grown successfully, and of fine quality.

Fruits—Peaches, apples, pears, grapes, chestnuts, and nearly every kind of fruit grown to great perfection.

Timber—Walnut, white pine, oak, poplar, hickory, ash, maple, cherry, chestnut and many other kinds of wood noted in the fine arts.

Minerals—Mica and other valuable minerals are found in this county. Mineral and iron springs abound. The water-power is unsurpassed.

TOWNS AND POST OFFICES.

	POP.		POP.
Acton,	25	Gudger's Mills,	20
Alexander,	60	Hominy,	200
Alto,	10	Inanda,	25
Arden,	100	Juno,	20
Asheville (C H),		Jupiter.	50
	13,000	Leicester,	250
Avery's Creek,	25	Limestone,	35
Barnardsville,	50	Luther,	50
Beech,	30	Mascot,	25
Bell.	35	Meganna,	25
Biltmore,	300	Morgan Hill,	20
Bl'k Mountain,	100	Mt. Mitchell,	—
Busbee.	20	New Found,	30
Buena Vista,	—	Owenby,	25
Candler,	30	Pinnacle,	25
Canto,	50	Proviso,	15
Carrier's Springs,		Resthaven,	50
	100	Riceville,	20
Democrat,	50	Rockview,	35
Denmark,	—	Sandy Mush,	100
Dillingham.	20	Shope,	30
Dunsmore,	25	Skyland,	65
Emma,	50	Starksville,	50
Ewart,	25	Success,	25
Facerock,	50	Swannanoa,	150
Fairview,	75	Theodore,	—
Flat Creek,	30	Turnpike,	100
Foxville,	20	Tweed,	25
Gem,	10	Vanceville,	30
Glen Inglis,	25	Weaversville,	500
Grace,	20	W. Asheville,	
Glady,	15		1,000
Grantville,	70		

COUNTY OFFICERS.

Clerk Superior Court—J L Cathey.
Deputy Clerk—J McD Whitson.
Commissioners—J E Rankin, Chm; R C Claton, G M White, D M Gudger, J F Wells.
Coroner—L B McBrayer.
Register of Deeds—J J Mackey.
Solicitor Twelfth District—George A Jones.
County Attorney—Lock Craige.
Sheriff—J A Brookshire.
Surveyor—J M McKoy.
Standard Keeper—J S White.
Treasurer—John H Courtney.
County Examiner—J H Felmot.
Tax Collector—J H Weaver.
County Physician—E C Starnes.

COURTS.

Criminal Court—Fifth Monday before first Monday in March; eighth

Monday after first Monday in March; sixth Monday before first Monday in September, and seventh Monday after first Monday in September.

Superior Court—First Monday after first Monday in March; third Monday before first Monday in September; thirteenth Monday after first Monday in September.

TOWN OFFICERS.

ASHEVILLE—*Mayor*, W A Blair. *City Clerk*, F M Miller. *City Attorney*, J C Martin. *City Engineer*, B M Lee, *Chief of Police*, J H Carter. *Aldermen*, H B Carter, W F Snider, W H Westall, L V Terrell, D D Suttle, M H Fletcher. *Sanitary Inspector*, B F Rieves. *Treasurer*, S E Rankin. *Tax Collector*, H C Fagg. *Superintendent Water Works*—R J Stokely. *Superintendent Streets*, J T Bostic.

FIRE DEPARTMENT.

Chief, J B Sawyer.
Hose Company—H C Fagg, Captain; J H McDowell, First Foreman; F Stikeleather, Second Foreman; S Lepinsky, Secretary.
Hook and Ladder—E E Elliotte, Captain; John E Gay, First Assistant Foreman; John Stelling, Second Assistant Foreman; Wm Deaver, Secretary.
BILTMORE—*Mayor*, —— Champion.
KENILWORTH—*Mayor*, W P Cheesbrough.
LEICESTER—*Mayor*, —— ——.
MONTFORD—*Mayor*, J E Bonclough.
VICTORIA—*Mayor*, Chas McNamee.
WOLSEY—*Mayor*, Col T B Long.
WEAVERSVILLE—*Mayor*, —— ——.
Aldermen, F P Roberts, E Byerly. J A Reagan, S E Penland, D H Reagan.

TOWNSHIPS AND MAGISTRATES.

Asheville—T B Long, R B Justice, Wm Hamilton, Frank Carter, Justice Terrell, Chas Williams, J C Gentry, Jas Carson, K M Smith, M M Ledford, H C Jones, E T Belote, J M Davidson, D S Hildebrand, H C Hunt, C W Malone, John S Boggs, Geo H Bell, J B Womley, C J Woody, W B Cheesborough, W H Deaver, Wm Turner, J H Carter, M L Reed, Jas Reese. (Asheville.)
Avery's Creek—T J Carland, W B Cook, J B Cochran, R Ledbetter, E B Bishop, C W Ledbetter, J Ingram, W T Springs. (Avery's Creek.)
Black Mountain—T P Sutton, M M

Jones, Chas Cliff, G W Stepp, J T Morris, J A Walker, W H Burnett. (Black Mountain.)
Fair View—T J Young, S A Stroup, G W Conner, J W Heath, A H Pinkerton, J Will Jones, C G Dodson. (Fair View.)
Flat Creek—J R Brigman, J H Sams, R V Blackstock, Ch Haven, W G Blackwood, W T Roberts, Pitt Black, W E Clark, R A Pickens. (Flat Creek.)
French Broad—J N W Rogers, W M Allen, W H White, C A Nichols, A Goins, A H Martin, H D Buckner, J R Hughey, W H Hunter, J D Miles. (Alexander.)
Ivey—J N Morgan, J H Woodard, Thos S Dillingham, Geo W Cole, John E Herst, S M Riddle, J L Lay, M Whittemore, Wm Greenwood, J H Britter. (Ivey.)
Leicester—R C Wells, Wm H Henderson, D B Ford, B Swain, E West, J C Plemmons, C B Slader, C J Woody. (Leicester.)
Limestone—Burton Brown, J B Sumner, J W Brown, M A Rickmon, J M Rickmon, W S Murray, J R Lambert. (Arden.)
Lower Hominy—R C Crowell (Acton), A L Bright (Inanda), G W Ballard, A H Felmot, W L Henry, M N Roberts (Acton).
Ream's Creek—Chas Williams, R J Bronk, Ed F Vandiver, C P Weaver, J G Chambers, J L Weaver, W T Bradley. J H McDowell, G M Robinson, T H Weaver (Weaversville).
Sandy Mush—J H Reynolds, M L Robison, J M Rogers, J M King, W E Waldrop, A E Wells, J W Boling, J S Wells (Sandy Mush).
Swannanoa—S W Davidson, jr, J S Bartlett, J C Craig, S W Davidson, P H Folsom, J C Clark, W M Gudger (Swannanoa).
Upper Hominy—J K Hoyt (Luther), M V Cole, Geo F Brock, H A Luther (Candler), W P O'Kelly, W L Isral (Dunsmore), C Z Netherton (Candler), R L Luther, J E Morgan (Hominy Creek).

CHURCHES.

Names, Post Offices, Pastors and Denom.

METHODIST.

Acton—Acton, J A Clark.
Alexander's—Alexander, L E Stacy.
Asbury—Leicester, L T Cordell.
Balm Grove—Emma, J A Clark.
Bent Creek—Inanda, J A Clark.
Berea—Swannanoa— ——
Bethesda—Bell, Geo F Kirby.
Bethel—Asheville, J M Donnovin.

BUNCOMBE COUNTY.

Big Sandy—Sandy Mush, L T Cordell.
Big Ivy—Barnardsville, A L Marsh.
Biltmore—Asheville, J M Donnovin.
Brush Creek—Farview, J A Sronce.
Central—Asheville, H F Chreitzberg, D D.
Chestnut Grove—Alto, L T Cordell.
Church—Leicester, L T Cordell.
Church—Avery's Creek, G G Harly.
Church—Swannanoa—Geo F Kirby.
Church—Black Mountain, G F Kirby.
College Street—Asheville, E L Bain.
Dick's Creek—Leicester, L T Cordell.
Flint Hill—Flint Hill, L E Stacy.
French Broad—Alexander, L E Stacy.
Garrett's—Sandy Mush, L T Cordell.
Gillespie's Chapel—Leicester, L T Cordell.
Haywood Street—Asheville, W H Wells.
Laurel Hill—Hominy, J A Clark.
Montmerenci—Hominy, J A Clark.
Mt. Pleasant—Ramoth, L E Stacy.
New Found—New Found, L T Cordell.
North Asheville—Asheville, E L Bain.
Penland Chapel—Leicester, L T Cordell.
Pleasant Grove—Weaversville, L E Stacy.
Pleasant Hill—Hominy, J A Clark.
Ream's Creek—Vanceville, L E Stacy.
River View—Emma, J A Clark.
Sales—Rest Haven, Geo F Kirby.
Salem—Flat Creek, L E Stacy.
Sardis—Inanda, J A Clark.
Sharon—Fairview, J A Sronce.
Skyland—Skyland, Geo F Kirby.
Snow Hill—Candler, J A Clark.
South Fort—Foxville, L E S acy.
Tabernacle—Black Mountain, Geo F Kirby.
Turkey Creek—Leicester, L T Cordell.
Tweed's Chapel—Tweed's, J A Sronce.
West Chapel—Biltmore, Geo F Kirby.
Western Chapel—Leicester, L F Cordell.

METHODIST PROTESTANT.

Big Ivy—Morgan Hill, ——
Church—Sandy Mush, ——
Church—Swannanoa, ——
Church—Flat Creek, ——
Flint Hill—Alexander, —— Savage.
Ream's Creek—Weaversville, ——
Ridge—Weaversville, ——
Turkey Creek—Liecester, ——

N. METHODIST.

Bee Tree—Swannanoa, ——
Bull Creek—Swannanoa, ——
Bull Creek—Riceville, ——
Church—Avery's Creek, ——
Church—Asheville, ——
Davis' Chapel—Weaversville, ——
Glady Branch—Hominy, ——

BUNCOMBE COUNTY.

Mount Zion—Shufordsville, ——
Mt. Pisgah Lodge—Hominy, ——
Trull's Chapel, Hominy, ——

BAPTIST.

Antioch—Democrat, W L Justice.
Beaver Dam—Asheville, ——
Bent Creek—Vernon, Jas Plemmons.
Berea—Swannanoa, T K Brown.
Bethel—Hazel, ——
Big Ivy—Morgan Hill, Wm T Bradley.
Cane Creek—Fairview, ——
Chapel (col)—Asheville, ——
Church—Black Mountain, T K Brown.
Church—Avery's Creek, ——
Church—Morgan Hill, ——
Fern Hall—Best, E A Brown.
First Church—Asheville, J S Felix, DD
Flat Creek—Flat Creek, ——
French Broad—Asheville, M A Adams.
Gash's Creek—Biltmore, ——
Hominy—Hominy, ——
Macedonia—Owenby, ——
Mt. Carmel—Owenby, ——
Mt. Zion (col)—Asheville, R T Remley.
Nazareth (col)—Asheville, ——
New Salem—Busbee, ——
Sand Hill—Hominy, ——
Vernon Hill—Vernon, J E Morgan.
West End—Asheville, E A Brown.
White Rock—Cornelius, ——

FREE-WILL BAPTIST.

Big Ivy—Morgan Hill, ——
Church—New Found, ——
Mountain View—Alexander, F Boyd.
Ream's Creek—Vanceville, ——

EPISCOPAL.

Chapel (col)—Asheville, Jarvis Buxton, D D.
Ravenscroft Associate Mission—Asheville, ——
St. Andrews—Asheville, J H Postell.
St. Paul—Asheville, J H Postell.
Trinity Chapel—Asheville, ——
Trinity—Asheville, McNeely DuBose,

PRESBYTERIAN.

Church—Asheville, ——
Piney Grove—Vanceville, ——
Piney Grove—Swannanoa, ——
Red Oak—Refuge, ——
Sand Hill—Hominy, ——

N. PRESBYTERIAN.

Reams' Creek, Vanceville, ——

DISCIPLES OF CHRIST.

Church—Alexander's, —— Tipton.
Church—Asheville, ——

LUTHERAN.

St. Paul—Asheville, L Busby.

UNITARIAN.

Church—Asheville, H A Westall.

BUNCOMBE COUNTY.

CATHOLIC.

St. Lawrence Martyr—Asheville, Father Marion.

A. M. EPISCOPAL.

Church (col)—Asheville, ———

A. M. E. ZION.

Chapel (col)—Jarrett's, H B ———
Hopkins' Chapel (col)—Asheville, ———
Shiloh (col)—Asheville, ———

MINISTERS RESIDENT.

Names, Post Offices and Denominations.

METHODIST.

Atkins, James, jr., D D, Asheville.
Bain, E L, Asheville.
Byrd, Chas W, D D, Weaversville.
Chreitzberg, H F, D D, Asheville.
Clark, J A, Acton.
Cole, T M, Foxville.
Cordell, L T, Leicester.
Crook, J L, Emma.
Donnovin, J M, Asheville.
Kirby, Geo F, Asheville.
Hawkins, J M, Acton.
Marsh, V L, Barnardsville.
Miller, Geo W, Asheville.
Mitchell, W A, Weaversville.
Pease, L M, Asheville.
Pickens, R W, Weaversville.
Reagan, J A, D D, Weaversville.
Sronce, J A, Fairview.
Stacy, L E, Weaversville.
Starnes, A H, Acton.
Turner, H, Asheville.
Willis, W N, Asheville.

BAPTIST.

Adams, M A, Asheville.
Ammons, John, Morgan Hill.
Anderson, J W, Asheville.
Brown, T K, Black Mountain.
Connally, J K, Asheville.
Justice, A L, Emma.
Meanes I J (col), Asheville.
Morgan, E J, Candler's.
Morgan, E J, Morgan Hill.
Owen, S C, Candler's.
Partlett, G W, Black Mountain.

PRESBYTERIAN.

Campbell, R F, D D, Asheville.

N. PRESBYTERIAN.

Penland, Alfred, Vanceville.

EPISCOPAL.

DuBose, McNeely, Asheville.
McDuffie ——— (col), Asheville.
Stubbs, Alfred H, D D, Asheville.

B. M. E. ZION.

Gaither, Rufus (col), Asheville.
Jacobs, ——— (col), Asheville.

BUNCOMBE COUNTY.

HOTELS AND BOARDING HOUSES.

Names, Post Offices and Proprietors.

Battery Park Hotel, Asheville, W P McKissick, mgr.
Blackwell's Springs, Alexander, David Blackwell.
Boarding House, Black Mountain, Silas F Dougherty.
Boarding House, Black Mountain, G McKoy.
Boarding House, Fairview, John Merrill.
Boarding House, Fairview, Ashworth & Co.
Boarding House, Swannanoa, G N Alexander.
Everett House, Asheville, Mrs J M Seigler.
Hotel Alexander, Alexander, R B & J N Vance.
Hotel, Asheville, ———
Hotel, Biltmore, ———
Kenilworth Inn (1 mile south), Browning & Rhoades, Asheville.
Luther House, Hominy, LaFayette Luther.
Neville House, Asheville, Robert O Neville.
Oakland Heights, Asheville, C A Wood pro.
Reagan House, Weaverville, ———
Skyland Springs Hotel, Skyland, Otis Miller.
Slagle House, Asheville, J L Slagle.
Smathers, Turnpike, J E Smathers.
Swannanoa Springs, Swannanoa, R L Patton.
Swannanoa, Asheville, Rawls Bros.
The Berkley, Asheville, Langhorn & Bro.
The Oaks, Asheville, Samuel Reed.
Winyah House, Asheville, Dr Carl Von Ruck.

LAWYERS.

Names and Post Offices.

Adams, J S & Breese, Wm, jr, Asheville.
Arthur, John P, Asheville.
Atkinson, E B, Asheville.
Baird, Willie Lee Grace, Asheville.
Bourne, L M & Parker, H, Asheville.
Brown, W P, Asheville.
Brown, H B (col.), Asheville.
Candler, W G, Hominy.
Carter, Eugene D, Asheville.
Carter, H B & Weaver, Zeb V, Asheville.
Cobb, T H, Asheville.
Cooper, James H, Fairview.
Craig, Locke, Asheville.
Cummings, P A, Asheville.

BUNCOMBE COUNTY.

BUNCOMBE COUNTY.

Cushman, Walter S, Asheville.
Davidson, Theo F & Jones, Thos A, Asheville.
Gudger, Pritchard & Rollins, Marshall.
Gudger, J M, sr, & J E, Asheville.
Gudger, H A, Asheville.
Gwyn, W B, Asheville.
Johnston, Thos D, Asheville.
Jones, W W & Barnard, Alf S, Asheville.
Justice, G W, Asheville.
Lipscombe, —— (col.), Asheville.
Lusk, Virgil S, Asheville.
Luther, Dillon M, Asheville.
Lyman, A J, Asheville.
Martin, J C, Asheville.
McCall, R S & Rogers, J N, Asheville.
Merrimon, J G, Asheville.
Merrick, Duff, Asheville.
Moore, C A & Moore, Fred, Asheville.
Pearson, Richmond, Asheville, (member of Congress).
Reed, S H, Asheville.
Sondley, F A, Asheville.
Shuford, Geo A & W E, Asheville.
Stevens, Henry B, Asheville.
Summers, J W, Asheville.
Thomas, F W & Wells, R M, Asheville.
Tucker, J H, Murphy, J D & Erwin, M, Asheville.
Weaver, Wm E, Weaversville.
Webb, Charles A, Asheville.
Whitson, W R, Asheville.

MANUFACTORIES.

Kinds, Post Offices and Proprietors.

Asheville Cotton Mills, established in 1888; L Banks Holt, pres; George A Mebane, sec and treas; E C Barnhardt, supt. Capital stock, $250,000. Spindles, 8,448; looms, 42; daily consumption, 6,000 pounds; daily output, 30,000 yards colored cottons; hands, 350; average wages per day, $1.00.
Asheville Coal Co, Asheville, H T Collins & Co.
Asheville Ice and Coal Co, H T Collins, pres; W E Collins, sec and treas.
Blacksmithing and repairing, Asheville, J H Woody.
Blacksmithing and wheelwrighting, Asheville, H C Sexton.
Blacksmithing and wheelwrighting, Inanda, J C Sexton.
Blacksmithing and wheelwrighting, Weaversville, J M Davis.
Blacksmithing and wheelwrighting, Black Mountain, C P Kerlee.
Blacksmithing and wheelwrighting, Hominy, C P Hutchinson.
Boots and shoes, Asheville, A Fraeck.
Brooms, Brooks, Jesse Yeates & Co.

Building material (Wood Working Co), Asheville, Geo W Vanderbilt.
Buggies, wagons, &c, Asheville, J H Woody.
Brick, Asheville, D S Hilderbrand.
Brick, Asheville, W R Penniman.
Builder, Asheville, O D Revell.
Carriages, Asheville, W D Justice.
Contracting and building, Grantville, M Buckner.
Contracting and building, Black Mountain, E B & E R Kerlee.
Contracting and building, Weaverville, E Byerly.
Contracting and building, Asheville, J A Wagner.
Contracting and building, Asheville, J A Tennant.
Contracting and building, Asheville, A C Melton.
Fertilizer, Asheville, J F Woodberry.
Fertilizer, Asheville, Bone Fertilizer Co.
Furniture, Asheville, W A Blair.
Furniture, Asheville Furniture and Lumber Co; capital, $150,000; —— Barnhardt, manager; Dr Mebene, pres.
Ice and Coal Co, Biltmore, T J Reed; manager.
Iron foundry, Asheville, J J Cole.
Lime, Asheville, J R Garren.
Marble works, Asheville, W O Wolfe.
Millwrighting, Black Mountain, J W Dougherty.
Planing mill, Asheville, T L Clayton.
Roller flour mills, Asheville, Asheville Ice and Coal Co.
Saddles and harness, Asheville, T J Mitchell, manager.
Saddles and harness, Asheville, J M Alexander.
Sash, blinds and doors, Asheville, W M Jones.
Tannery, Weaverville, A J Gill.
Tannery, Asheville, W H Penland.
Tannery, Weaverville, W B Cheek.
The Skyland Furniture Co, Asheville, J P Sawyer, treas and manager.
Tobacco, smoking, Asheville, E L Holmes.
Wagons, Asheville, J R Dickerson.
Wagons, Asheville, T S Morrison & Co.
Woolen mills, Weaverville, John Carnes.

MERCHANTS AND TRADESMEN.

Name, Post-office and Line of Business.

ACTION.

Hawkins, J M,　　　　　　　G S

ALEXANDER.

Hunter, W H,　　　　　　　G S

BUNCOMBE COUNTY.		BUNCOMBE COUNTY.	
Morris & Sheppard,	G S	Cowan & Oates,	Livery
Nelson, W A,	G S	Cole, Miss M A,	Engraver
ARDEN.		Davenport, L E,	—
Hudson, J N,	G S	Davis, T J,	—
Summer Bros,	G S	Davis, A C,	Gro
Youngblood, R P,	G S	Deaver, R M,	G S
ASHEVILLE.		Dickerson, J E & Co,	H'd'r
		Dixon. J H & Co,	—
Abraham, Peter,	G S	Dixon, Isaac (col.),	Gro
Allen, W E,	G S	Doggett & Cowan,	Livery
Alexander, J M,	Harness	Doster, H (col.),	Gro
Alexander, M,	Jeweler	Drake & Owens,	—
Amis, J T,	Drugs	Drug Co,	Drugs
Asheville Ice and Coal Co,		Duckett, Thomas & Co,	—
	Ice, Coal and Wood	Ellick, M,	Furrier
Asheville Printing Co: John H		Elliott, E,	Plumber
Weaver, pres; Geo L Hack-		Evans, S J R,	—
ney, sec and treas and m'g'r;		Falk, C,	Pianos
Job Printers and Publishers		Falk's Music House: C Falk, Prop	
of the Epworth (semi-month-			Musical Mdse
	ly) News.	Farinholt, L A,	
Bagwell, W L,	—		Real Estate and Notary Public
Bailey, James,	—	Feinster, S,	Clo
Baird, C W & Co,	Gro	Field, A N,	Jeweler
Ballow, W A,	Banner Warehouse	Finestein, Sam,	—
Berman, R,	G S	Fitzpatrick, T W,	—
Blair, W A,	—	Fitzpatrick, R L,	Gro
Blair, W P,	Furn	Fitzpatrick & May,	Printers
Blanton, J D & Co,	Shoes	Flack, Wm (col.),	Gro
Blomberg, L, Sporting Goods,		Flemming, J M.	Gro
	Cigars, News and Stationers	Foller, J J,	—
Bostic, P L,	Sewing Machines	Forster, J S,	Gro
Boyce & Burton,	Plumbers	Forster, F M,	Gro
Boyd, J S,	Livery	Foster, Frank S,	—
Boykin, ——,	Repair'g Jewelry	Frick, T T,	—
Briggs, J,	—	Frick, A,	Shoes and Gro
Brown, R,	—	Fullam, J S,	Gro
Brown & Co,	—	Fullenwider, H E,	B and S
Brown, J C,	Tinware	Fulmer, Jacob,	—
Brown, J V & Son,	Undertakers	Furman, D W,	Printer
Brown, Northop & Co,	Hardware	Garrett Bros,	—
Brown, W,	Livery	Glaser & Silver,	—
Brown, Wiley R,	Livery	Glaser, I W,	Jeweler
Brown & Gudger,	Livery	Glenn Bros.	Gro
Bryson, A W,	Gro	Goldsmith. W W,	Repair'g Jewelry
Buncombe Coal Co,	Coal	Goosh, W D, Co,	Typewriters
Campbell, C H,	Soda Water	Grant, Mrs Lula S,	Drugs
Cannon, G W,	Gro	Green, Gay,	Gro
Carmichael, W C,	Drugs	Greer, G A,	Gro
Carolina Coal Co,	Coal	Gross, D,	—
Carrington, Jesse,	—	Halyburton & Trott,	—
Chambers, Weaver & Co,	Livery	Hamlin, Levi,	D G and Shoes
Chedester & Fortune,	—	Hamrick Bros,	Gro
Chedester, S H,	G S	Heinitsh & Reagan,	Drugs
Chedester, N P,	—	Helps, Wm.	—
Cigar Co,	Cigars	Heston, J M,	—
Clayton, Thos L,	Builder	Heston, B M.	Gro
Colley, Henry,	—	Higgins, C D,	Gro
Cosby, B H,	Jeweler	Hildebrand, D S	Brickmaker
Cook, J F,	—	Hill, W M & Co,	Butchers
Cook, A F,	Gro	Hines, Mrs E F,	—
Cook, J T,	Fruit	Holcomb, W T	—
Cooper, A D,	Gro	Hough, W J,	—
Cooper, C S,	Grain and Feed	Howell, Jno H,	Leaf Tobacco
Cowan, P L,	Jeweler	Hudson, R H,	Teas and Coffees

BUNCOMBE COUNTY.		BUNCOMBE COUNTY.	
Hughes, D H,	Meats	Monaur, Meyer,	—
Hunt, J H,	—	Monday, A C,	G S
Israel, W A,	G S	Moody, C E,	Tiles
Jackson, Frank,	—	Moore, M V,	Gent's Furn
Jackson, J T,	—	Morgan & Alexander,	—
Jarvis, Wiley,	—	Morgan, J N & Co,	Books and Sta
Jenkins Bros,	Gro	Morrison. T S & Co,	Fertilizer
Jesse R Starnes Undertaking Co, Ashe-		Mustin, Fakes & Co,	Brokers
ville, J J Yeates, D G Noland, J E		Myers, M,	G S
Dickerson and Mrs Jesse R Starnes		Nolan, D G,	—
(incorporators),	Undertakers	Noland, M C,	Gro
Johnson, L A,	—	Nolau, R B & Son,	Gro
Johnson, H C	G S	Northop & Brown,	—
Johnson, J B,	Furn	Oats & Cowan,	Livery
Jones, A V & Co, Stationers and News		O'Donnell, Frank,	—
Dealers and Fancy Goods		Owenby & Son,	Gro
Jones, A B & Co,	Books and Sta	Owenby. R L,	Gro
Jones & Payne,	Gro	Owenby, W A,	—
Jones, W C,	G S	Patton & Stikeleather (Kenilworth
Kelly, M H,	Hardware	Inn),	Livery
Kepler, S R,	Gro	Pelham, W E,	Drugs
Kenron Bros.	—	Penland, N L.	Gro
Kienle, A,	Jeweler	Penniman & Bros,	Hardware
Kroger, Wm,	Gro	Perkinson, T J,	Painter
LaBard, Miss Nellie,	Milliner	Perry, N L & Co,	Warehouse
Lance, J G & Co,	Gro	Postell, W J,	G S
Lang, Romezewiske,	—	Powell & Snider,	Whol and Ret Gro
Latimer, W A,	Gro	Powell & Snider,	G S
Laughran, J H,	Hotel	Quinn, Wm,	Mfr Rustic Furn
Law, J H	China	Randall J C (col),	Gro
Lee, Neil,	Sec.-hand Furn	Ray, J M,	Real Estate
Lee, Robt. H,	Painter	Ray, C F,	Tob and Cigars
Lepensky, S,	—	Raysor & Smith,	Drugs
Levy, M,	Shoes	Redmond. J W,	—
Levy R & Son,	—	Redmond, S M,	Gro
Lindan, Hough & Co,	G S	Redwood, H & Co,	G S
Lindsay, H A	—	Reeves, Thos,	—
Lindsay, H H,	Curiosity Shop	Revelle, O D, Architect and Builder
Lindsay, T H,	Photographer	Revell, T J,	G S
Lipinski, S	Bon Marche	Reynolds, Joe,	Livery
Lipe, J C,	—	Rice & Morris,	Gro
Lugere, J A,	Gro	Rich, J R,	Stoves
Lyman, A J, Real Estate and Loans		Riverside Undertaking Co: J M Ingle,
Marcus, Max,	Gent's Furn	pres; J G Mackey, vice-pres; F A
McChesney, Ed, mgr,	Fruits	Hull, sec and treas. Undertakers
McConnell. J H, Coffin Maker and		Roberts, W O,	—
Undertaker		Roberts & Haymond,	Printers
McConnell, J H,	Cabinet Maker	Rogers, H T; Books and Stationery
McConnell, W C,	Confec	Rogers, H Taylor,	Jeweler
McDonald, G L,	Gro	Rogers, Nat S & Co, Lumber Dealers
McDowell Bros,	—	Rogers. H Taylor,	Books
McDowell & Phillips,	—	Rumbough, J E & Co,	Com'n
McDowell & Dalton,	G S	Sawyer, J P,	Carpets
McDowell & Johnson,	G S	Schartle, H,	Tailor
McPherson & Clark,	Plumbers	Schartle, J N,	Merchant Tailor
McIntyre, Pat,	—	Schwartzburg, M,	G S
McIntyre, C B,	—	Scott, G F & Co,	Lumber
Meadows & Drake,	—	Seigler, J P,	Grocer
Meadows, J F,	Fruit	Sevier, J V,	Livery
Meares, G A,	G S	Shaffner, W H,	Jeweler
Mechaloo, S H,	—	Shinbaum, A,	Clo
Mechaloo, I	—	Shope, J B.	Harness
Melton, E L,	Builders	Simmons, T,	Gro
Mitchell, F E, Gent's Furn and B & S		Simmons, Geo H,	Gro
Mitchell, W A	—	Smith, S,	Gro

BUNCOMBE COUNTY.

Smith, S O & Co, No. 8 Lexington
    Avenue, Mdse Brokers
Smith, T C & Co,   Drugs
Spangenberg, J,   Shoes
Starnes, Jesse R,   Undertaker
Stephenson, G H,   —
Stewart & Bird,   Gro
Stikeleather, Chas,   Livery
Stoner Bros,   Racket Store
Stradley, W C,   G S
Stroup, W H,   —
Sumner & Co,   D G
Supply and F Co,   —
Swicegood, L,   Painter
Swink, J C,   Gro
Teacher, M W,   —
Tennent, J A,   Builder
Terrell, Theo F,   —
Terrell, T V,   D G
Theobold & Buckner,   —
Thomas, John,   —
Thompson & Carroll,   Gen'l Ins
Thrash & Howitt,   —
Thrash, T W & Bro,
    Stoves and House Furnishings
Tolbett, H A,   —
Treadway & Collins,   Com. Brokers
Treadway, J J,   G S
Treadway, J R & Co,   Gro
Trexler, B C,   Gro
Trifield, A,   Cigars and Tob
Tucker, G H,   Gro
Turner & Son,   Gro
Ulmer, Susie,   Gro
Vangilder & Son,   Real Estate
Waddell & Sluder,   Ins and Coal
Wagoner, J A,   Builder
Walker, Monroe,   —
Webb, W A,   Gro
Wesenberger, D S,   —
West, W W,   Ch School Committee
West, W W,   Real Estate
Westall, J M,   Builder
Westall, T C & Son,   Builders
Westall, W H,   Materials
Wexler, E,   Jeweler
Whitaker, F M,   —
White, J B,   Fruit
Whitlock, A, agent,   Clothing
Whitlock, G,   Clothing
Wiggins, J A,   Gro
Wilkinson, M B,   Lumber Dealer
Wilkinson, W M,   Lumber Dealer
Williamson, W B & Co,   Furn
Wilson, J B,   —
Wolfe, W O,   Marble Works
Wolsley, J B,   —
Walton, H S,   —
Wolfe, J,   Butcher
Woody, J H,   Foundry
Worthem, B S,   Drugs
Zagier, B,   Clo

AVERY'S CREEK.

Ingram, Joel,   G S
Ledbetter, Z T & Co,   G S

BUNCOMBE COUNTY.

BARNARDSVILLE.

Roberts & Maney,   G S
Whitmore, C C & J F,   G S

BEACH.

Chambers, Grigg,   G S

BELL.

Armstrong, R F,   G S
Bell, G H,   G S
Cordell, B L,   G S
Hildebrand, D S,   G S
Lindsay, G W,   G S
Miller, W R,   G S
Reed, M L,   G S
Rice, Joe,   Variety
Stepps, J F,   G S
Walden, A F,   G S
Williams, L M,   G S

BILTMORE.

Brookshire, J A,   G S
Brookshire, T J,   Variety
Brown, B C,   G S
Cauble, A L,   G S
Cline & Cornelius,   G S
Davis, E P,   G S
Davidson, J M,   G S
Griggs, W H,   G S
Hall, Charles,   G S
Jones & Payne,   Variety
Marlow, D M,   G S
McDowell, Phillips & Co,   Gro
Murphey, J H,   —
Patton, H C & Co,   G S
Penly, J A,   G S
Reed, J H & Bro,   G S
Reed & Clapp,   G S
Reed, T J,   G S
Roberts, J C,   G S
Roser, James,   G S
Sales, W H,   G S
Sales, W C,   G S
Smith, J B,   G S
Sorrells, G A,   G S
Stevens, R N,   G S
Stevens, F M,   Variety
Vanderbilt, Geo   G S
Wailey, G W,   G S
West, Aleck,   G S
Whitaker, Charles,   Variety
Wilson, T F,   Variety
Williams, W W, agent,   G S

BLACK MOUNTAIN.

Garrison, J H,   G S
McCoy, J M,   G S
Suttle, W H,   G S

BUENA VISTA.

Sumner Bros,   G S

CANDLER.

Bucknar, R D,   G S
Candler, E W & Co,   G S
Morgan, A L,   G S
Thompson, O F & Co,   G S

BUNCOMBE COUNTY.

CANTO.

Davis, J T,	G S
Randall Bros,	G S

COOPER.

Davidson, W F,	G S
Williams, L M,	G S
Wilson, N H,	G S

DUNSMORE.

Howell, T H,	G S

EMMA.

Ingle, F P,	G S
McLelland, D J,	G S

FAIRVIEW.

Ashworth Bros & Co,	G S
Jones, J W,	G S
Morgan, R A,	G S

FLAT CREEK.

Black, W P & Co,	G S

GLADY.

Howell, C W,	G S
Miller, G H & Bro,	G S

GLEN INGLIS.

Falsom, P H,	G S

GRACE.

Baird, I V,	G S
Baird, J S T,	G S
Baird, W A,	
Barnard, H E,	G S
Carter, Sol A.	G S
Carter, Sam T,	G S
Diamond, R F,	G S
Hines, W,	Variety
Killian, C M,	Variety
Kinberry, T M,	G S
Lamb, A H,	G S
Nelson, R L,	G S
Ramsay, W C,	G S
Smith, H B,	G S
Stradley, J A,	G S
Way, C B,	G S
Weaver, W T,	Variety
Wolfe, R O,	G S

GUDGER'S MILL.

Merrill, A J,	G S

HIGH KNOB.

Teague, R,	G S

HOMINY CREEK.

Gaston, R J,	G S
Muse, D F,	G S

INANDA.

Ingle, J B,	G S
Rhoades, E J,	G S

JUNO.

Brookshire & Foster,	G S
Hampton, J E,	—
Ingle & Welsh,	G S

JUPITER.

Roberts, M F & Co,	G S

BUNCOMBE COUNTY.

Roberts, C E & Co,	G S
Hunter, W C & Son,	G S
Pickens, Fair & Co,	G S

LEICESTER.

Brookshire & Foster,	G S
Brown, F P,	G S
Brown, J E,	G S
Carpenter, John,	G S
Dodson, Thos & Co,	G S
Gilbert, Wm,	Variety
Meares, Mrs C P.	G S
Merrill, A J,	G S
Penland & Sluder,	G S
Wilson, J B,	G S

MASCOT.

Ingle, F P,	G S
Wells, J S,	G S

MORGAN HILL.

Stockton, F M,	G S

NEW FOUND.

Wells, J S,	G S

OWENBY.

Hayes, J M & Son,	G S
Owenby, W N,	G S

REST HAVEN.

Brookshire, T J,	G S
Sorrells, J A	—
Waldrop, W E	G S

SKYLAND.

Case, A B & Bros,	G S

STOCKVILLE.

Blackstock, R V & Co,	C S

SUCCESS.

Ingle & Welsh.	G S

SWANNANOA.

Chambers & Co,	G S
Davidson & Sherrill,	—
Hallett, M H,	G S
Wilson, W H,	G S

TURNPIKE.

Smathers, V C,	G S

TWEED.

Young Bros & Co,	G S

VANCEVILLE.

Rice, J W,	G S

WEAVERVILLE.

Austin, J F & Son,	G S
Reagan, J A & Co,	Drugs
Reeves, T H,	G S
Roberts, F P,	G S
Robinson & Bro,	G S
Vandiver, J W & Co,	G S
Williams, R N,	G S

WEST ASHEVILLE.

Adams, J S,	G S
Boggs, J S,	G S

BUNCOMBE COUNTY.

BUNCOMBE COUNTY.

Butterick, Jas,   G S
Clayton, E E,   G S
Cockran, J W,   Variety
Cowan, Jas,   G S
Cowan, J T,   G S
Embler, R H,   Assorted
Garrett, J M,   G S
Henry, J L,   Variety
Ingle & Welch,   G S
Lammack, J W,   G S
Ledford, J M,   G S
McKimish, J H,   G S
Reynolds, J R,   G S
Rich, J L,   G S
Smith, J H,   Variety
Smith, Mark,   G S
Smith, R S,   G S
Wills, Rufus (col),   G S
Wolfe, Jas   G S

MINES.

Kinds, Post Offices and Proprietors.

Blackwell Iron, Alexander, D A Blackwell and others.
Eller Magnetic Iron, Alexander, owned by J M Heck's heirs, of Raleigh, and others; as a magnetic iron deposit second only in the State to Cranberry, the vein being 28 feet wide.
Gold, Hominy, W G Candler and others.
Gold, Asheville, C B Atkinson & Co.
Manganese, Asheville, Natt Atkinson's heirs and others.
Mica, Black Mountain Station, Lock Craige & Perry.
Mica, Asheville, Wm Bearden & Co.
Mica, Asheville, Henry Martin (col.).

MILLS.

Kinds, Post Offices and Proprietors.

Corn and saw, Fairview, L W Jones.
Corn, Asheville, Thos Reed.
Corn and saw, Hominy, W G Candler.
Corn and saw, Swannanoa, Mrs Dougherty.
Corn, flour and saw, Glady, Nelson Smathers.
Corn and flour, Limestone, Jno Young.
Corn and saw, Juno, Mr. Bucker.
Flour and saw, Brooks, Sam'l Brooks.
Flour and saw, Weaverville, ——.
Flour and saw, Weaverville, J R Brank.
Flour, corn and saw, Swannanoa, A B Fortune.
Flour and corn, Asheville, W A Baird.
Flour and corn, Asheville, R B Vance.
Flour and corn, Fairview, Thos Young.
Flour and corn, Sandy Mush, W E Waldrop.
Flour and corn, Democrat, Sam'l Carter.
Flour and corn, Alexander, A M Alexander.

Flour and corn, Hominy (roller), R J Gastor.
Flour and corn, Black Mountain, J W Dougherty.
Flour, Leicester, W H Penland.
Flour, Ramsey, Henry Penland.
Flour, Stocksville, —— Logan.
Flour, Democrat, J A Carter.
Flour and saw (roller), Candler, Mrs A A Cole, adm'r.
Merchant flour (roller), Asheville, H T Collins.
Merchant flour and corn (roller), Logan & Collins.
Merchant flour and corn, Turkey Cr'k, A M Gudger.
Merchant flour and corn, Turnpike, John Smathers.
Merchant flour and corn, Sandy Mush, John Boling.
Saw, New Found, J J Cole.
Saw and corn, Turkey Creek, J Frisly.
Saw and corn, Hominy, Benjamin Curtis' heirs.
Saw and corn, Hominy, Daniel Davis.
Saw and corn, Hominy, A Warren.
Steam saw, Barnardville, J Y Keyth.
Steam saw, Hominy, Penland & Rutherford.
Steam saw, Hominy, S J Joyce.
Steam saw, Sulphur Springs, D P Luther.

PHYSICIANS.

Names and Post Offices.

Alston, —— (col.), Asheville.
Baird, Harry, Asheville.
Baird, J S T, Ramoth.
Ballard, A M, Asheville.
Battle, S W, Asheville.
Barrett, John, Beech.
Bookhart, —— (dentist), Asheville.
Brock, Frank, Candler.
Bryant, R S (col.), Asheville.
Burgin, H F, Biltmore.
Burrough, J A, Asheville.
Chussboro, C P, Asheville.
Clark, Moses, Hominy.
Clark, W W, Candler.
Cliff, C F, Asheville.
Clebb, ——, Asheville.
Clontz, Joseph, Alexander.
Cooper, R W, Fairview.
Fletcher, Hall M, Asheville.
Gill, J N, Weaverville.
Gudger, D M, Hominy.
Harris, J A, Stocksville.
Hawthorn, —— (dentist), Asheville.
Hilliard, Walter L, Asheville.
Hilliard, W D, Asheville.
Hilliard, Charles, Asheville.

BUNCOMBE COUNTY.

Hughes, Wm, Leicester.
Jordan, Chas, Asheville.
Levin, Jo, Asheville.
Linn, —— Asheville.
Little, ——, Biltmore.
McBrayer, L B, Asheville.
Nerriweather, F T, Asheville.
Minor, Charles F, Asheville.
Nelson, Miss Olivia, Asheville.
Pierson, ——, Asheville.
Purefoy, G W, Asheville.
Ramsey, J F (dentist), Asheville.
Reagan, J A, Weaverville.
Reagan, W L, Weaverville.
Reeves, R H (dentist), Asheville.
Reed, George, Biltmore.
Qeynolds, John H, Sandy Mush.
Reynolds, C V, Asheville.
Roberts, —— (dentist), Asheville.
Rob, ——, Asheville.
Robinson, ——, Alexander.
Ruck, Carl Von, Asheville.
Starnes, Clingman E, Asheville.
Stephens, J M, Leicester.
Suier, Dan, Asheville.
Thrash, Geo. jr, Asheville.
Thrash, G H, Hominy.
Ware, A B (dentist), Asheville.
Weaver, H B, Asheville.
Whitson, G W (dentist), Asheville.
Whitaker, A S, Biltmore.
Whittington, W P, Asheville.
Wilson, Wm, Swannanoa.
Williams, J H, Asheville.
Woodcock, J H, Asheville.
Woodcock, Johnson, Asheville.

SCHOOLS.

Names, Post Offices, and Principals.

Academy, Leicester, Prof H F Ketron.
Asheville Graded School, Aheville, Prof J D Eggleston.
Asheville Home Industrial School, Asheville, under the care of the Board of Home Missions of the Presbyterian Church of America; Rev Thomas Lawrence, D D, Superintendent; Miss Florence Stephenson, Principal; 125 students; for the education of poor young women.
Asheville Normal and Collegiate Institute, for young women, Asheville; Rev Thos Lawrence, D D, President; under the auspices of the Executive Committee of the Woman's Board of Missions.
Beaver Dam, Ramoth, Prof C B Way.
Bent Creek High School, Demia, Prof Brock.
Bingham Military School, Maj Robt Bingham, Supt.
College Hill, Riceville, Rev H A Goff.
Collegiate Institute, Fairview, Prof W A G Brown.

BUNCOMBE COUNTY.

Episcopal School (col), Asheville, H S McDuffie, Principal.
Female College, Asheville, Rev James Atkins, D D, President.
Graded School (col, Asheville, E H Lipscombe, Principal.
Graded School (Orange St.), Asheville, R J Tighe, Principal.
Graded School (Bailey St.), Asheville, Mrs Fannie Featherston, Principal.
Graded School (Montford Avenue), Asheville, J S McIlwaine, Principal.
Graded School (Valley St., col.), Asheville. E H Lipscombe, Principal.
High School, Black Mountain, Misses Clemmons and Manly.
High School, Hominy, Rev S C Owens.
Livingston's Presbyterian Parochial School (col.), Asheville, Susie E Myers. If they are able to pay, the charge is $50 per annum; if unable, they are taken for what they can pay, or nothing.
Male Academy, Asheville, S F Venable, Principal.
Montanie Institute, Vanceville, Rev Alfred Penland.
Pine Crest Academy, Best, Prof B F Evans.
Primary, Asheville, Miss Mary Sawyer.
Ravenscroft Training School (Episcopal), Asheville;
School, Morgan Hill, Prof Poe.
School, Emma, E H Merrimon.
Skyland Institute, Asheville, J S Dickery.
Southern Business College, Asheville, M M Lemmond, President.
Weaverville College, Weaverville, Prof M A Yost, President.
Pulic Schools—White, 92; Colored, 23.

TEACHERS.

Names and Post Offices.

Eggleston, J D, Superintendent City Graded Schools.

LOCAL CORPORATIONS.

A. O. U. W., Asheville Lodge, No 2; meets every Thursday night.
Asheville Lodge A. F. and A. M., No. 410; meets third Thursday in each month.
Asheville Chapter, No. 25; meets second Thursday in each month.
Blackmer Masonic Lodge, No. 170, Weaverville; time of meeting, Saturday evening on or before each full moon.
Buncombe County Medical Society, Asheville; L B McBrayer, President; J H Woodcock, Secretary.
Buncombe Division, No. 1, Uniform Rank Knights of Pythias.

BUNCOMBE COUNTY.

County Hospital, Asheville.

Cyrene Commandery, No 5, Asheville; meets fourth Thursday in each month.

Gap Co, Asheville.

Good Templars; meet once a week.

Knights of Honor, Asheville; meet first and third Monday nights in each month.

Mission Hospital, Asheville; managed by a Committee of Ladies, Miss Walton. matron.

Mt. Hermon Masonic Lodge, No. 118, Asheville; time of meeting, first Thursday evening in each month.

Orphans' Home, Asheville; Mrs. Capps, matron; has about 40 children.

Pisgah Lodge, No. 32, Knights of Pythias, Asheville; meets every Monday night.

R. B. Vance Masonic Lodge, No. 293, Grantville; time of meeting, Thursday evening on or before each full moon.

Royal Arcanum, Asheville; meets second and fourth Monday nights.

Swannanoa Lodge, I. O. O. F., No. 56; meets every Tuesday night; J P Sawyer, N. G.

Sulphur Springs Street Railway Co.

The Asheville Street Railway Co, J E Rankin, Receiver.

The First National Bank of Asheville; capital stock, $100,000; W. E. Breese. president; R. R. Rawls, vice-president; W. H. Penland, cashier.

Western Carolina Bank, Asheville; Lewis Maddux, President; Lawrence P. McLand, Cashier.

Western Carolina Savings Bank.

NEWSPAPERS.

Asheville (evening, daily and semi-weekl) Citizen (democratic), published by the Citizen Company (incorporated).

Asheville News and Hotel Reporter, Furman & Messler publishers and proprietors; Nat S Rogers, editor.

Asheville Morning Gazette, Asheville (independent, daily), Jas E Norton, editor; published by Gazette Publishing Co.

Fuller's Gleaner, Asheville (variety, monthly), J M Fuller, editor and proprietor.

State Register, Asheville (Republican, weekly), Roberts & Brown, editors and publishers.

Southern Lutheran, Asheville (monthly denominational journal), Rev. L. E. Busby, editor; published by the Lutheran Publishing Co.

BUNCOMBE COUNTY.

The State Reporter, Asheville (non-denominational religious weekly), Prof J M E Hall, editor and proprietor.

The Colored Enterprise, Asheville (industrial weekly); Thos Leatherwood, editor and proprietor (colored).

The Epworth News, Asheville (semi-monthly, religious), Geo L Hackney, editor and proprietor; organ of Epworth Leagues for Asheville District.

The Southern Baptist, Asheville (denominational weekly), M P Matheny, editor and proprietor; organ of Baptists for Western North Carolina.

Tar Heel Knight, Asheville; organ of the Grand Lodge K of P; Furman & Messler, editors and proprietors.

FARMERS.

Names and Post Offices.

Action—J C Alexander, H N Alexander, G W Ballard, Harry Batterham, T J Bird, J P Bishop, Wilson Boyd, A L Bright, T D Brittain, S S Brigman, A H Britt, J W Bryson, J L Buckham, John H Buckner.

Alexander — D A Blacknell, R H Boyd, Wilson Brown, R H Embler, J H Frisby, W C Garrison, J A Gartney, J P Hughey, W H Hunter, W H Martan, John Martan, C A Nichols, W H Peck, B F Rogers, Tom Ruvis, J H Shepard, A M Snelson, J C Sprance, Jno Sprance. A W Stoder, R B Vance, W A Wagner, W H White, T S Woodson.

Arden—J W Beale. F R Blake, J B Frady, J R Garren, D S Graves, J W Hudson, T F Johnson, J Kyle, J A Lance, L A Lance, M A Lance, N Lanning, D Merrill. A Merrill, S A Murray, N D Murray, Monroe Pinner, Lee Pinner, W R Powers, W H Pressley, F M Pressley, O M Rutledge, M D Shuford, E N Stevens, F P Stroup, J N Suttles, J B Sumner, J F Tweed, J S Weston.

Avery's Creek—Isaac Bishop, S M Bishop, R S Brooks, Sam Brooks, W T Burnett, H W Cagle, M R Cagle, J B Carn, T J Carland, Jesse Case, G W Cavock, P J Cavock, Robert Clayton, Moses Cockran, W D Cockran, J B Cockran, W D Cook, M B Cothran. Wm Creasman, J B Creasman. T H Creasman, W V Creasman, C J Davis, H M Ducker, Mrs Martha Ducker, J H Ducker, Eli Glenn, M S Glenn, Z V Green, W J Hoxed, Joel Ingram, Jesse Ingram, J M Israel, L T Israel, Mrs M Israel, W H Jarrett, W C Johnson, M F Johnson.

Barnardville — J H Andrews, J G Andrews, C F Andrews, W C Baird,

A C Ball, J W Brigman, Joel Brigman, W P Buckner, I K Buckner, R F Buckner, J W Burnett, W H Burnett, M L Burnett, G D Carter, Flora Carter, J A Carter, Z J Carter, J H Carter, N F Carson, H S Carson, H D Carson, W K Chambers, A J Cole, J W Cole, J P Dillingham. T S Dillingham, D O Dillingham, J F Dillingham, T J Garrison, W E Goodson, J O Bragg, W A Bragg, B H Greenwood, W Greenwood, T D Harris, A J Harriwood, S T Holcombe, J C Hunt, W H Hunt, J S Hunt, A E Ingle, S J Ingle, E C Maney, T J McKinney, J S McKinney, T C Morgan, J B Morgan, Paily Robertson, J E Robertson, M E Roberts, J S Roy, J W Sams, S F Williams, C C Whitmore, G W Whitmore, J P Young.

Black Mountain—Byrd Adams, W R Alison, J E Alison, J M Bird, D C Briggs, T K Brown, Jno Cheesebourgh, Ella Goodlake, Charles Cliff, J K Connelly, L P Dacon, S F Daughtery, T A Daughtery, G M Fortune, W H Harris, J D Hemphill, S W Holman, L L Ingram, C P Kerlee, E J Kerlee, J M McCoy, James McNair, J M Moffitt, J H Pagett, W T Partin, C B Rymer, W N Stepp, G W Stepp, J L Stepp, K T Vance, J M Watkins, J P Walker, J A Walker, J W Walker.

Candler—T A Ballard, J C Bird, J H Brooks, D V Brooks, C B Brooks, B F Brooks, G W Brooks, Chas Brooks, T B Brooks, A H Bryson, R D Buckner, W G Candler, W H Cathey, J L Cathey, E L Clark, Levi Clark, J W Clapp, W V Cole, E C Cole, J Courtney, R A Curtis, Washington Curtis, J C Curtis, A M Curtis, J H Davis, W H Davis, H W Dour, A S Dour, A T Dour, H B Duckett, Sallie Fletcher, E C Foster, Wm Green, J W Green, A C Green.

Fairview—J R Allison, Jason Ashworth, Johnson Ashworth, B Barnwell, S B Barnesvill, M E Brank, J E Casey, R C Claton, D M Clemmonts, H W Corbell, J H Dotson, T L Duffy, Thomas Earwood, W C Early, Nancy Frady, Will Garron, Eli Garron, A W Gilmon, James Good, Thomas Harper, C F Harper, J L Jenkins, Mollie Jenkins, B A Jenkins, Maoma Jenkins, J M Lanny, L A Lanny, G W Lynch, A Lytle, T B Lytle, Milton Lytle, Lyton Lytle, J B Merrall, W A Merrall, Rebecca Miller, T J Miller, J C Mitchell, R A Morgan, F L Neslett, W C Neslett, O D Owenby, E M Owenby, A F Patton, R L Patton, A H Pinkerton, J A Ray, Hensey Reed, S P Reed, H M Reed, F M Reed, S C Robertson, O M Rutledge, E C Sales, J T Sherrill, J B

Sherrall, J L Smart, T L Smart, L C Sorrells, S A Stroup, Silas Stroup, Sal Sumner, Jas Trouthorn, J H Tweed, T W Tweed, M M Tweed, N Whiter, A Williams, J S Williams, B H Williams, B V Williams, W R Wright, J E Young, W H Young, Reb. Young, T C Young.

Flat Creek—L Allman, R D Allman, D S Arwood, George Bell, H C Blockstock, A M Brantt, Jas Buckloard, A W Carter, J B Chambers, W W Chambers, C E Chambers, J A Cole, R H Cole, M C Cole, M C Davis, J B Davis, A F Eller, J C Eller, M Garrison, T A Harris, C W Lankford, A L Logan, J W Pickens, T B Redman, Marion Roberts, G W Roberts, J G Roberts, J J Roberts, W S Roberts, G H Sams, H Sprinkle, W E Weaver, J A Whitted, G M White, J H Whittington.

Hominy Creek—T J Candler, E G Carrier, J Marion Cole, W W Crowell, J H Daniels, Mrs E Davis, T E Davis, A H Felmet, Mrs M E Gaston, T P Gaston, D M Gudger, N K Halcombe, J H Halcombe, R M Halcombe, T J Hawkins, W L Henry, T F Hunter, J M Hyatt, T W Jones, R L F Jones, J R Jones, A B Jones, H A Luther, S L Morgan, G W Morgan, W A McKinney, J M Miller, S M Morgan, James Nickles, S S Norman, G W Owenby, Robert Owenby, James Parker, Joe S Parker, G W Penland, Joe Pinley, J M Pettitt, Mrs M E Reeves, P C Reeves, Larkins Reeves, D A Rickman, M N Roberts, A H Starnes, C N Starnes, T A Starnes, Thomas Stradley, N J Tennant, W H Waters, C W Wilson, Robt Williams.

Inanda—J B Johnson, J W Johnson, C W Johnson, A T Jones, S M Jones, J H Jones, G P Jones, C M Jones, F M Kyle, R P Lance, W N Lance, Mrs S R Lance, J M Lance, J J Lance, T L Lance, S B Lance, M H Lance, R Ledbetter, Z T Ledbetter, G H Morris, M Morris, H P Morris, W C Morris, Mrs Mary Pinner, Jas Plemmons, Mrs S A Rice, G M Roberts, W P Shipman, J M Sliton, Mrs R Spain, W T Springs, G A Torrence, John Taylor, J W Walker, J H Webb, D F Wood.

Leicester—M A Beachloard, M M Blacknell, W M Bradburn, G D Brooks, C W Bridges, J F Brown, J L Brown, J S Brown, C A Brown, J E Brown, W M Broyles, H P Broyles, T P Broyles, H B Coffee, W Cole, J W Cole, D V Cole, W S Cook, M L Cullerson, P W Daves, W M Dover, W T Erwin, L D Felmet, J M Ford, D B Ford, W L Foster, J H Foster, J M W Frisbee, J M Garron, H W Gilbert, J Gillespie, T J Gillespie, J W Gillespie, G L Gilles-

|

pie, A M Gudger, B G Gudger, J H Hall, L N Hall, J E Hampton, M F Hampton, T N Hawkins, J C Hawkins, A N Hawkins, J F Hawkins, J M Hayes, E S Ingle, S P Ingle, T R James, S B Jones, A M Jones, S M Kerr, R D Kennon, H F Ketrion, J P King, J R Lanning, H L Lindsey, W Martin, L H Martin, J M Martin, S F Meadows, C P Meadows, M G Mears, A J Merrill, J H Miller, R P Moore, R C Morgan. E P Moss, M L Owenby, W D Patton, R P Penland, W H Penland, M Plemmons, John H Plemmons, Mrs M C Plemmons, J C Plemmons, J I Plemmons, Levi Plemmons, W E Powndere, J T Ratcliff, H M Ratcliff, M J Ratcliff, W D Redmond, D W Reynold, A A Reynold, J P Reynold, J A Robinson, G W Robinson, W L Robinson, R B Roberts, M Q Roberts, M E Roberts, N A Rodgers, J I T Rodgers, W A Rodgers, J M Sans, D H Shook, John Shook, R S Shook, G M Sluder, C B Sluder, M M Sluder, R E Sluder, W M Sluder, G W Sluder, J D Smith, M M Snelson, A L Snelson, M M Swain, D R Teague, D A Warlick, R C Wells, Mrs M E Wells, E West, W M White, M B Wild, W D Worley, Wm Wright.

Luther—W P Hampton, J B Haney, D Henson, J B Henson, C W Henson, F B Henson, T T Henson, T M Holford, R H Hyatt, J R Hyatt, J C Hyatt, W L Israel, L T Israel, W H Jamison, M H Jamison, M S Joyce, W F Justice, Root Joyce, J Koytt, W A Luther, R L Luther, S M Luther, J J Miller, W H Miller, L C Miller, Jacob Miller. W J Moore, S L Moore, G W Morgan, L W Morgan, J E Morgan, P P Morgan, J H Morgan, J L Morgan, E J Morgan, W L Penner, W L Peoples, J W Rice, J B Roberson, W J Roberson, S T Sawyer, J C Smathers, J A Taylor, W P Terrell, G M Warren, Harriett Warren, J B Warren, J T Warren, Miller Warren, J M Warren, M E Williams, J P Wolfe, J L Young, S F Young, Mrs Young.

Sandy Mush—J E Austin, Peter Ball, J P Black, Elizabeth Boyd, Z B Boyd, N Bramner, Violet Bradburn, C W Bridges, J W Carson. M S Clark, H F

Ducket, J B Ducket, T J Ferguson, C S Ferguson, John Garrett, E Garrett, D A Gillespie. B P Green, W J Haze, T H Hill, J M Ingles, A R James, S J Jones, T G King, M O King, M A King, J M King, J R Lusk, J G Lowery, J M Noland, R E Noland, J W Pounders, A C Randall, E R Randall, Jno Reeves, J H Reynolds, W M Rodgers, J M Rodgers, J D Robinson, D W Robinson, M L Robinson, O W Surratt, J P Surratt, W E Waldrope, D M Wells, J W F Wells, J F Wells, J S Wells, C L Wells, E A Worley, L Worley.

Swannanoa — C Alexander, M I Alexander, W R Alexander, G N Alexander, A N Alexander, W A Barnett, J S Bartlett, H H Bears, Walter Bingham, J M Brookshire, B I Burgan, W L Creasman, D C Clarke, J W Coggin, S W Davidson. S Brock Davidson, C F Davidson, P H Falsome, A B Fortune, W P Fortune, B F Fortune, J S Gash, J A Glass, L L Grant, J W Gragg, C P Gragg, W M Gudger. T L Harris, J H Hemphill, H C Hunt, F J Ingle, T J Jones, W L Kemball, C J McCope, Latilda McGimp, Alice Ogborn, J T Padgett, T M Paiter, R L Patton, J M Patton, Taylor Redman, J A Reed, W F Rice. A J Rice. J H Rice, J A Roy, J E Roy, W R Roy, W M Sawyer, W R Shope, H F Shope, D V Shope, J M Shope, M F Stevens, H E Swan. D H Swan, B S Tipton, Z B Vance, H Wilson. Wilson & Fry, W R Whitson.

Weaverville—J M Aikens, Z A Baird, J R Baird K Baird, D Ballard, Jno H Ballard, R B Brantt, Dr J Brantt, K Brigman, R Brigman, R P Britton, J B Chambers. K Chambers, J G Chambers, Gragg Chambers, F M Cole, Jno Capps, J M Davis. J B Garrison, T M Garrison, A J Gill, J D Harran, E W Hemphill. J Hemphill, J W McDavis, W A Davis, J H Money, S M Munday, M M Parker, J F Parker, J M Parker, D W Peake, G F Pendland, R W Picken, D W Roberts, F P Roberts, Joseph Roy, Jas Sawyer, J W Vandiver, W A Wagner, T W Wagner, C P Weaver, R H Weaver, F M Weaver, J S Weaver, P H Weaver, Rufe Weaver.

BURKE COUNTY.

AREA, 400 SQUARE MILES.

POPULATION, 14,939; White 12,378, Colored 2,561,

BURKE COUNTY was laid off from Rowan county in 1777, and named in honor of the celebrated English statesman and orator, Edmund Burke.

MORGANTON, the county-seat, is located immediately on the Western North Carolina Railroad, 197 miles west of Raleigh, and is called in compliment of General Daniel Morgan: it is the seat of the Western Insane Asylum and Institution for the Deaf and Dumb. Population 1,500.

Surface—Mountainous, with many rich valleys. The soil is rich, with clay sub soil, water excellent, and the scenery unsurpassed for beauty and sublimity in this or any other State. Morganton, and the mineral springs in its vicinity, are delightful places of summer resort.

Staples—Wheat, corn, oats, rye, barley, buckwheat, live stock and dairy products.

Fruits — Apples, peaches, pears, grapes, melons and all manner of small fruits.

Timber—Oak, hickory, ash, walnut, beach, white pine, chestnut, wild cherry, and many other varieties.

TOWNS AND POST OFFICES.

Bridgewater,	150	Linville's Store,	50
Brindletown,	50	Morganton	
Camp Creek,	25	(C. H),	1,500
Chamber's,	30	Pearson,	50
Chesterfield,	25	Penlope,	25
Connelly's		Rollins,	40
Springs,	150	Rutherford	
Dogwood,	40	College,	200
Enola,	20	Shoup's Ford,	40
Fonta Flora,	50	Table Rock,	75
Gibbs,	25	Valdese,	375
Glen Alpine,	100	Warlick,	25
Jonas Ridge,	25	Worry,	30
Joy,	15		

COUNTY OFFICERS.

Clerk Superior Court—P W Patton.
Commissioners—G P Irwin, chairman; H C Bennett, H W Connelly.
Coroner—Joseph Dale.
Register of Deeds—J H Cooper.
Sheriff—T M Webb,
Solicitor Tenth District—J F Spainhour.
Surveyor—T S Drury.
Standard Keeper—J H Pearson.
Treasurer— —— Waters.
County Examiner—Rev R L Patton.

COURTS.

Second Monday after the first Monday in March, and first Monday before the first Monday in September,

TOWN OFFICERS.

MORGANTON—*Mayor*, L A Bristol.
Commissioners—J A Dickson, chairman; Samuel Huffman, R K Pressnell, T J Gillam, J W Garrison, B F Davis. *Chief of Police*—John Wall. *Secretary and Treasurer*—W A Ross.

RUTHERFORD COLLEGE—*Mayor*, W E Abernethy.

TOWNSHIPS AND MAGISTRATES.

Icard—H A Adams, L F Warlick, W W Aiken, Lewis Warlick, James Hildebrand, A J Cook, James Martin, Ellis Cook, Will Jones (Morganton.)

Linville — C D Giles, John Gibbs, Davis Alexander, Sam B Moore, Sam A McCall, P P Mull, W N Wise, Robert Roper, John Fox (Linville's Store).

Lovelady—J A Ballinger, H W Connelly, J H Hoffman, John W Berry, jr, Jeff Abee, A A Shuford, Daniel Hudson, Wm Griffin, David Lowman (Morganton).

Lower Creek—Pink Corpening, J A Perrett, W B McDowell, Vance Powell, S C Kirby, James I Hood, S S Hallyburton, D H Peeler, Jno R McCall (Morganton.)

Lower Fork — Joseph Mull, J D Hoyle, N L Chapman, S A Carsnell, Ransom Cloud, John Snarp, Peter Buff (Morganton).

Morganton—J A Date, Geo L Phifer, W E Powe, N P Beck, L A Bristol, Jas R Howard, R A Cobb, D C Pearson, R C Wilner, Joseph Bowman, W A Wortman (Morganton).

Quaker Meadow—W M Winter, W T Hardison, Wm Wall, O M Aury, Jackson Miller, Peter Whisnant, Thos Causby (Morganton).

Silver Creek—W H Pool, C E Tate, H C Fisher, N M Hennesse, W N Thompson, J D Knott, John Waters, T L Eply, John Seals (Morganton).

Smoky Creek—J S Tillery, Avery Smith, Phillip Burnes, Harrison Benfield, J J Smith, E A Poe, Nelson Brown (Morganton).

Upper Creek—J A Cox, J L Sisk, Westley Joynes, Robt Patton, Thos

BURKE COUNTY.

Keller, Geo M Scott, W R Allen, S J Pearcey (Morganton).
  Upper Fork—R A Denton, F E Cook, J M Carsnell, Zachery Carswell, William Mace, J R Carsnell, J G Smith, Rufus Carswell, John Denton, Joseph Denton (Morganton).

CHURCHES.

Names, Post Offices, Pastors and Denom.

BAPTIST.

Abee's Chapel—Warlick's Mill, J A Rector.
Antioch—North Catawba, J A Rector.
Bethlehem—Enola, Z Carswell.
Church—Bridgewater, Dr M M Landrum.
Enon—Connelly Springs. ——
Fellowship—Camp Creek, A P Bumgarner.
Glen Alpine—Glen Alpine, ——
Harmony Grove—Brindletown, J C Sorrels.
Hopewell—Brindletown, J L Shinn.
Morganton—Morganton, R L Patton.
Mt. Gilead—Camp Creek, Wm Hull.
Mt. Olive—North Catawba, J A Rector.
Mt. Horne—North Catawba, J L Shinn.
Mt. Zoar—North Catawba, M L Clark.
New Prospect—Enola, J W Mull.
North Catawba—North Catawba, G W Thomas.
Pleasant Hill—Enola, J L Shinn.
Smyrna—Table Rock, J M Harris.
St. John's—Pearson, Wallace B Mull.
Zion—Morganton, J L Shinn.

METHODIST.

Ballinger—Rutherford College, W F Honeycutt.
Bethel—Morganton, J S Nelson.
Big Hill—Warlick's Mills, W F Honeycutt.
Chapel—Warlick's Mills, W F Honeycutt.
Church—Glen Alpine, J S Nelson.
Church—Morganton, —— Leith, D D
Fairview—Joy, —— Gantt.
Friendship—Connelly's Springs, W F Honeycutt.
Gilboa—Morganton, J S Nelson.
Linville—Linville Store, —— Gantt.
Macedonia—Enola, J W Houk.
Missionary Ridge—Morganton, J M Houk.
Morganton (col)—Morganton, J S Settle (Zion Meth).
Mountain Grove—Table Rock, —— Gantt.
Mt. Pleasant—Chesterfield, J S Nelson.
Nebo—Bridgewater, Jas Gibson.
Oak Forest—Morganton, J M Houk.
Oak Hill,—Morganton, —— Gantt.

Oleth—Gill's, —— Gantt.
Rutherford College—W F Honeycutt.
Pleasant Gap—Enola, J M Houk.
Providence—Morganton, J M Houk.
Salem—Morganton, J S Nelson.
Snow Hill—Bridgewater, J D Gibson.
Zion—Morganton, J S Nelson.

PRESBYTERIAN.

Anderson Chapel—Morganton, J M Rose.
Church—Morganton, J M Rose.
Quaker Meadow Chapel—Morganton, J M Rose.
Silver Creek—Glen Alpine Station, J M Rose.

EPISCOPAL.

Grace—Morganton, ——

LUTHERAN.

Church—Glen Alpine, ——

A. M. E. (METHODIST).

Church (col)—Morganton, W J Jordan.

MINISTERS RESIDENT.

Names, Post Offices and Denominations.

BAPTIST.

Bumgarner, A P, Cæsar.
Carswell, Z. Enola.
Clark, M L, Enola.
Hildebrand, J M, Enola.
Holloway, W W, Morganton.
Hull, W F, Wortman.
Patton, R L, Morganton.
Rector, J A. Table Rock.
Shinn, J L, Morganton.
Sorrels, J C. Bridgewater.
Thorpe, J W, Iredell.
Whitener, P A, Morganton.

METHODIST.

—— Gantt, Table Rock.
Goode, D B, Connelly Springs.
Hoyle, J T. Camp Creek.
Kaylor, F R. Morganton.
Nelson, J S, Morganton.
Payne, J N, Morganton.
Somers, J N, Worry.
Steele, M T, Dysartsville.

PRESBYTERIAN.

Rose, J M, Morganton.
Soulier, Barth, Valdese (Waldensian).

HOTELS AND BOARDING HOUSES.

Names, Post Offices and Proprietors.

Boarding House, Glen Alpine, Sidney Bright.
Boarding House. Glen Alpine, J J Sigmon.

BURKE COUNTY.

Connelly Springs Hotel, Connelly Springs, Major J C Jones.

Eagle Hotel, Morganton, Gabriel Pearcy.

Glen Alpine Springs, Glen Alpine, W B Morrison.

Jenkins House, Glen Alpine Station, J D Knott.

Mountain House, Morganton, J T Walton.

Piedmont Springs (16 miles north of Morganton), Piedmont Lum. Branch and Mining Co., J L Martin, Supt.

Restaurant, Morganton, W W McGalliard.

Restaurant, Morganton, Joe Avery (col).

Restaurant, Morganton, Jno Erwin (col).

Rose Villa, Morganton, D C Pearson.

LAWYERS.

Names and Post Offices.

Avery, A C, Morganton (Supreme Ct Judge).

Avery, I E. Morganton (Vice Consul at Shanghi, China).

Bynum, J G, Morganton (Superior Ct Judge).

Erwin, G P, Morganton (Pres. Piedmont Bank).

Ervin, W C, Morganton.

Erwin, I Ernest, Morganton.

Ervin, S J, Morganton.

McDowell, Frank, Morganton.

McKesson, C F, Morganton.

Pearson, W S. Morganton.

Perkins, J T, Morganton.

Silver, M, Morganton.

MANUFACTORIES.

Kinds, Post Offices and Proprietors.

Attocoa Cotton Mills. Morganton (proposed).

Blacksmithing and wheelwrighting, Garlick's Mills, Andrew Abee.

Blacksmithing and wheelwrighting, Warlick's Mills, J P Abee.

Blacksmithing and wheelwrighting, Glen Alpine Station, Jerry Garrison.

Blacksmithing and wheelwrighting, Morganton, John Navy.

Blacksmithing and wheelwrighting, Glen Alpine Station, Green Moore.

Blacksmithing and wheelwrighting, Warlick, Adam Whitt.

Brick, Morganton, M M & Trading Co.

Brick, Morganton. R R Pressnell.

Burke Tannery Co, Morganton, Kestler, Lash & Co of Boston; W F Camp, resident mgr.

Boots and shoes, Morganton, J J Pearson.

BURKE COUNTY.

Boots and shoes, Morganton, R Garrison.

Boots and shoes, Morganton, Jno Williams.

Carriage and wagons, Morganton, J H Coffey.

Carpentering, Warlick, John Martin.

Dunavant Cotton Mfg Co, Morganton, 3,300 spindles: Foster Cotton Mill Co.

Coopering, Warlick, Alex Lail.

Coopering, Warlick, J Brittain.

Contracting and building, Glen Alpine Station, M C Sigmon.

Contracting and building, Glen Alpine Station, J J Sigmon.

Contracting and building, Morganton, Frank Kaylor.

Contracting and building, Morganton, John R Martin.

Contracting and building, Morganton, H Setzer.

Contracting and building, Warlick, Jonas Martin.

Contracting and building. Morganton, C S Smith.

Contractor and builder, Morganton, Wm Sloan.

Hoisery and half-hose woolen mill, Valdese, John Meier, prop; 40 knitting machines.

Lumber and shingles, Morganton, Annis & Craig.

Machine Shops, Morganton, McRary & Gillelang.

Shingles and lumber, Connelly Springs, H W Connelly.

Shingles, Connelly Springs. S Deal.

Shingles and lumber, Gibbs, Joshua Gibbs.

Shingles and lumber, Morganton, Denton & Co,

Shingles and lumber, Morganton, W G Hogan.

Steam planing mill, Morganton, J W Garrison.

Tannery, Morganton, E P R Cline.

Tannery, Warlick, Alex Hood.

Tannery, Warlick, P M Warlick.

Tannery, Morganton, D McKenzie.

Tobacco (smoking), Morganton, Sallie Michael Tobacco Co, Laxton Bros.

MERCHANTS AND TRADESMEN.

Name, Post Office, and Line of Business.

BRIDGEWATER.

Barnett & Son,	G S and lumber
Bowers, S T,	G S
Hutchins, T C,	G S
Mills, J C,	Mining
McCall, S A,	G S
Rust, J R,	G S
Seals, T A,	G S

BURKE COUNTY.

BURKE COUNTY.

BRINDLETOWN.

Kirksey, W L, G S
Kirksey, S P, G S
Kirksey, E J, G S
Taylor, J Z, G S

CAMP CREEK.

Mull, J L, G S

CONNELLY SPRINGS.

Berry, D J, G S
Connelly, H W, Lumber
Coulter, J E (near), G S
Dorsey & McGilliard, G S
Dorsey, J W, G S
Goode, D P, G S
Johnson, D P, Miller

FONTA FLORA.

Giles, A H, G S
McGimpsey, J Thomas, G S

GLEN ALPINE SPRINGS.

Beach, J T, G S
Bright, T S, G S
Hennessee & Co, G S
Simpson Bros, G S
Simpson & Co, G S

LINVILLE'S STORE.

Summers, A F, G S

MORGANTON.

Annis & Craig, G S
Bailey & Duckworth, G S
Berry, W B, G S
Britton, F B & Co, Livery
Boger, W H, Jeweler and G S
Bush, Ernest, Florist
Buffalow, A R, Butcher and Grocer
Claywell & Bros, Furniture and Undertakers
Collett & Gilliam, Clothing
Davis, J L & Co, G S
Davis & Anderson, Who & Ret Gro
Davis, I I, Dry Goods
Ervin, Robt J, Civil Engineer
Forney & Co, Butcher and Gro
Gilliam, T I, Hardware
Halliburton, R J & Co, Gro
Hemphill, T L, Drugs
Hicks, Mrs A E, Milliner
Huffman, M & Co, G S
Huffman, S & Co, G S
Huffman, Amos, G S
Hunt, M T, Livery
Kibbler, M B, G S
Lazarus Bros, Clothing
LeFever, W E & Co, G S
McGalliard, W W, Butcher and Gro
Moore, T P, G S
Mull, D B & Co, G S
Newton, P F, Grocer
Payne, H F, Tel Op
Payne, J N, G S
Pearson, J H, Fire Ins
Poe, W T, Cane Mcht
Reid Hardware Co, W B Reid, Pres

Ross, W A, G S
Shuping, J A, Butcher and Gro
Turner, W G, Post Master
The Herald Book Store, Books and Sta
The Gash Co, Bicycles, etc
Tate, Frank P, Civil Engineer
Tull, Dr John, jr, Drugs
Walter, W E, Civil Engineer
Walton & Pressnell, G S
Ward & Goodson, Livery
Weber, H A, Baker
Wilson, G W, Depot Agt
Wilson, J H, Barber
Wright, J D, Jeweler
Wortman, W A, G S
Wortman, Frank, Grocer

ROLLINS.

Poteet, C A, G S

RUTHERFORD COLLEGE.

Cuthberston, D C, G S
LeFever, W E & Co, G S

SHOUP'S FORD.

Proctor, J G, G S

TABLE ROCK.

Sisk, J L & Co, G S
Ferguson, F C, G S
Berry, J M, Carriages

WARLICK'S MILLS.

Havener, R C, G S

WORRY.

Forney Bros, G S

MINES.

Kinds, Post Offices and Proprietors.

Gold (Penly), Perkinsville, owned by a Northern company,
Gold (Pax Hill), Perkinsville, Hill & Co.
Gold (Park Hill), Glen Apline Station,
Gold, Brindletown, J C Mills and others,
Gold, Brindletown, Queen Mining Co.

MILLS.

Kinds, Post Offices and Proprietors.

Flour and corn, Fonta Flora, J W Wilson.
Flour and corn, Warlick's Mills, ——.
Flour and corn, Joy, Gray Turner,
Flour and corn, Morganton, B A Berry.
Flour and corn, Morganton, J W Garrison.
Flour and corn, Bridgewater, H C Bennett.
Flour and corn, Worry, Mrs Cornelia Henderson,
Merchant flour (steam), Connelly Sp'gs, S Deal.

BUSINESS DIRECTORY. 135

BURKE COUNTY.

Roller mills, Morganton, W G Hogan.
Saw, Glen Alpine Springs, J D Pitts.
Saw, Shoup's Ford, G W Chapman.
Saw, Connelly Springs, J S Coulter.
Saw, Bridgewater, Austin Conley.
Shingle mill, Morganton. Hogan & Franklin.
Steam saw, Glen Alpine, Abel Pitts.

PHYSICIANS.

Names and Post Offices.

Anderson, J R, Morganton.
Jeter, J Peter (dentist), Morganton.
King, ——, Bridgewater.
Lanlancher, P P, Morganton.
Laxton, J L, Morganton.
Marlick, E S, Morganton,
Moran, G H, Morganton.
Mott, ——, Morganton.
Murphy, P L (Supt State Hospital), Morganton.
Pearson, R C, Morganton.
Ross, C E, Morganton.
Taylor, J M, Morganton.

SCHOOLS.

Names, Post Offices and Principals.

Amherst Academy, North Catawba, —— Moore.
Morganton Male Academy, Morganton, ——.
N C School for Deaf and Dumb, one mile southeast of court house, E McK Goodwin, supt.
Private school, Morganton, Mrs Wm R Marbut.
Private school, Morg'nt'n, Miss Emma Tate.
Private school, Morganton, Miss Mary Dickson.
Rutherford College, Rutherford College, Will E Abernethy, pres.
Table Rock Academy, Table Rock, A K Brahaw, prin.
Waldensian school, Valdese, M A Johier, prin.
West Morganton school, Morganton, R L Patton.
Public schools, white 55; colored 11.

BURKE COUNTY.

TEACHERS.

Names and Post Offices.

Abernethy, W E, pres. Rutherford College.
Benfield, Miss Mary, Jonas Ridge.
Betts, O A, Morganton.
Bumgarner, Mrs J P, Enola.
Chase, G F, Glen Alpine.
Druxy, F S, Morganton.
Goodwin, E McK, Morganton.
Haynes, Z W, Morganton.
Justice, W C, Bridgewater.
Marbert, Mrs W R, Morganton.
Moore, Mrs Emma, Rutherford College.
Rodrick, Miss Lillie, Morganton.
Rose, Miss Mattie, Morganton.
Peter, Jennie, Worry,

LOCAL CORPORATIONS.

Burke Tinning Co, Morganton, W F Camp, supt.
Chamber of Commerce and Industry, Morganton, I I Davis, pres.
Dunnivant Cotton Mills, Morganton, F P Tate, receiver. Capital stock, $75,-000.
Electric Light and Power Co, Morganton, M F Scaife, pres; W C Ervin, sec and treas.
Morganton Manufacturing and Trading Co, Morganton, J A Dickson, sec and treas.
Morganton Land and Improvement Co, W C Ervin, pres; S T Pearson, treas.
Tennessee River Land and Timber Co, Morganton, J T Perkins, agent.
The Herald Publishing Co, Morganton, W C Ervin, pres; S T Pearson, sec'y and treas; F B Davis, manager.
State Hospital for Insane, located one mile east of court house, Dr P L Murphy, supt.

NEWSPAPERS.

Gospel Mission Fan, Morganton (missionary monthly), Rev R L Patton, editor and prop.
Morganton Herald (dem, weekly) published by Herald Pub Co, W C Ervin, editor.
The Populist, Morganton, R A Cobb, editor and publisher,

CABARRUS COUNTY.

AREA, 488 SQUARE MILES.

POPULATION, 18,142; White, 12,683, Colored 5,459.

CABARRUS COUNTY was formed in 1792, from Mecklenburg county, and was so named in compliment of Stephen Cabarrus, a member of the Legislature from Chowan county and Speaker of the House of Representatives.

CONCORD, the county-seat, is on the North Carolina Railroad, and is 150 miles west of Raleigh;population 6,300.

A marble monument stands in the Court House yard, erected in the honor of the Confederate dead of the county.

Surface—This county has a pleasantly undulating surface. It is situated on Rocky river and its tributaries. The soil is generally good and much of it rich. The North Carolina Railroad passes directly through it. It is a thrifty county and a desirable place to live. Water-power fine.

Staples—Cotton, corn and wheat are the leading staples, and fine crops are produced.

Fruits—Apples, peaches, pears, cherries, plums, grapes, berries, melons, etc.

Timbers—Walnut, poplar, ash, hickory, oak, maple, etc.

Minerals—Cabarrus county is very rich in minerals, having many rich gold and other mines. See list of mines further on.

TOWNS AND POST OFFICES.

	POP.		PO.
Bost's Mills,	40	Harrisburg,	60
Clear Creek,	10	Klutts,	25
Coddle,	25	Leading,	26
Concord		Maximo,	25
(C H),	6,300	Mt. Pleasant,	550
Dry's Mill,	38	Nussman,	—
Flow's,	40	Pioneer Mills,	75
Furr's,	15	Rimer,	15
Garmond,	25	Saunders,	30
Georgeville,	75	Smith's Ford,	20
Govern,	20	Tulin,	5

COUNTY OFFICERS.

Clerk Superior Court—J C Gibson.
Commissioners—J Dove, ch; J W Foil. Wm Propst, J S Turner.
Coroner—J P Hornbuckle.
Register of Deeds—Wm M Weddington.
Solicitor 8th District—J Q Holton.

Sheriff—J A Sims.
Surveyor—J H Long.
Standard Keeper—W J Hill.
Treasurer—G E Kestler.
County Examiner—J F Shinn.

COURTS,

Sixth Monday before the first Monday in March and sixth Monday before the first Monday in September.

TOWN OFFICERS.

CONCORD—*Mayor*, L McKee Morrison; *Commissioners*, L D Duval, A M Brown, R F Coble, J C Fink, J K Patterson; G T Crowell, C W Swink; *Town Clerk and Treasurer*, J L Hartsell.

MT. PLEASANT—*Mayor*, A W Moose; *Commissioners*, L J Foil, H T J Ludwig, W H Fisher, L A Lentz, W R Kindly.

TOWNSHIPS AND MAGISTRATES.

No. 1—W H Oglesby, M T Stallings (Harrisburg), Jno A Barnhardt (Pioneer Mills), I M W Alexander, V C Parrish (Concord).

No. 2—J McCaldwell, W F Cannon, W L Morris (Concord) Z A Morris, (Harrisburg), S R Andrews (Tulin), Robt H Smith (Springville).

No. 3—E R Graham (Saunders) W B Smith, E M Feilds, W S Isenhour (Coddle),R C Harris,G A Bradford (Tulin) M A Emmerson, G C Goodman (Mill Hill).

No. 4—Rufus Cline, H W Blackwelder, C A Sherwood (Concord), E R G Plaster (Enochville).

No. 5—E K Misenheimer, W B Earnhardt, John Holdbrooks, C W Earnbardt, E P. Deal, Robt. H Patterson, W R Blackwelder (Concord)

No. 6—A Crowell (Mt. Pleasant), A J Lippard, W C Klutts, A H Penninger. M L K utts, J H D Walker (Rimer),W D Ritchie,J H Ritchie(Govern).

No. 7—J D Klutts, J L Peck. D L Barringer, G W Dry, John H Moose, J W Lentz,R T Honeycutt (Dry's Mills), C L Nussman (Nussman).

No. 8—D H Ridenhouse, H C McAllister, T A Moser, C D Barringer, M L Buchanan, A W Moose. G J Hurlocker (Mt. Pleasant), J W Blackwelder (Concord).

138   BRANSON'S NORTH CAROLINA

CABARRUS COUNTY.

No. 9—M H Lefler (Concord), C F Smith, M M Furr (Georgeville), Frank Barrier (Mt. Pleasant), Jas Harkey, Wm Smith (Bost's Mill).

No. 10—D W Turner (Smithford), W G Newell, F P Boger (Flows), H C Cook, J C McEachern, Ed P Black (Pioneer Mills). M C Gorman (Garmond).

No. 11—Adam Hagler, D E Cline, C A Robinson. W R Johnston. James B White, Asa Blackwelder, W V Kimminger (Concord).

No. 12—J A Kimmons, W J Hill, J N Brown, S E W Pharr, Jno W Alexander, C A Pitts, J M Burrage, W H Blume, W C Coleman, Jno McInnis (Concord).

NOTARIES PUBLIC.

J L Crowell, H I Woodhouse, L D Cotrane (Concord).

CHURCHES.

Names, Post Offices, Pastors and Denom.

BAPTIST.

Allison, Grove (col), Concord, ——
First Baptist Church—Concord, A J Pasour.
Old Field—Concord. ——

LUTHERAN.

Centre Grove—Concord, J Q Wertz.
Cold Water—Concord, H A McCullough.
Church (col)—Concord, N J Bokke.
Grace (col)—Concord, N J Bokke.
Holy Trinity—Mt. Pleasant, J H C Fisher.
Luther Union—Mt. Pleasant, J H C Fisher.
Mt. Carmel—Mt. Pleasant, ——
Mt. Hermon—Concord, H A McCullough.
Mt. Olive—Mt. Pleasant, P H E Derrick.
Prosperity—Mt. Pleasant, ——
St. Andrew's—Concord, H A McCullough.
St. Martin's—Bost's Mills, J H Price.
St. Stephen's—Gold Hill, P H E Derrick.
St. James'—Concord, M G G Scherer.
St. John's—Mt. Pleasant, S D Steffey.
Trinity—Enochsville. V R Stickley.

METHODIST.

Bethel—Clear Creek, M D Giles.
Boger's Chapel—Flow's. M D Giles.
Centre Grove—Bost's Mills, M D Giles.
Centre—Concord, W H L McLawin.
Central Church—Concord, R H Parker.
Church—Mt. Pleasant. M D Giles.

Cold Springs—Mt. Pleasant, M D Giles.
Forest Hill—Concord, M A Smith.
Mt. Carmel—Concord, W H L McLaurin.
Mt. Olivet—Concord, W H L McLaurin.
Ray's Chapel—Concord, A H McCullough.
Rocky Ridge—Concord, W H L McLaurin.
St. Paul's—Bost's Mills, M D Giles.

N. METHODIST.

Mt. Mitchell—Concord, ——
Mt. Moriah (col)—Concord. Alf Sherrill.

EPISCOPAL.

All Saints—Concord, J A Davis.
Church (col)—Concord, Rev. Stancel.

PRESBYTERIAN.

Bethpage—Mill Hill, W M Shaw.
Chapel—Concord, A K Pook.
Church—Concord, W C Alexander.
Poplar Tent—Springville, Roger Martin.
Rocky River—Harrisburg, —— Lancaster.
Zion—Concord, ——.

N. PRESBYTERIAN.

Westminster—Concord. F T Logors.

METH. EPISCOPAL.

Mt. Moriah (col)—Concord, Rev. —— Rogers.

A. M. E. ZION.

Bell's Mission (col)—Concord, J F Lee.
Bethel (col)—Concord, R A Simmons.
Church (col)—Concord, G L Blackwell.
Church (col)—Mt. Pleasant, J F Lee.
Church (col)—Springsville. ——
Ebenezer (col)—Flow's, R L Edwards.
Piney Grove (col)—Concord, R L Edwards.
Poplar Tent (col)—Springsville, R A Simmons.
Reeves' Chapel (col)—Bost's Mills. J F Lee.
Rock Hill (col)—Concord, R A Simmons.
Price Memorial Temple (col)—Concord, W H Abbott.
Zion Hill (col)—Concord, J L Blackwell

MINISTERS RESIDENT.

Names, Post Offices and Denom.

METHODIST.

Giles, M D, Mt. Pleasant.
Love, W T, Coddle Creek.
McLaurin, W H L, Concord.
Moose, J R, Concord.
Parker, R H, Concord.
Rush, Z, Concord.
Simpson, ——, Concord.
Smith, M A, Concord.
Smith, T W, Concord.

CABARRUS COUNTY.

LUTHERAN.

Bokke, N J, Concord.
Fisher, J H C, Mt Pleasant.
Fisher, C L T, Mt. Pleasant.
McCullough, H A, Concord.
Moser, T, Mt. Pleasant.
Price, J H. Concord.
Scherer, M G G, Concord.
Steffey, S D, Concord.

EPISCOPAL.

Davis; J C, Concord.
Stancel, —— (col), Concord.

PRESBYTERIAN.

Logan, F T, Concord.
Pressley, J E. Coddle Creek.

N. PRESBYTERIAN.

Satterfield, D J, Concord.

REF. PRESBYTERIAN.

Barringer, Paul, Mt. Pleasant.

A. M. E. ZION.

Abbott, W H, Concord.
Bailey, J B, Concord.
Edwards, R L, ——
Lee J F, Mt. Pleasant.
Simmons, R A, Concord,

HOTELS AND BOARDING HOUSES.

Names, Post Offices and Proprietors.

Boarding, Concord, Mrs J S Hill.
Boarding, Concord, Mrs W S Bingham.
Boarding, Concord, Mrs Alex Sapp.
Boarding, Concord, Mrs Dr M Holden.
Boarding, Concord, J A Cline.
Boarding, Concord, Mrs J H Henderson.
Boarding, Mount Pleasant, Mrs M A Dreher.
Boarding, Mt. Pleasant. D W Corzine.
Boaring, Mt Pleasant. A W Moose.
Boarding, Concord, Mrs J S Fisher.
Hotel, Mt Pleasant, L A Lentz.
Morris House, Concord, S L Klutz.
St Cloud, Concord, Mrs M E Dusenbery.

LAWYERS.

Names and Post Offices.

Caldwell, M H H, Concord.
Crowell, J L, Concord.
Means, W G, Concord.
Means, Paul B, Concord.
Montgomery, W J, Concord.
Puryear, H S, Concord.
Smith, W M, Concord.

MANUFACTORIES.

Kinds, Post Offices and Proprietors.

Blacksmithing, Concord, Dan Heathcock.

CABARRUS COUNTY.

Blacksmithing, Concord, Jno Sanders.
Blacksmithing, Concord, Jno Parnell.
Blacksmithing, Mount Pleasant, J A Lefler.
Blacksmithing, Mount Pleasant, Jesse Skien.
Boots and shoes, Concord, S G Murr.
Boots and shoes, Concord, G W Brown.
Boots and shoes, Concord, J F Shoemaker.
Boots and shoes, Concord, Dan Stiller.
Brick, Concord, T Chapman.
Brick, Concord, R A Brown.
Brick, Concord, D W Moore.
Cabinet, Concord, Samuel Sloop.
Carriages, Concord, W C Boyd.
Contracting and building, Concord, N Correll.
Contracting and building, Concord, A H Propst.
Contracting and building, Concord, D A Caldwell.
Contracting and building, Concord, G R P Miller.
Contracting and building, Concord, S D A Shuping.
Contracting and building, Concord, C A Luther.
Contracting and building, Concord, James Smith.
Contracting and building, Concord, J P Luther.
Cotton mill, Mt Pleasant. W R Kindly, sec and treas; cap $20,000.
Mlictric Light Co, Concord, J M Odell, pres; J W Cannon, sec and treas; cap $12,000.
Furniture, Concord, M E Castor.
Hair work, Concord, Mrs L Quantz.
Harness, Concord, W J Hill.
Kerr Bag Mfg Co, Concord, J M Odell, pres; W R Odell, sec and treas; cap $224,000; manufacture seamless bags, also bleach and finish goods for flour bags.
Manufacturing (cotton), Concord, G W Patterson, sec and treas.
Cannon Manufacturing Co, Concord, cotton yarns and sheeting: J M Odell, pres; J W Cannon, sec and treas; capital $200,000; incorporated 1887; spindles 17,000; looms 500; hands 400.
Cabarrus Cotton Mill, Concord, D F Cannon, pres: J W Cannon, sec and treas; spindles 4,500; looms 278; cap $100,000; hands 150.
Millwrighting, Concord, J T Pounds.
Odell Mfg Co; estab., old mill 1840, new mill 1882; cap $500,000; J M Odell, pres; W R Odell, sec-treas; spindles 28,500; looms for plaids, 1,326; looms for seamless bags, 12; output about 240,000,000 yards a year; hands 900; 5 mills in all.

CABARRUS COUNTY.

Patterson Mfg Co, Concord, W R Kindly, pres; G W Patterson, sec and treas; capital, $38,900; spindles, 2,080.
Patterson Mfg Co, China Grove; capital, $75,000; J W Cannon, pres; spindles 4,000, looms 130; hands 125.
Public gin, Harrisburg, Will Harris.
Public gin, Pioneer Mills, H B Parks.
Public gin, Concord, J M W Alexander.
Public gin, Concord, M L Goodman.
Public gin, Concord, J V Pethel.
Public gin, Mill Hill, J A Rankin.
Public gin, Harrisburg, J L Query.
Public gin, Harrisburg, Oglesby & Bro.
Public gin, Springsville, J B Harris.
Public gin, Mt Pleasant, C F Smith.
Public gin, Concord, G C Goodman.
Public gin, Concord, A F Hileman.
Public gin, Mill Hill, T A Flemming.
Public gin, Tulin, W F Carrigan.
Public gin, Tulin, E G Irvin.
Public gin, Concord, P M Morris.
Shoes, Concord, W W Gibson.
Shoes, Concord, G W Swan.
Steam gin, Concord, R A Brown.
Steam gin, Pioneer Mills, F F Starns.
Tannery, Mill Hill, Jacob Freeze.
Tannery, Mt Pleasant, E D Lentz.
Tannery, Concord, G W Brown.
Tin and sheet iron, Concord, W J Hill.

MERCHANTS AND TRADESMEN.

Names, Post Offices and Lines of Business

CODDLE.
Nesbit & Pressley, G S
CONCORD.
Alexander, Miss Annie, Millinery
Blackwelder & Cline, G S
Boger, R I, G S
Boger, M C, Conf and Gro
Boger, J I, G S
Bostian, D J, G S
Bracken, Miss Mary, Millinery
Brown Bros, Livery
Burrage & Son, G S and Lumber
Cannon & Fetzer, G S
Carl, M J, Livery
Carter, S D, G S
Caster, D B, Conf and Gro
Coleman, W C, G S
Cooke, J R, G S
Correll & Co, Jewelers
Corzine & Maxwell, Conf and Gro
Davault, D P, G S
Dore & Bost, G S
Dry & Wadsworth, Furniture
Fetzer, N D, Drugs
Fisher, W T, Conf and Gro
Foil, J W, G S
Furr, D C, G S
Gibson, Dr J P, Drugs

CABARRUS COUNTY.

Gibson & Morrison, G S
Glass, F W, G S
Hill, W J, Stoves and Tinware
Hurley & Barrow, Gen Ins
Johnston, D D, Drugs
Lowe, Dick & Alexander, G S
Lippard & Barrier, G S
Marsh, M L, Drugs
Maxwell & Corzine, G S
McConnell, Ross L, Tel Op
Miller, John, G S
Miller, J L, G S
Montgomery, C G, Cotton Buyer
Morrison, W F, G S
Odell Mfg Co, G S
Ould Mercantile Co, G S
Parish & Barton, G S
Patterson, J K, Gro
Patterson, G W, G S
Pounds, J T, Furniture
Richmond, G T, Gen Ins
Sappenfield, A L, Gro
Sherrill, J B, P M
Sides, W A, Conf and Gro
Sloop, S & Son, Furniture
Smith, Mrs J W, Conf and Gro
Smith, ——, Depot Agt
Smith, T W, Gen Ins
Swink, C W, G S
Waggoner, C B, Gro
Walker, D M, G S
Walter, J C, G S
Walter, M C, G S
Walker & Cline, G S
Walter & Walser, G S
Walton, M C, G S
White, C R, Hardware
Woodhouse & Harris, Fire Ins
York, Wadsworth & Co, Hardware
Yorke, J F, Jeweler

EASTFIELD.
Wallace, J R, G S

FLOW'S.
Bost, P B, G S
Flow, D W, G S
Gansley, R A, G S

GARMOND.
Hartsell, J M, G S
Kiser, J K, G S
Russell, J R, G S

GEORGEVILLE.
Windenhouse & Shinn, G S

HARRISBURG.
Alexander, J T, G S
Morrison, M M, G S
Oglesby Bros, G S
Spears, Wade, G S
Stallings Bros, G S

LEADING.
Herrin, M E, G S

CABARRUS COUNTY.

MILL HILL.

Brown, J L,   G S
Parks, A W,   G S

MT. PLEASANT.

Barringer, W G & Son,   G S
Buchanan, M L,   G S
Cook & Foil,   G S
Heilig & Hendrix,   G S
Moose, S W,   Drugs

PIONEER MILLS.

Barnhardt, John A,   G S
Carriker, J W,   G S

RIMER.

Barrier, W D,   G S
Safrit, J M,   G S

SAUNDERS.

Graham, E R,   G S

SPRINGVILLE.

Heglar & Motley,   G S

TULIN.

Andrew, S R,   G S
Wallace, J W,   G S
Wallace, R F,   G S

MINES.

Kinds, Post Offices and Proprietors.

Allison & Reed, 10 miles S E of Concord.
Bangle, 10 miles N E of Concord.
Babcock, 5 miles N E of Concord.
Moses Barrier, 10 miles E of Concord, Mt. Pleasant.
Wiley Biggers, 10 miles E of Concord.
McDonald Biggers, 10 miles S of Concord, Flow's Store.
Burton Blackwelder, 4 miles E of Concord, Flow's Store.
Reuben Blackwelder, 3 miles E of Concord.
Allen Boger, 8 miles S W of Concord, Flow's Store.
John Boger, 8 miles N E of Concord.
Boger, 10 miles S of Concord.
Billy Bost, 12 miles S of Concord, W A Smith, manager.
A W Bost, 10 miles S E of Concord.
G W Bost, 5 miles S of Concord.
Charles Bost, 8 miles S E of Concord.
Eph Bost, 15 miles S E of Concord.
Wm Bost, 15 miles S E of Concord.
Cabarrus, 11 miles E of Concord.
Christian Sossamon, 12 miles S E of Concord, Furr's Store.
Eph Tucker, 10 miles E of Concord.
Concord Mining Co, Concord, Senator Jones, Washington, D C.
Cruse, 8 miles E of Concord.
Cullen, 8 miles S E of Concord.
Duff, 10 miles E of Concord.
C H Erwin, 11 miles S of Concord.

CABARRUS COUNTY.

Faggart, 8 miles S E of Concord.
Fink, 8 miles E of Concord.
First National, 10 miles E of Concord.
Fisher, 8 miles E of Concord.
D W Flow, 10 miles S of Concord, Flow's Store.
Furners, 8 miles E of Concord.
Fuer Rachale (silver), 10 miles E of Concord.
Allen Fuer, 12 miles E of Concord, W A Smith, manager.
Gorman, 12 miles S E of Concord, W A Smith, manager.
Gold Arbor, 8 miles E of Concord.
H N Goodman, 4 miles E of Concord.
W S Harris, 10 miles N W of Concord.
Jas Heglee, 8 miles S E of Concord.
Cyrus Litaker, 4 miles S E of Concord.
J F Litaker, 4 miles S E of Concord.
Ludwick, 8 miles E of Concord.
Melcher, 5 miles E of Concord, W S Bingham, owner.
Michael, 6 miles E of Concord, Mount Pleasant.
Margaret Miller, 8 miles E of Concord.
Montgomery Mine, Concord, W A Smith, manager.
N C Smelting and Developing Co, Concord, J M Freck, pres. Pottsville, Pa.
Newell, 10 miles S of Concord, Flow's Store.
Phœnix, Concord, Phœnix Gold Mining Co.
Pioneer Mills, 10 miles S of Concord, Pioneer Mills.
Joe Reed, 1 mile E of Concord.
Taylor, 8 miles E of Concord.
The Reed, 12 miles S E of Concord, Dr J D Liles, manager, Georgeville, N C. Over 200 pounds gold taken from this mine in nuggets of 1 pound and over 28 pounds the largest.
The Means Mine, 11 miles E of Concord, Paul B Means.
The Buffalo, 10 miles S E of Concord, W A Smith, manager.
Vanderburg, 10 miles S of Concord.
M L Walter, 4 miles E of Concord.
J C Watts, 10 miles E of Concord, Mt. Pleasant.
Nat White, 5 miles S of Concord.
Widenhouse, 10 miles S E of Concord, W A Smith, manager.
A M Wilhelm, 10 miles S of Concord, Flow's Store.
Woods, 4 miles E of Concord.

MILLS.

Kinds, Post Offices and Proprietors.

Cabarrus Flour Mill (roller), Concord, Lippard & Co.
Corn, Tulin. D B Overcash.
Corn and gin, Concord, R A Brown.

CABARRUS COUNTY.

Fenix Roller Flour Mill, Concord, G T Crowell.
Flour and corn, Concord, W J Bradford & Co.
Flour and corn, Harrisburg, T F Pharr.
Flour and corn, Springville, J Cox.
Flour and corn, Concord, J Hileman.
Flour and corn, Mt. Pleasant, D F Barrier & Bro.
Flour, corn and saw, Mt Pleasant. C G Heilig.
Flour, corn and saw, Mt Pleasant, C D Barringer.
Flour, corn and saw (steam), Mt Pleasant, W R Kenley.
Flour, corn and saw, Mt Pleasant, D A Miller.
Flour, corn and saw, Pioneer Mills, John Morrison & Bro.
Flour, corn, saw and gin, Bost's Mills, M L Bost.
Sawmill and cotton gin, Bost's Mills, M L Bost.
Sawmill (steam), Dry's Mill, Reed Misenheimer.
Sawmill (steam), Mt. Pleasant, Barrier Bros.
Saw and gin, Springville, J S Harris.
Saw, Concord, G M Misenheimer.
Saw, Tulin, E G Erwin.
Saw and corn, Concord. G M Misenheimer.
Steam saw and gin, Flow's, Burleyson & Flow.
Steam saw and gin, Concord, J V Pethel.
Steam saw and gin, Mt Pleasant, Miller & Blackwelder.

PHYSICIANS.

Names and Post Offices.

Archey, L M, Concord.
Barnhardt, Chas, Mt Pleasant.
Barrier, P A, Mt Pleasant.
Black, J C, Pioneer Mills.
Caldwell, D G, Concord.
Dreher, A H (Dentist), Mt Pleasant.
Foil, M A, Mt Pleasant.
Gougar, Geo. Tulin.
Geier, S A, Harrisburg.
Haines, P J A, Mt Pleasant.
Herring, H C (Dentist), Concord.
Houston, W C (Dentist), Concord.
Jerome, J R, Georgeville.
Lafferty, J S, Concord.
Lilly, W H, Concord.
Montgomery, S L, Concord.
Pharr, L R, Mt. Pleasant.
Rose, L R, Mt Pleasant.
Smoot, J E, Concord.
Wilson, J R, Pioneer Mills.
Young, R S, Concord.

CABARRUS COUNTY.

SCHOOLS.

Names, Post Offices and Principals.

Academy, Georgeville, W M Brooks.
Bethel Academy, Clear Creek, H C Dunn.
Concord Female Academy, Holland, —— Thompson.
Evangelical Lutheran Grace School (col). Concord, Rev. N J Bokke, Prof E F Ralf, asst.
Graded School (white), Concord, J F Sherrin.
Graded School (col), Concord, E O. Woodward.
North Carolina College, Mt Pleasant, J T J Ludwig. chm board.
Odell Factory School, Concord.
Sunderland Hall, Concord, Rev. E F Green.
Scotia Seminary, Concord; estab. 1870; investment. $65,000; boarding school for colored girls on the Mt. Holyoke plan; domestic work done by pupils. Rev D J Satterfield, D D, pres; Mrs Satterfield, principal, with 14 assistant teachers; number students, 286.
Seminary (female), Mt Pleasant, Rev C L T Fisher.

TEACHERS.

Names and Post Offices.

Alexander, Sallie, Concord.
Bailey, J B (col), Concord.
Bailey, Mattie J, Concord.
Bailey, Nannie (col), Concord.
Boker, H T, Garmond.
Barnhard, G F, Concord.
Barnhardt, M L, Concord.
Barringer, Eudora, Rimer.
Blackwelder, G W, Concord.
Boger, Mattie C (col). Concord.
Bost, Rosa L, Bost's Mills.
Bost, R A. Bost's Mills.
Brooks, W M, Concord.
Brown, F P, Enochville.
Caddell, Delia (col), Enochville.
Caldwell, Eunice, Harrisburg.
Caldwell, Mattie L, Springsville.
Cannon, Eliza (col), Concord.
Castor, D B. Concord.
Cole, Mrs L P, Concord Graded School.
Cole, Mrs H P, Concord.
Cook, H C, Concord.
Cooper, Mattie L, Concord.
Currence, T C (col), Concord.
Daniel, W M, Concord.
Davis, Lillian B (col), Concord.
Davies, Lula, Harrisburg.
Deaton, Eunice, Concord.
Derrick, P H E, Concord.

CABARRUS COUNTY.

Dockery, Z A (col), Gold Hill.
Dodson, Miss Mollie, Concord.
Eaves, John K, Concord.
Edwards, R L (col), Concord.
Erwin, J R, Concord.
Foil, W A, Mt. Pleasant.
Fisher, Jas W, Concord.
Galloway, W B, Concord.
Gilmore, Wm A (col), Concord.
Glasscock, Mary A (col), Concord.
Gordon J D (col), Concord.
Greeley, A E (col), Concord.
Grier, M G, Harrisburg.
Harris, J G (col), Concord.
Hartsell, R L, Flow's.
Isenhour, Cora, Gold Hill.
Jarvis, Nicie (col), Concord.
Kimmons, Bessie, Mill Hill.
Lentz, D S, Concord.
Leslie, Miss Laura, Concord.
Liles, W K, Georgeville.
Lipe, L A, Concord.
Litaker, L A (col), Concord.
Little, C H. Georgeville.
Little, Maggie (col), Concord.
Little, D J, Georgeville.
Ludwig, S J, Mt Pleasant.
McAdoo, Emma (col), Concord.
Meares, Cora A M, Concord.
Meader, Miss Bessie, Concord.
Melcher, Fannie C (col), Gold Hill.
Meisenheimer, Hattie, Mt. Pleasant.
Meisenheimer, Mrs E C, Concord.
Montgomery, G V (col), Concord.
Moose, D G, Rimer.
Morris, W W, Concord.
Nussman, Lillie, Nussman,
Patterson, B L. Concord.
Patterson, Mary D (col), Concord.
Patterson, Miss Jennie, Concord.
Peck, H, Rimer.
Peeler, G H, Concord.
Penninger. A H, Rimer.
Pharr, S E W, Concord.
Pitts, C A, Concord.
Pope, Maggie, Huntersville.
Pope, Hugh G, Huntersville.
Prather, Emma (col), Concord.
Query, Dena, Harrisburg.
Ridenhour. V C, Mt. Pleasant.
Rogers, M C (col), Concord.
Sapp, J S, Concord.
Sapp, Jennie, Concord.
Shankle, Ella (col), Concord.
Sheeping, J L, Concord.
Shinn, J F, Concord.
Simmons, Rev R A (col), Concord.
Stafford, Miss Fannie. Concord.
Stansill, Oliver (col), Concord.
Swepson, W M (col), Concord.
Tolbert, T V, Pioneer Mills.
Tucker, P W, Mt Pleasant.
Weddington, Ida, Mill Hill.
White, Bettie C (col), Concord.

CABARRUS COUNTY.

Widenhouse, A P, Georgeville.
Widenhouse, M L, Georgeville.
Wilkinson, H B, Concord.

LOCAL CORPORATIONS.

Cannon Mfg Co., Concord, J M Odell, pres; J W Cannon, sec and treas.
Concord Nat Bank, J M Odell, pres; D B Coltrane, cash.
Electric Light Co, Concord, J M Odell, pres; J W Cannon, sec and treas.
I O O F, No 62, Cold Water, Concord, J M Burrage, N G.
Knights of Pythias. No —, Concord.
Masonic Lodge, No —, Concord.
Masonic Lodge (Patterson), No 307, Mt Pleasant, H M Cowan, Rep; time of meeting Saturday on or before full moon.

NEWSPAPERS.

The Concord Standard (weekly and daily), dem; J D Barrier & Son.
The Elevator (col) (weekly), fusion, Concord and Salisbury; J W Boger (col), ed and prop.
The Index, Concord, repub; J L Montgomery (col), ed and prop.
The Times (weekly), dem. Concord; J B Sherrill, ed and prop.
The Vestibule (weekly), Pop, Concord. G E Kestler and J Z Green, eds and props.

FARMERS.

Names and Post Offices.

Bost's Mills—J Barbee, C N Barbee, J B Barbee, S J Barbee, G H Barbee, W M Barrier, G F Barnhardt, J L Barhardt, R V Barnhardt, J R Barnhardt, G H Barnhardt, R Biggers, M C Biggers, W E Biggers, R F Biles. Martin Boger, D P Boger, A Boger, F P Boger, Allen Boger, M F Bonner, Davis Bonner, Wm R Bost, D M Bost. M B Bost, S C Bost, M L Bost, A W Bost, E Bost, Pharles Bost, Isaac Burleyson, M W Clayton, H D Clayton, G P Coggins, A M Cox, R Cox, R D Ccx. P W Dry, A M Eudy, Mrs E C Faggart, M M Furr, S C Furr, E A Furr, M L Furr, A M Furr, M Furr, W Furr, G H Gorman, M C Gorman, John D Gibbs. Columbus Goodman, Nathan Grady, M J Hartsell, J H Hartsell, G F Hartsell, John Hatley, J Hathcock, M M Heglan, J F Heine, A J Honeycutt, W P Honeycutt, H C Howell, G R Johnson, John M Kluttz, M H Lefler, L A Lentz, M Little, T F Little, Wm Linker, A Linker, Jackson Linker, M Linker Aaron Linker, R O S Miller, J M Mor-

CABARRUS COUNTY.

ton, H A Platt, T S Rinehard, C Sossamon, G W Shankle (col), J L Shinn, T J Shinn, W B Smith, S M Smith, R S Smith, C S Smith, F P Smith, M Stallings, E Tucker, M M Tucker, J C Tucker, D W Vanderbring, Mac White, P F Widenhouse, W L Widenhouse, D M Widenhouse, Martin Widenhouse, S P Widenhouse, Wm M Widenhouse, J W Widenhouse, M W Widenhouse.

Coddle—C A Archer, James Bell, Wm Carr, A J Erwin, W J McCraven, M F Nesbit, jr, B W Pressly, Mrs Jas Sims, James H Smith, Walt Smith.

Concord—Chas W Alexander, John P Allison, R W Allison, John A Barnhardt, G T Barnhardt, J J Barringer, R C Blackwelder, Noah Blackwelder, Robert Blackwelder, R M Blackwelder, H A Blackwelder, W H Bloom, Aaron J Bost, Francis Bost, A G Bost, Alex Bostian, W J Brafford, J R Brown, M L Brown, R A Brown, A M Brown, J M Caldwell, C P Caldwell, R V Caldwell, D T Cannon, W F Cannon, Chas Cannon, Rufus Cline, C P Cline, Robt F Cline, F Cline, A M Cook, J Cook, D Cook, David Corzine, W V Crimenger, D B Cross, J R Cruse, Mack Cruse, Geo H Cruse, Jacob Dave, D P Davault, D C Davault, Caldwell Deal, Pink Deal, Wash Earnhardt, C M Earnhardt, Jesse Earnhardt, C W Earhardt, W C Eddleman, C L Erwin, E S Erwin, John M Faggart, Frank Faggart, J F Faggart, E T Faggart, J A Fink, C A Fisher, E L Fisher, Daniel Foil, Burt Furr, R E Gibson, M M Gillon, F W Glass, M L Goodman, W F Goodman, G C Goodman, J A Goodman, C M Goodnight, J C Hileman, A F Hileman, R R Holdbrooks, D R Holdbrooks, C A Isenhour, John Iseshour, D M Isenhour, E H Johnston, M W Johnston, Reece Johnston, J A Johnson, G R Johnson, R M Kimmons, V A Kimmons, Laurence Klutz, D V Krimminger, John Leady, Alfred Lefler, Mike Lefler, M H Lefler, Dr W H Lilly, Asa Linker, Jack Linker, Moses Linker, D M Line, Est Lipe, J R Litaker, D T Litaker, J A Litaker, C W Litaker, D V Litaker, W N Litaker, Geo L Litaker, Caleb Littles (col), John Little, G M Love, H W Ludwick, Chas McDonald, D H McEachern, A S McNinch, Robert McRee (col), E K Misenheimer, A D Misenheimer, G W Misenheimer, W J Montgomery, D W Moore, W L Morris, J A Morris, P M Morris, W F Morrison, Pinckney Morrison, W O Nesbit, J M Odell, V C Parrish, G W Patterson, C M Petrea. F S Pharr, G A Propst, M A Propst, D H Ridenhour, W D Ritchie, G E Ritchie, J Rogers, Henry Safrit, Jackson Safrit,

CABARRUS COUNTY.

W S Sapp, D M Sides, John Slough, Wm Tolbert, John Loyton, J R Vanpelt, S E Vanpelt, Abner Walker, C L Walker, T J White, W S White, R B White, J R White, J B White, D H Wilkinson, W F Winecoff, M H Winecoff, Geo Winecoff, A B Young.

Dry's Mill—G W Barringer, G W Dry, C B Dry, C F Fisher, Wm B Banner, D L Barringer, John Cauble, W G A Cruse, J M L Culp, G A Culp, John L Dry, J M Dry, P A Earnhardt, C A Earnhardt, C S Fisher, G A M Fisher, J R Fisher, R B Hall, E T Hall, Y A Harkey, L T Hartman, R T Honeycutt, Edmond Honeycutt, Wilson Honeycutt, W G Honeycutt, J G Honeycutt, H M Isenhour, Daniel Isenhour, G L Klutts, P J Klutts, J D Klutts, G C Lentz, V C Lentz, J W Lentz, G J Lentz, Columbus Lentz, V T Melchor, Reed Missenheimer, D M Moose, H H Moose, J H Moose, John H Moose, A M Nussman, C L Nussman, J L Peck, M M Penninger, J D Redwine, F A K Smith, R M Troutman, W S Troutman, W A Troutman, W A Wilkinson.

Flow's—John Barbee, Geo Barbee, G W Barbee, R W Biggers, W M Biggers, Wm B Black, E P Black, E C Black, F P Boger, D P Boger, Martin Boger, Allen Boger, W H Bost, W A Bost, C M Bost, P B Bost, Jno E B st, D W Bost, S J Bost, M R Bost, C W Bost, Benj Burleyson, Isaac Burleyson, Ben Burleyson, R J Caldwell, J W Carriker, W M Chaney, W H Clay, H C Cook, W J Cook, J D Cox, John Dorton, W M Finn, R L Finn, H P Flowers, D W Flow, Henry Gorman, J C Gorman, M C Gorman, G H Gorman, B J Green, R D Gurley, R L Hartsell, W N Hudson, J M Hartsell, G T Hartsell, F M Hartsell, J C Hartsell, Mc J Hartsell, J H Hartsell, H C Howell, D A Klutts, L B Linker, John Newell, W G Newell, James S Russell, J C Sossamon.

Harrisburg—D L Alexander, J M W Alexander, L Alexander, F A Archibald, T M Barnhardt, John A Barnhardt, J C Barnhardt, John E Barrier, C A Black, Mrs A A Blair, B T Bost, G W Bost, Benjamin Burleyson, Mrs S N Caldwell, John M Caldwell, J E Caldwell, James Cochran, D B Cross, J A Davis, E H Davis, Will Heglar, E Harvey Davis, Martin C Davis, E P Davis, E C Davis, J M C Davis, J A Davis, Robert H Davis, J W Davis, Ed S Ervin, Mrs S V Ervin, A A Fink, Dr D W Flowers, S W Harris, W Ed Harris, S F Harris, M J Harris, A N Harris, Mc A Harris, J W Hartwick, Will Heglar, W H Heglar,

CABARRUS COUNTY.

J C Howie, B M Ingram, S N Johnston, J M Johnston, Mrs Dorcas Kimmons, John Lady, T A Linker, Jackson Linker, Jack Linker, J A Lipe, J L McCurry, D M McDonald, S S McWherter, Wm Morgan, L M Morrison, J P Morrison, Z A Morris. V C Parish, H B Parks, R H Pharr, T F Pharr, Mrs M M Pharr, S W Pharr, Mrs L L Platt, Nicholas Poplin, J L Query. L J Query, Mrs J V Query, J C Query, R W Query, J Russell, J G Smith, Cyrus A Snell, Christian Sossamon, L V Spears, Wade Spears, Wm N Spears, J H Spears, J L Springs, J L Stafford, S M Stafford P F Stallings, W H Stallings, Paul T Stallings, J W Stallings, F F Starnes, W C Taylor, Frank Teeter, M F Teeter, Logan Teeter, J C Thompson, J C Walker, L P White, D H White, R C White, R B White.

Mill Hill—J C Alexander, J F Bost, Jas Brown, A L Demarcus. James A Earnhardt, T A Fleming, A M Freeze, W D Gillon, J F Goodman, G C Goodman, C M B Goodnight, Wm Goodnight, R M Kimmons, Caleb Little, Jno McKinley, J A Rankin, C M Sedford.

Mt Pleasant—D D Barrier, John D Barringer, John H Barnhardt, J R Barnhardt, J T Brown, J A Cline, J D Cline, John Cook, Dan Faggart, W D Foil, Levi S Hahn, J D Hahn, A Hahn. W L Hahn. C G Heilig, W R Kindly, W A Kinley, Geo Lee, E D Lentz. H T J Ludwick, George H Miller, W N Misenheimer, Rufus Misenheimer, M M Misenheimer, T A Moser. J H Moose,

D H Ridenhour, J M Ridenhour, D W Shimpock, Willis Smith, R A Smith, F P Tucker, J W Walker, G H Walker, J D Walker.

Nussman—Geo L Kluttz, J D Kluttz, J W Lentz, C L Nussman, A M Nussman.

Pioneer Mills—Jno A Barnhardt, E C Black, Hiram Bost, Wm Bost, Henderson Clay, J W Cook, H C Cook, E C Davis, John C Gorman, James Hagler, J K Kiser, J C McEachern, S S McWhirte, Monroe Melchior, W W Morrison, J P Morrison, H B Parks. L M Pharr, F F Stearns, D B Parton.

Rimer—W D Barrier, H M Cress. John M Faggart, J W Faggart, J R Faggart, A H Penninger, J H D Walker.

Springville—C Barringer, Watt Barringer, T W Brumly, J C Brumly, T W Elliott, John Cox, Rufus Dees, J S Harris, J E Henderson, J C Johnson, S S Johnston, Joe Johnston, D R Little, Mrs Geo Ochler, J N Pharr, R H Smith, W M Stinson, G J Untz J R Wallace.

Tulin—R H Benson, G A Bradford, J R Bradford, W B Deweese, D R Ellis, M A Emerson, E G Erwin, J Faggart, Allan Grame, G C Goodman, Chas Hamilton, R C Harris, E M Holdbrooks, N Johnson, John H Johnston, John Morrison, John Mowerer, Mc Mowerer, C A Overcash, D B Overcash, Will R gers, John Seaford, J B Wallace, R F Wallace, J M Wallace.

10

CALDWELL COUNTY.

AREA, 450 SQUARE MILES.

POPULATION, 12,291; White 10,737, Colored 1,554.

CALDWELL COUNTY was laid off in 1841, from the counties of Burke and Wilkes, and was named in honor of Dr Joseph Caldwell, the first President of the North Carolina University.

LENOIR, the county-seat, is 200 miles west of Raleigh, and is beautifully situated among valleys at the foot of the Blue Ridge. It is a noted summer resort, and has a population of 965.

Surface—Hilly, and in places mountainous, lying under the eaves of the Blue Ridge; well watered, plenty of very fine water-power; land generally good and valleys rich. The scenery is very fine.

Staples — Wheat, corn, buckwheat. rye, oats, tobacco, grass and live stock. Large quantities of medicinal herbs and roots are gathered in this county and shipped to Northern markets.

Fruits—Peaches, apples, pears, apricots, grapes, melons and a great variety of small fruits.

Timbers—Walnut, white pine, oak, hickory, birch, ash and chestnut.

Minerals—Gold is found in a number of places.

TOWNS AND POST OFFICES.

	POP.		POP.
Baton,	—	Houck,	50
Blackstone,	25	Hudson,	150
Buffalo Cove,	20	Jumbo,	25
Cedar Valley,	40	King's Creek,	30
Collettsville,	60	Lenoir (C H),	965
Downsville,	25	Meadow Hill,	20
Draco,	30	Muttenz,	25
Emanuel,	20	McCall,	—
Gamewell,	40	North Catawba,	50
Glenburnie,	20	Patterson,	150
Globe,	25	Petra Mills,	20
Gragg,	—	Rippetoe,	40
Granite Falls	100	Risden,	15
Gunpowder,	—	Saw Mill,	50
Hartland,	40	Upton,	25
Hibriten,	50	Yadkin Valley,	35

COUNTY OFFICERS.

Superior Court Clerk—J V McCall.
Commissioners—John M Downs, E E Cline, D B Tuttle.
Coroner—W W Deaf.
Treasurer—A H Courtenay.
Sheriff—A H Boyd.
Solicitor Tenth District—J F Spainhour.

Surveyor—J L Isbell.
County Examiner—G D Sherrill.
Superintendent of Health—Dr A A Britt.

COURTS.

Fourth Monday after the first Monday in March; first Monday after the first Monday in September.

TOWN OFFICERS.

LENOIR—*Mayor*, J R Widby. *Commissioners*—Dr A F Houck, G W Conley, G H Harper. *Clerk and Treasurer*—G W Conley. *Marshal*—J A Bush.

TOWNSHIPS AND MAGISTRATES.

Globe—Alfred Wortman, Wm Gregg (Gragg), J B Phillips (Upton), Robert Green (Houck).

John's River—J H Dickson, I W Moore, J T C Hood, M N Harshaw, Pink Pruett, W A Setzer (Collettesville), R C Houck (Gamewell), J L Oxford (Muttenz).

King's Creek—Pickens Barlow, M L Green, John P Carlton, G M Isenhour, Alonzo Laxton, I W Dula, Thomas Livingston, A B Sanders.

Lenoir—M A Bird, J N Baird, R R Wakefield, J M Powell, Chas Sudderth (Lenoir), J M Tuttle, E H Crump (Hartland), J M Sudderth (Glenburnie), C M Sudderth (Gamewell).

Little River—W A White, L H Oxford, W L Payne (Downsville), J W West, Joseph Hartley, William Deal (Cedar Valley), W Palmer (Petra), Sid Whitner (McCall).

Lovelady—I J Yount (Petra), W H H Hartley (Hudson). D W Yount, C T Flowers (Granite Falls).

Lower Creek—Jason C Hartley (Hudson), E B Phillips, H G Powell (Hibriten), John G Ballew, J A Dula, A C Sherrill (Lenoir), H H D Hoover, J G Huntley (Emanuel).

North Catawba — W M Smith, O Kaylor, John P Harmon (Baton), D A Griffin, J P Bush (Rippetoe), A G Corpening (North Catawba), Geo Sullivan (Hudson).

Patterson—S F Harper, C P Abernathy, W A McCall, Julius Austin, John Spencer, W D Jones, sr, A E Nelson (Patterson).

CALDWELL COUNTY.

Yadkin Valley—I M Hawkins, R H Pipes, Jno Rollins (Buffalo Cove), Jno R Steele, Vincent Green, I B Lenoir (Yadkin Valley).

CHURCHES.

Names, Post Offices, Pastors and Denom.

BAPTIST.

Bethany—Patterson, Wm Knight.
Bethel—Hartland, J M Harris.
Blair's Fork—Lenoir, H C Marley.
Buffalo Cove—Buffalo Cove, ——.
Conway's Chapel—Muttenz, M L Clark.
Dudley Shoal—Petra, Alonza Downs.
Fleming's Chapel — Hartland, M L Clark.
Globe—Globe, E D Crisp.
Granite—Granite Falls, W R Bradshaw.
GreenValley—Collettesville, E D Crisp.
Green Rock—Yadkin Valley, ——.
John's River—Upton, E D Crisp.
King's Creek — King's Creek, I W Thomas.
Lovelady—Granite Falls, J F Shell.
Lower Creek—Lenoir, I W Thomas.
Mountain Grove—Baton, J F Crisp.
Mulberry—Risden, ——.
North Catawba—Cora, I W Thomas.
Piney Grove—Blackstone, J H Nelson.
Pisgah—Glenburnie, J F Crisp.
Rocky Springs — Collettesville, J H Nelson.
Sardis—Hudson, J M Harris.
Union—Cedar Valley, J M Shoner.
Union No 2—Risden, ——.
Yadkin—Patterson, C C Poole.
Zack's Fork—Lenoir, J F Crisp.

PRIMITIVE BAPTIST.

Globe—Globe, ——.
Philadelphia—Gamewell, ——

METHODIST.

Cedar Valley—Albert Sherrill.
Church—Lenoir Station, J O Shelley.
Collier's—Rippetoe, Albert Sherrill.
Ebenezer—Jumbo, Albert Sherrill.
Grace Chapel—Granite, Albert Sherrill.
Harper's Chpl—Patterson, L M Brower.
Hood's—Glenburnie, L M Brower.
Laurel Hill—Muttenz, L M Brower.
Littlejohn's—Hartland, L M Brower.
Morris' Chapel — Blackstone, L M Brower.
Mt Herman—Hudson, Albert Sherrill.
Mt Olive—Patterson. L M Brower.
Mt Zion—Emanuel, L M Brower.
Pisgah—Gunpowder, Albert Sherrill.
Rocky Mount — Gunpowder, Albert Sherrill.

PROTESTANT METHODIST.

Harris Chapel—Saw Mill, G D Moore.

CALDWELL COUNTY.

Shiloh—Patterson, G D Moore.

N. METHODIST.

Church—Petra, D A Lanier.
Smith's Chapel — Lenoir, David Connell.

EPISCOPAL.

Chapel Peace—Lenoir, Jarvis Buxton.
Church—Morganton, —— Henderson (col).
Church—Yadkin Valley, Jarvis Buxton.
St James—Lenoir Jarvis Buxton.

PRESBYTERIAN.

Church—Lenoir, C A Monroe.
Church—Hudson, C A Monroe.

SECOND ADVENTIST.

Church—Collettsville, W R Cottrell.
Tabernacle—Lenoir, G D Sherrill.
Yadkin—Patterson, G D Sherrill.

A. M. E. ZION.

Happy Chapel—Yadkin Valley, H S Roberts.
Slade's Ch'p'l—Morganton, — Holmes.
St Louis Chapel—Lenoir, H S Roberts

MINISTERS RESIDENT.

Names, Post Offices and Denominations.

BAPTIST.

Morley, H C, Lenoir.
Nelson, J H, Patterson.
Oxford, Isaac, Cedar Valley.
Shell, J T, Petra.
Shell, J W, Petra.
Shower, J M, Little River.
Thomas, I W, Lenoir.
Tillery, Edmund, Emanuel.

METHODIST.

Brower, L M, Lenoir.
Bush, J A, Granite Falls.
Healan, J L, Lenoir.
Holler, Martin, Hudson.
Kaylor, N H, Gamewell.
Shelley, J O, Lenoir.
Sherrill, Albert, Granite Falls.
Stimpson, D C, Lenoir.

N. METHODIST.

David Connell, Lenoir.

SECOND ADVENTIST.

Cathell, W R, McCall.
Gregg, S E, Collettsville.
Isbell, R L, Blackstone.
Isbell, John D, Blackstone.
Sherrill, G D, Lenoir.

EPISCOPAL.

Buxton, Jarvis, Lenoir.

PRESBYTERIAN.

Munroe, C A, Lenoir.

CALDWELL COUNTY.

CALDWELL COUNTY.

A. M. E.

Roberts, H S, Lenoir.

HOTELS AND BOARDING HOUSES.

Names, Post Offices and Proprietors.

Boarding House, Collettsville, C D Coffey.
Boarding House, Lenoir, W S Hamilton.
Boarding House, Lenoir, Jno W Dula.
Boarding House, Lenoir, Jno W Kirby.
Boarding House, Lenoir, Jacob A Bush.
Boarding House, Hudson, W M Morris.
Clark House, Lenoir, S M Clark.
Grier's Hotel, Patterson, Watt L Minnish.
Hotel, Granite Falls, ——
Hotel Jones, Lenoir, Dr W M Earnhardt.
Merchants' Hotel, Lenoir, T H Higgins.
Prospect Heights, Lenoir, Capt P J Johnson.

LAWYERS.

Names and Post Offices.

Bower, W H, Lenoir.
Crisp, B G, Granite.
Edmund, Jas, Lenoir.
Folk, G N, Lenoir.
Newland, W C, Lenoir.
Scott, W W, Lenoir.
Wakefield, W L, Lenoir.

MANUFACTORIES.

Kinds, Post Offices and Proprietors.

Blacksmithing and wheelwrighting, Lenoir, A J Allen.
Blacksmithing and wheelwrighting, Lenoir, J N McCrary.
Blacksmithing and wheelwrighting, Lenoir, J L Swanson.
Blacksmithing and wheelwrighting, Lenoir, S N Swanson.
Blacksmithing and wheelwrighting, Cedar Valley, Pinkney Deal.
Blacksmithing and wheelwrighting, Cedar Valley, Sidney Deal.
Backsmithing and wheelwrighting, Cedar Valley, F M McCrary.
Blacksmithing and wheelwrighting, Cedar Valley, L S Starnes.
Blacksmithing and wheelwrighting, Cedar Valley, J W West.
Boxes, Mattresses, etc., Lenoir, Blue Ridge Mfg Co, J R Waddy, mgr.
Caldwell Land and Lumber Co., Lenoir, Wm S Harvey, pres; John M Barnhardt, mgr.

Coach and wagon, Lenoir, N A Powell.
Contracting and building, Lenoir, P L Baker.
Contracting and building, Lenoir, Jno Hartley.
Contracting and building, Lenoir, Ed Martin.
Contracting and building, Lenoir, J A Montgomery.
Contracting and building, Lenoir, S M Whitener.
Contracting and building, Collottsville, J H Setser.
Coopering, Cedar Valley, J Chester.
Coopering, King's Creek, Martin Holler.
Cotton, Patterson (spindles, 1,808; looms, 19), Gwyn & Harper Mfg Co.
Cotton, Granite Falls, Granite Falls Mfg Co, A A Shepard, pres.
Lenoir Furniture Co, Lenoir, —— Wren.
Lackawanna Safe and Trust Deposit Co, Lenoir, J B Atkinson, mgr.
Millwrighting, Cedar Valley, E C Fox.
Planing, Sash, etc, Lenoir, J T Montgomery.
Tannery (steam), Lenoir, Julius Berg.
Woolen, Patterson, Gwyn, Harper & Co.

MERCHANTS AND TRADESMEN.

Name, Post-office and Line of Business.

BLACKSTONE.

Harrington, W J,	G S

CEDAR VALLEY.

Deal, M & Co,	G S

COLLETTSVILLE.

Coffey Bros,	G S
Moore, I W & Co,	G S
Pruett, C P,	G S
Wakefield, T C,	G S

DOWNSVILLE.

Downs Bros,	G S
Flower, J F,	G S

GAMEWELL.

Bradford, W W & Son,	G S
Tuttle, L H,	G S

GLENBURNIE.

Crisp, M E,	G S

GLOBE.

Cook & Coffey,	G S
Moore, J D,	G S
Moore, F P,	G S

GRANITE FALLS.

Flowers, Calvin T,	G S
Lertz, A A,	Mill
Moore & Hoke,	G S
Russel & Hickman,	G S

CALDWELL COUNTY.

Starnes, Hickman & Co,   G S
Starnes, S V,   G S

HARTLAND.

Courtney. M M,   G S
Crisp, J H,   G S

HUDSON.

Brown, J L,   G S
Hudson. D M,   G S
Lute, I T & Son.   G S
Morris, W M,   G S

KING'S CREEK.

Parlier, N E & J T,   G S
Parlier, J F & Co,   G S

LENOIR.

Abernethy, A S & Son,   Livery
Austin, Mrs W F,   Millinery
Bernhardt & Co.   G S
Cloyd & Johrson,   G S
Courtney, R G,   G S
Coartney. M M,   G S
Eps ein Bros,   G S
Franirer Credit,   Hardware
Grist, J F,   Grocer
Hamilton, S W,   G S
Haily, N H,   Dept and Ex Agt and Tel Operator
Harrison & Co,   Grocer
Harper & Co,   Bankers
Henkel, Craig & Cu.   Livery
Horton, Mrs M N,   Millinery
Johnson. P J,   Fertilizer
Lenoir Produce Co,   G S
Miller & Henry,   G S
Nelson, J L,   G S
Perry, D S.   Jeweler
Scott, Dr W W,   Drugs
Wright & Owens,   G S

MEADOW HILL.

Carlton, L L,   G S

PATTERSON.

Gwyn and Harper Mfg Co,   G S
Harris, John P,   G S
McCall, W A,   G S
Storie, J A,   G S

PETRA MILLS.

Field & Smith,   G S
Smith & Bowman,   G S

YADKIN VALLEY.

Radisell, L P (col.),   Grocer

MINES.

Kinds, Post Offices and Proprietors.

Asbestos, Lenoir, Wm Puett.
Ball Knob Mine, Hartland, Francis & Co.
Clarke Mine, Lenoir, John E Corpening.
Gold (Starnes), Hartland, B M & R G Tuttle.

CALDWELL COUNTY.

Gold, Lenoir, W A Tuttle.
Gold, Collettsville, S King.
Gold, Collettsville, Joseph Corpening.
Wallan & Bro, J N Barshaw, John Steele.

MILLS.

Kinds, Post Offices and Proprietors.

Corn, Patterson, E H Dobbin.
Corn and saw, Cedar Valley, John Flowers & Co.
Corn and saw, Lenoir, R R McCall.
Corn and saw, Lovelady, J & B W Sherrill.
Corn and saw, King's Creek, Crotz & Richard.
Corn, Fort Defiance, W B Coffey.
Corn, Globe, William Gragg.
Corn, Patterson, Joseph Green.
Corn, Globe, Daniel Green.
Corn, Patterson, Nathan Harrison.
Corn, King's Creek, Thos Livingston.
Corn, Fort Defiance, Ransom Triplett.
Corn, Lenoir, John Teague.
Flour, corn and saw, Patterson, C McD Dickerson.
Flour, corn and saw, Cedar Valley, Marcus Deal.
Flour, corn and saw, Petra Mills, B F Eaton.
Flour, corn and saw, Lenoir, Houk & Harper.
Flour and corn, Lenoir, R R & J McCall.
Flour and corn, Globe, David Moon.
Flour and corn, King's Creek, G D Sherrill & Co.
Flour, corn and saw. Patterson, S L Patterson.
Flour, corn and saw, Lovelady, J L Lierly & Co.
Flour, corn and saw, Lenoir, M A Barnhardt & Son.
Flour, corn and saw. Cedar Valley, Thomas G Sherrill.
Flour and corn, Collettsville, Harper, Idol & Co.
Flour and corn, King's Creek, Keturah Bradley.
Flour and corn, Lenoir, Jacob Bowman.
Flour, corn and saw. Lenoir, A J Corpening.
Flour and corn, Lenoir, J E Corpening.
Roller Mill, Granite Falls, —— Lutz, owner.
Saw, Lenoir, Dr W M Earnhardt.
Saw, Lenoir, J C Hartly & Co.
Saw, Lenoir, G W F Harper.
Saw, Lenoir, A D Lingle.
Steam roller flour mill, Lenoir, George Moore, manager.
Steam roller flour mill, Granite Falls.

CALDWELL COUNTY.

PHYSICIANS.

Names and Post Offices.

Blair, J C, Lenoir.
Carter, E H, King's Creek.
Flowers, G E, Granite Falls.
Flowers, Cyrus, Granite Falls.
Houk, A F, Lenoir.
Grey, W P, Lenoir.
Jones, A D, Granite Falls.
Kent, A A, Lenoir.
Moore, J K (Dentist), Lenoir.
Scott, W W, sr, Lenoir.
Spainhour, J M (Dentist), Lenoir.

SCHOOLS.

Names, Post Offices and Principals.

Barnes Academy, E L Barnes.
Davenport Female College, Lenoir, John D Merrick.
Globe Academy, Globe, W F Marshall.
Granite Academy, Granite Falls, E L Hughes.
Hibriten Academy, King Creek, Prof. E B Phillips.
Kirkwood Academy, Lenoir, Miss E L Rankin.
Lower Creek Academy.
Riverside Law School, Cillery, Col. George N Folk.
Wilson's Academy, Lenoir, E F Wakefield.
Public schools—White, 64; colored, 15.

TEACHERS.

Names and Post Offices.

Barnes, Prof E S, Hibriten.
Beach, Prof W R, King's Creek.
Boushelle, Miss Mariam, Patterson.
Clark, Miss Mamie, Lenoir.
Conoly, Miss Mattie, Lenoir.
Copps, Eddie, Collettsville.
Crist, W C, Glenburnie.
Crisp, Prof. B G, Granite Falls.
Deal, Miss Mamie, Cedar Valley.
Estes, Miss M E, Collettsville.
Glass, Miss L D, Patterson.
Greer, Prof. W L, King's Creek.
Halsclaw, N P, Lenoir.
Hoover, Prof H H D, Emanuel.
Howell, W B, Lenoir.
Isenhour, Prof G M, King's Creek.

CALDWELL COUNTY.

Jenkins, J A, Collettsville.
Malloy, Miss Mollie, Blackstone.
Miller, Miss Effie, Gamewell.
Minich, Prof John D, Lenoir.
Powell, Miss Clara, Lenoir.
Rand, Mrs S A, Hudson.
Rankin, Miss Emma, Lenoir.
Robbins, E T, Buffalo.
Sherrill, G W, Hickory.
Sherrill, W P, Lenoir.
Sherrill, Albert, Hibriten.
Sigmon, C A, Lenoir.
Sigmon, Prof B L, Granite Falls.
Steele, Finley, Cedar Valley.
Steele, Miss Sue, Yadkin Valley.
Thomas, Miss Jennie, Hibriten.
Wakefield, John A, Patterson.
Whitted, Mrs G E Lenoir.

LOCAL CORPORATIONS.

Bank of Lenoir, G W F Harper, pres; G L Bernhardt, vice pres; G F Harper, cash; J H Beale, asst cash.
Blue Ridge Furniture Co, Lenoir, E H Umstead, sec and treas.
Caldwell and Watauga Land and Timber Co, Lenoir, J L Nelson, pres; J M Spainhour, sec; capital, $20,000.
Chester and Lenoir Railroad, G W F Harper, pres; E F Reid, auditor, Lenoir; H A Beard, G F & P A, Yorkville, S C.; L T Nichols, sup, Chester, S C; N A Haley, claim agent, Lenoir, N C. Length of road, from Chester, S C, to Lenoir, N C. 109 miles.
Citizens Building and Loan Association, Lenoir, S L Bernhardt, pres; W W Scott, sec and treas.
Hibriten Masonic Lodge, No. 262, Lenoir; regular meetings, Thursday before full moon, Tuesday night of court, June 24, Dec. 27; J M Spainhour, W M; K R Wakefield, sec.
Lenoir Lodge, No. 45, I O O F, Lenoir, J R Widby, N G.
Private bank (not incorporated), total worth of partners, $60,000 to $75,000.

NEWSPAPERS.

The Topic (Dem, weekly); Lenoir, W W Scott, jr, editor and proprietor; R H Hairston, associate editor.

CAMDEN COUNTY.

AREA, 280 SQUARE MILES.

POPULATION, 5,667; White 3,347, Colored 2,320,

CAMDEN COUNTY was formed in 1777, from Pasquotank county, and derives its name from the Earl of Camden.

CAMDEN COURT HOUSE, the county-seat, is on the Pasquotank river, and is 220 miles northeast of Raleigh; population 350.

Surface — This county is situated along the east bank of the Pasquotank river, and extends from the Virginia line to the Albemarle Sound. The land is level, sandy loam, easily cultivated when drained, and very productive.

Staples—Corn, cotton, naval stores, fish and wild fowl. Sweet potatoes yield largely. Grapes are grown successfully, especially Scuppernong.

Truck farming is now extensive.

Fruits—Peaches, pears, apples, berries, grapes, melons, etc.

Timbers — Pine, cypress, juniper, gum, etc.

TOWNS AND POST OFFICES.

	POP.		PO.
Belcross,	50	Old Trap,	50
Borum,	25	Riddle,	25
Camden C H.	350	Shiloh,	110
Indiantown,	40	South Mills,	500
Lilly,	25		

COUNTY OFFICERS.

Clerk Superior Court—R L Forbes.
Commissioners—G H Riggs, ch'mn; Geo Beverly, W B Hughes, E G Sawyer, C S Wright.
Register of Deeds— W R Dozier.
Sheriff—W S Bartlett.
Solicitor 1st District—W J Leary, Sr.
Surveyor—John K Abbott.
Treasurer—George Jacobs.
County Examiner—H Spencer.
Standard Keeper—C S Sawyer.

COURTS,

First Monday after first Monday in March and first Monday after first Monday in September.

TOWNSHIPS AND MAGISTRATES.

Court House—E M Mercer, E S Mercer, T B Godfrey, J L F Sawyer, O L Pritchard, Willis Ferebee, H W Scott, P G Bray, T B Boushall, T G Bray (Camden).

Shiloh—G M Tillett, G C Barco, Jas E Burgess, J B Burgess, D G Bray, Felix Jones, W G Godfrey, S H Sawyer, S B Williams (Shiloh).

South Mills—William E McCoy, D T Pritchard, J A Spencer, J W Whitehurst, Marshall Daily, Wilson Sawyer, H C Brite, S R Edney, W R Dozier (South Mills).

CHURCHES.

Names, Post Offices, Pastors and Denom.

METHODIST.

McBride's—South Mills, S Pool.*
Mill Dam— ——, N H Guyton.
Old Trap— ——, N H Guyton.
Parksville—Indian Town, N H Guyton.
Sharon—South Mills, S Pool.
Trinity—South Mills, S Pool.

BAPTIST.

Ebenezer— ——, R R Overby.
Sawyer's Creek— ——, R R Overby.
Shiloh—Elizabeth City, O C Horton.

MINISTERS RESIDENT.

Names, Post Offices and Denominations.

METHODIST.

Guyton, N H, South Mills.
Pool, S, South Mills.

BAPTIST.

Overby, R R, South Mills.

EPISCOPAL.

Williams, ——, South Mills.
McBride, O S (col.), South Mills.

HOTELS AND BOARDING HOUSES.

Names, Post Offices and Proprietors.

Hotel, Camden, M B Hughes.
Hotel, South Mills, Robert Bullock.

LAWYERS.

Names and Post Offices.

Ferebee, C M, Camden.
Spencer, C H, South Mills.

MANUFACTORIES.

Kinds, Post Offices and Proprietors.

Blacksmithing, Shiloh, N G Sawyer.
Blacksmithing, Camden, H W Scott.
Blacksmithing, Camden, I M Forbes.

Blacksmithing, Old Trap, N Kyle.
Blacksmithing, South Mills, B Ferebee.
Cotton-gin, Shiloh, W N Gregory.
Cotton-gin, Redcross. A Sawyer.
Cotton-gin, Hasting's Corner, Noah Garrett.
Grist mill and cotton-gin, Camden, N W Stevens.
Grist mill, South Mills, Geo Beveridge.

MERCHANTS AND TRADESMEN.

Name, Post Office, and Line of Business.

BELLCROSS.

Godfrey, T D,   G S
Robertson, T S,   G S
Sawyer, A,   G S

CAMDEN C. H.

Bernard, Mrs Wilson,   G S
Bartlett, John A, (near,)   G S
Berry, George,   G S
Sawyer, C S,   G S and Postmaster
Scott, Henry,   Coachmaker

INDIAN TOWN.

Gregory, J D,   G S
Tatum, A W,   G S

LILLY.

Lynch, W,   G S and Lumber
Roper, J L,   G S and Lumber

NEW CANAL BRIDGE.

Beveridge, G D,   G S
Etheridge, C,   G S

OLD TRAP.

Burgess, James E,   G S
Mitchell, E,   G S

PIERCEVILLE.

Jones, C,   G S
Pearce, G W,   G S

SHILOH.

Cornell, W J,   G S
Garrett, P G,   G S
Gregory, W N,   G S
Jordan, T H,   G S
Morrisett, J H & Co,   G S
Lorksey, M B,   G S

SOUTH MILLS.

Beveridge, George,   G S
Foster, J P & Bro,   G S
Hinton, L E & C L,   G S
Jacobs, John,   G S
Lynch, W & Co,   G S
Pearce, C W,   G S
Pool, Jos W,   G S
Riggs, G H,   G S
Sawer, L,   G S
Williams, L P,   G S

SHIP YARD.

Bartlett, J A,   G S
Jones, C F,   Wagon and Repair Shop
Johnston, C P,   Undertaker

MILLS.

Kinds, Post Offices and Proprietors.

Corn, Shiloh, Marshall Torksey.
Corn, Shiloh, John Torksey.
Corn, Camden.
Grist, South Mills, W S Jones.
Mill, Old Trap, C L Sawyer.
Saw and grist, Old Trap, A K Surry & Co.
Saw and grist, Camden. N W Stevens.
Saw and grist, South Mills, Geo Beveridge.

PHYSICIANS.

Names and Post Offices.

Aydlett, H T, South Mills.
Brothers, ——, Camden,
Kellem, W D, Shiloh.
Mullen, F N, South Mills.
Pool, J H, South Mills.
Sawyer, C H, Belcross.

SCHOOLS.

Names, Post Offices and Principals.

Academy, South Mills, Wm Towe.
Creek Bridge Academy, Camden.
Jonesboro Academy. Camden, M B Hughes.
No. public schools—white, 12; colored, 12.

TEACHERS.

Names and Post Offices.

Burgess. C B, Shiloh.
Towe, William, Camden.

LOCAL CORPORATIONS.

Camden Lodge I O O F, No 80, Sawyer's Creek; time of meeting, Monday nights; G D B Pritchard, N G.
Fidelity Lodge I O O F, No 83, South Mills; meets every Tuesday night.
New Lebanon Masonic Lodge. No 314, South Mills; meetings first Friday in each month.
Shiloh Lodge I O O F, No 70, Shiloh; meets every Saturday night.
Widow's Son Masonic Lodge, No 75, Camden; regular meetings, 3d Saturday morning.

FARMERS.

Names and Post Offices.

Belcross—A Aydlett, Sam Bell, Willis G Ferebee, E Y Nash, G D B Pritchard, James Randall, R Roberly, E M Sawyer, J L F Sawyer, H A Tarkinton, J W Trafton.
Camden—G L Berry, Noah Burfoot, E M Deford, M D Dozier, C M Ferebee,

CAMDEN COUNTY.

CAMDEN COUNTY.

Adam Forbes, M B Hughes, H C Lamb, P G Morrisett, N W Stevens, Mrs J M Whitehurst.

Shiloh—Willam Bartlett, D Bray, S W Forbes, Silas Gregory, N S Gregory, H S Gregory, M D Gregory, Wm Perkins, W B Sanderlin, Luke Stephens, Nathan Stephens, Samuel Squires, J S Walston.

South Mills—J K Abbott, Samuel Brown, J E Burgess, Isaac Burnham, Jos Hodges, F M Mullen, P C Pearce, C W Pearce, J P Pearce, J B Pearce, G H Riggs, M N Sawyer, Wilson T Sawyer, J A Spencer, Jos N Spence, Henry Whitehurst, Wilson Whitehurst.

CARTERET COUNTY.

AREA, 520 SQUARE MILES.

POPULATION, 10,825; White, 8,528; Colored 2,297.

CARTERET COUNTY was one of the original precincts of the Lords Proprietors, and was called in honor of one of the Lords, Sir George Cartaret. It borders on the Atlantic Ocean for a distance of 75 miles, and is so near to the Gulf Stream as to make the climate quite equable all the year round.

BEAUFORT, the county-seat, is on Beaufort harbor, and is a town of growing importance. It is a delightful summer resort, 144 miles east of Raleigh, and has a population of 2,500.

MOREHEAD CITY, the terminus of the Atlantic & North Carolina Railroad, is a beautiful new city. It has a population of 1,365, and is a charming seaside home.

Surface—The land is low and level, much of it in swamps and marshes. It extends up and down the sound for seventy miles. A portion of the county in narrow strips, called The Banks, lies between the sound and the ocean. Much of the swamp is very rich, and very productive when well drained.

Staples—There are some very fine cotton lands in this county. The moisture of the climate has a tendency to produce a fine, soft fabric. Corn grows well, and in the western portion, along the sound, ground-peas are produced to perfection. Sweet potatoes are raised in large quantities of superior quality. The fisheries are extensive and often very valuable.

The last battle fought in the State with the Indians was fought in 1712, within one mile of the present town of Beaufort. Col. James Moore, of South Carolina, was in charge of the Colonial forces. The battle was with the Core Indians, who inhabited this county.

Fruits—Figs, apples, peaches, pears, grapes and melons to great perfection.

Timbers—Live oak, long-leaf pine, cedar, cypress, ash, gum and juniper.

TOWNS AND POST OFFICES.

	POP.		POP.
Atlantic,	25	Marshallberg,	50
Beaufort,	2,500	Merrimon,	25
Bogue,	50	Morehead	
Cedar Point,	25	City,	1,365
Davis,	50	Newport,	315
Harlowe,	100	Ocean,	50
Hollywood,	50	Peletier's Mills,	100
Lupton,	25	Portsmouth,	100
Roe,	50	Wildwood,	50
Smyrna,	100	Winthrop,	25
Springle,	25		
Stella,	25	Wit,	20
Straights,	50		

COUNTY OFFICERS.

Clerk Superior Court—L A Garner.
Commissioners — W L Arendell, chairman; C P Dey, O G Bell, W P P Weeks, J O Mason.
Coroner— ———
Register of Deeds—Nathan L Carson.
Sheriff—M A Hill.
Solicitor Sixth District—M C Richardson.
Surveyor—Richard Leffers.
Standard Keeper—Joseph P Roberson.
Treaurer—N W Taylor.
County Examiner—Joseph Pigott.
County Physician—D G N Emett.

COURTS.

Second Monday after the first Monday in March, and seventh Monday after the first Monday in September.

TOWN OFFICERS.

BEAUFORT—*Mayor,* Dr J B Davis.
Commissioners — W F Dill, E W Brooks, S A Blount (col), John Henry (col), Chas I Wallace, D Webb, W P Adams.
Clerk and Constable—Gilbert I Willis.
MOREHEAD CITY—*Mayor,* A J McIntyre.
NEWPORT—*Mayor,* L W Perkins.
Commissioners — Wiliam Bell, C Mann, J A Lee Murdock, J L Bell.
Clerk and Treasurer—C Mann.
PORTSMOUTH—*Mayor,* B R Dixon.

TOWNSHIPS AND MAGISTRATES.

Beaufort—J W Gillikin, S L Simpson, J H Davis, J B Davis, Ralph Honland, D E Langdale, S D Delamar, T R Pierce, W R Springle, Samuel Chadwick, C S Bell (Beaufort).
Hunting Quarters — S H Styron, Edward Meilson (Wit), Wm P Paul (Atlantic).
Morehead City—W W Willis, Allen

CARTERET COUNTY.

C Davis, J T Eaton (Morehead City), J H Watson (Wildwood), D S Sharp, R C Bell (Newport).

Newport—Jas R Bell, E D Hardesty, Jas C Graham (Harlowe), Rufus Garner, D McCain, J T Dennis, H D Wyatt, E W Hill (Newport).

Smyrna—Faren Willis. F P Davis (Davis), E B Salter, A G Davis (Smyrna) W Q H Graham (Marshalberg).

Straights—T M Gillikin, Wm Hancock, Cull Pigott (Straits). Eugene Teamans, V B Salter, C H Brady (Beaufort).

White Oak—J B Hanard, D S Weeks (Stella), Elijah Watson, R F Springle (Pelletier's Mill), J W Sanders (Ocean), W F Taylor, J W Guthrie, P M Russell (Bogue).

Merrimon—J T Carraway, A Lee, C S Nelson, John B Neil, J E McCless, E T Carraway, Josephus H Wallace, John N Hamilton (Merrimon).

CHURCHES.

Names, Post Offices, Pastors and Denom.

BAPTIST.

Church, Beaufort.
Church, Morehead City, —— Jenkins.
Church (col), Newport, Samuel Mann.
Church (col), Beaufort, N C Balentine.
Church (col), Morehead City, Samuel Mann.
North River, Straits.
Russell's, Beaufort, J B Russell.
St Luke, Morehead City.
Young Bethel, Harlowe.

METHODIST.

Adams' Creek, Merrimon.
Ann Street, Beaufort, R F Bumpass.
Becton, Harlowe.
Bethlehem, Sander's Store.
Brice Creek, Riverdale, P Greening.
Church, Portsmouth.
Church, (col), Havelock.
Church, Havelock. P Greening.
Church, Atlantic, E Erenton.
Church, Newport, P Greening.
Church, Morehead City, E C Glenn.
Harlowe's Creek, Harlowe, P Greening.
Hopewell, Peletier's Mills.
Little Branch, Morehead City.
Newport, Newport, P Greening.
North River, near Beaufort, R F Bumpass.
Shackelford Banks. Beaufort, E Erenton.
Smyrna. Smyrna.
Straits, Straits.

NORTH. METHODIST.

Harker's Island, Beaufort.
Star, Straits.

PRIMITIVE BAPTIST.

Cedar Island, Roe.
Church, Pelletier's Mills.
Church, Newport, —— Brinson.
Hunting Quarter, Atlantic.
Nelson's Bay, Atlantic.
North River, Beaufort.

FREE-WILL BAPTIST.

Davis' Shore, Davis Warden.

A. M. E. ZION.

Hull Swamp, Oglesby.
Jones' Chapel, Newport. Wm Bodges.
North River, Beaufort, S J Turner.
Purvis' Chapel (col), Beaufort, H P Walker.
Turner's Chapel (col), Morehead City, Wm Bodges.

CONGREGATIONAL.

Church (col), Beaufort, J P Simms.

EPISCOPAL.

Church (col), Beaufort, Frank Gibble.
St Paul's, Beaufort.

PRESBYTERIAN.

Church (col), Beaufort, Michæl Jenkins.

MINISTERS RESIDENT.

Names, Post Offices and Denominations.

METHODIST.

Abernethy, John T, Beaufort.
Bumpass, R F, Beaufort.
Greening, P, Newport.
Gurganus, ——, Atlantic.
Hancock, W B, Straits.
Perkins, Dr Edgar L, Newport.

BAPTIST.

Leary, T J, Harlowe.

PRIM. BAPTIST.

Gillikin, T M. Beaufort.
Smith, E C, Newport.

FREE-WILL BAPTIST.

Lewis, W, Beaufort.
Russell, J B, Beaufort.
Wade, Henry, Davis.
Willis, I F, Davis.

CONGREGATIONAL.

Jenkins, M (col), Beaufort.

HOTELS AND BOARDING HOUSES.

Names, Post Offices and Proprietors.

Arendall House, Morehead City, W L Arendall.
Atlantic. Morehead City.

Boarding, Morehead City, Mrs Wade.
Boarding house, Beaufort, George A Russell.
Boarding house, Newport, J L Bell.
Davis House, Beaufort, Miss Sarah A Davis.
Hotel, Newport, W D Harrison.
Horton House, Morehead City, Mr Horton.
Newbern House, Morehead City, John H Mann.
Ocean View, Beaufort, ——— .

LAWYERS.

Names and Post Offices.

Abernethy, Charles, Beaufort.
Doughty, Wm J, Newport.
Felton, C B, Beaufort.

MANUFACTORIES.

Kinds, Proprietors and Post Offices.

Blacksmithing, Newport, S H Newberry.
Blacksmithing, Beaufort, Jerry Fisher (col).
Blacksmithing, Sander's Store, Cicero Parker.
Boots and shoes, Beaufort, W Johnson.
Building and contracting, Harlowe, W F Becton.
Building and contracting, Harlowe, R M Weeks.
Building and contracting, Smyrna, C S Willis.
Building and contracting, Smyrna, G W Willis.
Building and contracting. Smyrna, J T Willis.
Building and contracting, Smyrna, R Willis.
Building and contracting, Smyrna, W F Willis.
Carriages, Newport, J P Mann.
Carriages, Newport, S H Newberry.
Coopering, Merrimon, G W Carraway.
Coopering, Harlowe, D H Dickinson.
Coopering, Beaufort, Wm Dickinson.
Coopering, Straits, M Goulding.
Coopering, Smyrna, W D Piner.
Cotton gin (steam), Sander's Store, Jno W Sanders.
Fish, scrap and oil, Davis, Daniel L Bell.
Fish, scrap and oil (steam), Beaufort, Dey & Bro.
Fish, scrap and oil, Beaufort, E W Brooks & Co.
Fish, scrap and oil (steam), Beaufort, Jones & Caffrey.
Lime, Hollywood, Fertilizing Co.
Millwrighting, Straits, W R Hancock.

Millwrighting, Atlantic, W L Salter.
Millwrighting, Smyrna, John T Willis.
Public gin, Newport, J D Bell.
Public gin (steam), Newport, J W Peletier.
Public gin (steam), Sanders' Store, J W Sanders.
Public gin, Beaufort, Thomas Thomas.
Public gin, Harlowe, J R Bell.
Public gin, Harlowe, F Taylor.
Repair shop, Newport, H D Wyatt.
Ship building, Beaufort, Capt Hall.
Turpentine distillery, Newport, J L Bell.

MERCHANTS AND TRADESMEN.

Names, Post Offices and Lines of Business.

ATLANTIC.

Chadwick, Thos,	G S
Hamilton, S E & Bro,	G S

BANKS.

Guthrie, A L, Banks,	G S
Hancock, T C, Banks,	Grocer
Hancock, Charles,	Grocer

BEAUFORT.

Bell, B J & Co,	G S
Blount, S A (col),	Conf
Chaplan, M,	Gro
Clawson, C A,	Baker and Gro
Congleton, James,	Gro
Congleton, R C jr,	Gro
Coughton, B B,	G S
Davis, Allen,	Drugs
Davis, Dr J B,	Drugs
Davis, P H (col),	Gro
Delamar, T B,	Drugs
Delamar, C F,	G S
Dey & Arrington,	G S
Dickinson, G M,	G S
Dill, W F & Son,	G S
Duncan, T & Bro,	Fish
Ersken & Dean,	Racket Store
Farlow, B C,	Milliner
Farlow, L S,	Hardware
Fulford, O B (near),	G S
Fuller, H W,	Tailor
Gaskill & Bro,	G S
Gilgo, Jonas,	G S
Guthrie, Mrs A,	G S
Hancock, S P,	G S
Henry, J E & Co (col),	G S
Herman & Bro,	Dry Goods
Ives, Geo N,	Oysters
Johnson, F F,	G S
Jones, B L & Sons,	G S
Jones, C D & Bro,	G S
Jones & Farlow,	G S
King, John F & Son,	G S
Mace, F D,	Drugs
Marshall, J I,	G S
Moore, J B & Co,	G S
Newport, O B,	G S

CARTERET COUNTY.

Norris, Thomas,	G S
Noe, James,	G S
Noe, T D,	Gro
Pierce, D & Son,	Conf and G S
Rice, William,	Photog
Richardson, G W,	Lumber
Robinson, C V, agt,	G S
Robinson, E D,	G S
Russell, J B,	G S
Sanders, D S,	G S
Sass, J B,	Dry Goods
Simpson, G W,	G S
Sharen, L & Co,	Fish
Smith, J S,	G S
Springle, R D & Co,	G S
Springle, J G W,	Gro
Taylor, N W,	G S
Taylor, S H,	Drugs and G S
Thomas, Thomas,	G S
Whitehurst, H A & Bro,	G S
Whitehurst, H W,	G S
Whitehurst, J E & Son,	Gro
Willis, W N,	G S

BOGUE.

Weeks, E P,	G S
Weeks, J A,	G S

CEDAR POINT.

Holland, H C,	Milliner
Saunders, Mrs Sallie	G S
Weeks, J S,	G S

HARLOWE.

Bell & Long,	G S
Bell, Oscar G & Co,	G S
Goodette. Carter & Co (col)	G S

LUPTON.

Daniels, J W,	G S
Lupton, Jas T & Co,	G S
Lupton, S,	G S
Potter, A,	G S

MARSHALLBERG.

Lewis, E P & Son,	G S

MERRIMON.

Stallings, J,	G S

MOREHEAD CITY.

Adams, W P,	G S
Arendell, W L,	Tobacco, Cigars and Fish.
Arthur, E D & Bro,	Whol Fish Dealers
Arthur, J M,	Whol Fish Dealer
Ballow, W A,	G S
Bell, Mrs Georgia V,	Millinery
Bell, Daniel, est,	G S
Bell, Mrs W P,	Milliner
Boyd, J J,	Whol Fish Dealer
Daniels, Thos,	Fish Dealer
Dean, Miss ——,	D Goods and Notions
Dixon, Miss Matilda,	Millinery
Dixon, W T & Co,	G S
Eaton, John H,	G S
Fennel, F (col),	Gro
Gaskill, Ferney & Co,	Whol Fish Dealers

Guthrie, W D,	G S
Hales, W J,	Gro and Notion
Ives, G N,	Whol Fish Dealers
Jones, B C,	Drugs
Jones, W H,	G S
Leary, L L & Bro,	G S
Leary, J L,	Confec
Lepper, Phillips,	Drugs, Gro and Confec
Manson, E F,	G S
Mason, W V,	Butcher and Vegetables
McIntire, A J,	Druggist
Morton & Webb,	G S and Fish
Robinson, C V,	Clothing
Smith, J X,	G S
Taylor, Bates,	Whol Fish Dealer
Taylor, Ed & Bro,	Fish Dealer
Wade, A F,	Fresh Meat and Vegetables
Wallace, C S,	Whol Fish Dealer
Watson, C T,	Whol Fish Dealer
Webb, T D & Bro,	G S and Fish
Webb, A H,	So Ex Agt
Willis, Needham,	G S
Willis & Bro,	G S

NEWPORT.

Bell, W S, jr,	G S
Bell, J L,	G S
Garner, P P,	G S
Garner, R C,	G S
Mann, Cicero,	G S
Mann, J B & Son,	G S
Wyatt & Edwards,	G S

OCEAN.

Smith, Michael,	G S

PORTSMOUTH.

Parson, H,	G S
Gilgo, G W,	G S
Robinson, Alex,	G S
Williams, W O,	G S

SANDERS' STORE.

Taylor & Weeks,	G S

SMYRNA.

Bell, H B,	G S
Bell, W B,	G S
Davis, A G,	G S
Fulcher, W P,	G S
Hamilton, S E & Bro,	G S
Willis, Alfonzo T,	G S

SPRINGLE.

Springle, R D,	G S

STELLA.

Kuhn, Wm,	G S
Maddox, J A,	G S
Pelletier, J Walter,	G S
Sabiston, J W,	G S
Sabiston, M J,	G S

STRAITS.

Chadwick, Guy C,	G S
Chadwick, A H & Bro,	G S
Harky, Jane H,	Millinery

CARTERET COUNTY.

CARTERET COUNTY.

WILDWOOD.

Murdock, M E,   G S

WINTHROP.

Lee, A,   G S

WIT.

Mason, L W,   G S
Nelson & Hamilton,   G S
Taylor & Bro,   G S
Taylor, J E,   G S
Willis, Wallace,   G S

MILLS.

Kinds, Post Offices and Proprietors.

Corn and gin (steam), Beaufort, Thos Thomas.
Saw and grist (water), Newport, F D Hervett.
Steam saw, Harlowe, J R Bell.
Steam saw, Stella, White Oak Lumber
Steam saw, Merrimon, Hostler & Co.
Steam saw, Beaufort, Whitcomb Bros.
Windmill, Portsmouth, M Ireland.
Windmill, Roe, M & J Lupton.
Windmill, Atlantic, Reuben Fulcher.
Windmill, Atlantic, Wm Hill.
Windmill, Atlantic, Freeman Lewis.
Windmill, Atlantic, Thos Gaskill.
Windmill, Straits, Chadwick & Bro.
Windmill, Straits, Leffers & Gillikin.
Windmill, Morehead City, Daniel Bell.
Windmill, White Oak, John Guthrie.
Windmill, White Oak, Jno W Sanders.
Windmill, Marshallburg, E P Lewis.

PHYSICIANS.

Names and Post Offices.

Clark, ——, Beaufort.
Davis, J B, Beaufort.
Delemar, T D, Beaufort.
Emmett, G W, Cedar Point.
Leffers, Richard, Straits.
Mason, C N, Harlowe.
Paul, Wm T, Atlantic.
Perkins, E L, Jr, Newport.
Perkins, E L, Sr, Newport.
Saunders, John, Saunders' Store.

SCHOOLS.

Names, Post Offices and Principals.

Academy, Beaufort, Rev J T Aberne- thy, Miss Annie Jones, assistant.
Academy, Newport, G W Mewborne.
Academy, Pelletier's, Miss Olive Garn- er.
Academy, Smyrna, W Q A Graham.
Harlowe Academy, Harlowe.
Morehead City High School, H W Reinhart, J F Brinson, ass't, and W N Webb, ass't.
Music School, Morehead City, Miss Mary Bell.
Primary School, Morehead City, H S Lee.
Rocky River Academy, Cedar Point, F K Koonce.
Seminary, Beaufort, A B Hill, Julia Bird, ass't.
Washburn Seminary (col.), Beaufort, Miss M E Wilcox.

TEACHERS.

Names and Post Offices.

Abernethy, J T, Beaufort.
Arendell, Thomas, Morehead City.
Arrington, B B, Beaufort.
Brinson, J F, Morehead City.
Davis, Miss Mary E, Smyrna.
Ellison, E W, Beaufort.
Fales, Miss Annie, Morehead City.
Fisher, Miss Mamie E. (col.), Beaufort.
Fisher, Miss Maggie (col.), Beaufort.
Garner, Olive, Newport.
Garner, L C, Newport.
Gaskill, Miss Anna B, Straits.
Gibble, Miss Lottie, Beaufort.
Gillikins, Cicero T, Straits.
Hartsell, Miss Laura, Morehead City.
Hardesty, Miss Matilda, Newport.
Hardesty, E D, Harlowe.
Hardy, Geo M, Portsmouth.
Hazel, Miss Maud E (col.), Beaufort.
Hill, Miss Gertrude, Newport.
Irving, Miss Della H, Beaufort.
Ireland, Medora, Beaufort.
Jerkins, Miss Nettie M, Beaufort.
Lawrence, Watson, Straits.
Lee, H S, Morehead City.
Leffers, Samuel, Straits.
Mason, E Z, Beaufort.
Matthewson, Miss Nannie (col.), Beau- fort.
Murdock, W C, Wildwood.
Parker, Miss Mary E (col.), Beaufort.
Piner, Henry O, Smyrna.
Russell, Irvin, Beaufort.
Slaughter, Wm H, Wildwood.
Simpson, Clarence, Beaufort.
Simpson, Vernon, Smyrna.
Smith, N L, Morehead City.
Starney, Mrs E L, Morehead City.
Stanton, Miss Mary V, Springle.
Willis, Anthony, Smyrna.
Public schools: white 27, colored 7.

LOCAL CORPORATIONS.

Carolina City Land Co: Office, New- bern.
Concordia, I O O F, Beaufort, A B Hill, N G. Time of meeting, Friday.
Franklin Lodge (masonic). Time of meeting, last Thursday evening in every month.

CARTERET COUNTY.

Morehead City Land Co, Jas T Morehead, of Greensboro, pres.

NEWSPAPERS.

Beaufort Herald, Beaufort, C T Abernethy, editor and prop; J T Abernethy, ass't.

FISHERIES AND OWNERS.

Bird Shoal, Ives C Chadwick.
Carrot Island, Davis Congleton and others.
Fort Macon Fishery, Davis and others.
Hard Scrabble, Seth Arthur.
Lenoxville, Congleton, Gaskill and others.
Mullet Pond, Howland Bros.
Rice Path, Styron and others.
Russell's, Russell and others.
Sandy Point, John Willis.
Starving Island, Dudley, Fulcher and others.
Steep Point, Howland Bros.
Tavern Rock, Fulford and others.
Wade Shore, Miss Pigott.
Wreck Point, Pigott and others.
Some others in the extreme western part of the county and on the banks, but the owners are unknown.

FARMERS.

Names and Post Offices.
Beaufort—Edward Chadwick, Sam'l Chadwick, J H Davis, Elizabeth Gilliken. Z J Howland, Lockhart Gibbs, B A Felton. D W Russell, Sam'l Thomas, E O Springle, J M Thomas, J F Wade.
Bogue—W F Taylor, C Taylor, B F

CARTERET COUNTY.

Taylor, G W Taylor, E B Weeks, P M Russell, R W Humphrey, M E Bell, C F Bell.
Cedar Point—H N Bell, W F Bell, Geo Dennis, Dr G N Ennett, L B Holland, D A Morton, Alex Weeks, J A Weeks.
Harlowes—W N Bell, Jas R Bell, W J Fodric, E D Hardesty.
Morehead City—Olive Adams, J T Eaton, T M Hall, W W Willis, R Ward.
Newport—J G Bell, F P Bell. G H Boland, J L Dennis, James Elliott, E C Garner, D B Garner, S M Garner, Zerneriah Garner, Reuben Garner, R C Garner, A R Garner, T M Garner, Wm Glancy, S G Gould, John Hall, Wendfield Hasket, T D Hewitt, I S Hill, T M Mann, D L Mann, D McCain, Frank Mason, Jas Midyett, S H Newberry, D S Quinn, Henry Simmons, H W Small, E S Smith.
Ocean—D S Bell Sr, D S Bell, Jr, G S Bell, Willis C Bell, Jere Cannon, Alex Dennis, Cicero Parker, James Pigott, Frank Sanders, J S Smith.
Pelletier's—Frank Morse, L F Pelletier, Willoughby Prescott, Elijah Watson, Jere Watson, Samuel Weeks, W P P Weeks.
Stella—W Barker, Thomas Dudley, Geo W Koonce, J W Pelletier.
Straits—Call Pigott, James Stewart, John S Smith, David W Willis, O C Whitehurst, Robt H Whitehurst.
Wildwood—W S Bell, T M Bell, Jos Elliott, Thos McCabe, A E Oglesby, L T Oglesby, Elijah Oglesby, W T Pelletier. Lewis Piner, T J Tolson, H Teasly, Michael Willis.

MARY POTTER MEMORIAL SCHOOL,
OXFORD, N. C.

The object of the School is to prepare colored young men and women for the practical duties of life by training the hands, heart and head—the hands to do with might and skill what they find to do, the heart to obey God's law, and the head to think.

The School is named in honor of the late Mrs. B. F. Potter, of Schenectady, N. Y., through whose influence the work was started.

The School is under the direct control of the Freedmen's Board, through whose hands come all donations, or who will be informed of all donations that come direct to us. It is also under the control of a local Board of Directors and Advisers.

It is supported by the Freedmen's Board, by personal friends through the Freedmen's Board, by the students, and by the people of both races here on the field.   REV. G. C. SHAW, A. M., PRINCIPAL.

CASWELL COUNTY.

AREA, 400 SQUARE MILES.

POPULATION, 13,028; White 6,639, Colored 6,389.

CASWELL COUNTY was created in 1777, out of Orange county, and takes its name from Richard Caswell, the first Governor of the State under the Constitution.

YANCEYVILLE, its capital (named in compliment of Hon Bartlett Yancey), is 69 miles northwest from Raleigh, and contains a population of 965.

Surface—Caswell county lies on the south bank of Dan river, and on small tributary streams. The surface is moderately uneven, and the soil generally good, especially for tobacco. There are probably no finer tobacco lands in America.

Staples—Tobacco is the great staple in this county. The leaf grown here is celebrated far and near. Wheat, corn and oats grow finely, but are not considered so profitable as tobacco.

Fruits—Apples, peaches, pears, and all the small fruits, melons.

Timbers—Oak, hickory, walnut, poplar, pine and various other kinds common to the middle part of the State.

TOWNS AND POST OFFICES.

	POP.		POP.
Allison,	50	Hycotee,	25
Anderson's,	150	Leasburg,	250
Ashland,	75	Locust Hill,	25
Bedford,	25	Milesville,	25
Blackwells,	75	Milton,	1,000
Blanch,	25	Osmond,	50
Cherry Grove,	25	Pelham,	50
Corbett,	25	Prospect Hill,	75
Eastland,	50	Purley,	50
Estelle,	50	Ridgeville,	25
Fitch's,	25	Semora,	20
Gannaway,	—	Stony Creek,	20
Gatewood,	25	Tony,	—
Hamer,	25	Yanceyville,	900
Hightowers,	40	Yarbro,	25

COUNTY OFFICERS.

Clerk Superior Court—S B Adams.
Commissioners — T W Corbett (ch).
Coroner—
Register of Deeds—F A Pierson.
Solicitor Fifth District—W P Bynum.
Sheriff—T T Donoho.
Surveyor—T A Williamson.
Standard Keeper—H T Henderson.
County Examiner—A E Henderson.
Treasurer—T H Harrison.

COURTS.

The Superior Court meets the fifth Monday after the first Monday in March; third Monday before the first Monday in September; and seventh Monday after the first Monday in September.

TOWNSHIPS AND MAGISTRATES.

Anderson—B F Hurdle, J F Dillard, John R Burton, Jas M Simpson, John S Miles (Anderson's Store).

Dan River—John F Walters, W H Connelly, G Lea, T M McCrary, T S Harrison (Yanceyville).

Hightowers—Charles B Crisp, D E Wilkinson, J T Malone, John A Johnston (Hightowers).

Leasburg—T L Lea, B F Stanfield, Gabriel L Walker, A B Newman, Robt P Smith (Leasburg).

Locust Hill—J C Allison, James A Williamson, Robt S Mitchell, John S Blackwell (Locust Hill).

Milton—L H Hunt, N T Raney, Jos N McCain, N M Richmond (Milton).

Pelham — James M Hodges, W C Swann, A K Pinnix, J M Hodges, W H Gatewood (Pelham).

Stony Creek—J O Simpson, J A Lea, Marcus A Turner, A J Thompson (Stony Creek).

Yanceyville—J P Poteat, N G Lindsay, Jos C Pinnix, H F Brandon, M Oliver (Yanceyville).

CHURCHES.

Names, Post Offices, Pastors and Denom.

BAPTIST.

Beaver Island—Mayo, D G Taylor.
Beulah—Horner, J E Armstrong.
Church—Milton, J E Armstrong.
Church—Yanceyville, J E Armstrong.
Elm Grove— ———.
Kerr's Chapel—Anderson's Store, T D Harris.
Prospect— ———, J H Shore.
Providence—Gatewood, S G Mason.
Shiloh, Hamer, T E Armstrong.
Trinity—Yanceyville, T D Harris.

PRIMITIVE BAPTIST.

Bush Arbor—Anderson's Store.
Church—Prospect Hill,
County Line—Yanceyville.
Ferrit Chapel—Purley.
Lynch's Creek—Prospect Hill.

CASWELL COUNTY.

Mill Church—Milton.
Pleasant Grove—Ashland.

METHODIST.

Bethel—Ridgeville, R H Broom.
Camp Spring—Ashland, M Rice.
Church—Yanceyville, J H Shore.
Church—Leasburg, R H Broom.
Connelly's—Milton, R Fox.
Harrison's—Purley, R Fox.
Hebron—Hightowers, R H Broom.
New Hope—Milton, R Fox.
Prospect—Yanceyville, J H Shore.
Shady Grove—Pelham, J H Shore.
Union—Leasburg, R H Broom.

PRESBYTERIAN.

Bethesda—Locust Hill.
Church—Yanceyville, W B Campbell.
Grier's—Hightowers, N B Campbell.
Red House—Milton, W S Campbell.

CHRISTIAN.

Concord—Cherry Grove, S Stroud.
Lebanon—Milton, J L Foster.

MINISTERS RESIDENT.

Names, Post Offices and Denominations.

CHRISTIAN.

Apple, Solomon, Milton.

BAPTIST.

Armstrong, J P, Milton.
Harris, J D, Yanceyville.

PRIMITIVE BAPTIST.

Oakley, F L, Anderson's Store.

METHODIST.

Shore, J H, Pelham.

PRESBYTERIAN.

Campbell, W S, Milton.
Campbell, N B, Yanceyville.

HOTELS AND BOARDING HOUSES.

Names, Post Offices and Proprietors.

Hotel, Yanceyville, T W Corlett.
Hotel, Yanceyville, J H Kerr.
Hotel, Milton, W H Connolly.
Hotel, Leasburg, H T Connolly.
Hotel, Purley, E G Carrington.
Restaurant, Milton, A J Owens & Son.

LAWYERS.

Names and Post Offices.

Anderson, G G, Yanceyville.
Henderson, A E, Yanceyville.
Johnston & Johnston, Yanceyville.
Warlick, L M, Milton.

11

CASWELL COUNTY.

MANUFACTORIES.

Kinds, Post Offices and Proprietors.

Blacksmithing, Yanceyville, H McGee.
Blacksmithing, Yanceyville, S D Crowder.
Cabinet-makers, Milton, Farley & Ferguson.
Carriages, Anderson's Store, J A & J H Hurde.
Cigars, Milton, W T Farley & Son.
Plows, Milton, N M Richmond & Son.
Plug and Twist Tobacco, Milton, N E Oliver.
Tobacco, Milton, C J Allen.
Tobacco, plug and twist, Milton, E D Winstead & Co.

MERCHANTS AND TRADESMEN.

Names, Post Offices, Lines of Business.

ANDERSON.

Baynes, J R,	G S
Hurdle, J H,	G S
Walker, L H & Son,	G S

ASHLAND.

Rice & Ware,	G S

BEDFORD.

Watlington, O O,	G S

BLACKWELL.

King, R A & Bro,	G S

BLANCHE.

Watkins, D G.	G S

CHERRY GROVE.

Miner, W A,	G S

CORBETT.

Corbett & Cooper,	G S

ESTELLE.

Brandon, Jas.	G S
Evans, Henry (col),	G S

EASTLAND.

Blackwell, R H,	G S

FITCH'S STORE.

Fitch, A N,	G S
Martin, G W T,	G S

GATEWOOD.

Carter, C L & Bro,	G S
Gatewood, A S & Bro,	G S
Gatewood, James E,	G S
Hodges, J L,	G S
Powell, J,	Drugs
Smith, J C,	G S
Watlington.	G S

HAMER.

Hubbard, G T,	G S
King, J C,	Mill
Smith, J C,	G S

CASWELL COUNTY.

HIGHTOWERS.

Hamlett, F H,	G S
Warren, J L,	Mill

HYCOTTE.

Stephens, S D,	G S

KILL QUICK.

Mitchell, R S,	G S

LEASBURG.

Connolly, H T,	G S
Malone, J Z,	G S
Pulliam, W J,	G S
Thomas, W L,	G S

LOCUST HILL.

Siddle, S W,	G S

MILESVILLE.

Miles, W & Son,	G S

MILTON.

Bowers, G F (col.),	G S
Connelly, W H,	Hotel
Dixon, R L,	Drugs
Farley, Mrs W T,	Millinery
Farley & Ferguson,	
Cabinet makers, Undertakers	
Featherstone, M M,	G S
Francis, Joseph,	Tinner
Frion & Fleming,	G S
Hunt, E,	Leaf Tobacco
Hurdle, J H,	Leaf Tobacco
Irvin, John L,	Leaf Tobacco
Jones, F B,	G S
Koklan, V & Bro,	G S
Lewis, J W & Son,	Tobacco
Milton Roller Mill Co,	—
Nethery, J C,	Harness
Owens, G H,	Butcher
Owens, H A & G,	Gro
Smith, W A,	G S
Walker, Lewis & Co,	Drugs
Walker, R L,	Fertilizer
Watkins, W M & Co,	G S
Yarborough, Joseph J,	Foundry

OSMOND.

Hutchins, J B,	G S

PELHAM.

Fitzgerald, J O,	G S
Pierce & Son,	G S

PROSPECT HILL.

Warren, W A,	G S

PURLEY.

Covington, E G,	G S
Slade, T D & Co,	G S
Woods, S G & Co,	G S

RIDGEVILLE.

Wilkinson, D E,	G S

SEMORA.

Adams, W E & Bro,	G S
McAden, John H,	G S

CASWELL COUNTY.

TONY.

Crawford & Dailey,	G S

YANCEYVILLE.

Florence, T J,	G S
Graves, Miss S,	Millinery
Harrelson, W N,	G S
Kerr, J H,	Hotel
Rockett, Miss M W,	Millinery
Lownes, B,	Carriage-maker
Neal, L M,	G S
Watson, A B,	Blacksmith
Wilson, Geo O & Co,	Drugs

MILLS.

Kinds, Post Offices and Proprietors.

Corn and saw, Yanceyville, W B Graves.
Corn and flour, Milton, W B Lewis.
Flour and saw, Anderson's Store, Bird & Eason.
Flour, Gatewood, A G Watson.
Flour, Hamer, King & Bro.
Saw, Eastland, J A & G O Williams.
Steam saw and grist, Hightower, G L Warren.

PHYSICIANS.

Names and Post Offices.

Anderson, James Q, Anderson's Store.
Budgett, J F, Blackwell's Store.
Dodson, H H, Milton.
Gunn, George, Purley.
Henderson, N S, Pelham.
Hester, James A (dentist), Anderson's Store.
Keesee, J J, Pelham.
Lea, C G, Hamer.
Oakley, T A, Hightower.
Spencer, W O, Yanceyville.
Thompson, J A, Leasburg.

SCHOOLS.

Names, Post Offices and Principals.

Public schools: white 35; colored 37.

LOCAL CORPORATIONS.

Merchants and Planters Bank, Milton, W H Thompson, pres; W W Lucke, cashier.

NEWSPAPERS.

Caswell News, Yanceyville, Poteat & Harris, eds and props.
Chronicle, Milton, M L King, editor.

FARMERS.

Names and Post Offices.

Anderson's Store—J Q Anderson, Q

CASWELL COUNTY.

T Anderson, T Y Baynes, J R Baston, Thos Baston, J S Barnwell, John Bird, Nathan Brown, J H Burton, Jos Dillard, J F Dillard, W Fitch, G S Fitch, E Florence, G W Florence, Eli Gooth, George Herndon, J E Herndon, W M Herndon, J H Hurdle, James Hurdle, James A Hurdle, W A Hughes, Levi Massey, P C Massey, Frank Massey, William McNeill, W W Miles, John S Miles, Warren Miles, C J Richmond, Ezekiel Sawyer, T N Smith, W H Stainback, M Walker, A B Walker, Abner Walker, L H Walker, W L Walker, Y C Walker, C Walker.

Blackwell's—T W Farrish.

Hightower—J R Burton, Thos Burton, F Burton, D Burch, N Covington, J W Jones, J Johnson, Benjamin Nick, J Riggs, W H Smith, T B Smith, T Smith, W Smith, J Smith, James Warren, F A Wiley.

Leasburg—W H Botton, Joseph T Bradshaw, Drury Burton, H T Connolly, L W Currier, Jerry Dixon, A B Fewman, F W Featherstone, Tom Fullington, A M Fuller, T J Gattis, Anderson Harris, A J Hester, John A Johnston, W H Johnston, T L Lea, Solomon Lea, E W Lea, S Lea, V L Martin, James Nelson, Lea Paterson, Wm Paterson, B G Pulliam, Henry Richmond, George A Rogers, H A Rogers, Levi Sawyer, John Sergent, J T Sergant, Robert Smith, W H Smith, Nash Stanfield, J A Stanfield, B F Stanfield, John Stephens, W Stephens, A Stephens, Henderson Stephens, Banks Talley, H S Thaxton, Thos Thompson. J A Thompson, J S Thompson, C A Warren, W S White, C S Winstead, jr.

Milton—William Bryant, Tom Connelly, Abi Daniels, David Elliott, Thos G Epps, Thos Hamlet, Eustace Hunt, Joe Hunt, Eustis Hunt, Jack Irvin, Sidney S Lea, J M Long, Jas McAden, Giles Mebane, Sam Moore, Jas New inart, Robt Phelps, N M Richmond, James Scott, W G Smith, Loftin Smith, J M Smith, William Smith, J

CASWELL COUNTY.

W Stephen, Weldon Stephen, J T Stevens, Joel Waters.

Pelham—J D Keesee, J W Neal, J D Neal, J W Nunnally, A B Pinnix, J A Pierce, J A Swan, W B Swan, Geo W Williamson, J A Williamson.

Prospect Hill—M S Allen, J Q Allen, W H Anderson, M G Anderson, W H Barnwell, Lorenza Baynes, R M Blacknell, L A Boon. Wm Burch, Lewis Burch, Ephraim Burch, Sandy Burch, Calvin Burch, J T Burton, R H Cearnal, J J Calmon, J L Compton, Allen Compton, W L Compton, William Cooper, W A J Cooper, H W Cooper, J T Compton, F L Cooper, C B Crisp, J B Daniel, A Domison, W C Harolson, N C Hester, Spivey Henslee, Bedford James, Calvin Jones, W M Lea, E H and J Malone, J B Malone, B Y Malone, J T Malone, W W Marrie. Haywood Malone, W W Miles, E G Mitchell, B T Morgan, G W Morgan, J C Murphy, W M Murphy, James Nelson, Ephraim Norris, Sidney O Brient, J L Phelps, A L Phelps, S T Prittard, Davis Prittard, H P Pope, C J Richmond, Ezekiel Sartin, W R Sharpe Jerry Smith, E R Smith, W J Smith, H H Stewart, W R Stewart, J B Terrell, W M Terrell, Wm Terrell, W T Vaughn, J B Warren, Y B Warren, B H Warren. John Warren, James Warren, F L Warren, J Q Warren, John Warren. William Warren, Wesley Warren, Brice Warren, B Wells, W T Wilson, A M Woods.

Purley—J M O'Briant, John Cobb, E G Covington, S S Harrison, T S Harrison, T J Hodges, W J Hodges, W T Hodges, H E Hodges, Nat Hunt, L F Hunt, T McBrag, J L Motley, Wm Slade, E Slade, John W Slade.

Ruffin—J B Blacknell, R A Blacknell.

Yanceyville—Jerry Graves, B Graves, J L Graves, B Grour, J L Grour, W B Johnston, Wm Lee, jr, Wm Lee, Rufus Lea, N L Lindsey, James Poteat, Jno G Wilson, Andy M Woods, J L Womack, Geo Williamson.

Hickory

MARCELLUS E. THORNTON, President.
O. M. ROYSTER,
A. A. SHUFORD,
M. E. THORNTON,
K. C. MENZIES,
} Directors.

Printing

PUBLISHERS OF

PRESS AND CAROLINIAN.

M. E. THORNTON, Editor.

Company,

GENERAL PRINTERS,

HICKORY, N. C.

THE PRESS AND CAROLINIAN is bright, crisp, breezy and pungent. Is a thoroughbred Democratic newspaper, published every Thursday. It is read by the people— also by the other side.

Hickory is a looming—not booming—young city, and is a competitive point, and the nucleus of nine counties. Think of it! Pretty good for a weekly newspaper of any sort of "git up and git."

Advertising Rates Very Reasonable for the Service!

This newspaper has a vein, or streak of humor permeating its interior, which has to be appreciated to be acknowledged. It always trusts to the public to see the point. They know as much about it as we do. Try a sample copy. Write for it.

CATAWBA COUNTY.

AREA 440 SQUARE MILES.

POPULATION, 18,689; White 16,073, Colored 2,616.

CATAWBA COUNTY was cut off from Lincoln county in 1842, and takes its name from the beautiful river which forms its northern boundary.

NEWTON, the county-seat. is directly on the Western North Carolina Railroad, and is 178 miles west of Raleigh. Population 1,656.

Surface—This county is situated in the bend of the Catawba river, which makes a curve around the north and east sides. The land is moderately uneven, and most of it quite productive; it is well watered, and plenty of water-power for immense macninery. Catawba is a prosperous county, out of debt, taxes low, and money in the treasury —a desirable place to settle. The celebrated Sparkling Catawba Springs are in this county.

Staples—Corn, cotton and wheat are the great staples, and large quantities are shipped to other counties. Irish potatoes and grass are grown with success. Live stock is profitable. This is among the best wheat growing counties in the State.

Fruits—Peaches, apples, pears, berries, grapes, plums.

Timbers—Black walnut, poplar, ash, gum, hickory, chestnut, wild cherry, elm and all the oaks.

Minerals—Iron, gold and alum are found in this county.

TOWNS AND POST OFFICES.

	POP.		POP.
Arnt,	—	Loretta,	—
Bandy,	20	Louise,	35
Blackburn,	50	Maiden,	300
Carson,	25	Millstone,	20
Catawba,	300	Monbo,	30
Catfish.	25	Mountain Cre'k,	50
Chestnut,	20	Mullgrove,	25
Chronicle,	40	Newton (CH)	1,660
Claremont,	50	Oxford Ford,	25
Conover,	500	Plateau,	25
Cook,	20	Rockett,	20
Drumsville,	30	Rudisill,	20
Edith,	25	Shawnee,	25
Flemming,	50	Sherrill's Ford,	28
Hayseed,	25	Sparkl'g Cataw-	
Hickory,	3,000	ba Springs,	150
Jacob's Fork,	25	Startown,	50
Jugtown,	130	Terrell,	25
Long Island,	25	Whitener,	50
		Yoder, 25	

COUNTY OFFICERS.

Clerk Superior Court—John W Rockett.

Commissioners—P A Hoyle, ch'mn; A A Shuford, John Sherrill.

Coroner—Q A Sitzer.

Register of Deeds—J F Hermon.

Sheriff—T L Bandy,

Solicitor 10th District—J F Spainhour.

Surveyor—C R Brady.

Standard Keeper— ——.

Treasurer—Noah Barringer.

County Attorney—M E Laurence.

County Examiner—J D Rowe.

Superintendent Health—Dr J M McCorkle.

Keeper of Poor—M L & J J Cline.

COURTS.

Second Monday before first Monday in March and fifth Monday before first Monday in September.

TOWN OFFICERS.

CONOVER—*Mayor*, J Hannaker.

HICKORY—*Mayor*, J D Elliott; *Aldermen*, A A Shuford, O M Royster, G H Gertiner, J S Abernethy, R A Yoder, J C Martin; *Clerk and Treasurer*, J H Bruns; *Chief of Police*, S T Campbell.

NEWTON—*Mayor*, A D Shuford; *Commissioners*, John P Yount, J B Little, A C Seagle, M A Davority; *Secretary and Treasurer*, A J Seagle; *Marshal*, W I Woodard.

MAIDEN—*Mayor*, H C Caldwell.

CATAWBA—*Mayor*, ——.

CLAREMONT—*Mayor*, ——.

TOWNSHIPS AND MAGISTRATES.

Bandy's—M F Hall (Mull Grove), J S Goodman, T J Leonard, R O Ramsaur (Jugtown), McClelland Hildebrand, John Johnson, J F Hudson (Jugtown).

Caldwell's—J D Caldwell, H H Caldwell (Loretta), J A Epps, J L Hewitt, W A Lee, L J Caldwell (Newton), Daniel Bandy (Bandy's).

Catawba—M J Cochran, R H Trollinger, J B Trollinger, L D L Witherspoon, S H Abernethy, T A Abernethy (Catawba). L H Shuford, Sam'l Turner (Monbo).

CATAWBA COUNTY.

Cline's—P G Herman (Conover) T H Bumgarner (Catawba Springs), P K Little, Jonas Cline (Catfish), John H Moser (Claremont), C S Little, W P Simon (Oxford Ford), W H Rockett (Rockett), D A Yount (Conover).

Hickory—J W Mouser, S E Killian, J;H Bruns, Abel Whitener, L H Yount, S V Cline, W H Mouser, J S Setzer, E L Whitener (Hickory).

Jacob's Fork—J M Clompett (Plateau), S T Wilfong, G M Yoder. David Ramsauer (Jacob's Fork).

Mountain Creek—C H Lester, Alley Gabriel (Sherrill's Ford), D P Smith, M M Gabriel (Mountain Creek), H H Harwell, F G McCall (Fleming's).

Newton—C W Herman, J Hunsucker (Conover), M A Thornburg, A D Shuford, J M Brown, James McRee, W P Fye, W C Caldwell (Maiden), M Hildebrand, H A Forney (Newton), C C Gall (Maiden).

CHURCHES.

Names, Post Offices, Pastors and Denom.

METHODIST.

Arney's Chapel-Hickory, W V Honeycutt.
Bethel—Jacob's Fort, E M Merritt.
Bethlehem—Catawba, J F England.
Center—Bandy, J F England.
Church—Hickory, J F England.
Church—Plateau, R E Abernethy.
Church—Maiden, M H Hoyle.
Church—Newton, M H Hoyle.
Concord—Catawba, J F England.
Ebenezer—Hall's X Roads, E M Merritt.
Fair Grove—Newton, M H Hoyle.
Fair Grove—Conover, M H Hoyle.
Friendship—Newton, M H Hoyle.
Friendship—Carson, M H Hoyle.
Hopewell—Catawba, J F England.
Marvin—Rockett, M H Hoyle.
Marvin—Newton, M H Hoyle.
May's Chapel—Newton, M H Hoyle.
May's Chapel—Maiden, M H Hoyle.
Mt Pleasant—Mountain Creek, J T Stover.
Nebo—Newton, M H Hoyle.
Oak Grove—Newton, M H Hoyle.
Pisgah—Catawba, J A England.
Plateau—Plateau, E M Merritt.
Prospect—Newton, M H Hoyle.
Rehoboth—Sherrill's Ford, J T Stover.
Wesley Chapel—Jacob's Fork, E M Merritt.
Wesley Chapel—Jacob's Fork, R S Abernethy.
Zion—Stamey's Store, R S Abernethy.
Zion—Stamey's Store, E M Merritt.

NORTH METHODIST.

Church—Hickory, L G McDonald.
Shiloh—Maiden, D A Lanier.

CATAWBA COUNTY.

LUTHERAN.

Church—Startown, H K Doermann.
Church—Conover, R Weirs.
Grace—Jacob's Fork, R H Yoder and J L Murphy.
Haas—Newton, J L Hunt.
Miller's—Hickory, C D Besch.
Mt Zion—Catawba Springs, J H Rexrode.
St Andrew's—Hickory, R A Yoder.
Piney—Arnt, J M Smith.
St James'—Newton, R A Yoder.
St John's—Conover, J H Rexrode and J H A Holshouser.
Mt Olive—Hickory, W P Cline.
St Mark—Claremonts, J H Rexrode.
St Paul's—Newton, J H A Holshouser, Jos Smith, J L Hunt.
St Paul's—Hickory, H K Doermann.
St Peter's—Sparkling Catawba Spr'gs, J M Smith.
Zion—Hickory, J C Moser.

BAPTIST.

Church—Maiden, J A Hoyle.
Church—Hickory, —— Cashwell.
Lebanon—Catawba, Jacob Hoyle.
Morning Star— ——, B F Watts.
Mt Rehamah—Loretta, J A Hoyle.
Olivet—Catawba, J B Marsh.
Providence—Catawba, J B Marsh.
Church (col)—Newton.

REFORMED.

Bethel—Hickory, Joseph L Murphy.
Corinth—Hickory, Joseph L Murphy.
Grace—Newton, Andrew Smith.
Memorial—Maiden, J C Clapp, D D.
Smyrna—Edith, H A M Holshouser.

PRESBYTERIAN.

Church—Hickory, J A Ramsey.
Church—Newton, J A Ramsey.
Church—Sherrill's Ford.

EPISCOPAL.

Church of the Ascension—Hickory, James A Weston.

FREE CHURCH.

Union—Sparkling Catawba Springs.

A. M. E. ZION.

Baring's Tabernacle—Jacob's Fork, A L Newby.
Baker's Mountain—Blackburne, N L Mills.
Matthew's Chapel—Conover, N L Mills
Mt Pisgah—Hickory, J M Henderson.
Snow Hill—Newton, A L Newby.
Spring Hill—Maiden, N L Mills.
Thomas' Chapel—Hickory, D C Covington.

ZION METHODIST.

Church (col.)—Conover.
Church (col.)—Newton.

CATAWBA COUNTY.

MINISTERS RESIDENT.

Names, Post Offices and Denom.

METHODIST.

Abernethy, M A, Newton.
Abernethy, R S, Plateau.
Drum, G P, Maiden.
England, J F, Catawba.
Hilton, Robt, Blackburn.
Hoyle, M H, Newton.
Killian, W L C, Killian.
Sherrill, Dr J A, Mountain Creek.
Townsend, F L, Hickory.
Lanier, D A, Bandy.
Merritt, E M, Plateau.

LUTHERAN.

Bookheimer, ——, Conover.
Cline, W P, Hickory.
Crouse, J L, Hickory.
Daw, W H T, Conover.
Dowman, H K G, Hickory.
Hunt, J L, Newton.
Moses, J L, Newton.
Romoser, G A, Conover.
Smith. J M, Conover.
Weiss, ——, Conover,
Yoder, Pres R A, Hickory.

REFORM.

Clapp, Dr J C, Newton.
Foil, J A, Newton.
Halshouser, H A M, Conover.
Murphy, J L, Hickory.
Smith, A H, Newton.

BAPTIST.

Anas, J A. Monbo.
Cashwell, W A, Hickory.
Hoyle, J A, Maiden,
Murdison, C M, Penelope.

PRESBYTERIAN.

Ramsay, J A, Hickory.

EPISCOPAL.

Weston, J A, Hickory.

A. M. E. ZION.

Covington, D C, Hickory.
Hyatte, S L, Catawba.
Mills, N L, Conover.
Newby, A L, Claymont.

HOTELS AND BOARDING HOUSES.

Names, Post Offices and Proprietors.

Boarding house, Hickory, H L Moore.
Boarding house, Hickory, Mrs J S Propst.
Boarding house, Hickory, Mrs Benj Seigle.
Boarding house, Hickory, W P Reinhardt.
Charter House, Hickory, Misses Evans.

CATAWBA COUNTY.

Commercial, Conover.
Elliott's, Sparkling Catawba Springs, E O Elliott.
Haynes' Hotel, Newton, C M Haynes.
Hickory Inn, Hickory, Frank Loughran.
Hotel, Catawba.
Restaurant, Hickory, Flanagan & Son.
Restaurant, Hickory, A W Chance.
St Hubert's Inn, Catawba. E E Pott.
Summerrow House, Newton, B J Summerrow.

LAWYERS.

Names and Post Offices.

Cilley, Judge C A, Hickory.
Cline, E B, Hickory.
Denny, H C (col), Hickory.
Huffham, T M, Hickory.
Jordan, Samuel H, Conover.
Lawrance, M E, Newton.
Lynch, A P, Newton.
McCorkley, George, Newton.
McCorkle, M L, Newton.
Self, W A, Hickory.
Thornton, M E, Hickory.
Witherspoon, L L, Newton.

MANUFACTORIES.

Kinds, Post Offices and Proprietors.

Blacksmithing, Hickory, P C Coons.
Blacksmithing, Jug Town, John Bullinger.
Blacksmithing, Sparkling Catawba Springs, D Haynes.
Blacksmithing, Jug Town, Emanuel Speagle.
Blacksmithing, Jug Town, Geo Wilson.
Black-mithing, Catawba, Fred Wike (col).
Building and Contracting, Hickory, J Worth Elliott.
Building Material, Hickory Mfg Co, A A Shuford, pres: G C Bonniwell, supt,
Building and Contracting. Jug Town, A Baker.
Building and Contracting, Sparkling Catawba Springs, Seth Baker.
Building and contracting, Claremont, Martin Hoke.
Building and Contracting, Newton. A H Sherrill.
Building and Contracting, Hickory, A D Elliott.
Building and Contracting, Hickory, Killian & Whitener.
Building and Contracting, Hickory, J C Fry.
Carriage and Buggy, Hickory, A S Abernethy.
Carriage and Buggy, Conover, J Balch.

| CATAWBA COUNTY. | CATAWBA COUNTY. |

Catawba River Lumber Co, Geo E Worey, pres; L S Lerch, vice-pres; Frank R Whiting, treas; Wm S Whiting, sec; capital, $50,000.

Coopering, Sparkling Catawba Springs, Monroe Reinhardt.

Coopering, Sparkling Catawba Springs, John Hynes.

Coopering, Sparkling Catawba Springs, Adam Hynes.

Cotton (Granite Shoal), Monbo, Turner Bros.

Cotton (Long Island), Catawba, Brown & Co.

Cotton (Newton Cotton Mills), Newton, Heath Bros.

Foundry, Hickory, Ellis & Robinson.

Foundry, Newton, Fisher & Pangle.

Furniture, Hickory, E & J E Heathcock.

Hickory Novelty Co, J A Lentz.

Maiden Cotton Mills, Maiden, L A Carpenter, pres.

Marble Yard, Newton, Geo E Coulter.

Millwrighting, Catawba, J H Irvin.

Millwrighting, Catawba, John Irvin.

Millwrighting, Catawba, J W Irving.

Millwrighting, Newton, A W Wilson.

Millwrighting, Hickory, J C Fry.

Millwrighting, Hickory, G C Bonniwell.

Plug Tobacco, Hickory, N Martin.

Providence Cotton Mills, D M Carpenter, pres.

Saddles and Harness, Newton, L Plonk.

Saddles and Harness, Newton, G W Lowe.

Saddles and Shoes, Hickory, Seagle Bros.

Saddles and Harness, Hickory, S A Abernethy.

Sash, Doors and Blinds, Newton, Finger & Dakin.

Shingles, Hickory, G M Whitener.

Shoes, Hickory, R N Harris.

Shuttle Block and Spoke and Handle, Newton, —— Parmalee.

Stoneware, Jug Town, Wade Johnson.

Stoneware, Jug Town, Henry Ritchie.

Stoneware, Jug Town, Thos Ritchie.

Stoneware, Jug Town, Frank Smith.

Tannery, Roseman, Hoke Bros.

Tannery, Sherrill's Ford, Gil Beaty.

Tannery, Roseman, W H Rocket.

Tannery, Hickory, A S Abernethy.

Tannery, Hickory, Geitner & Co.

Tannery, Catawba, John Smith.

Tannery, Jug Town, E F & R O Ramsaur.

Tannery, Jug Town, Reinhardt & Co.

Tannery, Newton, M J Rowe.

Union Cotton Mills, Maiden, D M Carpenter, pres.

Wagons, Hickory, Piedmont Wagon Co, E B Springs, pres; H C Dixon,

sec; H D Abernethy, treas; G H Geitner, mgr.

Wool Carding, Jug Town, Mosteller & Warlick.

MERCHANTS AND TRADESMEN.

Names, Post Offices, Lines of Business.

ARNT.

| Arnt, J M & Son, | G S |

BANDY.

| Bandy & Son, | G S |

CATFISH.

| Huitt, J H C, | G S |

CATAWBA.

Alley, A S,	G S
Boggs, A C,	Agr Implements
Drum, P B & Son.	G S
Erwin & Pitts,	Cotton Gin
Little, J D,	G S
Long, J W & Co,	G S
Massey, W F	Mill and Cotton
McNeil & Murray,	Millers
Pitts, J H,	G S
Reid, C A & Co,	G S
Smith, John J,	Tanner
Weisenfeld, J,	G S

CHRONICLE.

Dellinger, A C,	G S
Killian & Beal,	G S
Mullin, James,	G S

CLAREMONT,

Holler, Carpenter & Co,	G S
Setzer Bros,	G S
Sigmon Bros,	G S
White, W F,	G S

CONOVER.

Cline, W L,	Gro
Hunsucker, J,	G S
Isenhour, Cline & Co,	G S
Simmons, Robt S	Confec
Smith, P F,	G S
Smyre, Mrs C E,	Confec
Yount, J A,	G S
Yount, D McD,	Drugs

COOK.

| Brittain, ——, | G S |

CROSSING.

Hoke, W A,	G S
Holler, J H,	G S
Kelly, J D,	G S

FLEMING.

| Harnell & McCaul, | G S |

HICKORY.

Abernethy & Whitener,	Livery Stables
Abernethy & Whitener,	G S
Allen & Leonard.	G S
Bost & Co,	Butchers and Grocers
Bowles & Dall,	G S

CATAWBA COUNTY.

Bonniwell & Daughter, Architects
Clay, Miss Rosa, Dressmaker
Crouse, Rev A L, Insurance Agent
Clinard, F A, Insurance Agent
Deitz, F L, Barber
Deitz, J C, Barber
Denny, H C (col), Barber
Flanagan & Son, G S
Field, T E, G S
Groves, Chas A, Insurance Agent
Haithcock & Co, Furniture and Undertakers
Hall, J G, Insurance Agent
Hall, George, G S
Hass, H S, Foreman Paint Dep't Piedmont Wagon Co
Hay, L G & Son, Insurance Agents
Huffman, W P, Postmaster
Ingold & Johnson, Hardware
Johnson, R W, Agricultural Implements
Jones, W F, Foreman Wood Dep't Piedmont Wagon Co
Lawrence, J M, Jeweler
Little, J R, G S
Martin, J C, Merchant Tailor
Martin, J C, Clothing
Pope, J D, Butcher and G S
Reid, W X, Telegraph Operator
Roseboro, Miss Mary, Milliner
Royster, O M, Druggist
Seagle Bros, Shoes
Settlemyre, J G, Confections
Shuford & Whitener, G S
Shuford Hardware Co, Hardware
Shuford, E L, G S
Shuford & Setzer, G S
Sigmon, A Y, G S
Sigmon, W H, in charge of Lumber Dep't Piedmont Wagon Co
White, C M, Confections
Whitener, L S, Foreman Blacksmith Dep't Piedmont Wagon Co

JACOB'S FORK.

Blackburn, W H, Confections
Brittain, D M, D G
Props: Absalom, G S
Ramsour, E F & Son, G S

KEEVERSVILLE.

Heffner, A, G S
Keisler, J J, G S

LOUISE.

Shuford, D H, G S and Mill

MAIDEN.

Boyd, D M, G S
Gall, C C, G S
Robb, J F & Co, G S

MONBO.

Brown, O & Co, G S
Brown, James (near), G S
Monbo Mfg Co, G S
Turner & Wilson, G S

MULLGROVE.

Brittain, D M, G S

CATAWBA COUNTY.

NEWTON.

Abernethy, T R, Drugs
Carpenter, D J & Bro, G S
Corpening, A M & Co, Livery Stables
Coulter, G E, Marble
Finger, J F, Machine Shops
Foil, Mrs E F, Millinery
Gaither, W B, Furniture
Gaither, J R, G S
Garvin, J A, Racket Store
Harwell, John F, G S
Hardister, J W, Jeweler
Jones, M F, G S
Kirchner, Jacob, Cigars
Logenour, P F, Dentist
Lowe, W L, Musical Instruments
Lowe, George W, Saddles and Harness
Marlowe, W H, Tinner and Painter
Moose, D F, Agricultural Implements
Murray, J M & Son, Grocer
Newton Hotel Co, Co-partnership
Newton Hardware Co, Co-partnership
Plonk, Levi, Harness and Confections
Roseborough, Miss Mary, Millinery
Setzer, L L, Grocer and D G
Shelton, H D, Grocer
Smith, J A, Drugs
Smith & Haywood, Drugs
Smyre, Rhyne & Co, G S
Warlick, George A, Agricultural Implements
Wood, J L, Grocer
Zount & Shrum, G S

OXFORD FORD.

Smith, J M, G S
Smith & Little, G S

PENELOPE.

Mayo, R P, G S

PLATEAU.

Kisler, J J, G S
Shuford, C P & Bro, G S

RUDISILL.

Rudisill & Hoffman, G S

SHERRILL'S FORD.

Connor, L T & Co, G S
Sherrill, E L & Son, G S

SPARKLING CATAWBA SPRINGS.

Elliott, Dr E O, Hotel

TERRELL.

Connor, T F, G S

YODER.

Yoder, F A, G S
Yoder, A A, Depot and Ex Agt

MINES.

Kinds, Post Offices and Proprietors.

Alum, Hickory, M Lawrence.
Garnet, Hickory, J A Martin.

CATAWBA COUNTY.

Gold, Newton, G W Setzer.
Gold, Newton, Lanier's estate.
Gold, Maiden, D M Carpenter.
Gold, Hickory, Menzi, Crowel & Co.
Gold, Mountain Creek, Shuford, Mc-
    Corkle & Barringer.
Gold, Catwba, Williams & Tewkes-
    bery.
Gold, Sherrill's Ford, John Holdclaw's
    heirs.
Gold, Sherrill's Ford, Perkin Robin-
    son's heirs.
Gold, Newton, Noah Barringer.
Gold, Catawba, W A Sweet.
Gold, Catawba, M Rufty.
Gold, Mountain Creek, M A Sigmon.
Iron, Hickory, Shuford Hardware Co.
Iron, Drumsville, J W A Paine's estate.
Iron, Newton, Noah Barringer.
Iron, Hickory, William Hall.
Lime, Catawba, Mrs M B Trollinger.
Mica, Lincolnton, Northern Company.

MILLS.

Kinds, Post Offices and Proprietors.

Corn, Catawba, P Edwards.
Corn, Sparkling Catawba Springs, E
    O Elliottr.
Corn, Newton, M Huitt.
Corn, Hickory, J A Whitener.
Corn, Catawba, W Setzer.
Flour, corn and saw, Sparkling Cataw-
    ba Springs, E O Elliott.
Flour, corn and saw, Jacob's Fork,
    David Ramseur.
Flour and corn, Newton, Henry Setzer.
Flour and corn (roller mill), Newton,
    S Smyre.
Flour and corn, Roseman's, D Rose-
    man's heirs.
Flour and corn, Jacob's Fork, Reuben
    Yoder.
Flour and corn, Hickory, Mrs Junius
    Rowe.
Flour and corn, Catawba, R McKinsie
    & Murray.
Flour and corn (roller mills), Newton,
    J H McLeland.
Flour and corn, Newton, Rhyne, Houk
    & Co.
Flour and corn, Hickory, Lyerly &
    Suttlemyer.
Flour and corn, Catawba, Conner & Co.
Flour and corn, Conover, Shell, Her-
    man & Co.
Flour and corn, Plateau, Hudson,
    Ford & Co.
Flour and corn, Catawba, L L James.
Flour and corn, Jacob's Fork, Ramseur
    & Love.
Flour and corn, Hickory, Mrs L Rowe.
Flour and corn, Oxford's Ford, Hedrick
    & Son.

CATAWBA COUNTY.

Flour and corn, Hickory, Phœnix Mfg
    Co.
Flour and corn, Monbo, W T Massey.
Flour and corn. Sparkling Catawba
    Springs, T J Wagoner.
Lumber and flour, Hickory, Phœnix
    Mfg Co.
Roller-flour, Catfish, Hewitt & Co.
Roller-flour, Claremont, J W Setzer.
Roller-flour and corn, Newton, Newton
    Roller Mill Co.
Roller-flour and corn, Hickory, A Y
    Sigmon.
Saw, flour and corn, Hickory, Link,
    McCombs & Co.
Saw (steam), Hickory, A Y Sigmon.
Saw, Conover, Shell, Hermon & Co.
Saw, Catawba, W Setzer.
Saw, Hickory, Fry & Rowe.
Saw, Hickory, Bumgarner & Wagoner.
Saw, Sherrill's Ford, John Gabriel.
Saw, Sparkling Catawba Springs, E O
    Elliott.
Saw, Clineville, M Hunt.
Saw, Jug Town, Hudson & Wyant.
Saw, Hickory, Geo Whitener.
Saw, Catawba, Grim & Coulter.
Saw, Newton, Wilson & Robertson.
Saw, Oxford's Ford, Hedrick & Co.
Steam corn, Sherrill's Ford, E L Sher-
    rill.

PHYSICIANS.

Names and Post Offices.

Abernethy, Henry, Hickory.
Abernethy, W L, Hickory.
Baker, R B, Hickory.
Cambell, J R, Newton.
Elliott, E O, Sparkling Catawba
    Springs.
Falls, B F, Newton.
Foard, Fred T. Jug Town.
Johnson, J T, Hickory.
Klutz, P J, Maiden.
Lattimore, J L, Maiden.
Little, J B, Newton (dentist).
Long, Walter, Catawba.
Marler, W A, Hickory (dentist).
McCorkle, J M, Newton.
Ramsey, W B, Hickory (dentist).
Sherrill, J A, Mountain Creek.
Whiteside, B F, Hickory.
Whiteside. J C, Newton.
Wilson, W E, Sherrill's Ford.
Yount, D McD, Conover.

SCHOOLS.

Names, Post Offices and Principals.

Academy, Penelope, C M Murchison.
Academy, Maiden.
Academy, Plateau. Chas Long.
Catawba College (male and female),
    Newton, J C Clapp, D D, Pres.

CATAWBA COUNTY.

Catawba Valley Academy, Catawba, Prof —— Ridge.
Claremont College (female school), Hickory, Rev. Joseph L Murphy, A M, President.
Concordia College, Conover, Rev W H T Daw.
Female School, Hickory, Mrs J B Beard, Principal.
High School for Boys, Hickory, Rev J A Ramsey, Principal.
Lenoir College, Hickory, Rev R A Yoder, President.
Primary School, Hickory, Miss Teague.
Public School (col), Hickory, C O Crowell.
St Paul Lutheran Seminary (male and female), Hickory, Rev H R G Doermann, Rev F H Patzer, S M Honrick.
Public Schools—white, 75; colored, 19.

LOCAL CORPORATIONS.

Catawba Agricultural Association, Newton, H A Setzer, Secretary.
Catawba County Bank, W C Kenyon, Cashier; $25.000 capital.
First National Bank of Hickory, A A Shuford, President; —— Kenzies, Cashier; A H Crowell, Teller; capital stock, $50,000; surplus, $5,300.
Hickory Electric Co, Hickory; A A Shuford, President; J A Martin, Manager; capital stock, $12,000.
Knights of Honor, Newton.

CATAWBA COUNTY.

Knights of Honor, Hickory.
Knights of Pythias, No 54, Hickory; J A Ramsey, C C; J A Martin, V C; W X Reid, K R of S.
Lodge No 49, I O O F, Newton; Jas A Smith, N G; B J Summerrel, V G; J F Herman, Secretary; M S Deal, Treasurer.
Masonic Lodge, Hickory, No 343, at Hickory, J W Shuford, W M; time of regular communication, Monday evening before full moon, June 24th and December 27th.
Masonic Lodge, No 248, Newton, S L Rhyne, W M; A A Wood, Secretary.
Newton Roller Mill Co, Newton; G A Warlick, President.
Piedmont Wagon Co, Hickory; J D Hall, President; H C Dixon, Secretary; H D Abernethy, Treasurer; Capital, $100 000; capacity 12 wagons per day.

NEWSPAPERS.

College Visitor, Newton.
Mercury, Hickory (Populist weekly), J J F Click, editor.
Newton Enterprise (democratic weekly), F M Williams, editor.
Press and Carolinian, Hickory; Hickory Printing Company, publishers, (weekly, Democratic). M E Thornton, editor.

THE GUTHRIE HOUSE,

J. B. GUTHRIE, Proprietor.

SILER CITY, NORTH CAROLINA.

New Building, Nice Rooms, Good Meals Neatly Served. Hotel pleasantly and and conveniently located about one hundred yards south of the depot.

Attentive Servants. Nice Sample Rooms.

LOANING AND DISCOUNT HOUSE

—— OF ——

Box E. ISAAC H. SMITH, Newbern, N. C.

LOANING AND DISCOUNTING A SPECIALTY.

CHATHAM COUNTY.

AREA, 800 SQUARE MILES.

POPULATION, 25,413, WHITE, 17,214; COLORED, 8,799.

CHATHAM COUNTY was organized in the year 1770, and named after the celebrated English statesman, William Pitt, Earl of Chatham.

PITTSBORO, the county seat, is 33 miles southwest of Raleigh. Population, 588.

Surface—This county is undulating, some parts almost approaching mountainous. The uplands are susceptible of a high state of cultivation. The valleys along the streams are rich.

Staples—Corn, cotton, wheat, oats, rye, tobacco, potatoes, peas, grasses and nearly every kind of vegetable, and large quantities of butter, chickens and eggs.

Fruits — Apples, peaches, pears, plums, apricots, melons and berries.

Timbers—Oak, hickory, pine, gum and ash.

Water-power—There is an abundant water-power. Haw river enters the county at its northwestern boundary, and passes diagonally across, affording at almost every mile the finest water-power in the State. Deep river, running through the western and southern portions of the county, and Rocky river through the centre, afford a series of water-powers unsurpassed. In fact, it is believed that the water-power of Chatham county is superior to that of the whole State of Connecticut.

	POP.		POP.
Moncure,	100	Riggsbee's Store,	
Mt. V. Springs,	100		40
Mud Lick,	20	Roscoe,	20
Ore Hill,	100	Rose,	25
Osgood,	100	Rosewood,	30
Paschal,	25	St Lawrence,	135
Patmos,	—	Sandy Grove,	35
Pedlar's Hill,	20	Siler City,	1,000
Peoples,	20	Silkhope,	25
Pittsboro (C H),		Simmon Grove,	25
	588	Stork,	20
Pluck,	25	Sylvester,	30
Providence,	50	Tillman,	50
Rainbow,	20	Truth,	15
Rialto,	40	Tysor Mills,	20
Richmond,	75	Waldo,	30
Rives' Chapel,	50	Williams' Mills,	50

COUNTY OFFICERS.

Clerk Superior Court—R H Dixon.
Commissioners—C R Scott, chmn; W. T Williams, D Y White.
Coroner—Dr H T Copin.
Register of Deeds—J T Paschal.
Sheriff and Treasurer—J J Jenkins.
Solicitor Fifth District—W P Bynum.
Surveyor—J W Strowd.
Standard Keeper--Wm Haithcock.
Public Administrator—W N Straughan
County Examiner—A H Merritt.
Board of Finance—A H Perry, chmn; Jas B Atwater, E W Atwater.

TOWNS AND POST OFFICES.

	POP.		POP.
Ascend,	—	Goldston,	150
Beaumont,	125	Good,	50
Bellevoir,	80	Gravel Spring,	25
Boaz,	25	Grove,	65
Brayville,	20	Gulf,	200
Brush Creek,	35	Hackney,	25
Bryant,	15	Hadley's Mills,	100
Bynum,	200	Harper's X Roads,	
Cane Creek,	20		40
Colon,	25	Haywood,	100
Corinth,	20	Kimbolton,	30
Cumnock,	25	Lambsville,	50
Ebenezer,	—	Leeward,	10
Egypt Depot,	150	Leota,	30
Elm Grove,	75	Lindhurst,	90
Elmville,	20	Lockville,	100
Evans,	25	Lutterloh,	50
Fall Creek,	20	Manndale,	25
Glenaloon,	25	Merry Oaks,	150
Goff,	25	Millwood,	20

COURTS.

Third Monday before the first Monday in March. Third Monday after the first Monday in September.

TOWN OFFICERS.

SILER CITY—*Mayor*, D J Fox. *Town Marshal*, C K Wrenn. *Board of Commissioners*, F M Hadley, J C Wrenn, A J Jordan. W A Teague, Dr. G A Smith. *U. S. Dep. Marshal*, J M Pugh. *U. S. Com.* — —— Hanner.

TOWNSHIPS AND MAGISTRATES.

Albright's—W T Vestal, Obid Marshburn, Wm B Carter, S P Teague, W A Lineberry, D C Cox, W P Stout, W H Swing (Pittsboro).

Baldwin—W C Mann, L B Farrar, H M Love, A L Lambeth, C W Jus-

CHATHAM COUNTY.

tice, S Durham, P A Ferguson, A W
Norwood (Baldwin).
Bear Creek—J A Caviness, D Y
White, B A Phillips, Laban Moon, Ira
Phillips, S P Willet, R W Kidd, J H
Benner (Pittsboro).
Cape Fear—J E Bryant, John W Utley, J J Womble, Isham Rosser, Mumford Mann, W B Wilkie, A N Yarborough, J A Parham, H C Long (Pittsboro).
Centre—W N Straughn, Robt M
Burns, Wm J Womble, Wm Haithcock, J E Eubanks, W Moore, N S
Webster, P N Foushee, G A Thomas
(Pittsboro).
Gulf—G A Murchison, J M Stinson,
J M Edwards, J H Burk, Oran Hatch,
Geo C Coggin, S G Norwood, R W Taylor (Gulf).
Hadley—Oliver Clark, Thos S Perry,
Gaston Love, Henry Jones, Ira Braxton, Orlando Lindley, Seymour Lewis,
Thos Andrews (Hadley).
Hickory Mountain—Jas N Green, I
T Brooks, J A Alston, N B Dunlap, T
E Carroll, W C Burk, T R Green, E V
Cheek (Pittsboro).
Matthews—W F Dorsett, Jos A Gilaland, Jas M Jordan, J W McAldens,
J P Dark, W W Edwards, S J Perry,
N R Dixon, Jno Adcock (Pittsboro.)
New Hope—W T Edwards, J Q Bryant, W G Lassiter, D M Poe, J M Farrell, jr, T A Bland, M E Mann, J C
Davis, C F Pendergrass (Pittsboro).
Oakland—W H Wicker, R P Womble, E L Tyson, Wm S Gunter, H R
Harward, Carson Johnson, W H Burns,
A W Wicker, J H Tysor (Pittsboro).
Williams—A J Riggsbee, Wm A
Foushee, C S Holloman, B R Hargrove,
J M Riggsbee, H C Williams, M S Horton, Ed Farrington (Pittsboro).

CHURCHES.

Names, Pastors, Postoffices and Denom.

METHODIST.

Asbury—Egypt.
Bryan's Chapel—Lockville.
Buckhorn—Martha's Vineyard, E Pope
Cedar Grove—Snipe's Store.
Chatham Church—Pittsboro, W W
Rose.
Church—Siler City, E C Sell.
Corinth—Goldston.
Ebenezer—Elm Grove.
Haywood Church—Haywood, W W
Rose.
Hickory Mountain, Pittsboro, W W Rose
Mann's Chapel—Bellevoir.
Maroney's—Beaumont.
Merritt's Chapel—Chapel Hill.
Mt. Pleasant—Chapel Hill.

CHATHAM COUNTY.

Mt. Vernon—Silkhope, E C Sell.
Mt. Zion—Pittsboro, W W Rose.
Pleasant Hill—Beaumont, W W Rose.
Providence—Providence, E C Sell.
Providence—Moncure, W W Rose.
Sutphin's Chapel—Sutphin, E C Sell.

METH. PROT.

Centre—Cane Creek.
Church—Siler City, W W Amick.
Fair Mount—Snow Camp.
Flint Ridge—Mud Lick.
Hope—
Piney Grove—Rainbow.
Saplin Ridge—Hadley's Mills.
Springfield—Siler City, W W Amick.

N. METHODIST.

Union Grove—Mud Lick.
Freedom Hill—Sandy Grove.

BAPTIST.

Bear Creek—Bear Creek, O T Edwards.
Bell's—Grove, W A Smith.
Church—Pittsboro, N B Cobb.
Church—Siler City, K C Horner.
Church—Rives' Chapel, R C Horner.
Emmaus—Hadley's Mills, S Gilmore.
Fall Creek—Fall Creek, J L Smith.
Gulf—Gulf.
Gum Spring—Lockville, L R Dixon.
Hickory Mountain—Kimbolton, Stephen Gilmore.
Love's Creek—St Lawrence, O T Edwards.
Lystra—Rialto.
May's Chapel—Tysor's Mills, L R Dixon.
Mineral Springs—Mt Vernon Springs,
W H Lawhorn.
Moore's Chapel—Siler City, O T Edwards.
Mt Gilead—Grove, Manndale S Gilmore.
Mt Olive—
Olive Chapel—New Hill.
Rives' Chapel—Rives' Chapel, K C
Horner.
Rocky River—Mud Lick, J L Smith.
Rocky River—Simmon Grove, G W
Harman.
Wesley Chapel—St Lawrence, West
Marsh (col).

PRIM. BAPTIST.

Big Meadows—Hadley's Mills.
Gilbert's—Bear Creek.

FREE-WILL BAPTIST.

Bethel—Grove.

CHRISTIAN.

Antioch—Pedlar's Hill, J W Hatch.
Centre Grove—Tysor's Mill's, C A
Bone.
Chapel—Lockville.
Hank's Chapel—Pittsboro.
Martha's Chapel—
Mt Zion—Lockville, J D Wicker.

CHATHAM COUNTY.

New Elam—Merry Oaks, Dr W T Herndon.
O'Kelley's—Williams' Mills, Dr W T Herndon.
Pleasant Hill—Mud Lick.

PRESBYTERIAN.

Church—Haywood, —— McIver.
Church—Mount Vernon Springs, W F Thom.
Gulf Church—Gulf, W F Thom.
Mineral Springs—Ore Hill, W F Thom.
Pittsboro—Pittsboro, —— McIver.

FRIENDS.

Brown's Chapel—Hadley's Mills, W W Rose.
Cane Creek—Snow Camp.
Rocky River—Mud Lick.
South Fork—Hadley's Mills.
Spring—Saxapahaw.

EPISCOPAL.

St Bartholomew's — Pittsboro, C T Blane.
St James' Chapel (col)—W A Walker.
St Mark's—Gulf.

A. M. E. ZION.

Gee's Grove—Siler City, David Williams.

MINISTERS RESIDENT.

Names, Post Offices and Denominations.

METHODIST.

Avent, J W, Chalk Level, Harnett Co
Crousen, ——, Bynum's.
Guthrie, T T, Siler City.
Mann, Isaac N. Siler City.
Perry, A H, Kimbolton.
Phillips, John, Harper's X-Roads.
Rose, W W, Pittsboro.
Sell, F C, Siler City.
Stamey, ——. Goldston.
Thompson, W H, Leota.
Dixon, L R, Goldston.

BAPTIST.

Edwards, O T, Mt Vernon Springs.
Ferguson, P A, Lambsville.
Gilmore, Stephen, Goldston.
Horner, K C, Siler City.
Murchison, Duncan, Gulf.
Sears, D R, Siler City.
Smith, J L, Siler City.
Watson, J W, Chapel Hill.

CHRISTIAN.

Dixon, Milo, Snow Camp.
Hatch, J W, Pittsboro.

FRIENDS.

Buckner, Jesse, Hadley's Mills.

PRESBYTERIAN.

Thom, W F, Gulf.

CHATHAM COUNTY.

HOTELS AND BOARDING HOUSES.

Names, Post Offices and Proprietors.

Boarding, Siler City, A D Jordan.
Boarding, Siler City, Geo W Coble.
Boarding, Siler City, Wm Rand.
Boarding, Siler City, A W Jordan.
Boarding, Siler City, Wesley Lutterloh.
Boarding, Siler City, B N Mann.
Burke's Hotel, Pittsboro, Mrs Thomas Cross.
Exline House, Pittsboro, Mrs L R Exline.
Guthrie House, Siler City, J B Guthrie.
Hotel, Mt Vernon Springs, John M Foust.
Jordan House, Siler City, A C Jordan.
Johnson House, Siler City, C E Johnson.
Muse's Hotel, Egypt, J R Burns.
Womble's Hotel, Moncure, B G Womble.

LAWYERS.

Names and Post Offices.

Gilbert, A P. Goldston.
Haynes, R H. Pittsboro.
Ihrie, Harry R. Pittsboro.
Jackson, S S, Pittsboro.
Jackson, J J, Pittsboro.
London, H A, Pittsboro.
Rencher, J G. Pittsboro.
Womack, T B, Pittsboro.

MANUFACTORIES.

Kinds, Post Offices and Proprietors.

Blacksmithing, Goff, F G Laurence.
Blacksmithing, Sandy Grove, W G Murchison.
Blacksmithing, Bear Creek, T Phillips.
Blacksmithing, Bear Creek, J Tilman.
Blacksmithing, Bear Creek, W A Willett.
Blacksmithing, Sandy Grove, A Wills.
Blacksmithing, Goldston, Noah Cheek.
Blacksmithing, Sandy Grove, Owen Cottner.
Blacksmithing, Beaumont, Green & Ferguson.
Blacksmithing, Sandy Grove, Ira Hinshaw.
Blacksmithing, Mt Vernon Springs, J C Causey.
Blacksmithing, Mt Vernon Springs, W F Brooks.
Blacksmithing, Pittsboro, Wm Riddle.
Buggies and repair shops, Moncure, W J Bradshaw & Co.
Carriages and repairs, Pittsboro, A G Drake.

CHATHAM COUNTY.	CHATHAM COUNTY.

Carriages and repairs, Bynum's, Johnson & Neal.

Contracting and build'g, Sandy Gr've, John Coble.

Contracting and build'g, Sandy Grove, Alex Way.

Contracting and build'g, Sandy Grove, W B Hornady.

Contracting and building, Bellevoir, R R Hamlet.

Contracting and building, Lockville, T J Poe.

Contracting and building, Osgood, R B Webster.

Contracting and building, Bear Creek, D F Wilkie.

Coopering, Sandy Grove, Dan Stoner.

Cotton factory, Bynum's, J M Odell Mfg Co.

Cotton gin, Siler City, Hadley, Peoples & Co.

Cotton gin, Siler City, D G Fox & Co.

Cotton yarns, Siler City, Siler City Mfg Co, J C Gregson, manager.

Fruit canning, Silver City, D G Fox.

Fruit canning, Siler City, F M Hadley's Sons.

Furniture, Siler City, Lamb & Co, A A Lamb, manager.

Hats, Mt Vernon Springs, H Q Dowd.

Hats, Ore Hill, W D Andrews.

Hats, Egypt, Moses Barber.

Iron work, Siler City, —— Langley.

Iron and steel, Lockville, American Iron and Steel Co, Wilmington, Del, G G Lobdell, pres.

Iron foundry, Cane Creek, Fairmount Foundry Co.

Iron Foundry, Lockville.

Knitting mill, Pittsboro, W L London, pres; S M Holt, sec and treas.

Millwrighting, Rialto, P M Pearson.

Millwright'g, Sandy Gr've, W F Vestal.

Millwrighting, Sandy Gr've, M E Pike.

Saddles and harness, Sandy Grove, S H Carter.

Saddles and harness, Pittsboro, T B Fowler.

Sappona Iron Works, Ore Hill, S H Wiley (Salisbury).

Sash and blinds, Siler City, W L Hudson & Co.

Sassafras oil, Sandy Grove, John Britt.

Shoes, Haywood, H C Harris.

Shoes, Pittsboro, Mark Farrar.

Shoes, Siler City, John White.

Shuttle blocks, spokes and handles, Pittsboro, B Nooe, Jr.

Tannery, Mud Lick, Zimni Hinshaw.

Tannery, Harper's X Roads, William B Harden.

Tannery, Hadley's Mills, J&J Johnston.

Tannery, Hadley's Mills, H Henderson.

Tannery, Sandy Grove, Jno Overman.

Tannery, Sandy Grove, Peter Stuart.

Tannery, Bear Creek, Sam'l Thomas.

Tannery, Mud Lick, W S Anderson.

Wagons, Kimbolton, J S Campbell.

Wagons, Pittsboro, Isaac Womble.

Wheelwrighting, Haywood, J T Sauls.

Willow works, Pittsboro, B Riddle.

Wool-carding, Sandy Grove, William Thompson.

Wool-carding, Dixon's Mill, H & T C Dixon.

Wool-carding, Manndale, H M Love.

MERCHANTS AND TRADESMEN.

Names, Post-Offices, Lines of Business.

ASCEND.	
Farror, Wilson & Roberson,	G S
BEAUMONT.	
Rives, Geo W,	G S
BELLEVOIR.	
Thompson, J A & Co,	G S
BRYANT.	
Bright, W B & Co,	G S
BYNUM.	
Odell, J M, Mfg Co,	G S
CANE CREEK.	
Teague, D F,	G S
CARBONTON.	
Jones, J R,	G S
Tyson & Willcox.	G S
EGYPT.	
Langdon, Henzzy Coal Mfg Co,	G S
ELM GROVE.	
Council L P,	G S
Council, W L,	G S
FALL CREEK.	
Brewer, W H,	G S
GOFF.	
Barker, Gray & Co,	G S
Lawrence, J H,	G S
GOLDSTON.	
Bynum & Paschal,	G S
Headen, S W.	G S
Smith, G N.	G S
Womble, T N,	G S
GOOD.	
Marks, Jas A,	G S
GROVE.	
Womble, J N,	G S
GULF.	
McIntyre, J W,	G S
McIver, J M,	G S
Palmer, R W,	Drugs
Russell, W G,	G S
HADLEY.	
Henderson, H,	G S
Johnson Joshua,	G S
HARPER'S CROSS ROADS.	
Phillips, N F & Son,	G S

CHATHAM COUNTY.

LAMBSVILLE.

Lambe & Teer,   G S
Williams, T E,   G S

LOCKVILLE.

Barringer, John,   G S
Jordan, S & Son,   G S

MANNDALE.

Love, H M,   G S
McBane, M C,   G S

MERRY OAKS.

Edwards, R J,   G S
Lashley, T R & Co,   G S
Yates & Thomas,   G S

MONCURE.

Bell, John,   G S
Berlin & Bros,   G S
Bradshaw, W J & Co,   G S
Bryan, J E,   G S
Moore, S J,   G S

MUD LICK.

Edwards, Samson,   G S
Teague, T M,   G S
Thompson, W J,   G S

ORE HILL.

Cheek, C C,   G S
Farmers' Alliance Store,   G S
Strowd, O B,   Drugs
White, J J & Son,   G S

OSGOOD.

Yarborough, N G,   G S

PEOPLES.

Sharpe, C G,   G S

PITTSBORO.

Bynum & Headen,   G S
Council, George,   Variety
Council, John L,   Conf. etc
Farrell, F M,   G S
Gilbert, Alpha,   G S
Hearn, A G,   Gro
London, W L & Son,   G S
Poe, O S & Son,   G S
Polkington, G W,   Drugs
Terry, A P,   Saloon

RIALTO.

Stone, H P,   G S

RICHMOND.

Coggins, I P,   G S
Farmers' Alliance Store,   G S

SILER CITY.

Brooks, A L,   Post Master
Crutchfield, Mrs J J,   Milliner
Edwards & Smith,   Drugs
Edwards, W S,   Agt C F & Y V
        R R, Ex Agt and Tel Op
Farmers' Aliance Store,   G S
Hadley, Peoples & Co,   G S
Jordan, J M,   G S
Jordan, A C,   Livery
Lambe & Teague,   G S

CHATHAM COUNTY.

Mann, B N,   Gro
Overman, T F,   -   Photog
Riddle, C D,   G S
Stanley, D H,   G S
Pugh, J M,   Tan Yard
Womble & Wrenn Bros,   G S

TYSOR MILLS.

Hart, William,   G S
Lea, L L,   G S

WILLIAMS' MILLS.

Scott, C R & Son,   G S

MINES.

Kinds, Post Offices and Proprietors.

Coal, Gulf, Kohinoor Coal Co.
Coal, Gulf, Glendon & Gulf Mining
    and Mfg Co.
Coal, Egypt.
Iron and Slate (Richmond, N C), Chat-
    ham Mining Co; J L Boatwright, of
    Wilmington. pres.
Quarry, Egypt, A P Bryan, pres.
Quarry, Gulf, The Buff Brownstone
    Co (Norfolk, Va).
    [The sandstone at Gulf is of superior
    quality, and said to be similar to that
    used in the Fifth Avenue buildings of
    the city of New York. Found in abun-
    dance in this section. Considerable
    gold has been mined in the northern
    part of this county near Cane Creek.
    and in the southern part near Ala-
    mance county.]
White Soapstone Co—valuable quarry
    near Deep river.

MILLS.

Kinds, Post Offices and Proprietors.

Merchant flour and saw, Lockville,
    Heck & Co.
Merchant flour and saw, Richmond.
    Solomon Womble.
Merchant flour and corn, Evans, Had-
    ley & Dixon.
Merchant flour and corn, Green Level,
    M Williams.
Merchant flour and corn, Grove, J W
    Atwater.
Merchant flour and corn, Haywood,
    Davis & Co.
Merchant flour, corn and saw, Pitts-
    boro, W L London.
Merchant flour, corn and saw, Pitts-
    boro, J W Hatch.
Merchant flour and corn, Lambsville,
    O Lamb.
Merchant flour and corn. Hadley's
    Mills, R Love.
Merchant flour and corn, Bynum's, L
    B & C W Bynum.

CHATHAM COUNTY.

Merchant flour, Grove, M & S Baldwin.
Merchant flour, Hadley's Mills, Lnther Baldwin.
Merchant flour, Lockville, Silas Burns' estate.
Merchant flour, Ore Hill, Milo Dixon.
Merchant flour, St Lawrence, Jno Fox.
Merchant flour, Bellevoir, Pace & Peoples.
Merchant fiour, Cane Crek, Henly & Andrews.
Merchant flour, Hadley's Mills, T Love.
Merchant flour, Silkhope, Steph Henly.
Merchant flour, Snow Camp, Sol Dixon.
Merchant flour, Clover Orchard, —— Stockard.
Merchant flour, Snow Camp, J Stewart.
Merchant flour, Snow Camp, M Pike.
Merchant flour, Tyson's Mills, J H Tyson.
Merchant flour, Pittsboro, Stephen Henly.
Merchant flour, Beaumont, R M Green.
Merchant flour, Sandy Grove, H W Dixon.
Merchant flour, Beaumont, Samuel Brooks' heirs.
Merchant flour, St Lawrence, Thomas Dark.
Merchant flour, Mud Lick, Sam Siler.
Merchant flour, St Lawrence, D Murchison & Co.
Merchant flour, Snow Camp, H W & F C Dixon.
Merchant flour, Mud Lick, L T Teague.
Merchant flour, Mud Lick, A Whitehead.
Merchant flour, Mud Lick, Jacob Hobson.
Roller Mill flour, Siler City, Farmers' Alliance, Jordan & Jordan mgrs.
Roller Mill, Siler City, Farmers' Alliance.
Roller Mill, Lockville, John Barringer.
Roller Mill, Gulf, John McIver.
Roller Mill, Bynum, Bynum & Haughton.
Saw, Pittsboro, J W Hatch.
Saw and gin, Ore Hill, Sidney Tally.
Saw and corn, Bear Creek, Jno Bright.

PHYSICIANS.

Names and Post Offices.

Albright, D H, Sandy Grove.
Burns, W M, Beaumont.
Chapin, H T, Pittsboro.
Edwards, J D, Siler City.
Edwards, W S, Staley.
Gattis, R L, Bellevoir.
Hanks, Lucien A, Pittsboro.
Harris, West (dentist), Pittsboro.
Ihrie, J H (dentist), Pittsboro.

CHATHAM COUNTY.

Kirkman, J C, Mt Vernon Springs.
Lassiter, Dowd, Lockville.
Lutterloh, I A H, Hadley's Mills.
Mann, A W, Bellevoir.
McKee, W T, Farrington's Mills.
O'Kelly, James, Williams' Mills.
Palmer, Robert W, Gulf.
Roberson, C N, Grove.
Smith, G A, Siler City.
Smith, Geo W, Siler City.
Stroud, O B, Ore Hill.
Thompson, J, Lambsville.
Ward, E H, Hackney.
Watson, Wm, Rives' Chapel.
Webster, J D (dentist), Siler City.

SCHOOLS.

Names, Post Offices and Principals.

Academy, Osgood.
Academy, Mt Vernon Springs, Rev O T Edwards.
Academy, Sandy Grove.
Haw River High School, Bynum.
Haywood Academy, Haywood.
High View, Riggsbee's Store, R B Lineberry.
Holly Oak Academy, Rialto.
Moore's Chapel St Lawrence.
Music School, Pittsboro, Miss Carrie M Jackson.
Music School, Siler City, Miss Minnie Willis.
Pittsboro Academy, P A B Stalbey.
Primary School, Pittsboro, Miss Bessie Merritt.
Sylvan Academy, Snow Camp, D H Thompson.
Thompson School and Business College, Siler City, J A W Thompson, Superintendent; average enrollment, 180.
Yates' Academy, Green Level.
Public Schools—white 76; colored 42.

TEACHERS.

Names and Post Offices.

WHITE.

Albright, A A, Moffitt.
Atwater, Miss Lizzie B, Lambsville.
Beal, R P, Gulf.
Bray, T B, Fall Creek.
Broxton, James G, Snow Camp.
Brooks, W E, St Lawrence.
Bridges, John P, Lockville.
Burns, J I, Comnock.
Burch, C H, Rialto.
Burns, Miss Berta, Lockville.
Clegg, M B, Pittsboro.
Dismukes, J M, Comnock.
Dixon, N R, Siler City.
Dowd, D J, Tillman.

12

CHATHAM COUNTY.

Edwards, Rev O T,Mt Vernon Springs.
Ellis, Van E, Mt Vernon Springs.
Forrill, Miss S F, Lockville.
Forrill, W O, Pittsboro.
Frazier, D H, Liberty.
Gattis, F N, Bellevoir.
Gilbert, T H, Providence.
Goodwin, J A, Merry Oaks.
Gough, Miss Fannie, Goldston.
Gunter, Miss Myrtie, Merry Oaks.
Hardin, Miss Lucy, Staley.
Harrington, J M, Lonely.
Hargrove, Miss Flora, Williams'⁀Mill.
Hatch, Miss Josie, Pittsboro.
Hinshaw, Miss Ruth, Gravel Springs.
Johnson, J W, Paschal.
Johnson, Miss Ethel, Elm Grove.
Losater, T B, Patmos.
Lineberry, G E, Waldo.
Luther, J O, Merry Oaks.
McManus, W L, Harpers' X-Roads.
Marks, Miss Ellie, Lockville.
Merritt, Miss S E, Pittsboro.
Moore, A M, Liberty.
Morris, I J, Riggsbee.
Murchison, Miss Flora, St Lawrence.
Rives, J R, Goldston.
Richardson, H F, Siler City.
Robinson, R M, Pittsboro.
Sledge, Thos H, Hadley.
Smith, Miss Mary, Siler City.
Snipes, Miss Lucy, Lambsville.
Snipes, W F, Bellevoir.
Street, D M, Ore Hill.
Tally, Hugh, Gulf.
Teague, W E, Simmon Grove.
Thomas, Miss Sue, Richmond.
Underwood, S M, Hadley.
Watson, T M, Rives' Chapel.
Walters, A M, St Lawrence.
Welch, R O, Siler City.
Wicker, E M C, Bryant.
White, T E, Rosewood.

COLORED.

Atwater, J D, Riggsbee.
Beville, Mabel, Lockville.
Bookrum, Fannie E, Apex.
Crecy, Melissa, Gulf.
Cole, B H, Chapel Hill.
Cotten, Sophronia, Bynum.
Cotten, Thos W, Bellevoir.
Craven, G N, Cates' Store.
Dorsett, Loretta, Siler City.
Durham, Lucian, Bynum.
Edwards, R L, Bynum.
Graham, Rev W H, Ascend.
Goldston, Q H, Siler City.
Hackney, Rev L H, Chapel Hill.
Headen, May S, Bellevoir.
Holmes, Q, Gulf.
Jefferson, R J, Lockville.
McCallum, Rev A, Colon.
McDowell, Viola, Pittsboro.
McIver, Alice D, Comnock.

CHATHAM COUNTY.

Miles, Lula, Siler City.
Minter, Annie T, Jonesboro.
Perry, A N, Bynum.
Riggsbee, J H, Riggsbee.
Siler, J F, Siler City.
Sellars, Mittie, Bynum.
Smith, J A, Haywood.
Taylor, Alice, Taylor's Mills.
Taylor, Cora A, Ore Hill.
Turner, Rev B W, Millwood.
Watson, E B, Goldston.
Yates, Dillie B, Elm Grove.

LOCAL CORPORATIONS.

Chatham Co. Branch of the Farmers'
Mutual Fire Ins Association of North
Carolina, Hon M L Holt, pres; W L
London, sec and treas; Dr Wesley
Coble, local agent.
Siler City Lodge, No 403, A F & A M.
I N Mann, master.

NEWSPAPERS.

Chatham Record, Pittsboro, Henry A
London, editor.

FARMERS.

Names and Post Offices.

Ascend—E H Holleman, L J Laurence, A J Wilson, S G Wilson, Aaron Wilson.
Beaumont—G W Brooks, A J Burns, J W Green, T R Green, R N Green, J A Harris, W A Rives, J C Tysor.
Bellevoir—J J Baldwin, A A Burnett, A D Burnett, A Eubanks, J J Fearington, T W Gattis, Elias Harris, A W Norwood, J G Norwood, C T Norwood, Thomas Powell.
Bryant—Amos Bridgers, H C Farrell, J W Goldston, A G Marks, G F Smith, Taylor Wicker, Thos Wicker.
Brush Creek—A G Bray, J M Bray, Wm Brown, N J Dixon, J I Lane, J R Lane, James Myrick, J E Page, E M Welch, H B Welch.
Bynum—J B Atwater, L S Burnett, L B Bynum, C W Bynum, R W Bland, B G Lambeth, Geo Sellars, Wm Williams.
Carbonton—John Jones, H H Palmer, H D Tysor, C W Womble.
Colon—G W Riggsbee, A W Wicker, W H Wicker.
Corinth—Wm Avent, W D Harrington, Wm Laurence, J G Laurence, Jos A Marks.
Egypt—G W Burns, John B Burns, William H Burns, Orrin Dowdy, Jerry Ragland, T W Seagraves, R R Seagraves, John L Tysor.
Elm Grove—D G Beckwith, R J Bo-

ling, L P Council, Sidney Eubanks, S
H Horton, J E Johnson, J S Williams,
L F Williams.

Elmwood—Minter G Johnson, Zeb
McPherson, Blake Wicker.

Evans—J B Burke, Jas Clark, Alex
Cockman, Mark Cockman, W P Hadley, J L Ray, J H Straughan, Isaac
Womble.

Glenaloon — Isham Rosser, Donna
Rosser, Micajah Rosser, J E Yarborough. C M Yarborough, N G Yarborough.

Goff—T J Harrington, G W Harrington, H T Johnson, J H Laurence,
J R Marks, J J Thomas, J W Utley.

Goldston—W T Dowdy, J J Goldston, Thomas Goldston, Basil Gilmore,
O S Johnson, T W Moses, Josiah Tysor, Geo W Smith, Hugh Womble.

Good—W H Cross, James A Marks,
T Y Munns.

Grove—L F Baldwin, M T Baldwin,
N S Clark, J A Council, Mrs Mahala
Copeland, J W Horton, James Horton,
C P Stone, John Williams, Alfonso
Womble.

Gulf—J F Ansley, W H Andrews,
Stephen Moore, John M McIver, O A
Palmer, O D Palmer, J A Palmer, W S
Russell, C E Stewart.

Hackney—J M Burnett, W A Foushee, Rufus Johnson, Wm King, E H
Ward, J H Ward.

Hadley—Henry Clark, W A Cheek,
H D Jones, Columbus Johnson, Joshua
Johnson, A J H Lutterloh, Thos Lut-
terloh, Oliver McMath, M M Perry,
Jesse Richardson, A M Self, Hayes
Smith.

Harper's Cross Roads—Wm An-
drews, B Burroughs, Milo Councilman,
W B Hardin, W M Harper, E W Mc-
Manus, Jasper McManus, Ed Phillips,
B B Phillips, B A Phillips, Geo Smith,
L A Tyson, Emsley Welch, J W Welch.

Haywood—Matthew Drake, W C
Kimball, B A Spence, A F Thomas.

Kimbolton—Augustus Alston, John
Blair, Alfred Ferguson, I B Fergu-
son, James McMath, A H Perry, De
Wi t Roberts.

Lambville—W B Atwater, Matthew
Atwater, Thos Atwater, Luther Bald-
win, Oliver Lambe, Alvis Snipes, B F
Snipes, T A Seer, A J Wilson.

Leewood—Wm Brofford, John Buck-
ner, D S Duncan, Lucius Kirkman,
Alex Lineberry, J W Perry, Frank
Pike, Adam Smith.

Lockville—A T Lambeth, W C Mad-
dox, J A Pitkin, J J Taylor, J W Taylor W C Thomas, W D Thomas, J P
Thomas, G W Thomas, Calvin Wat-

son, Rufus Womble, J J Womble. W
Womack.

Merry Oaks—Richard Cotten, A
Holt, Alfred Johnson, W B Lasater, W
G Lasater, Sion Mitchell, R E Sturdi-
vant, John Sturdivant, J R Thomas,
H H Wilson, B H Wilson, R J Yates.

Moncure—J E Bryan, N McK Bryan,
M M Farrell, Burwell Utley.

Mt. Vernon Springs—H Q Dowd, J
C Dowd, J A Dowd, O T Edwards, J J
White, D Y White, R R Vann.

Mud Lick—Nicholas Bridges, Wm
Buckner, W A Duncan, Sampson Ed-
wards, M Fogleman, Geo Fox, Thos
Hargrove, Zimri Hinshaw, Alfred
Klapp, Sol Nelson, Taylor Pike, Alfred
Pickett, Sam Siler, J R Siler, Wm
Teague, O W Ward.

Ore Hill—Jno Q Carter, Jno Crutch-
field, Jacob Dixon, H K Dorsett, R W
Garreil, John Hanner, Mrs Andrew
Headen, S J Talley, Wm S Webster.

Paschal—A N Andrew, I Andrew, T
F Andrew, jr, A J Clark, N Marshall.

Putmos—J C Davis, R E Harris, Jas
Hearne, T B Lassiter, Marlon Womble.

Peoples—R M Burns, Ruffin Jones,
Paul Perry, H W Peoples.

Pittsboro—J A Alston, Jno B Burns,
J B DeGraffenreid, R S Eubanks, Jos
Eubanks, J M Griffin, J B Harris, W
B Hatch, W H Hatch, L J Houghton,
Lysander Johnson, G W Knight, J P
Thomas, M T Williams, W J Womble.

Pluck—W G Cheek, M T Elmore, J
H Fuquay, W A Glenn, Marion Perry,
Ed Perry, Atlas Perry, W F Stone.

Providence—T W Andrews, T P Andrews, J A Caviness, W H Ellis, Jas
Gilbert, N R Sanders.

Rainbow—L J Fox, W W Jones. Cicero Smith, J W Whitehead, Hiram
Vestal, W H Vestal.

Rialto—J W Atwater, J A W Cheek,
J C Horton, J L Horton, A Morgan, J
C Morgan, H F Stone, A Stone, J
A Stone, Alex Williams, W F Wynne,

Richmond—A B Bright, J R Coggins, G C Cozgins, W L Goldston, Gaston Ivey, S C Johnson, N B Phillips, G
F Phillips, Noah R Phillips, D F Wilkie, Sol Womble.

Riggsbee—L S Andrews, H J An-
drews, E W Atwater, A M Bennett,
J G Bennett, A E Cole, T S Cole, E M
Fearington, J W Goodwin, S L Hern-
don, P M Pearson, W C Pearson, W J
Riggsbee, E J Riggsbee, C C Riggsbee,
J M Williams, E W Williams, B J Wil-
liams,

Rosewood—D B Burns, H R Harwood
J A Knight, ST Womble, B F Williams.

Roscoe—Jno H Dark, Willis Dark,
Aaron Dark, Willis Durham, Seborn

CHATHAM COUNTY.	CHATHAM COUNTY.

Durham, Columbus Justice. Mangum Perry, Henry Petty.

Silk Hope—John D Dorsett, Jas D Dorsett, Isaac Headen, Stephen Henley, Geo W Perry, E V Stranghan.

Siler City—Jasper Bray, R L Dark, D M Fox, O S Hanner, J G Hanner, W C Jones, Abraham Lane, J R Paschal, D F Teague, R C Siler, G W Womble.

St Lawrence—Mrs Rue Alston. John P Dark, L J Dark, Laird Hackney, Hanks Jones, T B Rice.

Stork—J R Bright, W D Bright. Carrow Johnson. W F Johnson, David

Johnson, O W Stedman, J A Williams, Brantley Williams.

Tysor's Mills—N A Gilmore. J A Johnson. J H Tysor, J L Tysor, Jordan Tysor, jr. Calvin Vestal. J W White,

Waldo—H W Johnson, H C Johnson, W A Lineberry, James Stone, H T Terry. Wm Wright.

Williams' Mills—W A Barber. M B Barbee. J F Council, Charles Farrell. C S Holleman. Elbert Herndon, T C Lewter, L M Mason. L T O'Kelly, D F Parrish, C R Scott, Harmon Sears, J F Williams, H C Williams, L J Williams. C L Williams, J D Yates, Wm Yates. Lucien Yates.

CHEROKEE COUNTY.

AREA, 500 SQUARE MILES.

POPULATION, 9,929; White 9,655, Colored 274.

CHEROKEE COUNTY was formed in 1839, from the county of Macon, and was named for the tribe of Indians that formerly occupied the territory of which it forms a part. It is the extreme southwestern county of the State.

MURPHY, the county-seat, was named for Judge Archibald D Murphy; it is 367 miles west of Raleigh, and has a population of 600.

Surface—Hilly, in parts mountainous, rich valleys and splendid water power.

Staples—Corn, wheat, oats, rye, barley, buckwheat, tobacco, medicinal herbs, grass and live stock. As a grazing county it is one of the finest in the State.

Fruits — Apples, peaches, pears, melons and the small fruits.

Timbers—Oak, hickory, pine, poplar, walnut, chestnut and wild cherry.

Minerals—Gold, silver, iron, lead, manganese, corundum, mica, marble,

TOWNS AND POST OFFICES.

	POP.		POP.
Andrews,	60	Nottla,	—
Ballew,	—	Ogreeta,	—
Coalville,	—	Patrick,	—
Cobbs,	—	Peach Tree,	—
Culberson,	150	Persimmon	
Grape Creek,	—	Creek,	—
Hanging Dog,	—	Postell,	—
Hiwassee,	—	Ranger,	—
Hothouse,	—	Suit,	—
Kinsey,	—	Tomatola,	—
Letitia,	—	Turtletown,	—
Mamie,	—	Unaka,	—
Marble,	—	Vesto,	—
Murphy,	600	Wehutty,	—
Nina,	—	Wolf Creek,	—

COUNTY OFFICERS.

Clerk Superior Court—D L Watts.
Commissoners — R Lewis Jervar; chairman; A H Sudderth, H S Hayes.
Coroner—Jas Boyles.
Register of Deeds—T C McDonald.
Sheriff—S W Davidson.
Solicitor Twelfth District—Jas M Moody.
Surveyor—Hull Lovinggood.
Treasurer—Thos Payne.
County Examiner— ———.

COURTS.

Eleventh Monday after first Monday in March, and sixth Monday after first Monday in August.

TOWN OFFICERS.

MURPHY—*Mayor*, R L Cooper.
Commissioners—R H Hyatt, Ben Mayfield, J W Patton, S H Hughes, R A Akins, A A Fain.

TOWNSHIPS AND MAGISTRATES.

Beaverdam—G J Crow, T N Bates. J T Griffin, H T Hortense (Beaverdam).

Hothouse—W H Phillips, J M Gaddis, Joel Simmons, D Mack Watson, Stephen Lefeners (Hothouse).

Murphy—S W Davidson, W M Nest, T N C Lovinggood, Jno B Standridge, D W Deweese (Murphy).

Nottla—John Anderson, John Cobb, J C Deweese, Arnett Shields (Nottla).

Shoal Creek—J Leadford, P E Nelson, R L Johnson, Warren Allen, J P Burnett (Murphy).

Valley Town—Joseph Kinsey, John Parkee, J L Welch, Stephen Porter, W B Parker (Valley Town).

CHURCHES.

Names, Post Offices, Pastors and Denom.

BAPTIST.

Church—Hanging Dog,——Tredaway.
Church—Murphy, G W Lowing.
Church—Peach Tree,——Tredaway.
Marble Sprin—Marble,—— Tredaway.

METHODIST.

Church—Peach Tree.
Harshaw's Chapel—Murphy.
Whitaker's—Valley Town.

MINISTERS RESIDENT.

Names, Post Offices and Denominations.

BAPTIST.

Dweese, E, Cutherson.
Tredaway, Peach Tree.

METHODIST.

James, C M, Peach Tree.
Patten, Dr J W, Murphy.

CHEROKEE COUNTY.	CHEROKEE COUNTY.

HOTELS AND BOARDING HOUSES.

Names, Post Offices and Proprietors.

Boarding House, Murphy, M L Brittain.
Boarding House, Murphy, Lillie Hullard.
Cottage Park, Murphy, J D Abbott.
Fair View, Murphy, Wm Beal.
Hotel, Andrews', Sam Bryan.
Hotel, Cutherson, J L Ownby.
Hotel, Valley Town, Mrs Walker.
Hotel Hennesa, Murphy, J H Hennesa.
Murphy Hotel, Murphy, Samuel Henry.
Murphy Hotel, T C Dickey.

LAWYERS.

Names and Post Offices.

Axley, Felix P, Murphy.
Bell, M W, Murphy.
Cooper, R L, Murphy.
Cooper, J W, Murphy.
Manney, L E, Murphy.
Posey, Ben, Murphy.

MANUFACTORIES.

Kinds, Post Offices and Proprietors.

Blacksmith and wheelwright, Beaver, J Thompson.
Blacksmith and wheelwright, Tomatola, W B Sales.
Blacksmith and wheelwright, Beaver, Columbus Roberts.
Blacksmith and wheelwright, Murphy, James Palmer.
Blacksmith and wheelwright, Beaver, D T Davis.
Brickmason, contracting and building, Murphy, J L Wilson.
Brickmason, contracting and building, J F Patterson.
Contracting and building, Beaver, W G W Roberts.
Contracting and building, Murphy, W A Turnbull.
Contracting and building, Murphy, John Rector.
Contracting and building, Murphy, J J Phillips.
Contracting and building, Murphy, W Mingus.
Contracting and building, Murphy, John Leatherwood.
Coopering, Beaver, E H Nelson.
Coopering, Tomatola, E Arrowood.

MERCHANTS AND TRADESMEN.

Names, Post Offices and Line of Business.

ANDREWS.

Walker, W P,   G S

Whisenhunt, D W,   G S
CULBERSON.
Dickey, J B & Son,   G S
Owensby, J L,   ——
KINSEY.
Axley, A W,   G S
MARBLE.
Smith, A B,   G S
MURPHY.
Aikin, R A,   G S
Axley, A W,   ——
Allott, J D,   Hotel
Cooper & Co,   G S
Cooper & Woodburg,   Lumber
Carter, W J,   G S
Dickery, A B,   Livery
Dickery, Mrs Nettie,   Hotel
Elliott & Woods,   G S
Gurley & Co,   G S
Hall, R P (near),   G S
Hennesa, Mrs J H,   Hotel
Hyatt, R H,   Furniture and G S
King, M C,   Drugs
Lovinggood & Deweese, G S and Drugs
Palmer & Letzer,   Wagon M'f'rs
Wood & Gregg,   Hardware
NOTLA.
Dicky, J M,   G S
OGRETTA.
Griffin, W A,   G S
PEACH TREE.
Brittain, W P,   G S
King & McGuire,   G S
RANGER.
Dickey, John,   G S
Dickey, R R,   G S
VEST.
Vest, T W,   G S

MINES.

Kinds, Post Offices and Proprietors.

Copper is found in various parts of the county. Gold and silver are found in many places.
Marble and cotton rock are also found in the county, a ledge of the latter running entirely across it.
No 6, gold, one mile north of Murphy.
Gold, 8 miles east of Murphy, J Abernethy.
Gold, 10 miles east of Murphy, —— Parker.
Iron, 10 miles south of Murphy, Miss E Walker.
Iron, Hanging Dog Cr'ek, Mercer Fain.
Iron, Hanging Dog, Creek, Jos. Henson.
Iron, 8 miles north of Murphy, H & N Lovingood.

CHEROKEE COUNTY.

Iron, 5 miles south of Murphy, John Hartness.
Iron, 5 miles northeast of Murphy.
Iron and marble, 7 miles southeast of Murphy.
Lead, Murphy, Valley River Mining Company.
Lead, Murphy, E P Kinsey.
Marble quarry, 4 miles southwest of Murphy.
Muddy Creek, gold, east of Murphy.
Paint mine, 7 miles east of Murphy.
Talc and soapstone, 4 miles southwest of Murphy.

MILLS.

Kinds, Post Offices and Proprietors.

Corn, Valley Town, M Tatum.
Corn, Vest. T W Vest.
Corn, Turtletown, John Shearer.
Corn, Turtletown, Joseph Green.
Corn, Turtletown, R D Kilpatrick.
Corn, Valley Town, S Whitaker.
Corn, Peach Tree, D M Howell.
Corn, Hanging Dog, C C Gentry.
Corn, 8 miles north of Murphy, J W Patton.
Corn, 10 miles south of Murphy, Miss E Walker.
Corn, one mile northeast of Murphy, J C Axley.
Corn, 5 miles northeast of Murphy, J Kinsey.
Corn, 12 miles northeast of Murphy, Martin Parker.
Corn, 18 miles west of Murphy, A T Johnson.
Corn and saw. 5 miles south of Murphy, John Hartness.
Corn and wheat, Peach Tree, John McGuire.
Grist, Ogretta, G G Whitcomb.
Grist, Hothouse, M C King.
Grist, Hothouse, G W Walker.
Grist, Brasstown, George Hampton.
Grist, Hothouse, Isaac Rise.
Saw, Persimmon Creek, Robt Ingram.

PHYSICIANS.

Names and Post Offices.

Abernethy, Jacob F, Murphy.
Castell, ——, Andrews.
Henry, S B, Murphy.
Hughnay, S C, Murphy.
Mayfield, B F, Murphy.
Patton, John W, Murphy.
Walker, C F, Ranger.
Webb, ——, Andrews.
Whitcomb, G G, Ogretta.

SCHOOLS.

Names, Post Offices. and Principals.

Mt Pleasant Academy, Murphy.

CHEROKEE COUNTY.

Public schools: white 45, colored 3.

TEACHERS.

Names and Post Offices.

Cunningham, Mont, Brasstown.
Sherril, Clara, Murphy.
Sneed, Brent, Peach Tree.
Sparks, G S, Suit.
Stuart, Mrs Viena, Murphy.
Lattimer, W A (col.), Murphy.
Lawing, J W, Peach Tree.
Lovingood, James, Hanging Dog.
Mauney, L E, Murphy.
Parker, Jos, Marble.

LOCAL CORPORATIONS.

Cherokee Masonic Lodge. No 145, Murphy; time of meeting: Monday night on or before full moon.
Notla Masonic Lodge, No 312, Notla; time of meeting: third Saturday in each month at 10 o'clock A M.

NEWSPAPERS.

Cherokee Scout (weekly). Murphy, J S Meroney, Sr, and Dan Towns, editors and props.
Murphy Bulletin, Murphy, A A Campbell, editor.

FARMERS.

Names and Post Offices.

Beaver—T H Barton, Z T Barton, T A Bell, H G Burgess. T M Bryson, S Bryson, Wm Bryson. G Burgess, Wm Burgess, B L Cook, Jas Davis, A J Evans, John Evans, Chas Hall, D C Linderman, Riley Martin, J M Martin, L D McNabb, D Murphy, L P Payne, H Payne, Curtis Rodman, Wm Roberts, A J Roberts, S N Thompson, S A Winkler.

Hothouse—Isham Gaddis, E M Deweese, W G Payne, W H Phillips.

Murphy—J H Adams, Wm Arrowwood, G W Barker, T Barnard. W Beal. J B Brindle, P V Britton, Jesse Combs, S W Davidson, Wm Donaldson, W P Farmer, W E Furguson, Wm Fruit, Eliza Fruit, B B Harper, R A Harper, A M D Harshaw, H S Hayes, J H Hennessa, D M Howell, S H Hughes, J C Huskins, F M Hyde, B F Johnson, W H H Johnson, Augustus Johnson, W G W Johnson, E P Kiscaid, R D McCombs, G S McGuire, Thos McGuire, F W McKarney, R B Mannery, Remus Mannery, B B Meroney, Richard Moore, J D Parker, P M G Rhea, Wm Rogers, H W Rogers,

CHEROKEE COUNTY.

John Sneed, J H Stalcup, A E Sudderth, D T Sudderth, A H Sudderth, A G Vaughan, Wm Waldrop, S C Wright, Sidney Zimmerman.

Nottla—M E Brown, V G Ditmore, A E Evans, R P Hall, T H Hampton, J A Hartness, S M Hyatt, W W Loudermilk.

Persimmon Creek—Henry Cloutz, B M Collins, E M Deaver, John Hedrick, John Johnson, Jackson Ledford, T J Payne, W B Sutton.

Ranger—G W Akin, E B Akin, Robt Bruce, D M Collins, Lafayette Cox, Z T Ditmore, Willis Ditmore, A E Evans, W C Evans, T M Evans, Thos Hughes, A J Hughes, H B Hyatt, Jno J Johnson.

Suit—G F Burgar, Robt In ram Cain Jenkins, Andy McNabb, Wm Mc-

CHEROKEE COUNTY.

Nabb, Jesse Pate, Johnson Suit, I N Taylor.

Tomatola—S W Davidson, N N Hyatt, M A Hyatt, A J Leatherwood, Jas Rogers, W B Sales.

Turtletown—Neppa Adams, E H Berrong, W F Briant, Edmond McNabb, Theodore Kilpatrick, Washington Ledford, J W Shearer, T J Shearer, D H Shearer, Wm Torrence, J W West.

Valley Town—Ben Adams, Hugh Collett, C N Hickerson, Wm Newman, Willis Newman, Calvin Nichols, W P Palmar, Willis Parker, Willey Phillips, J Piles, Stephen Porter, J M Richardson, H B Stewart, James Tatham, G B Tatham, James Whitaker, Stephen Whitaker, Harrison Whitaker, Lafayette Whitaker, Jas Wright.

Vest—Lafayette Martin, Telman Quinn, R H Reed, Elbert Reed, R W Vest.

CHOWAN COUNTY.

AREA 240 SQUARE MILES.

POPULATION 9,166 ; White 4,010, Colored 5,156.

CHOWAN COUNTY was one of the original precincts granted by Charles II. to the Lords Proprietors, and derives its name from a tribe of Indians that once inhabited the territory.

EDENTON, the county-seat, is situated on the Albemarle Sound, 150 miles east of Raleigh. It was called in honor of Charles Eden, the Royal Governor of the Province in the year 1720. It was settled in the year 1716, and was first called Queen Anne's Creek. Population 2,010. Edenton is connected by railroad with Norfolk, Va.

Surface—Chowan county lies on the east side of Chowan river and extends south to Albemarle sound. Navigation very fine. Soil low, level and rich.

Staples—Cotton, corn, lumber and fish. In proportion to size this is one of the most productive counties of the State.

Fruits—Peaches, grapes, apples, figs, peanuts, etc.

Timbers—Cypress, juniper, ash, gum, long-leaf and rosemary pine, and some others.

TOWNS AND POST OFFICES.

	POP.		POP.
Amboy,	25	Gliden,	25
Barnitz,	40	Rockyhock,	35
Cisco,	20	Ryland,	50
Chowan,	25	Somerset,	10
Edenton		Tyner,	40
(c h),	3,560	Woodley,	—

COUNTY OFFICERS.

Clerk Superior Court—H C Privott.
Commissioners—Frank Wood, chm'n; A J Ward, E F Woff, W P Jones, J C Thompson.
Coroner—Dr T J Haskins.
County Attorney—Pruden & Vann.
Register of Deeds—T D Byrum.
Sheriff—L W Parker.
Solicitor 1st District—W J Leary.
Surveyor— —.
Treasurer—C S Vann.
County Examiner—Rev J E White.
Tax Collectors—D C Byrum and Richard Bunch.

COURTS.

Fourth Monday after first Monday in March and fourth Monday after first Monday in September.

TOWN OFFICERS.

EDENTON—*Mayor*, C S Vann; *Constable*, J W Spruill; *Treasurer*, A L White; *Town Collector*, R F Cheshire; *Councilmen*, W B Shepard, J A Woodard, I B Blount (col.), Isaac Blount (col.).

TOWNSHIPS AND MAGISTRATES.

Edenton—F W Curren, C Torkinton, F A White, Thomas Thompson, T M Small, B F Elliott, J C Warren.

Middle—R Bunch, W T Perry, R B Hollowell (Rockyhock), Isaac Layder (Tyner), W H Elliott, L D Evans (Cisco).

Upper—W C Ward (Ryland), M W Elliott, Edward Forehard (Amboy), W D Deans (Gliden), J S Chapel, Hosea J Lane (Dwight).

Yeopim—Edward Jordan, T W Harris, J E Smith (Edenton), M A Hughes, W E Hassell (Somerset).

CHURCHES.

Names, Post Offices, Pastors and Denom.

BAPTIST.

Ballard's Bridge—Amboy, W B Woff.
Centre Hill—Tyner, Josiah Elliott.
Chapel Hill—Tyner, Josiah Elliott.
Edenton—Edenton, J E White.
Green Hill (col.)—Edenton.
Macedonia—Edenton, J E White.
Warwick—Gliden, A W Burfoot.
Welch's Chapel—Amboy, Luke Elliott.
Yeopim—Edenton, A W Burfoot.

METHODIST.

Centre Hill—Tyner.
Edenton—Edenton, N M Watson.
Evans—Rockyhock.
Skinner's—Tyner.

EPISCOPAL.

St Paul's—Edenton, R B Drane.
St John the Evangelist (col.)—Edenton, W J Herritage (col.).

CATHOLIC.

St Anne's—Edenton.

A. M. E. ZION.

Edenton (col.)—Edenton, O W Winfield.

MINISTERS RESIDENT.

Names, Post Offices and Denominations.

BAPTIST.

Bogart, Dr C P, Edenton.
Tynch, J, Edenton.

CHOWAN COUNTY.

CHOWAN COUNTY.

METHODIST.

Watson, N M, Edenton.

EPISCOPAL.

Drane, R B, Edenton.

A. M. E. ZION.

Overton, E (col.), Edenton.
Winfield, C W (col.), Edenton.

HOTELS AND BOARDING HOUSES.

Names, Post Offices and Proprietors.

Bay View House, Edenton, F A White.
Boarding House, Edenton, —— Jones.
Boarding House, Edenton, Mrs E S Brindley.
Boarding House (col.), Edenton, Harrison Miller (col.).
Boarding House, Edenton, Emeline Dempsy (col.).
Woodward Hotel, Edenton, Mrs Ellen Woodard.

LAWYERS.

Names and Post Offices.

Bond, W M, Edenton.
Leary, W J, Edenton.
Pruden, (W D), Vann (C S) & Pruden, (J N), Edenton.
Wood, Julian, Edenton.

MANUFACTORIES.

Kinds, Proprietors and Post Offices.

Blacksmith and wheelwright, Edenton, George Harris.
Blacksmith and wheelwright, Edenton, I A Harris.
Blacksmith and wheelwright, Edenton, John Sutton.
Boots and shoes, Edenton, W E Burke (col.).
Boots and shoes, Edenton, L Tillery (col.).
Contracting and building, Edenton, Theo Ralp.
Dressed lumber, Edenton, J W Browning, manager.
Shuttle and box factory, Edenton, Browning Mfg Co.
Tinware. Edenton, J H Bell.
Undertaking, Edenton, L F Ziegler.

MERCHANTS AND TRADESMEN.

Name, Post Office, and Line of Business.

AMBOY.

Howell, J T,   G S
Hudson, J N,   G S
Twine, J E,   G S

CISCO.

Evans, Z W,   G S
Nixon, H C,   G S

EDENTON.

Abrams, Sarah,   Dry Goods
Baker, N,   Clothing
Bogue, Mrs M L,   Millinery
Bond & Jones,   Hardware
Bonner, J E,   Gro
Brinkley, E L,   Dry Goods
Brinkley, L L,   Post Master
Burton, Mrs I T,   G S
Bush, A T,   Gro
Byrum, W H,   G S
Byrd, J C,   G S
Coffield, W H,   Gro
Darden, O H,   Fisherman
Dixon, M H,   Gro
Elliott, J M,   Gro and News Dealer
Elliott, W O,   Dry Goods
Elliott, C B,   Gro
Hast, R L,   Gro
Hooper, H D B,   Drugs
Jones, T P,   Gro
Jordan, W E,   Gro
Leary, W I,   Drugs
Maguire, John,   G S
McClenny, Martin,   G S
McCurdy, Mrs M A,   Millinery
Mitchell, A C,   Dry Goods
Moore, L L,   Dry Goods
Moore, Mrs L L,   Millinery
Newman, D,   Dry Goods
Northcutt, J A,   Gro
Norman, E G,   G S
Perry, W T,   G S
Robertson, Thos H,   Drugs
Rosenstein Bros,   Clothing
Stermon, B H,   Dry Goods
Skinner, J M.   Gro
Summerell, T D & Bro,   Gro
Tarkenton, C,   Gro
Woodard, J A,   Gro
Zeigler, L F,   Undertaker and Furniture

GLIDEN.

Ward, A J,   G S

ROCKYHOCK.

Wilson, T I J,   G S

RYLAND.

Ward & Ward,   G S
Ward & Bunch,   G S
Ward & Spivey,   G S

SOMERSET.

Thompson, J,   G S

TYNER.

Chappell, J P,   Gro
Layden, Isaac,   G S

MILLS.

Kinds, Post Offices and Proprietors.

Corn and flour, Cisco, Dr R Dillard.

CHOWAN COUNTY.

Flour, corn and saw, Edenton, D W Raper & Co.

Steam, saw and grist, Edenton, M G Brown, mgr.

Steam, saw, planing and grist, Cisco, B W Eavns.

Steam saw, Ryland, Ward & Spivey.

Steam saw, Edenton, R E Coffield.

PHYSICIANS.

Names and Post Offices.

Bogart, C P (dentist), Edenton.
Cooper, W H (dentist), Edenton.
Dillard, Richard, Edenton.
Haskins, Thos J, Edenton.
McMullin, J H, Edenton.
Winborne, Robt H, Rockyhock.

SCHOOLS.

Names, Post Offices and Principals.

Academy, Edenton, C F Graves, prin.
Private school, Mrs Pattie Finch.
Public school, Edenton, Miss Mary Bell.
Public school (col), Edenton, W J Herritage.
Public schools—white, 19; colored, 13.

LOCAL CORPORATIONS.

Albemarle Steam Navigation Co, A L White, agent, Edenton.
I O O F, No ——
Masonic Lodge, Unanimity No 7; time of regular communication first Tuesday evening, Monday of Court, March and September.
Pease United Lumber Co, Edenton, J A Wilkerson, Superintendent.
The Bank of Edenton, Julian Wood, President; E L Woodard, Vice-President; Geo P Folk, Cashier; capital stock, $25,000.
The Browning Co, Edenton, J W Browning, Treasurer and Manager.

CHOWAN COUNTY.

United States Marine Hospital, port of Edenton, N C, R Dillard, contract surgeon.

NEWSPAPERS.

Fisherman and Farmer, Edenton (Democratic weekly; A H Mitchel, Editor and Proprietor.

FISHERIES AND OWNERS.

Avoca--W B Capehart, Nichols & Bro.

Barnitz—Edward Elliott, W J Holley.

Chowan—John Parrish.

Coleraine—Etheridge & Co, T D Holley, Wilson & Mizzell.

Columbia—John Pinner.

Edenton – John Blair, T B Bland, John C Bond, M F Bond, H A Bond, J C Copeland, Goodwin & Co, Moses Hobbs, Jerry Jones. Kader McLenny, J F Nixon, Ersist Woodard, Richard Wynn, Frank Wood, H G Wood, P L Rea, J K Rea, Charlton & Lipsety, Bond & Jones, F C Mitchel & Co, W Fettrick, A H Ramsey, C W Rea & Co, W C Rea, T H Shepard, J C Warren, J G Wood, J A Woodard, J Hertford, C E Burke, Norman Bros, J J Parrish, Benjamin Hatch.

Mackey's Ferry—Thos Wynn.

Mount Gould--J H Jernigan, George Womble.

Plymouth—W H Hampton.

Rockyhock--J B Ashley, Q Bass & Son, John E Bass, W F Boyce, K S Bunch, R L Bunch, Harrell & Webb, William P Jones, Morgan & Peal, William Nixon, Nixon & Layton, H C Nixon & Bro, Nixon & Goodwin, J W Simpson, Wm Smith, J W White & Co, T I J Wilson, T J Wilson.

CLAY COUNTY.

AREA 160 SQUARE MILES.

POPULATION: 4,297; White 4,155; Colored 142.

CLAY COUNTY is situated in the extreme southwestern portion of the State, and is bounded on the north and east by Macon County, on the south by Georgia, and on the west by Cherokee County.

HAYESVILLE is the county seat, and is 360 miles southwest from Raleigh. Population 150.

Surface—Moderately uneven, valleys rich, and it has abundance of water power.

Staples — Corn, wheat, rye, oats, grass and live stock, tobacco and buckwheat.

Fruits—Apples, peaches, pears, chestnuts, grapes and berries.

Timbers— Hickory, oak, chestnut, wild cherry, etc.

TOWNS AND POST OFFICES.

	POP.		POP.
Belgora,	—	Ledford,	—
Brasstown,	—	Shooting Creek,	35
Elf,	—	Tusquitee,	40
Hayesville,		Twine,	—
(C H),	400	Warne.	—
Irena,	—		

COUNTY OFFICERS.

Clerk Superior Court—T H Hancock.
Commissioners—E G Smith, chairman; W H McClure, J S Carter.
Coroner— ——
Register of Deeds—Geo M Fleming.
Sheriff—J M Johnson.
Surveyor—J W Crawford.
Treasurer—R G Ketron.
Solicitor Twelfth District—Geo A Jones.
County Examiner—J H Chambers.

COURTS.

Tenth Monday after the first Monday in March, and fifth Monday after the first Monday in September.

TOWNSHIPS AND MAGISTRATES.

Brasstown—G W Kinsey, Wm Waldroof, J H'Chambers, J H Green, R E Martin, Jno H Green (Brasstown).
Hayesville—J J Scroggs, E S Curtis, W T Robinson, L L Scroggs, W B Martin, L H McConnell. L H McClure, M L Cleman (Hayesville).

Hiwasse—W S Boone, J C McCrackin, R E Long, A C Thompson, M F Crawford, J A Chambers. W C Ledford, P Tigue (Hiwasse).
Shooting Creek—R W Davenport, J L Burch, N N Rogers C N Penland, J A Davenport. John Patterson (Shooting Creek).
Tusquitee—W P Moore, W H Johnson, J H Byers, W A Parker, J M Moss, W C Wilson, J S Shearer, G A Sellers, G A Moore (Tusquitee).

CHURCHES.

Names. Post Offices, Pastors and Denom.

METHODIST.

Bethel—Shooting Creek, J W Bowman.
Boyles Chapel—Brasstown, J W Bowman.
Church—Hayesville, J W Bowman.
Ledford's Chapel — Hayesville, J W Bowman.
Pleasant Hill—Hayesville, J W Bowman.
Tusquitee—Tusquitee, J W Bowman.

NORTH. METHODIST.

Marshall's Chapel—Shooting Creek.
Old Camp Ground—Elf.

BAPTIST.

Bethabara — Shooting Creek, Marion Morgan.
Bethel—Warne, M H Barker.
Bethesda—Hayesville, J W Reece.
Church—Hayesville, J W Lowing.
Church—Shooting Creek, Marion Morgan.
Fires Creek—Ledford, M H Barker.
Mt Pisgah—Warne, J W Lowing.
Pine Log—Warne, Jefferson Brown.
Pleasant Hill—Elf, W C Standridge.
Tusquitee—Tusquitee, J T Platt.
Shady Grove—Hayesville, J J Kinsey.

PRESBYTERIAN.

Church—Hayesville.

MINISTERS RESIDENT.

Names, Post Offices and Denominations.

METHODIST.

Bowman, J W, Hayesville.
Brooks, J S, Hayesville.
Carter, Isaac, Hayesville.
Curtis, C H. Hayesville.
Ketron, R G, Hayesville.

CLAY COUNTY.

Richardson, S L, Hayesville.

BAPTIST.

Camp, T C, Hayesville.
Deitz, T F, Warne.
Platt, J T Warne.
Prater, F L, Tusquittee.
Reese, J W Warne.

HOTELS.

Kinds, Post Offices and Proprietors.

McClure House, Hayesville, W H Mc
Clure, prop.

LAWYERS.

Names and Post Offices.

Kinnery, M R, Hayesville.

MANUFACTORIES.

Kinds, Post Offices and Proprietors.

Blacksmithing and Wagons, Hayes-
ville, G T Cheek.
Blacksmithing and Wagons, Tusquit-
tee, W H Poteat
Boots and Shoes, Hayesville, O D Price.
Cabinet Making, Hayesville, R M
Webb.
Saddles and Harness, Hayesville, Wm
Angel.
Tannery, Hayesville, J J Scroggs.

MERCHANTS AND TRADESMEN.

Name, Post-office and Line of Business.

BRASSTOWN.

Jenkins, J,   G S

ELF.

Hooper, L J & Son,   G S
Ledford, A B,   G S
Tigue, P N,   G S

HAYESVILLE.

Alexander, J W,   G S
Cherry, J P & Son,   G S
Walker, A M,   G S

WARNE.

Webb & Welsh,   G S

MINES.

Names, Post Offices and Proprietors.

Corundum, Elf, Herman Behr & Co.
Corundum, Elf, Hooper & Skipper.
Corundum, Shooting Creek, A H Isbell
Corundum, Shooting Creek, H S Lucas
Gold, Warne, Wooing & Co.

MILLS.

Kinds, Post Offices and Proprietors.

Corn, Tusquittee, J H Byers.
Corn and saw, Shooting Creek, J M
Galloway.

CLAY COUNTY.

Corn and saw, Ledford, D A Ledford.
Corn, Hayesville, J S Lovin.
Corn, Hayesville, R M Webb.
Corn and Flour, Warne, Platt & Co.
Corn and Flour, Brasstown, Miss Abel
Hyatt.
Corn and Flour, Elf, Penland & Butcher
Corn and Flour, Hayesville, Jno Erwin
Corn and Flour, Hayesville, Brooks &
Co.
Corn and Flour, Hayesville, J P Cherry
& Co.

PHYSICIANS.

Names and Post Offices.

Bristol, W G (Dentist), Hayesville.
Killian, Paul, Hayesville.
Nichols, ——, Warne.
Sanderson, W E Hayesville,
Sullivan, J M, Hayesville.
Thompson, Jno (Dentist), Hayesville.

SCHOOLS.

Names, Post Offices and Principals.

Hayesville Male and Female College,
Hayesville.
No. of Schools—White, 18; colored, 1.

TEACHERS.

Names and Post Offices.

Allison, A O, Hayesville.
Burch, Miss Anns, Tusquittee.
Chambers, John A, Elf.
Chastain, R B, Warne.
Crawford, Wiley, Elf.
Herbert W H, Hayesville.
Hood, John W, Brasstown.
Lunsford, M C, Tusquittee.
Matheson, Miss Laura, Hayesville.
Moore, J V, Tusquittee.
Moore, Miss Ida, Hayesville.
Padgett, Miss Minnie, Hayesville.
Phillips, Prof W H, Hayesville.
Passmore, Bowman Hayesville.
Roy, Miss Mary, Elf.
Smith, Chas L, Elf.
Thomasson, John, Ledford.
COLORED.
Buchanan, A, Elf.
Hurburt, Wm, Hayesville.
Hurburt, Geo W, Hayesville.
Moffitt, Chas, Shooting Creek.
Moore, Iva, Hayesville
Scroggs, Sallie, Hayesville.
Winchester, W J, Hayesville.

LOCAL CORPORATIONS.

Clay Lodge, No 301, A F and A M
Regular Communication, Saturday
on or before full moon, June 24 and
December 27.

CLEVELAND COUNTY.

AREA, 420 SQUARE MILES.

POPULATION, 20,394; White 17,301, Colored 3,093.

CLEVELAND COUNTY was formed in 1841, from Rutherford and Lincoln counties, and derives its name from Col. Benjamin Cleveland, of Wilkes county, who acted an important part in the battle of King's Mountain on the 7th of October, 1780.

SHELBY, the county-seat, is situated 215 miles west of Raleigh, on the Carolina Central Railway and C C R R, and O R & C R R, and has a population estimated at 2,500.

Surface—Hilly, and in places mountainous; well watered by the French Broad river and its tributaries; along these are many rich lowlands. The climate is very pleasant and salubrious; a great summer resort for health.

Staples—Cotton, wheat, corn, oats, grass and live stock. Tobacco grows finely.

Fruits — Apples, peaches, pears, plums, grapes, berries, melons, etc.

Timbers—All the hard woods indigenous to the Piedmont region, with pine and cedar in considerable quantities.

Minerals—Gold, mica and monozite are found in this county.

TOWNS AND POST OFFICES.

	POP.		POP.
Beam's Mills	20	King' Moun-	
Beattyville,	15	tain	1,200
Belwood,	50	Knob Creek,	40
Boiling		Lark,	15
Springs,	300	Lattimore,	100
Byarsville,	20	Lawndale,	—
Casar,	100	Metal,	25
Camp Call,	35	Milligan,	—
Cleveland		Mooresbro,	125
Mills,	200	New House,	20
Crocker,	—	Nicholsonville,	25
Darfer,	—	Ola,	—
Delight,	25	Patterson's	
Double Shoal,	100	Springs,	300
Durbro,	20	Pearl,	15
Dellinger,	—	Point,	10
Earl,	100	Polkville,	60
Elbethel,	10	Sharon,	25
Erwinsville,	20	Shelby(C H),	2,500
Fallstown,	100	Stice's Shoal,	20
Fancy,	25	Stubbs,	10
Grover,	50	Toluca,	10
Hodge,	15	Waco,	100
Holly Bush,	100	Waverly,	10

COUNTY OFFICERS.

Superior Court Clerk—D T Lattimore.
Commissioners—I W Garrett (cb), A B Peeler, W A Martin.
Coroner—Dr R E Ellis.
Register of Deeds—J F Williams.
Sheriff—F S Fortenberry.
Solicitor Eleventh District—J L Webb.
Surveyor—W P Beam.
Treasurer—I B Byers.
County Examiner—J A Anthony.
Superintendent of Health—Dr O P Gardener.

COURTS.

Superior Court meets sixth Monday after first Monday in March; and seventh Monday after the first Monday in September.

TOWN OFFICERS.

SHELBY — *Mayor*, J T Gardener. *Commissioners*, E M Beam, B B Blanton, H T Hudson, J J Murry. *Clerk*, J F Tiddy. *Treasurer*, J D Lineberger.

TOWNSHIPS AND MAGISTRATES.

No 1—D G Palmer, R L Byars, G A Ellis, James McGinnis. G V Jones, W S Wood, L C Lemmons (Byarsville).

No 2—T J Holland, T M Holland, R M White, J M Irvin (Boiling Springs), W B Moore (Mooreboro), A B Lee (Sharon).

No 3—N N Thomason, S D Radell, T C Elliott (Earl), W J Hogue, L A Beam, J A Roberts (Patterson).

No 4—G F Hambright, W W Whisnant, J Pagenstecher (Grover), J W Goforth, H P Allison, J W Brown (King's Mountain).

No 5—W M Harrelson, M P Harrelson (Waco), A J Gamble, T M A Oates, J N Landon (Fancy).

No 6—W J Roberts, J H McBrayer, S S Marks, E C Borders, H K Winslow, J F Tiddy (Shelby), W M Beatty (Beattyville).

No 7—B F Blanton, G W McSwain, J H Lee, Z R Walker (Mooreboro), A G Wiggins (New House), A M Lattimore (Lattimore).

No 8—J B Nolan (Lawndale), J O Whisnant (Holly Bush), J C Elliott, E Q Champion (Polkville) J A Beam (Ola), J A Ham (Double Shoal).

CLEVELAND COUNTY.

No 9—D R Hoyle (Cleveland Mills), J W Grigg (Lawndale), D C Rollins (Double Shoals).

No 10—William Williams, Robert Brackett, Wm Lane, H F White, D M Cline, J A Carpenter (Knob Creek), Peter Hamot (Toluca).

No 11—J F Morris, W H Hull, A P Bumgardner, W G Duinny (Casar), W J Morrison (Holly Bush), G W Peeler, J A Newton (Casar).

CHURCHES.

Names, Post Offices, Pastors and Denom.

METHODIST.

Bethlehem—Shelby, A B Surratt.
Beulah—Waco, R L Owenby.
Church—Double Shoals, J A Cook.
Church—King's Mountain, J D Arnold.
Church—Shelby, C G Little.
Church—Fallston, A R Surratt.
Church—Mooresboro, R L Owenby.
Church—Polkville, J A Cook.
Clover Hill—Casar, J A Cook.
Elbethel—King's Mountain, J D Arnold.
Elliott—Polkville, J A Cook.
Kadish—Belwood, A R Surratt.
Lee's Chapel—Holly Bush, J A Cook.
Mt Harmony—Polkville, J A Cook.
Palm Tree—Lawndale, J A Cook.
Pine Grove—King's Mountain, R L Owenby.
Rehoboth—Lattimore, J A Cook.
Sharon, Sharon, R L Owenby.
St Paul—Waco, A R Surratt.
St. Peter's—Belwood, A R Surratt.
Sulphur Springs—Patterson Springs, R L Owenby.

METH. PROTESTANT.

Church—Fallston, —— Norton.
Church—Polkville, I H Moton.
Kistler—Cleveland Mills, J H Moton.
Knob Creek—Belwood.
Laurel Hill—Toluca.
Mt Moriah—Hodge, J H Moton.
Mt Pleasant—Hodge.
Pleasant Hill—Belwood, A P Irister.

BAPTIST.

Beaver Dam—Shelby, Munroe Bridges.
Bethlehem—Whitaker, G M Webb.
Camp Creek—Byarsville.
Church—Lattimore, Isaac Hollafield.
Church—Boiling Springs, G P Hamrick.
Church—Shelby, J D Huffham, D D.
Double Springs—Lattimore, G P Hamrick.
Elizabeth—Shelby, Thos Dixon.
Hawkins—Casar, R L Limerick.
Mt Pleasant—Mooresboro, A C Irwin.
Mt Sinai—Stice's Shoal, R N Hawkins.

Mt Zion—Beam's Mill, I M Hollafield.
Newhope—Earl, Claude Garver.
New Prospect—Waco, T Dixon.
Pleasant Hill—Shelby, C B Justice.
Pleasant Grove—Shelby, G M Hollifield.
Ross Grove—Shelby, T Dixon.
Sandy Run—Mooresboro, A C Irwin.
Sandy Plain—Delight, A L Limerick.
Whitaker—Grover.
Zion Hill—Shelby.
Zion—Shelby, A C Irwin.

PRESBYTERIAN.

Church—Grover.
Church—King's Mountain.
Church—Shelby, T M Lowry.

LUTHERAN.

Church—King's Mountain.

EPISCOPAL.

Church of the Redeemer—Shelby.

REFORM.

Church—King's Mountain.

MINISTERS RESIDENT.

Names, Post Offices and Denominations.

METHODIST.

Arnold, J D, King's Mountain.
Hartsell, J C, Shelby.
Little, C G, Shelby.
Owenby, R L, Shelby.
Renn, J J, Shelby.
Rollins, V G, Double Shoals.
Surratt, A R, Belwood.
Smith, L L, Sharon.

BAPTIST.

Bridges, J M, Waco.
Dixon, T W, Shelby.
Ebeltoft, T W, Shelby.
Elam, P R, King's Mountain.
Hamrick, G P, Henrietta.
Hawkins, R N, Sharon.
Hunter, S (col), Shelby.
Huffham, J D, D D, Shelby.
Irvin, A C, Shelby.
Limerick, R L, Shelby.
Poston, R Shelby.
Webb, G M, Shelby.

HOTELS AND BOARDING HOUSES.

Names, Post Offices and Proprietors.

Blanton Hotel, Shelby, J A Blanton.
Boarding house (Sulphur Springs), Shelby, W G Patton.
Boarding house, Mooresboro, W W Gilbert.
Boarding, Shelby, Mrs J S Borden.
Boarding, Shelby, Mrs —— Quinn.
Cleveland Springs Hotel, Shelby, Wilson heirs.

CLEVELAND COUNTY.

Commercial Hotel, Shelby, Mrs M A Brice.
King's Mountain Hotel, King's Mountain, W A Falls.
Piedmont House, King's Mountain, R T Cansler.
Restaurant, Shelby, D S Smith.
Shelby Hotel, Shelby, Mrs J G Taylor.

LAWYERS.

Names and Post Offices.

Anthony, J A, Shelby.
Cabiness, Harvey, Shelby.
Frick, G A, Shelby.
Gidney, J W, Shelby.
Hudson, H T, Shelby.
Ryburn, R L, Shelby.
Schenck, J F, Cleveland Mills.
Webb & Webb, Shelby.

MANUFACTORIES.

Kinds, Post Offices and Proprietors.

Belmont Cotton Mills, Shelby, A C & R B Miller. 3,100 spindles. Capital $60,000.
Blacksmithing, Shelby, A W Eskridge.
Blacksmithing, Shelby, John Lineberger Son.
Boots and shoes, Shelby, Jno Wilkins.
Bricks, Grover, A R Eskridge, m'g'r.
Buffalo Mfg Co (cotton), Stubbs, capital $30,000, T D Lattimore, pres.
Cleveland Cotton Mills, Cleveland Mills, H F Schenck, pres; T J Ramsour, sec'y and treas.
Contracting and building, Shelby, Jasper Branton.
Contracting and building, Shelby, M A Griggs and E A Rudisell.
Cotton mills, Double Shoal, Morgan, Cline & Co. 2,000 spindles. Capital $100,000.
Cotton factory, Cleveland cotton mills, H F Schenck, pres; established in 1874; spindles 3,000. Capital $75,000.
Durham Shoals cotton mills, Boiling Springs, J A Carroll, pres; H D Wheat, sec and treas. Capital stock $200,000; 20,000 spindles, 500 looms; in process of construction.
Enterprise cotton mill, King's Mountain. Capital stock $30,000, F Dilling, pres.
Foundry, Shelby, B B Babington.
Gunsmithing, Shelby, A W Eskridge.
Gunsmithing, Shelby, A Wilson.
Harness, Shelby, Washburn & Co.
Harness, saddles and leather, Belwood, M D Gantt.
House and sign painting, Shelby, T P Alexander.

CLEVELAND COUNTY.

Laura Glenn, Shelby (3 miles south), R B Miller; 3,000 spindles. Capital $60,000.
Millwright, Grover, W S Wells.
Oil, Holly Bush, A C Whisnant.
Piedmont Mill Co (cotton), King's Mountain. Capital $500,000; F Dilling, pres.
Planing mill, Shelby, Weathers & Crowder.
Saddles and harness, Shelby, Washburn & Co.
Silversmith, Shelby, M L Putman.
Steam Planing Mill, Shelby, L E Powers.
Steam Planing Mill, Shelby, Griggs & Rudisil.
Tannery, Mooresboro, J L Edwards.
Tannery, Mooresboro, A B Blanton & Son.
Tannery, Belwood, Gantt & Co.
Tinware, Shelby, Shull & Co.
Tobacco, Mooresboro, J F Bland.

MERCHANTS AND TRADESMEN.

Names, Post Offices and Lines of Business.

BEAM'S MILL.

Gladden, A C,	G S
Stamey Bros,	G S

BELLWOOD.

Dixon, F M,	G S
Grigg, D A,	G S
Hoyle, L J,	G S

BOILING SPRINGS.

Green, R H, jr & Sons,	G S
Hamrick, C J & Son,	G S

BYARSVILLE.

Humphrey, S R,	G S

CLEVELAND MILLS.

Cleveland Cotton Mills,	G S

CROCKER.

Crocker, J L,	Grocer

EARL STATION.

Austell, W Q,	Fertilizer
Borden, Mike,	G S
Bridges, D F,	G S
Rippy & McSwain,	G S
Rippy, J H,	G S
Webber, D G,	G S
Webber & Gibbons,	G S

FANCY.

Morgan, E A & Co,	G S
Oates, T M A,	G S

FALLSTON.

Milligan, H P,	G S
Stamey Bros,	G S

GROVER.

Ellis, J A & Co,	G S

13

CLEVELAND COUNTY.

Forbes, W R,   Grocer
Hambright, C F & Co,   G S
Turner, S R,   G S
Turner, Martin,   G S

HODGE.

Price, J B & Bro,   G S

HOLLY BUSH.

Morrison, W J,   G S
Whisnant & Hunt,   G S

KING'S MOUNTAIN.

Carpenter Bros,   G S
Garrett, I W & Co,   G S
Mauney, W A & Bro,   G S
Mauney Bros & Plank,   Dry Goods
Suggs, R S & Co,   Drugs
Summitt, L M,   G S
Willeford, Mrs R B,   Dry Goods

KNOB CREEK.

Mull, Mrs S A,   Grocer
Warlick, A D,
                    Agricultural Implements

LATTIMORE.

DePreist Bros,   G S
Hamrick, D A F,   G S
Price, O D,   G S

MOORESBORO.

Blanton, J B,   G S
Martin & Bro,   G S
Royster, S S,   Drugs

METAL.

Hamrich, C J & Sons,   G S

NEW HOUSE.

De Preist, Thos B,   G S

PATTERSON SPRINGS.

Byers, J C,   Grocer
Putnam, M L,   Grocer
Roberts, R & Son,   G S

POLKVILLE.

DePreist & Philpeck,   G S

SHARON.

Blanton, J F,   G S

SHELBY.

Baker, D M,   Hardware
Baker, E C & Co,   Grocer
Beam, E M,   Hardware
Black & Co,   Dime Store
Blanton, A,   G S
Blanton & Eskridge,   Livery
Bridges, J J & Co,   Grocers
Conley, Mrs Lula,   Milliner
Conley, R M,   Notions
Conner, L P,   Grocer
Davis, ——,   Silvermith
Dellinger & Co,   G S
Doggett, C R,   Livery
Ebeltaft, T W,
        Books, Stationery and Grocer
Elam Orlando,   Furniture
Elliott, J M,   Grocer

CLEVELAND COUNTY.

Eskridge, A W,
        Wagons, Buggies and Repairs
Froman, Miss Belle,   Milliner
Fulenwider, E H & Co,   G S
Gardner, J T,   Drugs
Gillespie, S L,   Notions and Music
Green, Albert,
              Life and Fire Insurance
Green, S J,   Fire Insurance
Hendrick, F V & Co,   G S
Hull, L M,   G S
Kendrick & Kendle,   Drugs
Lineberger, J W & Son,
                   Buggies and Repairs
Martin, J S & Son,   Grocers
McBrayer & Wilson,   Drugs
Miller Bros,   Fire Insurance
Miller, R B,   G S
Morrison, J C,   Silversmith
Nelson, J P,   Grocer
Nix, W & S,   G S
Palmer, W B,   G S
Pope, L J,   Notions
Putnam, A M,   Groceries and Beef
Shull & Co,   Hardware
Suttle, C B & Son,   Grocers
Webb, C M,   G S
Whisnant, W C,   G S
Wray & Blanton,   Livery

STICE'S SHOALS.

Thomason, N N,   G S

SWANG'S.

Roberts, R & Son,   G S

WACO.

Beam & Hoyle,   G S
Miller & Putnam,   G S

MINES.

Kinds, Post Offices and Proprietors.

Cleveland Mineral Springs, two miles
   east of Shelby, Welson heirs.
Gold, King's Mountain, Gold Mining
   Co.
Mica, Shelby, W W Green.
Tin, King's Mountain, Tin Mining Co.

MILLS.

Kinds, Post Offices and Proprietors.

Corn and flour, White Plains, M L
   Ware.
Corn and flour, Fancy, C Wolfe.
Corn and flour, Fallston, Fallston Flour
   Mills Co.
Corn and Flour, Knob Creek, Carpen-
   ter & Lackey.
Corn and flour Knob Creek, J S Falls.
Corn and flour, Durbro, Quinn & Har-
   rell.
Flour and corn, Holly Bush, Mrs Hunt.
Flour and corn, Polkville, Lattimore
   & Packard.

CLEVELAND COUNTY.

Flour and corn, Holly Bush, R C Whisnant.
Flur and corn, Polkville, Hoyle & Palmer.
Flour and corn, Beam's Mills, Abernethy & Wright.
Flour and corn, Shelby, C C Beam.
Flour and corn, Double Shoals, E A Morgan.
Flour and corn, Mooresboro, Samuel Young.
Flour and corn, Shelby, Hord, Tucker & Co.
Flour and corn, Camp Call, M M Mauney.
Flour and corn, Shelby, Burwell Blanton.

PHYSICIANS.

Names and Post Offices.

Andrews, W P, Shelby.
Beam, J F, Shelby.
Champion, C O, Mooresboro.
Ellis, R C. Shelby.
Gardner, O P, Shelby.
Gold, R G, Cleveland Springs.
Goode, W, Waco.
Griggs, W T, Belwood.
Humbright, A F, Grover.
Harrell, J A (dentist), Shelby,
Holland, A B (dentist), Boiling Springs.
Hord, J S, King's Mountain.
Lee, L V, Lattimore.
Martin, J O, Camp Call.
McBrayer, J H, Shelby.
McBrayer, Victor, Shelby.
McBrayer, T E, Shelby.
McKay, —— Kings's Mountain.
Moore, Simpson (dentist), Shelby.
Morgan, R (dentist), Shelby.
Morrison, R H, Shelby.
Oates, Geo, Grover.
Osborn, J R (dentist), Shelby.
Osborn, J C (dent), Cleveland Springs.
Osborn, J E, Knob Creek.
Palmer, V J, Polkville.
Price, R B, Grover.
Royster, S S, Mooresboro.
Trent, J W, Earl.
Whisnant, Miller, Cleveland Springs.
Ward, J W, Boiling Springs.

SCHOOLS.

Names, Post Offices and Principals.

Academy, Boiling Springs, J H Quinn.
Academy, Waco, Sylvanus Erwin.
Academy, Fallston, J T Thompson.
Academy, Earl.
Academy, Mooresboro, J J Hasener.
Academy, Lattimore.
Graded school, Shelby, F H Curtise.
High school, King's Mountain, E Walter Hall.

CLEVELAND COUNTY.

High School, Belwood. J P Rogers.
Male and Female High School, Grover, Chas Elam.
Music School, Shelby, Mrs E Z Webb.
Shelby Female College, Shelby.
No. public schools 94—white, 76; colored, 18.

TEACHERS.

Names and Post Offices.

WHITE.

Anthony, S R, Durbro.
Baker, V C, Ellenboro, Rutherford co.
Boggs, J S, Lark.
Bolfine, R J, Grover.
Bostic, Miss Attie T. Shelby.
Bridges, J D, New House.
Bumgarner, A P, Casar.
Butler, R L, Beattyville.
Carpenter, C T, Fallston.
Covington, W J, Polkville.
Curtis, F H (supt graded school), Shelby.
Dellinger, Sidney, Cherryville.
Dinney, W G. Hodge.
Dorsett, Miss Mattie, Earl's.
Elliott, J D, Waco.
Elliott, Andrew, Waco.
Elliott, Miss Lizzie, Polkville.
Elliott, Lizzie L, Polkville.
Elliott, Miss Jennie, Earl's.
Eskridge, Miss Minnie, Shelby.
Eskridge, J D, Camp Call.
Falls, J D, Fallston.
Fineamon, Miss Effie, Cleveland Mills.
Gardner, Miss Adalaide, Shelby.
Gardner, V A, Beam's Mills.
George, John J, Perry, Gaston co.
Gidney, R M, Shelby.
Gidney, J Will, Shelby.
Glasco, Miss Maggie, Sharon.
Goode, Mrs Sallie E, Cleveland Mills.
Green, John, Moresboro.
Green, B P, Mooresboro.
Hamrick, T B, Lattimore.
Havener, J C, Shelby.
Havener, J J, Polkville.
Havener, J C, Knob Creek.
Hilton, W T, Knob Creek.
Holland, A B. Boiling Springs.
Holland, Williams, Boiling Spring.
Hopper, Mrs W W, Earl's.
Humphries, S M, Byarsville.
Hunt, A W, Casar.
Hunt, J S, Casar.
Irwin, Sylvanus, Waco.
Jackson, Mrs Rossie, King's Mountain.
Jones, A B, Sharon.
Jones, B F, Polkville.
Justice, R M, Shelby.
Langston, John C, King's Mountain.
Logan, G H, King's Mounain.
London, Miss Bessie, Fancy.

CLEVELAND COUNTY.

Long. Thos, Fallston.
Luckey. John H. Fallston.
Lynch, Lee W, Cleveland Mill.
McSwain. Julia, Boiling Springs.
Moss, W H, Waco.
Newton, W R, Casar.
Newton, W R, Cleveland Mills.
Palmer. Minnie, Byarsville.
Peeler. A B. Casar.
Price, Miss Jennie, Ellenboro, Rutherford co.
Putnam, D F, Lattimore.
Quinn, J H, Metal.
Randall, W A, Shelby.
Rodgers. J P (supt). Belwood.
Ross, P O, Cleveland Mills.
Rhyne, Jennie C, Fancy.
Smith, J B, Waco.
Sperling, Geo E. Stubbs.
Thompson, S C, Fallston.
Walker. Z R, Lattimore.
Wallis, Miss Minnie E, Knob Creek.
Ware, Miss Maggie G, Fancy.
Weaver, J A, Sharon.
Webb, Geo P. Stubbs.
White, M L, Polkville.
Wolfe, W I, Fancy.

COLORED.

Bridges, Monroe, Boiling Springs.
Floyd, T J, Shelby.
Franklin. J P. Mooresboro.
Gedney, F J, Polkville.
Grumling, J F, Byarsville.
Harrell, A, Knob Creek.
Harris, M L. Boiling Springs.
Henderson, Fannie, Shelby.
Lee, Mamie, Boiling Springs.
Logan, J V. Mooresboro.
Maroney, Lizzie, Polkville.
Martin, A L, King's Mountain.
Miller. David, Patterson Springs.
Roberts, W A. Shelby.
Roberts, R. Shelby.
Roberts, Ida. Shelby.
Shuford, J W. Casar.
Surratt, P C, Byarsville.
Turner, Geo E, Boiling Springs.
Veal, W C. Grover.
Webster, Mary E, Shelby.
Wells, Alice, Cleveland Mills.
Wellman, Mirtie, Fallston.
Wellman, J W, King's Mountain.
Wessen, Lyda. Patterson Springs.
Young, J C, Mooresboro.

LOCAL CORPORATIONS.

Boiling Springs Lodge, A F and A M.
Cleveland Lodge, No. 202, A F and A M, Shelby. Time of meeting, Friday evening on or before each full moon, and June 24th and December 27th. W L Damron, W M.

CLEVELAND COUNTY.

Double Shoals Lodge, No 356. A F and A M, Cleveland Mills. Time of meeting, Saturday evening on or before each full moon.
Fairview Lodge, A F and A M, No 339, King's Mountain. Time of meeting. Saturday evening on or before each full moon. and June 24th and December 27th. I W Garrett, W M.
Mooresboro Lodge, A F and A M, Meets on Saturday night before full moon. D W W Gilbert, W M.
State Line Lodge, No 375, A F and A M, Grover. Time of meeting, Saturday before each full moon, at 1 o'clock P M. R G Price, W M.

NEWSPAPERS.

Aurora (Dem. Weekly), Shelby; W H Miller, ed and pro; circulation, 2,450.
Cleveland Star (Dem. Weekly), Shelby; Clyde B Hoey, ed and pro.
Progressive Reformer (Pop), King's Mountain; H P Allison, ed and pro.

FARMERS.

Names and Post Offices.

Ream's Mills—R Allen, J F Beam, M Carpenter, J M Carpenter, L S Carpenter, P Costner, A Costner, J Costner, R W Gardner. L S Gardner, D A Hamrick. A A Hamrick, A A Hendrick, J C Hendrick, Juan C Hendrick, E Hendrick, M S Hoyle, J G Hoyle, W R Hoyle, Pink Hoyle, J S Hoyle, D R Hoyle, John Kistler, J J Kistler, Wm Lackey, J R Ledford. M L Lutz. D L Martin, W G Nand, A Nolan, C P Vaughn, Z Williams, K Williams, WW Williams, Perry Wright, L A Wright.
Beattyville—J T Beattie, W M Beattie, Mrs Geo Dogett, J B Philbeck, Jno Poston.
Belwood—D B Alexander, N E Boggs, A N Boggs, W Boggs, M P Gant, Jonathan Hoyle, W B Hoyle, Luther Lutz, H D Randall, J H Smith.
Boiling Springs—Asbury Webb, Jno Beasom, G W C Byars, Stansberry Champion, J H Champion, Jno Green, R H Green, J R Green. J K Green. Jabez Hamrick. A R Hamrick, D J Hamrick, G R Hamrick, J T Hamrick, O W Holland, G G Holland. T J Holland, Stanford Jolly, James McSwain, W B McSwain, W H McSwain, Geo McSwain, James Privett, J H Quinn.
Byarsville—B F Allison, W L Blanton, Preston Briggs, R L Byars, Mrs E Byars, W J Davis, K C Davis, J P Hamrick, Luther Humphries, S H

CLEVELAND COUNTY.

Humphries, J Humphries, S R Humphries, C Jones, J J Jones, J V Jones.

Casar—Joseph Bingham, Wm Brackett, Pete Buff, F L Dinney, W H Hull, Zero Mull, W S Newton, R H Newton, NlP Philbeck, John Pruett, M N Pruett, Albert Pruett, J B Toury, J H Toury, A A Warlick, 'John Wortman, P A Wright, E H Wright.

Camp Call—Mrs A Elliott, A H Philbeck, Wm Wiggins, P D Williamson.

Cleveland—Whit Blanton, D A Cline, A H Cline, O N Cline, T J Dixon, J Walter Grigg, Junius Grigg, Daniel Lattimore, Frank Lattimore, Cr ok Lee, A B Peeler, Geo Peeler.

Darfer—S H Hamrick, E L Jenkins, L A McSwain.

Delight—J F Esker, C B Lattimore, R G Wells.

Dellinger—J P Dellinger, A F Ellis, A W McCran, J S Grambling, J T Humphries, J D Humphries, P W Humphries, A L Palmer, W J Ruppe, D Ruppe, J C Ruppe, Samuel Ruppe, J H Spake, T R Wilkins

Double Shoals—A Foree, R Hourd, J R Hoyle, D C Peeler, O White.

Durbro—W B Lowry, William Putnam Cass Putnam, W W Whisnant.

Earl—W Q Austell, J H Austell, A P Austell, A E T Bechlter, A E Bettis, W Bridges, W D Earl, T E Elliott, J A Hardin, W W Hopper, J H Patterson, R S Randall, Miller Randall, P Roberts, Eli Roberts, J C Runyans, R H Runyans, J M Runyans, P Sepaugh, S B Turner, M Warren.

Fallston—David Beam, J Costner, Thomas Costner, J W Crowder, J R Dickson, W W Dickson, E D Dickson, T J Dickson, M A Dickson, T D Falls, J H Fartenterry, F S Fartenterry, Sylvanus Gardner, Rufus Gardner, J S Glenn, P D Griggs, J W Grigg, Levi Griggs, B Hendrick, E Hendrick, A A Hendrick, W D Lockey, LaFayette Martin

Fancy—J A Goode, Thomas Goode, J Z Hord, J N London, J B Rhyne, J B Wolfe, W C Wolfe.

Grover—B Barber, J F Bell, D R Bell, M Borders, F H Bridges, N A Camp, James Crocker, W W Dixon, John R Dour, James Dour, John Herndon, W H Herndon, J P Moss, E A Patterson, J Pagenstacker, D C Patterson, J W Sheppard, H C Sheppard, W R Sheppard, B F Turner, James A Wesson, S White.

Hodge—W G Page, J B Price, H R Richards, W P White.

Hollybush—J Black, J F Esker, J M Hoyle, C B Lattimore, W J Morrison, D Morrison, J Morrison, R G Wells.

CLEVELAND COUNTY.

King's Mountain—J H Alllson, S H Anthony, S P Baker, L J Dixon, P R Elam, C R Falls, J P Falls, J B Falls, W A Falls, H D Fulton, J W Goforth, S P Goforth, E Goforth, A F Hambright, R Hambright, A N Harmon, T W Harmon, G C Herndon, W A Herndon, A H Herndon, Mrs E S Logan, J J Logan, G S Mauney, W A Mauney, Isaac McGill, John Medlin, J C Morrow, A H Patterson, Rufus Patterson, E B Patterson, J M Phifer, William Plonk, M Plonk, E C Quinn, J O Simmons, T M A Ware, M L Ware, J A Ware, J W Ware, A F Ware, John Watterson, A V Wells.

Knob Creek—J Z Falls, W E Ledford, Julius Mull, N B Warlick, Wm Williams.

Lark—A Bumgarner, H T Bumgarner, John Bumgarner, W Hoyle, H J Willis, David Wortman.

Lattimore—Jno Bridges, I J Bridges, C Cabiness, A M Cabiness, M Crowder, B F Gold, John Gold, Lee Gold, H H Green, sr, H H Green, jr, T J Green, C Green, D A F Hamrick, B Hamrick, Chiras Washburn, W W Washburn.

Metal—C J Hamrick, E B Hamrick, Solon Hamrick, Wm Hamrick, D S Lovelace.

Milligan—E Divines, Miles Hamrick, H Roberts, R Roberts.

Mooresboro—J H Beam, J B Blanton, J W Bridges, W M F Green, B Green, R C Green, Wm H Green, G W McSwain, B F McSwain, J D McSwain, B McSwain, P H Pruett, John Pruett, J L Pruett.

New House—Lorenza Bridges, L A Bridges, Hamby Davis, C C Grigg, George Grigg, Hilliard Grigg, M P Philbeck, Jas P Philbeck, R L Washburn, J M Washburn, Thos Washburn, W G Whiteside, J M White, A G Wiggins.

Nicholsonville—M E Scruggs, A J Settlemyre, J D Simmons, T R Wilkins, H S Wood, T C Wood, W S Wood.

Ola—J A Beam, T F Elliott, J F Steckton.

Patterson Springs—R H Anthony, W P Anthony, H Borders, J M Bowin, M A Bowin, Tyrrell Camp, D T Dour, Alonzo Ellis, W A Hamrick, W K Hardin, Winfield Hardin, L Hendrick, Jesse Hogue, N A Jackson, T H Lowry, Ross McSwain, R J Neal, Geo Patterson, Hayne Patterson, John Pruett, L M Putnam, R Roberts, J M Roberts, M H D Roberts.

Polkville—W D H Covington, Wess Covington, Wm Hanes, F J Hicks, Geo Lattimore, D D Lattimore, W S Lattimore, J A Lattimore, J C Lattimore, M Mauney, V J Palmer, M L White.

Point—Robt Newton, A Pruett, Geo White.

Sharon—J H Blanton, J M Blanton, N D Davis, Amos Davis, Esley Davis, W A Lattimore, E L Ledbetter. C M Ledbetter, T G Lee, A B Lee, Mrs E Lee, M M Moore, J M Moore, Wm Morehead, J L Presott. L L Smith, W R Smith, E F Turner, W H Turner, J W Wesson, W W White, S J Weaver, L L Yarboro, J L Yarboro.

Shelby—E M Allen, W P Andrews, J H Anthony, C C Beam, W P Beam, sr, W H Blanton, B Blanton, J S Blanton, E C Borders, S E Bostic, L A Botts, D Branton, J C Byers, J B Byers, John Camp, J F Cline, M Comnaul, M M Crane, W P Diews, H P Dixon, T Dixon, C C Durham, R C Ellis, M G Eskridge, J A Gantt, O P Gardner, R M Gidney, J W Gidney, sr, E S Glasco, W F Gold, W T Goode, A Green. Thos Hamrick, L S Hamrick. C C Hamrick, S H Hamrick, W R

Hardin, S Harrell, T L Hendrick, F V Hendrick. A R Henry, E Howser, R R Hoyle, W H Jennings, J P Ledford, Aaron Mauney, D G Mauney, D G Mawney, P N Martin, J J McMurry, J W McMurry, R B Miller, J R Moore, J F Moore, M Parker, A Y Patterson, J O Poston, Pink Poston, Able Poston, Samuel Poston, W A Randall, Wm Roberts, Eli Roberts (col), R Rollins, Geo A Spake, W G Spake, Isaac Spurlin, J J Spurlin, C B Suttle, T C Vaughn, F Vaughn, J D Weathers, sr, C M Weathers, A G Weathers, J McWebb, W R Wellmon, W R Wellmon, jr, E C White, J M Wilson, P D Wilson, S A Wilson, J W Wray.

Stice—John Hopper. S D Randall, N N Thomasson, Wm Wiley.

Stubbs—D Alexander, Ambrose Cline, E Hamrick, Wm Speake, Scott Speake, A Spurlin.

Waco—J Baker, E E Black, M Borders, W T Divine, R W Elliott, Sylvanus Erwin, Ira Erwin, B J Eskridge, E Hamrick.

COLUMBUS COUNTY.

AREA, 750 SQUARE MILES.

POPULATION, 17,856; White, 11,804; Colored 6,052.

COLUMBUS COUNTY was formed in the year 1808, from Bladen and Brunswick counties, and is named for the great discoverer, Christopher Columbus.

WHITEVILLE, the county-seat, is named after James B. White, one of the first members of the General Assembly. It is 126 miles south of Raleigh, and contains a population of 950.

Surface—Level and much of it in swamps. Soil good when well drained. The Wilmington, Columbia and Augusta Railroad passes directly through the county.

Staples—Naval stores are produced largely and profitably. Shingles and lumber are worked largely. Cotton, corn and sweet potatoes are grown extensively.

Timbers—Pine of different varieties, cypress, gum, water oak, white oak and several other species.

Fruits— Berries, apples, peaches, cherries, plums, apricots, nectarines, grapes, melons, etc.

TOWNS AND POST OFFICES.

	POP.		POP.
Applewhite,	—	Kingsville,	—
Armour,	25	Lake Wacca-	
Botton,	75	maw,	50
Bug Hill,	30	Lebanon,	20
Byrdsville,	25	Leroy,	25
Cerro Gorda,	200	Mollie,	25
Chadbourn,	400	Old Dock,	35
Clarendon,	30	Orton,	40
Coleman,	—	Peacock Store,	25
Cronly,	100	Pireway,	20
Crooms,	30	Pocosin,	—
Doomore,	25	Prong,	50
Dothan,	20	Record,	20
Elbow,	150	Robeson,	50
Eoka,	15	Sue,	25
Evergreen,	100	Tabor,	125
Fair Bluff,	250	Tariff,	—
Grist,	50	Vineland,	325
Haddock,	50	West,	25
Hallsboro,	100	Whiteville (c h),	
Hub,	500		950
Iron Hill,	50	Wooten,	20

COUNTY OFFICERS.

Clerk Superior Court—A H Lennon.
Commissioners—S N Forme, chmn; M F Owen, L I Yates, E Blackman, G L Powell.

Coroner—Dr G F Harrell.
Register of Deeds—Dr B F Nance.
Sheriff—M J Ward.
Solicitor Seventh District—H F Seawell.
Surveyor—J D Long.
Standard Keeper—J A Lunsden.
Treasurer—J K Gore.
County Examiner—L W Stanly.
Supt. Health—Dr I Jackson.

COURTS.

First Monday before the first Monday in March. Seventh Monday before the first Monday in September.

TOWN OFFICERS.

CHADBOURN—*Mayor*, J B Chadbourn.
FAIR BLUFF—*Mayor*, G A Powell.
HUB—*Mayor*, A D Lewis.
WHITEVILLE—*Mayor*, J S Williamson. *Commissioners*—D P High, J L Wiggins, E B Branch, J R Maxwell, A F Powell. *Treasurer*, A J Maxwell. *Marshal*, J K Hammons.

TOWNSHIPS AND MAGISTRATES.

Bug Hill—J J C Gore, S W Reams (Bug Hill), J L Dice (Pireway), T J Stanly, M J Stevens, J B Cox (Bug Hill), J N Cox (Dothan) C B Stanly (Pireway).

Bogue—Thos Barefoot, N Powell, A P Sassar, J P Pierce, sr, G Maultzby, J E Thompson, H Wyche (Bogue).

Chadbourn—B F Yates, Ned A Edmonds, W G Frack, J M Byrd, I M Fowler, Thos Thompson, D E Greene, S L Hughes, Jos A Thompson, W G Nobles (Chadbourn).

Fair Bluff—T E Borden, W J Benton, P T Godwin, C F Benton (Cero Gorda), R Q Powell, E D Meares (Fair Bluff), Wm Strickland (Crooms).

Lee's—J W Gore (Old Dock), D J Jolly (Eoka), Forney Pierce, J P Hill, G A Mills, J P Reaves (Eoka).

Ransom—D S Cowan (Robeson) E W Wells, J M Hill, Alva Benson, H Lennon, J W Flynn, George W Applewhite, R C Applewhite (Applewhite).

Tatom—Ira Lennon (Orton), M G Williamson (Evergreen), J C Lennon (Orton), A D Williamson, E R Brown (Cero Gorda), George W Lennon, J Q McDugal, A M Benton (Orton).

COLUMBUS COUNTY.

Western Prong—W M Pridgen. W D Wooten, D P Brown, G English, J E Powell, J T Wooten (Wooten).

Welch's—R D Sessions, J L McKay (Whiteville), J R Baldwin, J E Campbell, J M Chipman, I M Brown (Elkton).

Waccamaw — M Campbell, D M Hobbs, W E Westbrook, H H Holton (Pocosin), J W Dickson, H B Short, J Hall (Lake Waccamaw).

Williams'—J M D Long, J M Hardy (Marley), J M Cox, John Skipper (Iron Hill), M M Harrelson, M Wright, Minos Meares, Simeon Simmons (Haddock), C W Brown (Mt Tabor).

Whiteville—A J Thompson, L W Stanly, J C Powell, T S Memory, sr, N W Friar, A Toon, H B Register, H C Moffitt, J T Best (Whiteville).

CHURCHES.

Names, Pastors, Postoffices and Denom.

FREE-WILL BAPTIST.

Beaver Dam—Lebanon, P Blackman.
Walker Mills—Grist.

BAPTIST.

Bogue Chapel—Hallsboro, J F Tuttle.
Cross Roads—Orton, Haynes Lennon.
China Grove—Chadbourn, C P Bullock.
Church—Fair Bluff, J A Smith.
Church (col)—Whiteville, D Gresham.
Church (col)—Lake Waccamaw.
Chuch—Whiteville, J F Tuttle.
Church—Mt Tabor, Joshua Soles.
Cherry Grove— —, Joshua Soles.
Church—Chadbourn. T J Cobb.
Hepsy Hill—Whiteville.
Iron Hill—Iron Hill, C P Bullock.
Lake Waccamaw — Flemington, T J Cobb.
Macedonia—Cerro Gorda.
Mt Moriah—Robeson.
Mi Sinai—Haddock, E R Bullock.
Mt Zion—Clarkton, T J Cobb.
New Hope—Leroy, G F Stanly.
Oakdale—Orton, T J Cobb.
Pireway—Bug Hill, A G Stocks.
Pleasant Plains—Eoka, E W Wooten.
Pine Forest—Grist, T J Cobb.
Pleasant Hill, Peacock's, C P Bullock.
Potter Swamp—Cerro Gorda, J F Tuttle.
Seven Creek—Pireway, A G Stocks.
Sweet Home—West, A G Stocks.
Western Prong—Wooten, J A Smith.
White Marsh—Whiteville, T J Cobb.

METHODIST.

Britt's Chapel—Whiteville, T J Browning.
Church—Whiteville, W H Townsend.

COLUMBUS COUNTY.

Church—Bolton, L S Etheridge.
Church—Fair Bluff, W H Townsend.
Church—Lake Waccamaw, L S Etheridge.
Church—Old Dock, J M Marlow.
Church—Peacock's Store, T J Browning.
Church—Cerro Gorda, T T Gordon.
Church—Evergreen, T J Browning.
Evergreen—Evergreen, T J Browning.
Lebanon—Lebanon, J M Marlow.
Hebron—Hallsboro, L S Etheridge.
Pine Log—Iron Hill, J M Barlow.
Porter Swamp—Cerro Gorda, J M Marlow.
Shiloh—Lake Waccamaw, L S Etheridge.
Shiloh—Eoka, J M Marlow.
Smith's Chapel—Elkton, L S Etheridge.
Wayman—Armour, L S Etheridge.
Wooten's Chapel—Prong, T J Browning.

PRESBYTERIAN

Church—Chadbourn, T H Newkirk.
Church (col)—Chadbourn, —— Johnson.
Church—Whiteville, T H Newkirk.
White Plains—Elkton, T H Newkirk.

MINISTERS RESIDENT.

Names, Post Offices and Denominations.

METHODIST.

Browning, T J, Whiteville.
Etheridge, L S, Wayman.
Greening, T J, Eoka.
Marlow, J M, Old Dock.
Townsend, W H, Whiteville.

FREE-WILL BAPTIST.

Green, D F, Chadbourn.
Sikes, J M, Whiteville.

BAPTIST.

Lennon, Haynes, Orton.
Soles, J, Mount Tabor.
Smith, J A, Fair Bluff.
Wooten, E W, Wooten.

PRIMITIVE BAPTIST.

Wright, M, Haddock.

HOTELS AND BOARDING HOUSES.

Names, Post Offices and Proprietors.

Boarding House, Vineland, E Howes.
Boarding House, Chadburn, J P Foulk.
Boarding House, Whiteville, J H Maxwell.
Boarding House, Vineland, Miss Ellen Brown.
Boarding House, Lake Waccamaw, Mrs M Carroll.

COLUMBUS COUNTY.

Boarding House, Fair Bluff, Mrs O H Drake.
Boarding House, Chadbourn, Mrs G Brown.
Boarding House, Hub, Dr J Hester.
Hotel, Hub, Mrs W M Powell.
Hotel, Whiteville, H C Moffitt.
Whiteville Hotel, Whiteville, Mrs F A Howell.

LAWYERS.

Names and Post Offices.

Allen, D C, Armour.
Burkhead, W G, Whiteville.
Lewis, D J, Whiteville.
Schulken, J Bion, Whiteville.
Williamson, J R, Whiteville.

MANUFACTORIES.

Kinds, Post Offices and Proprietors.

Acme M'f'g Co, Wilkes Morris, General Superintendent; Cronly & Morris (Wilmington), General Agents.
Blacksmithing and wheelwrighting, Fair Bluff, Scott & Goodyear.
Blacksmithing and wheelwrighting, Peacock's Store, J N Hayes.
Blacksmithing and wheelwrighting, Robeson, Wesley Webb.
Blacksmithing and wheelwrighting, Robeson, C Mitchell.
Blacksmithing and wheelwrighting, Robeson, S M Carroll.
Blacksmithing and wheelwrighting, Robeson, John Butler.
Blacksmithing and wheelwrighting, Robeson, K H Brady.
Blacksmithing and wheelwrighting, Whiteville, J K Hammons, F P Bourdeux.
Buggies and carts, Vineland, Murdock Frazier.
Contracting and building, Chadbourn, Patrick Rasberry.
Contracting and building, Chadbourn, Isham Howard.
Coopering, Robeson, D J Webb.
Coopering, Robeson, Joseph Webb.
Coopering, Robeson, Robert Webb.
Coopering, Robeson, Thomas Webb.
Fertilizers, pine-straw matting, pine straw oil, cotton, logging and shingle factory, Vineland, Scholkan & Co.
Shingles, Waccamaw, J H Springer.
Shingles and lumber, Lake Waccamaw, H B Short.
Shingles, Whiteville, Richards & Co.
Turpentine, Bugg Hill, M B Smith.
Turpentine and cotton-gin, Elkinville, L A Smith & Co.
Turpentine and gin, Prong, W D Smith.

COLUMBUS COUNTY.

Turpentine, Mt Tabor, C C Pridgen.
Turpentine, Old Dock, H M Blackman.
Turpentine, Lebanon, Pinkney Blackman.
Turpentine, gin and saw, Hallsboro, Flynn & Hall.
Turpentine, Pireway, S H Thomas.
Turpentine, Vineland, J B Singletary.
Turpentine, Pireway, J R Gore.
Turpentine, Mt Tabor, S H Boswell.
Turpentine, Pireway, F C Williamson.
Turpentine, Chadbourn, Chadwick E H Thompson.
Turpentine, Vineland, W A J Soles.
Turpentine, Fair Bluff, G N Powell.
Turpentine, Robeson, R C Applewhite.
Wine, Whiteville Wine Co, D P High, Manager.

MERCHANTS AND TRADESMEN.

Names, Post Offices, Lines of Business.

BOLTON.

Brinkley, Mrs M,	G S
Brinkley, R T,	G S
Farmer, H J,	G S

BUG HILL.

Smith, M B,	G S and Turpentine

CERRO GORDO.

Benton, Mrs W V,	G S
Harrelson, E J,	G S
Kelliham, H D,	Turpentine
Nance, M H,	G S
Williamson, J L,	G S

CHADBOURN.

Brown, R E L,	Lumber and G S
Thigpen, W E,	G S

CRONLY.

Applewhite, R C,	G S
Hand, D,	G S

DOTHAN.

Dothan Exchange,	G S

FAIR BLUFF.

Anderson, A H,	G S
Anderson, Mrs S C,	G S
Drake, M E,	G S
Elsenton, M D,	G S
Gregg, D M,	Grocer
Gregg, R J,	G S
Jenkins, A W,	G S
Powell & Smith,	G S
Rogers, J F & Co,	G S
Rogers, W K,	G S
Smith, J Fulton & Co,	G S

FREEMAN.

Applewhite, E L,	G S
Brinkley, J B,	G S

GRIST'S.

Powell, J W,	G S and Furniture

COLUMBUS COUNTY.

HALLSBORO.

Cooper, J L (col),	Grocer
Flynn & Hall,	G S
Wyche, H,	
Agent Farmer's Alliance, G S	

HUB.

Britt & Britt,	G S
Butler's Lumber Co,	Lumber
Rice & Floyd,	G S

IRON HILL.

Wright, L,	G S

LAKE WACCAMAW.

Dickson, J W,	G S
McDowell, H (col),	G S
Short, H B,	Lumber
Stern, C A,	G S

LEBANON.

Stanley, J P (near),	G S

OLD DOCK.

Blackman, H M,	Turpentine

TABOR.

Boswell, S H,	G S
Inman, C H & Co,	G S
Pridgen, C C,	Turpentine
Todd & Co,	G S

PIREWAY.

Butler, G C,	G S
Buttler, J G,	G S and Lumber
Gore, J K,	G S

PRONG.

Wooten, Shade,	Variety
Wooten, W D, Agent,	G S

VINELAND.

Best, John T,	Postmaster
Calder Bros,	G S
Culbreth, N M,	Postmaster
Dunn, John F, Manager Racket Store	
Lewis, R B,	G S and Turpentine
Millican, Haynes,	Jeweler
Powell & Co, J L Powell, M'g'r,	G S
Richardson, A C,	
Depot and Express Agent and Telegraph Operator	
Schulken & Co,	G S
Smith, J & Co (five miles south),	G S
Soles, W A J,	G S
Vineland Dry Goods Co,	
Powell, A F, Sec and Treas	

WHITEVILLE.

Harrell, Dr J F,	Drugs
High, Oscar,	Con and Sta
Jackson & Williamson,	Drugs
Maultsby, J D,	
Agent for Calder Bros,	G S
Maxwell, J H & Son,	G S
Memory Co,	
Memory, Mrs E S, Proprietor, G S	
Memory's, T S, Son,	G S
Merchandise Co,	G S

COLUMBUS COUNTY.

Mills, F T,	Livery
Powell, J C (near),	G S
Powell, R H, Agent,	G S
Powell & Powell,	G S
Richardson & Co,	G S and Shingles
Truelove & Co,	G S
Williamson & Co,	Livery

MILLS.

Kinds, Post Offices and Proprietors.

Corn, Robeson, George Webb.
Corn, Whiteville, E C Watkins.
Corn, Vineland, William Richardson.
Corn, Whiteville, M F Bright.
Corn, Whiteville, J D Maultsby, Agent.
Corn, Bogue, H B Hall.
Corn and saw, Pireway, J F Butler.
Flour and corn, Peacock's Store, Hughes & Co.
Steam saw, Hallsboro, H B Short.
Steam saw and gin, Whiteville, J D Maultsby, Agent.

PHYSICIANS.

Names and Post Offices.

Culbreth, N M (Dentist), Whiteville.
Floyd, A G, Fair Bluff.
Harrell, J F, Whiteville.
Jackson, Isaac, Whiteville.
Lucas, A B, Armour.
McGougan, J M, Cerro Gordo.
McKinnon, A, Chadbourn.
Rollins, ——, Cronly.
Thompson, ——, Chadbourn.
Williamson, J C, Whiteville.

SCHOOLS.

Names, Post Offices and Principals.

Academy, Cronly, Prof Carter.
High School, Whiteville, J L Woodard.
High School, Fair Bluff.
No. Public Schools—White, 43; colored, 37.

LOCAL CORPORATIONS.

Fair Bluff Lodge, No. 100, A F and A M, Fair Bluff. Time of meeting, second Saturday in each month at 1 o'clock P M, and the evening of December 27th.
Lebanon Lodge, No. 207, A F and A M, Whiteville. Time of regular communication, Saturday before each full moon at 3 o'clock P M, and on June 24 and December 27.

NEWSPAPERS.

Columbus News (Dem. weekly), Whiteville; A J Maxwell, ed and prop.

COLUMBUS COUNTY.

The Southern Truck Farmer, Chadbourn (weekly farm journal;) D H Hornby, mgr.

FARMERS.

Names and Post Offices.

Ammon—Henry Allen, D C Allen, A J Burns, Jno Collins, B Daniel, C M Daniel, J C Daniel, T S Evans, Robt

COLUMBUS COUNTY.

Green, Felix King, S B King, Robt Larkin, Joseph Lasaseur, J B Love, R S Love, J D Loyd, R E Loyd, Andrew Perry, G W Robeson, W Flinn.

Farmers' Turnout—James Ridley, G M Robbins.

Robeson—B C Allen, V Bird, D S Cowan, J Green, A B Lucas, L Malpass, J McCoy, D Morrell, W B Robeson, J C Rowell.

CRAVEN COUNTY.

AREA, 900 SQUARE MILES.

POPULATION, 20,533; White 7,175, Colored 13,358.

CRAVEN COUNTY was one of the original precincts of the Lord's Proprietors, and derives its name from William, Earl of Craven, to whom, with others, the charter was granted by Charles II.

NEWBERN, the county-seat, is named after Bern, in Switzerland, and is one of the oldest towns in the State; located at the junction of Neuse and Trent rivers, 110 miles east of Raleigh. Population, estimated, 9,000.

Surface.—This county is level. It is traversed by the Neuse river, running from northwest to southeast. On both sides of the river there is much bottom land that produces heavy crops when well drained. The advantages of water transportation are very fine.

Staples—Cotton and corn are the great staples. Shingles and lumber are manufactured profitably. Naval stores and fish are items of very considerable profit. Newbern is one of the finest fish markets in the State. Truck-farming, of late years, has be come extensive and profitable.

Fruits.—Apples, peaches, pears, apricots, nectarines, figs, melons, and nearly every species of small fruit.

Timbers.—Pine, cypress, poplar, gum, live oak, white oak, etc.

TOWNS AND POST OFFICES.

	Pop.		Pop.
Askin,	25	James City,	100
Bachelor,	50	Jasper,	25
Bellan,	25	Lima,	30
Cherry Point,	30	Maple Cypress,	27
Clark,	25	Newbern,	9 000
Cohooque,	35	North Harlowe,	50
Cove,	25	Perfection,	45
Croatan,	20	Riverdale,	20
Debruhl's,	25	Thurman,	20
Dover,	250	Tuscarora,	100
Ernul,	25	Vanceboro,	300
Fort Barnwell,	30	Zorah,	20
Havelock,	100		

COUNTY OFFICERS.

Clerk Superior Court—W M Watson.
Commissioners—Jas A Bryan, chmn; Ed W Smallwood, J A Meadows, W C Brewer, M H Carr.
Coroner—Dr N H Street.
Register of Deeds— ——

Sheriff—W B Lane.
Solicitor Second District— ——
Surveyor—Henry J Lovick.
Standard Keeper—Eugene Tucker.
Treasurer—Thos Daniels.
County Examiner—Rev John S Long.
County Physician—Dr. Joe Duguid.
County Home—Mrs Emma Williams, keeper.

COURTS.

Ninth Monday after the first Monday in March. Fourth Monday after the first Monday in September.

CRIMINAL COURTS.

Second Monday before the first Monday in March. Fourth Monday after the first Monday in September.

TOWN OFFICERS.

NEWBERN—*Mayor*, Wm Ellis. *Commissioners*, Ferdinand Aluch, Dr. Robt S Primrose. B B Neal, Anthony Wetherington (col), Wayne Eubank (col). *Clerk and Tax Collector*, Hugh J Lauck. *City Marshal*, J T Lewis. *City Physician*, Dr Claude Benton.

VANCEBORO—*Mayor*, E F White. *Commissioners*, Thos Buck, E A Askim, N A Person. *Constable*, S E Ewell.

NEWBERN FIRE DEPARTMENT.

Chief Engineer, L J Taylor. *First Assistant*, W D Barrington. *Secretary*, Herbert W Simpson. *Treasurer*, T A Green. Atlantic Steam Fire Engine Co., No. 1, J L Hartsfield, foreman; Newbern Steam Fire Engine Co., James Moore, foreman; S B Waters, assistant. Hook and Ladder Co., No. 1, (col).

U. S. OFFICERS.

Collector of Customs. S H Lane; Deputy Collector, B G Creddle; Deputy Collector U S Internal Revenue, W T Caho. U S Revenue Steamer, stationed at Newbern, Captain Abbey. Postmaster at Newbern, Matt Manly. Assistant Engineer in charge of river and harbor, Lieut Chadbourn.

TOWNSHIPS AND MAGISTRATES.

No. 1—E A Askins, H E Dawson, B F Dinkins. Jno A Jackson, C B Stubbs, Amariah Toler, Stephen F Hill, A M Williams (Vanceboro).

CRAVEN COUNTY.

No. 2—Jas A Ernest (Newbern), Jno A Everington (Ernul), Alfred Gaskins, S E Mitford (Zorah), J W Latham, Beverly Paul, W D Pettijohn (Newbern), Willis Toler (Zorah).

No. 3—A W Avery, John Biddle, M C Daugherty (Cove), J W Lane (Ft. Barnwell), Joe E Kornegay (Dover). R A Russell, J B Rouse, J B Wooten (Ft. Barnwell).

No. 5—B F Borden, C C Bell, L M Gilbert, Jesse P Godett, Jno S Morton, M F Morton, J L Taylor, Isaac Taylor (Harlowe).

No. 6—J H Barnes, Dock Cooper, A J Chestnut, J H Hunter, E H Hess, Jno D Pittman, B E Williams, Edward Russell (Havelock).

No. 7—Geo D Conner, Jno S Fisher, G L Hardison, Henry B Lane, N M Porter, H H Berry, W H Smith, Washington Spivey, H C Wood (Riverdale).

No. 8—W G Bunson, A A Bryan, F L Bray, Wm Collegian, C M Dockham, A R Dennison, G T Eubanks, Wm Eller, J L Hahn, Ben Hahn, Meyer Hahn, Lewis Ham, J M Harrison, R D Hancock, W W Lawrence, Thos F McCarthy, Robt G Mosley, F T Patterson, R S Primrose, S D Pope, W F Rountree, S R Street, E S Street, John U Smith, C J Schelkey, Nathan Tisdale, Ferdinand Ulrich, R P Williams, John B Willis, D R Williams (Newbern).

No. 9—John E Dougherty, L H French, Thos B Ipoch, W B Lane, J C Moore, Deems Perkins, Frank Rasberry, Stephen Scott, N T Weeks.

CHURCHES.

Names, Post Offices, Pastors and Denom.

METHODIST.

Adams Creek—Newbern.
Asbury Cove—Cove, A L Ormond.
Bethany—Closs, A L Ormond.
Broad Creek—Stonewell.
Birch Grove (near Newbern)—A L Ormond.
Core Creek—Stonewell.
Epworth—Cove, A L Ormond.
Goose Creek—Stonewell.
Hancock Street—Newbern, A D Betts.
Jackson—Stonewell.
Johnson Chapel—Dover.
Lane's Chapel—Closs, A L Ormond.
Smith Creek—Stonewell.
South River—Newbern.
Station—Newbern, L L Nash. D D.
Tuscarora—Tuscarora, A L Ormond.

ZION METHODIST.

St. Peter's (col)—Newbern, H C Phillips.

CRAVEN COUNTY.

AFRICAN METHODIST.

Bethel (col)—Newbern, Ed Chambers.
Clinton Chapel (col)—Newbern.

BAPTIST.

First Baptist (col)—Newbern.
First Baptist—Newbern, —— Porter.
Fort Barnwell—Newbern, —— Porter.
Second Baptist (col)—Newbern, John S Johnston.

PRIMITIVE BAPTIST.

Swift Creek—Newbern.
Milton—Newbern.
Alpha—Newbern.

DISCIPLES.

Bay Creek—Newbern.
Bethlehem—Newbern.
Broad Creek—Newbern.
Concord—Newbern.
Goose Creek—Newbern.
Hancock Street—Newbern, D L Brindle.
Kit Swamp—Newbern.
Lane's Chapel—Newbern.

PRESBYTERIAN.

Ebenezer (col)—Newbern, W A Byrd.
First Presbyterian—Newbern, C C Vardell.

EPISCOPAL.

Christ Church—Newbern, T M N George.
St. Cyprian's (col)—Newbern, G F Miller.

ROMAN CATHOLIC.

St. Paul's—Newbern, Father Quinn.

MINISTERS RESIDENT.

Names, Post Offices and Denominations.

METHODIST.

Betts, A D, Newbern.
Bishop, F A, Newbern.

BAPTIST.

Grimes, H, Newbern.
Johnston, Jno S (col), Newbern.
Jones, Henry, Newbern.
Lawson, C C, Newbern.
Moye, L W, Newbern.
Pelham, H F (col), Newbern.
Porter, ——, Newbern.

DISCIPLES.

Fulcher, W R, Newbern.
Holton, Alonzo, Newbern
Holton, J W P, Newbern.
Winfield, Henry, Newbern.

EPISCOPAL.

Bass, Alex (col), Newbern.
George, T M N, Newbern.
Long, Johnson S, Newbern.
Miller, G F (col), Newbern.

CRAVEN COUNTY.

Miller, —— (col), Newbern.

PRESBYTERIAN.

Byrd, W A (col), Newbern.
Vardell, Charles, Newbern.

A. M. E. (METHODIST).

Bass, Alex (col), Newbern.
Morris, B W, Newbern. [P E Raleigh District.]

A. M. E. ZION.

Phillips, H C, Newbern.

HOTELS AND BOARDING HOUSES.

Names, Post Offices and Proprietors.

Boarding house, Newbern (Front st), Mrs G F Cradle.
Boarding house, Newbrn (Craven st,) W F Hill.
Boarding house (col), Newbern, Sam'l Jackson.
Boarding house, Newbern (S Front st), B G Creddle.
Boarding house, Newbern (Hancock st), C T Hancock.
Boarding house, Newbern (S Front st), Wright Moore.
Hoarding house, Newbern (Pollock st), Mrs N S Richardson.
Boarding house (col), Newbern, John E Hussey.
Farmers' Inn, Newbern, Mrs Mary B Tucker.
Henderson House, Newbern, Mrs —— Smith.
Hotel Albert, Newbern (Middle st), M Patterson.
Hotel Chatauka, Newbern (S Front st), Dr F W Hughes.
Hotel Neuse, Newbern, R H Berry.
Neuse Hotel, Newbern (Broad st), F W Perry.

LAWYERS.

Names and Post Offices.

Bryan, H R (Judge Sup Court), Newbern.
Caho. W T. Newbern.
Clark, W W. Newbern.
Clark, C C, Newbern.
Clark, William E, Newbern.
Daniels, Thos, Newbern.
Gibbs, H L, Newbern.
Guion, O H, Newbern.
McCarthey, W T, Newbern.
McIver. W D, Newbern.
McSorley, Jos, Newbern.
Moore, L J, Newbern.
Nixon, R B, Newbern.
O'Hara, Jas E (col), Newbern.
O'Hara, Raphael (col), Newbern.
Pearsall, P M. Newbern.

CRAVEN COUNTY.

Pelletier, P H. Newbern.
Roberts, F C. Newbern.
Seymour. A S (Judge U S Court), Newbern.
Simmons, F M, Newbern [Gibbs & Pearsal].
Stevenson, H C, Newbern.
Stevenson, M D W, Newbern.
Thomas, C R, Newbern.
Ward, D L, Newbern.
Whitehurst, H C. Newbern.
White, Geo H (col), Newbern.
Williamson, R W, Newbern.

MANUFACTORIES.

Kinds, Post Offices and Proprietors.

Blacksmithing, Newbern, Sam'l Jackson.
Blacksmithing, Newbern, P Trenwith.
Boiler-making, Newbern, Crabtree & Co.
Candy, Newbern, John Dunn.
Candy, Newbern, Robt Duffy.
Carriages, Newbern, Winfield & Sons.
Carriages, Newbern, S Cook & Bro.
Carriage-maker, Newbern, Waters & Sons.
Cigars. Newbern (Middle st), John Thomas.
Contracting and building, Newbern, John B Lane.
Contracting and building, Newbern, Herbert W Simpson.
Cotton gin Co, Newbern, Newbern Cotton-gin Co.
Cotton-seed Oil Mill and Cotton-gin, A R Dennison.
Fertilizers, Newbern, E H & J A Meadows.
Furniture and mattresses, Newbern, Patterson & Gaskill.
Furniture, ——, John Suter.
Furniture, Newbern, T J Turner.
Gas works, Newbern, Newbern Gas Light Co.
Guns and locks, Newbern, J T Hall & Bro.
Machine shops, ——, Crabtree & Co.
Machine shops and foundry, Newbern, Atlantic and N C R R.
Planing, molding and brackets, Newbern, Stimson Lumber Co.
Rubber stamps and stencil plates, Newbern, W T Hill.
Saddles and harness, Newbern, W S Phillips.
Shingles, Newbern, Bradus & Co.
Shingles and staves
Shingle mill, ——, Warren Ellis.
Ship-building, Newbern, J A Meadows.
Steam engines and boilers, Newbern, Crabtree & Co.
Truck-box factory, Newbern, George Bishop.

CRAVEN COUNTY. | CRAVEN COUNTY.

Tinware, Newbern, Daniel Smaw.
Tinware, Newbern, L H Cutler.
Turpentine, Newbern, Mrs E B Ellis.
Turpentine, Newbern, A R Dennison.

MERCHANTS AND TRADESMEN.

Names, Post Offices, Lines of Business.

ARNOLD.

Arthur, E H,   G S
Atkins, Julia A,   G S

BACHELOR.

Temple, W G,   G S

BELLAIR.

Lane, Guy S,   Gro

CLOSS.

Pearce, Wm B,   G S

COVE.

Avery, E D,   G S
Davis, E Z R,   G S
Richardson, G W.   G S
Taylor, L F,   G S
Tyndall, W M,   G S
White, F W,   G S
White, J C & Co,   G S
White, Mrs Julia,   G S

DOVER.

Adler, A.   Gro
Barrow, H S.   G S
Daugherty, M C,   Gro
Daugherty, E E,   G S
Hawkins, R L,   G S
Haskins & Huggins,   G S
Hines Bro,   G S
Richard, Voss,   G S
Street, J A,   Supply Store
Tyndall, W M,   G S
West & Richardson,   G S
White & Hawkins,   G S
Whitley, Jos & Co,   G S
Woodhurt, Mrs Charles,   Milliner

ERNUL.

Askins, Mrs J A,   G S
Fulcher, Barney,   Gro
Fulcher, Alonzo,   Gro
Stewart, K B,   G S
Thomas, W A,   G S
Weatherington, H B,   G S

FORT BARNWELL.

Davis, H C,   G S
Love, M D,   G S
Sauls, W R,   G S
White, W C,   G S

HAVELOCK.

DeParte, John,   G S
Fisher, M N,   G S
Garrell, J L,   G S
Piver, E,   G S

JAMES CITY.

Butler, Albert (col),   Gro

JASPER.

Dawson, A B,   G S
French, T E,   Gro
Wetherington, E D,   G S

MAPEL CYPRESS.

Gardner, J B,   Grocer
Stokes, R B,   Drugs

MERRIMON.

Gilbert, L M,   G S
Lee, A,   G S

NEWBERN.

Allegood, R E,   Broker
Armstrong & Baxter,   G S
Barfield, J D,   Green Grocer
Barrington, A H,   Grocer
Barrington, W R,   Sewing Machines
Baxter, J J,   Dry Goods
Baxter, E B,   Jeweler
Baxter, Mrs T J,   Jeweler
Benton, J H.   Dentist
Berry, Mrs R (Pollock Street),
                                     Milliner
Berry, Richard,   Drugs
Bishop, E K,   Mdse Broker
Bishop, R H.   Machinist
Blake, John R,   Grocer
Blumgardt, S, Agent,   Clothing
Blumgardt, Mrs M,   Dry Goods
Boom, J A (col),   Grocer
Bowden, F M,
                   Groceries and Confections
Bradham, C D,   Drugs
Broaddus, R F,   Grocer
Bryan, W P M,
                 Agent Southern Express Co
Bryan, A A (col),   B and S
Bryan, H R, jr,   Comm
Burruss, Wm P,   Grocer and Com'n
Bynum, A L,   Grocer
Copeland, S.   G S
Chadwick, Edward, Ticket Agent
          A & N C R R, and Telegraph Operator
Chapman, M W (col),   G S
Churchill, Lee L,   Tin and Iron
Clark, Jas F,   Grocer
Cohen, Lee,   Dry Goods and Clothing
Collins, J C,   Grocer
Cox, W B,   Grocer
Cox, Frank (col),   G S
Cutler, L H & Co,   Hardware
Daniels, Thos,   Fish Dealer
Damenberg, H,   Bottler
Dill, Samuel L, Superintendent
                             A & N C R R
Dellinghan, Mrs E F,
                      Books and Stationery
Dissosway, R J,   Grocer
Dissosway, R J,   Mill Supplies
Draney, P M,   Hardware
Duffy & Hill,   Confections
Duffy, F S,   Drugs
Duffy, Harvey B,   D G and B and S

CRAVEN COUNTY.

Dukes, J W,   Tinners
Dunn, John, Wholesale and
                          Retail Grocer
Dunn, W T,   Jeweler
Faton, Sam K,   Jeweler
Eubank, J W,   Auctioneer
Finch, A J,   General Insurance
Fisher, E,   Grocer
Fowler, J L,   Livery and Feed
Fulcher, A,   Grocer
Fallman, C,   Hardware and Tin
Gallup, A,   Lumber
Gaskill, Twiney & Co,   Fish Dealers
Gaskins, Chas W,   G S
Gaskins, A J,   Grocer
Gaskins, Henry,   Grocer
Gerock, Ed,   Photographer
Geddeon, Harris,   Grocer
Gorham, A J,   Grocer
Graves, ——,   General Insurance
Green, J C,   Plumber
Greenbaum,   Oyster Packers
Gates & Oliver,   Cotton Buyers
Gertman & Mahr,   Dry Goods
Hackburn & Willett,
            Wholesale and Retail G S
Hackburn, J H,   Grocer
Hahn, M & Co,   Livery
Hall, Henry L,   Books
Hall, T J & Bro,   Gunsmith
Harper, E E, Editor Newbern Journal
Harrison, Jas M,   Grocer
Hartsfield, J S & Co,   Grocer
Hargett, D A,   Drugs
Hassell, D,   Confections
Hayes, Elias,   Grocer
Haven, E,   B and S
Henry, T A,   Drugs
Hilbord, A E,   Jeweler
Hill, Humphrey, Agent,
            Auction and Retail
Hill, S E & Co.   G S
Hill, Mrs W I & Co,   Rubber Stamps
Hill, C S & Co,   Grain and Feed
Hilliard, L A.   G S
Holland, Jos B & Co,   Dry Goods
Hollister, C S,
            Wholesale and Retail Grocer
Hollister & Cox,   Com'n
Holly, M P,   Tailor
Hough, W T,   Grocer
Howard, Milon, Pollock St,
                    General Insurance
Howard, J M,   Clothing
-Hussey, Jno (col),   Grocer
Ipock. Mrs M M,   Grocer
Ives Geo & Son,   Fish Dealers
Jackson, Samuel,   Repair Shop
Jarvis, D F,   Dry Goods
Jones, K R,   G S
Jones, B C.   Stationer
Jones, W P,   Furniture
Jones, J A, Livery and Sales Stables
Jones, Peter (col),   Wood
Jones, W P,   Furniture

CRAVEN COUNTY.

Jordan, J V, Estate,   Drugs
Kafer, Jacob,   Baker
Kellam, Jas,   Grocer
Lane, Mrs B B, Middle St,   Milliner
Lane, Miss Harriet,Pollock St, Milliner
Lane, Mrs S H, Pollock St,   Milliner
Lane, B B,   Fish Dealer
Lane, Mrs H,   Millinery
Lane, Miss Harriett,   Millinery
Latham, J E, Com Merchant
                    and Cotton Buyer
Lorch, Wm,   G S
Lovick & Co,   Racket Store
Lucas & Lewis,   G S and Bakers
Mace, W S,   Drugs
Manly, M E,   Postmaster
Mannix, John S, Gen Agent
                    W N & Norfolk R R
Marks, E & Son, Wholesale
                    and Retail Dry Goods
McCarthy, T F,   G S
McCotter, H,   Fruits
McDaniel & Gashill,   Grocers
McSorley, John.   Shoemaker
Meadows, E H & J A Co,   Com'n
Meadows, J A,   Miller and Grain
Merritt, E (col),   Grocer
Montgomery & Makely,   Fish
Moore & Brady, Oysters and
                    Fruit Packers
Moody & Co,   Grocers
Nunn, K & Co,   Confections
Oglesby, W B.   Grocer
Orlansky, Philip,   Dry Goods
Oliver, Wm H (South St),
                    Gen Insurance Agent
Parker, J R, jr,   Grocer
Parris, J A & Co,   Wholesale Grocer
Parson , J B, State Inspector
                    of Oysters
Parsons, Samuel,   Sailmaker
Patterson, M & Son,   Grocers
Peed & Griffin,   Grocers
Perkins & Sutton,   Shipyard
Phillips, S J,   Grocer
Phillips. W S,   Harness
Pope, J R,   G S
Pope, Guy W,   G S
Richardson, N S & Son,   Printers
Roberts & Bro,
            Wholesale and Retail Grocers
Roberts, M T,   Grocer
Roberts, I P.   Grocer
Rosenbaum, J,   Clothing, etc
Rose, R E L,   Grocer
Rose, W,   G S
Rosenberg, J,
            Dry Goods and Clothing
Rountree, W F,   Commission
Saunders, C M (col),   Jeweler
Sawyer, R (col),   Tailor
Scott & Co,   Grocers
Scott, Mrs M J,   Grocer
Schelky, C J.   Lumber
Shepard, Miles,   Cabinet Maker

CRAVEN COUNTY.		CRAVEN COUNTY.	

Slover Hardware Co,	Hardware	Williams, A M,	G S
Smallwood, E W,	Hardware	**ZORAH.**	
Smallwood, J W,	Grocer	Tolar, A,	G S
Smaw, D G,	Tinner		
Smith, B J,	G S	**MILLS.**	
Smith, A J,	Dry Goods		
Spencer, C L,	Grain	Kinds, Post Offices and Proprietors.	
Sperling, H,	D G and B and S		
Stewart, John W,	Livery	Steam saw, corn and flouring mill,	
Staub, Henry,	Cabinet Maker	Union Point, Newbern, J A Mead-	
Street, S R, South Front St,		ows.	
Gen Insurance and Auctioneer		Steam saw mill, cotton-gin, ship yard	
Street, E S,.	Livery	and steam marine railway, Newbern,	
Suter, John,	Furniture	J A Meadows,	
Swert, Bernard,	Green Grocer	Steam saw and planing mill, Newbern,	
Swindell, W B & Co,	Dry Goods	D Congdon & Son.	
Taylor, L F,	G S	Steam saw and planing mill, Newbern,	
Taylor, L J,	Grocer	Jo Clark.	
Taylor, Jas F,	Grocer	Steam saw and planing mill, Pamlico,	
Tilling, Mrs Kate,	G S	Dean Lumber Co.	
Tolson, J J,	Grocer	Steam saw and corn, Bay River. Ab-	
Tucker, Eugene,	G S	bott & Co.	
Turner, F D Hardware Co,		Steam saw mill, Cove, B Ipock.	
Hardware and Furniture		Steam saw mill, Newbern, Blades &	
Tyson & Co, Agents,	Grocers	Bro.	
Ulrich, Ferdinand,	Ship Chandlery	Steam saw mill, Newbern, Stimson	
Vincent, N F,	Grocer	Lumber Co.	
Wadsworth, A E,	G S	Steam saw mill, Newbern, D Congdon	
Wallum Bros,	G S	& S n.	
Watson, C T,	Fish Dealer	Steam saw mill, Newbern, D L Cooper.	
Waters, S B,	Confections	Steam saw mill, Newbern, John W	
Wetherington, H B,	G S	Moody.	
Whaley, Mrs Bettie,	Milliner	Steam saw mill, Smith's Creek, Kughle	
Whitehurst, M E,	Variety	& Bro.	
Whitty, J C & Co,		Steam saw mill, Swift Creek, Heath	
Hardware and Agr Implem'ts		& Co.	
Willis, Jos K,	Marble	Steam saw mill, Fort Barnwell, W C	
Willis, S W,	Grocer	Whit.	
Willis, David, Freight Agent		Steam saw mill, Dover, Whitt & Haw-	
A & N C R R		kins.	
Winstead, F S & Co,	——	Steam, grist and gin, Pollocksville, J	
PERFECTION.		C Whitley.	
Arnold, Mrs Matilda,	G S	Steam flour, corn and saw, Newbern,	
RIVERDALE.		J A Meadows.	
Fisher, John S,	Gro	Steam cotton-gin, Newbern, J L Rhem.	
Porter, M,	G S	Steam corn, Swift Creek. —— Dinkins.	
THURMAN.		Water corn, Swift Creek, —— Dinkins.	
Connor, G L & Co,	G S	Water corn, Newbern, Wm Foy.	
Hardison, G L,	G S	Water corn, Newbern, John W Whit-	
TUSCARORA.		ford's heirs.	
Dillon, Thomas,	G S		
Dillon, T A,	Gro	**PHYSICIANS.**	
Moore, J M,	P M and G S		
Wetherington, O H,	G S	Names and Post Offices.	
VANCEBORO.		Atmore, George, Bay River.	
Brown, W E,	G S	Bagley, G K (dentist), Newbern.	
Cline, Wm, jr, agt,	G S	Benton, J H, Newbern.	
Ipock, N B,	Gro	Benton, Claude, Newbern.	
Ipock, John M,	Gro	Clark, J D (dentist), Newbern.	
Ipock, W H,	Gro	Duffy, Leicester, Newbern.	
Willis, Samuel,	G S	Duffy, C & F, Middle st, Newbern.	
Willis, J J,	Variety	Duguid, Jos, Newbern.	
		Golberg, E H (dentist), Newbern.	
		Hughes, J B, Newbern.	

14

CRAVEN COUNTY.

Hughes, Frank, Newbern.
Jones, Jo, Cove.
Lassiter, —— (col), Newbern.
Peek, ——, Barnwell.
Potts, ——, Vanceboro.
Primrose, R S, Newbern.
Rhem, Jos, Newbern.
Street, N H, Newbern.

SCHOOLS.

Names, Post Offices and Principals.

Newbern Academy, (Newbern graded school), Hancock st; John Long, supt; Miss Rachel C Brookfield, chm of faculty; associate teachers—Mrs Mary Williams, Miss Annie Chadwick, Miss Emily Ferebee, Miss Mary Hendren, Miss Mary Brown, Miss Willie Ferrebee; twenty-three trustees; W M Watson, treas.
Newbern High School, Newbern (Hancock st); E P Mendehall, Mrs A B Ferrebee, Misses Cobb and Murchison; run by tuition fees.
Intermediate school, Newbern, Miss Leah Jones.
Music School, Newbern, Miss Hatchie Harrison.
Primary School, Newbern, Miss Mollie Heath.
Colored Graded School, Newbern (West st); C E Palmer, prin; E A V Dudley, Mary Jones, Susie V Havens, assistants.
Pres Parochial (col), Newbern, Rev W A Byrd.
St Cyprian Parochial (col), Newbern, Mrs M T Nhompson.
Public schools—white, 35; colored, 37.

TEACHERS.

Names and Post Offices.

WHITE.

Arnold, Victoria, Newbern.
Askins, Viola B, Newbern.
Brewer, Lida, Vanceboro.
Brooks, Lula, Newbern.
Brown, May, Newbern.
Brown, Mary S, Newbern.
Butchard, Monroe, Newbern.
Bynum, Rebecca A, Newbern.
Chadwick, Annie D, Newbern.
Charlton, Julia, Newbern.
Connor, Rena, Newbern.
Dinkin, Cora, Newbern.
Dinkin, Dollie L, Newbern.
Ernul, Cornelia, Ernul.
Ewell, Lula, Newbern.
Ewell, Elizabeth, Newbern.
Ferebee, Willie, Newbern.

CRAVEN COUNTY.

Ferebee, Emily, Newbern.
Hall, Bettie L, Newbern.
Heath, Sabra, Newbern.
Hendren, Mary L, Newbern.
Hunter, Maggie J, Newbern.
Jackson, John Allen, Vanceboro.
Lane, Jennie. Newbern.
Lane, Julia H, Newbern.
Lane, Wm H, Newbern.
Martin, Elizabeth, Newbern.
Pope, Myrtle, Newbern.
Porter, Elizabeth, Newbern.
Prescott, Olivia. Newbern.
Smith, Ellen, Vanceboro.
Stubbs, Chas F, Newbern.
Trenwith, Fannie, Newbern.
Tucker, Katie, Newbern.
Tucker, Bertha E, Newbern.
Tucker, Bessie, Newbern.
Wetherington, Leak. Vanceboro.
Williams, Mary N, Newbern.
White, Minnie L, Newbern.
White, Hattie. Newbern.
Wilcox, Geo, Newbern.
Willis, J K, Marble Works.
Wilson, Geo, Newbern.
Wingfield, J V, Newbern.

COLORED.

Cherry, John T, Newbern.
Diggin, Carrie E, Newbern.
Everett, Arthur, Newbern.
Fisher, Maggie W, Newbern.
Garris, Mary E, Newbern.
Palmer, C E, Newbern.
Physic, Chas E, Newbern.
Walker, Nancy J, Newbern.

NEWSPAPERS.

Journal (Dem, daily and weekly), Newbern; C L Stephens, ed and prop.

LOCAL CORPORATIONS.

Athenia Lodge, No. 8, K. of P. S B Waters, C C. Time of meeting, second and third Tuesdays in each month.
Blade's Lumber Co, Newbern; capital stock, $150,000; W B Blade, pres.
Calumet Encampment, No. 4, I O O F, Newbern, B B Neal, C P.
Citizens Bank, Newbern, Thos Green, pres; H M Graves, casher. Capital stock, $50,000; surplus and undivided profits, $17,500.
Clark Lumber Co., Newbern; capital stock, $75,000. J B Cloth, pres.
Cotton and Grain Exchange, Craven street. S W Smallwood, pres; Jas Redmond, sec; T A Green, treas.
East Carolina Fish, Game and Oyster Association, Newbern. Wm Dunn, pres; Chas Reizenstein, sec and treas.

CRAVEN COUNTY.

East Carolina Barrel Factory, Newbern; Thos Daniels, pres; B B Neal, sec and treas.

Elm City Band (col), Newbern; John Fisher, leader.

Eureka Lodge, No. 7, I O O F, T W Dewey, N G. Day of meeting, Monday.

Farmers and Merchants' Bank, Newbern; L H Cutler, pres; T W Dewey, cash.

Newbern Royal Arch Chapter, No, 46; F Ulrich, H P.

Newbern Gas Light Co, S Front street; Samuel W Smallwood, pres.

Newbern Electric Light and Power Co, R P Williams, owner.

Newbern Ice Co, Wm Dunn, pres; B S Guion, sec and treas and mgr.

Newbern Building and Loan Association, L H Hunter, pres; J R B Carraway, sec.

Newbern Lodge, No 443, K of H.

Royal Arcanum, W G Brinson, Regent.

Silver Cornet Band (white), Newbern, C A Cook, leader.

Star Band (col), Newbern, Sam Richardson, leader.

St. John's Lodge, No 3, A F and A M, Newbern, T A Green, W M. Time of meeting, second Wednesday in each month.

St. John's Commandery K T, No. 10, Newbern, J H Hackburn, E C.

Stimpson Lumber Co, Newbern, Z R Folsom, pres.

Telephone Co, John Dunn, mgr.

The National Bank of Newbern; capital stock, $100,000; surplus and undivided profits, $82,000. Jas A Bryan, pres; vice-pres, Thos Daniels; cash, G H Roberts; teller, J R B Carraway; clerk, Green Bryan.

The East Carolina Dispatch Line, Geo Henderson, agt.

Water Co of Newbern, P H Pelletier, pres; James Redmond, sec and treas.

STEAMERS PLYING TO THE PORT OF NEWBERN.

"Cardina," between Newbern and Contentnea Creek.

"Eaglet," "Vesper" (Eastern Dispatch Line), between Newbern and Elizabeth City.

"Florence" (Swift Creek Line), J M Ipoch, Captain.

"George H Stewart," between Newbern and Baltimore.

"Howard" (Independent Line), J J Lassiter, General Manager.

"Newbern," "Manteo," between Newbern and Norfolk.

CRAVEN COUNTY.

The "Trent" and "L H Cutler," "Neuse," "Kinston" and "Blondie" steamers owned by the Neuse and Trent River Steamboat Co, a regular line of river steamers runnig between Kinston, Jolly, Old Field's, Biddle's Landing, Newbern, Pollocksville, Oliver's Landing and Trenton; capital paid up. $40,000.

FARMERS.

Names and Post Offices,

Bellair—M W Carman, J R Cromwell, S W Ipock, Jas H Ipock, Chas McIlwain, G T Richardson, Joe Stevenson, D L E Street, Geo Wilcox.

Closs—Jas Brown, H C Davis, Wiley Hill, W B Pearce, Jas Rouse, Jas L West.

Cove—W T Hawkins, J H Hawkins, F N Hawkins, J C Hawkins, A B Hawkins, R B Heath, W H Heath, D T Heath, Thos B Ipock, L F Taylor, F D White, W W White, T W White, T F Wetherington, J T Wetherington.

Dover—Asa Barns, R M Brock, Henry Daugherty, W T Hines, L B Humphrey, J W Rhem, Wm Rhem, G A Richardson, Vass Richardson, H T Richardson, Geo West, Rich White, Furney White.

Fort Barnwell—Miss Lizzie Biddle, John Biddle, J W Biddle, Oliver Biggs, M W Carr, H T Croom, E P Hartly, Joel Kinsey, Jos Kinsey, E H Lane, J W Lane, Rich McGlowhorn, R A Russell, M W Sauls, Alexander Taylor, E J White, W C White, J H White, Jno B Wooten, B B Wooten.

Havelock—T W Brame, J A Bryan, John Deport, J H Hunter, W H Mallison, T H Mallison, Henry Marshall, W H Pittman, J D Pittman, Mrs Emeline Rone, A J Rone, E D Russell, J L Stevenson, Mrs Mary L Taylor, G T Tippett, V A Tolson, J P Voliver, B E Williams.

Jasper—A B Dawson, Wm Dawson, S R French, Silas Heath, Alex Herring, G F Hill, Ed Wetherington.

Lima—Drew Dickson, Geo Green, Josin House, J M Pate, Oliver Perry, Robt Wethersbee.

Mapel Cypress—J B Gardner, J F Gwaltney, Willie Kirkman, J W Kirkman, A E Kirkman, C C Kirkman, J F Kirkman, LaFayette Kirkman, Steven Kite, Sam Kite, L M Lancaster, Jacob Lancaster, J D May, Mrs Kate Moye, W T Smith, A A Smith, Mrs Lovie Spier, R B Stokes, H H Summerell, Spice Wetherington, Alex Wiggins, Fred Wiggins, Hermon Willis.

CRAVEN COUNTY.	CRAVEN COUNTY.

Newbern—W H Bray, W F Crocket, E R Dudley (col), Wm Dunn, Hackburn & Willett. J A Meadows, J L Rhem, Enoch Wadsworth, Watson & Daniels, A J Yeoman.

North Harlowe—J H George (col), Leander Gilbert, J P Godet (col), Jerry Godet (col), J T Morton, Ben Richards (col). T S Richardson (col), John Smith, Jos Smith, David Sparrow (col), W F Taylor, Nelson Taylor, Isaac Taylor, A B Taylor, W G Temple, Jesse P Troller.

Perfection—Stephen Arnold, Wm Arnold, Walter Cox, J B Ferand, L H French, Brice Ipock. Wm Ipock, Geo Ipock, W B Lain, Milton Lancaster, Fred Pate, D W Porter, Wm Porter. W W Prescott, A E Wadsworth. E W Wadsworth.

Riverdale—Geo Conner, Robt Davis (col). J F Hardison, W J Hardison. G L Hardison, Summerfield Hasket, Henry B Lane, Geo B Latham, Washington Miller (col), H H Perry, Washington Spivey (col).

Vanceboro—J S Jackson, Elias Anderson, Nathan Barrington, J L Bland, Isaac Boyd (col), J B Boyd, C R Brewer, C W Brewer, H E Brinkley, W E Brown, S W Brooks, G F Buck, J R Buck, Mrs Mary Dewey, G J Dudey, Thos Gaskins. Furney Jackson, W F Lancaster, J R Miller, W R Morris, L M Morris, W D Morris, Wesley D Morris, Wm Morris, Jno B Nelson. A W Nelson, Fenner P Nelson, O C Nobles, J B O'Neal. Wm Padrick, Jesse Peterson, Robt Phillips. Jno Powell, Geo D Pugh. J F Purser, J A Purser, Thos White.

CUMBERLAND COUNTY.

AREA, 900 SQUARE MILES.

POPULATION, 27,293, WHITE, 14,952; COLORED, 12,341.

CUMBERLAND COUNTY was formed in the year 1754 from the upper part of Bladen. It derives its name from the Duke of Cumberland, a popular and brave officer, at that time, in England.

FAYETTEVILLE, the county-seat, was settled in 1762, and was at first called Campbelltown, afterwards Cross Creek, and in 1784 its name was changed to Fayetteville, in honor of General Lafayette. Fayetteville is located on the Cape Fear river; it is sixty miles west of south from Raleigh, and contains a population of 8,000.

Surface—Cumberland is situated on the Cape Fear river and tributaries; land generally level, a d much of it quite productive when well drained—especially so along the streams.

Staples — Cotton and corn are the leading staples. Naval stores are still pr duced, but not as extensively as formerly, though still a source of considerable income to the county.

Fruits—Pears, apples, peaches, apricos, grapes (the Tokay vineyards are in this county), all the small fruits and melons equal to any, perhaps, grown in the State.

Timbers—Pine in abundance, oak, gum, hickory, cypress, etc.

TOWNS AND POST OFFICES.

	POP.		POP.
Alderman,	20	Hope Mills,	270
Antonia,	25	Idaho,	25
Argyle,	15	Ivernesss,	10
Beard,	25	Kyle's Landing,	10
Brunt,	32	Leavitt.	32
Buckhorn,	25	Little River	
Carlos,	25	Academy,	85
Carmichael,	33	Manchester,	1,200
Cedar Creek,	70	Montrose,	50
Clay Fork,	30	Pike,	20
Cornelia,	30	Raeford,	20
Cumberland,	40	Rhodes,	20
Dial,	15	Robin Hill,	50
Edonia,	25	Roslin,	25
Falcon,	23	Sherwood,	20
Fayetteville,	8,000	Starsburg,	40
Floyd,	25	Stedman,	—
Gillisville,	15	Vander,	—
Godwin,	150	Wade,	—
Gray's Creek,	80	Wicker,	—

COUNTY OFFICERS.

Superior Court Clerk—Cyrus Murphy. *Commissioners*—J M Lamb (ch), W Doug Smith. J F Sinclair, J Hector Smith, Morris Hall.
Coroner—Dr J F High Smith.
Register of Deeds—Alex McNeill.
Sheriff—M D Geddie.
County Physician—J H Marsh.
Solicitor 7th District—H F Seawell.
Surveyor—Wm Alderman.
Standard Keeper—C J Hedgepeth.
Treasurer—J B Troy.
County Examiner—H F King.
Keeper Jail—W W Autry.
County Home for aged and infirm—Alex Leslie, supt.

COURTS.

Superior Court meets seventh Monday after the first Monday in March; tenth Monday after the first Monday March; sixth Monday before the first Monday in September; and tenth Monday after the first Monday in September.

TOWN OFFICERS.

FAYETTEVILLE—*Mayor*, W S Cook; *Clerk*, D McD Gradie; *Treasurer*, H O Sedberry; *Marshal*, W H Thomas; *Tax Collector*. S W Tillinghast.

TOWNSHIPS AND MAGISTRATES.

Beaver Dam—D M Beard, C H Cogdell, Jas W Cogdell, C P Rollins, W J F Beard (Cedar Creek), J S Horne, Alex Simmons, J J Bullard, M H Bullard (Clay Fork).

Black River—Isaac Strickland, J C Bain, Nathan Williams, D J L McIntyre, W Dolly Smith (Godwin), W M Pope, Z Taylor (Dunn).

Carver's Creek—A McBuie, Wm B Ray, Walter A Tillinghast. W L Williams, W G Adams (Little River Academy), E L Collier, J M McFarland, M W King, R R Bell (Wicker).

Cedar Creek—Jno B Downing (Buckhorn), J B Bryant. J H Averitt (Stedman). N C Thaggard, John McP Geddie, H B Downing, A J Bullard (Vander), Guilford Horn (Idaho)

Cross Creek—W S Cook, C P Overby, R W Hardie, W D Gaster, J W Sellars, D N McLean, W P Wemyss, T B Newberry, W J Tolar, Geo W Lawrence, A J Deal (Fayetteville).

CUMBERLAND COUNTY.

Flea Hill—G A McDonald. W H H Wade, Nathan A Williams, R J Harrison, W J Sessoms (Wade), D J Bruce, P N Talbott, J D Geddie, E S Sanders, D B Autry (Fayetteville).

Gray's Creek—E H Evans, J B Carver, J P Thomas, William Clark (Sherwood), W A Gainey, J B Williams. W C Riddle (Alderman), James Pate, A Gainey (Edonia).

Little River—J J Wright, J H Smith, L C Johnson (Little River Academy).

Quewhiffle—D K McDuffie, D J Ray (Gillisville), J A McRae, N S Buie (Montrose), J C Currie, J D McLeod, J A Campbell, Eugene Lewitt, Nathan Patterson (Pike).

Rockfish—John Smith (Roslin), E A Poe (Fayetteville), Louchlin McDonald, J T Sellars, T J Gardner, Warren Carver, M L Patterson, D J Cashwell, G E Buie, D A McNeill (Hope Mills).

Seventy-first—Duncan Shaw, N D M Clark (Raeford), J A McPherson, D B Gillis, J T Townsend, Thos Bennett, J W S Smith (Argyle), J R Luther, R S Jenkinson (Manchester).

CHURCHES.

Names, Post Offices, Pastors and Denom.

PRESBYTERIAN.

Barbecue—Fayetteville, J P McPherson.
Bethlehem—Fayetteville, H G Hill.
Bethel—Raeford, O E White.
Bluff—Kyle's Landing, —— Hassel.
China Grove—Manchester, D Fairly.
Church—Fayetteville (Church st), A J McKelway.
Church (col)—Fayetteville.
Church of the Covenant—Manchester, D Fairly.
Galatia—Fayetteville, O E White.
Long Street—Argyle, D Fairly.
Long Creek—Manchester, D Fairly.
McPherson—Fayetteville, D Fairly.
Phillippi—Raeford, O E White.
Rockfish—Fayetteville, Stead. Black.
Sandy Grove—Fayetteville, D Fairly.
Sardis—Little River Academy, Steadman Black.
Shiloh—Pike.

METHODIST.

Beaver Creek—Fayetteville, — Whitaker.
Bethany—Steadman, D A Futrell.
Camp Ground—Fayetteville, — Whitaker.
Church—Fayetteville, R A Willis.
Church—Cedar Creek, — Whitaker.
Church (col) — Cedar Creek, Isham Williams.

CUMBERLAND COUNTY.

Cokesbury—Steadanm, D A Futrell.
Marion Chapel—Gray's Creek, —— Whitaker.
Parker's Grove—Little River Academy, —— Whitaker.
Salem—Fayetteville, D A Futrell.
St Andrew's—Fayetteville.
Tabor—Cedar Creek, D S Futrell.
White Sulpher Springs—Manchester, —— Whitaker.
Evan's Chapel—Fayetteville, —— Zion.

BAPTIST.

Antioch—Fayetteville, W R Johnson.
Cape Fear—Gray's Creek, A E C Pittman.
Church—Cedar Creek, R A Hedgepeth,
Church—Fayetteville, C A S Thomas.
Church—(First col), Fayetteville, G W Moore.
Concord—Steadman, R A Hedgepeth.
Judson—Fayetteville, R A Hedgepeth.
Magnolia—Steadman, R A Hedgepeth.
Manchester—Manchester, J W Cobb.

SEVENTH DAY BAPTIST.

Curch Cumberland—Dial, D N Newton.

EPISCOPAL.

Christ Church — Rock Fish, I W Hughes, Rector; Joseph C Huske, D D, assistant.
St John's—Fayetteville, I W Hughes.
St Joseph's—(col), Fayetteville, Joseph C Huske, D D.
St Luke's—(col), Fayetteville, E S W Simmons.

A. M. E. ZION.

Beaver Creek—(col), Fayetteville, J W Horr.
Church — (col), Manchester, Benson Hasty.
Clark's Chapel—(col), Tar Heel, C P S Harrison.
Evans' Chapel—(col), Steadman, Isham Williams.
Evans'—Metropolitan, Fayetteville, P L Cylor.
Flea Hill—(col), Wade, C S Smith.
Gardner's Chapel—(col), Wade, C S Smith.
Hugh Grove — Fayetteville, Benson Hasty.
Little Marsh—(col), ——, C P S Harrison.
Lock's Creek—(col), Steadman, Isham Williams.
Mt Hebrew—(col), Kingsbury, Benson Hasty.
Mt Hebron — (col), Hope Mills, J J Stitt.
New Bethel—(col), ——, J W Horr.
Snow Hill—(col), Fayetteville, J J Stitt.

CUMBERLAND COUNTY.

Spring Branch—(col), Tar Heel, C P S Harrison.
St Paul's—(col), Steadman, Isham Williams.
Swanns Grove—(col), Fayetteville, J W Horr.
Union Oak—(col), ——, J J Stitt.
Wesley's Chapel—(col), C S Smith.
Willis Creek—(col), Gray's Creek, C P S Harrison.
Zion Hall—(col), Fayetteville, —— McNeill.
Church [Af. Meth]—Fayetteville.

CATHOLIC.

St John's—Fayetteville.

MINISTERS RESIDENT.

Names, Post Offices and Denominations.

METHODIST.

Boone, J A D, Fayetteville.
Culbreth, Love, Blocker's.
Johnson, W J, Fayetteville.
McLean, D N, Fayetteville.
Sutton, T H, Fayetteville.
Willis, R A, Fayetteville.

BAPTIST.

Lebanon, Beard, Dr W B Harrell.
Lilly's Grove, Beard, Dr W B Harrell.
Moore, G W, Fayetteville.
Thos, C A S, Fayetteville.

PRESBYTERIAN.

McBryde, D D, Little River Academy.
McKilway, Fayetteville.

EPISCOPAL.

Hughes, I W, Fayetteville.
Huske, Joseph. C, D D, Fayetteville.
Simmons, E S W, Fayetteville.

A. M. E. ZION.

Cylor, P A (col), Fayetteville.
Hill, J M, P E (col), Fayetteville.
Hood, J W, Bishop, D D, LL D, (col), Fayetteville.
Kelly, Chesie (col), Fayetteville.
Keene, H L (col), Fayetteville.

A. M. E.

Moore, C F (col), Fayetteville.
Smith, D W (col), Fayetteville.
Jordan, P J (col), Fayetteville.
Grange, G W (col), Fayetteville.
Hill, J M (col), Fayetteville.

HOTELS AND BOARDING HOUSES.

Names, Post Offices and Proprietors.

Boarding House, Fayetteville, Mrs Archie Smith.
Boarding House, Fayetteville, Mrs Spencer.
Boarding, Fayetteville, Mrs Carson.
Boarding, Fayetteville, Mrs D Owen.
Boarding, Fayetteville, S J Walton.

CUMBERLAND COUNTY.

Goddard House, Fayetteville, J M Goddard.
Hotel LaFayette, Hay st, Fayetteville, M McG Matthews.
Ingram House, Fayetteville, Needham Ingram.
Martin House, Old st, Fayetteville, G M Martin.
Ourlaugh House, Green st, Fayetteville, A Ourlaugh.

LAWYERS.

Names and Post Offices.

Bidgood, C W, Fayetteville (Robinson & Bidgood).
Broadfoot, C W, Fayetteville.
Buxton, Ralph P (ex Judge S C), Hay st, Fayetteville.
Cook, Henry L, Fayetteville.
Johnson, Jas H, Hope Mills.
MacRae, J C (Judge S C), Fayetteville.
McRae. S H, Fayetteville (McRae, J C & S H).
Newton, Z B, Hope Mills.
Pope, W H, Fayetteville.
Ray, Neill W, Fayetteville.
Robinson, H McD, Hay st, Fayetteville.
Rose, Duncan, Fayetteville.
Rose, George M. Fayetteville.
Shaw, John D, Fayetteville.
Sinclair, N A, Fayetteville.
Sutton, Thomas H, Fayetteville,

MANUFACTORIES.

Kinds, Post Offices and Proprietors.

Bakery, Fayetteville, C M Watson.
Bakery, Fayetteville, W F Raiford.
Beer bottling, Gillespie st, Fayetteville, D R Huffiness.
Photographer, Fayetteville, Hay st, Rev J A D Boone.
Brick Manufactory, Gillespie st, Fayetteville, E A Poe & Co.
Carriages, buggies and harness. Person st, Fayetteville, McKethan & Son.
Carolina Baking Powders. Fayetteville, No 23 Hay st, H R Horne.
Carolina Machine Co, Fayetteville, Russell Bros.
Cotton factory (Beaver Creek and Bluff Mills); H W Lilly, president; E G Lilly, secretary; N. F. Holmes, superintendent; 8,056 spindles, 60 looms.
Candy, Fayetteville, Noel Wilson.
Candy, Fayetteville, Kenneth Cole.
Candy, Fayetteville, W F Raiford.
Candy, Fayetteville, A E Smith.
Cumberland Mills, Cotton. Cumberland, J C Buxton, pres; W K Parker, sup.

CUMBERLAND COUNTY.

Edge-tool manufactory, Hay st, Walter Watson.
Fayetteville Cider Works, Fayetteville, A A McKethan.
Fayetteville Ice Factory, Fayetteville, D P Wemyss and J W Johnson.
Fayetteville Cooperage Co, R M Nimocks, owner and manager.
Fayetteville Cotton Mills, Fayetteville, J P Thompson, pres; A A McKethan, sec and treas.
Fayetteville Cotton-seed Oil Mill and Fertilizer Co, J R Williams, mgr; N B Alexander, supt; capacity, 24 boxes of seed per day.
Foundry, Person st, Fayetteville, J N Emmitt.
Foundry and plow manufactory, Hillsboro st, Fayetteville, Thos Ward.
Furniture, Cool Springs st, Fayetteville, W H Newberry & Son.
Hope Mills, No 1 (cotton). Hope Mill; Hope Mills, No 2 (cotton). Hope Mill; S H Cotton, sup; W C Houston, Jr, Philadelphia, Pa, pres.
Manchester Mills (cotton), Manchester, John F Clark, owner and mgr.
Native wines (Tokay vineyard), Fayetteville, Wharton J Green.
Planing Mill, Fayetteville, Walter Watson.
Planing Mill, Fayetteville, W L Rankin & Bro.
Planing Mill, Fayetteville, Walter Watson.
Planing Mill, Fayetteville, C O Gunenwyer.
Planing Mill, Fayetteville, Rankin Bros.
Prior's Rheumatic Remedy, Market Square, Fayetteville, A J Cook.
Saddles and harness, Hay st, Fayetteville, H Whaley.
Saddles and harness, 46 S Person st, Fayetteville, C F Overby.
Sausage and candy, Gillespie st, Fayetteville, Raiford Bros.
Shuttle Block, Fayetteville, L A Weeden, prop.
Southern Telephone Co, Fayetteville, W R & B Hawkins.
Steam Laundry, Gillespie st, Fayetteville, S A E Waddell, mgr.
Turpentine, Endor, W D Cameron & Co.
Turpentine, Endor, L A Blue.
Turpentine, Endor, Neill S Blue.
Turpentine, Glen Echo, Alex Sessoms.
Turpentine stills, stoves and tinware, 54 Person st, Fayetteville, McMillan & Bros.
Turpentine distillery, Fayetteville, A H Slocumb.
Turpentine distillery, Benson, A E Rankin & Co.

CUMBERLAND COUNTY.

Wagons, etc, Sanford Kelly Bros.
Art Gallery, Person st, Fayetteville, J L Winburn.
Woodenware Co, Fayetteville, J W McNeill, Sr, pres; C L Taylor, sec and treas.
Wool carding, Fayetteville, Thos Bennett.
Wool carding, Franklin st, Fayetteville, J N Emmitt.

MERCHANTS AND TRADESMEN.

Names, Post Offices and Line of Business.

ALDERMAN.

Johnson. J D,	G S

BRUNT.

Nunalee, W L,	G S

BUCKHORN.

Carter, H H,	G S
Downing, H B,	G S

CEDAR CREEK.

Geddie, J McP,	G S

CLAY FORK.

Bullard, H M,	Lumber
Bullard, P M,	G S
Hale, H & G,	G S
Smith, Simon,	G S
Smith, A C,	G S
Vinson, Sam,	G S

CUMBERLAND.

Cumberland Mfg Co,	G S
Harrington, A A, jr,	G S
Holmes, W G,	G S

FALCON,

Tew, O L,	G S

FAYETTEVILLE.

Atkinson, Mrs A,	Millinery
Beasley, B F,	Jewelry
Bevill & Vanstory,	Livery
Blue, D A,	G S
Boone, J A D,	Photog
Bolton, H H,	Miller
Bowman, Chas (col),	Undertaker
Brady, A G,	Capitalist
Bryant, David (col),	G S
Burns, G A,	Livery
Burns, R,	Livery
Carmon, S J,	Gro
Clark, E L.	Gro
Clark, W G,	Gro
Cole, W W.	Gro
Cook, A J & Co,	Drugs
Cook, W S,	Prov and Com
Cook, J P & Co,	Variety Store
Crawford, W A,	Tailor
Culbreth, Jno,	Broker
Davis, John & Bro.	Gro
Downing, H B,	—
Dye, Mrs L R,	Millinery

CUMBERLAND COUNTY.		CUMBERLAND COUNTY.	
Elliott, C W,	Gro	Ray, D H & Co,	Gro
Emmett, J N,	Foundry	Raynor, M M,	Gro
Evans, J & O,	G S	Reinsburg, E L,	Marble Works
Evans, W,	Gro	Robinson, J H, jr,	Furn
Folb, M,	D G and Clo	Robertson, A J & Co,	Books
Garrison, A,	Gro	Saul Bros,	Gro
Gill, Thos,	Shoemaker	Scurlock, G C,	Gro
Glover, Chas,	Auctioneer	Sedberry, B E & Son,	Drugs
Goddard, J M,	Gro	Shaw, Mrs Jno,	Fancy Goods
Green, W J,	Tokay Vineyard	Sheets, S & Son, Furn and Undertaker	
Haigh, Chas,	Gro and Hdw	Sloan, W T,	Gro
Hardin, W V,	G S	Slocumb, A H,	Turp
Hall, I B (col),	G S	Smith, Miss Mary H,	Millinery
Hedgepeth, C S,	Gro	Starr, J B,	Com and Fert
Hedgepeth, C L,	Gro	Strickland, J M,	Gro
Henderson, G H,	Gro	Tatum, J L, agt,	Gro
Hiatt, J K,	Ice house	Taylor, B R,	Mdse Broker
Hollingsworth, B G,	Gro	Thompson, J C,	Gro
Holland & Hollingsworth,	Racket Store	Thompson, Geo A, Green st, Real Estate, Ins and Mdse Broker	
Homer, M G	G S	Tillinghast, W N,	Crockery
Horne, H R,	Drugs	Thornton, Frank W & Son,	D G and Clo
Huske, A A, agt,	Gro		
Huske, ——,	Hdw House	Teller, M A,	Jeweler
Jackson, Alex,	G S	Underwood, J B, jr,	Mdse Broker
Jackson, Isador,	D G and Clo	Vann, J C,	D G
Jackson, Wm,	G S	Vann, J M,	Tailor
Jackson, O J,	Gro	Vann, J A,	G G
King Bros,	Drugs	Vann & Co,	G S
Lamb, Jas M,	Florist	Ward, Thos,	Mfr Plows
Lambeth, J A, Livery and Carriages		Watson, C M (mgr),	Bakery
Lilly, E J,	D G	Watson, W,	G S
Lutterloh, T S,	Junk	Whaley, H,	Harness
Matthews, M McG,	G S	Whaley, J J,	Jewelry
McDuffie, W C, jr,	Drugs	Wilkerson, Geo A P (col),	Grocer
McMillan, D A,	G S	Wilkinson, G A R,	Gro
McMillan Bros, Hardware, Turp Stills		Williams, A B,	Brok and Com
McMillan Bros.	G S	Williams, J R Co,	Brokers
McFall, Jas D,	Miller	Williston, B B,	G S
McNeill, J R & Son (col), Undertakers and Paper Hangers		Williston, F D (col),	G S
		Winburn, J F,	Hhotog
Mc Lean, D N, Real Est Agt and Collector		Worrell, J D, jr,	G S and Turp
		Worrell, W A,	G S
Maultsby, J S,	D G		
Moore, T F,	Books	FLOYD.	
Newberry, W H & Sons,	Millers and Furn	Bullard, J J & Son,	G S
		GODWIN.	
Nimocks Bros, Whol Gro and Cotton		Demming, S E & Co,	G S
Novitsky, H R,	Clothing	Felton, Mrs E.	G S
Nunallee, W L,	——	McGullan, C C.	G S
Overbaugh, G A,	Real State	McNeill & Son,	G S and Turp
O'Daniel, J,	Gro	Pope, W M,	G S
Owen, Nat,	G S	GRAY'S CREEK.	
Pemberton, O J & Co, Books and Sta		Hair, John B,	G S
Perry, Jno L,	G S	Yarboro, F C,	G S
Phillips, S A,	Gro		
Powell, W H,	G S	HOPE MILLS.	
Powers, J F & Son,	Gro	Deaver, A,	G S
Prior, R M,	Gro	Harrington, A A, jr (agt),	G S
Prior, Warren & Son,	Jewelry	Hope Mills Mfg Co,	G S
Raiford, W F,	Gro	IDAHO.	
Raiford & Co,	Gro	Evans, J & O,	G S
Rankin, A E & Co,	G S		
Rankin, W L & Bros.	G S	KYLE'S LANDING.	
Rainor, M N,	Jeweler	Wade, J F,	G S

CUMBERLAND COUNTY.

LITTLE RIVER ACADEMY.

Adams, Jno C, G S
McCormick, ——, G S

MANCHESTER.

Clark, J F, G S
Frizell, Chas, G S
McArtan, Jno, G S

MONTROSE.

Hearne, S T, G S

PIKE.

Blue, J S, G S

RAIFORD.

McLaughlin, J W, G S and Naval Stores

SHERWOOD.

Thomas, Jas, G S

STEADMAN.

Sessoms, J D & Co, G S
Sessoms, Kelly, G S

VANDER.

Bullard, A J & Son, G S

WADE.

Baker, Duncan, G S
McAllister, D A, G S
Wilson, Allen, G S

MILLS.

Kinds, Post Offices and Proprietors.

Corn, Fayetteville, J M Goddard.
Corn, Steadman, Reuben Fisher.
Corn and saw, Steadman, — Maxwell.
Corn, Cedar Creek, V B Hare.
Corn and gin, Cedar Creek, J B Hare.
Corn and gin, Gray's Creek, Henry Jones.
Corn and rice, Vander, Bullard & McDaniel.
Corn, Wade, James McAlister.
Corn, Idaho, Horn & McDaniel.
Corn, Cedar Creek, H B Downing.
Corn and saw, Fayetteville, J H Currie.
Corn, gin and wool carding, Fayetteville, R T Bennett.
Corn and saw, Fayetteville, J S Raynor.
Corn and cotton gin, Fayetteville, C & J Martin.
Corn and gin, Manchester, J A R Howard.
Corn and gin, Little River Academy, D D McBryde.
Corn and gin, Fayetteville, W R King.
Corn and gin, Kyle's Landing, D McDonald.
Corn and gin, Cedar Creek, R A Melvin.
Corn, Fayetteville, Jas D McNeill.
Corn, Cedar Creek, J M Jessup.
Corn, Clay Fork, E E Fisher.
Corn, Fayetteville, Pate Bros.

CUMBERLAND COUNTY.

Corn, Fayetteville, John Buie.
Corn, Argyle, Allen Ray.
Corn, Cedar Creek, B M Smith.
Corn, Little River Academy, Mrs R C McNeill.
Corn, Little River Academy, Williams & Smith.
Flour and corn, Fayetteville, (Carolina Roller Mills), Nimrock Bros.
Flour and corn, Little River Academy, B E Byrd.
Merchant Mills, cor Green and Old sts, Fayetteville, J D McNeill.
Merchant flour and corn, Fayetteville, W H Newberry.
Planing Mill, Sanford, Jones Lumber Company.
Planing Mill, Sanford, Smith & Lane.
Saw, Fayet'eville, J D McNeill.
Saw and corn, Rhodes, Rhodes & McLellan.
Saw, corn and gin, Fayetteville, R L Williams.
Saw and corn, Manchester, Neill Black.
Shingles, Cedar Creek, David Clifton.
Steam saw, Vander, Carter & Carter.
Steam saw, Vander, Carter & Bullard.
Steam saw and gin, Steadman, K Sessoms & Co.
Steam saw, Clay Fork, M H Bullard.
Steam saw, Vander, A J Bullard.
Steam saw and gin, Cedar Creek, W R Johnson.
Steam corn and gin, Fayetteville, McD Giddie.
Steam saw, Fayetteville, McKethan & Monroe.
Steam saw and grist, Hope Mills, A A Harrington.
Steam saw, Manchester, J D Bruton.
Steam grist and gin, Sanford, J B Matthews.
Steam saw, Sanford, Smith & Lane.
Steam saw, mouth of Cross Creek, McElner, Grenenger & Co.
Steam saw, Swan Station, N A McArthur.
Steam saw, Fayetteville, J D McArthur.
Steam saw and gin, Fayetteville, W N Williams.
Steam saw and gin, Little River Academy, A Hatcher.
Steam corn and gin, Fayetteville, S C Godwin.

PHYSICIANS.

Names and Post Offices.

Averitt, K G, Cedar Creek.
Caviness, J E, Hope Mills.
Floyd, E (Dentist), Hay st, Fayetteville.
Haigh, Thomas D, Fayetteville.
Highsmith, J F, Fayetteville.

CUMBEBLAND COUNTY.

Hunter, T M (Dentist), n e cor Market Square, Fayetteville.
Lilly, H W, Fayetteville.
Marsh, J H, Fayetteville.
McGorgan, J Vance, Fayetteville.
McDougald, Alex, Hope Mills.
McDuffie, W C, Fayetteville.
McKimmon, Wm H, Hope Hills.
McNeill, J W, se cor Market Square, Fayetteville.
McSwain, H A, Kyle's Landing.
Mulchor, G N (col), Fayetteville.
Ray, Wm G, Argyle.
Register, Frank, Manchester.
Smith, F, Little River Academy.

SCHOOLS.

Names, Post Offices, and Principals.

Academy, Cedar Creek, Rev R A Hedgepeth.
Academy, Little River Academy.
Graded School, Fayetteville, Miss Della Matthews.
Military Academy, Fayetteville (Hay st), Col T J Drewry, prin.
Primary School, Fayetteville, Miss A Mallette.
School, Fayetteville, Miss K Marsh.
School, Fayetteville, Mrs Utley.
School, Fayetteville, Misses Ellison.
State Colored Normal School, Fayetteville, George H Williams, prin; Miss Lilly Leary and J F K Simpson, assistants.
Swain High School, Steadman, D W Carter, prin.
Public schools—white, 76; colored, 58.

TEACHERS.

Names and Post Offices.

WHITE.

Adams, Miss Lidie, Little River Academy.
Adams, Josie, Little River Academy.
Autrey, Lelia, Steadman.
Averitt, Leland, Steadman.
Bain, Walter W, Cornelia.
Beard, Mrs Ida M, Cedar Creek.
Belton, Lilly, Fayetteville.
Bayne, Geo A, Kyle's Landing.
Cain, Susie A, Fayetteville.
Carter, D W, Vander.
Carver, Miss Hattie, Sherwood.
Conaly, Parmelia, Edonia.
Ellis, Miss Flora, Hope Mills.
Frazzelle, Maggie, Manchester.
Gainey, Mrs Abram, Gray's Creek.
Gardner, Alice, Fayetteville.
Hall, Marcie E, Clay Fork.
Harrison, Dora E, Fayetteville.
Lindsay, A G, Fayetteville.

CUMBERLAND COUNTY.

Maxwell, Mrs M, Fayetteville.
McDonald, Christian, Roslin.
McDuffie, Miss Newell, Gillisville.
McFadgen, Miss Christian, Raeford.
McNeill, Miss Belle, Manly.
Newton, Miss P C, Fayetteville.
Page, H F, Godwin.
Patterson, M A, Gillisville.
Pope, P F, Rhodes.
Register, M Bettie, Manchester.
Royal, M W, Cornelia.
Spence, Nellie, Idaho.
Strickland, J A, Falcon.
Usher, E T, Gray's Creek.
Walker, W M, Little River Academy.
Ward, Virginia J, Fayetteville.
Warwick, Mamie E, Fayetteville.
Wicker, Ethel A, Wicker.

COLORED.

Anders, Maggie A, Idaho.
Andrews, Mary E, Idaho.
Bain, Mary L, Fayetteville.
Berry, Lizzie, Idaho.
Boykin, E W, Fayetteville.
Brinkley, Mary E, Manchester.
Bryant, Maude M, Fayetteville.
Carver, Peter, Raeford.
Cogdell, Fannie, Idaho.
Council, Emma J, Fayetteville.
Culbreth, Reuben, Fayetteville.
Drake, R D, Alderman.
Elliott, G E, Manchester.
Evans, Mary E, Fayetteville.
Evans, Edward, Fayetteville.
Evans, Mattie, Fayetteville.
Freeman, Hesther V, Fayetteville.
Gainey, Maggie, Sherwood.
Henderson, Eliza D, Fayetteville.
Holliday, Meta, Fayetteville.
Holmes, J H, Fayetteville.
Holmes, T F, Fayetteville.
Jacobs, Roena B, Fayetteville.
Jones, Katie F, Fayetteville.
Jones, Cornelia, Fayetteville.
Leary, Sarah M, Fayetteville.
Lloyd, C P, Dawson Landing.
McDougald, Mattie E, Manchester.
McDaniel, T G, Buckhorn.
McKay, Nina, Fayetteville.
McMillan, W H, Hope Mills.
McMillan, Luta, Edonia.
McNeill, Hattie G, Fayetteville.
McNeill, Sudie B, Fayetteville.
Melvin, Alice V, Cedar Creek.
Murphy, D L, Fayetteville.
Payne, Fannie D, Fayetteville.
Raiford, L, Alderman.
Raiford, O B, Alderman.
Rain, Kate M, Fayetteville.
Rone, Rena, Idaho.
Rone, Rosa A, Idaho.
Scott, Rosa W, Fayetteville.
Scott, Cora H, Fayetteville.
Scurlock, Mary F, Fayetteville.

CUMBERLAND COUNTY.

Scurlock, H C, Fayetteville.
Scurls, Clara B. Fayettville.
Smith, J T, Godwin.
Smith, Sallie, Godwin.
Smith, C H, Fayetteville.
Spearman, A M, Idaho.
Thornton, Mary K, Fayetteville.
Thornton, Hattie I, Fayetteville.
Thornton, Carrie L, Fayetteville.
Tucker, Josie, Fayetteville.
Tucker, Carrie, Fayetteville.
Whitehead, Fracinia, Dial.
Whitehead, Mary A, Dial.
Willston, Nettie, Fayetteville.
Williston, Katie, Fayetteville.
Williston, Lillie S, Fayetteville.
Williams, Alice, Manchester.
Williams, Henry M, Fayetteville.
Williams, R H, Fayetteville.
Williams, Thos H, Fayetteville.
Williams, G M, Hope Mills.

LOCAL CORPORATIONS.

Bank of Fayetteville, H W Lilly, pres;
    R P Buxton, vice-pres; J C Haigh,
    jr, cashier; E J Lilly, jr; book keeper;
    G G Myroner, clerk.
Bluff Mills Manufacturing Co (cotton),
    Fayetteville, H W Lilly, pres; capital
    stock $75,000.
Cape Fear and Yadkin Valley Railway
    Co, office Fayetteville; John Gill,
    Baltimore, Receiver; Hon Geo M
    Rose, Fayetteville, atty.
Cape Fear and People's Steamboat
    Line, steamer "A P Hurt," Capt
    Alex Robinson; leaves Fayetteville
    every Monday and Thursday at 7
    o'clock A M, and returning leaves
    Wilmington every Tuesday and Fri-
    day at — o'clock P M; W S Cook,
    manager.
Cotton-seed Oil Mill and Fertilizer Co,
    W H Williams, pres; N B Alexander,
    supt; capacity 24 boxes of per day.
Cross Creek Lodge, No 4, I O O F,
    Fayetteville; day of meeting Monday.
Cumberland Lodge, No 5, Knights of
    Pythias, Fayetteville, Dr J W Mc
    Neill, C C.
Cumberland County Agricultural So
    ciety, Fayetteville; W B Draughn,
    pres; George W Lawrence, secre-
    tary; A A McKethan, jr, treasurer.
Fayetteville Publishing Co, J A North,
    lessee.
Fayetteville Water, Light and Power
    Co, operated by Ferris & Richards,
    John Roddrick, supt.
Fayetteville Electric Light and Gas
    Co, Fayetteville; W N Tillinghast,
    pres; R J Marks, receiver; C B Led-
    better, supt; capital stock $50,000.

CUMBERLAND COUNTY.

Fayetteville Lodge, No 329, A F and
    A M; time of meeting second and
    fourth Friday evenings.
Fayetteville Independent Light Infan-
    try, organized August 23d, 1793,
    John C Vann, E L Penberton, senior
    captains; B R Huske, W C McDuffie,
    junior captains.
Golden Chain, Fayetteville, W C Mc-
    Duffie.
Hope Mfg Co (cotton), Hope Mills, S
    H Cotton, supt Mills No 1 and No 2.
Knights and Ladies of Honor, W N
    Tillinghast, protector.
Manchester Mills (cotton), Manchester,
    John F Clark, pres; capital stock
    $50,000.
Mystic Circle, Fayetteville, H E Sheets,
    sec and treas.
North Carolina Baptist Publishing Co,
    southeast corner market square, J T
    Winburn, proprietor; John A Oates,
    manager and editor.
Order of Charmed Friends, Fayette-
    ville, W C McDuffie, secretary and
    treasurer.
Phoenix Lodge, No 8, A F & A M, Fay-
    etteville; time of meeting, first and
    third Friday evenings, and June 4th
    and December 27th.
Phoenix Chapter, No 2, Royal Arch
    Masons, Fayetteville.
Shepherd Lodge, No 557, Knight's of
    Honor, Fayetteville, H R Horne,
    S P.
Steamer "Frank Sessoms," Capt. Irwin
    Robinson; leaves Fayetteville every
    Wednesday and Saturday at 7 o'clock
    A M; leaves Wilmington every Mon-
    day and Thursday at 2 o'clock P. M.

NEWSPAPERS.

Names, Post Offices and Proprietors.

Chronicle, Hope Mills, W F Blount,
    editor and proprietor.
Evening Daily Telegram (independent),
    Fayetteville, W E Clark, editor and
    proprietor.
Fayetteville Observer, Green st (Dem-
    ocratic weekly), E J Hall, editor and
    proprietor.
N C Baptist (weekly), Fayetteville, J T
    Winburn, proprietor; J A Oates, jr,
    editor.

FARMERS.

Names and Post Offices.

Beaver Dam—Morris Hall.
Buckhorn—Daniel Carter, Wash Car-
    ter, J B Downing, H B Downing, J M
    Pheddie.
Brunt—M Hall, W L Numalee.

CUMBERLAND COUNTY.

Clay Fork—P P Hall, Shep Hall, J M Jessup.

Cumberland Mills—John Buie, Gibb Buie, W J Johnson, James Pridgeon, Tate Rackley, Gibb Roy.

Dial—J R Luther, Jerry Luther.

Edonia—John D Johnson, Henry Marsh, Francis McMillan, John Smith, W J Smith.

Fayetteville—John Autry, M Bill, H C Bolton, A G Brady, D J Bruce, John Bruner, Daniel Buie, Quince Bunch, Archie Carmicle, J R Carter, D B Currie, J C Currie, J H Currie, Dan Culbreth, Henry Downing, W B Droughton, John Elliott, Theo Evans, J & O Evans, Fitzell Bros, Wm J Gardner, J C Gidie, McD Gidie, Wharton J Green (Tokay Vinyard), Sam Guy, R Harris, George H Hull, W W Huske, A Huske, J A Huske, Wesley Johnson, James M Lamb (florist and farmer), John Lambeth, G W Lawrence, Alex Leslie, J S Lutterloh, Herbert Lutterloh, Pink Martin, John M Martin, John F McArthur, A D McArthur, J A McArthur, A M McBuie, John P McLean, Sidney McDaniel, A D McGill, Geo A McKoy, J A McPherson, Wm McPherson, James D Nott, John Owen William Owen, E A Poe, E S Sanders, J W Sellars, John and James Smith, Henry C Smith, W D Smith, S H Strange, Bragg Talbot, P N Talbot, J N Talbot,

N C Hagard, Alex Hagard, C Vaughn, R Vaughn, Thomas Vaughn, Theo Whaley, David Williams, G o Williams, J M Williams, W N Williams, Robert Williams, A J Woodward.

Godwin's—W D Smith, W J Smith, J A Wade.

Hope Mills—N G Biggs, John Culbreth, Hector McNeill.

Idaho—F J Haywood, James McDaniel, Henry E Smith.

Little River—D D McBryde, B T McBryde, W L Williams, J A Williams.

Mantz—L J Blue, S J Cameron, D K McDupree, J D McLeod, David Ray, J T Sinclair.

Manchester—J F Clark, A K McDairmid, J A McFarland.

Patrick—John Birk.

Roslin—Herman Jones, John Smith.

Sherwood—Jesse Carver, L D Caviness, E H Evans, J A Gainey, Abner Gainey, D W Marsh, Wm Marsh, Neill LeRoy, John Smith.

Stedman—David Sessoms, Kelly Sessoms.

Vander—Alex Carter, Geo Goodwin, Alex Horne.

Vass—Neill McPhail, J H Smith, James Wright, Archie Wright.

Wade—T J Devane, Dr H A McSwain, J McPhail, H H Wade, W H H Wade.

CURRITUCK COUNTY.

AREA, 200 SQUARE MILES.

POPULATION, 6,747; White 4,731, Colored 2,016.

CURRITUCK COUNTY was one of the early precincts of the State, in 1729, when the Lords Proprietors surrendered their rights to the English Crown. It derives its name from a tribe of Indians who once inhabited and owned the county. It is situated in the extreme northeastern portion of the State, and is bounded on the north by the Virginia line, east by the Atlantic Ocean, south by the Albemarle Sound, and west by Camden county. The county, especially on Currituck Sound, is well adapted for truck-raising. Melons can be successfully grown from four miles above the court house to Powell's Point—a distance of thirty-four miles. The fishing and ducking interests, from November until March, is a source of considerable revenue to the thirty miles of territory above named, including the islands and beach. With the Albemarle and Chesapeake Canal and the N. S. Railroad, her shipping facilities are good; on the road her trucks, etc., can leave this evening and be in New York to-morrow morning. Moyock is quite a thriving little village on the N. S. Railroad.

CURRITUCK COURT HOUSE, the county seat, is beautifully located on Currituck Sound, and is 242 miles northeast from Raleigh. Population, including township, 2,000.

Surface.—Low and level, soil rich. The navigation advantages are very good.

Staples.—Cotton, corn, and fish. Trucking for the northern markets is extensively engaged in. Large quantities of live fowl are killed during the winter months, and find a ready sale at Norfolk and points farther north.

Fruits.—Apples, peaches, pears, berries, melons and grapes in great profusion.

Timbers.—Pine, cypress, juniper and gum.

TOWNS AND POST OFFICES.

	POP.		POP.
Coinjock,	100	Harbinger,	25
Corolla,	50	Jarvisburg,	25
Currituck (c h),		Kitty Hawk,	25
	2,000	Knott's Island,	200
Gregory's,	50	Moyock,	500
Poplar Branch,		Silgo,	25
	100	Snowden,	50
Powell's Point,	75	Tulls,	25
Shawboro,	50	Waterlily	—

COUNTY OFFICERS.

Clerk Superior Court—E W Ansell.
Commissioners—A M Willey, ch'm'n.
Register of Deeds—G W Williams.
Sheriff—Edward Tillett.
Solicitor 1st District—W J Leary.
Surveyor— ———.
Treasurer—Ed Tillett.
County Examiner—V L Pitts.

COURTS.

First Monday in March and first Monday in September.

TOWNSHIPS AND MAGISTRATES.

Atlantic—J B Owens, B F Tillett, W J Tate, Stark Harris, Daniel Hayman, Andrew Twiford, W R Perry, Daniel Scarboro (Currituck).

Crawford—Henry Welstead, A O Dey, Seth B Forbis, M R G R Gregory, A B Midgett, James Doxy, W H Snowden, Phillip Northan (Currituck).

Fruitville—Elias Williams, S J Waterfield, E D Bowden, John C Cason, J C Cason, J Jones, Wm Evans (Currituck C H).

Moyock—Thomas B Jones, Walter Stewart, Geo C Sanborn, J C Garrett, Step Mercer, J J Morse (Moyock).

Poplar Branch—V L Pitts, Alex Owen, C S Crank, W L Owen, Edward Baum, John Brock, W S Harrison, N J Walker (Poplar Branch).

CHURCHES.

Names, Post Offices, Pastors and Denom.

METHODIST.

Asbury —Coinyock
Baxter's Grove—Currituck C H.
Church—Knott's Island.
Church—Moyock.
Ebenezer—Poplar Branch.
Hebron—Powell's Point.
Mt Zion—Jarvisburg.
Perkins' Chapel—Shawboro.

BAPTIST.

Church—Knott's Island.

CURBITUCK COUNTY.

Church—Powell's Point.
Church—Poplar Branch.
Providence—Shawboro.
Rehoboth—Currituck C H.
Shady Grove—Moyock.

PRIM. BAPTIST.

Church—Powell's Point.
Old Conyock—Currituck C H.

DISCIPLES OF CHRIST.

Church—Powell's Point.

MERCHANTS AND TRADESMEN.

Name, Post Office, and Line of Business.

CHURCH ISLAND.

Hampton, W H,	G S

COINJOCK.

Berry, Thomas A,	G S
Everett, S K,	G S
Hall, T P,	G S
Midgett, A B,	G S
Turner, J L,	G S
Williams, C T,	G S

CURRITUCK.

Johnson & Co,	G S
Mathias, Mrs A,	G S

GREGORY'S.

Boswood, John H,	G S

HARBINGER.

Aydlette, C C,	G S
Coombs, M A,	G S
Gallop, L H,	G S
Owens, H,	G S
Parker, Samuel,	G S

INDIAN.

Tatum, Aug,	G S

JARVISBURG.

Gallop, P G,	G S
Owen & Forbes,	G S

CURRITUCK COUNTY.

Owens, S J & Bro,	G S
Scott, D R,	G S

KITTY HAWK.

Tate, J W & Co,	G S

KNOTT'S ISLAND.

Halstead & Munden,	G S
Jones & Boney,	G S

MOYOCK.

Cox, Jerome,	G S
Creekmore, W P,	G S
Van DeCarr. C R & Co,	G S

POPLAR BRANCH.

Doxey, L A & Co,	G S
Gallop, J C,	G S
Owens & Mathias,	G S
Upton, L J,	G S
Woodhouse, D W,	G S

POWELL'S POINT.

Banks, W G,	G S
Ethridge, R,	G S
Gibbs Bros,	G S

SHAWBORO.

Williams, T W,	G S

SILGO.

Bray, Mrs E V,	G S
Griffin Bros,	G S
Williams, T W,	G S

SNOWDEN.

Stephenson & Sanborn,	G S

TULL'S.

Flora, Mrs A G,	G S

MILLS.

Kinds, Post Offices and Proprietors.

Gin and Grist, Moyock, C R Van De-
Carr.
Grist, Snowden, Geo E Stephenson.

DARE COUNTY.

AREA 160 SQUARE MILES.

POPULATION: 3,768; White 3,362; Colored 406.

DARE COUNTY was organized in 1870 from Tyrrell, Hyde and Currituck, and was named in honor of Virginia Dare, the first white child born on the American Continent after its discovery by Columbus.

MANTEO, the county-seat, is 250 miles northeast from Raleigh, and derives its name from the chief of an Indian tribe that formerly occupied that portion of the State. Population of the town, 175.

Surface.—Dare county embraces a small area of high land, and large bodies of swamp and marsh. The surface is cut up by extensive collections of water, hence the principal occupation of the people is that of fishing.

Nag's Head on the east shore is a noted summer resort. Education and enterprise would make this one of the finest counties in the State. It is noted for its sea breezes and healthfulness. The first English settlement was made here in 1584. Virginia Dare, the first white child born on this Continent, first saw the light of day in this county, hence the name; and the first religious services of this country were performed on the banks of Roanoke Sound.

Staples.—Fish form the great staple of this county. The product of this item is estimated at over two hundred thousand dollars per annum. Rogers & Etheridge alone did a business of some seventy-five thousand dollars in one year. Corn, sweet potatoes and scuppernong grapes grow finely. This is the native home of the scuppernong.

Timbers.—Cypress, juniper, gum, water oak, live oak and others.

Fruits.—Figs, apples, peaches, cranberries and other small fruits.

TOWNS AND POST OFFICES.

	POP.		POP.
Avon,	500	Manteo (c h),	500
Buffalo City,	50	Mashoes,	100
Buxton,	400	Nag's Head,	200
Colington,	250	Rodanthe,	400
East Lake,	500	Skyco,	100
Hatteras,	500	Stumpy Point,	200
Mann's Harbor,		Wauchese,	500
	350		

COUNTY OFFICERS.

Clerk Superior Court—J B Jennett.

Commissoners—B T Daniels, chm; T J Fulcher; Z F Scarborough, C C Mann, J P Midgett, C J Dough, clerk,
Register of Deeds—C J Dough.
Sheriff—R W Smith.
Solicitor First District—W J Leary.
Surveyor— ——
Treasurer—S E Mann.
County Examiner—Dr F P Gates.

COURTS.

Ninth Monday after the first Monday in March, and ninth Monday after the first Monday in September.

TOWNSHIPS AND MAGISTRATES.

Croatan—W W Midgett, B F Gard (Mann's Harbor).

East Lake—Theo L Mann (East Lake)

Hatteras—J W Robinson, B F Whidbee, A G B Solter (Hatteras), C C Miller. J J Barnett (Buxton).

Kennakeet—J H Scarborough, jr. H C Miller, C F Williams (Avon), I B Midgett, T S Meekins, S T Midgett (Rodanthe).

Nag's Head—C J Dough, J W Ward, J B Hancock (Manteo), W S Davis (Wauchese).

CHURCHES.

Names, Post Offices, Pastors and Denom.

METHODIST.

Bethany—Wauchese, D G Langston.
Church—Rodanthe, —— Porter.
Church—Hatteras.
Church—Avon, —— Porter.
Church—Kitty Hawk.
Church—Nag's Head, —— Warlick.
Church—Colington, —— Warlick.
Church—Buxton, —— Porter.
Clark's—Rodanthe, —— Porter.
Mt. Carmel—Mann's Harbor, —— Warlick.
Mt. Pisgah—East Lake, —— Warlick.
Mt. Olive—D G Langston.
Nag's Head—Nag's Head, —— Warlick.
Shiloh—Stumpy Point, —— Warlick.

N. METHODIST.

Church—Buxton, —— Crowder.

BAPTIST.

Roanoke Island—Manteo,——Stallings.

DARE COUNTY.

PRIM. BAPTIST.
Church—East Lake.

DISCIPLES.
Church (col)—Manteo, —— Normal.

A. M. EPISCOPAL.
Church (col)—Manteo.

MINISTERS RESIDENT.

Names, Post Offices and Denom.

METHODIST.
Fulcher, G L, Hat'eras.
Jennett, J B. Manteo.
Payne, N O, R danthe.
Payne, S inderson, Manteo.
Price, A W, Avon.

DISCIPLES.
Barnes, Geo (col), Manteo.

HOTELS AND BOARDING HOUSES.

Names, Post Offices and Proprietors.

Boarding House, Nag's Head, ——
    Spruill.
Buffalo City Hotel, Buffalo City, W M
    Hatton.
Hotel, Hatteras, Mrs Inez Angell,
Nag's Head Hotel, Nag's Head, J B
    Brockett.
Tranquil House, Manteo, A V Evans.

LAWYERS.

Names and Post Offices.

Blount, R L, Manteo,

MANUFACTORIES.

Kinds, Post Offices and Proprietors.

Boat building, Manteo, Sanders Payne.
Boat building, Avon, A W Price.
Boat building, Avon, Z F Scarborough.
Boat building, Avon, J H Scarborough,
    Jr.
Boat building, Avon, J H Scarborough, Sr.
Boat building, Hatteras, J J Barnett.
Boat building, Hatteras, J M Stowe.
Boat building, Hatteras, J F Austin.
Boat building, Hatteras, W K Gaskill.
Boat building, Hatteras, B F Stowe.
Boat building, East Lake, Mr Bosnight.
Boat building, East Lake, C L Mann.
Boat building, Manteo, Otis Doyle.
Boat building, Manteo, W T Daugh.
Boat building, Manteo, J W Casey.
Boat building, Manteo, B H Creef.
Boat building, Manteo, Geo Washington Creef, Sr.

15

DARE COUNTY.

Boat building, Manteo, B T Daniel.
Boat building, Manteo, Geo W Creef.

MERCHANTS AND TRADESMEN.

Name, Post-office and Line of Business.

AVON.
Miller, H F,   G S

EAST LAKE.
Pinner, J B.   G S
Sanderlin, T M,   G S

HATTERAS.
O'Neal, Uriah,   G S
Rollinson, S M S,   G S
Stowe, A J & Bro,   G S
Styron, H W   G S

MANTEO.
Evans & Forbes,   G S
Evans & Mann,   G S and Furn
Griffin & Smith,   G S
Hassell, L D,   G S

RODANTHE.
Midgett, Thos P,   G S

SKYCO.
Daniels & Pugh,   G S

WANCHESE.
Daniels, E R,   G S

MILLS.

Names, Post Offices and Proprietors.

Steam saw, Buffalo City, East Carolina
    and Lumber Co.
Wind Mill, Avon, B P Miller.

SCHOOLS.

Names, Post Offices and Principals.

Academy, Rodanthe.
Academy, Manteo, Miss Minnie Gattis.
Croatan Academy, Manns Harbor, —.
Rollinson Academy, Hatteras, L O
    Wyche.
No. public schools—white, 21; colored, 1.

TEACHERS.

Names and Post Offices.

Gattis, Mrs Minnie, Manteo.

FARMERS.

Names and Post Offices.

East Lake—Lemuel Basnight, Jas
Basnight, J W Creef, H J Creef, Martin Creef, Daniel Holmes, Jerome
Holmes, A W Jones, C L Mann, T S

DARE COUNTY.	DARE COUNTY.

Owens, Damron Pugh, Felix Rogers, J A Sawyer.

Mann's Harbor—Thos R Mann, S E Mann, Samuel Mann, Samuel Midgett.

Manteo—C H Basnight, Jas Basnight, John E Berry, Mrs Mahal Blevin, Geo A Blevin, W C Brinkley, Mrs Lavina Brinkley, G W Creef, W B Daniels, J W Dough, sr, H E Dough, W A Dough, W T Dough, Richard Etheridge (col), D W Etheridge, A V Evans, J A Evans, J W Evans, E Griffin, James Howard, B F Meekin, Fields

Midgett. Geo R Midgett, N Shannon, Thos Tillett, John W Ward, J W Ward. Geo W Wescott.

Skyco—C J Dough, Isaac Hays, James Howard, C L Midgett, L N Midgett, T T Tolar.

Stumpy Point—L D Hooper, J H Wise.

Wanchese—Avery Daniels, B T Daniels, E R Daniels, T W Daniels, Steward M Daniels, Geo C Daniels, Spencer Daniels, Jesse T Etheridge, P S Gallop, J T Garrison, J N Hooker, Alex Simpson.

DAVIDSON COUNTY.

AREA 600 SQUARE MILES.

POPULATION, 21,702; White 18,174, Colored 3,528.

DAVIDSON COUNTY was formed in 1822, from Rowan county, and named in compliment of Gen William David son, who fell at the passage of the Ca tawba river at Cowan's Ford, during the Revolutionary war. It is situated in the Piedmont section of the State, and is intersected by the North Caro lina Railroad. Its water-power is scarcely surpassed by any county in the State, the Yadkin river forming its southern and western boundary.

LEXINGTON, the county-seat, is sit uated on the North Carolina Railroad, 117 miles west of Raleigh. Popula tion 2,500.

Surface—Undulating, well watered by the Yadkin river and its tributaries; much of the soil along the streams good, the hills susceptible of a high state of cultivation.

Staples—Tobacco, corn, wheat, grass and fruits in great variety.

Fruits—Peaches, apples, pears, ber ries, melons, grapes, and all the small fruits.

Timbers—Hickory, oak, black wal nut, pine, wild cherry, poplar, maple, and others.

Minerals—Gold, silver and copper.

TOWNS AND POST OFFICES.

	POP.		POP.
Abbott's Creek.	50	Jubilee,	50
Arcadia,	60	Levi,	20
Arnold,	150	Lexington,	2,500
Bagdad,	25	Light,	20
Bain,	25	Lilac,	35
Belfast,	20	Linwood,	100
Bethany,	25	McKee,	50
Bringles,	20	Marsh,	50
Carlisle,	50	Michael.	35
Churchland,	40	Midway,	50
Cid,	100	Orinoco,	20
Denton,	100	Pastook,	25
Enterprise,	100	Pinnix,	20
Fairgrove,	100	Reedy,	50
Fairmount,	50	Rowell,	35
Friedberg,	—	Sapona,	200
Handy,	20	Silver Hill,	100
Hanes,	—	Thomasville,	800
Hannersville,	40	Tyro Shops,	100
Healing Sp'ngs,	40	Wallburg,	50
Hopkins,	30	Welcome,	25
Ilex,	40	Yadkin Col-	
Jackson Hill,	125	lege,	150
Jimes,	20	Yokley,	25
Jones' Mine,	20		

COURTS.

Sixth Monday before the first Mon day in March; second Monday after the first Monday in March; thirteenth Monday after the first Monday in March; fourth Monday after the first Monday in September.

COUNTY OFFICERS.

Clerk Superior Court—Geo E Hunt.
Deputy Clerk—W H Walker.
Commissioners—J W Lee (ch), C A Davis, J W Fitzgerald.
Coroner—J A Sowers.
Register of Deeds—W C Harris.
Sheriff—F J Leonard.
Deputy Sheriff—W N Kinney.
Solicitor Eighth District—J Q Holton.
Surveyor—C H B Leonard.
Standard Keeper—E A Rathrock.
Treasurer—J W McRary.
County Examiner—Allen Jones.
Superintendent of Health—Dr John Thomas.

TOWN OFFICERS.

LEXINGTON —*Mayor*, J H Moyer; *Commissioners*, W F Henderson, H P Gallimore, R L McCrary, A C Harris. T F Larden; *Chief Police*, J A Pea cock; *Clerk and Treasurer*, A C Har ris.

THOMASVILLE—*Mayor*, J A Elliott; *Commissioners*, E W Cates, J R Mires, W B Rounsaville, E F Westmoreland.

YADKIN COLLEGE—*Mayor*, E L Green.

TOWNSHIPS AND MAGISTRATES.

Abbott's Creek—C P Hedgecock, J R Osborne, W Pickard, C H Teague, E H Hayworth, Jas Yokely, C M Wall, M D Raper (Abbott's Creek).

Alleghany—D L Cook, Wm M C Surratt, A O Lanier, S A Coggins, Stokes Varner. E M Reeves, John G Surratt, W M Walker (Lexington).

Arcadia—J R Evans, C C Welsner, T S Spaugh, D A Tesh, Jordan Shutt, David Miller, F F Knouse (Arcadia).

Boone—J H Barber, W D Simerson, L F Snider, Robert F Wilson, J W Hacher, George Sowers, M W Barber, C F Fitzgerald (Boone).

Conrad Hill—S J Finch, S B Lane, J M

DAVIDSON COUNTY.

Dorsett, Wm Grimes, A L Miller, J L Underwood, J Copple, W A Sullivan, S C Watford, D L Smith (Lexington).

Cotton Grove—J D Lookabill, A M Hunter, Franklin Younce, J A Fink, Robt L Frank, J F Sharp (Lexington).

Emmons—A J Beck, A G Surratt, B I Harrison, U L Peacock, Dan Ward, Dan Sexton, A G M rris, J W Hedrick (Lexington).

Jackson Hill—J C Skeen, S L Surratt, J C Surratt, Wm M Surratt, W A Reed, J W Hailey, N F Morgan, J L Thompson (Jackson Hill).

Hampton—W B Hampton, J S Nelson, L Ed Brewer, Ed Sink (Lexington).

Healing Springs—T H Daniels, C G Harris, J C Bear, jr, D F Kinney, S M Snider, E Logan, L A Tysinger, B C Cole, Jno A Kinney (Healing Springs).

Lexington—Wm A Hertman, D F Fritts, J H Moyer, R B McCrary, W A Berner, C L Conrad, D W Wagoner, J Smith, J G Kinney, D L Brinkley, Ransom Everhart, David Hinkle, notary public (Lexington).

Midway—Chas J Beard, D F Lindsay, D A Clodfelter, C R Wilson, J M Nifong, M R Shoaf, W N Thomas (Midway).

Reedy Creek—H D Hedrick, D C Ader, J F Hudson, J C Link, J S Michael, Franklin Crotts, H D Hedrick (Reedy).

Silver Hill—J I Stoner, W A Beck, Chas Sechrist, J F Carrick, G W Greer, Z B Tussey, Geo W Beck (Silver Hill)

Thomasville—John W Bowers, J H Lambeth, W A Mendenhall, J A Leach, C W Burton, R K Stone, J T Grimes, M R Harris, L L Conrad, J C Kennedy, S A Hoover, L W Elliott, notary public (Thomasville).

Tyro—H Helmstettler, W W Myers, J H Swicegood, R F Swicegood, Lee Link, H C Fritts, J R Michael, H H Hartley (Tyro Shops).

Yadkin College—J F Byerly, J T Williamson, J D Davis, H F Wilson, J S Phillips, Ed L Green, T S Dale, Z M Rea (Yadkin College).

CHURCHES.

Names, Post Offices, Pastors and Denom.

METHODIST.

Clemmonsville—Clemmonsville.
Ebenezer—Lexington, Leroy Johnson
Fair Grove—Thomasville.
Lexington—Lexington, J E Thompson.
Macedonia—Cotton Grove, Leroy Johnson.
Midway—Midway, —— Cannon.

DAVIDSON COUNTY.

Mt Pleasant—Thomasville.
Mt Vernon—Salem.
Olivet—Arcadia, —— Cannon.
Shady Grove—Shady Grove.
Thomasville—Thomasville, —— Irwin.
Wesley Chapel—Lexington, Leroy Johnson.
Zion—Thomasville.

BAPTIST.

Abbott's Creek—Abbott's Creek, Henry Sheets
Holloway—Silver Hill, Henry Sheets.
Jersey—Linwood, Thos Carrick.
Piney Church—Linwood, R G Morton.
Thomasville—Thomasville. —— Hall.
Tom's Creek—Jackson Hill, Henry Sheets.

ASSO. REFORM.

Bethany—Midway, Thos Long.
Beulah—Lexington, Thos Long.
Emanuel's—Thomasville.
Jerusalem—Lexington.
Mt Carmel—Lexington.
Pilgrim's—Lexington.
Pleasant Retreat—Lexington, Thomas Long.

LUTHERAN.

Beck's—Lexington, Thos Long.
Bethany—Thomasville, Prof Michael.
Cedar Bush—Lexington.
Sandy Creek—Tyro Shops, Professor Michael.

PRESBYTERIAN.

Lexington—Lexington, J Egb't Smith.
Church (col)—Thomasville.

EPISCOPAL.

Church of the Redemption—— Felter.

MINISTERS RESIDENT.

Names, Post Offices and Denominations.

METHODIST.

Cannon, ——, Arcadia.
Johnson, Leroy, Lexington.
Irwin, ——, Thomasville.
Koontz C A, Arnold.
Surratt, R't, Jackson Hill.
Thompson, J E, Lexington.

METH. PROTESTANT.

Dunn, J S, Lexington.
Garrett, J N, Yadkin College.

BAPTIST.

Carrick, Thos, Lexington.
Hall, ——, Thomasville
Morton, H, Thomasville.
Newton, ——, Thomasville.
Sheets, Henry, Lexington.

ASSO. REFORM.

Cecil, J W, Thomasville.
Leonard, J C, Lexington.

DAVIDSON COUNTY.

LUTHERAN.

Michael, D W, Tyro Shops.

HOTELS AND BOARDING HOUSES.

Names, Post Offices and Proprietors.

Boarding House, Lexington, J W S xton.
Boarding House, Jackson Hill, W M Surratt.
Hargrave Hotel, Lexington, Miss Bessie Hargrave.
Hotel, Thomasville, John Lambeth.
March House, Lexington, A A Springs.
Mock House, Thomasville, Mrs W P McIntyre.

LAWYERS.

Names and Post Offices.

Henderson, W F, Lexington.
McCrary, J R Lexington.
Pickens, R T, Lexington.
Phnex, M H, Lexington.
Robbins (F C) & Raper (E E), Lexington.
Walser, Z V, & Z I, Lexington.
Williams, S E, Lexington.

MANUFACTORIES.

Kinds, Post Offices and Proprietors.

Blacksmithing, Midway, G o Brummell.
Blacksmithing, Lexington, H H Caudle.
Blacksmithing, Arcadia, H J Disher.
Blacksmithing, Midway, John Eller.
Blacksmithing, Arcadia, John Nifong.
Blacksmithing, Linwood, G G Smith.
Blacksmithing, Lexington, D L Trexler.
Blacksmithing, Abbott's Creek, Peter Brown.
Blacksmithing, Thomasville, Frank Welborn.
Blacksmithing, Thomasville, Cal Taylor.
Blacksmithing, Denton, Robt Tysinger.
Blacksmithing, Abbott's Creek, W W Pickard.
Cabinet and undertaking, Lexington, J W McCrary.
Cabinet, Thomasville, Wm Foster's heirs.
Chairs (wholesale). Thomasville, D S Westmoreland's Sons.
Contracting and building, Midway, J M Nifong.
Contracting and building, Arcadia, Wm Woolsley.
Foundry, machine shops, sash and blinds, Lexington, C M Thompson

DAVIDSON COUNTY.

Furniture. Lexington, Lexington Furniture Co.
Furniture, Thomasville, Thomasville Furniture Co.
Millwrighting, Thomasville, B C Lambeth.
Millwrighting, Linwood, H P Feezor.
Roller mill merchant millers, Lexington, Grimes Bros.
Saddles and harness, Lexington, W B Hanner & Son.
Sash, doors and contracting. Thomasville, J W Gray.
Shuttle blocks and spoke billets, Lexington, Mendenhall & Wheeler.
Shuttle and blocks, Jackson Hill, John Hatley.
Tobacco (plug and twist), Yadkin College. T S Dale & Co.
Tombstones, Lexington, H J Hege.
Undertaker and cabinet, Jackson Hill, A W Surratt.
Wagons, Tyro Shops, Fitts & Sink.
Wagon shops. Lexington, Rothrock Bros.
Wagons, Abbott's Creek, S W Wall & Son
Wennonah Cotton Mills, Lexington, W E Holt, owner and proprietor.
Woolcarding, Midway, J B Siseloff.
Woolcarding, Bringle's, W P Stafford.

MERCHANTS AND TRADESMEN.

Names, Post Offices, Lines of Business.

ABBOTT'S CREEK.

Roper. O P,	G S
Wall Bros.	Wheelwright

ARCADIA.

Fairabee, B L,	G S

ARNOLD.

Erathardt, R & Co,	G S
Link, J E.	G S

BELFAST.

Harris. O R.	G S

BETHANY.

Brindle, Franklin,	G S
Lindsay, D F,	G S

BRINGLES.

Stafford, W P,	Machinery

CID.

Beck, A J.	G S
Lanier, N W,	G S
Plummer, J R & Son (near)	G S

CLEMMONSVILLE.

Ferrabee, T C.	G S
Strope, C & F,	Tanners
Strope, W C & Son (near)	G S

DENTON.

Elliott, H C,	G S
Frank & Anderson,	G S
Morris, A G,	G S

DAVIDSON COUNTY.	
ENTERPRISE.	
Tesh, D A,	G S
FAIR GROVE.	
Kenneday, J A,	G S
FAIRMONT.	
VanCannon, L A,	G S
Young, Thos & Son,	G S
HANDY.	
Morris, J W,	G S
HANNERSVILLE.	
Hanner, A P,	G S
ILEX.	
Whitner, B A & Co,	G S
JACKSON HILL.	
Badgett, J M,	G S and Tanner
Surratt, Alex,	Furn
Surratt, G S & Co,	G S
Surratt, W D & Bro,	G S
Surratt, W M,	Hotel
JONES' MINES.	
Fuller, Dr A,	G S
JUBILEE.	
Wilson, J W,	G S
Young, A A,	—
LEXINGTON.	
Bernheim, C H,	—
Caudle, H H,	Wagons
Clements and Hargrove,	G S
Cross Eli,	G S
Crouse, Geo W,	Agl Implements
Crouse, John,	Livery
Davis, Mrs Amanda,	Millinery
Davis, E P,	Jeweler
Dodson, J M,	Photog
Earnhardt, Miss M C,	Millinery
Gray, M B,	Lumber
Green, R S,	Miller
Grimes Bros,	Millers and Grain
Hamilton, S A,	Contractor
Hamner, W B,	Harness-maker
Hanes, C A,	Fertilizer
Hanes, L F,	Jeweler
Hedrick & Finch,	Millers
Hedge Bros,	Produce
Hedge, H J,	Marble
Heitman, W A,	Cabinet Maker
Hinkle, A A,	G S
Hix, W W,	Fert
Irvin & Bro (col),	Gro
Johnson, P H (near)	G S
Layden, John, agt.	G S
McCrary, J W,	Furn and Undert'k'r
McCrary, R L,	G S
Moffitt Bros,	Gro
Noe, Mrs M A,	Millinery
Owens, S L,	Gro
Peacock Hardware Co,	Hdw
Penry, R L,	G S
Penry, W G,	G S
Penry & Green,	Livery

DAVIDSON COUNTY.	
Redwine, W P & Son,	Hdw
Sink, A L,	G S
Smith, J B & Co,	Drugs
Smith, W D,	G S
Smith & Hankin,	G S
Thompson, W M, mgr Lexington Livery Co,	Livery
Thompson, C M,	Foundry
Ward, J F,	G S
Watson, H P,	Furn
Watson & Cecil,	Builders
Wood, A C & Bro,	Mill
LINWOOD.	
Fitzgerald & Raper,	G S
Smith, G F,	G S
Byerby Bros,	G S
REEDY CREEK.	
Penry, R L,	G S
SAPONA.	
Barber, M W,	G S
Haden, J W,	G S
SILVER HILL.	
Hedrick, J B,	Cooper
Shirley & Tysinger,	G S
THOMASVILLE.	
Cates, E W,	G S
Elliott, E W,	G S
Fife, Miss E C,	Millinery
Foster, Miss Sallie F,	Furn
Gray, J W,	Planing Mill
Grimes, J F,	G S
Harris, Theo F,	Hdw
Johnson, H L,	G S
Julian, C A & Co,	G S
Kennedy, J A,	G S
Kinney, J C & Co,	G S
Lambeth, D T,	G S
Lambeth, J W,	Hotel
Leach, Gas & Co,	Mfrs Shoes
Long, J T & Co,	G S
McIntire, Mrs Minnie,	Hotel
Mendenhall, G L,	Machines
Morris, J M,	G S
Myers, F J & J R,	G S
Shiplett, M H,	G S
Thompson, W E,	G S
Wagner & Ragan,	Livery
Welborn, W L,	G S
TYRO SHOPS.	
Kuntz, C E,	G S
Marsh, A H,	G S
Swicegood, J H,	G S
Thompson, R B,	G S
WELCOME.	
Brinkley, D L,	G S
YADKIN COLLEGE.	
Davis, J D,	G S
Grimes, A A,	G S
Hanner, R R,	G S
Williamson & Son,	G S

DAVIDSON COUNTY.

MINES.

Kinds, Post Offices and Proprietors.

Baltimore Gold and Silver Smelting Co, Thomasville.
Cid mine, Cid, owned by a Philadelphia company.
Conrad Hill (copper and gold), McKee, Conrad Hill Mining Co., Jas E Clayton, supt.
Consolidated Gold and Copper Co., Cid; owned by a Baltimore company.
Eureka (gold). Thomasville; owned by a Scranton (Penn.) company.
Silver Valley, Thomasville, Silver Valley Mining Co.; owned by a Baltimore company.
Roanoke Gold, Thomasville, E M Coldcleugh & Bro.
Silver, Silver Hill, Mrs A B Jones.
Ward Mine, Lick Creek, ——.
Welborn (gold), Lexington, ——.

MILLS.

Kinds, Post Offices and Proprietors.

Corn, flour and saw, Midway, Lindsay & Clinard.
Corn, Hannersville, Judah Summers,
Corn, flour and saw, Arcadia, D Hanes.
Corn, flour and saw, High Point, R Orrell.
Corn and flour, Tyro Shops, R & P Swicegood.
Corn, flour and saw. Arcadia, G W Burke's heirs.
Corn and flour, Jackson Hill, Redwine & Co,
Corn and flour, Jackson Hill. R Morris.
Corn, flour and saw, Tyro Shops, D J Swicegood,
Flour, corn and saw, Denton, Frank Bros,
Flour, corn and saw, Denton, A T Morris.
Flour, Lexington, L L Conrad.
Flour, Clemmonsville, The Forsyth Co.
Flour, Linwood, B F Haden.
Flour, Yadkin College, T W Hartley.
Flour, Linwood, J E Summer.
Flour, Jackson Hill, Wm Loftin.
Flour and saw, Arcadia, J R Evans & Co.
Flour, Thomasville, Jacob Wagoner.
Flour and corn, Clemmonsville, Alfred Douthit.
Flour and corn, Silver Hill, G T Vuncannon.
Roller flour mill, Thomasville, J E Sumner.
Roller flour mills, Lexington, Grimes Bros.

DAVIDSON COUNTY.

Saw and flour, Cotton Grove, O C Miller.
Saw and corn, Hannersville, Wm Wilson.
Saw and corn, Healing Springs, R L Holmes.
Saw, Lexington, S J Finch.
Saw, Hannersville, B F Copple.
Saw, Churchland, W H Simmerson.
Saw and corn, Lexington, Henry Swing.
Saw and corn (steam), Reedy Creek, Link & Hoover.
Wennonah Mills (cotton yarns and plaids), two mills, Lexington; W E Holt.

PHYSICIANS.

Names and Post Offices.

Anderson, J N, Lexington.
Anderson, A, Denton.
Atkins, G I, Jackson Hill.
Beall, J F, Linwood,
Buchanan, E J, Lexington.
Bulla, Alex, Jackson Hill.
Byerly, B C, Yadkin College.
Daniels, C (Dentist), Bringles.
Dorrett, H W, Bethany.
Fitts, H B, Tyro Shops.
Hill, David, Lexington.
Hill, Lee, Arcadia.
Hill, Joel, Lexington.
Julian, ——, Thomasville.
Myers, J A, Cotton Grove.
Riley, J M (Dentist), Lexington.
Rathrock, J M (Dentist), Thomasville.
Thomas, Jno, Lexington.
Thomss, R W, Thomasville.
Vestal, W J, Tyro Shops.
Walker, T C, Thomasville.

SCHOOLS.

Names, Post Offices and Principals.

Academy, Reed's Cross Roads, Rev J M Bennett.
Academy, Arcadia, Prof Hill.
Academy, Arnold, J B Leonard.
Academy, Jackson Hill. W S Surratt.
Academy, Denton, B I Harrison.
Baptist Orphanage, Thomasville, Rev. J B Boon, general manager,
High School, Bethany, R H Beesecker.
Holly Grove Academy, Ilex.
Hedrick's Grove Academy, McKee, Rev. McNary.
Lexington Seminary, Lexington, O E Mendenhall.
Perry Academy, Churchland, Mrs B I Harrison.
Pilgrim Academy, Lexington, Rev J C Leonard.

DAVIDSON COUNTY.

Thomasville Female College, Thomasville, Rev Hall and P L Ledford.
Yadkin College High School, Yadkin College, Geo W Holmes.
No. Public Schools—White, 94; colored, 25,

TEACHERS.

Names and Post Offices.

WHITE.

Andrews, D F, Light.
Auston, G W, Linwood.
Barnes, A L, Tyro Shops.
Beck, S W, McKee.
Beck, R L, McKee.
Beck, A L, Cid.
Beckerdite, J W, Salem.
Bennett, Rev. J M, Michael.
Bowers, D E, Pilgrim.
Bryant, S L, Midway.
Byerly, S W, Arnold.
Byerly, Vick, Yadkin College.
Carrick, John A, Fairmount.
Carver, W L, Michael.
Clinard, G W, Wallburg.
Cole, Miss Lillie, Bringles.
Conrad, John A L, Pilgrim.
Croon, M L, Enterprise.
Croner, Miss Alice D, Michael.
Croner, R G, Michael.
Croner, A P, Michael.
Curry, G L, Midway.
Dean, Miss Annie, Wallburg.
Feezor, A W, Fairmont.
Finch, P D, Lexington.
Garrett, Rev G N, Yadkin College.
Gibson, S A, Midway.
Glover, John, Jackson Hill.
Grimes, Miss E L, Arnold.
Harris, E L, Fuller.
Harris, Miss Troy, Denton.
Harrison, Mrs I, Denton.
Harrison, B I, Denton.
Hoitley, H H, Tyro Shops.
Hedgecock, E L, Abbott's Creek.
Hedrick, J M, Leah.
Hedrick, P F, Newton.
Hedrick, Miss Ida, Lexington.
Helmstetler, J L, Michael.
Hill, Nathan, Denton.
Holmes, Thos, Salisbury.
Hughes, Mrs E J, Belfast.
Kennedy, J C, Thomasville.
Kenerly, J E, Tyro Shops.
Kinney, John A, Bringles.
Koonce, Miss Sallie, Yadkin College.
Koonce, Miss Bertha, Tyro Shops.
Koontz, C A, Arnold.
Laden, Miss Jessie, Lexington.
Lanier, Mrs F M, Cid.
Lanier, John R, Cid.

DAVIDSON COUNTY.

Lanning, R F, Tyro Shops.
Ledford, P L, Thomasville.
Leonard, C B, Newton.
Link, J E, Arnold.
Link, Miss Nannie, Arnold.
Link, T C L, Michael.
Loftin, A G, Jackson Hill.
Loftin, M L, Jackson Hill.
Loftin, R L, McKee.
Loftin, C T, McKee.
Lookabill, J D, Fairmount.
Madison, A F, Yadkin College.
McNary, Rev W H, McKee.
Mears, Miss Essie, Linwood.
Michael, W E, Tyro Shops.
Michael, J P, Michael.
Miller, G W, Linwood.
Morrison, Miss Effie, Thomasville.
Myers, A E, Michael.
Nelson, Chas, Bonar.
Newsom, A L, Jackson Hill.
Newby, Miss Emma, Thomasville.
Palmer, W E, Silver Hill.
Palmer, W F, Silver Hill.
Palmer, Miss Alice, Linwood.
Peacock, S C, Marsh.
Peacock, James, Marsh.
Reagan, Ida, McKee.
Riley, Miss Minnie, Denton.
Roach, W C, Linwood.
Roberts, W M, Linwood.
Robbins, Miss Maggie, Lexington.
Sexton, Alonzo, Denton.
Siceloff, Miss Sue, Midway.
Smith, Daniel, Ilet.
Sowers, M L, Arnold.
Stokes, C W, Jackson Hill.
Stone, Miss Lula, Thomasville.
Surratt, M K, Jackson Hill.
Surratt, B D, Jackson Hill.
Surratt, W L, Jackson Hill.
Teague, E E, Thomasville.
Thomas, I G, Fulbre.
Vorner, S L, Flora.
Wike, Rev Jacob, Pinnex.
Wilson, W C, Bagdad.
Wilson, F A, Lexington.
Yokeley, C M, Midway.
Younts, Miss Alice, Ilex.
Zimmerman, R U, Enterprise.

COLORED.

Beck, Thos L, Abbott's Creek.
Bilding, Isabella, Lexington.
Crump, Taylor, Tyro Shops.
Crump, Wilden, Tyro Shops.
Ellis, Hampton, Linwood.
Gilchrist, Sarah, Lexington.
Green, Minnie, Arnold.
Hairston, P T, Tyro Shops.
Hairston, G W P, Sapona.
Hargrave, Fannie, Lexington.
Hargrave, Fannie E, Lexington.
Hargrave, J M, Lexington.
Kerr, John, Tyro Shops.

DAVIDSON COUNTY.

Lowe, J F, Lexington.
Moore, J J, Salisbury.
Payne, Chas H, Lexington.
Saunders, P B, Jackson Hill.
Wagoner, S L, Midway.
Walser, James, Michael.

LOCAL CORPORATIONS.

Bank of Lexington; J D Grimes, pres;
  Geo W Montcastle, cashier; capital
  $30,000.
Cid Mining Co, Cid; J D Muffley, pres.
Conrad Hill Mining Co, McKee.
Farmers' Sportsman Game Protective
  Club, Thomasville.
Lexington Livery Co, Lexington.
Lexington, Electric Light Co, Lex-
  ington.
Lexington Drug Co, Lexington.
Lexington High School, Lexington.
Lexington Lodge, No 374, A F and A
  M; Jas Dodson, W M; W D Biggers,
  sec.
Masonic Lodge, No 214, Richland,
  Thomasville; F S Lambeth, W M;
  time of meeting, Friday evening be-
  fore full moon, June 24th, December
  27th.
N C Smelting Co, Thomasville.
Pennsylvania Mining Co, Lexington.
Pittsburgh and N C Mining, Manufac-
  turing and Lumber Co, Lexington.
Silver Valley Mining Co, Cid, J M
  Prim, supt.
Silver Hill Mining Co, Silver Hill.
The Gray Finch Co, Thomasville.
Thomasville Shooting Club, Thomas-
  ville.
Thomasville Manufacturing Co, Thom-
  asville.

NEWSPAPERS.

Charity and Children, Thomasville
(Orphanage organ), Archibald Johnson, editor.
Davidson County News, Thomas
ville (Populist, weekly), J F Westmoreland, editor and prop.
Dispatch (dem., weekly), Lexington,
S E Williams and H B Varner, editors
and props.

FARMERS.

Names and Post Offices.

Bethany—Andrew Beckerdite, An-
drew Bodenhamer, G L Charles, Dr S
C W Dorsett, P W Leonard, D F Lind-
say, J P Long, A H Motsinger, M R
Shoaf, Cornelius Shoaf.
Jackson Hill—W H Badgett, C L
Badgett, W W Bailey, L C Bailey, C L

DAVIDSON COUNTY.

Bailey, S S Bailey, W M Burkhead, Eli
Carroll, J C Coggin, J D Coggin, D L
Cook, W G Doby, Isaac Doby, Osborne
Elliott, J M Frank, W L Fuzor, G W
Hall, Harris Harrison, Henry Hill, J L
Hill, Jane Ingram, Allison Johnson,
O P Johnson, W Kinney, Alfred Kin-
ney, J C Lanier, M F Lassiter, A B
Loflin, B T Loflin, W C Loflin, Isaac
Loflin, John Loflin, Wm Loftin, J W
Morris, L P Nance, A W Reed, D V
Reeves, E M Reeves, M J Redwine, N
H Sills, Burwell Skeen, J L Skeen,
Jerry Smith, Thos Smith, David Smith,
G W Smith, Jas Smith, Alfred Smith,
J B Smith. D F Stafford, G F Steed, J
M Stokes, James Stafford, W M C Sur-
ratt, Allen Surratt, J M Surratt, J G
Surratt. R L Surratt, Jas L Surratt, C
L Surratt, Alex Taylor, Eli Varner,
Wm Walker, J T Wood.
  Lexington—H R Berrier, W A Ber-
rier, J J Biesecker, W T Briles, Dan'l
Brinkley, Harrison Brinkley, J W
Brown, Josiah Brown, Geo L Byerly,
D K Cecil, J L Clodfelter, Adam Clod-
felter, DeWitt Clodfelter, Ransom
Clodfelter, L L Conrad, G W Conrad,
Wm F Curry, Francis Darr, Levi Easter,
Elisha Evans, Alex Evans, Lafayette
Everhart, A Everhart, Riley Everhart,
Felix Everhart, Michael Everhart, Sam
Everhart, J J Finch, Jno W Finch, T C
Ford, George Fritts, Henderson Fritts,
John Fritts, J S Green, C A Green,
Smith Green, Chas M Griffith, Grimes
Bros, Alex Grubb, Frank Hargrave,
Matt Hines, W C Harris, Col W F
Henderson, A S Hedrick, J H Hedrick,
S E Hedrick, W A Heitman, Willis
Hiatt, Emanuel Hinkle, J A Hinkle, P
S Hinkle, Geo E Hunt, L Kepley,
Michael Koonts, J F Koonts, J A Leo-
nard, Jesse Leonard, J F Leonard, P J
Leonard, Burgess Leonard, Mrs P D
Leonard, D C Link, Jos Link, Charles
Long, J L McCrary, Levi McCrary, H
J Michael, John Michael, Mary Mosely,
J L Peacock, W G Penry, David Pick-
ett, Hamilton Reed, D H Reed, F C
Robbins, Laura Shemwell, Robt Shoaf,
Alfred Shoaf, G D Sink, Mrs S A Sink,
Alfred A Smith, Peter Smith, Chas L
Snyder, R A Sowers, W F Thomason,
R D Thomason, Jacob Wagoner, J P
Wagoner, Geo Wagoner, J F Ward,
W A Watson, H F Williams, W J
Yokley, S L Yokley, J T Yarborough.
  Midway—T J Beard, Henry Crotts,
D Crotts, G W Eller, S F Eller, A L
Everhart, John Hartman, Thos Hill,
J M Jones, Felix Leonard, T H Liven-
good, D Long, Wiley Nifong, Julius
Nifong, P I Nifong, C W Rothrock, G
S Rothrock. Philip Siceloff, Edward

DAVIDSON COUNTY.

Siceloff, L C G Sink, Daniel Sink, C C Sink, W N Thomas, J C Thomas.

Salem—N A Beckerdite.

Thomasville—C W Albertson, R R Alexander, H B Arnold, Phillip Ball, Andrew Black, John Black. J P Black, A P Black. J F Black, A G Boggs, H L Bowers, Wm Bowers, Geo Bowers, W N Bowers, J W Burton, S S Burton, Jacob Burton, Rev S A Cecil, J B Cecil, Philip Clinard, H L Clodfelter. G A Clodfelter, John Collett, P C Cates, J T Cramer, Mrs Eliz Darr, J C Darr, James Edinger, J A Eller, Jesse Gossett, John Grubb, J R Harris. S R Harris, Wm Hedrick, Adam Hedrick, Zebulon Helton, Jas Helton, George Helper, W M Hiatt, Thomas E Hilton, P A Hoover, D E Imbler, David Imbler, F M Kanoy, L Lee Kanoy, A L Kennedy, Lewis Kennedy, Thos Kennedy, W Kennedy, Ceph Kennedy, J C Kinney, Geo Kinney, J H Lambeth, D T Lambeth, J A Leach, G M Leonard, J D Loftin, R C May, Jason Mendenhall, John Mendenhall, J H Mills, S G Morris, Robert Murphy, W L Myars, Alfred Payne, B A Payne, Sol Payne, Spencer Pope, Abagail Ragan, J A Richard, H F Rothrock, Frank Rothrock, Andrew Sechrist, Curry Shepard, B F Stone, J E Sumner, P C Thomas, G A Thompson, J M Tomlinson, Sam Tomlinson, Isham Tomlinson, John Varner, H Varner, S S Welborn, C H Welborn, D A Welborn, J W Wilson, Ralph Wright,

Tyro Shops—L F Barnes, H P Broadway, William Brown, J N Davis, J W Foster, H H Hastley, Ham Helmstetler, John H Koonts, Valentine Leonard, J A Leonard, J H Michael, W E Nance, Madison Shoaf, Geo Snider, J H Swicegood, Robt Swicegood, Franklin Swicegood, Alex Swicegood, Rob't Thompson, J L Waitman, G W Wyatt, J A Young.

DAVIE COUNTY.

AREA 300 SQUARE MILES.

POPULATION 11,621; White 8,769, Colored 2,852.

DAVIE COUNTY was formed in 1836, from Rowan, and named in honor of Gen. Wm. R. Davie, a resident of Halifax county, who acted a prominent part in the Revolutionary War.

MOCKSVILLE, the county seat, is 120 miles west of Raleigh, and contains a population of 525. It takes its name from the Mock family, who were prominent citizens of that portion of Rowan before the reparation.

Surface.—Moderately uneven; well watered by the Yadkin river and its tributaries. Soil rich; a fine farming country.

Staples.—This is one of the finest wheat-growing counties in the State Corn is grown largely. Grass is profitable. Of late years tobacco is grown with great success. Some cotton is raised, and the amount is increased yearly.

Fruits are those common to the middle section of the State—apples, pears, peaches, plums, cherries, etc. The melons of the Yadkin Valley are noted for their flavor.

Timbers—Oak, hickory, elm, poplar, maple, and some walnut and pine.

TOWNS AND POST OFFICES.

	POP.		POP.
Advance,	200	Fulton,	75
Augusta,	100	Hall's Ferry,	20
Bailey,	50	Holman,	20
Calahaln,	75	Jerusalem,	75
Cana,	25	Kappa,	20
Cornatzer,	25	Mocksville (c h),	
County Line,	50		700
Dulings,	25	Nestor,	30
Dutchman,	20	Pino,	30
Elbaville,	25	Redland,	50
Ephesus,	20	Sheffield,	30
Farmington,	100	Smith's Grove,	150
Felix,	15	Tennyson,	20
Fork Church,	75		

COUNTY OFFICERS.

Clerk Superior Court—A T Grant.
Commissioners—N A Peebles, ch'm'n; H E Avertson, Isaac Roberts.
Coroner—P M Bailey.
Register of Deeds—G W Sheek.
Sheriff—W P Williams.
Solicitor 9th District—M L Mott.
Surveyor—S J Tatum.

Standard Keeper—W A Griffin.
Treasurer—Dr Jas McGuire.
County Examiner—Leon Cashe.

COURTS.

Fifth Monday after the first Monday in March, and the third Monday after the first Monday in September.

TOWN OFFICERS.

MOCKSVILLE.—*Mayor,* Will X Coley. *Commissioners.* H C Meroney, J H Meroney, J W Bailey, H P Brinegar, O T Williams.

TOWNSHIPS AND MAGISTRATES.

Calahan—L B Walker, J D Walker, G E Horn, J S Ratledge, Rich Stroud, James Moore (Calahaln).

Clarksville—N A Stonestreet, J G Pool, Jesse Richardson, G L White (Mocksville).

Farmington—M D Kimbrough, E C Smith, James Taylor, R T Swing, W F Furches, T A Bunch (Farmington).

Fulton—J R Williams, sr, Wm F Merrill, H C Pasten, W D Mason, J H Peebles (Fulton).

Jerusalem—P S Stewart, E H Morris, P W Booe, H H Swicegood, M A Foster (Jerusalem).

Mocksville—M R Chaffin, J A Kelly, P M Bailey (Mocksville).

Shady Grove—T E Allen, H T Smithdeal (Mocksville).

CHURCHES.

Names, Post Offices, Pastors and Denom.

METHODIST.

Anderson's—Calahan, —— Hardison.
Bethlehem—Redland, R T N Stevenson.
Bethlehem, Smith's Grove, R T N Stevenson.
Centre—Mocksville, —— Hardison.
Church—Farmington, R T N Stevenson.
Church—Fork Church, R T N Stevenson.
Church—Mocksville, —— Mann.
Church—Smith's Grove, R T N Stevenson.
Concord—Ephesus, —— Hardison.

DAVIE COUNTY.

Fulton—Advance, R T N Stevenson.
Liberty—Jerusalem.
Oak Grove—Mocksville, - — Hardison.
Olive Branch—Farmington.
Salem—County Line, —— Hardison.
Shady Grove, Advance, R T N Stevenson.
Smith's Grove—Smith's Grove.
Wesley Chapel—Farmington, R T N Stevenson.

METH. PROTESTANT.

Union Chapel—Mocksville.
White Oak—Elbaville.

BAPTIST.

Bear Creek—Clarksville.
Cedar Creek (col)—Farmington.
Cnurch—Mocksville.
Cnurch—Jerusalem.
Eaton—Farmington
Fork—Fulton.
New Bethel (col)—Jerusdem.
Poplar Grove (col)—Fork Church.
Sandy Level (col)—Fork Church.

PRESBYTERIAN.

Cnurch—Mocksville.
Cnurch (col)—Mocksville.
Mt Zion (col)—Mocksville.
Second (col)—Mocksville.

MORAVIAN.

Macedonia—Farmington.

LUTHERAN.

St Matthew's—County Line.

AF. METHODIST.

Church (col)—Mocksville.

N. METHODIST.

Piney Grove (col)—Advance.
St John's Chapel (col)—

ZION METHODIST.

Bethany (col)—Farmington.
Bingham (col)—Smith's Grove.
Liberty (col)—Jerusalem.
Main (col)—Mocksville.
Mt Sinai (col)—Elbaville.
New Zion (col)—Smith's Grove.
Palmetto (col)—Holdman's Cross.
Poplar Springs (col)—Calahaln.
St John (col)—Mocksville.

MINISTERS RESIDENT.

Names, Post Offices and Denominations.

METHODIST.

Hardison, ——, Mocksville.
Mann, ——, Mocksville.
Murchison, A K, Farmington.
Stevenson, R T N, Farmington.
Walker, Vincent, Calahaln.

BAPTIST.

Clark, A B (col). Catawba.

Hargrove, J D (col). Lexington.
Hariston. T H (col), Fork Creek.
Rich, J H. Farmington.
Stallings, D, Mocksville.

PRESBYTERIAN.

Crawford, James H (col). Mocksville.
Dalton, P H. Mocksville.

LUTHERAN.

Ketchie, R W, County Line.

METH. PROTESTANT.

Reminger ——. Mocksville.

MORAVIAN.

Leinbach, ——, Farmington.

ZION METHODIST.

Campbell, —— (col), Mocksville.
Carter, Sandy (col), Smith Grove.
Hauser, Henry (col), Panther Creek.
Miller, J A (col), Linwood.

AFRICAN METHODIST.

Campbell, T S (col), Mocksville.

NORTH. METHODIST.

Joiner, T W (col), Advance.

HOTELS AND BOARDING HOUSES.

Names, Post Offices and Proprietors.

Bahnson House, Farmington, Mrs J A Bahnson.
Davie Hotel, Mocksville, Jas A Kelly.
Boarding, E M Saicegood, Mocksville.

LAWYERS.

Names and Post Offices.

Anderson, R S, Calahaln.
Bailey, T B, Mocksville.
Chafin, T W, Mocksville.
Cain, Robert L, Felix.
Gaither, Ephraim L, Mocksville.
Morris, E H, Advance.
Stewart, Jacob, Mocksville.

MANUFACTORIES.

Kinds, Post Offices and Proprietors.

Tobacco, Mocksville, Sandford & Williams
Tobacco, Farmington, W F Jones.
Tobacco, Farmington, Rufus Bowles.
Tobacco, Farmington, J B Cornelison.
Tobacco, Mocksville, J L Sheek.
Tobacco, Fulton, Peebles Bros.

MERCHANTS AND TRADESMEN.

Names, Post Offices, Lines of Business.

ADVANCE.

Allen, T C,	G S
Davis, A H,	G S

DAVIE COUNTY.		DAVIE COUNTY.	

Ellis, Mrs W R & Co, Millinery
Foster, J M & Son, Furn and Und't'g
Hartman & Jones, G S
Morris & Co, G S
Orrell, W H, G S
Smithdeal. H T, G S
White, W G, G S

CALAHALN.
Anderson, A A, G S.

CANA.
Cain, Jas H, agt, G S
Frost, E, agt, G S

CORNATZER.
Cornatzer, J & Son, G S

COUNTY LINE.
Crater & Gaither, G S
Eaton, J T, G S
Lowery, M L. G S

ELBAVILLE.
Ellis, T J, G S

EPHESUS.
Foster, M A, G S

FARMINGTON.
Bahnson, C F, Jeweler
Conrad & Co, G S
James, W F, G S
Jarvis S A & Co, G S
Johnson, W G, agt. G S
Sparks, H F, G S

FORK CHURCH.
Carter & Carter, G S
Carter, J C, G S
Davis. D V & E J, G S
Smith, J B, G S

HALL'S FERRY.
Sheek, L A, G S

HOLMAN'S.
Coon, J F, G S
Holman B C. G S

JERUSALEM.
Bernier, F L G S
Charles, F W, G S
Foster. M A G S
Hobson, W H G S

MOCKSVILLE.
Bailey, W H, G S
Blount, J M, G S
Brown, F. agt. Gro
Clement. W A, G S
Grant, Miss Annie, Milliner
Griffin, Mrs W A. Millin r
Haines. Mrs Jane, Milliner
Horn & Bro, Millers
Hunt, C E. Furn and Coffins
Roberson. H E & Son, Tob
Sandford. C C. G S
Sanford & Williams, Tob
Sheek, Jas, M'f'r Tob

Stewart, J H, —
Young, T M, G S
Willis, A B, Drugs

NESTOR.
Langston, W A, G S

PINO.
Eaton, D, G S

SMITH GROVE.
Foster, J H & Co, G S
Tobias, J, G S

TENNYSON.
Hendrix & Thompson, G S

MILLS.

Kinds, Post Offices and Proprietors.

Corn, Fulton, J H Hanes.
Corn and flour, Mocksville, Philip Hanes.
Corn and flour, Kappa, W R Ketchie.
Corn and flour. Mocksville, G E & L G Horn.
Flour and corn, Mocksville, Sheaf & Sanford.
Flour and corn, Calahan, ——.
Flour and corn, Mocksville, Horn Bro.
Flour, corn and saw, Jerusalem, Tillett Lefler.
Flour, corn and saw, Fulton, J Hanes.
Flour, corn and saw (Clarksville), Mocksville, H Critz.
Flour, corn and saw, Smith Grove, J M Summer.
Flour. corn and saw, Farmington, A W Ellis.
Flour, corn and saw, Jerusalem, P W Hairston.
Saw, County Line, R W Ketchie.
Saw and corn, Mocksville, Brown & Bro.
Steam corn and flour, Farmington, A W Ellis.
Steam corn and flour, Cana, J W Etchison.
Steam saw, Mocksville, Call & Howard.

PHYSICIANS.

Names and Post Offices.

Anderson, John. Calahaln.
Arderson, C F, Fork Church.
Cain, John M, Mocksville.
Cash, L H. Smith Grove.
Kimbrough, M D, Smith Grove.
Lippard, G H. Advance.
Martin, W C, Mocksville.
McGuire, James, Mocksville.
Moore, W H, Farmington.
Wiseman, A W, Jerusalem.
Wiseman, J W, Farmington.
Strickland, ——, Advance.

DAVIE COUNTY.

SCHOOLS.

Names, Post Offices and Principals.

Academy, Smith Grove, Prof S Hutchins.
Academy, Farmington, Mrs Weathersbee.
Fork Church Academy, Fork Church.
Male and Female Academy, Mocksville, Miss Mattie M Eaton and Prof. E Barnett.
Public schools: white 38, colored 17.

LOCAL CORPORATIONS.

Farmington Lodge, No 265, A F and A M, Farmington; time of meeting: second Friday evening. June 24th and December 27th.
Knights of Honor, Mocksville; meeting: first Monday evening of each month.
Mocksville Lodge, No 134, A F and A M, Mocksville; time of meeting: 3rd Friday evening of each month, Tuesday evening of court, and June 24th and December 27th.

NEWSPAPERS.

Davie Times, (dem. weekly), W X Coley, editor and prop.

FARMERS.

Names and Post Offices.

Advance—T C Allen, C G Bailey, W A Bailey, Jacob Conatzer, W R Ellis, W B March, Geo Markland, Matthew Markland, Tom Nail, F M Phillips, H E Robertson, George Siddon.
Calahaln—C J Anderson, Pink Beck, Robert Blackwell, Isaiah Byerly, E P Casey, W M Davault, J W Dwiggins, John Foster, Denton I James, W Koonce, W R Ketchie, M A Neely, Pink Ratledge, Scott Smoot.
Clarkville—Dr J Anderson, G W Baity, J P Beck, H H Blackwelder, John C Bowe, J Q R Butler, P H Cain, J P Casey, Wm Clany, J G Clifford, Chas Collett, C L Cook, A J Cranfill, H Critz, Jas Cuthrell, A T Davis, Jas Eaton, Thos Eaton, J F Frost, E Frost, L A Furches, J A Gray, P P Green, F M Hendricks, J C Howell, J C Kinvam, W J Leach, Simpson Ledford, W Mason, J P Mason, B L McDaniel, W C Perdee, Gilliam Ratlege, D J Ratlege, S P Ratlege, D Ratlege, M G Richards, J I Smith, Thos M Smoot.
Elbaville—Richmond Bailey, Alphia Caton, Wm Clark, L A Crouse, W R Ellis, W J Ellis, J B Ellis, Jno S Lyon,

DAVIE COUNTY.

Wm Lyon, G W Markland, Z Minor, James Myers.
Farmington—B R Allen, W G Allen, John Bailey, Charles F Bahnson, B U Barneycastle, J M Beauchamp, Joel M Beauchamp, J A Beauchamp, S W Bowden, C A Bowden, R E Brock, R C Brown, T A Brunt, A B Butner, Walter Chaffin, J F Cuthrell, James Cutsell, Stephen Douthitt, E J Douthitt, Noah Dunn, Daniel Eaton, J V Eaton, Jordan Eaton, Wesley J Eaton, A W Ellis, Joseph Cuthrell, Thomas A Ferebee, R M Ferebee, John Fulcher, Matthew Fulford, L A Furches, W G Furches, S V Furches, J M Furdees, W F Furdees, S A Gaither, C F Griffith, C A Hall, J W Hauser, H H Hanes, G A Hartman, J H Hauser, Thos Horn, S A Jarvis, B F Sums, F R McMahon, H H McMahon, L L Miller, A K Murchison, Willie Murchison, J M Perry, S C Rich, T M Sain, L A Sheek, J G Sheek, A R Sheek, D S Sheek, C B Smith, Jonathan Smith, H H Smith, C H Smith, E C Smith, Green Tatum, R Q A Teague, J L Ward, F M Ward, F B Ward, J W Wiseman.
Fulton—B R Bailey, C G Bailey, L A Bailey, J D Barty, F L Berrier, J C Carter, Jacob Connatzer, P J Cope, L Davis, J H Deadman, Coleman Foster, H M Foster, J G Foster, P L Foster, P M Foster, Richard Foster, Samuel Foster, A M Garriwood, Jas Garriwood, P W Hairston, Jane Hanes, John W Hanes, M J Hanes, W P Hanes, N A Hendricks, Dan'l Hendrix, Pink Hendrix, W D Mason, W F Merrell, Zerrel Minor, J N Myatt, J N Myers, Elizabeth Peebles, John Peebles, N A Peebles, F M Phillips, J B Smith, E D Stewart, Mrs Fannie Williams, J R Williams, Jack Zimmerman.
Hall's Ferry—A B Butner, G W Chaffin, C A Hall, R G Sheek.
Jerusalem—H J Baker, G E Barnhart, Henry Beck, T M Bessent, T B Bessent, J W Bessent, J N Charles, W B Clement, J N Click, Sr, J N Click, Jr, John Cope, Jas A Crump, J C Daniel, Josiah Daniel, C A Davis, E L Davis, J R Deadman, T J Deadman, Frank Everhart, J C Foard, H L Foster, W D Foster, George Fowler, A T Grant, Jonas Graves, P W Hairston, J A Hendrix, G W Hendrix, W H Hobson, Mrs Ann Hobson, J D Hodges, T C Hudson, J A Kelly, Robert Lindsay, Tillett Lefler, E S Morris, H G Pack, W F Smith, H H Swicegood, Ezra Tatum, E W Taylor, I Tatum.
Mocksville—W J Atkinson, R M Austin, Wiley Bailey, James Bowles, G W Boles, J L Bowles, T B Brinager,

DAVIE COUNTY.

Hampton Brinager,C S Brown,Brown, Sanford & Co, P H Cain, S M Call, H R Call, E P Casey, J A Cheshire, C A Clement, M J Clement, Geo Clement, W A Clement, John H Clement, J F Coon, W C Denny, Wm Douthitt, S A Dula, Joseph Eaton, R T Van Eaton, Miles Foster, Samuel Foster, Albert Foster, B Foster, J D Frost, George Freezor, E L Gaither, James Gaither, Ephraim Gaither, G W Gaither, L G Gaither, G G Graves, Philip Hanes, J D Hayes, H H Helper, W A Hendrix, F M Hendrick, H C Holman, Mrs Mary E Holman, Mrs Sarah Howell, G B Ismes, F M Johnston, N D Johnston, W B Jones, James Jordan, T F Keller, J D Keller, A C Kelly, CS Kerfeese, J P Kerfeese, Peter Kerfeese, C F Kerfeese, J B Lanier, David Leach, Elijah Martin, George C McClamrock, John McClamrock, Jas McGuire, W F McMahan, W W Miller, F A Miller, E W

DAVIE COUNTY.

Mooring, G E Mumford, A M Nail, B F Nichols, W C Arrender, B W Parker, E H Pass, J F Ratlege, Isaac Roberts, Caspar Sain, Sr, J M Sain, J F Sain, Wiley E Sain, Andrew Sain, C W Seaford, Jacob Shoaf, W F Smith, O H Spencer, B R Steelman, J H Steward, John Stonestreet, W H Stonestreet, B F Stonestreet, P H Snider, W D Snider, A Z Taylor, Pinkney Turner, Frank Wagoner, J M Wellman, W F Whitaker, N H C Williams, Jerry Willman, R L Willson, D C Wilson, A S Womack, John J Woodruff, W T Woodruff, S A Woodruff, W M Wyatt.

*Smith Grove—*Dr L H Cash, L B Cook, John A Clouse, L A Clouse. Sr., G M Call, B B Cornelius, H W Dulin, John W Hanes, M A Haskins, W H Hodges, W T Jones, H F Sparks, Jas Taylor, J W Walker, W G Ward, Jas Williams, W F Williams, J T Wilson.

DUPLIN COUNTY.

AREA, 670 SQUARE MILES.

POPULATION, 19,488; White 11,588; Colored 7,900.

DUPLIN COUNTY was formed in 1749, from the upper part of New Hanover county. Its early settlers were Irish, and the name reminded them of Dublin.

KENANSVILLE. the county-seat, was named for the Hon James Kenan. and is situated 75 miles southeast of Raleigh. Population, 528.

Surface—Duplin county is situated mostly on the east side of the Wilmington and Weldon Railroad, and on the head waters of the Northeast Cape Fear river; it is level and much of the land good. The location and surface are such as to make it susceptible of a high state of cultivation.

Staples — Cotton is the great staple, and is cultivated with intelligence and marked success. Corn and sweet potatoes are profitable crops. Naval stores are still produced in considerable quantities, and some years bring in large amounts of money. The scuppernong grape is perfectly at home here, is grown extensively, and of the finest kind. Of late years trucking is attracting considerable attention.

Fruits — Grapes, melons, apples, peaches, pears, and almost all the smaller fruits common to this latitude.

Timbers—Long leaf pine, oak, gum, cypress, dogwood, maple, etc.

TOWNS AND POST OFFICES.

	POP.		POP.
Albertson,	25	McGowen,	50
Beulaville,	20	Magnolia,	300
Bowden's,	40	Myrts,	28
Branch's Store,	55	Natural Wells,	25
Cabin,	15	Outlaw's	
Cavenaugh,	30	Bridge,	50
Chinquapin,	32	Pasley,	30
Corine,	26	Pearsall,	35
Dolph,	25	Resaca,	25
Faison,	250	Rose Hill,	50
Hallsville,	75	Safe,	25
Humphrey,	50	Sarecta,	25
Joford,	20	Sloan,	50
Kenansville—		Teachey's,	150
(C H).	500	Wallace,	200
Leon,	30	Warsaw,	500
Lyman,	50	Xenia,	20

COUNTY OFFICERS.

Clerk Superior Court—J A Gavin.

Ch. Commissioners—I F Hill.
Register of Deeds—Thad Jones.
Solicitor Sixth District—M C Richardson.
Sheriff—Daniel Moore.
Treasurer—Daniel Moore.
County Examiner—

COURTS.

Second Monday before first Monday in March; fourth Monday before first Monday in September.

TOWNSHIPS AND MAGISTRATES.

Albertson— N B Stroud, W H Grady, F H Sutton, J B Outlaw, Joe Maxwell, J Lafayette Outlaw, J McR Grady, R G Maxwell (Albertson)

Cypress Creek—D M Sholar, M T Horne, E W Brown, E T Lanier, Jacob James, Micanor James, P F Davis, H R Henderson, J M Henderson (Kenansville).

Faison—H J Faison, Chas R Millard, J H Fonville, I N Hightower, J F Shine, Geo Giddens, W P Faison, B B Carr, J R Oliver (Faison).

Glisson—B F Bonnett, S M Waller, W B Herring, J H Westbrook, J D Kornegay, Gaston Kelly, W C Jones (Kenansville).

Island Creek—D T McMillan, J O Carr, J D Teachey, L L Millard, W S Bonet, J T Teachey, A D Rogers, E F Barlow, J C Millard, G S Carr, jr, J E Farrior (Kenansville).

Kenansville—B F Pearsall, R J Fermell, A F Williams, J S Rouse, J W Miller, J H Hamilton, F Sutherland, Samuel Ferrell, S B Newton (Kenansville).

Limestone—L A Kennedy, S O Middleton, M W Brown, F P Cox, George Edwards, Frank Kennedy, Robt Sandlin, John Swinson, Dr D A Williams (Kenansville).

Magnolia—J H Heath, A W Wells, W W Wilson, M J Carlton, Colin S aw, D D McMillan, J F Wilkins, Joshua West, sr, J C Boone, W J Hall (Magnolia).

Rockfish—I J Johnson, N F Register, I P Alderman, W R Hufham, J J Ward, J L Williams, S H Colwell, F L Johnson, Ira Band (Kenansville)

Smith's—T Q Hall, J R Miller, sr, Hiram Howard (Kenansville).

DUPLIN COUNTY.

Warsaw—J F Woodard. Leonidas Middleton, W H Williams, B L Blackmore, J F Williams, Levi Moore, J B Winders, Samuel Gavin, R F Pollock (Warsaw).

Wolfscrape — R D Bennett, D R Brown, J N Southerland, J L Kornegay, G W Goodson, D H Garner, Thad Jones, sr, Kinsey Jones, Daniel Jones, David Brown (Kenansville).

CHURCHES.

Names, Post Offices, Pastors and Denom.

BAPTIST.

Bear Marsh—Mt Olive.
Beaver Dam—Magnolia.
Berea—
Chinquapin—
Concord—
Corinth—
Dobson Chapel—
Dorum (col)—Wallace.
Hallsville—Hallsville.
Island Creek—
Johnson Grade—
Johnston—Warsaw.
Warsaw—Warsaw.

FREE-WILL BAPTIST.

Holly Hill—Branch's Store.

METHODIST.

Carlton's Chapel—
Charity Chapel—
Friendship—
Kenansville—Kenansville.
Magnolia—Magnolia.
Providence—
Wesley Chapel—

ZION METHODIST.

Zion's Hill (col)—Waycross.

AF. METHODIST.

Magnolia (col)—Magnolia.
Merritt's (col)—Waycross.
Rock Fish (col)—Wallace.
Teachey's (col)—Teachey's.

PRESBYTERIAN.

Beulah—
Chinquapin—
Grove—Kenansville.
Mt Zion—Teachey's.
Rockfish—Wallace.
Union—Faison.

EPISCOPAL.

Christ's—Rockfish.
St John's—Faison, J M Hillyar.

MANUFACTORIES.

Kinds, Post Offices and Proprietors.

Cotton-gin, Warsaw, Levi Moore.

16

DUPLIN COUNTY.

Crate factory, Warsaw, T B Pearce.
Crate factory, Faison, J W Mallard.
Turpentine, Sloan, Mary C James.
Turpentine, Leon, Branch Williams.
Turpentine, Rose Hill, Scott & Grisham.
Turpentine, Hallsville, O W Scott.
Turpentine, Chinquapin, W H Sloan.
Turpentine, Chinquapin, G B D Parker.
Turpentine Beulaville, J N Grisham.

MERCHANTS AND TRADESMEN.

Names, Post Offices and Lines of Business.

BEULAVILLE.

Grisham, J W, G S and Turpentine
Houston, W A, G S
Sandlin & Wilkins, G S
Williams, A, G S

CABIN.

Bishop & Smith, G S
Kennedy, W J, G S

CAVENAUGH.

Kilpatrick, T & Co, G S

CHINQUEPIN.

Cottle, J L, Agt, G S
James, Robt (near), G o
Parker, G B D (near), Turp and G S
Pickett, J L, G S
Sloan, W H, G S and Turp

FAISON.

Darden, I G, G S
Faison, Jno M, Drugs
Giddens, J L, G S
Hawley, W C, G S
Hill, S M (col), Gro and Confec
Hill & Bro, G S
Hollingsworth, J N, G S
Lee, Lovett (near), G S
Lewis & Hines, G S
Perrett, Thos. G S
Smith & Lucas (near), G S
Smith & Southerland, G S
Westbrook, Jas S & Co, Nursery
Witherington, B B, G S

HALLSVILLE.

Middleton, S O, G S
Ribbins, P D (col), Miller
Rhodes & Swinson, G S
Scott, O W, G S and Turp

HANSON.

Brown, E C, G S

JOFORD.

Williams, J B, G S

KENANSVILLE.

Blount, Dr J W, Drugs
Bryan, W R, Agt, G S
Farrior, D L, Live Stock

DUPLIN COUNTY.

Farrior, Miss E J,   Millinery
Grimes & Co.   G S
Jones, Dr A J,   Drugs
Kelly, J B,   G S
McGowan, A D (near),   G S
Sprunt, N H,   G S

KORNEGAY'S BRIDGE.

Cavenaugh, J A, Agt,   G S
Core, D L,   G S

LEON.

Williams, B F,   G S
Williams, Branch,   G S and Turp

MAGNOLIA.

Croom, J F & Bro, Miller and
                      Tuberose bulbs
Gaylor, C P,   G S
Mathis, J A,   Gro
Newberry, H E,   G S and Livery
Scott, Croom & Co,   G S

NATURAL WELLS.

Boone & Wells,   G S

PEARSALL.

Bryan, Mrs S A P,   G S

ROSE HILL.

Carr, J W,   G S
Fussell, W H (near),   G S
Fussell & Mallard,   G S
Scott & Grisham,   G S and Turp
Steinmetz, C M,   Lumber
Southerland, W B,   G S

SAFE.

Carr, J G,   G S

SARECTA.

Kennedy, W J, jr,   G S

SLOAN.

James, Mary C,   G S and Turp
Powell, D R,   Gro and Confec

TEACHEY'S.

Carter, Z J,   G S

DUPLIN COUNTY.

McMillan, J C, jr,   G S
Teachey, M W,   G S

WALLACE.

Carr & Carr,   G S
Carter & Brice,   Live Stock
Cavenaugh, J Q,   G S
Hall, T Q,   G S
Mallard, L L,   G S
Robinson, L W,   Drugs
Scott & Co,   G S

WARSAW.

Best, L P,   G S
Brown. Isaac,   G S
Hill, W L.   Fertilizer
Hines, S E,   G S
Hussey, C E,   G S
Johnson, A T (col),   Gro and Confec
Middleton & Cooper,   G S
Murray, M T,   Gro
Pierce, T B,   G S
Winders, J B,   G S
Williams, Holly (col),   G S
Woodard, J F,   G S

XENIA.

Carr, R D,   G S

MILLS.

Names, Post Offices and Proprietors.

Saw, Faison, H J Faison & Bro.
Saw, Magnolia, J H Baker.
Saw, Sarecta, Albertson Bros.

NEWSPAPERS.

Names, Post Offices and Proprietors.

Southern Christian Herald and News
Digest, Kenansville, Rev A R Raven,
editor.

DURHAM COUNTY.

AREA, 364 SQUARE MILES.

POPULATION, 18,000; White 10,671, Colored 7,329.

DURHAM COUNTY was formed in 1881 from parts of Orange and Wake counties, and takes its name from the principal town and county-seat, formerly known as "Durham's Depot," on the North Carolina Railroad, and which took its name from the Durham family residing at that place.

DURHAM, the county-seat, is known as one of the most flourishing and enterprising towns in the State, having risen, since the war, from a mere hamlet of half a dozen houses to its present dimensions of some 9,000 inhabitants, and is the headquarters of the world-renowned " Durham Smoking Tobacco," besides many other important enterprises. It is twenty-six miles northwest of Raleigh.

Surface.— Moderately undulating; water-power good; climate healthy.

Staples.—Corn, wheat, cotton, oats, rye, tobacco and vegetables.

Fruits.—Apples. peaches, pears, plums, damsons, berries, etc.

Timbers.—All the hard woods, pine and cedar, poplar, etc.

TOWNS AND POST OFFICES.

	POP.		POP.
Bahama,	50	McConn,	30
Dayton,	35	Nelson,	25
Durham,	9,000	Red Mountain,	150
E. Durham,	1,500	Rougemont,	50
Fish Dam,	300	South Lowell,	100
Flat River,	100	Stagville.	25
Galveston,	50	Umbra,	50
Gorman,	25	W. Durham.	1 000
Luster,	45	Willardville,	100
Lyndover,	20		

COUNTY OFFICERS.

Clerk Superior Court—W J Christian.
Commissioners—C B Green, chmn; J G Latta, John Suit, W F Hopson, W G Howard.
Register of Deeds—W W Woods.
Sheriff—John N Riggsbee.
Solicitor Fifth District—W G Bynum.
Treasurer—T J Holloway.
Surveyor— ——
Coroner— ——
County Examiner— —— Blalock.

COURTS.

Tenth Monday after the first Mon-day in March, and the fifth Monday after the first Monday in September.

TOWN OFFICERS.

DURHAM—*Mayor*, T L Peay. *Board of Aldermen*, T H Martin, C C Taylor, M A Angier. L A Carr, F J Riggsbee, W M Yearby. *Treasurer*, Patrick Lunsford. *City Clerk*, J W Woodward. *Chief of Police*, Jacob Woodall. *Street Commissioner*, J B Christian. *Clerk of Market*, W L Giddens. *Health Officer*, W M Mannin . *Tax Collector*, J R Patton.

WEST DURHAM—*Mayor*. B L Duke. *Commissioners*, H E Leaman, A J Draughan.

TOWNSHIPS AND MAGISTRATES.

Durham Township—D L Belvin, W R Suit, J W Shields, W L Cooper, Wm Lipscombe, J L Watkins, A F Faucette. D C Mangum, J S Durham, J C Wilkerson, C F Vickers, W A Jenkins, John W Ferrell, J S Mangum, R T Howerton, W T Neal, M H Ellen, W H Wilkins (Durham).

Mangum—A G Roberts, G C Hampton, J F M Terry, E G Gray, Victor Umstead (Mangum's Store).

Patterson—G A Barbee, John C Terrell, Paschall Cook, O J W Perry, W J Blackwood, P A Brown, Patrick Massey (Durham).

Oak Grove—S H Davis (Fish Dam), A M Sorrell (Nelson). Duane Carpenter, W G Gage, W H Perry (Durham).

Lebanon—Thos Lipscombe (Galveston), Samuel Flinton (Orange Factory), Kinch Halloway, W L Garrard, J E Rogers, J O Latta (Durham).

Cedar Fork—Jos Green, W B Hopson, J L Talley, G M Creen, Jos Shipp, Hugh Green, J R Page (Nelson).

CHURCHES.

Names, Pastors, Postoffices and Denom.

METHODIST.

Bethany—Durham, W B Doub.
Church—West Durham, R W Bailey.
Carr Church—East Durham, N E Coltrane.
Duke's Chapel—Durham, S T Moyle.
Fletcher's Chapel—Fish Dam, S T Moyle.

DURHAM COUNTY.

Main Street—Durham, W B Doub.
Massey's Chapel—Durham, S T Moyle.
McMannen Chapel—Durham, S T Moyle.
Old Bethel—Bahama, S T Moyle.
Orange Church (Chapel Hill, Orange co)—S T Moyle.
Orange Factory—Willardsville, S T Moyle.
Pleasant Green—Hillsboro, S T Moyle.
South Durham—Durham, B R Hall.
Sylvan—Stagville, S T Moyle.
Trinity—Durham, J N Cole.

AFRICAN METHODIST.

Church (col)—Durham, H H Hall.

BAPTIST.

Berea—Durham.
Cedar Fork—Nelson.
Cedar Grove (col)—Barbee's Store, Sam Hunt.
First Church—Durham—W C Tyree.
Mt. Moriah—Chapel Hill.
Piney Grove—Durham, J F McDuffy.
Roberson Grove—Fish Dam, —— Stevenson.
Rose of Sharon—Durham—G J Dowell
Sandy Level—Barbee's Store, G J Dowell
Second Church—Durham, G J Dowell.
Third Church—East Durham.
White Rock (col)—Durham, —— Eaton
Yates' Chapel—Durham, G J Dowell.

PRIMITIVE BAPTIST.

Enon—Durham, Samuel Terry.
Lebanon—South Lowell, Samuel Terry
Primitive (col)—Durham, Wesley Henderson.

PRESBYTERIAN.

Church—Durham, D B Turnbull.

CHRISTIAN.

Church—Durham, J W Wellons.

EPISCOPAL.

St. Philip's—Durham.

MINISTERS RESIDENT.

Names, Post Offices and Denominations.

METHODIST.

Bailey, H W, West Durham.
Doub, W B, Durham.
Gattis, Z J, Durham.
Cole, John N, Durham.
Coltrane, N E, East Durham.
Kilgo, J C, North Durham.
Massey, P H, Durham.
Merritt, A H, West Durham.
Moyle, S T. Durham.
Pegram, W H, West Durham.
Troy, Thad L, West Durham.
Walker, Alex, Durham.
Yates, E A, D D, Durham.

DURHAM COUNTY.

AFRICAN METHODIST.

Hall, H H (col), ——.

BAPTIST.

Dowell, Q J, Durham.
Tyree, W C, Durham.

PRIM. BAPTIST.

Monk, T Z, South oLwell.

PRESBYTERIAN

Turnbull, L B, Durham.

HOTELS AND BOARDING HOUSES.

Names, Post Offices and Proprietors.

Boarding House, Durham, Mrs R Hobgood.
Boarding House, Durham, J H Wood.
Boarding House, Durham, Mrs Royster.
Boarding, Durham, Mrs J A Cox.
Boarding, Durham, Mrs J T Watts.
Boarding, Durham, Mrs Yearby.
Central Hotel, Durham, Mrs Beavers.
Hopkins House, Durham, Miss Malissa Hopkins.
Hotel Carrolina, Durham, Howell Cobb.
Stuart House, Durham, Mrs Stuart.

LAWYERS.

Names and Post Offices.

Boone, T A, Durham.
Boone, R B, Durham.
Briggs, P M, Durham.
Cannady, —— (col), Durham.
Foushee, H A, Durham.
Fuller, Thurston & Fuller, Durham.
Fuller, Frank L, Durham.
Fuller, W W, Durham
Green, F A, Durham.
Guthrie, Will B, Durham.
Guthrie, W A, Durham.
Holton, S M, Durham.
Mangum, A, Flat River.
Manning, James S, Durham.

MANUFACTORIES.

Kinds, Post Offices and Proprietors.

Banner Warehouse, Durham, Lea Warren & Co.
Blackwell's Durham Co-operative Tobacco Co, Julian S Carr, pres: M W Reid, bus. mgr and supt: T B Fuller, head book keeper; H N Snow, cashier: W L Hall, time keeper; P M Briggs, book-keeper: R L Lindsey, stenographer: Alex Walker, leaf tobacco buyer; W M Wahab, shipping clerk.

DURHAM COUNTY.

Blacksmithing, Durham, T Amy (col).
Blacksmithing, Durham, Chris Holloway (col).
Blacksmithing, Durham, W H Holloway.
Brick, Durham, D Z and P P O'Brient.
Brick, West Durham, R B Fitzgerald (col).
Building and contracting, Durham, T. S Christian.
Cheroots and cigars, Durham, J T Malloy Cheroot Co.
Cigars, Durham, W P Henry & Co.
Cigars, Durham, Sam Cramer.
Cigars and cheroots, Durham, J T Mallory & Co.
Cigars, Durham, W L Henry & Co.
Coaches, carriages, etc, Durham, C P Howerton.
Cigarettes and smoking tobacco, Durham, W Duke, Sons & Co.
Cotton ginning, Durham, Jas H Gainey.
Cotton yarns and cloth, Orange Factory, Willard M'f'g Co.
Durham Fertilizer Co, S T Morgan, pres: J S Carr, vice pres; L A Carr, sec and treas.
Foundry, Durham, Louis Alberzett.
Granulated smoking, long and cut tobacco, Durham, Z I Lyon & Co (E J. Parrish, sole owner).
Hosiery, Durham, Durham Hosiery Co.
Ice, Durham, Jarman Ice Co.
Machine Shops, Durham, J T Keir.
Plaids & Yarns, Durham, Pearl Cotton Mill Co.
Plaids and Yarns, West Durham, Erwin Cotton Mill Co.
Plug and twist tobacco, Durham, Jas. G Whitted.
Roller Flour, Durham, Cox & Christian.
Saddles and harness. Durham, B R Woodall & Co.
Sash and blinds and planing mill, Wm. Mangum.
Sash, doors, blinds, etc, Durham, Wortham Wooden Mills.
Soap, Durham, Durham Soap Works.
Thread and Hose, East Durham, Commonwealth Cotton Mill.
Tinware, Durham, C C Taylor.
Tinware, Durham, George E Lougee.
Tobacco bags, cloth, and chambrays, East Durham, Durham Cotton M't'g Co, J M Odell, pres; W H Branson, sec and treas,
Undertaker, Durham, R T Howerton.
Wagons and repairs, East Durham, W R Dupree.

MERCHANTS AND TRADESMEN.

Names, Post Offices, Lines of Business.

BAHAMA.

Hall, W E.	G S
Tilley, A W,	G S

DURHAM COUNTY.

DAYTON.

Coldclough, C C,	G S
Weatherly, A C,	G S

DURHAM.

Adams, T,	Shoemaker
Anderson, S C, Mgr Dep't F	B D Tobacco Co
Andrews, J G,	Gro
Bagwell & Herndon,	Gro
Baldwin, J J,	——
Barbee, F M,	G S
Barbee, R H,	Gro
Bass, J H & Co,	Leaf Tobacco Dealer
Belvin, O W,	Gro
Berry, J H & Co,	
	Confections and Fruits
Bernstein, S,	Dry Goods
Blacknall, R & Son,	Drugs
Blackwell, W T,	Postmaster
Bradsher & Parish,	Tobacco Brokers
Broom, A J,	G S
Burch, Geo W, Mgr Dep't A	B D Tobacco Co
Birton, R C,	Leaf Tobacco Dealer
Carrington, W T,	Leaf Tob Dealer
Carrington & Hutchings,	
	Leaf Tob Dealers
Carlton, F M,	Gro
Cheatham, R I, Gen Agt D and N R R	
Cheek Furniture Co,	Furniture
Christian, J T,	Gro
Cole, J L & Co,	Dry Goods
Cole & Flinton,	Gro
Colly, W F,	Gro
Davis, Mrs B,	Dry Goods
Doud, J W, Mgr Dep't E, B D Tob Co	
Daughan, A J,	Gro
Duke, W,	Leaf Tob Dealer
Duke, B L,	Leaf Tob Dealer
Eakes, M.	Fruit and Confections
Ellis, Stone & Co,	Dry Goods
Elliott, A G,	G S
Enoch, B,	G S
Fivell, L,	G S
Floral Nursery,	Seeds and Flowers
Follett, Mrs C M,	Millinery
Forsyth, J S,	Gro
Gattis, T J & Son,	Booksellers
Gladstein, M & Co,	G S
Graham, E M, Gen Agt	
	Norfolk and Western Railway
Green, A M.	G S
Green, J T & Co,	Gro
Griswood, W J.	Mdse Broker
Halliburton, J H, Mgr Dep't H	B D Tob Co
Hanks, W H, Mgr Dep't I, B D Tob Co	
Hart, S R,	G S
Harden, G M, jr,	Livery
Heartt & Farthing,	Drugs
Herndon & Bagwell,	G S
Hopkins & Patterson,	Gro
Holmes, Walter, Agt Singer	
	Sewing Machine Co

DURHAM COUNTY.

Hyams & Lewitt, Furniture
Jenkins, J, G S
Jenkins, Miss Minnie, Millinery
Jennings, Mrs R W, Millinery
Jones, M H, Jewelry
Kelly, J B & Co, G S
Kirk, W M, Agt Singer
     Sewing Machine Co
Kramer, A, Leaf Tob
Lambe, T J, Clothing
Lea, J T, Leaf Tob Dealer
Leathers, S F, Mgr Dep't N, B D Tob Co
Leading Racket Store, Dry Goods, etc
Levy, S, Dry Goods
Lloyd, E A & Co, Hardware
Lyon, Mrs M C, Millinery
Lyon, Z I & Co, Leaf Tob Dealer
Lyon, E H, Leaf Tob Dealer
Mangum, Wm & Son, G S
Markham, H H, G S
Martin, T H, Leaf Tob
Massey, Rufus, Gro
Max, A, G S
McGary, W B, Mgr Dep't G, B D Tob Co
McGowan & Watts, Livery
Melvin, J L, G S
Mesley, J S, Tailor
Miller, M & Co, Gro
Miller, S, Dry Goods
Moffitt, E A, Dry Goods
Morgan & Carr, Coal
Morris, R, Gro
Morris, Jno, Mgr Dep't B, B D Tob Co
Morris, R F & Son Mfg Co,
     Leaf Tob Dealers
Murray, Joseph, Agt
    New Home Sewing Machine Co
New York Racket Store, ——
Morris, W J, G S
Owens, J E & Co, Confections
Parrish, E J, Leaf Tob Dealer
Peay, T L, Leaf Tob
Perry, D W, Gro
Pinnix, J T & Co, Leaf Tob Dealers
Piper, J G, Mgr Dep't D, B D Tob Co
Postley, C T, Jewelry
Rowland & Cooper, Leaf Tob Dealers
Pridgen & Jones, B and S
Pridgen, J D, Shoes
Proctor, W H, Gro
Rawls Bros, G S
Rawls, Q E, Dry Goods
Reams, C F, Tob
Reams, H A, agt, Tob
Reams, J M, Tob
Redwood & Summerell, Livery
Redmond, W T, U S Stamp Office
Richardson & Carver (col), Gro
Riggsbee, A M, Gro
Rochelle, C W, Photog
Rochelle, J A, Gro
Rollins, W P, Mgr Dept J, B D Tob Co
Rosemand & Co, Gro
Rowland & Cooper, Leaf Tob
Royal & Borden, Furniture

DURHAM COUNTY.

Sanders & Co, Gro
Sanders, W T, & Co, Gro
Satterwhite, S R, & Co, Gro
Scoggins, R O, G S
Sears, A A, Livery
Shelburn, Wm, Photog
Slater, W A, & Co, Clothing
Smith & Co, G S
Smith, P S, & Co, Gro
Smith, Miss Ada, Millinery
Smith, H M, Mgr Dep't K, B D Tob Co
Smith, J W, & Co, Leaf Tob Dealers
Snead & Thomas, Drugs
Southern Educator Co,
     Printing and Binding
Stokes, A H, Leaf Tob
Stroud, W D, Gro
Stroud, T E, Dist Mgr Singer
     Sewing Machine Co
Styron, E, Leaf Tob Dealer
Suit, J E (near), G S
Summerfield, C, Dry Goods
Surles, W B, G S
Tatum, J A, G S
Tatum, J W, G S
Taylor, C C, Tinware
Thaxton, Mrs J J, G S
Thompson, W H, G S
Tilley, Harwood, Miller
Umstead, A K, Leaf Tob Dealer
Vaughan, P W, Drugs
Walker & Kilby, Brokers
Walker, J B, Tob
Walker, Henry, Leaf Tob Dealer
Walker, W L, & Co, Leaf Tob Dealer
Weatherspoon, W H, Gro
Whitmore, J L, Baker and Conf
Whitaker, T J, Gro
White, J A, Gen Agt So R R
Whitted, J G, Leaf Tob Dealer
Williams & Hughes, China,
     Glassware, etc
Womble, John T, Hardware
Wyatt, J M, Harness
Yearby, W M, Drugs

EAST DURHAM.

Brady, Henry, G S
Crutchfield, W H, G S
Dickerson & Co, G S
Edwards, M D, ——
Ellis, E M, G S
Ellison, A M, G S
Flinton, G W, & Co, G S
Fowler, A T, G S
Green, Thos L, Gro
Kelly, T D, & Co, G S
Kelly, J D, G S
Matthews, A B, Drugs
Owen, J R, & Co, G S
Scoggins, R O, & Co, Gro
Smith, T B, Gro
Stroud, W D, Gro

FISH DAM.

Barber, J W, ——

DURHAM COUNTY.		DURHAM COUNTY.	
Holloway, W T,	G S	Bodie, N B, Durham.	
Ward, M P,	G S	Brown, J C (dentist). Durham.	
FLAT RIVER.		Cain, James, Durham.	
Hampton, G C,	G S	Carr, A G, Durham.	
Hampton, W B,	G S	Cheatham, Arch, Durham.	
GALVESTON,		Clark, M H P (dentist), Durham.	
Cole & Flinton,	G S	Durham, W J H, Durham.	
GORMAN.		Fitch, W E, Durham.	
Holloway, W G, & Co,	G S	Henderson, L B (dentist), Durham.	
LUSTER.		Hicks, W N, Fish Dam.	
Bowling, Wm,	G S	Holloway, R L, West Durham.	
NELSON.		Holt, E M, Orange Factory.	
Morris, W A,	G S	Johnston, N McC, Durham.	

SCHOOLS.

Names, Post Offices and Principals.

Classical Male School, Durham, L T Buchanan.
Colored Graded Schools, Durham, J A Whitted, prin: three assistants.
Female school, Flat River, Miss M P Mangum.
Graded school, Durham, C W Toms.
Mixed school (col), Durham.
Moring Star Academy, Fish Dam.
Music School, Durham, Miss Willie Smoot.
South Lowell Academy, South Lowell.
Trinity College, Durham, Jno C Kilgo, president.

MILLS.

Kinds, Post Offices and Proprietors.

Corn and saw, Durham, W W Mangum.
Flour and corn, Durham, Ed Cole.
Flour and corn, Durham, F C Greer.
Flour and corn, Durham, Cox & Christian.
Flour and corn, Durham, P C Cameron and heirs.
Flour and corn, Durham, S H Johnson and heirs.
Roller Flour and corn, South Lowel, R G Russell.
Flour and corn, Flat River, A Mangum.
Flour and corn, Durham, Asa Pickett.
Flour and corn, Luster, A Umstead.
Merchant flour and corn, Luster, Wm Bowling.
Saw, Luster, Flinton & Co.
Saw, Durham, T G Riggsbee.

TEACHERS.

Names and Post Offices.

WHITE.
Anderson, Miss J M, South Lowell.
Bailey, Miss M Lula, Dayton.
Barbee, C W, East Durham.
Benling, Miss Lzzie. Luster.
Breeze, Miss Laura, Durham.
Burch, Miss Ella, Durham.
Carpenter, W D, Fish D m.
Christmas, Miss Ida, Durham.
Clomerson, J W, East Durham.
Couch, N S. Durham.
Craigg, M E. University Station.
Davis, Miss Arizona, South Lowell.
Ellen, Rev M H, East Durham.
Gray, Miss Ella, Willardsville.
Hall, James N, E Durham.
Hicks, J T, Durham.
Holloway, Miss Ella, East Durham.

PHYSICIANS.

Names and Post Offices.

Battle, L W, Durham.

DURHAM COUNTY.

Johnson, Miss Julia, Durham.
Jones, Mrs Lizzie H, Gorman.
Latta, Miss Sadie. Durham.
Laws, Miss Maggie, East Durham.
Leathers, Miss Annie. South Lowell.
Lee, Miss Ida, Durham
Lyon, W F. Durham.
Norwood, Hassell. Durham.
Robertson, N E, East Durham.
Stewart, Vera L4, Durham.
Suitt, Spencer M, Dayton.
Suitt, W R, West Eurham.
Thompson, Miss Ida S. Durham.
Tilley, Pervis, Knap of Reeds.
Walton, E. Nelson.
Warren, C C, Durham.
Yates, W T. Durham.
Young, W E, East Durham.

COLORED.

Barbee, Dora, Nelson.
Bumpass, Eugene, Durham.
Cain, Cora L, Nelson.
Cannady, R B, Luster.
Carlton, I J H, Durham.
Carlton, Hattie J. Durham.
Day, Parthenia. Durham.
Dawkins, P W. Durham,
Dixon, Frank W. Durham.
Evans, J R. Durham.
Faucette, Nannie A, Durham.
Fitzgerald, Sadie A, Durham
Fitzgerald, M P, Durham.
Freeman, Katie R, Durham.
Geer, Clara P, Durham.
Gilmer, Fannie P, Durham.
Green Mollie M. Nelson.
Green, D B. Durham.
Hackney, Rev L H, Chapel Hill.
Holloway, Mary E, East Durham.
Hargrove. R B. Chapel Hill.
Harris, H E, Flat River.
Hester, Moses M. Durham.
Hopkins, B F. Chapel Hill.
Husband. F T. Durham.
Miller, Ella C. Durham.
Miller. Lilla, Durham.
Morgan, Mary W, Durham.
Morgan, Sallie E. Durham.
Page, E R, Nelson.
Page, Mary E, Durham.
Pearson, J L, Durham.
Pearson, Minnie I. Durham.
Satterfield, Maggie L, Durham.
Sellers, Maggie M. Durham.
Strudwick, Lucy E, East Durham.
Tucker, T R, Durham.
Warren. Mary J Durham.
White, B J, Durham.
Whitted, Pearly M. Durham.
Whitted, Lillie M, Durham.
Whitted, W O. Durham.
Whitted, Anderson, Stagville.
Young, Martha, Durham.

DURHAM COUNTY.

LOCAL CORPORATIONS.

Alma Lodge, No. 5. Daughters of Re-
bekah. Durham. Mrs Ella M Fuller,
N G; M J D Goodwin, V G; Miss
Alice Woody, R S; Mrs W E Wood,
F S; Mrs J A Stout, Treas.
Blackwell Durham Co-operative To-
bacco Company. Julian S Car, Pres-
ident; capital, $1,000,000.
Building and Loan Association, Dur-
ham; Alex Walker, Pres; James
Southgate, Sec; Leo D Heartt, Treas;
W A Guthrie, attorney.
Colored Band, Durham.
Durham Board of Trade: ———, pres;
Lucius Tilley, sec.
Durham Fertilizing Company, Dur-
ham; S T Morgan, pres; J S Carr,
vice-pres; L A Carr, sec and treas.
Durham Lyceum, Durham; Rev. H T
Darnell, sec.
Durham Lodge. No. 352. A F and A M,
Durham: W M Wall, W M. Time of
meeting. second and fourth Tuesday
nights, and June 24th and Decem-
ber 27th.
Durham Cornet Band, Durham.
Eno Lodge. No. 210, A F and A M,
Durham; John L Markham, W M.
Time of meeting. fourth Saturday.
Knights and Ladies of Honor, Durham.
R F Morris & Son. Mfg Co, Durham;
W H Willard. pres; S F Tomlinson,
sec and treas.
Tobacco Association, Durham, T H
Martin. pres.
The Fidelity Bank, Durham; capital,
$100,000; B N Duke, pres; A E L
Lloyd, vice-pres; J F Wiley, cashier.
The First National Bank of Durham,
N C; Julian S Carr, pres; Leo D
Heartt, cashier; capital. $150,000.
The Morehead Banking Co, Durham,
W H Willard, pres; T J Pinnix, vice-
pres; W Morgan, cashier; capital
stock, $150,000.

NEWSPAPERS.

Daily Sun (Dem). Durham; J A Rob-
inson, ed and pro.
Recorder (Dem. Weekly). Durham.
The Morning Herald (Independent),
Durham; Herald Pub Co.
The National Tobacco and Grocer, Dur-
ham, (monthly); pub by Tobacco &
Grocer Co.
Trinity Archive (monthly), organ of
Trinity College.

FARMERS.

Names and Post Offices.

Bahama—A W Ball, M Ball, F W

DURHAM COUNTY.

Ball, W J Ball, W E Hall, J W Harris, D D Harris, L H Loyd, L L Lunsford, Wesley Neeley, J D Oakley, W K Parrish, L D Roberts, A J Roberts, D B Roberts, J K Stagg. Radford Stagg, T D Sutherlin, J S Teasley, J F M Terry, Robt C Filley. A W Filley, Marcus Filley, Bauman Tilley, W S Wilkins.

Chapel Hill—Algernon Daniel, R J Emerson, J A Fowler, Wm Fowler, J R Hutchings, H B Jones, Ruffin Jones, A J Lloyd, F P Lint, Willis Peter.

Dayton—A F Evans, W A Evans, W W Evans, W H Mavton, J A Mavton, W T Mavton, J E Nichols, H W Nichols, Dr R E Nichols, D B Nichols.

Durham—Josiah Atkins, Sr, Josiah Atkins, Jr, N H Atkins, Paul A Brown, H T Barbee, A L Barbee, R A Barbee, Thos C Barbee, G A Barbee, A P Barbee, Jackson Barbee, John W W Barbee, Willis A Barbee, Geo E Barbee, H M Barbee, Sidney Barbee, Jno W Barbee, W R Barbee, Simeon Barbee, Jas G Barbee, R S Blalock, J H Blackwood, J W Cameron, James Carden, J S Carr, A G Carr, L A Carr, O T Carver, R B Carrington, W T Carrington, W M Carrington, Jno W Carlton, F W Carlton, H T Car ton, Spencer W Chamberlain, L L Chamberlaine, W B Chamberlaine, Jno B Christian, J M Christian, Thos Christian, Charles E Christian, T S Christian W J Christian, Mathew Christmas, J H Clements, J F Clements, W T Cole, J W Cole, J Ed Cole, J L Cole, James Cole, G Ed Cole, Jno A Cole, J H Cole, W d Cole, Paschall Cook, W R Cooper, W L Cooper, J H Copley, John H Couch, W E Couch, C Couch, J F Corbett, A B Cox, Jno A Cox, R C Cox, B H Cozart, A N Crabtree, Johnson Craig, J S Crutchfield, R H Crumpacker, A M Culberson, J P Cutts, Jno Cutts, Alex Cutts, Jas R Day, J H Dodd, G J Dowell, W M Dollar, W W Dunegan, E C Dunlap, A J Draughan, B N Duke, Washing on Duke, B L Duke, M Eakes, J H Edwards, A J Ellis, H F Edwards, A M Ellison, W W Ellington, H H Elliott J W Elliott, C M Enliss, W W Erwin, W R Erwood, G C Farthing, Robt Faucett, A P Faucett, Geo Faucett, T W Ferrell, W A Ferrell, W L Ferrell, Jno W Ferrell, J C Ferrell, W E Fitch, R B Fitzgerald, S G Flinton, G W Flinton, J S Forsythe, W J Fowler, Howard Foushee, A B Foushee, W L Freeland, W F Freeland, J F Freeland, T B Fuller, F L Fuller, W G Gainey, J H Gainey, Sam'l Garrard, W L Garrard, S G Garrard, S H Garrard, M J Garrett, J B Gates, S P Gooch, Claude A Gattis, W A Gattis, W R Gattis, F C Geer, J F Glenn, T H Glenn, P P Glenn, F W Glenn, W E Glenn, E T Glenn, Hileman Glenn, A J Glenn, Taban Green, A W Green, Abe Goldsmith, J W Goodson, Thomas Gorman, Paul Graham, W A Guthrie, M S Hackney, Ed C Hackney, W A Hall, W J Hall, W P Hailey, W Hall, J J Hall, W J Hall, W H Hanks, J A Harris, Geo M Hardin, A C Hayes, W G Harward, P B Herndon, Dr L B Henderson, J A Henderson, Dr W N Hicks, J H Hodges, R bt Holloway, S M Holton, J A R Hopkins, C P Horner, J M Hornedy, C P Howerton, R T Howerton, J W Hutchings, Tonev Inscore, Nathan Jacobs, L uis Jenkins, W A Jenkins, Dr N M Johnson, Robt M Jones, Chas Jordan S W King, W H King, W J Kirkland, Albert Kramer, Sam Kramer, S W Ladd, S M Ladd, J T Ladd, F J Lambe, J O Latta, G A Latta, J G Latta, Jno R W Latta, F S Leathers, W A Lea, J T Lea, Wesley Lee, R S Leigh, Jno W Leigh, L W Leigh, C M L wt r, E G Lineberry, P E Linnett, A E Lloyd, Geo E L ugee, R C Lowe, Pat Lunsford, J Ed Lyon, T B Lyon, G W Lynn, S H Lynn, J W Macklin, Moses McCown, W H McCabe, J A Malone, Sr, J S Mangum, N T Mangum, Wm Mangum, H B Mangum, D C Mangum, T H Martin, Jno W Markham, Isham Markham, N C Markham, G D Markham, H H Markham, M F Markham, J L Markham, O D Markham, W C Mason, J B Mason, P H Massey, C Massey, Rufus Massey, Rev P H Massey, Jno H Massey, B W Mathews, —— Mayes, Jno Merrick, J C Michie, Philip Moore, S T Morgan, W M Morgan, Mrs Lucy Morehead, J S Murray, W R Murray, W E Muse, W A Muse, W S Newton, W T Neal, C H Norton, Paul A Noell, C O'Briant, W T O'Brien, Dr Wm Owen, L L Pamplin, E J Parrish, R D Patterson, C H Parrish, T L Peay, J S Perry, S R Perry, Wiley Philpot, V H Pickett, Jas Pickett, Mark Pickett, Asa Pickett, J T Pinnix, L G Pickett, R C Pleasants, G E Pope, E Pope, Jackson Pope, S W Pope, J W Pope, J B Proctor, W H Proctor, O K Proctor, N A Ramsey, Q E Rawls, I M Reams, H A Reams, W T Redmond, G A Rhodes, A M Riggsbee, T J Riggsbee, J V Riggsbee, Dr J D Roberts, E T Rollins, W A Rochell, J E Rogers, W H Rogers, H M Rosemond, J R Ross, C J Ross, W H Rowland, T H Scoggins, A A Sears, H E Seaman, J K Shambley, Jno W Shepperd, C A Shepperd, Jas M Shepperd, T A Shepperd, Jno W P

DURHAM COUNTY.

Smith, Jno W Smith, Henry N Snow, A H Stokes, R C Stanard, J M Tatum, C C Taylor, G W Teer, J J Thaxton, E E Thompson, Dennis Tilley, S F Tomlinson, James Turner, J J Tyson, A K Umstead, Jas W Umstead, Jno A Umstead, G Upchurch, W A L Veazey, Jno A Vickers, Jas H Vickers, W G Vickers, G W Vickers, J H Vickers, W T Vickers, Chas Vickers, W D Vickers, W D Vickers, Jr, H H Vickers, W M Wahab, Jno B Walker, Rev Alex Walker, James Walker, W L Wall, James Warren, Dr M P Ward, J T Watts, S E Watts, W T Watts, G W Watts, S A Watts, Wm Weatherspoon, W W Whitted, R M Whitted, Sam Whitted, J C Whitted, C C White, J L Whitmore, J L Wilkerson, W A Wilkerson, Chas Wilson, W H Wilkins, R W Winston, T J Winston, J T Womble, J H Woods, G W Woodard, Thos H Wright, Rich H Wright, M B Wyatt, W J Wyatt, Jno M Wyatt.

East Durham—J W Evans

Fish Dam—T H Allen, H M Bailey, C Barbee, J B Belvin, Thos Bragg, J M Carpenter, Devane Carpenter, J T Colclough, Wm Crabtree, J W Creech, S H Davis, W H Davis, C M Dhew, W R Ellis, Sidney Ferrell, L S Ferrell, J W Fletcher, R D Fletcher, J D Fletcher, D S Fletcher, N C Freeman, O M Freeman, J A Holloway, L W Husketh, E H Husketh, F M Norwood, S A Olmstead, W G Page, W H Perry, R L Rogers, W J Sherron G C Stallings, W J Smith, Dr L P Sorrell, A M Sorrell, David Thompson, L C Thompson.

Flat River—Robt Adcock, J J Adcock, K R Mangum, A Mangum, Wm Mangum, J T Mangum, W P Mangum, Nelson Parrish, sr, J T Parrish, J W Parrish, W H Parker, J T Parker, Ellis Roberts, Haywood Roberts, Wm Roberts, F M Tilley, Simpson Tilley, W P Tilley, C F Umstead, Jno W Umstead, E V Umstead, R C Umstead, Hampton Umstead, L L Umstead, D C Umstead, A W Umstead, E H Veazey, V Wheeler.

Gorman—G S Curtis, W T Holloway, J H Holloway.

DURHAM COUNTY.

Hampton—C H Carrington, N M Carrington, A R Copley, I B Copley, Jas Copley, H M Jones, Geo Green, W B Hampton, Z T Hampton, G C Hampton, D B Johnson, Jno Meadows, J A Mitchell, W L Nichols.

Knapp of Reeds—D H Forsythe, Adolphus O'Key, F J Veazey, Joseph Woods, Wm Woods.

Luster—Dr E H Bowling.

Nelson—W S Burroughs, G W Barbee, A C Barbee, C D Edwards, R A Evans, A J Ellis, J W Ferrell, R A Evans, W H Edwards, W H Hopson, R F Green, Chas Guess, Asa Green, S F Hopson, J P Hopson, Paschall Herndon, W H Hopson, G S Hopson, W A Jenkins, J W King, W R Laurence, H B Lenter, Sanders Lynn, J J Lynn, W M Lowe, Wm Markham, W H Morris, Henry O'Briant, W H O'Briant, Ransom O'Briant, J B O'Briant, Rufus Page, Columbus Page, W A Page, L A Page, W H Page, J R Page, Aaron Roberts, W M Rich, Jos Rich, R T Shipp, J H Shipp, W D Stowe, M L Sorrell, Sol Thompson, E Walton, W H Weatherspoon.

Red Mountain—A A Parker, Pinkney Weaver.

Rougemont—J R Blalock, D W Blalock, Wm Blalock, B P Bowling, Wm. Bowling, H T Bowling, J W Bowling, S Bowling, W J Chambers, I F Cothran, Jno Crabtree, Z Dickey, W B Duke, E W Thacker, J L Wilson.

South Lowell—Henry C Bacon, Scott H Bowman, J F Cain, Jr, D K Hill, R D Hill, R L Jordan, J H Pool, A L Riggs, J S Rogers, J E Rogers, L W Rogers, R G Russell, Jacob Simson, W S Terry, J W Thompson, G W Tilley, J G Tilley, C P Warren.

Staggville—B Cameron, W D Turrentine, A C Vaughan.

Willardsville—A N Blalock, A G Cox, P A Flinton, W H Harris, E P Holt, Thos Lipscomb, Hawkins Maynard, Wm Monk, Phil Sutherlin, H L Umstead.

EDGECOMBE COUNTY.

AREA, 500 SQUARE MILES.

POPULATION, 24,075; White 8,475. Colored 15,600.

EDGECOMBE COUNTY was formed from Craven in 1733, by the then Governor Burrington and his Council, and was confirmed by the Legislature, which met in Edenton in 1741 The name is Saxon, and according to Bailey's Dictionary, means "a valley surrounded by hills."

TARBORO, the county seat, is situated on the Tar river, from which it takes its name, and is 76 miles east from Raleigh. Population, 2,500 — white, 1,300; colored, 1,200. Tar or Taw is the Indian name for "health."

Surface—This county is situated on both sides of Tar river; lies well; soil good, much of it rich—plenty of marl convenient for use on almost every farm. Edgecombe is in a higher state of cultivation than almost any other county in the State. Railroad and navigation facilities are fine.

Staples—Cotton is the great staple of this county. Corn, grapes and sweet potatoes are produced to a considerable extent; also, peas, rice and chufas.

Timbers—Pine and cypress, oak, hickory, gum, etc.

Fruits—Peaches, apples, pears, cherries, plums and the small fruits.

TOWNS AND POST OFFICES.

	POP.		POP.
Battleboro,	—	Mildred,	100
Coakley,	25	Old Sparta,	200
Conoetoe,	200	Penelo,	50
Crisp,	—	Rocky Mt,	2,500
Doehead,	20	Saint Lewis,	30
Epworth,	50	Speed,	—
Gethsemane,	—	Tarborough,	3,500
Lancaster,	50	Turnage,	50
Lawrence,	—	Whitakers,	425
Leggett,	25	Wrendale,	25

COUNTY OFFICERS.

Clerk Superior Court—Ed Pennington.

Commissioners — Owen Williams, chm; Geo L Wimberly, S T Cherry, J T Howard, Robt Watson.

Coroner— ——

Register of Deeds—B F Dawson.

Sheriff—Wm T Knight.

Solicitor 2d District—W E Daniel.

Surveyor— ——

Standard Keeper— —— Watson.

Treasurer—S S Nash.

County Examiner—F S Wilkinson.

County Physician — Donald Williams.

COURTS.

Third Monday before the first Monday in March, sixth Monday after the first Monday in March, fifth Monday after the first Monday in September, ninth Monday after the first Monday in September.

TOWN OFFICERS.

PRINCEVILLE—*Mayor*, H N Cherry.

TARBORO—*Mayor*, W E Fountain.

Chief of Police—Wood Winborn.

Clerk and Treasurer—Jas M Spraggines.

Commissioners — H T Bass, J F Shackelford, T H Gatlin, J H Baker, G M Fountain, John R Pender.

TOWNSHIPS AND MAGISTRATES.

No 1—W L Barlow, S E Speight, J W Charles, C W Jeffreys, Turner Prince, Y D Garrett, J B Keech, Rayford Liles, E Zoeller, J B Carlisle, J B Lloyd, F B Lloyd, Battle Bryan (Tarboro), R A Watson, David Williams.

No 2—W G W Leigh, E C Knight (Conetoe), Ruben Sanders (Mildred), Robt Brown (col), W A Williams, R C Warren, John E Howard (Conetoe), D E Cobb, J A Harris, F M Leigh (Mildred), Reuben Bryant, Gray Brown, J A Harris (Tarboro).

No 3—Thos L Mayo (Conetoe), W G Turner, N J Mayo, Geo W Howard, J R Satterthwaite, Samuel Howard (col), F L Savage, W H Savage (Coakley).

No 4—L B Knight (Tarboro), Wm Braswell, V B Knight, John H Hyde, F B Bellamy (col), J H Edwards, M P Edwards, A D Knight, W J Lawrence (Lawrence).

No 5—J D Hargrove (Tarboro), W C Bradley, Ebert Bryan, M W Pittman, J B Barnes, W T Mayo, Jordan W Johnson, C H Spivey (Leggett).

No 6—W H Cobb, J B Latham, A Braswell, jr, W F Draughan, J M Cutchin, W T Braswell, W Knight (Whitaker), L L Lyon (Leggett), R H Speight (Wrendale).

EDGECOMBE COUNTY.

No 7—D H Barlow (Deehead), J K Lawrence, Wm Johnson (col), J W Phillips, Jno R Vick, F M Rawlings, Jos Ruffin, G W Stewart, Gaston Battle, W W Vick, F S Baker, H E Odum, M C Braswell (Battleboro), W D Lancaster, H S Bunn (Wrendale).

No 8—W E Sugg, S R Moore J J Hearne, W G Harrell, J T Dupree, C H Jones, W J Peace (Sparta), J A Davis, W L Stallings, W J Peace. Frank Dew (Tarboro).

No 9—H C Turnage (Turnageville), Amos Wooten, W S Crisp, B F Harris, Alfred Reid, W H Thorne. Amos Harrell, Henry Corbitt, S M Crisp, J A B Thorne, Hickman Ellis, Eli Webb (Crisp).

No 10—W F Walston, B C Pitt, W A Bridgers, V P Sharpe. S W Crisp, F D Massey.

No 11—S L Hart, W E Page, D T Britt, David Lawrence, Jno R Pitt, Robt Hester. R M Brown, H C Bourne, R G Hart (Tarboro), N B Killibrew (Rocky Mount).

No 12—C L Killibrew, Ed Gorham, J B Barnes, W H Renfrow, A B Nobles. A J Williams. J N Worsley, Walter Thigpen, J H Chapman, W O Bullock (Rocky Mount).

No 13—Frank Cherry, W J Lancaster (Tarboro), J H Thorne, Jesse Proctor, P H Edge (Rocky Mount), W P Wilkins, Guilford Moore, John Lancaster, W A Hinton, John O Oates (Lancaster's Store), B B Barron (Elm City).

No 14—Fenner Gay, S H Thorne, Z H Weaver, Joshua Bullock, J I Killibrew, O B Proctor, Ellis Bird, Meter Proctor, W E Bradley, W H Lancaster (Rocky Mount).

CHURCHES.

Names, Post Offices, Pastors and Denom.

BAPTIST.

Church—Battleboro, W V Savage.
Eagles—Crisp, W V Savage.
Church—Battleboro.
Church—(col), Rocky Mount, R A Wales.
Church—Rocky Mount, W V Savage.
Church—Battleboro, Geo M Duke.
Church—(col), Whitaker's, T T Eaton.
Mill Branch—(Nash county), Rocky Mount, D Armstrong.
Mildred—Mildred, W V Savage.
Morning Star—Battleboro, C B Gibbs (col).
Red Oak—(Nash county), Rocky Mt.
Shiloh—(col), Whitaker's, G A Norwood.
Tarboro—(col), Tarboro, M D Mathewson.

EDGECOMBE COUNTY.

PRIM. BAPTIST.

Church—Tarboro, P D Gold.
Church—Whitaker's, A J Moore.
Church—Rocky Mount, P D Gold.
Cross-Roads—Tarboro.
Falls Church—Rocky Mount, P D Gold.
Few in-Number—Tarboro, A Wooten (col).
Fishing Creek—Hickory Hill, Wm Staton.
Little Creek—Tarboro.
Otter's Creek—Old Sparta, Wm L Wiggins.
Pleasant Hill—Rocky Mount, W Jackson.
Taylor's Hill—Rocky Mount, H Taylor.
Town Creek—Old Sparta, B Cooper Pitt.
Williams'—Wrendale.
Williams'—Whitakers's Jordan W Johnson.

METHODIST.

Bethesda—Old Sparta, S A Cotton.
Church—Battleboro. —— Fisher.
Church—Whitaker's, —— Fisher.
Church—Rocky Mt, —— Underwood.
Church—Tarboro, J A Lee.
Church—Battleboro
Church—Conetoe, S A Cotton.
Epworth—Epworth.
Jones' Chapel—Tarboro, S A Cotton.
McKendree Chapel-Tarboro, — Twilly
St Louis—Elm City, —— Twilly.
Temperance Hall—Toisnot, — Twilly.
Whitaker's Mill (Nash Co), Whitaker's.

PROTESTANT METHODIST.

Hilliard Chapel (Nash Co)—Rocky Mt, —— Williams.
Red Oak (Nash Co)—Rocky Mt, —— Williams.
Speight Chapel—Wrendale, —— Williams.
Temple—Whitaker's.

ZION METHODIST.

Zion (col,)—Tarboro,

EPISCOPAL.

Calvary—Tarboro, M L Poffenberger.
Church—Battleboro, Gaston Battle.
Eliza Battle Pittman—Laurence, M L Poffenberger.
Good Shepherd—Rocky Mount, Gaston Battle.
St Luke's—Tarboro, Jno W Perry (col.)
St Mary's Chapel—Coakley, M L Poffenberger.
St Mark's (col.)—Wilson, Jno W Perry (colored)
St Stephen's (col.)—Tarboro. — Tillery.

DISCIPLES OF CHRIST.

Bethel—Wrendale.

PRESBYTERIAN.

Church—Tarboro, —— Morton.

Church—Rocky Mount, Fred Thomas.
Leggett—Leggett's —— Morton.
St Paul's (col.)—Rocky Mount.

MINISTERS RESIDENT.

Names, Post Offices and Denominations.

BAPTIST.

Burgess, A (col.), Battleboro.
Eaton, T T (col.), Whitaker's.
Mathewson, —— (col.), Tarboro.
McSwain, L H, Whitaker's.
Powell, ——, Rocky Mount.
Savage, W V, Tarboro.

PRIMITIVE BAPTIST.

Jackson, John, Rocky Mount.
Moore, A J, Whitaker's.
Pitt, B C, Old Sparta.
Taylor, H, Rocky Mount.
Wooten, A (col.), Tarboro.

METHODIST.

Cotton, S A, Conotoe.
Fisher, ——, Battleboro.
Lee, J A, Tarboro.
Underwood, ——, Rocky Mount.

EPISCOPAL.

Cheshire, Jos B, D D, Tarboro.
Perry, John W (col.), Tarboro.
Poffenberger, M L, Tarboro.

PRESBYTERIAN.

Morton, ——, Tarboro.

HOTELS AND BOARDING HOUSES.

Kinds, Post Offices and Proprietors.

Boarding House, Rocky Mount, R H
  Gorham.
Boarding, Rocky Mount, W H Ren-
  frow.
Boarding, Rocky Mount, Mrs McCall.
Boarding House, Tarboro, Mrs J E
  Porter.
Boarding, Tarboro, Mrs. Dr. Williams.
Boarding, Tarboro, Mrs. J T Vines.
Bryan House, Tarboro, L H Lyon.
Bullard House, Rocky Mount, Misses
  M E & Z Bullock.
Dickens Hotel, Rocky Mount, Paine
  Dickens.
Gray House, Rocky Mount, Misses Bul-
  lock.
Hammond House, Rocky Mount, Mrs
  T A Marriott.
Hotel, Rocky Mount, Paine Dickens.
Hotel Woodward, Rocky Mount, Mr
  Woodward.
Hotel, Whitaker, M J Carr.
Hotel Farrar, Tarboro, Mrs Bettie Pon-
  der.
Hotel, Battleboro, James Hobgood.
Restaurant, Tarboro, Fred Carpenter
  (col).

Restaurant, Tarboro, Ruffin Thorp
  (col).
Restaurant, Rocky Mount, Robt Ham-
  mett (col).
School boarding, Tarboro, F S Wilkin-
  son.
School boarding, Tarboro, D G Gilles-
  pie.
Woodard Hotel, Rocky Mount, Mrs S
  E Edge.

LAWYERS.

Names and Post Offices.

Battle, Jacob, Rocky Mount.
Battle, Thomas H & Thomas T T,
  Rocky Mount.
Battle, Dorsey, Rocky Mount.
Bridges, J L & Baker, J H, Jr, Rocky
  Mount.
Bunn, B H & Conner, H G, Rocky
  Mount.
Gaskill, J R, Tarboro.
Gilliam, D & Gilliam, H H, Tarboro.
Howard, W O, Tarboro.
Howard, Geo, Tarboro.
Johnston, Wm H, Tarboro.
Jones, Paul, Tarboro.
Martin, J J, Tarboro.
Pinder, Jas, Tarboro.
Philips, Fred, Tarboro.
Pippin, J P. Tarboro.
Staton, H L & Johnson, Perry, Tar-
  boro.
Thorpe, Wm L, Rocky Mount.
Worthington, D, Rocky Mount.

MANUFACTORIES.

Kinds, Post Offices and Proprietors.

Agricultural Implements, Tarboro;
  Edgecombe Agricultural Works, Geo
  Howard, pres.
Barrels, Tarboro, H S Watson.
Barrels, Rocky Mount, Walter Hen-
  derson.
Blacksmithing, Whitaker, A K Pen-
  der.
Blacksmithing, Battleboro, A D Hearne
Blacksmithing, Battleboro, Jas Gard-
  ner.
Blacksmithing, Battleboro, Robt Bras-
  well.
Blacksmithing, Tarboro, F D Dancy
  (col).
Blacksmithing, Tarboro, I B Palla-
  mountain.
Blacksmithing, Rocky Mount, B C
  Taylor.
Boots and shoes, Tarboro, Joshua Bunn
Boots and shoes, Tarboro, M T Gwalt-
  ney.
Brick, Tarboro, Jeffrey Herman.

EDGECOMBE COUNTY.

Building and contracting, Battleboro, I M Neil.
Building and contractor, Tarboro, Thos Newton (col).
Carriages, Tarboro, John B Hyatt.
Carriages and harness, Tarboro, M L Hussey.
Carts and wagons, Rocky Mount, W H Flowers.
Creamery works (butter), Tarboro, J W Powell.
Creamery works (butter), Tarboro, C H King.
Creamery works (butter), Tarboro, L L Staton.
Coaches and buggies, Rocky Mount, Hackney & Co.
Coffins, etc., Tarboro, B C Carlisle.
Cotton-seed oil and meal, Tar River Oil Co, Dr. L L Staton, pres.
Edgecombe Cotton-seed and Oil Co, Tarboro, Wm Newton Smith, pres.
Fertilizers, Tarboro, F S Royster & Co.
Foundry, Battleboro, J Hobgood & Bro.
Foundry and iron works, Rocky Mt, Rocky Mt Iron Works.
Ginning, Battleboro, Moses Moore.
Ginning, Rocky Mt, Newsom & Hunter.
Ginning, Rocky Mt, E H Cockrell.
Ginning, Rocky Mt. Jacob Baker.
Ginning, Rocky Mt, W C Trevalthan.
Ginning, Rocky Mt, J H Hunt.
Ginning, Red Oak, S R Hilliard.
Ginning, Tarboro, Geo Harward.
Harness, saddles, etc, Tarboro, J H Brown.
Oil Mill, Conetoe, J Newton Smith, pres.
Riverview Knitting Mills, Tarboro, J F Shackelford.
Rocky Mount Iron Works, Rocky Mt, S K Fountain, prop and mgr.
Rocky Mt Lumber Co, Rocky Mt, I K Howell.
Rocky Mt Cotton Mills, Rocky Mt, T H Battle, pres; J H Ruffin, supt and treas.
Shoes and boots, Rocky Mt, William Soden, jr.
Shoes, Tarboro, M T Gwatney.
Stoves and tinware, Tarboro, George Howard, jr.
Stoves and tinware, Rocky Mt, Geo R Dixon.
Stoves and tinware, Tarboro, L C Terrell.
Swift Creek Oil Mill, Battleboro, Dr R H Speight.
Tarboro Cotton Mills, Tarboro, A T N Fairly, supt.
Tarboro Knitting Mill, J T Shackelford; works 110 hands.

EDGECOMBE COUNTY.

Tar River Oil Co, cotton-seed oil, etc. Tarboro, Dr L L Staton, pres; E V Zoeller, sec treas.
Tinware, Tarboro, L C Terrell.
Tobacco flues, Tarboro, The Pender, Hyman Hardware Co.
Tobacco flues, Tarboro, Howard & Co.
Tobacco hogsheads, Tarboro, Frank Hodges.
Undertaking, Tarboro, J E Simmons.
Wheelwrighting, Rocky Mt, — Gear.
Wheelwrighting, Battleboro, H Ward.

MERCHANTS AND TRADESMEN.

Names, Post Offices and Line of Business.

CONETOE.

Bullock, J E & Co,	G S
Bullock, W B,	G S
Dawson, N B,	G S
Evans, Glagon,	Gro
Horrell, J O,	Gro
James, M A,	G S
Statton, Cherry & Bunting,	G S

CRISP.

Eagles & Crisp,	G S

COAKLEY.

Hyman, H H,	G S
Jones, John J (col),	Gro

EPWORTH.

Anderson, Dr J H,	G S
Pittman, B,	G S

GETHSEMINE.

Pittman, O L,	G S

KINGSBORO.

Lancaster, John,	G S
Lancaster, W J,	G S
Thigpen, E K & Co,	G S

LANCASTER.

Lancaster, W J,	G S

LAWRENCE.

Bellamy, F B (col),	G S
Kninght, V B & Co.	G S
Parker, C,	G S
Smith, L W & Bro,	Gro

LEGGETT'S.

Fountain, L H,	G S

MILDRED.

Evans, G,	G S
Lee, Battle & Co (col),	Gro
Parker, C (near),	G S
Parker, Henry (near),	G S
Parker, H M (near),	G S
Sanders, —,	G S

OLD SPARTA.

Brown & Co,	G S
Carr, Elias & Son,	G S
Cumming, J B,	G S
Dunford, W T,	G S

Shaw, H H,   G S
Webb, W G,   G S

PENELO.

Hart, R G,   G S
Hash, R G,   G S

PITT'S CROSS ROADS.

Warren, W C,   G S

ROCKY MOUNT.

Abram, D,   G S
Anthony, D,   Butcher
Arringt n, A W,   G S
Baily, Draughn & Co,   G S
Barnes, Mrs M k,   Millinery
Barnes, J H,   G S
Battle, L L (col),   Gro
Bennett, Mrs——,   Dressmaker
Bennett & Burns,   G S
Bradley, ——,   Grocer
Braswell & Sherrod,   Leaf Tob
Brewer, H E.   Broker
Brown, J T & Co,   Gro
Browning, E D,   Gro
Bunn, B H.   Postmaster
Carlisle, W F,   Civil Engineer
Clay, J H (col),   Grocer
Cockran & Spears,   Clothing and D G
Cuthrell, J W.   G S
Doughtridge & Rollins,   G S
Davenport, J W,   Grocer
Davis, B.   Tob Warehouse
Dawes, W R (near),   G S
Dixon, G W,   Tinner
Downing, E D,   G S
Dunkles, C,   Gunsmith
Eason, W M,   G S
Ellen, C F (near),   G S
Farmer, Jesse,   Grocer
Fountain. S K,   Ice
Furkins, W H,   Shoemaker
Garvey, A,   Restaurant
Gravely, J O W,   Tob Warehouse
Griffin, Mrs A E,   Millinery
Griffin, J M,   Druggist
Hales & Edwards,
          Wholesale Grocers and Brokers
Hammond, C W,   Gro
Hines, M M (col.),   Grocer
Hines, J W,   Tob
Holden. Drake,   Barber
Horne, Pompey (col.),   Blacksmith
Howe, W H.   Grocer
Huffins, T R & Co,   Furniture
Jeffries Bros,   Tob Warehouse
Jenkins & Timmons,   Grocers
Jones. G F,   G S
Jones, J R,   G S
Jones, G T,   Grocer
Kyser, ——,   Druggist
Lancaster, W J (near),   G S
Lewis, J B,   Phœnix
Mathews, C L R,   Grocer
Mathews, S W,   Grocer
Mathews, C A & L,   Grocers

Mayo, R O,   Butcher
Middleton, W L,   Racket Store
Miller, Alex,   Baker
Moore, J R,   Painter
Nichols, James,   Restaurant
Odom, J D,   Livery
Parker, G L,   Jeweler
Parker, George,   Barber
Reynolds, W G.   Livery
Rocky Mount Mills Store,   G S
Sessoms, Isaac (col.),   Grocer
Sessoms, James, Jr (col.) (near),   G S
Short, J H & Co,   D G
Silly, G W (col.),   Gro
Skinner. R L,   Grocer
Smith, E W,   Leaf Tob
Sodom, Wm, Jr,   G S
Standard Hardware Co,   ——
Summerfield, R,   G S
Taylor, J A & Son,   Livery Stables
Taylor, B C,   Blacksmith
Thorn, G M,   Barber
Thorpe & Ricks,   Tob
Turner, Jesse,   G S
Ward, H H (col.),   Grocer
Williford, W T.   G S
Winstead, George,   Barber
Worsley, W H & Bro,   Grocers
Worth, ——,   Ice Dealer
Young Bros,   D G
Young, W B,   ——

SPARTA.

Webb, W G & Son,   G S

SPEED.

Satterthwaite, J W,   G S

ST. LEWIS.

Pitt, E L,   G S

TARBORO.

Allen, Mrs M H,   Gro
Anderson, Dr J H,   G S
Anderson, Thomas   G S
Andrews, L J,   Grocer
Arnheim, W M,   Grocer
Austin. C J,   Grocer
Battle. J W B,   G S
Bell, J H.   Jeweler
Bourne, H C.   G S
Brown, J H,   G S
Bridgers. D F,   G S
Bryan, E C (col.),   G S
Bryan, Mrs M S,   Millinery
Burnett, O,   Livery
Carlisle, B C.   Furniture and Undertaker
Clark, W S,   G S
Cobb, J E,   G S
Cobb, J E,   G S
Constantine, M L,   Confec
Cooper, S,   D G
Cooper, T,   G S
Davis, M L,   G S
Davis, J A & Co,   G S
Day & Hedges,   Livery

EDGECOMBE COUNTY.

Denton, Frank,   G S
Denton, Cicero,   G S
Exum, L (col.) (near),   G S
Faithful, J L (col.),   Grocer
Fander, Joe,   D G
Fouller, W H & Bro,   Stationery
Garrett & Cherry (col.),   Grocers
Gaskill, James R,   Fertilizer
Gatlin, T H,   D G
Givatney, M T,   Shoemaker
Hammond, A L (col.),   Gro
Harrison, J,   G S
Harrell, Alonzo,   Grocer
Hask, Edmond (col.),   Grocer
Heilbrower & Co,   D G
Heilbrower, M,   Jeweler
Howard & Co,   Hardware
Hyman, J G (col.),   Grocer
James, Owen (col.),   Grocer
Jenkins & Co,   Mdse Brokers
Jenkins, R P (near),   G S
Keech, B J,   G S
Lancaster, W D (near),   G S
Lancaster, W J,   G S
Lesosby, D (near),   G S
Lichenstein, D & Co,   G S and Furn
Lloyd, Geo (col),   Grocer
Lloyd, John W (col),   Grocer
Mallett & Mehegan,   Grocers
McNair, W H,   Druggist
Meyer & Co,   G S
Morris & Co,   Clo and Shoes
Murphy, Jenkins,   Com Merchant
Nash, S S,   Cotton Buyer
Orlinsky, ——,   Clothing
Pamlico Insurance and Banking Co.
Parker, R H,   Grocer
Pender, J Robert,   Grocer
Pender, Hayman, Hardware Co,   Hardware
Pender, F H,   Grocer
Pender, R J,   G S
Pittman, B,   Grocer
Pittman, O L,   G S
Powell, J A,   G S
Rawles, ——,   Jeweler
Redman, Geo,   G S
Robinson, Hugh (col),   Grocer
Rosebloom Bros,   D G
Rowe, Mrs R H,   Millinery
Royster, F S & Co,   Grocers
Satterthwaite, J W,   G S
Shackelford, J E,   Com Merchant
Shaw, H H,   Butcher
Simmons, J E,   Undertaker
Smith & Newton,   G S
Smith & Bro,   Oil Mill
Spraggins, B F & Co,   Grocers
Staton & Zoeller,   Druggist
Terrell, I C,   Hardware
Teiserer, Mrs H,   Millinery
Thomas, Geo B,   Grocer
Turner, A,   Green Grocer
Wallaman, E,   G S
Webb, W G & Son,   G S

EDGECOMBE COUNTY.

Whitley, Wm (col),   Grocer
Williams, D L,   G S
Williford, W T,   G S
Zander, Jos,   G S
Zoeller, W H,   Stationery

TURNAGE.

Jefferson, R L & Co,   G S

WHITAKER.

Cutchin, F H (agt),   G S
Cutchin, N S,   G S
Knight, W S (agt),   G S
Oursheet, W F & Co,   Grocer
Watson, J M (col),   Grocer

WRENDALE.

Lancaster, W D,   G S

MILLS.

Kinds, Post Offices and Proprietors.

Edgecombe Cotton-seed Oil Co, Tarboro and Conetoe, W N Smith, pres and mgr.

Flour, corn and saw, St Louis, Riley Phillips.

Flour and corn, Whitaker, J H Pippin

Flour and corn, Whitaker, A Braswell

Flour and corn, Sharpsburg, E G Eagles

Flour and corn, Enfield, Geo Howard.

Flour and corn, Sharpsburg, Robins & Bailey.

Public Gin, Tarboro, Geo Howard,

Steam saw, Whitaker, C W Land & Son.

Steam saw, Whitaker, Dr. W T Mayo.

Steam saw, flour and corn, Battleboro, Jos Hobgood.

Steam flour and corn, Mildred, B F Shelton.

Steam corn and gin, Tarboro, John W Charles.

Steam saw and corn, Conoho, John D Taylor.

Steam saw and grist, Leggett, Theodore Fountain.

Steam saw, Wrendale, Swift Creek Mfg Co.

Steam saw, Penelo.

Steam saw, Speed, A S Dunn.

Steam saw, Hartsboro, S L Hart.

Steam and water corn and gin, Rocky Mount, Nettles, Killebrew & Bros.

Steam saw, Tarboro, A A Nichols.

Steam flour and corn, Rocky Mount, W S Battle & Son.

Steam flour, corn, saw and gin, Rocky Mount, Thomas Watson.

Tar River Lumber Mill, Tarboro, A A Nichols.

Water flour and corn, Rocky Mount, David Proctor.

17

EDGECOMBE COUNTY.

PHYSICIANS.

Names and Post Offices.

Anderson, J H, Tarboro.
Battle, J J, Rocky Mount.
Baker, J M, Tarboro.
Baker, Jos H, Tarboro.
Barnes. Wright, Toisnot.
Barnes, E D (Dentist), Tarboro.
Barrow, Chas, Toisnot.
Bass, H T, Tarboro.
Braswell, M. Rocky Mount.
Braswell, J C. Whitaker.
Braswell, M R, Rocky Mount.
Battle, ——, Rocky Mount.
Carr, I N (Dentist), Tarboro.
Hall, Stuart, Lawrence.
Hilliard, S P (Dentist). Rocky Mount.
Jenkins, Jeff D, Elm City.
Jenkins. Chas L. Conetoe.
Jones, J W, Tarboro.
Killebrew. Chas. Rocky Mount.
Marriott. H B, Battleboro.
Mayo, W T. Whitaker.
Mercer, W P, Toisnot.
Nobles, A B, Rocky Mount.
Norfleet, L E, Tarboro.
Pitt, M B, Old Sparta.
Speight, R H, Tarboro.
Staton, L L, Tarboro.
Thorpe, F J, Rocky Mount.
Whitehead, W H, Rocky Mount.
Williams, D, jr, (Dentist) Tarboro.
Williams, Donald, Tarboro.
Wimberly, G L, Rocky Mount.
Wynn, T P, Tarboro.

SCHOOLS.

Names, Post Offices. and Principals.

Academy, Whitaker's, Rev A J Moore.
Academy, Rocky Mount, ——.
Academy, Battleboro, ——.
Graded School, No 1, Tarboro, Robt
    Davis, supt.
Graded School (col), Tarboro, John C
    Jones.
Female Academy, Tarboro, Prof D G
    Gillespie.
Logan School (col). Rocky Mount, Is-
    rael D Hargett, prin.
Male Academy, Tarboro, F S Wilkin-
    son.
Primary School, Rocky Mount, Miss
    Bettie Whitehead.
School (col), Tarboro, Rev J W Perry.
School, Wrendale, Dr Robt Speight.
Tarboro Institute, Tarboro, Miss Mary
    Whitehurst.
University School, Rocky Mount, Wil-
    liam Holmes Davis. A B, prin.
Wilkinson Female Institute, Tarboro,
    F S Wilkinson, pres; Mrs A E
    Hughes, principal.
Public schools—white, 34; colored, 37.

EDGECOMBE COUNTY.

TEACHERS.

Names and Post Offices.

Arrington, Mary Jones, Rocky Mount.
Avera, Florida A, Rocky Mount.
Chapman, J J, Rocky Mount.
Chapman, J Henry, Rocky Mount.
Checkley, Constance M, Rocky Mount.
Davis, Wm Holmes, Rocky Mount.
McSwain, Isabel, Rocky Mount.
Worthington. Bessie H, Rocky Mount.

LOCAL CORPORATIONS.

American Legion of Honor, D Abram
    commander.
Bank of Rocky Mount, T H Battle,
    pres; L F Tillery, cashier.
Concord Lodge, No 58, A F & A M,
    Tarboro; time of meeting, first Fri-
    day evening and third Saturday
    morning in each month.
Corinthian Lodge, No 230, A F and A
    M, Rocky Mount; time of meeting,
    first Thursday evening in each
    month: J G Snider, W M.
County Farmers' Alliance, Elias Carr,
    pres; J C Powell, sec.
Edgecombe County Medical Society,
    Tarboro; Dr J H Baker, pres; H T
    Boss, sec.
Golden Belt, No 47,163, I O O F; E G
    Smiih, N G.
Hamilton R R and Lumber Co, Hamil-
    ton; Frank Hitch, gen mgr. (Road
    22 miles long.)
I O B B, Zanoah Lodge, No 235; meets
    first and third Sunday A M; J Blum-
    enthal, pres; Meyer Morris, sec.
Old Dominion Line. John Myer's Sons,
    general agents. Washington.
Knights of Pythias, Queen City, No.
    47: E W Smith, C C.
Knights of Honor, No 1118; D Abram,
    Protector.
Knights of Honor, Edgecombe Lodge,
    No 504; meets first and third Tues-
    day nights; D Pender, dictator; B F
    Spragins, sec.
Knights and Ladies of Honor, Chrey-
    tos, No 192; B R Arrington, pro-
    tector.
Legion of Honor, Tar River Council,
    No 186; meets second and fourth
    Tuesday evenings; D Fender, com-
    mander; J V Paris, sec.
Mount Moriah Lodge, No 350, A F and
    A M, Battleboro; time of meeting,
    second Wednesday in each month.
Old Dominion Steamboat Line, from
    Tarboro to New York; John B Kuch,
    agt.
Pamlico Insurance and Banking Co,
    Tarboro; H L Staton, pres; Job Cobb,
    cash; capital stock, $113,200; $33,960
    paid; surplus, $36,000.

Repiton Encampment, I O O F; J H Brown, C P; Ed Pennington, Scribe.

Rocky Mount Eastern North Carolina Agricultural Fair, Rocky Mount; J J Battle, pres; J D Jenkins, sec; B H Bunn, treas.

Royal Arcanum, meets first and third Thursday evenings; E Zoeller sec; Ed Pennington, regent.

The Clyde Line, H H Shaw, agent, Tarboro.

The Tarboro, Greenville and Washington Telegraph Company, Tarboro; W E Fountain, general mgr.

Thompson Orphanage Guild, Tarboro; S S Nash, pres; C E Bernace, sec.

Tarboro Board of Trade, W E Fountain, pres; Hon Geo Howard, 1st vice-pres; Dr N J Pittman, 2d vice-pres; John F Shackleford, sec and treas.

Tarboro Bank, J F Shackelford, pres; James Mehegan, cashier ; capital stock, $30,000.

Tarboro Cotton Factory, $164.450 capital; raw material annually, 3,600 bales of cotton; work about 250 hands; S S Nash, pres; A M Fairley, treas and supt.

Tar River Oil Co, Tarboro; Dr L L Staton, pres; E V Zoeller, sec and treas.

U S B F, Una Council, No 12, meets second and fourth Friday evenings in each month; R C Brown, commander; H H Nash, sec.

Welcome Lodge, No 40, K of P, Tarboro, R E L Cook, C C; W O Howard, V C; J R Gaskill, K of R & S.

Winchester Lodge, No 16, I O O F, Rocky Mount; day of meeting, Friday; J C Allen N G; C W Jeffreys, sec.

Y M C A, F S Royster, pres; E T Bynum, 1st vice-pres; W E Fountain, 2d vice-pres; Laura Weddell, sec; B F Lipscombe, treas.

NEWSPAPERS.

Argonant, Rocky Mount, J A Campbell, editor.

Rocky Mount Phœnix, Rocky Mount (Democratic weekly), J B Lewis, editor and proprietor.

Southerner (Democratic weekly), Tarboro, J G Charles, editor and proprietor.

FARMERS.

Names and Post Offices.

Battleboro—R D Armstrong, T W Battle, Mrs Mary P Battle, Mrs Lizzie P Battle, R H Battle, T P Braswell &

Son, Mrs Bettie J Bryan, Mrs Annie Bryan, W B Bullock, H S Bunn (agt), Joel P Daughtry, Maggie C Farmer, J K Lawrence, Theo Lawrence, Mrs W G Lewis, R H Lewis, J W Mason, Mrs A Merriott, R H Moore, H E Odom, J B Phillips, J W Powell, W H Powell (agt), G L Wimberly.

Coakley—Fred Boyett, G E Brown, S T Carson, J L Cherry (agt), Miss Lucy Cherry, J Brinkley Cherry, W P Council, Jesse Crisp, W T Davis (agt), Joseph Downing, M G Edmondson, John H Harrell, Charles Harrell, H H Hyman, Mrs M E Jones, S M Pender, L R Purvis, T W Robinson, J B Staton, Felix Staton, Nick Staton, C Staton, J D Taylor, B H Taylor, C W Taylor, C G Thigpen, W G Turner.

Conetoe—W H Andrews, G L Brown, Mrs E E Bunting, F L Castex, Gray Cobb, Bettie D Crisp, T J Crisp, E C Crisp, N B Dawson, F J Dozier (agt), J T Dupree, M G Ford, Geo Grimes, John Hardy, W S Hicks, J T Howard, Mrs C H Jenkins, S P Jenkins, Dr C L Jenkins, Mrs Hannah Jenkins, E C Knight, R A Knight, Lam Lawrence, Mrs Mariah Lawrence, F M Leigh, W G H Leigh, G A Little, R H Mays, T L Mays, John Mays, J A Robinson, B B F Shelton, J N Shelton, H H Shelton, C J H Stancil, G W Stancil, F L Thigpen, Mrs Hattie Thigpen, John Walston, G M Walker, N S Walker, W O Warren, John Warren, sr, Eli Warren, R C Warren, J M Wichard, Jas Whitehurst, W A Williams, Mays Worsley, Arnold Worsley.

Crisp—J J Atkinson, J G Cobb, J H Corbett, W J Corbett, S M Crisp, W S Crisp, B F Eagles, J W Edwards, Job Felton, J C Forbes, Mrs B B Lewis, R T Lewis, Wm Norville, J G Owens, W H Owens, W R Owens, H R Owens, Benj Phillips, B B Pittman, Arthur Reid (col.), J A B Thorn, Elwell Webb, Jarrett Webb, A B Wooten.

Doe Head—D H Barlow.

Elm City—J L Horne, Jno H Horne.

Gethsemene—O L Pittman.

Lancaster—Walter Brown, H C Bullock, E V Bullock, W A Hinton, B P Jenkins, John Lancaster, W J Lancaster, Mrs W B Parker.

Leggett's—Theo Fountain, C H Spivey, J H Thigpen.

Mildred—L G Harris, Wm Harrell, P M Mays, J D Mays, Mrs Mary A Sanders, J L Thigpen.

Norfolk, Va—Rountree & Co.

Rocky Mount—Thos H Battle (trustee), A J Batchelor, J F Bishop, J D Bowman, J B Bradley, W E Bradley, A B Braswell, J L Brake, Jesse Brake,

EDGECOMBE COUNTY.

J D Brake, W O Bullock, J E Calhamer, James H Chapman, W R Cox, M F Doughtridge, E L Doughtridge, J P Doughtry, W H Fly, Ed Gorham, Frank Gorham, W O Griffin, John Hines (col.), Battle Howard, A B Jenkins, G F Jones, N B Killebrew, C L Killebrew, J I Killebrew (agent), B F Lancaster, W H Lancaster, J B Lancaster, Jos Long, A B Nobles, C W Proctor, M W Proctor, R E Thomas, John J Thorne.

Sparta—W H Brown, J D Brown. Elias Carr, J B Coleman, R Cobb & Reason, J T Cobb and wife, Staton Cummings, H B Edwards, John S Gray, Elisha Hales, J J Hearne, Mrs M V Johnson, Reuben Keel, R J Lewis, D V Mercer, S R Moore; W A Norville, J B W Norville, Offey Pitt, M B Pitt. Mrs S E Porter, Mrs M A Ricks, W M Savage. Mrs Della Staton, W L Stallings. E S Stallings. W O Thigpen, Frank Thorp (col), W G Webb, Mrs Kate Williams, Daniel Wimberly (col), B C Wooten.

Speed—W J Davenport, W R Howell, J W Howard, J A Long, Mrs W S Long, J W Satterthwaite, J T Savage, B C Sharp.

St Lawrence—E M Bryan, J E Cobb, J H Edwards (agent), Wm Hodges, Eli Howell, J M Howell (agent), V B Knight, W J Lawrence, O B Sharp.

St Lewis—M B Atkinson, Dr W Barnes, W W Cobb, J L Cobb, A J Cotton's heirs, J A Corbett, Thomas Felton, B C Pitt, Robt Pitt, R E Pitt, G P Sugg, L M & I Sugg, Robt Walston, W E Warren, F B Webb, Cenry Winborne

Tarboro—Thomas Anderson, C J Austin, J M Baker, Dr J H Baker, R H Banks, W L Barlow, J W B Battle, Octavo Battle, J H L Best (agent), C H Blocker, D B Botts, G W Bottoms, W C Bradley, John L Bridgers, D F Bridgers, Bridgers & Redmond, D T Britt, Battle Bryan, Gray Bryan, G R

EDGECOMBE COUNTY.

Bullock, W J Burnett, J W Charles. S T Cherry, Henry N Cherry (col.), W S Clark, C D Coker, Job Cobb, Mrs M E Colton, R E Corbett, Mrs P B Cox, Mrs M A Cromwell, J R Crumis, J B Cummings, Mrs B C Daniel, J A Davis, Frank Denton, Frank Dew (col.), W M Edmundson, A M Fairly, Mrs R G Farrar, Charles Fly, Lawrence Fountain, E D Foxhall, G R Gammon. G W Garrett, D G Gillespie, A Hask, Mrs M V Hask, W A Hask (agent), J D Hargrave, S L Hask (agent), N J Pitman's heirs, M W Hines, J J Hines, B G Howell, Geo Howard, jr, T W Howard, George Howard, Orren James (col), Jordan W Johnson, Dr J W Jones, B J Keech, C H King, E E Knight, W T Knight, L B Knight, Mrs Martha A Knight, Patrick Lane, T B Lloyd, Sherrod Mays, N J Mays, C W Mays, W T Mays (agent), John P McDonell, W P Mercer, J O Oats, Fred Philips, Mrs M A Pippen, Miss Minerva Pittman. Mrs M E Pittman, Mrs C A Porter, J H Purvis, J S Quinely, T H Ruffin, Jas H Ruffin. Jno F Shackelford, Harry Smith (col), S E Speight, J L Spragins, Thomas R Stallings, H L Staton. Lucy C Staton, P S Sugg, Mrs Mary Walston. M H Wetherlee, Jos W Weeks, J W Wells, T J White, J L Wiggins, C G Wilkerson, Mrs M L Wimberly.

Turnage—H C Turnage.

Wrendale—W D Lancaster.

Whitaker's—M J Battle, H T Bell, S C Bellamy, Dr John T Bellamy, S B Bradley, J R Bradley, A Braswell, J E Braswell, J W Braswell, W T Braswell, Mrs D W Bullock, J C Carlisle, C C Cherry, Henry Cokes, B E Cutchin, J M Cutchin, J S Dixon (agt), W F Draughan, J M Johnson, V W Land, H L Lyon, W S Knight (agt), Hardy Oneal, W D Pitman, J W Sherrod & Bro, R H Speight, James W Taylor, H J Weaver.

FORSYTH COUNTY.

AREA, 340 SQUARE MILES.

POPULATION, 28,434; White 19,333 Colored 9,101.

FORSYTH COUNTY was formed in 1848, from Stokes county, and was named in honor of Colonel Benjamin Forsyth, of Germanton, Stokes Co.

WINSTON is the county-seat. Population (estimated) 13,500.

Salem, settled by the Moravians over one hundred years ago, and adjoining Winston contains a population estimated at 5,500.

Surface—Moderately hilly, and watered by many small streams. Much of the soil is good and susceptible of a high state of cultivation.

Staples—Corn, wheat, oats and dried fruit. Tobacco has recently become one of the leading crops, and the large number of tobacco factories and ware houses in Winston has given an impetus to the culture of tobacco in the county almost unprecedented. Forsyth is one of the finest fruit-growing counties in the State.

The Fruits of this county are apples, peaches, pears, apricots, nectarines, cherries, plums and the small fruits. The export of dried blackberries from this county is immense.

Timbers of this county consist of oak, hickory, poplar, walnut, pine, chestnut, and other kinds common to the Piedmont counties of the State.

TOWNS AND POST OFFICES.

	POP.		POP.
Alspaugh,	25	Lewisville,	75
Belew Creek		Oak Summit,	50
Mills,	—	Okav,	—
Bethania,	160	Pfafftown,	100
Blakley,	—	Rural Hall,	105
Bower,	—	Ruth,	25
Clemmonsville,	—	Salem,	5,500
Crater's,	10	Salem Chapel,	45
Daisy,	15	Sedge Garden,	25
Donnoho,	25	Seward,	30
Dosier,	50	Tobaccoville,	25
Goodwill,	15	Vienna,	45
Hulon,	15	Walkertown,	150
Jolliet,	25	Whiteroad,	20
Kernersville,	1,025	Winston,	13,500

COUNTY OFFICERS.

Clerk Superior Court—N S Wilson.
Commissioners—M D Bailey, chm'n; E W Hauser, R S Linville.

Coroner—Dr A G Linville.
Register of Deeds—J F Miller.
Sheriff—R M McArthur.
Solicitor 9th District—M L Mott.
Surveyor—H W Morris.
Standard Keeper— —— Beck.
Treasurer—J F Griffith.
County Examiner—Dr A S Davis.
County Physician—D N Dalton.

COURTS.

Second Monday before the first Monday in March; tenth Monday after the first Monday in March; fourth Monday before the first Monday in September; thirteenth Monday after the first Monday in September.

TOWN OFFICERS.

WINSTON—*Mayor*, P W Crutchfield; *Mayor pro tem.* S F Vance; *Commissioners*, T J Wilson, Jesse Riggs, W B Pollard, C A McGalliard, Wm Tavis, Frank Carter, A J Gale, R A Mills, S F Vance, W H White, Henry Pendleton, C H Tavis, J J Hopper, R I Dalton, A L Snipes; *Secretary and Treasurer*, T J Wilson; *Chief of Police*, J M Willson; *Tax Collector*, O W Hanner.

SALEM—*Mayor*, C S Hauser; *Secretary and Treasurer*, ——; *Chief of Police*, —— Spainhour; *Tax Collector*, Frank Kulin.

Rough and Ready Fire Co, Salem; John Schote. captain; (one steamer and two hand engines).

TOWNSHIPS AND MAGISTRATES.

Abbott's Creek—J A Holder, G H Idol, R F Idol, L P Mathews, J L Phipps, S J Sapp, J F Tucker, J H Whicher (Kernersville).

Belew's Creek—E B Linville (Belew's Creek), E S Linville (Goodwill), J K P Carter, Fulton Fervel, J E H Hester, H A Lewis, Marshall Crawford, A G Vass, M W Vance (White Road).

Bethania—J N Anderson, A P Styers. J C Butner, R B Flynt, E T Kapp, F H Lash, E T Strupe (Bethania), R L Cox, Houston Hunter (Winston).

Broadbay—H L Beckerdite (Winston), Samuel Long, Chas Rothrock, W R Rominger, W L Sink, L L Smith (Salem).

FORSYTH COUNTY.

Kernersville—J S Vance (Okay), Henry Barrow, J I Crews, L F Davis, J M Guyer, F H Morris. N W Sapp, N H Smith, T B Wilson (Kernersville).

Lewisville—D A Binkley, T J Conrad, I O Hart, Albert Jones, G F Mock, T W Reynolds, W R Wagoner, E H Wright (Lewisville).

Middle Fork—W A Beason, R W Hedgecock, R S Kinnamon, P T Lehman, M F Masten (Winston), W H Cox (Oak Summit), J W Jones, E W Linville (Walkertown).

Old Richmond—W T Holt, E W Nash (Donaho), N B Holder, C R Orender, David Snider, J B Vest (Tobaccoville), Ellis Long (Dosier), H J Peddicord (Bethania), Oliver Spainhour (Seward).

Old Town—F N Pfaff. Thos Thacker (Bethania), J W Bullard, J I Craft, A C Davis, F E Shamel, C T Whicher, C S Walker (Winston), C H Hauser (Joliet).

Salem Chapel—J L Grubbs (Walkertown), T N Marshall, Sam'l Wagoner (Sedge Garden), T P Dalton. J F Grubbs, T M Marshall, J B Merritt, D G Walker (Salem Chapel).

South Fork—A B Atwood. G A Jones, C S Ryan (Crater's), W L Fishell, J J Shore, E D Sides. C S Spach (Salem), Theo Kimmell (Hulon).

Vienna—E C Dull (Lewisville). A E Conrad, A D Stimpson (Blakely), A S Conrad (Pfafftown), W H Goslen, G H Hauser, R C Lineback, L S Lehman, C F Mickle (Vienna).

JUSTICES OF THE PEACE.

Winston Township—H W Barrow, J C Bessent, J L Beard, G H Cox, J P Stanton, M E Teague, J S White, J A Warner, R A Womack, J B Whitaker, Jr, (Winston), C B Brooks, T B Douthit, S A Hege, A S Jones, A Litchenthaler, J McCuiston (Salem).

Clemmonsville Township — Frank Cook, T W Griffith, C L Johnson, U S Laurence, M C Nelson, A Phelps, J A Sheek, J C Womack, A C Wharton (Clemonsville.)

CHURCHES.

Names, Post Offices, Pastors and Denom.

MORAVIAN.

Bethabara—Bethania. R P Lineback.
Centreville—Salem. J F McCuiston.
Christ's Chapel—Salem.
Church—Salem. E Rondthaler. D D.
Church (col.)—Salem, J F McCuiston.
Church—Kernersville.
Church—Bethania, R P Linebach.

Church—Friedberg, J E Hall.
East Salem—Salem. J F McCuiston.
Elm Street Chapel—Salem, J F McCuiston.
Enon—Friedberg, James E Hall.
Friedland—Friedberg, J E Hall.
Hope—Friedberg, James E Hall.
Philadelphia—Bethania. E P Greider.
Reservation Chapel—Salem, A D Threber.

METHODIST.

Bethel—Kernersville. J A B Fry.
Bethel—Winston, J H Fitzgerald.
Bethlehem—Dennis, W C Wilson.
Brooktown—Vienna, M C Field.
Bunker Hill—Kernersville, W C Wilson.
Burkhead—Winston, S D Stamey.
Centenary—Winston, W S Creasy; A W Plyler, ast.
Church—Kernersville, W C Wilson.
Church—Lewisville. M C Field.
Church—Rural Hall. M H Vestal.
Church—Clemonsville. M C Field.
Concord—Kernersville, M C Field.
Doub's Chapel—Bethania. M C Field.
Grace—Winston, W M Curtis.
Love's—Walkertown, W C Wilson.
Marvin—Winston, J H Fitzgerald.
Mt Tabor, Winston, J H Fitzgerald.
Mt Vernon—Kernersville, J J Ecles.
New Hope—Bethania, J H Fitzgerald.
Pine Grove—Kernersville, J H Fitzgerald.
Sharon—Vienna, J H Fitzgerald.
Shiloh—Germantown, M H Vestal.
Union——Vienna. M C Field.

METH. PROTESTANT.

Church—Winston, L L Albright.
Hickory Ridge—Winston.
Maple Spring—Winston.
Pleasant Hill—Bethania.
Tabernacle—Bethania.

LUTHERAN.

Augsburg—Winston. W A Lutz.
Nazareth—Salem, E P Parker.
Shiloh—Salem, E P Parker.
Spanish Grove—Salem, E P Parker.

BAPTIST.

Beck's—Sedge Gareen, R W Crews.
Broad St—Winston, N S Jones.
Church—Lewisville, R W Crews.
Church—Waughton, W J Mathews.
Church—Kernersville. Henry Sheets.
Church—Clemmonsville, Rev Mason.
Church—Walkertown, Henry Sheets.
First Baptist—Winston, H A Brown.
First Faptist (col)——-, G W Holland.
Friendship—Salem, Henry Sheets.
Goodville—Sedge Garden, W J Mathews.

FORSYTH COUNTY.

Macedonia—Tobaccoville, Judson Vipperman.
Mission—North Winston.
Red Banks—Germantown, W H Wilson.
Union Hill—Lewisville. Rev Mason.
Valley—Walkertown, Henry Sheets.
Waughtown—Salem, Henry Sheets.
Baptist (col)—Winston, G W Johnson.

PRIM. BAPTIST.
Middle Fork—Winston.

PRESBYTERIAN.
First Church—Winston, R E Caldwell.
Second Church (mission)—Winston.
Church (col)—Winston, J C Alston.

CHRISTIAN.
Salem Chapel—Salem, W T Walker.

EPISCOPAL.
St Paul's—Winston, J F George.

DUNKARD.
Clemmonsville—Salem.
South Fork—Salem.

A. M. E. ZION.
Church (col)— ——, W H Gater.

A. M. E.
Church (col)— ——, J T Tate.

COL. METH. EPISCOPAL.
Church (col)— ——, E T Mayo.

METH. EPISCOPAL.
St Paul's (col)— ——, A H Newsom.

MINISTERS RESIDENT.

Names, Post Offices, Pastors and Denom.

METHODIST.
Albea, W W, Winston.
Craft, A W, Lewisville.
Creasy, W S, D D, Winston.
Curtis, W M, Winston.
Doub, J B, Vienna.
Edes, J J, Kernersville.
Field, M C, Bethania.
Fitzgerald, J H, Kernersville.
Fry, J A B, Kernersville.
Jefferson, J J, Wins'on.
Long, S, Salem.
Pegram, T H, Winston.
Petre, J E, Old Town.
Plyler, A W, Winston.
Stamey, S D, Winston.
Vestal, M H, Germanton.
Wilson, W C, Kernersville.
Wood, F H, D D, Winston.

METH. PROT.
Albright, L L, Winston.

BAPTIST.
Brown, H A, Winston.
Conrad, S F, Winston.

FORSYTH COUNTY.

Crews, R W, Germanton.
Gourley, Robt, Winston.
Holland, G W (col), Winston.
Jones, N S, Winston.
Mason, ——, Clemmonsville.
Matthews, N J, Sedge Garden.
Sheets, Henry, Salem.
Vipperman, Judson, Tobaccoville.

MORAVIAN.
Clewell, J H, Salem.
Hall, Jas E, Friedberg.
McCuiston, J F, Salem.
Rondthaler, E, D D, Salem.
Stoltz, T S, Rural Hall.
Threber, A D, Salem.

PRESBYTERIAN.
Alston, J C, Winston.
Caldwell, R E, Winston.

DIS. OF CHRIST.
Poindexter, Richard, Reeds.
Wilson, V A, Vienna.

CHRISTIAN.
Pinnix, J W, Kernersville.

EPISCOPAL.
George, J F, Winston.

HOTELS AND BOARDING HOUSES.

Names, Post Offices and Proprietors.

Boarding, Winston, Mrs Lizzie Rierson.
Boarding, Winston, Mrs Julian.
Boarding, Winston, Mrs Williams.
Boarding, Bethania, Jas Grabbs.
Boarding, Winston, Mrs N J Terry.
Boarding, Winston, Gen Barringer (col).
Boarding, Winston, Mrs F J Hardy.
Boarding, Salem, H D Lott.
Boarding, Winston, Andrew Gilliam.
Boarding, Winston, Mrs J W Alspaugh.
Boarding, Winston, Christian Reed.
Eating Saloon, Salem, Mrs Graham.
Hanes House, Winston, Mrs Hanes.
Hotel Phoenix, Winston, Efird Bros & Brown.
Hotel, Kernersville, J G Kerner.
Hotel, Kernersville, B J Sapp.
Hotel Jones, Winston, J L Jones.
Kiser House, Rural Hall, E L Kiser.
Kiser House, Winston, E C Rominger.
Select Boarding House, Salem, B F Crosland.

LAWYERS.

Names and Post Offices.

Baldwin, F T, Winston.
Blair, W A, Winston.
Bodenhamer, M J, Kernersville.
A R Bridges, (col), Winston.

FORSYTH COUNTY.

Buxton, J C, Winston.
Eller, A H, Winston.
Fitts, J S (col), Winston.
Glenn, R B. Winston.
Gray, E E, Winston.
Griffith, E A, Winston.
Grogan, J S, Winston.
Henderson, W M, Winston.
Holton, A E, Winston.
Jones, E B, Winston.
Lanier, J S (col), Winston.
Manly, Clement, Winston.
McNeil, J W, Winston.
Mott, D P, Winston.
Nowell, Lorenzo, Winston.
Patterson, J L, Winston.
Rayle, B G, Winston.
Starbuck, H R (Judge Superior Court), Winston.
Swink, L M, Winston.
Watson, Thos W, Winston.
Watson, C B, Winston.

MANUFACTORIES.

Kinds, Post Offices and Proprietors.

Arista Cotton Mills, Salem, F & H Fries, est 1840, old machinery sold and new mill built in 1880; run by steam engine –225 horse power; spindles, 5,200; looms, 180; daily consumption, 3,300 pounds; daily production, 9,000 yds sheeting; number of hands, 125; lighted by Weston's patent electric light.
Blacksmithing and wheelwrighting, Bethania, Transon & Grabs.
Boots and shoes, Winston, Jesse Riggs.
Brick & Tile Co, Winston, Brick & Tile Co.
Brick, Winston, W A Byerly.
Brick, Winston, J H Masten.
Brick, Winston, Sheppard & Carter.
Brick, Winston, Will Masten.
Brick, Winston, A H Motsinger.
Brick, Winston, Robt Hedgecock.
Brick, Winston, Nick Whitfield.
Brick, Winston, Green Newsom.
Brick, Winston, Sanford Snider.
Broom Factory, Salem, C F Jenkins, mgr.
Buggies and carriages, Kernersville, Lewis & Huff.
Buggies, Salem, F C Mienung.
Cabinet works, Kernersville, J L Plunket.
Cabinet work, Salem, A C Vogler & Son.
Candy, Salem, Mrs C A Winkler.
Canning, Kernersville, Edwards & Stone.
Canning, Salem, C F Jenkins, mgr.
Carriages and buggies, Winston, J S White & Son.

FORSYTH COUNTY.

Casing Machine Co, Winston.
Cigarette Machine Co, Winston, Cigarette Machine Co.
Cigarettes, Winston, W F Smith, Sons & Co.
Cigars, Winston, Dr V O Thompson.
Cigars, Winston, J D King.
Cigars, Winston, Liipfert & Jones.
Cigars, Winston, W J Liipfert & Co.
Contracting, Salem, H E McIver.
Contracting, Winston, Styers & Lohman.
Contracting, Winston, J C Miller.
Contracting, Winston, Piles & McKnight.
Contracting and building, Winston, H E McIver.
Foundry, machine and well fixtures, Winston, C H Tise.
Furniture, Winston, A C Green & Bro.
Guns and locks, Salem, Wm Detmar.
Guns and locks, Winston, W E Beck.
Iron works, Salem, C A Hege & Co.
Iron works, Winston, Kester Bros.
Iron working, machine shop and foundry, cor First and Depot sts, J A Vance.
Machine shops, Winston, Kester Bros.
Marble works, Winston, J A Bennett.
Merchant tailor, Winston, R D Johnston.
Millwrighting, Kernersville, C Sapp.
Millwrighting, Kernersville, J S Harmon.
Millwrighting, Kernersville, Newell Sapp.
Millwrighting, Salem, J L Nissen.
Nissen Wagon Co, Winston, S J Nissen.
Nissen Wagon (Waughtown), Salem, Geo E Nissen & Co, established 1834.
Pottery and clay pipes, Salem, Daniel Crouse.
Pump Works, Winston, C H Tise.
Saddles and harness, Winston, Hine & Shipley.
Salem Iron Works, Salem, C A Hege & Co.
Salem Cotton Mills, Salem, F & H Fries.
Sash, blinds and doors, Salem, Fogle Bros.
Sash, doors and blinds, contracting and building, Winston, Miller Bros.
Smoking Tobacco, Winston, T F Leak.
Southside M'f'g Co, Salem, H E Fries, pres and treas; E W Lehman, sec; capital, $125,000; daily consumption, 5 bales cotton; spindles, 5,000; hands, 60.
Tannery, Kernersville, J Kerner.
Tannery, Old Town, L J Hine.

FORSYTH COUNTY.	FORSYTH COUNTY.

Tannery, White Road, G V Fulp & Sons.

Tannery, Bethania, E M C Doub.

Tinware, Salem, W O Senseman, Brickenstein.

Tobacco, Kernersville, Beard & Roberts.

Tobacco Kernersville, B A Brown.

Tobacco, Kernersville, Greenfield & Galloway.

Tobacco, Kernersville, W A Torney & Son.

Tobacco Works, Winston, Liberty Tobacco Co.

Tobacco, Winston, Moseley & Martin.

Tobacco, Winston, W E Walker & Co.

Tobacco, Winston, W W Wood & Co.

Tobacco, Winston, W C Lassiter & Co.

Tobacco, Winston, Walker Bros.

Tobacco, Winston, T F Williamson & Co.

Tobacco, Winston, H B Ireland & Co.

Tobacco, Winston, M L Ogburn.

Tobacco, Winston, Dalton, Ellington & Co.

Tobacco, Winston, Harvey & Rintels.

Tobacco, Winston, Casey & Wright.

Tobacco, Winston, W S Clarey & Co.

Tobacco, Walkertown, T E Crews.

Tobacco, Salem, Casper, Efland & Co.

Tobacco, Winston, Dalton, Farrow & Co.

Tobacco, Winston, N S & T J Wilson.

Tobacco, Winston, P H Hanes & Co.

Tobacco, Smoking, Eagle Brand, Winston, S Byerly & Son.

Tobacco, Winston, M A Walker & Co.

Tobacco, Winston, Bailey Bros.

Tobacco, Winston, Brown Bros Co.

Tobacco, Winston, Hamlin, Liipfert & Co.

Tobacco, Winston, Kerner Bros.

Tobacco, Winston, W A Whitaker.

Tobacco, Winston, T L Vaughn & Co.

Tobacco, Salem, Reynold Bros.

Tobacco, Winston, F M Bohannan.

Tobacco, Winston, Ogburn, Hill & Co.

Tobacco, Winston, R J Reynolds.

Tobacco, Walkertown, W D Sullivan.

Tobacco, Winston, Blackburn & Harvey,

Tobacco, Winston, J A Bitting.

Tobacco, Winston, R L Chandler & Co.

Tobacco, Winston, W B Ellis & Co.

Tobacco, Winston, Hodgin Bros and Lunn.

Tobacco, Winston, B F Hanes & Co.

Tobacco, Winston, Taylor Bros.

Tobacco, Winston, Lockett, Vaughn & Co.

Tobacco, plug and twist, Kernersville, Stafford Bros.

Tobacco, Winston, S A Ogburn.

Tobacco, plug and twist, Bethania, O J Lehman & Co.

Tobacco, plug and twist, Winston, Brown & Williamson.

Tobacco, plug and twist, Salem, S F Nissen.

Tobacco, plug and twist, Old Town, M L Ogburn.

Wagons and Buggies, Kernersville, B Y Clark.

Wagons, Kernersville, Pendry & Phillips.

Wagon works, Bethania, W A Stoltz.

Wagon works, Winston, S W Farrabee.

Wagons, carts and barrows (Waughtown), Salem, C F Nissen & Co; established in 1881.

Wagons and buggies, Winston, S W Farabee.

Wagons, Salem, Chamberlain & Smith.

Wagons (Waughtown), Salem, Spach Bros; established 1856.

Wagons, Vienna, Transon Bros.

Wagons, Bethania, Transon & Stoltz.

Woodworking Co, Salem, J A Vance.

Wood Manufacturing Co, Salem, Fogle Bros.

Wood Manufacturing Co, Winston, Miller Bros.

Woolen Mills, Salem, F & H Fries; established 1840; spindles, 760; looms, 40; daily consumption, 700 pounds; daily production, 1,150 yards; number of hands employed, 100; electric lights of Edison's patent used.

MERCHANTS AND TRADESMEN.

Name, Post Office, and Line of Business.

BELEW'S CREEK.

Pegram, E H,	G S
Robison, J A,	G S

BETHANIA.

Lehman, O J & Co,	G S and Tob Mfg

BLAKELY.

Conrad A E	Ferry

CLEMMONSVILLE.

Idol I Wesley,	Ferry
Strupe, W C & Son,	G S

DAISY.

Pennight, Sid,	G S
Westmoreland, J W,	G S

DONNAHO.

Chiplin, Jas,	G S
Spainhour & Flynn,	G S
Speas, J W & F E,	Merchants
Sprinkle, C A,	Ferry

DOSIER.

Long, J M,	G S

FORSYTH COUNTY.

FORSYTH COUNTY.

JOLIETT.

James Bros,   G S

KERNERSVILLE.

Beard & Roberts,   G S
Crews & Lindsay,   G S
Davis, L F & Sons,   G S
Fulp & Linville,   G S
McKaugh, C M & Co,   G S
Sapp, B J.   G S
Sapp, N W,   Drugs

LINVILLE.

Wright, E H,   G S

PFAFFTOWN.

Pfaff, J H,   G S

RURAL HALL.

Gunn, A M,   G S
Kiser, E L,   G S and Hotel
Miller J F & Co,   G S

SALEM CHAPEL.

Haizlip, H,   G S

SALEM.

Allen, J F,   Livery
Berrier, L P,   G S
Bodenhamer, J P,   G S
Conrad & Vogler,   Gro
Crews, R S,   G S
Douthit, T B & Co,   G S
Douthit, Mrs T B,   Millinery
Giersch, H A,   G S
Hampton, C S,   Gro
Hopper, H C.   G S
Hudson, W D,   G S
Jones, C A,   G S
Linebach, J A,   Fire Insurance
Morgan, T,   Gro
Nissen, C F & Co,   G S
Parks, Jas,   G S
Pitts & Joyce,   G S
Pope, C T,   G S
Senseman & Brickenstein,   Plumbers
Shaffner, J F,   Drugs
Shore, H W,   Gro
Sink, Andrew,   Livery
Sink & Knome,   G S
Smith, Lee,   Barber
Spaugh, D A,   G S
Spaugh, ——,   Gro, Meats
Twin City Grocery Co,   Gro
Vogler, E L,   G S
Vogler, A C & Son,   Furn, Und't'k'r
Wattlington, F H & Bro,   G S
Winkler Bros,   G S
Yokely, W L,   Sales Stables
Yokely, C L,   Livery

SEWARD.

Doub, J F,   G S

TOBACCOVILLE.

Long, J A,   G S

VIENNA.

Speace Bros, Ferry.

WALKERTON,

Carmichael, I N,   G S
Lewis. J S   G S
Martin & Sievers,   G S

WHITE ROAD.

Marshall, E C,   G S
Mickie, C F,   G S

WINSTON.

Allen, S E,   Hardware
Allen, P E & Co,   G S
Archbell & Mann,   G S
Ashcraft & Owens,   Drugs
Banks, F B,   G S
Bedee, R H,   Music, etc
Beck, C O,   Bicycles and Sundries
Beck, W E,   Plumbing
Bell & McKnight,   Notions
Bennett & Co,   Gro
Bessent. J C,   Fire Ins
Blum. Geo.   Gro
Blum, G W,   G S
Brewer, Samuel,   Barber
Briggs, J E,   Pawnbrokers
Brown, Rogers & Co,   Gro and Hdw
Brown, Frank C,   Gro
Brown, C N,   Jeweler
Brown & McCrary,   Gro
Cash, C B,   Barber
Cater & Allen,   Gro
Coble, E F,   G S
Conrad, J F,   G S
Crater, R J,   G S
Crawford, R B & Co,   Gen Hardware
Crittenbaum, A M,   G S
Crittenbaum, J,   G S
Cronfer Bros & Co,   Who Gro
Cummings, J R,   G S
Davis, E J, Fire Ins and Sec Merchants and Traders' Union
Davis, A O, Auc'r Brown's Warehouse
Day, F N,   Jewelry
Drye, A,   G S
Dinglehoff & Bissinger,   G S
Dull, G L & Co,   Grain and Feed
Efird Bros,   Gro
Eller & Nading,   Fire Ins
Farrar, J H,   General Repairing
Franklin, Hauser & Co,   Gen Ins and Real Estate
Franklin, W L & Co,   G S
Gilmer, Marler & Co,   D G
Gray, Eugene E,   Fire Ins
Griffith, J F,   G S
Grizzard, A P,   G S
Grubbs & Hedgecock,   G S
Hampton, C T,   G S
Ham, Rev W R P,   G S
Hawkins, K H,   G S
Hester, J W,   Gro
Hill, W L,   G S
Hine, G C,   Harness
Hopper, H B,   Gro
Hubard, Mrs A,   G S
Hudson, W J.   Gro

FORSYTH COUNTY.		FORSYTH COUNTY.	
Huntley & Fordham,	G S	Thompson, V A,	Drngs
Jacobs, Joe,	Clothing	Tolliver, Sam,	G S
Joyner, J T,	G S	Vaughn & Co,	Whol Gro
Justice & Browder,	Books	Vogler, W T & Son,	Jeweler
King, D H,	Coal and Ice	Wachovia Loan and Trust Co, General	
Kurfees, J F,	Gro		Insurance
Lambe, P R,	Gro and Hides	Wall & Huske,	Hardware
Lassiter, Mrs M D,	Millinery	Webb, E G, Auc'r Piedmont Warehouse	
Leonard, W H.	Jeweler	White, J A,	G S
Levi, R.	Clothing	Wilson, J T. Auc Star Warehouse	
Lloyd, H,	G S	Williams, W E,	Confectionery
Lloyd, C H,	G S	Wright N Nealy,	Shoes
Lloyd, J S,	G S	Young, John G, Fire Ins and Mdse	
Long, S L (col),	Undertaker	Young, John G, Coal, Provisions	
Marsha, R,	G S		and Grain
Martin, Watt,	Com Merchant	Young, Y W,	G S
Martin, D C,	G S		
Martin & Rose,	G S	**LEAF TOBACCO DEALERS.**	
Martin, J F,	G S		
Masten, Matthias,	Gro	Barber, Thos.	
Matlock, C S, Auc'r Farmers' Ware-		Brown & Carter (Brown's Warehouse).	
	house	Burton, T J.	
Messick, W,	Gro	Clark, R D.	
Messick, A F,	Gro	Coleman Bros.	
Mick, J & Co,	G S	Coles, J E.	
Miller & Penry,	G S	Edmund, E C & Co (Pres of Tobacco	
Miller, J A L,	G S	Board of Trade).	
Miller & Penry,	Gro	Gorrell & Son (Farmer's Warehouse).	
Mills, Miller & Co,	G S	Hill, J H.	
Morse, B C,	Furniture	Jessup, J M.	
Moseley, R D,	Junk Dealer	Jones Bros.	
Moseley, J B & Co,	Coal	King, J D & Co.	
Neale, W H,	Gro	King, J W.	
Neale, L,	Gro	Matlock, C S.	
Newman & King,	Notions	Morgan, J L & Co.	
Noe, E O,	Blacksmith	Norfleet, M W & Co (Piedmont Ware-	
Norman, J J (agt)	Com Merchant	house).	
Nott, Robt,	G S	Riggins, H L.	
Palmer, W A,	Merchant	Schaum, F G.	
Pegram & Reed,	G S	Sheppard, B J & Co.	
Penny, Albert,	G S	Shoaf, C J & Co.	
Pearce, N B,	G S	Spencer, J.	
Pipkin, C C,	G S	Swink, D A.	
Poindexter, H D,	G S	Tise, Webster & Co (Star Warehouse).	
Pollard, Samuel,	G S	Walker, M A & Co.	
Reed, D S.	G S	Walker, G I.	
Roberts, W J, Mgr R G Dun & Co		Williamson, M N.	
Robinson, E,	G S		
Rogers, McDowell & Co,	Clothing	**MILLS.**	
Rose, Kenny,	D G		
Rosenbacher & Bro,	G S	Kinds, Post Offices and Proprietors.	
Saddler, W A,	G S		
Scales, Pess,	G S	Corn and flour, Vienna, A E Conrad.	
Schonler, D D,	G S	Flour and corn, Salem, J E Mickey.	
Scott, J H,	Gro	Flour and corn, Bethania, T J Kapp's	
Seabolt, L W,	G S	heirs.	
Shappira Bros,	G S	Flour and corn, Kernersville, B Beeson.	
Smith, S H (agt),	Drugs	Flour, corn and saw, Salem, A W	
Smoak & McCreary,	Livery	Bevel.	
Stanton, Mrs L K,	Milliner	Flour and corn, Belew Creek, J A	
Standfield, Mrs M,	G S	Robertson.	
Stephenson, A L,	G S	Flour and corn, Kernersville, Kerner	
Styers, J I.	G S	& Co.	
Styron, T P,	Gro	Flour, corn and saw, Joliett, Henry	
Sams, Wm,	Carpenter	Styers.	

FORSYTH COUNTY.	FORSYTH COUNTY.

Flour and corn, Bethania, Kapp & Miller.

Flour and corn, Rural Hall, C W Wall.

Flour and corn, Kernersville, J S Harmon.

Merchant flour and corn, Salem, Dove & Shore.

Roller Mills, Kernersville, Wm Hepler.

Roller Mills, Salem, H E Fries.

Roller Mills, Winston, L E Brewer.

Saw, Salem, G E Nissen & Co.

Saw, Lewisville, Laughenour & Nissen.

Saw, Kernersville, J F & E Kerner.

Saw, Salem, Johnson Vest.

Steam saw, Winston, John Boyer.

Steam Saw. Salem, Fogle Bros.

Wachovia Flouring Mill, Salem, F & H Fries; capacity 75 bbls of flour daily; 3 runners on corn.

PHYSICIANS.

Names and Post Offices.

Ashworth. W C, Kernersville.

Bahnson, H T. Salem.

Blum, J A, Winston (dentist).

Bynum, John, Winston.

Conrad, W J (dentist).

Dalton, D N, Winston.

Davis, A P, Winston.

Davis, S D, Vienna.

Dicks, W P, Walkertown.

Ector, J G, Winston.

Fearington, J P. Winston.

Flint, S S, Rural Hall.

Gray, R F, Winston.

Griffith, J F, Clemonsville.

Hall, H H (col), Winston.

Hamlin, ——, Winston.

Hammock, J C, Walkertown.

Holt, W T. Donnoho.

Hoton, H V, Winston (dentist).

Horton, P E, Winston (dentist).

Hunter, J W, Salem (dentist).

Jones, R H, Winston (dentist).

Jones, J W (col), Winston.

Linville, A Z, Salem.

Lott, H S, Winston.

Montague, S J, Winston,

Morris, J H, Kernersville.

Sapp, B J, Kernersville.

Shaffner, J F, Salem.

Siewers, N G, Salem.

Strickland, E F. Bethania.

Summers, C L, Winston.

Thomas, H J, Winston.

Watkins, C J, Winston (dentist).

Williams, J D, Lewisville.

SCHOOLS.

Names, Post Offices and Principals.

Academy, Rural Hall, S G Sutton and E A Thomas.

Conference School, Kernersville, H L Coble.

Davis Military School. Winston, Col J Davis, supt; Lieut W E Shipp, U S Army, Instructor in Military Science and Tactics.

Graded School, Salem, F D L Messer, principal.

Graded Schools, Winston, J J Blair, supt.

Graded School (col), Winston, G H Willis.

Primary School, Salem, Miss S A Vogler.

Primary, Winston, Mrs W W Albea.

Private School, Salem, Miss Jane Welfare.

Private School, Bethania, A J Butner.

Private School, Winston, Miss A Spiller.

Salem District School, Salem, F D L Messer, principal.

Salem Female Academy, Salem, Rev J H Clewell.

Salem Male Academy, Salem, Prof J F Brower.

The Slater Industrial Academy and State Normal School, Winston; S G Atkins, pres; six assistants.

Public schools—white, 69; colored, 20.

TEACHERS.

Names and Post Offices.

WHITE.

Blackburn, W E, Lewisville.

Brinkley, D A, Lewisville.

Butner, Miss Effie, Salem.

Carmichael, V, Walkertown.

Clinard, A W. Salem.

Conrad, R C, Craters.

Conrad, L I, Craters.

Cook, Frank, Clemonsville.

Crawford, Lizzie, Winston.

Crews, G W, Kernersville.

Doub, Ola, Vienna.

Dull, G V, Lewisville.

Endsley, Maggie, Winston.

Gordan, W E. Tobaccoville.

Gorder, Ida, Tobaccoville.

Grubbs, J F, Sedge Garden.

Grubbs, J L, Sedge Garden.

Hege, S A, Salem.

Holder, J A, Kernersville.

Holder, L C, Seward.

Holder, H B, Tobaccoville.

Holt, Julia P, Donnaho.

Huff, Laura, East Bend.

Idol, G H, Kernersville.

Johnson, Chapman, Abbott's Creek.

Johnson. C L, Bower.

Kreger, W N, Rural Hall.

Leak, Della, Kernersville.

Linville, R F, Goodwill.

Linville, C L, Goodwill.

Longueortt, Ed, Salem.

FORSYTH COUNTY.

Long, W O, Dosier.
Long, A F, Carlisle.
Long, W O, Dosier.
Lowry, Annie E, Kernersville.
Medearis, Lula, Goodwill.
McCuiston, Annie L, Salem.
McKaughn, M C, Salem.
McKaughn, L C, Salem.
Messer, F D L, Salem.
Mickey, Annie, Salem.
Mock, Mabel, Clemonsville.
Moir, Bettie, Walkertown.
Morris, Elmira G, Walkertown.
Moser, J H, Lewisville.
Motsinger, J M, Salem.
Murray, J W, Sedge Garden.
Nelson, J L, Carlisle.
Nelson, W L, Carlisle.
Newsom, W L, Rural Hall.
Pfaff, Lou, Pfafftown.
Pinnix, J W, Kernersville.
Poindexter, Bessie, Germanton.
Poindexter, J T, Donnaho.
Raper, Lula L, Salem.
Richardson, Mattie, Winston.
Ring, R W, Kernersville.
Rothrock, C W, Midway.
Sapp, H O, Salem.
Sheets, Nora, Winston.
Sheets, Mamie, Winston.
Sides, E D, Salem.
Smith, N H, Kernersville.
Spaugh, Ada, Salem.
Spease, W A, Rural Hall.
Spease, W C, Vienna.
Sprinkle, C P, Vienna.
Sprinkle, J A, Donnaho.
Thomas, E A, Rural Hall.
Tise, J M, Winston.
Trexler, H A, Rural Hall.
Wadkins, E R, Clemonsville.
Waggoner, W R, Lewisville.
Walker, I N, Winston.
Warren, J W.
Watkins, Annie.
Whicker, J N, Winston.
Whicker, P E, Salem.
Woosley, J T, Freidburg.
Yarborough, Loy, Bethania.

COLORED.

Adams, S A, Winston.
Bingham, S T, Winston.
Boger, C W, Salem.
Boger, G W, Lewisville.
Brown, A J, Winston.
Byers, J H, Winston.
Dalton, Wm, Winston.
Davis, J W, Kernersville.
Eldridge, Wm, Sedge Garden.
Glenn, J D, Lewisville.
Grady, W B, Winston.
Graham, J E, Winston.
Hairston, Mary.
Harris, Wade C, Winston.

FORSYTH COUNTY.

Harris, William, Winston.
Haskins, Eliza E, Winston.
Headen, C W, Kernersville.
Howard, Kerr, Winston.
Johnson, Cornelia, Kernersville.
Kimbrough, J E, Winston.
Lash, J Z, Bethania.
Lash, J L, Bethania.
Matthews, W E, Winston.
Miller, Alex, Bethania.
Mitchell, Addie L.
Murrell, C R, Bethania.
Penn, G W, Winston.
Taylor, R B, Winston.
Walker, A L, Oak Summit.
Wright, W A, Winston.

LOCAL CORPORATIONS.

Ancient Order of United Workmen, Winston, A B Gorrell, M W; W E Franklin, secretary.
Central Land Co, Winston.
Chamber of Commerce, Winston; J L Patterson, pres; W B Pollard, first vice-pres; J B Vaughn, second vice-pres; W A Blair, secretary and treasurer.
Congregation of United Brethren (Moravian), of Salem, N C, and its vicinity; managed by a board of six trustees, viz: Dr J W Hunter, pres; H A Giersch, J W Fries, Dr N S Siewers, C H Fogle, W A Lemly, J T Lineback, secretary and treasurer, in charge of property belonging to Salem Moravian Congregation.
Damon Lodge, No 41, K of P, Winston; O B Eaton, Lib.
First National Bank, Winston; P W Crutchfield, as't cash'r; surplus and undivided profits $15,000; capital $100,000.
Forsyth Canning and M'f'g Co, Salem; H E Fries, pres; G F Jenkins, secretary and treasurer; capital $10,000.
Forsyth Riflemen, Co A, 3d Reg N C S G; J C Bessent, captain.
Forsyth County Abstract Co, Winston; J L Patterson, pres; A T Hanes, secretary and treasurer.
Inside Land Co, Winston; Dr J F Shaffner, pres; W A Blair, secretary and treasurer.
Knights of Honor, No 1673; T B Douthit, dictator.
Knights of Pythias, Bethania.
Lodge, No 56, K of P, Salem.
Loyal Legion, Susie Williams, supt; O Williams, pres; Kate Hanes, sec.
Men's League, Salem, Rev A D Thaeler, president; C W Thaeler, secretary.
Merchants and Traders' Union, Winston-Salem; J M Rogers, pres; Dr V

FORSYTH COUNTY.

O Thompson, first vice-pres; E J Davis, secretary and Treasurer.

Museum in connection with the Young Men's Missionary Society of Salem.

National Building, Loan and Protective Association; Col A B Gorrell, pres; B B Owens, sec: P W Crutchfield, treas.

Norfolk & Western R R; principal office in Roanoke. Va; completed from Winston to Roanoke, Va; 110 miles; C H Fogle, treas.

North Winston Development Co.

Order of Chosen Friends; E E Gray, treas.

Piedmont Commandery, No 6, Knights Templar; Samuel H Smith, E C; W B Pollard, treas.

Salem Water Supply Co, Salem; F H Fries. pres; H F Shaffner, sec and treas; resevoir capacity 2,000,000 gallons.

Salem Orchestra, Salem; Prof W J Peterson, musical director.

Salem Lodge, No 36, I O O F, Winston; E Spaugh, N G; day of meeting, Monday.

Salem Lodge, No 289, A F and A M; E A Eberr, W M; time of meeting, first Thursday evening in each month and evenings of June 24th and December 27th.

Salem Home, Salem; Mrs H T Bahnson, pres; Mrs J F Shaffner, treas.

Salem Cemetery Company, John W Fries. pres.

Salem Band, Salem, S T Mickey, director.

Salem Literary Society, Salem, C W Thaeler, pres; W A Gasten, sec.

Salem Lodge, No 56, K of P.

Southside Land and Investment Co, Winston, A H Eller, pres; W A Blair, sec and treas.

The Peoples' Nat Bank of Winston, N C, J W Fries, pres; W A Blair, vice-pres; T A Wilson, cash; capital stock, $100.000; surplus, $15,000.

Tobacco Board of Trade, Winston, F A Coleman, sec: W B Pollard, treas.

Twin City Club, R L Crawford, pres; W A Blair. sec and treas.

Twin City Hospital, Mrs J A Bitting. pres; Mrs E E Shelton, treas; Miss M E Spach, matron.

Twin City Investment Co, Winston, J A Gray, pres; W A Blair, treas.

Union Grove Temperance Reform Club, J W Kennedy, pres; Jas Johnson, sec.

Wachovia National Bank, Winston, W A Lemly, pres; J A Gray, cash; capital, $150,000; surplus and profits, $150,000.

FORSYTH COUNTY.

Wachovia Land Office or Board of Provincial Elders of the Southern Province of the Moravian church or United Brethren, managed by a board of six members, viz: E Rondthaler, D D, Rev J H Clewell, Dr N S Siewers, Rev J E Hall, J H Kapp, Jas T Lineback, sec and treas, in charge of land and property belonging to the Moravian church in North Carolina.

Wachovia Loan and Trust Co, Winston, F H Fries, pres; J A Gray, vice-pres; H F Shaffner, sec and treas; authoriz d capital, $1,000,000.

W C T U, Winston branch, Mrs Phebe J Ector, pres.

West End Hotel and Land Co, J C Buxton, pres; T L Vaughn, sec and treas.

Winst n Electric Light and Motive Power Co, F W McClement, supt.

Winston Lodge A F & A M, No 167, Wi ston; N S Wilson, W M. Time of meeting, second Monday evening of each month.

Winston Royal Arch Chapter, No 24, Winston; D P Mast, H P.

Winston Lodge, K of P.

Winston Development Co, Winston, J A Gray, pres; E J Davis, sec.

Winston and Salem Building and Loan Association, J C Buxton, pres; H E Fries, vice-pres; G A Failin, sec and treas; capital. $200,000.

Y W C T U, Winston, Mrs Minnie Efird, pres; Susie E W Williams. rec sec.

Y M C A, Winston Salem, A W Hicks, sec; W T Spaugh, vice-pres.

NEWSPAPERS.

Business Guide, Winston; M I Stewart, ed.

Farmers' and Planters' Almanac, Salem, 68th year; Blum's Almanac Co, eds and props.

News (Dem. weekly), Kernersville; W C Stafford & H L Coble, eds and props.

North State Endeavorer, Salem, Rev A D Thaeler, ed.

Piedmont Presbyterian, Winston; Rev R E Caldwell, ed.

Silver Advocate, Kernersville; Anderson & Anderson, eds.

Southern Tobacco Journal, Winston; H E Harman, ed.

The Academy (monthly), Salem; Rev J H Clewell, ed.

The Schoolteacher (monthly), Winston.

Union Republican (Rep weekly), Winston; J W Goslen, ed; pub by Union Republican Pub Co.

18

Wachovia Moravian, Salem; Right Rev E Rondthaler, D D, ed.

Western Sentinel (dem weekly and daily). Winston; W F Burbank and J B Whitaker, eds and props.

FARMERS.

Names and Post Offices.

Alspaugh.—W A Alspaugh, R L Alspaugh, J Henderson Cox, W W Kapp, Florina Reich, Jas Reich, Isaac Reich, W W Reich, L M Reich, H A Styers, Samuel Styers.

Belew's Creek.—Boot Cook (col), C Flynn, T A Flynn, J W Freeman, T D Fulp, J S Gude, Patrick Hairston, J S King, M D King, J F Landreth, E B Linville, Joe Nelson, C W Neal, P H Neal, J E Preston, T J Preston, T W Pierce, J A Robertson, J R Self.

Bethania.—V I Berk, J H Chadwick, Jas Conrad, R B Flynt, Wm Grabbs, A A Grabbs, D B Jones, L G Jones, J H Kapp, E T Kapp, T H Lash, W E Lehman, E I Lehman, Edgar Lineback, J I Lineback, Peter Marshall, G J Moore, H T Moser, J F Norman, Mrs Ella Ogburn, G W Parker, J J Petree, F M Pratt, H A Peddycord, F N Pfaff, Paul Raymans, Jessie Shouse, Jesse Spears, W A Stoltz, G M Stoltz, W E Stauber, W A Strupe, E T Strupe, Jno Tise, Eugene Tise, I J Thacker, Albert Transou, R E Transou, Ransom Walker, Ed Wear, R L Yarborough.

Bower.—Junius Blackburn, A S Clinard, Jacob Cornish, Lewis Cornish, Andrew Davis, W H Davis, J A Douthit, John W Ellis, Lewis Ellis, E M Fishel, I W Idol, Bryan Jarvis, Chas E Johnson, H E Long, Enoch Mullican, Eb W Mullican, N C Nelson, Uriah Nelson, Ruffin Phelps, Uriah Phelps, Alvin Phelps, Edmund Sink, James Sink, John Watkins, H A Watkins, Wm Weaver, —— Wommack.

Clemmonsville.—Albert Blackburn, Milton Blackburn, Henry Bower, J W Bower, Albert Bratton, Jas E Craver, Thos Craver, Frank Cook, Alex Cook, James Cook, Benjamin Doty, Wm Doty, James Eccles (col), T C Ferabee, Anderson Franks, T W Griffith, Francis Hanes, Wesley Jones, Frank Jones, Y S Lawrence, J W Miller, W B Miller, Levi Sides, Frank Strupe, E C Strupe, Frank Swain, T D Welfare, Reuben Welfare, A C Wharton.

Crater—Jas A Alspaugh, W E Alspaugh, S W Alspaugh, Sarah Alspaugh, A W Bevel, J E Britner, L T Conrad,

G D Conrad, R J Crater, Geo Flynt, W E Griffith, J E Johnson, T F Jones, F M Jones, Lew Ketner, J A Nifong, C E C Reich, W J Satterfield, Frank Sailer, J E Shutt, S A Shutt, D A Shore, T D Speas, L F Thomas, W J Transon, H C Transon, J P Transon, N W Vest, A C Vogler, Frank Woosley.

Daisy—J B Bodenhamer, C F Day, John F Day, C L Day, T S Davis, Joseph Davis, Thos Fisher, W T Flynt, W P Hampton, John F Hampton, George W Hammock, E V Hester, J H Hester, Robert H Linville, Willis Marshall, James W Marshall, T J Pettis, Sidney Pendry, J P Sell, E M Sell, John M Vanhoy, T C Walker, R B Walker, P M Westmoreland, J W Westmoreland, T T Westmoreland, R Z Winckler, R T Winckler, Richard Zeglar (col).

Donnaho—Wm A Butner, G L Butner, Thos Flynn, J C Fleming, Isaac Hauser, W B Hauser, R L Hendrix, L A Hendrix, S L Hendrix, A H Long, R N Rayner, A C Reid, J W Shamel, J H Shamel, W N Shamel, J A Scales, A D Scott, J H Scott, S W Scoott, J W Scoott, T E Spease, J W Spease, C A Sprinkle, J B Sprinkle, H T Waller, S J Waller.

Dosier—E Doub, A E Hunter, J H Hunter, T M Hunter, A R Hunter, J W Long, E M Long, M C Long, W H Long, J M Long, J P Sprinkle, C O Sprinkle, J H Sprinkle, P A Sprinkle, J C Vogler, E C Vogler. L V Vogler, W W Vogler, J W Whitman, J A Whitman.

Goodwill—Chas Barrow, R S Brown, J G Fulton, John Hester, Emanuel Linville, E W M D Linville, R S Linville, W W Linville, Jef Lowe (col), J A Lowrey, W M Meaders, M D Meaders, E H Pegram, E J Warren.

Hulon—W A Ererage, J E Faw, Lewis Fishel, E S Fishel, Theo Kimel, J C Patterson, C P Patterson, C W Patterson, A H Patterson, C A Padgett, Wm Reich, J H Reich, J F Reich, Louis Spaugh, A E Spaugh, Jas L Spaugh.

Jolliet—W W Clayton, E L Crowser, T R Hunter, J C Hunter, J M Hunter, C B Hutchins, Frank James, S A James, E F Kiger, B R Kiser, R L Lawrence, W L Lawrence, John Lawrence, J H Miller, W H Spease, J H Sprinkler, Wm Sprinkler, W H Shouse, Aurelius Shouse, C B Zeiglar.

Kernersville—M Ballard, H S Barrow, T R Barrow, Jno A Baker, R T Blackburn, Hugh Beeson, J H Beeson, J W Bend, W W Bowman, Wm Brown, L T Carmichael, W R Clinard,

T B Campbell. J W A Cook, T A Crews, Joseph Crews, J T Crews, J M Crews, E W Crews, Yancy Crews, M C Dean, B Y Duggins, Samuel E Duggins, D B Duggins, R L Dwiggins, N A Dwiggins. H C Edwards, Jno Eagleson, B G Elliott, W W Frazier, J H Frazier, L W Fulton. Moses Fulp, W W Fulp, J A Fulp, H C Hedgecock, Alfred Hedgecock, W H Hester, D R Hester, J Hester, J W Harrold, J W Hasken, P S Hasken, J C Holder, H H Holder, Jno A Holder, W R Hopkins, J Hunter, G H Idol, J B Idol, A J Idol, T W Ingram, J R Jones, R P Kerner, J G Kerner, Israel Kerner, G F Kerner, D P Kerner, D C Kerner, A Lewis, W S Linville, Jas Linville, Moses Linville. W J Little, Jno Macy, W H Marshall, M M Mastin, O G Mastin, D L Mastin, W H Manuel, D C Mathews, L P Mathews, J B McGee, I H McCown, J H Meecum, W T Morris, F H Morris, R H Morris, J L Motsinger, Joseph Nelson, E W Nelson, R S Nelson. T H Nelson, V W Perry, H B Perry, O L Pegg, B F Pegram, J W Phinnix, J P Pitts, J Q Pitts, Wm M Phillips (col), J L Phipps, J M Ragland, S G Ring, Robt W Ring, W T Robinson, J C Robst. J P Robbins, D E Robbins, R F Roberson, E J Sapp. C M Sapp, H W Sapp, S E Stafford, A H Stafford, D R Stafford, J H S afford, R A Stafford, M D Stafford. C M Stafford, F M Stafford. W C Stafford, C F Stoellron, H D Shirlas, David Shirlas, J I Smith, Dan Smith, D Smith, I Smith, Jno E Snider. E T Snider, Jno Stockton. Newell Soff, N H Smith. M V Smith, J W Smith, John A Secrest, A Stanley, W W Stewart, J T Stigall, E B Teague. J M Teague, J H W Tucker, W C Vanhoy, W M Vance, J S Vance, D M Vance, Charles Warren, R R West, Alo Williard, J M Williard, Sam Whitt. W J Willis, G W Wilson, Tnos B Wilson, J N Whicker, G W Whicker, W F Winfrey.

Lewisville—A L Blackburn, W S Black, J W Brinkley, D A Brinkley, D C Brinkley, J Brinkley. Burton Brinkley, M Brinkley, C W Brinkley, W F Brandon, C M Brown, A N Brown, W Clingman (col.), F W Cooper (col.), E A Conrad, J S Conrad, Jr, J T Craft, Rev A W Craft, S W Craft, J W Craft, P L Doub, C B Doub, Geo E Dull, G H Dull, Geo P Dull, E C Dull, S Dull, W H Finch, J A Freeman, V L Franklin, W E Griffith, Robt Griffith, J W Harper, C E Harper, L M Harper, W A Harper, George W Harper, I O Hart, W G Hauser, P A Hauser, Jr, Alex Hege, Edin Hege, F M Hire, J E Hold

er, J E Jarvis. A W Jones, P F Jones, T J Ketner, Wm M Ketner, J J Kiger, A W Laurence, J J Marshall, F A Miller, F W Miller, George F Mock, P T Mock, P W Moser, H P Moser, John A Moser, J R Moser, L F Phillips, D W Reynolds, E P Rights, W H Sheets, Lewis Sheets, J B Spaugh, L P Spaugh, P D Spears, J A Tise, David Todd, W F Vogler, L M Vogler, J B Warner, M V Warner, W R Wagoner, W H Watkins, E H Wright, J Wharton. J L Whitman, P N Whitman, N E Whitman.

Old Richmond—S T Kiger, C T Spainhour, W W Spainhour.

Oak Summit—W H Cox, T E Grubbs, H H Grubbs, Jas W Marshall.

Pfafftown—A S Conrad, J B Conrad, J P Conrad, A E Conrad, J W Conrad, R S Fulk. Aug Fulk, John H Kerney, Henry T Long, E P Pfaff, A E Pfaff, J H Shouse, P H Stimpson, A E Transou. J A Transou, V A Wilson.

Rural Hall—Ira Alderman, J N Anderson, E G Anderson, B L Bitting, Z B Bitting. J E Banner. R A Bodenhamer, W L Bowles, J W Bostic, A M Burk, M C Clayton, J F Fulk, Cnarles Griffin, J R Griffin, John Grubbs, F N Hartgrove, H S Helsabeck, C H Kapp, J W Kapp, E D Kiger, H W Kiger, Adam Kiger, O A Kiger, Tandy Kiser, W A Kreeger, H T Laggins. T L Magee, J T Miller, S A Miller, J T Moore, A L Nussum, James W Nussum, A L Payne, A N Spease, E E Spease, E H Spease, T S Spease, W A Spease, J L Spease, E F Shore, E H Shore, E D Shore, E D Styers, S E Styers, J H C Stoltz, C C Stoltz. Walter Stoltz, E A Shouse, J Mc Tuttle, A L Tuttle, F A Tuttle, C T Wall, O T Westmoreland, J C Zimmerman.

Ruth—J B Merritt, A L Parill, N F Sullivan.

Salem—C R Adkins, H T Bahnson, H L B ckerdite, C M Beckler, R T Beeson, I P Bodenhamer, Alex Brewer, Albert Brindle, Jesse Brown, Jno Burk, W T Butler (col), E B Cassell, J H Chamelin, sr, J H Chamelin, jr, Lewis Chamelin, V L Charles, G L D Charles, J P Charles, J H Clinard, C M Clutts, Harrison Crouse, Jno Ebert, Geo Ebert, Henry Enocks. A M Enocks. Elias Evans, C Faw, W S Fishel, Zac Fishel, Jacob Fishel, Thos Fishel, S J Fishel, Fogler Bros, Jno D Foltz, W H Glascoe, A O Griffin, R A Harrell, F C Hastin, Amos Hattle, A H Hedgecock, Samuel Hege, Jno H Hege, S A Hege, E J Hine, J N Hine, Noah Hine, H F Hine Eli E Hine, R A Jenkins, G W John'

BRANSON'S NORTH CAROLINA

FORSYTH COUNTY.

FORSYTH COUNTY.

son. Ben Johnson. J L Johnson, Henry Johnson, J P Jones, L C Kimel, Erastus, Kimel, Geo Kimel, P E Leight, B X Linville, E C B Linville, J S Long, Reuben Longworth, Reuben Lorg. C Martin, J R Masten. J W McCoin, J F Mendenhall, L L Mendenhall. C A Mendenhall. J F Mendenhall. L B Mendenhall, G A Miller, T D L Missen, G Missen, C F, Missen. V Motsinger, J R Myers, Wm Myers. W J Myers, J H Nading, G A Nading. W E Nading. W R Petree, W F Pitts, A J Pitts, N Pope, G L Pope, G C Pope, C T Pope, L M Reed, C C Reed, G L Reed, Phillip R R ed, A L Reed, Jas A Reed, Samuel Reed, Jno G Reed, David Reed, C A Reynolds, Geo D Reynolds (col), Henry Reynolds (col), Wm Rol insen. W H Rollins, W R Rominger, E A Rominger, F M Rothrock, Jacob Sells, Emcry Shields, David Shoaf. J F Shaffner. J J Shore. F J Shore, E B Shore, N W Shore, Eli Sides, E D Sides, Ranson Sink, Samuel Sink. L Sink. J R F Sink. Phelix Sink, L V Smith, Andrew Smith, L L Smith, J C Smith. W R Snider, Wm Snider. L S Snider, J C Spach. C A Spach, E J Spach, D A Spaugh, C S Spaugh, F Spaugh, W B Stafford. John L Stewart, W M Stewart, M M Stewart, Thos W Stewart, J H Stockton, Wm Z Swain, Andrew Swain, Edward Swain, Chas Swain, Levi Swain, Erastus Swain. W L Swain, S W Swain, J H Teague, J O Teague, L H Teague, C F Thomas, Jos A Thomas, T J Thornton, J F Tucker, J A Tucker, W A Weavil, H H Weavil, Eli Weavil. L J Weavil. L F Weavil, C E Welbon, Geo H Williard, L O Williard, Jos Williard. C H Williard, David Williard. G Williard, J H Williard, Jno W Williard, J J Williard. J D Wilson, L H Wilson, Lewis Wilson, A H Yokely. W T Yokely, Jackson Yokely (col). J H Zeverly, David Z mmerman.

Salem Chapel—J F Andrews, E P Bowman. J R T Coffey, J F Coffey, M D Coffey. J S Crews, Reuben Crews, T P Dalton. J D Dalton, S M Davis. J C Grubbs, Jesse F Grubbs, T H Grubbs. H Hazelip, D M Johnson, J H Marsl all, T M Marshall, E N Marshall, J W Marshall, King Massey. S H Morris, G W Reed. Edmund Reed, Henry Reed, Wm Reed, H F Samuels, J D Sharp. T M Tuttle, J D Waddell, J E Young, J D Young.

Sedge Garden— C F Davis, L R Davis. Alex Davis, Robr Eldridge (col), M R Fulp, R W Grubbs, J F Grubbs, W H Grubbs, J C Grubbs, J E Grubbs, J W Grubbs, P A James Sandy Marshall. W J Marshall. T N Marshall, L C Mer-

ritt, F M Morris, J W Southern, J H Vanhoy, Sam Waggoner. D G Walker, J L Walker, L B Walker.

Seward—J S Anderson, J D Anderson, J W Bowen, Edward Cline, O W F Doub. J C Doub, S G Doub, J M Doub, W C Holden. P F Holden, W A Hunter, A T Kreeger, G A Leinback, L W Leinback, W J Masencup, Thos Moser, James Reed. A E Shore, Benj Sprinkle, J F Spainhower, J B Tate. J W Wall. J O Wall, J R Waldravin, J E Warner.

Tobaccoville— W A Briggs, E Cape, W W Doub, E L Gordwin, W W Gourcey. J M Gorder, Dr R A Hauser, H B Holden. J W Hunter, D O Hunter, W Johnson, J H Johnson, J M Kapp, J J Kruger, W L Love, J H Long, sr. H H Long, E A Moser. Martin Moser, Amos Moser, Alf Moore, G W Newsom, C R Orender, W H Pedre, C A Spainhower, W N Vest. J B Vest, Jesse Wall, J A Wolff.

Vienna—J A Alspaugh, J A Apper son, J W Atwood, G F Reck. J W Beck, W D Clodfelter, Sandford Clodfelter, Philip Clodfelter, S D Davis, Alex Davis (col), J W Doub, I A H Doub, E M C Doub, W B Doub, I C Doub, J Farrington, W M Franklin, J L Franklin, W H Goslen, H J Hauser, E W Hauser, George Hauser, R C Leinback, D S Lehman, J H Mock, J C Mock, J S Shore. J A Sink, J W Sink. E W Sink, J S Spease, J W Spease, Wm Sprinkle, W G Windingt n. Jno Yates, F L Zeigler, G S Zeigler.

Walkertown—J A Besson, W P Dix, Smith Frazier, Robert Gourley, T B Hanimock, Jordan Huff, C C Huff. J W Jones. W T Jones, C W Jones, R L Joyner, P V Lewis. H A Lewis, J M Lewis, E W Linville, J C Magee, W H Martin, J C Martin, S T Marshall. A M Meecum, M B Meecum. John A Mitchell (col). J S Moir, R J Morris, M H Morris, H A Morris, J L Morris, Ralph Parish, J H Parnell. J T Smith, N D Sullivan. N W Swain. W H Swain. D F Vanhoy, Alex Vanhoy, R V Waggoner. J M Wood.

White Road.—R N Adams. A H Adams, M N Adams, J K P Carter, W B E Crutchfield, J H Fair, J W Flyn, J A Fulp, J W Fulp, J W Fulton, H C Fulton, F Fulton, D S Ham. J M Ham, W M Lancaster, E W Leshly, R A Linville, G deon Magee, J L Martin, J T Martin, G A Pegram. Lewis Starbuck, J F P Thomas, A G Vass, N D Vance.

Winston.—J W Alspaugh, F P Alspaugh, W E Axson, Franklin Ball, John Brewer, John Boyer, Timothy

FORSYTH COUNTY.

Booze, J F Bumgardner, W L Brown, T J Brown, Brown Bros, David Brown, S A Burke. E W Burke. Branson Beeson, John Beeson, W A Beeson, R F Byerley, W A Byerley, J C Conrad, L K Chamberlain, E F Coble, Ham Cornish, R L Cox, E B Crawford, J T Craft, J A Crews, J P Crews, C E Crews, G P Crews. Calvin Crews, Allen Crews, M H Dawson, A J Dilworth, Wm Ebert, David Endoley, J F Frazier, Rufus Galoway (col), Andrew Gillam, Granville Glenn (col), Major Green (col), M H Goines (col), A R Griffith, J L Grubbs. Benj Hampton, Jacob Hart, R W Hedgecock. Edward T Henning, Elijah Hester, F T Hine, J

J Hine, L C Hine. T F Hine, L T Hine, W M Hinshaw, C Hamlin, C H Hauner, S A Hauser. N P Holloman, N A Holloman, J R Idon, J M Garrick H W Johnson, Albert Lashmett, John W Lashmet, W W Livengood, C W Masten, Junius Miller, A B Mock, Abram Myers, Henry J Myers, W L Myers, M L Ogburn, L A Ogburn. Jas W Ogburn. C L Peddicord, R J Reynolds. J F Robinson, C H Robinson, F E Sharnel, D D Shelton, L E Sides, Ivison Smith, L A Snider, J C Stutt, R L Tally, J O Tesh, E A Thomas. Dr V O Thompson, Jacob Tise, A G Whick, R L Whitfield, Emory White.

M. H. PINNIX,

Attorney and Counsellor at Law and Solicitor in Bankruptcy,

LEXINGTON, N. C.

Practices in the Courts of Davidson, Randolph, Forsyth and Guilford Counties

Prompt attention given to the collection of claims in all

parts of the State.

H. L. STEVENS,
Warsaw, N.C.

L. A. BEASLEY,
Kenansville, N. C.

STEVENS & BEASLEY,

Attorneys and Counsellors at Law.

PRACTICE IN ALL THE COURTS.

Claims Investigated.   COLLECTIONS PROMPTLY MADE.

FRANKLIN COUNTY.

AREA 420 SQUARE MILES.

POPULATION 21,072 ; White 10,737, Colored 10,335.

FRANKLIN COUNTY was formed in 1779, from what was, prior to that time, Bute county. In that year the General Assembly obliterated the name of Bute and formed from it territory which now constitutes Franklin and Warren counties. Franklin was named in honor of the philosopher and sage, Benjamin Franklin, who rendered his country important services in a civil capacity during the Revolution.

LOUISBURG, the county seat, is situated on Tar river, 35 miles northeast from Raleigh, and has a population of 1,200.

It was a common saying of this part of the State, during the Revolution, "There are no Tories in Bute."

Surface—Franklin county is situated on Tar river and tributaries; is moderately undulating, well watered and soil generally good. It is nearly on the dividing line between the cotton and tobacco sections; is a pleasant country and has a thrifty population.

Staples—Both cotton and tobacco are produced successfully, and may be called the leading staples. Corn, wheat, oats, clover, grasses, and sweet potatoes are profitable crops.

Fruits—Apples, peaches, pears and the small fruits, melons, etc.

Timbers—Oak, hickory, pine, gum, beech, walnut, etc.

TOWNS AND POST OFFICES.

	POP.
Cedar Rock, John Coppidge, p m,	—
Centreville, P G Alston.	35
Franklinton, E W Morris, p m,	700
Ingleside, Chas Macon,	50
Justice, Lawrence Bowden,	50
Katesville, Robt Jones,	25
Laurel, E C Jones.	50
Letha, Thos Whitaker,	25
Louisburg, J J Barrow,	1,200
Mapleville, Jno H Uzzle,	20
Mitchener, John Mitchener,	50
Moulton, Jno G Meyrick.	50
Oswego, Wesley Burnett,	60
Pilot, ——	15
Pocomoke, Andrew Hasnell.	50
Privett, ——	56
Pugh's, Mrs Ben Wilson,	10
Ransom's Bridge, Col Sturges,	25
Riley's Cross Roads, W H Perry,	20
Royal, Julius Clifton.	—
Stallings, Haywood Stallings,	—
Sutton, Sid Williams.	—
Youngsville, Dr J G Riddick,	325

COUNTY OFFICERS.

Clerk Superior Court—R R Harris.
Commissioners—T S Collie, ch'mn; Jno H Uzzle. Jno C Winston, J A Burt, John R Alford.
Coroner—W S Pruitt.
Register of Deeds—W K Martin.
Sheriff—H C Kearney.
Solicitor 3d District—Claude M Bernard, Greenville, N C.
Surveyor—John Moore.
Standard Keeper—L T Horton.
Treasurer—B F Wilder.
County Examiner—J N Harris.
County Attorney—C F Cook.
Chairman Board of Education—N Y Gulley.

COURTS.

Sixth Monday before the first Monday in March, and seventh Monday after the first Monday in September.

TOWN OFFICERS.

LOUISBURG — *Mayor*, W M Person. *Commissioners*. G H Cooper, ch'mn; R G Hart, R Y Yarboro, W H Macon. *Clerk*. Geo S Baker. *Treasurer*, W H Macon. *Attorney*. F S Spruell. *Chief of Police*. D C High. *Tax Collector*, J R High.

FRANKLINTON—*Mayor*, N Y Gulley. *Commissioners*. R W Heck, H A Bobbitt. A B Hester, W H Hester, H A Mitchell.

TOWNSHIPS AND MAGISTRATES.

Cedar Rock—Thos Gill, J J May, Jno W Webster, W T Davis. J T Justice. W T Dean, G B H Stallings, Jno Sykes, S H Moses. J S Ross (Cedar Rock).

Dunn—L S Ballentine, Ransom Dodd, Jonas Pearce. W K Phillips. J M Brantly. A C Privett, Burwell Baker, J J Williams, W R Yancey (Sutton).

Franklinton—J J Wilder, C D Butt, T B Harrington, J J May, R T Edwards, J J Muse, J R Mitchener, W H Byrum, J H Cook, E W Morris, W H Mitchell (Franklinton).

FRANKLIN COUNTY.

Freeman's—W S Strickland, J T Harris, Wm Freeman, J R Harrington, Thos J King, J C Winston, F P Pearce, J S King, B Hobgood, J R Johnson (Youngsville).

Gold Mine—Henry Gripton, J M May, James Upchurch, J B Denton, Peter Collins, J T Neal, W J Jenkins (Centerville).

Harris'—R C Penry, Chas Richardson, Jno W Yancy, N B Young, A J P Harris, M W Peroy (Sutton).

Hayesville—T H Whitaker, J E T Aysene (Letha).

Louisburg—D C Harrington, W T Wilder, A H Baker, J H Benton, M E Joyner, L S Salford (Mapleville), E N Dent, J H Mitchell, G L Aycock, G S Baker, B T Wilder, W N Fuller, O L Ellis, M S Davis, Jno W Pittman, R H Strickland (Louisburg).

Sandy Creek—S J Mann, R S Foster, C G Steven, Andrew Green, J R Debnam (Ingleside), Thos D Farrer, W C Bobbitt, R B Carr, E C Jones, E M Gupton, O P Gupton (Laurel).

CHURCHES.

Names, Post Offices, Pastors and Denom.

METHODIST.

Chapel Springs-Louisburg. J T Draper.
Church—Louisburg, — Shepherd (col)
Church—Louisburg, G F Smith.
Church—Franklinton, W S Davis.
Church—Youngville, J T Draper.
Cook's Chapel—Louisburg. J T Draper.
Ebenezer—Franklinton, W S Davis.
Leah Chapel—Louisburg, J T Draper.
Plank Chapel—Franklinton, WSDavis.
Prospect—Louisburg, J T Draper.
Trinity—Franklinton, W S Davis.
Wesley—Franklinton, W S Davis.

BAPTIST.

Church—Louisburg, R G Walden (col).
Church—Louisburg, H B Disanay(col).
Church—Franklinton. Joseph Harrell.
Church—Youngville, Wm Royal.
Church (col)—Franklinton.
Church—Louisburg, W B Morton.

PRESBYTERIAN.

Church—Louisburg, E Thacker.
Church—Louisburg, J F Jordan (col).
Church—Franklinton.

EPISCOPAL.

St Paul's—Louisburg, J B Avent.

CHRISTIAN.

Church—Franklinton.

FRANKLIN COUNTY.

MINISTERS RESIDENT.

Names, Post Offices and Denominations.

METHODIST.

Bobbitt, E A, Cedar Rock.
Davis, W S, Franklinton.
Draper, J T, Youngville.
Hester, W H, Kittrell.
Smith, G F, Louisburg.

BAPTIST.

Morton, W P, Louisburg.
Walden, R I, Louisburg.

EPISCOPAL.

Averitt, B, Louisburg.
Delanay, H B (col.), Louisburg.

PRESBYTERIAN.

Thacker, E, Louisburg.
Jordan, J F (col.), Louisburg.

CHRISTIAN.

Klapp, P T, Youngville.

HOTELS AND BOARDING HOUSES.

Names, Post Offices and Proprietors.

Boarding House, Louisburg, J W Williams.
Board'g House, Louisburg, Miss Mary Harris.
Boarding House, Louisburg, B D Pennell.
Boarding House, Louisburg, Mrs W K Martin.
Hotel, Franklinton, E M Ward.
Hotel Meadows, Louisburg, Dr J S Meadows.
Restaurant, Franklinton, Henderson Person.
Restaurant, Franklinton, E W Mayfield.
Restaurant, Louisburg, Rob't Yarboro.
Restaurant, Louisburg. Mitchell & Adams.
Restaurant, Louisburg, Julia Littlejohn.
Restaurant, Louisburg, Boney Hawkins.
Restaurant, Louisburg, Joe Perry.
Restaurant, Louisburg. Isham Green.

LAWYERS.

Names and Post Offices.

Bickett, ——, Louisburg.
Bullock, B F, Franklinton.
Cook, P H, Louisburg.
Cook, C M, Louisburg.
Gulley, N Y, Franklinton.
Person, W M, Louisburg.
Spruill, J S, Louisburg.
Timberlake, E W, Louisburg.
Wilder, T B, Louisburg.

FRANKLIN COUNTY.

Yarborough, W H, Jr, Louisburg.	

MANUFACTORIES.

Kinds, Post Offices and Proprietors.

Coaches. Franklinton, Wm Dunston.
Coaches, Franklinton. Allen & Brown.
Cotton-ginning, Franklinton, I H Kearney.
Cotton-ginning, Franklinton, A S Joyner.
Creamery, Laurel, J F Jones.
Cotton mills, Laurel. J F Jones.
Cotton mills, Franklinton. Sterling Cotton Mills (incorporated). Capital stock $50,000; Col W F Green, pres; S C Vann, sec and treas; J C Fogleman, supt. No spindles 2,080; daily consumption 1,400 lbs. cotton; production 1,260 pounds yarns; number hands 25.
Wheelwright'g. Youngsville, Jo Harris.
Blacksmithing, Youngsville, Hicks & Young.
Tannery, Franklinton, Geo F Smith
Tobacco factory, Franklinton, R R Holmes.
Wagon factory, Laurel, J F Jones.

MERCHANTS AND TRADESMEN.

Name, Post-office and Line of Business.

CENTREVILLE.

Alston, A W,	G S
Griffin, R H,	G S

FRANKLINTON.

Ally T J.	Blacksmith
Ballard. B W & Co,	G S
Cade, Maggie,	Millinery
Candell, ——,	Gro
Cheatham, T J,	W U Tel Op
Cooke, Robt,	Blacksmith
Cooke, B F & Co,	G S
Furman. H S,	Drugs
Hester, W H,	Barber
Hight, L R,	Farm Implem'ts
Hight, P R,	G S
Hight T J,	Furn and Undertaker
Hight, T J.	G S
Hobbs, H B,	Livery
Howard, I H,	Blacksmith
Joyner, T C,	Postal Tel Op
Joyner, T C.	Drugs
Joyner, A S,	Gro
Lowery, H S,	Gro
McGhee, W L,	G S
McKnight. G T,	Blacksmith
Mitchell, W J,	M'f'r Tob
Morris, E W.	Shoes
Pearce, H E,	G S
Pearce, S E,	G S
Ratly, S S,	Gro
Ratly, Sylvester (col),	Shoemaker

Roberson, J A & Co,	G S
Staunton, J G,	G S
Vann, S C.	G S
Ward, T T.	Gro
Wester, A B.	G S, Farm Implem'ts
White, Turly.	Blacksmith
Whitfield, G L,	G S
Wilder, L J.	G S
Winston, R W,	Drugs

INGLESIDE.

Mocon, Chas,	G S

LAUREL.

Bobbitt, J R,	G S
Jones, J F.	G S

LOUISBURG.

Alston, Walter,	Barber
Aycock & Co.	Drugs, etc
Baker, Geo S.	Life, Fire & Ac. Ins. agt
Barrow & Byrd,	Life and Fire Ins Agts
Carlyle. R T,	G S
Crenshaw. Hicks & Allen,	G S
Conway. W B,	Wheelwright
Cooke, D F & Co,	G S
Crenshaw, Hicks & Allen,	G S & Hdw
Dietz, Aaron,	G S
Dunston, Alex,	Shoemaker
Edwards, M J (near),	G S
Egerton. F N & R J,	G S
Ellis, S F, Jr,	Photographer
Ellis & Joyner,	Furn
Ellis, Dr O L,	Drugs
Evans, Jake.	Shoemaker
Faulkner, J A,	Jeweler
Ford, G W,	G S
Frazier, H B,	Jeweler
Green & Yarboro.	G S
Green. John.	Livery and Sale Stable
Hall, Mrs A M (Racket),	G S
Hart, R G,	Tob
Hartsfield, ——,	Jeweler
Harris, J H & Co,	Liv. & Sale Stables
Haynes & Fuller,	Liv. & Sales Stables
Hill, R P & Co,	G S
Hughes. W T,	Tobacco Warehouse
Hughes & Hart,	Tobacco Warehouse
Hughes & Hart,	Harness
Hughes & Hart.	Undertaker
Hunt, T T & Co,	G S
Jones & Cooper,	G S
King & Macon.	G S
Lancaster. M V & Co,	Family Gro
Lehman, Julius,	Clothing
Littlejohn, Julia,	G S
Louisburg Music Co,	Musical Mdse
Louisburg Shoe Store,	Shoes
May, N & D,	Shoemakers
Neal, W P & Co,	G S
Orleans, Nathan,	G S
Pleasants, W H & Co,	Tob Wareh'se
Portis, Ed.	Barber
Roberson & Whitfield,	G S
Stokes & Ferguson,	G S
Taylor, H C,	Wheelwright

FRANKLIN COUNTY.

The Leiser Oberdorfer Co,   G S
Thomas, W G,   Drugs, etc
Thomas, J B,   Tobacco Warehouse
Timberlake, J P (near),   G S
Webb, Wm P,   G S
West, Moses,   Shoemaker
Widler, F B,   Fire and Accident Ins Agt
Wilder, R N (near),   G S
Winston, J P,   G S
Yarboro, James,   Barber
Yarborough, Edward F,   Life, Fire and Accident Ins Agt

MAPLEVILLE.

Cooke, W B & Co,   G S

MOULTON.

Myrick, Jno G,   G S

OSWEGO.

Burnett, W,   G S

PILOT.

Rivett, A C & Co,   G S

POCOMOKE.

Keith, D M,   G S

PUGH'S.

Kearney, S H & Son,   G S

RANSOM'S BRIDGE.

Powell, J S,   G S
Shearin, J S,   G S

RILEY'S CROSS-ROADS.

Perry, W W,   G S
Phillips, W K,   G S
Privett, J B,   Gro

ROYAL.

Clifton, J A,   G S

STALLINGS.

Stallings, J M,   G S

YOUNGSVILLE.

Alford, Moses,   G S
Baker, Jno O,   G S
Burnett, A C (near),   G S
Duke, Joe,   G S
Johnson, J R,   Gro
Mitchell, I W,   G S
Moss & Woodlief,   G S
Patterson, John,   G S
Perry & Patterson,   G S
Pierce Furney,   G S
Pierce, Elman,   G S
Riddick, I G,   Drugs
Stell, C N, agt,   G S
Strickland, Chas,   G S
Timberlake, N G,   G S
Timberlake, J L (near),   G S
Timberlake, James,   G S
Williams, Peter,   G S
Williams, S D,   G S
Winston & Son,   G S
Woodlief, M,   G S

FRANKLIN COUNTY.

PHYSICIANS.

Names and Post Offices.

Clark, D Wm, Kittrell.
Clifton, J B, Louisburg.
Dugger, J E (dentist), Louisburg.
Ellis, O L, Louisburg.
Floyd, R P, Sutton.
Foster, E L, Louisburg.
Foster, P S, Ingleside.
Harris, J H, Franklinton.
Hatch, P R, Youngsville.
Jackson, J W, Mapleville.
King, R E (dentist), Louisburg.
Klapp, ——, Youngsville.
Malone, J E, Louisburg.
Moss, J T, Franklinton.
Nicholson, W H, Louisburg.
Perry, Sam, Centreville.
Riddick, I G, Youngsville.
Riddick, J G. Youngsville.
Wheeless, J R, Centreville.

SCHOOLS.

Names, Post Offices and Principals.

Baptist School (col), Franklinton, T O Fuller.
Christian College (col), Franklinton, N Del McReynolds.
Good Shepherd (col), Miss Sallie Alston, John H Williamson.
Louisburg Male Academy, S McIntyre, principal.
Louisburg Female College, Rev J A Green, pres.
Parochial School, Louisburg, J F Jordan, principal.
Primary School, Louisburg, Miss Josie Jones.
Primary School, Louisburg, Miss Fannie Yarborough.
Public Schools, Louisburg, Misses Yarborough and Foote.
State Normal Albian (col), Franklinton, J A Savage.
Training School (col), Franklinton.

LOCAL CORPORATIONS.

Bank of Louisburg; Wm P Nell, pres; Jas L Webb, cashier.
Farmers and Merchant's Bank, Louisburg; W P Bailey, pres; J S Barrow, cashier.
Knights of Pythias, Excelsior Lodge, No 72 J E Malone, C C; W J Barrow, K of R and S.
Louisburg Lodge, I O O F; R G Hart, N G.
Royal Lodge, No 413, A F and A M; R G Hart, W M; Geo S Baker, sec.

FRANKLIN COUNTY.

NEWSPAPERS.

Franklinton Weekly, Franklinton, W F Marshall.

Franklin Times, Louisburg, Jas A Thomas.

Our Farms (weekly), Franklinton; Baylus Cade.

Searchlight (weekly), Franklinton; R C Gulley.

The Crumb (weekly), Louisburg; J W Pittman, editor and proprietor.

FARMERS.

Names and Post Offices.

Centreville.—Garland Davis, P A Davis, A N Davis, Al Davis, A T Dorsy.

Clifton's Mill.—B R Chamblee, J L Cheers, B R Clifton, John T Clifton, T W Cook, Sam Curtis, Sherwood Denton, A J P Harris, S E Horton.

Franklinton.—Robert Alston, Jas Ball, R W Baliarp, Rev W O Barrett, Thos Bebby, J S Blackly, W T Blanks, H A Bobbitt, B B Botten, T W Bragg, T H Braikly, L A Brooks, S B Brooks, B F Bullock, L H Bunn, W M Bust, S H Collett, Isaac Callett, Wm H Cannady, Jim Cannady, Joe Cannady, R G Cheatham, C H Clifton, J H Convers, R L Conyers, T J Conyers, J H Cook, A H Cook, A Dickerson, P F Dickerson, W C Duke, H C Duke, C F Farrer, J P Feilds, A F Fort. W J Fort, Henry Freeman, George Fuller, Jackson Fuller. W O Fuller, A G Fuller, W H Garner, J O Green, W F Green, W W Green, T H Griffin, Geo Griffin, N Y Gully, Ben Harris, Alonzo Harris, H H Harris, W H Harris, W E Harrison, George Hatch, Frank Hawkins, G W Hawkins, J C Hight, T J Hight, B J Holden, Charles Holden, R R Holmes, Jno W House, S D Jenkins, W D Jones, J R Jones, J J W Jones, Geo D Kearney, G G Kearney, H C Kearney, H D Kearney, K Kearney, J H Kearney, J A Kearney, L C Kearney, S F Kearney, W H Kearney, W W King, L W Levister, Norman Long, Robt Long, S P Lowry, J H McGhee, John Y McGhee, S J McGhee. W S McGhee, J S Mitchell, S Mitchell. T H S Mitchell, A D Mitchener, Jno R Mitchener, R S Mitchener, W. P Montgomery, R F Morris, Moses Neal. Caleb Nicholson, C J Outlaw, Allen Pearce, J A Pearce, Chas Perry, Jno A Perry, Jacob N Perry, K J Perry. M L Perry, W P Perry, W T Perry, R O Pinell, Toney Pugh, W S Pruitt, Calvin Pritchard, R M Ricks, T M Reeves, C H Sanderlin. J C Sanderlin, H H Shrood, J M Shrood, L N B Shrood, G

FRANKLIN COUNTY.

B Smith, J D Speed, R A Speed, jr, W D Spruill, F W Stiky, J P Struthers, G G Struthers, B B Tomlinson, D Ursey, S C Vann, H Wilder, J H Wilder, C S Williams, B H Winston, E S Winston, Hendren Harris, Thomas Harris, T J Winston, W A Winston. J S Yarboro.

Ingleside.—M J Ball, O J Ball, Ephraim Blacknell, John Blacknell, J H Blacknell, J B Bledsoe, W C Bobbitt, J J Bridges, Thomas Burnett, Joseph Burnett, Wiley Burnett, R C Burnett, G W Bunn, Peter Carroll, B S Carroll, M L Clapton, G E Collins, E T Cook, W P Cook, E C Cook, W B Cook, F G Dean, J E Debnam, J R Debnam, P J Dement, Ed Dement, Rufus Dickerson, Henry Dickerson, R G Dickerson, Charles Dorsy, W H Edwards, H V Edwards, Thomas Edwards, M D Edwards, P H Edwards, Benj R Evans, G W Evans, J H Evans, M G Falkner, Charles Falkner, W H Falkner, Ernest Falkner, L D Falkner, John S Falkner, N H Falkner, R E Falkner, G M Falkner, W M Falkner, John N Falkner, Thos D Farrar, J M Finch, G W Finch, Isaac Finch, Henry Foster, R S Foster, Wm Frazier, T L Frazier, R J Frazier, D T Fuller, T H Fuller, J F Guscore, Geo R Guscore, B C Guscore, T H Guscore, C C Guscore, Norfleet Guscore, J L Jackson, John Joyner, A P Joyner, W D Joyner, S Y Macon, W O Mitchell, J R Smith, Jno Smith, jr.

Kittrell—L Carroll, J E Carroll, H V Champion, W T Clark, G W Duke, P V Duke, G M Duke, Allen Duke, Alex Fuller, P J Fuller, R F Gill, T L Gooch, Dock Gooch, Ellis Greenway, D R Gupton, Charles Johnson, Walter Johnson, R T Johnson, H J Johnson, J W Johnson, E D Johnson, W Z Johnson, W A Johnson, B C Perry, Charles Perry, Henry Person, W R Smith, W J Stokes, Chas G Stokes, J W Stokes.

Laurel—D A Alston, E T Alston, A T Alston, J A Andrews, G R Anderson, D E Aycock, G T Ayscue, J S Ayscue, G W Ayscue, Joseph Ball, J H Ball, Walter Bobbitt, Ed Bobbitt, Willis Boddie, Preston Breedlove, W D Breedlove, S P Burt, J A Burt, R B Carr, A J Carr, J A Champion, J C Clapton, W T Cooper, J J Cooper, Wm Cooper, J W Demint, A A Demint, Green Dickerson, W D Dorsy, W L Dorsy, R H Duke, P W Falkner, J J Foster, R E Foster, J C Foster, Munroe Fuller, Stephen Gupton, R H Gupton, P L Gupton, E M Gupton, E R Gupton, J T Gupton, Paul Gupton, N W Gupton, H H Gupton, E A Gupton, Peter Gupton, P W Gupton, Jno Gup-

FRANKLIN COUNTY.

ton, W L Gupton, R E Gupton, J W Gupton, S T Harper, J H Harper, Benj Harris, J E Harris, Wade Harris, Jas Hawkins, G W Hicks, Theo Hudson, T T Hunt.

Leathe—Jas Garrett, Bud Garrett, James Goodson, A J Green, J W Pace, J R Pace, A W Pace, B W Pace.

Louisburg—John J Allen, Mrs Dora Allen, William Allen, J M Allen, F G Ally, Fred Alston, Riddick Alston, S H Barly, Frank Ballard, C A Battle, E E Bennett, D E Best, R H Bobbitt, S C Carelett, J B Clifton, C M Cooke, Alex Coppedge, H A Crenshaw, E A Crudup, Oscar Davis, M S Davis, F M Davis, Whitner Dickerson, F N Eaton, W Z J Eaton, O Z Edwards, Wiley Edwards, H D Egerton, W W Ellis, C B Ellington, John A Evans, N O Evans, T M Flemming, G W Ford, W H Freeman, W N Fuller, S N Fuller, R F Fuller, G G Gill, R R Harris, O H Harris, B D Harris, Paul Hazelwood, A P Hedgpeth, M T Hedgpeth, W T Hight, Redding Hight, W H Hill, L T Horton, William Inscore, J R Inscore, Norfleet Inscore, J O Inscore, J W Jackson, A W Jackson, Geo W Jones, L H Jones, M H Jones, Joe Jones, W A Jones, J F Jordan, R W Lancaster, N H Macon, Charles Macon, W J Macon, Adkin May, T T May, H C May, J H Mitchell, Jacob Mitchell, W G Munford, A W Nelson, sr, J A Nelson, B L Nester, G W Newell, W S Parker, John Perry, W H Perry, Henry Perry, Thomas Perdew, T Z Perdew, Jno Pitman, W H Pleasants, James Perry, C W Roberts, W H Rudd, A S Sherrod, J H Sledge, Sherrod Sledge, Jno H Smith, E B Smith, J R Spencer, J L Spencer, C H Stamp, W S Stamp, J W Stamp, Sid Strickland, D C Tharrayton, John Thomas, J P Timberlake, G R Underhill, J H Upperman, W L Vaughan, T J Wiggs, A W Wilson, jr, Nick Wright.

Mitchener.—L C Mitchener.

Oswego.—R F Anderson, C G Ayscue, L G Ayscue, J E T Ayscue, W H Bledsoe, W A Burnett, Wesley Burnett.

Pugh.—J R Kearny, S H Kearny, L Kimble, T W Lassiter, Jno H Lasstter, Jas Lassiter, J R Lassiter, L H Lassiter, J Lassiter.

FRANKLIN COUNTY.

Riley's Cross Roads.—Ransom Dodd, Edward Driver, A P Faison, Ben Faison, J E Knight, T A Lee, Wesley Lewis, Alonzo Lloyd, J H Massey, A Moye, J R S Pearce, Kearney Pearce, J C Pearce, Paul Pearce, Will Pearce, J L J Pearce, M P Pearce, Abe Pearce, Bryant Pearce, Ben Pearce, J B Perry, W H Perry, E S Perry, W K Phillips, J H Ray, Wm Rogers, Allen Thomas, Ambrose Upchurch, J W Upchurch, Turner Vick, J R Weatherly, J J Weatherly, W S Weatherly.

Sutton.—G S Alford, J C B Alford, B Baker, J B Baker, W J Baker, Ben Baker, J C Baker, J A Baker, Jones Bell, W B Bunn, J C Bunn, J D Bunn, C H Bunn, Thos E Bunn, W B Chamblee, J H Cheers, A D Crudup, James Gay, W J Gay, James Glover, N D Green, J Griffin, J H Griffin, R Griffin, Henry Haywood, W F Jackson, Isaac Jones, M T Jones, J M Medlin, J C Mullens, B H Murray, J D Pace, J W Pace, G W Pace, Burnell Perry, K W Perry, Wesley Pippin, J A Pippin, J T Pippin, C Pippin, J B Pruitt, C T Pruitt, W R Pruitt, A C Pruitt, W E Pruitt, W J Stallings, E W Stallings, E R Stallings, O L Strickland, Jno Strickland, J J Tant, Richard Tant, Cordy Tant, W H Tant, Clinton Tant, A J White, J C White, J M White, S T Williams, Floyd Williams, J F Williams, J W Williams, W H Williams, Daniel Yeargan.

Wake Forest.—J C Fuller.

Youngsville.—W T Alford, J B Allen, A T Beddingfield, J M Champion, Geo Cook, R J Covers, T J Crocker, J W Davis, A D Davis, L W Dent, M J Dent, J A Ellis, W J Freeman, C A Garner, S W Gill, Lee Gill, T S Gill, W T Glenn, R F Green, W H Green, M S Gripton, J E Hale, S T Hale, A M Harris, J O Harris, W J Harris, J T Harper, R M Hicks, E L Hicks, W W Hill, Allen Hodge, J M Holden, Simon Holden, Thos Holden, R T Holden, F C Holden, M D Holmes, C F Holmes, G W Hunt, J R Johnson, W E Johnson, N S Johnson, J H Jones, Aaron Jones, Robt Jones, C W Jones, L A Jones, G B King, J L King, J E Knight, J T Lancaster, G T Levister, W B Levister, Tobe Long, J H Mangum, Jordan May, C B May, A M May, Victor Minger, L C Mitchener.

GASTON COUNTY.

AREA, 340 SQUARE MILES.

POPULATION, 17,676; White 12,839, Colored 4,837.

GASTON COUNTY was formed in 1846, from Lincoln county, and was named for William Gaston, of Craven county. who was formerly one of the Judges of the Supreme Court.

DALLAS, the county-seat, was named for Vice-President George M. Dallas, of Philadelphia. It is 200 miles southwest of Raleigh, and has a population of 1,000.

Surface—Moderately uneven; land generally good; water-power very fine. Manufacturing obtains, and especially in cotton and iron.

Staples—Corn and wheat are the leading staples. Tobacco grows well. Cotton can be raised profitably. Stock-raising is remunerative.

Fruits—Peaches, apples, grapes, pears and melons of fine quality. The grasses are profitable, and nearly all the small fruits are abundant.

Timbers—Hickory, dogwood, oak, pine, maple and walnut.

Minerals—Gold, iron and manganese.

TOWNS AND POST OFFICES.

	POP.		POP.
Alexis,	50	Lowell,	200
All Healing,	100	Lucia,	30
Begonia,	40	Lufty,	35
Belmont,	100	McAdenville,	1,500
Bessemer City,	500	Mountain	
Bethesda,	75	Island,	500
Carpenter,	20	Mount Holly,	1,500
Cherryville,	250	Old Furnace,	25
Costner,	60	Perry,	25
Crowder's Cr'k,	30	Pleasant Ridge,	25
Dallas,	1,000	Snapp,	28
Gastonia,	2,260	South Point,	25
Gould,	25	Stanley,	400
Harden,	200		

COUNTY OFFICERS.

Clerk Superior Court—G H Davis.
Commissioners—C Pason, chm'n; J T Carpenter, J R Connell, G R Patrick, J F Thomas.
Coroner—J W Abernethy.
Register of Deeds—J J Ormand.
Sheriff—A K Loftin.
Solicitor 11th District—J L Webb.
Surveyor—A W Hoffman.
Standard Keeper—Ed Mason.
Treasurer—Lee B Stowe.
County Examiner—L G Cathey.

COURTS.

Superior Court meets second Monday before the first Monday in March and the second Monday after first Monday in September.

TOWN OFFICERS.

DALLAS—*Mayor*, T Lee Wilson; *Commissioners*, J R Lewis, E E Summery, J C Puett, L M Hoffman.

MT HOLLY—*Mayor*, W B Rutledge; *Commissioners*, J C Rankin, R B Ballington, A P Lentz, C W Upton.

TOWNSHIPS AND MAGISTRATES.

Cherryville—Jacob Kiser (Cherryville), L H J Houser (Snapp), John T Carpenter (Carpenter), J T R Damron, John E Jones, W L Aderthoidt, J J Carpenter, J B Houser, Moses Stroup, F A Workman, Sidney Carpenter (Cherryville).

Crowder's Mountain—Rich'd H Garrett (King's Mountain), J A Neil, Jno T Oates, S M Wilson, J B Carson, J T Smith, R J Kennedy, J A Smith, J W Walker, C A Hampton, C A Thornburg (Dallas).

Dallas—M D Friday (High Shoals), A P H Rhyne (Dallas), Jonas Pasour, Gary Rhyne, P M Rhyne, Frank W Thompson, Ellis Parsons, D H McKown, S D Brown (Dallas).

Gastonia—B G Bradley (Gastonia), John Rutledge (Harden), W A Pearson, A C Strout, W M Noten, J A Huss, B C Bradley, William Bell, E P Lewis, Geo Dixon, L L Jenkins, S M Asbury, Wiley Hanna (Gastonia).

River Bend—J M McIntosh (Dallas), W B Rutledge, W C Snerrill, W P Eddeman, J L Wallace, R E Lineberger, R M Johnson, J A Morris (Dallas).

South Point—L H Stowe, A R Andrews, W T McLean, C C Cornwell, John A Gullick, J M Huffstellar, Lawson Stowe, W W McLean, J M Sloan, J M Huffman (South Point).

CHURCHES.

Names, Post Offices, Pastors and Denom.

METHODIST.

Baker's Mill—King's Mountain, J W Roberts.

GASTON COUNTY.

Bethesda—Lonell, M TSteel.
Church—Lonell, M T Steel.
Church—Gastonia, W M Bagby.
Church—Dallas, R M Taylor.
Church—Mountain Island, S M Davis.
Sanders' Chapel—Carpenter.
Church—Stanley's R M Taylor.
Church—McAdensville. M T Steel.
Church—Mt Holly, G W Callahan.
Church—Bessemer City. J W Roberts.
Concord—Cherryville, J D Arnold.
River Bend—Lucia, W F Womble.
Snow Hill—Lowell, G W Callahan.
South Point—Belmont, R M Taylor.
Yates' Chapel—Bessemer City, J W
  Roberts.

LUTHERAN.

Church—Mt Holly, —— Moser.
Christ Church—Stanley's. J R Patter-
son.
Luther's Chapel—Dallas.
Philadelphia—Dallas.
St. Mark's—Cherryville

N. METHODIST.

Bradley's Chapel—Gastonia.
Concord—Cherryville. —— Daniel.
Smyrna—Cherryville.

PRESBYTERIAN

Church—Dallas, R C Johnston.
Church—Gastonia, R P Smith.
Church—Stanley's, Jonas Barclay.
Goshen—Mt Holly, Jonas Barclay.
Hope—South Point.
Long Creek—Old Furnace, J J Ken-
nedy.
Olney—Pleasant Ridge.
Union—Begonia, J M McLean.

BAPTIST.

Church—Dallas.
Fellowship—Belmont, D W Thompson.
Long Creek—Dallas, G M Webb.
Mt Zion—Cherryville, A C Grier.
Mt Zion (2d)—Stanley's, J F Morris.
Sandy Plain—Begonia, J F Morris.
Shady Grove—Cherryville, Jacob L
  Hoyle.

MINISTERS RESIDENT.

Names, Post Offices and Denom.

METHODIST.

Bagly. W M, Gastonia.
Callahan, G W. Mt Holly.
Carpenter, M L Carpenter.
Davis. S M. Mountain Island.
Roberts. J W. Bessemer City.
Steele. M T Lowell
Taylor. R M. Stanley's.

BAPTIST.

Hicks E D (col), Stanley's.
Morris, J F, Stanley's.
Thomason, D W, Belmont.

GASTON COUNTY.

PRESBYTERIAN.

Barclay, Jonas, Mt Holly.
Kennedy, J J, Gastonia.
McLean, J M, Gastonia.

LUTHERAN.

Moser, —— Mt Holly.
Petterson, J R. Dallas.

ASSO. REFORMED.

Boyce, E E, Gastonia.

HOTELS AND BOARDING HOUSES.

Names, Post Offices and Proprietors.

American Hotel, Dallas, Jonas Hoff-
man.
Central Hotel, Mount Holly, Mrs M A
Hutchison.
Dallas Hotel, Dallas, J R Durham.
Falls House, Gastonia, J L Falls &
Son.
Healing Springs, All Healing, Cuzzens
& Thomas.
Hotel, Bessemer City, J R Durham.
Hotel, Cherryville, S S Mauney.
Hotel, Stanley's, J L Rutledge.
Hotel, Mountain Island, J S Craig.
Hotel, McAdenville. Miss Webb.
Hotel, Dallas, J Hoffman.
Matthews Hotel, Dallas, Hal McDon-
ald.
Merchants' Hotel, Gastonia, Jno John-
son.
Riverview, Mt Holly, C B Holland.
Stowe Hotel, Belmont, Pink Stowe.

LAWYERS.

Names and Post Offices.

Durham, ——, Dallas.
Hoffman, L M, Dallas.
Lewis, ——, Gastonia.
Mangum & Lewis, Gastonia.
Mason, O S, Dallas.

MANUFACTORIES.

Kinds, Post Offices and Proprietors.

Albion Mfg Co (cotton), Mt Holly, A P
Rhyne. pres; W T Love, sec; capital
stock, $115,000; value of plant, $54,-
000; daily consumption 3,000 pounds
raw cotton; daily production, 2,600
pounds yarns; number of hands, 60;
average wages, 60c. per day.
Blacksmithing, Dallas. R O Costner
Blacksmithing, Gastonia, Wm Jenkins.
Blacksmithing Stanley's, —— Jenkins.
Blacksmithing, Stanley's, R M Brown.
Blacksmithing, Mt Holly, Henry Pat-
terson.
Boots and shoes, Dallas, L Costner.
Brick, Mt Holly, R M Jenkins & Son.

GASTON COUNTY.

Canning factory, Belmont, Hall & Stone.

Carriages, etc., Gastonia, Stultz & Starns.

Contracting and building, Mt Holly, J C Hamlet.

Contracting and building, Dallas, W G Morris.

Cotton mills, Stanley's, J G Morrison.

Cotton mills, Cherryville, J M Rhodes, mgr.

Cotton mills, King's Mountain, J S Mauney, mgr.

Cotton mills, Crowder's Creek, P S Baker, mgr.

Cotton mills, Dallas, J O Rankin, mgr.

Cotton mills, Bessemer City, J A Smith, pres.

Dilling Cotton Mills, King's Mountain, F Dilling, mgr.

Gaither's Mills, Belmont, Thomas H Gaither, prop; number spindles, 1,400.

Gastonia Cotton Mfg Co, Gastonia, R C G Love, pres; G A Gray, supt; Jno F Love, sec-treas; cap stock, $200,000; 4,000 bales cotton used annually; 9,300 spindles; 136 looms; 1,500,000 yarns per year; 500,000 yards cloth annually; 275 hands.

Gastonia Cotton Mills, Lowell, J H Wilson, jr, prop; established in 1876; capital stock, $60,000; number of spindles 4,000; daily consumption 5,000 pounds; daily production 4,000 yards; number of hands 60.

Harden Mfg Co, Harden, O D Carpenter, mgr.

Harness, Gastonia, Craig & Wilson.

Hooper, W J, Mfg Co, Mountain Island.

Mattresses, Dallas, R Jackson.

McAden Cotton Mills, McAdenville, R R Ray, mgr.

Millwrighting, Dallas, M P Clemmer.

Modena Cotton Mills, Gastonia, J D Moore, mgr.

Mountain Island Cotton Mills, Mountain Island, W T Jordan, mgr.

Mountain Island Plaid Mills, Mountain Island, W J Hooper, prop; estab in 1848; daily consumption 3,000 lbs; number spindles, 6,000; looms, 250; hands, 75.

Mount Holly Mills, Mt Holly, A P Rhyne & Co; number of spindles, 2,800, capital stock, $55,000; daily consumption, 1,500 lbs raw cotton; daily production, 1,300 lbs yarns; number of hands, 55; average daily wages, 75 cents.

Mims Cotton Mfg Co, Mt Holly; capital stock, $25,000; M R Dewstar, pres; C E Hutchison, sec-treas; 2,000 spindles; daily consumption 1,500 lbs;

production about 1,200 lbs yarns; 75 hands—average wages 75 cents.

River Bend Cannery, Stanly Creek, R M Johnston.

Roller flour mills, Mt Holly, R M Jenkins.

Saddles and harness, Dallas, J W Bean.

Saddles and harness, Gastonia, R L Johnson.

Sash, doors and blinds, Gastonia, J B Broomfield.

Sash, doors and blinds, Gastonia, J B Beal & Co.

Stanley Creek Cotton Mills, Stanley's, A P Rhyne, pres; E L Pegram, sec and treas; capital stock, $33,000; No. spindles, 2,200; raw material daily, 1,800 lbs; daily production, 1,500 lbs yarns; No. of hands, 55; average daily wages, 85 cents.

Stowesville Cotton Mills, Belmont, T H Gaither, treas.

Tannery, Gastonia, —— Arrowood.

Tannery, Dallas, J E Rhyne.

Tannery, Gastonia, G Rolinson.

Tannery, Cherryville, J T Carpenter.

Tannery, Cherryville, A A Mauney.

Trenton Cotton Mills, Gastonia, G W Ragan.

Tuckaseege Cotton Mills, Mt Holly, A P Rhyne, pres; A C Lineberger, sec and treas; capital invested, $125,000; daily consumption 5,500 lbs raw cotton; daily production 4,750 lbs yarns; hands 85; average wages 85 cents.

Wheelwrighting, Stanley's, W C Sherrill.

Wilson Cotton Mills, Lowell, J L Lineberger, treas.

Woodlawn Cotton Mills, Mt Holly, A P Rhyne, pres.

MERCHANTS AND TRADESMEN.

Names, Post Offices, Lines of Business.

BEGONIA.

Huffstetter, J M & Sons,	G S
Johnson, S C & Co,	G S

BELMONT.

Armstrong, J W,	Gro
Fite & Neagle,	G S
Gaither, T H, Cotton Mill and	G S
McKnight, J E,	G S
Smith & Ragan,	G S
Stowe, J P, Shoes and	Gro
Stowe Bros,	G S

BESSEMER CITY.

Bell, R C,	G S
Smith, J T & Co,	G S
White Bros & Ormond,	G S

CHERRYVILLE.

Berry, E M,	G S

GASTON COUNTY.

Bess, W B & Co, G S
Carpenter, M & Son, G S
Goode, T V & Co, Drugs
Leonharkt, T B, G S
Long, A T & Son, Tinware
Mauney, S S & Bro, G S
McGinnis, W J, G S
Moore. W A, G S
Rudisill & Alderholdt, G S

COSTNER.

Costner, E S & Co, G S

DALLAS.

Brown, S D, Gro
Gemayel, A J, G S
Hoffman, G W & Co (col), G S and Confections
Lewis, J R & Co, G S
Moore, M A, Drugs
Pasour, E, G S
Puett, John C, Mill and Fertilizer
Rawlings, G R & Co, Gro

GASTONIA.

Armstrong Furniture Co, Co-partnership
Beale Mfg Co, Sash and Blinds
Beards, J B, Marble
Bradley, B G, Fertilizer, etc
Costner, Jones & Co, G S
Craig & Wilson, Harness and Livery Stables
Curry & Kennedy, Drugs
Davis, O W, Fertilizer and Feed
Douglas, J E, G S
Elder & Sanders, G S
Falls, J L, Hotel
Gallant, Whiteside & Co, G S
Gastonia Coffin Co, Corp
Gastonia Jewelry Store, Co-partnership
Heath, L D, Baker
Heath, P T, G S
Heath & Howell, Bakers
Howell & Strickland. Gro
Hunter, J A, Books and Stationery
Lineberger, E N, G S
Long Bros, Stoves and Tinware
Love, John F, Dry Goods
Love, R C G & Son, Cotton and Gro
Marshall, W F, Newspaper
McMean, R C, Gro
Morris Bros, agts, G S
Page, J E & Co, Sash and Doors
Torrence, Frost & Co, Drugs
White, W M, Marble
Williams, A C & Co, Dry Goods and Shoes

HARDIN.

Carpenter Bros, G S
Carpenter, M M, G S
Harding Mfg Co, Cotton Goods

LOWELL.

Cornwell, C C & Co, G S

GASTON COUNTY.

McAden Mills, Cotton Goods
Ragan, J D, G S
Rankin, R P, G S
Reed, J R & Co (near), G S
Robinson, S M. G S

MACADENVILLE.

McAden, Henry, G S

MT. HOLLY.

Bollinger, S L, G S
Cathey, J L & Co, Gro
Dellinger, A C, G S
Eddenman, H M & Co, Gro
Fite & Garrison, G S
Hutchinson & Ashbury, G S
Lentz, A P, G S
Rhyne, A P & Co, G S

MOUNTAIN ISLAND.

Abernethy, R L, G S
Farrar Bros. G S
Jordan, W T & Co, G S

OLD FURNACE.

Hovis, J J, G S

PLEASANT RIDGE.

Fall, T G, G S

SOUTH POINT.

Gulick, J A, G S

STANLEY.

Abernethy & Co, G S
Abernethy & Kincaid, G S
Broom. R M, Blacksmith
Carpenter B F, G S
Lineberger & Thompson, G S
McLurd, R L, & Bro, G S
Pegram, E L. jr, G S
Sherrill, W C, Carriage Maker
Summey, J E, Gro

MINES.

Kinds, Post Offices and Proprietors.

Gold, King's Mountain. T M A Talcott.
Gold, Dallas, Stanford M'f'g Co.
Gold, Stanley's Creek. J F Cannon.
Gold, Mt Holly, A P Rhyne.
Gold, Dallas. Bynum & Grier.
Gold (Rhodes Mine), Dallas, J C Puett.
Iron (Ormand Ore Bank), Mountain, Bessemer Mining Co.
Iron, Dallas, Bynum & Grier.
Iron, Stanley's Creek, J F Cannon.
Tin, King's Mountain, King's Mountain Improvement Co.

MILLS.

Kinds, Post Offices and Proprietors.

Cotton, King's Mountain, Delling Cotton Mills.
Cotton, Gastonia, R C G Love & Co.
Cotton, King's Mountain, I W Garrett & Co.

GASTON COUNTY.

Corn, Stanley Creek, I R Stroupe.
Flour, corn and saw, Mt Holly, W C
  Abernethy.
Flour, corn and saw, Cherryville, E
  Aderholdt.
Flour, corn and saw, Gastonia, Mor-
  row & Co.
Flour, corn and saw, Dallas, White &
  Jenkins.
Flour and corn, Crowder's Creek, Jno
  F Wilson.
Flour and corn, King's Mountain,
  White & Kiser.
Flour and corn, Mountain Island, W J
  Hooper.
Flour and corn, Old Furnace, Ransom
  & Wilson.
Flour and corn, Harden, J F Plank.
Flour and corn, South Point, J G Gul-
  ick's heirs.
Flour and corn, McAdensville, R Y
  McAden.
Flour and corn, Gastonia, G F Mc-
  Langhorn.
Saw, Dallas, L A Thornburg & Co.
Saw, Cherryville, Dellinger & Carroll.
Saw and grist, Mt Holly, R M Jenkins.
Saw, grist and gin, Lucia, J M & M A
  McIntosh.
Steam saw, Harden, O D Carpenter.
Steam flour, corn, saw and gin, Stan-
  ley Creek, Hili Abernethy.

PHYSICIANS.

Names and Post Offices..

Adams, Chas, Gastonia.
Davis, W W, Belmont.
Eddleman, M H, Mt Holly.
Glenn, Frank (dentist), Gastonia.
Howell, W A, Cherryville.
Jenkins, John, Dallas.
Lattimer, Thomas, McAdensville.

GASTON COUNTY.

Patrick, G R, Begonia.
Robinson, Frank, Lowell.
Torrence, J W, Pleasant Ridge.
Wilson, W H, Gastonia.

SCHOOLS.

Names, Post Offices and Principals.

Academy, Stanley's.
Gaston College, Dallas, S A Wolf.
High School, Gastonia, J M Douglas.
Olney, Pleasant Ridge.
Mt Holly High School, —— Lippond.
St Mary's College, Belmont, Rev P Leo
  Haid.
Union Academy, Begonia, M L Arro-
  wood.
Public School—white, 66; colored, 28.

TEACHERS.

Names and Post Offices.

Arrowood, M L, Dallas.
Douglas, ——, Gastonia.
Haid, Rev P Leo, Belmont.
Wolf, S A, Dallas.

LOCAL CORPORATIONS.

Gastonia Lodge, No 263, A F and A M,
  Dallas. Times of meeting, Friday
  evening after full moon: Monday
  evening of court; June 24th and December 27th.

NEWSPAPERS.

Bessemer City Messenger, Bessemer
  City; J A Smith, ed and prop.
Gazette, Gastonia (dem weekly); W F
  Marshall, ed and prop.

GATES COUNTY.

AREA, 360 SQUARE MILES.

POPULATION, 10,246; White, 5,533 Colored 4,713.

GATES COUNTY was formed in 1779, from Hertford, Chowan and Perquimans counties. It was named after General Horatio Gates, the victorious commander at Saratoga in 1777.

GATESVILLE, the county-seat, is situated 180 miles northeast from Raleigh, and has a population of 300.

Surface.—Low, level, and soil rich; lies north and east of the Chowan river. This is really a desirable county, and its proximity to the Norfolk and Baltimore markets will always insure abundant reward to the agriculturist.

Staples.—Corn and cotton are great staples of Gates county. Sweet potatoes, fish and naval stores are items of pecuniary profit.

Fruits.—Grapes, melons, peaches, pears, apples, plums and the small fruits generally. Scuppernong grapes are here at home.

Timbers.—Juniper, cypress, sweet and black gums, pine, oak and a variety of the shrubs.

TOWNS AND POST OFFICES.

	POP.		POP.
Adoir,	100	Sandy Cross,	25
Bosley.	100	Sarem,	25
Corapeake,	100	Sunbury,	200
Dort,	20	Trotville,	10
Drum Hill,	50	Vivian,	20
Eure,	10	Wiggins' Cross	
Gatesville (c h),	300	Roads,	30
Hobbsville,	100	Willeyton,	50
Merchant Mills,	40	Willow,	25
Reynoldson,	45		

COUNTY OFFICERS.

Clerk Superior Court—W T Cross.

Commissioners—S I Harrell, chmn.

Coroner—Dr J W Costen.

Register of Deeds—Lycurgus Hofler.

Sheriff—R O Riddick.

Standard Keeper—W R Hayes.

Surveyor—W F Eason.

Superintendent Public Schools—J A Walton.

Treasurer—H B Cross.

County Board of Education—Jos T Wall. T W Costen, sr, Franklin Mathews,

Keeper of the Home for the Aged and Infirm—Mrs Martha E Eure.

COURTS.

Fifth Monday after the first Monday in March, and fifth Monday after the first Monday in n September.

TOWNSHIPS AND MAGISTRATES.

Gatesville—J H Hofler, Wm Smith, B F Willey, R O Riddick, T E Jenkins, J S Whidbee, jr, B F Willis, W H Standin, T A Brown, R S Riddick (Gatesville).

Hall—Henry Carter, Jno S. Felton, J A Sparkman (Eure), W K Lawrence, D B Lee, R R Carter, John E Askew, T J Sparkman, R B Harrell, Kindred Parker (Gatesville).

Hastett—E J Freeman, N R Felston (Willeyton), H Clay Williams, Wiley Wiggins, W W Walters, Nathaniel Newsome, W S Rogers, T H Rountree, J W Parker, W S Benton (Gatesville).

Holly Grove—G J Costen, W C Jones, John R Hill, C W Costen, T M Pearce (Sunbury), Thos Costen, Laban Pearce, W H Mathias, J R Parker, S S Mears (Gatesville).

Hunter's Hill—W H Cannon, George W Rountree, J R Eason, R W Simpson, T J Riddick (Trotville), Moses Byrum, E B Spivey, H L Brown, Jno R Hinton (Gatesville).

Mintonsville—Alex Carter, John M Trotman, Thos B Walton, J A Roberts, Joen B Walton, Hill J Reid, J H Freeman, W S Wiggins, T J Costen (Gatesville).

Reynoldson—W M Daughtry, W D Langston, E L Smith, Wm McP Goodman, D S Harrell, Thos J Felton, M J Lawrence (Reynoldson).

CHURCHES.

Names, Post Offices, Pastors and Denom.

METHODIST.

Church—Gatesville, C R Taylor.
Fletcher's—Gatesville, C R Taylor.
Harrell—Gatesville, C R Taylor.
Kittrell—Willeyton, G G Hardy.
Parker's—Sunbury, G G Hardy.
Philadelphia—Sunbury, C R Taylor.
Savage's—Willeyton, G G Harley.
Zion—Willow, C R Taylor,

BAPTIST.

Church—Gatesville, C B Williams.

19

GATES COUNTY.

Cool Springs—Reynoldson, W B Waff.
Middle Swamp—Gatesville, W B Waff.
Piney Grove—Reynoldson, W B Waff.
Sandy Cross—Sandy Cross,T T Speight.

EPISCOPAL.

St Mary's—Gatesville, —— Wingate.
St Peter's Mission—Gatesville, ——
Wingate.

CHRISTIAN.

Damascus—Sunbury, H H Butler.

MINISTERS RESIDENT.

Names, Post Offices and Denominations.

BAPTIST.

Spelght. T T, Sandy Cross.
Waff, W B, Reynoldson.
Williams, C B, Gatesville.

METHODIST.

Harley, G G.
Taylor, C R, Gatesville.

EPISCOPAL.

Wingate, ——, Gatesville.

CHRISTIAN.

Butler, H H, Sunbury.

LAWYERS.

Names and Post Offices.

Fostin, T W, jr., Gatesville.
Smith, L L, Gatesville.

MANUFACTORIES.

Kinds, Post Offices and Proprietors.

Blacksmith, wheelwright and general
    mechanic, Adair. James R Rooke.
Blacksmith, wheelwright and under-
    taker, Sunbury, B F Pearce.
Blacksmithing and wheelwrighting,
    Bosley, Jesse Yeates.
Blacksmithing and wheelwrighting,
    Gatesville, Billie Mitchell.
Blacksmithing and wheelwrighting,
    Sunbury. Alfred Hofler.
Blacksmithing and wheelwrighting,
    Sunbury, C R Howell.
Blacksmithing and wheelwrighting,
    Sunbury, J W Speight.
Blacksmithing and wheelwrighting,
    Gatesville, W H Peland (col.).
Blacksmithing and wheelwrighting,
    Gatesville, W H Standing.
Brick-makers, Eure, Story & Gatling.
Coach and harness, Gatesville, W H
    Standing.
Coach dealers, undertakers, black-
    smith and wood work, Gatesville,
    The Gatesville Carriage Co.
Coach and wagon, Sunbury, T Parker.

GATES COUNTY.

Coopering, Gatesville, J L Taylor.
Coopering, Reynoldson, James Rooks.
Cotton-gin, Sunbury, E E Harrell.
Cotton-gin and saw mill, Willow, Geo
    W Rountree.
Cotton-gin, Gatesville, R M Riddick &
    Co.
Cotton-gin, Willeyton, Parker & Cross.
Cotton-gin, Sunbury, Mills Benton.
Cotton-gin, Sunbury, Cross & Co.
Cotton-gin, Gatesville, A Carter.
Distillery (apple brandy), Reynoldson,
    Riddick Gatling.
Distillery (apple brandy), Gatesville,
    James Russell.
Manufacturer of pine lumber, saw and
    grist mill. planer, etc, cotton-gin,
    Merchant Mills, W H Edwards.
Shoes, Gatesville, A Green.
Shoes, Gatesville, H Savage.
Undertaker and wood workman, Mer-
    chant Mills, George F Eason.

MERCHANTS AND TRADESMEN.

Names, Post Offices and Lines of Business.

ADAIR.

Evans, R F,	G S
Jenkins, T E,	G S
Smith, M W & Bro,	G S

BOSLEY.

Cockey, W W,	G S
Fitchell & Hofler,	G S
Wilson & Fitchett,	Lumber

BUCKLAND.

Hayes & Co,	G S
Wilkins, W S,	G S

CORAPEAKE.

Brinkley, J J,	G S
Jones & Pearce,	G S
Jones, W C,	G S
Jones, J B & Son,	G S
Small, Eugene,	G S

DENNIS.

Nichols, Truitt & Co,	Lumber

DRUM HILL.

Cross, W E,	G S
Parker, J W,	G S

EURE.

Downs, W D,	G S
Eure, Nathaniel,	G S

GATESVILLE.

Brown, J A,	G S
Brown, T A,	G S
Cowper, R B G,	G S
Cross, C W & Co,	G S
Hayes, B R,	Confec and Gro
Laurence, B D,	Furniture
Parker & Co,	G S
Riddick, R M,	G S
Riddick, W E,	Confec
Roberts, A R,	Drugs

| GATES COUNTY. | GATES COUNTY. |

GATLINGTON.

Goodman, W McP,   G S

HOBBSVILLE.

Byrom, Jos,   G S
Hathaway & Rountree,   G S
Hollowell, D & Co,   G S
Hobbs, A & Son,   G S
Hobbs, P L,   G S
Rountree, R & Son,   G S

HOLLY GROVE.

Jones & Son,   G S

MERCHANT MILLS.

Eason, G F,   Undertaker
Edwards, W H,   G S
Wolfley, H A,   Liquors and G S

REYNOLDSON.

Waff, Jos T,   G S

SANDY CROSS.

Russell, E D,   G S

SAREM.

Eason & Parker,   G S
Holland, J T,   G S
Parker, C E,   G S

SUNBURY.

Alphin, J L,   G S
Benton, M,   G S
Copeland, C F,   G S
Cross & Co,   G S
Dennis, R,G,   G S
Dennis, Truitt & Co,   G S
Harrell, O C,   G S
Harrell, E E,   G S
Savage, R T & Co,   G S

TROTVILLE.

Trotman, J M,   G S

VIVIAN.

Williams, H C,   G S

WIGGINS' CROSS ROAD.

Morgan, James E,   G S
Saunders & Co,   G S

WILLEYTON.

Parker & Cross,   G S

WILLOW BRANCH.

Hathaway, Rountree & Co,   G S
Hudgins, A S,   G S
Rountree, G W,   G S

MILLS.

Kinds, Post Offices and Proprietors.

Grist mill, Sunbury, Cross & Co.
Grist mill, Mintonsville, W H Speight.
Saw mill, Sunbury, M Buxton.
Saw mill, Adair, Powell & Edwards.
Saw mill, Gatesville, Hofler & Trotman.

PHYSICIANS.

Names and Post Offices.

Brooks, G C, Sunbury.
Corbell, E T, Sunbury.
Costen, I W, Gatesville.
Horton, ——, Hobbsville.
Lee, W O P, Reynoldson.
Smith, R C, Gatesville.

SCHOOLS.

Names, Post Offices and Principals.

Academy, Reynoldson, M O Carpenter.
High School, Gatesville, C E Cross.
Private School, Gatesville, John R Walton.
Private School, Wiggin's Cross Roads, Miss M A Parker.
No. Public Schools—White, 32; colored, 29.

TEACHERS.

Names and Post Offices.

WHITE.

Carpenter, Prof M O, Reynoldson.
Cross, C E, Gatesville.
Costen, M J, Sunbury.
Cowper, Miss Annie, Gatesville.
Felton, John S, Gatesville.
Hudgins, Miss Rebecca, Willow.
Rountree, L A, Hobbsville.
Russell, Jennie, Sandy cross.
Riddick, Miss E G, Gatesville.
Smith, Miss Beatrice, Willeyton.
Smith, William, Gatesville.
Walton, Miss Margaret, Gatesville.

LOCAL CORPORATIONS.

Occidental Lodge, No. 33, I O O F, Gatesville; time of meeting Wednesday before the 2d and 4th Sunday in each month.
Lilly Valley Lodge, No. 252, A F & A M, Sunbury; time of meeting fourth Saturday in each month.

FARMERS.

Names and Post Offices.

Adair—R C Cowper, Willie S Eure, Elisha Jenkins, Nathaniel Newsom, James R Rooks (col), W S Wilkins, J B Willey.

Bosley—J H Briggs, jr, Moses Bynum, J R Hinton, jr, Leroy Jones, Noah Rountree, L C Rountree, Charles White.

Sorapeake—S D Ballard, W C Brinkley (col), B W Franklin, W C Jones,

GATES COUNTY.

B W Jones, J B Jones, John R Lassiter, Thomas Mathias, J E L Morgan, T M Pearce.

Dort—Jesse Eure, W McP Goodman, W H Howell, W D Langston, T H Langston, M J Lawrence, Stephen Williams.

Drum Hill—D O Collins, P H Cross, E J Freeman, J W Howell, J E Howell, W W Walters.

Gatesville.—K E Baines, F E Baines, John Brady, R B G Cowper, T E Cross, W F Eason, H A Eure, J H Hofler, T W Lawrene, C M Lawrence, J W Lilley, J M Outland, James Parker, Asbury Reed (col), R M Riddick, G K Riddick, A G Rountree, L L Smith, Henry Stallings (col), T B Walton.

Hobbsville—Joseph Bunch, N W Hobbs, D H Hobbs, John Hobbs, Jesse Hobbs, D Hollowell, W H King, Solomon Riddick, A F Rountree, J F Russell, Josiah Spivey, Elbert Winslow, Allen Wood.

Merchant Mills.—Dr R H Riddick, James Russell.

Reynoldson—Hugh Collins, J R Cross, E S Cross, J A Edwards, Geo R Eure, Gilbert Fanny, H Fanny, Henry Fowler, E J Freeman, R Freeman, J J Gatling, Riddick Gatling, J D Goodman, W H Goodman, Warren Green (col), J R Jones, R M Savage, A Smith, J T Waff, B T Weston, B F Wiley, J B Wiley, M Williams.

Sandy Cross.—J R Eason, T W King, T G McCotten, Jas Riddick, Nathan Riddick, Q E Russell, W H Stallings.

GATES COUNTY.

Sarem.—R Gatling, J J Gatling, M C Lawrence, J W Parker, Augustus Wolffey.

Sunbury.—R E Barnes, Wm Beaman, Geo Benton, E S Brooks, C W Costen, J G Costen, T W Costen, J F Cross, Thos Ellis, W T Ellis, S I Harrell, E E Harrell, James Harrell, G T Harrell, J A Harrell, Wm P Harrell, James R Hare (col), Whit Hill, John R Hill, J R Hinton, Robert Hinton, Riddick Hofler, Thos Hunter (col), Wells Jones, T H Lassiter, W M Manning, C M Manning, Wm Nixon, jr, J A Parker, L M Pearce, B F Pearce, Jos Rayner, W W Rice, J A Rountree, James Seawell, Jas W Speight, Jacob White.

Trotville—W H Cannon, R E Cochrane, L A Hobbs, J T Overman, James W Riddick, F H Russell, R W Simpson, J M Trotman, N O Ward.

Wiggin's Cross-Roads—T W Babb, L L Goodman, E H Matthews, Franklin Matthews, Dr H A Morgan, J E Morgan, John W Morgan, D W Parker, W Riddick, T W Riddick, W H Riddick, C O Riddick, T H Rountree, Mrs Alice Savage, Carlton Savage, J S Whidbee, jr.

Willow—J C Blanchard, Elisha Blanchard, A O Brown, W D Burke, C W Hudgins, F P Lassiter, J R Moore, Orin Wright.

Wileyton—Elisha Cross, R W Eason, J C Eggleston, G W Kittrell, J F Willey, H Clay Williams.

GRAHAM COUNTY.

AREA, 250 SQUARE MILES.

POPULATION, 3,362; White 3,137; Colored 225.

GRAHAM COUNTY was set off from Cherokee County by the Legislature of 1871-'72, and named after William A Graham, who was Governor of the State in 1845. He was once Secretary of the Navy, and always noted for his integrity and statesmanship.

ROBBINSVILLE, the county-seat, is situated 309 miles west of Raleigh, and has a population of 75.

Surface—Hilly, and in many places mountainous, with rich valleys and splendid water power.

Staples — Corn, wheat, oats, rye, buckwheat, medicinal herbs, grass and live stock. This is a very fine grazing county.

Fruits—Peaches, apples, pears, berries, and almost all the small fruits.

Timbers—Black walnut, white pine, black locust, chestnut, wild cherry, poplar, the oaks, and a great variety of the shrubs.

TOWNS AND POST OFFICES.

	POP.		POP.
Cheoah,	30	Robb'ville (C H)	75
Fairfax,	60	Stecoah,	100
Homestead,	45	Tulula,	50
Johnson,	65	Yellow Creek.	50

COUNTY OFFICERS.

Clerk Superior Court—T A Carpenter.

Commissioners—W D Crisp, W B West, J A Wiggins.

Coroner—D E Hyde.

Register of Deeds—W F Mauney.

Sheriff—J A Ammons.

Solicitor Ninth District — Geo A Jones.

Surveyor—H P Hyde.

Treasurer—S B Rose.

County Examiner—J A Hyde.

COURTS.

Thirteenth Monday after the first Monday in March, and ninth Monday after the first Monday in September.

TOWNSHIPS AND MAGISTRATES.

Cheoah—N C Phillips, T J Wakfield, J D Rogers, J R Calvard, W M Barnes (Rollinsville).

Robbinsville—Reuben Rogers, F J Wakefield, John Dston (Robbinsville).

Stecoah—M A Crisp, W H Crisp, D A Taylor, Daniel R Welch, C F Sawyer (Stecoah).

Yellow Creek—W M Barnes, James Rimer, Wm Garrison, A Wall, Clinton Millsap (Yellow Creek).

CHURCHES.

Names, Post Offices, Pastors and Denom.

BAPTIST.

Cneoah—Robbinsville, W C Morgan.
Sweet Water——————, Wm Pruett.
Stecoah—Stecoah, Wm Pruett.
Tutula—Robbinsville, W C Morgan.
Yellow Creek—Yellow Creek, Geo Orr.

METHODIST.

Crisper—Welch, Alford Foster.
Robbinsville—Robbinsville, Alford Foster.

MINISTERS RESIDENT.

Names, Post Offices, Pastors and Denom.

BAPTIST.

Green, P G, Stecoah.
Hooper, L D, Robbinsville.
Hooper, G W, Robbinsville.
Jordan, Samuel, Robbinsville.
Morgan, W C, Robbinsville.
Pruett, Wm, Robbinsville.

METHODIST.

Cooper, J C, Robbinsville.
Wiggins, J A, Robbinsville.

HOTELS AND BOARDING HOUSES.

Names, Post Offices and Proprietors.

Junaluska, Robbinsville, J W King.
Lovejoy, Robbinsville, N M E Slaughter.
Mauney House, Robbinsville, W F Mauney.

MANUFACTORIES.

Kinds, Post Offices and Proprietors.

Furniture, Robbinsville, P P Harwood.
Furniture, Robbinsville, W P Phillips.
Wagons, Robbinsville, W C Morgan.

MERCHANTS AND TRADESMEN.

Name, Post Office, and Line of Business.

JOHNSON.

Carden, S J,　G S

ROBBINSVILLE.

Robinson, J W,　G S
Walker, W P & G B,　G S

STECOAH.

Crisp, J L,　G S
Crisp, Joel L,　G S

WELCH.

Crisp, W H,　G S

MILLS.

Kinds, Post Offices and Proprietors.

Flour and corn, Stecoah, M A Crisp.
Flour and corn, Stecoah, Joel L Crisp.
Flour and corn, Stecoah, M B Crisp.
Flour and corn, Yellow Creek, Z T Ditmore.
Flour and corn, Welch, J S Bradshaw.
Flour and corn, Yellow Creek, Henry Grant.
Flour and corn, Robbinsville, J L Hyde.
Flour and corn, Robbinsville, J P Adams.
Flour, corn and saw, Robbinsville, P P Harwood.
Flour, corn and saw, Robbinsville, W B Wiggins.
Flour and corn, Robbinsville, C C Jordan.
Grist, Robbinsville, Samuel Larne.
Grist, Stecoah, J D Harwood.
Grist and saw, Stecoah, P P.Harwood.
Grist, Johnson, Robert Stratton.
Grist, Johnson, P L Jenkins.
Grist, Robbinsville, J A Hyde.
Grist, Homestead, James M Crisp.
Grist, Robbinsville, Thos Shepard.
Grist, Robbinsville, W M Maynor.
Grist, Robbinsville, J A Stewart.
Grist, Robbinsville. Charles Gregory.
Planing, Robbinsville, W C Phillips.
Saw, Robbinsville, Hampton, McElray & Co.
Saw, Robbinsville, James Baker.
Saw, Stecoah, James Lisenby.

PHYSICIANS.

Names and Post Offices.

Davis, C C, Robbinsville.
Ghormley, D C, Robbinsville.
Maxwell, M T, Robbinsville.

SCHOOLS.

Public schools—white, 18; colored, —.

FARMERS.

Names and Post Offices.

Homestead—Samuel Ammons, T J Bradshaw, A A Edward, John Marcus, I J Sawyer, Galliman Sawyer, Daniel Welch.

Johnson—F M Caringer, A J Caringer, P C Caringer, B P Grant, P L Jenkins, Samuel Lene, Josiah Phillips, J R Stratton.

Robbinsville— J T Adams, Jno Adams, J L Ammon, D K Blanton, John Cody, N F Cooper, Jas Calvard, R Calvard, S J R Calvard, J M Calvard, J J Calvard, Thomas Carver, R Carver, J B Crisp, J C Cooper, N F Cowper, P Campbell, B B Campbell, John Davis, M T Davis, M F T Davis, J M Dawes, Jno Dawes, W Ellis, W W Flemming, D C Ghormley, R E Hampton, W W Hampton, R S Harper, L S Harper, J O Holloway, G W Hooper, W H Hyde, J L Hyde, J S Hyde, H P Hyde, Wm Jenkins, W B McCracken, W C Morgan, G W Orr, A J Patton, Andrew Phillips, P L Phillips, A R Phillips. G P Rice, N W Rice, D R Roberts, Reuben Rogers, A H Sherrill. M S Sherrill, R H Sherrill, N M E Slaughter, I J Slaughter, John Taylor, J D Taylor, T J Wakefield, W B West, John M Whisenhunt, W B Wiggins, J A Wiggins.

Stecoah.—Dick Aldridge, T J Ammons, W J Ammons, P S Calvard. R S Calvard, P A Cable. A M Cable, J M Crisp. Joe Crisp, M B Crisp, W D Crisp, J L Crisp, Phillip Crisp. Joel Crisp,* John M Crisp. W D Crisp, James M Carver, J S Gunter, P C Gunter, J S Gunter, R P Harwood, P P Harwood. S P Harwood, J C Holloway, G P Rice, J S Hyde, D E Hyde, John Jenkins, Philip Jenkins. J D Jenkins, D F Johnson, Phil Lanin, W R McLean, N M. Pilchentan, P L Phillips, J B Taylor, D A Taylor, W B West, P A Wiggins, W C Wiggins.

Welch.—J S Bradshaw, N Crisp, J M Crisp, Frank Mealin, John Sawyer, T J Welch.

Yellow Creek.—J G Brooks, Riley Calvin, J B Caringer, J D Carrington, F M Carrington. S T Ditmore. C Fairley, Wm Garrison, Varnel Grant, Jacob Shope, J Shope, Geo Shuler, C P Williams, A Williams.

GRANVILLE COUNTY.

AREA, 750 SQUARE MILES.

POPULATION 24,461; White 12,101, Colored 12,360.

GRANVILLE COUNTY was formed in 1746, from Edgecombe county, and was named in honor of the British nobleman who was created Earl of Granville and held the land under a grant from Charles II.

OXFORD, the county-seat, is 36 miles north from Raleigh, and has a population estimated at 4,000. It is situated on the Oxford and Clarksville and the Oxford and Henderson railroads.

Surface—Pleasantly undulating; well watered by the head branches of the Tar river; and generally remunerative. This is altogether a fine county, and contains a thrifty population.

Staples—Tobacco is the great staple. The weed is produced to perfection and manufactured largely. Wheat, corn, oats, sweet potatoes, etc., are grown extensively and profitably.

Fruits—Peaches, apples, grapes, berries, pears, melons and a variety of other small fruits.

Timbers—Hickory, oak, pine, ash and poplar.

TOWNS AND POST OFFICES.

	POP.		POP.
Adoniram,	—	Hester,	50
Berea,	125	Jacho,	25
Big Rock,	25	Knapo' Reeds,	100
Blue Wing,	20	Lyons,	75
Brownsville,	25	Mount Energy,	20
Buchanan,	50	Noblin,	25
Bullock,	100	Northside,	20
Clay,	50	Oak Hill,	60
Cornwall,	60	Oxford,	4,000
Cozart,	55	Pleasants,	25
Creedmoor,	100	Satterwhite,	35
Culbreth,	50	Stem,	100
Dean,	26	Stovall,	150
Dexter,	—	Sunset,	50
Dutchville,	25	Tar River,	100
Fairport,	85	Whitestone,	50
Grissom,	20	Wilkins,	50
Hampton,	20	Welton,	75
Hargrove,	25	Zacho,	25

COUNTY OFFICERS.

Clerk Superior Court—J M Sikes.
Commissioners—T D Waller, G B Royster, B I Breedlove, W H Garner, J P Thomas.
Coroner—J W Branen.
Sheriff—W S Cozart.

Register of Deeds—C F Crews.
Solicitor 5th District—W P Bynum, Jr.
Standard Keeper—S V Ellis.
Surveyor— ——.
Public Administrator—B S Royster.
Treasurer—A S Peace.
County Examiner—W H Jenkins.

COURTS.

Fifth Monday before first Monday in March; seventh Monday after first Monday in March; sixth Monday before the first Monday in September; twelfth Monday after the first Monday in September.

TOWN OFFICERS.

OXFORD—*Mayor*, B S Royster; *Commissioners*, J F Edwards, L B Booth, J M Currin, J C Horner, J B Hall, W L Mitchell; *Town Clerk*, E T Crews; *Chief of Police*, J A Renn; *Constable*, D A Moore.

TOWNSHIPS AND MAGISTRATES.

Brassfield—J D Davis, Jno H House, W A Blackley, W P White, W P Lyon, G L Allen, J M Davis, W H Sikes, (Oxford).

Dutchville—M L Coley, W T Adams, J V Roberts, J D Tillery, E E Lyon, L A Wilkins, J M Taylor, B Beasly (Dutchville).

Fishing Creek—E C Montague, Wm A Parham, C A Bryan, W D Blackley, R M Height, S J H Mayes, L P Wortham, Alex Baker (Oxford).

Oak Hill—B F Winston, W T Eakes, W T Chandler, J S Pool, M S Daniel, J W Downey, S S Henderson, William Raker (Oak Hill).

Oxford—W L Thomas, A C Parham, R J Mitchell, J W Brown, A J Dalby, A S Peace, B W Hicks, N D Hobgood (Oxford).

Sassafras Fork—Wilkins Stoval, S J Curran, W H Gregory, R A Gill, Wm Davis, Alford Bullock, S L Daniel, James R Callahan (Oxford).

Tally Ho—Radford Gooch, W T Allen, James R Walters, D C Farabow, Durell Johnson, G T Walters, H G Lilly (Oxford).

Salem—C F Crews, J B Parham, A L Gooch, J R Wilson, J W Wilson, H

GRANVILLE COUNTY.

C Gill, W N Hicks, Rufus Puckett (Oxford).

Walnut Grove—G S Latta, John G Shotwell, B H Hester, J N Hobgood, J F Cole, G T Murray, N J Woodlief, Thomas Cash (Oxford).

CHURCHES.

Names, Pastors, Postoffices and Denom.

METHODIST.

Banks' Chapel, Franklinton, N H D Wilson.
Bethel, Oxford, G P Perry.
Bullock's, Hester, B C Allred.
Calvary, Knap of Reeds, B C Allred.
Church, Oxford, J B Hurley.
Church, Stem, B C Allred.
Gray Rock, Clay, G B Perry.
Grove Hill, Franklinton, N H D Wilson.
Hebron, Sunset, W S H ster.
Herman, Carlton, G B Perry.
Moore's, Stem, B C Allred.
Mount Tabor, Flat River, B C Allred.
Rock Spring, Grissom, N H D Wilson.
Salem, Oxford, G B Perry.
Shady Grove, Oxford, G B Perry.
Trinity, Berea, N E Coltrane.

METH. PROTESTANT.

Antioch (Vance county), Oxford, W Harris.
Mt. Olivet, Oxford, —— Dozier.

BAPTIST.

Amis Chapel, Buchanan, P H Fontaine.
Bethany, Stem, —— Hairfield.
Brassfield's, Wilton, G T Watkins.
Church, Stovall, J A Stradley.
Church, Oxford, J S Hardaway.
Concord, Dutchville, —— Davis.
Corinth, Clay, J A Adkinson.
Fellowship, Beck's, J A Adkinson.
Grassy Creek, Adoniram, R H Marsh.
Hester's, Sunset, R H Marsh.
Mountain Creek, Cornwall, —— Riddick.
Mount Zion, Berea, J A Stradley.
Pleasant Grove, Mt Energy, J E Smith.
Rock Spring (Vance county), Townsville, J A Stradley.
Tally Ho, Stem, J E Smith.

PRESBYTERIAN.

Church, Oxford, J E Thacker.
Church, Oak Hill, W T Walker.
Church (col), Oxford, G C Shaw.
Church (col), Henderson, G C Shaw (Vance co).
Geneva, Culbreth, C W Wharton.
Grassy Creek, Stovall, C N Wharton.
Shiloh, Stovall, W T Walker.

GRANVILLE COUNTY.

EPISCOPAL.

St. Paul's, Oak Hill (Goshen).
St. Stephen's, Oxford, Junius Moore Horner.

CHRISTIAN.

Mt Carmel, Wilton, J W Wellons.

MINISTERS RESIDENT.

Names, Post Offices and Denominations.

BAPTIST.

Cozart, J R (col), Berea.
Devin, R I. Oxford.
Gregory, Wm (col), Stovall.
Hardaway, J S, Oxford.
Henderson, S S (col), Buchanan.
Hunt, J A (col), Oxford.
Marsh, R H, Oxford.
Patillo, W A (col), Oxford. (Vance county).
Ransom, M C (col), Oxford.
Reavis, W D (col), Oxford.
Stradley, J A, Oxford.

METHODIST.

Floyd, J B, Wilton.
Hester, W S, Oxford.
Hurley. J B, Oxford.
Perry, G B, Oxford.
Turner, L T, Wilton.

PRESBYTERIAN.

Shaw, G C (col), Oxford.
Thacker, J E, Oxford.

EPISCOPAL.

Horner, J M, Oxford.

HOTELS AND BOARDING HOUSES.

Names, Post Offices and Proprietors.

Exchange, Oxford, Mrs T H Jones.
Freeman House, Creedmore, E E Freeman.
Hotel, Oak Hill, John D Wilkinson.
Irwin Place, Oxford, Mrs L W Meadows.
Osborn House, Oxford, C D Osborn.

LAWYERS.

Names and Post Offices.

Amis, J S. Oxford.
Biggs, J, Crawford (Winston, Fuller & Biggs).
Cannady, N B, Oxford.
Edwards, L C, Oxford.
Field, Alex J, Oxford.
Graham, P C (Graham & Graham), Oxford.
Graham, A W (Judge Superior Court), Oxford.
Hayes, John W, Oxford.

GRANVILLE COUNTY.

Hicks, A A, Oxford.
Jenkins. Willis H, Oxford,
Lanier, T. Oxford.
Lanier, M V, Oxford.
Royster, Beverly S, Oxford.
Shaw, H M, Oxford.
Sikes, J M, Oxford.

MANUFACTORIES.

Kinds, Post Offices and Proprietors.

Blacksmithing, Dexter, Jordan Ourby.
Blacksmithing, Berea, Lottie Nemson (col).
Blacksmithing, Oxford, Sandy Parham.
Blacksmithing, Stovall, Geo Young (col).
Blacksmithing, Grissom, J V Allen.
Blacksmithing. Berea, John T Murray.
Blacksmithing, Grissom, Pleas Priddy.
Blacksmithing, Grissom, Josiah Wheeler.
Blacksmithing, Berea, W P Slaughter & Bro.
Brick, Oxford, B H Cozart.
Candy, Oxford, S W Jackson.
Contracting and building, Sassafras Fork, William Fain.
Contracting and building, Sassafras Fork, Daniel Armistead.
Contracting and building, Sassafras Fork, Collins Pettiford.
Contracting and building, Sassafras Fork, Thomas Flagg.
Contracting and building, Blue Wing, T S Wilkinson.
Contracting and building, Berea, Stephen M Slaughter.
Foundry and plows, Stem, D W Wheeler.
Foundry and grist mill, Oxford, W S Hundley.
Furniture and undertaking, Oxford, J K Wood, agt.
Sash and blinds, Oxford, Hundley Bros & Co.
Tannery, Dutchville. G W Pool.
Tobacco Flues and Tinware, Oxford, Edwards & Winston.
Tobacco orderer, Oxford, W S Hundley.
Wagons, Buchanan, Wm Seat.
Wagons, Oxford, B F Taylor.
Wagons, Oxford, W B Glenn, mgr Clipper Wagon Co
Wood and Iron, Stovall, J W Patterson.

MERCHANTS AND TRADESMEN.

Names, Post Offices and Line of Business.

ADONIRAM.

Peace, Alex (col),   G S
Royster, L A,   G S

GRANVILLE COUNTY.

BEREA.

Casa & Murray,   G S
Fuller, J N & Bro,   G S

BLUE WING.

Pannebaker & Ford,   G S

BUCHANAN.

Norwood, Mrs S D,   G S

BULLOCKS.

Royster, Mrs J A & Son,   G S
Royster & Tolly,   G S

CLAY.

Daniel, J W,   G S

CORNWALL.

Watkins. J W,   Fertilizer and G S
Wright & Hester,   G S

COZART.

Chappell, J P & E E,   G S
Beck, A C,   G S

CREEDMOOR.

Cross, L H.   Harness
Dupree, W R,   G S
Fleming, R H,   G S
Freeman, E E,
   Boarding House and Livery Stables
Longmill, L H,   G S
Lyon, S C,   G S
O'Briant, J R,   G S
Rogers, R H,   G S
Rogers, S H & Co,   G S
Tingden, J H,   G S
Wagstaff, D P,   G S

CULBRETH.

Jones, S H,   G S

DEAN.

Rice, W L (agt),   G S

DEXTER.

Green, W H,   G S
Heck, Patterson & Co,   G S

DUTCHVILLE.

Cozart, W W,   G S

FAIRPORT.

Williams, J D,   G S

GRISSOM.

Hockaday, W P,   G S
Lloyd, A B,   G S
Sikes, W H & Co,   G S
York, E T (near),   Tobacco

HAMPTON.

Eastwood, C D,   Undertaker
Gooch, W H,   G S
Hampton, W B,   G S

HARGROVE.

Jones, R S & Co,   G S

HESTER.

Barley, Mrs M E,   G S
Bryan, J J,   Drugs
Burnett, C F,   G S

GRANVILLE COUNTY.

Hester, W A,   G S
Pittard, J C,   G S

KITTRELL.

Williams, J D,   G S
Woodlief, J M & Co,   O S

KNAP OF REEDS.

Bullock Bros,   G S
Waller, J A,   Fertilizer

LYONS.

Green, Gwyn,   G S

MT. ENERGY.

Bullock, J T,   G S

NOBLIN.

Noblin, J T,   C S

NORTH SIDE.

Fleming & Cooley,   G S
Cash, W A,   G S
Fleming & Beck,   G S

OAK HILL.

Thorp, P, jr,   G S

OXFORD.

Adams, W A D & Co,   Tobacco Stem-
                                     mers
Adams, W A & Co,   Leaf Dealers
Alston, A D,   G S
Ballott, W B,   Tobacco Stemmers
Biggs, W C,   Tel Op Postal Tel Co
Bobbitt, W A,   Leaf Dealer
Booth & Hunt,   Warehousemen and
                              Leaf Dealers
Booth, J B,   Tob Buyer
Bowling, J R,   Auctioneer
Brinkley, J D,   Photographer
Brooks, J D & Co,   G S
Brown, J S,   Gro
Bryant, A A,   Painter
Bullock, J D,   Leaf Dealers
Bullock & Mitchell, Owners and props
   Banner Tobacco Warehouse; also
           Commission and Brokerage
Carroll, C A,   G S
Chapman & Co,   Saloon
Cheatham, D S (near)   Miller
Clayton, M F,   G S
Council, H J, Cabinet and Upholstering
Crews, W H, jr (col),   G S
Crews, E T,   Auctioneer
Currin, A B,   Livery Stables
Currin Bros,   Tobacco
Currin, J M,   Leaf Dealer
Currin, E G & Bro,   Leaf Dealer
Cutchen, G A,   Cabinet and Uphols-
                                 tering
Daniel, G S,   G S
Davis, J C,   Grocer
Day L F,   Harness
Day, R W,   Livery Stables
Day, J N,   Leaf Dealers
Dusenberry, Gowan,   Agt So R R
                          and So Ex Co

GRANVILLE COUNTY.

Dusenberry, G S,   Agt O & C R R
Edwards & Winston,   Hardware
Foster, Grant (col),   Butcher
Fuller, J W,   Gro
Gooch, D J,   Gro
Hall, J S,   Harness
Hall, J G,   Drugs
Harris, E C (near),   G S
Howell, T L & Bro,   G S
Hughes, D (col),   Barber
Hunt, W H,   Ins Agt
Jackson, S W,   Conf and Baker
Jones, W W,   Books and Str
Knott & Cooper,   Minor Warehouse
Knott, G W,   Post Master
Knott, H T,   Leaf Tob
Kronheimer, Misses L & C,   Millinery
Kronheimer, B F,   G S and Clothing
Landis & Easton,   Dry Goods and G S
Long Bros,   Dry Goods
Lynch, W D,   Jeweler
Lyon, Thos & Co,   Meadows' Ware-
                                 house
Lyon & Lyon,   Leaf Dealers
Meadows, John,   Leaf Dealer
Medford, J J,   Racket Store
Mitchell, R J,   Miller
Orphan's Friend,   Job Printing
Osborn, Job,   Com Mcht
Osborn, E,   Leaf Dealer
Osborn, C D,   Livery
Paris Bros,   Dry Goods
Parker & Hunt,   Fert and Lumber
Pendleton, T B,   Baker and Conf
Pitchford, R L,   Gro
Pitchford, W J & Son,   G S
Public Ledger,   Job Printing
Randolph & Co,   G S
Ragland, R B & W L,   G S
Rawlins, E T,   Dry Goods
Robinson, Banister, jr,   G S
Roller, J R & Son,   Gen Ins Agts
Royster, J F,   Livery
Sizemore, J T & Co,   Gro
Smith, S H,   Hdw and Vehicles
Spencer, Frank,   Exp Agt and Tel Op
Starke, L W,   Auctioneer
Stedman, J P,   Drugs
Stegall, Mrs A B,   Gro
Terry, H (col),   Barber
Ward, C J,   Com Mcht
Warsham, A T,   Wheelwright
Webb, John,   Leaf Dealer
Webb, Joseph A,   Fertilizers
Webb, J A,   Furniture
White, J F,   Leaf Dealer
White, E T,   Leaf Dealer
Wilkinson, W I,   Tob Warehouse
Wood, J K,   Coffins, Furniture and
                         U S Commissioner
Wright, L E & Co,   Dry Goods

SATTERWHITE.

Evans, J H & Co,   G S
Evans, S M,   G S

GRANVILLE COUNTY.

STEM.

Bailey, Mrs M E,   Millinery
Booth, R E,   G S
Burnett, J R,   G S
Cash & Washington,   G S
Gooch, J H,   G S
Gooch, W G,   G S
Jones & Washington,   G S
Moyes, J B,   Livery
Weeb & Gooch,   G S

STOVALL.

Daniel, Mrs G E T,   G S
Daniel, G S,   G S
Gregory, Dr F R,   Drugs
Stovall, T W,   G S
Taylor, R A & Co (col),   G S
Young & Smith (col),   G S

TALLY HO.

Sanders, J L,   G S

TAR RIVER.

Burnett, J A,   G S
Crews, L L,   Fert
Harris, B T & T C,   G S

WHETSTONE.

Frazier, B F & Bro,   G S

WILTON.

Burnett, Ira A,   G S
Cannady, T L,   G S
Cannady, J F,   G S
Harris, J W, agt,   G S
Rogers, T C,   G S

WILKINS.

Roycroft and Bros,   G S

MINES.

Kinds, Post Offices and Proprietors.

Copper, Blue Wing, Blue Wing Copper Co.
Copper, Oak Hill, James Norwood.
Gold, Young's X Roads, Robert Elliott.
Gold, Young's X Roads, Thos. Chandler.
Iron, Berea, Lewis Thorpe, Jr.
Rockbrook Mineral Spring, Oxford, Dr E T White, proprietor.

MILLS.

Kinds, Post Offices and Proprietors.

Corn and saw, Knap of Reeds, Waller Bros & Co.
Corn, flour and saw, Oxford, R J Mitchell.
Corn, flour and saw, Oxford, T G Cheatham.
Corn, flour and saw, Tar River, R T Crews.

GRANVILLE COUNTY.

Corn, flour and saw, Oxford, D J Gooch.
Corn, flour, saw and carding, Hargrove, W D Kimball.
Corn, flour and saw, Wilton, E B Lyon & Co.
Corn and flour, Oxford, H C Herndon.
Corn and flour, Clay, Jas Howell.
Corn and flour, Clay, Simeon Tippett.
Corn and flour, Oxford, Edward Hicks.
Corn and flour, Wilton, Lyon & Floyd.
Corn and flour, Oak Hill, Dr William Thorp.
Corn and flour, Wilton, W H Cannady's heirs.
Corn and flour, Sassafras Fork, L E Amis.
Corn and flour, Sassafras Fork, James Buchanan.
Corn and flour, Sassafras Fork, C A Gregory.
Corn and flour, Sassafras Fork, J L Gregory.
Corn and flour, Young's X Roads, J J Speed's estate.
Corn and flour, Berea, Pinck Meadows.
Corn and flour, Dutchville, Green & Lyon.
Corn and flour, Grissom, Haswell & Bailey.
Roller flour, Sassafras Fork, Hubert Gregory.
Saw, Dutchville, Green & Lyon.
Saw and corn, Blue Wing, G A Harris & Sons.

PHYSICIANS.

Names and Post Offices.

Atwater, R S, Knap of Reeds.
Baskerville, W O, Oxford.
Booth, Robert (druggist), Stem.
Booth, J W, Stem.
Booth, S D, Oxford.
Booth, Thomas, Oxford.
Bryant, ——, Stem.
Cannady. S H, Oxford.
Cozart, W W, Dutchville.
Fort, C D H (dentist), Oxford.
Gregory, T R, Stovall.
Harris, A C, Stovall.
Hardee, P R, Virgilina.
Hays, B K, Oxford.
Henderson, R B, Wilton.
Laurence, ——, Wilton.
Morris, ————.
Sanford, J L, Creedmore.
Sikes, G T, Grissom.
Sweaney, John, Berea.
Taylor, L C, Oxford.
Thorp, William, Oak Hill.
Williams, J B, Oxford.

GRANVILLE COUNTY.

SCHOOLS.

Names, Post Offices, and Principals,

Academy, Stovall, Miss Minnie Holden,
Academy, Dutchville.
College St Seminary, Oxford, Mrs M A
Faucett.
Francis Hilliard School, Oxford, Misses
M & C Hilliard.
Graeed School, Oxford, M C Kausan,
(col).
Mary Potter Memorial School, Oxford,
G C Shaw.
Mathematical and Classical, Oxford,
J C Horner and J M Horner (military).
Orphan Asylum (masonic), Oxford, N
M Lawrence, supt.
Orphan Asylum (col), Oxford, A R
Shepard.
Oxford Female Seminary, Oxford, F P
Hobgood, pres.
Primary, Oxford, Miss Bettie Jordan.
Tar River Academy, Hargrove, W T
Allen.
Public Schools—white, 43; colored, 73.

LOCAL CORPORATIONS.

Adoniram Lodge, No 149. A F and A M,
Brownsville; meets Saturday before
second Sunday at 2 o'clock P M.

GRANVILLE COUNTY.

Bank of Granville, Oxford; E T White,
pres; J B Roller, cash'r; F W Hancock, teller; C S Easton, b'k'p'r.
Banking House of Oxford, J C Cooper
& Sons; H G Cooper, cash'r.
Berea Lodge, No 204, A F and A M,
Oxford; meets Saturday before 4th
Sunday, and June 24th and December 27th at 2 o'clock P M.
Knap of Reeds Lodge, No 158, A F and
A M, Knap of Reeds; meets Saturday before third Sunday, and December 27th.
Mount Energy Lodge, No 140, A F and
A M, Mount Energy; meets first
Saturday at 2 o'clock P M, and December 27th
Oxford Chapter, No 8; Dr E C White,
H P.
Oxford Lodge, No 396, S H Smith,
W M.
Tuscarora Lodge, No 122, A F and A M,
Oxford; meets first Monday evenings;
in December on second Monday evening.

NEWSPAPERS.

Names, Post Offices and Proprietors.

The Public Ledger, Oxford (Democratic weekly); John T Britt, editor
and prop.
The Orphan's Friend, Oxford; W B
Tarkinton, editor; E W Jones, mgr.

GREENE COUNTY.

AREA 300 SQUARE MILES.

POPULATION, 10,039; White 5,281, Colored 4,758.

GREENE COUNTY was formed in 1799, from what was, prior to that time. Glasgow county. It was named in compliment of Gen Nathaniel Greene, who was one of the bravest, most sagacious a· d most successful officers of the Revolution, and the saviour of the South from the invasions of the British. He was a native of Rhode Island, where he was born in 1741. Glasgow (now Greene county) and Lenoir originally formed Dobbs county, extinct since 1791.

SNOW HILL, the county seat, is situated 76 miles east of Raleigh, and has a population of 510.

Surface—Greene county is situated on Contentnea creek, and is level; lands rich and very productive when well drained. The population is a thrifty one, and the section is a good one for agriculture.

Staples—corn, cotton, tobacco sweet potatoes and naval stores. Cotton is grown systematically, and with great success; also wheat, oats and rye are being grown successfully.

Fruits — Apples, peaches, pears. grapes, melons. plums, and other small fruits.

Timbers—Pine, oak, cypress, hickory, ash and poplar.

TOWNS AND POST OFFICES.

	POP.		POP.
Appletree,	10	Lizzie,	30
Bull Head,	25	Ormondsville,	40
Castoria,	30	Ridge Spring,	25
Contentnea,	15	Shine,	40
Fieldsboro,	25	Snow Hill	
Fountain Hill,	50	(CH),	510
Glenfield,	80	Speight's	
Hardeesville,	—	Bridge,	25
Hookerton,	179	Willow Green,	25
Jason,	25		

COUNTY OFFICERS.

Clerk Superior Court — John W Blount.

Commissioners— W E Best, ch'm; Lawrence Bryant. W D Mewborn.

Coroner—Jas B Jones.

Register of Deeds—C A Lasiter.

Sheriff—B W Edwards.

Solicitor 5th District—W C Richardson.

Standard Keeper—B F Albritton.

Surveyor—Pinkney Arthur.

Teasurer—John Sugg.

County Examiner—E A Darden.

Supt of Health—Dr J E Brinkley (Speight's Bridge).

COURTS.

First Monday before the first Monday in March, third Monday before the first Monday in September, and twelfth Monday after first Monday in September.

TOWN OFFICERS.

SNOW HILL—*Mayor*. J A Albritton; *Chief of Police*. H D Potter; *Clerk and Treasurer*, L D Morrell; *Commissioners*, Joshua Potter. Joe Exum, L V Morrell. G E Dail, William Caraway, S E Moore.

TOWNSHIPS AND MAGISTRATES.

Names and Post Offices.

Bull Head—W D Spence, R D S Dixon, Jno W Taylor. J F Britt, A J Edmonson, Lemuel Dawson (Bull Head).

Carr's—W G Walston, W M Caraway, W G Cair, J W S Beamon, J H Beamor, J H Newell, J T Parker, B F Moore (Snow Hill).

Hcokerton—Jno F Hooker, J E W Sugg, D V Dixon, W H Johnson, G B Pate, J P Hill, J C Pridgen, J A Aldridge, Pinkney Arther (Hookerton).

Jason—L J H Mewborn, Rufus F Hadley, I R Baker, A A Moye, Geo M Carter, E Mitchell, B T Mooring, P M Harrison (Jason).

Olds—J T Barrett, T E Barrow, J M Patrick, A T Grimesly, W E Murphey, L S Hardy, J W Speight (Ormondsville).

Ormondsville—T J Worthington, E A Coward, W T Dixon, C C Hardy, W H Phillips, J R Patrick, J A Newell (Ormondsville).

Shine—Z L Smith, J W Taylor, Ben Taylor, jr, Taylor Barrow. Monroe Lancaster. J A Frazier, H H Best (Castoria).

Snow Hill—Arvil Sugg, John Grant, C P Sauls. J T Holmes, J T Sugg, W P Ormond, Everett Taylor, Jno Lynch (Snow Hill).

GREENE COUNTY.

Speight's Bridge—J F Dildy, J H Garris, W R Gay, J A McKeel, B R Gay, A L Darden, W M Darden (Speight's Bridge).

Willow Green—J A Davis, J R Spier, W D Jenkins, A E Denton, W L May, Thomas Bowens, Ferdinand Robinson (Willow Green).

CHURCHES.

Names, Post Offices, Pastors and Denom.

METHODIST.

Chapel—Ormandsville, D L Earnhardt.
Church—Snow Hill, D L Earnhardt.
Church—Hookerton, D L Earnhardt.
Howell's Swamp—Speight's Bridge, D L Earnhardt.
Jerusalem—Snow Hill, D L Earnhardt.
Lebanon—Appletree, D L Earnhardt.
Mt Herman—Lizzie, D L Earnhardt.
Rainbow—Hookerton, D L Earnhardt.
Tabernacle — Speight's Bridge, D L Earnhardt.

FREE-WILL BAPTIST.

Church—Hookerton.
Free Union—Snow Hill, E B Hart.
Friendship—Snow Hill.
Grimesley—Snow Hill, E B Hart.
Howell's Swamp—Speight's Bridge, E B Hart.
Little Creek, Scuffleton, Fred McLawhorn.
Little Creek (col)— ———
Old Free Union (col)—Speight's Bridge.
Oaky Grove (col)—Hookerton, Ellis Dixon.
Waterside (col)—Willow Green.

DISCIPLES OF CHRIST.

Church—Hookerton.
Edenton—Shine.

A. M. E. ZION.

Church (col)—Snow Hill.
Falling Creek—Shine.
New Zion (col)—Ormondsville.

MINISTERS RESIDENT.

Names, Post Offices and Denominations.

DISCIPLES OF CHRIST.

Davis, Jesse, Ormondsville.

METHODIST.

Edwards, J A, Hookerton.
Earnhardt, D L, Snow Hill.

FREE-WILL BAPTIST.

Blount, Dan'l (col), Willow Green.
Dixon, Ellis (col), Hookerton.
Joyner, Alexander (col), Scuffleton.
Moore, Thomas, Snow Hill.
Sugg, Chas (col), Snow Hill.
Taylor, Richard, Ormondsville.

GREENE COUNTY.

A. M. E. ZION.

Conrad, Alfred (col), Ormandsville.
Moore, ——— (col), Hookerton.

HOTELS AND BOARDING HOUSES.

Kinds, Post Offices and Proprietors.

Boarding House, Hookerton, J Taylor.
Boarding House, Snow Hill, Mrs Frank Harrell.
Hotel, Snow Hill, Haywood Dail.
Hotel, Snow Hill, J J Potter.

LAWYERS.

Names and Post Offices.

Blount, John W, Snow Hill.
Edwards, Theo, Snow Hill.
Lindsay, Geo M, Snow Hill.
Morrell, L V, Snow Hill.

MANUFACTORIES.

Kinds, Post Offices and Proprietors.

Building and contracting, Snow Hill, Owen Silivant.
Coach, Snow Hill, McD Pate.
Coach, Hookerton, Jas Moore (col.).
Shingles, Snow Hill, Wiley Singleton.

MERCHANTS AND TRADESMEN.

Names, Post Offices, Lines of Business.

APPLETREE.

Bryant, W R, Jr,	G S
Crocker, J W,	G S
Scott, W L,	G S

BROWN TOWN.

Arthur Pinkey,	G S

BULL HEAD.

Taylor, R W,	G S

CASTORIA.

Beaman, J H,	Grocer
Carr, T W,	G S
Phillips, Jesse,	Grocer
Wooten, Simeon,	G S

CONTENTNEA.

Dixon, R D S,	G S

FIELDSBORO.

Baker, A J,	G S
Fieldsboro, W R,	G S
Peoples & Moore,	G S
Turnage, Henry C,	G S

FOUNTAIN HILL.

Wood & Coward,	G S

GLENFIELD.

Hooker, H A,	G S

GREENE COUNTY.

HARDEESVILLE.

Hardee, H M,   G S

HOOKERTON.

Dixon, D V,   G S
Dixob, D H & Co,   G S
Dixon, W O,   G S
Edwards, Mrs J J & Co,   Millinery
Edwards, J J,   G S
Edwards, D N,   G S
Harper, R M & Co,   G S
Rouse, R C,   G S
Tunstall, J S,   G S

JASON.

Hardy & Mewborn,   G S

LIZZIE.

Lassiter & Bro,   G S
Tunstall, Bros (near),   G S

ORMONDSVILLE.

Hardee, Henry M,   G S
Turnage & Ormond,   G S

RIDGE SPRING.

Holton & Spier,   G S

SHINE.

Best, B J & R E,   G S
Frazier & Smith,   G S and Gin
Jones & Herring,   G S
Lancaster, L A,   G S

SNOW HILL.

Dail, G E & Co.   Grocers
Exum, Josiah & Co,   Grocers
Grimsley, Dr J E,   Drugs
Jordan, W J,
             Fire, Life and Accident Ins
Lehman, E M & Co,   D G
Pate, M,   Carriage Mfr
Patrick, D W (near),   G S
Potter, Miss Emma,   Millinery
Sauls, C D (col.),   Grocer
Sugg & Dail,   G S
Sugg, L A,   Postmaster
Sugg, G W,   G S
Sugg & Bro (near),   G S
Warren, Miss Ellen,   G S

SPEIGHT'S BRIDGE.

Beaman, R E & R J W,   G S
Williams, H G,   G S

WILLOW GREEN.

Carr, F,   G S

MILLS.

Kinds, Post Offices and Proprietors.

Corn, Snow Hill, Aquilla Sugg.
Corn, Snow Hill, R C D Belmont's
   heirs.
Corn, flour and saw, Jason, R H Hardy.
Corn, flour and saw, Snow Hill, Thos
   Moore.
Corn, flour and saw, Hookerton, Mrs
   T E Hooker.

Flour and corn, Hookerton, W W Or-
   mond.
Steam saw and grist, Snow Hill, J E
   W Sugg.
Steam saw and grist, Snow Hill, Eli
   Dargan.
Steam grist and gin, Castoria, J H
   Newell.
Steam saw and gin, Scuffleton, Hol-
   ton & Spiers.
Steam saw, Castoria, Jesse Philips.
Steam saw, Ormondsville, Herbert Or-
   mond.
Steam saw and grist, Speight's Bridge,
   R J Rodman.

PHYSICIANS.

Names and Post Offices.

Derring, John, Speight's Bridge.
Edwards, C C, Hookerton.
Grimsley, J E, Snow Hill.
Hornaday, E H, Willow Green.
Jordan, Thos A, Hookerton.
Powell, W E, Castoria.
Sugg, Ed, Snow Hill.
West, W T, Fieldsboro.

SCHOOLS.

Names, Post Offices and Principals.

Academy, Snow Hill.
Academy, Male and Female, Hooker-
   ton.
Glenwood Academy, Snow Hill.
Primary, Castoria.
School, Ormondsville, Miss Emma
   Parker.
School, Glenfield, Miss Willie Hooker.
Snow Hill Female Seminary, Miss Car-
   rie Dail.
Public Schools—White, 24; colored, 22.

TEACHERS.

Names and Post Offices.

Albritton, Miss Mattie, Snow Hill.
Barwick. J F, Hardeesville.
Barnes, Miss E, Eureka, (Wayne co).
Bennett J S (col), Farmville (Pike co).
Best, C H, (col), Snow Hill.
Best, L L A (col), Snow Hill.
Brown, John L (col), Grifton (Pitt co).
Brown, Geo A (col), Snow Hill.
Bushee, Miss Maude (col), Snow Hill.
Cooper, Miss Lula A (col), Snow Hill.
Cotton, Mrs M A (col), Farmville (Pitt
   co).
Dail, Miss Carrie, Snow Hill.
Dixon, Miss Bettie, Fountain Hill.
Dupree, E W (col), Farmville (Pitt co).
Edwards, W M, Hookerton.
Field, Edward (col), Hookerton.

GREENE COUNTY.

GREENE COUNTY.

Grimsley, Miss Minnie, Snow Hill.
Gregory, J L (col), Snow Hill.
Gully, Miss Annie, Snow Hill.
Hazel, Rev P V (col), Appletree.
Hooker, Miss Willie, Glenfield.
Hughes, Miss Mabel C, Lizzie.
Jones, Fort (col), Eureka (Wayne co).
Joyner, Miss Josie, Lizzie.
Kilpatrick, Miss Susie, Hookerton.
Lane, Miss Dolly, Appletree.
Lewis, Miss Amanda, Dongola (Pitt co).
Loftin, Miss Carrie, Lizzie.
May, Miss Pattie, Speight's Bridge.
Mewborn, Miss Ada, Jason.
Mewborn, J P, Jason.
Mewborn, Mrs G, Glenfield.
Mewborn, D A, Dongola (Pitt co).
Moore, A M, Saratoga (Wilson co).
Moore, John J (col), Hookerton.
Monroe, Miss Mattie A W (col), Castoria.
Murphy, Miss Etta J (col), Snow Hill.
Murphy, Adrian (col), Snow Hill.
Moore, Miss Lizzie J, Glenfield.
Parker, Miss Emma, Ormondsville.
Partis, Cora P (col), Appletree.
Rouse, Miss Mattie A (col), Hardeeville.
Silivant, Miss Lillie, Snow Hill.
Smith, Miss Julia B (col) Jason.
Stanford, J T, Hookerton.
Taylor, Miss Nannie E, Snow Hill.
Taylor, Miss Alice, Bull Head.
Williams, Miss Lila, Snow Hill.
Whitted, Mrs C A E (col), Lizzie.
Wooten, Miss Estelle, Speight's Bridge.
Wooten, John C, Speight's Bridge.

LOCAL CORPORATIONS.

Radiance Lodge, No 132, A F & A M, Snow Hill; meets 1st Friday 11 A M; L V Morrill, W M.
Jerusalem Lodge, No 95, A F & A M, Hookerton; meets second Saturday; Owen Frizzell, W M.
Knights of Honor, Hookerton; E H Hornady, dictator.

NEWSPAPERS.

Free-Will Baptist, weekly, Ormondsville; J M Barfield and W E Move, eds and props.

FARMERS.

Names and Post Offices.

Appletree—Hiram Best, W R Bryan, Lawrence Bryan, Wm Condon, J W Crocker, Haywood Edmundson, Mrs Lydia Edmundson, Mrs William H Edwards, C P Farmer, Kinchen Heath, George W Lane, William Randolph,

David Spence, R W Taylor, I M Williams.
Bull Head—W Barrow, E C Cobb, A J Edmundson, Theo Edwards, C C Pope, Andrew Rose, John Rose, S Shackelford, W Charles Taylor, R W Taylor, B W Taylor, J W Taylor.
Castoria—J H Beaman, T W Carr, W R Gay, B J Gay, William Harrell, F L Hardison, Adam Hinson, H D Hinson, J H Newell, W E Powell, W R Shackelford, Robert Shirley, Rufus Shirley, Wm Shirley, W J Wooten, Shade Wooten, Marcellus Walston.
Contentnea—Edward C Cobb, A L Darden, Pinkney Darden, R P S Dixon, Thomas Dawson.
Fieldsboro—A J Baker, J J Dildy, J F Dildy, E Dildy, B Fields, jr, S G Fields, W R Fields, Isham Gay, B F Moore, J T Ward, W T West.
Fountain Hill—Joseph Dixon.
Hookerton—W L Churchill, William Coward, W L Coward, W Dixon, jr, Q Dunn, J A Edwards, sr, W L Harper, E W Hart, Albert Hooker, John Hooker, Frank Hooker, Paton Hooker, Travis Hooker, J J Moore, Jas Moore, John Patrick, Peter Patrick, Samuel C Sugg, A Sugg, Benj Sutton, John Silervant, Jesse Taylor.
Jason—Carson Cobb, Mrs E R Hardy, R H Hardy, Jesse Hardy, McD Pate.
Newsom—I P Britt, J S Newsom, Mark Smith.
Ormondsville—Walter Barfield, J M Barfield, R A Carr, Lawrence Carr, W L Churchill, Wm Coward, J T Davis, W T Dixon, Wm F Edwards, C T Edwards, R Faulkner, J T Frizzell, A Frizzell, H H Frizzell, Owen W Frizzell, P J Grimsby, J H Hardie, F M Hardie, A M Hardie, Whitman Hardie, F J Hardie, Wm May, W E Ormond, Herbert Ormond, Marvin Ormond, John C Ormond, G T Ormond, Cnas Stocks, John Silervant, Elias Turnage, W Tunstall, W T Worthington, Thos Worthington.
Scuffleton—T H Foust, A R Holton, John McLanhorn, James G Worthington.
Shine—James Best, J A Frazier, J B Jones, S L Lynch, David Smith, V L Smith.
Snow Hill—Haywood Reaman, Haywood Best, W E Best, H H Best, J G Britt, Thos Caraway, J W Creech, A L Darden, Ellis Dixon, Josiah Dixon, Jas B Faircloth, J D Grimsby, J F Harper, P S D Harper, Luly Harper, R H T Harper, R F Harper, W J Jordan, Patrick Lynch, Thomas Moore, C T Moore, Samuel Moore, Abner Murphy, D W Patrick, J M Patrick, Mrs S E Patrick,

GREENE COUNTY.	GREENE COUNTY.
Jas Potter, C D Sauls, A H Sugg, J E W Sugg, S C Sugg, O Sugg, John Walston, Susan V Whitehead, J B Williams, Mrs E Wood.	Harrison, J O W Jones, M P McKeel, Silas McKeel, Samuel McKeel, A P McKeel, Rufus McKeel, J R Moore, B A Ruff, Wm Speight, James P Speight,

Speight's Bridge—A J Baker, R J W Beaman, Wm Corbitt, S J Daniel, R E Beaman, John J Beaman, John Eason, J B Faircloth, W M Darden, E A Darden, W H Derring, J H Garris, J J

J B Speight, Henry Walston, J H Whitley, W J Whitley, Wm Wooten.
Willow Green—R A L Carr, R R Carr, F T Carr, P L Carr. R A Darden, W A Darden, Jr, James Darden.

LEVI M. SCOTT,

ATTORNEY AT LAW,——•

GREENSBORO, N. C.

ROBERT M. DOUGLAS,

GREENSBORO, N. C,

ATTORNEY AT LAW.

STANDING MASTER IN CHANCERY AND EXAMINER OF THE UNITED STATES CIRCUIT COURT.

Attorney for the following Corporations:

Greensboro Chamber of Commerce, The Piedmont Bank, Peoples' Five Cents Savings Bank, South Greensboro Investment Company, The Union Land Company, Oak Hill Roller Mills, The Bain Building Company, Life Insurance Company of Virginia, Baltimore Building and Loan Association, Washington National Building and Loan Association, Cape Fear Manufacturing Company.

BYNUM & BYNUM,

ATTORNEYS AT LAW,

JOHN GRAY BYNUM.
WM. P. BYNUM, JR.

GREENSBORO, N. C.

20

GUILFORD COUNTY.

AREA, 680 SQUARE MILES.

POPULATION, 27,868; White 19,645, Colored 8,223.

GUILFORD COUNTY was formed in 1770, from Rowan and Orange counties. It was called in compliment of Lord North, who, in 1770, succeeded the Duke of Grafton as First Lord of the Treasury and Prime Minister. He was heir to the title of Guilford and eventually succeeded to it as Earl of Guilford.

GREENSBORO, the county-seat, is 82 miles northwest of Raleigh, at the junction of the Richmond & Danville and Cape Fear & Yadkin Valley Railroads, and was named in honor of General Nathaniel Green. Population (estimated) 9,000.

Surface — Pleasantly undulating—hilly, but not mountainous; soil good, water-power very fine. Deep river and other smaller streams supply abundant water, and the central location makes it a desirable county for residence. It contains a thrifty population.

Staples—Tobacco, corn, wheat and fruits in abundance and in great perfection. Several nurseries have been in operation for many years and have accomplished much for the interest of fruit-growing. Grass-growing is also profitable.

Fruits—Apples, pears, peaches, cherries, grapes, quinces, melons, plums, and other small fruits.

Timbers—Pine, oak, hickory and poplar.

TOWNS AND POST OFFICES.

	POP.		POP.
Allamance,	30	Gilmer's Store,	25
Battle Ground,	—	Greensboro,	9,000
Brick Church,	160	Guilford	
Brown's Sum-		College,	1,000
mit,	100	High Point,	2,500
Cascade,	50	Hillsdale,	40
Centre,	60	Hinton,	60
Climax,	100	Holt,	25
Colfax,	70	Jamestown,	100
Company's Mill,	40	Julian,	50
Crystal,	40	Kernersville,	25
Danamora,	50	Lacrosse,	45
Danville,	25	Lamont,	50
Deep River,	30	Lego,	20
Dennysville,	55	Liberty Store,	25
Freeman's		Longview,	30
Mills,	125	McLeansville,	30
Friendship,	90	Oak Ridge,	75
Gibsonville,	130	Plain,	40

	POP.		POP.
Pleasant Gar-		Summerfield,	60
den,	30	Sumner,	30
Pomona,	150	Tabernacle,	60
Rathbone,	50	Vandalia,	100
Scalesville,	25	Westminster,	40
Shaw's Mills,	50	Whitsett.	250
Stokesdale,	500		

COUNTY OFFICERS.

Clerk Superior Court—E L Ragan.
Commissioners—J H Millis, chm'n: John C Brend, W E Bevel, N A Harmon, Wm P Wharton.
Coroner—J T Welker.
Register of Deeds—Abel G Kirkman.
Sheriff—Joseph A Hoskins.
Solicitor 5th District—W P Bynum, Jr.
Surveyor—Joseph Worth.
Standard Keeper—T A Mathews.
Treasurer—John A Hodgin.
School Examiner—Simeon Hodgin.

COURTS.

Superior Court—Second Monday before first Monday in March and first Monday before the first Monday in September.
U. S. Court—Held at Greensboro, first Monday in April and October; R P Dick, U S Dis Judge; S L Trogden, Clerk.

UNITED STATES OFFICERS.

Judge U. S. District Court—R P Dick, Greensboro.
Clerk U. S. District Court—Samuel L Trogden, Greensboro.
Master in Chancery and Examiner in Equity U. S. Court—R M Douglas, Greensboro.
U. S. Marshal—Thomas J Allison.
Postmaster—James W Forbis, Greensboro.
Clerks in Post Office—Will Russ, R A Foard, S S Willey, —— Stewart.
Janitor—J R Pearce.
Laborer—James Apple.
Free Mail Delivery.

TOWN OFFICERS.

GREENSBORO—*Mayor*, Jno J Nelson; *Commissioners*, S C Dodson, J W Scott, J N Nelson, P D Price, Neil Ellington,

GUILFORD COUNTY.

J L King, W E Bevill, George S Seargeant, James F Jordan, J A Odell; *Clerk of Board*, J D White; *Clerk*, A M Scales; *Treasurer*, Neil Ellington; *Police*, R M Reese, chief; T D Andrews, W S Lyon, M A Whittington; *Chief Fire Department*, C D Benbow.

HIGH POINT—*Mayor*, W H Snow; *Town Clerk*, R J Lindsay; *Treasurer*, J H Mills.

TOWNSHIPS AND MAGISTRATES.

Centre Grove—L A Walker, J W Winchester, Jas A Grant, J F Highfield, Thompson Johnson, Henry W Gordon, J C Hilton (Hillsdale).

Claey—D H Coble (Tabernacle), V B Donnell, C C Causey (Gilmer's Store), W H C Shaw, W A Welker, R B Foust (Lamont).

Deep River—J W Sapp, W L Gibbons (Kernersville), A B Dillon, W E Bowman (Friendship), John Davis, S W Sechrist, E B Atkinson. T C Starbuck (Colfax).

Fentress—Wesley Coble, W R McMasten, D G Neeley, Thomas Taylor, Clark Hackett, A M Lewis (Pleasant Garden), Jas T Hodgin (Centre).

Friendship—J W Knight, B F White, Henry Wakefield, John D Hunt, M H Ballinger, Marshal Dunday, Lee G Cummings, Jesse H Stanley, D F Huffiness (Guilford College).

Gilmer—John E McKnight, F M Keith, Eugene Eckel, John Brodnax, G T Glasscock, J A Hodgin, H L Moffitt, W O Stratford (Greensboro).

Greene—J H Bowman, J F R Clapp (McLeansville), Lewis Holt, Nathan Kime, Frank Grason, John Corsbee (Kimesville).

High Point—W R Richardson, J M Sechrist, W H Snow, D Hedgecock, D A Stanton, B F Hayworth, D S Gurley, Marshal Hiatt, M B Williams (High Point).

Jamestown—T H Hodson, J S Gray, E A Guyer, M C Hatton, Samuel Stack, A W Jones, C A Vickery, G Will Armfield (Jamestown).

Jefferson—W T Wharton, Julius M Dick, Wm Summers, W H McLean, J A Cobb, J W Forbes, J H Montgomery, W G Cobb (McLeansville), James Whitt (Snow's Mills).

Madison—J R Moore, Edward L Fields, J H Rudd, L E Howerton (Brown's Summit), Jesse L May (McLeansville), A J Lambeth (Brown's Summit).

Monroe—W J Ector, John Schoolfield, Wm Andrews, G W Wyrick, R

GUILFORD COUNTY.

L Schoolfield (Greensboro), Jas L Pitsford (Rathbone), B G Chilcutt (Brown Summit).

Morehead—W G Balsby, C H Hancock, Jere Cox, Tyre Glenn, A A Hinton, E F Shuber, Sid Leonard, J P Ogment, A Hinshaw, W J Benbow, J H Johnson (Greensboro).

Oak Ridge—H L Gant, J M McMichael, M F Blylock, Geo W Elliott, P H Pegram, J J Hilton, John A Lowery, John M Bowman (Oak Ridge).

Rock Creek—J C Clapp, D T Faust (Faust Mills), Albert Ingle, J M Raney, J G Moses (Brown Summit), G W Clapp (Greensboro), P G W Walker (Hillsdale).

Summerfield—Jere Highfill, J L Ogburn, W H Case, J M Lee, Wm Debal, F M Medearias, J M Burton, Wm Canada (Summerfield).

Sumner—W R McCuiston, G V Lamb, John T Hodgin, A O Newman, John F Anthony, W M Kirkman, David S Hodgen, A C Morrow (Centre).

Washington—C A Tickel, Mebane Apple, Alfred Apple, D E Wagoner, John J Williams (Gibsonville).

CHURCHES.

Names, Post Offices, Pastors and Denom.

METHODIST.

Bethany, Liberty, S F Barber.
Bethlehem, Climax, S F Barber.
Centenary, South Greensboro, W M Bagley.
Center, Hillsdale, J A B Fry.
Church, Summerfield, T L Gibson.
Church, Jamestown, J A B Fry.
Church, High Point, S H Hilliard.
Church, Oak Ridge, J A B Fry.
Friendship, Friendship, J A B Fry.
Gethsemane, Hillsdale.
Goshen, Stokesdale.
Holt's Chapel, Greensboro, W S Hales.
Lee's Chapel, Busick, W S Hales.
Mt Pleasant, McLeansville, W S Hales.
Muir's Chapel, Guilford College, J A B Fry
Pisgah, Martinsville, W S Hales.
Pleasant Garden, Pleasant Garden, S F Barber.
Rehobeth, Greensboro, S F Barber.
Shady Grove, Freeman's Mill.

METH. PROTESTANT.

Oi, Oak Ridge, C A Pickens.
Benedict's, High Point.
Bethel, Oak Ridge, T J Ogburn.
Brown Summit, Brown Summit, C E M Raper.
Fairfield, Jamestown, C A Pickens.
Flat Rock, Summerfield, T J Ogburn.

GUILFORD COUNTY.

Friendship, Brown Summit, C E M Raper.
Grace, Greensboro, J Samuel Williams.
Hickory Grove, Jamestown, C A Pickens.
Lebanon, High Point, C A Pickens.
Mitchell's Grove, Jamestown, C A Pickens.
Moriah, Greensboro, J E Hartsell.
Mount Pleasant, Crystal, J R Hutton.
Oak Ridge—Oak Ridge, T J Ogburn.
Piney Grove — Kernersville, T J Ogburn.
Pleasant Union—Crystal, J R Hutton.
Red Hill—Greensboro, C A Pickens.
Sandy Ridge, Colfax, C A Pickens.
Spring Hill—High Point, T F McCulloch.
Tabernacle—Tabernacle, J E Hartsell.

WES. METHODIST.

Bundy's Chapel — Jamestown, J C Johnston.
Oak Hill—High Point, J C Johnston.

NORTH. METHODIST.

St Matthew's (col)—South Greensboro, R C Campbell.

METH. EPISCOPAL.

Church (col)—High Point.
St Matthew's (col)—Greensboro, R C Cameron.

BAPTIST.

Abbott's Creek—Abbott's Creek, Wm Turner.
Buchanan—Greensboro, E P Ellington.
Church—Summerfield, W H Wilson.
Church—Greensboro.
Church (col)—High Point, A W Wellborn.
High Point—High Point, J J Farris.

FRIENDS.

Center—Center.
Church—Greensboro, Jas R Jones.
Concord—Sumner, J S Cox.
Davis—Colfax.
Deep River—Deep River.
N C Yearly Meeting House — High Point.
New Garden—Guilford College, Albert Peel.

CHRISTIAN.

Hines—Brown's Summit, J W Patton.
Pleasant Ridge—Holt, J W Pinnix.

PRESBYTERIAN.

Church—High Point, W P McCorde.
First Pres—Greenboro, Dr J Henry Smith; Dr Egbert W Smith.
Springwood—Whitsett, H D Legnex.
Westminster—S Greensboro, S O Hall.

GUILFORD COUNTY.

EPISCOPAL.

St Barnabas—Greensboro, Alfred H Stubbs, Rector.
St James' Mission (held in Jones' hall) Louis L Williams.

LUTHERAN.

Frieden's—Gibsonville, E P Parker.
Sharon—Gibsonville, E P Parker.
Frieden's Cong.— Gibsonville, V T Boozer.
Trinity—Brick Church, H M Brown.
Zion—Julian, H M Brown.

GERMAN REFORMED.

Whitsett—Whitsett, J D Andrew.

MINISTERS RESIDENT.

Names, Post Offices and Denominations.

METHODIST.

Bagbey, W M, Greensboro.
Blair, H M, Greensboro.
Carraway, P J, Greensboro.
Cunninggim, J A, Greensboro.
Grissom, W L, Greensboro.
Groom, P, L, D D, Greensboo.
Keith, F M, Greensboro.
Thomas, J C, Greensboro.
Weaver, J H, D D, Greenboro.

METH. PROTESTANT.

Causey, J W S, Crystal.
Hartsell, J E, Greensboro.
Hutton, J R, Climax.
Kennett, W F, Kernersville.
McCulloch, J F, Greensboro.
Michaux, J L, Greensboro.
Ogburn, T J, Summerfield.
Rapier, C E M, Lego.
Williams, J S, Greensboro.
York, P P, High Point.

METH. EPISCOPAL.

Bowman, G W, Crystal.
Matton, W C, High Point.

WES. METHODIST.

Johnson, J C, High Point.
Jones, Miss Martha, High Point.

FRIENDS.

Blair, Mrs Solomon, High Point.
Cartland, Mrs Mary E, pres State W C T U, Concord.
Frazier, John Gurney, High Point.
Purdy, E R, High Point.
Richardson, Wm, High Point.

PRESBYTERIAN.

Dinwiddie, J C, High Point.
Hall, S O, Greensboro.
Smith, J Henry, D D, Greensboro.
Smith, Egbert, D D, Greensboro.

EPISCOPAL.

Green, ——, Greensboro.

Miller, ——, Greensboro.
Williams, Louis L, High Point.

CHRISTIAN.

Hines, Henry, Elon College.
Roach, W H, High Point.

BAPTIST.

Ellington, E P, Greensboro.
Moore, R R, Greensboro.
Thomas, C A G, Greensboro.

LUTHERAN.

Brown, H M, Brick Church.
Parker, E P, Gibsonville.

HOTELS AND BOARDING HOUSES.

Names, Post Offices and Proprietors.

Bellevue Hotel, High Point, George T
  Leach, owner and prop; J N Camp-
  bell, manager.
Benbow House, Greensboro, B J Fisher.
Boarding House, Greensboro (Elm st),
  Mrs Pemberton.
Boarding house, Greensboro (West
  Market st), Mrs Lillie Ellis.
Boarding house, Greensboro (Sycamore
  st), Mrs Nannie Sholer.
Boarding house, Greensboro (Church
  st), Miss Sallie Brent.
Boarding house, Greensboro (North
  Elm st), Mrs N A Brown.
Boarding house, Greensboro (near de-
  pot), Mrs E C Watlington.
Boarding house, Greensboro, John H
  Rankin.
Boarding house, Greensboro, Mrs A
  Dilworth.
Boarding house, Whitsett, Mrs M
  Sharp.
Central House, Whitsett, Dr J C Clapp.
Cooper House, Greensboro, Mrs Cooper
Hotel European, Greensboro, Will
  Clegg.
Jarrell's Hotel, High Point, Mrs Jar-
  rell.
McAdoo House, Greensboro, B J
  Fisher.
Moore House, Greensboro (Elm st),
  Mrs Morgan.
Munroe House, Greensboro, Mrs Mun-
  roe.
Park House, Whitsett, Wm M Clapp.
Restaurant, High Point, Hinton Wills
  (col).
Wharton House, Whitsett, C A Whar-
  ton.
Whitsett Inn, Whitsett, J D Oldham.
Winstead House, Greensboro (West
  Market st), Mrs M Winstead.

LAWYERS.

Names and Post Offices.

Barringer, J A, Greensboro.
Boyd, James E, Greensboro.

Bynum, W P, jr, (Bynum & Bynum)
  Greensboro.
Bynum, Judge John Gray (Bynum &
  Bynum), Greensboro.
Caldwell, James S, Greensboro.
Dillard & King, Greensboro.
Douglas, R M, Greensboro.
Forbis, J W, Greensboro.
Keogh, Thomas B, Greensboro.
Michaux, John S, Greensboro.
Morehead, James T, Greensboro.
Scales, A M (Shaw & Scales), Greens-
  boro.
Schenck, David, jr (Schenck &
  Schenck), Greensboro.
Scott, L M, Greensboro.
Shaw, T J (Shaw & Scales), Greens-
  boro.
Sharp, B, Greensboro.
Steele, Edwin D, High Point.
Taylor, Z V, Greensboro.
Turner, J A, High Point.
Wade, T W, Greensboro.
Wilson, John N, Greensboro.

MANUFACTORIES.

Kinds, Post Offices and Proprietors.

Blacksmithing, Greensboro, Jno Lewis.
Brickmaking, Greensboro, Jas Dean
  (col).
Cabinetmaking and undertaking, Rob-
  ert Parker, High Point.
Cape Fear M'f'g Co, Greensboro, O R
  Cox, pres; T D Sherwood, sec and
  treas.
Greensboro Candy Co, Greensboro, J
  N West.
Catarrh Cure, Greensboro, Rev J W
  Blosser, M D.
Contracting and building, Greensboro,
  W C Bain.
Contracting and building, Greensboro,
  John Y Smith.
Contracting and plastering, Greens-
  boro, F M Keith.
Contracting and building, High Point,
  Wesley Welburn.
Contracting and building, High Point,
  John Payne.
Contracting and building, High Point,
  Lindsay Davis.
Contracting and building, High Point,
  Pinkney Smith.
Contracting and building, High Point,
  J T Edwards.
Empire Plaid Mills, High Point, E H C
  Field, sec and treas; capital $30,000;
  112 looms.
Furniture and Undertaking, Greens-
  boro, F F Smith.
Greensboro Gas Co, R R King, pres;
  R H Marks, treas; capital $20,000.

GUILFORD COUNTY.

Greensboro Sash and Blind Co, Greensboro, J R Mendenhall and J W Mc-Nairy.

Guilford Lumber Mfg Co, Greensboro, C A Reynolds, pres; W D Mendenhall, sec and treas; capital $35,000.

Harness, saddles and collars, Greensboro, J H Harris.

Harness, High Point, F J Horney.

High Point Furniture Co, E A Snow, pres; J H Tate, supt; T F Wrenn, sec and treas; capital $9,000.

High Point Machine Works, J Elwood Cox, pres; O N Richardson, sec and treas; R B Boren, supt; capital $3,000.

High Point Canning Co, E E Beason, mgr; G A Matton, sec and treas.

Iron Foundry, Greensboro, Eagle Foundry Co, M J Teague, mgr.

Iron Foundry, Greensboro, J T Glasscock & Son.

Iron Foundry and Machine Shop, Greensboro, Sergeant Mfg Co.

Mattress-maker, High Point, C F Call.

Modern Barn Smoking Tobacco, High Point, Modern Smoking Tobacco Co, W H Snow, pres.

Mt Pleasant Mfg Co (cotton) Liberty, J W Scott, pres; W M Kime, sec and treas.

Oak Hill Roller Mills, Greensboro, D F Caldwell, pres; S Williams, sec and treas.

Oakdale Mfg Co (cotton), Jamestown, J S Ragsdale, agt; capital $86,000.

Odell Hardware Co, Greensboro, J A Odell, pres; C H Ireland, sec and treas.

Plug and Twist Tobacco, Greensboro, J L King & Co.

Plug and Twist Tobacco, High Point, J H Jenkins & Co.

Saddles, Harness and Saddlery Goods, Greensboro, J H Harris.

Sash, doors and blinds, and dressed lumber, High Point, Snow & Dalton.

Sash, doors, etc, Greensboro, Thos Woodruffe.

Shoes, High Point, N E & J J & W M Allred.

Shoes, Deep River, S H Mendenhall & Co.

Shuttle-blocks, spokes, etc, High Point, J Elwood Cox.

Shuttle-blocks and spoke billets, Columbia Factory, J Elwood Cox.

Shuttle-blocks, etc, Staley, J Elwood Cox.

Suttle-blacks, etc, Julian, J Elwood Cox.

Shuttle-blocks, etc, Summerfield, J Elwood Cox.

Snow Lumber Co, High Point (incorporated); $25,000 capital; R E Dalton, pres; E A Snow, supt.

GUILFORD COUNTY.

Spoke and Bending Works, Greensboro, Scott, Eldridge & Glenn.

Spokes and handles, Greensboro, B H Merrimon.

Tannery, Guilford College, Edgerton & · Bro.

Tannery, Guilford College, Samuel W H Smith.

Tannery, High Point, Ragan & Millis.

Tannery and harness, Deep River, S H Mendenhall & Co.

Tar Heel Liniment, Greensboro, Houston & Emerson.

Tobacco boxes, Oak Ridge, J L King.

Tobacco (plug and twist), High Point, W P Pickett & Co.

Wagons, Greensboro, J N Lewis.

Wagons, High Point, Beeson Bros.

Wool carding, Frilling and Dyeing Works, shuttle-blocks, etc, Centre, D S Hodgen.

MERCHANTS AND TRADESMEN.

Names, Post Offices, Lines of Business.

ALAMANCE.

Foust, D P,		G S

BATTLE GROUND.

Oakley Bros,		G S

BRICK CHURCH.

Huffman, D S & Geo,		G S

BROWN'S SUMMIT.

Conway, S W,		G S
Hopkins, J W,		G S
Jones, J W,		G S
Richardson, J H & Co,		G S

CASCADE.

Wheeler, G C,		G S

CENTRE.

Hodgin, J A,		G S

CLIMAX.

Hatton, J R & Co,		G S

COLFAX.

Bohannon, B,		G S
Gray, J W,		G S

DANVILLE.

Shaw, W S,		C S

FRIENDSHIP.

Dudley, T T,		G S

GIBSONVILLE.

Davidson, B,		G S
Jordan, Dr J E,		G S
Leonard, W A,		G S
Minneola, Mfg Co,		G S
Steele, H W,		G S

GREENSBORO.

Aiken & Clapp,	Grocer
Alderman, Sid L,	Photographer

GUILFORD COUNTY.   GUILFORD COUNTY.

Armfield, Ridge & Victory, D G
Barker, John, G S
Berger, H C & Co, Leaf Tobacco
Boon, O L, Gro
Bevill & Walker, Leaf Tobacco.
Bowldin, B B, US Rev Agt, Div N C and S C
Brockman, C J, Music and Stationery
Brockman, A J, Gro
Brooks, R W, Whol Lumber Dealer
Brooks, T T, Receiver of Bain Bldng Co
Coldcleugh & Bro, Crockery
"Candy Kitchen," Confectionery
Cape Fear Mfg Co, Lumber
Carr, O W & Co, Gen Ins Agts
Cartland, H H, Tailor
Cator, Mrs Annie, Milliner
Causey, R E, Rev Agt
Cobb, H W, Leaf Tobacco
Cobb, J S & Co, Leaf Tobacco
Collins, W, Undertaker
Cox, Ferree & Co, D G
Daniel Hardware Co, Hdw
Darden & Bro, Shoes
Devin W A, Rev Clerk
Donnell, J & Co, Gro
Duffee, L E, G S
Epps, O, Architect
Farrar, W B & Son, Jewelry
Fields, W A, Tob Factory
Fisher, B J, Benbow Hotel
Fishblate, E R, Merch Clothier
Gilmer & Smith, Canning
Gilmer, D J (col), Gro
Glasscock, G L, Foundry and Machine Shops
Gorrell. Mrs C C, Milliner
Greensboro Book Store, Books and Stationery
Groom, J M, G S
Hamner, Miss Rosa M, Milliner
Hendricks, J M & Co, D G and Notions
Hiatt & Lamb, G S
Hodgin & Pegram, G S
Hodgin & Hunt, G S
Hodgin, J W & Co, G S
Holley, W E (col), G S
Holton, C E, Drugs
Houston & Bro, Gro
Howard. Mrs, Bookstore
Hudson, S E & Co, Grocers
Hunter & Tucker, Grocers
Hunter, & Co, G S
Johnson & Dorsett, D G
Jones, John W, Grocer
Jordan, J T & Co, Leaf Tobacco
Keeling, S P, Grocers
Keeling, J L, Whol and Ret Grocers
King, J L & Co, Tobacco
Kivitt, W S. Gro and Con
Knight, J W, Marble
Landreth, J W, G S
Landreth, C E, G S
Lachie, M, Cloth
Lea & Tate, Tob

Leak Bros & Hasting, Tob
Lewis, Mrs D W, Milliner
Lewis, J, & Co, Blacksmith
Love, Wm, Lumber
Mason, J E, Gro
McCracken & Clarida, G S
McCracken, R A, G S
McDuffie, N J, Furniture and Crockery
McLane, C, Rev Agt
McLane, T G, G S
Means, Geo W, Rev Agt
Moore, W S, Musical Instruments and Millinery
Morris & Co, Racket Store
Neese, J H, Marble
Nelson, Anderson, Builder and Contractor
Newell & Matthews, Carriages, etc
O'Connor, Jno, Gro
Odell Hardware Co, Hardware
Ozment, J K, G S
Pearce, O F, Grocer
Pegram, S J, & Co, Tobac
Phipps, J H, G S
Phœnix, J J, Gro
Pickard, T M, & Co, Gro
Piedmont Drug Co, Drugs
Pretzfelder & Co, Dry Goods and Shoes
Pugh & White, Gro
Racket Store, Dry Goods, etc
Rankin. J T, & Bro, G S
Rawls & Bro, G S
Reese & Elam, Printers
Richardson & Farris, Drugs
Ridge & Sherwood, Dry Goods and Shoes
Royster, Geo H, Dry Goods
Scarborough, S W, Gro
Schiffman Jewelry Co, Jewelry
Scott, J W, & Co, Wholesale and Retail Gro and Wholesale Dry Goods
Sikes, J H, Gro
Siler. N J, Jeweler
Smith & Gardner, Drugs
Smith. F F, Furniture and Undertaking
Smithdeal, L A, Books, Sta and Conf
Stewart, M L, Livery Stables
Stratford, W O, Fert
Stone & Reid, Job Printers
Tatum & Taylor, Livery Stables
Tatum & Matthews, Wood and Coal
Thacker & Brockman, Dry Goods and Shoes
Thomas, D E, Gro
Thomas, C F, Printer
Thornton, J J, Jeweler
Trupler & Law, G S
Vandiford. T H. Rev Agt
Vanstory & Donnell, Livery
Vanstory, C M, & Co, Clo
Vuncannon & Co, G S
Wakefield Hardware Co, Hardware

GUILFORD COUNTY.

Walker & Omohundro.	Milliners
Ward, G W,	Drugs
Ward, J W, & Co,	Nursery
Wharton, J W, sr,	
	Agr Imp, Wagons and Lime
Wharton Bros,	Books
Wharton, Jackson & Co,	Ice
Whitt, J H, & Co,	Tobac Warehouse
Wilson, H M, & Co,	
	Millinery and Fancy Goods
Wilson, A G,	Gro
Wilson & Wilson,	Gro
Wordruffe, Thos, & Co,	
	Contractors and Builders
Workman & Christian,	Gro
Wyrick, Geo W,	G S

GUILFORD COLLEGE.

McCracken, John T,	G S
Smith, Lee S, & Co,	G S
Smith, S W H,	G S
Stanley & Ballinger,	G S

HIGH POINT.

Alexander, H,	G S
Allred Bros,	G S
Beeson Hardware Co,	Hardware
Bodenhammer & Gurley,	
	Livery Stables
Callum, J C,	G S
Campbell, J N,	G S
Campbell, J P,	G S
Charles, R C,	Gro
Clark, Mrs B A.	Milliner
Clinard, J A,	G S
Cox, E J.	Shuttle B'ocks
Davis & Son,	G S
Flagler, L,	Gro
Gordy, McDaniel,	Tinner
Gulley, Frank,	Books
Hiatt, W J,	G S
Hoskins, D A,	G S
Ingram, Mrs M J,	Dry Goods
Johnson, P H.	G S
Jones, J C. & Son,	G S
Jordan, B F,	Marble
Knight, John,	Baker
Keaber, Mrs L J.	G S
Lindsay, J A,	G S
Matton, Geo A,	Drugs
Moore & McKinsey,	Clo
Parker, J R,	Undertaker
Pickett, J R,	G S
Pitts & Brown,	Livery
Ragan, W H & Co,	G S
Ragan & Mills,	G S
Rankin, W T,	Dry Goods
Sapp, A V & Co,	Racket Store
Sechrest, F W,	Gro
Sechrest, J M,	G S
Shell, J E,	Jeweler
Shiplett & Marsh,	G S
Smith, Miss Venetia.	Milliner
Smith, M A,	Drugs
Snow Lumber Co,	Lumber
Suits, J T,	Gro

GUILFORD COUNTY.

Umstead, E H,	G S
Walker, Lindsay Co,	Clothing
Welch, J C,	Livery Stables
Welch & Co,	G S
Welch, W P.	Jeweler
Wrenn, M J,	Dry Goods
Younts, A L,	G S

HILLSDALE.

Florence, G T,	G S

HINTON.

Wilson, A G & Co,	G S

JAMESTOWN.

Corralt, J D.	G S
Johnson & Bro,	Shoemakers
Moore, D W.	G S
Ragsdale. J S & Bro,	Nursery
Raper, S E & C E M,	G S
Wharton, J M & Co,	G S

JULIAN.

Bowman & Schoffner,	G S
Coble, O,	Fert
Hardin & Co,	G S
Stout & Co,	G S

KERNERSVILLE.

Garrett & Wrightsell,	G S
Kinnen, N,	G S
Mt Pleasant Mfg Co,	G S

LAMONT.

Hunter & Co,	G S

MACLEANSVILLE.

Foust, J C,	G S
Reitzel, M A,	G S
Tate, J A,	G S

OAK RIDGE.

Baynes, W T.	G S
Bowling. A J,	G S
Donnell, W O,	G S
Williams, R S,	G S

PLEASANT GARDEN.

Ross, J F,	G S

POMONA.

Lindley, J Van,	Nursery and G S

SHAW'S MILLS.

Foust, J C,	G S
Mebane, J R,	G S

STOKESDALE.

Gant, J M,	G S
Gant, H L,	Undertaker
Gentry, R,	G S
Gentry, W B,	G S
Hilton, Dr J J,	Drugs
Vaughan, J W.	Gro
Vaughan, W M,	Gro

SUMMERFIELD.

Brittain. H C,	G S
Ogburn, N W,	G S
Summer, J T.	G S

TABERNACLE.

Neece, C C & Co,   G S

WHITSETT.

Oldham & Green,   G S

MILLS.

Kinds, Post Offices and Proprietors.

Flour and corn, High Point, Payne & Brown.

Flour and corn, Oak Ridge, J L King.

Flour and corn, Oak Ridge, Rev R M Stafford.

Flour and corn, Gibsonville, Miss Nora Summers.

Flour and corn, Alamance, Clapp Bros.

Flour and corn, Alamance, D P Foust.

Flour and meal, Whitsett, Clapp's Mill.

Greensboro Mills, Greensboro, Greensboro Mill Co.

Grist, Greensboro, J T Morehead.

Lumber and laths, Whitsett, W M Clapp.

Merchant corn and flour, Deep River, Payne & Brown.

Merchant flour mill, Jamestown, Oak Mfg Co.

Merchant flour and corn, High Point, W H Ragan.

Merchant flour and corn, High Point, Hammer & Brown.

Oak Hill Roller Mill, Greensboro, D F Caldwell, pres.

Planing mills, Greensboro, Thos Woodroffe.

Roller flour mill, Gibsonville.

Roller flour mill, Greensboro, North & Watson.

Roller flour mill, Gibsonville, O L Huff.

Steam saw, Greensboro, Wm Love.

MINES.

Kinds, Post Offices and Proprietors.

Armfield Gold and Copper, High Point.

Ferabee Gold and Copper, High Point.

Fisher Hill, Greensboro, A M Farnum.

Gardner Hill Mining Co, ——, Frank Osgood, prop, New York.

Guilford Gold Copper Co, Jamestown, James Palmer, agt.

Lindsay Gold and Copper, High Point.

North State Gold and Copper Comp'ny, Jamestown, Dr Jos Wilkins, Baltimore, Md, pres.

Soapstone quarry, High Point, Wm Wheeler.

Tuscarora Iron and Steel, Friendship, Thomas Graham.

PHYSICIANS.

Names and Post Offices..

Beall, W P, Greensboro.
Broadnax, J G, Greensboro.
Clapp, J C, Whitsett.
Cox, J J, High Point.
Gregory, R K, Greensboro.
Griffith, J W (dentist), Greensboro.
Hayes, J M, Greensboro.
Jones, W O (dentist), High Point.
Logan, ——, Greensboro.
Marley, H B S, Greensboro.
McCanless, A L, Trinity College.
Michaux, E R, Greensboro.
Pitts, H C (dentist), High Point.
Powers, J K, Willard.
Richardson, ——, Greensboro.
Rone, Walter W (dentist) Greensboro.
Stanton, D A, High Point, (Cox & Stanton).
Tate, R W, Greensboro.
Whitsett, G W (dentist), Greensboro.

SCHOOLS.

Names, Post Offices and Principals.

A M College (col.), Greensboro, W H Crosby, pres.
Belleview Institute, Lee T Blair.
Bennett Seminary, Greensboro.
Fairview Institute and Commercial College, Whitsett, W T Whitsett, Ph D, supt, with five assistants.
Graded school (col), South Greensboro.
Graded school (col), Greensboro, Frank Logan.
Greensboro Female College, Greensboro, Dred Peacock, pres.
Guilford College, Guilford College, L L Hobbs, pres.
High Point Classical Institute, High Point, Prof J M Weatherly.
Kent Home (industrial department of Bennett), Mrs D Snow, supt.
Oak Ridge Institute, Oak Ridge, J A & M H Holt.
Public school, High Point, Gurney Frazier, prin.
State Normal and Industrial School, Greensboro, Chas D McIver, A B, LL D, pres.
Public schools: white 91, colored 37.

TEACHERS.

Names and Post Offices.

Albright, Nina, Greensboro.
Amick, Eugenia, Kernersville.
Amick, G L, Kernersville.
Ballinger, Dora, Guilford College.
Barnhardt, Amelia, Whitsett.
Blair, James, Guilford College.

GUILFORD COUNTY.

Bowman, J H, Shaw's Mills.
Briggs, Minnie, Greensboro.
Burgess, J R, Tabernacle.
Campbell, Mrs Mary, Tabernacle.
Causey, J W S, Crystal.
Causey, Jesse, Crystal.
Clapp, Bobbie, Brick Church.
Clapp, Maria L, Whitsett.
Coley, Georgia, Lamont.
Cox, W O, Gibsonville
Craven, R K, Summerfield.
Cranford, Fannie, Pleasant Garden.
Credalelough, C A, High Point.
Cude, E S, Colfax.
Cude, H C, Colfax.
Cude, Will, Colfax.
Cude, Stephen, Colfax.
Cude, Rosa, Colfax.
Cude, Charles, Colfax.
Dalton, Kate, Summerfield.
Darnell, Mary, Greensboro.
Darnell, Lizzie, Greensboro.
Davidson, Laura, Gibsonville.
Denny, M A, Centre.
Ector, Elmore, Greensboro.
Ector, Norella, Greensboro.
Edgerton, Annie V, Guilford College.
Enoch, R A, Pleasant Garden.
Fields, Mamie, Greensboro.
Foust, S J Shaw's Mills.
Gamble, C W, Summerfield.
Gladson, R M, Greensboro.
Gray, Hattie, Pleasant Garden.
Hackett, Ellen, Centre.
Hackett, J C, Centre.
Hammer, V R, Deep River.
Hancock, J R, Greensboro.
Hoskins, Elmer, Greensboro.
Hodgin, David, Greensboro.
Hodgin, R E, Greensboro.
Hodgin, R W, Guilford College.
Hodson, Bertha, Centre.
Hodson, Ila, High Point.
Holt, J R, Dennysville.
Johnson, N M, Summerfield.
Johnson, Jane, Oak Ridge.
Johnson, C F, Summerfield.
Kearns, R M, High Point.
Ledbetter, J A, Julian.
Lindley, J W, Jamestown.
Lineberry, J B, Greensboro.
Lowrie, Annie, Oak Ridge.
May, Jas M, Brick Church.
McCullock, John, Pleasant Garden.
Mendenhall, Davey, Kernersville.
Meredith, Elsie, Westminster.
Merritt, Alice, Jamestown.
Millis, A T, Guilford College.
Montgomery, E E, Greensboro.
Morphews, Dora, Westminster.
Murray, Ora, Greensboro.
Ogburn, Lizzie, Westminster.
Osborne, Borsene, Centre.
Osborn, Susanah, Centre.
Osborn, Lindley, Greensboro.

GUILFORD COUNTY.

Parker, Jas P, Guilford College.
Patterson, Beulah D, Whitsett.
Pegg, Mamie, Colfax.
Rankin, W C, Greensboro.
Roach, T J, Climax.
Rutzell, M A, McLeansville.
Socknell, Belle, Greensboro.
Stack, J W, Greensboro.
Staley, J T, Crystal.
Stanley, Callie, Centre.
Stanly, Emma, Centre.
Stewart, W B, Greensboro.
Teague, Mary, Tabernacle.
Teague, Bettie, Tabernacle.
Weatherby, D M, Greensboro.
Wharton, Collie, McLeansville.
Wiley, S S, Jamestown.
Wiley, Annie, Jamestown.
Woody, W E, Shaw's Mills.
Whitsett, Lizzie E, Whitsett.
Hammer, D E, Whitsett.
Joyner, J H, Whitsett.
May, J M, Whitsett.
Woods, Elmer, Kernersville.

LOCAL CORPORATIONS.

Buena Vista Lodge, No 2, I O O F, Greensboro; R B Beall, N G; —— Crutchfield, V G; Robert W Murray, sec; H H Cartland, treas; Levin C Howlett, fin sec.

Central Land Co, Greensboro; J W Fry, pres; J M Scott, sec and treas.

Greensboro Water Co; D R Schenck, pres; Fred K Hubbell, sec and treas; Col W W Taylor, supt and builder; Jas D Glenn, receiver.

Greensboro Electric Light and Power Co; R L Vernon, pres; C P Vanstory, vice president; C D Benbow, sec and treas; E P Wharton, gen mgr; capital $35,000.

Greensboro Industrial and Immigration Association; H W Cobb, pres; W E Stone, sec and treas.

Greensboro Chamber of Commerce; J R Mendenhall, pres; W E Buill, 1st vice pres; J W Fry, 2d vice pres; Thos Woodroffe, 3d vice pres; W C Carr, sec and treas; R M Douglas, attorney.

Greensboro Land and Improvement Co, J A Odell, pres.

Greensboro Security and Investment Co; J T Tate, pres; Charles W Tate, sec and treas.

Guilford Battle Ground Association; Hon D M Schenck, pres; Col Thos B Keogh, Dr D W C Benbow, J W Scott, directors. Owns 65 acres of land where the battle was fought.

High Point, Randleman and Ashboro Railroad, Capt —— Nichols, supt.

GUILFORD COUNTY.

High Point Machine Works; $3,000 capital; J Elwood Cox, pres; O N Richardson, sec and treas; R B Boren, supt.

High Point Furniture Co; capital, $9,000; J H Tate, supt; E A Snow, pres; T F Wrenn, sec and treas.

National Bank of High Point; W J Armfield, pres; A J Sapp, vice-pres; C W Worth, cash; capital stock, $50,000.

North Carolina Steel and Iron Co, Greensboro; J A Odell, pres; Dr D W C Benbow, vice-pres; J D Kase, sec and treas.

Paisley Encampment, I O O F, No 10, Greensboro.

Peoples Five Cents Savings Bank, Greensboro; J W Scott, pres; S S Brown, 1st vice-pres; J H Harris, 2d vice-pres; J A Odell 3d vice-pres; J A Hodgin, treas; H H Cartland, sec; R M Douglas, atty.

South Piedmont Land Co, Greensboro.

South Greensboro Investment Co; J M Scott, pres; J S Hunter, sec and treas.

Southern Stock Mutual Insurance Co; Dr J M Worth, pres; E P Wharton, vice-pres; A W McAllister, sec and treas; capital stock, $100,000.

The Piedmont Bank of Greensboro, N C; J M Walker, pres; Samuel Trogden, vice-pres; R G Vaughn, cash; R M Douglas, atty; E L Sides, teller.

The Keeley Institute of N C, Greensboro; Wm H Osborn, pres; Leo D Heartt, sec and treas; A K Umstead, G W Watts, Rev Alex Walker, directors; Dr Williams, physician in charge; Judge W H Eiler, sec; Wm Lipscomb, bookkeeper; Jas R Day, steward.

The National Bank of Greensboro; capital stock, $100,000; surplus fund, $33,000; Neil Ellington, pres; W S Hill, vice-pres; A H Anderson, cash; W E Allen, teller; M S Sherwood, clerk; A H Alderman, bookkeeper.

The North State Improvement Company, Greensboro; J D Williams, pres; ——, vice-pres and gen mgr; R Percy Gray, sec and treas; paid up capital, $250,000.

The Bank of Guilford, Greensboro; D F Caldwell, pres; Dr W P Beall, vice-pres; W B Bogart, cash; L M Scott, attorney; W F Bogart, teller; R M Murray, bookkeeper.

NEWSPAPERS.

Carolina Methodist (col), Greensboro.

College Message, Greensboro, Greensboro Female College organ.

Christian Advocate Publishing Co., established 1855; office, Odd Fellows' building, Greensboro, N C; Rev P L Groom, D D, pres; Rev W L Grissom, sec and treas; directors, W L Grissom, P L Groom, Dred Peacock, M A Smith, A J Williams.

The High Point Enterprise (weekly, industrial); J J Farris, editor.

The Greensboro Patriot (weekly, Democratic), W M Barber, editor and prop.

The Greensboro Record (daily and weekly), Reece & Elam, editors and props.

Guilford Herald (ind weekly), W M Sherrill, editor.

FARMERS.

Names and Post Offices.

Alamance—A C Boon, Curtis Caldwell, Jacob Z Clapp, G A Clapp, J A Coble, J F Foust, D P Foust, G W Foust, J H Rankin, Cyrus Wharton.

Battle Ground—Bob Dennis, W D Dennis, Jas Dennis, J H Lambeth.

Brick Church—J T R Clapp, G M R Clapp, F Z Clapp, Jno E Clapp, Henry M Coble, G W Coble, Joe V Coble, Bob C Coble, R A Coble, W A Coble, D M Coble, S F Coble, J F Coble, Wilbert C Coble, W H Fogleman, W A Fogleman, James Greeson, A J Greeson, M N Greeson, D L Greeson, G W Greeson, W A Hammer, D F Huffman, Jno R Huffman, M A Huffman, D L Huffman, George Huffman, Elisha May, D A May, W L May, R B May, Jno F May, Jas M May, J R May, Jno M Phillips, Simeon Shepherd, W R Shepherd, David Shepherd, W C Shepherd, S R Shepherd, J H Shoffner, J R Shoffner, Geo Shoffner, D J Shoffner, T B Shoffner, G T Shoffner, Thos Shoffner, Jno H Shoffner, W H Shoffner, Jacob Shoffner, H B Shoffner, Thos A Smith, D L Smith, H W Steel, Jacob Summer, A G Thomas.

Brown's Summitt—D C Akin, Madison Beville, Bob C Beville, J M Bowman, J J Busee, G N Buchanan, Jas W M Cordeza, Branch Chilcutt, R L Chilcutt, J A Coble, T V Colman, Jno Davis, R K Denny, W O Doggett, J T Doggett, C R Doggett, E T Field, J H Fryer, Robt A Geringer, Jno S Geringer, Pinkney Gordon, W A Greene, G W Greene, Geo D Greene, Isaac Greeson, W M Greeson, J L Hawkins, J W Hopkins, David Hopkins, Jas D Huffins, W L Huffins, D R Huffins, J D Johnson, David Kernodle, J R Kernodle, G W Lemons, W D Lambeth, J A Lambeth, Jas W Lambeth, Jas A May, David E McMicheal, Alfred A McMichael, G W McMicheal, P M McMcMicheal, Jno McMicheal, Walter M McMicheal, David A Maxwell, Jas

|

Miles, Jas H McNeil, G R Moore, J W Phillis, W H Pitchford, J L Pitchford, Isaac Pritchett, W H Rankin, Cicero H Beedd, W M Scott, Jno Shon, Robt L Small, J M Small, G W Small, Isaiah Smith, Jno W Smith, Robt R Smith, J D Smith, Jno Smith, J R Smith, Henry Smith, D B Smith, J M Summers, Jacob H Summers, Jerry Terry, Isaac Troxler, Geo R Troxler, Jacob Wagoner, W T Wagoner.

Centre.—J C Armfield, J P Bishop, A L Blair, Lindsay Coltrane, Jas A Davis, Jas M Davis, F S Davis, John Dillon, T B Farrington, W E Field, C J Fowler, W D Frazier, Jno Frazier, T T Glenn, S B Glenn, H L Gray, J S Murrow, J A Murrow, A C Murrow, J A Newman, Jonathan Ozment, Lewis Reynolds, Henry Shepherd, Enoch Shelby, J F Shelby, W R Smith, R M Sniggett, David Stack, R C Swain.

Climax.—John P Coble, Nathan Coble, Dr. Jas a Curtis.

Colfax.—Jas Atkins, S J Atkins, E B Atkins, Jno Baker, H R Barrow, R A Blalock, Jno M Brookbank, J H Brookbank, G W Charles, J L Charles, C C Clark, B T Clark. M L Cude, J A Davis, D L Davis, J D Davis, S H Davis, R J Dillon, A B Dillon, J A Edwards, H C Edwards, S W Farrington, Stephen Fussy, Seth Gardner, Sol Gard- J D Gardner, Geo T Gossett, Jesse Gray, Wm Gray, A A Gray, D L Gray, J M Guyer, N P Henley, E B Jacob, G B Jacob, Henry Jones, Henry McCollum, Elwood Morgan, G N Payne, M H Pegg, Isaiah Pegram, John F Pegram, Jas F Pegram, Sam'l Pitts, J P Raper, W W Shields. G W Snider, J C Smith, J J Smith, Jeffrey Smith, J H Staples, J R Staples, W C Stafford, Ed L Stafford, J H Stanley, T C Starbuck, E J Stewart, B F Sullivan, A W Thornton, W B Tucker, E A Tucker, J R Welborn, D W Welborn, M L Welborn, C H Whitehead, C A Wood.

Company Mills.—P H Apple, Cyrus Apple, Mehane Apple, Cornelius Apple.

Crystal—Reily Brown, J W S Causey, G W Ephlin, David Farmer, G W Farmer, John B Farmer, Simpson Fields, P V Foster, Frank Freeman, Henry Garrett, Fred Garrett, David Garrett, Jesse Garrett, Wm Garrett, Peter Garrett, W R Gerringer, James Gerringer, J E Greison, Jno T Greison, J N Layton, D N Layton, H H Layton, T S Layton, David Layton, John Layton, R W Layton, Wm Layton, Oliver Staley.

Friendship—Jas N Blalock, Jno M Blalock.

Gibsonville—W J Brooks, Berry Davidson, J S Davidson, W T Davidson, Ezekiel Devault, A R Foust, J S Smith, Jno M Summers. Peter Summers, J V Wagoner, Peter Wagoner, D E Wagoner, W N Wright.

Gilmer's Store—V B Donnell, B H Fields, D Q Foust, W H Phipps, Sam'l R Phipps, L A Phipps, S W Phipps, M C Shaw, J M Thorn.

Greensboro—C E Albright, Wm Albright, Jasper Alred, W L Andrews, Jno C Andrews, O C Anthony, Logan Anthony, L D Aydlett, N Ballinger, R H Ballinger, W J Benbow, J F Bennett, O N B nnett, A L Boon. Geo R Briggs, Sidney Brown, W H Brothers, Jas H Buchanan. J C Buson, Alex Cabel, Jno C Cannon, John A Cobb, Westley Coble, P R Coble, J R Cocklerees, W A Coe, C C Copps, A A Crutchfield, G A Denny, Robt Dennis, J M Dick, S O Dick, T B Donnell, Edwin Donnell, Jas Donnell, John Donnell, Geo Donnell, W J Ector, Eugene Eckle, W M Edwards, C H Fields, Ashley Ford, R R Fryer, J D Gammon, Jas M Gant, Wm Gant, J C Gilbreth, R A Gilmer, D L Gilespie, Robt Gilchrist, G M Glass, W P Glass, J A Groome, Z L Groome, W J Groome, C A Groome, Emesley Gullett, Nathan Hanner, J L Hendrix, Thos A Hill, W G Holt, O C Holt, J B Hughes, D H Hunter, Wm Jeldings, W R Jenkins, J H Johnson, G W Kenley, C E Landreth, J F Lanier, I D Lewis, Rev A W Lineberry, David May, J E McKnight, S D McLeon, Webb McNairy, J D McNairy, Rufus McNeely. Zack Melvin, A S Moore, A H Murray, A L Ozment, Cyrus Parker, W H Patterson, H C Phillips, R S Phipps, J A Rankin, N E Rankin, W C Rankin, George Rich, Henry Rust, Walker Scott, J C Sharp, J W Sharp, W A Sharp, B A Smith. Geo A Smith, W R Smith, Arnelines Stack, Jno A Starr, Jno R Stewart, E W Stratford, J S Sumners, M C Taylor, Phillip Thomas, C A Tucker, W C Tucker, A S Vass, M T Ward, John Weatherly, C H Weatherly, J W Webb, W D Wharton, A T Whitsett, J D White, Ellis White, T J Welles, Henry Wilson, James M Wood, A B Wray, Joseph Wright, Jno A Young.

Guilford College—S C Barber, Adison Boren, Wm Bowman, W E Smith, S W H Smith, R S Smith, J H Stanley. T A Stewart, Dal I Worth.

High Point—Tho E Anderson, Joel Anderson, Joshua Anderson, W J Armfield, C A Barker, C A Bartell, S J Blair, Uriah Beeson, J B Bodenhammer, A C Davis, Dougan Davis, W R Davis, E H C Fields, J M Gordon, J W

GUILFORD COUNTY.

Gwyer, E A Gwyer, T B F Hayworth, M F Hayworth, Zeb Hiatt, John H Hedgecock, Jno W Hedgecock, David M Hedgecock, James Hedgecock, J P Horney, H W Horney, C D Horney, J D Horney, W H Idol, A M Idol, H C Kearns, S H Mendenhall, Samuel Mendenhall, James Meredith, Jesse Moore, M M Motsinger, A M Payne, W D Pitts, A L Mendenhall, Amos Ragan, Sol A Raper, Robt Richardson, W R Richardson, J P Snider, W H Snow, Z S Weavell, M H Weavell, Cyrus Welch, E J Welch, W D Welborn, J W Welborn, S C White, J H White, P W Willard, Geo W Williams, M S Williams, W B Williams.

Hillsdale—Alford Amick, O F Busie, J H Gant, R P Gordon, H W Gordon, Wm Harris, J F Highfill, Thos L Johnson, B F Jordan, J A Lambeth, H W Lee, W L Miles, Jas A Morgan, W D Moore, W R Pearson, R T Scott, Thos J Styers, W H Warren, Jesse Wilson, R W Wilson, J W Winchester.

Hinton—D L Boon, J R Pritchett.

Jamestown—Z Groome, C A Groome, W J Groome, A A Holton, J S Ragsdale, A W Reece, S C Robins, Jno A Robertson, W H Rule, Jas F Rush, B F Rush, W G Sapp, E S Thornton, A L Vickery, C A Vickery, S H Ward, Charles B Wilson, W M Wiley, B F Wiley, Jas Yates.

Julian—R C Downing, C K Downing.

Kimesville—G W Amick, John C Amick, W A Amick, John Black, Jno R Bowman, W T Bowman, Jno H Bowman, W A Bowman, Jno M Brown, W A Clapp, M A Clapp, M A Fogleman, Z M Fogleman, Peter Fogleman, Emsley Fogleman, R B Foust, Z M Foust, Eli Foust, H E Friddle, E J Friddle, Levi Humble, Jno A Humble, Alfred Humble, William Humble, W B Humble, D M Humble, David Humble, P W Humble, Fogleman Johnson, Alfred Johnson, Geo B Johnson, Henry A Johnson, Adam Johnson, Jno N Kime, M N Kime, W A Kime, R M Lineberry, J A Lineberry, W A Lineberry, W D Lowe, Cyrus Lowe, Washington Lowe, M E May, Amick Mendenhall, C M Mendenhall, J H Thomas, W M Thomas, C W Thomas, R C Wood, J R Woods, R D Wright.

Lamont—Isaac Amick, Daniel Bowman, J P Green, J W Holden, J L Holt, J R Holt, W S Holt, Isaac Holt, W M Holt, W C Hornaday, J T Huffman, W A Ingold, R D Ingold, Jno W Ingold, Henry Iseley, A E McNairy, D N Neese, W G Neese, Jno B Neese, J F Neese, Alfred Neese, David Neese,

GUILFORD COUNTY.

T M Neese, D L Neese, Wm Patterson, J D Patterson.

Liberty Store,—Jno S Barber, Jno P Boon, N H Brown, W A Brown, J J Busie, Peter Cobb, W R Cummings, J M Gerringer, Peter Gerringer, J H Gilliam, Gregory Kernodle, R B Kernodle, Dock Kernodle, Wm Kirkman, Jno Loman, John R Loman, D A Thomas, Brooks Wallington.

McLeansville.—J C Browning, Geo T Buchanan, T P Clapp, Luke Carman, Jno R Carman, H K Carman, Jacob Cobb, John C Cobb, Feter Cobb, S W Cobb, W G Cobb, Henry Cobb, Rankin Cummings, Jos Denny, A C Denny, J C Dick, Franklin Dick, J W Forbis, A F Forbis, J M Foust, Gideon C Foust, J C Foust, Jno Forsyth, Wm Forsyth, J H Fryer, G W Glass, A L Gilmer, J H Gilmer, W M Gannon, Wm Gray, Jas H Gray, J G Hackett, Wm Heath, Jno P Heath, A S Hanner, J R Hanner, G L Hobbs, Sam'l Hfliness, D B Huffiness, Dr A P McDaniel, Dr J A McLean, Walter McLean, Alfred Michael, J A Montgomery, Jno W Paisley, J R Paisley, Henry Reece, M A Reitzel, Lewis Shepherd, Middleton Lockwell, R S Stewart, D C Stewart, Dan M Starr, J W Summers, Peter Summers, David Sackwell, C A Tickle, W F Thorn, Henry Wagoner, Phil Wayrick, Jno S Wayrick, G W Wharton, W P Wharton, Dr Alfred Whitsell, Eli Wilson, C H Woolers, W A Wyrick.

Oak Ridge—John Angel, Henry Anthony, W H Ball, Thomas J Benbow, Jesse Benbow, W E Benbow, C R Benbow, M F Blalock, John M Bowman, J A Bowman, J M Bowman, J S Brookland, J J Brookland, Rufus Browning, L M Dean, Charles Case, Jas H Clark, A S Clark, W O Donnell, Thos Fuller, N W Gernon, R A Greegon, H B Johnson, S B Jones, Caleb Jones, Dennis Gulley, W T Linville, S Lowery, Jno A Lowery, Geo S Nelson, Jno C Pegram, W A Pegram, J H Pegram, F M Pegram, C J Pegram, A W Pegram, C F Perry, W W Roberts, A J Rolling, E F Rumley, Thos J Rumley, J W Stafford, R M Stafford, Jas R Stanley, H D Vass, Rufus Warren.

Pleasant Garden — D M Causey, Daniel Coble, Jordan Crawford, A H Crawford, Rev J F Craven, Wm Fentress, M W Fentress, R F Fentress, T C Fentress, David C Field, John Field, Roddy Field, R A Field, R L Field, C G Field, J T Gassett, Thos N Gladson, W D Hardin, C V Hardin J W Heath, T F Hendrix, M C Hendrix, Joseph Herbin, W B Hackett, C E Hackett,

GUILFORD COUNTY.

GUILFORD COUNTY.

John E Hackett, M C Hodgin, Robt L Hodgin, P C Hunt, Alston Jones, J Frank Kennett, Robt L Kennett, J C Kennett, W F Kirkman, W D Kirkman, Jas S Kirkman, Daniel M Kirkman, Peter V Kirkman. Ed Kirkman, W C Kirkman, Robt M Kirkman. H T Kirkman, Jas E Leaman, A A Lewis, Henry Macy, Calvin McCullock, John M McCullcck, Rev T F McCullock, A E McCullock, W R McMasters, D C Neely. R C Pattonson, W Calvin Rankin, W D Ross. Julius F Ross, J Frank Ross, John A Royall, S J Scott. John Smith, D W Swain, Thos W Taylor, Wm Taylor, John R Tucker. A M Underwood, S W Vickery, J W Wertherly, John Whitley, W B Witty, D N Woodburn, H B Wolf, S N Wolf.

Pomona—H L Bergman, Geo T Larne, J Van Lindley, W H McCormack.

Scalesville—Geo W Barber, W H Clayton, Jas E Blackburn, H C Brown, Jas H Brown, G T Florence, B J Moore, W P Wall, J W Wharton, A M Whitsett, G A Williams.

Shaw's Mills—D M Hubbard, C M Jobe, D C Jones, Thos Jones, W M Shaw, W H C Spaws.

Stokesdale—J R Dwiggins, Geo B Elliott, Daniel Frazier.

Summerfield—J H Barker, Chas Bevill, W J Bevill, H C Brittain, Thos Brookland, J C Bunch, W H Bunch, Wm Canada, A C Case, W H Case, M C Crews, S H Coltrane, Robt L Coltrane, R E Coltrane, W C Debon, T W Doggett, J G Evans, Sewell Frazier, J W Gourley, R H Gourley, J Lee

Hall, P H Harris, Henry Hayworth, Jerry Highfill, Jonathan Hodgin, J A Hodgin, David Hodgin, J L G Hodgin, Jno T Hodgin, R E Hodgin, A M Hodgin, Geo Hoskins, J A Hoskins, Jesse Hoskins. Nicholas Jennings, C F Jones, David Jones, Jefferson Jones, B W Johnson, Geo Kernodle, G W Kirkham, G A Kirkham, A G Kirkman, W M Kirkman, N M Knight, Julius Knight, J W Knight, Shedal Land, T C Lamb, Jas A Leonard, Robt Leonard, Jas Lee, F M Lee, J S Lloyd, W R Marsh, J L Marsh, Jas Massey, J M McMichael, Archibald McMichael, Jesse C McMichael, Jesse F McCracken, H G Moore, Rufus Newell, Abson Oakley, J L Ogburn, N W Ogburn, Geo Oliver, Green Pass, Albert Peel, A R Pegram, J L Pitts, Raleigh Richardson, Thos J Smith, J B Smith, J C Shrauer, D L Stafford, Moses Stafford, Jas R Stapleton, T A Wilson, P L Wilson.

Tabernacle—Davis F Coble, S P Coble, Orlanda Coble, Robt L Coble, W Allen Coble, J Henry Coble, Alson G Gorrell, Thos R Gruson, Jesse E Hanner, M Harper, W D Hardin, P H Hardin, Simpson Hemphill, J A Hockett, Jno R Jones, W H May, J S Merritt, H E Rankin, H B Shaffner, Robt A Starr, J A Stewart, John W Stewart, David Wilson, Cornelius Wilson, Jeter Wilson, N D Woody.

Whitsett—L Barnhardt, C A Boon, T G Boon, A L Boon, John Clapp, A G Clapp, Mrs L Foust, A J Greeson, B F Law, Jas Oldham, J H Rankin, Mrs M P Summers, E B Wheeler, Joseph Whitsett.

HALIFAX COUNTY.

AREA 680 SQUARE MILES.

POPULATION: 24,868; White 19,645; Colored 5,223.

HALIFAX COUNTY was formed in 1758, from Edgecombe county, and in this year the court house for the counties of Edgecombe, Granville and Northampton was moved from Enfield to the town of Halifax. It derives its name from the Earl of Halifax, who in 1758 was the first Lord of the Board of Trades.

HALIFAX, the county-seat, is 83 miles northeast from Raleigh, on the west bank of the Roanoke river, and also on the Wilmington and Weldon Railroad. Population 500.

Scotland Neck, 21 miles southeast of Halifax, has a population of 1,400.

Surface—This county is located on the west side of the Roanoke river; generally level and soil rich. Convenient railroad and river transportation make it very desirable for farmers. This is doubtless one of the finest counties in the State.

Staples—Cotton is the great staple. Corn and sweet potatoes are profitable crops, and tobacco is grown successfully in the northern part of the county. Plenty of water-power and timber.

Fruits—Apples, peaches, pears, cherries, grapes, plums, melons and a great variety of small fruits.

Timbers—Pine, oak, hickory, poplar, maple, cypress and juniper.

TOWNS AND POST OFFICES.

	POP.		POP.
Airlie,	—	Neal,	—
Aurelian		Newsom,	—
Springs,	60	Norfleet,	—
Brinkleyville,	200	Palmyra,	150
Chockoyotte,	—	Panacea	
Crowell's,	160	Springs,	80
Dawson,	75	Ringwood,	200
Enfield,	1,500	Roanoke R'pids,—	
Essex,	—	Romola,	—
Glenview,	—	Scotl'd Neck,	1,400
Halifax	700	South Gaston,	275
Heathsville,	35	Springhill,	—
Hobgood,	—	Thelma,	—
Ita,	—	Terrapin,	—
Kitchin,	—	Tillery,	80
Littleton,	500	Veni,	—
Medoc,	—	Weldon;	1,500

COUNTY OFFICERS.

Clerk Superior Court—S M Gary.

Commissioners—R W Brown, chm'n; M H Clark, R B Britt, W C Daniel, Ed W Hyman.

Coroner—B F Gary.

Register of Deeds—J Frank Brinkley.

Sheriff—Samuel Clark.

Solicitor-2d District—Walter C Daniel.

Surveyor—W R Neville.

Treasurer—W F Parker.

County Examiner—Aaron Biscott.

County Superintendent of Health— Dr T E Green.

COURTS.

Twelfth Monday after the first Monday of March, the thirteenth Monday after the first Monday in September.

TOWN OFFICERS.

HALIFAX — *Mayor,* Jeff Grizzard; *Commissioners,* H J Canady, E L Travis, J H Fenner, R G Reid; *Constable,* C H Wilcox.

LITTLETON—*Mayor,* T N Harrison; *Commissioners,* G B Hackett, J Hall, J W Northington, S Johnston, M V Perry, J A McCraw; *Clerk,* J W Nottingham; *Chief of Police,* B C King; *Treasurer,* S Johnson; *Constable,* H T Macon.

SCOTLAND NECK—*Mayor,* J A Perry; *Commissioners,* G W Bryan, E W Hyman, J W Leggett, J Stern; *Chief of Police,* W C Dunn; *Treasurer,* R C Josey.

WELDON—*Mayor,* J T Gooch; *Treasurer,* Dr A B Pearce; *Constables,* J H McGee and Wm Roberts; *Commissioners,* Dr A B Pierce, W H Capell, W A Daniel.

TOWNSHIPS AND MAGISTRATES.

Brinkleyville—F M Parker (Enfield), S S Norman (Brinkleyville), W P Sledge, W V Bobbitt, R A Hardy, W R Harvey, R J Harvey, Norman Keen, J C Marks (Ringwood).

Butterwood—B B Nicholson, E A Thorne, L H Allen, W E Bowers, J E Rue, Wm Bowser, J K Dickens (Littleton), C J Smith, A T Dickens (Aurelian Springs).

Conoconary—N Fitzpatrick (Crowell's), W M Crump, C F Hancock, J R Weeks, W B Barnhill, John Barkley,

HALIFAX COUNTY.

J M Pittman, R L Berry, J G Powell (Tillery).

Enfield—J H Whitaker, B C Dunn, C P Simmons. John J Robertson, D C Thrower, M V Barnhill, J D Wood, M W Sykes, B E Bradley, H P Williams (Enfield).

Faucett's—W H Hap, W R Newill, K E Kilpatrick, W K Pittman, John E Anderson, A J Pittman, Lewis Williams (Aurian Springs), J D White head (Halifax), W H Hayes (Heathsville).

Halifax—H J Carraway, M H Clark, J J Daniel, W A Wilcox, J H McIver, M Whitehead, J H Fenner, Wade Carter, Jas H Batchelor, C Bradley, Edgar Barkley, Edward Cheek, James H Arrington.

Littleton—W M Martin, W E Spruill, T W Myrick, J E Johnston, John R Johnston, Eugene Johnston, D S Moss, T N Harrison, R J Lewis, A G Bobbitt, G E Harris, W F Young (Littleton).

Palmyra—J L Philpott, B T Harrell, L C Bell, R J Shidds, K Leggett, W K White. Ivy M Parker, Stewart Hardy, F J Savage (Hobgood).

Roseneath—R H Parrington, Stewart Strickland, M T Savage. W T Whitehead, W T Vaughan, M B Pitt. A B White. Dennison Harrell, L E Griffin (Scotland Neck).

Scotland Neck—J H Darden, J B Neal, R E Hancock, W F Butterworth, A C Liverman, J A Perry, A A White, C A Camp, C C Baker, W T Askew, M Shields, Thad Shields (Scotland Neck).

Weldon—B F Gary, T L Emry, W H Harrison, J T Gooch J W Rook, B A Pope, W A Pierce, S Trueblood, G A Branch, H Tucker, J J Wood, V M Burton (Weldon).

CHURCHES.

Names, Post Offices, Pastors and Denom.

BAPTIST.

Antioch (col)—Scotland Neck, H H Hall.

Cherry's Chapel (col)—Hobgood.

Church—Tillery, J A McKanghan.

Church—Dawson's Cross Roads, J A McKaughan.

Church—Scotland Neck, R T Vann.

Church—Littleton, J K Fant.

Church—Hobgood, J R Pace.

Conoconarie—Enfield, J A McKaughan.

End Street (col)—Scotland Neck, Jo Rawls.

Enon (col)—Littleton, Jack Mayes.

HALIFAX COUNTY.

First Church—Weldon, H W Harman.

First Church—Enfield, J A McKaughan.

First Church (col)—Littleton, M E Hall.

Kehakee (col)—Scotland Neck, Chas Smith.

Long's Chapel (col)—Hobgood, Jesse Williams.

Mary's Chapel (col)—Scotland Neck, M D Matthewson.

Mt Gilbert (col)—Spring Hill, J A Hill.

Oak Grove—Littleton.

Pleasant Hill (col)—Scotland Neck, Sandy Fenner.

Shiloh (col)—Scotland Neck, Milson Brown.

Williams' Chapel (col)—Scotland Neck, Jo Rawles.

Zion Hill (col)—Panacea.

PRIM. BAPTIST.

Kahakee—Scotland Neck, Elder Andrew J Moore.

METHODIST.

Bethlehem—Littleton, E H Davis.

Bethel—Littleton, E H Davis.

Beulah—Littleton, E H Davis.

Calvary—Littleton, E H Davis.

Church—Halifax, E E Rose.

Church—Enfield, E E Rose.

Church—Littleton, E H Davis.

Church—Weldon, R P Troy.

Church—Palmyra, H M Jackson.

Ebenezer—Enfield, —— Frizzell.

Haywood's—Enfield, E E Rose.

Pierce's Chapel—Halifax, H M Jackson.

METH. PROTESTANT.

Bear Swamp—Enfield, Vernon T Anson.

Moriah—Enfield, J Paris.

Olive Branch—Littleton.

Roseneath—Scotland Neck.

EPISCOPAL.

Chapel of the Cross—Littleton, W M Phelps.

Church (col)—Littleton, V N Barnes.

Grace Church—Weldon.

Old Trinity (one mile north)—Scotland Neck, Walter J Smith.

St Mark's—Brinkleyville.

St Mark's—Halifax, Walter J Smith.

Trinity—Scotland Neck, Walter J Smith.

PRESBYTERIAN.

Church—Littleton, —— Wharton.

First Church (col)—Littleton, John Mayo.

Nahala—Scotland Neck, R W Hines.

Second Church—Weldon, — Waldron.

MINISTERS RESIDENT.

Names, Post Offices and Denom.

METHODIST.

Black, W S, D D, Littleton.
Davis. E H, Littleton.
Frizelle, ——, Aurelian.
Grady, L G, Halifax.
Jackson, H M, Scotland Neck.
Kilpatrick, J A B. Brinkleyville.
Rose, E E, Enfield.
Smith, Walter J A, Scotland Neck.
Troy, R P, Weldon.

METHODIST PROTESTANT.

Northington, J H, Littleton.
Whitaker, C C, Enfield.
Wills, W H, Ringwood.

ZION METHODIST.

Davis, W A (col), Weldon.

BAPTIST.

Fant, J K, Littleton.
McKaughan, J A, Enfield.
Vann, R T, Scotland Neck.

HOTELS AND BOARDING HOUSES.

Names, Post Offices and Proprietors.

A C L Hotel, Weldon, John Gall, gen
  manager.
Boarding House, Weldon, Mrs Ida Wil-
  kins.
Boarding House, Weldon, Mrs J T
  Evans.
Boarding. Littleton, W H Bobbitt.
Boarding, Littleton, S T Thorne.
Boarding, Littleton, Mrs M J Miles.
Boarding, Littleton, M E Newsom.
Boarding House, Scotland Neck, Mrs
  Brown.
Boarding, Littleton, Mrs C B Heptin-
  stall.
Bon Air, Littleton, J C Brown.
Central, Littleton, J W Johnson.
Eating-house, Weldon, W A Davis
  (col).
Eating-house, Littleton, W W White.
Eating-house, Littleton, Winfield
  Young (col).
Hotel, Enfield, Mrs B T Whitaker.
Hotel, Roanoke Rapids, R M Brown.
Hotel, Scotland Neck, C A Camps.
Hotel, Enfield, D D Bryan.
Hotel, Littleton, J H Hann.
Hotel Panacea, Panacea, Mrs A H A
  Williams.
Littleton Hotel, Littleton, J L Shaw.
Main Street, Scotland Neck, Mrs Fanny
  L Sills.
Southern Hotel, Halifax, Mrs C P
  Tillery.
Spring Park Hotel, J L Shaw.

LAWYERS.

Names and Post Offices.

Alston & Faulcon, Littleton.
Alsop, S S, Enfield.
Bell, David, Enfield.
Clark, Edward, Weldon.
Collins, J H (col), Halifax.
Daniel, S G. Littleton.
Daniel, W E. Weldon.
Day, W H, Weldon.
Dunn. W A, Scotland Neck.
Faulcon. Walter B, Littleton.
Finch, Wm C. Ringwood.
Furgerson. McMurray M, Littleton.
Grizzard. James M, Halifax.
Hawkins, Thos W, Littleton.
Hilliard, E E, Scotland Neck.
Hill, Thomas N, Halifax.
Kitchin, W H, Scotland Neck.
Kitchin, Claude, Scotland Neck.
Ransom, Robert, Weldon.
Smith. R H. Scotland Neck.
Whitaker, T E, Scotland Neck.

MANUFACTORIES.

Kinds, Post Offices and Proprietors.

Blacksmithing, Ringwood, Stephen
  Threewits.
Brickyard, Weldon, T L Emry.
Brick, Scotland Neck, J A Madree.
Buggies, Scotland Neck, J E Woolard.
Building and contracting, Enfield,
  Warren Hartwell.
Building and contracting, Littleton,
  Robert Crenshaw.
Building and contracting, Ringwood,
  George Hunt.
Building and contracting, Scotland
  Neck, H G Jones.
Building and contracting, Weldon,
  Geo Lewis, (col).
Building and contracting, Weldon,
  Bugg Parker (col).
Cabinet and upholstering, Scotland
  Neck, D G Haskett.
Canning (fruit), Littleton, J L Tate.
Carriages and buggies, Aurelian
  Springs.
Coaches, Scotland Neck, E K Hassell.
Coaches, etc, Brinkleyville, Johnson &
  Pulley.
Coaches, etc, Tillery, W M Crump.
Coaches, Enfield, Dennis & Horne.
Cotton ginning, Enfield, J C Clark.
Cotton ginning, Enfield. J B Hunter.
Cotton ginning, Enfield, D F Whitaker.
Cotton ginning, Enfield, Joe Witley.
Cotton ginning, Littleton, B R Brown-
  ing & Son.
Cotton ginning, Littleton, J L Shaw.
Cotton ginning (steam), Littleton, W
  A Johnston.

HALIFAX COUNTY.

Cotton Factory, Enfield, J T Bellamy.
Cotton Mills, Roanoke Rapids, Roanoke Rapids Co.
Iron and woodwork, Brinkleyville, David Clark.
Iron and woodwork, Littleton, David Mitchell (col).
Iron and woodwork, Weldon, Wm Pearce.
Iron and woodwork, Dawson Cross Cross-Roads. F M Wallace.
Knitting Mills, Scotland Neck, Scotland Neck Cotton Mills Co.
Machine Shops, Scotland Neck, J L Kitchen.
Machine Shops, Littleton, J L Tate.
Repair Shops, Littleton. J J Williams.
Repair Shops, Littleton, Jeff Hall.
Saddles and Harness, Scotland Neck, E Shields.
Saddles and Harness, Littleton, J K Harris.
Saddles and Harness, Littleton, W C Hewlett.
Shingles, Enfield, W F Farker.
Southern Sweet Gum Co, Scotland Neck; N B Josey, pres; A McDowell, sec and treas; J K McIlheny, mgr,
Undertaking and Carriages, Weldon, W R Vick.

MERCHANTS AND TRADESMEN.

Names, Post Offices, Lines of Business.

AIRLIE.

Thorne, S T, jr,	G S

AURELIAN SPRINGS.

Brinkley, A (near),	G S
Jenkins, W T,	G S

BRINKLEYVILLE.

Harrison, N M & Co,	G S
Hunter, J E, agt for wife,	G S
Norman & Co,	G S
Vinson, J H,	G S

CROWELL'S.

Gregory, F W,	G S

ENFIELD.

Britt, J L,	G S
Curtis, Geo B & Co,	G S
Cuthrell, Mrs S C,	G S
Dennis, F J,	Coachmaker
Dickens, F M,	Gro
Gunter, R E L, agt,	Gro
Harrison, Dr A S,	Drugs
Leon, I,	G S
McGrugar, C E,	G S
Meyer, S, agt,	Gro
Millikin & Merritt,	Millinery
Moore, D P,	G S
Parker, W F,	G S and Shingles
Pender, N J (col),	G S
Shields, C W,	G S

HALIFAX COUNTY.

Stallings, O P,	G S
Whitaker, J J,	G S
Whitaker, Dr L T,	G S

ESSEX.

Sexton, Geo W,	G S
Williams, Sid,	G S
Wood, C G,	G S

GLEN VIEW.

Hales, E G,	G S

HALIFAX.

Aycock, C P,	G S
Brown, John N,	G S and Drugs
Daniel, W C,	G S
Enfield Lumber Co,	Hor. Phillips mgr
Froelich Trading Co,	G S
Grady, L G,	Jeweler
Hale Bros,	G S
Hale, C H,	G S
Howard, G H,	Gro
Howerton, C H B, agt,	Gro
Webb, W N J,	Gro

HOBGOOD.

Hyman, Mise Sue A,	Millinery
Leggett, W A & Co,	Drugs
Moore, H H,	Gro
Shields, R J,	G S

ITA.

Pridgen, R H & Co,	G S

LITTLETON.

Bobbitt, J H,	G S
Bobbitt, E A,	G S
Bobbitt, W S,	G S
Browning, B R & Son,	Cotton and G S
Cordle, H J,	Jeweler
Cutchin, Miss Mary,	Tel Op
Cutchin, J,	Depot and Exp Agt S A L
Ferguson, G W,	Prop Furgerson Mineral Springs
Gibson, P B,	Printer
Harris, W G & Co (col),	G S
Johnston, W A,	Livery
Johnston, W A,	G S
Johnston, S,	Cotton and G S
Johnson, A H.	G S
Johnson, S & A M,	Machinery
Littleton Drug Co, Howard Browning, Mgr,	Drugs
Little, Mrs E A,	G S
Mayo, H D (col),	G S
Moore, C Y,	G S
Moseley, A J,	Gro
Myrick, J D, agt,	G S
Newsom, M E & Sons,	G S
Newsom, A M,	Night Tel Op
Northington, J W,	G S
Owens, W T (col),	Gro
Perry, E B & Co,	Drugs
Perkinson, E Z,	G S
Shaw, J L,	G S
Shaw, Mann,	G S
Shearin, N H,	G S
Skinner & Co,	G S

| HALIFAX COUNTY. | HALIFAX COUNTY. |

Stallings, F P,	Gro and Conf
Stallings, S J,	Cotton, G S and
	Undertaker
Thornton, J W,	Livery and Feed
Wise, A Z,	G S
Young, W F (col),	Conf and Fruits

MEDOC.

| Garrett, C W & Co, | Vineyard |

NORFLEET.

| Laurence & Co, | G S |

PALMYRA.

Baker & Robinson,	G S
Bell, L C,	G S
Edmondson, T H,	G S
Wilkins, Robt (col),	G S

PANACEA SPRINGS.

| Sexton, J T & Son, | — |

RINGWOOD.

McGuigan, W H,	G S
Matthews, H C,	Gro
Pridgen, W H (near),	G S
Vinson, L,	G S

SCOTLAND NECK.

Allsbrook, J L,	G S
Allsbrook, W,	G S
Anthony & Co (col),	G S
Biggs, N, & Johnson, R M,	
	Horses, Guano, etc
Bryan, G W,	Depot and Ex Agt
	and Tel Op
Cook, Jo,	Shoemaker
Cook, M C,	G S
Dunn, C W,	Chief Police (Dept
Sheriff), and Tax Collector
Futrell, J H.	Gro
Grady, Mrs L G.	Milliner
Gray, John,	Livery Stable
Griffin, L E,	G S
Hill, J D,	Butcher
Hoffman & Bro,	G S
Hyman, Aquilla,	G S
Hyman, E W,	G S
Jenkins, K,	G S
Johnson, R M,	Fert
Jones, W W & Co,	G S
Josey, N B,	D G and Gro
Josey, R C & Co,	G S
Lawrence, C W,	Gro
Lawrence, Jas H,	Grain
Morrisett, J M & Son,	Livery Stables
Powell, E E,	G S
Purrington, A L,	G S
Robertson, John (col),	Shoemaker
Savage, J Y,	Fruit Trees
Shields, Ed.	G S
Skepwith, John (col),	Shoemaker
Smith, Peter E,	Civil Engineer
Smith, R H,	Post Master
Tillery, Miss Kate G,	Milliner
White, W H & Co,	Merchandise
	Brokers
White & Powell,	G S

| Whitehead, E T & Co, | Drugs |

SOUTH GASTON.

Bradley, W F,	G S
Cohen, J & Co,	G S
House, J A & Bro,	G S
Iles, D E,	G S
King, J J & Co,	G S
Mayo, G (col),	G S
Moody, H S.	G S
Shaw, Mann,	G S
Sledge, J L.	G S
Valentine, W H & Bro,	G S
Vincent, A J, sr, agt,	G S
Wilkins, E W & Sons,	G S

SPRINGHILL.

| Riddick, J T, | G S |
| Weeks, J R, | G S |

TERRAPIN.

| Duke, W M, agt, | G S |

TILLERY.

Barkley, Chas R,	with B F Tillery
Randolph, W H & Co,	G S
Tillery, B F,	G S
Tillery, J R,	Lumber

WELDON.

Anderson, Wm (col),	G S
Biggerstaff, Mrs W,	Clo
Clark, E.	G S
Clark, T A,	G S
Cohen, W M,	Drugs
Edmondson, Lucy,	G S
Emery & Pierce,	G S
Harrison, W H (near),	G S
Hart. The M F Co Corporation,	G S
Judkins J L.	Gro
Lewis, Mrs P A,	Milliner
Moseley, J L.	Jeweler
Pair, Mrs M C,	G S
Parker, W T,	Gro
Pepper, T J (near),	G S
Rooks, J T (near),	G S
Smith, W D (col),	Gro
Spears, H C.	G S
Stainback. P W,	G S
Tillery, W H,	G S
Vick, Mrs H A,	Gro
Vick, W R,	Coach-maker
Zollicoffer, Dr A R,	Drugs

MINES.

Kinds, Post Offices and Proprietors.

Portis' Gold. Littleton, —— Sturgess

MILLS.

Kinds, Post Offices and Proprietors.

Corn, Scotland Neck, W A Staton.
Corn, Littleton, W H Thorne.
Corn (steam), Enfield, John Goodrich.
Corn, Enfield, John Bellamy.

HALIFAX COUNTY.

Corn, Palmyra, N B Jones.
Corn and gin, Weldon, Mrs H T Ponton.
Corn, flour and saw, Littleton, J P Leach.
Cotton gin, merchants flour and corn, Littleton, S Johnson.
Flour and corn, Littleton, S Johnston.
Flour and corn, Scotland Neck, W A Staton.
Merchant flour and corn, Littleton, G B Alston.
Mill, South Gaston, Johnston Sterling.
Mill, Littleton, G B Alston.
Mill, Littleton, J W Heptinstall.
Public gin (steam), Littleton, J L Shaw.
Saw (steam), Weldon, T L Emry.
Saw, Enfield, Samuel Ford.
Steam gin, Littleton, J H Harris.
Steam gin, Littleton, E W Furgerson.
Steam corn mill and gin, Littleton, S Johnston.
Steam saw and planing, Littleton, J H Harris.
Steam saw, Littleton, A M Johnston.
Steam saw and planing and lumber mills, Tillery N C Lumber Co; Dr Harold H Fries (New York), pres; —— McRackin, local mgr; S F Dunn, timber inspector.
Steam grist and gin, Halifax, T L Emery.
Steam saw, Tillery, W H Randolph & Co.
Steam flour grist gin and saw, Aurelian Springs, A Brinkley.
Steam corn, Scotland Neck, W H Smith.
Steam corn, gin and planing mills, Scotland Neck, Dunn & Coughanour.
Steam saw, Scotland Neck, J H Allsbrook.
Steam saw, Scotland Neck, J E Condrey.
Steam corn and gin, Scotland Neck, G W Grafflin.
Steam saw and planing mill, Scotland Neck, John Coughanour.

PHYSICIANS.

Names and Post Offices.

Alston, Willis, Littleton.
Browning, B Ray, Littleton.
Clements, W W, Gaston.
Collins, J A, Enfield.
Drake, Frank, Ringwood.
Furgerson, H B, Halifax.
Green, I E, Weldon.
Harris, T W (dentist), Littleton.
Hill, James C, Tillery.
Leggett, K, Hobgood.
Liverman, A C, Scotland Neck.
Matthews, G E, Ringwood.

HALIFAX COUNTY.

McDowell, M O, Scotland Neck.
McGuigan, John A, Enfield.
O'Brien, John, Aurelian Springs.
Perkins, W M, Aurelian Springs.
Picot, L J, Littleton.
Pierce, A B, Weldon.
Pope, J R, Scotland Neck.
Ross, T T (dentist), Weldon.
Savage, M T, Scotland Neck.
Shields, J E (dentist), Weldon.
Ward, W J (dentist), Enfield.
Whitehead, F W, Scotland Neck.
Wood, W R, Scotland Neck.
Zollicoffer, A R, Weldon.

SCHOOLS.

Names, Post Offices and Principals.

Academy, Spring Hill.
Academy, Enfield, Miss Clara Whitaker.
Baptist Primary, Littleton, Miss Edna Hudson.
Episcopal Parish School, Littleton, Miss Lucy G Capehart.
Episcopal Mission School (col), ——, V N Bond.
High School (male), Littleton, L W Bagley.
Littleton Female College, Littleton, Rev J M Rhodes.
Littleton High School (male), Littleton.
Male Academy, Scotland Neck, D M Prince and C W Wilson, prins.
Nahala Academy, Scotland Neck.
Primary School, Littleton, Mrs Marion Johnston.
Primary School, Enfield, Mrs Lizzie Bass.
Primary School, Scotland Neck, Miss Etta Allsbrook.
Primary School, Littleton, Mrs E A C Jackson.
Private school, Littleton, Miss Susie S Spruill.
Private school, Littleton, Miss Lucy Williams.
Private school, Littleton, Miss Rosa Johnson.
School, Scotland Neck, Miss Margaret Savage.
Seminary, Halifax, Mrs H J Carraway.
Supplimentary (col), Littleton, Rev M E Hall.
Vine Hill Female Academy, Scotland Neck, Miss Lena Smith, prin; Miss Sadie Perry, Miss Evie Caldwell, Miss Bettie Hill and Miss Reta Johnson, teachers.

LOCAL CORPORATIONS.

Atlantic Coast Line, Weldon, Mr Goul.

HALIFAX COUNTY.	HALIFAX COUNTY.

Good Samaritans, Enfield, Rufus Bennett, pres.

Knights of Honor, Weldon, ——— dictator.

Knights of Honor, Littleton, N E Jenkins, dictator.

Legion of Honor, Enfield.

Legion of Honor, Scotland Neck, ——— dictator.

Palmyra, No 338, A F and A M, Palmyra; time of meeting first Wednesday at 2 P M.

Roanoke Lodge, No 203, A F and A M, Weldon; W G Whitfield, W M; time of meeting first Thurday at 8 P M.

Roanoke and Tar River Agricultural Association, Weldon, T L Emery, pres; ———, sec.

Roanoke Navigation and Water Power Co, Weldon; R T Arrington, pres (Petersburg, Va).

Royal White Hart Lodge, No 2, A F and A M, Halifax; time of meeting second Wednesday, June 24th and December 27th, and second Monday in each month.

Scotland Neck Lodge, No. 61, I O O F.

Scotland Neck Lodge, No. 68, A F and A M, Scotland Neck. Time of meeting, first and third Saturdays, June 24th and December 27th.

Scotland Neck Bank, A McDowell,

pres; F P Shields, cash; A B Hill, asst cash; capital stock, $5,000; surplus, $3,500.

The Scotland Neck Cotton Mills, N B Josey, pres; A McDowell sec and treas and gen mgr; capital, $60,000.

Weldon Manufacturing and Navigation Co, Weldon; capital stock, $25,-000; owned by Arrington & Bro, Petersburg, Va; Wm Mahone estate, and Don Cameron, U S Senator Pennsylvania.

Weldon Building and Loan Association, Weldon; G T Gooch, sec and treas.

Weldon Lodge, No 1, I O O F, Weldon; W H Brown, N G.

NEWSPAPERS.

Daily Railroad Ticket, Weldon; Mrs J A Harrell, ed and prop.

Railroad Ticket, Weldon, H B Harrell Publishing Co.

Roanoke News, Weldon (Dem weekly); J W Sledge, ed and prop.

The South, Weldon (immigration quarterly), Mrs J A Harrell, ed and prop.

The Courier, Littleton (Dem weekly), G W Charlotte & Son, eds and props.

The Democrat, Scotland Neck (Dem weekly), E E Hilliard.

HARNETT COUNTY.

AREA, 540 SQUARE MILES.

POPULATION, 13,657; White 9,437, Colored 4,220.

HARNETT COUNTY was set off from Cumberland county in the year 1855, and was named in honor of Cornelius Harnett, a distinguished patriot during the Revolutionary war.

LILLINGTON, the county-seat, is situated 28 miles southwest from Raleigh, and has a population of 150.

Surface.—Level, sandy, much of it thin and not productive—good land along the streams. The Cape Fear river runs directly through the county, affording some fine water-power.

Staples.—Cotton, corn, wheat, chufas, rye, oats, peas, &c. Sweet potatoes are produced in large quantities and of fine quality.

Fruits. — Grapes, melons, apples, pears, peaches and most of the small fruits.

Timbers.—Long-leaf and other pine, poplar, oak, hickory, ash, maple, etc.

Minerals.—Iron; sulphur and iron springs have been discovered of valuable quality.

TOWNS AND POST OFFICES.

	POP.		POP.
Averasboro,	38	Linden,	—
Barclaysville,	—	May,	50
Bovie's Creek,	20	Mohawk,	25
Bradley's Store,	60	Norval,	30
Bunn's Level,	25	Paolia,	—
Chalk Level,	65	Poe's	100
Chopin,	40	Polk,	—
Dickinson,	40	Spout Springs,	50
Dunn,	821	Summerville,	100
Fish Creek,	—	Troyville,	20
Harrington,	150	Turlington,	25
Key,	15	Variety Grove,	20
Leaflet,	20	Westville,	25
Legal,	—	Winston,	10
Lillington (c h)		Wythe,	30
	150		

COUNTY OFFICERS.

Clerk Superior Court—Felix M McKoy.
Commissioners—J M Hodges, ch'm'n; Ed Smith, F J Swann, W J Long, W F Marsh.
Register of Deeds—J M K Byrd.
Sheriff—John H Pope.
Treasurer—Geo D Spence.
Coroner—Duncan Darrock.
Surveyor—J O A Kelly.
County Examiner—L B Chapin.
Entry Taker—D A Faucett.

COURTS.

Second Mounday before the first Monday in March, and first Monday in September, and twelfth Monday after the first Monday in September.

TOWN OFFICERS.

DUNN—*Mayor*, H C McNeill. *Marshal*, M L Wade. *Commissioners*, P T Massingill, D H How, Eldridge Lee

LILLINGTON—*Mayor*, B F Shaw. *Commissioners*, H T Spears, W J Parker, D J McNeill. *Town Constable*, H L McNeill.

TOWNSHIPS AND MAGISTRATES.

Anderson's Creek—Duncan Shaw, H R Buie, John Shaw, Alex West, D J McCorquicke.

Averasboro—H S Jackson, W H Norris, J B Holland, L M Ragals, S Parker, A E Norris.

Black River—A H Gregory, B F Williams, J S Gardner, R H Dewar, Perrion Huneycutt.

Barbecue—H D Cameron, R W Byrd, John McLane, John Darrock, M A McFarland.

Buckhorn—N T Johnson, A T Arnold, D H Wheeler, T E Smith, T H Thomas.

Gregory—A N Sexton, W A Green, J D Long.

Grove—C Hodges, R M Parker, L L Turlington, S R Wilson, J A Stewart, A F Grimes.

Hector's Creek—W G Marcom, A B Betts, G D Spence, D L Matthews, D H Senterly, D E Green.

Johnsonville—R C Bolden, D P McDonald, A C Buie.

Lillington—G S Byrd, Jno W Pipkin, Z T Kivett, Henry McLean, K M McNeill, B F Shaw.

Neill's Creek—A D Byrd, H H Poe, L H Markes, J R Gregory.

Stewart's Creek—Duncan Darrock, Bryant Smith, D S Williams, J F Byrd, J A Colvin.

Upper Little River—W M Patterson, Jno A Hanley, C H Nordon, J L Byrd, R J Patterson, Paul McKoy.

HARNETT COUNTY.

HARNETT COUNTY.

CHURCHES.

Names, Post Offices, Pastors and Denom.

METHODIST.

Aure's School House—Dunn, Langdon Leitch.
Church—Dunn, Langdon Leitch.
Church—Averasboro, Langdon Leitch.
Cokesbury—Chalk Level, B B Hoder.
Cool Spring—Jonesboro, —— Galloway.
Lillington—Little River Academy, W F Craven.
Olive Branch—Chalk Level, B B Hoder.
Pleasant Planes—Dunn, Langdon Leitch.
Spring Hill—Little River Academy, W F Craven.

BAPTIST.

Antioch—Pine Forest, A M Campbell.
Cumberland Union—Jonesboro, C V Brooks.
Friendship—Poe's, J A Campbell.
Holly Springs—Holly Springs, — King.
Little River—Swann's Station, H W Graham.
Mill's Creek—Lillington, J M Holleman.
New Life— —— Dennis.

PRIMITIVE BAPTIST.

Dunn—Dunn, Bernice Wook.
New Hope—Troyville, Thos Coats.
Sandy Grove—Troyville, Thos Coats.

PRESBYTERIAN.

Barbecue—Little River Academy, D D McBryde.
Dunn—Dunn, A H Hassell.
Flat Branch—Little River Academy, D D McBryde.
Pisgah—Jonesboro, —— McLoud.
Summerville—St Paul, J S Black.

FREE-WILL BAPTIST.

Dunn—Dunn, R H Jackson.
Prospect—Dunn, R H Jackson.
Old Field—Dunn, R H Jackson.

DISCIPLES OF CHRIST.

Dunn—Dunn, J J Harper.

MINISTERS RESIDENT.

Names, Post Offices and Denominations.

BAPTIST.

Campbell, A M, Poe.
Campbell, J A, Poe.
Collins, ——, Winslow.
Graham, H M, Dunn's Station.
Harrell, W B, Dunn.
Spence, J B, Ballentine Mills.

METHODIST.

Coat, Thomas, Troyville.
Holder, B B, Chalk Level.

Leitch, Langdon, Dunn.
McNeil, David, Harrington.

PRIMITIVE BAPTIST.

Hood, W B, Dunn.

HOTELS AND BOARDING HOUSES.

Names, Post Offices and Proprietors.

Dunn, Dunn, John Oates.
Jackson House, Dunn, S M Jackson.
Harnett Hotel, Lillington, J T Rogers.
Lillington Hotel, Lillington, Mrs A E Atkins.
Restaurant, Dunn, J F P Stewart.

LAWYERS.

Names and Post Offices.

Best, L J, Dunn.
Chapin, L D, Lillington.
Jones, F P, Dunn.
McLean, D H, Lillington.
Spears, J A, Lillington.
Spears, O J, Lillington.

MANUFACTORIES.

Kinds, Post Offices and Proprietors.

Blacksmithing, Chalk Level, Jesse Morgan.
Blacksmithing, Chalk Level, B Avent.
Blacksmithing, Chalk Level, S M Carpenter.
Blacksmithing, Lillington, Clinton McNeill.
Coopering, Chalk Level, John Griffin.
Millwrighting, Lillington, W L Washburn.
Saw, grist and merchant miller, Cokesbury, Allen Mathews.
Spirits turpentine, Turlington, Taylor & Slocumb.
Spirits turpentine, Spout Springs, Consolidated Lumber Co.
Spirits Turpentine, Legal, Faucette & McLean.
Spirits turpentine, Dunn, Young & Barnes.
Spirits turpentine, Winslow, J & B F Williams.
Spirits turpentine, Lillington, John McArtan.
Turpentine distillery, Benson, A T Lee.
Tannery, Lillington, D J McDonald.
Tannery, Harrington, M A McLean.
Tannery, Lillington, D C McLean.

MERCHANTS AND TRADESMEN.

Names, Post Offices and Line of Business.

AVERASBORO.

Parker, F A,   G S

HARNETT COUNTY.

BARCLAYSVILLE.

Gregory, A W,   Postmaster and G S
Johnson, James A (near).   G S
Matthews, J A,   G S

BRADLEY'S STORE.

Bradley, O G,   G S
Matthews, James,   G S
McKinney, L D,   G S

BROADWAY.

Douglass, R B & Co,   G S

BUNN'S LEVEL

Allen, W W,   G S
Smith, Ed   G S

BOUIE'S CREEK.

Johnson, Frank,   G S
Johnson, J A,   G S

CHALK LEVEL

Avent, W A,   Fertilizer
Champion, J A,   G S
Dewar, John,   G S
Dorsett, L & W,   Lumber Dealers
Hunter & Co,   G S
Johnson, J J,   Auctioneer
Prince & Spence,   G S
Rollins, E,   G S
Rollins & Spence,   G S
Rollins, Gaston,   G S
Spence & Price,   G S

DUNN.

Anderson, H B,
Bass, W E.   G S
Braswell, T W,   Painter
Burke, J H,   G S
Cox, G W & Son,
       Ins Agts and Dealers in Guano
Cox & Balance,
       Livery and Sale Stables
Creel, J N,   Carpenter
Culbreth, J A.   G S
Demming & Higgs,   G S
Dupree, J Q,   G S
Gainey & Jordan,   Jewelers
Grantham & Petim,   Job Printers
Gregory, J W,   G S
Hales, R A,   G S
Harper & Hood. Drugs and Millinery
Hood, N B (Harper & Hood),
                           Druggist
Hood, D H,   Drugs
Jackson, W S. Agt,   G S
Jeffreys. P J, Depot Agt, Southern
       Express Agt, and Tel Operator
Jernigan. H W & Co,   G S
Jordan, J E.   G S
Johnson, J A,   Carriage Shops
Jones, M J & Bro,   Gro
Lane, Mrs C,   G S
Lee Hardware Co,   Gen Hardware
Massengill, J A & Co,   G S
McDaniel, E J,   G S
McDonald, Chas,   Barber
McKoy, Miss Lou,   Postmistress

HARNETT COUNTY.

McNeill, H C,   Gro
Parker, E L,   G S
Parker, S V,   G S
Phillips, J F,   Stables
Pope, Mrs J H,   Millinery
Shell & Co.   G S
Strickland. J H,   Furniture
Sutton & Creel,   G S
Stewart, J F P,   Gro
Taylor, R G,   G S
Underwood, T W,   G S
Wade, J J,   G S
Wilson, J J,   Buggies and Harness
Williams, J A & Bro,   G S
Young, E F,   G S

LEAFLET.

Brown, J H,   G S

LEGAL.

Faucett & McLean,   G S

LILLINGTON.

Burke, J H,   G S
Johnson, A F,   G S
Legum. Simon,   G S
Rodgers, J F & Co.   G S
Shaw, B F,   Ins Agt
Waddell, Byrd,   Jeweler

MAY.

Burt & Robbins,   G S
Rollins & Spence,   G S

PEACOCK'S CROSS-ROADS.

Rose & Bro,   G S and Turp

SPOUT SPRINGS.

Britton & Johnson,   G S

WINSLOW.

Williams, J C & B F,   G S

MINES.

Kinds, Post Offices and Proprietors.

Buckhorn (coal), Chalk Level, Brown
    & DeRossett.
Cape Fear (steel and iron), Chalk Level,
    Cape Fear Steel and Iron Co.

MILLS.

Kinds, Post Offices and Proprietors.

Corn and saw, Lillington, J Rich.
Corn and flour, Winsboro, E D Smith.
Flour, Harrington. Harrington Bros.
Flour and corn, Chalk Level, Gaston
    Robbins.
Flour and corn, Chalk Level, J W
    Avent.
Flour and corn, Winslow, P J Wray.
Saw and grist, Barclaysville, Wm
    Johnson.
Saw, Barclaysville, T Fowler
Saw, Barclaysville, A J Turlington.
Saw, Winslow, E D & R W Smith.

HARNETT COUNTY.

Saw (steam), Lillington, J A Green.
Saw, flour and corn (steam), Averasboro, H C Avera.
Saw, flour and corn (steam), Averasboro, Thos Fowler.
Woolen, Chalk Level, W L Morris.

PHYSICIANS.

Names and Post Offices.

Denning, O L, Dunn.
Goodwin, J C (dentist), Dunn.
Harper, M W, Dunn.
Holden, M, Dunn.
McDougald, J A, Harrington.
McKay, J F, Dickerson.
McKay, A M, Summerville.
McKay, J A, Dickinson.
McNeill, W M, Dickinson.
Moore, F T, Dunn.
Pipkin, J W (dentist), Lillington.
Rodgers, J T (dentist), Lillington.
Sexton, C H, Dunn.
Smith, F, Bunn's Level.
Spence, R G, Chalk Level.
Withers, J H, Summerville.

SCHOOLS.

Names, Post Offices, and Principals.

Bonie's Creek Academy, Rev J A Campbell, prin.
Cokesbury Academy, Chalk Level.
Lillington Academy, Lillington.
Progressive Institute, Dunn, D B Barker, prin.
Public Schools—whites, 60; colored, 29.

TEACHERS.

Names and Post Offices.

Betts, B, Barclaysville.
Briggs, C H, Poe's.
Bryan, Jas E, Summerville.
Byrd, W P, Poe's.
Campbell, Mrs J A, Poe's.
Cameron, J A, Chalk Level.
Crowder, Miss Leola, Poe's.
Gardner, Miss Ella, Barclaysville.
Gardner, Eddy, Barclaysville.
Grimes, A F, Troyville.
Harrington, T W, Harrington.
Johnson, Miss Florence, Poe's.
Johnson, A A, Bradley's Store.
Kenedy, R T, Troyville.
Kivet, Miss Emma, Lillington.
Marsh, Miss Lena, Lillington.
McLeod, W G, Harrington.
McKay, Miss Mary (music), Summerville.
Page, J M, Mohawk.
Patterson, Jas, Mohawk.

HARNETT COUNTY.

Patterson, H M, Mohawk.
Pearson, J S, Poe's.
Poe, E C, Poe's.
Rich, Chas, Lillington.
Rodgers, John, Lillington.
Senter, D H, Bradley's Store.
Shaw, Miss Lena, Lillington.
Spears, John A, Lillington.
Spence, Miss Ida, Poe's.
Spence, Miss Mariam, Bradley's Store.
Smith, Miss Bettie, Bradley's Store.
Smith, H Z, Bradley's Store.
Smith, Lonnie, Bradley's Store.
Stephenson, C T, Benson.
Stephenson, J Q, Barclaysville.
Stewart, D N, Barclaysville.
Taylor, Miss Alice, Poe's.
Withers, Mrs J H, Summerville.
Withers, Sam W, Summerville.
Withers, Dr J H, Summerville.
Williams, Joseph, Barclaysville.

LOCAL CORPORATIONS.

Cokesbury Lodge, No 235, A F and A M, Chalk Level; time of meeting Saturday before first Sunday, and June 24th and December 27th.
Evergreen Lodge, No 303, A F and A M, Swann's Station (Moore co); time of meeting 3d Saturday at 2 P M.
Harnett Lodge, No 258, A F and A M, Winston; time of meeting Friday evening before first full moon, and June 24th and December 27th.
Lillington Lodge, No 302, A F and A M, Lillington; time of meeting first Saturday before the Sunday in each month at 4 P M, and June 24th and December 27th.
Palmyra Lodge, No 147, A F and A M, Dunn; time of meeting 3d Saturday and June 24th and December 27th.
Pine Forest Lodge, No 186, A F and A M, Harrington; time of meeting Saturday on or before full moon.

NEWSPAPERS.

County Union, Dunn, Grantham & Pittman, eds and props.

FARMERS.

Names and Post Offices.

Averasboro—J C Adams, W G Adams, H C Avera, J F Byrd, J L Byrd, Geo D Elliott, Thomas Fowler, James P Hodges, J M Hodges, James Hodges, W B Hodges, J A Hodges, B A Hodges, A H Hodges, Arch McBryde, D McN McKay, W B McKay, W H Pope, J H Pope, Henry Pope, Mrs Mary Smith, I D Smith, J M Stewart, N S Stewart,

Daniel Stewart, E Stewart, A J Turlington.

Barclaysville—John Gregory, Alex Gregory, A W Gregory, J P Honeycutt. J M Langdon, D Stewart, E Stewart, S R Wilson.

Benson—Willis Bailey, Lem Bailey. J A Ennis, Hinton Ennis, Alonzo Ennis, James Ennis, Cornelius Hodges, C D Stewart, Edmond Stewart, Daniel Stewart.

Bouie's Creek—J A Johnson, W A Johnson, W J Johnson, Reuben Matthews, Thomas Matthews, Hugh McLean, N D McLeod, H H Poe, William Sexton, L Ferrell, Jake Williams.

Bradley's Store—A D Bradly, S S Bradley, C H Coffield, Wm Collins, D E Green, Willis Johnson, P Johnson, N Johnson, William Jones, Joseph Matthews, P A Norris, William Parker, T W Spence, Dr Robert Spence, G D Spence.

Bunn's Level—M H Allen, Lewis Bailey, B J Bell, Hervey Bone, James Bone, Romulus Byrd. Josiah Byrd, G S Byrd, J S Byrd, R E Byrd, L W Byrd, Willis Byrd, A Byrd, James Covington, J C Dollar, J T Dollar, T Heath, C Hobbs, Benjamin Hobbs, John Johnson, William Jones, M L Jones, James A Jones, J C McDougald, Neill McDougald, Henry McKay, A McNeill, John McNeill, Stokes McNeill, Nelson McNeill, Reuben McNeill, W A Parker, James Parker, Alex Parker, D J Parker, F Smith, J S Smith, J L Smith, Lawrence Smith, Gaston Surles, S A Truelove, Simeon Truelove, Henry Turner, Jacob West. Aaron Wilson, P Williamson, John Williams, Joseph H Williams.

Chalk Level—D Abernathy, A D Arnold, William Arnold, W A Dewar, J P Harrington, B F Harrington, S Harrington, J S Harrington, Allen Matthews, M V Prince, William Senter.

Dunn—John Avery, L H Byrd, Jas Byrd, John H Byrd, B M F Coats, Dr M W Harper, H A Hodges, G R Hodges, G F Hodges, Bud Hodges, Burrell Hodges, A D Jones, Pierce Jones, Ed Jones, A T Lee, E Lee, J B Norris, W H Norris, J H Pope, Henry Pope, J L Ryales, Loyd Ryales, T Spence, Henry Tart, Moses Trip, J J Wade.

Harrington—Jas Cameron, J Harrington, John Maxwell, Dr J McCormick, J A McDougald, Neill McLeod, M McLeod, D Minnum, W W Salmon.

Lillington—J H Atkins, G W Byrd, J A Cameron, Neill Clark, J R Grady, J A Green, B Johnson, W F Marsh, W B McKay, Dr N McKay, Neill McKay, T N McLean, J W McNeill, M R Morgan, K Murchison, E J Pipkin, J W Pipkin.

Mohawk—Lewis Byrd, Ed Byrd, Jno Byrd, Sherod Patterson, W M Patterson, W D Patterson, E S Smith.

Poe's—A D Byrd, A J Byrd, W J Ennis, A J Ennis, W V Ennis, W F Gregory, Jams Gregory, J R Gregory, W R Gregory, B F Hamilton, H H Harmon, F B Harmon, Wm Johnson, L H Marks, R M Mitchell, Wm Morgan, Jas Pearson, John Pearson, W R Pearson, Wm Pearson, H H Poe, W R Spence. W A Stewart, G D Stewart, J A Stewart, A W Stewart, E B Taylor.

Spout Springs—W J McDairmid, A K McDirmaid.

Troyville—Neill Barnes, C M Beasley, W F Beasley, A W Denning, J M Denning, John Denning, T G Hays, J R Kennedy, R Parrish, Mack Stewart, Thos D Stewart, J A Stewart, J K Stewart, Jas Stone.

Wythe—Richard Bullock, Robert Johnson, John Johnson, Willie Johnson, Jas Johnson, B Johnson, Daniel McLeod, J A Morgan, Benj Upchurch, J C Upchurch, H Wanderey.

HAYWOOD COUNTY.

AREA 740 SQUARE MILES.

POPULATION 13,331; White 12,814, Colored 517.

HAYWOOD COUNTY was formed in 1808 from Buncombe county, and was named in honor of John Haywood, who was, from 1787 to 1827, Treasurer of North Carolina.

WAYNESVILLE, the county-seat, is 292 miles west of Raleigh, and on the line of the Western North Carolina division of the Southern Railway, and is situated at the base of the great Balsam Mountains, the highest rail-town east of the Rocky Mountains, and one of the finest summer resorts in the world, on the projected line of the Carolina, Knoxville and Western Railroad. Population, 1,000.

Surface.—Out-edges, mountainous; finely watered by the Big Pigeon river and branches, running north and north-west through the centre of the county, and forming a beautiful, rich valley. Scenery enchanting.

Staples.—Wheat, corn, tobacco, oats, potatoes, grass, medicinal herbs and live-stock. This is particularly a fine wheat, tobacco and grass county. The finest apples in America are grown in this county.

Fruits.—Apples, peaches, pears, grapes and small fruits.

Timbers.—Oak, chestnut, ash, hickory, gum, birch, buckeye, balsam, hemlock or spruce, walnut, locust, wild cherry and poplar.

Minerals.—Mica, copper and iron magnetic ores are found in this county.

TOWNS AND POST OFFICES.

	POP.		POP.
Canton,	200	Lavinia,	45
Cataloochee,	100	Mt. Sterling,	100
Clyde,	50	Palm,	50
Cove Creek,	50	Pant,	25
Crabtree,	25	Peru,	50
Cruso,	50	Plott,	25
Dellwood,	75	Retreat,	30
Dutch Cove,	25	Sonoma,	50
Ella,	50	Split Mountain,	
Fannie,	20		100
Ferguson,	100	Springdale,	50
Line's Creek,	100	Teague,	25
Forks of Pigeon,		Tuscola,	35
	50	Waynesville (c h),	
Garden Ceeek,	50		1,000
Iron Duff,	25	Western,	50
Jonathan	35		

COUNTY OFFICERS.

Clerk Superior Court—J K Boone.
Commissoners—J M Tate, chmn.
Register of Deeds—H B Moore.
Solicitor Twelfth District—G A Jones.
Sheriff—W J Haynes.
Treasurer—W J Hannah.
County Examiner—A J Garner.

COURTS.

Fifth Monday after the first Monday in March. First Monday after the first Monday in September.

CRIMINAL COURTS.

Seventh Monday before the first Monday in March. Sixteenth Monday after the first Monday in March.

TOWNSHIPS AND MAGISTRATES.

Beaver Dam—J M Blalock, Parker McGee, J N Mease, J L Moore, Chas Wells, J M Curtis, Jos Christopher, Wiley Johnson (Waynesville).

Cataloochee—E T Harrell, Hiram Caldwell, E M Misser, D Caldwell, Ezekiel Harrell, C M Jarrett, Drewry Craig, Andy Hall (Cataloochee).

Clyde—A G Osborne, W W Medford, K V B Rinehart, H C Shook, T S Green, Wm Jarrett, Dock Smathers (Clyde).

Crabtree—Lawrence Walker, O O Sanford, Jas Swayngum, M A Kirkpatrick, J E Swayngum, E E McCracken, E M Ferguson, W H Silvers, Winfield Ferguson (Crabtree).

East Fork—Fidelo Howell, T R Pless, W L Massie, J M Gwyn, Baylus C Clark, J A Crawford (Waynesville).

Fine's Creek—H L Kingsmore, J M Noland, C M Rogers, S L Teague, Hiram Rogers, R V Hawkins, Lee Ferguson, Harrison Ferguson (Fine's Creek).

Iron Duff—J M Queen, J F Murray, M G Downs, H H Garner, Z C Davis, Andy Ferguson, Jesse Noland (Iron Duff).

Ivy Hill—W L Justice, C M Carpenter, J L Queen, Jos Liner, W R Davis, W G B Garrett, R L Owen, W A Campbell (Waynesville).

Jonathan Creek—J C Leatherwood, A H Justice, Harrison Davis, L M Dempsey, H S L Moody, David Nelson (Jonathan).

Pigeon—J W Long, Jas Cathey, Wm Ledbetter, David Vance, M D Kinsland, Jos Singleton, Thos Wells, Burton Crawford, J W Reece (Waynesville).

Waynesville—W H Faucett, J R Cowan, R Q McCrackin, A M Ratcliff, W M Crymes, M J Overby, A E Ward, K Howell, W H McClure, J H Mull (Waynesville).

CHURCHES.

Names, Post Offices, Pastors and Denom.

METHODIST.

Bethel—Circuit, W M Baring.
Church—Waynesville, R D Sherrill.
Cross Roads.
Fine's Creek—Haywood Circuit, W A Jacobs.
Killian's Chapel—W G Malone.
Morning Star—W G Malone.
Parker's Chapel—W G Malone.
Pigeon River—W G Malone.
Conton.
Shady Grove—West Haywood Circuit.
Shook's Camp Ground, —, J T Stover.
Turpins Chapel—W M Baring.

BAPTIST.

Bethel Forks—Pigeon River.
Church—Waynesville, —— Jones.
Clyde—Geo Wharton.
Crabtree—Jonathan's Creek.
Locust Field—Canton, R A Sentell.

PRESBYTERIAN.

Betel.
Church—Waynesville.

EPISCOPAL.

Church—Waynesville, F W Way.
Dellarod—Caldwell, Thos Frisbee.

MINISTERS RESIDENT.

Names, Post Offices and Denominations.

METHODIST.

Howell, D C, Jonathan.
Miller, Geo, Forks of Pigeon.
Phillips, B R, Conton.

BAPTIST.

Sentell, R A, Clyde.

PRESBYTERIAN.

Towles, D T, Crabtree.

EPISCOPAL.

Way, F W, Waynesville.

HOTELS AND BOARDING HOUSES.

Kinds, Post Offices and Proprietors.

Battle Hotel, Waynesville, Wm Rhinehart.

Boarding House, Retreat, T B Edmonston.
Boarding House, Conton, Mark Mews.
Gilmer House, Waynesville, R D Gilmer.
Haywood White Sulphur Springs, Wayesville, G W Williams & Bro.
Hotel, Waynesville, Mrs Emma Willis.
Hotel, Waynesville, Wm Rhinehart.
Hotel, Clyde, Bailey Jones.
Hotel, Conton, L F Miller.
Howell House, Waynesville, A Howell.
Love House, Waynesville, Mrs M H Love.
Merchants' Hotel, Waynesville, J Willis.
National Hotel, Waynesville, W H Nelson.
Ratcliff House, Waynesville, L J Ratcliff.
Reeves House, Waynesville, A J Reeves.
Skyland House, Waynesville, J L Williams.
Tate House, Waynesville, Mrs R N Tate.
Hotel, Clyde, Bailey Jones.
Hotel, Conton, L F Miller.

LAWYERS.

Names and Post Offices.

Crawford, W T, Waynesville.
Ferguson, G S, Waynesville.
Ferguson, W B, Waynesville.
Ferguson, J W, Waynesville.
Ferguson, H R, Waynesville.
Green, T L, Waynesville.
Gudger, J C L, Waynesville.
Howell, A A, Waynesville.
Holcombe, M L, Waynesville.
Moody, J M, Waynesville.
Norwood, W L, Waynesville.
Smathers, George, Waynesville.
Welch, S C, Waynesville.

MANUFACTORIES.

Kinds, Post Offices and Proprietors.

Blacksmithing, Waynesville.
Blacksmithing, Waynesville, Allen Brown.
Blacksmithing, Canton, James Anderson.
Blacksmithing, Sonoma, T E J Edwards.
Blacksmithing, Fine's Creek, W G B Green.
Blacksmithing, Clyde, W J Jenkins & W M West.
Coopering, Crabtree, W M Wilson.
Coopering, Garden Creek, Wesley Henson.
Coopering, Garden Creek, Wm Henson.

HAYWOOD COUNTY.

Cheese factory, Waynesville, Capt A Howell.
Cole wood works, Waynesville, W H Cole.
Furniture, Waynesville, F Poindexter.
Harness and saddles, Waynesville, C W Miller.
Hardware Mfg Co, Waynesville, B F Smathers, sec'y.
Insular pin factory, Waynesville, Hellams & Ellis.
Leather and Harness Co, Waynesville, C W Miller.
Lumber, Waynesville, A C Cogle.
Millwrighting, Waynesville, W P Feronis.
Pin and stave, Waynesville, Hillams & Ellas.
Richland Woolen Mills, Waynesville, D Drayton, Perry & Co.
Tanning, Waynesville, W A Herrin.
Tannery, Waynesville, C W Miller.
Tannery, Forks of Pigeon, W S Terrell.
Woolen Mill, Waynesville, D D Perry.
Wagon Company, Waynesville, McKeehan & Co.
Waynesville Hardware M'f'g Co.
Wood Company, Waynesville, C E Satterwaite.

MERCHANTS AND TRADESMEN.

Names, Post Offices and Lines of Business.

CANTON.

Hampton, W J,	G S and Fert
McGee, W F P,	G S
May, J A,	Nursery
Mease & Mease,	Drugs
Perry, Mrs Mittie,	Milliner
Sharp, W T,	G S
Well, C T,	G S
Winfield & Mears,	G S

CATALOOCHEE.

Palmer, J F & Co,	G S

CLYDE.

Dotson, E R & Co,	G S
Hill & Collins,	H'd'w
Jarrett, C M,	G S
Jarrett, W H,	Drugs
Morgan, J L & Co,	G S
Morgan, J W,	G S

COVE CREEK.

Cagle, D M & Co,	G S

CRABTREE.

McCracken, J M L,	Live stock
McCracken, W D,	Live stock
Silver, W H,	G S

CRUSO.

Trull, J R,	G S

DELLWOOD.

Davis, W R & Co,	G S

HAYWOOD COUNTY.

FERGUSON.

Ferguson, W R,	G S
Noland, D R & Co,	G S

FINE'S CREEK.

Walker, N P,	Miller

GARDEN CREEK.

Massey, W L,	G S

FORKS OF PIGEON.

Ledbetter, ——,	G S
Terrell, W S,	G S

IRON DUFF.

Rogers, L V,	G S

JONATHAN'S CREEK.

Howell, D A,	G S
Howell & Son,	G S
Moody, A A,	Live Stock

PANT.

Noland, R & Co,	G S

SONOMA.

Terrell, W S,	G S

SPLIT MOUNTAIN.

Ferguson, W R & Co,	G S

WAYNESVILLE.

Aldrich, ——,	Lumber
Clay, H C,	Lumber
Cogdell, S C & J G,	G S
Cole, W H,	G S
Campbell, W A,	Lumber
Davis, J M,	Jeweler
Davis, R L,	G S
Davis, Hay & Co,	Drugs
Farmer, Mull & Co,	G S
George, Osborne,	Beef Market
Garrison, J W,	Beef Market
Hall, J E,	Tob
Herrin, W A,	Tanner
Herrin, J P,	G S
Lee, W T & Co,	G S
McCracken & Co,	G S
Miller, C W,	Saddler
Morgan, D C & Co,	Bookstore
Ray, C E,	G S
Ray, C H,	G S
Reeves & McClure,	G S
Rogers & Clayton,	G S
Satterthwaite & Smathers,	Drugs
Satterthwaite, S C,	Lumber
Schulhofer, S J,	G S
Shepherd, Mrs W E,	Milliner
Smathers, Killian & Co,	Millers
Swift, J P,	Livery
Waynesville Dispensary.	
Waynesville Steam Laundry.	
Welch, J C,	Miller
White & Lewis,	Stoves and Hardw
Wilburn, G W,	Jeweler
Williams, G W & Bro,	G S

MINES.

Kinds, Post Offices and Proprietors.

Copper, Crabtree, S Furgerson & Co.
Mica, Waynesville, W W Stringfield.
Mica, Waynesville.

HAYWOOD COUNTY.

MILLS.

Kinds, Post Offices and Proprietors.

Corn and flour, Fine's Creek, J H Noland.

Corn and flour, Canton, C S Thompson & Son.

Corn, flour and saw, Crabtree, H McCracken.

Corn, flour and saw, Garden Creek, Erwin Henson.

Corn, flour and saw, Waynesville, N Howell.

Corn, flour and saw, ——, Jas Moore.

Corn, flour and saw, Forks of Pigeon, J A Blalock.

Corn, flour and saw, Jonathan's Creek, D A Howell.

Corn and saw, Canton, Jas Moore.

Corn and Saw, Canton, Jesse Smathers.

Corn and flour, ——, J M Hall.

Corn and flour, Cove Creek, D M Cogle & Co.

Flour and corn, Waynesville, W P Francis.

Flour and corn, Waynesville, Smathers & Killian.

Roller corn and flour, Waynesville, Howell Mill Co.

Roller corn and flour, Clyde, J L Morgan & Co.

Saw, Waynesville, E P Hyatt.

Saw and corn, Waynesville, Q A Harison.

Saw and corn, Cruso, Reece & Wharton.

Saw, flour and corn, Fine's Creek, N P Walker.

PHYSICIANS.

Names and Post Offices.

Abel, J F, Canton.
Allen, R L, Waynesville.
Bennett, M E, Palm.
Davis, I M, Iron Duff.
Ferguson, W R, Ferguson.
Fitzgerald, I A, Dellwood.
Kilpatrick, W L, Crabtree.
McCracken, C M, Clyde.
McFaden, H L, Waynesville.
Mease, J M, Canton.
Medford, R C, Iron Duff.
Medford, S B, Clyde.
Roberts, C B, Clyde.
Rogers, H M, Waynesville.
Russell, J H, Clyde.
Walker, Robert L, Clyde.
Way, J H, Waynesville.
Wells, H N, Waynesville.
Wilson, J E, Sonoma.

SCHOOLS.

Names, Post Offices and Principals.

Bethel High School, Fork of Pigeon.
Clyde High School, Clyde, R A Sentell.

HAYWOOD COUNTY.

Crabtree Institute, Crabtree, Rev D T Towles.

Wayne School, Waynesville, T G Harbison.

TEACHERS.

Names and Post Offices.

WHITE.

Boyd, J R, Fannie.
Clark, Miss ——, Teague.
Crymers, Nettie, Waynesville.
Davis, Miss Carrie (music), Waynesville.
Ector, Miss Mollie, Waynesville.
Fitzgerald, Mary, Waynesville.
Garner, A G, Peru.
Hahn, G W, Tuscola.
Harbison, T G, Waynesville.
Hoke, W A, Dellwood.
Hyatt, R A L, Waynesville.
Kelly, John, Crabtree.
McGee, E E, Waynesville.
McCracken, Sallie, Peru.
McCracken, Mary, Peru.
Owen, Charles, Dellwood.
Pless, Wattie, Springdale.
Pless, D H, Springdale.
Ratcliff, A M, Waynesville.
Roland, Miss ——.
Sentell, R A, Clyde.
Siler, Miss Hattie, Waynesville.
Siler, Miss Iola, Waynesville.
Towles, Rev D T, Crabtree.

LOCAL CORPORATIONS.

Chosen Friends, Waynesville.
Kimball tannery plant, Waynesville, W W Cole Lumber Co.
Knights of Pythias, Waynesville; meets every Tuesday evening.
Knights of Honor, Waynesville; meets 2d and 4th Monday evenings in each month.
Odd Fellows, Waynesville, meets every Thursday evening.
Royal Arcanum, Waynesville, meets 1st and 3d Monday evenings in each month.
Southern Ry Co, completed and in operation.
Waynesville Lodge, No 259, A F and A M, Waynesville; time of meeting Friday evening on or before full moon.
There are agricultural clubs and societies in each township.

FARMERS.

Names and Post Offices.

Canton—W R Burnett, John Cabe, J Christophers, Calvin Clark, C R Clark, George Cook, J M Curtis, W P Ford, A J Hall, L W Hall, H P Haynes,

HAYWOOD COUNTY.

R T Harris, L H Hipps, J G Hipps, Wiley Johnson, E E Johnson, W H Johnson, J T Kinsland, J B Mann, J A May, J M Mease, J L Moore, J H Moore, A J Murray, J Noland, J S Patton, W A Pharr, C B Phillips, B R Phillips, L F Pinner, Wm Renno, M F Renno, W R Rhodamer, R D Rice, J H Russell, H A Smathers, Jasper Smathers, James Smathers, John Smathers, G M Smathers, W B Smathers, J D Smathers, Allen Shoop, C S Thompson, James Thompson, Thomas Timmons, M L Warley, M L West, John Williams, Dock Williams, Robert Williams, R Winfield, J Woods, J A Woods.

Cataloochee—Andy Caldwell, J Caldwell, D L Caldwell, H Caldwell, W A Caldwell, D C Carroll, D Craig, B C Messer, G L Palmer, W Palmer, D L Palmer, G N Palmer, Thos Palmer, Robt Palmer, S L Woody, T Woody.

Clyde—D H Byers, D C Clark, W P Fincher, T M Green, J M Haynes, F C Haynes, J H Haynes, J A Jones, P L Jones, W W Medford, N Medford, J A Medford, J M Osborne, T F Osborne, A J Osborne, G N Penland, W P Robinson, John Robinson, M N Robinson, Wiley Shook, D L Smathers, Levi Smathers, C L Smathers.

Cove Creek—H H Bradley, D M Cogle, T W Crawford, W P Davis, D C Davis, L M Dempsey, J K Howell, G T Long, J S Marrow.

Crabtree - Pink Best, W R Ferguson, Riley Ferguson, G W Ferguson, R M Ferguson, T M Ferguson, Eli Ferguson, A J Fisher, D J Garner, Thos Garrett, T S Gillett, J B Harris, L P Hipps, David James, T H James, A J Justice, M A Kirkpatrick, J T Kirkpatrick, W M Mason, E E McCracken, H McCracken, D V McCracken, J M McCracken, J M L McCracken, L McCracken, L P McCracken, W D McCracken, M J McCracken, Riley Medford, Henry Messer, Allen Noland, J W Robertson, R L Rogers, Jno Rogers, J H Sanford, James Sanford, Oscar Sanford, J E Swatengim, J L Walker, Albert Walker.

Dellwood—J L Buchfield, John H Boyd, R L Campbell, W A Campbell, Alex Carpenter, W R Davis, J A Ferguson, W G B Garrett, J R Henry, L N Henry, J B Henry, R P Haynes, Mack Jones, Jacob Lowe, J L Moody, W L Moody, W H Nichols, R L Owen, D W Owen, D J M Owen, R H Plott, N W Rathbone, J C Rich, Jacob Setzer, J B Turkin.

East Fork—W H Brown, S P Brown, J M Burnett, B Clark, F H Cogburn, J Cody, J M Gwyn, P Howell, F Howell,

H C Ivester, M J McCracken, J C Osborne, J H Pless, Henry Pless, Rowly Pless, T H Pless, B H M Trull.

Fine's Creek—Y A Bennett, W G Bennett, J N Bennett, C C Clark, Ben Clark, Spate Clark, B F Clark, E L Ferguson, W H Ferguson, A J Ferguson, Z T Ferguson, J L Ferguson, J L Fisher, Silas Green, James Green, G B W Green, R V Hawkins, J W Hooker, John James, W P James, J P Jarrett, M N Justice, H L Kingsmore, W F McCrary, T B McCracken, J H Noland, Jos Noland, Randolph Noland, J M Noland, T M Noland, M M Noland, J W Noland, Wm Rathbone, P Rathbone, Jesse Rathbone, S M Redmond, H Rogers, Robert Rogers, A T Rogers, R W Rogers, H M Rogers, J M Rogers, J L Rogers, J E Rogers, J W Teague, M E Trantham, E H Walker, N P Walker, Wm Williamson, G W Williamson, James Williamson.

Forks of Pigeon—E H Blalock, J A Blalock, K C Cathey, J K Cathey, J W Cathey, W K Cathey, Lewis Chambers, N H Chambers, T B Edmondson, B M Edwards, A E Edwards, J M Edwards, W S Evans, J H Evans, C D Evans, W B Henson, Henry Henson, sr, Elisha Henson, Wesley Henson, Alfred Henson, Turner Henson, W J Holland, J J Justice, James Kelley, M D Kinsland, J Kinsland, W S Kinsland, S Kirby, R C Kirby, William Ledoetter, T N Long, J W Long, J P Mann, M Mease, G W Mease, L D Mease, W J Moore, J W Moore, L L Moore, P P Plott, D Vance, Julius Welch, J A Wells, T C Wells.

Garden Creek—F B Evans, James Evans, J M Evans, W H Hartgrove, L L Moore, R R E Osborne, A J Osborne, W T Readsleave, George A Smathers.

Jonathan's Creek.—J H Allison, M S Allison, M I T Allison, W J & G B Boyd, J R Boyd, Mrs F A M Boyd, W R Davis, L J Ferguson, Geo Garrett, E H Howell, D C Howell, C D Howell, E J Howell, D A Howell, Asbury Howell, Mrs Mark Howell, A H Justice, Caswell Leatherwood, Robt Leatherwood, J R Leatherwood, J C Leatherwood, Jos Liner, H S L Moody, J B Moody, E T Moody, A A Moody, D A Owen, Will Owen, M H Owen, James Parker, James Parks, A M Parton, Calvin Parton.

Lavinia.—Robt Bingham, A B Crawford, Henry Franklin, R R Penland, Jerry Reece, M B Rhodes.

Waynesville.—J M Allen, W H Allen, R L Allen, J F Bass, G F Boggs, J K Boone, Joseph Brendle, John Bren-

HAYWOOD COUNTY.

dle, Ed Bright, H M Bright, Wesley Brown, Mrs Laura Coman, Vaugh Coman, R W Corzine, B A Felmet, Joshua Fitzgerald, W B Ferguson, H R Francis, J A Francis, Josiah Francis, T L Francis, W P Francis, A J Fulbright, Chas Goodyear, Joseph Hall, Frank Hall, J L Herren, Alden Howell, Nelson Howell, E Howell, Luke Howell, R A L Hyatt, H C Hyatt, E P Hyatt, J D Hyatt, P E Hyatt, R E Hyatt, M Kelly, D M Killion, W H Leatherwood, L B Leatherwood, Pink Leatherwood, W T Lee, R D Lee, Charles Lee, Thos Liner, Henry Liner, J R Long, R C Long, G L Love, H C Marshall, W H

HAYWOOD COUNTY.

McClure, R Q McCracken, M B McCracken, David McElroy, Abel McElroy, R E Medford, A B Medford, Snell Medford, Israel Medford, W E Miller, F C Moody, Wm Morsey, Henry Plott, E P Plott, Mont Plott, J L Queen, R E L Ratcliffe, J N Ratcliffe, A M Ratcliffe, W J Ratcliffe, D L Ratcliffe, W T Reeves, Jas Robinson, J K Rogers, M S Russell, S J Shelton, T S Siler, J B Siler, J P Swift, R C Smathers, B F Smathers, W W Stringfield, J M Tate, Philip Turner, P T Turner, V A Turpin, D H Turpin, W M Turpin, W P Underwood, Dr R V Welch, L M Welch, W A Withers.

22

HENDERSON COUNTY.

AREA, 360 SQUARE MILES.

POPULATION 12,507; White 11,129, Colored 1,378.

HENDERSON COUNTY was formed in 1838, from Buncombe, and named in compliment to Leonard Henderson, late Chief Justice of the Supreme Court of the State.

HENDERSONVILLE, the county-seat, is 250 miles west of Raleigh. It is a beautiful and thrifty town, with a population estimated at 2,000. It is directly on the Spartanburg and Asheville Railroad.

Surface—Henderson county is situated on the head branches of the French Broad river, and embraces a beautiful valley on the west side of the Blue Ridge. The location could hardly be surpassed for elegant scenery and good land.

Staples—Corn, wheat, cabbage, the grasses, rye, oats and live-stock. Hendersonville ships from two to three million pounds of cabbage annually. A good farming county and a desirable place to live.

Fruits — Apples, grapes, peaches, cherries, pears, melons, and almost every variety of the small fruits.

Timbers—Oak, pine, black walnut, wild cherry, poplar, ash, linden, hickory, etc.

TOWNS AND POST OFFICES.

	POP.		POP.
Angeline,	50	Hillgirt,	50
Balfour,	40	Horseshoe,	25
Bat Cave,	50	Lead,	30
Baxter,	36	Maxwell,	50
Bear Wallow,	35	Mill's River,	100
Blue Ridge,	50	Money,	50
Bollston,	25	Osteen,	25
Bowman's Bluff	75	Pinkbed,	50
Dana,	25	Pump,	40
Delmont,	25	Rugby,	25
Dewitt,	30	Sitton,	25
Edneysville,	100	Splendor,	20
Flat Rock,	300	Upward,	50
Fletcher,	100	Yale,	20
Fruitland,	50	Zirconia,	25
Gypsy,	50		

Hendersonville (c h), 2,000

COUNTY OFFICERS.

Clerk Superior Court—C W Pace.
Commissioners—A Cannon, chm'n.
Register of Deeds—J B Arledge.
Solicitor Eleventh District—J L Webb.

Sheriff—J G Grant.
Treasurer—W J Davis.
County Examiner—C J Edney.

COURTS.

Eleventh Monday after the first Monday in March; twelfth Monday after the first Monday in September.

CRIMINAL COURTS.

Sixth Monday after first Monday in March and fifth Monday after first Monday in September.

TOWNSHIPS AND MAGISTRATES.

Blue Ridge—H P King, C A Case, M S Justice, E J Edney, J F Jones, W P Blackwell, Thos Gibbs (Blue Ridge.)

Clear Creek—G W Love, J H Fletcher, John Jackson, A J McMinn, J T Jackson, J B Freeman, E M Merrell, J W Freeman, J J Fisher (Hendersonville).

Crab Creek—Charles S Orr, C S Orr, A L Patterson, Jos Hamilton, K W King, J M Mace, T M Anderson (Hendersonville).

Edneyville—M L Edney, Geo Lyda, J T Freeman, G W Ledbetter, R J Brown, J A Merrell, J M Owenby, G B Hill (Edneyville).

Greene River—J W Ward, J T Staton, John Ward, W F Pace, M F Arledge, J M Hart, P J Hart, J W Ward, John Staten (Hendersonville).

Hendersonville—Geo Holmes, John P Patton, M S Johnson, A B Freeman, W A Hood, J C Drake, L C Patterson, J H Ripley, J N Bowen (Hendersonville).

Hooper's Creek—W G McDowell, J N Russell, N J Lance, W J Baldwin, M L Sumner, W M Maxwell, C M Fletcher, Jos Youngblood (Hendersonville).

Mill's River—A E Posey, Sr, J T Osborne, J S Rhodes, M M Stewart, S C Lilton, J L Whitaker, J H Crawford, M D Barnett (Mill's River).

CHURCHES.

Names, Pastors, Postoffices and Denom.

METHODIST.

Ball's Chapel—Hill Girt, J A Sronce.
Blue House—Blue Ridge, J A Peeler.

HENDERSON COUNTY.

Brown's Chapel—Hendersonville.
Church—Hendersonville, J W Jones.
Church—Edneyville, J A Peeler.
Church—Mills River, G G Harley.
Cross Roads—Blue Ridge, J A Peeler.
Cross Roads—Upward.
Holly Springs—Boilston.
Johnson's Chapel—Fletcher.
Mills River Chapel—Mills River.
Mann's Grove-Henderson, J A Sronce.
Patty's Chapel—Fletcher, J A Sronce.
Reedy Patch—Bat Cove, J A Peeler.
Round Top—Hill Girt, J A Sronce.
Shaw's Creek—Horse Shoe, G G Harley.

BAPTIST.
Beulah—Horse Shoe.
Crab Creek—Delmont.
Ebenezer—Hendersonville.
French Broad—Hendersonville.
Green River—Green River.
Hendersonville—Hendersonville.
Holly Springs—Hendersonville.
Hooper's Creek—Shufordville.
Mountain Page—Saluda (Polk co.).
Mt Moriah—Edneyville.
Mud Creek—Hendersonville.
Refuge—Blue Ridge.
Sycamore—Mills River.

PRESBYTERIAN.
Hendersonville—Hendersonville.
Mills River—Hendersonville.

EPISCOPAL.
Flat Rock—Flat Rock.
Hendersonville—Hendersonville.

MINISTERS RESIDENT.

Names, Post Offices and Denominations.

METHODIST.
Harley, G G, Mills River.
Jones, J W, Hendersonville.
Peeler, J A, Blue Ridge.
Sronce, J A, Hendersonville.

HOTELS AND BOARDING HOUSES.

Names, Post Offices and Proprietors.

Hotel, Fletcher, G W Fletcher.
Hotel, Flat Rock, M S Farmer.

MANUFACTORIES.

Kinds, Post Offices and Proprietors.

Blue Ridge Canning Co, Dana, P T Ward & Co.
Building, Hendersonville, W F Edwards.
Contracting, Hendersonville, J T Pruden.
Canning Co, Horse Shoe, W B Ledbetter.

HENDERSON COUNTY.

Canning Co, Hendersonville, J P Shepard.
Carolina Knitting Mills, Flat Rock, P W Hart & Co.
Carolina Canning Co, Flat Rock, P W & R R Hart.
Flat Rock Knitting Co, Flat Rock, Hart Bros.
Lumber and Mfg Co, Hendersonville, J P Shepard.
Tannery, Hendersonville, J C Morgan.
Tannery, Hendersonville, Taylor & Williams.
Wood Co, Zirconia, W T Davis & Co.

MERCHANTS AND TRADESMEN.

Name, Post Office, and Line of Business.

BAT CAVE.		
Dewall, J P,		G S
Freeman, J T,		G S
Owenby, J M & Co,		G S
BEAR WALLOW.		
Conner, G W,		G S
Freeman, F M,		G S
BLUE RIDGE.		
Hyder, H M,		G S
Justice, H D,		G S
BOWMAN'S BLUFF.		
Matlock, A D & Co,		G S
DANA.		
Case & Ward,		G S
EDNEYVILLE.		
Brown, W G B & Co,		G S
Edney, Rufus & Son,		G S
Justice, Isaac,		G S
FLAT ROCK.		
Carolina Canning Co,		G S
Patton, J P,		G S
Ripley, J H,		G S
FLETCHER.		
Cunningham, W E,		G S
Fletcher, G W,		G S
Morris, Thos A,		G S
FRUITLAND.		
Hyder, H D,		G S
GYPSY.		
Lance Bros,		G S
Moore, O E,		G S
HENDERSONVILLE.		
Allen, T A & Son,		G S
Davis, J D,		Gro
Dermid, J D & Co,		G S
Fletcher & Manders,		G S
Hart, Mrs A E,		Milliner
Hawkins, W H,		Jewelry
Hollingsworth, J W,		Racket Store
Jackson & Russell,		G S

HENDERSON COUNTY.		HENDERSON COUNTY.	
Justus, M T & Co,	H'd'w	HORSE SHOE.	
Justus, W H,	G S	Allen, M J,	G S
Kenyon, C M,	Printer	Davenport, A L & L E,	G S
Laughter, I T & Sons,	G S	Johnson, H F,	G S
Liverett, G P & Co,	Livery	MILLS RIVER.	
Lyda, J B,	Gro	Allen, J L & Bro,	G S
Lyda, J F,	Gro	Jones & Warlick,	Drugs
Morris, K G,	Books	UPWARD.	
Pruden, J T,	R R Contractor	Case & Waters,	G S
Ray, W H,	G S		
Richman, J P,	G S	ZIRCONIA.	
Shepherd, M M,	G S	Hart, J P & Co,	G S
Stagg, B F,	Tinner	Hughston, T E,	G S
Stepp & Orr,	Livery		
Streatman, J W,	Drugs	**LOCAL CORPORATIONS.**	
Thomas, David,	G S		
Wilson, C E,	G S	State Bank of Commerce, Henderson-	
HILL GRIT.		ville; Geo H P Cole, pres; J A Mad-	
Edwards & Edwards,	G S	drey, cashr; capital stock, $30,000; surplus and profits $5,000.	

HERTFORD COUNTY.

AREA, 340 SQUARE MILES.

POPULATION, 13,851; White 5,897, Colored 7,944.

HERTFORD COUNTY was formed in 1759, from Chowan, Bertie and Northampton counties. It was named in compliment to the Marquis of Hertford, an English nobleman, a friend of liberty, an elder brother of Lord Conway, who, in 1766, moved in the House of Lords the repeal of the Stamp Act. Hertford is a name of Saxon origin and signifies the "Red Ford."

WINTON, the county-seat, was named after the Wynn family; it is situated 155 miles northeast from Raleigh, on the Chowan river, and has a population of 800.

Surface—Level and sandy, soil good; watered by the Meherrin and Chowan rivers.

Staples—Cotton, corn, peanuts and fish. Being near the Norfolk market, trucking might be profitable.

Fruits — Apples, peaches, scuppernong grapes, pears, melons, and the small fruits.

Timbers —Juniper, cypress, pine, oak, ash, the gums and the usual eastern growth.

TOWNS AND POST OFFICES.

	POP.		POP.
Agate,	50	Mapleton,	100
Ahoskie,	100	Menola,	50
Anneta,	50	Murfr'sboro,	1,200
Bethlehem,	25	Riddicksville,	100
Como,	20	St. John,	25
Earley's,	50	Tunis,	600
Harrellsville,	200	Union,	100
Lotta,	25	Winton,	800

COUNTY OFFICERS.

Clerk Superior Court—Thos D Boone·
Commissioners—Wm T Brown, chm.
Register of Deeds—Geo A Brown.
Sheriff—Wm E Cullins.
Solicitor—W J Leary.
Treasurer—W E Collins.
County Examiner—S M Aumac.

COURTS.

Sixth Monday after first Monday in March; sixth Monday after first Monday in September.

TOWNSHIPS AND MAGISTRATES.

Harrellsville—Wm J Lloyd, S M Aumac, C N Pruden, Edmund Jones, J H Evans, T Q Copeland, John Sharp, J W Holloman, N T Freeman (Harrellsville).

Maney's Neck—S P Winborne, L F Lee, Blount Ferguson, E G Sears, Dr H T Britte, J H Picot, J G Majette, R J Taylor (Murfreesboro).

Murfreesboro—Uriah Vaughan, J C Vinson, Thos E Hines, J T Griffith, A M Darden; J T Benthall, L C Lawrence, Ebenetus Curl, J A Parker, Wm Reed (Murfreesboro).

St John's—Lee Tayloe, C W Parker, J N Holloman, W H Mitchell, H D Godwin, S Parker, W H Castellow, W E Jenkins (St John's).

Winton—James H Matthews, J L Anderson, J A Copeland, Geo T Harrell, G H Mitchell, J F Newton, Robt Overton (Winton).

CHURCHES.

Names, Post Offices, Pastors and Denom.

METHODIST.

Bethel—Harrellsville.
Church—Murfreesboro.
Murfreesboro—Murfreesboro.
New Hope—Como.
Union—Union.
Winton—Winton.
Vann's—St John's.

BAPTIST.

Ahoskie—Union.
Brantley's Grove—Winton.
Bethlehem—Bethlehem.
Buckhorn—Como.
Church—St John's.
Church—Union.
Church (col)—Winton.
Church (col)—Murfreesboro.
Church (col)—Harrellsville.
Jordan's Grove (col)—Winton.
Meherrin—Murfreesboro.
Mill Neck (col)—Como.
Mt Moriah (col)—Winton.
Mt Tabor—Mapleton.
Murfreesboro—Murfreesboro.
New Bethlehem (col)—Bethlehem.
Pleasant Plains (col)—Winton.
Pleasant Grove—St John's.

EPISCOPAL.

St Barnabas'—Murfreesboro.
St John's—Winton.

HOTELS AND BOARDING HOUSES.

Names, Post Offices and Proprietors.

Hotel, Bethlehem, J P Britton & Son.
Hotel, Murfreesboro, Mrs Kate H Boyette.
Hotel, Winston, Jordan & Parker.

HERTFORD COUNTY.

LAWYERS.
Names and Post Offices.
Cooper, Geo, Winton.
Lawrence, L J, Murfreesboro.
Shaw, W P, Winton.
Vann, J E, Winton.
Winborne, B B, Murfreesboro.

MANUFACTORIES.
Kinds, Post Offices and Proprietors.
Cabinet making, Union, M A Proctor.
Coaches, Aboskie, W S & J C Duke.
Coaches, Murfreesboro, G W Hines.
Globe Manufacturing Co, Murfreesboro, F Ferguson.
Harness, Winton, P A Patterson.

MILLS.
Kinds, Post Offices and Proprietors.
Mill, Murfreesboro, Brown, Jessup & Co.
Saw, Winton, W P Taylor & Bro.
Saw and grist, St John, J J Brown & Bro.
Saw, Murfreesboro, E C Worrell.
Saw, Murfreesboro, G E Carman.

MERCHANTS AND TRADESMEN.
Names, Post Offices, Lines of Business.
AHOSKIE.

Copeland, J A & Co,	G S
Downs, W D & Bro,	G S
Duke, W S & J C,	Coach maker
Haggard, C C,	G S
Holloman, Robt,	G S
Mitchell, J H,	G S
Newsome, M E,	G S
Parker & Hill,	G S
Powell, F,	G S

BETHLEHEM.

Adkins, A B,	G S
Britton, J P & Son,	G S
Haggard, P J,	G S
Shaw, W P & Co,	G S

COMO.

Picot, G C,	G S
Taylor, J C,	G S

EARLY'S.

Early, J D & Bro,	G S
Gurly, J & Co,	G S

HARRELLSVILLE.

Askew, J O,	G S
Cotton, James,	G S
Holloman, W A,	G S
Sharp, H C,	Fertilizer
Williams Bros,	Gro

MAPLETON.

Boyette, E T, agent,	G S
Britt, E,	G S
Parker, J D,	G S
Parker, J H,	Gro

MENOLA.

Benthall, R C,	G S
Brown, W H,	G S
Futrell, J H,	G S

HERTFORD COUNTY.

Futrell, J H & Co,	G S
Liverman, J H & Son,	G S
Parker, C W,	G S
Parker, Wiley,	G S

MURFREESBORO.

Balb, J D,	G S
Balb, Mrs J D,	Millinery
Barnacasel, J B & Co,	Jewelers
Benthall, C R,	G S
Boyette, C E,	G S
Boyette, Mrs Kate,	G S
Britt, T A,	G S
Day, D A,	Gro and Confec
Deloatch, K S,	G S
Evans, R.	Tin and Stoves
Futrell, W P,	G S
Jones, E L (col.),	Notions
Lawrence, J N,	G S
Liverman, B F,	G S
Nicholson, T H,	D G
Parker, J B,	G S
Parker, P C.	G S
Payne, Geo D & Co,	G S
Rice, E F & Co,	G S
Sewell, Rinsaler,	Gro
Skinner, J M (col.),	G S
Spencer, W B,	Drugs and Sta
Spencer Drug Co,	Drugs
Underwood, Wm,	Gro
Vaughan, C T,	G S
Vaughan, T J,	G S
Vaughan, Uriab,	G S
Watson, W,	G S
Welser, Mrs E C,	Sewing Machines
White, B K (near),	Gro
Wise, M W, agent,	Fertilizer
Wynne, J N,	G S

RIDDICKSVILLE.

Johnson, A E & Co,	G S
Riddick, J D,	G S

ST. JOHN.

Benthall, Mary E,	G S
Best, J J,	G S.
Joyner, D C & Bro,	G S

UNION.

Darden, J H,	G S
Dukes, H E,	G S
Eley & Co.	G S
Freeman, J P,	G S
Mathews, J E,	G S
Modlin, Henry,	G S
Wynn & Sears,	G S

WINTON.

Carter, J C,	Gro
Daniel, S S,	Drugs
Holloman, L,	G S
Jones, E R & Co,	G S
Jordan & Parker,	G S
Miller, D C.	G S
Mitchell, J P,	G S
Newsom & Jones (col.),	Gro
Odon, Mrs N F,	Millinery
Patterson, P A,	Harness
Shaw, W D,	G S
Vann, H B,	G S

HYDE COUNTY.

AREA, 430 SQUARE MILES.

POPULATION, 8,899; White 4,958, Colored 3,941.

HYDE COUNTY was one of the original precincts of North Carolina, and existed previous to 1729, when the Lords Proprietors (except Lord Granville) surrendered their rights to the Crown. It was called in honor of Edward Hyde, who was Governor of the Colony. His commission is dated January 24, 1711.

SWAN QUARTER, the county-seat is situated at the head of Swan Quarter Bay, 160 miles east of Raleigh, and has a population of 253.

Surface.—Level, and in places is swampy; soil very rich, especially around Lake Matamuskeet.

Staples.—Corn, cotton, wheat, sweet potatoes and fish.

Fruits. — Apples, peaches, pears, grapes, plums and other small fruits. The celebrated Matamuskeet apple grows to perfection around the lake, from which it derives its name.

Timbers. — Cypress, gum, maple, holly, juniper, pine, cedar and oak.

TOWNS AND POST OFFICES.

	POP.		POP.
Engelhard,	150	Ocracoke,	100
Fairfield,	500	Scranton,	—
Lake Comfort,	125	Sladesville,	175
Lake Landing,	125	Swan Quarter	
Makelyville,	150	(c h),	500
Middletown,	175		

COUNTY OFFICERS.

Clerk Superior Court—J H Wahab.
Commissioners—G B Watson, chmn; E O Spencer, H H Swindell, J C Simmons, A B Credle.
Coroner— ——
Register of Deeds—L H Swindell.
Sheriff—R D Harris.
Solicitor First District—W J Leary.
Standard Keeper—W R Gibbs.
Treasurer—C F Benson.

COURTS.

Tenth Monday after the first Monday in March, and tenth Monday after the first Monday in September.

TOWNSHIPS AND MAGISTRATES.

Currituck—A J Smith, E B Cutrell, S S Lupton, W A Buss, J M Lupton, B L Dunbar, W M Smithwick (Swan Quarter).

Fairfield—S B Sadler, T M Watson, W S Carter, T H B Gills, J C Simmons, H B Hixon, A G Hudson, Jas P Hudson, Jas P Flowers (Fairfield).

Lake Landing—R F Watson, H L Gibbs, W D Mann, F S Roper, Jas A Gibbs, Valentine Harris, C A Stokesbury (Lake Landing).

Ocracoke—Joseph O'Neal, W S Lindley, W H Tolson, P C Howard (Ocracoke).

Swan Quarter—Wm R Caranan, J M Watson, A Berry, Jas Hodges, C S Boonser, J B Credle (Swan Quarter).

CHURCHES.

Names, Post Offices, Pastors and Denom.

METHODIST.

Englehard—Englehard, C P Jerome.
Fairfield—Fairfield, J W Anderson.
Lake Comfort—Lake Comfort, D A Watkins.
Lake Landing—Lake Landing, C P Jerome.
Middleton—Middleton, C P Jerome.
Ocracoke—Ocracoke, J W Martin.
Sladesville—Sladesville, D A Watkins.
Swan Quarter—Swan Quarter, D A Watkins.

BAPTIST.

Fairfield (col)—Fairfield, Fred Long.
Lake Landing (col)—Lake Landing, Aaron Jones.
Lake Comfort (col)—Lake Comfort, Alexander Williams.
Sladesville (col) — Sladesville, Sam Hendley and Albert Bryan.
Swan Quarter (col)—Swan Quarter, A Bryan.

PRIMITIVE BAPTIST.

Beulah—Swan Quarter, L S Ross.
Fairfield—Fairfield, L S Ross.
Swan Quarter—Swan Quarter, L S Ross.

DISCIPLES OF CHRIST.

Middleton—Middleton, —— Winfield.
Pringo Chapel—J R Windfield.
Swan Quarter—Swan Quarter, W R Jennet.

EPISCOPAL.

Neal's Chapel— ——
St George—Lake Landing, S S Barber.
St John's—Makelyville, S S Barber.
Swan Quarter—Swan Quarter, S S Barber.

HYDE COUNTY.

MINISTERS RESIDENT.

Names, Post Offices and Denom.

METHODIST.

Anderson, H B, Fairfield.
Jerome, C P, Lake Landing.
Watkins, D A, Swan Quarter.

BAPTIST.

Jones, Aaron (col), Lake Landing.
Long, Fred (col), Fairfield.
Williams, Alex (col), Lake Comfort.
Windley, Samuel (col)—Sladesville.

PRIMITIVE BAPTIST.

Ross, L S, Swan Quarter.

DISCIPLES OF CHRIST.

Jennett, W R, Swan Quarter.

EPISCOPAL.

Barber, S S, Swan Quarter,

HOTELS AND BOARDING HOUSES.

Names, Post Offices and Proprietors.

Boarding house, Fairfield, J Mason.
Mulberry House, Swan Quarter, Jas
   W Hayes
Slaughter House, Swan Quarter, E O
   Spencer.
Swindell House, Swan Quarter, Bri-
   ner Bros.
Tooley's Tavern, Swan Quarter, W J
   Harris.

LAWYERS.

Names and Post Offices.

Mann, S S, Swan Quarter.
Mann, J S, Middletown.

MANUFACTORIES.

Kinds, Post Offices and Proprietors.

Blacksmithing and wheelwrighting,
   Makelyville.
Blacksmithing and wheelwrighting,
   Sladesville.
Blacksmithing and wheelwrighting,
   Swan Quarter, D J Mason, jr, L K
   Harris, J E Bridgman, John W Lis-
   ter and D J Mason.
Building and contracting, Fairfield, C
   E Swindell.
Building and contracting, Swan Quar-
   ter, E H Gaskill.
Building and contracting, Lake Land-
   ing, —— Cutrell.
Building and contracting, Makelyville,
   N D Manly.
Millwrighting, Fairfield, W D Murray.
Saddles and harness, Makelyville, ——
   Webster.

HYDE COUNTY.

MERCHANTS AND TRADESMEN.

Names, Post Offices, Lines of Business.

ENGELHARD.

Bonner, E C,	G S
Clayton, John M,	G S
Cox, T R	G S
Gibbs, A S,	G S
Gibbs, C E P,	G S
Gibbs, J B,	G S
Guthrie, C F,	G S
Spencer, S H & Co,	G S
Williams & Roper,	G S

FAIRFIELD.

Coffey, S W & Co,	G S
Chadwick, J A,	G S
Chadwick, Midgett & Co,	G S
Cuthrell, A L,	G S
Carter & Murray,	G S
Harris, J G & Co,	Jewelry
Lewis, Mrs D W,	Millinery
Mann, Dr J A,	Drugs
Mason, Jephtha,	G S
Midyett & Co,	G S
O'Neal, J S,	G S
Pue, L L,	G S
Sadler, S B,	G S
Simmons & Gibbs,	G S
Swindell & Co.	G S
Watson, Mrs H E,	G S
Williams, R,	G S
Young, R L,	G S

LAKE COMFORT.

Bell, E B,	G S
Benson, J & Co,	G S
Jennett, Robert,	G S
Sears, W J,	G S
Weston, Mrs H T,	G S

LAKE LANDING.

Ballance, ——,	G S
Boomer, B E,	G S
Boomer, L W,	G S
Bridgeman, G S,	G S
Caravan, C E,	G S
Credle, G T,	G S
Cuthrell, S T,	G S
Gaskins, S T,	G S
Gibbs, Jas A,	G S
Gibbs, L L & Co,	G S
Hall, W D,	G S
McKinney, J R,	G S
McKinney, P H,	G S
Midyette, B J,	G S
Selby, G A,	G S
Selby, Milton E,	G S
Watson, D M,	G S
Watson, George I,	G S
Young, S J,	G S

MAKELYVILLE.

Spring, A,	G S
Scranton & N C L L Co,	——

HYDE COUNTY.

MIDDLETON.

Burrus, R S,	G S
Gibbs, J M,	G S
Gibbs, E L,	G S
Gibbs, J W.	G S
Jennette, B E,	G S
Jennette, B F,	G S
Hall, J M,	G S
McKinney, W T,	G S
Rollins, S M,	G S
Weston, R B,	G S

OCRACOKE..

Fulcher, George,	G S
Howard, W E,	G S
McWilliams, J W,	G S
Pilland, M L,	G S
Sabiston, Wm,	G S
Taylor, Stephen,	G S

ROSE BAY.

Chadwick, R C,	G S

SCRANTON.

Bishop, J C & Sons,	G S
Bridgeman Bros,	G S
Lupton, J M,	G S
Richards, R H,	G S

SLADESVILLE.

Bell, F M,	G S
Bishop, J C,	G S
Bridgeman, W Y,	G S
Jarvis, T R,	G S
Jordan, J B,	G S
Lupton, S S,	G S
Lupton, J M,	G S
Newman, G G,	G S
Sparrow, Mrs L,	Millinery
Spring, Alex,	G S
Wahab, H W,	G S

SWAN QUARTER.

Berry Bros,	G S
Brinn Bros,	G S
Chadwick, R C,	G S
Credle, G V,	G S
Hudson, Garrison,	Fish
Swindell, A B,	G S
Swindell, W M,	G S

MILLS.

Kinds, Post Offices and Proprietors.

Corn and flour, Leachville (Beaufort co), Caleb Clark.

Corn and flour, Leechville (Beaufort co), N B Satterthwaite.

Saw, Makelyville, Scranton & North Carolina Lumber Co.

Wind-mill (corn), Lake Comfort, M G Fisher.

Wind-mill (corn), Middleton, W F Raper.

Wind-mill (corn), Swan Quarter, Berry & Gaskill.

Wind-mill (corn), Ocracoke, Eli Howard.

Wind-mill (corn), Middletown, Allen Burrus.

Wind-mill (corn), Middletown, W P M Burns, S A Johnson, Thomas Spencer.

Wind-mill (corn), Fairfield, W D Murray and Murray & Harris.

PHYSICIANS.

Names and Post Offices.

Cartwright, A, Fairfield.
Clark, Edward, Middletown.
Credle, O S, Lake Comfort.
Gibbs, O H, Middletown.
Hooten, G B, & Windly, Clem, Sladesville.
Jones, E H, & Statesbury, C A, Lake Landing.
Long, S A, Lake Landing.
Mann, J A, Fairfield.
Mann, C E, Middletown.
Murray, M M, Lake Comfort.
Weston, B L, Lake Landing.
Windley, Samuel, Lake Landing.

SCHOOLS.

Names, Post Offices and Principals.

Chapel Hill, Academy, Lake Landing.
Fairfield Academy, Fairfield, Miss Simmons.
Middletown Academy, Middletown.
Nebraska Academy, Lake Landing.
Swan Quarter Academy, Swan Quarter, Miss M A Webb.
Public schools—white, 32; colored, 20.

TEACHERS.

Names and Post Offices.

WHITE.

Bell, John D, Sladesville.
Bell, Mrs Maggie, Sladesville.
Benson, James M, Juniper Bay.
Credle, Mrs Lucy, Sladesville.
Credle, I R, Swan Quarter.
Davis, C W, Enlelhard.
Gaskill, Mrs Sarah, Ocracoke.
Jennett, W R, Middletown.
Mann, C A, Lake Landing.
Raper, George E, Engelhard.
Sadler, James R, Fairfield.
Simmons, Miss Mary, Fairfield.
Smith, Miss Mary D, Leechville (Beaufort county).
Swindell, Louis L, Fairfield.
Watson, R F, Engelhard.
Watson, Miss Lena G, Lake Landing.

COLORED.

Branch, Mrs Florence J, Washington.

HYDE COUNTY.

Burns, Benj, Jr, Fairfield.
Clark, T W, Pantego (Beaufort co).
Clark, W A, Leechville (Beaufort co).
Collins, J R, Engelhard.
Collins, J C, Pantego (Beaufort co).
Fleming, W S, Newbern.
Green, W H, Jr, Swan Quarter.
Green, John E, Swan Quarter.
Hutson, Mrs Ritta, Newbern.
Mosely, D G, Newbern.
Smith, Geo W, Sladesville.
Smith, Dennis, Leechville (Beaufort county).
Spencer, George W, Engelhard.
Spencer, Seth A, Middleton.
Swindell, Anson D, Lake Landing.
Swindell, Major Lewis, Swan Quarter.
Walker, S R, Newbern.
Willie, D S, Sladesville.
Wyman, F J, Sladesville.

LOCAL CORPORATIONS.

Atlantic Lodge, No 294, A F & A M, Swan Quarter; time of meeting: second Saturday, Tuesday evening of Court.

Mattamuskeet Lodge, No 328, A F & A M, Engelhard; time of meeting: fourth Saturday, at 10 o'clock A M.

FARMERS.

Names and Post Offices.

Englehard—Sam'l L Baum, Anson Bidds, W Pell Burrus, D H Carter, T M Davis, J B Gibbs, T L Gibbs, B F Gibbs, J M Mann. John Midyett, John Northam, Geo E Roper, W W Spencer, Thos Spencer, P P Spencer, J B Watson, Israel B Watson.

Fairfield—E Baum, A Baum, Allen Burrus, W P Burrus, G S Carter, D M Carter, H C Carter, W S Carter, T H B Gibbs, Henry Jones, Dr J S Mann, T Mann, T C Mann, W F Midgett, W D Murray, Dr P H Simmons, C Simmons, L Swindell, R Tunnell, Samuel Tunnell.

Lake Comfort—M V Benson, John H C Berry, Jas E Berry, John Berry, W W Boomer, Y Emery, S Emery, M G Fisher, S B Harris, R B Harris, Dr E H Jones, M M Murray, E Simmons, J W Spencer, W S Spencer, B Stokesbery, L H Styron, George Weston.

Lake Landing—J M Benson, C F Benson, T R Benson, G S Bridgman,

M Fisher, R Jennett, A McJones, S A Long, J S Mann, S M Mann, W D Mann, W P Midgett, T P Pugh, A B Tunnell, Geo G Watson, J W H Watson, Dr Samuel Windley.

Makelyville—A Green, W G Ruffin, S L Snell, Alexander Spring.

Middletown—Dr E Clark, J H Davis, W Farrow, B F Gibbs, Milton Gibbs, J W Gibbs, B F Jennett, W H Lucas, J M Mann, Thos Mann, E L Mann, W F Roper, W S Swindell.

Scranton—N A Armstrong, O M Bishop, W B Bishop, J C Bishop, G Brown, S A Bridgman, W R Cutrell, W R Carawan, R C Chadwick, W B Dunlar, W K Eanuls, Z J Fortune, J L Gourn, Will Hodges, Jas Hodges, W H Hays, R O Harris, J M Lupton, J L Palrids, Geo R Richards, F S Spencer, Will Spencer, S Swindell, O Swindell, Sam Siluther, W B Watson, C M Watson.

Sladesville—Mrs Hettie Adams, J E Bell, B D Brinn, M S Burgess, J Credle, A B Credle, W M Credle, M B Davis, L S Dillon, W J Fisher, S Fisher, T M Fisher, Z T Fortescue, Mrs Nan Fortescue, W R Harris, Wiley Hodges (col), R W Hollowell, W T Hooten, E Howard (col), Thos R Jarvis, M W Jarvis, Wm O Jordan, J B Jordan, J W Lupton, Pat Lupton, S S Lupton, W A Maning, W P Mydgett, Geo G Newman, S Northam, Richard Oats (col), Daniel Roberson, C H Russell, D H Sawyer, N B Selby, W W Silverthorn, A J Smith, W E Spencer, J H Spencer, E H Tovly, Geo Wade, J H Wahab, R P Wahab, D Wahab.

Stencil House—A Baum, S Baum, J Baum, T M Gibbs, W D Murray, W A Williams.

Swan Quarter—J E Bridgman, H Brown, M S Credle, E S Credle, I R Credle, W M Credle, David Credle, T F Credle, J E Credle, G T Credle, J E Donnell, E D English, Wm M Farrow, E H Gaskill, R F Green, R W Harris, J S Harris, T B Harris, Robt D Harris, Daniel Harris, T E Harris, D E Harris, David Hudson, D S Jarvis, Nat Jarvis, B Jarvis, J W Jester, E J Lovick, D J Mason, sr, Y Mason, Oliver O'Neal, N S Warner, J M Watson, E C Williams, A H Williams.

IREDELL COUNTY.

AREA, 600 SQUARE MILES.

POPULATION, 25,413; White 19,474, Colored 5,939.

IREDELL COUNTY was formed from Rowan in 1788, and called in honor of James Iredell, Sr, late Associate Justice of the Supreme Court of the U. S.

STATESVILLE, the county-seat, is 145 miles west of Raleigh, and immediately on the Western North Carolina Railroad at the junction of the Atlantic, Tennesse and Ohio Railroad. Population, 3,000. It is a growing mountain town, in the centre of a fine farming section.

Surface — Moderately uneven; soil generally good; well watered by the South Yadkin river and tributaries. Water power abundant and very fine. This county contains a thrifty population.

Staples—Corn, cotton, rye, tobacco, oats, wheat, grass, butter and live stock. This is one of the best wheat sections in the State. Large quantities of medicinal herbs are shipped to Northern markets from Statesville.

Fruits—Apples, pears, grapes, cherries, peaches, melons, and a great variety of small fruits.

Timbers—Oak, poplar, hickory, dogwood, black walnut, cherry, maple, etc.

Minerals—Iron, corundum and gold.

TOWNS AND POST OFFICES.

	POP.		POP.
Abernethy,	25	Net,	—
Amity Hill,	30	New Hope,	50
Armfield,	25	New Sterling,	40
Banton,	25	Nicholson's	
Barium		Mills,	25
Springs,	250	Oak Forest,	25
Bryantsville,	50	Olin,	50
Clio,	25	Ostwalt,	115
Cool Spring,	50	Perth,	25
Doolie,	25	Pressly,	50
Dunlap,	30	River Hill,	35
Eagle,	70	Rock Cut,	25
Elmwood,	160	Scott's,	30
Eupeptic		Settle,	25
Springs,	25	Shrimsville,	—
Evelin,	30	Sigma,	—
Fancy Hill,	30	Snow Creek,	40
Granite Hill,	50	Statesville,	3,000
Harmony,	50	Staphel,	—
Houstonville,	30	Sweet Home,	125
Jennings,	25	Troutman's,	150
Longford,	25	Turnersburg,	100
McCurdy,	25	Vance,	50
Mayhew,	25	Watts,	—
Miller,	25	Waugh,	35
Mooresville,	1,200	Weisner,	25
Mount Mourne,	93	Williamsburg,	25

COUNTY OFFICERS.

Clerk Superior Court—H V Furches.
Commissioners—J A Cooper, ch'm'n; Dr L Harrell, J C Gray, A P Clark, R R Hill.
Coroner—W L Harbin.
Register of Deeds—M E Ramsey.
Deputy Register—R V Tharpe.
Sheriff—M A White.
Solicitor 8th District—L Q Holton.
Surveyor—R O Lazenby.
Standard Keeper—J U Lamprecht.
Treasurer—W A Wright.
County Examiner—R V Tharpe.
Deputy Sheriffs—J R Abernethy, P D Atwell. J W Long, jr, U I Roseman, W W Tharpe, W V Williams.
Jailer—W M Nicholson.
Superintendent of Chain Gang—Jas Patterson.
Superintendent of County Home—W D Eastey.
Constable—W G Karcher.

COURTS.

Fourth Monday before the first Monday in March; eleventh Monday after the first Monday in March; fourth Monday before the first Monday in September; ninth Monday after the first Monday in September.

TOWN OFFICERS.

MOORESVILLE—*Mayor*, F J Brawley. *Clerk and Treasurer*. W J Freeze. *Constable*, Espey McLean.
STATESVILLE——*Mayor*, L C Caldwell. *Aldermen*, W H Allison, J C Turner, R R Cowles, J U Lamprecht, J A Brady, J C Steele, W F Hall, jr, C B Webb. *Clerk and Treasurer*, E B Stinson. *Tax Collector*, D C Rufty. *Chief of Police*, W C Henry. *Superintendent of Streets*, J A Conner. *Keeper of Cemetery*, P R Patterson. *Superintendent of Electric Lights*, J D Cochrane. *Chief of Fire Department*, J F Armfield. *Cotton Weigher*, J P Cathy. *Graded School Trustees*, Dr L Harrill, ch'mn. *Superintendent Public Schools*, D Matt Thompson.

TOWNSHIPS AND MAGISTRATES.

Barringer's—C L Shinn, J C Shinn, W H Marsh (Shinnsville), A L Wagner (Troutman's), J H Brown (Amity).

IREDELL COUNTY.

Bethany—W C Wooten (Armfield), W H Crawford, G W Morrison (Statesville), J A Haynes, A L Fox, W H Adderholdt (Dunlap), J W Harper (Armfield).

Chamberburg—J D Click (Elmwood), G W McNeely, S A Hoover, G R Mills (Amity), J F Eagle, T T Conyer (Statesville), J F Dotson (Oak Forest).

Coddle Creek—D W Lamance, A M Walker, C V Voils, T C Beatty, J L Bradley, E L Clominger (Granite Hill), E L Goodman (Amity), J H Reed (Mt Mourne).

Concord—J H Scroggs (Clio), J T Murdock, J S Morrison (Pressly), J R Guey, E F Morrison (Scott's), J A Davis (Statesville), W B Gibson (Fancy Hill), R A Stone (Armfield).

Cool Springs—J A Harper (Oak Forest), W C Blaylock (Sigma), J C Turner, W F Reece, W S Page (Cool Springs).

Davidson—T O Brawley, J B Cornelius, J H Thompson (Mt Mourne), J A Mills, A S McKay, J A Sherrill (Doolie), J A Alexander, J A Black (Mayhew).

Eagle Mills—E E Smith, E W Johnson, E H Powell (Settle), J T Cash (Eagles), T W Johnson, J L Cain (Nicholson's Mills), I Angle (Houstonville).

Fallstown—J M Patterson, W H Evans (Troutman's), D R Howard (Rock Cut), E W Putnam (Perth).

New Hope—O G Williams, J P Williams, A G Myers, H E Sloan, P C Fletcher, J W Williams (Evalin), M H Shoemaker, E L McHargue (Eupeptic Springs).

Olin—I A Cowan, T J Osborne, D C Rhyne, W B Campbell, J M Davis, J A Stikeleather (Olin), J E Headen (Turnersburg).

Sharpesburg—A A Hines, R J Bryant (Bryantville), A R Bowles, R P Patterson (Sweet Home), W P A White (McCurdy), R T Campbell, jr (Snow Creek).

Shiloh—J F Stewart, A L Alexander, J C Brown, A T Smith (New Sterling), M L Moose (Statesville), I A Johnson (Pressley).

Statesville—J P Bradley, W G Lewis, G C White, W P Coone, J C Kimball, A D Parks, W C Mills, T S Barkley (Statesville).

Turnersburg—L C Mullin, J T Baggarly (Turnersburg), J A Butler, J H Thorpe (Harmony).

Union Grove—N G Jurney, W M Parks, E M Sale, A A Rast, J C Templeton (Jennings), D I Hegler (Eupeptic Springs), J E Colvert (Olin), D F Weisner (Weisner).

IREDELL COUNTY.

CHURCHES.

Names, Post Offices, Pastors and Denom.

METHODIST.

Bethel—Catawba, J O Shelly,
Bethlehem—Statesville, J O Shelly.
Chapel Hill—Statesville, T L Triplett.
Church—Eagle Mill, A E Wiley.
Church—Turnersburg, A E Wiley.
Church—Mooresville, J A Bowles.
Church—Snow Creek.
Church—Olin, A E Wiley.
Clarksburg—County Line, A E Wiley.
Connelly's Chapel—Statesville, J O Shelly.
Hoqewell—Olin, A E Wiley.
Knox Chapel—Amity, T L Triplett.
Macedonia—Williamsburg, A E Wiley.
McKendrick's Chapel—Mahew, R G Tettle.
Moss—Olin, A E Wiley.
Mt Bethel—Turnersburg, A E Wiley.
Mt Moriah—Eagle Mills, J F Craven.
New Salem—Oak Forest, J O Shelly.
Pisgah—Sweet Home, J O Shelly.
Pleasant Grove — Fountmore, T L Triplett.
Providence—Watts, J O Shelly.
Rocky Mount—Troutsman, T L Triplett.
Salem—Mt Mourne, J A Bowles.
Statesville — Statesville, Daniel Atkins, D D.
Trinity—Liberty, J O Shelly.
Vanderourg—Graniteville, T L Triplett.
Wesley—Troutsman, T L Triplett.
West End—Statesville, R G Barrett.

METH. PROTESTANT.

Union Grove—Olin.

LUTHERAN.

Church—New Sterling, W L Darr.
Sharon—Waugh.
St John's—Statesville, W L Darr.
St Michael's—Troutsman, B S Brown.
St Martin's—Troutsman, W L Darr.
St Paul's—Statesville, B S Brown.

A. M. E. ZION.

Bethesda (col)—Mooresville, Wm Johnston.
Catawba (col)—Mooresville, Wm Johnston.
Church (col)—Statesville, P A McCorkle.

BAPTIST.

Bethel—Cool Spring.
Bethel—Troutman's, J B Marsh.
Church—Statesville, G H Church.
Church—Mooresville.
Church—Zion, Thomas Parrish.
Holly Spring—Williamsburg, W P Gwaltney.

IREDELL COUNTY.

New Bethany—Catawba, J B Marsh.
New Hope—Cool Spring, J B Marsh.
Sandy Spring—Eagle Mills, Nathan Chaffin.
Society—Cool Spring, W F Fulford.
Vernon—Olin, —— Myers.

PRESBYTERIAN.

Bethany—Dunlap, W R McLelland.
Bethesda—Statesville, W R McLelland.
Centre—Mt Mourne, Wm W Pharr.
Church—Mooresville, J M Whary.
Church (Fourth Creek)—Statesville, Wm Wood, D D.
Church (col)—Mooresville, J G Murray.
Church (col)—Statesville, S F Wintz.
Clio—Statesville.
Concord—New Stirling.
Fifth Creek—Cool Spring, J E Summers.
New Salem—Statesville.
Old Salem—Statesville.
Prospect—Mooresville, W W Pharr.
Shiloh—Statesville.
Tabor—Olin.

EPISCOPAL.

St James—Granite Hill.
Trinity—Statesville.

ASSO. REFORM.

Amity—Statesville, J H Presley.
Coddle Creek—Spring Grove, W T Love.
New Perth—Troutman's, W T Love.
New Sterling—Statesville, J C Boyd.

MINISTERS RESIDENT.

Names, Post Offices and Denominations.

METHODIST.

Adkins, Dan, D D, Statesville.
Barrett, R G, Statesville.
Bowles, J A, Mooresville.
Rone, J C, D D, Statesville.
Rowe, G P, Statesville.
Shelby, J O, Statesville.
Smith, E E, Settle.
Somers, J N, Statesville.
Triplett, T L, Mooresville.
Triplett, L H, Mooresville.
Tuttle, R G, Mt Mourne.
Wiley, A E, Olin.
Willson, Jas, Statesville.

BAPTIST.

Baker, A W, New Hope.
Church, G H, Statesville.
Green, J B, New Hope.
Logan, R P, Sweet Home.
Marsh, J B, Catawba.
Moore, A C, Catawba.
Paris, T W, Eagle Mills.

IREDELL COUNTY.

Redman, A, New Hope.
Way, G (col), Nicholson's Mills.

LUTHERAN.

Brown, B S, Troutman's.
Darr, W L, Statesville.
Fesperman, J H, Barium Springs.
Stiehecker, T H, Barium Springs.

PRESBYTERIAN.

Pharr, W W, Mooresville.
Wood, Wm A, D D, Statesville.

ASSO. REFORMED.

Presley, J E, Coddle Creek.
Pressley, J H, Statesville.

HOTELS AND BOARDING HOUSES.

Names, Post Offices and Proprietors.

St Charles, Statesville, I G Green & Sons.
Cooper House, Statesville, J W Gray.
Eupeptic Springs, Olin, J A White.
Female College (summer), Statesville, Mrs Fannie Walton.
Goodman House, Mooresville, W M Robinson.
Henry House, Statesville, George H Henry.
Johnston House, Mooresville, C A Johnston.
Hotel, Troutman, A D Troutman.
Hotel, Olin, H L Gill.
Boarding, Statesville, Mrs M Neely.
Boarding, Barium Spring, Mrs Lippard.
Boarding, Barium Spring, W M Dayvault.
Boarding, Statesville, Mrs P B Chambers.
Boarding, Statesville, Mrs Quincy Sharpe.
Boarding, Statesville, Mrs Robina Jamison.
Boarding, Statesville, J S McRary.
Boarding, Statesville, Mrs W H Morrison.
Boarding, Statesville, Mrs M V Reed.
Boarding, Statesville, Mrs J D Winslow.
Boarding, Statesville, Mrs M J Daniels.
Boarding, Statesville, W M Nicholson.

LAWYERS.

Names and Post Offices.

Armfield (C H), Turner (W D) & Armfield (R F), Statesville.
Armfield, J B, Statesville.
Burke, H, Statesville.
Furches (D M), Supreme Court Judge, & Coble (A L), Superior Court Judge, Statesville.
Connelly, J B, Statesville.

IREDELL COUNTY.	IREDELL COUNTY.

Cowles, A D, Statesville.
Gamble, J F, Statesville.
Grier, H P, Statesville.
Hartness, J A, Statesville.
McLoughlin, R B, Statesville.
Robbins (W M), Long (B F) & Long (Frank), Statesville.
Scales, J L, Statesville.

MANUFACTORIES.

Kinds, Post Offices and Proprietors.

Barrels and kegs, Statesville, H W Miller & Co.
Barrels and kegs, Statesville, J A Wise
Barrels and kegs, Statesville, L C Wagner & Co.
Brick, Mooresville, J W Brown.
Brick, Mooresville, Hudson & Lourance.
Brick, Statesville, H M Mills.
Brick, Statesville, W E Morrison.
Brick, Mooresville, Troutman & Cloaninger.
Brick, Statesville, Isidore Wallace.
Brick machines, Statesville, J C Steele & Son.
Brooms and mattresses, Statesville, J B Watson.
Building and contracting, River Hill, D M Campbell.
Building and contracting, Vance, J F Hare.
Building and contracting, Amity Hill, G R Mills.
Building and contracting, Statesville, W F Munday.
Building and contracting, Mooresville, J W Brown.
Canning, Troutman's, J C Collins.
Cigars, Statesville, Louis Clark.
Cotton mills, Statesville, Paul Bigelow, pres.
Cotton, sheeting and yarns, Turnersburg, Stimpson & Steele; looms, 10; spindles, 650; established in 1849; capital, $26,000; consumes 350 pounds of raw cotton daily.
Cotton mills, Statesville, Will Wallace, pres; T D Miller, sec and treas. Capital, $200,000; 180 looms, — spindles.
Creamery, Statesville, Dr. J J Mott.
Foundry and machine shop, Statesville, J C Steele.
Granite quarry, Mooresville, — Johnson.
Harness and collar works, Statesville, S A Sharpe.
Harness and shoes, Mooresville, W A Wilson.
Harness, Statesville, T C Anderson.
Harness, Statesville, J T Murdock.
Harness, New Sterling, W R Summers.
Iron and wood work, Vance, E W Sills.

Iron and wood work, Statesville, L C Dietz.
Iron and wood work, Troutman's, A D Troutman.
Iron and wood work, Spring Grove, F Vance.
Iron and wood work, Statesville, M J Deitz & Co.
Iron and wood work, New Sterling, Q Adams.
Iron and wood work, New Sterling, J F Murdock.
Iron and wood work, Olin, J Litton.
Iron and work work, Olin, G W Weir.
Iron and wood work, River Hill, D Gaither.
Iron and wood work, River Hill, W T Stroud.
Iron and wood work, Mayhew, H Hager.
Iron and wood work, Turnersburg, G L Henderson.
Iron and wood work, Turnersburg, T T Hilliard.
Iredell Granite Co, Mooresville.
Iron and wood work, Mayhew, Moses Heileg.
Lowenstein & Co, Chillcure, Statesville.
Linseed oil, Eagle Mills, John Anderson.
Linseed oil, Williamsburg, J Stock.
Leather Co, Mooresville, W C Patterson.
Marble Works, Statesville, C B Webb.
Machine Works, Statesville, J C Steele & Son.
Millwrighting, Sweet Home, A Summers.
Millwrighting, Sweet Home, N G Sloan
Millwrighting, Amity Hill, Arthur Wallace.
Millwrighting, Oak Forest, J F Dotson.
Millwrighting, Olin, N T Summers.
Mott's Dairy, Statesville, Dr J J Mott.
Mooresville Cotton Mill, J E Sherrell, pres; G C Goodman, sec and treas; capital, $100,000.
Saddles and harness, New Stirling, W P Harrison.
Saddles and harness, Statesville, S C Anderson.
Sash, doors and blinds, Statesville, Overcash & Sons.
Spoke and handles, Statesville, Stock Co
Shoes, Statesville, W T Bowen.
Soda Water, Statesville, W S Phifer & Sons.
Tannery, Mooresville, W C Patterson.
Tannery, River Hill, O Henley.
Tannery, Statesville, S A Sharpe.
Tanning, Harmony, F Tomlinson.
Tannery, Clio, W F Millsap.
The Jimtown Dairy, (near).
Tinware, Statesville, S W Stinson.

| IREDELL COUNTY. | IREDELL COUNTY. |

IREDELL COUNTY.

Tinware, Mooresville, R H Tomlinson.
Tobacco, Mooresville, Benson & Plyler.
Tobacco, Statesville, Rankin Bros.
Tobacco, Olin, J H Tatum.
Tobacco (plug and twist), Statesville, Miller & Clifford.
Tobacco, Statesville, Ashe & Sons.
Tobacco (plug, twist and smoking), Statesville, L Harrell, mgr; Iredell Tobacco Co.
Tobacco, Statesville, Clark, H, & Sons.
Tobacco (plug, twist and smoking), Statesville, Irwin & Poston.
Tobacco, Statesville, Kee & Co.
Tobacco, Statesville, Stafford Bros.
Tobacco, Statesville, J Stephany.
Tobacco (plug and twist), Mooresville, W L Caldwell.
Tobacco boxes, River Hill, B Gaither.
Tobacco, Houstonville, P B Kennedy.
Tobacco, Statesville, J H McElwee.
Tubs and boxes; Statesville, C L Wagoner.
Wool rolls, Olin, Summers & King.
Wool rolls, Eagle Mills, Morrison, Gaither & Co.
Wool rolls, Cool Spring, J B Holman.
Wool rolls, Statesville, Jno Wise.

MERCHANTS AND TRADESMEN.

Name, Post-office and Line of Business.

ADAMS.

| Weston, W F, | G S |

ABERNATHY.

| Abernathy, M A. | G S |

AMITY.

| Goodman, J T, | G S |
| Templeton, G W, | G S |

CLIO.

Brown, E R,	G S
Hager, W B & Co,	G S
Hager, J W,	G S
Lackey, L A,	G S

BRYANTVILLE.

| Bryant, R J, | G S |

COOL SPRINGS.

| Sartin, D P, | G S |

DOOLIE.

| McKay, A G, | G S |

DUNLAP.

| Summers, W H H, | G S |

EAGLE MILLS.

| Stimpson, A L, | G S |

ELMWOOD

| Long, J J & Son, | G S |

EUPEPTIC SPRINGS.

| Goforth, W A, | G S |
| Hagler, D I, | G S |

IREDELL COUNTY.

EVELIN.

| Williams, O G & Sons, | G S |

FANCY HILL.

| Gibson, W B, | G S |

GRANITE HILL.

| Simmons & Co, | G S |
| Smith, H A, | G S |

HARMONY.

Grose, C A & Bro,	G S
Hays, C N.	G S
Thorp, J H,	G S

JENNINGS.

| Jennings, T L & Son, | G S |

MAYHEW.

| Mayhew, J W, | G S |

MILLER.

| Caldwell & Hubbard, | G S |
| Miller, E C, | G S |

MOORESVILLE.

Butler, J W,	Gro
Deaton, J C & Son,	Livery
Freeze & Co,	G S
Goodman, Geo C & Co,	Drugs
Harris, J S,	G S
Harris, Sherrill & Co,	G S
Johnston, H M & Co,	Furniture
Johnson, W C & Co,	Gro
Johnson, W N,	Gro
Kistler, J W & Co,	G S
Ludwig, H A,	Gro
McLean, J C.	Gro
McNeely, B W & C K,	Livery
Mills, J P.	G S
Neill, W M & Co,	Gro
Rankin, S C.	G S
Tomlinson, R H,	Stoves and Tinware
Voils, C V & Co,	Gro
Walter, J H,	Jeweler

MT. MOURNE.

| Bell Bros, | G S |
| Thompson, J H, | G S |

MT. ULLA.

| Upwright, W L, | G S |

NET.

| Barnard Bros, | Gro |
| Thorp Bros, | G S |

NEW STIRLING.

| Bradford, D L, | G S |

OAK FOREST.

| Gunn, J A, | G S |

OLIN.

| Holland Bros, | G S |
| Holland, J W & Co, | G S |

RIVER VIEW.

| Nixon, T I, | G S |

ROCK CUT.

| Wilhelm & Waugh, | G S |

IREDELL COUNTY.	IREDELL COUNTY.

SCOTT'S.

Hunter, J L & Co,	G S
Morrison, J S,	G S

SETTLE.

Smith, E E,	G S

SHINNVILLE.

Shinn, J C,	G S

STATESVILLE.

Allison, W H,	Variety
Anderson, W E,	Grocer
Ary, D J,	Confectionery
Bailey, R D,	Boarding
Barron & Nicholson,	Furniture
Bell, Miss Emily,	Millinery
Browley & Sloan,	Clothing
Carson & Woods (col),	Livery
Chambers, P B,	Boarding
Cooper & Gill,	Groceries
Copeland & McDougald,	G S
Cowan, Wycoff & Mills,	Livery
Cox Bros,	Grocers
Daniels & Sullivan,	Livery
Dietz, R O & Co,	Grocers
Flanigan & Son,	Hardware
Gray, J W, Cooper House, Cigars, etc	
Green, Rev Richard,	Hotel
Hall, W F, jr,	Drugs
Harrison, N,	Clothing
Henry, G H,	Henry House
Jamison, Mrs A W,	Boarding House
Jenkins, D F,	Grocer
Key, P B & Co,	Mfrs Tobacco and Snuff
Lerry, D,	Clothing
Lewis, W G,	Fire Ins
Marshall, J W,	G S
Miller, H W,	Boarding
Mills & Wycoff,	Livery
Mills, N B & Co,	G S
Mitchell, J M,	G S
Moore & Miller,	Grocers
Moore, R L & Co,	Jewelers
Morrison, J K & Co,	Whol Grocers
Moses, S,	D G
Murdock, R B (col),	Boarding
Perry, J T,	Grocer
Phifer, W S & Co,	Grocers
Parton, Bro & Neill,	G S
Propst, C E,	Confectioner
Reid, Mrs M N,	Boarding house
Rickert, R H,	Jeweler
Rufty, D C,	Grocer
Schiller, L,	Furniture
Sharp, J M,	G S
Sherrill, W F,	Grocers
Sherrill, F A & Co,	G S
Smith, Frank (col),	G S
Stimpson & Anderson,	Drugs
Stimpson, S W,	Stoves and Tinware
Thomas, W A & Co,	Hardware
The Wallace Bros Co,	Whol Dry G, Roots and Herbs
Tunstall, N R,	Drugs

Turner, W P & Co,	Grocers
Turner, F H,	Boarding
Walton, & Gage,	D G
Westmoreland, R L,	Livery
White, J W,	Undertaker
Wilhelm & Mills,	D G
Willison, Jas,	Grocer
Wright, W G,	Grocer

TROUTMAN.

Wagner & Brown,	G S

TURNERSBURG.

Stimpson & Steel,	G S

WILLIAMSBURG.

Baity, G A,	G S

MINERAL SPRINGS.

Barium Springs, Barium Springs, Donald McRae, owner.

Cresswell's Springs, Mooresville, Mrs J R McNeeley, owner.

Eupeptic Springs, ——, W E Current, owner.

Lithia Barium Springs, Statesville, Isidore Wallace, owner.

Strohecker's Barium Springs, Barium Springs, Rev T H Strohecker, owner.

MILLS.

Kinds, Post Offices and Proprietors.

Corn, Rock Cut, Dr W W Wilhelm.
Corn, Evelin, P C Fletcher.
Corn, Mooresville, R S Kennerly.
Corn, Miller, Barkley & Kelley.
Corn, Mt Mourne, J B Cornelius.
Corn, Granite Hill, H A Neill.
Corn, Toutman, Wagner & Smith.
Corn, Olin, C S Holland.
Corn, Rock Cut, R L Moose.
Corn, Rock Cut, C R Roseman.
Corn, Statesville, Jacob Bostain.
Corn, Turnersburg, W T Shaver.
Flour and corn, Eagle Mills, S W Little.
Flour and corn, Statesville, Mrs E H Davis.
Flour and corn, Evelin, M H Shoemaker.
Flour and corn, Evelin, J W Williams & Son.
Flour and corn, Coddle Creek, Nesbit & Pressley.
Flour and corn, Statesville, J M Sharpe.
Flour and corn, Statesville, T A Watts & Bro.
Flour, corn and saw, New Stirling, Carter Bros.
Flour and corn, Turnersburg, T P Martin.
Flour and corn, Sweet Home, J B King.

IREDELL COUNTY.	IREDELL COUNTY.

Flour and corn, Cool Spring, Turner Bros & Co,

Flour and corn, Troutman's, Jno Oustwalt.

Flour and corn, Olin, Summers & King.

Flour and corn, Olin, A C Tomlin.

Flour and corn, Statesville, White Bros.

Flour and corn, Statesville, W E Morrison.

Flour, corn and saw, Oak Forest, C C Barrier.

Flour, corn and saw, McCurdy, W P A White.

Flour, corn and saw, Sweet Home, R F Canter & Co.

Flour, corn and saw, Abernethy, Ray-Bros.

Flour, corn and saw, Abernethy, Stewart Bros.

Flour, corn and saw, Nicholson's Mills, John Anderson.

Flour, corn and saw, Watts, N P Watts & Co.

Flour and corn, Ostwalt, J W Arthur, sr.

Flour and corn, Ostwalt, J W Ostwalt.

Flour and corn, Elmwood, C C Barrier.

Flour and corn, Amity, G J Turner.

Flour and corn, Amity, W L Poston.

Flour and corn, Oak Forest, P R Houpe.

Flour and corn, Mayhew, J L Caldwell.

Steam saw, corn and gin, Mooresville, Melchor Bros.

Flour and corn, Jennings, T L Jennings.

Flour and corn, Jennings, Miss Alice Campbell.

Flour and corn, Jennings, J R Hines.

Flour and corn, Statesville, White Bros.

Flour anp corn, Harmony, J A Butler.

Flour and corn, New Sterling, Carter & Smith.

Flour and corn, Waugh, Morrison & Stewart.

Flour and corn, Statesville, Watts Bros.

Flour and corn, New Hope, J W Harmon.

Flour and corn, Eupeptic Springs, J E Myers.

Flour and corn, Clio, J M Sharpe.

Flour and corn, Bryantsville, Canter, Myers & Co,

Flour and corn, Snow Creek, S C Crater.

Flour and corn, Williamsburg, G A Baity.

Flour and corn, Jennings, Myers, Davis & Co.

Roller Mill, Harmony, J A Butler.

Roller Mill, Mooresville, Templeton, Williams & Co.

Roller Mill, Cool Springs, Turner & Holeman.

Roller Mill, Eagle Mills, J E Simpson.

Roller Mill, Scott's X-Roads, Morrison & Co.

Roller Mill, Long Ford, Troutman & Co.

Roller Flouring Mill, Statesville, Henry Gilbert.

Roller Mill, Troutman's, J S Troutman's estate.

Roller Mill, Statesville, Mott & Sullivan.

Roller Mill, Turnersburg, Simpson & Steele.

Roller Mill, Scott's, J L Hunter & Co.

Roller Mill, Statesville, Miller, Rayner & Co.

Roller Mill Waugh, H L Gilbert.

Saw, Sweet Home, A Summers.

Saw, Nicholson's Mills, Geo Anderson.

Saw, Ostwalt, J W Arthurs, jr.

Saw, Harmony, Cheshire, White & Co.

Saw, Net, J L Forcum.

Saw, Fancy Hill, Gibson & Vickory.

Saw, Sweet Home, N F Hartness.

Saw, Rock Cut, Kincard & Bro.

Saw, Perth, Lambert & Collins.

Saw, Granite Hill, R D Moore.

Saw, Jennings, Morris & Sale.

Saw, Granite Hill, H A Neill.

Saw, Oak Forest, Smith & Fox.

Saw, Snow Creek, T P Summers.

Saw, Statesville, Wagner & Overcash.

Saw, Evelin, J P & M E Williams.

Steam saw, Troutman's, T K & A T Ostwalt.

Steam gin and corn, Troutman's, Wagner & Smith.

Steam saw, Cool Spring, A L Fox.

Steam saw and planing, Harmony, Stikeleather & Chesire.

Steaw saw, Statesville, W F Bailey.

Steam saw, corn and gin, Mooresville, Melchor Bros.

PHYSICIANS.

Names and Post Offices.

Adams, M R, Statesville.

Adams, J R B, Statesville.

Anderson, T E, Statesville.

Angle, J B, Net.

Caldwell, R J, Mooresville.

Campbell, Arch, Snow Creek.

Carlton, J F, Statesville.

Chenault, W F, Elmwood.

Douglas, B F, Scotts.

Gaither, F B (dentist), Harmony.

Hall, E A, Dunlap.

Harrill, L, Statesville.

Hill, M W, Statesville.

23

IREDELL COUNTY.	IREDELL COUNTY.

Hill, W J, Statesville.
Holler, O L, New Sterling.
Houston, George, Mt Mourne.
King, J E, Snow Creek.
Klutz, E E, Troutman.
Langenour, P F (dentist), Statesville.
Lawrence, R L (dentist), Mooresville.
Little, S W, Harmony.
Long, J F, Statesville.
Long, N F, Statesville.
McCorkle, J R, Mooresville.
McLaughlin, J E, Cool Spring.
McLelland, J R, Mooresville.
Mills, R W, Troutman.
Mott, W B, Mt Mourne.
Mott, H G, Mt Mourne.
Nicholson, W G, Harmony.
Parks, W P, Olin.
Stevenson, S W, Mooresville.
Turner, C A (dentist), Statesville.
Vaughn, ——, Cool Spring.
White, L (dentist), Statesville.
Wilhelm, W W, Statesville.
Williams, J V, Settle.
Young, James, Mooresville.

SCHOOLS.

Names, Post Offices and Principals.

Academy, Troutman, Prof J L Bost.
Academy, Olin, Prof Sherrill.
Academy, Mooresville, Prof C L Grey.
Academy, Mooresville, Rev W T Totten.
Academy, Harmony, Prof J N Baron.
Academy, Clio, Prof E S Millsaps.
Fairview Academy, Pressley.
Graded Schools, Statesville.
Graded Schools (col), Statesville, Prof D Matt Thompson, supt.
Male Academy, Statesville, Prof V J Hill.
Music School, Mrs F L Page.
Music School, Statesville, Miss Jennie Culur, Miss E V Comelins, Miss Jennie Fowler.
Orphans' Home, Barium Springs, Rev R W Boyd.
Public schools—white, 97; colored, 38.

TEACHERS.

Names and Post Offices..

WHITE.
Adderbolt, R M, Statesville.
Ary, Chas C, Elmwood
Barrow, J N, Harmony.
Barkley, E L, Miller.
Bell, J E M, Mt Mourne.
Bost, J L, Troutman's.
Braidy, E D, New Sterling.
Branley, Jessie A, Mooresville.
Brandon, Ada, Sigma.

Brown, Bettie, Troutman.
Brown, J J, Catawba.
Brown, J C, Catawba.
Campbell, W A, Evaline.
Carson, Nannie, Statesville.
Crawford, J C, Statesville.
Crater, A J, Williamsburg.
Deaton, T J, Amity.
Elliott, J T, New Sterling.
Elliott, W F, Bryantsville.
Gilreath, Jennie, Rock Cut.
Goforth, S T, Eupeptic Springs.
Goodwin, W C, Bryantville.
Hall, Bettie. Mooresville.
Harbin, J F (band instructor), Statesville.
Howard, Maggie, Statesville.
Hill, Mary A, Clio.
Holland, Bettie, Weisner.
Holland, W W, Weisner.
Kimball, Mattie, Statesville.
Lentz, R E, Mooresville.
Little, Maggie, Cuddle Creek.
Luckey, Maggie, Oak Forest.
McNeely, Mary, Mooresville.
McKarpee, C, Mooresville.
Mitchell, David A, Net.
Moose, Carrie, Statesvile.
Morrison, Jennie, Scott's.
Morrison, Minnie, Scott's.
Myers, David A, Nicholson Mill.
Patterson, Fannie, Troutman.
Patterson, Will, Mooresville.
Scruggs, Mattie, Statesville.
Sherrill, Alda, Raman.
Shoemaker, Della, Evelin.
Somers, C H, Clio.
Stevenson, H L, Fancy Hill.
Steele, J A, Mooresville.
Thorp, J H, Harmony.
Thorp, J E, Net.
Thompson, H B, Elmwood.
Thomas, M G, Rock Cut.
Trivett, W R A, Eagle.
Trontis, M C, Mooresville.
Wagner, Carrie, Troutman.
Watson, Mary, Statesville.
Watts, J P, Pressley.
Williams, Lola, Evelin.
Williamson, W W, Troutman.
Windsor, J W, Buck Shoals.
Wood, W B, Statesville.
Wooten, W C, Statesville.

COLORED.
Alexander, B H, Statesville.
Alexander, Lelia, Watts.
Allison, J A, Turnersburg.
Allison, Lucy, Turnersburg.
Bailey, Addie, Statesville.
Barker, L B, Statesville.
Blackburn, M B C, Statesville.
Bruner, B K, Turnersburg.
Carter, A G, Statesville.
Carver, B, Clio.

IREDELL COUNTY.

Clark, Wm, Mt Mourne.
Dobson, Mattie, Statesville.
Hampton, Mary E, Statesville.
Haynes, G T, Statesville.
Lynch, Mattie V, Statesville.
Metz, W L, Watts.
Miller, J W, Elmwood.
Murdock, Mary J, New Sterling.
Murdock, R B, Statesville.
Murdock, Creole, Watts.
Parks, J F, Statesville.
Phifer, H A, Statesville.
Phifer, Maggie, Elmswood.
Pnifer, J S, Cleveland.
Radford, C E, Statesville.
Robinson, Annie, Statesville.
Smith, J A, Dunlap.
Steel, M C, Statesville.
Steel, P W, Statesville.
Trusure, J E, Statesville.
Wallace, Maggie, Statesville.
Watts, Bruner, Miller.
White, P C, Statesville.
Wilson, J H, Omega.
Wood, Maggie E, Statesville.

LOCAL CORPORATIONS.

Building and Loan Association, States
ville; J C Irvin, pres; L Harrill, sec
and treas.
Campbell Lodge, No 374, A F and A
M, Amity Hill; time of meeting, first
Saturday and June 24th and Decem-
ber 27th.
County Line Lodge, No 225, A F and
A M, River Hill; time of meeting,
Friday on or before full moon.
First National Bank, Statesville, J A
Cooper, pres; J C Irvin, vice-pres;
G H Brown, cashier; capital stock,
$50,000.
Hunting Creek Lodge, No 299, A F
and A M, Eagle Mills; time of meet-
ing, Friday evening on or before full
moon.
Iredell Lodge, No 362, A F and A M,
Mooresville; time of meeting fourth
Saturday at 2 P M.
—— Lodge, No 1552, Knights of Honor,
Mooresville; S W Stevenson, dicta-
tor.
Mount Mourne Lodge, No 347, A F and
A M, Mt Mourne; time of meeting,
Saturday before second Sunday.
Snow Creek Lodge, No 345, A F and
A M, Snow Creek; time of meeting.
Friday evening on or before full
moon.
The Key Mfg Co, Tobacco and snuff,
Statesville.
Wilson Lodge, No 226, A F and A M,
Olin, time of meeting, Thursday on
or before full moon, and June 24th
and December 27th.

IREDELL COUNTY.

NEWSPAPERS.

Landmark, Statesville (democratic,
semi-weekly); J P Caldwell and A R
Clark, eds and props.
Our Fatherless Ones (orphan asylum
paper), Barium Springs; Rev R W
Boyd, ed.
Piedmont Sun, (col republican), States-
ville; R B Murdock, ed and mgr.
Simple Testimony (religious monthly),
Catawba; Rev J H Booth, ed.
The Record (dem weekly), Mooresville;
F S Starrett.
The Mascot (dem weekly), Statesville;
J A Hartness, ed and prop.

FARMERS.

Names and Post Offices.

Abernethy—M P Abernethy, Jacob
Blackwelder, T J Christopher, R F
Cline, Peter Little, R C Little, H L S
Lollar, G A Moore, J A Moore, S H
Moore, Raymer Brothers, Henry Set-
zer, Mrs L M Shook, J F Stewart, J R
Stewart, S N Thomas, A J K Thomas,
C A Troutman, E M Young.
Amity Hill.—A J Bass, J L Deaton,
B C Deaton, Turner J Goodman, C A
Haithcox, S A Hoover, Miss A C King,
J W Leatz, S L Madden, G W Mc-
Neely, G R Mills, S M Moore, J C Mor-
ton, Peter Smith, G W Templeton, W
J Upright, Geo White.
Armfield.—M A Femister, T J Gib-
son, S Gross, H Hartness, R S Hart-
ness, W B McClelland, J L McLallard,
L M Morrow, W F Morrow, N V Pearce,
Wesley Privett, G F Robb, J W Robb,
Theo Sharpe, J W Sides, Sides Broth-
ers, R A Stone, W H Summers, Asa
Summers, P M Summers, E D Wade,
J A White.
Clio.—Mrs E Adams, W M Adams,
R L Bailey, T A Bailey, R M Bruce, R
R Hill, H S King, C S King, A L Mil-
ligan, J F Millsaps, W F Millsaps, J D
Patterson, C F Rickert, J A Scroggs.
Cool Springs.—W A Balock, W M
Campbell, B Colvert, N C Crickmore,
Wm Fraley, N J Gaither, G Hendrix, J
B Holman, S G Holton, D J L Knox,
R C Knox, B R Knox, L W Knox,
Burt Knox, C W Leckie, W T Mont-
gomery, E T Montgomery, Geo T Nib-
lock, N F Gwings, D J Page, A R
Reece, Mrs M C Ricket, J A Reid, H
Reid, Jas Roid, J L Shepherd, N C
Summers, P B Summers, P W Swann,
Mrs M A Turner, J C Turner.
Doolie.—J B Atwell, J W Ballard, D
H Brantly, H A Brawley, T O Braw-
ley, T S Byers, John Collins, Mrs E E
Cornelius, C M Cornelius, J H Corne-
lius, J B Cornelius, J S Deaton, J S

Fisher, D F Fisher, R A Harwell, F O Henson, M D Hobbs, W L Kennedy, Jas Mayhew, T F McRary, S F Parker, R C Plyler, G L Rankin, J A Sherrill, M L White.

Dunlap.—J A Gray, T P Gillespie, J A Haynes.

Eagle Mills—S Angle, G A Balty, John Barnard, James A Barnard, Lee Carson, P B Kennedy, J B Patterson, Jno Revis, J E Stimpson, Z R Thorpe, D D Tally.

Elmwood—E E Arey, B E Arey, W F Bailey, J F Beard, W S Clendening, J D Click, W W Click, T J Conger, R T Cowan, H L Fleming, J J Gilbert, J A Gunn, W W Hair, W Y Hair, H S Hair, E Hair, W H Honeycutt, J M Long, B F Phifer, G F Shepherd, Eli Sills, M O Steele, B T Steele.

Eupeptic Springs—W M Goforth, J W Greenwood, John Myers, A Rhyne, Robt Rhyne, D C Rhyne, S T White.

Evelin—B F Barker, E F Cass, Levi Dacons, Thalons Dacons, Alex Davis, R B Edwards, P C Fletcher, C C Fletcher, J C Fletcher, J W Holland, I C Holland, Jos Kemp, William Marlow, J F McLain, M F Privett, Wesley Redman, A Redman, R D Redman, H C Redman, G W Redman, J N Roupard, W H Shoemaker, J L Shoemaker, J W Williams, J P Williams, G W Williams, Alex Williams, S A Williams, L S Williams, T S Williams, O G Williams, J D Williams, M E Williams, H F Williams, E C Williams, M O Williams, R D Williams, J W Younger.

Fancy Hill—J N Dellinger, W R Ervin, R D Ervin, R W Gibson, W B Gibson, G E, Harris, F Hedrick, R M Lewis, A E McLelland, W J McLelland, M J McLelland, S C Millen, L F Stevenson, Mrs T C Stevenson, Wm Stikeleather, J G Whitesides.

Granite Hill—J A Allison, George Bogar, J L Brady, D S Chandler, Henry Cloaninger, T M Cook, H W Davis, A A Gabriel, W P Gabriel, F M Gant, J W A Kerr, J A Mills, W M Mills, Miss M L Mills, J W Mills, A R Moore, J R Moore, R D Moore, H A Neill, T B Neill, J D Oliphant, Wm Overcash, W A Overcash, John Owens, L C Perry, D A Perry, J W Poteat, R A Ramsey, Wm Rea, G H Upright.

Harmony—T R Albea, J A Feimister, A B F Gaither, W L Gaither, A F Gaither, Martin Gaither, Wiley Gaither, S A Hayes, D P Heath, Milburn Heath, S T Heath, Z M Heath, C C Holland, R Q Holmes, E C Holmes, O N Holmes, J M Holmes, J L Padgett,

J L Parris, J T Tharp, F G Tharp, J E Tharp.

Houstonville—J L Cain, Mrs M C Dalton, Milton Ellis, P B Kennedy, Dr S W Little, E H Powell, J W Reavis, E W Shaw, Amos Wright.

Jennings' Mills—J W Bowlin, Sanford Crater, J J Crater, D I Hegler, J C Holland, P J Holland, J R Huie, T L Jennings, T L Jurney, J E Jurney, P W Jurney, N J Jurney, R Lowe, Jas Mitchell, E Mitchell, S Mullis, J Myers, L C Myers, W C Privett, Jacob Privett, A A Rash, John Rash, Thos Templeton, W G Templeton, S S Templeton, M Templeton, T M Walker, D F Weisner, S A White, F White, D J White, Thomas Wooten, C C York.

Longford—A N Allison, W L Allison, Mrs J E Brown, C H Brown, W S Brown, J W Clark, A P Clark, Mrs E C Clark, T A Kerr, J C Setzer, H P Sherrill, T S Shelton, Mrs J S Troutman.

Mayhew—Miss Jane Alley, J B Atwell, J A Alexander, W A Cashion, G A Hager, A A Holtzhouser, J B Mayhew, R F Mayhew, J W Mayhew, E W Mayhew, J J Mayhew, W A Mayhew, H T Mayhew, Oscar Turleyfill.

McCurdy—Jere Bowles, Thos Brotherton, Ned Graham, R M Grant, N F Harkness, C A Lockey, Andrew Myers, W C Myers.

Miller—D A Barkley, W A Caldwell, J S Johnston, J H Johnston, P A Kelly, A A Kelly, J H Kelly, E C Miller, Bruce Thornburg, J B White, E S White.

Mooresville—Mrs I R Alexander, C J Alexander, W R Allison, J B Atwell, R S Atwell, W S Ballard, T C Beaty, T F Beaty, J L Bradley, D H Brantley, J J Brawley, R F Brawley, Mrs N E Brawley, J V Brawley, D C Brawley, R S Brawley, J S G Brown, J McBrown, J H Brown, J A Brown, W L Caldwell, E L Cloaninger, J H Cloaninger, A W Colston, M W Cornelius, J H Cornelius, W N Creswell, J C Deaton, J M Eudy, Henry Eudy, J C Gray, D J Gray, J A Harris, Isaac Harris, J L Harris, S B Harris, C A Johnston, J A Jones, J A Kennerly, L L Kennerly, Samuel Kerr, Mrs M C Kerr, Noah Ketchie, G L Kistler, R M Kistler, D W Lawrence, R W Lawrence, S A Lawrence, James Linker, G N Lipe, E S Lipe, J R McCorkle, D L McKey, R W McKey, W A McLean, W B McLean, C K McNeely, E M McNeely, W J McNeely, J R McNeely, R H McNeely, Mrs J E McPherson, J V Melchor, Mrs N J Mellon, J P Mills, R

L Moore, J C Neel, Mrs M M Overcash, J P Patterson, A D Plyler, M E Ramsey, S C Rankin, J F Rodgers, W A Sloop, T N Steele, J A Steele, B F Sumrow, J T Templeton, J A Templeton. R S Templeton. W L Turner J C Wallace, J B Wallace, F H Wallace, W Willaford, T J Williams, B F Young.

Mount Mourne—Mrs M B Alexander, D N Alexander, Bell Bros, J A Black, T J Caldwell, J F Caldwell, H F Caldwell, A F Cathey, T G Christie, H C Davidson, R A Duckworth, J F Irvin, R M Evans, Jack Gillespie, J W Gudger, A L Hobbs, Dr G J Houston, J E Knox, S A McConnell, S F McRary, S W Morrow. John Morrow, W B Mott, H Y Mott, W A Potts, J M Potts, J H Reid, W L Regan, J A Sherrill, S L Sherrill, J M Shook. J M Templeton, W T Thompson, J S Thompson, M W White.

New Hope—N I Jolly, D L McHargue, E L C McHargue, J W McHargue, W A Millsaps, R M Myers, J M Shaven, J G Weatherman.

New Stirling—A L Alexander, Peter Beaver, Mrs Mary S Bost, D O Bost. W R Bradford, N L Bradford, Milas Brady, D J Brawley, J C Brown, J A Deal, David Deal, G H Deal, M D Fink, E L Freeze, E D Fry, J H Fry, R H Gray, M L Hall, Henry Harris, R N W Hart, Jacob Hefner, I A Johnson, J E McFarland, J A McFarland, David Mock, R W Moose, D H Moose, James Morrison. J M Morrison, R A O Morrison, A F Morrison, H G Morrison, R M Morrow, J A Morrow, J A Pope, R P Pope, W F Pressly, H B Reece, C P Roseman, R P Scroggs, J B Sherrill, M W Shook, C A Shook. M L Shook, A M Smith, A T Smith, Peter Smith. R W Stevenson. H C Summers, J M Sumpter, W T Watt, A M White, J H Yount, F W Yount.

Nicholson's Mills—T W Johnson, M L Nicholson.

Oak Forest—J R Abernethy, T B Adkins, J F Dotson, H M Foust, G W Gay, J K Gay, C C Gay, J F Houpe, J A Houpe, P R Houpe, H M Hughey, W C Jones, E T Montgomery, W A Murdock, A C Robinson, J W Stevenson.

Olin—W H Barnesley, N V Cowan, J M Davis, A A Dobbins, H A Femister, Q D Femister. Mrs Eliza Femister, T M Femister, A C Femister, S A Fowler, H L Gill, D A Harmon, J F Holland, T S Holland, J M Jurney, F P Martin, Isaac Pope, Mrs F E Redman, R R Reid, J J Robertson, J S Sharpe, J C Siceloff, N J Summers, J H Tattum,

T W Tomlin, H W Tomlin, A C Tomlin, J H Vanstory, M G Vanstory, Mrs M O Walker.

Pressly—Miss M C Boyd, G A Brown, J F Burgess, Mrs M S Douglass, Mrs F A Femister, R W H Femister, R Q Frery. J R Guy, P L Guy, J O Guy, Amos Guy, N L Lewis, J F Moore, J W Moore, Samuel Moore, A B Moore, J H Morrison, J A Morrison, Mrs C Morrison, J T Morrison, J Sid Morrison, J C Morrison, H L Morrison.

River Hill—C W Campbell, Milas Campbell, T B Campbell. Lewis Campbell, Mrs M Elam, C T Elam, Mrs M E Gaither, T W Gibson, O Henly, Casper Kinder, E Nichols, J F Nichols, J K Reid, J W Rives, R J Stroud, C C Stroud, J B Stroud, G P Stroud, W S Turner, Mrs R Ward.

Rock Cut—Levi Bost, Chalmers Bost, Mrs R S Clark, J A Ingram, J G Ingram, B Ingram, R M Ingram, Mike Josey, S W Josey, J S Norris, W H Norris, F M Oswalt, Peter Oswalt, R C Plott, S R Rimmer.

Scotts—E C Browning, R R Combs, R B Combs, D E Douglass, W M Fleming, J O Guy, Amos Guy, J R Guy, G W Harris, J S Moore, S Moore, W P Morrison H L Morrison, J H Morrison, John Sloan.

Settle—J C Fletcher, E W Joiner, J C Joiner, J H Joiner, H C Joiner, G W Smith, E E Smith, J M Smith, W H Smith, Sanford Steelman.

Snow Creek—Dr R T Campbell, Jas Clark, W H Cowan, Mrs M Cowles, R B Dobson, Mrs J A Foote, J E King, King, Mrs D J King, J T Perry, T P Summers, R H Summers, W F Wasson, G W Weber, D B White.

Statesville.—J F Armfield, P I Ayers, A P Barkley, T Scott Barkley, A P Barron, W M Blackwelder, H A Bost, Jacob Bostian, J P Bradley, P C Carlton, P B Chambers, Mrs Lizzie Cornelius, J H Cornelius, H C Cowles, J M Crawford, H M C Davidson, Mrs Esther Davidson, R Q Davidson, J A Davidson, W R Day, W M Dulin, J F Eagle, W A Eliason, J S Fleming, H H Freeze, J S Fry, W M Gibson, W H H Gregory, W F Hall, sr, A A Hampton, Miss M M Harris, J A Hartness, J M Hoke, W W Houpe, J R Houpe, F W Houpe, D M Howard, R B Joyner, A D Kestler, J C Kimball, J A King, J C Lentz, J A Lippard, I S Lippard, W H Lippard, Henry Lippard, J M Lippard, M Litaker, F L Lofland, Dr J F Long, E A McLaughlin, J L McLelland, J A Milligan, W A Moore, T F Morris, J S Morrison. M E Morrison, Lee Morrow. Dr J J Mott, A P Murdock, W M Mur-

IREDELL COUNTY.

dock, T A Murdock, S L Nicholson, J
J Nicholson, E B Nicholson, W W
Nicholson, Mrs Ellen Parker, W M
Ramsey, W W Redman, Jere Richard-
son, A J Rominger, R M Rumple, G G
Rumple, W E Setzer, J M Sharpe, A C
Sharpe, Sharpe Bros, S A Sharpe, W
C Sowers, J A D Stephenson, Steven-
son Bros, J H Stevenson, Miss L A
Stikeleather, J C Sullivan, J J Sulli-
van, R B Talley, J D Troutman, A C
Troutman, J L Troutman, A Turner, T
W Vickery, W J Vickery, J W Vickery,
I G Warren, J S Watts. Wetts Bros, J
A White, M A White, M W White, O
A Woods, F F Wooten, W T Wooten.

Sigma—W B Brandon, T N Holland,
E P Lazenby, R G W Lazenby, D O
Lazenby, S O Lazenby.

Stophel—A L Barringer, M L Bar-
ringer, P A Barringer. J A Galligher,
D M Haithcox, C W Hoover, T M
Hoover, Robt Lipe, J C Plyler, S H
Plyler, Hugh Plyler, Wm Winecoff.

Sweet Home—Jesse Barkley, A D
Goodin, B G Goodin, S S Ham, E L
Harmon, W F Harmon, J W Harmon,
P W Harmon, Richard Hendren, A A
Hines, W W Johnson, W C Johnson,
J B King, J A Lackey, K A Marshall,
G W Martin, J W McLelland, W A
McLelland, J O Moore, W P Morton,
A P Sharpe, F W Sharpe, Jere Sloan,
W A Summers, Mrs S E Wilson.

Troutman's—A J Aldredge, J W
Arthurs, J F Arthurs, S A Campbell,
John Cavin, John Y Cavin, J D Col-
lins, J C Collins, Henry Collins, J D

IREDELL COUNTY.

Cook, A L Darr, J T Eudy, W H
Evans, D Hartline, P Hartline, D R
Howard, J F Kerr, C Kestler, F Kyles,
J P Lawson, T B Lemly, R R Leonard,
Peter Lippard, J M Lippard, Jr, R W
Mills, A A Murdock, F K Ostwalt, T A
Ostwalt, J F Ostwalt, J M Patterson,
T L Patterson, J A Rimmer, A Rim-
mer, J W Rimmer, Jas Scroggs, A H
Setzer, A D Troutman, H M Trout-
man, R L Troutman, J J Waugh.

Turnersburg—Mrs L Bailey, J W
Codie, J M Codie, J M Godby, Wm
Green, R P Holmes, J L Lazenby, D O
Lazenby, P R Lazenby, M K Steele, T
M Stikeleather, D H Stimpson, Mrs R L
Stimpson, L T Stimpson, Mrs L Thom-
as, Leander Thorpe, R L Tomlin, W L
Tomlin, A R Tomlinson, Wm Turner.

Vance—M P Beard, L A Beaver, M N
Beaver, H A Beaver, Wm Knox, P M
Little, T J Murdock, W W Turner, J C
Turner, D L Webb.

Watt—N P Watt.

Waugh—J Q Alexander, J A Elliott,
J D Elliott, J N Hoke, J F McLean, F
M Miller, R R Patterson, W A Rhyne,
T A Stewart, H B Stewart, T J Stewart,
W I Warren.

Weisner—S C Crater, John Current,
P W Eagle, W S Eagle, D F Edison,
R W Holland, R S Lowrence, L W
Pierce, J P Shoemaker.

Williamsburg—G A Baity, J L Bar-
nard, J E Colvert, A A Colvert, L H
Fraley, J E Fraley, D F Missick, W F
Parks, John L Parris, W D Thorpe,
F A Trivitte.

Trenton High School,

TRENTON, N. C.

W. H. RHODES, Principal.

Miss SALLIE KINNEY,
Music Teacher.

Mrs. W. H. RHODES,
Assistant.

JACKSON COUNTY.

AREA, 290 SQUARE MILES.

POPULATION, 9,183; White 8,665; Colored 518.

JACKSON COUNTY was formed in 1850, from Haywood and Macon counties, and organized in 1852. It was named in honor of Gen. Andrew Jackson.

WEBSTER, the county seat, is situated 326 miles west of Raleigh, and has a population of 267.

Surface—A beautiful and rich mountainous country, watered by the Tuckaseegee and Oconeeluftee rivers, which run through the central part of the county, forming one of the finest valleys of the west.

Staples—Corn, wheat, oats, buck wheat, hay, Irish potatoes and medicinal herbs.

Fruits—Apples, peaches, pears, cherries, melons and a great variety of the small fruits.

Timbers — Oak, chestnut, poplar, black walnut, maple, dogwood, white pine, holly and laurel.

TOWNS AND POST OFFICES.

	POP.		POP.
Addie,	20	Fernhurst,	50
Balsam,	50	Georgetown,	20
Barker,	25	Glenville,	20
Bessie,	28	Harris' Mine,	100
Beta,	25	Norton,	15
Big Ridge,	25	Oscar,	25
Big Spring,	40	Painter,	30
Cashier's,	45	Quallatown,	75
Cathey,	35	Sapphire,	30
Cowarts,	40	Scott's Creek,	50
Cullowhee,	40	Speedwell,	40
Dillsboro,	100	Sylva,	35
East La Porte,	75	Tuckaseegee,	20
Effie,	35	Webster (c h),	267
Erastus,	25	Whiteside Cove,	50
Fall Cliff,	20	Wilmot,	25
Fidelity,	60	Wolf Mountain,	25

COUNTY OFFICERS.

Clerk Superior Court—H C Cowan.
Commissioners—S H Bryson.
Register of Deeds—J R Long.
Sheriff—J E McLain.
Solicitor 12th District—Geo A Jones.
Treasurer—A V P Bryson.
County Examiner—John Wilson.

COURTS.

Seventh Monday after the first Monday in March and third Monday after the first Monday in September.

TOWNSHIPS AND MAGISTRATES.

Barker's Creek—J B Raby, S C Allison, W P Jones, W W Jones, Thomas Brown, Joseph Bumgarner, R Nations, C Gibson, J Turpin (Barker).

Canada—H R Brown, A J Parker, H F Beard, J A Galloway, John Alexander, Luther Owens, John H Mathis, J C Wood (Webster).

Cany Fork—Robert Coward, J E Norton, W A Brown, Wiley Henson, H H Wood, J H Painter, Jacob Wood, M Parker, E M Coward, Brag Hooper (Webster).

Cashier's Valley—L M Dillard, W H C Rice, T D Alley, D M Wike, J Rochester, John Truit, H Heaton, C Long, M Hooper (Cashier's).

Cullowhee—W C Norton, D D Bavies, J T Wike, Z V Watson, Jos Buchanan, John Long, Sr, E M Painter (Cullowhee).

Dillsboro—C W McDade, J J Mason, J W Sherrill, Frank Garratt, H R Snider, Jos Queen, R P Potts, S P Conner (Dillsboro).

Hamburg—J P Stewart, John Collins, L A Wilson, E Watson, T L Jameson, E C Heddin, Hosea Morrison, Wm Henderson, Newton Jennings (Webster).

Mountain—J S Leapard, J J Moss, R H Stewart, Geo B Bumgarner, T V Henderson, B M Peck; W F Moody, W J Henderson.

Quallatown—C A Bird, S W Cooper, A M Bennett, C C Ashe, R L Hyatt, Stephen Byck, J M Whorley, Wm B Sherrell, J H Battle, M Zachary (Webster).

Riser—Alford Galloway, J T Jackson, M M Wike, John Cope, Lambert Hooper, Hit Wike, H Queen, H Moses, J A Hooper, John Moody (Webster).

Savannah—J C Reed, W C Tathum, Wm Sutton, W C Buchanan, J J Deitz, H C Cannon, E C Ashe, John Cagle, N Cole, Jasper Buchanan, Charlie Buchanan (Webster).

Scott's Creek—S R Cook, Robt Fisher, J T Carson, J M Sutton, Joseph Hoyle, R G Snider, S H Queen, L Snider, J M Queen, Andrew Henson (Scott's Creek).

Sylva—Walton Allen, J W Dendbiss, M Buchanan, A M Parker, J B Enesby, J R Love, J R Crofford, R A Painter (Sylva).

Webster—Wm Rhineheart, J A Wild, A V P Bryson, W D Frizzell, E H Cagle, A J Long, Jno Stillwell, Jr, P Brindle, W P Allman, Jule Snider (Webster).

CHURCHES.

Names, Post Offices and Denom.

BAPTIST.

Cullowhee—Painter.
Dillsboro—Dillsboro.
East Fork—Barker.
Hamburg—Glenville.
John's Creek—Cowarts.
Oscar Hill—Balsam.
Saul's Creek—Cathey.
Savannah—Barker.
Scott's Creek—Addie.
Shoul Creek—Qualler.
Sylva—Sylva.
Webster—Webster.
Zion Hill—Barker.

METHODIST.

Cashiers—Cashiers.
Cullowhee—Painter.
Dillsboro—Dillsboro.
Qualler—Qualler.
Sylva—Sylva
Webster—Webster.

HOTELS AND BOARDING HOUSES.

Kinds, Post Offices and Proprietors.

Boarding, Webster, Mrs L C Hall.
Boarding, Cashiers, Geo M Cole.
Boarding. Cashiers, Riley Hooper.
Forest Hill, Cullowhee, D D Daves.
Glen Hotel, Glenville, E C Hedden.
Hotel, Sylva, Mrs Steadman.
Hotel, Dillsboro, Frank Jarrett.
Mountain View, Webster, F H Leatherwood.
Mt Buta, Dillsboro, W A Dills.

LAWYERS.

Names and Post Offices.

Cowan, C C, Webster.
Thompson, E R, Sylva.
Hooper, J J, Webster.
Moore, W E, Webster.

MANUFACTORIES.

Kinds, Post Offices and Proprietors.

Blacksmithing and wheelwrighting. Sylva, Jeff Rhoe.
Blacksmithing and wheelwrighting, Dillsboro, E Allen.
Blacksmithing and wheelwrighting, Barker, E C Ash.

Blacksmithing and wheelwrighting, Webster, J B Witt.
Building and contracting, Painter, J Painter.
Building and contracting, Webster, Allen Parris.
Building and contracting, Dillsboro, L Bumgarmer.
Building and contracting, Dillsboro, Wilson Sutton.
Building and contracting, Dillsboro, S Early.
Building and contracting, Webster, Lawrence Cowan.
Building and contracting, Webster, Joseph Cowan.
Building and contracting, Harris' Mines, W A Stillwell.
Building and contracting, Webster, W P Allen.
Building and contracting, Webster, James Cowan.
Building and contracting, Webster, J F Stillwell.
Building and contracting, Big Spring, W P Jones.
Corundum wheels, Sylva, Hofman & Co
Kaolin clay, Equitable Mfg Co, Sylva, Brocker & Co.
Kaolin clay, Carolina Clay Co, Dillsboro, C J Harris, pres.
Leather, Webster, Jas Marshall.
Locust Pine, Equitable Mfg Co, Dillsboro, C J Harris, pres.
Lumber, Blue Ridge, Lumber Co, Dillsboro.
Saddles and harness, Barker, M W Bryson.
Saddles and harness, Webster, Henry McKee.
Saddles and harness, Webster, A V P Bryson.

MERCHANTS AND TRADESMEN.

Names, Post Offices, Lines of Business.

ADDIE.	
Clayton, W A,	G S
BARKER.	
Ashe, D H,	G S
BETA.	
Allen, L W,	G S
CASHIER'S.	
Adams & Co,	G S
Cole, Geo M,	G S
Reese, Miss Alma,	G S
COWART.	
Coward, E M & E G,	G S
Coward, L,	G S
DILLSBORO.	
Chandler, Dr J M,	Drugs
Cunningham, D C & E K,	Livery

JACKSON COUNTY.

Enloe & Chase, G S
Hunnicot & Co, Grocers
Jarrett, R H & Sons, G S
Jarrett Co, The Frank, G S
Sherrill, J W, Gro
Spoke, G W, Gro
Watkins, J C, C S

EAST LA PORTE.

Davis, J, G S

GLENVILLE.

Adams & Co, G S
Brown, H A, G S
Fowler, W A, G S

HARRIS' MINES.

Harris, C J, G S

PAINTER.

Long, J B & J R, G S
Smith & Long, G S

QUALLATOWN.

Moody & Burchfield, G S

SAPPHIRE.

Jacobs, A S, C S

SCOTT'S CREEK.

Knight, D T & M L, G S

SPEEDWELL.

Hooper, Lee, G S

SYLVA.

Baum, A E, Marble
Devilbiss, J W, Livery
Dills, A B, G S
McKee & Cowan, G S
Potts, A B, G S
Rigdon, J M, G S

TUCKASEEGEE.

Moses, H & Co, G S

WEBSTER.

Allison, T B, G S
Hooker, Jos J, Loan and Real Est
Leatherwoop, Mrs A C, G S
Long & Brown, G S
Long & Brown, Painters

WILMOT.

Cooper, S W, G S
Miller & Boone, G S

MINES.

Kinds, Post Offices and Proprietors.

Corundum, Barker, W H Buchanan.
Corundum, Cullowhee, Hofman, Hecker & Co.
Corundum, Sylva, Aluminum Copper Co.
Cullowhee Copper, Cullowhee, D D Davis & Co.
Georgetown Gold, Cashiers, Sappire Valley Co.
Jackson Kaoline, Sylva, J H Wooff.

JACKSON COUNTY.

Kaolin, Sylva, Equitable Mfg Co.
Kaolin, Harris Mines, C J Harris, prop.
Mica, Harris Hines, Geo Springs, jr.
Mica, Webster, E Bowers & Co.
Sugarloaf copper, Cullowhee, D D Davis & Co.
Webster Mica, Webster, Hofman & Co.
Webster Kaoline, Webster, Shuler & Co.

MILLS.

Kinds, Post Offices and Proprietors.

Flour and corn, Glenville, A Bryson.
Flour and corn. East La Porte, C B Zachary.
Flour and flour, Painter, O Painter & Son.
Flour and corn. Barker, E C Ashe.
Flour and corn, Qualla, S Enloe.
Flour and corn, Addie, Jesse Jones.
Flour and corn, Beta, L W Allen.
Flour and corn, Dillsboro, H R Snider.
Flour and corn, Webster, Jas Cowan & Co.
Saw, Speedwell, John Holder.
Saw, Tuckasegee, A J Parker.
Saw, Sylva, T C Bryson & Son.
Saw, Webster, Joseph Cowan.

PHYSICIANS.

Names and Post Offices.

Bennett, A M, Quallatown.
Candler, J M, Dillsboro.
Nicholson, J J, East La Porte.
Might, ——, Sylva.
Queen, W A, Fidelity.
Self. Wm, Webster.
Siler, F L, Dillsboro.
Tompkins, W F, Webster.
Woolfe, J H, Sylva.

SCHOOLS.

Names, Post Offices, and Principals.

High School, Cullowhee, R L Madison.
Normal School, Cullowhee, B B Brown
Normal High School, Glenville.
Public schools: white 37; colored 3.

TEACHERS.

Names and Post Offices.

Brown, B B, Painter.
Madison, R L, Painter.
Rogers, Miss Fannie, Webster.
Smith, Miss Ida, Painter.
Wike, D, Georgetown.
Wilson, John, Speedwell.

JACKSON COUNTY.

LOCAL CORPORATIONS.

East La Porte Lodge, No 385, A F and A M, East La Porte.

Enneker Lodge, No 268, A F and A M, Webster.

Dillsboro Lodge, No —, A F and A M, Dillsboro.

NEWSPAPERS.

The Herald, Webster; W C Tompkins, editor.

Tuckaseegee Democrat, Sylva; F A and Nellie P Lusk, eds and props.

FARMERS.

Names and Post Offices.

Big Spring—S C Allison, Jesse Brown, Wm Bumgarner, Lane Gunter, John Natrons, David Turpin, A H Ward.

Cashier's—George Hawkins, W M Hooper, E F Bell, W Lusk, D M Wike, T H Zachary.

Cowarts—Robert Coward, James Coward, G W Hawkins, J N Hunlee.

Cullowhee—D Bryson, D Coward, T A Cox, D D Davis, Lee Hooper, Wm Norton, David Rogers, Wm Wilson.

East LaPorte—Jarvan Davis, Henry Jackson, John Moody, Ed Norton, J T Wike, M M Wike, Lee Wike.

Glenville—R A Enloe, W A Fowler, A Gribble, John Henderson, T W Jamison, T S Jamison, T S Monteith, A T Moody, W R Owen, E Watson, Alfred Watson, Thomas Wilson.

Sylva—C W Allen, J D Allen, D Z Dillard, B F Dillard, R W Fisher, H P Holland, J M Love, R O Phillips, W H Rhoe, B H Woodfin.

Tuckaseegee—L C Hooper, D W Middleton, Hosea Mose, D T Shelton.

Webster—W P Alman, Jas Cowan, E P Davis, A J Long, sr, C C Lowe, W W Rheinhart, D Snider.

Wilmot—D G Bigham, W P Jones, Virgil King, H Moody, J M Varley.

JOHNSTON COUNTY.

AREA 670 SQUARE MILES.

POPULATION: 27,211; White 19,889, Colored 7,322.

JOHNSTON COUNTY was formed in 1746, from Craven county, and named in honor of Gabriel Johnston, who was Royal Governor at that time.

SMITHFIELD, the county-seat, is situated on Neuse river, at the terminus of the Midland N C R R, twenty-five miles southeast of Raleigh, and has a population of 950.

Surface—Level, sandy loam, generally good, and much of it very productive when well drained.

Staples—Cotton, corn, sweet potatoes, chufas, wheat, rye, oats and peanuts. This is a fine cotton county. Naval stores are yet produced, but not so largely as formerly.

Fruits—Apples, peaches, scuppernong and other grapes, melons, pears and nearly all the small fruits common to this climate.

Timbers—Oak, long-leaf pine, hickory, maple and gum and ash.

TOWNS AND POST OFFICES.

	POP.		POP.
Abell's,	40	Itiner,	30
Archer,	40	Kenly,	60
Atfa,	25	Leachburg,	175
Bagley,	30	Lunsford,	50
Banner,	40	Micro,	25
Benson,	400	Overshot,	50
Bentonville,	95	Penny,	35
Bismark,	40	Pine Level,	300
Candills,	25	Polenta,	90
Clayton,	675	Pratt,	40
Earpsborough,	80	Preston,	—
Elevation,	200	Princeton,	595
Emit,	25	Ramon,	50
Ezra,	40	Rome,	60
Four Oaks,	40	Selah,	45
Gift,	20	Selma,	375
Glenmore,	40	Smithfield,	950
Glenwood,	40	Spilona,	40
Hare's Store,	20	Stephenson,	—
Harper's,	35	Wilson's Mills,	200

COUNTY OFFICERS.

Clerk Superior Court—W S Stevens.
Commissioners—P H Dupree, chm; L P Creech, J R Barnes, J J Young, J T Whitington.
Coroner—Dr J D T Williams.
Register of Deeds—Allen R Smith.
Sheriff—J T Ellington.
Solicitor Fourth District—E W Pou.

Standard Keeper—Isaac W Grice.
Surveyor—F B McKinney.
Treasurer—T R Hood.
County Attorney—L R Waddell.
County Supt of Health—R J Noble.
County Examiner—Ira T Turlington.

COURTS.

Superior Court meets second Monday in March, last Monday in August, and the tenth Monday after the first Monday in September.

TOWN OFFICERS.

CLAYTON—*Mayor*, N Y Gulley; *Commissioners*, R B Whitly, J E Page, A Julian Barbour; *Clerk*, V B Tomlinson; *Chief of Police*, D L Barbour.

SELMA—*Mayor*, N E Edgerton; *Clerk*, W H Hare; *Constable*, J A Hinnant; *Commissioners*, T H Whitly, J W Futrell, Chas Talton, R J Noble.

SMITHFIELD—*Mayor*, Seth Woodall; *Commissioners* J A Morgan, H L Graves, C L Eason, J L Davis, J T Avera, F J Williams, W H Brown (col), R J Noble (col); *Chief of Police*, J C Bingham.

TOWNSHIPS AND MAGISTRATES.

Banner—D M Ivey, I J Smith, N H Lucas, E H Woodall, N T Barefoot, N T Ryals, Jo M McLamb, E J D Boykin, E L Hall (Benson).

Bentonville—Robt Strickland, Leonidas Eason, Rufus Sanders (Glenmore), R B Ezell (Bizzell's), J A Cole, H C Williams, J M Beasley, G H Toler (Bentonville).

Beulah—H H Richardson, E G Barnes, Ransom Hoyles, J T Edgerton, G F Woodard (Kenly), J T Parker, D H Hinnant, Silas Edgerlee (Bagley).

Boon Hill—Lewis Braswell, W D Phillips, J T Capps, J D Massey, J W Snipes, W F Parrish, J T Creech, J M Oliver, J D Finlayson (Princeton).

Clayton—L F Austin, M G Gulley, J M Turley, J H Johnson, A R Duncan, Robt Stansil, J D Adams (Clayton).

Cleaveland—A M Sanders (Preston), F M Weeks, S E Creech, David M Lee (Polentee), W B Godwin, R B Leach (Leachburg).

Elevation—J H Smith, W A Lassi-

JOHNSTON COUNTY.

ter, R E Creech, McD Langdon (Spilona), J W Stephenson (Atfa), D D Medlin (Banner).

Ingrams—A O Keen, E Creech, E D Sneed, J H Adams, Phillip Lee, John Sanders, John W Oliver (Four Oaks), G W Massingill (Glenmore).

Meadow—J Q Johnson, J G Smith, D J Wood, B B Broughton, Elam Lee, T T Lee (Rome), G P M Fort (Glenwood), J J Bose (Overshot), J W Wood (Rome).

O'Neal's—W D Brown, J W Hocutt (Earpsboro), L H Boykin, J B Whitley, E Raper, A R Bailey, J E Winston, I Renfrow (Hare's Store).

Pleasant Grove—A R Stansill, Lynn B Grimes, J R Coats, R H Stephenson, Jo Stephenson, Elijah Parrish, H H Johnson (Pratt's), R A Sanders (Polenta).

Selma—C F Kirby, A M Noble, E S M ore, Thos Hinnant, P B Corbett, W H Hare (Selma), W F Gerald. Gibson Fitzgerald, D B Oliver (Pine Level).

Smithfield—Robert Sanders, Jesse Daughtery, T S Thain, G S Wilson, Z L Lemay, C A Wallace, Aden Powell, D J Wellons, Seth Woodall (Smithfield).

Wilson's Mills—T R Youngblood, G L Jones, J A Wilson, N R Mitchener (Wilson's Mills).

Wilder's—J B Reaves, C T Faison, N H Whitley, Wiley Hood, J D Jeffreys, Otis Marshburn, J W Hilliard (Archer Lodge), J W Hocutt (Earpsboro).

CHURCHES.

Names, Post Offices, Pastors and Denom.

BAPTIST.

Baptist Centre—Clayton, G N Cowan.
Blackman's Grove—Gift, W M Page.
Bethany-Hare's Store, Worley Creech.
Bethel (col.)—Clayton, C Sanders.
Carter' Chapel-Selma, Worley Creech.
Church—Four Oaks, J G Pulliam.
Church—Benson, G N Campbell.
Church—Pine Level, W M Sorrell.
Church—Princeton, J G Pulliam.
Church—Wilson's Mill, O C Horton.
Church (col.)—Clayton. A A Jones.
Church (col.)—Selma, E B Blake.
Church (col.)—Kenly, E B Blake.
Church (col.)—Benson, J J Robinson.
Church—Clayton, G N Cowan.
Church—Smithfield, J G Pulliam.
Church—Bethesda. H W Norris.
Church—Selma, J G Pulliam.
Clyde's Chapel—Shotwell, G W Coppage.
Corinth—Archer Lodge, G W Coppage.

JOHNSTON COUNTY.

Gallilee (col.)—Smithfield, U Thompson.
Lee's X-Roads (col.)—Clayton, ——— Peterson.
Live Oak—Selma, Worley Creech,
Mt Moriah—Clayton, O L Stringfield.
New Hope—Smithfield, Robert Strickland.
Oakey Grove (col.)—Smithfield, A A Jones.
Piney Grove (col.)—Clayton, T O Fuller.
Pisgah—Smithfield, J G Pulliam.
Sardis—Smithfield, J G Pulliam.
St Amanda (col.)—Lemay, H Thompson.
Shiloh—Polenta, A C Cree.
St Mary's (col)—Wilson's Mills, A A Jones.
Watson's (col)—Smithfield, J J Robinson.
White Oak—Archer Lodge, G W Coppage.

PRIM. BAPTIST.

Bethany—Pine Level, H F Peedin.
Beulah—Pine Level, H F Peedin.
Church—Smithfield, J A T Jones.
Clements—Smithfield, Lewis P Adams.
Creech's—Selma, H F Peedin.
Fellowship-Smithfield, Moore Stephenson.
Hannah's Creek—Smithfield.
Hickory Grove—Rome, — Westbrook.
Juniper—Four Oaks, J B Parker.
Rehobeth—Bismarck, Moore Stephenson.
Union—Princeton, H F Peedin.

FREE-WILL BAPTIST.

Black Creek—Smithfield.
Hopewell—Smithfield.
Little River—Princeton.
Stony Fork—Ezra.
St Mary's Grove—Bismarck, J S Ellis.
Williams' Springs (col)—Lemay.

METHODIST.

Antioch—Glenmore, J W Ashley.
Church—Selma, Solomon Pool, D D.
Church—Earpsboro, N H Guyton.
Church—Elevation, — Cain,
Church—Clayton, J M Ashley.
Church—Princeton, Sol. Pool, D D.
Church—Bentonville, J M Ashley.
Ebenezer (Wayne co)—Princeton, R A Bruton.
Elizabeth—Smithfield, J M Ashley.
Mary's Chapel— ———, R A Bruton.
Mt Zion—Smithfield, J M Ashley.
Phillip's Chapel—Princeton, R A Bruton.
Sanders' Chapel—Smithfield, R B Bruton.
Smith's Chapel—Princeton, R A Bruton.
Zion—Kenly, R A Bruton.

JOHNSTON COUNTY.

DISCIPLES OF CHRIST.

Eureka — Grantham's Store (Wayne co), J H Johnson.
Mill Creek—Harper's, J H Johnson.
Wilson's Mills—Wilson's, J J Harper.

PRESBYTERIAN.

Church—Kenly, J A McMurray.
Church—Smithfield, J A McMurray.
Oakland—Clayton, J A McMurray.

CHRISTIAN.

Church—Spilona, —— Jones.
Pleasant Hill—Smithfield, Lewis Mangum.

A. METH. EPISCOPAL.

Church (col)—Clayton, —— Roberts.
Church (col)—Smithfield, J E Haynes.
Watson (col)—Smithfield, J E Haynes.
Wesley's Chapel (col) — Smithfield, —— Roberts.

A. M. E. ZION.

Avery's Grove (col—Beulah.

MINISTERS RESIDENT.

Names, Post Offices and Denom.

BAPTIST.

Creech, Worley, Hare's Store.
Pulliam, J G, Smithfield.
Woodward, W L H, Selma.

PRIMITIVE BAPTIST.

Braddy, S H, Princeton.
Brown, Wm, Princeton.
Jones, J G T, Gully's Mills.
Parker, J B, Four Oaks.
Stephenson, Moore, Bi-marck.

FREE WILL BAPTIST.

Worley, Jas, Pine Level.

METHODIST.

Ashly. J M, Clayton.
Oglesby, G A, Selma.
Pool, Solomon, D D, Smithfield.

DISCIPLES OF CHRIST.

Harper, J J, Smithfield.
Johnson, J H, Bentonsville.

A. M. E.

Haynes, J E, Smithfield.

HOTELS AND BOARDING HOUSES.

Names, Post Offices and Proprietors.

Boarding, Clayton, Stanford Creech.
Boarding, Clayton, Dr J B Robertson.
Boarding, Princeton, Geo T Whitley.
Grice House, Smithfield, S A Grice.
Hotel de Gurley, Smithfield, J G Gurley.
Page Hotel, Selma, Mrs —— Page.
Restaurant, Smithfield, Julia George (colored).

Restaurant, Clayton, James Hilliard.
Winston House, Selma, Mrs G A Tuck.

LAWYERS.

Names and Post Offices.

Abell, E S (Waddell & Abell), Smithfield
Edgerton, C W, Kenly.
Massey, P T, Smithfield.
Morgan, J M (Wellons & Morgan), Smithfield.
Narron, J A, Smithfield.
Pou (J H) & Pou (E W), Smithfield.
Waddell, L R (Waddell & Abell), Smithfield.
Wellons (J A) & Morgan (J M) Smithfield.

MANUFACTORIES.

Kinds, Post Offices and Proprietors.

Blacksmithing and wheelwrighting, Smithfield, M Avera (col).
Blacksmithing and wheelwrighting, Smithfield, S B Brooks (col).
Blacksmithing and wheelwrighting, Clayton. J E Page.
Blacksmithing and wheelwrighting, Pine Level, W C Little.
Blacksmithing and wheelwrighting, Elevation, J S Jones.
Blacksmithing and wheelwrighting, Hare's Store, Wm Hicks.
Blacksmithing and wheelwrighting, Selma, John Graham.
Blacksmithing and wheelwrighting, Princeton, Jesse Pearce, Sr.
Blacksmithing and wheelwrighting, Princeton, J H Howell.
Blacksmithing and wheelwrighting, Princeton, John Bucker.
Blacksmithing, Clayton, W J Davis (colored).
Carriages, wagons, etc, Smithfield, Willard Woodall.
Carriages, blacksmithing and wheelwrighting, Clayton, J M Barbour.
Contracting and building, Archer Lodge, Wall & Mitchell.
Contracting and building, Pine Level, R W Crumpler.
Contracting and building, Hare's Store, G Manning.
Contracting and building, Princeton, D H Howell.
Contracting and building, Pine Level. B Crocker.
Contracting and building, Four Oaks, K L Barbour.
Contracting and building, Smithfield, H M Barnes.
Distillery (turpentine), Pine Level, W B Oliver.
Patent Chill Cure, etc, Selma, M V Green.

JOHNSTON COUNTY.

JOHNSTON COUNTY.

Sash, doors and blinds, Wilson's Mills,
   J H Wilson & Co.
Shoemaking, Clayton, I W Johnson.
Shoemaker and grocer, Clayton, D H
   Williams.
Steam planing mill, Selma, Lynn Bros.
Turpentine, Clayton, Alford & Thomas.
Undertaking, Clayton, J E Page.

MERCHANTS AND TRADESMEN.

Names, Post Offices and Lines of Business.

ARCHER.
Barnes, E C,   G S
Richardson, C W,   G S

ATFA.
Barbour, G W,   G S
Cannady, J H,   G S
Stephenson, L G,   G S

BENSON.
Allen, Seth, & Bro,   G S
Anderson, Mrs C A,   G S
Barnes, C C,   G S
Benson, J W,   Druggist
Bingham, Miss Mary,   Millinery
Braddy, R B,   G S
Cavenaugh, Hall & Co,   G S
Hudson & Co,   G S
Johnson, C T,   G S
Jones, G F,   G S
Lucas, Mrs D W,   Millinery
Marshburn, T J, & Co,   G S
Parks, N W,   G S
Rankin, A E, & Co,   G S
Ryals, C C,   G S
Weekes, W M,   G S
Wood, M, & J W,   G S
Woodall, E H,   G S
Woodall, Alice L,   Millinery
Woodall, Phœbe,   G S

BENTONSVILLE.
Beasly, J M,   G S
Stevens, Julius,   G S

BIZZELL'S.
Bizzell, James,   G S

CLAYTON.
Alford & Thomas,   G S
Austin, Fletcher,   G S
Barnes, H L,   G S
Barnes, W A,   G S
Barbour, J G & Son,   G S
Davis, S G,   G S
Ferrall, T L,   G S
Green, J R,   G S
Horne, A,   G S
McCullers, W H, sr, & Sons,   G S
McCullers, D O,   Druggist
Mitchell, H W,   G S
O'Neil, E L,   G S
Oxford & Thomas,   G S
Page, J E,   Undertaker
Smith, S T,   G S

Stephenson, S T,   G S
Williams, D H,   G S
Yelvington, B H,   G S

EARPSBORO.
Creech, J W,   G S
Whitley, R B,   G S

EVELATION.
Dixon, A,   G S

EMIT.
Griswold, S,   G S

FOUR OAKS.
Adams, C R & Co,   G S
Cole, J T,   G S
Creech, Mrs E & Co,   G S
Denson, J E,   G S
Johnson, Julius,   G S
Keen, J W,   G S
Lassiter, Mrs R I,   G S
Sanders, J W,   G S
Young, Dr S R,   Druggist

JEROME.
Ward, P G & Co,   G S

KENLY.
Boykin, J T,   G S
Davis Bros,   G S
Edgerton, J T,   G S
Edgerton, G G & Son,   G S
Hales, G H & Co,   G S
Hinnant, J W & Co,   G S
Joyner, S V,   G S
Morris, G M,   G S
Richardson, J S,   G S
Slocomb, A H,   Turp
Winer, B,   Dry Goods

LEACHBURG.
Barnes, Jno J,   Dry Goods
Bridges, R S,   G S
Gower, Anderson,   Prov and Tob
Holland, C H,   G S
Wood, Jesse,   G S

LEMAY.
Gowen, O,   G S
Wynn & Wynn,   G S

MICRO.
Ward, P G & Co,   G S

PENNY.
Smith, D T,   G S

PINE LEVEL.
Britt, W G,   G S
Creech, W S,   Gro and D G
Creech, K W,   G S
Crocker, B,   G S
Fields, D A,   G S
Goodwin, B,   G S
Hughes, J W,   G S
Jones, J D,   G S
Oliver, W B,   G S
Oliver, T T,   G S
Stallings, W H,   G S

JOHNSTON COUNTY.

POLENTA.

Booker, E T & Co,	G S
Yelving, J W,	G S

PRATT.

Johnson, J L,	G S

PRINCETON.

Edwards, W T & Son,	G S
Edwards, J H & Co,	G S
Finlayson, J D,	Racket Store
Jones, Frances,	G S
Ledbetter, J R,	G S
McKinnie, D E,	G S
Perry, J W,	G S
Strickland, Robt,	G S
Wallace, Mrs M J (near),	G S
Woodard, B C,	G S

ROME.

Mashburn, T J & Co,	G S
Massengill, R S,	D G and Gro

SELMA.

Barbour, C C,	Cotton Buyer
Bunn, B H (col),	Barber
Driver, W B,	Gro
Driver, W B,	G S
Edgerton, N E,	Depot Agt A C L
Edgerton & Hare,	Drugs
Etheridge, W H,	G S
Graves, D H,	Cotton Buyer
Graham, John (col),	Blacksmith
Land, J W,	W U Tel Op
Lyles, J W,	G S
Lynn & Bro,	G S
Massey, J B,	Agt S Ry
Miles, J W,	G S
Oliver & Futrell,	G S
Parker, J H,	Cotton Buyer and G S
Pate, E F,	Night Op W U Tel
Richardson, N D,	G S
Snipes, N B & Bro,	G S
Snipes, N B,	Market and Groceries
Spice J W,	W U Tel Op
Talton, Chas,	Jewelry
Whitley, T H,	G S

SMITHFIELD.

Alford, Polly,	G S
Cohen, S,	Dry Goods
Cotter, R O & Co,	G S
Duncan, W H,	Racket Store
Fuller & Lemay,	Livery Stable
Holt, E J & Co,	Hardware
Hood Bros,	Druggists
Hudson, J B,	Broker
Jones, B R,	G S
Littman, Louis,	G S
Massey, D T,	Fertilizer
Morgan, S R,	Furniture
Morgan, J A,	Undertaker and Furniture
Parham, J T,	G S
Parker, J H, jr,	G S
Peeden & Garner,	G S
Sanders, W M,	G S

JOHNSTON COUNTY.

Smith, A W (col),	G S
Watson, G H,	Fish and Oysters
Woodall, W L,	Racket Store
Woodall, S,	G S
Woodall, Willard,	G S
Yelvington, W G,	Dry Goods

SPILONA.

Lassiter, P G,	G S

WILSON'S MILLS.

Holt, John,	G S
Vinson, J W,	G S

WOODS.

Blackman, Jernigan,	Grocer

MINES.

Kinds, Post Offices and Proprietors.

Iron (near Smithfield), B A Jones.

MILLS.

Kinds, Post Offices and Proprietors.

Corn and gin, Smithfield, Dan Thomas (col).

Corn and gin, Benson, Moses Grey.

Corn and saw (steam), Smithfield, P S Heath.

Corn and saw, Wilson's Mills, J A Wilson & Co.

Corn, flour and saw, Rome, W H Smith.

Corn, flour and saw, Four Oaks, James Webb.

Corn, flour and saw, Pine Level, T T Oliver.

Corn, flour and saw, Pine Level, J D & R H Creech.

Corn, flour and saw, Benson, Adams Bros.

Corn, flour and saw, Godwin's, J G Rayner.

Corn, flour and saw, Rome, Powell Black's heirs.

Corn, flour and saw, Princeton, R H Baker.

Corn, flour and saw, Princeton, J Dixon.

Corn, flour and saw, Princeton, W A Smith's heirs.

Corn and flour, Smithfield, Mrs J W Myatt.

Corn and flour, Smithfield, Mrs E B McCullers.

Corn and flour, Clayton, Mrs B T Barbour.

Corn and flour, Hare's Store, T H Atkinson.

Corn and flour, Archer Lodge, C W Richardson.

Corn and flour, Leachburg, John R Coats.

Corn and flour, Harper's, C M Rose.

Corn, Harper's, W R Weaver's heirs.

JOHNSTON COUNTY.

Corn and flour, Pratt's, Joe Massingill.
Corn and flour, Smithfield, John R Creech.
Corn and flour, Bentonville, P H C Dupree.
Corn and flour, Rome, W H Smith.
Corn and flour, Selma, J W B Watson.
Cotton gin, Clayton, Ashley Horne.
Cotton gin, Clayton, J G Barbour & Sons.
Cottou gin, Abell's, Egerton Bros.
Flour, corn and saw, Princeton, E J Holt.
Gin, Preston, Claude Sanders.
Grist mill, Selma, James Holt.
Public-gin, Hare's Store, Aquilla Narron.
Public-gin and saw, Polenta, C Stephenson & Son.
Public-gin, saw and grist, Four Oaks, E J Holt.
Public-gin, saw and corn, Smithbfield, B R Jones.
Public gin, Benson, J W Creech.
Public-gin, Four Oaks, D W Adams.
Public-gin, Elevation. Jno R Denning.
Public gin, Spilona, Rob't G Lassiter.
Public-gin, Elevation, James Creech.
Public-gin, Leachburg, Anderson Gower.
Public-gin and saw, Leachburg, Jesse Wood.
Public gin, Smithfield, W L Johnson.
Saw, Pine Level, W B Oliver.
Steam saw, Polenta, Parrish Bros
Steam saw and gin, Gift, Sorrell Wood.
Steam saw, corn and gin, Spilona, D L Flowers.
Steam flour, corn. saw and gin, Benson, M Wood & Hudson.
Steam corn and saw, Clayton, H A McCullers.
Steam saw, Hare's Store, Thos Davis.
Steam saw, Emit, J H Glover.
Steam saw and corn, Benson, J H & H W McClarn.
Water, flour and grist, Barnes, Godwin Bros.

PHYSICIANS.

Names and Post Offices.

Booker, E N, Polenta.
Hood, G A, Kenly.
Lassiter, D B, Spilona.
McLean, R H, Benson.
Noble, R J, Selma.
Parker, George, Benson,
Roberson, G J, Smithfield.
Roberson, J B, Clayton.
Sasser, L L. Smithfield.
Seawell, F H. Earpsboro.
Strachan, J B. Princeton.
Turlington, W E, Benson.
Vick, J W, Selma.

JOHNSTON COUNTY.

Wall, E L, Bagley.
Wellons, J D T, Four Oaks.
Young, S R, Four Oaks,

SCHOOLS.

Names, Post Offices and Principals.

Academy, Benson, P D Woodall.
Eutopian Institute, Clayton, J W Williams.
High School, Glenwood, R L Hamilton.
Johnston Academy, Leachburg.
Pleasant Hill Academy, Elevation, Z V Turlington.
Pine Hill Academy, Earpsboro.
Preparatory (col), Smithfield, J W Byrd.
Preparatory (col), Clayton, Q C Mial.
Primary School, Princeton, Miss Lola McKoonce.
Primary School, Smithfield, Miss Fannie Higden.
Primary School, Smithfield, Mrs Sarah Helme.
Princeton Academy, Princeton, J H Skinner.
Selma Academy, Selma, Palmer Dalrymple.
Turlington Institute, Smithfield, Ira T Turlington, prin.
Wentworth Academy, Rome.
Public Schools—white, 90; colored, 33,

TEACHERS.

Names and Post Offices.

WHITE.

Adams, Miss Anna, Smithfield.
Adams, Miss Minnie R, Smithfield.
Atkinson, Joseph R, Selma.
Atkinson, A S J, Selma.
Atkinson, Jas R, Bagley.
Atkinson, J R, Selma.
Auston, W H, Pratt.
Austin, W B, Elevation.
Barbour, Miss Lucy A, Ezra.
Barbour, R H, Ezra.
Barbour, Alonzo, Ezra.
Barham, Miss Maie, Smithfield.
Batten, Ira, Micro.
Boykin, Ashley, Kenly.
Britt, A R. Bentonville.
Britt, Miss Annie. Bentonville.
Byrd, John W. Smithfield.
Canaday, Jas P, Benson.
Corbett, C A, Selma.
Creech, John L, Benson.
Creech, Miss Zorah, Spilona.
Creech, D T, Pine Level.
Creech, W L, Pine Level.
Creech, J W. Smithfield.
Dalrymple, Miss Annie, Selma.

JOHNSTON COUNTY.	JOHNSTON COUNTY.

Earp, H E, Selma.
Edgerton, J P, Kenly.
Eldridge, Julius, Rome.
Garner, Jesse, Selma.
Garner, Elisha, Selma.
Garner, James, Selma.
Garner, James P, Smithfield.
Garner, E A, Selma.
Hales, Ransom, Kenly.
Hollowell, Miss Dora, Bagley.
Harper, Miss Fannie Smithfield.
Helme, Miss Hollie, Smithfield.
Hocutt, J I, Earpsboro.
Hudson, T L, Glenwood.
Hudson, J E, Glenwood.
Johnson, L A, Rome.
Johnson, A C, Ezra.
Johnson, Charlie, Rome.
Johnson, P E, Rome.
Johnson, P B, Rome.
Jones, Elder J A T, Gully's Mill.
Jones, Miss Nannie T, Gully's Mill.
Lee, R E, Smithfield.
Lee, Miss Frances, Smithfield.
Lee, S P J, McKoy.
Lee, Miss Lorah, Smithfield.
Mear, T C, Clayton.
Moore, Miss Minnie H, Selma.
Mozing, J B, Selma.
Narron, Ivey, Emit.
Neighbors, Joseph W, Benson.
Oliver, Miss Lillian, Four Oaks.
Parker, J D, Benson.
Parker, D P, Benson.
Parker, John W, Smithfield.
Parker, D A, Smithfield.
Parker, Miss S Anna, Benson.
Parker, R P, Hare's Store.
Peacock, Miss Mary, Micro.
Penny, Miss Alma, Penny.
Penny, Miss Azzie, Penny.
Peterson, Miss Amelia, Smithfield.
Powell, Miss Bettie, Smithfield.
Price, Haywood, Hare's Store.
Reaves, L E, Benson.
Richardson, C E, Princeton.
Richardson, Charles, Selma.
Richardson, Nannie, Selma.
Richardson, Cora, Selma.
Rose, H L, Harper's.
Rose, Miss Annie M, Bizzell.
Row, A M, Overshot.
Sanders, W G, Smithfield.
Smith, L C, Pratt.
Smith, R W, Rome.
Smith, J W, Clayton.
Smith, Miss Mattie, Four Oaks.
Snead, E D, Four Oaks.
Stallings, Miss Maggie, Clayton.
Strickland, C B, Glenmore.
Surles, R T, Benson.
Stancill, Miss Annie, Selma.
Stancill, George, Selma.
Stancill, Alonzo, Selma.
Stancill, Miss Sarah, Lucoma.

Stancill, A C, Selma.
Stuart, C D, Benson.
Strickland, Geo B, Glenmore.
Talton, Miss Mary J, Princeton.
Typett, B W, Hare's Store.
Tuck, Miss Julia, Selma.
Turlington, Zeb V, Benson.
Underhill, Wingate, Selma.
Westbrook, C B, Blackman's Mills.
Whitley, Miss Sarah, Smithfield.
Whitley, Mis Zelphia, Smithfield.
Whitley, Miss Jennie, Archer Lodge.
Williams, J R, Clayton.
Wood, Miss Ella, Rome.
Wood, Joseph, Rome.
Woodard, Miss Sallie, Smithfield.
Woodall, ——, Preston.
Woodall, J L, Benson.
Woodall, Miss Lillian, Smithfield.
Woodall, P D, Benson.
Woodall, Miss Bessie, Benson.
Woodard, John R, Pine Level.

COLORED.

Allen, Gabrilla B, Smithfield.
Atkinson, Lucy, Smithfield.
Atkinson, Laura J, Selma.
Atkinson, Rosa B, Selma.
Beckwith, Geneva L, Smithfield.
Brown, W H, Smithfield.
Brown, Minnie, Smithfield.
Bunn, Roberta, Selma.
Byrd, J W, Smithfield.
Byrd, T B, Clayton.
Cole, H R, Harper's.
Hines, A H, Wilson's Mills.
Hines, C H, Wilson's Mills.
Hocut, J E, Heflin.
Holden, Sarah A, Smithfield.
Jones, J D, Clayton.
Linceford, Annie, Smithfield.
Lockhart, Lougenia, Selma.
Sanders, John W, Penny.
Skinner, J H, Princeton.
Smith, John E, Smithfield.
Smith, J A, Selma.
Thomas, Mary E, Smithfield.
Whitfield, Jennie G, Smithfield.
Whitly, E R, Smithfield.
White, J H, Palmer.
Williams, James L, Pine Level.
Williams, G L F, Four Forks.

LOCAL CORPORATIONS.

Archer Lodge, No 165, A F and A M,
  M, Clayton. Time of meeting, first
  Saturday, June 24th and Dec 27th.
Beulah Lodge, No 257, A F and A M,
  Pine Level. Time of meeting, Sat-
  uday before the fourth Sunday, and
  June 24th and December 27th.
Fellowship Lodge, No 84, A F and A
  M, Smithfield. Time of meeting sec-
  ond Saturday and Tuesday evenings
  of Court week. Elisha Rose, W M,

24

JOHNSTON COUNTY.

Good Templars Lodge, No. 33, Clayton. J C Ellington, W C T.

Granite Lodge, No 191, A F and A M, Clayton. Time of meeting, third Saturday.

Johnston County Medical Society, G J Robinson, pres, Smithfield; R J Noble, sec and treas, Selma.

Odd Fellows' Lodge, No —, I O O F, Clayton; N R Richardson, N G.

Olive Branch Lodge, I O O F, No 37, Smithfield; R G Noble, N G. Meets Monday evenings.

Selma Lodge, No 320, A F and A M, Selma. Time of meeting, third Friday night.

Webster Lodge, No 222, A F and A M, Elevation. Time of meeting, fourth Saturday at 10 o'clock A M.

NEWSPAPERS.

Weekly Herald, Smithfield (Dem); Beaty & Harrison, eds and props.

FARMERS.

Names and Post Offices.

Abell's.—J S Fulghum, E I Pearce, L B Richardson, J S Starling.

Archer Lodge—H H Anderson, J H Barham, W A Barnes, J W Barnes, D L Barnes, E G Barnes, J R Barnes, L O Battin, J A Battin, E A Battin, N B Battin, H A Biggs, J R Carroll, W R Carroll, R D Christman, R J Castleberry, H W Eason, E Y Eatman, C T Faison, R H Green, B D Hilliard, Wm Hilliard, H Hinnant, Jesse Hinnant, W P Hinnant, Almay Hinnant, L B Hinnant, E W Holder, W H Hocutt, sr, Caswell Hocutt, J W Hocutt, J D Jeffreys, Jas Jeffreys, J A Liles, W M Murphrey, Josiah Pulley, W E Pulley, J B Reeves, R E Richardson, W W Richardson, A H Richardson, O W Richardson, J H Robertson, W J Smith, J R Wall, N J Whittey, A T Whittey, J H Whittey, W H Whittey, R B Whittey, H H Whittey, N G Williamson, J B Woodard.

Atfa.—J D Barbour, J H Cannady, B A Coats, B P Coats, W R Coats, D L Flowers, E A Johnson, J M Langday, John Stephenson, D S Stephenson, J W Stephenson, Cornelius Stephenson.

Bagly—J E Atkins, A B Atkins, Josiah Aycock, Elias Aycock, S H Bagly, D H Bagly, Wesly Patten, G T Boyett, B Brown, Thos Brown, Henry Cockerell, J H Cockerell, G G Edgerton, Silas Edgerton, W R Edgerton, H Garner, H F Gerald, T T Godwin, Gilles Hales, Elias Hales, Hiram Hatcher,

JOHNSTON COUNTY.

Jesse Pully, Alvin Rains, J T Stancill, Windsor Watkins, Barna Woodard, Ben Woodard, J I Woodard.

Barnes' Store—L H Boykin.

Benson—J P Adams, J T Adams, J G Allen, J B Allen, W L Barber, R A Barber, J E Barber, W C Benson, A M Benson, J W Benson, J R Benson, B A Benson, L S Byrd, J E Byrd, W H Cannady, R H Creech, J W Creech, L W Creech, J R Dening, B D Dening, J A Hodges, H A Hodges, Ben Hudson, D N Ivey, Moses Ivey, J J Jernigan, W H Jernigan, Ben Mathews, Isham McLaw, J D McLaw, J M McLaw, J E Morgan, Henry Morgan, J D Parrish, Ransom Ryals, N T Ryals, W D Ryals, C C Ryals, R S Ryals, J W Ryals, I J Smith, Y Stancill, Dr W E Turlington, John Whitmore, William Wood, Isham Woodall, W R Woodall, Thos Woodall, J A Woodall, Henry Wheeler.

Bentonsville—E O Beasly, J M Beasly, G R Britt, J A Cole, Willie Cole, W T Cox, M T Cox, M Cox, P H C Dupree, Green Flowers, W J Jennett, W R Joyner, Joseph Lee, N B Stevens, Jno Stevens, Julius Stevens, S B Thain, E T Westbrook, S W Weaver, J J Williams.

Bismarck—A G Austin, R M Byrd, J H Cannady, J W Coats, B F Langford, McD Langdon, A McGee, L Y Stephenson.

Bizzell—R B Ezzell.

Candill—M F Candill, L B Grimes, D A King, J C Ogburn, J E Smith, H A Stephenson, J D Stephenson, J H Stephenson.

Clayton—Geo Avers, Henry Austin, Jones E Austin, Joseph Austin, Vick Austin, D L Barbour, A J Barbour, S T Barbour, D W Boone, W W Cox, A Creech, H C Crocker, A R Duncan, J H Eason, C P Ellis, R H Gower, M G Gulley, V G Gulley, E R Gulley, J D Gulley, G G Gulley, J F Hall, J H Harrison, J R Harrison, I B Harrison, W R Hinton, D T Honeycutt, A Horne, H Horne, J H Johnston, A D Jones, J W Jones, M H Jones, J G Jones, J C Jones, E S Lancaster, W H Lancaster, W R Long, W H McCullers, jr, D H McCullers, E B McCullers, A S Pool, W R Pool, N R Pool, W H Pool, Paschal Pool, J C Pool, J A Pool, D C Pool, J F Sanders, S V Smith, J B Stallings, W T Stallings, W J Y Thurston, J T Vinson, J A Vinson, C R Wallace, J T Wiggs, J H Wood, Ransom Yelventon, B H Yelventon.

Cockerell—J R Creech.

Earpsboro—J S Brewer, W D Brown, J W Brown, Floyd Brown, Heff Brown, L D Dednam, C M Holloman, J E Pulley, C W Richardson, J W Hocutt, Dempsy Hocutt, J C B Hocutt, Wyatt Whitley.

Elevation—D M Coats, J E Dixon, J P Dixon, Ben Dixon, Abram Dixon, Haywood Dixon, P G Godwin, P F Godwin, S W Johnson, G W Johnson, J H Massengill, K Morgan, J D Stevens, D H Surles.

Emit—J S Atkinson, T H Atkinson, L G Bailey, H P Bailey, J B Bailey, H R Bailey, G T Barham, Robert Battin, L G Boyett, J B Boykin, R R Creech, Jesse Creech, W H Creech, J B Creech, Cullen Creech, Bennett Creech, J B Creech, J H Creech, Charles Creech, Worley Creech, J M Corbett, Joshua Edwards, Joseph Edwards, J M Edwards, J H Glour, H R Godwin, J H Godwin, J J Hall, H H Hare, Willis Hales, A P Holster, A B Laurey. Robt Morgan, Wiley Narron, W G Narron, Borden Narron, Aquilla Narron, Troy Narron, Jesse Narron, Loyd Narron, J W Narron, Iredell Narron, Carson Oneal, R L Oneal, J W Oneal, W R Oneal, F M Oneal, J B Oneal, Gideon Price, Green Price, J I Reufrow, J I Richardson, J W Robertson, J H Stancill, Joseph Talton, J W Talton, J E Winston.

Ezra—Josephus Johnson, A T Johnson.

Four Oaks—L P Adams, D W Adams, A G Adams, Hardy Adams, F L Adams, J W Allen, S W Allen, W P Allen, Jas G Allen, R J P Baker, T D Barbour, J M Blackman, S W Bryant. J G Coats, E Creech, Amos Dunn B S Evans, J C Keen, G W Keer, Gideon Keer, A R Keer, J A Lee, J H Lee, John W Moore, J W Oliver, J I Parker, J B Parker, N R Parker, Y E Parker, O R Rand, John Sanders, J D Smith, W B Stanly, W R Stanly, J H Stanly, B E Strickland, J A Strickland, S E Temple, W R Tool, D L Tool, Bython Wallace, J S Wood.

Glenmore—Gainey Coats, J R George, B J Grant, W N Jordan, W F Lee, Lit Lee, Rufus Lee, John Lee, Jas E Lee, I Massengill, R S Massengill, D E Massengill, G W Massengill.

Glenwood—Wm Eldridge, J T Hudson, S P M Tart, L M Underwood.

Gulley's Mill—J A T Jones.

Harper's—W B Cole, John Harper, G W Langston, W A Langston, J S Massengill, S W Morris, J E Thornton, N B Toler.

Itiner—S A Barnes, B A Benson, R M Byrd, H W Godwin, J B Hardee, C R Johnson, A D Johnson, J D Jones, L H McGee, G W Pleasant, J T Whittington.

Kently—B D Dixon, J M Ballance, Daniel Ballance, Joshua Dixon, Henry Flowers, G H Garner, Eli Godwin, J H Holland, P D Holland, Thos Holland, Garry Horne, N T Jackson, E P Jones, Henry Kirby, Zeno Langsly, B D Parrish, J R Pearce, J B Pearce, L M Peeden, M T Pittman, W H Pittman, Miles Radford, H H Richardson, Henry Rose, Henry Starling, J H Watkins, C W Williams, B T Woodard, J B Yelverton.

Leachburg—C H Holland, R B Leach.

Lemay.—H A Barbour, R S Bridgers, C B Bridgers, A Gower, T W Lemay.

McKay.—Nathan Barefoot, Julius Barefoot, L D Johnson, C B Johnson, Jas Johnson, David Lee, Westbrook Lee, W J Morgan, A D Tart.

Micro.—Wesley Batton, Ephraim Batton, W H Blackman, Kader Creech, N B Hinnant, J W Mazingo, S D Pearce, Alfred Pearce, C D Fearce, Jonas Pittman, E F Pittman, Jas W Pittman, R W Radford, P G Ware.

Overshot.—J B Hood, Alonzo Hood, J J Rose, W A Rose, W N Rose, jr, C M Rose, J W Rose.

Penny.—L F Austin, Ransom Penny, Caleb Penny, A C Penny, D T Smith.

Pine Level.—John Batton, D A Bizzell, Simon Brown, Geo Chestnut, J R Cresch, B Crocker, D A Fields, Gibson Fitzgerald, T R Fulgham, E T Futrell, J W Futrell, W F Gerald, B Godwin, J W Lamb, T T Oliver, W B Oliver, J U Oliver, S A Peeden, S C Peeden, W J Peeden, A W Peeden, S R Peeden, T E Wellons.

Polenta—Dr E N Barker, F T Booker, H H Finch, H T Garrard, John Jones, J W Myatt, Thad Stevens, A D Taylor, R R Weeks, F J Williams, W G Wren, J T Wood, Jesse Wood, J W Yelverton, J H Yelverton, J J Young.

Pratt—W H Coats, J R Coats, M D Coats, L B Grimes, H H Johnson, L P King, B King, C H King, J C Ogburn, R I Ogburn, W A Ogburn, C H Wood.

Preston—A M Barbour, A M Sanders, E S Sanders, C L Sanders, Willis A Sanders, W J Smith, Mack Smith, J B Tomlinson.

Princeton — Alex Braswell, Jacob Braswell, Isaac Crow, L P Creech, D W Creech, E J Creech, C R Daughtry, W T Edwards, W T Hinton, J C Holt, P M Holt, Jake Holt, R M Howell, A Langly, W H Langly, Wm Lane, W H Lindsay, Geo W Martin, Wes Massey, J I Massey, A J Massey, C P McCauley, Wiley Mitchell, A W Oliver, N G Oliver, H B Pearce, H F Peeden,

JOHNSTON COUNTY.

J W Perry, W D Phillips, Levi Radford, W B Raines, J T Raines, Haywood Raines. Clem Richardson, J G Rone, T H Sasser, J H Sasser, W P Sellars, C W Smith, J W Snipes. G B Stallings. D H Thompson. P D Thompson, J R Thompson, J M Th mpson. H J Thompson. A R Thompson, S O Wellons, W G Whitly, G W Wiggs, W G Woodard, R W Woodard, A F Woodard. Kedor Woodard, Daniel Woodard.

Rome—M V Barefoot. N G Barefoot, Nathan Barefoot, Handy Barefoot, Hassell Blackman. W S Eldridge, Tony Eldridge. Lovett Eldridge, J L George, W J Hudson. J J Hudson. Joshua Johnson. H M Johnson. John Johnson A P Johnson. D G Johnson, James H Johnson, J O Johnson, R J Kinsey. Elam Lee, Monroe Lee, J C Lee, W A Lee, T T Lee, S D Lee. Jerry Lee. West. Lee, Jesse Lee, G W McLarret N McLarret,O B Morgan, Frank Parker, J W Parker, J G Raynor, C M Rose. J G Smith, W H Smith. Y B Smith, W T Tart, Y A Tart, John Tart. J W Wood, D J Wood.

Selma — J A B'ackmore, Barney Creech, J G Eason, C F Kirby, W T Kirby, E S Moore, Dr R J Noble, A M Noble, B Oneal, J H Parker, Hill Peedin, W R Peedin, F G Price, W M Pittman, R Pittman, N Pittman, H Pittman. B S Pittman. Jack Rains, J C Scarborough, Riddick Stancill, J A Underhill, J W Vick. C B Waddell

Smithfield—Mrs J W Avera. J A Ballard, W R Creech, D T Creech. A S Creech. June Cullons Jesse Daughtry, B D Daughtry, L Eldridge, J L Eld-

rigde, D W Fuller. Pollie Gardner, N B Grantham, H L Graves, L L Hamilton, J J Harper, P S Heath, H W Higgins, S C Higgins, B P Hood, W B Johnson. G B Johnson, Walter Johnson, W L Johnson, Lee Johnson. S W Johnson, P P Johnson. M D Johnson, Joe Johnson, Alex Johnson, Edmond Johnson. J W Johnson, B P Johnson. Perrin Jones, Geo L Jones, H J Lane. R D Lunsford, D T Lunsford, D T Massey, P T Massey, John Massey, G H Morgan, Alex Mims. J S Ogburn, Eli Olive, M G Olive, G S Peterson, H A Peterson. H L Peterson. Thos Pittman, G T Pool. J H Pou. E W Pou, E E Powell, John Powell, C S Powell. Adin Powell. C Radford, C B Sanders, Robert Sanders, J K Sanders, John Smith, T S Thain. Cicero Thompson. A G Thompson, J D Underwood, A Wallace, C A Wallace. R I Wallace, E Wallace, D J Wellons, J W Wellons, Adam Whitley. W H Whitley, P T Whitley, F P Whitley, G S Wilson. B B Yelvington.

Spilona—A M Barbour, R C Barbour. D L Flowers, Esron Johnson, R I Lassiter, Dr D B Lassiter, Joseph Lassiter, W L Lassiter, H S Lassiter.

Stephenson—Monroe Fry. Wm Jones, R I Ogburn. C B Ogburn, O R Stancill, T H Stephenson, H A Stephenson.

Wilson's Mills—J H Allen, Willis Allen, N B Mitchener. A T Uzzle, G F Uzzle, J M Vinson. D V Vinson, Dury Vinson, A B Vinson, J W Vinson, D T Vinson, J A Wilson, J M Wilson, C M Wilson, W E Wilson, J H Youngblood, R N Youngblood, T R Youngblood.

JONES COUNTY.

AREA, 450 SQUARE MILES.

POPULATION, 6,899; White 3,381; Colored 3,518.

JONES COUNTY was formed in 1779, from Craven county, and was named in honor of Willie Jones, who was so distinguished a patriot and useful citizen.

TRENTON, the county-seat, is 129 miles southeast from Raleigh, and has a population estimated at 500.

Surface—Jones county lies on both sides of Trent river, which leads into the Neuse at Newbern. The land is level, and much of it quite rich. Owing to the fine soil and beautiful location of the land, farming is the great business of this county.

Staples—Cotton is the great staple. Corn and sweet potatoes are produced in large quantities. Rice is grown largely on some of the lowlands. The piney lands produce abundant naval stores.

Fruits — Apples, peaches, pears, plums, grapes, strawberries and the small fruits.

Timbers—Pine, oak, ash, birch, gum, cypress, juniper, hickory and poplar.

TOWNS AND POST OFFICES.

	POP.		POP.
Bonus,	25	Pollocksville,	50
Comfort,	60	Trenton (C H),	500
Fowle,	30	Tuckahoe,	65
Maysville,	30	Whitford,	30
Oliver's,	25		

COUNTY OFFICERS.

Clerk Superior Court—S E Koonce.
Commissioners—J A Smith, F M Dixon, F A Whitaker.
Coroner—William Querries.
Register of Deeds—Aug Haskins.
Sheriff—J H Bell.
Solicitor Sixth District— —— Richardson.
Standard Keeper—S Banner.
Surveyor—A Becton.
Treasurer—Lewis King.
County Examiner—T J Whitaker.

COURTS.

Third Monday after the first Monday in March, and eighth Monday after the first Monday in September.

TOWNSHIPS AND MAGISTRATES.

Beaver Creek—J F Noble, F Green, J S Rose (Trenton).

Cypress Creek—Bug Brock, A F Cox, R N White (Trenton).

Pollocksville—H C Foscue, Franklin Fog, J N Foscue, Haywood A White, J P Harper, L T Smith, John Mercer (Pollocksville).

Trenton—Thos Wilcox, T J Whitaker, John W Wooten, J W Mallard, J W Bryan, W H Cox (Trenton).

Tuckahoe—C C Fordham, I John Small, B F Huffmann, Luther King (Tuckahoe).

White Oak—Lewis Bynum, Cyrus Foscue, Ken Hay, Amos Heath, C P Foy, Ken Parsons, C F Hadnot (Trenton).

Chinquepin—M E Haskins, J E Harrison, Joe Small, W J Penny (Trenton).

CHURCHES.

Names, Post Offices, Pastors and Denom.

METHODIST.
Church—Trenton, H E Tripp.
Cypress Creek—Comfort, H E Tripp.
Lee's Chapel—Pollocksville, H E Tripp.
Oak Grove—Pollocksville, H E Tripp.
Shady Grove—Kinston (Lenoir co), H E Tripp.

DISCIPLES OF CHRIST.
Church—Tuckahoe.
Deep Springs—Trenton.
Haskin's Chapel—Bonus.
Pleasant Hill—Tuckahoe.

BAPTIST.
Piney Grove—Trenton.

PRIMITIVE BAPTIST.
White Oak—Pollocksville.

FREE-WILL BAPTIST.
Friendship—Trenton.

PRESBYTERIAN.
Mill Creek—Pollocksville.

MINISTERS RESIDENT.

Names, Post Offices and Denominations.

BAPTIST.
Isler, Henry (col), Trenton.

METHODIST.
Tripp, H E, Trenton.
Morris, — (col), Trenton.

PRIMITIVE BAPTIST.
Porter, A J, Trenton.

DISCIPLES OF CHRIST.
Tingle, ——, Tuckahoe.

JONES COUNTY.

HOTELS AND BOARDING HOUSES.

Names, Post Offices and Proprietors.

Hotel, Trenton, John P Brogden.
Hotel, Trenton, Jas A Smith.
Hotel, Trenton, Jas M Pollock.

LAWYERS.

Names and Post Offices.

White, A H, Pollocksville.

MANUFACTORIES.

Kinds, Post Offices and Proprietors.

Blacksmithing and wheelwrighting, Pollocksville, Addison & Berry.
Blacksmithing and wheelwrighting, Comfort, Brown & Atkinson.
Blacksmithing and wheelwrighting, Comfort, B F Huffman.
Blacksmithing and wheelwrighting, Trenton. J B Stanley.
Blacksmithing and wheelwrighting, Trenton, Jarman & Gardner.
Blacksmithing and wheelwrighting, Maysville, Curtis Hay & Bro.
Building and contracting, Comfort, Levi Rhodes.
Building and contracting, Comfort, J M F Rhodes.
Building and contracting, Comfort, B F Gardner.
Building and contracting, Trenton, G E Andrews & N J Leary.
Coaches and undertaking, Trenton, —— Gardner.
Millwrighting, Comfort, B F Gardner.
Wagons, Trenton, J B Stanley.

MERCHANTS AND TRADESMEN.

Name, Post-office and Line of Business.

MAYESVILLE.

Bynum, Lewis,　　　　　　　G S
Collins. A J,　　　　　　　G S
Maysville Supply Co,　　　　G S
Mayes, C D,　　　　　　　G S
Mills, F L,　　　　　　　　G S
Sabeston, M R,　　　　　　G S
Sanders & Bell,　　　　　　G S
Shepard, W L,　　　　　　G S
Foy, C D, Jr,　　　　　　　G S
Hadnot, C E.　　　　　　　G S
Madnot & Provow,　　　　　G S
Mattocks, W F,　　　　　　G S
OLIVER.
Parker, J C & Son,　　　　　G S
Simmons, J J,　　　　　　　G S
POLLOCKSVILLE.
Bell, T A & Bro,　　　　　　G S

JONES COUNTY.

Bender Bros.　　　　　　　G S
Chadwick, H A,　　　　　Drugs
Harrell & Co,　　　　　　　G S
Lee, J H,　　　　　　　　　G S
Lee. T R,　　　　　　　　　G S
Register, J E,　　　　　　　G S
Scott, J W,　　　　　　　　G S
Shepard, James W,　　　　　G S
Smith, W B,　　　　　　　　G S
Whitly, Charles,　　　　　　G S
TRENTON.
Barker, S,　　　　　　　　G S
Brogden. John P,　　　　　G S
Coble, W M,　　　　Photographer
Ca·tet, F,　　　　　　　　　G S
Heritage, J D,　　　　　　　G S
King, Lewis,　　　　　　　G S
Kinsey, W C,　　　　　　　G S
Whitaker. T C,　　　　　　G S

MILLS.

Kinds, Post Offices and Proprietors.

Corn, rice and saw, Tuckahoe, Willoughby Jarman.
Corn, flour and gin, Pollocksville, Jno Pearce.
Flour, corn and gin (steam), Pollocksville.
Flour, corn and gin (steam), Pollocksville, J C Bryan.
Flour, corn and gin, (steam), Pollocksville, M N Harriott.
Flour, corn, gin and saw, Oliver, —— Simmons.
Flour and corn, Maysville. — Bynum.
Flour and corn, Tuckahoe, Frank Brown.
Flour and corn. Trenton, J P Brogden.
Flour and corn, Pollocksville, J Pierce.
Flour and corn, Tuckahoe, H F Brown.
Saw (steam), Trenton, Lewis King.

PHYSICIANS.

Names and Post Offices.

Hughes. G R, Pollocksville.
Whitaker, R A, Trenton.

SCHOOLS.

Names, Post Offices and Principals.

Trenton High School, Trenton; W H Rhodes, prin; Mrs W H Rhodes, ass't; Miss Sadie Kinney, music.
Vance Academy, Pollocksville; —— Burrus.
Public schools—white, 22; colored, 23.

TEACHERS.

Names and Post Offices.

Bryant, Amos, Dour.

JONES COUNTY.

Burney, J, Tuckahoe.
Burney, Margaret H, Tuckahoe.
Burt, Orlena H, Bonus.
Collins, J B, Maysville.
Foscue, Lillian E, Pollocksville.
Foy, Lavinia, Trenton.
Gray, Nannie D, Barrus.
Green, Thos (col), Trenton.
Hargett, Ida J, Trenton.
Harrison, Annie C, Bonus.
Hicks, D L (col), Maysville.
Isler, Nannie, Kinston, (Lenoir co).
Jones, R B, Maysville.
King, Bettie L (col), Kinston (Lenoir co).
Kinsey, E M (col), Maysville.
Kinsey, Mamie, Tuckahoe.
Koonce, Ora L, Comfort.
Moore, Catherine J (col), Pollocksville.
Murrill, D W, Pollocksville.
Noble, Mattie L, Trenton.
Pearce, Nellie, Pollocksville.
Pollock, Nannie Z, Bonus.
Willie, Laura, Pollocksville.

LOCAL CORPORATIONS.

Pleasant Hill Lodge, No 304, A F & A M, Kinston; time of meeting, first Saturday.
Pollocksville Lodge, No 175, A F & A M, Pollocksville; time of meeting, first Wednesday, and June 24th and December 27th.
Stella and Pollock-ville Telephone Co; R E Terry, pres; Cyrus Foscue, treas; D S Barnes, general manager. The line extends from Pollocksville, in Jones county, to Jacksonville, in Onslow county, via Maysville and Stella; length, 36 miles.
Zion Lodge, No 81, A F & A M, Trenton; time of meeting, third Saturday.

FARMERS.

Names and Post Offices.

Bonus.—Jas Bryan, S Cox, Jas Cox, W Dail, Nathan Gilbert, Dock Gooding, Isaac Gooding, John Gray & Bro, D H Harrison, Jas Harrison, Mark Haskins, Lewis H Haskins, Elijah Haskins, W O Haskins, Ed Martin, S H Philips, Sylvester Small, Jas Taylor, Dr. F A Whitaker, J F Westbrook, Jas Westbrook.
Comfort.—A Askew, J Borden, Benj Brown, Benj Brock, Isaac Brock, Tur-

JONES COUNTY.

ney Brock, John W Coombs, A F Cox-Wm C George, A G Gooding, E L Hardee, John L Hardee, L A Haywood, W H Hammond, Wm Huffman, J W Huffman, Amos Jenkins, Chas Jones, G R Jones, F King, H C Koonce, Jno C Koonce, Levi Rhodes, J M F Rhodes, Wm Shiver, J B Westbrook.
Fowle.--Cyrus Foscue, Ed Godwin, J F Maides.
Maysville.—Lewis Bynum, Wm Bynum, I W Collins, B B Collins, John Collins, E S Dixon, C D Foy, Ken Foscue, Jas E Hay, Curtis Hay, Ken Hay, Amos Heath, S W Maides, Mrs Rebecca Oldfield, S Waters.
Oliver.—John W Andrews, Geo Barrow, A G Barrow, L P Edwards, J P Harper, J L Harrison, John F Heath, Benj Henderson, B F Henderson, Elvin McDaniel, Jas McDaniel, J C Parker, C M Pollock, W W Pollock, J T Pollock, Willie Rouse, J J Simmons E B Simmons,
Pollocksville—J B Banks, B F Banks, Bryan Bender, J C Bryan, D S Burrus, E F DeBruhl, C I DeBruhl, B F Dillahunt, A F Duval, G H Duval, H C Foscue, J N Foscue, Franklin Foy, S Hudson, Geo Harriett, M N Harriett, Abner Hargett, John Hargett, B Hargett, R R Jones, C J Mattocks, John Pearce, E F Sanderson, W H Scott, G W Scott, A H Scott, A L Simmons, Charles Simmons, L T Smith, Stephen Taylor, John H Whitley, Hardy Whitford, N M White, Augustus White, H A White, F Wilcox.
Trenton—Lewis Andrews, Charles Andrews, Peter Andrews, John Andrews, J P Brogden, J W Bryan, L Dillahunt, John P Gray, John Griffin, J R Hargett, J Howell, J L Hawkins, W M Hawkins, L A Haywood, F Jones, Wm Jones, Lewis King, S E Koonce, F S Koonce, Z T Koonce, L H Mallard, John W Mallard, Geo Mallard, Wm H Mallard, D L Mallard, E P McDaniel, L F McDaniel, E G McDaniel, William McDaniel, J F Noble, F S Noble, Ed H Pollock, H Pollock, I H Scott, Jos A Smith, Thos Wilcox, J W Wooten.
Tuckahoe—Isaac Brown, H F Brown, Mrs Matilda Brown, J W Eubanks, C C Fordham, A J Fordnam, W G Fordham, Willoughby Jarman, E M Jarman, W C Jones, Felix King, Isaac Koonce, Job Metts, George H Miller, Martin Noble, John Small, A T Uzzell.

Mecklenburg Iron Works, Charlotte, N. C.

Teed Turbine Water-wheels, Gearing, Shafting, Pulleys and Belting.

LENOIR COUNTY.

AREA, 420 SQUARE MILES.

POPULATION, 14,859; White 8,497, Colored 6,362.

LENOIR COUNTY was formed in 1791, from what was Dobbs county at that time. It was named in honor of Gen. William Lenoir, who was distinguished for his Revolutionary and civil service.

KINSTON, the county seat, is 80 miles east of Raleigh. It is located on the Neuse river and Atlantic & N. C. Railroad. Population, 3,500.

Surface—Level, sandy loam, generally rich—very productive when well drained. Lenoir is naturally a rich section and many farms are under a high state of cultivation.

Staples—Cotton, tobacco, rice and corn are the great staples of this county. Sweet potatoes are produced largely and to perfection. The scuppernong grape grows luxuriantly. Rice is now an important crop. This is a fine trucking section.

Fruits—Apples, peaches, strawberries, cherries, grapes, plums and the other small fruits common to this section.

Timbers—Pine, oak, hickory, gum, ash, cypress and maple.

TOWNS AND POST OFFICES.

	POP.		POP.
Cadez,	25	Institute,	100
Closs,	25	Kinston (ch),	3,500
Coahoma,	25	LaGrange,	675
Deep Run,	20	Pink Hill,	50
Falling Creek,	85	Repose,	30
Fields,	32	Strabane,	30
Grainger's,	25	Woodington,	30
Hugo,	25		

COUNTY OFFICERS.

Clerk Superior Court—S H Bright.
Commissioners—Dr Henry Tull, chm'n; B C Turner, W A Jones, Josiah Sutton, jr, W O Mosely.
Coroner—Ira S Davis.
Register of Deeds—E S Pittman.
Sheriff—T R Hodges.
Solicitor 6th District—M C Richardson.
Standard Keeper—Geo B Webb.
Surveyor—E P Loftin.
Treasurer—John H Dawson.
County Examiner—E G Tyndall.

COURTS.

Ninth Monday after the first Monday in March, and tenth Monday after the first Monday in September.

TOWN OFFICERS.

KINSTON—*Mayor*, J B Temple; *Commissioners*, Dr R H Lewis, A R Miller, E F Cox, B W Candy, Geo B Webb; *Chief of Police*, J E Dupree.

LAGRANGE—*Mayor*, H E Dillon; *Commissioners*, H M McDonald, H V Williams, Geo L Taylor, Shade Wooten, Robt Jones, Josiah Wells.

TOWNSHIPS AND MAGISTRATES.

Contentnea Neck—R W Pope, J M Phillips, C L Rountree, W J Pope, Peter Phillips, J E Cameron, T J Allott, John Langston (Contentnea Neck).

Falling Creek—Dempsey Wood, E E Rouse, W L Kennedy, E L Sutton, W J Warters, J W Daily, W E Askew, C P Davis (Falling Creek).

Institute—J K Aldridge, A T Dawson, J E Turnage, Franklin Dail, F M Harrison, A S Fields, John Phelp, Wm O Pelletier (Institute).

Kinston—Wirte Saunders, L Harvey, W C Fields, B F Nunn, W W Hinton, J F Mewborne, C F Dunn, E H E Perry, Star Hicks, J F Parrott, J P Tucker, J H Sugg, W Saunders, L W Dawson, E W Bordon (Kinston).

Mosely Hall—K E Sutton, Daniel Hines, G L Capell, R W Moore, John Fields, jr, Albert Miller, U S Uzzell, J W Sutton, John Warters (LaGrange).

Neuse—E G Tyndall, R F Hill, Jesse Jackson, W J Barrett, Benjamin Sutton, W A Croom, Jesse Holland (Kinston).

Pink Hill—George Turner, W B Nunn, J R Howard, J W Tyndall, W H Bird, J H Taylor, J R Tyndall, J B Smith (Kinston).

Sand Hill—J W Taylor, G V Richardson, Seth West, J A Tilgham, D T Warters, J F Vance, W B Avery, Rowlin Hood (Kinston).

Southwest—E P Loftin, S M Wooten, J E Moore, Jerry Warters, C E Kennedy, J T Ward, jr, J I Vance, W K Baker (Kinston).

Trent—A W Whitfield, Wendel Harper, W W Rouse, W E Wooten, Nathan Hill, Alonzo Brown (Kinston).

Vance—Lemuel Taylor, R F Church-

LENOIR COUNTY.

ill, R C Hill, B F Parrott, B F Scarboro, L A Mewborne, J T Askew, J H Sugg (Kinston).

Woodington—Frank King, C A Dudley, Z nus Gooding, E P Hauser, S C Gooding, E F Oglesby, Jesse Harper, jr, S D Parrish (Woodington).

CHURCHES.

Names, Pastors, Postoffices and Denom.

METHODIST.

Bethel—Shine (Greene co), George T Simmons.
Church—Kinston, J O Guthrie.
Cnurch—Lenoir Institute, George T Simmons.
Church—La Grange, Geo T Simmons.
Church—Beston, Geo T Simmons.
Piney Grove—Seven Springs, Geo T Simmons.
Trinity—Falling Creek, G T Simmons.

METHODIST PROTESTANT.

Church—La Grange, —— Swain.
Field's Chapel—La Grange, —— Swain.

PRESBYTERIAN.

Church—Kinston.
Church—La Grange. Fred Thomas.
Church (col.)—La Grange, Dr Rutherford.

BAPTIST.

Church—La Grange.
Church—Kinston, —— Spillman.
Church—La Grange, —— Rose.
Church (col.)—La Grange.
Union—Kinston.

FREE-WILL BAPTIST.

British Chapel—Kinston, H Cuninggim.
Christian's Chapel—Kinston.
Deep Run—Kinston, Haskett Jones.
Loosing Swamp—Kinston.
Woodington—Kinston, H Cuninggim.

PRIMITIVE BAPTIST.

Bear Creek—T B Lancaster.
Church—La Grange, —— Langston.

DISCIPLES OF CHRIST.

Bethel—Kinston.
Church—La Grange, —— Petree.
Church—Kinston, —— Petree.
Southwest—Kinston.
Wheat Swamp—Kinston, Sam'l Snmmerell.

EPISCOPAL.

St Mary's—Kinston, Allan Gravis.

A. M. E. ZION.

Church (col.)—La Grange.

LENOIR COUNTY.

MINISTERS RESIDENT.

Names, Post Offices and Denom.

METHODIST.

Guthrie, G O, Kinston.
Hooker, N A, Kinston.
Simmons, Geo T, La Grange.
Webb, J B, Kinston.

FREE WILL BAPTIST.

Carey, J H (col.), Kinston.
Cuninggim, H, Deep Run.
Jones, Haskett, Kinston.
Taylor, I J, Kinston.

DISCIPLES OF CHRIST.

Cherent, Isaac.
Howard, C W.

EPISCOPAL.

Greaves, Albion, Kinston.

UNION BAPTIST.

Grubbs, J T, Grifton.

A. M. E. ZION.

McKennie, —— (col.), La Grange.

BAPTIST.

Rose, ——, La Grange.
Spillman—Kinston.

PRESBYTERIAN.

Rutherford, ——, La Grange.
Swain, ——, La Grange.

HOTELS AND BOARDING HOUSES.

Names, Post Offices and Proprietors.

Boarding, Kinston, M r s Needham Moore.
Boarding, LaGrange, J W Sutton.
Central Hotel, Kinston, Ivey Brown.
Fields Hotel, LaGrange, J H Fields.
Hotel Bailey, Kinston, Mrs H C Bailey.
Hotel Tull, Kinston, Junius Stevenson.
Nunn's Hotel, Kinston, B F Nunn.

LAWYERS.

Names and Post Offices.

Allen, O H, Kinston
Collins, Plato, Kinston.
Jackson, J Q, Kinston.
Loftin, A J, Kinston.
Perry, D E, Kinston.
Pollock, W D, Kinston.
Rouse, N J, Kinston.
Shaw, H E, Kinston.
Wooten, T C, Kinston.
Wooten, J F, Kinston.

MANUFACTORIES.

Kinds, Post Offices and Proprietors.

Barrels and truck boxes, Kinston, White & Murphey.

LENOIR COUNTY.	LENOIR COUNTY.

Blacksmithing and wheelwrighting, LaGrange, S Taylor.
Boots and shoes, Kinston, S B Clayton.
Boots and shoes, Kinston, L J Hill.
Brick, Kinston, S H Abbott.
Building and contracting, LaGrange, B F Fuller.
Building and contracting, LaGrange, J H Kinsey.
Building and contracting, LaGrange F M McKoy.
Buggies, Kinston, Ellis Carriage Works.
Carriage Factory, Kinston, C T Randolph.
Coaches, Kinston, Ellis Carriage Works, H E Ellis.
Crackers and candy, Kinston, Mrs C E McRae.
Distillery (turpentine), Kinston, A Harvey.
Machine shops and foundry, Kinston, E M Hodges.
Machine shop work and machine supplies, Kinston, E M Hodges.
Orion Knitting Mill, Kinston, J F Taylor, sec and treas.
Repair Shops, Kinston, Bell & Sons.
Saddles and harness, LaGrange, Asa McCoy.
Shingles, Kinston, J A Harvey.
Shingles, Kinston, Nottingham & Renn
Turpentine, Kinston, Davis & Taylor.

MERCHANTS AND TRADESMEN.

Names, Post Offices and Line of Business.

CADEZ.
Wooten, D F, G S

CLOSS.
Cobb, Stephen, Gro
Pierce, W B, G S
West, Seth, G S

DEEP RIVER.
Sparrow, Ora D, G S

FALLING CREEK.
Creech, E A, G S
Fields, B F, G S
Haskins, J T, Gro
Hill, J N C, G S
Murchison & Sutton, G S
Rouse, F L B, G S
Rouse, E E, G S
Sutton, W H, G S

GRANGERS.
Hamilton, D W, G S

GRIFTON.
Long, E, G S

HUGO.
Harris, R F, G S

INSTITUTE.
Brothers, W J, G S
Dawson, A T, G S

KINSTON.
Abbott, S H, G S
Alphen, S & Co, G S
Bailey, C, Jeweler
Ball, J T, Tob
Barrow, D S, Sale Stables
Beasley, T A, Gro
Becton, J O, Gro
Becton, Mrs F B, Dry Goods
Bond, W R, Butcher
Bond & Hartsfield, Mrs, Millinery
Bond, W R, Gro
Borden, E W W (col), Gro
Borden, P R (col), Gro
Borden, J L, Gro
Broxton, ——, Butcher
Bull, J T, Gro
Burnett & Co, Brokers
Canady, B W, Hardware
Caraway, Stephen, Gro
Collins, J W, Hardware
Cox, L B, Gro
Cummings, J B, G S
Dawson, Gus, Gro
Dawson, F H, Gro
Denmark, K, Jewelry
Desmond, A, G S
Dunn, C F (col), G S
Dunn, Henry, Drugs
Einstein Bros, Dry Goods
Fields, W C, Cotton Dealers and Fertilizers
Fields, B F, Livery
Fields & Bros, Gro
Grady, Lewis, Fruits
Grainger, J W, Engines, Guano, etc
Grimsley, W H, G S
Hargett, J C (col), G S
Harper, W G, Livery
Harvey, Misses B & K, Millinery
Harvey, J A, Shingles
Harvey, L & Son, Gen Life and Fire Insurance
Harvey, C F, Leaf Dealer
Hartsfield & Bond, Millinery
Hartsfield, Mrs T L & Co, Millinery
Harper, W G, Livery
Hicks, O R, Grocer
Hicks, L, G S
Hickson, W H, Fire Insurance
Hill, R C (near) G S
Hodges, E M, Carriages
Hollowell, A L, G S
Holland, Jesse, Gro
Holloway, T B, Gro
Hood, J E, Drugs
Hyatt, Dr H O, Drugs
Joyner, E R (col), Gro
Kornegay, Geo E, G S
La Roque, A P, Sale and Livery
La Roque, F M (agt), Gro

LENOIR COUNTY.

La Roque, W A, G S
Loftin, L H. G S and Bank
Lowery, W (col), G S
Marks, Mike, Dry Goods
Marks, Moses, Dry Goods
Meachan, Thos J, Agt A C Line
McKinnie, H W, Gro
McRae, Mrs C E, G S
Mewborne, John F, Leaf Dealer
Mewborne, T W & Co, Gro
Miller, A R, G S
Mitchell, A, Sale Stable
Moore, W F, Gro
Moore, L J, Cotton Buyer
Moore, J H, Fruits
Moore, Mrs N T, Boarding House
Myers, N D, Gro
Nunn, B F, Hotel
Nunn, L P, Gro
Oettinger Bros, G S
Patrick, Mrs M S, Stationery
Parrott, Jas F, Gro
Patrick, Jordan, Boarding House
Pearce, W B (near) G S
Pridgen & Cox, G S
Quinn, O W, G S
Quimberly, M H, Gro
Randolph, C T, Carriages
Rayner, W D. Gro
Rountree, S H, jr, Gen Life and Fire Insurance
Skinner, J T, Gro
Smith, J B, G S and Turpentine
Stanley, H D, Agt steamer Vanceboro
Stanley, Mrs M E, G S
Stevenson, Junius, Express Agent
Strickland, John, Butcher
Stricklin, Joe, Sale Stable
Strowd, J F. Gro
Strowd & Sparrow (near), G S & Turp
Temple, R H. Drugs
Topp, L T & Co, Tob Warehouse
Webb, Geo B. Undertaker
Whitfield, W H, Gro
Whitehurs, Irvin, Butcher
Williams, Mrs A V & Co, Gro
Williams & Bro, G S
Wooten, M H Agt A & N C R R
Wooten, J M. G S
Wooten, John C, Postmaster

LA GRANGE.

Barrow, C P, G S
Best, W T, G S
Burke, W H, Gro
Davis, Jesse, Boarding House
Dillon, H F, G S
Foss, J W (near), G S
Harper, R M. G S
Harper, W H. Livery
Hardy, Ida P. G S
Kennedy, A W, G S
Kinsey, P B, G S
Kinsey, R M. G S
McDonald, H M, Drugs

LENOIR COUNTY.

Murchison, D C, G S
Pitts, Mary D. Boarding House
Pulley, M. Gro
Rouse, T R, G S
Smith, Samuel, Cotton Weigher
Stanton, D M, G S
Sutton, A J, G S
Sutton, S I, Agt A & N C R R [and Ex Agt
Sutton, Miss Alice, Tel Operator.
Sutton, K E & Co, G S
Taylor, Mrs S, G S
Taylor, O, G S
Wells, Jas. Confect
Wooten, S & Co, G S
Wooten, S, Gro

PINK HILL.

Carter, B C, G S
Taylor & Davis, G S
Tyndall, L P, G S

REPOSE.

Tyndall, W J & Co, G S

SEVEN SPRINGS.

Hines, D L, G S
Waller, J H, Gro

MILLS.

Kinds, Post Offices and Proprietors.

Corn and flour, Kinston, J P Davis.
Corn and flour, Kinston, J P Kelley.
Corn and flour, Kinston, Mrs J T Askew.
Corn and flour, Kinston, Herbert Davis.
Corn and flour, Pink Hill, R K Nobles
Corn and flour, Pink Hill, Harper Bros.
Corn and flour, LaGrange, Mrs L J Joyner.
Rice Mill, Kinston, Richard Noble.
Steam saw, Kinston, J L Nelson.
Steam saw, Kinston, Sam Taylor.
Steam saw, Kinston, J B Temple.
Steam saw, Grifton, Hellen & Brooks.
Steam saw, Kinston, J W Dail.
Steam saw, Grifton, Nottingham Renn.
Steam saw, LaGrange, O H Pearce.
Steam saw, LaGrange, J T Daily.
Steam saw, Kinston, Waller Bros.
Steam saw, Kinston, W H O'Berry.
Steam saw and dry kiln, Kinston, W H Hickson.
Steam saw and planing, Kinston, A McF Cameron.
Steam Saw, LaGrange, J W Sutton.

PHYSICIANS.

Names and Post Offices.

Davis, Ira S. Serecta.
Denny, W W, Pink Hill.

LENOIR COUNTY.

Falkner, T H, Kinston (dentist).
Hadley, J M, LaGrange.
Harper, H D, Kinston (dentist).
Hodges. J M, LaGrange.
Hyatt, H O, Kinston.
Kirkpatrick, J M, LaGrange.
Lofton, P B, Grifton.
Parrott, James. Kinston.
Woodley, C B, Kinston.
Pollock, W A J. Kinston.
Pollock, J A, Kinston.
Rutherford, —— (col), LaGrange.
Tull, Henry, Kinston.
Weyler, V E, Kinston.
Wooten, R L, Coahoma.

SCHOOLS.

Names, Post Offices and Principals.

Bethel Academy, Kinston, Miss McGowan.
Kinston College, Kinston, R H Lewis.
Kinsey's Female Seminary, LaGrange, Joseph Kinsey, prin, with seven assistants.
Male Academy, LaGrange, Prof Guire.
Primary School, Kinston, Miss Dora Miller.
Primary School, Kinston, Mrs H Archibald.
Primary School, Kinston. Miss Emma Webb.
Primary School, LaGrange, Miss Lula Whitfield.
Seminary, Kinston, Misses Jennie and Hunnie Patrick.

TEACHERS.

Names and Post Offices.

Archibald. Mrs H, Kinston.
Aldridge, Miss Nina Z (col), LaGrange.
Aldridge, Lizm E (col), LaGrange.
Barrow, Miss Lucy, Jason
Bright, Miss Daisy, Kinston.
Bright, Miss Delia. Kinston.
Boyan, Miss Mary, Institute.
Carroll, J C (col), LaGrange
Cobb, Miss Lula (col), Kinston.
Cobb, Miss Sue May, Kinston.
Cobb, Miss Emmie, Kinston.
Coleman. Miss Lilian C (col), Kinston.
Croom, Miss Fannie A (col), LaGrange.
Cox, Lewis (col), Kinston.
Davis, Miss Hattie (col), Kinston.
Edwards, Miss Leula, Kinston.
Fisher, Jas H, Kinston.
Gilbert, Miss Lizzie, Grifton.
Guver, Saml J, (Professor Male Academy), LaGrange.
Hardee, Miss Sadie, Kinston.
Harper, W F, Grifton.
Harper, Miss Blanch. Kinston.
Harper, James H (col), Kinston.

LENOIR COUNTY.

Harris, Miss Mary (col), Kinston.
Hill, Miss Lizzie, Institute.
Hines, Miss Bertha (col), LaGrange.
Hodges, Miss Irene, LaGrange.
Hood, John D (col), Falling Creek.
Huggins, Miss Bertha, Strabane.
Jarman, Miss Dora. Kinston.
Jennings, Miss Lucy (col), Kinston.
Kennedy. S G, Coahoma.
Kinsey, Miss Mamie, Tuckahoe.
Kinsey, Miss Bettie, LaGrange.
Kinsey, J H, LaGrange.
Kilpatrick, Miss Mary, Kinston.
King, F R (col), Kinston.
Lewis, R H, Kinston.
Loftin, Miss Carrie, Kinston.
Loftin, Miss Rosa. Kinston.
Maxwell, G M, Ressacca.
Mewborn, Miss Mary F (col), Kinston.
McGowan, Miss Leta C, Grifton.
Miller, Miss Dora, Kinston.
Moore, Miss Pattie A (col), Kinston.
Murrill, Miss Edith (col), Kinston.
Parrott, Miss Pattie, Kinston.
Patrick, Miss Virginia, Kinston.
Patrick, Miss Hennie, Kinston.
Patterson, Lettise L (col), Kinston.
Pierce, W J (col), Kinston.
Pittman, Miss Anna, Grifton.
Pope, Miss Julia, Fields.
Queson, G G, Seven Springs.
Simpkens, E A, Kinston.
Smith, Miss Lillie A (col), Kinston.
Smith, I B, Repose.
Spruill, Isaac (col), Kinston.
Strowd, Phill p, Kinston.
Strowd, Miss Rebecca, Kinston.
Sutton, John H (col), Kinston
Sutton, Miss, Darlie, Kinston.
Taylor, Miss Lyle E, LaGrange.
Taylor, Miss Delsie (col), LaGrange.
Taylor, Miss Mollie (col), LaGrange.
Thompson, Miss Ida A (col), Kinston.
Tyndall, H G, Repose.
Tyndall, N A, Repose.
Uzzell, Essie, Seven Springs.
Vaughn, Mary E (col), Institute.
Webb, Mrs Emma, Kinston.
Weeks, Alford (col), LaGrange.
Whitfield, A (col), LaGrange.
Williams, Miss Clara (col), Kinston.
Wooley, Miss Lola, Pink Hill.
Wooten, Miss Berenice, Kinston.
Wooten, Miss Ethel, Kinston.

LOCAL CORPORATIONS.

Chosen Friends, Kinston, J L Hartsfield.
Knights of Honor, No 160, J P Hasket, sec, Kinston.
Kinston Lodge, No 316, A F and A M; time of meeting, first and third Monday evenings; S H Rountree, sr, W M.

LENOIR COUNTY.

LENOIR COUNTY.

Knights and Ladies of Honor, Kinston; G F Cox, sec.

Lenoir Lodge, No 233, A F and A M. LaGrange; time of meeting, first Thursday.

Mystic Circle, Kinston.

Odd Fellows, Kinston.

Private Bank, Kinston, S H Loftin.

Royal Arcanum, No 640, G L Hodges, sec, Kinston.

Rountree Lodge, No 243, A F and A M, Bell's Ferry; time of meeting, first Saturday 10 o'clock A M.

St John's Lodge, A F and A M, Kinston; time of meeting, second Wednesday, June 24th and December 27th.

NEWSPAPERS.

Kinston Free Press (Democratic semiweekly), W S Herbert, ed and prop

School Girl, LaGrange (monthly), organ of Kinsey School

FARMERS.

Names and Post Offices.

Cadiz —Sam Taylor, jr. B C Turner, B F Wooten.

Closs—J W Daugherty, G L Daugherty, R T Daugherty, Emanuel Daugherty, G F Evans, W L Field, Abram Hargett, H C Harrison, J A B Heath, J W Kilpatrick, J C Kilpatrick, Jesse B Noble, S ephen McCoy, J L W Pearce, J W Rhem, T L Russell, Geo West, L D West.

Coahoma.—C C Hunter, J P Kelly, Mrs H Kennedy, J H Sutton, W H Sutton, R W Wooten, N B Wooten, J M Wooten.

Deep River.—Frank Cauley, H Cunninggim, S W Noble, Jesse Noble, I B Smith, F M Smith, Silas Taylor.

Dover.—W T Hines, G V Richardson.

Falling Creek.—Wm Arthur, W L Arthur, Isaac Boswick, J W Creech, Wiley Dawson, A J Grant, J L Kennedy, W R Kennedy, R W Kennedy, Madison Lamb, G F Parrott, Jerry Sutton, W F Sutton, Rich Sutton, Wm Warters, Dempsey Wood, Jesse Wood.

Fields.—R W Pope.

Glenfield—Clarence Bright, Claude Bright, S W Bright, B F Daugherty, J F Daugherty.

Goldsboro (Wayne Co).—E W Bizzell, H Wiel.

Grifton.—L D Abbott, F G Abbott, F J Abbott, sr, Chas Abbott, sr, Mrs Lucy Abbott, A A Albri ton, W A Aldridge, N A Boswick, J H Boswick, J F Braxton, E J Brooks, H F Brooks,

Henry Cameron, J E Cameron, Mrs H E Carr, A G Coward, W C Coward, L B Cox, J H Craft, S W Dawson, Alonzo Dunn, C C Dunn, J C Edwards, J J Edwards, Benj Faulkner, Elijah Fields, J A B Garris, W P Gilbert, J T Grubbs, A S Griffin, J C Griffin, E W Hamilton, J E F Harper, R F Harris, E L Hazelton, E G Hoof, J L Ives, I F Johnson, Jos Johnson, W F Jones, Lewis Kirkpatrick, L J Langston, B N Langston, R T Langston, Robt Nelson, J L Nelson, Joel Patrick, A L Patrick, Lucy Phillips, W H Phillips, J M Phillips, H E Phillps, W H Rountree, H B S ith, R B Speight, Moses Spivey, An y Summerell, S H Taylor, J L Tucker, J F Turnage, E W Warren, G Whitman, B F Wiggins, J A Wiggins, D W Wood.

Hugo—W J Pope.

Institute—N J Allen, J L Arthur, W L Arthur, J W Brothers, W Burfield, Lemuel Byrd, M B Creech, B S Creech, Franklin Dail, A T Dawson, J T Dawson, C N Dozier, S J Dupree, John T Gray, Henry Gregory, B M Hardy, S P Hardy, W A Hardy, — Hartsell, R L Herring, J E Hill, Webb Hill, J T Hill, L Hines, A G Hines, W E Hires, Maj Jackson, W E Kennedy, Jas Measley, Luly Measley, B T Parrott, J M Patrick, Berry Smith, J N Stallings, Elias Sullivan, W F Sullivan, A R Sutton, J S Tilghman, J W Tilghman, L Tindall, J E Turnage, E Vause, H B Warters, J H Williams, J J Wilson, T D Wilson.

Kinston—S H Abbott, A O All ritton, John T Aldridge, J N Alexander, D C Alexander, R W Alexander, C S Andrews, Allen Arnold (col.), J T Askew, W K Baker, R F Bland, R P Bright, C A Broadway, J F Brown, G T Brown, T B Brown, J H Bruton, B H Canady, W W Caraway, Robert Casey, E F Cox, J G Cox, T R Cuninggim, J W Darby, J H Darden, Josh Dawson, W W Dunn, J E Dupree, Furney Dupree, H A Edwards, Z Ed wards, W E Faulkner, I A Faulkner, Ben F Faulkner, Mrs Nancy Faulkner, W C Fields, Zenas Gooding, J W Grainger, Durham Gray, M A Gray, George Gray, J P Hardee, J C Hartsfield, J E Harper, Jesse Harper, J J Harper, L Harvey, Jesse Heath, Jos Herring, W J Herring, R C Hill, J B Hill, J W C Hill, L J Hill, J F Hill, John Hill, S H Humphreys, S E Hodges, F R Hodges, E M Hodges, B L Hodges, Mrs S E Holland, G W Holland, C W Howard, Jesse Jackson, J C Jackson, Gilf Johnson, N B Johnson, B F Jones, W P Jones, A T Kennedy, Geo L Kilpatrick,

LENOIR COUNTY.

Richard King, W A La Roque, W L Lewis, S H Loftin, Samuel Loftin, Jno B Loftin, C B Loftin, E P Loftin, S H Loftin, F C Loops, Scott McArthur, J A McDaniel, L A Mewborn, Sr, J F Mewborn, L A Mewborn, Jr, J M Mewborne, Frank Miller, N F Miller, A Mitchell, W H Moore, T W Moore, Geo L Moore, E T Moseley, J F Moseley, W T Moseley, J W Moseley, L A Moseley, L C Moseley, W O Moseley, Jacob Murphy, R K Noble, B F Nunn, J P Nunn, W F Nunn, Sr, Oettinger Bros, Redmon Parker, C H Parker, S D Parrish, J F Parrott, S C Parrott, B F Parrott, L L Parrott, A D Parrott, J M Parrott, D E Perry, J R Phillips, N M Phillips, C C Phillips, S W Phillips, J A Pollock, John W Pool, J A Pridgen, G P Robinson, S H Rountree, Sr, W B Rouse, J E Rouse, R T Rouse, J F Rouse, E R Rouse, Wright Saunders, B F Scarborough, E L Schrierckorb, Simeon Simons, M H Smith, W B Smith, J G Smith, R P Smith, J J Smith, W F Stanley, B E Stanley, M E Stanley, Joseph Stricklin, Wm Stroud, Philip Stroud, Grey Stroud, Amos Stroud, J H Sugg, Josiah Sugg, Mrs W P Sutton, E L Sutton, Emett Sutton, Jas O Sutton, J D Sutton, Bony Sutton, W E Sutton, R G Sutton, F G Taylor, R B Taylor, D W Taylor, G G Taylor, M P Taylor, D G Taylor, Lemuel Taylor, H S Taylor, J W Taylor, Sam Taylor, Sr, J H Taylor, R H Temple, J B Temple, Alex Tilghman, Sr, J A Tilghman, J P Tucker, Geo W Tull, Dr H Tull, Mrs W R Tull, E R Tull, A J Tyndall, J I Vance, J F Vause, Dock Wallace, J H Waller, Jr, W H Worth, R B West, Miss Tiffany West, Seth West, L T West, E F White, C Whitfield, W H Whitfield, D W L Wilkins, David Williams, J L Williams, R A Wooten, E M Wooten, J F Wooten, J C Wooten.

LaGrange—J K Aldridge, J W Aldridge, T M Aldridge, jr, J H Aldridge, Joseph Allen, Rhenlin Almore, W T Best, N E Best, M J Boswick, J F Boswick, B C Brewer, Benjamin Britt, Jesse Brown, G L Cople, J H Cokes, J W Colie, R C Croom, J T Daily, Joshua Daily, J P Daily, E F Daily, L A Davis, Thos Dawson, A L Dawson, W J Dawson, J H Dawson, H T Dawson, A J Dawson, H E Dillon, Joel Elmore, J H Elmore, T J Emerson, A S Fields, A G Fields, J H Fields, W M Fields, H Fields, J E

Fields, J M Fields, M E Fields, E J Fields, John Fields, jr, J W Fields, T B Fields, Noah Fields, J W Foss, Wiley Gerganus, Ransom Gorris, G W Gorris, Percy Gorris, Alford Graddy, J M Hadley, E E Hadley, I P Hardee, T B Henderson, B F Herring, E M Herring, N W Herring, J J Herring, Levi Hill, T P Hill, Daniel Hines, J M M Hodges, James Holland, Daniel Isler, S Jackson, Emanuel Jarman, J P Joyner, L J Joyner, C W Joyner, A W Kennedy, J M Lassiter, Stephen Lassiter, L C Lassiter, W H Lassiter, Albert Miller, Willie Miller, F J Moore, L J Moore, H L Pate, B T Pelletier, C E Phillips, M Pulley, J H Rhodes, J W Rice, Hester Rollius, Noah Rouse, Alex Rouse, J A Rouse, W L Rouse, A E Rouse, J E Rouse, M A Rouse, L H Russell, Luke Russell, M J Sasser, J W Spruill, D M Stanton, J A Sutton, J N Sutton, J E Sutton, Clarence Sutton, N G Sutton, J W Sutton, sr, J W Sutton, jr, E A Sutton, Alex Sutton, J Sutton, Josiah Sutton, sr, W N Sutton, M Sutton, F M Sutton, B F Sutton, jr, Octavius Taylor, Geo Taylor, J L Todd, W S Uzzell, O K Uzzell, J D Walters, David Walters, N J Warters, Geo W Warters, James Warters, John Warters, Austin Williams, H V Williams, J M Wood, E E Woolard, C S Wooten, S I Wooten, K T Wooten, Nancy Wooten.

Pink Hill—W H Bird, W A Boyett, L H Carter, Jr, A Davis, J J Davis, S H Davis, E G Davis, R Howard, Sr, Stephen Howard, Geo Howard, W A Jones, J W Kinsey, M C C Lawson, H R Maxwell, J E B Noble, Geo Turner, S S Tyndall, Grey Whaley, J W Whaley.

Repose—Richard Strowd, Isaac Strowd.

Seven Springs—S A Bird, A H Daily, S H Davenport, M G Koonce, S A Kornegay, G W Mershaw, J E Outland, J D Quinn.

Strabane—J B Davis, H W Davis, J M Davis, T E Elmore, W L Hardy, Windal Harper, James Hill, Sr, Nathan Hill, Jonas Hill, Sr, W C Hines, Joel Howard, R H Jones, G W Jones, W W Rouse, T E Smith, Ira Smith, Lott Strowd, Louis Strowd, N B Whitfield, E D Wooten.

Willow Green—R A Darden.

Woodington—J H Waller, W H Waller, E W Waller, M F Waller.

LINCOLN COUNTY.

AREA, 270 SQUARE MILES.

POPULATION 12,579; White 10,021, Colored 2,558.

LINCOLN COUNTY was formerly called Tryon, but in 1779 the name was changed to Lincoln in honor of Benjamin Lincoln, who, at the time, was fighting the battles of his country against the British at Charleston.

LINCOLNTON, the county seat, is 182 miles west of Raleigh. Population, 1,500.

Surface.—Moderately uneven; soil good, valleys rich, scenery fine; well watered by the Catawba river and branches, furnishing abundant water-power.

Staples—Wheat, corn, oats and minerals. Iron ore is abundant; mica is mined profitably in the western part of the county.

Fruits—Apples, grapes, peaches, pears, and a variety of other fruits.

Timbers—Oak, pine, hickory, chestnut, poplar, ash, walnut and maple.

Minerals—Gold, iron, copper, mica, oil stone, asbestos, with lime and sulphur springs; Monozite (abundant), plumbago and garnet.

TOWNS AND POST OFFICES.

	POP.		POP.
Crimsic,	40	Lincolnton,	1,500
Crouse,	100	Long Shoals,	—
Derr,	20	Lowesville,	150
Denver,	300	Loyd,	25
Hagers,	—	Machpelah,	30
Harvey,	—	Mariposa,	20
Henry,	30	North Brook,	50
Hull's Cross		Orleans,	50
Roads,	50	Reepsville,	75
Iron Station,	150	Reinhardt,	25
Johnstown,	—	Sains,	15
Kidville,	50	Triangle,	30

COUNTY OFFICERS.

Clerk Superior Court—G A Barkley.
Commissioners—H E Ramseur, chm'n; P H Thompson, J E Reinhardt, D A Coon, W L Baker.
Coroner—J T McLean.
Register of Deeds—J F Killian.
Sheriff—C H Rhodes.
Solicitor 11th District—J L Webb.
Standard Keeper—Geo Bullinger.
Surveyor—O C Thompson.
Treasurer—D Luther Yount.
County Examiner—L A Abernethy.

COURTS.

Superior court meets fourth Monday after first Monday in March, and sixth Monday after first Monday in September.

TOWN OFFICERS.

LINCOLNTON—*Mayor*, S W McKee; *Commissioners*, H W Burton, D T F Costner, J B Ramseur, H S Kestler, J C Quickle; *Marshal*, J R Cline; *Secretary and Treasurer*, J C Quickle.

DENVER — *Mayor*, John F Davis; *Commissioners*, Dr H N Abernethy, H S Kids, B D Bollick; *Marshal*, M J Shelton.

TOWNSHIPS AND MAGISTRATES.

Catawba Springs—D A Lowe (Lowesville), John Davis, L A H Wilkinson (Denver), A King, R H W Barker (Harvey), D H Parker (Machpelah), R A Keever (Kidsville).

Howard's Creek—Henry Warlick, T F Crowell, G E Crowell (Lincolnton), M M Lutz (Henry). W H Hoover (Crouse), Henry Houser (Lincolnton).

Ironton—S S Morris, R H Dallinger, Bartlet Stroup. W F Huggins (Iron Station), J Mullen (Derr), S V Goodson (Lincolnton),

Lincolnton—S T Sherrill, J T De-Lane, A C Shrurn, J O Allen, J A C Barckley, H J Crooks (Lincolnton).

North Brook—T M Foster (North Brook), F J Leatherman (Hull's X Roads), J F Sain (Reepsville), C L Brown, W C Childress (North Brook). C Z Hoyle (Hull's X Roads).

CHURCHES.

Names, Post Offices, Pastors and Denom.

METHODIST.

Antioch—Crouse, J P Reynolds.
Asbury—Lincolnton, W F Womble.
Bethlehem—Lincolnton, E M Merritt.
Church—Lincolnton, W F Womble.
Friendship—Beattie's Ford, J C Mack.
Hill's Chapel—Lowesville, D M Litaker.
Laboratory—Lincolnton, J P Reynolds.
Marvin—Lincolnton, W F Womble.
Marvin—Denver, J C Mock.
McKendric Chapel—Lincolnton, W F Womble.

LINCOLN COUNTY.

New Hope—Lowesville, D M Litaker.
Palmtree—Henry, E M Merritt.
Pisgah—Lincolnton, W F Womble.
Pleasant Grove—Lincolnton, J P Reynolds.
Trinity—Lincolnton, W F Womble.
Salem—Lowesville, D M Litaker.
Zion—Lincolnton, E M Merritt.

NORTH. METHODIST.

Hebron—Sains.
Keever's—Beattie's Ford.
Laurel Hill—Sains.

METHODIST PROTESTANT.

Bess Chapel—Lincolnton.

ZION METHODIST.

First Church (col), Lincolnton.

EPISCOPAL.

Christ Church—Lincolnton, W R Wetmore, D D.
St Cyprian (col)—Lincolnton, W R Wetmore, D D, Dean.
St John's—Beattie's Ford, W R Wetmore, D D.
St Luke's—Lincolnton, W R Wetmore, D D.
St Paul's—Lincolnton, W R Wetmore, D D.
St Stephen's—Lincolnton, W R Wetmore, D D.

LUTHERAN.

Bethpage—Lincolnton, J C Wesinger.
Cedar Grove—Hull's X Roads, J C Wesinger.
David's Chapel—Hull's X Roads, J C Wesinger.
St Luke's—Lincolnton, John Moses.
Trinity—Henry's, J C Wesinger.

BAPTIST.

Church—Lincolnton, —— Austin.
Macedonia—Iron Station, Bart Mc Clure.
Salem—Iron Station, J F Morris.
Union—Lowesville.

LUTHERAN AND GERMAN REFORM.

Daniels—Lincolnton, D J Sachs and Dr Klapp.
Salem—Lincolnton, D J Sachs and Dr Klapp.

GERMAN REFORM.

Emanuel—Lincolnton, Dr Klapp.
Matthews—Lincolnton—Dr Klapp.

PRESBYTERIAN.

Church—Lincolnton, R J Johnston.
Second Church (col)—Lincolnton, —— Baker.
Ironton—Iron Station, R Z Johnston.
Unity—Beattie's Ford.

LINCOLN COUNTY.

MINISTERS RESIDENT.

Names, Post Offices and Denominations.

METHODIST.

Hake, F C, Cherryville.
Litaker, D M, Lowesville.
Reynolds, J P, Lincolnton.
Womble, W F, Lincolnton.

BAPTIST.

Gower, ——, Lincolnton.
Leatherman, John, Hull Cross-Roads.
McClure, Bart, Alexis.

PRESBYTERIAN.

Johnston, R Z, Lincolnton.
Kennedy, J Z, Lowesville.

EPISCOPAL.

Bynum, W S, Lincolnton.
Wetmore, W R, DD, Lincolnton.

HOTELS AND BOARDING HOUSES.

Names, Post Offices and Proprietors.

Boarding, Lowesville, W C Withers.
Boarding House, Denver, M J Shelton.
Boarding, Iron Station, Calvin Dellinger.
Hinson House, Lincolnton, P D Hinson.
North State Hotel, Lincolnton, P D Hinson.

LAWYERS.

Names and Post Offices.

Brevard, Alexander, Iron Station.
Childs, C E, Lincolnton.
Cobb, B C, Lincolnton.
Finley, L G, Lincolnton.
Hoke, Alexander (Judge Sup. Court), Lincolnton.
Justice, B A, Lincolnton.
McBee, V A, Lincolnton.
Robinson, D W, Lincolnton.
Wetmore, L B, Lincolnton.

MANUFACTORIES.

Kinds, Post Offices and Proprietors.

Blacksmithing and wheelwrighting, Denver, Henry Brevard (col).
Blacksmithing and wheelwrighting, Lincolnton, John Cornwell.
Blacksmithing and wheelwrighting, Lincolnton, J R Dettor.
Blacksmithing and wheelwrighting, Kidsville, J T Punch.
Blacksmithing and wheelwrighting, Lowesville, M S P Hagar.
Blacksmithing and wheelwrighting, Lowesville, Moses Conner.
Brooms, Lincolnton, John Warlick.

25

LINCOLN COUNTY.	LINCOLN COUNTY.

Building and contracting, Triangle, A W L Hager.
Building and contracting, Lincolnton, E H Cauble.
Building and contracting, Lincolnton, Motz & Wells.
Building and Loan Association, Lincolnton, Hugh Jenkins, sec.
Carriages, Lincolnton, John Ramsey.
Elm Grove Cotton Mills, Lincolnton, Reinhardt & Smith.
Foundry, Lincolnton, A Costner.
Furniture factory, Lincolnton, C Motz & Wells.
Laboratory Cotton Mills, Lincolnton, D E Rhyne.
Lime, Lincolnton, Lawson Keener.
Lincolnton Cotton Mill, Lincolnton, J A Abernethy & Co; capital stock, $150,000; spindles. 5,000.
Long Shoals Cotton Mills, Lincolnton, Mauney & Crouse; capital stock, $100,000; No of hands, 100.
Marble works, Lincolnton, J Thomas McLean.
Morrison Cotton Mill, Moreposa, J G Morrison; capital, $75,000.
Owen Flour Mills, Iron Station, R S Reinhardt.
Planing, furniture and flour mills, Lincolnton, Ed James.
Pottery, Seagle's Store, Dan'l Hartzog.
Pottery, Seagle's Store, Goodman & Seagle.
Shoes, Lincolnton, Alfred Thompson (col).
Shoes, Lincolnton, Wm Schenck (col).
Tannery, Triangle, D A Lowe.
Tannery, Triangle, L A Kaylor.
Tannery, Lincolnton, P W Ramseur.
Wagons, etc., Lincolnton, J R Blackburn.
Willow Brook Cotton Mill, Lincolnton, J L Kestler & Co; cap. stock $75,000; 2,500 spindles; No of hands, 50.
Wool carding, ——, T P Jenks.

MERCHANTS AND TRADESMEN.

Names, Post Offices, Lines of Business.

BEATTIE'S FORD.

Proctor, J W,	G S

CROUSE.

McLurd, J W,	G S
Mauney, T H & Bro,	G S
Moore & Rutledge,	G S
Quickle, J C,	G S

DENVER.

Kids, F S,	Hardw and Gro
Kids, J A,	G S
McCaul, Dr C L,	Drugs
Proctor, H C,	G S
Proctor, A M,	Drugs

Proctor, W C,	G S
Rankin, W W,	G S
Thompson, P A,	G S

DERR.

Lehmons, M A,	G S
Mullen, J & Son,	G S
Perkins, Lee,	G S

HARVEY.

King, J O,	G S

HENRY.

Havner, C L,	Dry Goods
Hinkle. Wm O,	G S
Hoyle & Sons,	Dry Goods
Hoyle, W L,	G S
Shuford & Bass,	G S
Spake, G W,	G S
Wood Bros,	G S

HULL'S CROSS-ROADS.

Baker, W L,	G S
Jenks. T P,	G S
Sain. Samuel,	G S
Thompson, O C,	G S

IRON STATION.

Randleman & Smith,	G S
Reinhardt & Co,	G S

JOHNSTOWN.

Dellinger, J C,	G S
Best, P B,	G S
Brown, J J,	G S

KIDSVILLE.

Kids, J A,	G S
Puntch, J S,	G S

LINCOLNTON.

Barr, P A.	G S
Childs, E T,	Dry Goods
Cobb, John L,	Dry Goods
Crouse, W L & Co,	Drugs
Edwards, W R,	Gro
Elm Grove Cotton Mills,	G S
Green Bros,	Livery
Griggs, B F,	Gro
Hinson, P D,	Gro
Hoffman, C P L,	G S
Hoke, E W,	Livery
Houser, R A,	Tinware
Jenkins Bros,	Dry Goods
Kids, F S,	Gro
Kistler, J L,	Dry Goods
McLean, C L,	
McLean, J Thomas,	Gro
Micheal, Robt M,	Hardw
Motz, W H,	Miller
Pate, P J,	Agt C C R R
Quickel, J C,	Dry Goods
Ramsaur & Burton,	Hardw
Ramsaur, J B,	Gro
Reedy, A W,	Gro
Rhyne, G P,	G S
Robinron, H S & Co,	G S
Roseman, R M,	Agr Implements

LINCOLN COUNTY.

Rudisill, L M (near),   G S
Sherrill, J F,   Harness
Sowers, Robt,   G S
Sumner, Miss Eva,   Postmaster
Toby, F A,   Dry Goods
Warlick, Jno C,   G S
Wilkie, J L,   G S

LONG SHOALS.

Long Shoal Cotton Mills,   G S

LOWESVILLE.

Kincaid, D,   Live Stock
Lowe, D A & Son,   G S
Lowe, Mrs S H & E M,   G S
Lowe, E M & Co,   G S

MACHPELAH.

Bisener, J B,   G S
Goodson. G W,   Grocer
Goods, A F,   G S
Lane, J W,   G S

MARIPOSA.

Morrison, J G,   G S
Summey, J E,   Grocer

NORTH BROOK.

Brown, C L,   G S
Jenks, O B & Son,   G S

ORLEANS.

Baxter, T H,   Grocer

REEPSVILLE.

Holly, W S,   Dry Goods
Rhyne, G P,   G S
Rudisill, L M,   G S
Warlick, Max,   Miller

RHEINHARDT.

Morrison, J G,   G S

SAIN.

Sain, L E,   G S
Sain, Samuel,   G S

TRIANGLE.

Kincaid, Limbarger,   G S
Morrison & Cherry,   Millers
Nance, W B,   G S
Nixon, J A & Co,   G S
Trim, S W,   G S

MINES.

Kinds, Post Offices and Proprietors.

Gold, Beattie's Ford, Miss F C Burton.
Gold, Lincolnton, L Keener.
Gold, Lincolnton, R M Beal.
Gold, Macpelah, W A Graham.
Gold, Mackpelah, McKnight & Morrison.
Gold, Lincolnton, H W Burton.
Gold, Lincolnton, Hoke & Burton.
Gold, Lincolnton, W A and Miss S B Hoke.
Gold, Reinhardt, J F Reinhardt.
Iron, Iron Station, J M Smith's estate.
Iron, Iron Station, J E Reinhardt.
Iron, Iron Station, A F Brevard.

LINCOLN COUNTY.

Mica, North Brook, Dr A A Thompson.
Mica, Loyd, Thos Baxter.
Mica, North Brook, J F Bess.
Sulphur, Kidsville, J M Kids.

MILLS.

Kinds, Post Offices and Proprietors.

Corn and flour, Machpelah, J F Brevard.
Corn and flour, Lincolnton, J A Killian.
Corn and flour, Lincolnton, L W Hoyle.
Corn and flour, Lowesville, D A & S H Lowe.
Corn and flour, Sains, Hoyle & Co.
Corn and flour, Derr, J B Hoke.
Corn and flour, Iron Station, R S Reinhardt.
Corn and flour, Lincolnton, W H Motz.
Corn and flour (roller mill), Lincolnton, John Rudisill.
Corn and flour, Reepsville, Jacob Warlick.
Corn and flour (roller mill), Lincolnton, Thos Finger.
Corn and flour (roller mill), Lincolnton, A Costner.
Corn and flour, North Brook, J D Hollman & Co.
Corn and flour, North Brook, George Beam.
Corn and flour, Orleans, Thomas Bess & Co.
Corn and flour, Triangle, G D Abernethy.
Corn, flour and saw, Triangle, Morrison & Cherry.
Corn, flour and saw, Crouse, W W Noland.
Corn, flour and saw, Kidsville, W A Smith.
Flour and saw, Denver, T H Proctor.
Gin and saw (steam), Lincolnton, Ed James.
Planing, saw and furniture, Lincolnton, E H Cauble.
Saw, Iron Station, R S Reinhardt.
Steam saw, Lincolnton, L & C Shrum.
Steam saw, Hull's Cross Roads, Bess & King.
Steam saw, Lincolnton, W A Rudisill.
Steam saw, North Brook, Dellinger & Bean.
Steam saw, Henry, Wood Bros.
Steam saw, Henry, Yount & Beam.
Steam saw, Lincolnton, Henry Huss.

PHYSICIANS.

Names, Post Offices and Principals.

Abernethy, H N, Denver.
Alexander, A W (dentist), Lincolnton.

LINCOLN COUNTY.

Bean, J Lee, Crouse.
Bess, W C, North Brook.
Bess, C L (dentist), North Brook.
Costner, T F, Lincolnton.
Crouse, W L, Lincolnton.
Crowell, Eli, Lincolnton.
Davidson, John, Triangle.
Davidson, Sinclair, Triangle.
Gains, J W, Lincolnton.
Houser, E A, Orleans.
Kiser, William, Reepsville.
McCann, C L, Denver.
McLean, R A, Lowesville.
Munday, J D, Denver.
Noland, W W (dentist), Crouse.
Reedy, J A, Lincolnton.
Smith, Augustus, Iron Station.
Thompson, Samuel, Orleans.
Thompson, W A, North Brook.

SCHOOLS.

Names, Post Offices and Principals.

Academy, Lowesville, Rev — Litaker.
Academy, Denver, S J Whitener.
Colored School, Lincolnton, H H Mulgrow,
High School, Iron Station.
Paper Mill School, J O Allen,
Piedmont Seminary, Lincolnton, L W Dick.
Public schools: white 55; colored 12.

TEACHERS.

Names, Post Offices and Principals.

Abernethy, J S, Henry.
Abernethy, L A, Lowesville.
Bayler, B B, Hardin.
Camp, L V, Iron Station.
Camp, R E, Iron Station.
Chambers, Hall, Lincolnton.
Craft, W L, Reepsville.
Davison, J W, Iron Station.
Dellinger, R H, Lincolnton.
Detter, Loula W, Henry.
Diet, L O, Lowesville.
Diggs, J D, Machpelah.
Dixon, Miss Dora C, Lowesville.
Edon, D E, Machpelah.
Forney, E W, Henry.
Franklin, J P, Iron Station.
Graham, Flora L, Lincolnton.
Graham, Miss Flora L, Hardin.
Hager, Miss Della, Lowesville.
Hallman, W C, Iron Station.
Hauser, D P, Reinhardt.
Harper, D H, Lowesville.
Harly, Flora, Hardin.
Headen, F C, Kidsville.
Heavner, A S, Kidsville.
Heitt, A N, Lincolnton.
Hoover, C C, Machpelah.
Hoover, J C, Lowesville.

Hoover, C H, Henry.
Hugans, W H, Hardin.
Johns, J T, Chronicle.
Johnson, Loula, Iron Station.
Johnson, Forney, Kidsville.
Johnson, D J, Machpelah.
Lutz, T M, Lowesville.
Lynhardt, Henry D, Iron Station.
Mansteller, E C, Iron Station.
McGee, Carrie, Lincolnton.
McGinas, E L, Lincolnton.
Morrison, Marra G, Iron Station.
Monroe, H H, Lowesville.
Nixon, Miss Sallie, Lincolnton.
Nixon, Miss Sallie, Lowesville.
Pope, L J, Chronicle.
Ramsour, Mrs George, Lowesville.
Reinhardt, Jas R, Reinhardt.
Reinhardt, Thos F, Iron Station.
Reinhardt, Jas R, Kidsville.
Rudisill, J H, Henry.
Seff, Lee R, Reinhardt.
Seff, Lester L, Iron Station.
Setzer, Emma, Lincolnton.
Shuford, W S, Lowesville.
Sullivan, R B, Lincolnton.
Wallict, Hattie, Lowesville.
Wallict, J Frank, Henry.
Westberger, J E, Lincolnton.
Whitner, S J, Machpelah.
Wilkinson, J D, Lincolnton.
Willis, Geo H, Machpelah.
Wilson, Miss Sallie, Lincolnton.

LOCAL CORPORATIONS.

Heptasoph Lodge, Lincolnton.
I O O F, Lincolnton, A M Wingate, sec.
Knights of Pythias, Lincolnton, Hugh Jenkins, C C; P J Pate, K of R & S.
Knights and Ladies of Honor, Lincolnton, J B Huin, Pro.
Knights of Honor, ——, R M Roseman, Dic; C E Childs, Rep.
Lincolnton Lodge, No 137, A F and A M, Lincolnton; A Nixon, W M; C E Childs, Sec; time of meeting, first Monday of Court week, and June 24th and December 27th.
Rock Springs Lodge, No 343, A F and A M, Denver; time of meeting, Saturday on or before full moon, and June 24th and December 27th.

NEWSPAPERS.

Lincoln Democrat, Lincolnton (Democratic weekly), C L Coon & G G Finley, editors and proprietors.
Lincoln Patriot, Lincolnton (Republican weekly), Gasque Printing Co.
Lincoln Courier, Lincolnton, T S Starrette.

FARMERS.

Names and Post Offices.

Chronicle—J F Moore, A F Moore.

Crouse—James Getange, P A Reep, J Warlick, David Warlick.

Deer—J B Armstrong, D M Armstrong, J W Armstrong, Robt Armstrong, W H Abernethy, C Frank Abernethy, D L Abernethy, James Abernethy, Kail Abernethy, D F Abernethy, Chas Abernethy, L A Abernethy, C Abernethy, Dora Abernethy, Wm Abernethy, J H Alexander, J W Alexander, J H Anton, Mason Ash, Levi Baker, Dan Baker, S P Beal, B V Beal, T F Beam, Larkin Boyd, Little Boyd, Jim Bradshaw, Brice A Bradshaw, Alexander Bradshaw, V A Bradshaw, F R Bradshaw, J F Bradshaw, B S Bradshaw, W R Bradshaw, Jack Brevard, R J Brevard, A F Brevard, J B Burk, Winslow Bynum, A A Bynum, D A Crouse, J C Crouse, D E Crouse, G S Goodson, Jas A Goodson, Milton Goodson, M L Goodson, W A Goodson, John Hoyle, F C Lawing, T A Lawing, Wesley Lawrence, J C Lee, J F Lee, J C Lynch, E M Lynch, J W Marsh, S A McBee, J Miller, J O Mullen, Geo S Mullen, J Mull, W C Mullen, J L Perkins, J F Perkins, W M Perkins, Lee Perkins, Make Pool, G R Potts, W C F Punch, J A Queen, M G Rheinhardt, J E Rheinhardt, Wm Rhodes.

Henry—Henry Baxter, J Baxter, W J Beam, W R Beam, T Bess, H L Bess, G Bess, J M Briant, Noah Brown, E H Burr, L S Burr, Geo Cancer, J Carpenter, E Carpenter, Ed Crowell, C C Dellinger, T M Foster, W L Hovle, Lee Heavner, M L Heavner, Geo Heavner, Cane Heavner, E Hoover, I Hoover, C Hoover, J E Hoover, Dr —— Killian, Manuel Lantz, Chas Leonard, J Miller, Lawsen Peter, A C Plunk, John Quincle, Melchi Rhodes, T E Rhodes, A D Robinson, J Sain, Andy Sain, George Sain, Ralph Shroutz, Dan Shuford, Jno Shuford, John Werchnel, L Werchnel, Tim Yount.

Iron Station—J Abernethy, L M Ballard, R H Ballard, J H Ballard, S M Ballard, R B Ballard, J S Ballard, W H Ballard, J D Ballard, John Barnett, J Benedict, J H Bisinger, S A Bisinger, J B Black, E C Black, A Black, J A Brown, J F Brown, Wm Brown, Geo Brown, Noah Brown, J B Buck, Alonzo Bynum, J S Bynum, W G Bynum, C E Bynum, L B Camp, C T Carpenter, Jno S Carpenter, M S Carpenter, J A Carpenter, W S Carpenter, O D Carpenter, M M Carpenter, D M Cashion, D H Clanton, C H Clanton, David Clippard, D A Clippard, D V Clippard, J E Crowland, J H Daily, J D Dellinger, A P Dellinger, M A Dellinger, D H Dellinger, J C Dellinger, Lawson Dellinger, M P Dellinger, L L Dellinger, A A Dellinger, H S Dellinger, R H Dellinger, J W Dellinger, C L Dellinger, John Dellinger, G W Edwards, Mrs Erson, J B Ewing, M O Ewing, W F Finger, J C Finger, Wm Finger, V P Friday, S V Goodson, J S Holliman, J P Harkins, W A Hoke, J C Hovis, M S Hovis, H B Hovis, J F Hovis, M L Hovis, Henry Hovis, M Hovis, L L Hovis, H W Hovis, N F Hovis, Will Keeve, J C Link, E F Link, W M Link, G P Rhyne, Peter Stump.

Johnstown—W L Baker, Peter Bess, Lansen Bess, Marvin Goldhill, Will Poh, Hessie Saine, Levi Saine, Sam Saine, John Scism, Geo Stiller, P C Thompson, O A Thompson, S Yount.

Kidsville—J O Hackans, S J Hackans, Frank Hackans, L A Hartsue, S L Hartsue, R P Harkey, C C Jones, G M Michael, Jas Michael, J M Michael.

Lowesville—J J Heavner, Marcus Hallard, J S Lawing, W A Lawing, Rob't Lawing, D C Lawing, R M Lowe, H W Loftin, M L Loftin, C P Miller, E Miller, J Nance, P W Ramsaur, J B Smith, R M Smith.

Lincolnton—E M Aderholt, Capt.— Alexander, J H Anton, John Beker, Frank Barns, Nelce Bass, H P Beal, Pley Beam, P Bess, J Bigerstaff, Sam Burgan, M Burton, W A Caldwell, A A Caldwell, W H Caldwell, Milton Campbell, E Campbell, Geo Caner, J R Carpenter, D W Carpenter, Alex Carpenter, A M Carpenter, P Carpenter, Jules Carpenter, Cavin Carpenter, John Carpenter, T C Childs, Wiley Childs, J Clark, Henry Cline, J K Cline, Dave Coon, Mark Coon, A S Coon, Ambers Costner, W A Costner, A Costner, Matt Costner, John Cribb, L D Dellinger, Monroe Dellinger, W R Edwards, T Finger, W P Garrison, Calvin Goodson, R F Goodson, B F Grigg, R B Harrill, S G Harrill, J B Harrill, A G Harrill, Sam Harrill, A Hauss, J Hauss, C Hauss, Wm Havner, John F Haynes, Laban Hoyle, George Heavner, D W Heaver, Moses Heavner, E Hedict, L S Hicks, Geo Hines, P P Hinson, J B Hoke, Cavyn Hoover, Lee Huffman, J Huffstetter, T Hall, B Hall, T P Jinks, A N Jones, E Jones, L W Keener, W A Keener, Louis Keener, C C Keener, David Keener, Dank Keener, P Keener, Wm Keener,

LINCOLN COUNTY.	LINCOLN COUNTY.

E W Keener, W M Keener, Daniel Keener, D A Kelly, W F Kelly B J Kenney, L P Killian, N P Killian, O King, J O King, H King, Harris King, J S Lantz, Prince Lantz, C C Leadford, Noah, Leatherman, J R Link, A Link. Mames Loar, J C Martin, E I Mastiller, W McClurd, Vard McGhee, W F Miller, W H Miller, A C Miller, S S Morris, C C Moore, W Motz, John Motz, George Movner, J Movner, F J Nantz, Albert Nantz, Wm Nantz, A Nixon, R M Nixon, C L Noles, John Parker, F H Parker, N M, Parker, J C Plunk, M C Plunk, Sidney Poovey, T Ramsour, E Ramsour, John Ramsour, D Rankin, W F Reinhardt, J H Reinhardt, R O Reinhardt, E M Reinhardt,

C H Rhodes, W Rhyne, J A Roberts, J A Robinson, David Robinson, R M Roseman, Guss Rudisill, Al Rudisill, J Self, R Self, J P Sherrill, Geo Shufford, J L Shrum, L O Shrum, C Shrum, Levi Shrum, Henry Shrum, Samuel Shrum, R Silver, John Sisk, J Smith, J Stamey, John Stamey, Chalers Sumner, Geo Sumroe, Peter Sumroe, Mann Taylor, Bill Taylor, J H Tothure, Josh Tothure, Jacob Willams, B C Wood, D L Yount.

Machpelah — G W Goodson, R E Goodson, T N Graham, O S Hollman, W O Henke, F L Howard, J W Lane, John Laney.

Reinhardt — R S Reinhardt, J B Robinson.

MACON COUNTY.

AREA, 650 SQUARE MILES.

POPULATION, 10,085; White 9,420, Colored 665.

MACON COUNTY was formed in 1828 from Haywood county, and named in honor of Hon. Nathaniel Macon, of Warren county, who was so long the representative in Congress from the Warren district.

FRANKLIN, the county seat, is 331 miles west of Raleigh, romantically situated on the Little Tennessee river. Population, 425.

HIGHLANDS is a town situated 20 miles northeast from Franklin, and is 3,700 feet above the level of the sea.

Surface— Moderately uneven, with occasional mountains; water-power splendid, scenery fine; watered by the Tennessee river.

Staples—Wheat, corn, oats and medicinal herbs—also live-stock.

Fruits— Apples, peaches, plums, cherries and other small fruits.

Timbers—Oak, hickory, black walnut, poplar, cherry, buckeye and locust.

TOWNS AND POST OFFICES.

	POP.		POP.
Aquona,	—	Millshoal,	—
Burningtown,	—	Nonah,	—
Crawford,	—	Otto,	—
Cullasaja,	—	Parrish,	—
Ellijay,	—	Pineland,	—
Etna,	—	Roane's Mill,	—
Flats,	—	Saquilla,	—
Franklin (c h),	500	Scaly,	—
Higdonville,	—	Shortoff,	—
Highlands,	200	West's Mill,	—
Knoll,	—	Wikle's Store,	—
Leatherman,	—		

COUNTY OFFICERS.

Clerk Superior Court—Lee Crawford.
Commissioners—John Amons, chm'n.
Register of Deeds—J S Sloan.
Sheriff—C T Roane.
Solicitor 12th District—Geo H Jones.
Treasurer—C T Roane.
County Examiner—L H Garland.

COURTS.

Ninth Monday after the first Monday in March, and fourth Monday after the first Monday in September.

TOWNSHIPS AND MAGISTRATES.

Burnington—P C Wild, C S Ray, Geo Parrish, Joseph Morgan, David Vance, Jr (Burnington).

Cartoogeehaye— W B Setser, Jesse C Weaver, T M Slagle, Mack Gillespie, Harrison Dills, Caleb Dalrimple (Franklin)

Cowee—A B Dalton, J B Carden, W J Jenkins, H D Dean, G T Bryson, E C Sturman (Franklin).

Ellijay—R A Jacobs, N J Rush, John B Gray, W L Higdon, J T Henry, J R Bryson (Ellijay).

Franklin—John Reid, Geo McPherson, J P Campbell, J M Carpenter, H H Jarrett, J M Farmer, N P Rankin (Franklin).

Highlands—T B White, W R McCall, Marion Wright, T J Smith, Mack Wilson, H M Roscure, T H Hill, T B White (Highlands).

Mill Shoals—John Elmore, J W Parker, J B Elmore, W M Haskett, Thos W Angel, J T Berry, J H Young (Mill Shoals).

Nantahala—Jason Morgan, J A Baldwin, J W Harris, S J May, Z Barnes, A N Wood, R P Garrison (Franklin).

Smith's Bridge—W J Grist, J J McConnel, Tervel Bradley, Zeb Angel Jack Foster (Franklin).

Sugar Fork—J B Bryson, W W Moss, Isaac Peek, J M Kenner, Jno Corbin, J L Strain (Franklin).

CHURCHES.

Names, Post Offices and Denominations.

METHODIST.
Asbury—Franklin.
Bethel—Franklin.
Buck Creek—Franklin.
Church—Highlands.
Church—Franklin.
Clark's Chapel—Franklin.
Cowee—Franklin.
Iotlee—Franklin.
Mt Zion—Franklin.
Shepherd's—Franklin.
Tessentry—Franklin.
Union—Franklin.
Watauga—Franklin.

N. METHODIST.
Church—Highlands.

MACON COUNTY.

MACON COUNTY.

BAPTIST.

Brush Creek—Franklin.
Buck Creek—Franklin.
Burningtown—Franklin.
Cartoogechaye—Franklin.
Church—Franklin.
Cold Springs—Franklin.
Cowee—Franklin.
Ellijay—Franklin.
Liberty—Franklin.
Nantahala—Aquone.
Sugar Fork—Franklin.
Watauga—Franklin.

PRESBYTERIAN.

Church—Highlands.

UNITARIAN.

Church—Highlands.

HOTELS.

Names, Post Offices and Proprietors.

Hotel, Franklinton, D C Cunningham.
Hotel, Highlands, David Norton.

MANUFACTORIES.

Kinds, Post Offices and Proprietors.

Millwrighting, Franklin, R A Wood.
Nantahala Lumber and Mfg Co, Jarrett's.
Saddles, Franklin, W A McConnell.
Saddles, Franklin, J P Angel.
Wagons, Franklin, Palmer & Phillips.

MERCHANTS AND TRADESMEN.

Name, Post Office, and Line of Business.

AQUONE.

Baird, Zeb,   G S

CULLASAGA.

Bidswell & Co,   G S

ELIJAH

Berry, John T,   C S
Henry & Berry,   G S
Hiddon, W H,   Mill
Barker, J W & Co,   G S

ETNA.

Morgan, Jas,   G S

FRANKLIN.

Angel, Jas P,   Saddler
Angel, Thos,   Miller
Barnard, J Lee,   G S
Cunningham, Mrs D C,   Hotel and
                                   Livery

Cunningham, J B & Co,   G S
Franks & Pendergrass,   G S
Jarrett, R H & Son,   G S, Hotel and
                                 Livery
Lyle & Garland,   Drugs
McConnell, W A,   Saddler
Munday, A P,   Mill
Palmer & Phillips,   Wagons
Porter, R L,   G S
Potts, W T,   G S
Robinson, Mrs J L,   Books
Smith, C C,   G S
Trotter, H G,   G S
Waldroup, Jacob,   Miller
Welsh, J W,   Miller
Wood, R A,   Millwright
Wright, John C,   G S

HIGHLANDS.

Bascom, H M,   G S
David, Mrs M A,   Hotel
Henry, A,   Livery
Partridge, Wm.   Grist Mill
Paul, H M & Son,   G S
Rideout & Co,   G S
Smith & Miller,   G S
Waleen, T D,   Banker
White, T Baxter,   G S

JARRETT'S.

Jarrett, L A,   G S
Nantahala Lumber and Mfg Co.

NONAH.

Arthur, T S,   Miller

ROANE'S MILL.

Roane, H C,   G S and Mill

SKEENER.

Hodgin, C,   G S

WEST MILLS.

Hall, J A,   G S

MINES.

Kinds, Post Offices and Proprietors.

Corundum, Callasaja, Dr H S Lucas.
Lead and silver, Franklin, Brooks & Co
Mica, Franklin, Dr H S Lucas.
Mica, Franklin, C D Bowers.
Mica, Franklin, Arnold & Campbell.
Mica, Burningtown, C Bowers.
Quartz gold, Franklin, Arch. Gregory.

MILLS.

Kinds, Post Offices and Proprietors.

Grist mill, Elijah, W H Hiddon.
Mill, Franklin, A P Munday.
Grist mill, Highland, Wm Partridge.
Roane's mills, Roane's Mills, H C Rosne

MADISON COUNTY.

AREA 450 SQUARE MILES.

POPULATION 17,080 ; White 9,080, Colored 8,000.

MADISON COUNTY was formed in 1850, from Buncombe and Yancey counties, and was named in honor of James Madison, the fourth President of the United States.

MARSHALL, the county-seat, is situated on the French Broad river and the Western North Carolina railroad. Population estimated at 325.

Surface — Mountainous, with rich valleys interspersed, watered by the French Broad ; scenery unsurpassed for beauty and grandeur.

Staples—Tobacco, wheat, corn, butter, medicinal herbs, grass, clover, oats, etc, and live stock. No tobacco was produced in this county prior to 1872, the adaptability of the soil to its growth being unknown. It is now an important staple.

Fruits—Apples, peaches, pears, cherries, grapes, plums, berries and other small fruits.

Timbers-Oak, pine, ash, poplar, hickory, birch, walnut, chestnut, bynn, buckeye, sycamore, buck blackgum, dogwood and sourwood.

Minerals—Iron, mica and several valuable mineral springs.

TOWNS AND POST OFFICES.

POP.		POP.
Alleghany,		Leonard,
Barnard,		Little Fine Creek,
Big Laurel,		Luck,
Big Pine,		Lynch,
Bluff,		Marshall (c h), 700
Briggsville,		Mars Hill,
Buckner,		Outlook,
California Creek,		Paint Fork,
Croprock,		Paint Rock,
Endlish,		Peck,
Faust,		Ray,
Friezeland,		Sandy,
Grapevine,		Sexton,
Halewood,		Spring Creek,
Hot Springs,		Stackhouse,
Ivey,		Theta,
Joe,		Trailbranch,
Kind,		Walnut Run,
Laurelton,		White Rock,
Lee,		

COUNTY OFFICERS.

Clerk Superior Court—M A Chandley.
Commissioners—Jasper Ebbs, chmn.
Register of Deeds—R F Fox.
Sheriff—Jas H White.
Solicitor Twelth District- Geo H Jones.
Treasurer—Enoch Rector.
County Examiner—W P Jervis.

COURTS.

First Monday after the first Monday in March, and fifth Monday before the first Monday in September.

TOWNSHIPS AND MAGISTRATES.

No 1—M Davis, G W Waldrop, J J Redmond, L M Sprinkle, Henry Brown. J F Bryan, Jake M Ramsey, G M McDowell, L M Bryan, B Fortener (Marshall).

No 2—Kelsey Prigman, J S Tweed, S S Shelton. Jas Rice, W R Shelton, J C Chanley, W S Rice, J S Tweed, Jas Haynie, B W Gahagan (Laurelton).

No 3—M F Roberts, H J Chambers, S O Deaver, W P Jarvis, J L Phillips, W C Ray, R W Guthrie, W C Ammons, C N Jarvis, N H Rice (Marshall).

No 4—Don Anderson, H L McLean, N W Anderson, J G Holcombe, L B Metcalf, Wm Taylor, L H Rice, A W Arrowood, L E Briggs (Marshall).

No 5—W P Bryan, T M McPeeters, Jas Ramsey, J B Sprinkle, Wm George, J H Buckner, Wm M Edwards, Robert Ponden, Alfred Sprinkle (Marshall).

No 5—M M Treadway. M Teague, J B Bellew, J W Randall, Edward Teague, Berry Clark (Sandy).

No 7—J B Roberts, Logan Lunsford, Willis Payne, Joseph Payne, S J Kent, A J Roberts, Enoch Rector, jr, R F Payne (Little Pine Creek).

No 8—J P McLean, A E Brown, R H Hipps, T L Plemmons, W A Melton, W H Plemmons. Van Brown, J B Balding (Spring Creek).

No 9—W F Ramseur, B W Hill, I C Mooneyham, Z W Harris, H H Trent, Thos Garrett, John Harrison, R N Branson, A V Lawson (Hot Springs).

No 10—Joe Bishop, J M Wallen, Reuben Ramsey, James Rice, J E Rice, Eli H Jarrett (Big Laurel).

No 11—J C Davis, J S Ponder, F M Marshbanks, A Metcalf, Geo Marshbanks, Mack English, O B Holcombe (Marshall).

No 12—G Wild, A J Roberts, E P

MADISON COUNTY.

Goforth, N Buckner, Marion Sawyer, R G Wild, Wm Reese (Little Pine Creek).

No 13—M J Balding, W G Gregory, J L Williamson, E L Haynes, J G Reynolds, R M Hicks, John Keener (Marshall).

No 14—George Brown, S S Coats, Whitt Owens, C C Bruce, Jos Saylor, J F Tilson, Jeff Sams, John B Goswell (Grapevine).

CHURCHES.

Names, Post Offices, Pastors and Denom.

METHODIST.

Antioch—Paint Rock, W D Sasser.
Bolin Grove—Bluff, T McCurdy.
Big Pine—Big Pine, H C Sprinkle.
Church—Marshall, H C Sprinkle.
Chapel Hill—Laurel, H C Sprinkle.
Church—Paint Rock, W D Sasser.
Church—Spring Creek, T B McCurdy.
Church—Little Ivey, V L Marsh.
Church—Weaverville, L E Stacy.
Hot Spring—Hot Spring, W D Sasser.
Little Sandy—Sandy Marsh, L T Cordell.
Meadow Fork—Bluff, T B McCurdy.
Ottinger's—Hot Spring, W D Sasser.
Poplar Gap—Bluff, T B McCurdy.
Rector's—Marshall, H C Sprinkle.
Roaring Fork—Bluff, T B McCurdy.
Walnut Creek—Marshall, H C Sprinkle.

BAPTIST.

Bethel—Ivey.
Big Pine Creek—Marshall.
Bull Creek—Marshall.
Cane Fork—Marshall.
Fairview—Marshall.
Laurel Hill—Big Laurel.
Little Ivey—Ivey.
Little Pine Creek—Marshall.
Middle Fork—Ivey.
Mount Zion—Ivey.
Paint Gap—Ivey.
Spring Creek—Spring Creek.
Sagar Camp—Marshall.
Upper Laurel—Big Laurel.
Walnut Creek—Marshall.

FREE-WILL BAPTIST.

Fairview—Marshall.
Sodom—Marshall.
Union—Marshall.

LAWYERS.

Names and Post Offices.

Hendricks, John A (Gudger & Hendricks), Marshall.
Marshburn, C B, Marshall.

MADISON COUNTY.

McElroy, J S, Ivey.
McElroy, P A, Marshall.
Rumbough, H T, Hot Springs.
Zackary, W W, Marshall.

MERCHANTS AND TRADESMEN.

Names, Post Offices, Lines of Business.

ALLEGHANY.

Shelton, W R,	G S

BARNARD.

Haynie & Wilson,	G S
Miles, D P,	G S
Trammel, W A & Co,	G S

BIG LAUREL.

Redmond, Lance & Co,	G S
Rice, W S & Bro,	G S

BIG PINE.

Lance, Robert & Co,	G S

BRIGGSVILLE.

Briggs, L E,	G S

BULL CREEK.

Edwards, J H, & Co,	G S

GRAPE VINE.

Brown, W H,	G S
Cragile, C W,	G S

HALEWOOD.

Bruce, M,	G S
Whitt Bros,	G S

HOT SPRINGS.

Ebbs, F C,	G S
Lance, N J,	G S
Lance, R M & Co,	G S
Laurel River and Hot Springs	Supply Co
McFall & Tainter,	G S
Mountain Park Hotel,	Corp
Ross, Dr W F,	Hotel

IVY.

Clouse, W M,	G S
Gibbs & Clouse,	G S

LEE.

Balding, J B,	Mill
Brown, S W,	G S

LEONARD.

Gudger, J M, & Co,	G S

LIME ROCK.

Lawson, Thomas, & Co,	G S

LITTLE PINE CREEK.

Kent, S J (near),	Miller
Roberts, A J,	G S
Worley, Henry, & Son,	G S

LYNCH.

Fribee, D G & Son,	G S
Rolen, G W & Son,	G S

MARS HILL.

Baird & Edwards,	G S
Ramsey, O H, & Son,	G S

MADISON COUNTY.

MADISON COUNTY.

MARSHALL.

Edward, B B,	G S
Fisher Bros,	G S
Gudger, J M, & H A,	Tob
Gudger, W J,	G S
Gudger, Wallin & Co,	G S
Haynie, G C, & Co,	Jeweler
Hudgins, P M & Co,	G S
Lance, M W,	G S
Lance, West & Co,	G S
Lawson Bros,	G S
Lawson & Rector,	G S
McKay, Bryant & Co,	G S
McKay & Smart,	G S
McPheeters, C L,	G S
Nelson, John B (near),	G S
Nelson Bros,	G S
New England Southern Timber and Land Co	
Nichols, J A,	G S
Perkins. J J,	G S
Rector, E, & Co,	G S
Redmond Bro & Co,	G S
Redmond & Brown,	Drugs
Rogers, John,	G S
Tweed, Tillery, Hess & Co,	G S
West, J N, & Co,	G S
White & Roberts,	G S

OUTLOOK.

Edwards, J H & Co,	G S
Sprinkler Bros,	G S

PAINT ROCK.

Brown, J M & Son,	G S
Haworth, M L,	G S
Scion & Frey,	G S

RAY.

Hall, E S,	G S

SANDY BOTTOM.

Runion, W F & Son,	G S
Wetzell, W B & Co,	G S & Lumber

SEXTON.

Rice, N H,	G S

SPRING CREEK.

Woody, C J,	G S

STACKHOUSE.

Stackhouse, A,	G S

TAPATAMEE.

Teague, M,	G S

TRAIL BRANCH.

Ward, R H & Co,	G S

WALNUT CREEK.

Runion & Roberts,	G S

WHITE ROCK.

Shelton, W G & Bro,	G S
Tweed Bros,	G S

MINES.

Kinds, Post Offices and Proprietors.

Copper, Marshall, A S Freeman & Co.
Mica, Marshall, J K Hardwick & Co.

MILLS.

Names, Post Offices and Proprietors.

Mill, Lee, J B Balding.
Saw mill, Marshall, W B Ramsey.
Steam saw mill, Marshall, Riggs & Barber.

MARTIN COUNTY.

AREA, 500 SQUARE MILES.

POPULATION, 15,216; White 7,833, Colored 7,383.

MARTIN COUNTY was formed in 1774 from Halifax and Fayette counties, and named in honor of Josiah Martin, then the Royal Governor (and the last) of the colony of North Carolina.

WILLIAMSTON, the county-seat, is situated on the south bank of the Roanoke river, 100 miles east of Raleigh, population 900.

Surface.—Low, marshy; lies on the south side of Roanoke river, and is generally rich and very productive when well drained.

Staples.—Cotton, corn, peanuts, shingles, lumber, naval stores and fish.

Fruits.—Apples, peaches, grapes, berries and other small fruits.

Timbers.—Oak, pine, cypress, maple and birch.

TOWNS AND POST OFFICES.

	POP.		POP.
Amhurst,	15	Hassell,	—
Conoho,	50	Jamesville,	500
Darden,	—	Parmele,	200
Dymond City,	10	Robersonville,	400
Everett,	150	Williamston (c h),	
Gold Point,	80		900
Hamilton,	800		

COUNTY OFFICERS.

Clerk Superior Court—N S Peel.
Commissioners—J B Coffield, chmn, S L Wallace, B F Godwin, J B Roberson, Justus Everett.
Coroner—Thos L Whitley.
Register of Deeds—J A Teel.
Sheriff—W J Hardison.
Solicitor Third District—C M Bernard.
Standard Keeper—J G Swain.
Surveyor—Sylvester Peel.
Treasurer—S R Biggs.
County Examiner—Sylvester Hassell.
County Physician—W H Harrell.

COURTS.

Superior Court meets second Monday after the first Monday in March, and the first Monday in September.

TOWN OFFICERS.

HAMILTON—*Mayor*, T B Slade. *Commissioners*, H D Cask, Geo Blount, Eli Gurganus, W A Ellison, Mack Rhodes. *Constable*, J W Watts.

WILLIAMSTON—*Mayor*, Alex H Smith. *Constable*, C N Bellamy. *Commissioners*, C H Baker, Thos H Pritchard, J B Williams, W B Gardner, J B Anthony. *Clerk*, C H Baker. *Treasurer*, Thos H Pritchard.

TOWNSHIPS AND MAGISTRATES.

Beargrass—J F Bailey, W L Bailey, W H Jones, L T Holliday, J S Peal, R S Rogerson, David Gurganus (Williamston).

Cross-Roads—H W Holliday, J B Burroughs, J D Simpson, John Bailey, G D Gurganus, J D Ayers, H D Cowan, Stanley Ayers (Williamston).

Goose Nest—J T Hyman, H Brown, S T Burnett, J J Long, J L Davenport, W E Garrett, J L Hines, W L Ruffin, Wash Moore (Williamston).

Griffin—D R Daniel, J A Lilly, S R Hardison, G W Griffin, P Peal, S T Peal, G E Peal, J E Peal, C C Coltraine (Williamston).

Hamilton—T W Ward, R H Salsbury, Geo E Brown, T B Slade, W T West, H A Nicholson, L A Bailey, Calvin White, Calvin Griffin, Geo Harrison, A E Weatherbee (Hamilton).

Jamesville—C C Waters, J L Ward, E W Auge, G M Burroughs, C C Fagan, S H Spruill, J P Butler, Stewart Auge (Jamesville).

Poplar Point—J R Ballard, Jason Tice, J G Taylor, J A B Lane, G R L Roebuck, Henry Smith, Robt Leggett (Williamston).

Robersonville—M A Roberson, B R Jenkins, J A Coburn, W G Whitfield, J H Grimes, J R Smith, J O Keel, W W Andrews (Robersonville).

Williams—N T Riddick, S E Hardison, H P Gibson, W S Manning, M L Andrews, W E Daniel (Williamston).

Williamston—J L Ewell, A L Mizell, W H Robertson, W J Riddick, G S Whitley, B B Watts, J R Mobley, T L Green, W H Wilson (Williamston).

CHURCHES.

Names, Post Offices and Denominations.

METHODIST.

Bethlehem (col)—Williamston.
Cedar Branch—Jamesville, R T Wyche.
Church—Jamesville, R T Wyche.

MARTIN COUNTY.

Church—Hamilton, A J Parker.
Church—Williamston, A J Parker.
Chuech (col)—Dymond City.
Church (col)—Jamesville.
Holly Springs — Williamston, R T Wyche.
Jones Chapel—Hamilton. A J Parker.
Siloam—Jamesville, R T Wyche.
Taylor's Chapel — Jamesville, R T Wyche.
Welch's Creek—Jamesville,R T Wyche
Williams' Chapel—Hamilton, A J Parker.

BAPTIST.

Church—(col), Hamilton, A Cooper.
Church—(col), Williamston.
Church—Williamston, J E Edwards.
Church—Hamilton, J E Edwards.
Church—(col), Jamesville.
Pine Forest—Everett's, J E Edwards.

PRIMITIVE BAPTIST.

Bear Grass—Williamston, John N Rogerson.
Church—Jamesville, Henry Peele.
Church—(col), Williamston, Elijah Brown.
Church—Conoho, M T Lawrence.
Church—Hamilton, M T Lawrence.
Flat Swamp—Robersonville, J D Roberson.
Hamilton—Hamilton, M T Lawrence.
Kenarky—Williamston, S Hassell.
Peter Swamp—(col), Williamston, Geo Rollins.
Smithwick's Chapel — Williamston, Henry Peel.
Spring Green—Hamilton, G D Roberson.

DISCIPLES OF CHRIST.

Church—Jamesville, J D Davis.
Church—Robersonville, —— Summerson.
Cross Roads—Everett's, S Ayers.
Lebanot —Hassell, —— Summerson.
Macedonia—Williamston, S Ayers.
Poplar Run—Jamesville, J D Edwards.

EPISCOPAL.

Church of Advent—Williamston.
Mission—Jamesville.
St Martin—Hamilton, W J Smith.

MINISTERS RESIDENT.

Names, Post Offices and Denom.

PRIMITIVE BAPTIST.

Brown, Henry (col), Robersonville.
Hassell. S, Williamston.
Lawrence, T H, Hamilton.
Mizzell, A D, Williamston.
Outerbridge, Willis (col), Conoho.
Peele, Hyman, Williamston.
Peele, Henry, Williamston.

MARTIN COUNTY.

Robertson, G D, Robersonville.
Smith, M P, Robersonville.

BAPTIST.

Fagan, Frank, Williamston.

METHODIST.

Cherry, J L. Williamston.
Eborn, W R, Robersonville.
Harrell, W H. Palmyra.
Parker, A J, Williamston.
Whitley John (col), Williamston.

DISCIPLES OF CHRIST.

Ayers, S, Everett's.

HOTELS AND BOARDING HOUSES.

Names, Post Offices and Proprietors.

Boarding, Enretta, Mrs S P Everett.
Boarding, Hamilton, Mrs Jane Jarvis.
Conoho House, Hamilton, Mrs T E Darden.
Hassell House, Williamston, Mrs Ida Hassell.
Hotel. Jamesville, Mrs Florence J Kemp.
Hotel, Jamesville, Mrs Dennis Taylor.
Hotel, Robersonville, ——.
Roanoke Hotel, Williamston, Blount & Bro.

LAWYERS.

Names and Post Offices.

Moore (J E) & Stubbs (H W), Williamston.
Morton, W Z, jr, Robersonville.
Smith (A H) & Martin (Wheeler), Williamston.
Waldo, Jos T, Hamilton.

MANUFACTORIES.

Kinds, Post Offices and Proprietors.

Blacksmithing and wheelwrighting, Williamston, J H Hatton.
Building and contracting, Dymond City, Nelson Warters.
Building and contracting, Dymond City, J E Lordly.
Carriages, Robersonville, R L Roberson.
Cheap bedsteads, Williamston, Martin & Briggs.
Coaches, Hamilton, Slade, Jones & Co.
Cypress shingles and elm hoops, Hamilton, Boyle Mfg Co.
Sawed lumber and shingles, Williamston, Dennis Simmons Lumber Co.
Dressed lumber, Everett's, Martin Lumber Co.
Dressed Lumber Co, Parmalee, Parmalee Eccleston Lumber Co.

MARTIN COUNTY.

Lumber and shingles, Williamston, Dennis Simmons Lumber Co.
Lumber and shingles, Williamston, B R Whitley.
Sawed Lumber, Parmelee, North State Lumber Co.
Sawed Lumber, Everett's, Martin County Lumber Co,
Shingles and lumber, Hamilton, J P Boyle.
Shingles and lumber, Williamston, Godwin & Roberson.

MERCHANTS AND TRADESMEN.

Names, Post Offices, Lines of Business.

DARDEN.

Broughton. W T & Co,	G S
Waters & Barden,	G S

DYMOND CITY.

Nolan, H P,	G S

EVERETT'S.

Barnhill, W S,	G S
Barnhill & James,	G S
Clark, W B,	G S
Clark, W H,	G S
Wynn, L B,	G S

GOLD POINT.

Coburn & Roberson,	G S
Johnson, B L & Co,	G S
Roberson, J E & Son,	G S

GOOSE NECK.

Gladstone, R K & Bro,	G S
Harrell, H K,	G S
Ross, S H,	G S
Ross, W B,	G S

HAMILTON.

Cherry, McG,	Shoemaker
Gladstone, F L,	Grocer
Jones, D C,	Livery
Long, Dr B L,	Drugs
Robertson, F H,	Drugs
Sherrod, A & Baker, C K,	G S
Sherrod, B B,	G S
Slade, Jones & Co,	G S
Thompson, O T,	G S
Thompson, M (col.),	Gro

HASSEL.

Cooper, G L & Son,	G S
Nicholson, H A,	G S
Salisbury, Mrs A E,	G S

JAMESVILLE.

Allen, J B & Co,	G S
Berry, T A,	G S
Brown, L M,	G S
Burras, H M,	G S
Clark, W W,	G S
Collopy, J W,	G S
Cooper, G F,	G S
Ellison, J R,	R R Agent
Gainer, R H,	G S
Hamilton, S A,	G S

MARTIN COUNTY.

Hassell & Co,	G S and Fish
Johnson, J L,	G S
Kemp, G L,	G S
Lilly, W B,	G S
Mann, L A (col.),	G S
Mann, R P (col.),	G S
Mays, Dr W R,	Drugs
Owens & Co,	G S
Parker, M F,	Gro
Peele, M G & Bro,	G S
Peele, R J,	G S
Price, Kemp & Son,	G S
Stallings, H T,	G S
Stallings, N S,	G S
Stallings, W L,	G S
Vaughan, W W,	Gro
Wallace, S L,	G S
Ward, Mrs Mary A M,	G S

PARMELEE.

Andrews & Purvis,	G S
Andrews, J C,	G S
Bellflour, A L,	G S
Harper, W H,	G S
Gaynor & Peely,	G S
Jones, W M & Co,	G S
Parmelee, Eccles Lumber Co,	Lumber
Parmelee Commissary Co,	G S
Powell, D S & Co,	G S
Powell, W M,	G S
Purvis, Bryant & Co,	G S
Whitly, Thomas,	Confec

ROBERSONVILLE.

Everett, M,	Gro
Everett, W A,	G S
Hardison, N H,	G S
Hardison & Co,	G S
Hargrove, Dr R H,	Drugs
Keil, W D,	G S
Peel, Mrs M R & Co,	G S
Roberson, A G & Co,	G S
Roberson, A S & Co,	G S
Roberson, G D,	G S
Roberson, G E & J C,	G S
Roberson, Mrs H B,	Millinery
Roberson, J E & Son,	G S
Roberson, M A,	G S
Ross, H & Co,	G S
Ross, S L,	G S
Taylor, S G,	G S
Taylor, R T,	G S

WILLIAMSTON.

Anderson, J W & Bro,	G S
Ballard, M W,	G S
Biggs, S R,	Drugs
Blount & Bro,	G S
Carstarphen, C D & Co,	G S
Cherry, J B,	G S
Daws, M B,	G S
Ewell, J L,	Hay and Grain
Ewell, P,	Jeweler
Godard, Jos G & Bro,	Gro
Godwin & Robertson,	G S
Griffin, W E (near),	G S
Gurganus & Crawford,	G S

MARTIN COUNTY.

Hassell, W H.   Livery
Hodges, F K,   G S
Johnson, A (col),   Livery
Leggett, J D,   G S
Leggett, W H,   G S
Lilley, K (near),   G S
Mizell, A J,   G S
Powell & Clark,   G S
Sprewell, P S (col),   Gro
Watts, B B & Co,   G S

MILLS.

Kinds, Post Offices and Proprietors.

Corn and flour, Williamston, J L Roberson.

Corn, saw and gin (steam), Robersonville, M A Roberson.

Flour and corn, Williamston, H A Coltraine.

Flour and corn, Williamston, Mobley & Taylor.

Flour, corn and saw, Dymond City, W H Daniel.

Saw (steam), Williamston, R H Rogerson.

Saw (steam), Everett's, M L James.

Saw (steam), Everett's, Henry Wynn.

Saw (steam), Williamston, K Lilley.

Steam saw, Jamesville, W L Stallings.

Steam saw, Williamston, M Burroughs.

Water saw and grist, Jamesville, F B Hardison.

Water grist, Everett's, John R Leggett.

PHYSICIANS.

Names and Post Offices.

Clark, H I, Palmyra.
Coke, L C, Hamilton.
Gurkin, G S, Jamesville.
Hargrave & Nelson, Robersonville.
Hargrave, Robert, Robersonville.
Harrell, W H, Williamston.
Hassell, W S, Jamesville.
Jenkins, J C, Everett.
Knight, J P H, Williamston.
Lewis, D W, Hamilton.
Long, B L, Hamilton.
Mayo, W R, Jamesville.
Sherrod, J W, Hamilton.
Yates, L S, Williamston.

MARTIN COUNTY.

SCHOOLS.

Names, Post Offices, and Principals.

Academy, Williamston, Mrs Walter Hassell.
Academy, Hamilton, L W Seawell.
Academy, Jamesville, J R Peel.
Academy, Robersonville, S W Outerbridge.
Academy, Everetts, Prof Neal.
Primary, Hamilton, Miss Jennie Boyle.
Public schools—white, 36; colored, 25.

LOCAL CORPORATIONS.

Conoho Lodge, No 131, A F & A M, Hamilton; time of meeting, first Wednesday at 2 P M, and third Wednesday at 7 P M; Dr H G Clark, W M.

Hamilton Star Lodge, No 92, I O O F, Hamilton.

Knights of Honor, No —, Hamilton, T B Haskill, dictator.

Knights of Honor, Williamston, J A Teel.

Knights and Ladies of Honor, Hamilton, J T Waldo, protector.

Legion of Honor, Hamilton.

Lodge, No —, Knights of Honor, Jamesville, ——, dictator.

Norfolk & Southern Railroad; steamship from Williamston to Edenton, daily.

North State Lodge, I O O F, Parmelee.

Roanoke Lodge, No 83, I O O F, Williamston, W T Crawford, N G.

Roanoke and Tar River Steamboat Co, Dennis Simmons, pres; J D Briggs, sec.

Shewarkey Lodge, No 90, A F & A M, Williamston; time of meeting, second and fourth Tuesday evenings at 7 P M; H W Stubbs, W M.

Stonewall Lodge, No 296, A F & A M, Robersonville; time of meeting, third Saturday at 1 o'clock P M; J A Whitly, W M.

FARMERS.

Names and Post Offices.

Hamilton—Mrs N J Best, J P Boyle, J L Davenport. B P Davenport, Mrs M E Davenport, D W Lewis, J R Purvis, J H Purvis. L K Purvis, A J Purvis, P R Rives, G R L Robuck, F J Robuck, W L Sherrod, J H Sherrod, A Sherrod, Henry Slade, M G Taylor, V R Taylor, J I Taylor, Jason Tice.

M. A. NEWLAND,

Attorney at Law,

MARION, N. C.

P. J. SINCLAIR,

MARION, N. C.,

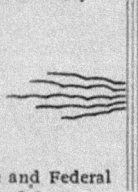

ATTORNEY AND COUNSELLOR AT LAW.

Practices in the Supreme and Federal Courts, and Superior Courts of the State. Collections in all parts of the State.

Counsel for Ohio River and Charleston Railway.

J. L. C. BIRD,

MARION, N. C.,

Attorney and Counsellor at Law.

NOTARY PUBLIC.

Practices in all the Courts of the State, and in the United States Circuit and District Courts. Prompt personal attention given to all business entrusted to him.

E. J. JUSTICE,

ATTORNEY AT LAW,

MARION, N. C.

OFFICE OPPOSITE COURT HOUSE.

McDOWELL COUNTY.

AREA, 440 SQUARE MILES.

POPULATION, 10,903; White 9,078, Colored 1,825.

McDOWELL COUNTY was formed from portions of Rutherford and Burke counties, in 1842, and was named in honor of Col. Joseph McDowell, a distinguished officer of the Revolution.

MARION, the county seat, is situated on the Western North Carolina Railroad, also the O. R. & C. terminates at this place, 230 miles from Raleigh. Population, 1,000.

Surface—The outer edges mountainous, the central part moderately hilly and watered by the head branches of the Catawba river, forming many beautiful and rich lowlands—the scenery enchanting.

Staples—Wheat, corn, oats, peas, rye, tobacco, butter, medicinal herbs and live stock.

Fruits—Apples, peaches, pears and berries.

Timbers—Pine, oak, hickory, poplar, walnut, chestnut and mountain birch.

Minerals—Iron, copper, gold, silver, lead, also fine monozite, with sulphur springs.

TOWNS AND POST OFFICES.

	POP.		POP.
Armstrong,	—	Nealsville,	100
Ashford,	20	Nebo,	125
Broad River,	20	North Cove,	20
C aig,	20	Old Fort,	300
Denning,	25	Patten,	25
Dills,	10	Rocky Pass,	15
Dysartville,	100	Round Knob,	15
Garden City,	25	Stone Mount'n,	10
Greenlee's,	20	Sugar Hill,	35
Glenwood,	—	Tom's Creek,	10
Marion,	1,000	Vein Mountain,	10
Montford,	25		

COUNTY OFFICERS.

Clerk Superior Court—B B Price.
Commissioners—John Carson, chm'n; R H Moore, Geo C Conly.
Coroner—N H Jameson.
Register of Deeds—J C Brown.
Sheriff—Geo H Garden.
Solicitor 10th District—Joseph F Spainhour.
Surveyor—J B Burgin.
Standard Keeper— ——
Treasurer—G H Gardin.
County Examiner—J F Wilson.

COURTS.

Superior Court meets first Monday in March, third Monday before the first Monday in September.

TOWN OFFICERS.

MARION—*Mayor*, M F Mosphew; *Commissioners*, Wm Sweeny, A R Gilkey, W M Martin, J L Morgan; *Clerk and Treasurer*, M A Newland; *Marshal*, J M Patton.

UNITED STATES OFFICERS.

MARION — *Collector*, S L Rogers; *Chief Deputy*, W O Conner; *Stamp Deputy*, Gilmer Brenizer; *Dep. Col.*, P M Hudgins, J S Robinson, J S Coleman, J M Roberts, F T Waleer, F A Rogers, R B Vance, A Rankin; *Clerk*, R V Williams; *Messenger*, J A Wild; *Stenographer and Typewriter*, B A Wicker.

TOWNSHIPS AND MAGISTRATES.

Bracket's—W C Rabourn, Robt Rhour, J F Bright, B G Gaden Thurmel City).

Broad River—J H Garrison (Black Mountain), W J Nesbitt, Z V Hudgins, J B Gilliam (Broad River), J M Shuford (Stone Mountain).

Crooked Creek—J H Gilliam, J L Bird, I W Davis, W J Gilbert, A B Holford, J W Nesbitt (Old Fort).

Dysartsville—W A Laughridge, J A Laughridge, J P Whisnant (Dysartsville), Samuel Morgan, D Patton (Patton).

Finlay's—J W Ballew, J M Simmons (Bridgewater), J F Wilson, T J Hemphill, G M Annis (Nebo).

Higgins—W A Goforth, J G Pratt (Nealsville), W S Freeman, J L Padgett (Rocky Pass).

Marion—J H Huskins (Tom's Creek), W B Ratcliff, W F Craig, H Heathsteiner, Wm Sweeney, W M Jones, B W Craig, T J Flemming (Marion).

Montford's Cove—J R Harris (Montford), W L Fortune (Craig), J C Crawford, E W Marlow (Sugar Hill).

North Cove—J D Conley (Woodlawn), W J English, W B McCall, R W Brown (Ashford), Geo W Conley, R J Lonon (North Cove), D M Washburn (Grassy Creek).

26

McDOWELL COUNTY.

Old Fort—J C Sandlin, M G Pendergrass, W M Marshburn, W J Southers, J H Blalock, J R Kelley, O H Blocker (Old Fort).

CHURCHES.

Names, Post Offices, Pastors and Denom.

METHODIST.

Bethlehem—Old Fort, James Carpenter.
Bethel—Old Fort, James Carpenter.
Church (near)—Marion, M L Kaylor.
Church—Old Fort, James Carpenter.
Concord—Ashford, M L Kaylor.
Glenwood—Nealsville, James Gibson.
Green Mountain—Tom's Creek, M L Kaylor.
Marion—Marion, J T Rogers.
Murphy's Chapel—Marion, Jas Gibson.
North Catawba — North Cove, M L Kaylor.
Providence—Marion, Jas Carpenter.
Thompson's Chapel — Marion, James Carpenter.
Trinity—Dysartsville, James Gibson.

NORTH. METHODIST.

Green Hill—Marion, —— Ratchford.
Salem—Old Fort, —— Ratchford.

BAPTIST.

Bethel—Nealsville, J C Sorrell.
Bethlehem—Old Fort, J C Sorrell.
Dysartville—Dysartville, B B Harris.
Harmony Grove—Marion, B B Harris.
Marion—Marion, Dr M M Landrum.
Turkey Cove—Turkey Cove, J C Sorrell.
Walnut Grove—Ashford, J C Sorrell.

PRESBYTERIAN.

Church—Old Fort, W H White.
Drucilla—Dysartville.
Marion—Marion, W H White.
Pleasant Retreat—Marion, W H White.
Silvan—Greenlee, W H White.

EPISCOPAL.

Church—Old Fort, J C Phelps.
St John—Marion.

A. M. E. ZION.

Zion—Marion, S M Pharr.
Zion—Old Fort.
Church—Old Fort.

MINISTERS RESIDENT.

Names, Post Offices, Pastors and Denom.

METHODIST.

Allison, James, Old Fort.
Brown, J C, Greenlee.
Carpenter, James, Old Fort.
Gibson, James, Tom's Creek.
Kaylor, M L, Marion.

Rogers, T J, Marion.

CON. METHODIST.

Brookshire, R R, Marion.

BAPTIST.

Denton, J R, Dysartville.
Harris, ——, Dysartville.
Landrum, Dr M M, Marion.
Marshburn, Burton, Nealsville.
Settlemire, George, Old Fort.
Sorrell, J C, Nealsville.

PRESBYTERIAN.

Greenlee, John M, Marion.
White, Wm, Marion.

HOTELS AND BOARDING HOUSES.

Names, Post Offices and Proprietors.

Blocker, Old Fort, O H Blocker.
Eagle Hotel, Marion, J G Grant.
Fleming House, Marion, —— Gruber.
Hotel, Old Fort.
Hotel, Round Knob, Railroad Co.

LAWYERS.

Names and Post Offices.

Bird, J L C, Marion.
Eaves, G G, Marion.
Haney, L A, Deming.
Hudgens, D E, Marion.
Justice, E J, Marion.
Morphew, J F, Marion.
Morris, James, Marion.
Newland, M A. Marion.
Sinclair, P J, Marion.

MANUFACTORIES.

Kinds, Post Offices and Proprietors.

Coaches and wagons, Marion, T A White.
Furniture, Marion, Marion Furniture Co, D R Roper, mgr.
Harness and saddles, Marion, J S Dysart.
Locust Pins, Marion.
Millwrighting, Nebo, Wm Culbertson.
Tannery, Marion, J L Morgan.
Tannery, Turkey Cove, Yancy Bros.
Tobacco, Marion, Crawford & Morgan.
Undertaking, Marion, J L McCoy & Co.
Wool-carding, Dysartsville, P P Price.

MERCHANTS AND TRADESMEN.

Names, Post Offices and Lines of Business.

ASHFORD.

McCall, W B,   G S

DEMMING.

Sprouse, J J,   G S

McDOWELL COUNTY.

DYSARTSVILLE.

Dysart, W W,	G S
Denton, J R,	G S
Kirkey, E T,	G S
Taylor, Geo D,	G S

GLENWOOD.

Bright, A L,	G S
Brockett, T W,	G S
Brown, S J,	G S

GREENLEE'S.

Williams, L W,	G S

MARION.

Atkins, J A,	Real Estate Agt
Blanton, A B & Co,	G S
Dellinger, J F,	G S
Dysart, J S,	G S
Gilkey, G W,	Furniture
Gilkey, J Q,	Tel Operator
Gilkey, A B & Son,	Gro and Livery
Gilkey, A B.	Gro
Hemphill, J H,	Marble Yard
Jones, W P,	Hardw
Landis, W E.	Agt O R & C R R
Lee, Geo E, Agt Southern R R	and Express Agt
Lenon, D N,	G S
Martin Bros,	G S
McCall & Conley,	G S
McCoy, J L,	Painting
McCurry, J C,	Postmaster
McCurry, J C,	G S
McDonald & Norton,	Millinery
McDonald, J A & W,	Livery
McFodyer, A H,	Job Printer
Meld, Thos,	Variety
Morphew & White,	Drugs
Neal, J G,	Undertaker
Nichols, J G & Bro,	G S
Norton, Miss Loula,	Millinery
Norton, Jas P,	Gro
Ratliff, W B.	Gro
Swindell, J B,	G S
Trexler, R E,	Night Tel Operator
Welsh, ——,	Gro

MONTFORD.

Harris, J R & Bro,	G S

NEALSVILLE.

Brackett, T W & Co,	G S
Bright, A L & Bro,	G S
Brown, S J & Son,	G S

NEBO.

Annis, G M,	G S
Snipes, T E,	G S

NORTH COVE.

Lenon, R J,	G S

OLD FORT.

Blacklock, J H,	Confections
Bradley, J S,	G S
Crawford, J R,	G S

McDOWELL COUNTY.

Disoway, W H,	Drugs
Sandlin. W C & Co,	Drugs
Thomason, G B.	G S
Westerman Bros,	G S

ROCKY PASS.

Holler, I J,	G S

VEIN MOUNTAIN.

Kirksey, S P,	G S

MINES.

Kinds, Post Offices and Proprietors.

Gold, Marion, A K Weaver.

Gold, Dysartville.

Gold, Vein Mountain, Allen Schwark, prop; B G Godin, supt.

Gold. Deming. Col Demming; J J Sprouse, mgr.

White Marble, Town Creek, O H Blocker & Co.

MILLS.

Kinds, Post Offices and Proprietors.

Flour, corn and saw, Marion, H C Bennett.

Flour, corn and saw, Nebo, J W Hunter.

Flour, corn and saw, Rocky Pass, P J Sinclair.

Corn and flour, Marion, J C Pool.

Corn and flour, Marion, D A Knip.

Corn, Nealsville, Wilson Allen.

Corn and flour, Dysartville, —— Nix.

Corn, Dysartville, J R Patton.

Corn and flour, Old Fort, Mrs D C Salsburg

Corn. Marion, Geo C Conly.

Corn and flour, North Cove, W A McCall.

Corn and flour, North Cove, R W Brown.

Corn and flour, Marion, Dysart & Conly.

Corn, flour and saw, Nebo, G W Dobson.

Corn, flour and saw, Marion, W D Summers.

Corn and saw, Old Fort, Hiram Kelly.

Corn and saw, Broad River, J W Lancaster.

Corn, Dysartville, P P Price.

Corn and flour, Marion, Carson & Morgan.

Corn and flour, Old Fort, G B Thomason.

Corn and flour, Town Creek, J H Greenlee.

Corn, flour and saw, Dysartville, R E Patton.

Corn, Dysartville, W J Allen.

McDOWELL COUNTY.

McDOWELL COUNTY.

PHYSICIANS.

Names and Post Offices.

Cheek, B A, Marion.
Jones, W P, Marion.
Morphew, M F, Marion.
Noblett, W B, Old Fort.
Reed, J F, Old Fort.
Simmons. J O, Dysartville.
White, Geo I, Marion.

SCHOOLS.

Names, Post Offices and Principals.

Academy, Old Fort, Prof Roberson.
Belle Fort Academy, Old Fort, Prof Tate.
Male and Female Academy, Marion, Prof Guy, Mrs Guy and Misses Guy.
Public schools—White, 42; colored, 11.

LOCAL CORPORATIONS.

Commercial Bank of Marion, B B Price, pres; Geo I White, cash. Capital, $10,000.
Marion Lodge, No 47, I O O F, Marion; Wm Sweeney, N G; J G Nichols, sec.
Mt Ida Lodge, No 58, K of P, Marion; J B Swindell C C; W W Cooper, K of R and S.
Mystic Tie Lodge, No 37, A F and A M, Marion; B B Price, W M; G W Crawford, sec.

NEWSPAPERS.

Free Lance, Marion, Sam'l Archer, ed.
Marion Record (Dem. weekly); A H McFadyen, ed and prop.
The Revolution. Marion.

FARMERS.

Names and Post Offices..

Armstrong—J A Autrey, T L Bailey, H M Baucome, F R Baucome. R P Buchanan, A A Buchanan, W A Buchanan, J H Buchanan, G W Byrd, D S Byrd, J N Cox, T H D Gillespie, Sam'l Good, J S Hallifield, J W Hallifield. Jesse Hallifield, J G B Hallifield W E Hallifield, B P Hallifield, A M Hallifield. Reuben Harvey. Sam'l McPeters, J A McGee, Jas Odear.
Ashford.—J A Audry, J H Brown, Sam'l Brown, S L Brown, R W Brown, W T Burnett, H Chapman, Henry Chapman, Peter Chapman, S E Conley. Martin Denney, G W Denney, J English, E English, W B McCall, J P McCall, W R McGee, Bryson McGee. W S Minnish, T G Williams.

Bridgewater.—G W Ballance, D R Brown, Mrs Thos Hemphill, A E Rouse, J R Russ, jr, Mrs M E Thornton
Broad River.—W C Bailey, D L Clements, W E Curry, A A Dalton, S Freeman, T C Ledbetter, R E Ledbetter, T B Ledbetter, J Ledbetter, T J Owensby, D R Owensby, J W Reed.
Denning—Levi Arrowood, W D Arrowood, J A Arrowood, Erwin Bright, J F Bright, J B Davis, J J Davis, T W Earley, B G Gaden, James Gallim, Jos Kayter, J F Landing, Daniel Landing, J L Laughridge, W C Rabum, J M Rabum, Robert Rhour, Joe Seaman, J J Sponce, Jethron Ward.
Dysartville—J W Allen, Wm Bailey, G W Bates, Sam'l Biggerstaff, J M Biggerstaff, John Carson, J H Cooper, R H Cowen, Hamp Cowen, A F Cowen, J F Cowen, H B Crawley, Alex Crawley, J A Curtis, W S Cuthbertson, D L Daves, C M Daves, J R Denton, C H Dixon, A G Dixon, T C Dixon, W W Dixon, W F Duval, J L Dysart, J R Dysart, W W Dysart, G T Effs, G C Ellington, E J Foster, R R Gellys, FW Gellys, J A Gellys, Jas Glass, J M Goforth, J H Green, Noah Green, J M Hemphill, T B Hemphill, R Higgins, J D Hogan, R G Honerst, J G Landis, J B Landis, T B Landis, J A Laughbridge, J M Laughbridge, C W Laughbridge, D M Laughbridge, W A Laughbridge, R G Margum, T J McDaniel, S B Morgan, R E Patton. J F Patton, J C Price, P P Price, J W Price, Harvey Price, J F Pyatt, T P Satterwhite, L M Simmons, R H Sisk, L A Smart, S P Tate, A G Tate, M T Tate, W H Taylor, H H Taylor, J W Taylor, G D Taylor, W L Taylor, J D Taylor, A B Taylor, W S Walker. David Walker, J W Walker, W R Walker, L L Walker. J Webb Walker, J Q Waters, G S Waters. J P Whisnard, N C Wilson.
Garden City—Mrs D E Butt, W E Byrd, Geo Byrd, A C Cerdell, T T Cerdell, L A Chapman, G W Chapman, R C Chapman, S P Custis, Jno Custis, Job Efftee, Spencer Elliott, Jno S Elliott, J L Elliott, W C Elliott, T J Fleming, H A Gibbs, J P Gowan, Jas Hedgepeth (col), H L Johnson, G W Johnson, Jas Morris. J Z Page, W S Pyatt. J P Snipes, E D Stroud, J A Stroud, J H Stroud, W C Stroud, T B Young.
Greenlee—Jno C Brown, S Duncan, R V Duncan. R L Greenlee, E L Greenlee, Dr J A Greenlee.
Kirksey—E J Kirksey, J R Kirksey.
Marion—Thos Barnes, Mrs S E Barnes, Fred Barnes, Robt Barnes, Mrs M A Barnes, J W Biddy, W A

McDOWELL COUNTY.

Brockett, J C Brown, W E Brown, Wm McD Burgin, A Burgin, S M Burgin, Dr R J Burgin, Jas Byrd, P F Cannon, Mrs R J Cannon, J C Cannon, G M Carson, J R Carson, Jno Carson, D W Cansley, C C Clentz, W L Conly, H A Conly, J E Conly, W A Conly, Austin Conly, G C Conly, L J Conly, C D Corpening, B F Corpening, Mrs M A Corpening, W B Craig, J W Craig, G W Crawford, C W Crews, T O Custis, M I Custis, G B Custis, Samuel B Custis, J H Davis, J A Davis, J W Davis, J G Davis, Emanuel Davis, Wm D llinger, Samuel Dobbins, R C Dobbins, J S Duncan, J S D sart, G W Early, G G Eaves, F A Effey, J H Effey, Gus Elliott, Robt Elliott, Jno G Elliott, Jas S Elliott, Jno Ellis, J S Finley, J C Finley, A L Finley, J Y Finley, L C Fortune, C W Godfrey, C G Godfrey, M H Grant, J M Greenlee, D W Greenlee, M s M Greenlee, Mrs M M Hall, J M Hall, W F Hall, J P Hall, E Y Hall, J H Hawkins, S M Hawkins, T F Hawkins, H H Hawkins, J C Hemphill, W W Hemphill, J O Hensey, A M Hensley, A Y Hicks, T M Hicks, W H Holland, J W Horton. Amos Horton, Cyrus Huffman, K M Jarrett, J L J Jeanison, C F Kraws, W E Landis, F Ledford, Geo Lentz. Emanuel Lewis, sr, Daniel Lucas, J W Marsh, J C McCurry, R L McCurry, Wm McCurry, sr, Wm McCurry, jr, G W McCurry, Abe McGee, Willard McNeely, Jno McNeely, G W Nichols. R B Nichols, L J Noblet, W H Moody, J L Morgan, J R Morgan, Jetaro Morgan, Wm Morgan, J L M sseller, W H Odom, E H Odom, D W Odom, Chas H Odom, Wm Parker, J C Pool, M B Poteat, L A Poteat, G P Poteat, S L Poteat, S A Poteat, Jno B Poteat, G L Po eat, J A Poteat, sr, S M Proctor. Isaac Queen, J P Ray, J P R el, G W Shellum, W S Smith, J W Smith, R L Smith, P J St Clair, H A Tate, G S Tate, J S Thompson, Jas Turner, Oliver Turner, Rich Turner, W C Wall, J L Walsh, C H Walsh, A K Weaver, Mark Whitstile, Mrs S A E Yancey, Andy Yount.

Montford—J F Allen, J W Al en, R I Bird, Jos A Bird, Henry B ight, M B Bright, Jas Bright, A L Bright, John A Bright, J O Burdges, I C Cannon, H B Conley, S C Early, Peter Eflee, W S Fortune, J S Grant, M L Grayson, J W Grayson, C M Hall, J R Harris, M J Harris, A W Hogan, N C Jones, J H C Kanipe, Geo Kaylor, J G Koon, Gurard Lail, R Ledbetter, R L Ledbetter, J B Ledbetter, E V Luding, J A Luding, G Landing, G J Marlow, E W

McDOWELL COUNTY.

Marlow, A B Marshburn, J F Morgan, M W Morgan, G G Morgan, G R Morgan, J C Morgan, R P Morris, E L Morris, Lee Morris, Z V Morris, C W Morris, J H Morris, Thos Morris, J R Neal. J W F Nichols, Thos Parker, I A Reel, G W S agle, Geo W Sellory, J R Simmons, S J Simmons, M M Sisk, C H Snipes, E W Strowd, J A Swan, A Wilkerson, C F Williams, J C Wilson. W G Wilson, T W Wilson, E M Wilson.

Nealsville—J L Bidgett, T W Brackett, A L Bright, S J Brown, J L Dobson, Mick Elliott, A C Gardin, J H Gardin, M B G irdin, E G G forth, A L G forth, W A G forth, D W Haney, N C Hayes, Nim Holland, M L Kaylor. W S Miller. A V Miller, A F Mo le, W C Pyatt, G W Seagle, P J Sinclair, J C Sorrells, Noah Turner, T L Upton, G W White, C A Withro.

Nebo—G M Annis, Z T Anderson, Levi Austin, J F Bailey, J W Bailey, Ed C nley, W A Conley, Joe Craig, T C Cuthbertson, W A Cuthbertson, C H Cuthbertson, J H Cuthbertson, M L Dale, I A Davenport, D W Dobson, Geo W Dobson, J A D le, A D Erwin, J P Finley, J C Finley, W J Gibson, J F Gibbs, W S Gray, S N Gray, A G Gray, J E Gray, S D Halliburton, T J Halliburton, W N Hefner, T J Hemphill, J C Hensley, N Holland, W G Hunter, J C Hunter, J B Hunter, N H Jimison, D W Jimison, T M Jones, W C Jones, J B Jones, J T Jones, John S Louis, J A Mason, W S Masters, S C McNeely, S D Pyatt, James Pyatt, J T Queen, T B Ray, J A S agle, J M Simmons, A J Simmons, A H Simmons, J C Simmons, T E S ipes, J K Stacy, T W S acy, S N Stockton, J W Tate, G L Wilson, J F Wils n, J W Wilson.

North Cove—J G Brown, W E Brown, Hugh Derault, H A Hefner, W B Hefner, T E Hefner. J W Hensley, W R Hennessee, J P Hennessee, Joe Hoffes, E B Hoffes, W C Huskins, D W Jarrett, R J Lenon, O N Lenon, J B Lenon, J T Lenon, Thos Lindsay, Robt McCall, Sam'l McCall, W A McCall, Wm McCall, Henry McKinney, R E McKinney, T M McKinney, Jas Medfred, M L Snipes, Jas Swoffud, J P Swoffud, D M Washburn, E S Wiseman, Thos Wiseman.

Old Fort—R S Allison, T H Allison, W W Bailey, A L Bird, J L Bird, C M Bird, C A Bird, G V Bird. C A Blackwelder, L C Blackwelder. W M Blackwelder, O H. Blocker, C C Bradley, J W Bradley, J S Bradley, J M Bradley, H Bradley. G W Bradley, Rev John C Brown, C C Burgin, J B Burgin, C S

McDOWELL COUNTY.	McDOWELL COUNTY.

Burgin, J L Burgin, A B Burgin, R M Burgin, R H Burgin, R L Burgin, J D Burgin, W W Clark, L P Crawford, M A Dalton, J L Davis, P E Davis. J H Davis, J A Dula, J T Durham, J C Finch, L A Gentry, J W Gibson, J M Gilbert, M J Gilliam, W R Gilliam, J H Gilliam, A W Gilliam, W H Gilliam, J L Goley, W M Goodson, W D Gray, W H Greenlee, T Y Greenlee, R L Greenlee, A B Halford, J W Hemphill, T Y Hemphill, B P Hensley, C Hoyle, W M Hoyle. A P Jardin, J A Jarrett, A Kelley, H Kelley. J R Kelley, H Kyle. C C Linley, J H Lytle, L I Lytle, M P Lytle, T Y Lytle, J L Lytle, G W Lytle, J J Mackey, C P Mackey, W M Mashburn. Amos McCurrey, J C McKoy, M A Minzie, W L Moffitt, J W Moffitt, R H Moore, J Q Morrison, W J Morris, E A Nesbitt, T W Noblitt, W T Noblitt, W B Noblitt, A W Padgett. J Parker, Wm Parker, W D Parish, T C Parks, M G Pendergrass, T A Postel, B Ricketts, A L Ricks. D L Robertson, J H Ross, J C Sandlin, C Sandlin, T J Silver, Alex Silver, John Silver, Alf Silver, J M

Silver, W J Souther. F M Stipp, R A Tate, H M Taylor, W P Terrill, B F Tisdale, G B Thomason, J W Walker, J R Walker, James Webb, J C Whitson, L W Williams, M A Young, J M Young.

Patton—J W Mode, S E Morrison, J W Morrison, J D Patton, J R Patton, Robt Patton.

Rocky Pass—I G Hollar, J D Jarrett.

Stone Mountain—S A Fortune, J L Fortune, A D Fraley, J C Garrison, J H Garrison, J B Gilliam, J P Gilliam, O W Gilliam, I V Stroud, R C Warren, C W White.

Tom's Creek—J D Conly, Mary E Craig, Odom Gibson, H W Gibson, C W Godfrey, Chas Godfrey, J C Hensley, J M Hicks, J H Huskins, G W Huskins, C M Huskins, W Huskins, Mills Lackey. Geo Lackey, M V Lackey, J F Poteat, G W Proctor, W Queen, T P Quinn, W B Quinn, Mrs A M Reid, John C Strowd, J G Yancey, John Yancey, S H Yancey.

Turkey Cove—D W Greenlee, J M Greenlee.

MECKLENBURG COUNTY.

AREA 680 SQUARE MILES.

POPULATION: 42,424; White 22,898, Colored 19,526.

MECKLENBURG COUNTY was formed in 1762, from Anson county, and named in honor of the new Queen, Princess Charlotte, of Mecklenburg.

CHARLOTTE, the county-seat, is at the junction of five railroads, and is 180 miles southwest from Raleigh. Population (estimated) 16,500, or 19,000 including suburbs. At Charlotte, May 20, 1775, the Mecklenburg Declaration of Independence was promulgated—hence it is called the birth-place of liberty.

Surface—Moderately uneven; lies on the eastern shore of the Catawba river; is well watered, plenty of water-power, and soil generally remunerative.

Staples—Corn, wheat, oats, cotton, tobacco, fruit and live-stock.

Fruits—Apples, peaches, pears, cherries, plums, melons, berries, and other small fruits.

Timbers—Oak, pine, hickory, walnut, ash, poplar and locust.

Minerals—Gold, silver, and other ores.

TOWNNS AND POST OFFICES.

	POP.		POP.
Arlington,	50	Madge,	35
Biddleville,	100	Martindale,	30
Bristow,	50	Matthews,	300
Burdett,	25	Mint Hill,	100
Caldwell's,	35	Monteith,	40
Charlotte		Nevin,	45
(C. H.),	16,500	Newell,	100
Cluster,	25	Nimrod,	—
Cottonwood,	60	Paw Creek,	50
Cowan's Ford,	500	Pineville,	400
Croft,	30	Query's,	40
Davenport,	50	Ranaleburg,	50
Dadvidson		Rankin,	25
College,	500	River View,	30
Delos,	55	Sago,	25
Derita,	100	Sandifer,	100
Dixie,	25	Sardis,	25
Eastfield,	50	Shamrock,	25
Fennimore,	30	Shera,	35
Griffith,	30	Shopton,	100
Harrison,	50	Spurrier,	50
Hebron,	25	Steel Creek,	50
Hood's,	60	Stevens,	60
Hopewell,	50	Tampa,	30
Hornet,	30	Uncas,	20
Huntersville,	250	Unity,	22
Kingwood,	40	Wailes,	40
Lodo,	50		

COUNTY OFFICERS.

Clerk Superior Court—J M Morrow.
Deputy Clerk—L F Osborne.
Commissioners—Jno R Erwin, chm'n; J H Soaler, W F Kreykendal, J H McClintock, P C Hilkerson.
Coroner—A A Cathey.
Register of Deeds—J W Cobb.
Deputy Register—A S Anderson.
Sheriff—Z T Smith.
Deputy Sheriffs—F M Bisaner and E O Johnson.
Solicitor 11th District—J L Webb.
Standard Keeper—C O Keuster.
Surveyor—C A Spratt.
Tax Collector—Z T Smith.
Treasurer—E H Walker.
Superintendent of Health—Dr H M Wilder.
County Examiner—M A Gray (Huntersville).

COURTS.

Superior Courts meet sixth Monday before first Monday in March; second Monday after first Monday in March; thirteenth Monday after first Monday in March and fourth Monday after first Monday in September.

Criminal Court meets sixth Monday after first Monday in March and first Monday in September.

United States Circuit Court, Charlotte, R P Dick, Judge, Greensboro; courts meet fourteenth Monday after first Monday in March; Circuit and District Court, fourteenth Monday after first Monday in September.

UNITED STATES SIGNAL STATION.

Charlotte, — Dosher, in charge; signal reports by telegraph, received and forwarded three times a day.

UNITED STATES ASSAY OFFICE.

Charlotte, W E Adrey, Assayer in charge; Geo B Hanna, Ass't; established by an Act of Congress, March 3, 1835, and opened October 19, 1837; annual appropriation for all purposes, $4,750; burned in 1844, rebuilt and opened October 1, 1846; assays about $275,000 each year.

MECKLENBURG COUNTY.

TOWN OFFICERS.

CHARLOTTE—*Mayor*, J H Wheddington; *Aldermen*, Geo A Howell, Major Praten, G A Howell, J B McLaughlin, W W Allen, W L Long, D O Donoghee, H M Wilder, T Garibaldi, E P Williams, Joseph Siler, W G Berryhill, W B Kidd, T S Franklin; *Clerk and Treasurer*, Fred Nash; *City Tax Collector*, W B Taylor; *Chief of Police*—W S Orr; *Cotton Weigher*, J S Withers; *Cotton Inspector*, Warren Roach; *City Attorney*, Burwell & Walker; *Keeper of Elmwood Cemetery*, Moses Thomas; *Keeper of Pinewood Cemetery*, A Phifer (col.);*Supt Streets*, W H Hall; *Chief of Fire Department*, W E Culpeper.

DAVIDSON COLLEGE — *Mayor*, Z A Hovis; *Commissioners*. S R Neal, Prof Graves, R W Shelton, J W Summers, J L Query; *Clerk*, S R Neal; *Treasurer*, S C Scofield; *Marshal*, M W Crawford.

HUNTERSVILLE — *Mayor*, H K De Armon; *Commissioners*, J T Mayberry, J B Nicholson, A Darby, G F Steele; *Clerk and Treasurer*, J W Mullen; *Chief of Police*, J H Holler.

MATTHEWS—*Mayor*, D J Bruner.

PINEVILLE—*Mayor*, J A Younts.

TOWNSHIPS AND MAGISTRATES.

Berryhill—Geo L Sadler, H D Stowe, S S Herron, W S Herron (Dixie), W S Clanton (Charlotte), W G Ford (Lodo), H L Sloan, W M Long (Charlotte).

Charlotte Township—A J Gormley, R P Moring, S H Hilton, W F Buchanan, Wade H Harris, R E Young. A L Smith, E S Williams. J S Myers, L J Walker, W R Terry, Ed McDonald, J W Brown. J J Lewis, Jos H Welsor, J F Correll. R Brewer (Charlotte), J A Williams, E M Crowell, W D McCorkle, J B Clanton, J B Alexander, R E Cooper. A Brady, T J Keith, T A Austin. W J Hutchinson, J C Dowd, D P Hutchinson, D G Maxwell, H C Severs, D H Wolfe, W W Phifer, M C Mayer, S W Davis, Walter Brem, B P Boyd (Charlotte).

Clear Creek—J L Campbell, J P Flow, J E Henderson (Mint Hill), W J Miller, F M Hinson (Arlington), C J Biggers (Hood).

Crab Orchard—J M Reid (Cluster), John C Orr, J C Kirk, J Newell (Newell's), G C L Junker (Ringwood), J R Utley, Leander Query (Query's), A S McClelland (Burdett).

Deweese—J B Thomasson, W S Caldwell. T E Potts. C E Bost (Caldwell), J Lee Sloan, jr, R L Query. S H Brady (Davidson).

Huntersville—A J Hunter, W B Barnett, J M Knox, G F Steele, W J Ransom, C F Alexander, A Darby (Huntersville).

Lemley—J M Wilson, John H Fuller, (Sheba), F M Worsham, W A Potts (Davidson), Egbert Davidson, W A Alexander, R D Alexander (Hopewell).

Long Creek—R D Whitly, M B Alexander, Thomas Gluyan (Martindale), W R Craven, W M Martin, J C Hutchinson (Bristowe), Jas A Wilson, Abner Alexander (Hopewell).

Mallard Creek—R H Flow, A S Kirk, John Graham Alexander, J G Alexander, N Gibbon (Derita), D Frank Davis, W O Cochrane (Monteith), W E Alexander (Croft).

Morning Star—S B Smith, W H D Wager, T J Irwin, J C Stewart, J S Grier. A P Nesbit, J W Phillips (Matthews), J W Hood (Hoods).

Paw Creek—R B Abernethy, G A McCord, E W McGinn, J M Grice, W W Gileson (Sanderford), J F Abernethy, E R Spurrier (Spurrier's), J F Frazier (Saco).

Pineville—M A Edwards, Oswold Alexander, J H Barnett, W E Younts, F C Harris, G F Grier, J D Culp (Pineville).

Providence—W M Matthews, N B Williamson, Wm Morton, H D Rea, J F Bowers (Davenport), H Bryant, W M Ardrey (Hebron), T S Squires (Matthews).

Sharon—W Henry Hunter (Sardis), J Watt Kirkpatrick (Griffith), W S Pharr (Charlotte), W N Alexander C T Brown, H T Reid (Rankin), C T Elliott, W D Beatty (Griffith).

Steel Creek—J C Smith, R A Grier (Shopton), J L Kendrick, J L Mulwee (Ranalsburg), J B Watt, W N Peoples, S W Reed (Steel Creek), H D Smith (Ranalsburg).

CHURCHES.

Names, Post Offices, Pastors and Denom.

METHODIST.

Big Spring—Lodo, —— Howie.
B Street—Charlotte, J E Hoover.
Church—Paw Creek, —— Howe.
Church Street—Charlotte, H L Atkins.
Church—Pineville, T C Smith.
Church—Harrison, T C Smith.
Church—Hebron, T C Smith.
Church—Matthews, Z Paris.
City Mission and Seversville—Charlotte, J F Butt; Geo A Page, asst.
Hickory Grove—Charlotte, Z Paris.
Marvin—Monteith, T C Smith.
Moore's Chapel—Paw Creek, G W Calahan.

MECKLENBURG COUNTY.

Mt Zion—Davidson College, J S Nelson.
Prospect—Charlotte, —— House.
Trinity—Martinsdale, —— H)wee.
Trinity—Charlotte, S B Turrentine.
Tryon Street—Cnarlotte, W W Bays.
D D.

METH. EPISCOPAL.

Church (col)—Charlotte.
Wesley Chapel (col)—Charlotte, ——
Davis.

PRESBYTERIAN.

Amity—Charlotte, S W Newell.
Bethel—Davidson College, J M Grier.
Church—Pineville, J R McAlpine.
Church—Paw Creek.
Church—Huntersville, J M Grier.
Church—Steel Creek, —— Little.
Church (col)—Huntersville, O W King.
Church (col)—Davidson College, D S
Baker.
Church—Matthews, R C Morrison.
Church (col)—Charlotte, R P Wyche.
Church—Steel Creek, —— Little.
Caurch—Davidson College, —— Graham.
First Cnurch—Charlotte, John A Preston, D D.
Graham Street Chapel—Charlotte, ——
White.
Hopewell—Huntersville, — Stempsay.
Mallard Creek — Alexandria, Roger
Martin.
Mulberry—Charlotte.
Philadelphia—Hoods. J J Harrell.
Pleasant Hill—Ranalsburg, J R McAlpine.
Providence—Matthews, Jesse Siler.
Ramah—Huntersville, J M Grier.
Robinson—Shamrock, J J Harrell.
Second Church—Charlotte, J W Stagg.
Sharon—Charlotte.
Sugar Creek—Charlotte, J L Williamson.
Williams' Memorial—Charlotte.

BAPTIST.

Ebenezer—Charlotte, G A White.
First Baptist (col)—Charlotte, A A
Powell.
Independence—Alexandria.
Second Baptist (col)—Charlotte. C L
Davis.
Tryon Street—Charlotte.
West Trade Street—Charlotte.

ASSO. REFORMED.

Black Creek—Query's, G McLaughlin.
Central Creek—Charlotte, R L Grier.
Church—Charlotte, J T Chalmers.
Church—Huntersville, W W Orr.
Ebenezer—Charlotte, G R White.
Gilead—Huntersville, W Z Love.
Prosperity—Alexandria, W M Hunter.
Sardis—Charlotte, R G Miller.

MECKLENBURG COUNTY.

EPISCOPAL.

All Angels—Cnarlotte, P P Alston.
St Mark s—Hopewell, Frank Lea.
St Martin—Cnarlotte, J B Austin.
St Michael's (col)—Charlotte, P P Alston.
St Peter's—Charlotte, C L Hoffman.

LUTHERAN.

Morning Star—Matthews, I Conder.
St Mark's—Cnarlotte, G W Bowman.

CONGREGATIONAL.

Church (col)—Charlotte, G H Haynes.

ROMAN CATHOLIC.

St Peter's—Charlotte, F Francis.

A. M. E. ZION.

Biddleville (col)-Hopewell, R D Dawry.
Center Grove (col)—Center Grove, L
H Wyche.
Church (col)—Street Creek, W Morgan.
Clinton Chapel (col)—Charlotte, R H
Simmons, D D.
Grace (col)—Charlotte, R B Bruce.
Hopewell (col)—Hopewell, W L Alexander.
Little Rock (col)—Charlotte, G W Clinton, D D.
Moore's Sanctuary (col)—Lodo, Fab
Alexander.
Mowing Glade (col)— Hornet, H B
Bennett.
Torrence Chapel (col)—Davidson College.
Weeping Willow (col)—Hebron, H B
Bennett.

MINISTERS RESIDENT.

Names, Post Offices and Denom.

PRESBYTERIAN.

Alexander, Charlotte.
Baker, D S (col), Davidson College.
Beatty, S J, Charlotte.
Cochran, J B, Huntersville.
Foster, W C, Cnarlotte.
Graham, ——, Davidson College.
Harrell, J J, Matthews.
King, G W (col), Huntersville.
Little, ——, Cnarlotte.
Martin, Rogers, Query's.
McAlpine, J R, Pinesville.
Shearer, J B, D D, LL D, Davidson
College.
Stagg, J W, Charlotte.
Williamson, J L, Cnarlotte.
White, ——, Charlotte.
Wyche, R P (col), Charlotte.

METHODIST.

Overcash, G A, Charlotte.
Overcash, Elias, Charlotte.
Paris, Zodok, Matthews.
Williams, W P, Davidson College.

METHODIST PROT.

Welborn, John W, Pineville.

CONGREGATIONAL METHODIST.

Ledwell, Thomas, Charlotte.

A. M. E. ZION.

Alexander, W L. Hopewell.
Alexander, Fab (col), Lodo.
Bennett. H B (col), Charlotte.
Bruce, R B (col), Charlotte.
Davidson, John, Charlotte.
Davidson, Edward, Charlotte.
Massey, W M (col), Charlotte.
Moseley, Henry, Charlotte.
Musgraves, G G (col), Charlotte.
Rives, R S. Charlotte.
Simmons, R H (col). Charlotte.
Wyche, L H (col), Charlotte.

BAPTIST.

Beasley, J J, Matthews.
Davis. C L (col), Charlotte.
Williams, E C, Matthews.

ASSO. REF.

McDonald, C E. Charlotte.
Miller, R G. Sardis.
Hunter, W M. Huntersville.
Orr, W W. Huntersville.
White, G R, Griffith.

LUTHERAN.

Bowman, J W, D D, Charlotte.
Conder, I, Matthews.

ROMAN CATHOLIC.

Francis, F, Charlotte.

HOTELS AND BOARDING HOUSES.

Names, Post Offices and Proprietors,

Arlington, Charlotte.
Boarding, Charlotte. D F Dixon.
Boarding. Charlotte, Mrs E B Laird.
Boarding, Charlotte, John B Ross.
Boarding, Charlotte, Mrs A J Bagley.
Boarding, Charlotte, Mrs Griffith.
Boarding, Charlotte, Mrs Baitey.
Boarding, Charlotte, Mrs C L Hunter.
Boarding. Charlotte. J M Goode (col).
Boarding, Charlotte, W F Snider.
Boarding, Charlotte. S J Brown.
Boarding, Davidson College, Mrs C H
  Lefferty.
Boarding, Davidson College, R L
  Query.
Boarding. Charlotte, Mrs Marshall.
Buford Hotel, Charlotte, Eccles & Bryant.
Caldwell House, Charlotte, Mrs William Caldwell.
Central Hotel, Charlotte, Campbell &
  Gresham.
Charlotte Hotel, Charlotte. W J Moore.
Cochran Hotel, Huntersville, Mrs Livingston.

Dixon House, Charlotte, D F Dixon.
Dodge House, Charlotte, Mrs Sloan.
Hotel, Pineville, Mrs Hannah Garrison.
Hotel, Davidson College, H P Helper.
Hotel, Matthews, T V Henry.
Queen City Hotel, Charlotte, W J
  Moore.
Railroad Hotel, Charlotte, C C Gresham.
Steward's Hall. Davidson College, Mrs
  Mary E S ewart.
Tryon House. Charlotte, 202 N Tryon
  st. Mrs J F Alexander.
Williams House, Davidson College, W
  P Williams.

LAWYERS.

Names and Post Offices.

Bison, G F, Charlotte.
Bell, J A Charlotte.
Brown. Morrison, Charlotte.
Burwell, A. Walker, P D, and Cansler, E T, Charlotte.
Clarkson, H, Charlotte.
Dowd. C. Charlotte.
Duls, C H (Clarkson & Duls), Charlotte.
Harris, Hugh W, Charlotte.
Jones (H C) & Gillett (C W), Charlotte.
Maxwell, Wm C, Charlotte.
McCall, J D, Charlotte.
Nixon, B, Charlotte.
Osborne, F I (Osborne & Maxwell), and
  Kearns, J W, Charlotte.
Pharr, H N, Charlotte.
Shannonhouse, F M, Charlotte.
Sprinkle, T H, Charlotte.
Wilson, G E, Charlotte.
Yates, W K, Charlotte.

MANUFACTORIES.

Kinds, Post Offices and Proprietors,

Ada Cotton Mills, Charlotte, M C Meyer,
  pres; J J Gormley, sec and treas,
  Capital, $128,000. Consumes 14 bales
  cotton per day. 450 lbs each; produces about 6,000 lbs yarn, Number
  hands, 200; average wages, 64 cents
  per day,
Alpha Cotton Mills, Charlotte; C Scott,
  pres; W S Mallory, sec and treas.
  Capital stock, $100.000.
Artificial Ice, Charlotte; Standard Ice
  and Fuel Co.
Atherton Mills, Charlotte; D A Tompkins, president; R M Miller, jr, vicepres and treas; W W Moore, supt.
  Capital stock. $170,000. Daily consumption, 15 bales cotton; production (daily), 3,330 lbs yarn; 24 looms;
  Number hands, 300.

| MECKLENBURG COUNTY. | MECKLENBURG COUNTY. |

Bellows contracting, and sash, doors and blinds, Charlotte, Berryhill & Newcomb.

Blacksmith bellows (wholesale), Newcomb & Berryhill, prop.

Blacksmithing and wagon building, Charlotte, Page & Medlin.

Blacksmithing, Alexandria, J P Hawkins.

Blacksmithing, Huntersville, Frank Caldwell (col).

Blacksmithing, Charlotte, N L Savage.

Blacksmithing, Charlotte, A Harris.

Boots and Shoes. Charlotte, Mack Taylor (col).

Boots and shoes. Charlotte, P McKane.

Boots and shoes, Davidson College, S Jamison.

Boots and shoes, Davidson College, R James.

Buggies and carriages, Charlotte, J W Wadsworth & Sons.

Building and contracting, Charlotte, M A Stauffer.

Broom Factory, Charlotte.

Building and contracting, Charlotte, J Asbury.

Building and contracting, Tissur Bros.

Building and contracting, Charlotte, F W Ahrens.

Building and contracting, Charlotte, G A Lawing.

Building, Charlotte, D A Long.

Building, Charlotte, Asbury & Finger.

Building, Charlotte, J W Brown.

Building and contracting. Charlotte, H C Herring & W L White.

Buggy and Wagon Repair Shop, Charlotte, D E Sharar.

Cabinet and undertaking, Davidson College, J M Johnson.

Cards and leather belting, Charlotte, Southern Card Clothing Co, J C Leslie.

Charlotte Paint and Oil House, Charlotte, Wheeler Wall Paper Co,

Charlotte Clothing and Mfg Co, Charlotte, Burroughs & Dula.

Carriages, Alexanders. Robt Hawkins.

Charlotte Sash, Door and Blinds Mfg Co, R E Cochrane, pres: Wm Tiddy, sec and treas.

Charlotte Cotton Mills, R M Oates, pres; D W Oates, sec and treas; capital, $131,500; daily consumption, 5.000 lbs cotton; number of hands, about 200; average wages per day, 60c.

Charlotte Machine Co, H S Chadwick, pres and treas, (incorporated); engineers, contractors and dealers in machinery.

Charlotte Broom Co, F W Carnehan, prop.

Cigars, Charlotte, E L Martin.

City Rock Quarry, Charlotte.

Cotton Mill Machinery, Charlotte, The D A Tomkins Co.

Cotton-seed oil, meal, lint and hulls, Charlotte, N C Cotton Oil Co, T J Davis, mgr.

Cotton ginning, Davidson College, J D Brown.

Cotton-ginning, Davidson College, W A Brown.

Cotton gins and presses, Charlotte, Liddell Co.

Cotton-ginning, Davidson College, Dr J M Wilson.

Cotton gins and presses, Charlotte, Mecklenburg Iron Works.

Cotton gin, Huntersville, J S Sossamon & Bro.

Cotton gin, Huntersville, Ransom & Bro.

Cotton gin, Huntersville, T H Brown.

Crawley's Weave Mill, Charlotte, towels, quilts and dress goods; consumes about 1,000 lbs of yarns daily; average number of hands, about 50; average wages, $1 per day.

Electrical apparatus and supplies, The Westinghouse Electric and Mfg Co.

Feed-water pumps, Park Mfg Co.

Furniture, 220 Eighth st, Elliott Furniture Co.

Galvanized iron fronts, finials and cornice and general sheet metal work, slate and tin roofing, Charlotte, J M McCausland & Co.

Gold Crown Hosiery Mills, Charlotte, R M Oates, Jr; prop. Capital, $45,-000: consumption, 500 pounds yarns daily; no. hands, 100; average wages 60 cents per day.

Harness, Charlotte, P A Osborne.

Highland Park M'f'g Co. cotton ginghams, Charlotte, W E Holt. pres; G W Johnston, treas. Capital stock, $198,000.

Honey-comb, Davidson College, C E Bost.

Ice factory, Charlotte, Geo L Baker.

I X L Broom Co, Charlotte, Rossler Hyams.

Iron foundry, Charlotte (Dilworth), —— Moffitt.

Iron founders and machinists, Charlotte, Mecklenburg Iron Works; Jno Wilkes, manager; J Frank Wilkes, supt.

Knitting mills, Charlotte, Gold Crown Hosiery Mill, R M Oats, Jr, prop.

Leader Broom Co, Charlotte, C H Wilson.

Liddell Company, incorporated; W S Liddell, pres; F B McDowell, vice-pres; J L Chambers, sec'y and sup't; engines, saw-mills, cotton presses, cotton-gins. Capital stock $100,000.

MECKLENBURG COUNTY.

Machine shop, cotton mill repairs, Charlotte, The D A Tompkins Co.

Machine card clothing and other cotton mill supplies, Charlotte, (Dilworth) Southern Card Clothing Co, prop; James Leslie, manager.

Machine shops, Huntersville, J S Sossamon & Bro.

Marble and granite works, Charlotte, R H Moore & Son.

Marble works, Charlotte, —— Elliott.

Mattress manufactory, Charlotte, E M Anderson.

Mecklenburg mill (roller), Charlotte (Dilworth), Lee H Battle, pres; T W Harris, sec and treas. T B Ronald's head miller; capacity, 100 pounds flour daily (incorporated).

Mecklenburg Mills, roller flour, Charlotte, Battle & Harris, props.

Mecklenburg iron works, Trade street and R and D passenger depot, Charlotte; engineers, founders and machinist.

Myrton Hosiery Mills, Charlotte, R M Oates, Jr.

N C Cotton Oil Co, Charlotte, T J Davis, manager.

"Observer" Printing House, Charlotte, Caldwell & Tompkins, proprietors.

Oil and Fertilizer Co, Charlotte, Fred Oliver, pres and treas.

Plumbing and gunsmithing, Charlotte, A R Willman.

Planing mill, Charlotte, Asbury & Finger.

Planing mill, Charlotte, F W Ahren.

Planing mill, Charlotte, J Asbury.

Planing mill, Davidson College, Allison & Brittain.

Robbins' Sash Cord mill, Charlotte, (at Dilworth), —— Robbins, prop.

Roller coneing, Charlotte, The D A Tompkins Co.

Sash, doors, blinds and mantles, Charlotte, Asbury & Finger.

Sash cord, Charlotte, J H Robbins.

Shirts, drawers and overalls, Charlotte, Miller & Davis.

Shoes, Charlotte, William Holt.

Shoes, Alexander's, S Hawn.

Shoes, Huntersville, N C Frazier.

Shuttle-blocks, Charlotte, —— Cox, prop.

Soda Water, Charlotte, C Voler & Co.

Southern Newspaper Union, Charlotte, Charles S Donaldson, mgr.

The Atherton Mills, Charlotte, D A Tompkin, pres; B M Miller, jr, vice-pres and treas; Geo L Krudger, sec; capital stock $175,000.

MECKLENBURG COUNTY.

The D A Tompkins Co, counsulting and contracting engineers, S College and Fourth sts, Charlotte.

The Dixie Paint Factory, E Trade st, J Hershinger & Co, Charlotte.

The Queen City Printing and Paper Co, Charlotte; printing, binding and wholesale stationery, H A Murrill, pres and treas; G L Dooley, sec.

The Alpha Mills, Charlotte; C Scott, pres; W S Mallory, sec and treas; W H M Woods, supt; capital $100,000; raw material daily 2,700 lbs; daily proportion about $2,500 lbs warps and yarns; number hands 65; average wages 72 cents per day.

The Charlotte Trouser Co (at Dilworth), R J Brevard, pres; J F Robertson, vice-pres; W R Talliafero, sec and treas; capacity of 600 pair of pants daily.

The Charlotte Supply Co, general supplies and manufacturers of leather belding; E A Smith, pres; J P Wilson, sec and treas.

The Park Mfg Co, Charlotte (Dilworth), Latta, Pharr & Moffitt, props; boilers, feed-pumps and heaters.

The Shaw-Howell Harness Co; W E Shaw, pres; G A Howell, sec and treas; m'f'rs collars, saddles, harness and farmer and bicycle dealers.

Towells, Crowley Mfg Co, Charlotte; J H Crowley, pres and treas; capital stock $40,000.

Trouers Co, Charlotte; ——, pres; W R Talliaferro, treas.

Victor Cotton Mills, Charlotte; Geo E Wilson, pres; A C Hutchison, sec and treas; capital stock $150,000; daily consumption about 12 bales; produces daily about $4,000 lbs yarn; number of hands 180; average wages daily 60 cts.

Wagons, Huntersville, C W Ritch.

Wagons, Huntersville, Holler & Darly.

Wheelwrighting, Pineville, J H Spencer.

Whitin Machine Works (branch office), S W Cramer, Southern Agt.

Wagons, etc, Davidson College, P P Maxwell.

MERCHANTS AND TRADESMEN.

Names, Post Offices and Line of Business.

CHARLOTTE.

Alexander, Dr J B,	Drugs
Alexander, I K A,	G S
Alexander, R B,	Gro
Alexander, T L, Son & Co,	G S
Andrews, E M,	Furn
Andrews, F M & Bro,	Pianos and Organs

MECKLENBURG COUNTY.	MECKLENBURG COUNTY.
Andrews & Co, Undertakers	Durham, J A & Co, Wholesale Gro
Anthony, J T, Whol Prov and Feed	Duval, J E, Electrician
Anthony, J T & Co, Meats, etc	Eccles & Bryan, Hotel
Asbury, Josiah, Contractor	Eddins, J R, agt, Books
Asbury & Finger, Builders	Elam, R B, Job Printer
Asbury & Shafer, Gro	Elliott, T L, Marble Yard
Austin, J D, Gro	Emery, J H, G S
Baker, James C (near), G S	Farrior, John, Jeweler
Baruch, H, Whol and Retail	Fa-nacht. J A Baker and Confec
Dry Goods and Carpets	Field, R H, Wholsale and Retail Gro
Baruch, J & Co, Dry Goods	Frank, Max, Jeweler
Baumgarten, H, Photo	Gaither, Thomas H, Com
Beattie, A M. Gro	Garabaldi, T, Tinner and Roofer
Beattie, R A, Gro	Goodman, R, Gunsmith
Berryhill, Jno A, Gro	Gray, Mat, G S
Belk Bros. G S	Gresham, C, Restaurant
Bethine & White, Gro	Gryder, J L, Gro
Blair Bros, Drugs	Hall, Geo S, Green Gro
Borney & VanNess, Gro	Hales, A. Jeweler
Boyte, T L, G S	Hannon, J C, Gro
Brem & Co. Real Estate and Ins	Harris & Keisler, D G
Brem, Walter, Fquitable Life Ins,	Hayes, C C, agt, Gro
[City Hall.	Hayes & Austin, Gro
Bresse, O F & Sons, Mutual Life Ins	Heath Bros. Bankers
[Co, City Hall	Henderson, W L & Bro, Gro
Bridges & Co, Gro	Hicks. F A, Stoves
Brockenborough, G H, Mdse	Hirst, Miles, Gro
Brown & Jones, Organs	Holtsclaugh, D S, Gro
Brown, Weddington & Co, Hdw	Holtsclaugh, Geo M, Gro
Bryan, B K. Gro	Holton, Chas S, G S
Butner, D H, Furn	Hook, Chas C, Architect
Burwell & Dunn, Drugs	Hooper, E, Gro
Burroughs & Duls, M'f'rs Plant	Houser, W H, Builder
Butt, C N G & Co, Fire and Accident	Howell, Orr & Co, Cotton
[Ins, City Hall	Irwin, H C, Gro
Calder, John. Gro	Johnson Pope (S College st),
Caldwell, R B, G S	Plumbing
Cates, V H, Shoemaker	Johnson, Jas A, Marble
Chadwick, H S. Pres and Treas	Johnson & Morris, Furn
[Charlotte Machine Co.	Johnson Bros, G S
Charlotte News, Job Printing	Jones, C Furber, Sec Carolina Mut
Charlotte Observer, Job Printing	Fire Ins Co
Charlotte Brick and Tile Mfg Co.	Jordan. R H & Co, Drugs
Charlotte Cotton Compress Co.	Justus Hardware Co, Hdw
Charlotte Gas Light Co, Corp	Kaufman, W & Co, Clothing
Charlotte Electric Light and Power Co	Kennedy, H B (col), G S
Charlotte Granite Co, Corp	Kidd, W B, Gro
Charlotte Oil and Fertilizer Co, Corp	Kirby, M F, Gro
Clinard, J A, Gro and Com	Kirkpatrick, J M (near), G S
Cochrane & Barnhardt, Flour, Grain	Knox, Henry E, Hydraulic Engi-
Collins, J D,	neer, City Hall
Cramer & Bigelow, Engineers and	Kraus, C A, Painter
[Contractors	Lance, P L, Auctioneer and Va-
Crowell, A H, Lumber	riety Store
Culpepper, Rowlin, Jr, Gro	Long, Tate & Co. Clothing and
Davidson, T R, Livery	Gents Furnishing Goods
Davidson & Wolfe, Gro	Lawing. Geo A (near), G S
Davis, J L & Co, Gro	Liddell Co, Foundry and
Doud, F W, Machinery	Machine Works
Duls, N, Gro	Link, H G, Gro
Duncan, R A, Gro	Litchenstien, M, Tailor
Durham, F R, Gro	Little, J M, Conf
Durham, I W & Co, Marble	Littlejohn, R N, Com Mcht
	Long, W M, G S

MECKLENBURG COUNTY.

Lubinsky & Schieller, Variety Store
Lubinsky & Co, Installment Furn
Magill, T R, Gro
Malone, John C, Real Est, Life and Fire Ins
Margolin & Co, Bagging
Martin, E L, Tob and Cigars
Mayer & Ross, Whol Gro
McAden, Dr John H, Drugs
McCausland, J N, Stoves
McGinn, G H & Co, Gro
McKenzie, Wm, Gro
McKnight, F A, Gro
McLaughlin & Warlick, G S
McLaughlin, J B, jr, & Co, Gro
Mensing, H C, Mercht Tailor
Mills & Davis, Wholsale Shirts, Drawers and Overalls
Mesenheimer, Mrs Delila, G S
Moore, W J, Hotel
Moore, R H, Marble
Morse, R H & Son, Marble Yard
Mullen, W N, Pat Med
Nash, Fred, Fire Ins
Nathans, H M, Clothing
Newcomb, Mrs G, Millinery
North Carolina Granite Co, ——
Northey, J D, G S
Oliver, Fred, Pres Charlotte Oil and Fert Co
Oliver Oil Co, Corp
Orders, John Y, G S
Osborne, P A & L W, G S
Overcash, W J A, Butcher
Oznient, J J, Cabinet Maker
Palamountain, J C, Jeweler
Parnella, G A, Fruit
Pegram, M P, jr, Gents' Fur Goods
Phillips, J S, Mcht Tailor
Phœnix Drug Co, C A Walker, Manager, Drugs
Plummer, J M, Gro
Prather, W N, Gro and Conf
Queen City Printing Co, Job Printing
Queen City Drug Co, Drugs
Rebman, F T, Gro
Reid, J S & Co, Crockery and Glassware
Reese & Robertson, Drugs
Rhyne, A S & Bro, Com Mcht
Roessler, J, Com Mcht
Rogers Clothing Co, Clothing
Ross, R C, Book Store
Byland & Gresham, Gro
Surratt & Blakely, Gro
Savin, F A, Drugs and Conf
Schiff & Co, Whol Gro
Schorch, T E, Whol Gro
Scott, John M & Co, Whol Drugs
Seigle, T L & Co, Dry Goods
Shannonhouse, J G, agt, Gro
Shaw, W E & Co, Corp
Shell, J E, Jeweler
Sherrill, J L, Jeweler
Sims, J M, Gro

MECKLENBURG COUNTY.

Sloan, J H, Cotton Buyer
Smith, Vale & Tompkins, Machinery
Smith & Flournoy, Crockery
Spratt, J B, County and City Engineer, City Hall
Springs, E B & Co, Fert
St Catherine Gold Mining Co, ——
Stevens & Stevens, G S
Stokes, A R, Sec N C Building and Loan Asso, City Hall
Stone & Barringer, Books and Sta
Taylor, J P, G S
Taylor, W B, Conf
The Charlotte Supply Co, Mill Sup
Thomas, J S, Life and Accident Ins
Thomas & Maxwell, Furn
Thompkins, The D A Co, Corp Machinery
Thomason, W H, Gro
Todd, John W, G S
Valer, C & Co, Soda Water
VanNess, J H, Photo
Victor Cotton Mills, Corp
Vita, A, Conf
Vogel, John, Tailor
Vogler, J A, Printer
Wadsworth, J W, Livery
Wadsworth, J W & Son, Carriages
Walker, L J, Drugs
Ward, W W, Lime and Grain
Watts, Harrison, Cotton Buyer
Wearn, J H & Co, Lumber
Wearn, W S, Carriage Maker
Weddington, J H & Co, Wholesale and [Retail Hardware
Wheeler Wall Paper Co, [C P Wheeler, prop
Whitaker, Miss Mattie A, Stenogra-[pher and Type-writer
White, R M & Sons, Gro
Williams, Hood & Co, Racket Store
Willis, J H, Res
Willman, A R, Plummer and Gun-[smith
Withers, B F, Building Material and [grain
Withers, B T, Lime and grain
Withers, John T, Confec
Young, J B, Gro
Young & Pope, Gro

CLEAR CREEK.

McEachern, J C, G S

COWAN'S FORD.

Alexander, R D & Co, G S
Derr, A J, G S

CROFT.

Henderson & Howie, G S
Woodruff, G E, G S

DAVIDSON.

Allison, James, G S
Brown, W A (near), Saw Mill
Cornelius Cotton Mills, Corp

27

MECKLENBURG COUNTY.		MECKLENBURG COUNTY.	
Crawford, M W & Co (near),	G S	MONTEITH.	
Dupuy, Dr J J,	Drugs	Lamond & Hunter,	G S
Howard & Co,	G S	NEWELL.	
Johnson, J R,	G S		
Linden Mfg Co. (corp),	Cotton Mills	Newell, J A,	G S
Neil, S R,	G S	NIMROD.	
Sherrill, W F,	Gro and Hdw	Long, W M,	G S
Sloan, J L, sr,	G S		
Sloan & Sherrill.	G S	PINEVILLE.	
Stough, Cornelius & Co,	G S	Bailes, W O (near),	G S
		Bryant, Henry,	G S
DAVENPORT.		Fisher Bros,	Cotton gin
Grier, J S,	G S	Medlin, Hoover & Co,	G S
Matthews & McManus,	G S	Rodman, Heath & Nevens Co,	G S
		Rome, J J,	Drugs
DERITA.		Spencer & Heath,	Coachmakers
Hunter, J P,	G S	Yount, J A, agt,	G S
Jordan, W R,	G S	Yount, W E, agt,	G S
DIXIE.		RANALSBURG.	
Collins & Freeman,	G S	Stroup, J P,	Blacksmith
Marshall, R A,	G S		
		SANDIFER.	
EASTFIELD.		Cathey, A F,	G S
Wallace, J R,	G S	Sadler Bros,	G S
GRIFFITH.		SHOPTON.	
Kilpatrick, J M,	G S	Hayes, J R,	—
HARRISON.		Spratt, J B,	—
McGinn & Son,	G S	SPURRIER.	
HEBRON.		Spurrier, E R,	G S
Benton, J M,	G S	Williams, J A, & Co,	G S
HOPEWELL.		STEELE CREEK.	
McElroy & McNeely,	G S	Hayes, J R,	G S
HORNET.			
Harris, W H,	G S	**MINES.**	
HUNTERSVILLE.		Kinds, Post Offices and Proprietors.	
McConnell, Steele & Co,	G S		
Choat, J L, & Co,	G S	A G Wilson Mine, gold, Indian Trail,	
Milholland, N T,	Marble	J D Yount.	
Mullen, J W, & Co,	Drugs	Alexander, gold, Charlotte, J P Mc-	
Walker, C A, & Co,	Drugs	Combs.	
McConnell & Co,	G S	Arlington, gold, Charlotte.	
LODO.		Black, gold, Charlotte, J W Wads-	
Bigham & Berryhill,	G S	worth's estate.	
Hoover, Sadler & Co,	G S	Blair vein, Harmet, Mrs —— Blair.	
		Capps, gold, Charlotte, John Wilkes.	
MARTINDALE.		Cathey, gold and copper, Charlotte,	
Alley, W H,	Saw Mill	Green C Cathey.	
MATTHEWS.		Cathey, gold and copper, Charlotte,	
Barrett & Grier,	G S	W H Frost (Charleston, S C.)	
Black & Funderburk,	G S	Chapman, gold, Charlotte, R P Chap-	
Funderburk & Renfrow,	Cotton-gin	man.	
Heath & Reed,	G S	Clark, gold, Charlotte, J H Carson.	
Henly, D J,	G S	Davidson, Charlotte, J W Wads-	
Hooks, S J,	Fert	worth's estate.	
Hosey, F V, & Co,	Drugs	Dunn, gold and copper, Charlotte, H D	
Irvin, T G,	Drugs	Wallbridge, Washington, D C, mgr.	
McLaughlin & Warlick,	G S	Elliott, gold and copper, Charlotte; J	
Medlin & Funderburk,	G S	A Elliott, mgr.	
Stevens & Stevens,	G S	Ferris, gold, Charlotte, Dr J P Mc-	
MINT HILL.		Combs.	
Henderson, J M,	G S	Frazier Mine, Charlotte, E C McDow-	
		ell, mgr.	

MECKLENBURG COUNTY.

Garris, gold, Charlotte, Dr J P Mc-Combs.

Henderson, gold, Charlotte, C A Rollins, supt.

Hopewell, gold and copper, Charlotte, M Cohen, Baltimore, Md.

Howell Mine, Charlotte, S M Howell, owner.

Hunter, gold, Huntersville, A H Hunter, mgr.

Icyhour, gold, Charlotte, S H Hilton.

Maxwell Mine, Charlotte, John Wilkes.

McGinn, gold and copper, Charlotte.

Means, gold, Charlotte, E W Howey.

Point Mine, gold, Charlotte, H W Clark, supt.

Poplin vein, Charlotte, Poplin estate, Baltimore, Md.

Ray, gold, Charlotte, Baltimore and N C Gold Mining Co, Thos W Hooper, sec and treas.

Rea, gold, Charlotte.

Rudisill, gold, Charlotte, J H Carson, manager.

Simpson mine, Charlotte.

Smith & Parker mine, Charlotte, S P Smith, manager.

St Catharine, gold, Charlotte, G W Pitcher.

Stephen Wilson mine, J T Clark, mgr.

Surface Hill, Arlington, E H Hinson, manager.

Taylor, gold, Charlotte, S H Hilton.

Trotter, gold, Charlotte; H D Wallbridge, Washington, D C.

MILLS.

Kinds, Post Offices and Proprietors.

Corn and flour, Davidson College, Mellon & Graham.

Corn and flour, Alexander, W D Alexander.

Corn and flour, Paw Creek, —— Terepaugh.

Corn and flour, Monteith, R B Cochran.

Corn and flour, Nimrod, Beatty & Long

Corn and flour, Charlotte, R A Grier.

Corn, saw and gin (steam), Caldwell, M Dove.

Corn, saw and gin (steam), Davidson College, W Brown.

Corn, saw and gin (steam), Davidson College, Dr J B Alexander.

Corn and saw, Huntersville, Sossamon Bros.

Corn (steam), Davidson College, Allison & Bratton.

Corn (steam), Mint Hill, Robert Henderson.

Corn (steam), Hooe's, J B Morris.

Corn and gin, Charlotte, John Garabaldi.

MECKLENBURG COUNTY.

Corn and flour, Hopewell, R D Whitley.

Corn, gin and flour (steam), Matthews, J B. Williamson.

Corn, gin and saw, Derita, John P Hunter.

Corn, gin and flour, Pineville, Lee Fisher.

Corn and gin, Arlington, F M Hinson.

Flour and saw, Pineville, T J Downs.

Flour, corn and saw, Monteith, R B Cochrane.

Flour and corn, Charlotte, Stewart's heirs.

Mecklenburg Flour Mills (roller), Charlotte, Battle & Harris.

Saw, Matthews, Funderburk & Co.

Steam saw and gin, Lodo, Sloan & McDonald.

PHYSICIANS.

Names and Post Offices.

Abernathy, J A, Bristow.

Alexander, H S, Tampa.

Alexander, Annie L, Charlotte.

Alexander, J B, Charlotte.

Alexander, C L (dentist), Charlotte.

Bland, M A (dentist), Charlotte.

Bland, C A (dentist), Charlotte.

Boyte, C, Paw Creek.

Brevard, R J. Charlotte.

Brevard, E M, Charlotte.

Bruner, J, Matthews.

Byers, J W, Charlotte.

Caldwell, J Ed, Huntersville.

Craven, W P, Hopewell.

Crowell, M. Kingwood.

DeArnid, Mc, Mint Hill.

Dupuy, J J, Davidson College.

Gibbon, Robert, Charlotte.

Gibbon, R L, Charlotte.

Graham, William A, Charlotte.

Graham, G W, Charlotte.

Graham, Joseph, Charlotte.

Henderson, J M, Charlotte.

Henderson, S, Croft.

Herron, I W, Dixie.

Herron, J Mc, Dixie.

Houser, W H (col), Charlotte.

Hunter, M C, Huntersville.

Irvin, J R, Charlotte.

Irvin, T G, Matthews.

Jones, S B. Charlotte.

Keerans, E P, Charlotte (dentist).

Kell, Thomas, Pineville.

Knox, John, Ranalsburg.

McManaway, C G, Charlotte.

McCoy, ——, Bristow.

McCombs, J P, Charlotte.

Meisenheimer, C A, Charlotte.

Montgomery, J C, Charlotte.

Moore, Nick, Pineville.

Monroe, J T, Davidson College.

MECKLENBURG COUNTY.

Monroe, J P. Davidson College.
Neal, T C, Derita.
O'Donohue, D, Charlotte.
Petree, A L, Charlotte.
Pharr, William, Newells.
Pope, J T (col), Charlotte.
Reed, T N, Matthews.
Register, E C, Charlotte.
Rone, J J, Pineville.
Strong, Charles M. Charlotte.
Strong, J M. Steele Creek.
Wakefield, W H, Charlotte (destist).
Walker, H J, Huntersville.
Walker, Chas J. Huntersville.
Wilder, H M, Charlotte.
Wilson, J M, Caldwell.
Williams, J T (col), Charlotte.
Winchester, F M, Charlotte.
Wooley, W T, Charlotte.
Wooten, ——, Davidson College.

SCHOOLS.

Names, Post Offices and Principals.

Academy, Matthews, Miss Cora Vale.
Academy of Medicine, Charlotte, Dr
  Robert Gibson, pres.
Biddle University (col) for young men
  (Presbyterian), Charlotte, Rev D J
  Sanders, D D, pres; faculty, Rev A P
  Burrell, PhD, S B Priddy, A M, Geo
  E Davis A M, Rev W F Brooks, D D,
  I D Martin, D D.
Charlotte Commercial College, Jackson
  & Haynard.
Conservatory of Music and Art, Char-
  lotte. Prof Carl S Gaertner, princi-
  pal; Mrs Gaertner and Miss Carrie
  Motz, assistants.
Davidson College (Presbyterian), Da-
  vidson College, B Shearer, D D, LL
  D, pres; faculty; C R Harding, Har-
  ry Smith, Prof Currett. Prof Graves.
Female Seminary, Charlotte, Miss Lil-
  lie Long.
Graded School, Alex Graham.
High School, Providence, Miss Mettie
  Weaver.
High School, Davidson College.
High School, Huntersville Gray &
  Crosby.
High School, Hopewell, Prof J W
  Sample.
Hudson's Business University, Char-
  lotte, J E Hudson.
Military Institute. Charlotte, J G Bond,
  supt; W F Harding, asst supt.
School (Music and Art), Charlotte, ——
  Giertner.
Sharon Academy, Charlotte, Professor
  Roseboro.
Welborn School, Pineville, Rev John
  W Welborn.
Public Schools—white, 89; colored, 64.

MECKLENBURG COUNTY.

LOCAL CORPORATIONS.

Biddle University (col), D J Sanders,
  D D, pres; established in 1867; capi-
  tal invested, $125,000; $30,000 endow-
  ment; number students, 260.
Chamber of Commerce, Charlotte, J L
  Chambers, pres; R N Tiddy, sec and
  treas.
Charlotte Lodge, No 88, I O O F, Char-
  lotte, Walter Brem, N G; day of
  meeting, Monday.
Charlotte Commandery, No 2, Knight
  Templars, T R Robertson, E C.
Charlotte Chapter. No 39, Royal Arch
  Masons, Charlotte. Meets 2d and 4th
  Tuesday evenings of each month.
Charlotte Water-works, Charlotte, R J
  Brevard, pres; D P Hutchinson, supt.
Charlotte Cotton Mills, Charlotte; es-
  tablished in 1880; R M Oates, pres; D
  W Oates, treas; capital stock, $125,-
  000; number of spindles, 6,240; daily
  production, 2,400 pounds yarn; num-
  ber hands employed, 80.
Charlotte Gas Co, Charlotte, S E Lin-
  ton, mgr; capital stock paid in, $37,-
  000.
Charlotte Cotton Compress Co, Char-
  lotte, ——, supt.
Charlotte Building and Loan Association, Charlotte.
Commercial National Bank of Charlotte; capital stock, $175,000; undi-
  vided profits, $185,000; J S Spencer,
  pres; A G Brenizer, cashier; D H Anderson, Teller.
Craighead Lodge, No 366, A F and A
  M, Huntersville, J W Mullen, W M.
  Time of meeting, 1st and 3d Friday
  nights.
Dixie Lodge, No 108, I O O F, Char
  lotte; J K Purefoy, N G. Day of
  meeting, Friday.
Excelsior Lodge, No 261, A F and A M,
  Charlotte. Time of meeting, 1st and
  3d Tuesday evenings.
First National Bank of Charlotte; cap-
  ital stock, $300,000; R M Oates, pres;
  M P Pegram, cashier; John F Orr,
  teller.
Heath Brothers' Bank, Charlotte, W
  H Twitty, cashier; capital, $50,000.
Law Library Association, Charlotte,
  Geo F Bason, pres.
Loan and Savings Bank, Charlotte, S
  Wittkowsky, pres; D A Tompkins,
  vice-pres; — Battle, cash; A Graham,
  jr, asst cash; capital, $100,000; sur-
  plus, $600.
Lodge, Knights of Honor, Davidson
  College, W P Williams, dictator.
Mechanics Perpetual Building and
  Loan Association, Charlotte; S Witt-

MECKLENBURG COUNTY.

kowsty, pres; R E Cochrane, sec and treas; capital stock, $100,000

Mecklenburg County Bible Society; Geo B Hanna, pres; S W Reed, s-c.

Mecklenburg Lodge, No 176, A F and A M, Davidson College; time of meeting, Thursday, on or before full moon; and June 24th, and Decemlber 27th.

Mecklenburg Declaration Lodge, No 9, I O O F, Charlotte; Thos L Gednell, N G; day of meeting, Tuesday.

Mecklenburg Lodge, No 2682, Knights of Honor, Huntersville; J S Sossamon, dictator.

Mutual Building and Loan Association, Charlotte; P M Brown, Pres; A G Brenizer, sec and treas; capital stock, $226,700.

Mystic Shrine, No 1, W S Liddell.

North Carolina Building and Loan Association, Charlotte.

People's Building and Loan Association, Charlotte; ——, pres; R J Sifford, sec and treas.

Phalanx Lodge, No 31, A F and A M, Charlotte; time of meeting, second and fourth Mondays; A R Scott, sec.

Royal Arch Chapter, No —, Charlotte.

The Merchants and Farmers National Bank of Charlotte; capital stock, $200,000; J H McAden, pres; J M Miller, cash; C N G Butt. teller.

The First National Bank of Charlotte; capital stock, $300,000; surplus, $100 000; R M Oates, pres; M P Pegram, cash; W R Myers, vice-pres.

Thompson Orphanage, Charlotte; Episcopalian; Rev E A Osborne. supt.

Underwriters Association, Charlotte; Dr E Nye, Hutchinson.

MECKLENBURG COUNTY.

NEWSPAPERS.

Afro-American Presbyterian, Charlotte (weekly religious), Rev D J Sanders, D D, editor and prop.

Charlotte Observer (daily and weekly Democratic); Caldwell & Tompkins, proprietors; J P Caldwell, editor.

Charlotte Democrat, Charlotte (Democratic weekly), J P Strong, editor and prop.

Davidson Monthly, Davidson College; (literary).

Mecklenburg Times, Charlotte, W C Dowd, editor and prop.

Southern and Western, Textile Excelsior, Charlotte (industrial), John Cuthbertson and C S Donaldson, editors and proprietors (John Cuthbertson & Co).

Southern Newspaper Union, College st, Charlotte, M L Yeager, mgr.

Spirit of the South, Charlotte (Republican), W R Terry.

The Charlotte Medical Journal, Drs E C Register and J C Montgomery, editors and props.

The Evening News, Charlotte (daily, except Sunday), W C Dowd, editor and proprietor.

The Messenger (col), Charlotte (weekly Republican), W C Smith, editor and prop.

The People's Paper, Charlotte (Populist weekly), J P Sossamon, editor and prop.

The Star of Zion, Charlotte (organ of the A M E Zion Church in America; Rev G W Clinton, D D, editor.

MITCHELL COUNTY.

AREA, 240 SQUARE MILES.

POPULATION, 12,784; White 12,231, Colored 553.

MITCHELL COUNTY was formed in 1861, from the counties of Burke, McDowell, Caldwell, Watauga and Yancey, and was named in honor of Rev Elisha Mitchell, D D, who for a number of years was a Professor in our State University, and who was accidently killed in making a scientific exploration of the highest peak of the Black Mountain. His body was finally interred on the summit of Mount Mitchell, the highest peak east of the Rocky Mountains.

BAKERSVILLE is the county-seat, and is situated 250 miles west of Raleigh. Population 850.

Surface—This county is situated on the north side of the Nollichucky river, and between the Blue Ridge on the east and the Iron Mountain on the west, forming a valley rich and beautiful beyond description.

Staples— Wheat, corn, rye, oats, medicinal herbs, butter and live stock. Mitchell is one of the finest wheat counties in the State.

Fruits--Apples, pears, grapes, peaches, etc.

Timbers—Poplar, wild cherry, hickory, white pine, oak, chestnut, walnut and ash.

Minerals—Iron, mica, manganese, asbestos. plumbago, corundum, samarikite, gummite, pitchblende, mineral springs.

TOWNS AND POST OFFICES.

	POP.		POP.
Altamont,	50	Kawana,	50
Bakersville		Ledger,	25
(C H),	850	Lineback,	30
Bandana,	30	Linville,	300
Brighton,	100	Little Rock-	
Brummett,	50	creek.	50
Cloudland,	100	Magnetic City,	150
Cranberry,	150	Mica,	50
Crossmore,	50	Minneapolis,	55
Elk Park,	400	Montezuma,	50
Elsie,	25	Penland,	60
Estaton,	40	Plumbtree,	40
Frank,	50	Redhill,	25
Glen Ayre,	100	Relief,	30
Hale,	50	Senia,	25
Herrell,	50	Spear,	35
Hollow Poplar,	50	Sprucepine,	50
Ingalls,	25	Valley,	60

COUNTY OFFICERS.

Clerk Superior Court—J C Bowman.
Commissioners—A A Wiseman, chm'n.
Register of Deeds—R M Davis.
Sheriff—G K Pritchard.
Solicitor Tenth District—J F Spainhour.
Treasurer—W S Daniels.
County Examiner—I T Turlington.

COURTS.

Ninth Monday after first Monday in March, and sixth Monday after the first Monday in September.

TOWNSHIPS AND MAGISTRATES.

Bakersville—T T Baker, Peter Grindstaff, R F McKinney, H T Wilson. S J Moore, D S Elliott, Jno Dale, Dock Gage. Will Seagle, Chas Stevens, Coleman Pannell (Bakersville).

Cranberry—Robt Ellis, Ed Young, David Mourning, A C Gaultney, L E Clark, Jas Stewart. H T Morrison, J R Pritchard, G F Vance, W A Ellis, David Perry, Wm Buchanan (Cranberry).

Fork Mountain—Gilbert Sparks, Will Edwards, Jno McKinney, Geo Young, Hay Green, Chas McKinney, jr, E B Gibbs, H R Hughes (Bakersville).

Grass Creek—Calvin Wood, Wm Davenport, D F Blalock, Chas Sparks, J A Bailey, R J Bailey, R B Harris, Alfred McBee, Massey Sorrell, Wm Hollifield, Fowler Hall, Harry Worthen (Bakersville).

Harrell's—A K Hall, Thos Greene, Wm Buchanan, Jas Garland, J W Phillips. Tilman Arrowood. Harrison Street, Wm Bennett, A G Wetherly, Allen Butler, David Street (Bakersville).

Hollow Poplar—David Tipton, Sanders Hughes, Jno Tipton, Jno Flanning, T M Cooper, Elbert Bailey, L C Webb, Jno N Peterson, Hiram Tipton, Clingman Whitson, Jno Miller (Hollow Poplar).

Linville—W E Blackburn, M W Clay, T W Wright. Leroy Franklin, J C Carpenter. Jas Carroll, Rube Carpenter, J W Farthing, Jno A Riddle, Jno Carpenter, Brown Hughes, Thad Braswell, Jack Blalock, Harry Johnson (Linville).

MITCHELL COUNTY.

Little Rock Creek—Jno Edwards, W A Burleson, Alex Buchanan. Jacob Ayres, John Burleson, W L Young, Cain Freeman, Jake Randolph, Sanders Young, Starlin Buchanan (Little Rock Creek).

Red Hill—T G Phillips, Henry Masters, G M Young. Chas Whitson, Jos Garland, Geo Byrd, Thos Garland, Augustus Masters (Red Hill).

Snow Creek—Jas Phillips, S R Hensley, J R Gouge, S F Hensley, Jas Buchanan, D W Greene, Jno Ellis, Whitfield Sparks, Lon Conley, Wm Willis (Bakersville)

Toe River—A A Wiseman, Jas Mace, A G Childs, Edward Wiseman, LaFayette Wiseman, W H Ollis, J L Wiseman, Tilman McCurry, Howard Stafford, Wm Hay, Chas McKinney (Bakersville).

CHURCHES.

Names, Post Offices, Pastors and Denom.

METHODIST.

Beaver Creek—Spruce Pine.
Big Rock Creek—Herrell's.
Church—Bakersville.
Little Rock Creek—Bakersville.
Phillips—Bakersville.
Piney Grove—Elsie.
Pisgah—Elsie.
Shiloh—Red Hill.
Silver's—Bakersville.
Snow Creek—Bakersville.

N. METHODIST.

Church (col.)—Bakersville.
Hunter's Chapel—Elsie.
Little Rock Creek—Bakersville.
Mine Creek—Bakersville
Pisgah—Elsie.
Shiloh—Red Hill.
Snow Creek—Bakersville.
Spring Creek—Herrell's.

BAPTIST.

Bear Creek—Bakersville.
Beaver Creek—Flinty Branch.
Beech Mountain—Cranberry Forge.
Big Meadow—Elsie.
Big Rock Creek—Herrell's.
Bush Creek—Elsie.
Buck Mountain—Cranberry Forge.
Cane Creek—Bakersville.
Church—Bakersville.
Elk River—Cranberry Forge.
Fork Mountain—Bakersville.
Grassy Creek—Flinty Branch.
Liberty Hill—Flinty Branch.
Lilly Branch—Bakersville.
Linville—Plumtree.
Little Rock Creek—Bakersville.
Mine Creek—Bakersville.

MITCHELL COUNTY.

Mt Pleasant—Elsie.
Providence—Red Hill.
Roan Mountain—Bakersville.
Yellow Mountain—Plumtree.

FREE-WILL BAPTIST.

Bean's Creek—Herrell's.
Brummett's Creek—Red Hill.
Church—Red Hill.
Cub Creek—Bakersville.
Linville—Elsie.
North Toe River—Elsie.
Spring Creek—Herrell's.
Squirrel Creek—Elsie.
Toe Hill—Red Hill.

HOTELS AND BOARDING HOUSES.

Names, Post Offices and Proprietors.

Hotel, Bakersville, R J Young.
Hotel, Cloudland, Roane Mount Hotel Company.
Hotel, Cranberry, Wallace Hahn.
Hotel, Elk Park, V B Bowers.
Watauga Inn, Linville, Mrs — Penly.

LAWYERS.

Names and Post Offices.

Black, Samuel, Bakersville.
Bowman, J C, Bakersville.
Bowman, Jacob W, Bakersville.
Greene, Jere H, Bakersville.
Lambert, W, Bakersville.
Love, Thomas A, Bakersville.
Turner, Samuel J, Bakersville.

MANUFACTORIES.

Kinds, Post Offices and Proprietors.

Furniture, Linville, J M McCampbell.
Harness, Bakersville, J W T Quinn.
Sash, doors and blinds, Elk Park, H L Brinkley.

MERCHANTS AND TRADESMEN.

Name, Post-office and Line of Business.

BAKERSVILLE.

Name	Line
Bailey, I H,	G S
Bailey, J W & Son,	G S
Berry Bros.	G S
Deyton & Wilson,	G S
Gauge, J H,	G S
Green & Poteat,	G S
Howell, Jas C (near),	G S
Johnson. Wm,	G S
Poteet, J S,	G S
Prestwood. Dr R L,	G S
Quinn, J W T,	Harness
Wilson, L,	G S
Wilson, J S,	G S
Wilson, S S,	Drugs

MITCHELL COUNTY.	

BRIGHTON.

Ayers, J M,   G S

ELK PARK.

Banner, E J,   G S
Bowers, V B,   G S
Brinkley, H L,   G S
Council, Taylor & Co,   G S
Elk Park Boot and Shoe Co.

ESTATOE.

Jimerson, J E,   G S

GLEN AYRE.

Edwards, Frank,   G S

HALE.

Heaton, J M & Co,   G S

HERRELL.

Buchanan, C M,   G S

HOLLOW POPLAR.

Griffin & Peterson,   G S

INGALLS.

Kay & Keener,   G S

LEDGER.

Garvin, J R.   G S
Phillips, J C,   G S

LINEBACK.

Hughes, M B,   G S

LINVILLE.

McCampbell, J M,   Furn
Richseeker, Chas H,   G S
Teal, Cornelius,   Drugs

LITTLE ROCK CREEK.

Ayers, J M,   G S

MAGNETIC CITY.

Arrowood, Tilman,   G S
Blevens, D L,   G S
Parker, L G,   G S

MICA.

Hyams, M A,   G S

MONTEZUMA.

Lovin, J G,   G S

PLUM TREE.

Burleson, C W & Son,   G S
Jones, Mica J & Co,   ——

RELIEF.

Griffith, R H,   G S
Whitson & Son,   G S

SPEAR.

Banner, J L,   G S

SPRUCE PINE.

Bailey, J A & Bro,   G S
Berry, L A,   G S

MINES.

Kinds, Post Offices and Proprietors.

Abestos, Bakersville, D A Bowman.
Iron, Magnetic City, Roan Mountain Iron and Steel Co.
Iron, Cranberry Forge, Cranberry Iron and Coal Co, —— Pardee, pres.
Mica, Plumtree, English, Burleson & Co.
Mica, Penland, D H Robeson.
Mica, Bakersville, Rorrison & Abernethy.
Mica, Snow Creek, Gould & Watson.
Mica, Plumtree, Samuel Lander.
Mica, Bakersville, J K Irby.
Mica, Spruce Pine, Grier, Gregory & Co.
Mica, Spruce Pine, —— Griffith.
Mica, Elsie, Dellinger & Co.

MILLS.

Names, Post Offices and Proprietors.

Flour mill, Bakersville, Moses Young.
Flour mill, Herrell, Gibbs Garland.
Mill, Relief, R H Griffith.

MONTGOMERY COUNTY.

AREA, 570 SQUARE MILES.

POPULATION, 11,223; White 8,966, Colored 2,257.

MONTGOMERY COUNTY was formed in 1779, from Anson county, and was named in honor of G-n. Richard Montgomery, who was a distinguished officer of the Revolution, and who fell fighting in his heroic attack upon Quebec, 31st December, 1775.

TROY, the county seat, named in honor of John B. Troy, is 115 miles southwest from Raleigh. Population, 500.

Surface—Uneven and, in places, very hilly and rocky; soil good along the streams. Water-power fine; mineral resources very valuable.

Staples—Corn, cotton, wheat and oats.

Fruits—Apples, peaches, pears, cherries, plums, grapes and other small fruits.

Timbers—Oak, pine, hickory, dogwood, maple and ash, pine predominating and very fine.

Minerals—Gold, copper, silver, iron chalybeate and sulphur springs.

TOWNS AND POST OFFICES.

	POP.		POP.
Alco,	25	Martin's Mill,	25
Allenton Ferry,	75	Milledgeville,	100
Allred's,	25	Montgomery,	20
Asbury,	10	Mount Gilead,	250
Blaine,	25	Nalls.	20
Cagle's Mill,	25	Okeewernee,	25
Candor,	150	Onvil,	20
Carl,	20	Onward,	25
Carmel,	20	Ophir,	25
Chandler,	10	Pekin,	25
Dry Creek,	15	Pantop,	50
Eldorado,	100	Queen,	25
Endicott,	10	Scarboro,	30
Erie Mills,	30	Star,	100
Ether,	30	Sulphur	
Filo,	25	Springs,	25
Fly,	30	Swift Island,	25
Glenbrook,	20	Troy (c h),	500
Harrisville,	20	Wadeville,	60
Macedonia,	50		

COUNTY OFFICERS.

Clerk Superior Court—J S Lewis.
Commissioners—J T Wade, chm'n; W C Wallace, J W Colton.
Coroner—W M Bostick.
Register of Deeds—G S Beaman.
Sheriff—D E Erwin.
Solicitor 8th District—J Q Holton.

Standard Keeper—J M Deaton.
Surveyor—N M Thayer.
Treasurer—D A Erwin
County Examiner—Jas W Dixon.

COURTS.

Fourth Monday after the first Monday in March, and fourth Monday after the first Monday in September.

TOWN OFFICERS.

TROY—*Mayor*, J I Sanders.
Commissioners—A R Morris, I M Deaton, J C Bruton, C C Wade, Dr A F Thompson.
Town Clerk—I M Deaton.
Chief of Police—A F Saunders.

TOWNSHIPS AND MAGISTRATES.

Cheek Creek—James Thompson, K E McAuley, J H LeGrand, Charles Brookshire, R T Rush, J E Steele, James Covington, J G Skinner, D L Parson (Troy).

Eldorado—J F Cotton, W G Redwine, Alex M Russell, G B Coggin, D M Ross, L T Russell, Jr (Eldorado).

Hill—J F Deaton, E K Auman, Spinks Maness, Hiram Freeman, Ora Stewart, Ellis Leach, J M Barnwell, W L Freeman (Troy).

Hollingsworth—J M Fox, D M Hunsucker, Neil Leach, W F McMaster, A B McCaskill, J W Ewin, D A McLeod, R B Sutton, Raleigh Green, Z T Wright (Troy).

Little River—N J Enry, J C Cornelison, Nixon Lucas, D B Allen, W S Moore, P G Deaton (Troy).

Mount Gilead—E M Williams, Jas A McAulay, James M Robinson, J R Scarboro (Mount Gilead).

Ophir—W G Davis, Jacob Reynolds, T H Coggin, C C Calicot, P P Hall (Troy).

Pee Dee—W K Beachner, A R Moore, H P Montgomery, C W Wooley, Jr, D F Robinson, G M Bruton (Troy).

Rocky Springs—S T Usher, W T Raper, J B Erwin, B F Rush, Ell Wooley, D I Erwin.

Troy—C C Wade, J M Reynolds, G W Morris, D A Leach, C W Wooley, Sr, W F Wooley, D E Pemberton, J M Deaton (Tr y).

Uwharrie—P C Saunders, J W Thompson, W F Hearne.

MONTGOMERY COUNTY.

MONTGOMERY COUNTY.

CHURCHES.

Names, Pastors, Postoffices and Denom.

METHODIST.

Bethlehem—Sulphur Springs, — Joyner.
Center—Blaine.
Church—Ophir, J W Wallace.
Church—Troy, J W Wallace.
Church—Mt Gilead, J E Thompson.
Flint Hill—Ophir, J W Wallace.
Lane's Chapel—Chandler's, J W Wallace.
Macedonia—Eldorado, J W Wallace.
Pine Grove—Ridge Creek.
Pleasant Hill—Sulphur Springs.
Prospect—Nall's, J W Wallace.
Sardis—Sulphur Sp'ngs, J B Thompson.
Shiloh—Troy, J W Wallace.
Zion—Montgomery, J E Thompson.
Zoah—Eldora, J W Wallace.

METHODIST PROTESTANT.

Church—Millegeville.
Lovejoy—Queen, J W Tarlton.

METHODIST EPISCOPAL.

Chandler's Grove—Chandler's, — Earnhardt.
Church—Blaine, — Earnhardt.
Church—Parson's, J E Evans.
Church—Eagle Spring, J E Evans.
Elliott's Grove—Blaine, — Earnhardt.
Mt Olivet—Troy, J E Evans.
New Bethany—Blaine, — Earnhardt.
New Home—Candor, J E Evans.

BAPTIST.

Church—Troy, G L Merrell.
Bethel—Edinboro.
Big Creek—Glenbrook.
Blackwood's Chapel—Pekin, G L Merrill.
Church—Mt Gilead, W H Lawhon.
Forks of Little River—Okeewernee.
Laurel Hill—Troy, W M Bostick.
Mt Carmel—Carmel, Wesley Littleton.
New Union—Wadeville, J L Morton.

PRESBYTERIAN.

Church—Wadeville, A McLauchlin.
Macedonio—Pekin, K McIntyre.
Sharon—Mt Gilead, A McLauchlin.

CONGREGATIONAL.

Church (col)—Pekin.
Church—Troy, O Faduma.

CHRISTIAN.

Shady Grove—Martin's Mill, Jno Lawrence.

MINISTERS RESIDENT.

Names, Post Offices and Denom.

METHODIST.

Joyner' ——, Star.

Strider, W J, Troy.
Thompson, J E, Mt Gilead.
Thompson, J B, Candordo.
Wallace, J W, Eldorado.

METH. EPISCOPAL.

Beaman W B, Troy.
Evans, J E, Eagle Spring.
Lamar. Nelson, Chandler.

METH. PROTESTANT.

Tarlton, J W, Mt Gilead.

BAPTIST.

Bostick, W M, Onvil.
Henderson, F W, Chandler.

PRESBYTERIAN.

McIntyre, K M, Troy.
McLauchlin, A, Mt Gilead.

HOTELS AND BOARDING HOUSES.

Names, Post Offices and Proprietors.

Allen House, Troy, G W Allen.
Boarding, Mt Gilead, J A McCaulay.
Hotel, Star, Mrs A Leach.
Hotel, Candor, Neil Leach.
Troy Hotel, Troy, A R Morris.

LAWYERS.

Names and Post Offices.

Blair, J R Troy.
Dixon, J W, Troy.
Hurley, Elias, Uwharie.
Jordan, Allen, Troy.
Sanders & Fry, Troy.
Simmons, B F, Troy.
Smith (J W) & Rush, (Wiley), Troy

MANUFACTORIES.

Kinds, Post Offices and Proprietors.

Building and contracting, Allreds, W C Kerns.
Building and contract'g, Martin's Mill, A P Leach.
Blacksmithing and wheelwrighting, Allreds, T W Vuncarmon.
Blacksmithing and wheelwrighting, Allreds. L W Freeman.
Blacksmithing and wheelwrighting, Troy, A B Moore.
Blacksmithing and wheelwrighting, Allreds, Hiram Freeman.
Cotton, Milledgeville, Yadkin Falls Mfg Co.
Iron and wood works, Pennington, J R Everhardt.
Lumber, Ether, Hiram Freeman.
Millwrighting, Erie Mills, John Scarborough.
Millwrighting, Allreds, A P Leach.
Millwrighting, Troy, J L James.

MONTGOMERY COUNTY.

Sash and blinds, Troy, N C Build'g and Supply Co.
Turpentine, Troy, J C Bruton.
Turpentine, Clark's Mills, J C Currie.
Turpentine, Candor, J T Tomlinson.
Turpentine, Troy, W D Clark & Bros,
Turpentine, Troy, S J Smitherman.
Turpentine, Troy, A L Ledbetter.
Turpentine, Troy, Blue & McNeil.
Turpentine, Troy, J F Suggs.
Turpentine, Star, Hector McLeod.
Turpentine, Filo, A C Ray.
Turpentine, Candor, J C Currie & Bro.
Turpentine, Candor, D D Bruton.
Turpentine, Candor, R B Sutton.
Turpentine, Fly, A D Clark & Bros.
Wool-carding, Troy, J L Hall.

MERCHANTS AND TRADESMEN.

Names, Post-Offices, Lines of Business.

ALLENTON FERRY.
Lilly, G H A,   G S

ASBURY.
Cagle, W S;   G S
Steed, J W,   G S
Steed, H L,   G S

BLAINE.
Morris, B E,   G S

BRANCHVILLE.
Currie, J C & Bro,   G S
Nixon, Lucas,   G S

CANDOR.
Campbell, M L,   G S
Currie, J C & Bro,   G S
McCaskill, A B,   G S
Petty, J H,   G S
Shamburger, Dr J B,   Drugs
Stewart, J O,   G S
Sutton, R B, Jr,   G S
Tomlinson, J G,   G S

CARMEL.
Ledbetter, A L,   G S
Parnell, D S,   G S

CLARK'S MILLS.
Currie, J C,   G S

CRAIGROWINE.
Blue, D D & L S,   G S

ELDORADO.
Tayer, N M,   G S

ENDICOTT.
Green, Eli,   G S

ETHER.
Freeman, Hiram,   G S
Freeman & Melton,   G S

FLY.
Clark, A D & Bro,   G S
Blue, A A,   G S

MONTGOMERY COUNTY.

GLEN BROOK.
Russell, G L,   G S

LOVEJOY.
Spencer & Allen,   G S

MORATOCK.
Morris, G W,   G S

MOUNT GILEAD.
Byrd, L P,   G S
Haywood Bros,   G S
Ingram, Dr C B,   Drugs
McAuley, J A,   G S
McAuley, ——,   G S
Martin, M S,   Hiller
Overton, J M,   G S

O'NEIL.
Bruton, J C,   G S

OPHIR.
Davis, W G,   G S

PEKIN.
Cox, C L,   G S
Shamburger, M E,   G S

STAR.
Allen, J A,   G S
Currie, J C & Bro,   G S
Ingram, H C,   G S
Leach, A,   G S
Owens, W B,   G S
Stewart & Allen,   G S

TROY.
Allen, G W,   Hotel
Allen, Geo,   Livery
Atkins, W M,   G S
Blue, A A,   G S
Clark, W D & Bro,   G S
Hall, John L,   Miller
Hearne & Morris,   Livery
Morris, A R,   G S
Morris, G F, jr,   G S
Smitherman & Batton,   G S
Suggs, J F,   G S
Wade, C L,   Mining

UWHARRIE.
Stout, H L,   G S

WADEVILLE.
Furr, A T,   G S
Harwitz & Harwitz,   G S
Parker & Bruton,   G S
Robinson, J M,   G S
Wade, J T & Co,   G S

MINES.

Kinds, Post Offices and Proprietors.

Apalachian, Glenbrook, Guilford Iron Works.
Beaver Dam, gold, Flaggtown, Smith Wilson.
Bettie Hearne mine, Eldorado, Scott & Co.

MONTGOMERY COUNTY.

Carter, gold, Troy, Smitherman & Harris.
Collicott, Ophir, J R Blair.
Cotton, gold, Pontop, J F Cotton.
Christian, gold, Mt Gilead, J A Mc-Cauley.
Cox, gold, Troy, J R Blair.
Dark Spring, Eldorado, Col J H Davis.
Denson, gold, Troy, Moore & Moore.
Dry Hollow, Uwharrie. C C Wad-.
Genesee Mine, Ophir, H H Warner.
Grandman Mine, Eldorado, Scott & Co.
Iron Mountain, Troy, Blair & McKen-non.
Kron, Pontop, Miss Addie Kron.
Moratuck, Moratock, Hipple & Co, of Phila.
Morris Mountain, Eldorado, Thompson & Co, of New York.
Peartree, Moratock, Miss Addie Kron.
Russell, gold, Glenbrook, Dr Brand-rith, of New York.
Riggin Hill, Glenbrook, H McCoy.
Sanders mine, Moratock, Seaton, Spoon-er, Taylor & Hurst.
Spencer Creek, gold, Troy, Jno Bea-man and A Moran.
Stone Mt, gold, Try, C C Wade.
Worth, gold, Nall's, H A Taylor.

MILLS.

Kinds, Post Offices and Proprietors.

Corn, flour and saw (steam), Mt Gilead, Frank McCauley.
Corn, flour and saw, Wadeville, C C Wade.
Corn and flour, Sulphur Springs, W P & J S Lewis.
Corn and flour, Star, Stuart & Allen.
Corn and flour, Troy, J L Hall.
Corn and flour, Milledgeville, Valen-tine Mauney.
Corn and flour, Dry Creek, J G Tom-linson.
Corn and flour, Ophir, Boyles & Craw-ford.
Corn and flour, Eldorado, N M Thayer.
Corn and flour, Mt Gilead, M S Martin.
Corn and flour, Troy, S J Smitherman.
Corn and flour, Allenton Ferry, James Livingston.
Corn and flour, Martin's Mill, B L Allen.
Corn and flour, Nalls, M A Smith.
Corn and flour, Troy, R Johnson.
Corn, Wadeville, J E Parker.
Corn and flour, Wadeville, E DeBerry.
Corn and flour, Cagle's Mills, A J Cagle.
Corn and flour, Swift Island, C A Arm-strong.
Corn and flour, Allred's, F Allred.

MONTGOMERY COUNTY.

Corn and flour, Milledgville, Yadkin Mfg Co.
Corn and flour, Glenbrook, Harry Mc-Kay.
Corn and flour, Eldorado, H McCoy.
Corn and flour, Mt Gilead, W S In-gram.
Mill, Star, A Leach.
Saw (steam), Allret's. Jesse Freeman & Son.

PHYSICIANS.

Names and Post Offices.

Allen, James, Star.
Asbury, F E, Asbury.
Boyles, A C, Eldorado.
Deaton, J B (dentist), Star.
Ingram, C B, Mt Gilead.
Shamberger. J B, Star.
Simmons, W A, Troy.
Thompson, F A. Troy.

SCHOOLS.

Names, Post Offices and Principals.

Academy, Troy.
Academy, Mt Gilead, R H Skeen.
Eldorado Academy, Eldorado.
High School, Wadesville, D Scott Pool.
Lovejoy Academy, Queen.
Peabody Institute (col), Troy, Rev O Foduma.
Public schools—white, 37; colored, 14.

TEACHERS.

Names and Post Offices.

WHITE.

Allen, W D, Star.
Allen, Pattie, Allenton Ferry.
Bernett, M A, Clark's Mills.
Carter, Miss J B, Nalls.
Cochran, George, Endicott.
Cornelison, W L, Eagle's Mills.
Cotton, C L, Pontop.
Cotton, James G, Eldorado.
Cotton, John W, Flagton.
Dabney, Mrs L P, Mt Gilead.
Dunn, J J, Wadesville.
Green, E A, Endicott.
Harris, Eugene, Wadeville.
Ingram, Miss Alla, Star.
Ingram, J R, Star.
Leach, Miss Nannie, Candor.
Leach, W A, Martin's Mills.
Lilly, Miss C C, Allenton Ferry.
McAuley, G T, Mt Gilead.
McMillan, H A, Martin's Mills.
Moore, Miss Viola, Queen.
Moore, Miss Fannie, Queen.
Morris, P C, Carmel.

MONTGOMERY COUNTY.

Paisona, Miss R A, Onvil.
Pool, D S, Wadeville.
Pool, H S, Clark's Mills.
Reynolds, J M, Queen.
Reynolds, D R, Queen.
Russell, L F, Eldorado.
Sanders, J F, Ophir.
Scarboro, A D, Mt Gilead.
Scarboro, Miss Laura, Mt Gilead.
Searboro, R B, Mt Gilead.
Shepperd. H H, Troy.
Strother, W C, Wadeville.
Thompson, Miss Bertha, Mt Gilead.
Williams, Carmel.
Williams, E M, Erie Mills.
Wooly, A O, Troy.
Wright, L A, Martin's Mills.

COLORED.

Baldwin, John, Fly.
Deberry, W C. Scarboro.
Dockery, Sarah. Nalls.
Green, Katie, Dry Creek.
Green, Molsie, Pekin.
Leak, Washington, Erie Mills.
McNeill, C M. Wadeville.
Morris, G R, Erie Mills.
Powell, Martin R. Dry Creek.
Robinson, ——, Mt Gilead.
Sanders, J H, Ophir.
Sanders, B H, Nalls.
Smitherman, Ada, Troy.
Tyson, C L, Mt Gilead.

LOCAL CORPORATIONS.

A F and A M, Star, J L Stuart, W M.
Blackmer Lodge, No 127, A F and A
   M, Mt Gilead. Time of meeting,
   Saturday on or before full moon, at
   2 P M.

NEWSPAPERS.

The Trojan (independent Democratic
   weekly); D Scott Pool, ed and prop.

FARMERS.

Names and Post Offices.

Allred's—W L Auman, Elisha Bur-
roughs, John F Burroughs, Harrison
Freeman, Jesse Freeman, Jacob Jor-
dan, Alex Jordan, J P Leach, Joshua
Maness, J More, Jno Needham, E H
Needham, J W Steed.
   Chandler's Grove—K Chandler, W
G Chandler, Simon Coggin, J W Cot-
ton, Thos Cotton, Pinkney Hall, J S
Pennington, J W Reeves, J Russell, L
F Russell, C Taylor.
   Dry Creek—K C Chisholm, J P Em-
erson, Rod Holton, Wm Roper, A F
Rush, Rod Rush, B F Rush, D C Rush.

MONTGOMERY COUNTY.

Edinborough—D B Allen, Lawrence
Ballard, W B Ingram, E T R Living-
ston, Bost Lisk, M Matheson, Alex
Russell, T S Williams.
   Endicott—J M Beam, Calvin Cagle,
W T Gillis, M Gillis, Eli Green, R C
Green, C L Hicks, G M Lammonds, T
M McAskill, K M McIntyre, R B Munn,
D Parsons, D R Pittman, Aaron
Wright.
   Eldorado—J F Cotton, J G Cotton,
J A Crawford, J H Davis, J D Harris,
B Harris, Wm Henderson, Jacob Lef-
ler, G H Morgan, Nelson Russell, W A
Russell, E Russell, Alex Russell, L M
Russell, J W Stafford, M W Thayer,
N M Thayer, J M Tucker.
   Harrisville—J B Ewing, J M Green,
R E Green, Wm Harris, R E Harris,
M L Harris, J C Harris, S Parsons, T
Poole, Wm Rush, R T Rush.
   Hunsucker's Store—John Allen, Jesse
Freeman, M Leach, A Leach, Alsey
Many, Wm Smith, John Stewart.
   Martin's Mill—John H Allen, B L
Allen, P G Allen, David Allen, A J
Cochran, B F Kerns, A P Leach, E C
Martin, D K McLeod, G W McLeod, J
L McMillan, M McMillan, B F Reyn-
olds, Jacob Vuncannon, L A Wright.
   Milledgeville—A M Loftin, J S Pen-
nington, W G Redwine, W H Taylor,
Harris Taylor.
   Mt Gilead—L P Byrd, D H Cook,
Wm Haywood, T F Haywood, Edmund
Hearne, W S Ingram, J A Ledbetter, J
T Lilly, W T Lisk, M S Martin, W F
McAuley, J A McAnley, G W McAu-
ley, R L McKinnon, Jas Robinson, J R
Scarboro, H M Scarboro, C W Wooley.
   Pontop—J F Cotton, J W Cotton, T
J Cotton, D Tolbert.
   Scarboro—W T Bruton, Rob Mathe-
son, J C Tolbert, E F DeBerry, A R
Moore.
   Pekin—B W Brookshire, G M Cov-
ington, C L Cox, D Green, R Harris, jr,
J T Jenkins, P T Kearns, C W Leether,
D D Mackay, J M McKenzie, J R Mc-
Kenzie, D L Parsons, Martin Rush, M
E Shamburger, J G Skinner, R T Steele
   Ridge's Creek—J M Bean, J C Bru-
ton, Calvin Cagle, Neill Gillis, W T
Gillis, M Gillis, Eli Green, R C Green,
C L Hicks, A N Lammonds, T M Mc-
Askill, A B McAskill, K M McIntyre,
R B Munn, D Parsons, D R Pittman,
Aaron Wright.
   Star—A Leach, Alsey Maness, Spinks
Maness, J A Maness, W W Nall, John
Stewart.
   Sulphur Springs—Duncan Clark, D
I Ewing, W T H Ewing, T P Harris,
E D McCallum, Thomas Parsons, J F
Whitlock, Eli Wooten.

MONTGOMERY COUNTY.	MONTGOMERY COUNTY.

Swift Island—C A Armstrong, G M Bruton, W T Bruton, A M Moore, A R Moore, W H Robinson, Geo Smith.

Troy—G W Allen, Wm Atkins, D B Batten, R Beaman, J Beaman, John A Beaman, A J Beaman, H T Blake, Jno C Bruton, B T Coggin, Saml Fountain, N Gillis, J Hurley, W B Hurley, W B Hurley, E B Jordan, Jas Morris, Cal vin Morris, A R Morris, G F Morris, B

Russell, B F Simmons, S J Smitherman, J C Smith, T Suggs, C C Wade, W F Wooly.

Uwharrie—L Dennis, Rich'd Dennis, Geo Morris, J T Morris, Jas Morton, Thomas Mullinix, John Mullinix, J L J L Sanders.

Wadeville—J R Dunn, W F Green, R McKinnon. J L McKinnon, D D, J M Robinson, W T Wade's estate.

MOORE COUNTY.

AREA, 800 SQUARE MILES.

POPULATION 20,464; White 13,985, Colored 6,479.

MOORE COUNTY was formed in 1784 from Cumberland county, and named in honor of Hon. Alfred Moore, one of the Associate Justices of the Supreme Court of the United States.

CARTHAGE, the county-seat, is situated 65 miles southwest of Raleigh. Population, 1,200.

Surface—Moderately uneven; in the northern part of the county clay foundation, land good; southern part of the county sandy, with heavy pine forests; western portion hilly, consisting of minerals, gold mines, millstones, etc.; water-power in the county very good, with never-failing streams; timber in abundance. Facilities for reaching maskets good, the Cape Fear and Yadkin Valley Railroad and the Raleigh and Augusta Air Line Railroad together crossing the county. These roads connect with the Carolina Central Railway. Branch road from Cameron to Carthage.

Staples—Corn, cotton, wheat, oats, rye, minerals and naval stores.

Fruits—Apples, peaches, pears, cherries, melons, and a variety of small fruits.

Timbers—Pine, oak, hickory, maple, dogwood, persimmon, etc.

Minerals—Gold, copper and very superior millstone and soapstone.

TOWNS AND POST OFFICES.

	POP.		POP.
Aberdeen,	1,000	Flynn,	—
Antler,	—	Forkade,	—
Bensalem,	75	Gale,	—
Big Oak,	125	Gilbert,	—
Blink,	—	Glendon,	—
Broadway,	65	Greenwood,	100
Burlew,	—	Grotto,	—
Caledonia,	43	Horner,	50
Cameron,	450	Ireland,	—
Carbonton,	51	Jackson Springs,	
Carter's Mills,	123		40
Carthage (c h),	1,200	Jessup,	650
		Jonesboro,	—
Chiloe,	—	Keyser,	250
Clark's Mills,	40	Lawhon,	—
Coffer,	—	Lemon Springs,	45
Currensville,	40	Lonely,	—
Eagle Springs,	—	Long Leaf,	—
Emily,	—	Manly,	275
Euprhonia,	25	Mooshaunee,	25
Fair Haven,	80	Mt Carmel,	45

	POP.		POP.
Noise,	45	Sanford,	700
Old Stores,	—	Southern Pines,	
Ollie,	—		750
Parkewood,	50	Spencer,	—
Patterson's Bridge,	20	Swann Station,	75
		Swinton,	—
Pine Bluff,	—	Tempting,	—
Pocket,	20	Tnagardville,	—
Prosperity,	45	Tyra,	44
Quiet,	50	Vass,	—
Rise,	—	Victor,	—
Rockway,	—	Villanon,	—
Robison,	—	West End,	—

COUNTY OFFICERS.

Clerk Superior Court—D A McDonald.
Commissioners—John Shaw, ch'm'n, J A McIver, H A Page, Evander Matheson, J M Wright.
Coroner—D G McLeod.
Register of Deeds—D S Ray.
Sheriff—John L Currie.
Solicitor Seventh District—H F Sewell.
Surveyor—H C Stutts.
Treasurer—Dr K M Ferguson.
Superintendent Public Schools—W N McNeill.
Superintendent Board of Health—Dr G M McLeod.

COURTS.

Seventh Monday before first Monday in March. First Monday in March. Third Monday before first Monday in September. Fourteenth Monday after first Monday in September.

TOWN OFFICERS.

ABERDEEN—*Mayor*, R N Page. *Commissioners*, N A Page, A C Campbell, F A Ordway, T B Creel. *Marshal*, David Knight.

CAMERON—*Mayor*, Dr K M Ferguson. *Commissioners*, W H Britton, W M Kennedy, Hugh McPherson.

CARTHAGE *Mayor*, H A Foote, Jr. *Commissioners*, T B Tyson, S T Fry, C H Graves, W W Mills, J E Waddell. *Marshal*, I N Clark.

JONESBORO—*Mayor*, J R Watson. *Commissioners*, Dr E P Snipes, A J Sloan, J L Godfrey, G W Avent, Jas Dalrymple.

432   BRANSON'S NORTH CAROLINA

MOORE COUNTY.

MANLY—*Mayor*, J E Buchan. *Commissioners*, W C Petty, W O Robinson, W D Morris, T B Sinclair, W M Byrd.
SANFORD—*Mayor*, T L Bass. *Commissioners*, S M Jones. W S Hunter, W B Moffitt, A P McPherson, O M Kelly.
SOUTHERN PINES—*Mayor*, Dr L T Smith. *Commissioners*, W E Poe, O T Johnson, I L Hamlin. *Clerk*, B H B H Burroughs. *Treasurer*, Philander Pond.

TOWNSHIPS AND MAGISTRATES.

Bensalem—J M Denton, J C L Monroe (Swinton), J C Stutts (Old Store), W M McKenzie (Inland), H A Kelly, H B Currie (Caledonia), A P Fry (Mt Carmel), J G Seawell (Bensalem), Josiah Allen (Tyra), J F Reynolds (Eagle Springs).
Cape Fear—M M Watson, W A Campbell, A H Thomas, J Harwood, (Broadway), Geo W Avent (Jonesboro), B W Hunter (Forkade).
Carthage—M M Frye, Neill McKay, A S McIntosh, Jesse Try, J King, H A McCollum (Carthage), J J Richardson (Carriesville), Emmerson Jones (Mt Carmel).
Deep River—M Campbell, J N Edwards, T H Herrington, Ed Paschall (Quiet), R Street, Baxter Street (Fair Haven), J W Cole (Carthage).
Greenwood—Gorrie Jackson, S E Johnson (Cameron), J W Cole, J W R McDonald (Greenwood), T M Cross, A A McPhail, J J Edwards (Lemon Springs), V N Seawell (Villanow).
Jonesboro—N McK Dalrymple, G S Cole, T N Campbell, H S Cox, W I Brooks, Alex Hand, J R Perry, J B Watson (Jonesboro).
McNeill's—W P Smith, A J Keith (Vass), P Pope, T D McLean, A A Roy (Autler), S N Rockwell (Southern Pines).
Mineral Springs—W W Cole (Rubicon), Daniel Blue, W A Clark, I F Peterson, M Brown, Robt McFarland (West End), James L Currie (Jackson Springs), M M Thomas (Clark's Mills).
Pocket—Wm McLeod, C C Underwood (Jessup), A M Wicker (Sanford), Geo Cole (Corbanton), W A Wadsworth (Greenwood), W S Temple, Thos Gross, O B Murchison, T C Campbell (Pocket).
Ritters—A P Davis (Fair Haven), G L Finnison (Prosperity), B L Matthews (Parkwood), Thomas Horner (Horner's), J T Seawell (Mooshaunee).
Sand Hills—C W Shaw (Southern

MOORE COUNTY.

Pines), R N Page, J McN Johnson, J W Fagan (Aberdeen), John Campbell (Ryser).
Sanford—John D McIver, G W Temple, T J Hornaday, James L McNeill, James Kelly (Sanford).
Sheffield—Calvin McNeill (WhyNot), Robt Melton, H T Melton, J W McKenzie (Spencer), J R Marley (Carter's Mills), John W Moore, John Kennedy (Noise).

CHURCHES.

Names, Post Offices and Denominations.

PRESBYTERIAN.

Bensalem—Carthage, K M McIntyre.
Bethesda—Jackson Springs, J W Johnson.
Buffalo—Sanford, M D McNeill.
Buffalo—Carthage, M D McNeill.
Church—Pocket, M D McNeill.
Church—Sanford, M D McNeill.
Church—Carthage, G L Wolf.
Church—Cameron, G L Wolf.
Church (col)—Sanford, W H Montgomery.
Church (col)—Carthage, H D Wood.
Church—Sanford, —— McNeill.
Church (col)—Sanford.
Culdee's Chapel—Carthage.
Euphronia—Jonesboro.
Mineral Springs—Jackson Springs.
Salem—Broadway, K M McLeod,
Sassafras (col)—Carthage, H D Wood.
St Andrew's—Swann's Station, K M McLeod.
Union Church—Carthage.
White Hill—Villanow.

METHODIST.

Bascomb Chapel—
Centre—Carthage, A McCullen.
Church—Carthage, A McCullen.
Church—Sanford, L J Holden.
Church (col)—Jonesboro.
Church—Jonesboro, L J Holden.
Church—Cameron, A McCullen.
Church—Manly, Jesse H Page.
Church—Sanford, L J Holden.
Cool Springs—Quiet, A McCullen.
Fair Promise—Carthage, H G Stamey.
Morris' Chapel—Jonesboro, L J Holden.
Mt Carmel—Carthage, H G Stamey.
Mt Olive (col)—Carthage.
Philadelphia— ——
Pleasant Hill—Carter's Mills.
Poplar Spring-Jonesboro, L J Holden.
Reeves' Chapel (col)—Carthage.
Smyrna-Carthage, H G Stamey.
St Augusta (col)—Carthage, George H Miles.
Tabernacle—Carthage.
Thyatira—Carthage.

MOORE COUNTY.

BAPTIST.

Bethlehem—Carthage, K W Horner.
Church—Carthage, C J F Anderson.
Church—Jonesboro, C J F Anderson.
Church—Manly, —— Newton.
Church—Sanford, —— Anderson.
Church (col)—Sanford.
Cool Spring—Sanford.
Crain's Creek—Cameron.
Deep Creek—Aberdeen.
Dover—Spencer,
Friendship—Mooshauner.
Mechanics—Carter's Mills, K W Horner.

CHRISTIAN.

Acorn Ridge—— ——.
Bear Creek—Moffitt's Mills (Randolph co), W R Brown.
Brown's Chapel—Brower's Mills (Randolph co), J W Lawrence.
Grace Chapel—Jonesboro, G R Underwood.
Moore Union — Haywood (Chatham co), C A Boon.
Mt Zion—Brower's Mills (Randolph co), J W Lawrence.
New Providence—Brower's Mill (Randolph co), J W Lawrence.
Shallow Well—Jonesboro, Geo Underwood.

A. M. E.

Church (col)—Manly, Rev Mr Morris.
Church—Sandford.

A. M. E. ZION.

Church—Sanford.
Church—Jonesboro, —— McKay.

CATHOLIC.

Church—Southern Pines, Father Marion.

CONGREGATIONAL.

Church—Southern Pines, G R Ransom.

EPISCOPAL.

Church—Sanford, —— Bland.
Emanuel — Southern Pines (supplied from Raleigh).

MINISTERS RESIDENT.

Names, Post Offices and Denominations.

METHODIST.

Chaffin, W S, Jonesboro.
Klapp, P S (col), Sanford.
McNeill, D, Swann's Station.
Phillips, Lewis, Fair Haven.
Sanders, Hardy, Big Oak.
Williams, D (col), Carthage.
Williams, W (col), Carter's Mills.
Womack, D (col), Sanford.

PRESBYTERIAN.

Colton, J D, Jonesboro.

28

MOORE COUNTY.

McIntyre, K, Jackson Springs.
McNair, E, D D, Jackson Springs.
McPherson, J P, Jonesboro.
McQueen, James, Swann's Station.
Montgomery, F L (col), Sanford.

CHRISTIAN.

Boon, C A, Haywood (Chatham Co).
Brown, W R, Moffitt's Mills (Randolph co).
Lawrence, J W, Brown's Mills (Randolph co).
Nelson, A G, Caledonia.
Smith, Isham, Brown's Mills (Randolph co).
Underwood, George, Jonesboro.

BAPTIST.

Judd, H D, Jonesboro.
Lawhon, W H H, Carthage.

HOTELS AND BOARDING HOUSES.

Names, Post Offices and Proprietors.

Barnes House, Jonesboro, Mrs R Barnes.
Boarding House, Southern Pines, Irving L Hamlin.
Boarding House, Southern Pines, Fred Dixon.
Boarding House, Southern Pines, R S Marks.
Boarding House, Southern Pines, Philander Pond.
Boarding, Carthage, Mrs Julia Ritter.
Boarding House for school, Sanford.
Boarding, Carthage, Mrs J M L Kelly.
Boarding, Jonesboro, W E Murchison.
Boarding, Carthage, L P Tyson.
Boarding, Carthage, Mrs A D Muse.
Boarding, Jonesboro, George Avent.
Boarding, Jonesboro, Mrs E R Partridge.
Covington House, Covington.
Cole House, Jonesboro, Geo S Cole.
Grove Cottage, Southern Pines, Miss Lizzie Brown.
Hotel Ozone, Southern Pines, R M Couch.
Hotel, Carthage, Mrs C J Shaw.
Hotel, Keyser, Mrs Register.
Hotel, Manly, Mrs S J Kelly.
Hotel, Cameron, M Britton.
Hotel, Carthage, A W Campbell.
Page Hotel, Sanford, J H Harris; Miss Mattie Harris, mgr.
Piney Woods Inn, Southern Pines, J T Patrick, mgr.
Prospect House, Southern Pines, Mrs W R Raymond.
Southern Pines House, Southern Pines, Dr Day, owner; Geo H Crogan, Mgr.
The Central, Southern Pines, D W Lowell.

LAWYERS.

Names and Post Offices.

Adams, W J, Carthage.
Black, J C, Carthage (Black & Adams).
Burns, R L (Dockery & Burns), Carthage and Rockingham.
Douglass, W C, Carthage, (Douglass & Spence).
Dunlap, N M, Curriersville.
Ihrie, H R (Seawell & Ihrie), Carthage.
Kennedy, Mack, Eagle Springs.
McIver, J D, Carthage (Judge Superior Court, 7th District).
McNeill, W H (Robinson, Dunlap & McNeill), Carthage.
McNeill, A L, Sanford.
Murchison, W E, Jonesboro.
Seawell, H F (Seawell & Ihrie), Carthage.
Seawall. A A F, Jonesboro.
Spence, U L, Carthage.

MANUFACTORIES.

Kinds, Post Offices and Proprietors.

Blacksmithing, Sanford, Kelly & Hornaday.
Blacksmithing and wheelwrighting, Swinton, Isham Sanders.
Blacksmithing and wheelwrighting, Pocket, Ira L Nall.
Blacksmithing and wheelwrighting, Swinton, L B Munroe.
Blacksmithing and wheelwrighting, Jonesboro, W A Thomas.
Blacksmithing and wheelwrighting, Jonesboro, J A Stewart.
Blacksmithing and wheelwrighting, Jonesboro, J I Kelly.
Blacksmithing and wheelwrighting, Jonesboro, A E Kelly.
Blacksmithing and wheelwrighting, Burlow, A A Kelly.
Blacksmithing and wheelwrighting, Jonesboro, W H Humber.
Blacksmithing and wheelwrighting, Keyser, J L Caddell.
Blacksmithing and wheelwrighting, Greenwood, A H Cameron.
Blacksmithing and wheelwrighting, Big Oak, E S Brown.
Boots and shoes, Carthage, W W & T Hunsucker.
Brick-making, Sanford, Jno and David Womack (col.).
Brick-making, Sanford, J C Wicker.
Buggies, Jonesboro, W A Thomas.
Building and contracting, Greenwood, R Salmon.
Building and contracting, Greenwood, L C McDonald.
Building and contracting, Greenwood, D C Lemons.
Building and contracting, Pocket, Jos Oldham.

Building and contracting, Sanford, G W Gilmore.
Building and contracting, Pocket, W B Campbell.
Building and contracting, Aberdeen, D J Campbell.
Building and contracting, Jonesboro, Jos Wicker.
Building and contracting, Jonesboro, A J Sloan.
Building and contracting, Jonesboro, Henry Parker.
Building and contracting, Jonesboro, M M Brooks.
Building and contracting, Jonesboro, H Bobbitt.
Building and contracting, Big Oak, M C McDuffie.
Coaches and wagons, Carthage, R A McLaughlin.
Coaches and wagons, Carthage, Tyson & Jones Buggy Co.
Contracting, Carthage, John Ray (col).
Contracting, Carthage, D J McRae (col).
Contracting, Sanford, G W Gilmore.
Coopering, Greenwood, Wadsworth & Bro.
Coopering, Jonesboro, Wm Davis.
Cotton-ginning, Sanford, D N McIver.
Cotton-ginning, Sanford, Levi Gunter.
Cotton-ginning, Sanford, Thos Campbell.
Cotton-ginning, Sanford, D E McIver.
Cotton-ginning, Cameron, J C Ferguson.
Cotton-ginning, Cameron, M Britton.
Cotton ginning, Cameron, A J Keith.
Cotton-ginning, Carter's Mills, C L Allred.
Cotton ginning, Prosperity, W K Jackson.
Cotton-ginning, Sanford, J C & D C Gilmore.
Cotton-ginning, Sanford, A D McIver.
Cotton-ginning, Sanford, J D McIver.
Cotton-ginning, Sanford, Mrs W McIver.
Cotton-ginning, Quiet, McRae & Campbell.
Cotton-ginning, Pocket, Thos Campbell.
Cotton-ginning, Pocket, Dr W Arnold.
Cotton-ginning, Jonesboro, W Underwood.
Cotton–ginning, Jonesboro, W O Thomas.
Cotton-ginning, Jonesboro, M Dalrymple.
Cotton ginning, Jonesboro, Geo H Thomas.
Cotton-ginning, Fair Haven, R Street.
Cotton-ginning, Carthage, D M Sinclair.
Cotton-ginning, Carthage, H Fields.
Cotton-ginning, Manly, J W M Caskill.

MOORE COUNTY.

MOORE COUNTY.

Cotton-ginning, Carthage, J P Seawell.
Cotton-ginning, Carthage, E Kelly.
Cotton-ginning, Carthage, S R McIntosh.
Distillery (turpentine), Eagle Springs, K M McDonald.
Distillery (turpentine), Keyser, John Campbell.
Distillery (turpentine), Union Church, Blue & Co.
Distillery (turpentine), Aberdeen, W A McKeithan.
Distillery (turpentine), Aberdeen, N S Blue.
Distillery (turpentine), Aberdeen, John Blue.
Distillery (turpentine), Carthage, A McMillan.
Distillery (turpentine), Carthage, Currie & Rowan.
Distillery (turpentine), Patterson's Bridge, Mr Gillis.
Distillery (turpentine), Manly, W C Petty.
Distillery (turpentine), Vass, Dr J A Leslie.
Distillery (turpentine), Manly, J E Buchan.
Distillery (turpentine), Manly, Duncan A Blue.
Distillery (turpentine), Cameron, M Britton.
Distillery (turpentine), Cameron, Muse Bros.
Distillery (turpentine), Condor (Montgomery co), John C Currie.
Distillery (turpentine), Eagle Springs, K M McDonald.
Distillery (turpentine), Curriersville, M D McCrumer.
Distillery (turpentine), West End, McDonald Bros.
Dressed Lumber, Sanford, Smith & Lane.
Dressed Lumber, Sanford, Jones Lumber Co; S D Jones, pres.
Foundry and machine shops, Sanford, Moffitt Bros.
Foundry, Jonesboro, Kelly Bros.
Harness. Carthage, James Larkins.
Hats, Jonesboro, John T Kelly.
Mfg Fruit Cates and wood turning, Southern Pines, I F Chandler.
Millwrighting, Jonesboro, A J Sloan.
Millwright'g, Greenwood, Reuben Salmon.
Millwrighting, Jonesboro, B N Hunter.
Millwrighting, Pocket, W B Campbell.
Pottery, Jonesboro, Jonesboro Pottery Company.
Potteries, Carter's Mills, J D Craven.
Saddles and harness, Carthage, Tyson & Jones.
Saddles and harness, Carthage, J N Clark.

Saddles and harness, Cameron, N A McFadyen.
Saddles and harness, Jonesboro, L H Fitchett.
Sash and blind factory, Sanford, Sanford Sash and Blind Co. Capital stock, $6,000; J W Scott, Sr, pres; J B Makepeace, sec and treas.
Sash and blind, Jonesboro, W A Thomas & Co.
Sash and blinds, Sanford, J B Makepeace & Co.
Tanneries, Jonesboro, A H Gross.
Tanneries, Prosperity, Peter Councilman.
Tanneries, Jonesboro, McIntyre & Oliver.
The Niagara Grape Co, Southern Pines, C E Mabon, manager.
The Petty Fruit and Canning Co, near Cameron, H T Petty.
Wine, Carthage, N G S Marley.
Wine, Cameron, H T Petty.

MERCHANTS AND TRADESMEN.

Names, Post Offices, Lines of Business.

ABERDEEN.

Aberdeen Drug Co,	
Blue, D D & L S,	G S
Blue, John & H S,	G S and Turp
Cameron, W D & Co,	G S
Graham & Gillis,	G S
Hill & Benoy,	G S
Leavitt & Leavitt,	G S
Long, N V,	
McKeithan, J A,	G S
McKeithan, N A,	G S
McLauchlin, Keith & Co,	G S
Ordway & Tarbell,	G S
Page, R N,	Lumber
Petty, W C & Bro,	G S and Turp
Pleasant, C E,	G S
Upchurch, J C & Co,	Lumber
Tarbell & Mallonee,	G S
Webster, J T,	Jeweler

BENSALEM.

Seawell, S P,	Agr Imp.

BIG OAK.

Monroe, F & C,	Naval Stores
Williamson, C D,	G S

BROADWAY.

Douglass, R B & Co,	G S
Holmes, J E,	G S
Kelly, C B,	G S and Turp
Thomas, J C,	G S
Watson, M M,	G S

BURLOW.

Buchanan, M B,	G S
Kelly, A A,	G S

CAMERON.

Britton, Moses,	G S and Turp

MOORE COUNTY.

Gilchrist & Johnson, Gro and Lumber
McClenny, J A,   G S
McFadgen, N A,   G S
McKeithan, M McL,   G S
McKeithan, Mrs M McL,   Millinery
Muse Bros,   G S
Phillips, J E,   G S
Rogers, Wm & Co,   G S
Turner, Dr H & Co,   Drugs

CARBONTON.
Jones, J R,   G S
Thomas, Wesley,   G S
Tyson & Wilson,   G S

CARTER'S MILLS.
Carter, W G,   G S
Horner, G W,   G S
Hunsucker, C L,   G S

CARTHAGE.
Anderson, Mrs E W,   G S
Blue, Martin & Bros,   Lumber
Bryan & Wicker, Mrs,   Millinery
Cole, Chas & Co,   Drugs
Cole, Rich A,   Miller
Currie & Rowan,   G S
Fields, R T,   G S
Graves, G C,   G S
Hales, A C & Co,   Lumber
Hannon, Archibald,   G S
Hurnitz & Hurnitz,   G S
McAuley, J R,   G S and Turpentine
McIver, B J,   G S
McNeill, W H,   Notary Public
McNeill, A H,   Notary Public
McMillan, A,   G S and Turpentine
Mills, W W,   Lumber and G S
Muse, H J & A D,   G S
Shaw, Mrs C J,   Hotel
Tyson, L P & Son,   G S
Upchurch, T B & Bro,   G S
Warner, M F,   G S
Williamson, J W,   G S

CURRIERSVILLE.
Dunlap & McIntosh,   G S
Mills, W O,   G S
McCrummin, M D,   G S
Taft, C W,   G S

EAGLE SPRINGS
Allred, C L,   G S
Bensalem Farmers' Alliance Exchange, N Brewer, mgr,   G S
Graham, T A,   G S
Kennedy Bros,   G S and Turpentine
Matheson & Bro,   G S and Turpentine
McDonald Bros,   G S
McNeill Bros,   G S

FAIRHAVEN.
Glen Haven Mills, R G Glenn, pres
Jones, A J,   G S

FORKADE.
Hunter, B W,   G S

GLENDON.
Jones, A J,   G S

MOORE COUNTY.

GREENWOOD.
Craven, C A,   G S

INLAND.
Hall, Thos M,   G S

JONESBORO.
Arnold, D H,   G S
Buchanan, J B,   Gro
Buchanan, S H,   Banker
Burroughs, Miss Mary,   Millinery
Coddell, G B,   G S
Cox, P S,   Livery
Fooshee, L M,   G S
Godfrey, T J,   G S
Gunter, J D,   G S
Kelly, A A (near),   Gro
McIver & Dalrymple,   G S
Mann, L F,   G S
Murchison, W E,   Notary Public
Perry, J R,   G S
Smith, A,   Gro and Furniture
Snipes, E P & Co,   Drugs and G S
Vick, A C,   G S
Watson & Godfrey,   G S
Watson, Gunter & Co,   Lumber

KEYSER.
Blue, D C,   G S and Turpentine
Blue, J & N S,   G S and Turpentine
Blue, L A & J A (near),   G S and Turpentine
Campbell, John,   G S
Currie, J A,   Turpentine
Fagan, J W,   Editor
Hall, T M,   Lumber
Harris, P J,   G S
Holland Bros,   G S and Saw-mill
Jeffrees Bros,   G S
McLeod & Son,   G S and Turpentine
McLeod, A H,   Turpentine
Mase, G H,   G S and Turpentine
Upchurch, T B & Bros,   Lumber

LEMON SPRINGS.
Edwards, J J & Co,   G S
Guess, D S,   G S
Smith, Geo W & Co,   G S

LONELY.
Howard, A S,   G S

LONG LEAF.
Garner, G F,   G S

MANLY.
Blue & Keith,   G S
Blue, J A & Co,   G S
Buchan, J E,   G S & Turp
Butler, Willie,   Jeweler
Cameron, D D F,   G S
Kelly, D P,   Lumber
Petty, W C,   G S and Turp

NOISE.
Horner & Stutts,   G S
Howard, S,   G S
Leonard, W L,   C S

MOORE COUNTY.

PHARSALIA.

| Exchange, Farmers Alliance, | G S |
| Monroe, L B & Son, | G S |

PINE BLUFF.

| Packard, L L, | G S |
| Patrick, J T, | G S |

POCKET.

Worthy & Murchison, G S and Turp

PROSPERITY.

| Garner, A C & Co, | G S |
| Parks, T W, | G S |

QUIET.

Edwards & Knight, G S

RISE.

Baldwin, H T,	Wagon-maker
Cagle, W S & Co,	G S and Turp
Melton, H T,	G S

RUBICON.

Lewis, C L, G S

SANFORD.

Boss, T L,	Agt C F & Y V R R
Bowling, J E,	Jeweler
Bowers, J R & Co,	G S
Brewer, S W,	Butcher
Britt, H H,	G S
Buchanan, W T,	G S
Clark Bros,	G S
Cole, B,	Job Printer
Cox, D Z,	G S
Davis, G A,	Marble Works
Mdens J D,	Tel Op S A L
Gout, M W,	Billing Agt C F & Y V
Hunt, Mrs M H,	Milliner
Jones, R D,	Billing Agt S A L
Jones, S D,	G S, Turp, Livery
Jones, S M,	G S
Kelly, O M,	G S and Livery
McIvers, Theo,	G S
McNeill, A L,	Notary Public
McPherson & Weatherspoon,	G S
Mann & Watson,	Gro
Moore & Cox,	G S
Monroe, W A,	Drugs
Perry, S B,	Livery
Peoples, W F,	Yard Master C F & Y V
Redding, J F,	Livery
Reitzel, J F,	Tel Op C F & Y V R R
Sanford Farmers' Alliance,	G S
Scott, John W, Jr,	Postmaster
Scott, J P,	Agt
Smith & Lane,	Lumber
Stephens, Mrs J M,	Millinery
Strowd Bros,	G S
Thomas, A J,	Drugs
Thomas, A J,	G S
Watson, C P,	G S
Wicker, J,	G S
Williams, J C,	Furn

SOUTHERN PINES.

Blue & McQueen, Livery and Feed
Stable

MOORE COUNTY.

Burroughs, B H,	R R Agt, Ex Agt and Tel Op
Chatfield, F & Co,	G S
Clark, A M & C F,	Livery
Clark, A M,	Livery, Feed and Sale Stables and Real Estate Agt
Cobb, E C & Co,	G S
Couch, R M,	Agt N C Home, Ins Co and Real Estate Agt
Johnson, O P,	Hay, Feed, Vegetables and Fuel
Moffitt, T S,	Builder
Patrick, John T,	Mgr of the New England Mfg, Mining and Est Co
Pond, Philander,	Real Estate and Ins
Raymond, Mrs L A,	Hotel
Ruggles, A S & L P,	Grocers
Ruggles, Hamlin & Co,	Lumber
Saddleson, Dr G H,	Drugs
Schram, Mrs H A,	Hotel
Shaw, Tom,	G S
Southern Pines Supply Co, Dr L T Smith, mgr,	G S
Tarbell, C H,	G S
Thomas, S S,	Gen Repair Shop
Utley, A,	G S
Wilson, John T & Co,	G S
Young, Mrs L W,	Post Mistress

SPENCER.

Baldwin, F M, G S

SWANN'S STATION.

Graham, J A,	G S
Gross, A H,	G S
Sikes, Wm H,	G S
Swann, J Q,	G S

VASS.

Cameron, A & Co, G S and Turp

WEST END.

Bryant & Markham,	Lumber and Turpentine
Hall, Thos,	Lumber
Jones & Clark,	G S and Turp
Jones, S K,	G S
McDonald Bros,	G S
Wade, C C & Son,	Lumber
West End Drug Co,	Drugs

GRAPE AND FRUIT GROWERS.

Names and Post Offices.

Bilyeu, H P, Southern Pines, grapes
 fruit.
Conch & Murray, Southern Pines,
 grapes and fruit.
Huttonhower John, Southern Pines,
 grapes and fruit.
Newton, Ed, Southern Pines, grapes
 and fruit.
Tarbell, C D, Southern Pines, grapes.
Thomas, S W, Southern Pines, grapes
 and fruit.

MOORE COUNTY.

MOORE COUNTY.

Weaver, Dr C W, Southern Pines, grapes and fruit.

Whipple & Co, Southern Pines, grapes and fruit.

MINES.

Kinds, Post Offices and Proprietors.

Aldrich Stone Co, Sanford, J E Malloy, supt.

Bell gold, Carthage, Harrison & Linton (Charlotte).

Brown, gold, Carthage, Smith & Co (Greensboro).

Brown sandstone quarry, Sanford, S Witherspoon.

Brown sandstone quarry, Sanford, J W Scott, jr,

Brown sandstone quarry, Sanford, J M Wicker.

Brown sandstone quarry, Sanford, J G Foushee.

Brown sandstone quarry, Sanford, H A Bland.

Burns, gold, Carthage, J F Burns and others.

Cut stone, Sanford, Phila Red and Brownstone Co; Geo Stewart, Phila, pres; John Radcliff, local mgr.

Cut stone, Sanford, Carolina Brownstone Co; C J Thorpe, local mgr.

Cagle, gold, Carter's Mills, T C Overton (New York).

Chambers, coal (on Deep river), Northern company.

Coal, Sanford, M C Stanback.

Coal, Sanford, John Dye and heirs of W W Dye.

Copper (on Deep river), Amos Wade and heirs.

Cotton, gold, Carthage, Hon J Manning.

Foushee, coal (on Deep river), G W Foushee's heirs, Gulf.

Gold, Sanford, Alexander Wadsworth's heirs.

Gold, Prosperity, W K Jackson.

Gold, Prosperity, D A McDonald and others (Carthage).

Gold, Carter's Mills, Columbian Gold Mining Co (Washington City).

Grampers, gold, Carthage, A H McNeill and others.

Kaolin, Carthage, D A McDonald.

Kaolin, Carthage, A H McNeill.

Millstone quarry, Carthage, N C Millstone Co.

Murchison, coal (on Deep river), Northern Company.

Sandstone grits (in abundance on McLendon's creek, a branch of Deep river).

Sandstone, Carthage, A H McNeill.

Sandstone quarry, Sanford, Southern Red Brownstone Co.

Sandstone quarry, Sanford, Carolina Brown Stone Co.

Sandstone quarry, Sanford, Stuart and others.

Shields, gold, Carter's Mills, H B Shields and others.

Silver, Carthage, Massachusetts Company.

Soapstone, Carthage.

Soapstone, Carthage, New York Company.

Streets, coal, Carthage, A H McNeill.

Tyson, coal (on Deep river), W G Tyson.

Wilcox, coal (on Deep river), Alex McIver, Pittsboro.

MILLS.

Kinds, Post Offices and Proprietors.

Corn and flour, Blink, H H Martin.

Corn and flour, Glendon, N M Dunlap and others.

Corn, saw, gin and planing, Jonesboro, Watson & Gunter.

Corn and flour, Jonesboro, John Godfrey.

Corn and flour, Jonesboro, W A J Thomas.

Corn and flour, Jonesboro, J S Thomas.

Corn and gin, Cameron, McNeill & Muse Bros.

Corn and flour, Carter's Mills, C L Aldred.

Corn and flour, Carter's Mills, E Shuffield.

Corn and flour, Carbonton, O D Palmer & Co.

Corn, Jonesboro, E R Partridge.

Corn, Jonesboro, D Oliver.

Corn, Sanford, Moffitt Bros.

Corn and saw, Jonesboro, John Dalrymple.

Corn and saw, Jonesboro, D Cox.

Corn and saw, Curriersville, McDonald & Allen.

Corn (steam), Cofer, J W McDuffie & Co.

Corn, flour and saw, Noise, Howard & Sheffield.

Corn, flour and saw, Carter's Mills, Isaac E Sheffield.

Corn, flour and saw, Jonesboro, Lawrence, Hunter & Co.

Corn, flour and saw, Prosperity, W K Jackson.

Corn, flour and saw, Jonesboro, A R Thomas.

Corn, flour and saw, Jonesboro, Watson & Gunter.

Corn. flour and saw, Jonesboro, N McKay's heirs.

Corn, flour and saw, and gin, Carthage, J W Cole.

Corn, flour and saw, Rubicon, R A Cole.

MOORE COUNTY.

Corn, flour and saw, Carthage, L Grimm's heirs.
Corn, Carthage, W M Black's heirs.
Cotton-gin, Jonesboro, Dalrymple, Partridge & Co.
Dry and planing mills. Carthage, W W Mills.
Flour, corn and gin, Cameron, M Ferguson.
Flour, corn and saw, Caledona, H Sanders.
Flour, corn and saw, Sanford, McIver & Gilliam.
Flour, corn and saw, Caledonia, L B Monroe.
Flour and corn, Swann's Station, F L Swann.
Planing mill, Southern Pines, Ruggles. Hamlin & Co.
Saw, Jonesboro, W O & H B Thomas.
Saw, Big Oak, J C McDuffie.
Saw, West End, W T Wade & Bro.
Saw, Carthage, T B Upchurch & Bro.
Saw and grist, Jonesboro, W J Brooks.
Shingles, Carthage, R S Shields.
Steam saw, corn and gin, Jonesboro, Willett Bros.
Steam saw, Cameron, James Gilchrist & Son.
Steam saw, Eagle Springs, Tom L Hall.
Steam corn, saw and gin, Victor, D D Kelly.
Steam saw and gin, Jonesboro, Dr Jno McIver.
Steam saw, Harrison's. C L Lewis.
Steam saw, Carthage, Martin Blue & Bro.
Steam saw, Carthage, A C Hales & Co.

PHYSICIANS.

Names and Post Offices.

Arnold, Wm.
Ballentine, J N (Dentist), Jonesboro.
Caviness, J E, Sanford.
Cox, J L, Jonesboro.
Ferguson, K M, Cameron.
Hayes, W A, Carbonton.
Leslie, J A, Vass.
McIver, John, Jonesboro.
McLeod, Gilbert, Carthage.
McNeill, J N, Victor.
Monroe, A J, Jonesboro.
Monroe, W A, Sanford.
Newby, G C, Sanford.
Saddleson, G H, Southern Pines,
Seawell, V N, Vellanow.
Shaw, John, Carthage.
Sheppard, J L, Jonesboro,
Shields, H B, Carthage.
Snipes, N P, Jonesboro.
Swett, Wm P, Southern Pines.
Turner, H, Cameron.
Weaver, C W, Southern Pines.

MOORE COUNTY.

SCHOOLS.

Names, Post Offices and Principals.

Academy (col), Sanford.
Academy, Southern Pines, Mrs Rockwell.
Academy, Vass, Misses Florence and Lillie Leslie.
Academy, Greenwood.
Academy, Carbonton, Allen Jones, jr.
Academy, Jackson Springs.
Academy, Aberdeen, Miss Emma Page.
Carthage Institute, Carthage: W S Snipes, L R McIver, Mrs Mary C Bagwell.
Classical School, Cameron.
Colored School, Sanford.
High School, Sanford.
High School, Broadway, M A McLeod.
High School, Jonesboro, Prof H T Boggs.
High School, Dover.
High School, Pocket, Prof Hughes.
High School, Ingram Branch, S D Cole.
High School, Sanford.
Oak Grove Academy, Bensalem, T M Langley.
Primary School, Southern Pines, Mrs E A Rockwell.
Primary School, Southern Pines, Miss Mary Terry.
The Building and Southern Pines Trades College (col); Rev Joshua Brockett, D D; J S Williams, asst; Mrs Joshua Brockett.
Union Home School for both sexes, Victor, John E Kelly.
Public schools—White, 68; colored, 31.

TEACHERS.

Names and Post Offices.

WHITE.

Allen, Lockie, Tyro.
Arnett, J M, Antler.
Avent, Miss Fannie, Jonesboro.
Barrett, R C, Mt Carmel.
Barrett, W C, Carthage.
Blackman, N R, Greenwood.
Blue, A P, Carthage.
Blue, Miss Kittie, Antler.
Blue, Florence, Antler.
Boggs, H P, Jonesboro.
Bradshaw, Miss Ollie, Aberdeen.
Coddell, A N, Curriersville.
Caligan, J A, Cameron.
Cameron, J B, Cameron.
Campbell, Miss Irene, Pocket.
Campbell, Miss Rosa, Pocket.
Caveness, W B. Villanow.
Caveness, L G, Villanow.
Clegg, I N, Carthage.
Cole, D B, Bensalem.
Cole, James L, Carthage.
Cole, S B, Gilbert.

MOORE COUNTY.

Cole, Miss Ella, Carthage.
Cole, Robt, Carthage.
Cole, S D, Carthage.
Cole, E W, Carthage.
Comer, J R, Spencer.
Crutchfield, Miss Callie, Villanow.
Dalrymple, Miss Jane, Jonesboro.
Davis, R L, Spencer.
Davis, Miss Ursala, Spencer.
Deaton, B, Swinton.
Dowd, Clement, Eagle Springs.
Fry, W F, Carthage.
Furr, C R, Carter's Mills.
Garner, G F, Long Leaf.
Gilliam, Miss Ellen, Tempting.
Harrington, J M, Broadway.
Harrington, Miss F C, Broadway.
Henly, Minnie, Jonesboro.
Horner, W B, Carter's Mills.
Humber, Miss Ada, Carthage.
Kelly, J C, Burlow.
Kennedy, John H, Noise.
King, J H, Villanow.
Jows, J S, Mt Carmel.
Langley, T M, Bensalem.
Leslie, Miss Florence, Vass.
Liles, Rev J D, Cameron.
McDonald, H M, Aberdeen.
McDonald, J M, Villanow.
McIntosh, L C, Carthage.
McIntosh, D M, Curriersville.
McIntosh, Lillie, Carthage.
McKinnon, D C, Bensalem.
McQueen, J R, Carthage.
McQueen, Alice, Swan's Station.
Melton, Stephen, Spencer.
Oliver, J J, Burlow.
Perry, J K, Jonsboro.
Petty, Miss Nora, Carthage.
Pierce, Miss S C, Cameron.
Ray, Miss Bella, Antler.
Ray, Miss E J, Antler.
Roberts, Miss Mollie, Carbonton.
Robertson, Minnie, Jonesboro.
Seawell, L W, Carthage.
Seawell, Miss Annie, Jonesboro.
Sheppard, R M, Broadway.
Steadman, Miss Mattie, Sanford.
Stewart, Miss May, Carthage.
Stutts, W L, Carter's Mills.
Stutts, J F, Horner's.
Stutts, A H, Carter's Mills.
Thomas, W D, Swan's Station.
Williams, Miss Sarah, Parkwood.
Williams, J G, Carter's Mills.
Williamson, E, Carter's Mills.
Womble, Miss Lydia, Fair Haven.
Woody, T N, Prosperity.

COLORED.

Barnes, M H, Carbonton.
Barrett, Vance W, Pharsala.
Barrett, C H, Carthage.
Faust, C W, Gendon.
Jackson, Fannie, Carthage.
Matthews, Ella, Carthage.
McIver, Alice D, Egypt.

MOORE COUNTY.

Minter, Annie P, Jonesboro.
McIver, Fannie, Southern Pines.
McIver, Leita T, Jonesboro.
McKinnon, Florence, Carthage.
McLauchlin, Sarah, Carthage.
McNeill, Bettie, Carthage.
Miles, Lula C, Carthage.
Parsons, Nettie, Cameron.
Persons, Bertha, Carthage.
Ramseur, Rev J A, Jonesboro.
Rieves, L E, Carthage.
Rieves, S J, Tempting.
Stanford, Rev S A, Carter's Mills.
Stone, Martha, Kyser.
Taylor, Rayia, Carthage.
Taylor, Robt L, Carthage.
Taylor, Cora A, Carthage.
Tyson, Marie L, Carthage.
Wallace, Shuford, Carter's Mills.
Westbrook, J W, Aberdeen.
Miles, Rev G H, Carthage.
Wood, Mrs Annie M, Carthage.
Wood, Rev H D, Carthage.

LOCAL CORPORATIONS.

Douglass Manor Farm, C F Surbury, sup, Southern Pines.
J Van Lindley Orchard Co; 350 acres under cultivation (60,000 trees); E B Hodgin, sup, Southern Pines; J Van Lindley, pres; W C Boren, sec and Treas, Pamona, N C.
McCormick Lodge, No 228, A F & A M, Broadway; time of meeting, third Saturday at 2 o'clock P M.
Odd Fellows Lodge, No 110, Carthage; meets every Saturday night at 8 o'clock.
Southern Pines Fruit Growing and Canning Co; Rev J W Johnstone, mgr, Aberdeen.
White Hill Lodge, No 321, A F and A M, Greenwood; time of meeting, third Saturday evening and June 24 and Dec 27.

NEWSPAPERS.

Carthage Blade, Carthage (Democratic weekly), H A Foote, Jr, editor and prop.
Express, Sanford (Democratic weekly), P H & D L St Clair, editors and props.
Progress (Ind weekly), Jonesboro, S N Liles & Son.
Republican (weekly), Carthage, W H Battley, editor and prop.
Sand (monthly), Pine Bluff.
Sanford Express (Democratic weekly), Sanford, P H & D L St Clair, editors and publishers.
The Telegram (Democratic weekly), Aberdeen, J W Fagan, editor.
Yankee Settler, Southern Pines (monthly); published by Southern Pines Publishing Co.

NASH COUNTY.

AREA, 520 SQUARE MILES.

POPULATION, 17,731: White 9,418; Colored 8,313.

NASH COUNTY was formed from Edgecombe in 1777, and named in honor of General Francis Nash, of Orange county, who fell that year at the battle of Germantown, bravely fighting for the liberties of his country.

NASHVILLE, the county-seat, is 45 miles east of Raleigh, on the Nashville branch of the Wilmington and Weldon Railroad, ten miles west of Rocky Mount. It was laid out in 1820, and after many years of slow growth, has recently taken on a new growth, stimulated by the opening of a good tobacco market.

Surface—Moderately uneven; much of the soil good and remunerative when well cultivated.

Staples—Corn, cotton, tobacco, wheat, oats, peas, sweet and Irish potatoes, peanuts and sugar cane.

Fruits — Apples, peaches, pears, grapes, melons and the small fruits

Timbers—Pine, oak, cypress, gum, hickory and dogwood.

Minerals—Gold and building stone.

TOWNS AND POST OFFICES.

	POP.		POP.
Argo,	—	Nashville,	500
Battleboro,	350	Oakland,	—
Castalia,	200	Red Oak,	—
Drywells,	—	Rocky Mt	
Duke's,	—	Mills,	500
Eatman,	—	Sharpsburg,	—
Finch,	100	Stanhope,	—
Glover,	—	Springhope,	550
Goldrock,	50	Union Hope,	—
Heflin,	—	Town of Rocky	
Hilliardston,	—	Mt (partly in	
Hunt's,	—	Nash Co),	2,500

COUNTY OFFICERS.

Clerk Superior Court—Meedy M Williford.

Commissioners—Thomas Westray, T V Avent. Gilliam Lewis, C W Ward, W B Harper.

Sheriff—John P Arrington.

Register of Deeds—John H T Baker.

County Treasurer—E J Braswell.

Coroner—Dr J J Mann.

Surveyor—J C Beal.

Standard Keeper—S H Griffin.

County Examiner—Maj L M Conyers.

Solicitor 3rd District—C M Bernard.

COURTS.

Superior Court meets the eighth Monday after the first Monday in March. and eleventh Monday after the first Monday in September.

TOWNSHIPS AND MAGISTRATES.

Bailey's—Z R Bissett, David Daniel Eatman), R P Driver (Dry Wells)), Joseph D Farmer (Eatman), John R Morris (Heflin). A A Morgan (Glover), J B Smith (Heflin), J P Underwood (Eatman).

Castalia—C F Boddie (Nashville), A O Braswell, T J Braswell (Castalia), Gideon Coggin (Nashville), A Hinton, J D Melton, W H May, D S Rice, J S Terry (Castalia).

Cooper's—J N Bone, R W Bone, J L Bell, James P Cooper, R C Dixon, W C Ferrell (Nashville). G M D Langley (Sharpsburg), G W Strickland (Nashville).

Ferrell's—A Bryant, Kinchen W Ballentine (Dry Wells), Tobias Brentley, D E Cone (Springhope), W M Ethridge (Dry Wells), D H Finch (Glover), G S Murray. Z T Strickland (Stanhope).

Griffin—Thos P Alford, Miles Bobhitt (Ita). R S Critcher, R O Critcher, Geo B Cooper (Hilliardston), A C Griffin, Chas P Harper (Duke's), W T Shearin, J R Saunders (Ita), John W Walker (Nashville).

Jackson—S H Brantley (Finch), J F Brantley (Stanhope), Bennett Brantley, F F Eure, J H Strickland (Finch), I J Williams (Wilson).

Manning's—Mack Brantley, J R Boone, J J N Edwards, J T Fulford, B L Holland (Springhope), J L Hinton (Nashville), V B Mathews (Springhope), J J Marshbourne (Hunt's), G Rice (Spring Hope).

Nashville—C H Baines, N C Cooper, M S Griffin, S H Griffin, J C Harper, J P Jenkins (Nashville), W H Jones (Duke's). J R Stone, D A Taylor, Willie Womble (Nashville).

Rocky Mount—V B Carter, G R Dixon, Daniel Everett, W T Griffin, jr, J A Hilliard, W D Joyner, W G Reynolds, C R Robbins, R J Weaver (Rocky Mount), Geo W Williams, H C Williams (Sharpsburg).

NASH COUNTY.

Stoney Creek—J W Barrett, W L Batts, R L Bullock, G T Coley, J J Coley, E A Hunter, John A Joyner (Rocky Mount), P A May (Red Oak), J H Ruffin, W B Rose (Rocky Mount).

North Whitaker's—R W Arrington, B J Archbell, Lawrence Battle, W R Mann, T E Powell (Gold Rock), D B Sumner (Hilliardston), W C Taylor, J H Wheless (Whitaker's).

South Whitaker's — E T Barkley (Gold Rock), J A Beal (Red Oak), W P Davis (Battleboro), C F Ellers, S R Hilliard (Gold Rock), John Stokes (Red Oak), J A Whitaker (Gold Rock).

CHURCHES.

Names, Post Offices and Denominations.

BAPTIST.

Church—Battleboro, J C Pace.
Church—Castalia, W C Nowell.
Crocker's Chapel — Nashville, J W Sledge.
Elm Grove—Nashville, J E Hocutt.
Ephesus—Springhope, G W Coppedge.
Fishing Creek, Ita, J R Pace.
Hickory—Whitaker's, W C Nowell.
John's Chapel—Glover, J E Hocutt.
Lee's Chapel—Drywell, A A Pippin.
Missionary Baptist—Rocky Mount, W V Savage.
Nashville—Nashville, W C Nowell.
North Rocky Mount—Rocky Mount, J K Howell.
Oak Level—Nashville, W C Nowell.
Philadelphia—Dukes, G W Coppedge.
Peach Tree—Springhope, G M Duke.
Pleasant Grove—Oakland, A A Pippin.
Rehoboth—Red Oak, A A Pippin.
Stony Creek—Rocky Mount, W C Nowell.
Springhope—Springhope, J E Hocutt.
Stanhope—Finch, A A Pippin.
Samaria—Stanhope, J E Hocutt.

PRIMITIVE BAPTIST.

Church—Castalia, Jos Collins.
Falls of Tar River—Rocky Mount, P D Gold.
Mill Branch—Sharpsburg, Cooper Pitt.
Sappony—Nashville, M B Williford.
Sandy Grove—Stanhope, Burt Williams.
Salem—Whitaker's, J D Armstrong.

FREE WILL BAPTIST.

Barnes Hill—Nashville.
Flood's Chapel—Finch.
Rocky Chapel—Castalia, J L Strickland.
Stony Hill—Glover.
White Oak—Wilson, B H Boykin.

METHODIST.

Belfsrd—Castalia, R L Davis.

NASH COUNTY.

Bethlehem—Nashville, R L Davis.
Church (col.)—Castalia.
Dozier's School House—Nashville, J E Underwood.
Gold Valley—Springhope, R F Taylor.
Horne's—Wilson, R F Taylor.
Mt Pleasant—Stanhope, R F Taylor.
Mt Zion—Elm City, R F Taylor.
Nashville—Nashville. R L Davis.
Rockville—Finch, R F Taylor.
Rocky Mount—Rocky Mount, J E Underwood.
Sandy Cross—Nashville, R F Taylor.
Springhope—Springhope, R F Taylor.
Sharon—Nashville, R L Davis.
White Oak—Springhope, R F Taylor.
Whitaker's Mill—Gold Rock, G W Fisher.
York's Chapel—Hilliardston, R L Davis.

METHODIST PROTESTANT.

Harmony—Ita, —— Davis.
Hilliard's Chapel—Red Oak, — Davis.

PRESBYTERIAN.

Church—Rocky Mount, Fred Thomas.
Strickland's—Wilson.

DISCIPLES OF CHRIST.

Pig Basket—Nashville, Isaiah Carver.

EPISCOPAL.

Church—Rocky Mount, Gaston Battle,

MINISTERS RESIDENT.

Names, Post Offices and Denom.

BAPTIST.

Bridgers, J A, Rocky Mount.
Hocutt, J E, Nashville.
Nowell, N C, Nashville.
Pippin, A A, Finch.

FREE-WILL BAPTIST.

Matthews, T H, Nashviile.
Strickland, J L, Finch.

PRIM. BAPTIST.

Armstrong, J D, Rocky Mount.
Williford, M B, Nashville.

METHODIST.

Davis, R L, Nashville.
Eure, F F, Finch.
Taylor, R F, Springhope.
Underwood, J E, Rocky Mount.

PRESBYTERIAN.

Thomas, Fred, Rocky Mount.

DISCIPLES OF CHRIST..

Carver, Isaiah, Nashville.

EPISCOPAL.

Battle, Gaston, Rocky Mount.

HOTELS AND BOARDING HOUSES.

Names, Post Offices and Proprietors.

Hammond House, Rocky Mount, Mrs T A Marriott.
Boarding House, Rocky Mount, —— Gorham.
Farmers' Hotel. Nashville, B H Sorsby.
Collins House, Nashville, J H Collins.
Drake House, Nashville, Mrs M C Drake.
Pernell House, Nashville, Mrs V A Pernell.
Owens House, Springhope, Mrs E M Owens.
Taylor House, Springhope, Mrs R F Taylor.
Boarding House, Argo, Mrs W H Cullifer.

LAWYERS.

Names and Post Offices.

Austin, S F, Nashville.
Battle, Jacob, Rocky Mount.
Battle, Thos H, Rocky Mount.
Baker, J H, jr, Rocky Mount.
Bunn, B H, Rocky Mount.
Binley, W S, Nashville.
Cooley, R A P, Nashville.
Thorp, W L, Rocky Mount.
Thorne, T T, Rocky Mount.

MANUFACTORIES.

Kinds, Post Offices and Proprietors.

Blacksmithing, Castalia, Frank Williams.
Blacksmithing, Castalia, Dennis Avent.
Blacksmithing and wheelwrighting, (Nashville), C E Barnes & Son.
Blacksmithing and wheelwrighting (Nashville), M M Gupton.
Building and contracting (Nashville), Sprague and Davidson.
Building and contracting (Nashville), B W Batchelor.
Buggies and wagons (Rocky Mount), Taylor & Odom.
Blacksmithing and wheelwrighting (Stanhope), E B Finch.
Blacksmithing and wheelwrighting (Stanhope), Dr R W Finch.
Coaches and wagons (Battleboro), A J Hearne.
Cotton, yarns and sheeting (Rocky Mount), Rocky Mount Mills.
Harness and saddles (Nashville), L W Hedgepeth.
Tin and sheet iron (Rocky Mount), G R Dixon.

Machinery and repairing (Springhope), J R Lewis.
Buggies and wagons (Springhope), Edwards & Collins.
Tobacco flues (Nashville), V B Batchelor.

MERCHANTS AND TRADESMEN.

Name, Post Office, and Line of Business.

ARGO.
Campbell & Lyon, G S
BATTLEBORO.
Braswell, T T & Son, G S
Phillips, C W, G S
Rawlings, F M, G S
Stewart, J P & Co, Saloon and G S
CASTALIA.
Bartholomew, S J, G S
DRY WELLS.
Kinchen, W, Ballentine, G S
DUKE'S.
Duke Bros, G S
Harper, Mrs L M, G S
FINCH.
Brantley, C H, Drugs
Harper, S B, G S
Harper, G H, G S
Roberson, W R, G S
GLOVER.
Glover, J P, G S
GOLD ROCK.
Edwards, T E, G S
Lyon, Sandy, G S
Pope, J W, G S
Smith, R L, G S
Whitley, R A, G S
HILLIARDSTON.
Avent, T V, G S
Clark, W T, G S
Clark & Cyrus, G S
Woodley, Wm, G S
HUNTS.
May, W H & Co, G S
NASHVILLE.
Bissett & Arrington, G S
Bone, T A, G S
Bone, R W, G S
Batchelor, V B, G S
Boddie, J B, Saloon and G S
Boddie, Ward & Co, G S
Brooks, R U, G S
Bass, W C, G S
Cooper, F B, G S
Floyd, B F & Co, Saloon
Griffin, W G, G S
Griffin, S S, Gro
Johnson, W H, Gro
Joyner, D S, G S

NASH COUNTY.

Pernell, Mrs V A,   G S
Ricks Bros,   G S
Robbins, F B & Co,   G S
Smith, G W,   Saloon and Gro
Schenn, B & S,   Saloon
Tyson, J W,   Saloon and Gro
Vestner, B H B,   G S
Wood, W R,   Merchandise Broker
Yarboro, M C & Co,   Drugs

OAKLAND.

Overby, A G & Co,   G S

ROCKY MOUNT.

Abram, D,   G S
Arrington, A W,   G S
Bremer, H E & Co,   Gro
Cuthrell, J H,   G S
Dixon, G R,   Stoves and Tinware
Dames, W R,   G S
Davenport, J W,   G S
Eason, W M,   G S
Gupton & Co,   G S
Hammond, C W,   Gro and G S
Hackney, T J,   Buggies and Harness
Hill, M E,   Gro
Middleton, W L,   G S
Proctor, C G,   Saloon
Rocky Mount Mills,   G S
Robbins, J H,   Saloon
Sessoms, James,   G S
Standard Hardware Co,   Hardware
Simms, Dallas,   G S
Timmans & Co,   G S
Turner, Jesse,   G S

STANHOPE.

Beard, A R,   G S
Griffin, W H,   G S
Hopkins, S C,   G S

SPRINGHOPE.

Bunn, Geo W,   G S
Bergeron, J N,   Saloon and Gro
Edwards, J H A,   G S
Finch, Richardson & Co,   G S
Lamm & Co,   Saloon and Hardw
Lamm, S L,   G S
Luper, J D,   Saloon
May, T C,   G S
Manning & Bass,   G S
Morgan, A T,   Saloon
Strickland, J D,   G S
Spivey, J J & Co,   G S
Sanders, C T,   G S
Upchurch & Earl,   G S
Wheless, S M & Co,   G S
Wheless, Yarboro & Co,   Drugs

UNION HOPE.

Murray, C J,   G S

WHITAKER'S (EDGECOMBE CO.).

Bullock, W B,   G S
Davis, Mrs L J,   G S
Downing, H J,   Gro
Greene, Alex,   G S
Taylor & Co,   G S

NASH COUNTY.

MINES.

Kinds, Post Offices and Proprietors.

Argo Gold Mine, Argo, Arrington Gold Mining Co, W D Wood, pres.

MILLS.

Kinds, Post Offices and Proprietors.

Corn and flour, Nashville, G A Winstead.
Corn and flour, Nashville, V B Batchelor.
Corn and flour, Castalia, W H Arrington.
Corn and flour, Wilson, B E Thompson
Corn and flour, Wilson, N R Strickland.
Corn and flour, Nashville, Josiah Baker
Corn and flour, Hilliardston, J J Harper.
Corn and flour, Rocky Mount, R J Weaver.
Corn and flour, Gold Rock, J A Whitaker's ex'r.
Corn and flour, Gold Rock, S R Hilliard.
Corn and flour, Springhope, J T Webb's estate.
Corn and flour, Nashville, Mrs N W Boddie.
Corn and saw, Wilson, A B Williams.
Corn and saw, Eatman, J D Bailey.
Corn and saw, Wilson, Peyton Bissett.
Corn and saw, Finch, Wm Dickerson.
Corn and saw, Stanhope, Edw'd Finch.
Corn and saw, Finch, S H Brantley.
Corn and saw, Springhope, T C May & Son.
Saw, Nashville, W C Bass.
Saw, Nashville, Smith & Griffin.
Saw, Nashville, J B Joyner.
Saw, Nashville, W A Pittman.
Saw, Nashville, R W Bone.
Saw, Whitaker's, C C Vinerett.
Corn and flour, Rocky Mount, Noah Vinerett.
Corn and flour, Springhope, John W Murray.
Saw, Springhope, Strickland, Bryant & Creech.

PHYSICIANS.

Names and Post Offices.

Brantley, C H, Finch.
Brantley, Hassell, Springhope.
Battle, J P, Hilliardston.
Braswell, M R, Rocky Mount.
Edwards, Wm, Springhope.
Hilliard, S P (dentist), Rocky Mount.
Harper, W B (dentist), Castalia.
Marriott, H B, Battleboro.

NASH COUNTY.

Matthews, T A, Castalia.
Mann, J J, Nashville.
Ross, T T (dentist) Nashville.
Sills, D N, Castalia.
Thorp, F J, Rocky Mount.
Strickland, J T, Nashville.
Whitehead, W H, Rocky Mount.
Whitaker, H H, Hilliardston.

SCHOOLS.

Names, Post Offices. and Principals.

Carolina Collegiate Institute, Nashville, S E Eure.
Spring Hope Male and Female Academy, Spring Hope, Griffin & Cornwell.
Stanhope Male and Female Academy, Finch. A A Pippin.
Dortch's Academy, Rocky Mount, J A Bridges.
Mount Pleasant Academy, Glover, Miss Martha Chamblee.
Nashville Colored High School, Nashville, J P Murphrey.
Public Schools—white, 65; colored, 45.

TEACHERS.

Names and Post Offices.

Allen, Miss Esther, Oakland.
Anderson, L T, Stanhope,
Anderson, Zanie (col). Stanhope.
Arrington, Sallie M. Hilliardston.
Arrington, Bettie, Argo.
Arrington, Mrs S N. Hilliardston.
Arrington, Miss Mary, Nashville.
Arrington, C F (col), Ita
Arrington, J G (col), Springhope.
Baines, C H, Nashville.
Baines, G T, Oakland.
Baines, S H. Oakland.
Battle, A W, Nashville.
Battle, Amanda, Wilson.
Battle, C W, Battleboro.
Battle, J D, Nashville.
Barnes, Miss Minnie. Elm City.
Barnes, Miss Bettie, Wilson.
Britt, Miss Claudie E, Rocky Mt.
Boyles, S F, Finch.
Burnett, Miss Rosa. Whitaker's.
Baxter, John E, Rocky Mt.
Bridges, J A, Rocky Mt.
Bridges, Mrs John, Rocky Mt.
Brantley, T B. Springhope.
Bryant, G B, Dukes
Batchelor, Britton, Nashville.
Bolden, Miss Florence, Wakefield.
Blackwell. Mrs Loula B, Rocky Mt.
Collins, Miss Florence, Nashville.

NASH COUNTY.

Coghill, Miss Mamie, Red Oak.
Collins, Miss Anna, Castalia.
Collins, Miss Missouri D, Nashville.
Cooper, Frank, Argo.
Crenshaw, R C, Whitaker's.
Crenshaw, Sudie, Whitaker's.
Chamblee, Miss Martha. Glover.
Chamblee, J P. Union Hope.
Drake, Mrs M R, Castalia.
Drake, B F, Gold Rock.
Deans, Miss Patsie, Finch.
Dickerson, O P, Finch.
Earl, Miss Tassie, Nashville.
Eure. S E. Nashville.
Edwards, Miss Florence, Hunt's.
Edwards. Miss Bettie, Rocky Mount.
Eatman, Miss M N, Glover.
Eatman. Miss R A, Glover.
Ferrell, O C, Nashville.
Ferrell, Miss Pearl S, Springhope.
Green. W T. Dry Wells.
Glover, J E W, Glover.
Green, Miss Anna, Rocky Mount.
Griffin, M A, Springhope.
Griffin, W T, Nashville.
Grant, Walter. Whitaker's.
Harper, G T, Castalia.
Horne, Miss Theodosia, Rocky Mount.
Hunt, Miss Annie V, Stanhope.
Hocutr, J E, Nashville.
Jenkins, Miss Rosa, Nashville.
Kemp, Miss Ina S. Wakefield.
Key, Miss Annie M, Enfield.
King, W S, Springhope.
Lucas, C L. Finch.
Lewis, W C. Springhope.
Lewis. Miss Anna H, Rocky Mount.
Lucas, Miss Mary E, Rocky Mount.
Lucas, Mariah, Rocky Mount.
Murphrey, J P, Nashville.
Murphrey. Miss Rachel E, Nashville.
Peace, W G, Springhope.
Pitts, Miss Lillie, Springhope.
Pearce, C C, Finch.
Pearce, Miss Mattie, Rocky Mount.
Parker, Miss Cornelia, Rocky Mount.
Rice, A N, Springhope.
Snakenburg. Miss Alice, Wilson.
Stone. J P, Hunt's.
Strickland, H S, Union Hope.
Taylor, Miss Anna M. Wilson.
Thorp, Mrs S E, Rocky Mount.
Valentine, J A, Springhope.
Watson, J W, Whitaker's.
Whitley, Miss M P, Stanhope.
Wilkins, Miss Martha, E, Springhope.
Winstead, J T, Elm City.
Whitehead, Miss Bettie, Battleboro.
Warren, N C, Springhope.
Win-tead, Miss Etta, Nashville.
Whitaker, Miss Louisa, Gold Rock.
Whitaker, Miss Rebecca, Gold Rock.
Whitaker, Miss Alliene. Gold Rock.
Woods, Miss M C. Red Oak.
Watkins, G W, Dry Wells.

NASH COUNTY.

TOBACCO WAREHOUSES.

Cooper's, Rocky Mount, C C Cooper.
Graveley, Rocky Mount, Graveley &
Petty.
Davis, Rocky Mount, Buckner Davis.
Jeffreys', Rocky Mount, T B Jeffreys.
Banner, Nashville, Lawson, Griffin &
Co.
Farmers', Nashville, Ward, Jones & Co.

LOCAL CORPORATIONS.

Carolina Collegiate Institute, Nashville,
S E Eure, prin.
Central Cross Lodge, No 187, A F and
A M, Springhope.
Corinthian Lodge, No 230, A F and A
M, Rocky Mount.
Morning Star Lodge, No 85, A F and A
M, Nashville.
Rockville Lodge, No 411, A F and A
M, Finch.
Rocky Mount Agricultural and Me-
chanical Association, Rocky Mount.
Argo Gold Mining Company, Argo,

NEWSPAPERS.

Dixie Optic, Nashville (Dem weekly),
O C & W A Ferrell, eds and props.
The Argonaut, Rocky Mount (Dem
weekly), Campbell & Logan, props;
W A Campbell, ed.
The Phœnix, Rocky Mount (Dem
weekly), John B Lewis, ed and prop.

FARMERS.

Names and Post Offices.

Argo—A C Griffin, W H Wood, A
W Cooper, M E Felt, Wm Gay, W B
Howerton, E H Jenkins, W H Callifer.
Battleboro—T P Braswell, E J Bras-
well, W P Davis, A L Harper, J B
Phillips, Carter Pope, G W Ward, F
M Rawlings.
Castalia—W H Arrington, B L Ar-
rington, Merritt Batchelor, T J Bras-
well, J M Braswell, James Harper,
Samuel Harper, J A Matthews, J D
Melton, S W Kittrell, W H Drake, W
T Taylor, John T Taylor, T A Sills, Dr
D N Sills, J F Terry, Jos Privett, D S
Rice, Wm Rich, W H May, W H
Mitchell, J W Wheless, S J Bartholo-
mew, Jas I Pleasants.
Duke's—W B Bunting, T G Bunting,
C E Hedgepeth, C P Harper, G L Win-
stead, W W Strickland, W P Parrish,
J T D Avent, Thos H Drake, W P Tay-
lor, Mrs L M Harper, J B Cooper, Jno
T Duke.
Dry Wells—K W Ballentine, A Bry-

NASH COUNTY.

ant, J R Morris, Carson Strickland,
Calvin Strickland, R P Driver, J H
Johnson.
Eatman's—Taylor Eatman, J P Un-
derwood, J D Bailey, P J Bissett, Z R
Bissett, Geo W Finch, Exum O'Neal,
W I Renfrow, J D Farmer, G W
Perry.
Finch—G W Baines, J M Baines,
Thomas Westray, Ed Dilliard, G D
Ricks, C D Bunn, J H Strickland, Wm
Dickerson, W H Brantley, S H Brant-
ley, Haywood Perry, Manly High, H
O Strickland, J L Finch, G H Harper,
S B Harper, Josiah Bissett.
Glover—V A J Glover, W H Glover,
G W Morgan, D H Finch, Miles Bis-
sett, J P Glover, M Bissett, W D
Brown.
Gold Rock—A H Ricks, J H Exum,
T E Powell, G W Powell, W T Bryan,
B J Archbell, W R Mann, J A Whita-
ker, Malchus Whitaker, P E Edwards,
Jefferson Cobb, John W Ellen, W L
High, J H Green, A O Wadford, W H
Sexton, B F Drake, R M Moore.
Hilliardston—T V Avent, B P Cooper,
W G Jones, R W Arrington, D E Sum-
ner, D B Sumner, B B Ricks, R P Fox,
Mrs Bettie York, W M York, J W
York, G B Cooper, W G Hedgepeth,
Thos Dean, B Freeman, Alex Tisdale,
J T Tisdale, R O Critcher, R L Critcher.
Hunt's—G R Marshburne, G A Gard-
ner, S C Edwards, J J H Edwards, J
D Bunn, Geraldus Rice, A Thomas,
Geo Coppedge, A H Wester, R V Col-
lins.
Nashville—V B Batchelor, S A Bat-
chelor, Everson Cobb, C W Ward, J
B H Boddie, C F Boddie, L W Boddie,
Geo Ricks, S B Ricks, J W Harper, W
R Felts, Mrs N W Boddie, C J Odom,
R H Buchanan, J P Jenkins, J W
Henry, N C Cooper, W H Robbins, M
Rose, W T Sellars, J W Braswell, W L
Sykes, J R Harper, H N Snell, W L
Dozier, F M Dozier, J R Dozier, J W
Stone, M J Hedrick, T A Bane, J N
Bane, J W Vanhook, T R Batchelor,
Jas W Batchelor, R C Dixon, R W
Bane, Geo W Strickland, G J Joyner,
H E Joyner, M S Joyner, J B Joyner,
C C Smith, S H Griffin, J A Clark, J
H Gordon, Dr T T Ross, L M Conyers,
J J Cockrell, H C Mason, W C Bass, B
H Sorsby, J H Smith, J W Pettit, J L
Hinton.
Oakland—A S Baines, J H Win-
stead, G A Winstead, W T Batchelor,
Cooley Boddie, Jas Weaver, J H Hol-
lingsworth, Nick Collins, B L Holland,
A A Turner, D M Turner.
Red Oak—J T Jones, J R Jones, J C
Beal, J K Beal, J D Griffin, M S Grif-

NASH COUNTY.

fin, J A Edwards, M W Drake, G W Gay, P A May, Ira May, W H Johnson, R B Melton, J I Everett, R C Edwards, H C Rose, W D Barnes, H B Jenkins, J S Beal, R H Whitfield.

Rocky Mount—R H Ricks, R H Bunn, D W Thorp, J H Griffin, W D Joyner, W T Griffin, Jr, J L Boone, J H Hunter, John Dilliard, D B Ricks, J R Barnes, Robert Barnes, J W Barrett, W L Batts, J J Coley, David Everett, G W Guy, E J Joyner, W D Joyner, G W Price, W B Harper, C C Ricks, J H Thorp, Mrs E B Lewis, Mrs Pattie Winstead, W C Weaver, W S Treventham, G W Culpepper, Joel B Whitley, H A Whitley, J L Woodruff, W J Newby, J N Griffin, Jr, C F Ellen, W A Hunt.

Sharpsburg—J J Sharp, J D Robbins, T J Robbins, Buddy Davis, G W Williams, W H Pridgen.

Springhope — S J Batchelor, M C Brantley, W H Culpepper, A J Deans, J W Floyd, D M Johnson, W D Lamon, Simon Jones, S S Hendrick, Jacob Lamon, W P Lamon, S L Lamon, W W

Manning, W E Manning, E M Manning, J H Pitts, B G Sanders, J D Strickland, Henry Wilkins, E H Wilkins, Exum Wester, B T Strickland, Britton Wood, W W Batchelor, D L Gilliam, Dr Wm Edwards, W F May, Alford Edwards, H M Warren, W M Warren, Seymour Warren, W R Batton, P V Renfrow, C B Brantley, Z T Strickland.

Stanhope—William Baines, Hardy Brantley, W S Brantley, W H Griffin, E B Finch, D R W Finch, W J R Finch, Monroe Griffin, Samuel Murray, W H Murray, Henry J Murray, C M J Strickland, Henry Whitley, Ruffin Whitley, Wm Cove, L R Whitley, Iredell B Vick, J W Turner.

Union Hope—E C Vick, C J Murray, Orren Brantley, D S Cove.

Whitaker's—Lawrence Battle, J C Bellamy, J H Burnett, J H Wheless, J H Exum, Jr, Theo Hunter, W B Hunter, J H Overstreet, W C Taylor, K C Taylor, A L Taylor, John Baker, Alex Greene.

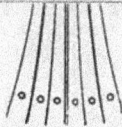

NEW HANOVER COUNTY.

AREA, 80 SQUARE MILES.

POPULATION, 25,586; White 11,649, Colored 13,937.

NEW HANOVER COUNTY was formed in 1728, and named in honor of the House of Hanover, then on the English throne.

WILMINGTON, the county-seat, was named in honor of the Earl of Wilmington, the nobleman to whose patronage Governor Johnson (in 1739) was indebted for his office. It was originally called Newton, and is situated at the head of ocean navigation, on the Cape Fear river, 148 miles south of Raleigh. Population, 24,968.

Surface—New Hanover county is situated between Cape Fear river and Onslow Bay, and lies in the shape of a cone with the apex extending south to New Inlet. The county of Pender took the greater portion of the former territory of New Hanover. The land is level and much of it swampy—quite rich, and very productive when well drained. The advantages of navigation are very fine.

Staples—Cotton, corn, rice, ground-peas, vegetables, naval stores and fish.

The climate and soil of New Hanover make it very valuable for trucking, vegetables being at least twenty-five days earlier than at Norfolk and points further north.

This is the banner county of the State in the production of ground-peas, a very profitable crop to the planter.

Fruits—Peaches, grapes, berries and other small fruits.

Timbers—Pine, cypress, gum and live-oak.

TOWNS AND POST OFFICES.

	POP.		POP.
Castle Hayne,	50	Wilmington,	
Wrightsville,	250		24,968

COUNTY OFFICERS.

Clerk Superior Court—Jno D Taylor.
Commissioners—Horace A Bagg, chairman; D G Worth, E L Pierce, J C Stevenson, B S Montford.
Coroner—D J Jacobs (col).
Register of Deeds—John Haar.
Sheriff—Elijah Hewlett. *Deputies*, Wm H Shaw, W W King, J A Sutton, R H Holmes.
Solicitor Fourth District-M C Richardson, Clinton.

Solicitor Criminal Court—M C Richardson.
Criminal Court Judge—O P Mears.
Surveyor— ———
County Examiner—M C S Noble.
Standard Keeper—J W Perdew.
Treasurer—S Van Amringe.
County Physicians—R D Jewett and J C Shepard.
Clerk Committee of Andit and Finance—Jas G Burr (col).
Chief Deputy Sheriff--Geo Z French.
Jailer—W W King.
Superintendent of Poor House—S Hill Terry.

COURTS.

Superior Court meet sixth Monday before first Monday in March; sixth Monday after first Monday in March; third Monday after first Monday in September, and fifth Monday after first Monday in September.

Criminal Court meets first Monday in January; third Monday in March; third Monday in May; third Monday in June; third Monday in July; third Monday in September, and third Monday in November.

UNITED STATES DISTRICT COURT.

Aug S Seymour, District Court Judge; residence, Newbern, N C.
C B Aycock, District Attorney; residence, Goldsboro.
Sol C Weill, assistant; residence Wilmington.
W H Shaw, Clerk; residence, Wilmington.
R Bunting, Deputy Marshal.
Court meets first Monday after fourth Monday in April and October.

CONSTABLES.

Federal Point Township—L C Williams.
Harnett Township—J A Hewlett.
Wilmington Township—J W Millis.

CITY OFFICERS.

WILMINGTON—*Mayor*, S H Fishblate.
Board of Aldermen, W E Springer, J O Nixon (col), W C Van Ghlan, W N Harris, John Maunder, W H Northrop,

NEW HANOVER COUNTY.

NEW HANOVER COUNTY.

jr, R W Hicks, Dan'l Cameron, Thos J Gore, A J Walker (col). *City Physician*, Andrew H Harris. *Chief of Police*, J R Milton. *Clerk, Treasurer and Tax-collector*, F B Rice; John E Taylor, assistant. *City Attorney*, D B Sutton. *Chief of Fire Department*, Martin Newman; Chas Schnilben, assistant. *Captain of Police*, R M Capps. *Board of Audit*, Wm Calder, chairman; Chas Ganzer, Jas Hanby. Henry C McQueen, C W Yates, John Cowan, clerk. *Clerk of Front Street Market*, John W Galloway. *City Standard Keeper*, J W Perdew. *Surveyor* — J D McRee. *Weigher of Beef Cattle. and Clerk of Fourth Street Market*, W J Styron.

In the Police Department there is one chief, one captain, four sergeants, thirty policemen, two janitors and one messenger.

UNITED STATES OFFICERS.

Weather Bureau Office United States — Third floor U S Court House and Post Office building, observer in charge. F L Graham; assistants, J F Newsom and S G Stevens.

U S Eng'r office, Wilmington. River and Harbor Improvements; Maj W S Stanton, corps of eng'rs, U S A, in charge; Lieut E W Van, C Lucas, corps of eng'rs, U S A, assistant; J C Loder, chief clerk; Henry J Clark, stenographer.

Internal Revenue, U S, in U S Court House and post office building; D H Wallace, deputy collector; Thos A Brown, U S Internal Revenue Gauger.

Wm H Shaw, Clerk of U S District Court and Deputy Clerk of U S Circuit Court, second floor U S Court House and Post Office building.

ASYLUMS AND HOSPITALS.

City and County Hospital, between North Tenth and Eleventh, Walnut and Red Cross sts, Dr W W Lane, surgeon in charge.

United States Marine Hospital, Eighth, cor Church st, Dr S D Brooks, surgeon in charge; office in Custom House.

FOREIGN CONSULS, WILMINGTON.

W M Cummings, Haytien, Princess st.
William L DeRossett, Vice-Consul of Portugal, N Water st.

George Harris, Vice-Consul of Argentine Republic, N Water st.
R E Herde, Vice-Consul for Denmark, Sweden and Norway, 9 S Water st.
F J Lord, Spanish Vice-Consul, N Front st.
O G Parsley, Brazilian Vice Consul, N Front st.
Edward Perchaw, German Vice-Consul, 204 N Water st.
James Sprunt, British Vice-Consul, 231 Nutt st.

CEMETERIES.

Bellevue, Seventeenth st, cor Chesnut, E W Manning, pres; N M McEachem, sec and treas.
Oakdale, between Thirteenth and Seventeenth and Savage and Miller sts, R J Jones, sec and treas.
Pine Forest (col), between Sixteenth and Seventeenth and Rankin sts.
Roman Catholic, Market st, one half mile from city limits.
United States Military, Market st, outside city limits, —— Lacy, supt.

TOWNSHIPS AND MAGISTRATES.

Cape Fear — James Cowan, Luke Grady, W M Hansley, Lewis Hollingsworth, Jos T Kerr, Levi Nixon, Jno P Quetch.

Federal Point — J A Biddle, J W Canady, J H Davis. A L Freeman, G E Green, Stephen Keyes, H A Kine.

Harnett — W B Canady, Walker Garrett, B B Humphrey, L R Mason. J N Melton, Jordan Nixon. Auringe Van.

Masonboro — Benj Farrar, D J Fergus, Jere J Hewlett, Jas J Hewlett, E A Orrell, D W Trask.

Wilmington — Sam'l Bear, jr, L S Belden, B Bellews, Jno H Brown, R H Bunting. J L Cantwell, W H Chadbourn, W C Craft, M H Curran, J B Dudley, S H Fishblate, F W Foster, G Z French, J W Galloway, W H Gerken, Lewis Geyer, W H Gilbert, B F Hall, Geo Harris, W N Harris, John Holloway, Dan Howard, Valentine Howe, Jno H Howe. C M D Humphrey, J G Love, J F Maunder, Caleb M Martin, Washington McNeill, H C McQueen, J M McGowan, M C S Noble, F W Ortman, W M Poisson, Geo W Price, N B Rankin, F B Rice, F P Risley, Charles Schinbben. W H Shaw, W H Strauss, Walker Taylor, M E Taylor, Thos Thayer, Wm Ulrich, T E Wallace, A J Walker, Jno H Webber, Louis Weill, Isaiah West, F W Westerman, Silas P Wright.

450   BRANSON'S NORTH CAROLINA

CHURCHES.

Names, Post Offices, Pastors and Denom.

METHODIST.

Bladen St—Cor Bladen and Fifth,Wilmington, J F Butt.
Bethany—(8 miles southeast), Wilmington, M T Plyer.
Fifth Street—Fifth between Nun and Church sts, W L Cuninggim.
Grace—N cor Fourth and Mulberry sts.
Herring's Chapel—Long Creek, A R Raven.
Market St—cor Market and Ninth sts, M T Plyer.
Mt Zion—(col), Fifth st, between Swann and Nixon.
Oak Hill—Wilmington, A R Raven
Rocky Point—Rocky Point,A R Raven.
Trinity—cor Seventh and Brunswick.
Union—Scotts Hill (Pender Co), A R Raven.
Wesleyan Chapel—Scott's Hill (Pender Co), A R Raven.

ZION METHODIST.

St Matthew's Mission — 12th between Dock and Orange, L B Blackledge.

BAPTIST.

Brooklyn—cor Fourth and Brunswick, R E Peele.
Central—(col), cor Seventh and Red Cross sts, L T Christmas.
Ebenezer — (col), Seventh, between Ann and Orange sts.
First Baptist—(col), Fifth, cor Campbell st, Joseph Spells.
First Baptist—cor Fifth and Market sts, W B Oliver.
Mt Calvary—cor Ninth and Bladen sts, C B Waters.
Second Adventist — Sixth, between Church and Castle sts, Jos P King.
Shiloh—(col), cor Walnut and McRae st, P F Maloy.
South Side—cor Fifth and Wooster sts, J B Harrell.

PRIMITIVE BAPTIST.

Baptist Chapel—Castle, between Fifth and Sixth sts.

PRESBYTERIAN.

Chestnut St (col)—Chestnut, between Smith & Eighth sts, W A Alexander.
First Church—Third, cor Orange st, Peyton H Hoge, D D.
Immanuel Chapel—South Suburb, J M Rawlings, D D.
Immanuel—Front, between Queen and Wooster.
St Andrew's—cor Campbell and Fourth, A D McClure.

EPISCOPAL.

Chapel of the Good Shepherd—Sixth and Queen, Robert Strange.
St James—Third, cor Market st, Robert Strange.
St John's—cor Red Cross and Third sts, Jas Carmichael, D D.
St Mark's (col)—cor Sixth and Mulberry sts.
St Paul's—cor Fourth and Orange sts, F W Skinner.

LUTHERAN.

St Matthew's—Fourth, above Bladen, G D Bernheim, D D.
St Paul's—cor Market and Sixth, K Boldt.

FREE.

Seamen's Bethel—Front and Dock sts, Jas Carmichael, D D, and A D McClure, chaplains.

ROMAN CATHOLIC.

St Thomas—Dock, between Second and Third sts, P Moore.

JEWISH SYNAGOGUE.

Temple of Israel—cor Market and S Fourth sts, S Mendelssohn.

CONGREGATIONAL.

Christ Church (col)—Ann, bet Sixth and Seventh sts.

AFR. METH. EPISCOPAL.

Mt Olive—Second st, Ed Robertson.
St Stephen's—Red Cross st, cor Fifth, E J Gregg.
Mt Zion—Fifth, bet Swan and Nixon sts, L B Sims.

MINISTERS RESIDENT.

Names, Post Offices and Denom.

METHODIST.

Bailey. J B, Mulberry st.
Butt, J F, Fifth and Bladen st.
Capart —— (col), 1112 N 5th st.
Craigg, J W, 6th bet Orange and Ann.
Cunninggim, W L, 415 S 5th.
Plyler, M T, 316 North W.
Ricaud, T Page, Mulberry.
Roan, W S, Mulberry bet 4th and 5th.
Telfair, Jas W (col), 615 Walnut st.

ZION METHODIST.

Hooper, J, 708 Church st.
Small, J B, cor Seventh and Church sts.

BAPTIST.

Alexander, W A (col), Chestnut st.
Christmas, L T (col), 710 Red Cross st.
Conway, A M (col), 508 Campbell st.
Harrell, J B, South st, bet Queen and Wooster.
Jackson, —— (col), 601 Mulberry st.
King, Jos P, 619 Queen st.
Malloy, P F (col), 713 Red Cross st.
Moore, D J (col), 505 South 7th st.

NEW HANOVER COUNTY.

Oliver, W B, 3d st south.
Spells, Jos, 508 Campbell st.

PRESBYTERIAN.

Bonner, J A (col), 714 Chestnut st.
Hoge, Peyton H, 3d bet Nunn and Church sts.
McClure, A D, cor Campbell and 4th.
Morrelle, Daniel, 420 Orange st.
Rawlings, J M, D D.
Sanders, D J (col), 711 Princess st.

LUTHERAN.

Bernheim, G D, D D, Mulberry, near Sixth street.
Boldt, K, 12 N Sixth.

EPISCOPAL.

Morrell, Daniel, cor Orange and Fifth.
Skinner, F N, Fourth street, near Church.
Watson, A A, D D, Bishop of Diocese of East Carolina, 511 Orange st.
Wootten, Edward, 812 Orange st.

HEBREW.

Mendelsohn S, 411 Chestnut st.

CONGREGATIONAL.

Sims, F W (col), 600 Ann st.

AF. METH. EPISCOPAL.

Edwards, D J (col), Taylor st.
Gregg, E J, 516 N Sixth.
Parker, J J, 817 S Front st.
Robinson, Edward (col), 908 South Second st.
Sims L B (col), 508 N Seventh st.

A. M. E. ZION.

Moore, Alexander (col), 405 South Sixth st.

METH. EPISCOPAL.

West, S P (col), 615 Brunswick st.

HOTELS AND BOARDING HOUSES.

Kinds, Post Offices and Proprietors.

Atlantic Cafe, cor Front and Red Cross sts, Geichen Bros.
Boarding, 108½ Market st, Ed Sutton.
Boarding, Second st, bet Martin and Princess sts, Miss Julia Hill.
Boarding, 123 N Market st, Mrs S D Hankins.
Boarding, 516 N Front st, J A King.
Boarding, 504 N Front st, Mrs E B King.
Bonitz House, 129 Market st, J H Bonitz.
Boarding, cor Fourth and Red Cross sts, Mrs Davis.
Boarding, cor Fifth and Princess, Miss Morrison.
Boarding, cor Front and Mulberry, Mrs Sam Collier.
Boarding, N Front st, Mrs John E Pigford.

NEW HANOVER COUNTY.

Boarding, Church st (between Front and Second), Mrs Thos Smith.
Boarding House, 114 Dock st (between Front and Second), R M Wescott.
Boarding House, Second st (between Market and Princess), Mrs Bell.
Fulton House, 22 North Front st, Neill McIntosh.
Hotel, Brunswick, Southport, C T Bennett.
Purcell House, 18 and 20 N Front st, M E Springer & Co, owners.
Rock Spring Hotel, 12 Chestnut st, Mrs Bagwell.
The Orton, Front st (between Chestnut and Princess) J E Montague, mgr.
Victor House, N Front st, Mrs W J Bergen.
Ocean View Hotel (Wrightsville), E W Manning.
Stokeley's House (Wrightsville Sound), W H Stokeley.

LAWYERS.

Names and Post Offices.

WILMINGTON.

Bellamy, Marsden & Son, 210 Princess st.
Bellamy, J D Jr, room 5 Smith building.
Blue, L A, Water st.
Bryan, E K, 118 Princess st.
Cutlar, DuBrutz, sr, 114 Princess st.
Cutlar, DuBrutz, Jr, 114 Princess st.
Davis, Junius, 116 Princess st.
Davis, George, 116 Princess st.
Empie, S M, Princess st (between Front and Second sts).
Howell, Geo H, city court-house.
Latimer, W & E S (Ins. building), Princess st.
Lockey, C P, 8 N Second st.
Marshall, A J, 212 Princess st.
Martin, E S (Allen building), Princess st.
McClammy, Herbert, 103 Princess st.
McKay, R H, Court House.
McKay, W B, 209½ Market st.
Meares, O P (Judge Criminal Court), 218 Market st.
Meares, Iredell, Princess st.
Peschaw, G L, 114 Princess st.
Ruger, A W, Wilmington.
Ricaud (A G) & Weill (Sol), corner Front and Chestnut sts.
Rountree, Geo, Allen building.
Russell, D L (ex-Judge Sup Court) 118 Princess st.
Stokes, J G, Allen building.
Strange, T W, Princess and Front sts.
Sutton, D B, 118 Princess st.
Waddell, Alfred M, Court House.

MANUFACTORIES.

Kinds, Post Offices and Proprietors.

Barrels,Chestnut st, bet 10 and 11, R M Ninmocks.

Blacksmithing and wheelwrighting, Princess st, opp City Hall, James A Lowrey.

Blacksmithing and wheelwrighting, 106 N Second st, D Quinlivan.

Blacksmithing and wheelwrighting. S W Cor Third and Princess streets, Thomas Quinlivan.

Book-binding, 21 N Front st, Jackson & Bell.

Book-binding, 11 Princess street, W H Bernard.

Boots and shoes, 208 N Water street, B Thompson.

Boots and shoes, 903 N Fourth st, J L Williams.

Boots and shoes, Second bet Princess and Market sts, J Y Taylor.

Boots and shoes, 418 N Water street,A Stewart.

Boots and shoes, 613 N Fourth st, T J Sterling.

Boots and shoes, 105 Queen street, M C Parker.

Boots and shoes, 705 N Fourth st, S W Oden.

Boots and shoes, N Cor Front and Mulberry sts, Charles Johnson.

Boots and shoes, Mulberry, bet Front and Water sts, J E Farrow.

Boots and shoes, 301 N Front st, Amos Boston (col.).

Boots and shoes, bet N Front and Second st, J Baker.

Boots and shoes, 12 N Second st, John Bauman (col.).

Bottling works, 20 N Second st.

Bottling works, 614 N Fourth st, W Genaust.

Brick, near the city, W H Alderman.

Brickyard, near the city, Roger Moore.

Brick, 13th, bet Orange and Ann sts, Preston Cummings.

Brick, 13th, bet Orange and Ann sts, Daniel Lee.

Building and contracting, 517 S Third st, J W Howe (col.).

Cabinet, Market, bet Second and Third sts, C D Murrill.

Cabinet, Third, bet Princess and Chestnut streets, J W Woolvin.

Candy, Cor Front and Market sts, Mrs E Warren & Son.

Carriages and wagons, 101 and 102 Princess and Second sts, C B Southerland & Co.

Carolina Oil Co, Church and River sts, L Hanson.

Champion Cotton Compress, 423 Nutt

st, foot of Red Cross st, Compress and Warehouse Co.

Cigars, N Front st, L Simon & Co.

City Electric Laundry, Market and 2d sts, L B Pennington prop.

Clothing, 33 Front st, A David.

Clothing, 2 Water st, Sol Bear.

Coopering, Nutt st, cor Brunswick st, Morton Hall.

Coffins, 105 N Third st, J W Woolvin.

Cotton mill, foot of Dawson st, W A French, pres; James H Chadbourn, vice-pres; Ed Tennant. sec and treas; Richard Edwards, supt; capital stock, $80,000; number of spindles, 6,000; daily consumption, 30 bales of cotton; daily production, 6,000 yards prints; number of hands, 150.

Cotton Compress, 901 Nutt, foot of Harnett st, Wilming Cotton Compress and Warehouse Co.

Distillery (turpentine), 719 Nutt st, Morton & Hall.

Dyes and chemicals, foot Dawson st, Dalton Chemical Co; T S Clark, mgr.

Fertilizers. 101 N Water st, Navassa Guano Co.

Fertilizers, pine hair. pine matting or carpeting; office cor Princess and Water sts; factory at Cronly, Columbus co.

Fertilizers, 102 N Front st, E J Powers.

Lubricating oils, brewers pitch and ready-mixed paints, 111 N Water st, W A Martin & Co.

Marble and granite, 225 N Front st, John Maunder.

Marble and granite, Front near Chestnut, H A Tucker.

Mattresses, Market bet 2d and 3d sts, B F White.

Peanut cleaning, Front near Orange. E A Blake.

Peanut cleaning, Princess st. B F Mitchell & Son.

Pearl hominy, meal, etc, 316 Nutt st, Boney & Harper.

Peregay Lumber Co, near Hilton.

Picture frames, 107 Market st, M S Heinsberger.

Picture frames, 119 Market st, C W Yates.

Planing mill, Water bet Castle and Queen sts, S & W H Northrop.

Planing mill, Fourth near Ashe st, Parsley & Wiggins.

Planing mill, Water, cor Princess st, E Kidder & Son.

Planing mill, foot Harnett st, J H Chadbourn.

Planing mill, at Hilton, Peregay Lumber Co.

Saddles and harness, 10 S Front st, H L Finnell.

NEW HANOVER COUNTY.

Saddles and harness, Third, bet Market and Princess, P Hayden.

Sash, doors and blinds, near Front st, Devine & Chadbourne.

Sellers sash and blinds, cor Sixth st, R R Core & Foster.

Sellers sash, doors and blinds, 12 S Front st, N Jacobi.

Shingle factory, foot of Harnett st, Wilmington Shingle Co, Victor B Britton, mgr.

Shingles, Surry st near Castle, H A Cook.

Ship building, foot of Castle st, S W Skinner.

Shirts, 27 Market st, J Elsbach.

Southern Chemical Works, wood, alchohol and disinfectants, foot of Dawson st, Franklin S Clark, supt.

Spiritine Chemical Co (Malmo, Brunswick Co), L Hansen, prop; office Wilmington; plant for factory $10,000.

Terra Cotta Lumber, Smith building, Princess st, Hairson & Smith.

Tinware, Market, between Second and Third sts, E G Polley.

Tinware, S Front st, Jas H Taylor.

Turpentine, near depot, Manton & Hall.

Turpentine, west side Cape Fear, Alfred Martin.

Upholstering and picture frames, Second, cor Princess st.

Wilmington Lumber Co (near Hilton).

Wilmington Steam Laundry, cor Orange and Front sts.

Wilmington Iron Works, E P Bailey, pres; H A Burr, sec and treas.

Shingles, near Carolina Central depot, Parker & Brinson.

MERCHANTS AND TRADESMEN.

Names, Post Offices and Lines of Business.

WILMINGTON.

Angel, H W, Clerk A C L

Atkinson & Son, 113 N Water st, Gen Ins Agent

Boatwright, J H, Water st, Fire and Life Ins

Bell, Miss M Lee, Gen Delivery Clerk P O

Bonitz, H E, 129 Market st, Architect and Supt

Brown Asa A, Clk Worth & Worth

Callihan, J L, Engineer P O

Carroll, Dan M, Stamper P O

Collins, J W, Cash'r Worth & Worth

Covington, C C & Co, N Water st, Who Gro

Craft, W C, Asst P M

Cutts, A H, Flagman A C L

Darley, Miss M C, Money Order Clk P O

NEW HANOVER COUNTY.

Davis, E H, Stamper P O

Dick, Wm A, Clk A C L

Dixon, G T, Carrier P O

Doyle, Geo, Ship loading contractor

Harris, H G, Watchman, A C L

Harris, Wm W, Water st, Fire and Life Ins Agt

Harker, Mrs Fannie, Char Woman P O

Hawkins, J A, Watchman A C L

Heide, A S, 9 S Water st, Ship Chandler

Honord, B W, Carrier P O

Hodges, Wm W, Nutt st, Fire and Life Ins Agt

Holloway, John M, Night Mailing Clk P O

Keen, J W, Clerk A C L

Keen, John T, Asst Agt A C L

Moore, John, Mailing Clk P O

Morton, Geo L, Postmaster

Myers, Elmer K (Special Delivery), Messenger P O

Murchison, J W, agt, Who and Ret Hardware

Neil, J W, Carrier P O

Norwood, W H, Carrier P O

Oterson, W G H, Carrier P O

Pennington, L B, cor 2d and Market, Prop City Electric Laundry

Post, Thos R, Cash'r A C L

Prempert, Arthur, Carrier P O

Roberts, W W, Clk Worth & Worth

Rutland, Walter (office foot Red Cross), Agt A C L

Sampson, Alex, Carrier P O

Silsa, John E, Janitor P O

Sheehan, John, Sub-Carrier P O

Smith, A W, Clk A C L

Smith, T J, Clk A C L

Smith & Gilchrist, Water st, Who dealers in Fertilizers

Jmith, J D, & Robinson, C H jr, Life and Fire Ins Agts

Stedman & Worth, Princess st, Fire Insurance

Story, A L, Clk Worth & Worth

Swann, Jas G, Clk Worth & Worth

Taylor, Walker, Water st, Fire Ins Agt

Telfair, J S, Sub-Carrier P O

Toon, W P, Bkpr Worth & Worth

Ubirch, Wm, Chief Clerk P O

Ward, C H, Clk A C L

Wellons, J H, Carrier P O

Williams, J S, Clk A C L

Willard, M S, Princess st, Fire, Marine and Life Ins

Willis, B E, & Co, Water, bet Market and Dock sts, Fish, Oysters, &c

Worth & Worth (B G, D G & C W), Mulberry and North Water sts, Com Mchts and Who Gro and Importers

Yarborough, C D, Clk A C L

MILLS.

Kinds, Post Offices and Proprietors.

WILMINGTON.

Corn (steam), 12 Dock st, W P Oldham & Co.
Corn (steam), 9 N Water st, B B Mitchell & Son.
Grist, South suburbs, W H Turlington.
Rice, 13 Chestnut st, Giles, Norwood, Gales & Co.
Saw (steam), foot Castle st, S & W H Northrop.
Saw (steam), N Water, cor Princess st, Kidder & Sons.
Saw (steam), 1011 N Front st, J H Chadbourne & Co.
Saw and planing (steam), foot Ashe st, Hilton Lumber Co.
Steam corn and pearl hominy, Nutt st, Boney & Harper.

PHYSICIANS.

Names and Post Offices.

WILMINGTON.

Bellamy, W J H, 205 Orange st.
Burbank, T S, Fourth and Dock sts.
Browne, Mrs L Hughes (col), Princess st (between Seventh and Eighth sts).
Galloway, W C, 2 Post Office Park.
Lane, W W, City Hospital.
Love, Wm J, Fourth and Chestnut sts).
McDonald, A D, 411 N Fourth st.
Pigford, E S, 107 Mulberry st.
Schomwald, J T, 506 N Fourth st.
Storm, W E, 222 Market st.
Thomas, Geo G, 315 Market st.
Von Sant, John, U S Marine, Hospital.
Wright, S P, 613 N Fourth st.

DENTISTS.

Names and Post Offices..

WILMINGTON.

Alston, J H (col), Fourth and Hanover sts.
Baldwin, A M.
Bell, C D, Fourth and Campbell sts.
Bullock, D W, 45 N Front st.
Dreher, J H, cor Front and Princess sts.
Durham, J H, 108 Princess st.
Hallett, A P, Bank New Hanover building.
Hall, Wright, 125 S Front st.
Harris, A H, Sixth and Market sts.
Jewett, R D, 305 N Fourth st.
Kea, James E, 520 N Fourth st.
Mask, T R (col), 12 N Second st.

Matthews, J F, Market st.
Reynolds, R A (col), 12 N Second st.
Russell, F H, 212 Market st.
Shepard, J C, 218 Market st.
Smith, W L, cor Princess and Front sts.
Stokes, W F, 123 S Front st.

SCHOOLS.

WILMINGTON.

Public schools: white, 13; colored, 14.

LOCAL CORPORATIONS.

WILMINGTON.

Acme M'f'g Co, foot of Princess and Water sts.
American Legion of Honor, H McClammy, com.; A L DeRossett, vicecom.
Association of Officers of the Third North Carolina Infantry, Col W L DeRossett, pres; Col J L Cantwell, sec; organized February, 1886.
Atlantic Coast Line Road, T M Emerson, general agent.
Bellevue Cemetery Company, John Bellamy, pres.
Brunswick Bridge and Ferry Co, E S Tennent, pres; W M Cummings, sec and treas. Capital stock, $16,000.
Campbell Encampment, No 1, I O O F; J N Jacobi, C P; B J Jacobs, scribe.
Cape Fear Lodge, No 2, I O O F, Jos N Jacobi, N G; A D Yopp; day of meeting: Tuesday.
Cape Fear Club, cor Front and Chestnut streets, Wm Latimer, pres; J D Munds, sec.
Carolina Inter State Building and Loan Association, Charles E Borden, pres; W P Toomer, sec; W G Whitehead, treas. Capital stock, $5,000,000.
Carolina Yacht Club, Wrightsville, Wm Latimer, commodore; F A Lord, purser.
Champion Compress and Warehouse Co, Walter Smallbones, sec'y and treas. Capital stock, $100,000; capacity, 750 bales of cotton per day.
Cherokee Tribe, No 9, Improved Order of Red Men, S P Wright, V G I; J M Branch, sachem; J D H Klander, K of W; meets every Thursday night in Red Men's Hall.
Clarendon Water Works, John F Divine, pres; Geo W Kidder, sec'y and treas; J C Chase, supt and engineer. Capital stock, $100,000; pump capacity, 3,000,000 gallons per day.

NEW HANOVER COUNTY.

Concord Chapter, No 1, M S Willard, H P; W A Martin, sec.

Cunard Steamship Co (limited), 6th S Water st, Heide & Co, agents.

Express Steamboat Co, Water near Market.

Eysta Tribe, No 5, Improved Order of Red Men, D D Cameron, sachem; J M McGowan, C of R; E R Wooten, K of W; meets Wednesday night in Red Men's Hall.

Germania Lodge, No 4, K of P, John Myers, C C; J W Gerdts, K of R and S.

Hanover Lodge, No 145, I O O F, C B Allen, N G; S G Hall, sec.

Hibernian Benevolent Scoiety; D O Conner, pres; John L Cantwell, sec and treas.

Hibernian Association, ——, pres; Jas Corbett, sec; T Doulan, treas.

Historical and Scientific Society of Wilmington; J G Burr, pres; ——, vice-pres; S A Story, sec and treas.

Knights of Honor, J D Bellamy, jr, dictator; Samuel G Hall, reporter.

Navassa Guano Co, D G Worth, pres; C E Borden, gen'l mgr and vice-pres; Col W L DeRossett, treas; capital stock $200,000; capacity 12,000 tons per annum; office cor Princess and Water sts.

New York and Wilmington Steamship Line, 201 N Water st, H G Smallbones, supt.

Orion Lodge, No 67, I O O F; day of meeting, Wednesday; E T Mason, N G; L T Bowden, sec.

Orient, No 395, A F and A M; time of meeting, first Wednesday; M C S Noble, W M; H G Smallbones, sec.

Plantagenet Commandery, No 1, K T; W E Storm, E C; M C S Noble, Recorder.

Produce Exchange, 103 N Water st; Henry C McQueen, pres; D L Gore, vice-pres; John L Cantwell, sec and treas.

Royal Arcanum, ——, regent; John Cowan, sec.

Southern Express Co, 106 N Front st, J R Williams, mgr.

Southern Mercantile Association; E S Sennent, mgr; P B Manning, attorney; credit reports and collections; office Wilmington, Smith building, Princess st.

St John's Lodge, No 1, A F and A M; J C Stout, W M; time of meeting, second Tuesday evening; W M Poisson, sec.

Stonewall Lodge, No 1, K of P; J L Dudley, C C; S T Potts, K of R and S.

The Cape Fear and People's Steamboat Line; Woody & Curry, agts; James Madden, gen mgr.

The Chamber of Commerce, 103 N Water st, F W Kerchner, pres; Edward Perchaw, first vice-pres; Donald MacRae, sec vice-pres; John L Cantwell, sec and treas.

The Citizens Building and Loan Association; W H Chadbourn, pres; H G Smallbones, vice pres; J D Bellamy, jr, sec and treas; nine series of stock, par value $100

The National Bank of Wilmington, cor Front and Princess st, John S Armstrong, pres; F R Howes, acting cashier; capital $100,000; undivided profits $6,000.

The Wilmington Homestead and Loan Association, C H Robinson, pres; J C Stevenson, vice-pres; C C Brown, sec and treas; first series of stock, two thousand shares; second series, five hundred shares; par value of shares $100.

The Wilmington Street Railway Co, J D Bellamy, jr, pres.

Third North Carolina Infantry; W L DeRossett, pres; J L Cantwell, sec.

United Society of St George and St Andrew, H G Smallbones, pres. Walter Outlaw, local freight agent; A Weil, soliciting agent.

Wilmington and Point Caswell Steamboat Co, 102 N Water st.

Wilmington and Southport Steamboat Line, foot Market street, Capt J W Harper, mgr.

Wilmington & Weldon and Wilmington, Columbia and Augusta Railroads; —— Elliott, pres; John F Divine, gen supt; T M Emerson, gen freight and pass agt; J F Post, treas; W A Riach, gen auditor; John S Latta, asst auditor; James Knight, master of trans; John Bisset, master mechanic; B R Dunn, chief engineer; C R Clowe, master car builder.

Wilmington Telephone Exchange, 19 N Front st, E T Coghill, mgr; J R Williams, agent.

Wilmington Sewerage Co, W P Toon, pres; R R Bellamy, vice-pres; R M McIntyre, sec and treas.

Wilmington Sea Coast Railroad Company; capital stock, $100,000; Geo B French, pres; W H Chadbourn, vice pres, John H Daniel, gen mgr.

Wilmington Savings and Trust Company, Princess and Front sts; J W Norwood, pres; Geo Sloan, cash.

Wilmington Produce Exchange, 113 W Water st; H C McQueen, pres; J H Currie, vice-pres; John L Cantwell, sec and treas.

Wilmington Steam Laundry, cor Front and Orange sts (Wilson & Bliss).

Wilmington Medical Society, Dr W J Love, pres; Dr W J H Bellamy, sec.

Wilmington Lodge, No 319, A F and A M; time of meeting, third Tuesday evening; R H Grant, W M; H G Fennell, sec.

Wilmington Light Infantry; armory, City Hall; W H Northrop, Jr, captain.

Wilmington Library Association, Market st; Col A M Waddell, pres; T C Diggs, sec and librarian.

Wilmington Gas Light Co. 114 Princess st; E S Martin, pres; R J Jones, sec and treas.

Wilmington Compress and Warehouse Co, H G Smallbones, pres; Walter Smallbones, sec and treas; capital stock, $85,000; capacity, 1,000 bales of cotton per day.

Wilmington City Opera House, 309 Princess st; J W Cronly, lessee.

Wilmington Chamber of Commerce, 113 N Water st; F W Kerchner, pres; Edward Peschau, first vice pres; Donald MacRae second vice-pres; John L Cantwell, sec and treas.

Wilmington Lodge, No 139. I O O F, W C Smith, N G; J M McGowan, sec.

Wilmington Cemetery Co, Princess st, J C Stevenson, pres.

Western Union Telegraph Co, 19 N Front st, C C Brown, mgr.

Wilmington Telegraph Co, W P Toomer, sec and treas (ten miles, from Wilmington to Atlantic Ocean).

Young Men's Christian Association, Market st.

NEWSPAPERS.

Daily Review, 110 Market st (evening, Democratic); Josh T James, editor and prop.

Morning Star, 9 and 11 Princess st (Democratic morning daily and weekly); W H Bernard, ed and prop.

North Carolina Presbyterian, 21 Front st (weekly); John McLaurin, editor and prop.

North Carolina Medical Journal, cor Chestnut and Second sts (monthly); Dr R D Jewett, editor.

The Bulletin of the North Carolina Board of Health (monthly); published at Wilmington by the N C Board of Health.

The Dispatch (evening daily), Water st.

The Messenger (Dem. morning daily and weekly), 21 N Front st, Jackson & Bell, editors and proprietors.

Wilmington Journal, 110 Market st (weekly), J T James, ed and prop.

FARMERS.

Names and Post Offices.

WILMINGTON—POST OFFICE OF ALL THE FARMERS.

Wm Ashley, col., L B Batson, col., Isaac Bissell, col., London Bissell. col., Sam'l Blossom, Wm Blossom, Noah Boney, col., Jas Boney, col., Benj. Bonham, col., R W Bordeaux, E E Bordeaux, John Bradley, col., F J Brownwell. col., Harvey Brown, col., Isaiah Brown, col., Anna Brown, col., Bun Bryant, col., Isaiah Bryant, col., Owen Bryant, col., Richard Bryant, col., Eliza Burgwyn, col., Judy Burgwyn, col.. Geo Canady, col., Barbara Carr, col., John Casteen, Chas Casteen, Isaac Carver, col., M G Chadwick, Henry Clark, col., Thos Clark, col., Alex Collins, col., M P Costin, Jas Cowan, Wm Cromwell, Geo Davis, col., James Davis, col., Minerva Davis, col., F J Dempsey, J B Dempsey, Cicero Dickson, col., Wm Dickson, col., Wright Dickson, col., Jas A Dorsett, col., W A Drake, M M Faircloth, Jere Fonville, col., Wm Fonville, col., Mingo Foy, col., Nathaniel Foy, col., Thos Futch, Jno F Garrell, Clarissa Grady, col., Geo Grady, col, Holly Grady, col., Luke Grady, col., Plent Grady, col., Jake Green, col., Lewis Hall, col., W M Hairsley, Owen Hairsley, Thos Harrell, col., Frank Hawkins, col., Daniel Hawkins, col., W J Hawkins, C H Heide, Henry Henderson, Amy Hill, col., J F Hines, James Holmes, sr, col., James Holmes, col., Fred Hooper, col., Jesse James, col., J G Johnston, col., Isabella Jones, col., Hillary Jones, col., A B Jones, John Jordan, col., Richard Jordan, col., Willis Jordan, col., Ben Judge, col., Henry H Kelly, col., Leak Kelly, col., Jas A Kerr, Joe T Kerr, J N Kerr, Sol King, col., Ben Laspeyre, col., Peter Lawrence, col., Alex Ledley, col., Simon Lewis, col., Hays Litlow, col., Edward Marshall, col., Robt Martin, Abram Marbles, col.. Wm Mallet, col., Judy Maxwell, col., Jas H Merrick, Virtue McFarland, col., G G McGhee, col., Wm McIntire, Alonzo Miller, col., T C Miller, col., Richard Montgomery, col., Andrew Moore, col., Dennis Moore, col., Cornelius Moore, col., Jas M Moore, col., John Moore, col., Joshua Moore, col., Louisa Moore, col., D J Morgan, James L Moseley, col., Zeb Moseley, col., J Edward Moseley, col., Ann Mott, Perry S Murray, R S Murray, J W Murray, Geo Murray, col., Essex Newkirk, col., Haywood Newkirk, col., Titus Newkirk, col., Wm Newkirk, col., Richard Newsom, col., Levy Nixon, col., Betsy Nixon, col , Andrew Nixon, col., Owen Nixon, col., Robt Nixon, sr, col., Prince Nixon, col., Sam'l N Nixon. col., Susan Nixon (heirs), col., Jas Nobles, Jere Patterson, col., Warren Peebles, col., Nancy Peebles, col., John B Quelch, John P Quelch, John W Quinn, Alcenia Reed, col., William Ripley, col., D D Rivenbark, col., W T Ritter, G F Scitter, C F Scitter, Agnes Schriver, Franklin Scott, col., Selina Sharpless, col., Paul B Sharpless, col., Henry Sharpless, col., Edward Sharpless, col., Joseph A Sharpless, col., Wm Hunter Simpson, Wm Smith, col., E P Smith, Hector Smith, col., Arthur Smith, col., Frank Solomon, Rosa Spear, col., Barten Spellman, col., G W Spicer, col., J W St George, col., E M Surles, H C Tait, col., Chas Tait, col., Robt Tait, col., Dennis Thomas, col., Robt Thomas, col., Joseph F Walker, col., Murphy Ward, col., Mary I Watson, D G Westbrood, Peter Wilber, col., William Blackwell, col , Berkeley Williams, col., Benj Williams [heirs], col., Dan'l Williams, col., Geo Williams. col., Isaac Williams, col., Joe Williams, col., Richard Williams, col., C V Willis, Mrs Jane N Wilson, col., Jas Wilson, col., Mag Wooten, col., B G Worth, Henry C Wright, Wm Wright.

Federal Point Township—C a r l S Bache, Jno A Biddle, Jas M Blackledge, Cæsar Blackledge, col., John T Blackledge, col., Chas T Bonham, Edward T Bowsman, Robt S Bowsman, David Brothers, col., Alex Bryant, col., Alfred Bryant, col, Thos J Burnet, W H Burnet, col., Jos N Burriss. Jos N Burriss, Jr, John H Canady. J F Clark, John Cooper, col., Wm Cooper, col.. Chas W Craig, Eugene Craig, Jesse J Craig. Walter F Craig, Wm M Davis, col., Thos A Davis, col., Theo Davis, col., Jos H Davis, col., Henry G Davis, col., E W Davis, C W Davis, col., Jas F Dixon, Jno W English, Jas T English, Isaac Evans, col., Frank Farrier, Moses Faison, col., Archie L Freeman, c o l , Dave W Freeman, c o l , J N Freeman, col., R B Freeman, col., R V Freeman, c o l , R B Freeman, jr. c o l , R S Fulford, George H Graham, col., Geo C Green, col., Chas B Grissom, Nelson Hawks, Enoch Hausley, col., Alfred Harris, col., Joseph Harris, col., Jno C Harris, col., Nathan Harris, col., Wm Highsmith, col., Alfred Hill, col., Chas Hill, col., Chas A Hill. col., James A Hines, Thos Jacobs, col., Chas James,

col., Louis James, col., Wm James, col., Wm H James, Wiley Johnson, col., Chas W Jordan, col., Jno F Keys, Stephen T Keys, Wm J Keys, Wm J King, Henry R Kuhl, Wm R Lewis, col., Geo A Lowe, col., Jesse C Lowe, col., Jno H McDonald, col., Henry McDonald, col., Edward J McMillan, col., Jas H McNeil, col., Wm McNeil, col., M C McKeithan, Richard D McQuillan, col., Theo E McQuillan, col., Wm Mitchell, col., Jas J Mitchell, col., Jno Mitchell, col., David W Moore, col., Elijah Moore, col., Pary Pickett, col., Geo Rhodes, col., Wm D Rhodes, Jno Roberson, col., Jno M Roberson, col., Geo W Rogers, Edgar W Rogers, Lee Samuel. col., Cuffee Sanders, col., David W Sanders, col., Rich C Sanders, Hiram C Southerland, James D Southerland, Jno D Southerland, W A Southerland, W K Southerland, W J Taylor, Steward Taylor. col., Henry Taylor, A M Teachey, Wm Turley, D M Wade. col., Louis Wade, col., Chas Walker, col., Amos Wheeler, col., Sam'l M Wiggins, Henry B Williams, Heywood Wilson, col., M S Winner, Wm Wright, col., Abram Wright, col.

Harnett—N T Alexander, C H Alexander, R T Alford, Wm Alford, John H Alford, R C Bell, Wm Bonham, D N Bullard, York Ballard, Richard Ballard, col., U R Barksdale, Wm H Batton, Susan Batton, O P Batton, Jno U Berry, col., John Blanton, Hansley Blanton, L A Blue, Hezekiah Bonham, C M Bonham, Demps Botts, col., Mrs H M Bowden. Thos Boykin, col , Henrietta Bradham. Stephen S Brock, Henry Brown, Thos H Brown, Jackson Brown, A D Brown, J H Brown, N N Bryan, C B Bullock, col., Louis Burns, Chas Bush, col., H F Canady, Jas T Canady, W B Canady, W T Canady, J R Canady, R W Carney, C T Carney, T B Carney, J B Castine, T Harnett, Harry Chadbourn, col., Fred L Clark, col., George W Clay, col., L J Cottle, S S Conoway, S T Conoway, Lavinia Conoway, Jno M Capps. Laura Corbett, O F Corbett, Jno L Corbett, Benj Davis, col., Bettie Davis, col., David Davis, col., Jas Davis, col., Jas Edward Davis, col., Nelson Davis, col., H L Deans, A B Dewar, W G Dizar, T L Downing, C H Edens. C N Edens. Eugene Edens, H C Ellears, Wm Thos Ennett, col., Thos Ennett. Mrs M F Ennett, C L Ennett, Rich'd Everett, col , Stokely Everett, col., Vann Everett, col.. Jas M Fail. Fannie Fail, Larry Faison, col., Israel Faison, col., Edward Farrow, col., John Farrior, col., C C Fennell heirs, Fletcher Flowers, col., Edward Foy, col., J T Foy, David Taylor, col., Andrew Foy, col., Thos Franks, col., Simrell Franks, col., Christopher Franks, Moses Franks, col., C Frederick, Ben Fulton, col., Harry Fritch, col.. Alex Galloway, col., Mary Eliza Galloway, col., J B Garrett, J F Gause, J E Garvey, Jos Gibbs, col., Thos Gillespie, col., Quarker Golden, col., Geo Golden, R F Gore, Wm Green, col., J H Gurganus, Herbert B Hankins, Jas Hansley, col., Jane Harper, Mrs M A Hayden, Jno S Harris, Jno D Howlett, Ann M Hewlett, J M Hewlett, J H Highsmith, Caspar Hill, col., Church Hines, col., Isaac Hines, col., Louis Hines, col., J A Holt, Dave Howard, col., B B Humphrey, Mrs T A Humphrey, M J Jackson, London Jacobs, col., Jno James, col., Jno S James, Jos M Jarrott, Isaac Jarrott, Jas F Jarrott. J H Jones, Buck J Jones, S J Jones, D J Joyner, jr, Mrs J T Kenan, W F Kerr, J T Kerr, C C Ketchum, J C Kirkham, D F Klein, Mrs M A Klein, H N Lamb, W O N Lee, Jas Livingston, col., David Loftin, col., John Loftin, col., J H Lowery, col., Evelina Mack, col., Jere Mack, col., Geo Maids, col., Mrs M F Manning, Geo Mandy, John Martin, col., Thomas Mashburn, J F Mason, L R Mason, C R Mason, L J Mason, C D McCabe, col., D & N McEachern, Anthony McClammy, col., H R McGrath, Owen McKinney, col., R H McKoy, Jas McRae, col., Mrs M C Mebane, Henry Melton, Harry Merrick, col, C S Miller, W H Mills, J L Mills. Jno W Monk, Thomas Moore, col., Archy Moore, col., Jas Moore, col., Nick Moore, col., Horace Moore, col., Geo Moore, Delaware N Moore, Perry Murray, H D Murrill, Jas Nichols, col., Anthony Nixon, col., T Harnett N N Nixon, R B Nixon, Thos Nixon, col., Geo Nixon, col., Jordan Nixon, col., J D Nixon, col., S W Nobles, R J Padrick, A R Padrick, J E Phillips, Eliza A Polley, C H Pottey, Geo R Parker, J E Peadrick, Holly Pearce, col., Ashley Peders, col., Sim Peden, col., J A Perry, Jos Pickett, jr, col., Jos Pickett, col., W R Piner, J J Piner, R D Piner, W A Piner, Jas Rhue, S R Rhue, W E Rhue, Mrs M A Robinson, W F Roberts, Jas C Roderick, Geo H Rogers, W F Rogers, W L Rogers, Cnas Rogers, S A Rogers, Cyrus Ross, col., W B Scattergood, E H Schoot, J W Scott, B H Scott, Beverly Scott, col.. Henry Shepard, J N Shepard, W T Shepard, Hosea Shepard, H B Shepard, Geo T Shepard, I Shrier, John Sidbury, col., Marcus Sidbury, col., Burrilly Sidbury,

col., Wesley Sidbury, col., Burrill Sidury, sr., col., Sarah Sidbury, col., N A Sidbury, col., Delaware Sidbury, Jos Silva, Geo Simpson, col..Wm Sinclair, Brinson Singletary, col., Jno F Soll, Mrs C B Southerland, W T Southerland, Henry J Southerland, Jno Southerland, R O Spooner, Wm M Stanley, cal., Jno R Stedman, col., Mrs Alex Stedman, col., Alex Stedman, Mrs C C Stevens, Abel St. George, col., John T Stokely, Mrs M A Stokely, Louisa C Swann, col.. W H Sneeden, Stephen Sneeden, T V Sneeden, O T Swinson, T J Tart, W A Taylor, John Taylor, col., Chas Tietgen, Burney Thomas, col., N B Tompkins, Henry W Tompkins, H A & D R Tucker, Henry Waddell Jno G Wagner, Joseph Wagner, col., Sandy Wallace, col., C H Walker. Gwen Walker, col., C W Watters, Maria T Walker, Gerrit Walters, G W Westbrook, Mary E Wood, H Weritzensen, L B Whitledge, Gilbert Whitfield, col., C N D Whitehurst, col., A E White, col., Ives White, col., C C Williams, Geo D Williams, col., Larry Williams, col., Frank Williams, col., Geo Williams, jr, col., Jos Williams. col., D A Williams, col , Jesse S Williams, J B Williams, C G Williams, Mrs E F Williams, C C Williamson, Eliza Williamson, David Williamson, V F Williamson, M S Willard, Handy Willis, col. Wm Winters, col.

Masonboro—Jos Albro, H S Barnes, col., Cæsar Barker, col., Eugene Barker, col., Geo R Bate, M F Beasley, col., L B Benjamin, Virgil Berry, H P Biddle, col , Abram Bishop, C H Bishop, col., Chas H Buckley, col., Geo M Burnett, col., C L Burriss, col., F D Capps, J M Capps, H H Castine, J W Castine, J L Castine, J D Cottle, W S Craig, S G Craig, Louis Craig, Jno H Craig, C T Craig, Chas Craig, jr, Jno M Cullen, col., Louis Davis, col., Ben Dickerson, col., Joseph Doane, col., J T Edens, Julia Everett, Jas B Fails, Benj Farrow, Benj Farrow, jr, C H Farrow, J A Farrow, J J Farrow, N G Fergus, D J Fergus, T T George, D D George, A B George, Thos Gladen, J E Grissom, W T Grissom, Narcissa Hawkins, R E Heide, Alonzo Hewlett, Elijah Hewlett, J B Hewlett, Jno J Hewlett, Wm Hollis, Jas Hollis, Benj Hollis, G R Holt, J T Holt, H S Horne, G H Johnson, J J Johnson, J H King, Stanley King, J J King, E G King, N A Layton, W H Lumsdon, J E Mapes, Henry Martindale, E S McGowan. Sophia McKinney, col., R H McKoy, Wm McLaurin, col., Wm Melton, W M Mintz, A E Mohr, J P Montgomery, B

NEW HANOVER COUNTY.

S Montford, W P Oldham, E A Ovell, T N Price, Henry Risley, G W Rogers, Mrs E L Rush, Jos Smith, Eli Southerland, Lat Southerland, D Steljes, C M Stokley, Jas W Telfair, col., Louis Todd, D W Trask, W H Turlington, W H Waddell, col., Cate Waddell, col., Jno G Wagner, Jas P Walton, Seth Walton, M S Warrock.

Orton plantation, 15 miles below Wilmington, on the west side of the Cape

NEW HANOVER COUNTY.

Fear river is owned by K M Murchison; 325 acres in rice; size of plantation, 10,000 acres.

Lilliput & Kindal plantation, adjoining the Orton, owned by Fred Kidder, of Wilmington, cultivation and growth about the same as the Orton—both in Brunswick county.

Rice, 50 to 55 bushels per acre, price this year, $1 to $1.15 per bushel; mostly sold in Wilmington. Cost of milling or hulling, 10 cents per bushel.

NORTHAMPTON COUNTY.

AREA, 510 SQUARE MILES.

POPULATION, 21,242; White 9,224, Colored 12,018.

NORTHAMPTON COUNTY was formed from Bertie county by the Legislature of 1741, which met at Wilmington. The origin of its name is unknown.

JACKSON, the county-seat, is 115 miles from Raleigh, and was named in honor of Andrew Jackson, the hero of New Orleans, and the sixth President of the United States. Population 450.

Surface—Pleasantly undulating, lies along the Roanoke river, is well watered, plenty of water-power, land generally good and productive when well drained and cultivated.

Staples—Cotton, tobacco, corn, potatoes, wheat, peanuts and naval stores.

Fruits—Apples, peaches, pears, melons, berries and other small fruits.

Timbers — Oak, pine, hickory, ash and cypress.

TOWNS AND POST OFFICES.

	POP.		POP.
Bryantown,	25	Milwaukee	25
Conway,	100	Pendleton,	100
Creeksville,	30	Pleasant Hill,	100
Eagletown,	25	Potecasi,	100
Garysburg,	125	Rehobeth,	25
Gumberry,	50	Rich Square,	300
Ingram,	30	Seaboard,	275
Jackson (C H),	450	Severn,	50
Lasker,	75	Thomas,	25
Margaretts-		Vultare,	—
ville,	125	Wildcat,	—
Meherrin,	—	Woodland,	250
Miami,	25		

COUNTY OFFICERS.

Clerk Superior Court—J T Flythe.
Commissioners—W P Vick, chmn, E Baugham, Jos A Garris, W E Harris, B D Stancell.
Coroner—Thos Duke.
Register of Deeds—Millard F Stancell.
Sheriff—W H Buffaloe.
Solicitor Second District—W E Daniel.
Standard Keeper—Edwin Wright.
Surveyor—E W Conner.
Treasurer—J A Burgwyn.
County Examiner—A J Conner.

COURTS.

Fourth Monday after first Monday in March; fifth Monday before first Monday in September.

TOWNSHIPS AND MAGISTRATES.

Gaston—D B Zollicoffer, B M Pugh, W L Stanley, Jno A Snow, J H Crews, J R Carstarphan, J I Pope, W H Lee, W M Jordan, F A Ingram, Wiley Baker (Jackson).

Jackson—Jeremiah Gay, J E Moore, G P Burgwyn, J T Peebles, J A Parker, T C Parker, Exum Futrell, J H Bradley, J T Gay, C J Bradley (Jackson).

Kirby—J A Garris, D N Stephenson, B F Martin, J Q Parker, W H Madrey, John Futrell, K I Martin, J R Beale, J B Stevenson, S K Edwards, J R Martin, John A Parker (Jackson).

Occoneechee—W H Joyner, Bennett Stephenson, L M Long, G S Urquhart, E L Sumerell, J J Stephenson, C H Pate, J H Ballard, M L Parker, Bennett Stephens (Jackson).

Rich Square—W T Baughan, H C Edwards, E P Outland, S M Lassiter, Isaac Carter, J B Bryan, J E Blanchard, A McDaniel, G H Parker, J W Conner, W J Parker, E E Roberts (Rich Square).

Roanoke—C W Brittain, Wm Grant, A J Conner, A Grant, W E Woodruff, I P Baker, H T Griffin, H R Deloatch, P S Parker (Jackson).

Seaboard—W R Hart, A H Reid, J J Wheeler, R S Stephenson. N A Parker, G F Gray, J L Harris, W R Harris, W C Coats, J W Drewett, L A Jordan, J M Palmer (Seaboard).

Wiccama—J D Bottoms, Kinchen Davis, J P Parker, T A Lanier, J H Garris, Turner Britton, John Lewter, J T H Garris, J W Flythe, B P Long, G E Outland, Jas Talton (Wiccama).

CHURCHES.

Names, Post Offices, Pastors and Denom.

METHODIST.

Church—Woodland, J T Harrison.
Church—Seaboard, J R Tillery.
Church—Jackson, Z T Harrison.
Church—Garysburg, J R Tillery.
Concord—Seaboard, J R Tillery.
New Hope—Jackson, Z T Harrison.
Magnolia—Jackson, Z T Harrison.
Pinner's—Rich Square, Z T Harrison.
Oak Grove—Garysburg, J R Tillery.
Pleasant Grove—Jackson, J R Tillery.
Providence — Murfreesboro (Hertford Co), P Greening.

NORTHAMPTON COUNTY.

Rehobeth—Jackson, Z T Harrison.
Sharon—Margarettsville, P Greening.
Shiloh—Garysburg. J R Tillery.
Willow Oak—(col). Rich Square.
Zion—Conway, P Greening.
Zion—(col), Conway.

BAPTIST.

Allen's Chapel—(col). Jackson.
Branch's Chapel—(col), Bryantown.
Chapel Hill—(col), Rich Square.
Church—(col), Garysburg.
Church—Jackson, A Cree.
Church—Margarettsville,J N Haggard.
Church—Rich Square, A Cree.
Church—Seaboard, A Cree.
Elam—Seaboard, Mr Green.
First—(col), Rich Square.
Gallatea—Margarettsville, J N Haggard.
Hebron—Woodland. Dancy Cole.
Jerusalem—(col), Woodland.
Mt Carmel—Jackson, A Cree.
Pine Forest—Garysburg, Mr Green.
Potecasi—Potecasi, Dancy Cole.
Roanoke—Lasker, Dancy Cole.
Roberts' Chapel—Pendleton, Chas W Scarborough.

FRIENDS.

Cedar Grove — Woodland, Benj P Brown.
Church—Rich Square, Henry Outland.

EPISCOPAL.

Church of the Savior—Jackson, W T Pickard.

MINISTERS RESIDENT.

Names, Post Offices and Denominations.

METHODIST.

Flythe, Jesse, Creeksville.
Greening, P. Margarettsville.
Harrison, Z T. Jackson.
Tillery, J R, Garysburg.

BAPTIST.

Cale, Dancy, Potecasi.
Cree, A, Seaboard.
Fleetwood, J C, Margarettsville.
Haggard, J N, Pendleton.

FRIENDS.

Brown, Benj P, Woodland.
Outland, Henry, Rich Square.

EPISCOPAL.

Pickard, W T, Jackson.

HOTELS AND BOARDING HOUSES.

Names, Post Offices and Proprietors.

Boarding. Rich Square, Mrs S M Lassiter.
Cleveland House, Jackson, James S Grant.

NORTHAMPTON COUNTY.

Hotel, Jackson, Jas Scull.
Hotel, Seaboard, Mrs H P Duke.
Hotel, Garysburg, W T Kee.
Hotel, Pendleton, Turner Lee.

LAWYERS.

Names and Post Offices.

Bagley, Willis, Jackson.
Calvert, S J, Jackson.
Gay, B S. Jackson.
Harris, F R, Jackson.
Mason, T W, Garysburg.
Peebles, R B, Jackson.
Peebles, W W. Jackson.
Peebles, C G (Peebles & Son), Jackson.
Ransom, T R, Jackson.
Ransom, M W, sr, (U S Minister to Mexico), Garysburg.

MANUFACTORIES.

Kinds, Post Offices and Proprietors.

Blacksmithing and wheelwrighting, Woodland, F S Muldor.
Blacksmithing and wheelwrighting, Jackson, Wright Bros.
Blacksmithing and wheelwrighting, Ingram, F A Ingram.
Blacksmithing and wheelwrighting, Rich Square, J J Manley.
Blacksmithing and wheelwrighting, Seaboard, J E Cuthrell.
Blacksmithing and wheelwrighting, Seaboard, T W Rose & Bro.
Blacksmithing and wheelwrighting, Woodland, Samuel Whitley.
Blacksmithing and wheelwrighting, Rich Square, W R Conwell.
Blacksmithing and wheelwrighting, Margarettsville, J W Cocke & Son.
Blacksmithing and wheelwrighting, Rich Square, Joshua Conwell.
Building and contracting, Jackson, Henry Stewart.
Building and contracting, Woodland, J T Mulder.
Building and contracting, Woodland, Jos Peele (col).
Coaches and carriages, Jackson, Moore & Cocke.
Millwrighting, Murfreesboro (Hertford co), D C Park.
Millwrighting, Woodland, F S Mulder.
Saddles and harness, Jackson, W T Picard.
Tannery, Woodland, J P Blanchard.
Tannery, Rich Square, A McDaniel.

NORTHAMPTON COUNTY.

MERCHANTS AND TRADESMEN.

Name, Post-office and Line of Business.

CONWAY.

Britt, J T, jr,	G S
Futrell, Dr M A,	Drugs
Hedgepeth, J Q,	G S
Lassiter & Flythe,	G S
Reid, Henry & Co,	G S

CREEKSVILLE.

Davis, J A,	G S

DOGWOOD.

Baird, Mrs M A,	G S

EAGLETOWN.

Elliott, J T & Co,	G S
Smith, J P,	G S

GARRYSBURG.

Collier, J B (col),	G S
Ellis & Bro,	Gro and Conf
Garner, McNeil & Co,	G S
Harding, T J,	G S
Hawks, J A,	G S
Jordan, L A,	Gro
Joyner, W T,	Machinery
Reese, Robt R, agt,	G S
Suiter, J L,	G S
Zollicoffer, D B,	G S

GASTON.

Bradley, W E (near),	G S

GUMBERRY.

Kell, F,	G S

JACKSON.

Barrow, Wm,	G S
Burgwyn, Geo P,	G S
Burnett, J J, Conf and Fancy	Gro
Buxton, J A & Co,	G S
Deloatch, W R, agent,	Gro
Edwards, M T,	G S
Flythe, J M,	G S
Moore, W P & Co,	Drugs
Scull, James,	G S
Weaver, R A & Bro,	G S

LASKER.

Conner & Vaughan,	G S
Lassiter, W E,	G S
Parker, J J,	G S

MARGARETTSVILLE.

Garris & Bridgers,	G S
Lanier, B H,	G S
Norvell, W T (near),	G S
Spivey, A B,	G S
Stephenson, W U,	G S

MEHERRIN.

Pruden Bros & Co,	G S

MIAMI.

Parker, J Q,	G S

PENDLETON.

Beale, J R,	G S
Britt, T A,	G S
Edwards, D K,	Gro and Livery
Stevenson & Sikes,	G S

NORTHAMPTON COUNTY.

PLEASANT HILL.

Alston & Harris,	G S
Smith, R L,	G S
Williams, W H (near),	G S

POTECASI.

Baugham, B F,	Guano Agent
Griffin, C H,	G S
Harrell, C R,	G S
Johnson, Mrs E L,	G S

REHOBETH.

Lassiter, S C & Co,	G S

RICH SQUARE.

Baugh, J H,	G S
Bishop & Powell,	G S
Bolton, Dr M,	Drugs
Baughman, J,	G S
Boyce, L W,	Gro
Brown, P B,	G S
Buxton & Baughan,	G S
Gay, E J,	G S
Leak, J R,	G S
Leak, J R, Jr,	G S
Outland, W C & Son,	G S
Spivey & Bros,	Lumber
Weaver & Lassiter,	G S

SEABOARD.

Buxton & Stevenson,	G S
Crocker, J G S,	G S
Duke, H P & Co,	G S
Grubbs, W F,	G S
Harris, M D L (near),	Undertaker
Hart, W R, agent,	G S
Joyner, H L, agent,	G S
Maddrey, J T,	G S
Pruden, W S & Co,	G S
Stephenson, Dr M R,	Drugs
Wheeler, J J,	Gro

SEVERN.

Edwards, R M,	G S
Howell, W H,	G S
Pruden, W H & G W,	Dumber
Stephenson, Henry (col.),	G S
White, B K,	G S

WOODLAND.

Benthall, J A (near),	G S
Blanchard, J P, Lumber and Guano	
Blanchard, R W & Co,	G S
Brown, A W,	G S
Brown, B P & Son.	G S
Griffin, J B, G S and Lumber	
Jacobs & Edmonds,	G S

MILLS.

Kinds, Post Offices and Proprietors.

Corn, flour, saw and gin, Rich Square, E D Spivey.

Corn and flour, Boykin, Va, Sykes & Stevenson.

Corn and flour, Potecasi, C Lassiter.

Corn and flour, Garysburg, E J Thomas.

NORTHAMPTON COUNTY.

Corn and flour, Margarettsville, Vick & Bridges.
Corn and flour, Woodland, Griffin & Harrell.
Corn and flour, Margarettsville, W J Rogers.
Corn and flour, Margarettsville, W P Vick.
Corn and flour, Margarettsville, Stancell & Gay.
Corn and flour, Rich Square, Thomas C Reele.
Corn and flour, Rich Square, Jas Futrell & Co.
Corn and flour, Jackson, G P Burgwyn.
Corn and flour, Jackson, J L Deloatch.
Corn and flour, Jackson, M W Ransom, jr.
Cotton gin, planing machine, engines repaired, etc, Lasker, C Parker.
Saw, Potecasi, Lassiter & Peel.
Saw, Severn, Pruden Bros.
Saw, Garysburg, Daniel & Gordon.
Saw, Rich Square, J F Futrell & Co.
Saw and grist, Jackson, J E Moore.

NORTHAMPTON COUNTY.

Saw, Jackson. Lassiter & Bro.
Saw, Rich Square, J R Leek.
Saw, Rich Square, Jas Baugham & Co.
Saw, Rich Square, J T Elliott.

PHYSICIANS.

Names and Post Offices.

Bolton, M, Rich Square.
Brown, —— (dentist), Woodland.
Ellis, A J. Garysburg.
Futrell. M. Conway.
Gary. R H, Pendleton.
Griffin, Ephraim (dentist), Woodland.
Griffin, ——, Woodland.
Joyner, R W, Woodland.
Lewis, H W, Jackson.
Moore, W P (dentist), Jackson.
Morehead, ——. Lasker.
Outland, J L, Woodland.

NEWSPAPERS.

Patron and Gleaner (ind weekly), Lasker. A J Connor, editor.

ONSLOW COUNTY.

AREA 640 SQUARE MILES.

POPULATION 10,303; White 7,392, Colored 2,911.

ONSLOW COUNTY was formed in 1734, from New Hanover county, and named in honor of Arthur Onslow, then Speaker of the British House of Commons.

JACKSONVILLE, the county-seat, is situated on New river, 105 miles southeast from Raleigh. Population, 450.

Surface—Low, level, and in places swampy; much of the land very rich, and very productive when well drained.

Staples—Cotton, corn, sweet potatoes, ground peas, live-stock, naval stores and fish.

Fruits—Apples, peaches, scuppernong grapes, etc.

Timbers—Pine, oak, hickory, ash, juniper and cypress.

TOWNS AND POST OFFICES.

	POP.		POP.
Aman's Store,	—	Marines,	50
Angola,	25	Palo Alto,	50
Bay View,	50	Peanut,	50
Catharine Lake,	75	Promise,	45
Charles,	—	Quincy,	25
Cyrus,	25	Richlands,	150
Dixon,	35	Silver Dale,	40
Duck Creek,	25	Snead's Ferry,	40
Flox,	50	Sparkman,	25
Gum Branch,	40	Springer,	—
Holly Ridge,	25	Stump Sound,	25
Hubert,	25	Swansboro,	300
Jacksonville,		Tar Landing,	75
(c h)	450	Verona,	25
Lanier,	25	Ward's Mills,	40
Loco,	50		

COUNTY OFFICERS.

Clerk Superior Court—Chas Gerock.
Commissoners—D J Saunders, chm'n; A N Sandlin, G D Matocks, John Gurganus, G H Simmons.
Coroner—B L Kellan.
Register of Deeds—C C Morton.
Sheriff—F W Hargett.
Solicitor 6th District—MC Richardson.
Standard Keeper—J S Gardner.
Treasurer—J F Cox.
County Examiner—E M Koonce.
County Physician—E L Cox.
County Home—Mrs Margret Thomas.

COURTS.

Fourth Monday after the 1st Monday in March, and the 9th Monday after the first Monday in September.

TOWNSHIPS AND MAGISTRATES.

Jacksonville—L L Hoyt, John Z Gardner (Jacksonville), G J Scott, L A Jones, G T Walton, Wm King, James Gurganus (Sparkman), H H Shepard (Cyrus).

Richlands—J R Francks, F D Shaw, U W Mills, I G Barbee, R D Thompson (Richlands), Col S B Taylor, J K P Batchelor, Thos Bryant (Catharine Lake), E J Newbold (Gum Branch).

Stump Sound—W C Allen, W P Walton, George King, J E Topp, R C Davis, D E Humphrey (Verona), V Sidberry, H E King (Peanut), J B Grant (Snead's Ferry).

Swansboro—L O Fonville, sr (Duck Creek), D A Freshwater, G W Kellum. jr, H E Morten (Hubert), D G Ward, W W Russell, Geo W Ward (Swansboro), E W Fornell (Ward's Mills), Lewis Marine (Marine's).

White Oak—John L Morton (Jacksonville), S L Gerock, A A Eubanks (Mayesville), E B Hargett (Silverdale), D W Smith (Loco), Joseph Henley, Ralph Bender, Dr W J Montfort (Ward's Mills).

TOWN OFFICERS.

JACKSONVILLE—*Mayor*, J W Burton; *Commissioners*, Frank Thompson, J F Koonce, L S Avery, George E Songer; *Clerk and Treasurer*, Frank Thompson.

SWANSBORO—*Mayor*, John A Pittman.

RICHLANDS—*Mayor*, H B Koonce; *Commissioners* L W Hargett, C Mills, N Sylvester, J H Aman; *Clerk and Treasurer*, C Mills.

CHURCHES.

Names, Pastors, Postoffices and Denom.

BAPTIST.

Church—Snead's Ferry.
Church—Jacksonville, M C Walton.
Church—Catharine Lake.
Church—Richlands, L V Tillery.
Enon—Duck Creek, J W Nobles,
Half Moon—Gum Branch, Ben Ward.

ONSLOW COUNTY.

Piney Grove—Swansboro, Ben Ward.
Southwest—Sparkman, Isaac Jones.

PRIMITIVE BAPTIST.

Haws Russ—Sparkman.
Northeast—Jacksonville, Job Smith.
Stump Sound—Peanut.
Wardville—Duck Creek, Job Smith.
Yopp's—Snead's Ferry.

METHODIST.

Church—Swansboro, Daniel Reid.
Haw Branch—Flox, J T Kendall
Mt Lebanon—Swansboro, Daniel Reid.
Queen's Creek—Hubert, Daniel Reid.
Richlands—Richlands, J T Kendall.
Tabernacle—Palo Alto, Daniel Reid.
Trinity—Jacksonville, Daniel Reid.

DISCIPLES OF CHRIST.

Chapel—Catharine Lake.
Church—Richlands, —— Howard.

PRESBYTERIAN.

Church—Richlands, J W Wood.

FREE-TO-ALL.

Church—Jacksonville.

MINISTERS RESIDENT.

Names, Post Offices and Denom.

BAPTIST.

Nobles, J W, Ward's Mills.

PRIMITIVE BAPTIST.

Brown, C C, Snead's Ferry.
Rhodes, A H. Tar Landing.
Smith, Job, Palo Alto.

MISSIONARY BAPTIST.

Ward, Ben, Marines.

METHODIST.

Henderson, I N, Hubert.

HOTELS AND BOARDING HOUSES.

Names, Post Offices and Proprietors.

Boarding, Jacksonville, W S Downs.
Boarding, Jacksonville, G W Gurganus.
Boarding, Jacksonville, J A Wood.
Boarding, Jacksonville, W H Jarman.
Boarding, Jacksonville, Mrs M M Grimsley.
Boarding, Jacksonville, Mrs Laura Shepard.
Boarding, Jacksonville, Jacob Rochelle.
Hotel, Swansboro, T D Lindsey.
Hotel, Richlands, Geo E Brock.
Hotel Gilma, Jacksonville, Mrs E V Wooten.
Murrell House, Jacksonville, Charles Gerock.
New River Inn, near mouth of New river, E M Koonce & Co.

30

ONSLOW COUNTY.

LAWYERS.

Names and Post Offices.

Duffy, Rodolph, Catharine Lake.
Gilman, T E, Jacksonville.
Koonce, Frank D, Richlands.
Thompson, Frank, Jacksonville.

MANUFACTORIES.

Kinds, Post Offices and Proprietors.

Buggies and carts, Verona, R W Sandlin.
Carriages, etc, Jacksonville, John Z Gardner.
Carts, etc, Richlands, John H Aman.
Carts, etc, Jacksonville, S C Evans.
Lumber and shingles, Holly Ridge, C M Whitlock.
Lumber, Jacksonville, Parmele, Eccleston Lumber Co.
Public gin, Jacksonville, W B Murrill.
Public gin, Verona, L A Guy, mgr.
Public gin and turpentine distillery, Tar Landing, B F Hall & Co.
Rough and dressed lumber, Mayesville, Stempson Lumber Co.
Rough Lumber, Swansboro, Swansboro Lumber Co.
Turpentine distillery, Hubert, Slocum & Co.
Turpentine distillery, Marines, W N Marine.
Turpentine distillery, Catharine Lake, J F Boggs.
Turpentine distillery, Catharine Lake, Sim B Taylor.
Turpentine distillery, Catherine Lake, O B Cox.
Turpentine distillery, Sparkman, Geo W Blake.

MERCHANTS AND TRADESMEN.

Names, Post Offices, Lines of Business.

BAY VIEW.

Bay View Farm, Bay View, J S Westbrook & Co.

CATHARINE LAKE.

Boggs, R H,	G S
Boggs, J F,	G S
Cox, O B,	G S
Taylor, Col S B,	G S

FLOX.

Williams, Jonas (col.),	G S
Williams, John,	G S

HUBERT.

Slocum, A H & Co,	G S

JACKSONVILLE.

Avery & Gardner,	Undertakers

ONSLOW COUNTY.

Brown, J E,　　　　Cigars and Tob
Cox, Dr E L,　　　　　　　　Drugs
Gibbs, Amos (col.),　　　　　　G S
Goldberg, A.　　　　　　　Clothing
Hall, B F & Co,　　　　　　　　G S
Harrell, E D & J T,　　Cigars and Tob
Henderson, B M,　　　　　　Livery
Jarman, H A,　　　　　　　Livery
Humphrey, J D.　　　　　　　G S
Marim Bros & Co,　　　　　　G S
Murrill, W B,　　　　　　　Trucker
Parmele Eccleston Lumber Co,　G S
Reece, A,　　　　　　　　　G S
Sabiston, E W.　　　　　　　G S
Scherr, B H & S,　　Cigars and Tob
Taylor, Geo W,　　　　　　　G S
　　　　MARINE.
Koonce, A F,　　　Cigars and Tob
Marine, W N,　　　　　　　G S
Marine, Lewis,　　　　　　　G S
Marine, Lewis, Wholesale Fish
　　　Dealer and Oysters
Smith, E S,　　　　　　　　G S
　　　　PALO ALTO.
Morton, E H,　　　　　　　G S
Sabiston, M R,　　　　　　　G S
Shepard, N S,　　　　　　　G S
　　　　PEANUT.
Batts, P D,　　　　　　　　G S
Everitt, M V D,　　　　　　G S
Harrell, Geo,　　　　　　　G S
Sidberry, V,　　　　　　　G S
　　　　RICHLANDS.
Cooper, B F,　　　　　　　G S
Mills, J W.　　　　　　　　G S
Steed, M B,　　　　　　　　G S
Sylvester, N,　　　　　　　G S
　　　　SNEED'S FERRY.
Canady, J S,　　　　　　　G S
Canady, U G,　Who Fish and Oysters
Justice, O F. & J H,　　　　　G S
Shepard, P P,　　　　　　　G S
　　　　SPARKMAN.
Justice, F M,　　　　　　　G S
　　　　STELLA.
Sanders & Bell,　Cigars and Tobacco
　　　　TAR LANDING.
Hall, B F, & Co,　　　　　　G S
Rhodes, A H,　　　　　　　G S
　　　　VERONA.
Guy, L A,
　Mgr of T A McIntyre's Stock Farm
Hardison, C W,　　　　　　G S
Humphrey & Sandlin,　　　　G S
Landen, L M, Who Fish & Oyster Deal
McIntyre, T A,　　　　Stock Farm
Morton, E H,　　　　　　　G S
　　　　WARD'S MILLS.
Wynn, W S,　　　　　　　G S
　　　　SWANSBORO.
Dennis, W N,　　　　　　　G S
Moore, D J,　　　　　　　G S
Pittman, J A,　　　　　　　G S
Ward, D G,　　　　　　　G S
Watson, J E,　　　　　　　G S

ONSLOW COUNTY.

MILLS.

Kinds, Post Offices and Proprietors.

Corn, Jacksonville, Isaac Kellum.
Corn and saw, Hubert, I N Henderson.
Corn and saw, Catharine Lake, Jno P
　Cox.
Corn and gin, Richlands, R D Thomp-
　son.
Corn and gin. Sneads Ferry, T J Capp.
Corn, Catharine Lake, J F Cox.
Corn, Richlands, Ferney Jarman.
Corn, Flox, Jas Shivers.
Corn, flour and gin, Richlands, J W
　Mills.
Corn, Richlands, Cyrus Thompson,
Corn and gin, Hubert, I N Henderson.
Corn, Catharine Lake. J F Cox.
Corn (wind), Sneads Ferry, John Hill.
Corn, Ward's Mills, W J Montfort.
Corn, Swansboro, James Holland.
Corn, Jacksonville, E H Morton.
Corn, Jacksonville.
Corn, Gum Branch, J F Cox.
Corn, Gum Branch, Ben Marshburn
　& Bro.
Saw and gin, Sparkman, M L Ward.

PHYSICIANS.

Names and Post Offices.

Blount, F H, Swansboro.
Cox, E L, Jacksonville.
Hoyt, M C. Jacksonville.
McClenden. E G, Sneads Ferry.
Montfort, W J, Ward's Mill.
Nicholson, J L, Richlands.
Thompson, C, Richlands.
Ward, R W, Verona.

SCHOOLS.

Names, Post Offices and Principals.

Academy, Catherine Lake, John S
　Hargett.
High School, Richlands, L V Tillery.
High School, Jacksonville.
Public Schools—white, 38; colored, 13.

LOCAL CORPORATIONS.

LaFayette Lodge, A F and A M, No 87,
　E M Koonce, W P; L L Hoyd, sec.
Mercantile Land and Improvement Co,
　Jacksonville, Chas M Whitlock, pres
　and gen mgr.
New River Lodge, No 20, I O O F,
　Jacksonville; I E Kitchurm, N G;
　L L Hoyd, sec.
Seaside Lodge, A F and A M, No —,
　Dr W J Montford, W M; D J Moore,
　sec.

NEWSPAPERS.

Jacksonville Times (Democratic week-
　ly), H Whitely, editor and prop.

ORANGE COUNTY.

AREA 670 SQUARE MILES.

POPULATION: 14,948; White 9,705, Colored 5,243.

ORANGE COUNTY was formed in 1751, from Granville, Johnston and Bladen counties, and was named in honor of the House of Orange, which, in the persons of William and Mary in 1692, filled the English throne.

HILLSBORO, the county-seat, is situated on the North Carolina Railroad, 40 miles west of Raleigh. It was originally called Childsburg, but was changed to the present name in honor of the Earl of Hillsboro. Population 1,050.

Surface—Hilly, but not mountainous; water-power very fine; good lands along the streams.

Staples—Tobacco, wheat, grass, corn and fruits in great variety. Tobacco, of late years, has become an important staple of this county.

Fruits—Apples, peaches, pears, cherries, plums and the small fruits.

Timbers—Oak, hickory, pine, walnut, poplar, maple and gum.

Minerals—Iron, with traces of coal, mica and copper, with eight chalybeate and sulphur springs.

TOWNS AND POST OFFICES.

	POP.		POP.
Blackwood,	25	Hillsboro,	1,050
Border,	20	Joppa,	25
Bradshaw,	25	Laws,	25
Breeze,	—	Lindsay,	25
Caldwell In-		Meredith,	—
stitute,	119	Oaks,	75
Carr,	—	Rock Spring,	25
Cedar Grove,	65	Teers,	—
Chapel Hill,	1,063	Tolers,	—
Faucett,	25	University	
Gath,	40	Station,	50

COUNTY OFFICERS.

Clerk Superior Court—D F Crawford.
Commissioners—D H Hamilton, chm'n; W A Maddry, M W Moore.
Coroner—W R Faucette.
Register of Deeds—John Laws.
Sheriff—John K. Hughes.
Solicitor 5th District—W P Bynum.
Surveyor—James M Neville.
Standard Keeper—C F Crabtree.
Treasurer—W F Jackson.
County Examiner—Milton Craig.
County Physician—D C Parris.

COURTS.

Second Monday after the first Monday in March; fourth Monday before the first Monday in September; eighth Monday after the first Monday in September.

TOWN OFFICERS.

CHAPEL HILL—*Mayor*, A S Barbee; *Commissioners*, Elmore Woods, D J Ezzell, Wilson Caldwell (col.), Jas F Craig, T M Kirkland.

HILLSBORO — *Mayor*, J A Harris, *Commissioners*, W W Webb, George Overacre, Dr C C Jones, D M Laws, J T Shaw, F R Faucette, Frank Nash; *Constable*, Robert Christmas; *Clerk*, Calvin Parish; *Treasurer*, O D Hooker.

TOWNSHIPS AND MAGISTRATES.

Bingham—S S Webb (Oaks), D M Durham, G P Cheek, J S Neville (Gath), D M Sykes, John Holmes, W F Dodson (Rock Spring), J P Teer (Teer's).

Cedar Grove—John McCracken (Cedar Grove), John R Kenion (Toler), S J Hall, Charles P Forrest, B C Patton, James H Dollar, W A Jordan (Cedar Grove).

Chapel Hill—Hinton Tilley, A S Barbee, Charles W Johnson, E H Wilson (Chapel Hill), D A Clayton (University Station), W R Faucett (Faucett), J D Dodson (Hillsboro), W M Sugg (Chapel Hill).

Hillsboro—M L Efland (Efland), Thos D Tinnin, Jas W Riley, Jno Kirkland, Wm Strain, E L Cooley (Hillsboro), James McCauley (University Station), Henry O Jobe (Mebane), Geo F Crutchfield (Hillsboro).

Little River—A L Holden, J P Lockhart, R C Hill (Hillsboro), H Y Harris, J A Wilkerson, Wm S Gray (Caldwell Institute), W E Hall (Rougemont).

CHURCHES.

Names, Post Offices, Pastors and Denom.

METHODIST.

Cedar Grove—Cedar Grove, D N Caviness.
Chapel Hill—Chapel Hill, L S Massey.
Hillsboro—Hillsboro, D N Caviness.
Mt Lebanon—Mebaneville (Alamance co), B C Thompson.

ORANGE COUNTY.

New Bethel—Rougement, D N Caviness.
New Sharon—Hillsboro, D N Caviness.
Old Bethel—Flat River (Durham co), S T Moyle.
Orange—Chapel Hill, S T Moyle.
Pleasant Green—Hillsboro, S T Moyle
Walnut Grove—Cedar Grove, D N Caviness.

METHODIST PROTESTANT.

Ridge—Hillsboro, M W Pike.
Union Grove—Hillsboro, M W Pike.

BAPTIST.

Bethel—Chapel Hill, J P Mason.
Cane Creek—Hillsboro.
Church—Chapel Hill.
Church—Hillsboro, N B Cobb.
Cool Spring—Rock Spring.
Mars Hill—Hillsboro.
Mt Carmel—Gath.
Mt Hermon—Hillsboro.
Mt Moria—Chapel Hill.

PRIMITIVE BAPTIST.

Mt Lebanon—South Lowell, Andrew Hall.

PRESBYTERIAN.

Bethlehem—Oaks.
Chapel Hill—Chapel Hill.
Eno—Hillsboro.
Fairfields—Hillsboro, H S Bradshaw.
Hillsboro—Hillsboro. H S Bradshaw.
Little River—Hillsboro, H S Bradshaw.
Mebane—Bingham School.
New Hope—Hillsboro.

EPISCOPAL.

Chapel of the Cross—Chapel Hill.
St Matthew's—Hillsboro, B S McKenzie.
St Mary's—Hillsboro, B S McKenzie.

MINISTERS RESIDENT.

Name, Post Office and Denomination.

METHODIST.

Caviness, D N, Hillsboro.
Martin, J B, Chapel Hill.
Massey, L S, Chapel Hill.

METH. PROTESTANT.

Hayes, T C, Hillsboro.

BAPTIST.

Hume, Thos H, D D, Chapel Hill.
Vernon, ——, Cedar Grove.

PRIM. BAPTIST.

Hall, Andrew, South Lowell.
Monk, Yancey, South Lowell.
Terry, Samuel, South Lowell.

PRESBYTERIAN.

Bradshaw, H S, Hillsboro.
Currie, Archie, Hillsboro.

EPISCOPAL.

McKenzie, B S, Hillsboro.

ORANGE COUNTY.

HOTELS AND BOARDING HOUSES.

Kinds, Post Offices and Proprietors.

Grand Central, Chapel Hill, S M Barbee.
University Hotel, Chapel Hill, ——— Pickard.
Occoneechee Hotel, Hillsboro, Mrs. I Hassell.
Boarding, Hillsboro, S Cole.
Boarding, Hillsboro, Henry Richards.
Boarding, Caldwell Institute, S A Jordan.
Boarding, Caldwell Institute, H Y Harris.
Patterson Hotel, Chapel Hill, N G L Patterson.
Robeson Hotel, Chapel Hill, A A Kluttz
University Inn, Chapel Hill, W W Pickard.

LAWYERS.

Names and Post Offices.

Gattis, Samuel L, Hillsboro.
Graham, J W, Hillsboro.
Manning, John, Chapel Hill.
Mason, Jas B. Chapel Hill.
Nash, H K, Hillsboro.
Nash, Frank, Hillsboro.
Parish, C E, Hillsboro.
Turner. Chester, Hillsboro.
Turner, Josiah, jr, Hillsboro.

MANUFACTORIES.

Names, Post Offices and Proprietors.

Alliance Tannery, Hillsboro, Farmers' State Alliance.
Alliance Shoe Factory, Hillsboro, Thad Ivey, mgr for Alliance.
Blacksmithing, Hillsboro, John Ray.
Blacksmithing and wheelwrighting, Chapel Hill, John Huskey.
Blacksmithing and wheelwrighting, Chapel Hill Andrew Marshall.
Blacksmithing and wheelwrighting, Caldwell Institute, D S Allison.
Boots and Shoes, Hillsboro. R L Faucette.
Boots and shoes, Hillsboro. Thomas C Hayes.
Brick, Hillsboro, J D Whitaker.
Buggies and wagons, Hillsboro, Chas Crabtree.
Eno Cotton Mills, Hillsboro, Jas Webb, jr; capital stock, $100,000.
Plug and twist tobacco, Hillsboro, N W Brown & Co.
Shoes, Hillsboro, Abel Payne (col).
Smoking tobacco, Hillsboro, H F Jones & Co.

ORANGE COUNTY.

Staves, Hillsboro, T D Tinnen.
Tannery, Rock Spring, D & John T
Sikes.
Tannery, Caldwell Institute, Joe Burton.
Tinware, Hillsboro, John Laws & Son.

MERCHANTS AND TRADESMEN.

Names, Post Offices, Lines of Business.

BORDER.

| Berry, J R, | G S |
| Brown, W T, | G S |

CALDWELL INSTITUTE.

Gattis, S F,	G S
Harris, H T,	G S
Jordan, T M & Co,	Drugs
Wilkerson, J T,	G S

CARR.

| Corbett & Cooper, | G S |

CEDAR GROVE.

| Patton, B C, | G S |
| Simmons, W S & Bro, | G S |

CHAPEL HILL.

Bunch, T W,	Grocer
Cates, J W & Bro,	Undertaker and Lumber
Eubanks, R A,	G S
Foister & Ezzell,	G S
Hester, W H,	Grocer
Hagon & Hutchings,	Livery
Klutz, A A,	Confections, etc
Lindsay, C L,	G S
Lindsay, W E,	G S
Lloyd, W C & Co,	G S
McCooley, D,	G S
Nunn, Von,	Grocer and Confec
Patterson, H H,	G S
Pritchard, W N,	G S
Robeson, A B,	Drugs
Sorrell, W B,	Grocer
Sorrell, W B,	Watches and Jewelry
Tankersley, W L,	Grocer
Temple & Hearn,	Grocer
Webb, J D,	Grocer

HILLSBORO.

Brown, N W,	Books and Stationery
Brown, N W & Co,	G S
Carter & Co (col),	Confec
Cole, J W,	G S
Cooley, C L,	Furniture
Christmas, John,	G S
Faucett & Whitted (col),	G S
Forest, O J (Exchange),	G S
Hassell, Eugene,	Postmaster
Hayes, W A,	Drugs
Hooker, J W,	Livery
Jones, Jos E,	G S
Laws, Geo,	Furniture
Newman & Smith,	G S
Parks & Hedgepeth,	G S
Parish, H L,	G S

ORANGE COUNTY.

Paries & Show (Hillsboro Drug Co, Drugs	
Rosemond, E A,	G S
Rosemond, E A,	Livery
Shaw, J T,	Jeweler
Sherrill, ——.	Depot Agt and Tel Op
Taylor, Mrs M L,	Millinery
Webb, James, jr. & Bro,	Who and Ret G S

LAWS.

| Laws, James, | G S |

TEER.

| Teer, J P, | G S and Miller |

UNIVERSITY STATION.

Blackman, J T,	G S
Shumaker, J F,	G S
Stroud, H M,	G S
Stroud, W M,	G S

MINES.

Kinds, Post Offices and Proprietors.

Iron, Chapel Hill, Hoke & Co.
Gold, Oaks, A J Ruffin.
Slate, Hillsboro, Jas Webb.

MILLS.

Kinds, Post Offices and Proprietors.

Corn and flour, Rock Spring, Oldham & Teer.
Corn and flour, Rock Spring, D F Thompson & Co.
Corn, flour and gin, Chapel Hill, Thos F Lloyd.
Corn and flour, Chapel Hill, Baxter King.
Corn, flour and saw, Caldwell Institute, C R Miller.
Corn and flour, Caldwell Institute, Winstead & Miller.
Corn, flour and saw, Chapel Hill, G W Purefoy's heirs.
Corn and flour, Chapel Hill, A J Brockwell.
Corn and flour, Chapel Hill, M J W McCauley.
Corn and flour, Border, J K Hughes.
Corn, flour and saw, Hillsboro, Mrs E Dimmock.
Corn, flour and saw, Hillsboro, W W Cox.
Corn, flour and saw, Hillsboro, T H Holden.
Corn and flour, Hillsboro, Sam'l Wilson.
Corn and flour, Rock Spring, H C Thompson & Co.
Corn and flour, Lindsay, Pritchard Bros.
Corn and flour, Oaks, Morrow & Co.
Corn, saw and gin, Gath, Thompson & Co.

ORANGE COUNTY.

Corn and flour, Hillsboro, Jackson Crabtree.

Corn and flour, Hillsboro, Hall & Taylor.

Corn and flour, Hillsboro, A F Faucett's heirs.

Corn and flour, Hillsboro, Sam'l Crawford.

Corn and flour, Hillsboro, M L Efland,

Corn, flour and saw, Cedar Grove, G W Parker.

Corn and flour, Cedar Grove, F L Warren.

Corn and flour, Cedar Grove, A C Compton.

Corn and flour, Cedar Grove, George Parker.

Saw, Caldwell Institute, W R McKee.

Saw and corn, Chapel Hill, C W Johnston.

Saw and corn, Chapel Hill, Robt Patterson.

Saw and Grist, Hillsboro, Jesse Miller.

Saw, Hillsboro, W D Woods.

Saw, Cedar Grove, Wm Hawkins.

Steam corn and saw, Chapel Hill, W R Lloyd.

Steam corn and flour, Chapel Hill, Thos F Lloyd.

Steam saw, Hillsboro, J F Thompson.

PHYSICIANS.

Names and Post Offices.

Jones, C D, Hillsboro.
Jordan, Thomas, Cedar Grove.
Jordan, A C., Caldwell Institute.
Patterson, John, Chapel Hill.
Parris, D C. Hillsboro.
Roberson, A B, Chapel Hill.
Spurgeon, J S (dentist), Hillsboro.
Strudwick, William, Hillsboro.
Wilson, T J, Chapel Hill.
Whitehead, Prof, Chapel Hill.

SCHOOLS.

Names, Post Offices and Principals

Academy, Cedar Grove.
Academy, Hillsboro, Mrs Carrie Jones (col).
Academy, Chapel Hill, H C Andrews.
Caldwell Institute, Caldwell Institute, J N McCracken.
Female School, Oaks.
Female Institute, Hillsboro, Misses Kollock.
Mission School Congregational (col).
Orange Presbytery, Mebane, Herbert Bingham.
Orange Academy, Hillsboro.
Primary School, Hillsboro.
Primary School, Hillsboro, Miss Alice Heartt and Mrs Mary Bragg.

ORANGE COUNTY.

University of North Carolina, situated at Chapel Hill, Orange co, 28 miles northwest from Raleigh and 11 miles from University Station, o n the North Carolina Railroad, and the present terminus of the Chapel Hill Railroad,

Public schools—white, 35; colored, 30.

TEACHERS.

Names and Post Offices.

Andrews, W V, Faucette.
Andrews, John W, Rock Springs.
Andrews, Henry C, Faucette.
Andrews, Ella B, Cedar Grove.
Atwater, John D (col), Lindsay.
Browning, Allan, University Station.
Bacon, Vesta V, Hillsboro.
Berry, A W (col), Hillsboro.
Byers, Leonora C (col), Mebane.
Burwell, W H (col), Hycote.
Berry, M D (col), Hillsboro.
Bowling, E S, Rougemont.
Canaday, J P, Chapel Hill.
Cates, Walter L, Rock Spring.
Claylor, C L, Caldwell Institute.
Crawford, L A. Teer's.
Claytor, C E, Caldwell Institute.
Cuningham, K C, Roxboro.
Cole, J A, Chapel Hill.
Foust, M E, Hillsboro.
Gray, Vitura L, Efland.
Hughes, S F, Mebane.
Haughawant, A H, Hillsboro.
Haskins, H L, Mebane.
Hackney, L H, Chapel Hill.
Howard, Martha, Hillsboro.
Holt, James E, Mebane.
Hughes, James L, Mebane.
Hester, C A, Roxboro.
Jones, C E, Chapel Hill.
Johnson, H H, Chapel Hill.
Kenan, Alonzo W, Hillsboro.
Kirkland, Wm E, Blackwood.
Morrow, Emeline, Oaks.
Moore, Aaron W, Gordonton.
Murray, Alice J, Mebane.
Moore, Mary E, Mebane.
Martin, G W, Greensboro.
Parker, D S, Laws.
Pool, O B, Roxboro.
Richmond, L D, Mebane.
Scholz, H, Lindsay.
Scott, L E, Mebane.
Thompson, Lillian, Joppa.
Turner, Annie L, Caldwell Institute.
Thompson, Florabelle, Rock Spring.
Thompson, Ida, Rock Spring.
Tasley, Bessia A, Caldwell Institute.
Terrell, Leonie M, Cedar Grove.
Tate, Wm A, Mebane.
Tucker, T R, Durham.
Whitted, L A (col.), Chapel Hill.

ORANGE COUNTY.

Watson, J W, Chapel Hill.
Wagner, A F, Ai, Person county.
Wood, W H (col), Mebane.
Wood, C M (col), Mebane.
White, B J (col), Durham.
Whitted, A A (col), Hillsboro.

LOCAL CORPORATIONS.

Eagle Lodge, No. 71, A F and A M, Hillsboro, Dr D C Parris, W M.
N C Farmers' Alliance, Richlands, Dr Cyrus Thompson, pres; W S Barnes, sec and treas, Hillsboro; T Ivey, state business agent; Central Office, Hillsboro, N C.
Oaks Lodge, No 255, A F and A M, Oaks; time of meeting, Saturday before the 3rd Sunday at 5 o'clock P M.
University Lodge, No 408, A F & A M.

NEWSPAPERS.

Alliance Weekly, Hillsboro; W S Barnes, editor.
Chapel Hill News; N B Thompson, ed and prop.
Orange County Observer, Hillsboro; (Democratic weekly) Joseph A Harris, ed and prop.
University Magazine, Chapel Hill; monthly; edited by Literary Societies.

FARMERS.

Names and Post Offices

Blackwood — Malcolm Blackwood, Thos J Burroughs, Gilbert Craige, Leroy Craige. James Hicks, T J Hogan, Wm J Kirkland, I J Kirkland, W E Kirkland, Nelson Kirkland, Jno Kirkland, M King, Wm May.
Border—R Hodge, J McAdams, W M and G H McAdams, J W Pickett, Robert K Rice, James A Smith, C T Smith, F A Terrell, W T Tate, R W Tate, B F White, W H Whitted,
Caldwell Institute—D S Allison, H Blalock, R N Hall, sr, R N Hall, jr, H Y Harris Weldon Hall, Wm Hall, Dr A C Jordan, W S Gray, S F Gates, W W Latta, Frank Laws, C R Miller. W R McKee, George McKee, H H McKee, Joe McKee, D J Nichols, W Terry, W D Villines, J T Wilson, C E Wilson, John Wilson, T H Wilson.
Carr—J A Ashley, R Byrd, George Christopher, G D Compstar, W A J Cooper, R Corbett (col), Price Haith (col), W R Hawkins, J A Hesse, Dr J R Hester, H A Murphy, Dr W E Murphy, R J Satterfield, W R Sharp, W A Sharp, J N Warren, M Ward, Charles Yeates.

ORANGE COUNTY.

Chapel Hill—Laban Andrews, H C Andrews, A J Brockwell, D W Burch, John T Burroughs, C C Carroll, Addison Cheek, W J A Cheek, R D Cheek, Jas Craig, G E Donnell, James Fipps, J W Fowler, Samuel Gattis, Oscar Hogan, D R Hogan, J C Hogan, Thos Hogan. Wm Harwood, J R Hutchins, Moses Hutchins, C W Johnson, Cicero Johnson, Baxter King, Thos Loyd, W R Loyd, Thadeus Loyd. Henry Loyd, W A Maddrey. J W McCauley, Cane McFarland. J Y Merritt, Wm H Merritt, Bryant Neville, W D Neville, R D Patterson, Alvis Pendergrass, Thos J Potts, Isaac W Pritchard, J C Roberts, H Q Strain, Thos Strain. R L Stroud, M Stroud, O B Tinney, J D Varner, W Weaver, J F Weaver, Thos Weaver, J T Weaver, W Weaver, J F Weaver, J Whitfield, Eugene Wilson, E A Wilson.
Cedar Grove—W H Anderson, R W Anderson, A C Anderson, W B Allison, A W Clark, F P Clark, A C Compon, W N Dollar, A T Finley, S J Hall, R D Hinton, J H Hughes, J K Hughes, John McCracken, W L McDade, H L McDade, A J McDade, R W Murray, H J Murray, J S Murray, H J Murray, Chas Oakley, Thomas Pittard, James Pittard, W R Stewart, L Vincent (col), Thomas J Walker, David Wells, Green Wright.
Efland—R D Bain, M L Efland, S T Forest. Mrs F J Freeland, D C McAdams, L W McAdams, B F Mebane, Frank Smith.
Gath—Wm Andrews, B Andrews, W F Andrews, A Cates, G P Cheek, Frank Cheek, Thomas M Cheek, G P Cheek, J M Copeland, J W Copeland, W H Copeland, S Durham, A J Durham, S C Durham, D M Durham, M Durham Wm Eubanks,W D Eubanks, W G Eubanks, A Floyd, Wm Lawrence, P O Landale, Wm Lloyd, C W Lloyd, Albert Lloyd, J Q Lloyd, M Lloyd, S C Lloyd, John Maner, James Maner, I J Oldham, G F Pickard, S Ray, J L Ray, Lee Smith, Enoch Sykes, J P Sykes, G W Thompson, A W Ward.
Hillsboro—Stephen Arch (col), J W Bacon, N D Bain, R D Bain, B H Bell, Dr John Berry, Cicero Berry, Lewis A Boggs, Duncan Brown, Wilson Brown, Wm Carroll, Harvey W Clark, T R Cole, J W Cole & Co, I J Carden, sr, W G Craig, W A Craig, W J Dickson, Elmore Faucette, S Forrest, Joseph Freeland, Wm Freeland. Woodson Garrett, A Gordon, J E Hanner. J U Hart, Mrs M Ruffin Hill, John R Hobbs, W H Holden, J T Jones, J V Jones,

ORANGE COUNTY.

L H Kinion, Ben Kinion, S P Kirkpatrick, Joseph Latta, S T Latta, H C McCauley, Jesse Miller, Geo A Miles, J H Norwood, Oconeechee Farm (J S Carr, owner), Wm Overaker, J H Parish, C E Parish, L A Pratt, Thos G Pratt, W M Reeves, J W Riley, W Riley, Evans Riley, J S Scarlett, R H Sharpe, W T Shields, J B Sikes, A A Smith, Sidney Strayhorn, Dr Wm Strudwick, J T Tapp, R L Tapp, E A Terrell, J F Thompson, J W Thompson, E C Thompson, David Thompson, D F Thompson, Guion Waddell, S M Wilkerson.

Laws—A W Breeze, J H Breeze, Jas Laws, jr, Geo W Parke, J Porterfield, Rufus Reed, H H Stewart.

Meredith—J R Berry, J C Turner. J H B Turner.

Oaks—H McDaniel, H M McIver. Frank Miner, M W Moore, Jesse Morrow, T J Oldham, D F Thompson, S S Webb.

Rock Spring—T S Cates, W Cates, A P Cates, N A Cates, Wm Clark, D F Crawford, Z T Snipes, Ed Snipes, W G Stanford, E H Stubbins, H C Thompson.

Toler—Jeff Horner, J R Kinion, R H McKee, D G Ray, Newland Smith, G W Smith.

University—B H Bell. W A Browning, W G Crabtree, J W Crabtree, J J Crabtree, E Crabtree, J T Hogan, Irvin Hogan, W L Latta, G W Lockhart, A Lynch, John McCauley, J L Neal, Fred Patterson (col), Geo Pratt (col), M Shields, W T Simpson, Robt Strayhorn, W G Strayhorn, W M Stroud.

PAMLICO COUNTY.

AREA, 360 SQUARE MILES.

POPULATION, 7,146; White 4,767, Colored 2,379.

PAMLICO COUNTY was formed in 1872 from Beaufort and Craven counties, and bears the name of the sound on its eastern and southern borders.

BAYBORO, the county-seat, is 140 miles from Raleigh, located on the Bay river, and takes its name from that stream. Population 500.

Surface—This county is low and level. It is traversed by Bay river. On both sides of the river there is much swamp land that produces heavy crops when well drained. The advantages of water transportation are fine. It is sufficient to say that this county makes the well-known "Bay River" section.

Staples—Cotton, rice, sweet and Irish potatoes and corn are the great staples. Fish is an item of very considerable profit. Newbern, one of the finest fish markets in the State, is soon reached, by land or by water, from any part of this county.

Fruits—Apples, grapes, melons and the small fruits.

Timbers—Pine, poplar, ash, gum, oak, holly and beech. Large quantities of pine timber are produced and shipped to the Northern markets.

TOWNS AND POST OFFICES.

	POP.		POP.
Alliance,	50	Maribel,	25
Arapahoe,	50	Merritt,	—
Baird's Creek,	25	Mesic,	25
Bayboro (c h),	500	Olympia,	25
Florence,	15	Oriental,	150
Grantsborough,		Pamlico,	75
	100	Reelsboro,	50
Hobucken,	25	S onewall,	250
Kershaw,	50	Vandemere,	150
Lowland,	25		

COUNTY OFFICERS.

Clerk Superior Court—Festus Miller,
Commissioners—Chas Fowler, chm'n; J F Harris, Samuel Campen, H A Reel, Jas Potter.
Coroner— ——
Register of Deeds—Alex Lee,
Sheriff—W J Parker.
Solicitor First District—W J Leary.
Surveyor—P T Tingle.
Standard Keeper— ——
Treasurer—J A Cooper.
County Examiner—T A Mozingo.

COURTS.

Eleventh Monday after first Monday in March, and eleventh Monday after first Monday in September.

TOWNSHIPS AND MAGISTRATES.

No 1—Geo Dees, D W Brinson, J B Sawyer, J P Tingle, J E Stapleford, J J Brinson, N H Banks, J S Caton, J F Paul (Bayboro).

No 2—W H Lewis, C R Cleese, Chas Harper, R L Woodard, W H Lewis, C R McCleese, Wiley Wharton, Wm Richardson, J Dean, J E Carson (Bayboro).

No 3—J W Miller, H W Cowell, W T Mayo, J W Miller, H W Cowell, W D Alfred, A Whealton, C A Flowers, J R Rice, Henry Mayo, Henry S Carraway (Bayboro).

No 4—J C Alcock, E B Credle, W J Mayo, J E Alcock, J C Alcock, R L Hopkins, H C Betts, W A Caraway, J S Leary (Bavboro).

No 5—Geo W Brinson, Isaac Lewis, A S Aldridge, Lovick Harris, G W Brinson, Isaac Lewis, P JDelamar, J B Martin, E L McCleese, A J Midgett (Bayboro).

Bayboro—W E Hooker.
Stonewall—T A Mozingo.

CHURCHES.

Names, Post Offices, Pastors and Denom.

METHODIST.

Barnes'Chapel—Vandemere,C P Snow.
Broad Creek—Olympia, C P Snow.
Church—Goose Creek, W A Keys (col).
Church—Bayboro, C P Snow.
Good Hope—Grantsboro, C P Snow.
Mt Hermon—Stonewall, C P Snow.
Pamlico—Pamlico, C P Snow.
Smith's Creek—Oriental, C P Snow.
Smith's Creek—Goose Creek, W A Keys (col).
Smith's Creek—Kershaw, C P Snow.
Stonewall—Stonewall, C P Snow.

FREE-WILL BAPTIST.

Bethany—Baird's Creek.
Goose Creek—Grantsboro.
Milton—Bayboro, B B Albritton.
Mt Pleasant—Pamlico, W Lewis.
Mt Zion—Vandemere, W Lewis.
New Bethlehem—Stonewall, B P Stilly.

PAMLICO COUNTY.

Pilgrim's Rest—Grantsboro, J Bennett.
Rock Zion———, B F Stilly.
Star of Bethlehem—Grantsboro, J Bennett.
St Paul Chapel—J S Cummins.
Warden's Grove—John W Leary.

BAPTIST.

Chapel Creek (col)—Bayboro, H Hooker.
Church—Bayboro, W F Frey.
Jerusalem (col)—Vademere, S Foscue.
Maja's Chapel (col)—Vandemere, A F Bryan.
Mt Maria (col)—Grantsboro, J C Blackman.
St Delight (col)—T Long.
Mt Sinai (col)—Stonewall, F Long.

PRIMITIVE BAPTIST.

Grantsboro—John T Roe.

DISCIPLES OF CHRIST.

Baird's Creek—Arapahoe, Henry Winfield.
Bay Creek—Mesic, Henry Winfield.
Bethany—Arapahoe, Henry Winfield.
Broad Creek—Olympia, Henry Winfield.
Church—Grantsboro, Henry Winfield.
Concord—Florence, Henry Winfield.
Dawson Creek—Arapahoe, Henry Winfield.
Star Bethlehem—Stonewall.

EPISCOPAL.

Church—Stonewall.

MINISTERS RESIDENT.

Names, Post Offices and Denominations.

BAPTIST.

Blackman, J B (col), Grantsboro.
Bryan, A F (col), Vandemere.
Fry, W F, Vandemere.
Long, L (col), Stoneville.

FREE-WILL BAPTIST.

Bennett, J, Reelsboro.
Miller, D P, Grantsboro.

METHODIST.

Holt, Moses (col), Baird's Creek.
Keys, W A (col), Goose Creek.
Snow, C P, Bayboro.

DISCIPLES OF CHRIST.

Holton, J W P, Reelsboro.
Holton, Jessie, Reelsboro.
Holton, A J, Olympia.

MANUFACTORIES.

Kinds, Post Offices and Proprietors.

Barrels, Bayboro, W H Sawyer & Co.
Blacksmith, Vandemere, Wm Holton.

PAMLICO COUNTY.

Carriages, Stonewall, Jos Skeyboosky.
Cotton gin, Stonewall, C H Fowler.
Cotton gin, Merritt, J T Davenport.
Cotton gin, Merritt, H J Kennedy.
Cotton-ginning, Baird's Creek, A C Brinson.
Cotton-ginning, Bayboro, Fowler & Cawdle.
Cotton-ginning, Vandemere, J C Muse.
Cotton-ginning, Reelsboro, J B Reel.
Cotton-ginning, Stonewall, C H Fowler & Co.
Lumber, Stonewall, Pamlico Lumber Co.
Lumber, Oriental, Oriental Lumber Co.
Oyster Factory, Vandemere, Stock Co.

MERCHANTS AND TRADESMEN.

Names, Post Offices, Lines of Business.

ALLIANCE.

Campen, A B,	G S
Campen, Samuel,	G S

ARAPAHOE.

Hardison & Bowden,	G S
Paul & Lee,	G S

BAIRD'S CREEK.

Brinson, A C,	G S
Reel, J E,	G S

BAYBORO.

Campen, A B.	G S
Cooper, John T,	G S
Daniels, L G,	Live Stock
Farnell, G T,	G S
Fowler & Cowell,	G S
Lupton, R G,	G S
Sawyer, W H,	G S
Turner, J B,	G S

FLORENCE.

Brabble, J F,	G S
Horton, G H,	G S

GRANTSBORO.

Banks, N H, agt,	G S
Dees, Geo,	G S
Paul, J F (near),	G S

HOBOKEN.

Allcock, F W,	G S
Clark, S J,	G S
Leary, ——,	G S
Watson, ——,	G S

KERSHAW.

Curtis, S S.	G S
Hodges, R D,	G S

LOWLANDS.

Allcock, ——,	G S

MARIBEL.

Fentress, J L,	G S
Rice, J R,	G S

PAMLICO COUNTY.	PAMLICO COUNTY.

MERRITT.

Davenport, John T,	G S
Kenedy, H J,	G S
Paul, E E,	G S
Small, Mrs,	G S

MESIC.

Jones, F B,	G S
Mesic, S R,	G S
Riggs & Mayo,	G S

OLYMPIA.

Wayne, W N,	G S

ORIENTAL.

Carson, Joseph,	—
Haskins, T C,	G S
Midyett & Co,	G S
Oriental Lumber Co,	G S and Lum

PAMLICO.

Paul, C E,	G S
Wharton, R P (near),	G S
Woodward, R L,	G S

REELSBORO.

Delamar, J E,	G S
Reel, John B,	G S and Mill
Reel, H A,	G S

STONEWALL.

Atmore, Dr G S,	Drugs
Baxter, Mrs V J,	G S
Ferebee, S W,	G S
Eowler, C H,	G S

TRENT CREEK.

Small, Mrs H,	G S

VANDEMERE.

Abbott, D H,	G S
Holton, U C,	C S
McCotter, S F & Bro,	G S
Muse, John W,	G S
Muse, J C & Co,	G S

MILLS.

Kinds, Post Offices and Proprietors.

Corn, flour and saw (steam), Baird's Creek, Alex C Brinson & Co.

Grist (water), Goose Creek, J E Delamar.

Saw (steam), Stonewall, Pamlico Lumber Co.

Steam saw, Arapahoe, Vendrick & Co.

Steam saw, Arapahoe, Hardison & Bowden.

Steam saw, Pamlico, Woodward & Son.

Steam saw, Kershaw, R D Hodges.

Steam saw, Oriental, Midyett & Delamar.

Steam saw (Pamlico Lumber Co) S W Ferebee, manager, Stonewall.

Steam saw, Bayboro, W H Sawyer.

Steam saw, Reelsboro, J B Reel.

Steam saw, grist gin, Alliance, Sam Campen.

Steam saw, Bayboro, A B Campen.

Steam saw, Oriental, Oriental Lumber Company.

PHYSICIANS.

Names and Post Offices.

Atmore, G S, Stonewall.
Jones, T F, Bayboro.
Lindsay, W A, Pamlico.
Redding, J P, Merritt.

SCHOOLS.

Names, Post Offices. and Principals.

Academy, Vandemere, Rev W F Fry.
High School, Bayboro, W W Cole.
 Public schools: white 19; colored 11.

TEACHERS.

Names and Post Offices.

Baxter, Amanda, Stonewall.
Brinson, Gracie, Grantsboro.
Brinson, Walter, Grantsboro.
Campen. Bethany, Bayboro.
Cary, John W, Florence.
Cary, Florence. Florence.
Cowell. Minnie, Alliance.
Dees, Daniel, Grantsboro.
Dees, Kitty D, Grantsboro.
Dees, Lucy E. Grantsboro.
Dixon, Nancy, Reelsboro.
Eaton, G A, Grantsboro.
Flowers, Nannie J. Vandemere.
Hardison, John. Alliance.
Heel, Zilpha, Grantsboro.
Holton, Rholanda. Olympia.
Ireland, George, Stonewall.
Ireland, Mollie, Stonewall.
Jones, Louis J, Merritt.
Keel. Charles, Grantsboro.
Lee, Isadora, Arapahoe.
Lewis, C W, Grantsboro.
Morris, Jos. Mesic.
Morris, Coolage. Vandemere.
Parker, Gertie, Lowland.
Paul, L Jennie, Grantsboro.
Paul, Smith, Grantsboro
Paul, Hughes, Grantsboro.
Rice, Amanda, Marabel.
Ross, E C. Arapahoe.
Sawyer, De Ella, Grantsboro.
Sawyer, Ella L, Bayboro.
Smithwick, J B, Grantsboro.
Spain, E W, Hobucken.
Tingle, J P, Grantsboro.
Wayne, Ida L, Olympia.

PAMLICO COUNTY.

LOCAL CORPORATIONS.

Bayboro Lodge, No 331, A F and A M, Bayboro; time of meeting, fourth Saturday at 10 o'clock A M.

Mt Vernon Lodge, No 359, A F and A M, Stonewall; time of meeting, second Thursday at 2 o'clock P M.

FARMERS.

Names and Post Offices.

Arapahoe—Leroy Dixon, R B Hardison, R W Hardison, Thos Land.

Baird's Creek—Berry Bennett, B F Brinson, G C Brinson, A C Brinson, Mitchel Paul, R W Fingle, E J Fingle, Joe Willis.

Bayboro—W D Alford, William Alford, Andrew Armstrong, H W Armstrong, Chas Bobbitt, Sam Campen, Frank Casey, Amos Cowell, A J Flowers, Cason Gibbs, Benjamin McCotter, Festus Miller, C W Miller. John C Muse, William Potter, W S Riggs, J L Riggs, J F Sawyer, S Sawyer, Quincey Sawyer, Wm Sawyer, John T Shipp, J W Stilley, Charles Swann, Burney Fingle.

Florence—James Broadwaters, J M Carey, Stephen Carey, Utley Carey, A J Leary, J P Redding, William Richardson. W H Sawyer.

Goose Creek Island—Joseph Alcock, W L Barnett, Marcus Carawan, Benjamin Carawan, Allen Daniels, R L Ireland, R B Lewis, T R Lupon, W J Mayo, M Potter, L J Potter, Graham Potter, Benjamin Potter, James Potter, Bryan Rice, F A Spain, B A Sadler, Bryan Wilkerson.

PAMLICO COUNTY.

Grantsboro—R E Barrington, H H Barrow, Jesse Boyd, D H Brinson, W C Brinson, Samuel Brinson, Elijah Casey, Hiram Cuthrell, George Dees, Samuel Delamar, John D Dixon, Geo Dixon, J B Ensley, Geo Lewis, Robert Lee, John Lindsey, D P Miller, J S Miller, Lewis Nelson, John B Reed, J B Sawyer, jr, Josiah Tingle.

Kershaw—M N Hooker, P C Delamar.

Lowland—Joseph Leary.

Maribel—A B Armstrong, Joshua Flowers, J W Furlaw, Leroy Harper, Jas T Lincoln, J M Weskut.

Merritt—Wm Bright, Geo Bright, F M Davenport, P J Daniels, Robert Jones, W H Powers, J R Sawyer, T J Sawyer, Mrs E P Small, Daniel Spruill, Jas Spruill, Edmond Tingle.

Mesic—Jno Mayo, W T Mayo, Jesse Riggs, J D Riggs, Ben Squires, James Whealton, Freeman Wise.

Olympia—A J Holton.

Oriental—A S Aldridge, Aquilla Aldridge, M N Hooker, John Mann, L B Midyett, R P Midyett, B J Johnson, E L McClure.

Pamlico—C M Caroon, Geo Caroon, Scott Caroon, J T Gooding, J W Paul, R P Wharton, B M Wise, Paul Woodward.

Stonewall—J O Baxter, Israel Boomer (col), Miller Caroon, jr, R M Daniels, S W Ferrelee, C H Fowler, J H Gaskins, Thos Gray, Stephen Harris, Haywood Lewis, W H Lewis, J C Ormond.

Vandemere—D H Abbott, Morris Alexander, Andrew Barnes, Abram Barnes, F P Caraway, W B Eastwood, C A Flowers, R Flowers, Jno R McCotter, Joseph Morris, John Morris.

PASQUOTANK COUNTY.

AREA, 240 SQUARE MILES.
POPULATION, 10,748: White 5,201, Colored 5,547.

PASQUOTANK COUNTY was formed in 1729 from one of the original precincts of Albemarle. It derives its name from the tribe of Indians who once owned the soil.

ELIZABETH CITY, the county-seat, is 215 miles northeast from Raleigh, and is located on the Pasquotank river and on the N. S. R. R. Population (estimated), 6,000.

Surface—Low, level, portions of it swampy, but a part in a high state of cultivation. Very rich and very productive. The county lies on the west bank of the Pasquotank river, and has very fine advantages for navigation. A daily line of steamers runs from the county-seat to Norfolk, and steam transportation lines from Norfolk to all points on the Pamlico and Albemarle sounds, and on the Chowan, Roanoke and Neuse rivers and other streams tributary to these sounds, touch at Elizabeth City. Besides the canal commerce, there is considerable coasting trade, while the railroad does an immense business. A hospitable population.

Staples—Cotton, corn, sweet potatoes, wheat, oats, rice and general trucking, shingles, lumber and fish.

Fruits — Apples, pears, peaches, grapes and the small fruits.

Timbers—Pine, oak, cypress, poplar, juniper, ash and gum.

TOWNS AND POST OFFICES.

	POP.		POP.
Elizabeth City,	6,000	Mumford,	30
		Nixonton,	100
Elisha,	50	Okisko,	35
Fauna,	25	Rosedale,	175
Kebukie,	50	Weekville,	100

COUNTY OFFICERS.

Clerk Superior Court—J P Overman.
Commissioners—G M Scott, chm'n; Fred Whitehurst, Frank Weeks, Jos E Harrell, Charles L Weeks.
Coroner—John Cartwright.
Register of Deeds—M B Culpepper.
Sheriff—T P Wilcox.
Solicitor First District—W J Leary.
Standard Keeper—W D Williams.
Surveyor—W F Pritchard.
Treasurer—John S Morris.
County Examiner—Gaston Pool.

UNITED STATES OFFICERS.

Clerk U. S. District Court—W C Brooks, Elizabeth City.
U. S. Commissioner—M B Culpepper, Elizabeth City.
Deputy Marshal U. S. District Court—W D Williams, Elizabeth City.

COURTS.

Superior Court — Second Monday before first Monday in March, and second Monday after first Monday in September.

U. S. Court—Seventh Monday after the first Monday in March; sixth Monday after the first Monday in September.

TOWN OFFICERS.

ELIZABETH CITY—*Mayor*, C C Pool. *Commissioners*, Palemon John, T A Commander, A B Seeley, B F Spence and W W Griggs. *Clerk*, Charles A Banks. *Treasurer*, Geo W Cobb. *Constable and Chief of Police*, William C Brooks. *Street Commissioner*, Reuben W Berry. *Fire Commissioners*, Allen Kramer and Fred H Ziegler. *Collector of Customs*, Jas C Brooks. *Postmaster*, E F Lamb. *Examining Surgeons of Pensions*, Drs. J E Wood, W W Griggs and W J Lumsden. Meet on the first and third Wednesdays of each month at the corner of Road and Church sts.

TOWNSHIPS AND MAGISTRATES.

Elizabeth City—H T Greenleaf, M B Culpepper, W G Underwood, J B Flora, C E Kramer, A B Keeley, Chas A Banks, Peter S Shipp, John Cartwright, M N Sawyer, M Sedgwick (Elizabeth City)

Mt Hermon—H C Wood, Elias Reed, J Walter Perry, W F Pritchard, Joseph A Wood, Joseph H Jackson, Joe E Harrell, John C Overman (Elizabeth City).

Newland—W J Williams, W S Temple, N A Jones, Wm G Temple, Alpheus Stafford, E J Spence, Wm J Spence, J J Richardson (Elizabeth City).

Nixonton—Alex Armstrong, Joseph H Dozier, J W Stokeley, Geo Waters,

PASQUOTANK COUNTY.

J E Lane, Geo D Pool, J D Price, E D Owens (Nixonton).

Providence—Simeon Pritchard, S N Morgan, R N Morgan, Wm F Pritchard, S Sawyer, Wm H Harris, L Jackson, John C Perry (Elizabeth City).

Salem—F M Newby, S P Wilson, Charles Snowden, F M Godfrey, J P Eaves, John T Davis, Edward Markham, W T Coppersmith (Elizabeth City).

CHURCHES.

Names, Post Offices and Denominations.

BAPTIST.

Berea—Elizabeth City, Josiah Ellisa.
Church (col)—Rosedale, John Dunn.
Church (col)—Rosedale I B Roach.
Church (col)—Elizabeth City, J K Faulk.
Church—Elizabeth City, C S Backwell.
Corinth—Elizabeth City, J B Ferebee.
Olivet—Elizabeth City, J B Ferebee.
Ramoth Gilead—Rosedale, T G Wood.
Salem—Weeksville, C S Blackwell.

PRIMITIVE BAPTIST.

Ridgefield—Kehukee.

METHODIST.

Church—Weeksville, J A Castel.
Church—Elizabeth City, John H Hall.
Hall's Creek—Nixonton, J A Castell.
Mt Hermon—Okisko, J A Castell.
Union—Elisha, J A Castell.

PRESBYTERIAN.

First Presbyterian—Elizabeth City, F H Johnson, D D.

EPISCOPAL.

Church—Elizabeth City, L L Williams.
Church—Weeksville, L L Williams.

A. M. E. ZION.

Church—Weeksville, A L Newby.
Church—Elizabeth City, H B Pettigrew.
Holly Grove—Elizabeth City, A L Newby.
Jerusalem—Rosedale, A L Newby.
Mt Zion—Elizabeth City, A L Newby.
Newland—Rosedale, A L Newby.
Pitt's Chapel — Elizabeth City, A L Newby.
Salem—Weeksville, A L Newby.

MINISTERS RESIDENT.

Names, Post Offices and Denom.

BAPTIST.

Berry, Z H (col), Elizabeth City.
Blackwell, C S, Elizabeth City.
Coleman, J C, Elizabeth City.
Faulk, J A, Elizabeth City.
Ferebee, J R, Elizabeth City.

PASQUOTANK COUNTY.

PRIMITIVE BAPTIST.

Meads, Chas, Kehukee.

METHODIST.

John, R B, Elizabeth City.
Hall, J H, Elizabeth City.
Hocutt, W E, Elizabeth City.
Sawyer, E F, Elizabeth City.

PRESBYTERIAN.

Johnston, F H, Elizabeth City.

EPISCOPAL.

Williams, L L, Elizabeth City.

A. M. E. ZION.

Newby, A L, Elizabeth City.
Pettigrew, H B (col), Elizabeth City.

HOTELS AND BOARDING HOUSES.

Names, Post Offices and Proprietors.

Boarding, Elizabeth City, Mrs Mollie Fearing.
Boarding, Elizabeth City, Mrs S Bell.
Boarding, Elizabeth City, J T Dalton.
Boarding, Elizabeth City, S T Williams.
Boarding, Elizabeth City, Mrs C A Smith
Boarding, Elizabeth City, Mrs H M Fearing.
Boarding, Elizabeth City, Mrs M Holmes.
Boarding, Okinco, M G Gregory.
New Albemarle House, Elizabeth City, Mrs M J Sawyer.
Pendleton Hotel, Elizabeth City, Dr A L Pendleton.
Swain's Hotel, Elizabeth City, G W Swain.

LAWYERS.

Names and Post Offices.

Albertson, J W, sr, Elizabeth City.
Albertson, J W. jr, Elizateth City.
Aydlett, E F, Elizabeth City.
Brooks, J C, Elizath City.
Creecy, R B, Elizabeth City.
Griffin, W J, Elizabeth City.
Godfrey, F M, Weeksville.
Lamb, E F, Elizabeth City.
Pool, Charles C, Elizabeth City.
Sawyer, J H, Elizabeth City.
Vaughn, Frank. Elizabeth City.
Ward, G W, Elizabeth City.

MANUFACTORIES.

Kinds, Post Offices and Proprietors.

Brick-making, Elizabeth City, F G Thompson.
Building and contracting, Okisko, H C Perry.

PASQUOTANK COUNTY.

Building and contracting, Elizabeth City, P S Ship.

Building and contracting, Elizabeth City, D S Kramer.

Cabinet-making, Elizabeth City, Ford Zeigler.

Cabinet-making, Elizabeth City, R Madrin.

Carriages and wagons, Elizabeth City, J F Sanders.

Cotton-ginning. Weeksville, G W Small.

Cotton-ginning, Elizabeth City, C C Allen.

Elizabeth City Cotton Mill, Elizabeth City, O McMullen, pres; I M Scott. vice-pres; D B Bradford, sec and treas; H F Smith, supt; capital stock, $80,000.

Elizabeth City's Net and Twine Factory, Elizabeth City; capital $18,000; number spindles, —; daily capacity 300 pounds; daily consumption 350; number hands, 25; I M Scott. pres; S S Fowler, sec-treas; F S Brown, mgr.

Ice factory, Elizabeth City, W E Dunstan, mgr.

Iron work, Elizabeth City, David Davis.

Iron and wood work, Elizabeth City, W K Carter.

Iron and wood work, Elizabeth City, Isaiah Cartwright.

Iron and wood work, Nixonton, John Linton.

Iron and wood work, Elizabeth City, Wm Morgan.

Iron work, Elizabeth City, W H Morris.

Iron and wood work, Elizabeth City, W F Cobb (col.).

Iron and wood work, Elizabeth City, Abram Jones (col.).

Machine shops and carriages, Elizabeth City, J F Sanders.

Mattress factory, Elizabeth City, P W Mellick.

Mattresses, Elizabeth City, C W Owen.

Mattresses, Elizabeth City, N R Parker.

N C Iron Foundry, Elizabeth City, N C Iron Works.

Planing mill, Elizabeth City, Kramer Bros & Co.

Sash, doors and blinds, Elizabeth City, Kramer Bros & Co.

Seines and nets, Elizabeth City, S S Fowler.

Shingles, Elizabeth City, W D Lathrop

Shingles, Elizabeth City, J Welkins.

Ship building, Elizabeth City, E S Wiley.

Ship-building, Elizabeth City, James F Snell.

Steam press brick, Elizabeth City, Elizabeth City Brick Works.

PASQUOTANK COUNTY.

Tin and sheet iron ware, Elizabeth City, H O Hill.

MERCHANTS AND TRADESMEN.

Names, Post Offices and Line of Business.

ELISHA.

Lister, C L.	G S

ELIZABETH CITY.

Applebaum, J H,	D G
Allen, T C,	Confec
Askew, R H,	Confec
Burgess, M R.	Confec
Benbury, L B,	Gro
Brothers, G W,	D G
Cartwright, J B,	D G and Gro
Daniels, Aaron,	Confec
Davis, J B.	G S
Davis, Fred	Coal
Davis, M U & Co,	Gro
Elinghaus Bros & Co,	Gro
Elliott, Henderson,	Gro
Etheridge & Etheridge,	Drugs
Flora, J B,	Gro
Fowler & Co,	D G
Garrett, Newell,	Gro
Garrett, W W.	Gro
Griggs, Dr W W & Son,	Drugs
Glover, W C,	Com
Graves, Mrs G,	Millinery
Godfry, H C,	Gro
Gray, James,	Gro
Grundy, N G,	Com
Harbor, Fred,	Confec
Harris, A J,	Gro
Hathaway Bros,	Jewelry
Heath, H W,	Gro
Hollowell, J A,	Gro
Hughes & Pritchard,	Gro
Jennings, G M & Co,	Gro
Jenkins. Mrs T M,	Gro and Confec
Jones & Roper,	D G
Jordan, W T,	
Jordan, T J,	—
Koch, Rich,	Bakery
Lane, B C,	Gro
Lavenstein & Son,	D G
Lawrence, Jas. & Son,	Gro
Lyon, W H,	Gro
Massel, H,	D G
Mathews, J A,	Gro
McCabe & Grice,	D G
McMullen, Dr Oscar,	Drugs
McMorne, Warren,	Con
Midbick, P W,	Books
Mitchell, R J,	D G
Morgan, Mrs V,	Gro and D G
Modlin, Samuel,	Gro
Morrisett, J T,	Tobacco
Neal, Mrs A S,	Millinery
Overman, C W,	Furn
Parker, N R,	Furn
Parsons, S B,	Con
Pinner, J R,	Gro

PASQUOTANK COUNTY.

Pritchard, J L,   Gro
Pruschanskin, F,   D G
Raulfs, C A F,   Tailor
Richardson, Geo,   Con
Robinson & Co,   Gro and D G
Racket Store,   D G
Sawyer, Jeremiah,   Gro
Sawyer, J L, & Co,   H'd'w
Salomonsky, R,   D G
Sartorious, Fred,   Jewelry
Sealy, A B, & Son,   Gro
Selig, Louis,   Jewelry
Shoobor & White,   H'd'w
Simpson, R F,   Gro
Smith, Mrs S E,   Oon
Spevies, Jas.   H'd'w
Stevenson, W H,   Confec
Walker, Mrs J W,   D G
Walker, Nathan,   Gro
Wadsworth, Alex,   Drugs
Waters, S, & Son,   Soda Bottlers
Weatherly & Friddy,   Confec
Weisel, Mrs R,   D G
Weisel, Mo-es,   D G
Wescott, M,   Tailor
White, R B,   Gro
Whitehurst, Nelson,   Confec
Wilson, Jos,   Gro
Williams & Gordon,   D G
Winder, L L, & Co,   Gro
Woodley, W J,   Gro
Wood, Dr J E,   Drugs
Wright, M G,   Gro

FAUNA.

Hinton, C L,   G S

MUMFORD.

Brothers, J S,   G S
Stafford, N T,   G S

NIXONTON.

Britt, Daniel,   G S

OKISKO.

Perry, D,   G S

ROSEDALE.

Etheridge. W K,   G S
Jackson, B C,   G S
Lynch, C S,   G S

WEEKVILLE.

Pendleton, N D,   G S
Perry, D C,   G S
Potter, Aug,   G S
Price, J W,   G S
Markham, H C,   G S
Raper. C,   G S
Small, J W,   G S
Weeks, C L,   G S

MILLS.

Kinds, Post Offices and Proprietors.

Corn (steam), Elizabeth City, Wm Paillin.
Corn and saw (steam), Weekville, Jno R Sawyer.

Corn and saw, Rosedale, Dr W S Temple.
Flour, corn and saw (steam), Elizabeth City, W W Griffin.
Steam saw, Elizabeth City (two mills), Elizabeth City Mill Co.
Steam saw, Elizabeth Oity, Elizabeth City Lumber Co.
Steam grist, Elizabeth City, Raper & White.
Steam saw, Elizabeth City, Jones Mfg Co.
Steam planing, Elizabeth City, Blade Lumber Co.
Steam planing, Elizabeth City, T A Commander & Sons.
Steam planing, Elizabeth City, Toadwine Lumber Co.
Steam grist, Elizabeth City, W T Wilhams.
Steam gin, Elizabeth City, M G Gregory.
Steam gin, Elizabeth City, C C Allen.
Steam saw and planing, Elizabeth City, Kramer Bros & Co.
Steam saw, Nixonton, F Davis.

PHYSICIANS.

Names and Post Offices.

Griggs, W W, Elizabeth City.
Griggs, J B, Elizabeth City.
Lowry, F, Weeksville.
Lumsden, W J, Elizabeth City.
McMullan, O G B, Elizabeth City.
Swindell, R B (dentist), Elizabeth City.
Temple, W S Rosedale.
White, H (dentist), Elizabeth City.
Wood, J E. Elizabeth City.

SCHOOLS.

Names, Post Offices and Principals.

Academy, Rosedale, Wm Lowe.
Academy, Weeksville, R B Creecy, Jr.
Atlantic Collegiate Institute, Elizabeth City, L S Sheep, prin; Prof Little, Mrs E G Thompson, Miss S E Martin, assistants.
City Public School, Elizabeth City, J R Fleming, prin; three assistants.
Classical and Mathematical, Nixonton, Miss Cox.
Music School, Elizabeth City, Mrs J W Albertson.
Primary, Elizabeth City, Mrs Alonzo Bell.
Primary, Elizabeth City, Mrs C C Pool.
Public school, Elizabeth City, W M Hinton.
Rosedale School, Miss Mary S Sawyer.
State Normal School, Elizabeth City, P W Moore, prin; J W Brown, Miss C N Kearny, J E Felton, assistants.
Public school—white, 18; colored, 16.

PASQUOTANK COUNTY.

TEACHERS.

Names and Post Offices.

WHITE.

Albertson, Miss Kate S, Elizabeth City.
Baker, Jas B, Elizabeth City.
Banks, Miss Mattie S, Elizabeth City.
Barclift, Miss Mamie A, Elizabeth City.
Bell, Miss Annie C, Elizabeth City.
Creecy, R B, jr, Kahukee.
Cox, Miss Sallie, Weeksville.
Davis, R N, Elizabeth City.
Eason, Miss Sallie E, Elizabeth City.
Evans, Miss Maggie L Elizabeth City.
Greaves, Miss Minnie, Elizabeth City.
Hinton, Wm M, Elizabeth City.
Hinton, Miss Berta, Elizabeth City.
Hood, Miss Lelia, Elizabeth City.
Jennings, W H, Elizabeth City.
Jordan, Geo T, Elizabeth City.
Newbould, J T. Okisko.
Parsons, Miss Mary, Weeksville.
Randolph, W G, Elizabeth City.
Sawyer, Miss Mary L, Elizabeth City.
Spence, Miss J Annie, Elizabeth City.
Stanton, Miss Susan, Weeksville.
Whitehead, J A, Elizabeth City.
Whitehurst, Fred, Elizabeth City.
Whitehurst, L m, Elizabeth City.
Wood, Miss Sophie N, Elizabeth City.
Wood, Miss M Alice, Elizabeth City.
Woodward, Miss Ellen, Elizabeth City.

COLORED.

Barrington, John, Elizabeth City.
Brockwell, Miss M E, Elizabeth City.
Brown, Mrs L A O'Kelly, Elizabeth City.
Cooper, E C, Elizabeth City.
Fleming, R F, Elizabeth City.
Fleming, Miss Annie G, Elizabeth City.
Griffin, Jas E, Elizabeth City.
Hollowell, Miss Isabella, Elizabeth City.
Hollowell, J C, Elizabeth City.
Holly, Miss Mary C, Elizabeth City.
Johnson, Miss Ada J, Elizabeth City.
Newby, Miss Fannie O, Elizabeth City.
Newby, Miss Mattie A, Elizabeth City.
Newby, Martin L, Elizabeth City.
Price, Miss Catharine, Elizabeth City.
Riddick, Mrs Susan F, Elizabeth City.
Riddick, Miss Lillian L E, Elizabeth City.
Spellman, Miles D, Elizabety City.
Skinner, Mrs Lizzie V, Elizabeth City.
Turner, Rooks, Elizabeth City.
White, Mrs Courtney A, Elizabeth City.
White, Z W, Elizabeth City.

LOCAL CORPORATIONS.

Albemarle Park Fair, Elizabeth City, W M Baxter, pres.
Albemarle Historical Society, Eliza-

PASQUOTANK COUNTY.

beth City, ——, pres; ——, first vice-pres; H A Gilliam, second vice-pres; J W Allerston, third vice-pres; R B Creecy, sec and treas.
Albemarle Fire Company, F H Ziegler.
Anchoree Lodge. No 14, I O O F, Elizabeth City, E F Sawyer, N G; day of meeting. Thursday.
Business Mens Club, Elizabeth City, Dr W W Griggs, M R Griffin, sec and treas.
Elizabeth City and Norfolk Telegraph Co, Geo W Cobb, sec and treas.
Eureka Lodge, Mo 317, A F and A M, Elizabeth City; time of meeting, first and third Tuesday evenings, and June 24th and December 27th.
First National Bank, Elizabeth City, Charles H Robinson, pres; W T Oldcash; capital stock $50,000; John G Wood, vice-pres.
Knights of Honor, Elizabeth City, Jno H Engle, dictator.
Naval Reserves, Elizabeth City, W J Griffin, lieut.
Private Bank, Elizabeth City, Guirken & Co.
Royal Arcanum, Teler Creek.
Council No 1209, Elizabeth City, T B Wilson, regent; J P Overman, sec.
Saw and planing mills, Elizabeth City, corporation.
The Elizabeth City Electric Light and Power Co, —— Dewey, mgr.
Woodmen of the World, No 11, Elizabeth City, F S Brown, council commander.

NEWSPAPERS.

North Carolinian (Republican), Elizabeth City, Palemon John editor and prop.
Semi-Weekly News, Elizabeth City (Democratic), T B Berry, owner and publisher; L E Chapman, editor.
The Economist, Elizabeth City (Democratic weekly), R B Creecy, editor; E F Lamb, joint prop.

FARMERS.

Names and Post Offices.

Elizabeth City — W W Albertson, Elisha Albertson, Alex Armstrong, A B Armstrong, E F Aydlett, Noah Baker, J E Bailey, W M Baxter, J H Beasley, Wm Blount, Wilson Bray, J A Brite, J R Brite, Simeon Brite, W T Brite, Jos E Brothers, Seth M Brothers, John F Brothers, J Walter Brothers, Wesley Brothers, W H Brothers, W H Buffkin, R E Buffkin, Ambrose Burgess, W K Carter, Ephraim Cart-

PASQUOTANK COUNTY.

wright, J J Cartwright, J M Cartwright, A M Cartwright, W H Cartwright, W T Cartwright, W A Cartwright, J A Cartwright, William Cartwright, Sr, William Cartwright, Jr, Exum Chapel, R H Commander, J C Commander, S W Cooper, W H H Cooper, William Corbett, Leroy Culpepper, Jasper Daily, C W Dance, E V Davenport, Samuel S Davis, John T Davis, Dr Sykes Davis, Joseph W Davis, Chas E Davis, Miles L Davis, David S Davis, J H Dozier, Augustus Eason, B F Emmett, Caleb Etheridge, John B Fearing, Malachi Fletcher, B H Forbes, Taylor Forbes, Jos Frew, Thos Godfrey, Toft Godfrey, Abram Granberry, W A Griffin, W T Halstead, W B Halstead, W H Harrell, J E Harrell, T C Harrell, Seth Harris, Robert Harris, Lemuel Harris, Dorsey Harris, Q T Harris, C T Harris, S Harris, L J Harris, M E Harris, Colley Harris, Elisha Harris, W T Harris, Clifford Harris, W H Harris, Gumbery Harris, S J Harris, Jos G Harris, Rich Harris, Judson A Harris, W C Harrison, Abram Haskett, C W Hollowell, W T Jackson, Lemuel Jackson, W S Jackson, J M Jackson, Jas Jennings, W G Jennings, B F Jennings, Thomas Jennings, Jerry Jennings, W F Jennings, Daniel Jennings, Carter Jennings, W A Jennings, J M Jennings, J N Jennings, J W Johnson, John H Johnson, Newton S Jones, Luther Jones, J S Knowles, John Lamb, E F Lamb, Dr A J Lumsden, Dempsey McMorrison, C H Meads, W G Miller, Seth N Morgan, R Nixon Morgan, Thos C Morgan, Seth Morgan, A G Morgan, A S Morgan, Henry Mullen, R H Murden, T J Murden, W A Only, T L Overman, Dennis Overman, Jahn C Overman, Chas Overman, J T Overton, E D Owens, Wm Pailin, N R Parker, W N Parker, Benoni Parsons, W K Parsons, Benj Pendleton, J D Perry, John C Perry, W G Pool, S D Pool, P G Pool, Geo D Pool, Jordan Pool, Cicero Pool, J M Pool, J H Price, Stephen Price, H M Pritchard, W F Pritchard, Simeon Pritchard, Stephen Pritchard, Peter Pritchard, Philip Pritchard, Richard Pritchard, Thomas W Pritchard, W F Pritchard, Jr, Arthur Pritchard, W P Pritchard, L J Pritchard, Clinton S Pritchard, Richard Pritchard, Jr, C A Pritchard, Miles R Pritchard, Philip G Pritchard, Henry Roper, J Reef, E W Reid, Geo E Riggs, Granville Riggs, C W Rogerson, Miles E Russell, I J Russell, W H Russell, Jas D Russell, R L Sanders, William Satterthwaite, David Savin, Jerry Sawyer, John M Sawyer,

Lowry Sawyer, S S Sawyer, G W Sowyer, J L Sawyer, Sanford Scott, Walter Scott, G W Scott, H W Scott, S W Scott, Rufus Scott, J W Sherlock, W H Sherlock, Jr, E L Sherlock, G D Sherlock, Isham Simpson, David Simpson, W R Speight, Enoch Speight, N Spellman, Jas E Spence, Moses Spence, Geo Spence, J W Stafford, W S Stafford, M C Stanly, W R Stephenson, J R Stokely, W F Stokely, H W Swann, B V Taylor, J A Taylor, Wilson Temple, Leroy E Temple, Timothy Temple, Jno Temple, Jas Thomas, J B Thornton, A V Thornton, I F Toxey, W F Toxey, H F Toxey, Isaac Volira, W H Walton, Sam'l Waters, J B Whedbee, Wallace Whitehurst, James M Whitehurst, Lemuel Whitehurst, B F Whitehurst, Elliott Whitehurst, Miles Whitehurst, Darius White, Paul White, B M White, J T White, A A White, George White, Virgil Williams, J H Wilson, G R Winston, J R Winston, I J Winston, H C Wood, W E Wood, L D Wood,

Elisha—Geo W Alexander, John T Davis, Elisha Lister, J S Lister.

Fauna—R L Hinton.

Kahukee—Jno C James, Thos Meads, Jno S Meads, C C Meads, Chas Meads, Crowder Meads, Jno A Overman, C T Parker, Jordan Parker, J M Parker, Mills Skinner, Chas Snowden, Thos Snowden, Jno T Snowden, J S Wilcox, Jerry Wilcox.

Mumford—J L Hinton, C L Hinton, Jno W Hinton, Jno H Hinton, W T Stafford, J McB Whitney, W N Williams.

Nixonton—Richard Barclift, Dan'l Britt, G W Cartwright, Bessour Cartwright. W B Coppersmith, N Dailey, Henry Freshwater, George Jackson, T W Hollowell, J H Jackson, John J Kenion, Jas E Lane, Jno H Long, Jno Luton, Jno S Morris, W A Price, J W Price, W H Reed, Elias Riddick, J W Sample, J H Sauls, J W Stokely, H C White.

Okisko—Noah Brite, sr, Robt Brite, G Brite, J C Bundy, J E Bundy, Nathan Bundy, W W Dudley, Jno Eason, M G Gregory, W C Gregory, H Grundy, Elisha Harris, jr, Jos H Haskett, Saul Jenkins, W E Jennings, J K Layden, N B Lowe, L D Munden, W H Munden, Jno L Murden, J C Munden, J T Newlott, H H Overton, T S Only, Elisha Only, Jesse M Only, Walter J Perry, F C Perry, Israel Perry, Bragg Perry, H G Randolph, W H Thompson, J H Tuttle, J H Whitehead, W T White, J A Wood.

Rosedale—W J Albertson, J W Albertson, J R Albertson, Chas Albert-

PASQUOTANK COUNTY.

son, R A Baker, W E Ballance, C S Ballance, Dora Ballance, W W Betts, Wilson Boyer, E C Brite, W H Brite, H W Brite, J R Brite, Hollowell Brite, Jack Brite, Miles W Brite, James W Brite, Palmer Brown, W N Brothers, N B Brothers, J E Brothers, J S Brothers, James Brothers, J J Brothers, J W Brothers, M W Buffkins, Jesse Bundy, Thos Burnham, Seth Butts, J G Carver, Samuel Carver, Stephen Carver, D G Daily, W E Daily, E G Davis, Daniel Deal, Elijah Edge, B F E iney, Jno W Edney, R B Edney, W K Etheridge, Geo W Etheridge, J A Evans, C W Evans, B J Forbes, W C Forbes, W T Freeman, Isaac Gallop, Lot Gallop, Alfred Gallop, Josephus Gallop, John Gallop, J W Granger, E B Granger, W J Gregory, Nelson Griffin, Elijah H Griffin, Albert Griffin, Lemuel Griffin, Allen C Griffin, Josiah Griffin, C W Griffin, W W Griffin, Isaac Griffin, H C Harris, J J Harris, G W Harris, Abram Hence, Henry Hewitt, T B Hewitt, Wm Hewitt, D H Hewitt, P A Hinton, J T Hunter, B C Jackson, W J Jones, Samuel Jones, T D Jones, Miles Jones, Lodwick Jones, J S Jones, J F Jones, Willie Jones, Jno R Jones, Josiah Jones, D S Jones, N A Jones, N E Jones, W C Jones, Jas A Key, Jas C Key, Jno Lowe, C S Lynch, Timothy McDonald, B F McDonald, Wm McDonald, Carey Moore, Isaac Moore, A J Moore, W E Moore, Peter Moore, Abner Morgan, R H Morgan, Geo W Morgan, S O Mullen, Chas Mullen, F W Mullen, jr, H E Nixon, J J Richardson, William Richardson, I B Roach, S H Roach, M V Rodes, L R Sawyer, M S Sawyer, J L Shorber, W J N Spence, E J Spence, J F Spence, W J Spence, Geo A Spruill, A N Stafford, M P Stokely, A S Temple, W J Temple, Dr W S Temple, J E Temple, J P Turner, Johnson Warden, Geo C

PASQUOTANK COUNTY.

Warden, James Warren, W J Williams. Isaac Williams, Seth Williams, W P Williams, Jno T Williams, A E Williams, Job W Williams.

Twiddy Mack—Cornelius Lister, Elisha Sanders, Hilliard Sessoms, Stafford Skinner, E G Swain, Geo W Trueblood.

Weeksville—Jesse Agason, Frank Albertson, L T Armstead, Jno L Bailey, John C Banks, John Baleman, David Bell, Richard Berry, Alfred Billups, H C Boyd, J M Brite, Paul Brothers, Geo W Cartright, J B Cartright, Benoni Cartright, Bright Cartwright Hellony Cartright, Wesly Cherry, J T Chary, W T Chary, Joseph Chary, J T Coppersmith, W G Coppersmith, Henry Coppersmith, B F Conell, C A Davis, W L Davis, W H Davis, B W F Davenport, M M Elliott, Henry Evans, W W Eves, J P Eves, Fax Fagan, Geo Fox, W H H Garrett, Geo Glover, F M Godfrey, E W Harrell, R L Jackson, B M Jackson, B T James, A J Jennings, W Q Jennings, S J Jennings, Thos Jennings, J M Jennings, J W Jennings, W F Jennings, E lmond Jennings, Ben C Johnson, Mark Johnson, Daniel Johnson, Wood Keaton, Patrick Keaton, Martin Lamb, Wm Lowry, R C Lowry, W R Luton, Wiley Meads, C Meads, Jno A Meads, H C Meads, R H Meads, Geo A Meads, F M Newby, J E Nichols, John Nichols, James Nichols, G L Overman, Nathan Pailin, W E Palmer, T E Palmer, John L Palmer, T F Parsons, H C Price, Geo H Reed, R D Roper, E l R ughton, Clifton Sawyer, Jno H Sawyer, W T Sawyer, Jas F Scott, C T Scott, W J Scott, W H Shirlock, R C Shirlock, W F Small, J W Snow, W J Symons, Joseph Thomas, C C Tnompson, J F Weeks B F Yates, C L Weeks. Laurena White, M M White, S S Wilson, S P Wilson, Jesse D Wilson, Henry Winston.

PENDER COUNTY.

AREA, 800 SQUARE MILES.

POPULATION 12,514; White 5,967, Colored 6,547.

PENDER COUNTY was formed in 1875 from New Hanover county, and was named in honor of Major General W. D. Pender, of Edgecombe, who was a distinguished officer in the Confederate army.

BURGAW, the county seat, is 112 miles from Raleigh. Population, 600.

Surface—Level, quite rich and very productive.

Staples—Cotton, corn, ground-peas, vegetables and naval stores.

The climate and soil make it very valuable for trucking, vegetables being at least twenty-five days earlier than at Norfolk and at points further north.

Fruits.—Apples, pears, grapes, etc.

Timbers—Pine, oak, hickory, cypress, ash and gum.

TOWNS AND POST OFFICES.

	POP.		POP.
Ashton,	30	Montague,	50
Atkinson,	50	Moore's Creek,	85
Bannerman,	45	Page,	25
Birta,	25	Point Caswell,	165
Burgaw (c h),	600	Rocky Point,	200
Currie,	25	Scott's Hill,	55
Daughton,	30	Sloop Point,	55
Grit,	25	South Washing-	
Harrison Creek,	55	ton,	100
Keith,	30	Topsail Sound,	100
Long Creek,	70	Viola,	50
Maple Hill,	80	Willard,	100

COUNTY OFFICERS.

Clerk Superior Court—W W Larkins.
Commissioners—J T Fay, chm'n.
Register of Deeds—J P Stringfield.
Sheriff—W W Alderman.
Solcitor Sixth District—M C Richardson.
Treasurer—W W Alderman.
County Examiner—T T Bland.

COURTS.

First Monday in March, and first Monday after the first Monday in September.

TOWNSHIPS AND MAGISTRATES.

Burgaw—R W Collins, A E McNeill, J T Collins, M M Moore, G F Jordan, A E Taylor, J W Bowen, R L Playler, G F Walker (Burgaw).

Caintuck—H M Durant, D J Corbett, G W Bonham, L D Bordeaux, W C Keith, J W West, J Q Herring (Burgaw).

Caswell—A L Hubbard, J H Colvin, E A Harves, F P Hunt, J F Simpson, Eli Larkins, J L Colvin, J N Henry, Mathis Malpass (Burgaw).

Columbia—S B Costen, J F Johnson, W G Moore, G A Herring, J L Pigford, Major Eakins, G W McMillar, W T Moore, Hally Jones (Burgaw).

Grady—J H Foyles, J H Brinson, T T Lockey, J J Malpass, W F Bell, J A Harmon (Burgaw).

Holly—J R Bennerman, K F Powers, W J Player, Henry Shaw, L W McKoy, J W Weeks, J W Rowe, Nathan Murray, A B Cowan (Burgaw).

Long Creek—W W Larkins, M I Bordeaux, J Q Bell, J W Keith, J B Scott, G Williams, J H Armstrong, D J Lewis (Long Creek).

Rocky Point—T A McLendon, J E Durham, D S Black, W W Miller, G P Duncan, C D Pearsall, Cato Hill (Rocky Point).

Topsail—J B Davis, L H McClammy, A J Garrison, J W Westbrook, W O Johnson, David Watkins, Alfred Loyd, L W Howard (Burgaw).

Union—Isaiah Carroll, J H Alderman, R W Rivenbark, A B Garriss, N W Powers, J H Newkirk, E M Johnston, J D Cavanaugh (Burgaw).

HOTELS AND BOARDING HOUSES.

Names, Post Offices and Proprietors.

Hotel, Burgaw, Mrs R M Croom.

LAWYERS.

Names and Post Offices.

Bland, John T, Burgaw.
Frayser, R B, Point Caswell.
Howard, L W, Topsail Sound.
McClammy, Herbert, Scottsville.
Ramsey, G A, Burgaw.
Shuford, Geo E, Point Sound.
Williams, Bruce, Burgaw.

MANUFACTORIES.

Kinds, Post Offices and Proprietors.

Turpentine, Atkinson, Hanes & Sellars.

PENDER COUNTY.

MERCHANTS AND TRADESMEN.

Name, Post Office, and Line of Business.

ASHTON.

Holly, J,	G S
Sidbury, S,	G S

ATKINSON.

Hawes & Sellers,	G S

BANNERMAN'S BRIDGE.

Bannerman & Murray,	G S

BURGAW.

Croom, W D,	G S
Hand, W M,	G S
Highsmith, G W,	G S
Johnson, J F, sr,	G S
Jones, Wesley (col),	G S
Moore, Jno F,	G S
Rivenbark, J W,	G S

CHAPEL'S POND.

Howard, A S,	G S

CURRIE.

Harman, J A,	G S
Orr, F B,	G S

HARRISON'S CREEK.

Westbrook, J W,	G S

KEITH.

Keith, W C,	G S
West, Jno W,	G S

LONG CREEK.

Bryant, G H,	G S
Croom, W C & Bro,	G S
Henry, J E,	G S
Larkins, W W,	G S

MAPLE HILL.

James, Gibson,	G S
Powell, D J,	G S

MARSHBURN.

Marshburn, J R,	G S

MONTAGUE.

Bullard, M M,	Gro

MOORE'S CREEK.

Herring, A T,	G S
Moore, W G,	G S
Woodcock, C C,	G S

PENDER COUNTY.

POINT CASWELL.

Hollingsworth, W J, agt,	G S
Hunt, E P & Bro,	G S
Sessoms, T & F,	G S
Sherman, Wm,	G S
Vollers, Ludwig, agt,	G S
Woodcock, Jas H,	G S

ROCKY POINT.

Hocut, W B,	G S
Jones, J C,	G S
Miller, W W,	G S
Sidbury, F P,	G S
Turner, J M,	G S
Westbrook, J H,	G S

SCOTT'S HILL.

Canady, W B,	G S
Foy, F M,	G S
Pearce, E L,	G S
Sidbury, Newton,	G S

SHAKING.

McKay, F,	G S

SOUTH WASHINGTON.

Croom, A B,	G S
Croom, T J (near),	G S
Croom & Pinner,	G S
Rivenbark, R W,	G S

TOPSAIL SOUND.

Pollock, G W,	G S
Sidbury, J W,	G S

VIOLA.

Corbett, D J,	G S
Dew, J A,	G S
Hillburn, A R,	G S
Smith, F A,	G S
Zebelin, J,	G S

WILLARD.

Bowen, W F,	G S
Johnson, J M & Co,	G S
Powers, K I,	G S

MILLS.

Kinds, Post Offices and Proprietors.

Grist Mill, Rocky Point, Berry & Corbett.
Saw, Hamstead, J T Bryant.

PERQUIMANS COUNTY.

AREA, 220 SQUARE MILES.

POPULATION, 9,293; White 4,719, Colored 4,574.

PERQUIMANS COUNTY was the earliest settlement in North Carolina, and derives its name from the tribe of Indians who were once owners of the soil.

HERTFORD, the county seat, is 194 miles northeast from Raleigh, on the Perquimans river. Population, 2,000.

Surface—Low and level, well watered by the Perquimans river and its tributaries—land uniformly rich, and convenient to navigation.

Staples—Cotton, corn, rice, wheat, grapes, lumber, naval stores and fish.

Fruits—Apples, peaches, grapes and a variety of the small fruits.

Timbers—Pine, oak, ash, gum, poplar, hickory, maple, juniper and cypress.

TOWNS AND POST OFFICES.

	POP.		POP.
Beech Spring,	20	Hertford (c h),	
Belvidere,	500		2,000
Burgess,	25	Jacock's,	—
Chapanoke,	200	Nicanor,	100
Durant's Neck,	150	Winfall,	400
Dwight,	—	Woodville,	400
Eva,	150		

COUNTY OFFICERS.

Clerk Superior Court—J Q A Wood.
Commissioners—C W Wood, chm'n; Anderson White, Lee Relph, Josiah Nicholson, Edmond White.
Coroner—Dr R H L Blount.
Register of Deeds—W O White.
Sheriff—A F Riddick.
Solicitor 1st District—W J Leary, sr.
Standard Keeper—W F Stokes.
Surveyor—Thos C Morgan.
Treasurer—J H Parker.
County Examiner—W G Gaither.
County Physician—John W Speight.
Keeper of Co. Hospital—R B Kirby.

COURTS.

Third Monday after the first Monday in March, and third Monday after the first Monday in September.

TOWNSHIPS AND MAGISTRATES.

Belvidere—H B Hudle, T H Nicholson, E G Simpson, John A Lane, Elisha Chappel, Elisha Benton (Belvidere), Jos D Winslow, James F White (Nicanor).

Bethel—T J Long, J Gatling, C F White (Eva), R A Perry, Theo White, W T Jones (Hertford), H H Griffin (Burgess).

Hertford—W W Speight, W R White, G W Barrow, T W Babb, Geo D Newby, Jos F Newby, Jas P Winslow, A J Sutton, Robt White (Hertford).

New Hope—B F Humphries, W F B Sawyer, B F Gregory, W F Trueblood (Durant's Neck), Geo H Wood, E R Whedbee (Woodville).

Parkville—T C Morgan, T J Nixon, A W Jordan, R B Kirby, Jos B Baker, E H Winslow (Winfall), T J McNider (Chapanoke).

CHURCHES.

Names, Post Offices and Denominations.

METHODIST.

Anderson—Hertford, —— Jones.
Bethany—Belvidere, —— Jones.
Cedar Grove—Winfall, —— Jones.
Church—Hertford, J L Ramley.
Concord—Durant's Neck, J L Ramley.
Oak Grove—Chapanoke, —— Jones.
New Hope—Durant's Neck, J L Ramley.

BAPTIST.

Bethel (col)—Eva.
Chapel Hill—Belvidere, Joseph Elliott.
Church—(col), Hertford.
Church—Woodville. Josiah Elliott.
Church—Hertford, Josiah Elliott.
Great Hope—Hertford, Josiah Elliott.
Mt Sinai—Winfall, —— Ferebee.
New Haven—(col), Burgess, Jerry W Ross.
Whiteville Grove — Belvidere, T T Speight, D D.

NEW BAPTIST.

Godwin's Mill—Belvidere, John Smith.
Piney Woods—Belvidere, Harvey Parker.

DISCIPLES OF CHRIST.

Berea—New Hope, J L Burns.
Bethlehem—Eva, J L Burns.

EPISCOPAL.

Church—Winfall, —— Wingate.
Holy Trinity—Hertford, —— Wingate.

FRIENDS.

Piney Woods—Belvidere.

A. M. E. ZION.

Bay Branch—(col), Nicanor.
Church—(col), Hertford.

PERQUIMANS COUNTY.

MINISTERS RESIDENT.

Names, Post Offices and Denom.

BAPTIST.

Babb, Thos W, Hertford.
Burfoot, A W, Hertford.
Elliott, Josiah, Hertford.

METHODIST.

Jones, ——, Winfall.
Ramley, J L, Hertford.

DISCIPLES OF CHRIST.

Burns, J L, Hertford.

NEW BAPTIST.

Smith, John, Beech Spring.

EPISCOPAL.

Wingate, ——, Hertford.

HOTELS AND BOARDING HOUSES.

Names, Post Offices and Proprietors.

Boarding, Woodville, Wm Wilson.
Boarding, Hertford, John Parish.
Boarding, Winfall.
Eagle Hotel, Hertford, Geo D Newby.

LAWYERS.

Names and Post Offices.

Picard, F Hertford.
Skinner, Thos G, Hertford.

MANUFACTORIES.

Kinds, Post Offices and Proprietors.

Blacksmithing and wheelwrighting,
 Woodville, James Gregory.
Blacksmithing and wheelwrighting,
 Winfall, F W Humphlet.
Blacksmithing, Belvidere, Jno A Vann.
Blacksmithing and wheelwrighting,
 Durant's Neck, George & Newby.
Building and contracting, Hertford,
 W F Stokes.
Building and contracting, Belvidere,
 Henry Knight.
Building and contracting, Belvidere,
 A Cartwright.
Building and contracting, Belvidere,
 Thos Knight.
Building and contracting, Belvidere,
 John Knight.
Building and contracting, Belvidere,
 Josiah Smith.
Building and contracting, Belvidere,
 Wm Knight.
Building and contracting, Chapanoke,
 Jos Morgan.
Building and contracting, Chapanoke,
 W Martin.
Building and contracting, Chapanoke,
 Caleb White.

PERQUIMANS COUNTY.

Building and contracting, Chapanoke,
 Andrew White.
Coaches, Hertford, Toms & McMullen.
Coaches, Hertford, W H Ward.
Millwrighting, Winfall, A J Bright.

MERCHANTS AND TRADESMEN.

Name, Post-office and Line of Business.

BEECH SPRING.

White, Thos E (near),	G S

BELVIDERE.

Green, W T (near),	G S
Hendricks, Mary,	G S
Hobbs, J H,	G S
Lane, W H,	G S
Nicholson, Josiah & Son,	G S
Rogerson, R Q,	G S
Smith, R (col),	G S
White, C F,	G S
White, Rufus,	G S
Whitehead, B G,	Undertaker
Winslow, J D,	G S
Winslow, B G,	Undertaker

BURGESS.

Cullipher. J B,	Gro
Griffin, H H,	G S
Howell, James,	G S
Morgan, C W & Co,	G S
Parker, J H,	G S

CENTRE HILL.

Chappell, J P,	G S

CHAPANOKE.

Haskett, Aaron M,	G S
Towe, James, jr,	G S

DURANT'S NECK.

Britt, Mrs S E,	Millinery
Eure, Daniel W,	G S
Goodman, H A,	G S
Gregory, B F,	G S
Mauden, Mrs,	Millinery
Meades, Charles,	G S
Perry, L B & Co,	G S
Webb, J C,	G S

DWIGHT.

Chappell, J,	G S

EVA.

Farmer, M L,	G S
Long, W N & Bro,	G S
Long, Wm N,	G S
Long, Wm C F & Co,	G S
White, J A,	G S
White, C F & Co,	G S

HERTFORD.

Baker, N,	Clothing
Barrow, Geo W,	G S
Blanchard, T C & Bro,	G S
Chappell, R E,	G S
Davis, Samuel,	Baker and Gro
Edwards, W F C,	G S
Faulk, W J (col),	Barber and Cigars

Fleetwood, Jackson,	G S
Goodwin, Jacob (near),	G S
Gregory, J E (near),	Mill
Harrell, R E,	G S
Harvey, Misses E and S E,	Millinery
Hertford Drug Co,	Drugs
Hoffler, T D & Co,	G S
Hoffler, T H (col),	G S
Koonce, Mrs,	Millinery
Madre, Wm,	G S
McMullen, W T,	Fert and Coal
Morgan, C W & Co,	G S
Newby, G H & Co,	G S
Newman, O,	G S
Norman, L W,	Broker
Overton, Alonzo,	Gro
Saunders, J R,	Gro
Shannonhouse, W R,	G S
Skinner, R Q,	Gro and Baker
Skinner, Johnson,	Com
Small, P H,	G S and Lumber
Speight, U W,	G S
Stokes, W F,	Undertaker
Sumner, C F,	Gro and Conf
Thatch, R B,	Mill and Gin
Thack, Job (col),	Tob
Tucker, N W,	G T
White, Mrs L B T,	Millinery

NICANOR.

Parker, J D,	G S
Riddick, B S,	G S
Smith, Robt,	G S
White, J M & Bro,	G S
White, Z,	G S

WINFALL.

Copeland, Martha (col),	G S
Edwards, W F C,	G S
Reed, O A (col),	G S
White, Jos,	G S

WOODVILLE.

Dail, W A,	Blacksmith and gin
Fletcher, M R,	G S
Lowry, W C, jr,	G S
Wilson, W, agt,	G S
Wilson, J C,	G S

YEOPIN.

Olds, J Y & W T,	Lumber

MILLS.

Kinds, Post Offices and Proprietors.

Corn and flour, Beech Spring, Rufus White & Co.
Corn and floor (water), Eva, C F White.
Corn and flour, Winfall, F Vix & Co.
Corn, flour and saw, Belvidere, R White & Co.
Corn, flour and saw, Belvidere, Walter White & Co.
Corn, flour and saw, Woodville, E R Whedhee.
Corn, flour and saw, Durant's Neck, David Newby.

Corn, flour and saw, Chapanoke, Andrew White,
Corn, flour and saw (steam), Winfall, A Winston.
Corn, flour and saw, Eva, J J Farmer.
Saw, Hertford, R B Thatch.
Saw, Winfall, G G Barber.
Saw and planing mill, Hertford, Majar & Loomis.
Steam grist and gin, Burgess, H Parker.
Steam saw, Hertford, Fleetwood, Jackson Lumber Co.

PHYSICIANS.

Names and Post Offices.

Blount, R H L, Woodville.
Cox, David, sr, Hertford.
McMullen, T S, Hertford.
Nixon, A C, Durant's Neck.
Riddick, W M, Hertford.
Riddick, T M, Woodville.
Speight, J W, Hertford.
White, T N, Belvidere.
Winslow, C, Winfall.

SCHOOLS.

Kinds, Post Offices and Proprietors.

Academy, Hertford, Prof J C Kittrell.
Academy, Belvidere, Mrs Josiah Nicholson.
Academy (col), Hertford.
Piney Grove Academy, Belvidere, Ann E White.
Up-river Academy, Belvidere, Mrs E A White.
Public Schools—White, 27; colored, 19.

TEACHERS.

Names and Post Offices.

Bell, R T, Chapanoke.
Clemmons, Mrs, Woodville.
Gatling, Hortense, Eva.
Modlin, Miss, Eva.
Parker, Anna M, Hertford.
White, Albertice, Hertford.

LOCAL CORPORATIONS.

County Alliance, Hertford, W A Newbold, pres.
Perquimans Lodge, No 103, A F and A M, Hertford. Time of meeting, every Friday evening, and June 24th and December 27th. W F Stokes, W M.
Private Bank, Hertford, J Elmo White, cash.

PERQUIMANS COUNTY.

NEWSPAPERS.

Eastern Courier, Hertford (Dem. weekly), edited by J Q A Wood.

Republican, C H Wharton, mgr; (Rep. weekly).

Record, Perquimans (Populist weekly), Rev Y W Babb, ed and prop.

FARMERS.

Names and Post Offices.

Belvidere—R R Baker, E Chapel, Obed Chapel, J R Darden, J R Goblief, Wm Jordan, Thos Layden, S A Layden, Edmond Laydon, Henry Newby, Josiah Nicholson, Stephen Nowell, Jno B Parker, J B Perry, E W Riddick, Edmond Riddick, W D Riddick, B S Riddick, F H Russell, C G Simpson, Dempsy Winston, Rufus White, E A White.

Burgess—W G Arrington, H H Griffin.

Chapanoke—S D Bagly, Wm Bright, John Harris, W A Jackson, T J McNider, Dr W Riddick, Christopher Simmons, Augustus Story, John M Simpson, James Towe, Jr, Wm W Towe, J U White, Frank Winston, J D A Wood.

PERQUIMANS COUNTY.

Durant's Neck—B S Banks, Richard Barden, B F Gregory, B Hoskins, E A Leigh, M Matthews, T J McNider, W H Perry, T G Skinner.

Eva—Geo Lane, T C Long, Peter Swain, A White.

Hertford—B A Berry, R Blanchard, Dr D Cox, J R Felton, J T Felton, T G Skinner, Trim Harrell, D J Jackson, W T Jones, Wm Mardrey, J H Parker, R A Perry, W R Shannonhouse, T J Sutton, R B Thatch, Beverly Tucker, M H White, J White, Theophilus White, Wm H White, C W Wood, S S Williams.

Winfall—H W Baker, S D Bradley, James Davis, T Jessup, A S Jordan, K R Newbould, Wm Nixon, Thomas Nixon, F Nixon.

Woodville—Harrison Bateman, John H Benton, Alphonso Blanchard, Dr R H L Blount, Thomas Blount, B F Bray, John Burcher, Joseph Crawford, Capt — Davis, M R Fletcher, John Hollowell, Isaiah Layden, Abner Nixon (col), Button Price, John Prince, Sr, Elias Pritchard, Wm Rogers, David Russell, Anderson Russell, Richard Russell, Jas Smith, Jr, T B Walters, E R Whedbee, J C Wilson, Wm Wilson, T F Winslow, Geo H Wood.

PERSON COUNTY.

AREA 400 SQUARE MILES.

POPULATION, 16,00; White 8,220, Colored 7,780.

PERSON COUNTY was formed in 1791, from Caswell county, and named in honor of Gen Thomas Person, of Granville county, who was a distinguished friend of popular rights.

ROXBORO, the county seat, is 54 miles north of Raleigh. Population 1,800.

Surface—Pleasantly undulating, soil almost uniformly good, and wonderfully adapted to the growth of tobacco —evenly and beautifully watered, a pleasant and good land.

Staples—Tobacco, corn, wheat, oats and live-stock.

Fruits- Apples, peaches, pears, plums, berries and other small fruits.

Timbers—Pine, poplar, ash, walnut and hickory.

Mineral Waters—Lithia, Iron and Sulphur.

TOWNS AND POST OFFICES.

	POP.		POP.
Ai,	—	Mill Creek,	80
Allensville,	20	Moriah,	30
Bethel Hill,	45	Mount Tirzah,	120
Bushy Fork,	—	Olive Hill,	50
Cates,	—	Roseville,	—
Ceffo,	30	Roxboro	
Centre Grove,	35	(C H),	1,800
Chublake,	40	Surl.	25
Cunningham,	80	Telephone,	49
Foster,	—	Timberlake,	35
Gordonton,	30	Winstead,	40
Hester's Store,	35	Woodburn,	60
Highview,	—	Woodsdale,	40
Holloway's,	35	Yancy,	30
Hurdle's Mills,	75		

COUNTY OFFICERS.

Clerk Superior Court—D W Bradsher.
Commissioners—T H Street, chm; W T Noell, C A Whitfield, J P Wade.
Coroner—W M Clayton.
Register of Deeds—H J Whitt.
Sheriff—J A Carver.
Solicitor Fifth District—W P Bynum.
Surveyor—J H Howard.
Standard Keeper—R K Daniell.
Treasurer—J C Pass.
County Examiner—W E Webb.

COURTS.

Sixth Monday after the first Monday in March, second Monday before the first Monday in September, and eleventh Monday after first Monday in September.

TOWN OFFICERS.

ROXBORO—*Mayor*, W H Long; *Commissioners*, W H Hambrick, R J Featherston, W J Johnson, W T Pass and S P Satterfield; *Treasurer*, W T Pass; *Chief Police*, J T Woody.

TOWNSHIPS AND MAGISTRATES.

Allensville—J S Garrett, W T Melton, R D Royster, Jas K Duncan, John L Gentry, Chas T Davis (Allensville).

Bushy Fork—J S Brooks, J S Coleman, Robert Malone, J L Brooks, E S Malone, John C Harris, Thos J Horner, S E Morton, J F Henderson (Bushy Fork).

Cunningham—P H Clay, J S Cunningham, J M Brady, T W Pass, R A Williams, W A Duncan, L B Scott, J M Bray, R B Bass, J L Dixon (Cunningham).

Flat River—W A Blalock, H H Nichols, W L Allen, T W Blanchard, J P Tengen (Roxboro).

Holloway's—G D Neal, William H Bailey, J C Humphries, W A Woody, Thos D Woody, Wm N Haskins (Holloway's).

Mount Tirzah—G G Moore, James S Noell, W A Malone, J S Coleman, A J Burton, Wm F Reade, H C Fogleman (Mount Tirzah).

Olive Hill—C M G Wagstaff, Thos J Stephens, A J Hester, G A Rogers, T J Stephens, W F Snipes, N L Wagstaff, T J Carver (Olive Hill).

Roxboro—Green Daniel, J C Vanhook, John O'Briant, W H Moore, G H Yarboro, J H Burch, L H Daniel (Roxboro).

Woodsdale—H C Claton, J S Robertson, Wm Jones, J J Brooks, E J Robertson, H G Claton, Buckley Walker, T T Harris (Woodsdale).

CHURCHES.

Names, Pastors, Postoffices and Denom.

METHODIST.

Allenville—Centre Grove.
Bailey's—Woodsdale.
Bethany (col.)—Woodsdale.

PERSON COUNTY.

Church—Roxboro, H M Tuttle.
Concord—Leesburg.
Lee's Chapel—Leesburg.
Mt Tirzah—Mt Tirzah.
Mt Zion—Roxboro.
New Salem—Bratcher's Store,
Oak Grove—Roxboro.
Providence—Cunningham.
Webb's Chapel—Mill Creek.

BAPTIST.

Antioch—Roxboro.
Bethel Hill—Woodsdale.
Cedar Grove—Roxboro.
Church—Mill Creek.
Clement—Woodsdale.
Ephesus Chapel (col.)—Dudley Williams.
Ephesus—Black Walnut (Va.).
Harmony—Roxboro.
New Bethel (col.)—Roxboro.
Olive Branch—Mill Creek.
Pleasant Grove (col.)—Woodsdale.
Providence—Roxboro.

PRIMITIVE BAPTIST.

Church—Roxboro, P D Good.
Ebenezer (col.)—Roxboro.
Flat River—Roxboro.
Shiloh—Daysville.
Storie's Creek—Roxboro.
Upper South—.

PRESBYTERIAN.

Church—Roxboro, Dr P C Morton.

HOTELS AND BOARDING HOUSES.

Names, Post Offices and Proprietors.

Boarding, Roxboro, J C Mastin.
Boarding, Roxboro, R J Featherston.
Boarding, Roxboro, C P Payler.
Boarding, Roxboro, D W Bradsher.
Boarding, Roxboro, Mrs S T Satterfield.
Dowdy Hotel, Roxboro, R H Dowdy.
Winstead Hotel, Winstead, S P Williams.

LAWYERS.

Names and Post Offices.

Boon, Merritt & Bryant, Roxboro.
Brooks, T C, Roxboro.
Kitchen, W W, Roxboro.
Lunsford, N, Roxboro.
Merritt, W D, Roxboro.
Satterfield, S P, Roxboro.
Winstead & Brooks, Roxboro.

MANUFACTORIES.

Kinds, Post Offices and Proprietors.

Blacksmithing and wheelwrighting, Hurdle's Mills, Logan Moore.
Blacksmithing and wheelwrighting, Hurdle's Mills, Dr J I Coleman.

PERSON COUNTY.

Blacksmithing and wheelwrighting, Bushy Fork, Joseph Humphries.
Blacksmithing and wheelwrighting, Centre Grove, Henry Webb.
Blacksmithing and wheelwrighting, Centre Grove, H H Duncan.
Blacksmithing and wheelwrighting, Roxboro, Warren Johnson.
Blacksmithing and wheelwrighting, Roxboro, R K Daniel.
Blacksmithing and wheelwrighting, Roxboro, Henry Jonhson.
Blacksmithing and wheelwrighting, Roxboro, C C Critcher & Co.
Brick-making and contracting, Roxboro, H T Rudder.
Building and contracting, Bushy Fork, William Roberson.
Building and contracting, Bushy Fork, A M Long.
Building and contracting, Bushy Fork, P Jordan.
Building and contracting, Centre Grove, R A Stanford.
Building and contracting, Centre Grove, Lucius Huff.
Building and contracting, Centre Grove, W F Heston & Co.
Building and contracting, Roxboro, Lee Farley.
Building and contracting, Roxboro, James Farley.
Building and contracting, Roxboro, Jeff Farley.
Cabinet-making, Roxboro, Critcher Bros.
Cabinet-making, Roxboro, R K Daniel.
Critcher's Buggy Co, Roxboro, C C & J S Critcher.
Cigars, Roxboro, Murphy Bros, props.
Iron foundry, Roxboro, Jos Younger.
Millwrighting, Roxboro, M Humphries.
Millwrighting, Centre Grove, Sol Mangum.
Planing and moulding, ——, Long & Carver.
Tannery, Bushy Fork, J W Hughes.
Tannery, Roxboro, N F Lewis.
Tannery, Roxboro, James Long.
Tannery, Blue Wing (Granville co), C A Tuck.
Tinware, Roxboro, J A Long.
Tobacco, Bethel Hill, W A Woody.
Tobacco, Roxboro, Stock Co.
Tobacco, Roxboro, J A Long.
Tobacco, Roxboro, W H Long.
Tobacco, Mount Tirzah, J R Gooch.
Tobacco, ——, Long & Hubbard.
Wagons and buggies, Roxboro, R E Daniel & Son.
Wagons and buggies, Roxboro, Cheek & Co.
Wheel and Buggy Co, Roxboro, Owen Bullard.

PERSON COUNTY.

TOBACCO WAREHOUSES.

Farmers', Roxboro, 80x180 feet.
Hyco, Roxboro, 60x120 feet.
Pioneer, Roxboro, 80x200 feet.

MERCHANTS AND TRADESMEN.

Names, Post Offices and Lines of Business.

AI.
Ashley, H & Son,   Saw Mill
Tingen, Joseph P,   G S
ALLENVILLE.
Harris, H W,   G S
BETHEL HILL.
Clayton & Dickerson,   G S
Walker, B.   Mill
Woody and Gentry,   G S
BUSHY FORK.
Bradsher, A L,   G S
Long, W H & Co,   G S
CATES.
Cates, J T,   G S
CEFFO.
Paylor, R L,   G S
CHUB LAKE.
Clayton, H G & Co,   G S
CUNNINGHAM.
Bass, R B,   G S
Cunningham, J S,   G S
GORDONTON.
Malone, E S & Son,   G S
Tobacco Oil Mfg Co,   Oil
HELENA.
Johnson, A F,   G S
HESTER'S STORE.
Newton, A E & J H,   G S
HOLLOWAY.
Winstead, J P,   G S
HURDLE'S MILLS.
Coleman, Dr J I,   G S
Long, W H & Co,   G S
MILL CREEK.
Harris, H W,   G S
Street, Thos H,   Grist Mill
MORIAH.
Biggs, B V,   G S
MT TIRZAH.
Bowling, S,   G S
Moore, G G & Co,   G S
Reade, E B,   G S
Reade, E W & Co,   Millers
Speed, D E A,   Drugs
OLIVE HILL.
Paylor, R L,   G S
Wagstaff, C M G,   Farmer
ROSEVILLE.
Moore, W H,   G S

PERSON COUNTY.

ROXBORO.
Barnett, A (col),   Gro
Barton, W A,   Miller
Berman & Goodfriend,   G S
Brooks, C B,   Leaf Tobacco
Black, J H & Co,   Gro and Shoes
Cheek, E D,   ——
Critchers Bros,   Whellwrights and
                             Cabinet Makers
Daniel, R K & Son,   Wheelwrights
Foushee, Stephen,   Leaf Tobacco
Garrett & Co,   G S
Hall, R J,   Saddler
Monard, Philip & Co,   G S
Hunter, C H,   G S
Johnson & Co,   G S
Long, J A & Co,   G S
Lukin & Long,   Hardware
Mastin, J C,   Painter
Morris, J D,   Drugs
Pass, J C,   Miller
Pass Bros,   G S
Thomas, W L,   G S
Tucker, J E,   G S
Wilson, C T & Co,   G S
Woody & Yancey,   G S
Yarboro, G H & Co,   Leaf Tobacco
Younger, Josephus,   Foundry
SURL.
Lunsford, N & Son,   G S
TELEPHONE.
Davis, Jones & Bros,   Millers
Davis, T P,   G S
TIMBERLAKE.
Laws, John, jr, & Bros,   G S
Timberlake, Bro & Co,   G S
Paylor, J W,   G S
Rogers, G R W,   G S
Winstead, C S, sr,   G S
Winstead, J W,   G S
WOODBURN.
Winstead, T A,   G S
Winstead & Walters,   Millers
WOODSDALE
Brooks, J J & Son,   G S
Clayton, J W & Co,   G S
Dickerson & Clayton,   G S
Robertson, E J,   G S
Walker, B,   G S

TOBACCO BUYERS—ROXBORO.

G W Bowen, J J Bowlden, A S De
Vlaming, Foushee & Stephens, R E
Long, Long & Hubbard, T A Noell,
Pass & Clayton, Walker, G H Yarboro
& Co.

MINES.

Kinds, Post Offices and Proprietors.

Gillis Copper, Mill, Creek, W A Gillis.
The World Mining Company.

MILLS.

Kinds, Post Offices and Proprietors.

Corn, flour and saw, Hester's Store, W A Warner & Co.

Corn, flour and saw, Woodburn, C S Winstead.

Corn, flour and saw, Roxboro, Samuel Winstead.

Corn, flour and saw, Roxboro, S B Winstead.

Corn, flour and saw, Winstead, C S Winstead.

Corn, flour and saw, Murdle's Mills, D W K Richmond.

Corn, flour and saw, Mill Creek, T H Street.

Corn, flour and saw, Roxboro, Stanford & Co.

Corn, flour and saw, Mt Tirzah, E R Moore & Bro.

Corn, flour and saw, Roxboro, C S Winstead.

Corn, flour and saw, Roxboro, J C Pass.

Corn, flour and saw, Roxboro, Winstead & Long.

Corn, flour and saw, Mt Tirzah, W A Burton.

Corn, flour and saw, Busby Fork, Burton & Warren.

Corn and flour, Bushy Fork, Nat Broach.

Lake Roller Mills, Roxboro, J A Long & Co.

Locke Lilly Roller Mills, Chublake, Winstead & Long.

Pass Roller Mills, Roxboro, J C Pass.

Steam corn, flour and saw, Roxboro, M M Tapp.

PHYSICIANS.

Names and Post Offices.

Baynes, R S. Bushy Fork.
Bradsher, C H, Hurdle's Mills.
Bradsher, J C, Roxboro.
Crisp, W B, Roxboro.
Dean, R C. Centre Grove.
Fuller, J T, Roxboro.
Merritt, Wm, Holloway's.
Morton, R A, Roxboro.
Nichols, C G, Roxboro.
Pritchett, P G. Centre Grove.
Sanford, L, Blue Wing (Granville co).
Speed, E A, Mount Tirzah.
Thaxton, J J, Olive Hill.

SCHOOLS.

Names, Post Offices and Principals.

Academy, Roxboro, W L Fousbee, prin; Mrs T Anna Harrison and T C Brooks, assistants; Trustees: S B Winstead, W E Webb, T H Street, A R Foushee; number students, 240.

PERSON COUNTY.

Female school, Winstead, Miss Mary Hester.

Female school, Bethel Hill, Mrs T A Harrison.

Male and female school, Roxboro, Mrs J A Carver.

Male and female school, Roxboro, Prof —— Thomas.

Male and female school, Roxboro, Mrs Sam Burnett.

Male school, Bushy Fork, Albert G Satterfield and S Y Brown.

School, Centre Grove, W H Royster.

School, Mt Tirzah, James W Tillett.

School, Allensville, J J Scarborough.

School, Bethel Hill, Rev J H Beam.

Public schools—white, 18; colored, 20.

TEACHERS.

Names and Post Offices.

WHITE.

Bradsher, Miss Eugenia, Roxboro.
Bradsher, Miss Eugenia, Olive Hill.
Brooks, T C, Roxboro.
Brooks, Miss Nannie C, Bethel Hill.
Brooks, Mrs Alma, Woodsdale.
Brooks, Mrs Bettie. Winstead.
Brown. Rev S Y, Hurdle's Mill.
Field, Mrs C, Roxboro.
Fowler, Miss Lillie, Centre Grove.
Hamlen, Miss Beulah T, Roxboro.
Holloway, G F, Roxboro.
Humphries, Miss Sue, Bethel Hill.
Humphries, J K, Bethel Hill.
McFarland, R A, Centre Grove.
Morgan, Miss Kittie, Blue Wing.
O'Brient, Miss Nora, Roxboro.
Pulley, Miss S W, Bethel Hill.
Raglan, L C, Mill Creek.
Stanford. Miss L O, Mt Tirzah.
Terry, Miss Lois, Roxboro.
Thomas, Miss Mary A, Centre Grove.
Vellines, N R, Bushy Fork.

COLORED.

Bailey, S E. Roxboro.
Barnett, Mrs M V, Roxboro.
Buchanan, I H, Roxboro.
Cook, Mrs Isabella, Roxboro.
Day, Miss C L, Allensville.
Duncan, Miss Ella, Allensville.
Edwards. Miss Ida J, Roxboro.
Foster, H H, Woodburn.
Harris, R H, Roxboro.
Harris, Wm O, Roxboro.
Harris, Miss Novella, Roxboro.
Hester, C A, Roxboro.
Hester, C H, Roxboro.
Johnson, Edward, Roxboro.
Johnson. L H, Roxboro.
Jones, Wm H, Roxboro.
Lyon, Isabella. Centre Grove.
Mason, Miss Ida, Cunningham.

PERSON COUNTY.

Mason, Mrs N V, Cunningham.
Moore, A W, Gordonton.
Peace, Miss Martha, Roxboro.
Pool, Miss Ophelia, Roxboro.
Ragland, Miss S A, Christie, Va.
Satterfield, A R, Roxboro.
Wade, Alex, Woodsdale.
Whitted, A A, Roxboro.
Whitted, Miss A B, Roxboro.
Williams, Mrs L A, Roxboro.

NEWSPAPERS.

Person County Courier, Roxboro; J A
Noell, editor; Noell Bros, publishers.

FARMERS.

Names and Post Offices.

Bethel Hill—Thos Baird, J C Brooks,
J M Brooks, John Brooks, S Crutch-
field, J B Day, B F Gentry, S Gentry,
S C Humphries, S Humphries, M Jones,
Thos Montague, H Morton, G D Neal,
J Nord, J D Nord, John Pool, William
Pulley, S Walker, J D Walker, J S
Walker, R A Walker, John Wiley,
Wm Williams, Jas Wood, Wm Wood,
Ruffin Woody, J R Woody.
Bushy Fork—S G Bradsher, D W
Bradsher, J O Bradsher, Y H Briggs,
J L Brooks, J A Burch, J S Coleman,
J H Henry, W H Long, E S Malone,
Alexander O'Briant, J W Villines, W
R Warren, W A Warren.
Ceffo—S A Barnett, Abner Dixon,
George W Jones, J M Jones, T J Jones,
J Pointer, N L Wagstaff, H S Wil-
liams, Mrs Ann Williams, G B Wil-
liams, R A Williams, H S Winstead.
Centre Grove—Jas Bullock, A H
Bumpass & Sons, R J Davis, T M
Davis, R G Denny, H H Duncan &
Son, S H Garrett, W F Hester & Son,
Webb Knott, J W Knott, Woodson
Lyon, Wm Mangum & Sons, DeWitt
McFarland, A D Moore, J M O'Briant,
R D Royster, A Sherman, J H Shot
well & Son, B A Thaxton & Co, Wood-
son Thomas, R S Thomas, C C Town-
send, Wilkerson & Bro, Richard Wood
& Bro, T W Wright.
Cunningham's Store—H T Barber,
E B Barber, J E Barber, Jos Barker, S
A Barrett, R B Bass, W F Boyd, A
Boyd, Robt Bracy, B Carter, John S
Cunningham, Green Evans, William
Faulkner, G B Featherston, J G Frank-
lin, J J Franklin, G Haigh, J W Ham-
let, T M Hamlet, G W Jones, J A
Jones, J J Jones, B T Jones, W Lock-
hart, Sid Lee, J D Lee, E A McLean, J
F Moore, Ann E Oliver, J M Oliver, J
H Pass, J B Scott, Geo Scott, W G

PERSON COUNTY.

Scott, Loftin Scott, Sol Smith, B H
Solomon, T D Terrell, A Williams.
Daysville—G Bailey, J J Brooks,
Moses Jones, W J Shotwell, J D Wal-
ker.
Hester's Store—B L Bradsher, J L
Brooks, W R Brooch, L C Hester, Jno
Newton, H A Rogers, Wm F Snipes.
Holloway's—Gabe Bailey, J B Day,
R W Jones, Wm Merritt, J D Walker.
Hurdle's Mills—H Blalock, C Bla-
lock, Alfred Blalock, J B Blackwell,
Walter Bradsher, Stephen Bradsher,
Ben Butler, J T Cates, J M Cates, J B
Cates, C C Cates, S H Cates, Eddie
Cooper, W R Cooper, F M Daniels, A
N Davis, John Denny, T J Hall, J E
Harris, C G Harris, F D Harris, C
Hawkins, J H Henry, John Jones. Geo
Jones, Wesley Laws, R M Malone, Wil-
son McCullough, Silas Moore, A V
Moore, A M Potterfield, Dave Potter-
field, D W K Richmond, —— Rich-
mond, J M Satterfield, Rob't Stanfield,
Willis W Villians, Miss Delia Watkins,
Edwin Whitfield, N T Williams.
Long's Cross Raads—J M Blalock,
W B Childers, W M Horton, J G
Thomas, J C Vanhook.
Mill Creek—James Beavers, William
Buchanan, Jno Chambers, W H Cham-
bers, B T Chandler, D Chandler, G B
Day, J B Day, T Dixon, Jas Holloway,
W H Lawson, J F Neal, John Ramsey,
William Ramsey, J G Slaughter, T H
Street, J T Yancey, T A Yancey, Sr,
W S Yancey.
Moriah—John Bumpass, A R Cash,
D C Cozart, W H Day, Thomas Ellis,
Squire Glenn, A M Mincey, B Riggs,
G W Yancey, W P Yancey, B Yancey.
Mount Tirzah—J A Allen, G An-
drews, Haston Blalock, Albert Blalock,
B Bowen, John Bumpass. R A Burton,
A J Burton, J R Cash, Wm Cathron,
W D Cathron, R Cathron, J I Cathron,
L M Cathron, Thomas Chandler. T D
Clayton, Thos S Clayton, C B Clegg,
S H Clement, S B Coleman, J Y Coz-
art, D C Cozart, Henry Day, Thos Ellis,
H Evans, Jesse Evans, J B Glenn,
Samuel Glenn, R S Glenn, J R Gooch,
Andrew Harris, Thos Harris, D Hill, O
J Kennedy, D C Lunsford, John Luns-
ford, W A Malone, Simeon Meadows,
A Mency, H J Montgomery, Sidney
Moore, R A Moore. S S Moore, G G
Moore, W T Noell, John Oakley, Geo
Oakley, S K Oakley, R Oakley, S B
Peed, D E Peed, J R Reade, E B Reade,
W F Reade, J M Speed, E A Speed, R
A Stanford, H C Siveaney, S Taylor.
Olive Hill—B B Brooks, P H Clay, J
A Thaxton, C M G Wagstaff, W E
Wagstaff, G C Wagstaff, C H Woods.

PERSON COUNTY.

Telephone—John A Baird, Sr, T P Davis, S C Humphries. J C Rogers, Neal & Woody, Samuel Woody.

Roxboro—H Ashley, C B Brooks, J H Burch, R C Carver, C C Clayton, J D Clayton, Jas Dixon, W A Ellison, H H Garrett, C G Mitchell, G W Moore, L S Morton, Ruffin Rhen, D Rogers, S A Rogers, W P Satterfield, J T Sergeant, J C Vanhook, J T Wagstaff, S B Winstead, T D Wright, J M Yarboro, David Yarboro, J Younger.

Winstead—D Y Bradsher, W G Bradsher, J O Bradsher, J T Bradsher, M Brooks, Wm Brooks, R Brooks, G Brooks, Thos Burch. H Burch, G W Burch, Jeff Carver, J W Carver, Wm Childress, Wm Clayton, Marion Clayton, Jas Clayton, J J Coleman, J E Coleman, Haywood Foushee, C N Frederick, P Frederick, A Gray, James Grubbs, A Harris, Joe Harris, Willis Harris, Benj Harris, A J Hester, J P Hicks, Jos Holsomback, W T Holsomback, Jno Horton, Joe Humphries, Jas Jacobs, Geo James, J H Lee. Stephen Lee, A Loftis, Gabe Loftis, Jno Loftis,

PERSON COUNTY.

Chas Loftis, Dan Long, Jno Long, W L Marshall. Jno Miles. Jno Nelson, N Oakley, H M Paylor, D Potterfield, B Pulliam, V Pulliam, G A Rogers, John Rogers, W H Rudder, Thos Sally, A P Sally, Jas Sally, Jno Sergeant, R W Sergeant, J T Sergeant, Wm Snipes, W F Snipes, T J Stephens, R Tapp, Monroe Tapp, Geo Tilman, Jno True, J B Wagstaff, Geo Wagstaff, J H Walker. P Westbrook, Geo Westbrook, H A Whitted, Geo Whitfield, W Wilkerson, C S Winstead, J F Winstead, J W Winstead, H J Winstead.

Woodburn—Rufus Betts. C Burnett, Lewis Cunningham, J L Dixon, G B Evans, W M Faulkner. Miles Featherston, J M Jones, E Walters, Henry Winstead.

Woodsdale—B T Barnett, J W Brooks, J J Brooks, J S Cunningham, J Chambers, J Hall, T H Hall, T T Harris, A J Hester. Moses Jones, Wm Jones, H T Mitchell, J S Robertson, G A Rogers, T J Stephens, J T Walker, B Walker, T P Walters. W H Williams, T A Winstead, C S Winstead.

PITT COUNTY.

AREA 820 SQUARE MILES.

POPULATION 25,519; White 13,192, Colored 12,327.

PITT COUNTY was formed in 1760 from Beaufort county, and named in honor of William Pitt, Earl of Chatham, who was so distinguished and devoted a friend to America in the English Parliament.

GREENVILLE, the county-seat is situated on Tar River, 89 miles east of Raleigh. Population, 3,500.

Bethel, on the A. & R. R. R., is a thriving town of 300 inhabitants.

Surface—Generally level and in parts swampy, lying on both sides of Tar river; soil usually rich and very productive when well drained; convenient to river navigation.

Staples—Tobacco, cotton, corn, sweet potatoes, rice, lumber and naval stores.

This is a fine tobacco county, and many of the farms are in a high state of cultivation.

Fruits — Apples, peaches, pears, plums, grapes, berries and other small fruits.

Timbers—Pine, oak, hickory, poplar, cypress and gum.

TOWNS AND POST OFFICES.

	POP.		POP.
Ayden,	800	Hill,	100
Bethel,	300	Johnson's Mill,	25
Black Jack,	25	Keelsville,	25
Calico,	25	Littlefield,	25
Clayroot,	—	Langley,	30
Coxville,	25	Oakley,	25
Dongola,	50	Pactolus,	100
Falkland,	200	Pineboro,	50
Farmville,	400	Quinerly,	25
Gardnerville,	100	Redallie,	50
Greenville (c h),		Rinston,	35
	3,500	Rountree,	20
Grimesland,	50	Rochdale,	40
Grindool,	50	Stokes,	25
Grifton,	700	Whichard,	25
House,	50	Winterville,	50
Hollands,	25		

COUNTY OFFICERS.

Clerk Superior Court—E A Moye.
Commissoners—Council Dawson, chm; Leonidas Fleming, S M Jones, J L Smith.
Coroner—Dr Chas O H Laughinghouse.
Register of Deeds—W M King.
Sheriff—R W King.

Solicitor Third District — Claude M Bernard.
Surveyor—J R Jenkins.
Standard Keeper—W M Moore.
Treasurer—J R Little.
Superintendent of Health—Dr F W Brown.
County Examiner—W H Ragsdale.

COURTS.

Eighth Monday before the first Monday in March, the first Monday in March, the fourth Monday after the first Monday in March, the second Monday after the first Monday in September, and the thirteenth Monday after first Monday in September.

TOWN OFFICERS.

BETHEL—Mayor, D C Moore.
AYDEN—Mayor, W B Moore.
PACTOLUS—Mayor, J M Davenport.
FALKLAND — Mayor, D J Morrill; Chief of Police, M G Bullock.
GREENVILLE — Mayor, Ola Forbes; Councilmen—1st Ward, W L Brown, W H Smith; 2d Ward, W T Godwin, Julius Jenkins (col); 3d Ward, T A Wilkins (col); Dempsey Rufin (col); Clerk, C C Forbes; Treasurer, W T Godwin; Chief Police, J W Perkins; Asst Police—Fred Cox.

TOWNSHIPS AND MAGISTRATES.

Beaver Dam—R L Nichols, J S Norman, J H Mourning, Ivy Smith, T E Little, H A Rountree, G T Tyson (Granville).

Bellevoir—W H Rives, J T Hodges, Godfrey L Stancil, D C Barrow (Hollands).

Bethel—F C Martin, R N Jones, W J Rollins, J L G Mourning, J C Taylor, J R Jenkins, McG Whitehurst, D C Moose (Bethel).

Carolina—J W Page, W H Williams, D N Nobles (Oakley), J H Woolard, J R Congleton (Whichard).

Chicod—H C Venters, R G Chapman (Calico), John M Cox, J W Smith, McG Bryan (Blackjack), S Williams, J J Laughinghouse (Grimesland).

Contentnea — John D Cox, W B Moore, Elias Braxton, E E Dale, Benj

PITT COUNTY.

Croft, John Nobles (Ayden), J R Johnson (Littiefield), S V Laughinghouse (Grifton). W H Williams (Ayden)

Falkland—E F Williams, R Williams, H S Tyson, W C Moore, W M Smith, F G Dupree (Falkland).

Farmville—Dr J N Bynum, A Horton, R L Joyner, A J Moye, J H Flanagan, A D Hill, D M Edwards (Farmville).

Greenville—L A Moye, F M Smith, G M Tucker, J A Long, Ola Forbes, W T Godwin, J J Perkins, S I Fleming (Greenville).

Pactolus—Thos H Langley, W B Carver, E P Daniel, Lunsford Fleming (Pactolus).

Swift Creek–N R Coley, Slade Chapman, E G Cox (Coxville), L B Mewborne (Quinerly), C P Gaskins, John Thompson (Grifton), J M Dixon (Gardner's).

CHURCHES.

Names, Post Offices, Pastors and Denom.

BAPTIST.

Church—Greenville.
Chuich—Pactolus.
Church—Bethel.
Church (col)—Bethel, —— Ruffin.
Sycamore Hill (col)-Greenville, A Roberson.

FREE WILL BAPTIST.

Bethany—Ayden.
Church—Marlboro.
Cross Roads Church—Falkland, Jo Tyson.
Elm Grove—Littlefield, —— Albritton.
Gum Swamp— Greenville, Thos H Barnhill.
Hickory Grove—Bethel, Thos H Barnhill.
Hickory Hill (col)—Greenville.
Little—Bethel.
Parker's Chapel-Greenville, G S Johnson.
Ready Branch—Greenville, Fred Mc-Glawhon.

PRIMITIVE BAPTIST.

Brier Swamp—Pactolus, John Ross.
Cross Roads—Bell's Ferry, John Williams.
Flat Swamp—Robersonville, Geo Roberson.
Gailoway—Grimesland, C C Bland.
Great Swamp — Greenville, Samuel Moore.
Hancock's-Johnson's Mills, C C Bland.
Red Banks—Greenville, C C Bland.
Tyson—Farmville, —— Mewborn.

METHODIST.

Berea—Greenville.
Bethlehem—Greenville.

PITT COUNTY.

Church—Greenville, N H D Wilson.
Church—Bethel, Albert Barnes.
Little's—Pactolus.
Mt Zion—Pactolus.
Salem—Greenville.
Shady Grove—Greenville.
Shiloh—Greenville.
Sparta—Old Sparta.
Tripp's—Greenville.

AFRICAN METHODIST.

African—Greenville, L Johnson.

ZION METHODIST.

York's Temple (col.)—Greenville, —— Fulford.

M. E. C. A.

Church (col.)—Bethel, L B Sims.

DISCIPLES OF CHRIST.

Antioch—Farmville, I L Chestnut.
Corinth—Greenville, I L Chestnut.
Mt Pleasant — Greenville, J W Mc-Namara.
Oak Grove—Keelsville, J L Winfield.
Red Oak—Greenville, I L Chestnut.
Rountree's—Ridge Spring, I L Chestnut.
Salem—Johnson's Mills, J W Howard.
Timothy—Johnson's Mills, J L Winfield.

PRESBYTERIAN.

Church—Greenville, R W Hines.
Church—Falkland, W M Morton.

EPISCOPAL.

Emanuel—Farmville.
St John's—Johnson's Mills, Alvin Greaves.
St Paul's--Greenville, Alvin Greaves.

MINISTERS RESIDENT.

Names, Post Offices and Denominations.

BAPTIST.

Grimes, George (col.), Pactolus.
Prichland, A (col.), Greenville.

FREE WILL BAPTIST.

Barnhill, T H, Grindool.
Craft, James, Greenville.
Fort, W H, Grindool.
Hathaway, E D, Holland.
Manning, T N, Greenville.
McGlawhon, Fred, Greenville.
Johnson, G S, Greenville.
Pollard, Thomas, Grindoll.

PRIM. BAPTIST.

Bland, C C, Coxville.
Ross, W A, Greenville.
Williams, J A, Johnson's Mills.

METHODIST.

Hearne, W B, Greenville.
Wilson, N H D, Greenville.

AFRICAN METHODIST.

Johnson, L (col.), Greenville.

32

PITT COUNTY.

HOTELS AND BOARDING HOUSES.

Names, Post Offices and Proprietors.

Bethel House, Bethel, M A Bullock.
Hotel Macon, Greenville, Chas Skinner.
King House, Greenville, Mrs W M King.
Ricks House, Greenville, Mrs J W Perkins.

LAWYERS.

Names and Post Offices.

Bernard, C M, Greenville.
Blount, J H, & Fleming, J L, Greenville.
Harding, F C (Woodard & Harding), Greenville.
Jarvis, T J, & Blow, Alex L, Greenville.
James, F G, Greenville.
King, George B, Greenville.
Long, W H, Greenville.
Moore, J G & L I, Greenville.
Moore, T W C (col), Greenville.
Skinner, H, & Whidleal, H W, Greenville.
Skinner & Latham, Greenville,
Sugg, I A, Greenville.
Tyson, B F, & Galloway, Greenville.

MANUFACTORIES.

Kinds, Post Offices and Proprietors.

Blacksmith and wheelwright, Hanrahan, Tobias Nelson.
Blacksmith and wheelwright, Johnson's Mills, Wm C Butler.
Blacksmith and wheelwright, Hanrahan, Henry Harrington.
Blacksmith and wheelwright, Hanrahan, Asa Garris.
Blacksmith and wheelwright, Falkland, Wm Whitehurst.
Blacksmith and wheelwright, Black Jack, James Adams.
Boots and shoes, Greenville, H T Harris.
Bricks, Farmville, M L Horton.
Building and contracting, Black Jack, L H White.
Building and contracting, Hanrahan, J D Hart.
Building and contracting, Greenville, W T Godwin.
Building and contracting, Greenville, J T Williams.
Building and contracting, Falkland, L Joyner (col).
Building and contracting, Falkland, H Gorham (col).

PITT COUNTY.

Carriages, Greenville, Pitt Co Buggy Co.
Carriages, buggies and harness, Greenville, John Flanagan Buggy Co.
Coach-making, Farmville, J J Whitehurst & Son.
Coach, Bethel, D S Leggette.
Coaches. Bethel, B L T Barnhill & Son.
Coopering, Black Jack, J F Hudson.
Coopering, Black Jack, Wm Haddock.
Coopering, Black Jack, Ellis Boyd.
Cox Cotton planter, Winterville, Amos G Cox.
Foundry and machine shop, Greenville, James Brown.
Harness and saddles, Greenville, Lawrence, J R Carey & Bro.
Locks and guns, Greenville, R L Hunter.
Lumber factory, Greenville, Greenville Lumber Co.
Machine and iron foundry, Greenville, R L Hunter.
Tannery, Black Jack, Robt Dixon.
Tinware and roofing, Greenville, S G Pender & Co.
Wheelwright, Grimesland, J O Proctor & Bro.

MERCHANTS AND TRADESMEN.

Names, Post Offices and Line of Business.

AYDEN.

Basden, W H,	G S
Cobb, J H,	G S
Garris, R H,	G S
Harrington, A L,	G S
Hart, W T,	G S
Holton & Spear (near),	G S
Lee, T R,	C S
Pollard & Hardy,	G S
Redditt, A T,	G S
Smith, J R & Bro,	G S
Stokes, J J,	G S

BETHEL.

Blount & Bro,	G S
Bullock, T R & Bro,	G S
Bullock, J D,	G S
Carson, S T,	G S
Cherry, Mrs P B,	G S
Grimes, M F,	G S
Grimes, M J & Co,	—
James, Dr F C,	Drugs
Knox & Co.	G S
Manning, W A & Co,	G S
Bollins & Carson,	Fert and G S
Staton, Cherry & Bunting,	G S
Whitehnrst, R B & Co,	G S

CLAYROOT.

Smith, W A & Co,	G S

COXVILLE.

Clark, Jesse,	G S
Koach, W S,	G S

PITT COUNTY.

FALKLAND.

Cotton, R K (near),	G S
Fountain, J L,	G S
Vines, C C,	G S

FARMVILLE.

Askew, Wm C,	Gro
Davis, R L & Bros,	G S
Horton, M T & Parker,	G S
Lang, W G,	Millinery
Lang, W M,	G S
Turnage, T L,	G S
Tyson & Rawles,	Bankers

GARDNERVILLE.

Gardner & Gardner,	G S

GREENVILLE.

Andrews, John A,	Gro
Bagwell, Dr W H,	Drugs
Brown, W L, Fire Ins, Com and Fert	
Brown & Hooker,	G S
Bryan & Allen,	Livery
Cherry, J B & Co,	G S
Cobb, J C & Son,	Livery
Cobb, Charles,	G S
Cory, J R,	Harness
Cox, J W (near),	G S
Evans & Co, Greenville Warehouse	
Edwards, J S & Bro (near),	G S
Ernul, M G,	Drugs
Evans, Joyner & Co, Eastern Ware-house	
Flannigan, John,	Undertaker
Forbes & Mays, Planters Warehouse	
Forbes, Alfred,	G S
Gorman Campbell Co, Leaf Dealers	
Griffin, A J,	Jeweler
Hasket, D D,	H'd'w
Hardee, D W,	Gro
Harris, G E,	G S
Harrington, W H,	Live Stock
Hearn, J L,	Life Ins
Higgs Bros,	D G
Higgs, Mrs M D,	Millinery
Hines & Hamilton,	G S
Hooker, H C,	G S
Horne, Mrs R H,	Milliner
Humbers, R L,	Machinist
Jackson, W J,	Wheelwright
Jenkins, J S, & Co,	Leaf Dealer
Jones, Geo,	Leaf Dealer
Joyner, O L,	Leaf Dealer
King, J F.	Livery Stables
Lang, M R, agt.	G S
Laughinghouse, E (col),	G S
Long, W H,	Fire Ins
Long, Jas,	Gro and Com
Mangum, W T, & Co,	Leaf Dealers
Morgan, J W, Buyer for A M Tob Co	
Moye & Harden,	Livery
Mumford, C T,	G S
Parham, B E, & Co,	Leaf Dealers
Pender, S E, & Co, Stoves & Tinware	
Perkins & Cox,	Livery Stables
Rawls, W S,	Jeweler

PITT COUNTY.

Reaves, J L,	Lightning Rods
Ricks, Taft & Co,	G S
Roberts, T E, & Co,	Leaf Dealers
Runstall, Brown & Co,	Star Warehouse
Smith, C D (near),	G S
Smith, D S,	Gro
Smith, J S,	Gro
Speight & Forbes,	Fert
Starkey, J L, & Co,	Gro
Studdard, ——,	Life Ins
Sugg, A L, Life, Fire and Accident Ins	
Tucker, G M (near),	G S
Tyson & Rawles,	Bankers
Walker, D J,	Leaf Dealer
Warren, Allen & Son,	Nursery
Weatherington, Mrs S F,	G S
White & Speight, Life, Fire and Accident Ins	
White, S T.	G S
White, W H.	G S
Wiggins, J W, & Co, Leaf Dealers	
Wilson, F.	G S
Wilson, W B,	Broker
Wooten, J L,	Drugs
Worthington & Bryan, Livery Stables	

GRIFTON.

Albriton, A A,	G S
Cobb, L A,	G S
Coward & Spivey,	G S
Dixon, W G,	G S
Garkins, C P,	G S
Harvey, J R, & Co,	G S
Patrick, J, & Bro,	Livery
Pittman, F M.	H'd'w
Quinnerly, J W, & Bro,	G S
Spier, Mrs A, & Co,	Millinery
Thompson & Bro,	G S

GRIMESLAND.

Grimes, J B,	——
Laughinghouse, J J,	——
Moore, T M, & Co,	G S
Proctor, H H, & Bro,	G S
Proctor, J O, & Bro,	G S

GRINDOOL.

Whitehurst, S C,	G S

HOUSE.

House, D E, & Bro,	G S
Proctor, W C, & Co,	——

JOHNSON'S MILLS.

Bland, Miss Mattie,	Millinery
Chapinaw, L J, & Co,	G S
Quinnerly, J W & Bro,	G S

LITTLEFIELD.

Garris, Asa,	G S

PACTOLUS.

Davenport, J R,	G S
Fleming, R T,	G S
Grimes, W B,	——
Little & Satterwaite,	G S
Overton, J R,	Gro
Rollins, J J, agt,	G S

PITT COUNTY.

PENNY HILL.

Hicks, W S,   G S
Stancill, G A,   G S
Warren & Shelton,   G C

RENSTON.

McLawhorn, L,   G S

ROCHDALE.

Smith, C D,   G S

STOKES.

Perkins, J L & C,   G S

WHICHARD.

Whichard, W R,   G S

WINTERVILLE.

Cox, A G,   G S
Manning, B F,   Dry Goods

MILLS.

Kinds, Post Offices and Proprietors.

Corn (steam), Greenville, Jas Briley.
Corn, flour and saw (steam), Coxville, A G Cox.
Corn. flour and saw (steam), Calico, G W Venters.
Corn, flour and saw (steam), Greenville, J J Noble.
Corn, flour and saw (steam), Keelsville, J R Congleton.
Corn, flour and saw (steam), Renston.
Corn, flour and saw (steam), Greenville, Bryant Tripp
Corn, flour and saw (steam), Grimesland, John Galloway.
Corn and flour, Pactolus, R S Tucker's estate.
Corn and flour, Johnson's Mills, E A Johnson.
Corn and flour, Falkland. —— Webb.
Corn and flour, Falkland, Wm T Harris.
Corn and flour, Greenville, Nash Forbes.
Corn and flour (steam), Ayden, Braxton & Harrington.
Corn and flour (steam, Greenville, J C Cobb & Son.
Corn and saw (steam), Penny Hill, G A Stancil.
Corn and grist (steam), Ridge Spring, C Dawson.
Corn and saw, Pactolus, Thos Sheppard.
Corn and saw, Ridge Spring, E C Carmon.
Corn and saw (steam), Hanrahan, R H Garris.
Corn and saw (steam), Grifton, Webb & Pittman.
Corn and saw (steam), Hanrahan, Mrs J A Hanrahan.
Corn and saw (steam), Quimerly, J P Quinnerly.
Corn and saw, Johnson's Mills, J Pitt-
Saw (steam), Hanrahan, John Hart.

Saw (steam), Greenville, R Tripp.
Saw (steam), Greenville, Thos Nichols.
Steam saw and grist, Bethel, M A James.
Steam corn, flour, gin, saw, planing and bracket, Bethel, Ward & Barnhill
Steam corn and gin, Falkland, W M King.

PHYSICIANS.

Names and Post Offices.

Bagwell, W H, Greenville.
Best, W L. Quinnerly.
Brown, F W, Greenville.
Brown, Zeno, Greenville.
Brown, J P, Greenville.
Brown, W M H, Greenville.
Bynum, J N, Farmville.
Chears, ——, Pactolus.
Cox, B Thaddeus, Coxville.
Dixon, Jo, Ayden.
Grimes. R J, Bethel.
James, F C, Bethel.
James, D L, Greenville (dentist).
Johnson, Hardy, Bell's Ferry.
Jones, C M, Grimesland.
Joyner, H A, Greenville (dentist).
Laughinghouse, C O H, Greenville.
Loftin, ——, Grifton.
Morrell, James, Falkland.
Morrell, Samuel, Farmville.
O'Hagan, C J, Greenville.
Warren, William E, Greenville.
Woods, S B, Bell's Ferry.

SCHOOLS.

Names, Post Offices and Principals.

Academy, ——, Falkland.
Academy, Coxville, Mrs Mary Smith.
Academy, Bethel, —— Hassell.
Academy, Keechville.
Centreville Academy, Johnson's Mills.
Farmville Institute, Farmville, Willie Newbern, prin; Lizzie Smith, asst.
Greenville Institute, Greenville, T D Bagley.
Music, Greenville, Miss Hortense Forbes.
Primary, Greenville, Mrs C M Bernard.
Primary, Greenville, Miss Bettie Warren.
Public schools—white, 96; colored, 56.

LOCAL CORPORATIONS.

Covenant Lodge, No 17, I O O F; meets every Tuesday night; O W Harrington, N G.
Greenville Lodge, No 284, A F and A M; meets every first Thursday and Monday nights, after first and third Sunday at Masonic Lodge; Zeno Moore, W M; D J Whichard, sec.

PITT COUNTY.

Insurance Lodge, 1169, K of H; meets
every first and third Friday nights;
D D Haskett, D.
Pitt Council, No 236, A F of H; meets
every Thursday night; C A White, C.
Temperance Reform Club, Greenville,
E C Glenn, pres; G E Harris, sec;
1,500 members in the county.
Tyson & Rawls, Bankers, Greenville;
capital stock $10,000.

PITT COUNTY.

NEWSPAPERS.

Eastern Reflector, Greenville (Democratic daily and weekly), D J Whichard, editor and prop.

Free-Will Baptist (denominational),
Ayden, J M Barefield, editor.

King's Weekly (Democratic), Greenville, W T King, editor and prop.

POLK COUNTY.

AREA, 300 SQUARE MILES.

POPULATION, 5,902; White 4,807, Colored 1,095.

POLK COUNTY was formed in 1855, from Henderson and Rutherford counties, and was named in honor of Col Wm Polk, of the Revolution.

COLUMBUS, the county seat, is 225 miles west from Raleigh, and was named in honor of the discoverer of America. Population, 256.

Surface—Moderately uneven; a fine, healthy country, situated on Green river; soil generally good, and scenery pleasant; water power good.

Staples—Corn, wheat, oats, rye, tobacco, flax, butter and live-stock.

Fruits—Apples, peaches, pears, grapes, berries, etc. are grown to perfection in the "Thermal Belt."

Timbers—Oak, pine, hickory, walnut and chestnut.

Minerals—Gold and iron, with several mineral springs.

TOWNS AND POST OFFICES.

	POP.		POP.
Bright,	50	Mill's Spring,	160
Clover,	—	Pea Ridge,	60
Collinsville,	48	Poor's Ford,	50
Columbus (c h),	300	Poplar Grove,	30
Decatur,	50	Saluda,	250
Dimsdale,	60	Sandy Springs,	35
Fish Top,	25	Tryon,	110
Green River,	50	Turner's,	50
Lynn,	50	Walker,	40
Melvin Hill,	40		

COUNTY OFFICERS.

Clerk Superior Court—N B Hampton.
Commissioners—C W Pearson, ch'm'n; John C Powell, P H Gross.
Coroner—J R Smith.
Register of Deeds—J W Newman.
Sheriff—W C Robertson.
Solicitor Eleventh District—J L Webb.
Surveyor—S B Edwards.
Treasurer—J R Gibbs.

COURTS.

Tenth Monday after first Monday in March, and eleventh Monday after first Monday in September.

TOWNSHIPS AND MAGISTRATES.

Columbus—R S Abrams, C C Hampton, H C Marguin (Columbus).

Cooper's Gap—B T Wilson, W F T Brown. Wm Gibbs (Dimsdale).

Green's Creek—J W McFarland, Thos Silas, T P Coviton (Poor's Ford).

Tryon—J W Whitney, Z E Pace, B T Turner (Tryon), A B Thompson, H L Hart (Saluda).

White Oak—W B Mills (Pea Ridge), Grayson Arledge, T F Thorn (Mills Spring.)

CHURCHES.

Names, Post Offices, Pastors and Denom.

METHODIST.

Bethel—Sandy Springs.
Bethlehem—Mills' Spring.
Church—Columbus.
Friendship—Tryon City.
Lebanon—Poplar Grove.
Rains' Chapel—Columbus.

ZION METHODIST.

Nelson's Chapel (col)—Mills' Spring.
St Paul (col)—Columbus.

BAPTIST.

Church—Sandy Springs.
Church—Columbus.
Cooper's Gap—Poplar Grove.
Friendship—Tryon City.
Green's Creek—White Oak Hall.
Green River—White Oak Hall.
Rock Spring—Poplar Grove.
Silver Creek—Bright's Creek.
White Oak—Mills' Spring.
Mountain Valley—Fish Top.

PRESBYTERIAN.

Sandy Plains—White Oak Hall, L R McAboy, D D.

GERMAN BAPTIST OR BRETHREN.

Mills' Creek—Dunbrand, G A Branscombe.

MINISTERS RESIDENT.

Names, Post Offices and Denom.

BAPTIST.

Case, C C, Columbus.
Tate, Jack, Sandy Springs.
Williams, Joseph, Clover.

METHODIST.

Beaman, A S, Columbus.
Madale, A, Columbus.

BRETHREN.

Bradley, E J, Fish Top.
Branscomb, G A, Melvin Hill.

POLK COUNTY.

POLK COUNTY.

HOTELS AND BOARDING HOUSES.

Names, Post Offices and Proprietors.

Boarding house, Saluda, Mrs J A Thorn.
Boarding house, Saluda, J L Hart.
Boarding house, Saluda, Mrs -- Heritt.
Boarding house, Saluda, J Ramburger
Boarding house, Saluda, R W Pace.
Boarding house, Saluda, Mrs L Tunstall.
Boarding house, Saluda, Mrs H C Tanur.
Boarding house, Saluda, A Tanur.
Boarding house, Tryon, Mrs Williams.
Boarding house, Columbus, N H Hill.
Hotel, Columbus, F A Chirarere.

LAWYERS.

Names and Post Offices.

Carson, C A, Columbus.
Manison, Thomas F, Columbus.

MANUFACTORIES.

Kinds, Post Offices and Proprietors.

Building and contracting, Fish Top, Jos Newman.
Building and contracting, Saluda, E B Gelett.
Building and contracting, Tryon, J B Lindsay.
Building and contracting, Mill Spring, W R Turner.
Building and contracting, Columbus, H E Gray,
Coopering, Columbus, Benj Greene.
Iron and wood work, Dimsdale, V Thompson.
Iron and wood work, Saluda, J I Davis.
Iron and wood work, Tryon, Robert Gaines.
Iron and wood work, Mill Spring, Michael Corel.
Iron and wood work, Columbus, A Jackson.
Iron and wood work, Columbus, W M Corel.

MERCHANTS AND TRADESMEN.

Names, Post Offices, Line of Business.

CLOTER.
Putnam, J M,

COLLINSVILLE.
Cannon, A,   Lumber
Ezell, D F,   G S
Putman, J M,   —

COLUMBUS.
Cameron, W A,   G S
Fowles, C V,   G S

Jackson, A,   G S
McFarlan & Cannon,   G S
Pope, G S & Co,   —

DUKE.
Green, W S,   G S

DIMSDALE.
Burnett, Wm,   G S
Williams & Whiteside,   G S

GREEN RIVER.
Bigerstaff, I W,   G S
Sevier, W V,   G S

MELVIN HILL.
Branscomb, Geo,   G S
Shields, Wm M,   G S
Walker, Thomas M,   G S

MILL SPRING.
Baynard, O T,   G S
Boon, Mrs A M & Son,   G S
Mills, W B,   G S
Shankle, Dr H D,   Drugs
Thorne, Thos V & Bro,   G S
Wilson, W B & Co,   G S

PEA RIDGE.
Mills, W B,   G S

POPLAR GROVE.
Brown, Wm F T,   G S

SALUDA.
Garlet, Dr,   Drugs
Hart, J L,   G S
Morris, L D & Co,   G S
Staton & Robertson,   G S

SANDY SPRINGS.
Lancaster, D B,   G S

TRYON.
Ballenger, Wilson & Co,   G S
Hill, A,   G S
Livingston, J B & Co,   G S
Smith, G W & Co,   G S

MINES.

Kinds, Post Offices and Proprietors.

Double Branch, gold, Sandy Plains, Hoyt & Co, New York City.
Gold, Mill Springs, R L Hamilton.
Gold, Dimsdale, O A Lynch.
Gold, Columbus, W L Prince.
Gold, Skynker, David Stevens.

MILLS.

Kinds, Post Offices and Proprietors.

Corn and wheat, Columbus, Abrams & McFarland.
Corn and saw, Columbus, A Jackson & Son.
Flour and corn, Clover, Mrs J C Camp.
Flour and corn, Clover, H C Morgan.
Mill, Tryon, L F Thompson.

POLK COUNTY.

PHYSICIANS.

Names and Post Offices.

Gollett, E R, Saluda.
Grady, Earl, Tryon.
Kinnarthy, T C, Tryon.
Muldins, G S, Tryon.
Shankell, H D, Mill Springs.

SCHOOLS.

Names, Post Offices and Principals.

Academy, Columbus, A S Beaman, prin.
Academy, Saluda, Mrs M C Phelps, prin.

TEACHERS.

Names and Post Offices.

Allhands. J M, Columbus.
Arledge, Massie, Columbus.
Beaman, A S, Columbus.
Garron, Etha, Saluda.
Gills, J K, Columbus.
Higgins, J B, Mill Springs.
Higgins, H Z, Mill Springs.
Jackson, J F, Dimsdale.
Lollar. M W, Saluda.
Taylor, W S, Poplar Grove.

POLK COUNTY.

Thom, Maud, Mill Springs.
Whiteside, W M, Uree.
Widmer, Floyd, Columbus.
Williams, Oleo, Mill Springs.

FARMERS.

Names and Post Offices.

Columbus — John Carpenter, N B Hampton, J W Hampton, D V Rhoads, James Ridings, J T Waldrop, F L Weaver.
Dimsdale — Eli Bardly, Thom Edgerton, Wm Gills, R L Hamilton, B T Wilson.
Mill Springs — Grayson Arledge, A C Boone, M C Clark, L T Jackson, Wm Justice. J A Thom.
Sandy Springs — J C Campt, M O Cornwell, J B Giles, J R Simpson.
Saluda — H B Bradly, John Dalton, John W Edwards, J Faister, A W Garren, Wm Henderson, John McMurry, R L Newman, James Newman, T E Pace, J R Rhodes, D M Rollins, H K Thompson, Wm Thompson, B F Turner.
Tryon — Charlie Cox, John Garrison, R N Johnson, Adolphus Newman, D Pace, F Palwine, L F Thompson, G G Weaver. R L Wilcox.

RANDOLPH COUNTY.

AREA, 720 SQUARE MILES.

POPULATION, 25,195; White 21,848, Colored 3,347.

RANDOLPH COUNTY was formed in 1779, from Guilford and Rowan counties, and named in honor of the Randolph family of Virginia, distinguished for patriotism and talents.

ASHEBORO, the county seat, is 72 miles west from Raleigh, at the terminus of the High Point, Randleman, Asheboro and Southern Railroad. It was named in honor of Governor Ashe. Population (estimated), 1,500.

Surface — Undulatling, hilly, and some small mountains—much of it rocky. It is well watered by Deep river, Uwharrie, and various small tributary streams. There are many small plots of land lying along the streams, known as bottom lands; these are generally rich. The county altogether is finely timbered, and abounds in good water-powers.

Staples—Corn, wheat, oats, rye, flax and fruits in great variety.

Fruits—Apples, peaches, pears, grapes, berries and other small fruits.

Timbers—Oak, pine, hickory, poplar and walnut.

Minerals—Gold, silver, copper, iron, with several mineral springs.

TOWNS AND POST OFFICES.

	POP.		POP.
Aconite,	—	Flora,	45
Archdale,	500	Flower Hill,	49
Asheboro (c h),		Fork Creek,	20
	1,500	Foust's Mills,	129
Bombay,	—	Franklinville,	390
Brower's Mills,	90	Fuller's,	50
Brown's,	45	Gladesboro,	45
Brunswick,	25	Glenola,	25
Buffalo Ford,	50	Gray's Chapel,	50
Bulla,	25	Hill's Store,	25
Bunch,	30	Hoover Hill,	75
Cape,	40	Hoyle,	25
Caraway,	25	Jackson's	
Cedar Falls,	300	Creek,	90
Central Falls,	150	Kemp's Mills,	68
Cheek's,	45	Kildee,	25
Coleridge,	150	Lassiter,	65
Cole's Store,	60	Level Cross,	68
Defiance,	25	Level Plains,	65
Eden,	60	Liberty,	200
Edgar,	—	Lytton,	50
Eleazer,	30	Marley's Mills,	40
Empire,	25	Martha,	—
Erect,	39	Maud,	50
Farmer,	45	Mechanic,	50

	POP.		POP.
Melanchton,	25	Riley's Store,	45
Millboro,	50	Salem Church,	60
Moffitt,	100	Sawyersville,	75
New Hope		Science,	75
Academy,	45	Soapstone Mt.,	55
New Market,	50	Sophia,	—
New Salem,	100	Spero,	—
Penson,	—	Staley,	100
Pisgah,	60	Strieby,	50
Post Oak,	25	Trinity,	300
Progress,	50	Ula,	—
Quirine,	—	Velna,	—
Rachael,	—	Wheatmore,	—
Ralph,	30	White House,	40
Ramseur,	275	Why Not,	45
Randleman,	2,500	Woodford,	—
Randolph,	50	Worthville,	250
Reitzel,	60		

COUNTY OFFICERS.

Clerk Superior Court—J M Millikan.
Commissioners—J E Walker, chm'n; B W Steed, O R Cox.
Coroner—D W Burrow.
Register of Deeds—T J Winslow.
Sheriff—G G Hendricks.
Solicitor 8th District—J L Holton.
Surveyor—J M Allen.
Standard Keeper—W F Birkhead.
Treasurer—J S Swaim.
County Examiner—N C English.
Jailor—J S Ferree
Superintendent of Health—T T Ferree.

COURTS.

Second Monday after the first Monday in March; eighth Monday before the first Monday in September; tenth Monday after the first Monday in September.

TOWN OFFICERS.

ARCHDALE — *Mayor*, W T Parker; *Marshal*, J T White; *Commissioners*, A J Tomlinson, J L Freeman. Thomas Folwell, Herb Tomlinson, W M Wilson.

ASHEBORO—*Mayor*, W J Gregson; *Commissioners*, W P Wood, Jos Redding, T J Moffitt, W F Redding, R W Frasier; *Treasurer*, W H Moring, jr; *Clerk*, H D Caudel; *Marshal*, O R Fox.

RAMSEUR—*Mayor*, Y M C Johnson; *Marshal*, J T Turner; *Commissioners*, Willis Luther, W N Whitehead, C S

RANDOLPH COUNTY.

Tate; *Treasurer*, H B Carter; *Secretary*, W H Wadkins.

RANDLEMAN—*Mayor*, J H Wilson; *Commissioners*, S G Newlin, W G Glass, J M Pugh, W H Lawrence, J W Parson; *Clerk*, J T Millikan.

WORTHVILLE—*Mayor*, H M Worth; *Commissioners*, A W Jenkins, J S McAlister, N T Grace.

TOWNSHIPS AND MAGISTRATES.

Asheboro—Jos Redding, A A Spencer, Franklin Pritchard (Asheboro).

Back Creek—Chapp Bulla, T F Robbins (Bull', N H Ferguson (Hoyle), J W Bean (Spero), David Farlow (Level Plains).

Brower—R H Sewall (Cheek's), Alfred Brady (Velna), Marshal Moffitt, J E Allbright, R K Brady (Erect).

Cedar Grove—Oscar Tadlock, L B Lowe, W H Parker, W E Yeargin, Jas Lowe (Science Hill), Levi Branson (White House).

Columbia—D M Frazier, —— Kinnery (Soapstone Mount), Henry Craven, J T Brower (Ramseur), W J Frazier (Staley).

Concord—W J Loftin, J F Horney, Robt F Steed (Farmer), L G B Bingham (Flora).

Franklinville—J H Pugh, J M Ellison Jos Ellison (Franklinville), A G Jennings (Cedar Falls), Allen Osborn (Central Falls).

Grant—R J Cox (Franklinville), H M Gardner (Flower Hill), Jas Smith (Kemp's Mills), D C Brown (Brown's Store) J M Allen (Ralph), J M Hinson (Empire).

Liberty—D M Holladay, J M Williams, Mink Hornady, W F Bowman (Liberty), Wm Freeman (Julian).

Newhope—J T Thornburg (Lassiter), Branson Sheets (Riley's Store).

New Market—J W Davit (Progress) S W Laughlin (Sophia), G E Stanton Level Cross), T L L Cox (Gladesboro), Elias Spencer (Edgar).

Pleasant Grove—J E Stout, Aaron Stout, (Buffalo Ford), Jno Loudermilk, E W Brown (Cheek's), C B Craven (Buffalo Ford).

Providence—W A Rauth, J C Coltrane (Gray's Chapel), Rufus Nesse, Jesse Skeen, J A Branson (Brunswick).

Randleman—J T Millikan, E P Hayes, W C Hiushaw, W F Tally (Randleman), T N Harris (Worthville).

Richland — H M Johnson, (Fork Creek), Jos E Harper (Whynot), Wm Russell, Wm Coble (Randleman).

Tabernacle—R C Welborn, Lafayette Briles, N S Bingham (Hoover Hill).

RANDOLPH COUNTY.

Trinity—J J White (Trinity) James Winslow (Maud), B F Blair, Joseph Clark (Progress), Jos G Dorsett (Wheatmore).

Union—Cummings King, J B Parks (Pisgah).

DEPUTY SHERIFFS.

Brady, J A, Velna.
Brown, A D, Brown's Store.
Cox, W L, Coleridge.
Elliott, L C, Bombay.
Frazier, Henry, Brunswick.
Free, S E, Cedar Falls.
Free, Jas F, Asheboro.
Hayworth, J M, Archdale.
Hancock, J F, Flower Hill.
Kivett, W P, Soaptone Mount.
Laughlin, Robt. Defiance.
Lawrence, W H, Randleman.
Laughlin, J F, Hoyle.
Owen, W B, Libetty.
Pearce, Thos G, Jackson's Creek.
Routh, D M, Level Cross.

CHURCHES.

Names, Post Offices and Denominations.

METH. EPISCOPAL.

Church—Ashboro.
Cedar Falls—Cedar Falls.
Church—Staley.
Church—Ramseur.
Church—Franklinsville.
Concord—Foust's Mills.
Concord—Farmers.
Concord—Coleridge.
Ebenezer—Gladesboro.
Gilead—Defiance.
Hopewell—Trinity.
Mount Zion—Brown's Mills.
Mount Olive—Erect.
Mount Lebanon—Science Hill.
Mount Vernon—Maud.
Mount Tabor—Jackson's Creek.
Naomi Falls—Randleman.
New Lebanon—Science Hill.
Old Union—New Market.
Pisgah—Pisgah.
Pleasant Grove—Fuller's.
Prospect—Trinity.
Salem—Salem Church.
Shepherd—Hoover Hill.
Saint Paul's—Randleman.
Union—Rachael.

METHODIST PROTESTANT.

Church—Asheboro.
Bethany—Worthville.
Bethel—Brunswick.
Brower's—Asheboro.
Cedar Falls—Cedar Falls.

RANDOLPH COUNTY.

Church—Liberty.
Davis Chapel—Spero.
Fair Grove—Why Not.
Flag Spring—Uhla.
Flint Hill—Hoyle.
Level Cross—Level Cross.
Liberty Grove—Liberty.
Mt Lebanon—Randleman.
Mt Pleasant—Hoover Hill.
Mt Zion—Defiance.
New Hope—Aconite.
New Union—Science Hill.
Pleasant Hill—Fork Creek.
Salem—Ramseur.

FRIENDS.

Archdale Church—Archdale.
Back Creek—Post Oak.
Bethel—
Hopewell—White House.
Holly Springs—Fuffalo Ford.
Marlboro—New Market.
Oak Forest—Progress.
Pine Ridge—Moffitt's Mills.
Plainfield—Sophia.
Science Hill—Mechanic.
Uwharrie—Hill's Store.

WESLEYAN METH.

Caraway—Hoyle.
Cedar Grove—Science Hill.
High Pine—White House.

A. M. E. ZION.

Red Church—Mechanic.

AFRICAN METHODIST.

Colored Church—Hill's Store.

NORTH. METH. EPISCOPAL.

Mountain View—Caraway.

COL. METH. EPIS.

Church—Staley.
Friendship—Ramseur.

CHRISTIAN.

Antioch—Moffitt's Mills.
Christian Union—Why Not.
Church—Staley.
Church—Randleman.
Church—Liberty.
New Centre—Why Not.
Parks' Cross Roads—Ramseur.
Patterson Grove—Soapstone Mount.
Pleasant Ridge—Empire.
Pleasant Grove—Cheek's.
Shiloh—Moffitt's Mills.

BAPTIST.

Cedar Falls—Cedar Falls.
Church—Fork Creek.
Church—Cedar Falls.
Church—Liberty.
Church—Ramseur.
Church—Randleman.
Church—Wheatmore.
Liberty Grove (col)—Trinity.
Moore's Chapel—Franklinsville.
Shady Grove—Staley.

RANDOLPH COUNTY.

PRIMITIVE BAPTIST.

Sandy Creek—Four miles west of Liberty.
Rock Hill—Science Hill.

PRESBYTERIAN.

Calah—Buffalo Ford.
Church—Asheboro.

CONGREGATIONAL.

Salem (col)—Martha.

HOTELS AND BOARDING HOUSES.

Names, Post Offices and Proprietors.

Banner Hotel, Ashboro, B B Burns.
Boarding, Trinity, Prof L Johnson.
Boarding, Trinity, Mrs J L Craven.
Boarding, Trinity, J R Means.
Boarding, Randleman, C M Vestal.
Boarding, Ashboro, Mrs Lou Bradshaw.
Boarding, Trinity, Benson Parker.
Boarding, ——, R H McIntire.
Boarding, Ramseur, W F Lane.
Boarding, Franklinville, M M Brown.
Boarding, Franklinville. J S Ritter.
Boarding, Trinity, Mrs Hensley.
Boarding, Ashboro. Mrs Brookshire.
Boarding, Hoover Hill, J Sneed.
Barding, Archdale, W M Wilson.
Hotel, Ramseur.
Hotel, Randleman, F N Ingold.
Hotel, Liberty. W B Pemberton.
Hotel, Franklinville, Mrs J R Ritter.

LAWYERS.

Names and Post Offices.

Blair, J A, Ashoboro.
Bradshaw, Geo S, Ashboro.
Britton & Sapp, Ashboro.
Gregson, W J.
Hammer, W C, Ashboro.
Robbins. M S, Ashboro.
Rush, W D, Ashboro.
Sapp, O L.

MANUFACTORIES.

Kinds, Proprietors and Post Offices.

The Randleman Mfg Co (including the Quinn Mill), O W Carr, pres; J H Feree, sec and treas; J O Pickard, sup; capital stock, $100,000; surplus, $92,000; raw material, 3,000 bales cotton a year; products, 4,000,000 yds plaids; 250 hands; average wages per day, 43 cents; shipping point. express and telegraph offices, Randleman.
The Plaidville Mfg Co, J H Ferree, sec and treas; J O Pickard and S G Newlin. directors; capital stock, $50 000;

RANDOLPH COUNTY.

material used annually, 600,000 lbs yarn; products, 3,500,000 yds plaids; 125 hands; average wages per day, 60 cents; shipping point, express and telegraph offices, Randleman.

Powhattan Mfg Co, O R Cox, pres; Jas E Walker, sec and treas; $30,000 capital stock; 224,500 pounds yarn annually; 1,300,000 yards colored cotton goods; shipping point, express and telegraph offices, Randleman.

Naomi Falls Mfg Co, capital stock, $108,550; S Bryant, treas; Amos Gregson, sup; raw material used annually, 2,200 bales cotton; 3,000,000 yards plaids, checks and stripes, and 600,000 seamless bags; 225 hands; shipping point, express and telegraph offices, Randleman.

Randleman Hosiery Mill, capital stock, $30,000; A N Bulla, sup; L A Spencer, sec and treas; S G Newlin, partner; raw material used annually, 50,000; pounds yarn; 30,000 dozen pairs hose and half hose; number hands, 40; average wages, 60 cents per day; shipping point, express and telegraph offices, Randleman.

The Worth Mfg Co (Mill No 1), Hal M Worth, sec and treas; H L Jackson, sup; capital stock, $100,000; raw material used annually, 2 500 bales of cotton; gross products, 3,000,000 yds sheeting. 300,000 salt and grain bags; shipping point, express and telegraph offices, Millboro and Randleman; 135 hands; $22,000 pay-roll per year, Worthville.

The Worth Mfg Co (Mill No 2), J M Worth, pres; Hal M Worth, sec and treas; J M Fowler, sup; capital stock, $100,000; gross material used annually, 2,000 bales of cotton; gross products, 1,800,000 yards of plaids; 300,000 pounds of warps; shipping point, express and telegraph offices, Millboro; 150 hands; $23,000 pay-roll per year; Central Falls.

Cedar Falls Mfg Co (incorporated 1877), capital stock, $75,000; Dr J M Worth, pres; O R Cox, sec and treas and supt of mill; 75 hands; average per day, 40 cents; raw material used annually, 1,800 bales cotton; products, 720,000 pounds of warps and fillings; Cedar Falls.

Franklinville Mfg Co, capital stock, $60,000 (incorporated); Hugh Parks, pres; Benjamin Moffitt, sec and treas; W C Russell, supt; raw material uses annually, $1,500 bales of cotton; products, 600,000 bags and 150,000 lbs of warps; number of hands, 180; average wages per day, 60 cents; Franklinville.

RANDOLPH COUNTY.

Randolph Mfg Co, capital stock, $30,000; surplus, $15,000 (incorporated 1862); John D Williams (of Fayetteville) pres; Hugh Parks, sec and treas, J A Luther, supt; raw material used annually, 850 bales of cotton; products, 3,000 yards of 4 4 sheeting daily and also cotton yarns; number of hands, 70; average wages per day, 60 cents; Franklinville.

Columbia Mfg Co, capital stock, $90,000; surplus, $55,000 (incorporated); J S Spencer, pres; A W E Caper, supt; W H Watkins, sec and treas; raw material used annually, 3,000 bales of cotton; products, 3,000,000 yards sheeting, 25,000 lbs ball sewing thread, 25,000 lbs of bundle yarn; number of hands, 180; average pay, 54 cents per day; Ramseur.

Enterprise Cotton Factory, established in 1833 by E A Moffitt, James A Cole, Daniel Lambert and W S Russell, and has been quite successful; capital stock, $15,000; Coleridge.

Staley Cotton Mill, R V Cox, proprietor; original cost, $13,000; produces cotton yarns and warps, Staley.

Boot and shoe making, A H Burgess, Franklinville.

Trinity Broom Works, Benson Parker, sec and treas and business manager, Trinity.

Carriage and buggy works, Hugh J Burns, Asheboro.

Brick and tile works, Tomlinson & Andrews, Archdale.

Brick factory, J F Allred, Franklinville.

The Alberta Chair Works (incorporated 1889), capital stock, $25,000; W H Watkins, pres; J S Spencer, vice-pres; A W E Capel, sec and treas; J C Marsh, sup; surplus, $5,000. This factory also manufactures a general line of brooms, Ramseur.

Brickyard, H F Church, Archdale.

Cigar factory, A F Eshelman. Trinity.

Chair and furniture factory, A G Jennings, Cedar Falls.

Franklinville Stoneware Company, E R Moffitt & Co, Franklinville.

Pottery work, L O Sugg, Erect.

Pottery works, E R Moffitt & Co, Franklinville.

Pottery works, M T Sugg, Erect.

Pottery works, M R Moffitt, Uhala.

Pottery shop, Evan Cole, Why Not.

Po tery works, J G Albright, Kemp's Mills.

Pottery works, M F Wren, Erect.

Pottery works. J M Yow, Erect.

Pottery shop, G W Teague, Erect.

RANDOLPH COUNTY.	RANDOLPH COUNTY.

Wood manufacturing, Wood Milling and Mfg Co; B L Lineberry, mgr; Trinity.

Sash and blind factory, Nathaniel Cox & Son; Moffitt's Mills.

Shuttle block factory, Turner Vancannon; White House.

Shuttle block factory, W A Grimes & Co; 180,000 annually; Asheboro.

Stove factory, McKendric Gray, Wheatmore.

Tomlinson Mfg Co (incorporated), S F Tomlinson, pres; E P Parker, vicepres; A J Tomlinson, sec and treas; tanners and shoe manufacturers; capital, $18,000; Archdale.

Horse collars, Tomlinson Mfg Co, Archdale.

Harness and saddles, E W Erazier, Archdale.

Tannery and harness factory, F L Hayworth, Moffitt's Mills.

Tannery, Stephen Howard, Moffitt's Mills.

Tannery, Calvin Cox, Buffalo Ford.

Wagons and smithery, T M Hendricks, Archdale.

Foundry and machine shop, G H Allred, Randleman.

Asheboro Wood and Iron Works, capital, $15,000; E A Moffitt, pres; J T Moffitt, sec and treas; C J Cox. J G Stone and E A Moffitt, directors; Asheboro.

Woodworking and blacksmithing, A W Sanders, Asheboro.

Wagon and smithing, W E Allred, Cedar Falls.

Wood Mfg and Milling Co, Prof W T Ganaway, pres; B L Lineberry, sec and treas and general mgr; capital, $4,000; Trinity.

Guilord Lumber and Mfg Co, branch factory at Asheboro; R S Hunter, mgr; main office, Greensboro, N C; C A Reynolds, pres; W D Mendenhall, sec and treas; Asheboro.

Asheboro Lumber and Mfg Co; capital stock, $25 000; S G Bradshaw, pres; C C McAllister, sec and treas; David Petty, supt; capacity for cutting 4,000,000 feet lumber annually; Asheboro.

MERCHANTS AND TRADESMEN.

Names, Post Offices, Lines of Business.

ARCHDALE.	
Llewellen, M C,	G S
Tomlinson, H A & Co,	G S
Tomlinson Store Co,	G S
Tomlinson, A U & Sons,	G S

ASHBORO.	
Ashboro Clothing,	G S
Auman, J,	G S
Bargain Store Co,	G S
Burkhead, J W,	G S
Blair, Mrs E T,	Millinery
Boyette & Richardson,	Drugs
Brower, J W & Co,	Gro
Burns Hunter Drug Co,	Drugs
Burns, B B,	Livery
Burns, J M,	Gro
Hammer, J C & Co,	G S
Kearns, E B,	—
Lassiter, E C,	Hdw
Lewis & Spencer,	G S
Lewis, J S,	Turp and G S
Miller, J W,	G S
Moragne, W F,	Jeweler
Moring, W H, jr, & Co,	G S
Morris & Scarboro,	G S
Presnell, Uriah (near),	G S
Pugh, A S,	G S
Riss & Rush,	Livery
Spencer, J A,	G S
Stedman, W D & Co,	Gro
Taylor, Waddell,	G S
Waddell & Co,	G S
Wood, W P & Co.,	G S
Worth Store Co,	G S

BROWN'S STORE.	
Allen, W H,	G S
Brown, Ira,	—
Hammond, H & Son,	—
Morris & Scarboro,	—

BRUNSWICK.	
Barker, G P,	G S
Dunn, Sam'l,	G S
Fields C,	G S

BULLA.	
Hammond & Co,	Lumber
McRary, W F & Son,	G S
Redding, T J,	Lumber

CAPE.	
Parks, J R,	G S

CARRAWAY.	
Farlow, E N & Co,	G S
Jarrell, J F,	Jeweler

CEDAR FALLS.	
Jennings, A G & S n,	Furn
Leonard Bros,	G S

CENTRAL FALLS.	
Duffie, Mrs L J,	G S
McAllister & Co,	G S
Osborne, A M,	—
York, E C,	—

CHEEK'S.	
Brown, Wm H,	G S
Caviness, A T,	G S
Leonard, L D,	G S

CLIMAX.	
Hutton & Hutton,	G S

RANDOLPH COUNTY.

RANDOLPH COUNTY.

COLERIDGE.
Scotton, A K & Bro,	G S
Yow, W H,	G S

COLE'S STORE.
Caviness, J M,	G S
Lambert, J T,	G S
Lane, J R,	G S

DEFIANCE.
Miller, J A & B T,	G S
Sawyer, E N,	G S

EDEN.
Kennedy, S J,	G S
Phillips, L C,	G S

EDGAR.
Wall & Spencer,	G S

ERECT.
Tysor, Thos B,	G S
Yow, J M,	G S

FARMER.
Lewis, Dr C H,	G S
Newby, N W,	G S

FLORA.
Morgan, J A,	G S

FORK CREEK.
Spencer, J W,	—
Yow, A M,	G S

FRANKLINVILLE.
Burgess, A H,	Gro
Ellison, J M & Co,	G S
Leonard Bros,	—

FULLER'S.
Fuller, A W,	G S
Phillips, L C,	G S
Skeen, N R & Son,	G S

GLADESBORO.
Stanton, I F,	G S

GLENOLA.
Goins, J D,	G S
Spencer, R B,	G S

GRAY'S CHAPEL.
Coltrain, J C,	G S
Dunn, Samuel,	—
McMasters, W R,	G S
Pugh & Lineberry,	G S
Routh, W M,	G S

HILL'S STORE.
Lewis, W R,	G S

HOOVER HILL.
Jarrett, A W,	G S
Pearce, J,	G S

HOYLE.
Beckerdite, R I,	Gro
Causy & Hale,	G S

JACKSON CREEK.
Hill, J C,	G S
Nance, Allen & Sons,	G S

JONES MINE.
Childer, P L,	—
Fuller, A,	—

JULIAN.
Stout, J R,	—

KEMP'S MILLS.
Allen, J J & Co,	G S
Hinshaw, Thomas,	G S

KILDEE.
York, W H & V,	G S

LASSITER'S MILLS.
Lassiter, J, (estate of A G Murdock), manager,	G S

LEVEL CROSS.
Fogleman, W D,	G S

LIBERTY.
Banks & Morgan,	G S
Bowman, N F,	Drugs
Brower, Mrs E N,	Millinery
Cash Store Co,	—
Griffin & Trogden,	G S
Hornaday, S M,	Livery and G S
Overman, J O,	Confec
Ray, J M (near),	G S
Wrightsell, John,	G S
Wrightsell, J & Co,	G S

MAUD.
Elder, W N,	G S

MARTHA.
Nance & Nance,	—

MECHANIC.
Howard & Co,	G S

MILLBORO.
Pugh, J W & Son,	G S

MOFFITT'S MILL.
Caveness, J M,	G S
McCoy, J W & Son,	G S

MULLEN.
Jones, Alfred,	G S

NEW HOPE ACADEMY.
Shaw, W S & Son,	G S
Strickland, H W,	G S

NEW MARKET.
Newlin, D,	Gro and Tinner
Spencer, R B,	G S

NEW SALEM.
Caudle, L M,	G S
Hayes, E P,	G S

PINSON.
Hill & Bro,	G S

PISGAH.
Cogle, A J,	G S
Cornelison, J C & Son,	G S
Lucas, J J,	G S
Parks, J W,	G S

PROGRESS.
Hendrix, G G,	G S

RANDOLPH COUNTY.

RAMSEUR.

Copeland & Marsh,	G S
Forrester, J O & Co,	Furn and Jeweler
Fox, Dr L M,	Drugs
Ramseur Store Co,	G S
Stout, W C,	Gro

RANDLEMAN.

Allred, J W,	Lumber
Bain, J C & Sons,	G S
Barker & Olive,	G S
Barzune & Bro,	G S
Caudle, L M,	G S
Clapp, J A,	—
Coltrane, Miss Minnie,	Millinery
Coltrane, J N,	Barber
Cox, N P,	—
Davidson, Jos,	Painter
Dean, T E,	Gro
Engleworth Store Co,	G S
Fergerson, ——,	G S
Fields, J L,	G S
Hayes, E P,	G S
Kirkman, S E,	G S
Klapp, J M,	Gro
Lineberry, Mrs M,	Gro
Lineberry, W A,	Gro
Mendenhall Bros,	Mdse Brokers
Mills, G W,	—
Naomi Store Co,	G S
Newlin, Dunk,	Tin Shop
Newlin, Samuel,	Bookkeeper
Randleman Store Co,	G S
Redding, W W,	—
Richardson, N C,	Gro
Russell, I A,	Barber
Spencer, L A,	G S
Spencer & Lamb,	G S
Stratford, D W,	Painters
Talley & Co,	—
Woollen, W A,	Drugs
Wood, Jno,	Barber
Wright, J A,	G S

RANDOLPH.

Parrish, M W & Co,	G S

RED CROSS.

Fields, C,	G S
Freeman, B H,	Miller

RILEY'S STORE.

Sheet, B J,	G S

SALEM CHURCH.

Nance & Nance,	G S
Thompson, Jno,	G S

SCIENCE HILL.

Parker, W H,	G S
Ridge, J W,	G S

SOAPSTONE MT.

Jones, Alfred,	G S
Kimrey, H L,	G S
McMasters, Wm R,	G S
Wrightsell, G W,	G S

SOPHIA.

Dix & Gregy,	—

RANDOLPH COUNTY.

Gray, F G,	G S
Laughlin & Hinshaw,	G S

SPERO.

Bean, J W,	G S

STALEY.

Brewer, A C & Co,	G S
Frazer, C G & Co,	G S
Teague, J F,	G S

STRIEBY.

Parks, J G,	G S
Strider, E J & Co,	G S

TRINITY.

Lineberry, B L,	G S
Miller, Misses T and R & M,	Millinery
Parker, B,	G S
Riddick, R W,	Agt Farm Alliance

ULA.

Moffitt, M R,	G S
Pressnell, Uriah,	G S

VELNA.

Leonard & Brady,	—

WHY NOT.

Allred, E C & Son,	G S
Auman, D,	G S
Yow, Henry,	G S
Yow, W H,	G S

WORTHVILLE.

Allen, A H,	—
Arnold, J O,	Gro
Coble, W C,	G S
Deep River Store Co,	G S
Harper, C E,	G S
Jenkins, Alex W,	—

MINES.

Kinds, Post Offices and Proprietors.

Gold Prospect—the Burrow Mine, Asheboro, Mrs Hannah McDowell.

Gold, the Fisher, Asheboro, B J Fisher.

Gold Prospect—Jones' Mine; W H Moring, mgr.

Hoover Hill Gold Mine, capitalized at $350,000; supposed to be one of the richest mines in the county; Hoover Hill; Capt Joseph Parkin, mgr; T H Reading, mine clerk.

Keystone Gold Mining Co, Jones Mine, has been worked successfully.

Herring Gold Mine, Jones Mine P O; Mr Lewis, Brooklyn, N Y.

Laughlin Gold Mine, Jones Mine P O, W N Laughlin.

Pierce Gold Mine, Jones Mine P O, Alfred Pierce.

Elder Hill or Brower Gold Mine, Jones Mine P O; Delk Mine, Jones Mine P O; Miller Mine, Jones Mine P O, Dr Alson Fuller.

RANDOLPH COUNTY.

Jones Gold Mines—Nos 1 and 2, Jones Mine P O; Parish Gold Mine, Jones Mine P O; Kindley Gold Mine, Jones Mine P O—lately bought by a syndicate of North Carolinians and Pennsylvanians.

B W Hill Gold Mine, Jones Mine P O, B W Hill.

Spencer Gold Mine, Fullers P O, Mr. Spencer.

Copple Gold Mine, Fullers P O, Mr Stoupe, of Pa.

Rush & Redding Gold Mine, Hoover Hill P O.

Kindley Gold Mire, Hoover Hill P O, lately sold by Stanley Redding.

Northern company own a gold prospect near High Point.

Stafford Gold Mine, New Hope Academy, James Shears.

Griffin Mine, New Hope Academy, Burwell Steed.

Uwharrie Gold Mine—not now operated—S rieby, Old North State Mining Co.

• Newby Gold Mine—not now in operation—Science Hill, Nathan Newby's heirs.

Gold—not in operation—Flower Hill, B H Cox & Co.

Gold—Barker Mine—Flower Hill; not in operation now; owned by Levi Cox.

Gold—Spoon Mine—has been operated successfully; Empire. Owned now by Jo Spoon's heirs.

Gold—has been operated successfully—Empire, Miss Elizabeth Porter.

Gold—now being opened—Progress, Lowe Bros.

Gold prospect, Science Hill, S H & Jno T Lowe.

Gold prospect, Science Hill, N M & S H Lowe.

Gold prospect, White House, Mrs Doub and others of Greensboro, N C.

Gold—Coltrane Mine—Carraway; was worked successfully some thirty years ago—now dormant; owned by Jesse Coltrane, of Gladesboro, N C.

Gold—has been successfully operated, but now dormant—Caraway, T J Redding.

Cagle Gold Mine, Gray's Chapel, Geo Cagle.

The Buckeye Gold Mining Co, White House. Hon L C Reeve, pres; Arthur L Reeve, sec and treas; John T Cramer. gen mgr; telegraph and express offices, Asheboro, N C.

Little Jones Gold Mine, Jones Mine—now being operated—owned by David Lines & Co.

Sawyer Gold Mine—formerly worked successfully; this mine has just been

RANDOLPH COUNTY.

sold to Western Pennsylvania parties, who will at once develop and operate on an extensive sale—Caraway, T J Redding and others.

Gold—the Julian—Cedar Falls, Redding Brothers.

Gold—the Rush Mine—White House; not regularly worked, Z F Rush, sr.

Gold—The Hammer's Creek, White House; was operated successfully before the war; 500 acres, owned by Jno B Gluyas.

Gold prospect—formerly worked—near Asheboro, Nat Steed's heirs.

Gold prospect—formerly worked, near Asheboro; Henry Davis' heirs, Jamestown.

Gold—Davis Mountain Mine, Asheboro; now in operation; Worth & McAlister.

Gold prospect—High Point, owned by a Northern company.

Gold prospect—Trinity College, Dr F C Frazier.

Gold prospect—Trinity College, Miss Sallie Frazier.

Gold prospect—not in operation; Archdale, Dr J M Tomlinson.

Gold prospect—not yet worked—Caraway P O; owned by Dr J M Tomlinson.

Gold mine—prospect—Hill's Store, Joseph Eddie.

Gold mine—prospect—Mechanic, Henry Sanders.

MILLS.

Kinds, Post Offices and Proprietors.

Asheboro Roller Mill, incorporated, capital stock, $10,000; Dr J M Worth, pres; R R Ross, sec and treas; A M Rankin, vice-pres; D F Caldwell, director; capacity, 50 barrels per day.

Archdale Roller Mill Co (incorporated), capital, $6,000; Jesse Frazier, pres; Geo R Miller, sec and treas; capacity per day of 50 barrels of flour; corn mills, capacity, 300 bushels per day, Archdale.

Flour and corn (roller mill), Fuller & Hughes. Fullers.

Flour and corn (patent roller), Enterprise Mfg Co, Coleridge.

Flour and corn (roller mill), Harris Johnson, Flora.

Flour and corn (roller mill), Cole & Co, Coleridge.

Flour, corn and saw (roller mill), Miller & Co, Defiance.

Corn and feed mill, Asheboro Lumber and Mfg Co, Asheboro.

Corn and flour (Staley mill), Staley.

Corn and saw mill and blacksmith shop, West Bros, Liberty.

Corn and flour, H B Carter & Co, Marley's Mills.

Corn, M Holt, Soapstone Mount.

Flour and corn, Calvin Cox, Buffalo Ford.

Flour, corn and saw, Steven Hinshaw, Hoover Hill.

Flour and corn, Thayer Williams & Co, Eden.

Flour and corn, Enoch Cox, Brunswick.

Flour, corn, saw and gin, J R Parks, Cape.

Flour, corn and saw, J J Lucus, Pisgah.

Flour, corn and saw, Dennis Cox, Pisgah.

Flour and corn, A J Yow & Son, Fork Creek.

Flour and corn, Franklinville Mfg Co, Franklinville.

Flour, corn and saw, Cox & Craven, Moffitt's Mills.

Flour, corn and saw, J J Allen & Co, Kemp's Mills.

Flour and corn, A J Bean, Buffalo Ford.

Flour and corn, Columbia Mfg Co, Ramseur.

Flour, corn and saw, Jonathan Trotter, Progress.

Flour and corn (the Branson mill), owned by Branson heirs and others, Level Cross.

Flour and corn, Robert Coble, Brunswick.

Flour and corn, Elwood Rush & Co, Hoyle.

Flour and corn, Shubal Loflin, Hoyle.

Flour and corn, W F McRary & Co, Bulla.

Flour and corn, James Spencer, Sawyersville.

Flour, corn and saw, J M Trotter, Progress.

Flour and corn, Jesse F Coltrane, Gladesboro.

Flour, corn and saw, J J Allen & Co Kemp's Mill.

Flour, corn and saw, W D Spoon & Mother, Brown's Store.

Flour and corn, J A Humble & Co, Ralph.

Flour, corn and saw, J J Lucus, Pisgah.

Flour and corn, Mr Birkhead, Salem Church.

Flour and corn, Adderton & Nance, Farmers.

Flour, corn and saw, Hill & Garner, Jackson's Creek.

Flour, corn and saw, Jeff Hinshaw, Hoover Hill.

Flour, corn and saw, Burt Fuller & Hughes, Fuller's.

Flour, corn and saw, Noah Sheen, Hoover Hill.

Flour, corn and saw, Dennis Cox, Aconite.

Flour and corn, James Lowe, Science Hill.

Flour and corn, John Kemp, Science Hill.

Flour and corn, Murdoch & Loftin, Lassiter's Mills.

Flour and corn, E L Burney, Eleazer.

Flour and corn, Alson Bean, Buffalo Ford.

Flour, corn, saw and cotton gin, J R Parks, Cape.

Flour and corn, J R Lane, Cole's Store.

Flour and corn, Wren & Lambert, Cole's Store.

Flour and corn, Nathaniel Cox & Son, Moffitt's Mills.

Flour, corn and saw, Cox & Craven, Moffitt's Mills.

Flour, corn and saw, H T Caviness & Co, Cheek's.

Flour and corn, Mrs E B Brower, Brower's Mills.

Flour and corn (Merchant Mill), David M Payne, Trinity College.

Flour and corn, John Kemp, Mechanic.

Flour, corn and saw, Riley Hill, Riley Hill.

Flour and corn, Jeremiah Johnson, Riley's Store.

Flour and corn, E L Burney, New Hope Academy.

Flour and corn, Jonathan Trotter, Progress.

Flour and corn (Thayer mill), Kennedy & Co, Eden.

Flour, corn, saw and gin, Frank Parks, Parks Cross Roads.

Flour, corn and saw, Thos Marley, mgr, Marley's Mills.

Flour and corn, Pleasant Siler, Staley.

Flour, corn and saw, A P Brown, Soapstone Mount.

Flour and corn, Ramseur Mfg Co, Ramseur.

Flour, corn and saw, Geo Rightsell, Soapstone Mount.

Flour and corn, Isaac Ruth, Gray's Chapel.

Flour and corn, John Kemp, Mechanic.

Flour and corn, Andrew Yow, Fork Creek.

Flour and corn, W T Birkhead, Farmers.

Flour, corn and saw, J W Morgan, Jackson's Creek.

Flour and corn, Daniel Lambert, Cole's Store.

RANDOLPH COUNTY.

Flour and corn (Foundry mill), Rush Bros, Maud.
Flour and corn (Walker mill), J T Bostic & Son, New Market.
Flour and corn, Jesse Coletrane, Glades, boro.
Flour and corn mill and cotton gin, Franklinville Mfg Co, Franklinville.
Flour and corn, Cedar Falls Mfg Co, Cedar Falls.
Flour and corn, John Rightsell, Soap-stone Mount.
Flour and corn (McMaster's), Pressly Brown, Soapstone Mount.
Flour and corn (Lambert mill), D H Lambert, Cole's S ore.
Flour and corn (Cox's mill), Calvin Cox, Buffalo Ford.
Flour and corn, Levi Cox, Empire.
Flour, corn and saw (Spoon's), Wm Spoon, Kemp's Mills.
Flour and corn (steam), J R Parks, Cape.
Flour, corn and saw (Lane's Mills), Jno R Lane, Brush Creek.
Flour and corn (Cheek's mill), H T Caviness & Co, Cheek's.
Flour and corn, Nathaniel Cox & Son, Moffitt's Mills.
Flour, corn and saw. Riley Hill, Union.
Saw mill (water), J D Hackett, Centre.
Long's mills, Staley & Dixon, two miles north of Liberty.
Corn, saw and cotton gin, Frank Parks, Park's Cross Roads.
Steam saw, Jas A Parks, Ramseur.
Steam saw, Jerrell & Thad Crowson, Defiance.
Saw and planing mill, Asheboro Lumber and Mfg Co, Why Not.
Steam saw, Spencer & Coltrane, Glen-ola.
Steam saw, A K Scatten & Co, Cole-ridge.
Steam saw, R L Hoover, Eden.
Steam saw, John W Gray, of Thomas-ville, Wheatmore.
Steam saw, Thos Everhart, Wheat-more.
Steam saw, Crowson & Walker, Maud.
Steam saw, Hill & Bros, New Hope Academy.
Steam saw, Henry Strickland, New Hope Academy.
Steam saw and gin, J Wellons Parks, Cape.
Steam saw, Allison Bean & Bro, Erect.
Steam saw, Amos Hinshaw, Erect.
Steam saw, Allen McDaniels, Science Hill.
Steam saw, John Plummer, Farmers.
Steam saw, Millis & Co, White House.
Steam saw, Harris Johnson & Sons, White House.

RANDOLPH COUNTY.

Steam saw, Henry Pool & Sons, Science Hill.
Saw and planing (steam), Lineberry & Co, Trinity College.
Steam saw, Cox & Lewellen, Flower Hill.
Saw and planing (steam), Flower Hill Foundry Co, Asheboro.
Steam saw, Stephen Kivett, Sophia.
Steam saw (spoke billets, etc), Spencer & Co, New Market.
Saw (water), J D Hackett, Centre.
Steam saw, Thayer & Co, Fuller's.
York mill, Aaron York, five miles southwest of Liberty.

PHYSICIANS.

Names and Post Offices.

Asbury, F E. Asbury (Montgomery co).
Bulla, A M, Bulla.
Bulla, A C, Bulla.
Bulla, Jeff D. Level Cross.
Caddell, S W. Empire.
Dowd, T D, Kemp's Mills.
Ferree, Rev T T. Asheboro.
Fox, M L, Ramseur.
Fox, W A, Randleman.
Fox, Thomas, Franlinville.
Frazier, Cicero (dentist), Trinity.
Fuller, Alson, Fuller's.
Gray, Clayborn. Level Cross.
Hayworth, M M, Franklinville.
Henley, S A, Asheboro.
Hubbard, C C, Worthville.
Henley, F A (dentist), Randleman.
Kirkman, ——. Starr (Montgomery co).
Lewis, C H, Farmer's.
Malone, R J, Brower's Mills.
McCanless, A L, Trinity.
Parker, D Reid, Trinity.
Patterson, A J, Liberty.
Phillips, C H, Fuller's.
Plunket, J R, Strieby.
Redding, A H, Cedar Falls.
Reeves, ——, Julian.
Sapp, L L, Randleman.
Staley, W J (dentist), Liberty.
Tate, C S, Ramseur.
Tomlinson, John Milton, Archdale.
Walker, J O, Randleman
Winslow, Thomas L. Maud.
Woollen, W A, Randleman.

SCHOOLS.

Names, Post Offices and Principals.

Ashboro Academy, Ashboro, G H Crowell.
Academy, Erect, R M Vestal.
Academy, Farmer's, W H Boone.
Academy, Shiloh, J R Miller.
Academy, Ramseur, D M Weatherly.

RANDOLPH COUNTY.

RANDOLPH COUNTY.

Academy, Why Not, J P Burroughs.
Trinity High School, Trinity, T A Smoot.
Public schools—white, 99: colored, 23.

TEACHERS.

Names and Post Offices.

WHITE.

Males—First Grade.

Baldwin, J A, Franklinsville.
Boone, W H, Farmer.
Brown, B F, Erect.
Burgess, R R, Liberty.
Burroughs, J P, Why Not.
Caviness, J A, Ramseur.
Cagle, J N, Brown's Store.
Cox, J H, Brown's Store.
Cox, C E, Brunswick.
Cox, J A, Ulah.
Coggins, J T, Flora.
Crutchfield, J B, Liberty.
Cude, S F., Randleman.
Cude, C S, Randleman.
Garner, G F., Longleaf.
Hammond, W C, Archdale.
Hancock, Q L, Brown's Store.
Hickett, J C, Centre.
Holliday, J M, Franklinsville.
Hughes, J F, Fuller's.
Johnson, O, Fork Creek.
Johnson, L, Trinity.
Kearns, B S, Salem Church.
Lanier, B, Level Plains.
Loftin, A G, Jackson Hill.
Miller, J R, Moffitt.
McMasters, E A, Soapstone Mount.
Morgan, M M, Flora.
Neice, W R, Brunswick.
Parrish, M W, Randolph.
Patterson, G C, Worthville.
Ridge, C E, Asheboro.
Roach, T J, Liberty.
Russel, C L, Quinine.
Scarboro, W B, Archdale.
Smith, J R, Liberty.
Stricklan l, W I E, New Hope Academy.
Thornburg, W P, Lassiter.
Trogden, J B, Kemp's Mills.
Vestal, R M, Erect.
Welch, J D, Pisgah.
White, J J, Trinity.
Wood, V C, Eden.

Females—First Grade.

Blair, Ruth C, Progress.
Coltrane, Lizzie R, Progress.
Cox, Louelva L, Brown's Store.
Henly, Martha J, Asheboro.
Hackett, Maggie, Centre.
Ingram, Lucy J, Trinity.
Johnson, Crissie J, High Point.
Johnson, Annie E, Farmer's.
Loudermilk, Lura, Fork Church.

Morris, Rena, Franklinsville.
Pickler, Annie, Norwood.
Redding, Martha, Asheboro.
Redding, Mollie, Sophia.
Smith, Mary, Siler City.
Staley, Etta, Staley.
Staley, Annie, Staley.
Vuncannon, Fannie, Science Hill.
Young, India C, Trinity.

Males—Second Grade.

Allen, J M, Ralph.
Allred, S A, Asheboro.
Chisco, Orlando, Brower's Mills.
Cox, H P, Brown's Store.
Farlow, David, jr, Hoyle.
Fruit, R L, Melancthan.
Johnson, A S, Trinity.
Lanier, S W, Maud.
Rachel, E G, Pinson.
Sexton, A L, Flora.

Females—Second Grade.

Bingham, Fannie, Randolph.
Cheek, Annie, Cole's Store.
Cox, Cordelia, Brown's Store.
Cox, Eva J, Climax.
Diffee, Gertrude, Central Falls.
Henley, Ora, Asheboro.
Kearnes, Jessie, Trinity.
Lynch, Amelia, Brown's Store.
Royals, Berta, Wheatmore.
Siler, Cora, Coleridge.
Siler, Lillie, Coleridge.
Stout, Davie, Ralph.
Varner, Etta, New Hope Academy.

COLORED.

Male—First Grade.

White, J H, Asheboro.

Males—Second Grade.

Foust, G H, Aconite.
Greene, R L, Kemp's Mills.
Lann, C J, Cedar Falls.
Lutterloh, J H, Liberty.
McRae, J A, Thomasville.
Spinks, A S, Aconite.

Females—Second Grade.

Brower, Cornelia, Asheboro.
Edmundson, Minnie, High Point.
Freeland, Alice, Graham.
Gray, Lillie, Trinity.
McLeod, Laura, Strieby.
McNair, Adaline, Franklinsville.
Pace, Katie, Trinity.
Scotten, Jennie, Mullen.
Simmons, Annie, Martha.
Skeen, Minnie, Fuller.
Staley, Nancy J, Mullen.

LOCAL CORPORATIONS.

Balfour Lodge, No 188, A F and A M, Ashboro; time of meeting: Friday night before full moon.

RANDOLPH COUNTY.

Christian Temperance Union, Randleman; S G Newlin, sec.

Deep River Lodge, No 184, A F and A M, Foust's Mills; time of meeting: Saturday evening before full moon, June 24th, December 27th.

Hanks Lodge, No 128, A F and A M, Franklinville; time of meeting: third Saturday evening, June 27th, December 27th.

Knights of Pythias meet every Thursday night.

Randolph Lodge, No 309, A F and A M, El Dorado (Montgomery county); time of meeting: Saturday on or before full moon.

NEWSPAPERS.

Ashboro Courier (Democratic weekly), Ashboro; W C Hammer, editor.

Piedmont Herald, Moffitt's; Rev P T Way, editor.

Randolph Argus, Ashboro; J A Blair, editor.

FARMERS.

Names and Post Offices.

Archdale—S J Blair, J M Blair, W L Boldin, J G Frazier.

Ashboro—R J Allred, J T Brittain, Nathan Brown, John Burrow, Henderson Burrow, Jacob Chrisco, W D Cross, John Davidson, R W Frazier, E W Hammer, W P Hamlet, E A Hammer, Henderson Jerrell, William Lewis, E Leadville, W F McDowell, J S Pough, Q F Pritchard, Tom Redding, Levi Tucker, Thos Tucker, J H Vestal, E S Vestal, J W Winningham, E Winslow, J M Worth.

Bombay—Martin Cranford, Nixon Ingram, T W Ingram, John Kearns, Chas Kearns, Frank Kearns.

Brown Store—Ira Brown, D C Brown, Rewlin Brown, E Brown, O P Brown, C F Cagle, J N Cagle, T H Cox, S S Cox, E C Phillips, W D Spoon.

Browers—W N Brown, W M Moffitt, Lee Richardson.

Brunswick—G S Allred, Orlando Chaviness, W R Neece, S Parker, T F Pugh, W S White, Wm Wilson.

Buffalo Ford—Gilbert Cox, Seth Cox, Henry Cox, Calvin Cox, W D Cox, Joe Ellis, Ed Stout, Aaron Stout, J M S out.

Cape—Charles Barker, J A Barker, J P Barrett, M O Brooks, Jas Brower, John Brower, Hugh Coward, John Duncan, W S Edwards, Wm Garner, W A Kivett, Wm Mann, Henry Rains, Brantley Vestal, M S Vestal.

RANDOLPH COUNTY.

Cedar Falls—J W Allred, W D Allred, J H Coward, D C Jennings, P M Julian, J F S Julian, C M Free, S E Free, Jacob Hendrix, Nixon Pre-well, M F Pugh, Tyson Trogdon.

Central Falls—Allen Hinshaw, Zeb Hinshaw, Noah Hinshaw, B B Julian, R L Winningham, E L York.

Empire—S E Allen, Ira Blair, Ben Brown, J C Brown, A M Ingold, W P Wright.

Erect—Wm Berk, J S Lawrence, W W Lawrence, L O Sugg, Taylor Sugg, George Teague, T B Tyson.

Farmer—Tom Fuller, Madison Hammon, J F Horner, Wm Ingram, J I Johnson, T C Johnson, Frank Kearns, C S Kearns, Aaron Lassiter, B B Lewis, Gideon Macon, M L Monroe, John Plummer, A J Rush, Bud Rush, Milton Skeen, B W Steed.

Flower Hill—R F Hancock, J C Rich, Allen Scott,

Flora—J W Bingham, J F Bisher, R D Harris, Emer Hoover, J W Johnson, W A Prevo, Columbus Ridge, H C Snider, Nelson Snider, Hill Wood.

Fork Creek—Calvin Bean, Henry Bean, J M Bower, H M Johnson, E Loudermilk, J Loudermilk, S R Richardson, W R Richardson, H S Wilson, R C Yaw, A J Yaw, E R Yaw.

Gladesboro—J nathan Anthony, J R Coletrane, Talton Cox, Stanton Davis, Madison Bivis, Frank Frazier, Solomon Frazier, Jesse Frazier, Jesse Frazier, jr.

Gray's Chapel—D H Allred, J C All-G S Allred, B D Allred, A G Hough, Jim Jones, J M Jones, A F Jones, P P Jones, Madison Jones, R A Lineberry, Scott Lowderry, J W Pugh, Wm Ruth, J A Ruth, P A Ruth, Orlando Walker.

Jackson Creek—Harris Hill, Alson Hoover, L vi McDowell, John Morgan, Ivy Pierce, Will s Ridge, Pen Ridge, Jas Riggins, C Riggins, Simeon Rush, Milton Small, Andrew Totter, Peter Yates.

Kemps Mills—A M Barker, Nathan Barker, Leroy Bean, H Bird, E H Bird, Jas Borroughs, Geo Borroughs, J W Brown, J C Cagle, B F Coffin, D A Cox, T S Graves, J M Leonard, Allen Macon, Thos Macon, Z S Moffitt, J H Smith, W M Smith, W D Spoon, A J Wright.

Lassiter's Mills—Lane Hish, Griffin Lassiter, Sam Lassiter, J e Luther, D H Miller, T L Miller, Alex Murdock, Nathan Sikes, Joe Thornburg, Chas Workman.

Level Cross—W F Brown, Ferry Dosier, Robert Dosier, B Hinshaw, Bob Lamb, J S Swain, R L Vickery.

Martha—S Crawford, Lee Haltum,

RANDOLPH COUNTY.

J O Kearns. S Kearns, W E Kearns, Jno Morris, Branson Nance, J C Nance.

Mechanic—E Barnes,W A Bingham, J L Bingham, Lewis Cagle, J M Cooper. E N Howard, R F Lassiter, W W Lassiter. M H Lassiter, Zeb Lewis, S H Lowe, David Lowe, N M Lowe, Wm Spence, T J Vuncannon, W S G Vuncannon.

Millboro—John Brown, Oliver Coble, Eli Ellis, V R Hackett, G S Julian, J G Julian, R L Julian, W R Julian. Sam Kirkman. J M Nelson, R W Pugh, Solomon Redding, C H Redding, J M Redding, W C Ruth, Henry Underwood, John Underwood.

Moffitt—B B Brooks, J M Caviness. S L Hayworth, D R Hayworth, Solomon Moffitt, Alfred Moffitt, J M Moffitt.

Newhope—Thos Crawford, Fletcher Hicks, John Laughlin, Ira Saunders, Wm Shaw, Jesse Shaw.

Pisgah—Wm Allen Willis Graves, Newton Luck, Wm Buck, Franklin Ocman. J B Parks. J W Parks. George Parks. Wm Parks, J B Slack, Claiborn Slack, Hinton Strider, E J Strider, Wm Strickmire, J J Welch, John Welch, Henry Williams.

Progress—John Aldridge, B F Blair, J A Blair, Jesse Davis, Gurney Davis, D B Davis, C C Floyd, J O Gray, R L G ay, D M Hahn, Sid Hill, Jno Hill, Watson, Ingram, G W Kirkman, A L Marsh. A C Peace, E W Pugh, A S Robbins J D Taylor, R L White.

Ramseur—H Allen, Wm Allred, Benj Cox, T D Chisholm, R V Cox, B Cox, Chas Cox, Cos Craven, Jackson Craven, Will Craven, G W Harrison, Wm Parks, Thomas Parks, W E Poe, Wm Smith, Kilida Stout, Calvin Stout, W H Watkins, Jos Welborn.

RANDOLPH COUNTY.

Randleman—J T Bostic, William Brown. John Buson, R L Coletrain, D F Dicks, Dr W A Fox, N T Hinshaw, Jesse Hinshaw. J D Hinshaw, T C Henley, Wm Ivey, Wm Jobe, A W Vickery. Dr W A Wootten.

Sawyersville—Calvin Bell, Alfred Bulla, James Coltrane, John Fuller, Wm M Hinshaw, Rob Kearns, Wm Kearns. Julian Kearns, El Kearns, Jim Miller, John Spencer, Lee Spencer.

Science—Alfred Hussey, Geo Hussey, Jno Kemp, Jas Law, Jno Law, J T Law, A H McDaniel, Henry Parker, W P Pickett, J S Ridge, Wm Varner, Jas Vuncannon, W E Yergan.

Trinity—Will Albertson, N C English S L English, Edgar Ganaway, E H Ingram, Thos Jordan, Wilson Kenady, Frank Leach, D M Pane, Anson Parker. Smith Reddick, B F Steel, Jesse Welborn, Joe Welborn, W K Welborn, Sam'l Younts, H Younts.

Ulah—N Brower, D E Brown, W R Cox, Newton Dawson, W A Dawson, C L Fry, A M Luck, R M Moffitt, Uriah Presnell, C S Saunders, S Williams. P A Williams.

White Road—L F Branson, E Cox, J M Cox, F J Dawson, W B Hammond, J C Hammond, A L Ham, S Ham, J Ham, E O Hussey, Wm Hussey, E Luck, N Luck, R Luck, C T Luck. J L Phillips, W H Presnell, J R Ridge, Mrs J C Vuncannon, J L Williams. J M Williams.

Why Not—Martin Cagle, A L King, J M King, J A Ocman, Dempsey Orman, Lem Spencer, J H Spencer, L V Spinks, Chas Stewart, H H Yaw, A L Yaw, Henry Yaw.

Worthville—Sam Fredon, Henry Hurley. T C Julian, W R Julian, J L Jiles, E P Trogdn.

RICHMOND COUNTY.

AREA, 860 SQUARE MILES.

POPULATION, 24,948: White 10,989, Colored 12,959.

RICHMOND COUNTY was formed in 1779, from Anson county. It was named in honor of the Duke of Richmond, who was an able advocate of the cause of America in the House of Lords.

ROCKINGHAM, the county-seat, is 105 miles southwest from Raleigh. Population estimated at 2,750.

Surface—Level, sandy loam, generally rich, easily cultivated, and very productive when well drained; lies on the eastern shore of the Pee Dee river, and has abundant water-power.

Staples—Cotton, corn, rice, naval stores and lumber.

Fruits—Apples, peaches, pears, berries, plums, grapes, melons, and other small fruits.

Timbers—Oak, pine, poplar and gum.

TOWNS AND POST OFFICES.

	POP.		POP.
Arolina,	—	John Station,	100
Bragg,	25	Laurel Hill,	100
Bostic's Mills,	50	Laurinburg,	1,450
Capel's Mills,	60	Little's Mills,	200
Conclave,	25	Lytch,	50
Covington,	75	McNair,	—
Diggs,	50	Malee,	30
Dockery's Store,	—	Mangum,	120
Ellerbe,	50	Odom,	25
Elmore,	—	Old Hundred,	75
Fairley's,	25	Osborne,	25
Fontcol,	25	Pegues,	100
Ghio,	58	Powelton,	30
Gibson's Mills,	25	Riverton,	—
Gitson's		Roberdell,	1,000
Station,	300	Rockingham	
Hamlet,	500	(C H),	2,750
Hasty,	75	Stewart,	—
Hoffman,	250		

COUNTY OFFICERS.

Clerk Superior Court—Z F Long.
Commissioners—W T Covington, chm'n; A L James, J T Little, J A Ingram, D Z Hardin.
Coroner—N D McDonald.
Register of Deeds—Claude Dockery.
Sheriff—John M Smith.
Solicitor 7th District—H F Sewell.
Standard Keeper—
Surveyor—James P McLean.
Treasurer—John M Smith.
County Examiner—M N McIver.

COURTS.

Third Monday before the first Monday in March; sixth Monday after the first Monday in March; second Monday after the first Monday in September; eighth Monday after the first Monday in September.

TOWN OFFICERS.

LAURINBURG—*Mayor*, ——; *Commissioners*, J W McNair, L A Monroe, D D McIntyre, J D Parks, W D B McEachin; *Clerk*, J L Bundy; *Treasurer*, J A Cook.

ROCKINGHAM—*Mayor*, W N Everett; *Commissioners*, J P Leak, M T Henson, Bright Holt, J C Stubbs, T B Covington; *Constable*, E J McDonald; *Clerk and Treasurer*, W L Scales: *Attorney*, C Morrison.

TOWNSHIPS AND MAGISTRATES.

Beaver Dam—W W Graham, W A Graham, Jas L McDonald, Augus Currier (Gibson's Mills), E C Whitaker, John W Butler, J C New, S M Pankey (Hoffman).

Black Jack—A C Benton, E N Ingram (Dudo), Neill A Graham, H W Cooper (Rockingham). E E Hamer, H I Quick, M J Thrower, S T Morse (Dockery's Store).

Laurel Hill—Hector McLean (Laurinburg), N A McNair, Charles McLeod (McNair's), P H Livingston, Fairley Murray (Laurel Hill), Henry Fairley (Fairley's), R H Gibson, John McLean (Elmore).

Marks Creek—N D McDonald, E A Lackey, Geo J Freeman, C C Smith, E C Terry (Hamlet), M Leviner (Osborn), John Livingston (Ghio).

Mineral Springs—Nelson McAskill, A D Spivey (Ellerbe), T T Bostick, I B Jenkins, J C McFadyen (Bostic's Mills), Richmond Long (Bragg), J M Hines (Malee), W M Upery (Capel's Mills).

Rockingham—A M McAuley, H C Wall, W F Long, J M Ford, Y C Morton, S T Cooper, John S Covington (Rockingham).

Spring Hill—Lauchlin McNeill, A J Connelly, A E Shaw, J L Cooley, W W Bullard (Fontcol), T L McNair (Laurel

RICHMOND COUNTY.

Hill), Abraham Wilkes (Pike), Jas P McLean (Laurinburg).

Steele's—H A Ledbetter, A J Little (Little's Mills), J S Matherson, Robert Ballard (Mangum), J L Baldwin (Erie Mills), D A Bruton (Malee), John Hutchinson (Powellton), W C Upery (Covington).

Stewartsville—Jas M Graham (Hasty), Jas P Roe, W P Evans, W W McEllwee, John F Walters (Laurinburg), A M McKinnon, J M McKinnon, D A Patterson, A H Currie (Maxton).

Williamson's—J C Mason, B F McGregor, W T Wright (Conclave), W F Gibson, Simeon Gibson (Gibson's Station), A S McNeill, M C Woodard, C H Kelly (Old Hundred).

Wolf Pit—John C Ellerbe J H Williamson, E M Boggan, J T Dawkins, L A Hall, D M Jackson (Rockingham), W H Roberts (Diggs), E W Manshep (Pegues).

CHURCHES.

Names, Post Offices, Pastors and Denom.

METHODIST.

Church—Pee Dee, J M Louder.
Church—Roberdel, —— Pott.
Church—Rockingham, J T Lyon.
Church-Laurinburg, F M Shamburger.
Caledonia— Laurinburg, Mike Bradshaw.
Concord—Rockingham, J M Louder.
Green Lake-Rockingham, J M Louder.
Ledbetter—Rockingham, —— Pott.
Mt Nebo—Hamlet.
Mt Pleasant—Bostick's Mills, J M Louder.
Mizpah—Rockingham, —— Pott.
Philadelphia—Rockingham.
Snead's Grove (col)—Laurinburg, F M Shamburger.
St John's Station—Laurel Hill, W S Davis.
St Paul—Diggs, —— Pott.
Tabernacle—Laurel Hill, J H Page.
Zion—Rockingham, J M Louder.
Church—Old Hundred, W S Davis.
Church (col)—Laurinburg.

BAPTIST.

Church—Laurinburg.
Church—Rockingham.
Church—Laurinburg, J T Wright.
Dockery's (col)—Rockingham.
Holly Grove (col)—Rockingham.
Shady Grove—Rockingham, J T Wright.
Spring Hill—Laurinburg, M L Kesler.

PRESBYTERIAN.

Bower's Chapel (co)—Laurinburg, W G Cates.
Chapel Hill (col)—Laurinburg, W G Cates.

RICHMOND COUNTY.

Church—Laurel Hill, A N Ferguson.
Church—Covington, N T Bowden.
Church —Lauringburg, W B Arrowood.
Church—Rockingham, W R Coppedge.
Mark's Creek—Hamlet.
McGill's—Hoffman.
Montpelier—Laurinburg, A N Ferguson.
Mt Carmel—Capel's Mills.
Smyrna—Laurinburg, A N Ferguson.

CATHOLIC.

St Augustine Chapel—Laurinburg.

MINISTERS RESIDENT.

Names, Post Offices and Denom.

METHODIST.

Ledbetter, R S, Rockingham.
Lyon, J T, Rockingham.
Shamburger, F M, Laurinburg.
Smith, N McN, Laurinburg.
Smith, J C, Rockingham

BAPTIST.

Covington, R (col), Rockingham.
Ferguson, A N, Laurinburg.
McMillan, A, Laurel Hill.

HOTELS AND BOARDING HOUSES.

Kinds, Post Offices and Proprietors.

Boarding, Rockingham, M Fullard.
Boarding, Rockingham, J C Coodle.
Central Hotel, Laurinburg, Isaac Williams.
Hotel, Hamlet, Mrs Frazier.
Hotel Richmond, Rockingham, L Weill.
Merchants' Hotel, Laurinburg, J C Morgan.
McDonald House, Rockingham, Miss Sallie McDonald.

LAWYERS.

Names and Post Offices.

Cox, W H, Laurinburg.
Dockery (O H) & Dockery (Claude), Rockingham.
Guthrie, T C, Rockingham.
Kitty, W M, Rockingham.
LeGrand, J T, Rockingham.
Neal, W H, Laurinburg.
Quick, W H (col), Rockingham.
Shaw, J D & Son, Rockingham.
Shaw, J D, jr, Laurinburg.
Stuart, D, Laurinburg.

MANUFACTORIES.

Names, Post Offices and Proprietors.

Barrels, John's Station, J T John, jr.
Cotton-seed Oil, Gibson's Station.

| RICHMOND COUNTY. | RICHMOND COUNTY. |

Great Falls Manufacturing Co, Rockingham; established 1869; W I Everett, pres; capital stock, $150,000.

Ida Mills (cotton), Laurel Hill, M Morgan, pres.

Ledbetter Mills, Rockingham; established 1882; T B & J S Ledbetter, props; capital stock, $25,000.

Laurinburg Oil Mill, Laurinburg, Robt Covington.

Richmond Mills, Laurel Hill; established 1873; Mark Morgan, prop; capital stock, $25,000.

Midway Mills, Rockingham; established 1881; Jas P Leak, pres; capital stock, $50,000; spindles, 6,000.

Pee Dee Manufacturing Co, Rockingham; established 1874; W C Leak, pres; capital stock, $125,000; spindles, 6,112; looms, 300; hands, 250.

Roberdell Mfg Co., Rockingham; established 1882; H C Wall, pres; capital stock, $125,000; Spindles, 6,000; looms, 300; hands, 250.

S. A. L. Shops, Hamlet, S. A. L. R. R.

Steele's Mill, Rockingham, R L Steele, pres; capital stock, $125,000; spindles, 10,304; looms, 300 (Northrop); hands, 125.

Springfield Mills, Laurel Hill, M Morgan, pres

State Line Oil Mills and Fertilizers, Gibson's, Marlboro Oil Milling Co.

Stewart Canning Co, No 1, Laurinburg, Stewart.

Stewart Canning Co, No. 2, Rockingham, A Stewart.

Stewart Canning Co, No. 3, Rockingham, T C Leak.

Turpentine John's Station J T Johu. jr.

Turpentine, Fairley, T L McNair.

Turpentine, Rockingham, H C Watson.

MERCHANTS AND TRADESMEN.

Name, Post Office, and Line of Business.

BOSTIC'S MILL.
| Bostic, S W & Co. | G S |
| Ingram, J A (agent), | G S |

CAPEL'S MILLS.
| Capel, P R & Son, | G S |

CONCLAVE.
| Mason Bros & Co, | G S |

COVINGTON.
Hutchison, J G,	G S
Hutchinson, C S,	G S
Parson, W Son & Co,	G S

DUDO.
| Ingram, E N, | G S |
| Reynolds, N T, | G S |

ELLERBE.
| Auman, A. | G S |
| Loftin, A L & Co, | G S |

| Reynolds, L R & Bro, | G S |
| Underwood, Mrs Sallie, | Millinery |

FAIRLEY'S.
| Fairley, Henry, | G S |

FONTCOL.
| McNeill, N, | G S |
| Shaw, J P, | G S |

GHIO.
| Cameron, J A, | Saw Mill |
| Peel, J F, | G S |

GIBSON'S MILLS.
| Gibson, J. | G S |

GIBSON'S STATION.
Adams, B B & Co (near),	G S
Fletcher, John S & Son,	G S
Gibson, D D,	G S
Gibson, E J,	Livery
Gibson, F B,	G S
Gibson, R F & Co,	G S
Gibson, Simeon,	G S
Gibson, W Z	Drugs
Gibson, J L,	G S and Min Water
Goodwin, E M,	G S
Mason, P R,	G S
Maxwell, N T & Co,	G S
Parker, W F,	G S
White, J R,	G S
Whight, W F,	G S

HAMLET.
Bridgers, J M,	Hotel
Cowan, Albert,	G S
Cowan, T J,	G S
Freeman, J S,	G S
Goodman, O T,	G S
Henry, R L & Co,	G S
McDonald, M D,	G S
Pounds, J J,	Gro and Conf

HASTY.
Fry, Mrs C,	G S
Medlin, J D,	G S
Tatum, F P,	G S

HOFFMAN.
Austin, A B & Son,	G S
Blue, D T,	G S
Butler & Windham,	G S
Butler, W P & Co,	Gro
Holland Bros,	G S and Mill
Jones, W M & Co,	G S and Naval Stores
McDonald, N M,	G S
Page, Alex & Bro,	Lumber
Page, A H,	Saw Mill
Yates, J W,	G S

JOHN'S STATION.
| John, J T, jr, | G S |

LAUREL HILL.
Gibson, A D.	G S
Ida Cotton Mills.	G S
McNair, J F,	G S
McNair, T L,	G S and Turp
Morgan, M.	G S and Cot Fac
Morgan, M & M L,	G S
Morrison, M,	Gunsmith
Smith, M B,	G S

RICHMOND COUNTY.

RICHMOND COUNTY.

LAURINBURG.

Beacham, W K, Agt,	Gro
Cameron, A,	Confec
Cameron, W,	G S
Clark, A T,	G S
Coble, C H.	G S
Evans, W P (col),	G S
Everington, G D.	Drugs
Fields & Bro,	Drugs
Fields, W L,	G S
Hammond, N,	G S
Ivey, W B,	Livery
James, W D,	D G
Lee, R E,	G S
Lytch, D C,	G S
McDougald, M A,	Furn
McIntire, D D,	G S
McKay, M G,	G S
McNair, J W,	G S
McRae, Rod.	Fert
Monroe, L A,	G S
Morgan, J C,	G S
O lom. Mrs C E,	G S
Phillips, R D & Co.	G S
Prince & Blue,	G S
Ratliff & Shaw (col),	G S
Roper, Eli (col).	G S
Sanford, Miss Mittie,	Millinery
Shaw, A B,	G S
Standard Gro Co,	——
Zackary, W,	Gro

LITTLE'S MILLS.

Little, J P,	Miller

MACNAIR.

McNair, E L,	G S and Turp
Russell, C L,	G S

MANGUM.

Patterson, D M,	Drugs

MONTPELIER.

Johnson, N D,	G S

OLD HUNDRED.

Beasley, J D.	G S
Woodward, J W, G S and Blacksmith	

OSBORNE.

Johnson, N A,	G S
Nicholson, M B,	G S

ROBERDELL.

Nordan, D M,	G S

ROCKINGHAM.

Baldwin, H D,	G S
Biggs, S,	Drugs
Blakey, Miss L E,	Millinery
Caudle, J F.	Broker
Caudle & Hinson,	G S
Covington, J W,	G S
Covington, T B,	G S
Covington, W L,	Gro
Covington, W T & Co,	G S
Covington, T L & Co,	G S
Cox & Cooper,	G S
Davis, E S.	G S
Dawkins, W & Co,	G S
Dockery, H C,	G S
Everett, W I,	G S
Fowlkes, W M,	Drugs

Fowlkes, W S,	Jeweler
Hinson, M L,	Livery and Gro
Jones, F M,	Gro
Leak Bros,	Clo and Shoes
Leak & Wall,	Hotel
Long, A M,	Livery
McDonald, A L,	Gro
McDonald, Miss Sallie,	Hotel
Nutall, E B,	Gro
Phifer, W T & Co,	G S
Rathf & Caudle,	D G
Sandford, C,	Gro
Sandford, Mrs S P,	Millinery
Smith, J C.	G S
Wall, E B.	Gro
Watson, H C,	G S
Weill, L.	Hotel and Livery
Whitlock, T M & Bro,	G S
Williams, W T & Co.	G S

MILLS.

Kinds, Post Offices and Proprietors.

Corn and flour, Laurinburg, D C Lytch

Corn and flour, Laurinburg, P McRae.

Corn and flour, Laurel Hill, Mark Morgan.

Corn and flour, John's Stat'n, J T John.

Corn and flour, Erie Mills, J A Leak.

Corn and flour, Gibson's Stat'n, Henry Gibson.

Corn and flour, Gibson's Station, Jas T Pate.

Corn and flour, Pegue's, Croslin & Everett.

Corn and flour, Dudo, E N Ingram.

Corn, flour and gin, Laurel Hill, Wm Gilchrist.

Corn, flour and gin, Laurinburg, N A McNair.

Corn, flour, saw and gin (steam), Capel's Mills, T R Capel & Son.

Corn, flour and saw, Rockingham, T B Ledbetter.

Corn, flour and saw, Covington, F T Baldwin.

Corn. flour and saw, Covington, Mrs J A Baldwin.

Corn, flour and saw, Gibson's Mills, J T Gibson.

Corn, flour and saw, Bostic's Mills, J Chappell.

Corn. flour and saw, Conclave, Mason & Coble.

Corn, flour and saw, Little's Mills, Jno P Little.

Corn and saw (steam), Laurinburg, J H Jones.

Corn and saw (steam), Laurinburg, Angus Fairly.

Corn and saw (steam), Hasty, J C Hamer.

Corn and saw (steam), Hasty, C S McArthur.

Corn and saw (steam), Mangum, T Le Grand.

RICHMOND COUNTY.

Corn, saw and gin, Laurinburg, W D McEachin.

Corn, saw and gin, Laurinburg, T J Wooten.

Corn, saw and gin, Laurinburg, H Lytch.

Cotton gin, Laurinburg, M M McKinnon.

Cotton gin, Laurinburg, Cotton Seed and Oil M'f'g Co.

Saw (steam), Laurel Hill, M B Smith.

Saw (steam), Hoffman, Whitaker & Whitaker.

Saw (steam), Hoffman, Whitaker & Company.

Steam saw, Rockingham, Everett & Coslin.

Steam saw (2 mills), Hoffman, Dolly Page.

Steam saw, Hoffman, J A Austin & Son.

Steam saw, Hoffman, Fitts & Austin.

Steam saw, Hoffman, Alex Page.

Steam saw, Hoffman, W M Jones & Co.

Steam saw, Old Hundred, Miller Lumber Co.

Steam saw, Hamlet, K C Cameron.

PHYSICIANS.

Names and Post Offices.

Blue, K A, Laurinburg.
Cole, Robt S (dentist), Rockingham.
Covington, J M, Rockingham.
Fowlkes, W M, Rockingham.
Garrett, Frank, Ellerbee Springs.
Gill, E J (dentist). Laurinburg.
Hamer, A W, Laurinburg.
Herron, A M, Laurinburg.
Herndon, Jno (dentist), Leach's.
Herndon, Will (dentist), Leach's.
Jewett, Francis, Fairly.
McKay, S S (col), Laurinburg.
McLean, N M, Gibson's Station.
Patterson, D N, Mangum.
Pole, W T, Gibson's Station.
Prince, D M, Laurinburg.
Shaw, Daniel, Fontcol.
Shaw, Wm, Fontcol.
Stancill, J M, Rockingham.
Steele, W H, Rockingham.
Steele, W L (dentist), Rockingham.

SCHOOLS.

Names, Post Offices and Principals.

Academy, Gibson's Station, Professor Wyche.
Academy, Ellerbee Springs.
Academy, Rockingham, Prof Rast.
Private school, Laurinburg, Mrs J A Parker.
High School, Laurinburg, W G Quackenbush.

RICHMOND COUNTY.

Jefferson School (col), Laurinburg, Miss Maggie Neal, Miss Ina Purcell and Miss Mary McKinnon.

Public schools—white, 45; colored, 34.

TEACHERS.

Names and Post Offices.

WHITE.

Adams, Miss Sallie, Gibson's Station.
Baldwin, Miss Sallie, Erie Mills.
Bennett, M A, Rockingham.
Betts, Miss Sallie P, Rockingham.
Bostick, J T, Conclave.
Bruton, G E, Malee.
Cameron, Miss Virginia, Old Hundred.
Chappell, A E, Covington.
Chambers, W F, Powelton.
Livingston, Miss Kathrine, Riverton.
Long, E Jennie, Rockingham.
McCormac, R I, John's Station.
McFarland, E J, Old Hundred.
McKinnon, M L, Laurinburg.
McNair, Lee, Laurel Hill.
McNeill, Miss Mary, Laurinburg.
Milikin, C B, Hamlet.
Milikin, J E, Hamlet.
Pool, R T, Rockingham.
Pool, C J, Stewart.
Reynolds, L R, Roberdell.
Russell, G H, Laurinburg.
Sanford, K, Roberdell.
Shepherd, N H, Pekin.
Stanback, Miss Pauline, Mangum.
St Clair, Miss Cornelia, Sanford.
Story, J C, Ellerbe Springs.
Terry, E C, Hamlet.
Wood, Miss Maggie G, Laurel Hill.
Yarboro, Miss Mary, Laurinburg.

COLORED.

Covington, A W, Rockingham.
Covington, Sallie J, Rockingham.
Covington, S P, Rockingham.
Catus, E S, Laurinburg.
Dockery, S W, Maxton.
Dockery, C W, Dockery's Store.
Dunlap, A M, Osborn.
Funderburk, Lila C, Mangum.
Griffin, Miss Sarah A, Rockingham.
Gardner, Tamor, Rockingham.
Hines, J J, Hasty.
Johnson, E E, Laurinburg.
LeGrand, Ann E, Mangum.
Love, Eva, Rockingham.
Love, S H, Rockingham.
McEachin, N F, Laurinburg.
McEachin, Carrie B, Laurinburg.
McKay, S S, Laurinburg.
McLean, M J, Maxton.
McLauchlin, T M, Maxton.
McLauchlin, A F, Laurinburg.
McLauchlin, J W, Laurinburg.
McLean, Miss M J, Maxton.

RICHMOND COUNTY.

McMillan, Vesa J, Laurinburg.
McMillan, Sarah E, Laurinburg.
Malloy, Miss Julia A, Maxton.
Mitchell, W M, Rockingham.
Morgan, Carrie, Powelton.
Morrissey, G R. Little's Mills.
Nicholson, Neill L.
Robinson, C D, Laurinburg.
Russell, W R, Rockingham.
Simons, Cornelius, Rockingham.
Stansell, Miss Bettie, Rockingham.
Stuart, C J, Ghio.
Stitt, J W, Rockingham.
Thomas, W S, Mangum.
Tyson, J A, Rockingham.
Wall, Fannie, Rockingham.
Williams, F J, Rockingham.
Woodard, W H, Rockingham.

LOCAL CORPORATIONS.

Bank of Pee Dee, Rockingham, T C
Leak, pres; W G Parsons, cash; capital, $25,000.
Bank of Laurinburg, A L Jones, pres; T J Hill, cash; capital, $20,000.
Chosen Friends, No. 3, Rockingham.
Excelsior Lodge, No. 1648, Knights of Honor, Laurinburg.
Knights of Honor, No. 1610, Rockingham.
Laurinburg Lodge, No. 305, A F and A M, Laurinburg. Time of meeting, Thursday evening on or before full moon, and December 27th.
Laurinburg Cornet Band, Laurinburg, C A Burns, leader.
Legion of Honor, Rockingham.
Richmond Lodge, No 560, Knights and Ladies of Honor, Rockingham.
Scotland Lodge, No 27, Knights of Pythias, Laurinburg; Will Cameron, C C.

NEWSPAPERS.

Laurinburg Exchange, Laurinburg (Dem. weekly); L L Bundy, ed and prop.
Post (Ind. weekly), Laurinburg; Neal McEachin, ed and prop.
Richmond Rocket, Rockingham (Dem. weekly); Jno Walsh, ed and prop.
Spirit of the South, Rockingham (Rep. weekly); W R Terry, ed and prop.
Southern Index (non-partisan weekly). Rockingham; A S Dockery, ed and prop,

FARMERS.

Names and Post Offices.

Bostic's Mills—R H Bennett, T T Bostick, S W Bostick, W F Brookshire, Joshua Chapel, B Chapel, J A Ingram, K H Lowdermilk, N G Nicholson.

RICHMOND COUNTY.

Capel's Mills—P R Caple, Duncan Cole.
Conclave—J C Mason, J B Mason, W J Mason, E J Mason, B F McGruder, M V McGruder, Mrs Mag McKinzie, A S McNeill, jr, D O Wright.
Covington—J A Baldwin, H C Lowdermilk, Wm Parsons, A T Tyson.
Diggs—D M Hay, Jno M Liles, W H Roberts.
Dockery's Store—B F Dockery, E E Homer, Mathew Thrower, Jno C Usry.
Dudo—A C Benton, Dan'l Henderson, W P Ingram, J A Ingram, jr, B S Ingram, E N Ingram, W R Reynolds, Geo Thomas, I W Webb, J H Webb
Ellerbe Springs—Dr F J Garrett, J T Hight, Nelson McCaskill, Mrs Isabel Nicholson W M Smith.
Elmore—C W Bullard, A J Cassoday, T J Elmore, R H Gibson, D Z Hardin, John McLean, L A McLaurin,
Fontcot—W W Bullard, J L Cooley, Harris Feals, Murdock McDuffie, Neal McKay, Jno McKay, A X McLauchlin, B F McLauchlin, Mrs Flora McLean, A A McNeill, Malcom Monroe, W J Pharis, John P Shaw, Dr Daniel Shaw.
Ghio—Mrs Delia Beverly, Anderson Gwinn, Fletcher Peele, Eb Quick, Alex Seals.
Gibson's Station—W F Bullard, Jos Gibson, S F Gibson, B F Gibson, W F Gibson, Henry Gibson, Wm M Gibson, J T Gibson, N Gibson, Jephtha Gibson, Robert Gibson, N N Gibson, Sim Gibson, Z B Gibson, Eli Gibson, L E Gibson, John W Graham, W F Lovin, Jas A McCaulman, J B McCaulman, N E McCaulman, Mrs S C McDonald, L B McLaurin, J H Pate, R H Peele, Barnabus Skipper, C B Terry, D T Wright, Geo Wright.
Hamlet—J A Cameron, Norman Campbell, G J Freeman, D M Henderson, M Laviner, Perry Laviner, John Allen McDonald, P D Milliken, R H Morrison, Alex Smith, Eli Smith, E C Terry.
Hoffman—Jas Blue, John W Butler, Thomas Butler, J B McDonald, Duncan McPherson, M L Morrison, John C New, Mrs Flora Patterson, James G Watson, Jas K Watson, J W Wilkes, J C Yates, J W Yates.
Laurel Hill—J D Beasley, Jesse Hargrave, Peter F Levington, D M Malloy (col), John D McDonald, John F McNair, T L McNair, Neil Monroe, Mark Morgan, Zeb Pate, Westbell Quick, Malcom Smith, Anderson Smith.
Laurinburg—Mrs A F B zzell, Berry Bryant, Ed Buchanan, R R Covington,

RICHMOND COUNTY.

Mrs L T Everett, A N Furguson, W D James, James Jones, Hiram Jones, Capt J T John, Jerry Lee, Hec Lytch, J A McBryde, R R McEachin, Dr B McEachin, W M McKinnon, W H Mc Laurin, J B McLaurin, Hector McLean, Peter McRae, J P McRae, Mrs D W Middleton, Jas H Morgan, W H Murphy, John Norton, Fairly Patterson, Sink Quick (col), G A Roper, A B Shaw, Dougal Stewart. S M Thomas, John Walters, Maj T J Wooten, Capt J M Wright.

Little's Mills—John F Ledbetter, J P Little, jr, Little & Bros.

Lytch—D C Lytch, Jno McCormick, P McKinnon.

Malee—F T Baldwin, D A Bruton, J M Hines, Mrs Annie Usry.

Mangum—Jas Baldwin, O H Dockery, J T LeGrand, W A Webster.

Maxton—Wm Gatelev, T P Joyce, Wiley A Lowe, Mrs S E M Cormick, John M McKinnon, McKay McKinnon, A M McKinnon, D A Patterson, D H Southerland.

Odom—Hugh Livingston, John Livingston, Archie McNeill, Younger Tweed, T H Walters, C J Wright.

Old Hundred—B F Carter Sam Cale, Monroe Livingston, D C McNeill, J A McNeill, M C Woodard, Jno Woodward.

RICHMOND COUNTY.

Pegues—J A Broach, E W Manship.

Riverton-A J Conley, Wm Johnson, Chas Johnson, Chas Livingston, A M McMillan, Duncan McNeill.

Roberdell—H W Cooper, Mrs Mattie Covington, Perry Dawkins, Geo Terry, E C Terry.

Rockingham—Seth Andrews, J S Andrews, John Brigman, J F Brower (col), J R Cooley, T S Cole, Jas A Covington, Crawford Covington, Jas P Covington, J B Covington, A A Covington, W P Covington, V B Covington, J E Covington, H H Covington, Walter M Covington, Thos P Covington, T E Diggs, Mrs H E Diggs, W E Crosslin, T W Ellerbe, W P Ellerbe, W W Ellerbe, M C Ellerbe. Geo Entwistle, W I Everett, A M Flowers, W A Graham, T R Graham, W T Hall, J F Hamer, Wm Hamer, J A Harrington, Jos H Haywood, W C Hicks, H C Hicks, M L Hinson, M T Hinson, T W Howell, D M Jackson (col), H C Jones. Dorgan Lampley, B S Ledbetter, R S Ledbetter, E T Long, D M Morrison. T C Morrison, Geo W Nichols (col), R L Nichols, J D Pence. Jacob Perkins. H J Rogers, L C Smith, J A Smith, W S Townsend, H C Wall, S W Wall, B W Watson, T M Whitlock, E D Whitlock, W A Williams, J T Wright, J D Yeates.

ROBESON COUNTY.

AREA, 950 SQUARE MILES.

POPULATION, 31,493; White 16,819, Colored 14,574.

ROBESON COUNTY was formed in 1786 from Bladen county, and was named in honor of Colonel Robeson, who distinguished himself in the battle of Elizabethtown, July, 1781.

LUMBERTON, the county seat, is situated on Lumber river, 95 miles southwest of Raleigh. Population (estimated). 1,200.

Surface—Low, level, and in many places swampy—lies on both sides of the Lumber river; much of the land is rich.

Staples—Cotton, corn, shingles, lumber and naval stores.

Fruits—Apples, peaches, pears, melons, grapes, berries and other small fruits.

Timbers—Pine, oak, hickory and cypress.

TOWNS AND POST OFFICES.

	POP.		POP.
Affinity,	100	Melrose,	25
Alfordsville,	100	Miliprong,	25
Allenton,	50	Morrosenean,	25
Alma,	100	Moss Neck,	75
Antioch,	25	Nye,	20
Ashpole,	100	Orrum,	25
Athens,	25	Parkton,	30
Barnesville,	25	Pate's,	50
Blanchard,	25	Pembroke,	50
Bowmore,	20	Purcepolis,	25
Branchville,	25	Purvis,	50
Brit's,	20	Queensdale,	25
Buie's,	50	Red Banks,	70
Charm,	20	Red Springs,	300
Cromartie,	25	Refuge,	30
Echo,	30	Rennert,	25
Elrod,	50	Rochester,	25
Floral College,	50	Rowland,	40
Fulmore,	46	Rozier,	50
Gaddysville,	25	Ryan,	25
Grady,	30	Saddletree,	30
Howellsville,	20	St. Paul,	100
Ionia,	40	Sessom,	50
Leesville,	30	Shannon,	50
Lowe,	40	Sim,	25
Lumber Bridge,	75	Stirling,	25
Lumberton (c h),	1,200	Tolarsville,	50
		Valere,	25
McArthur,	25	Vollers,	30
McNatt,	50	Wakulla,	20
Maxton,	1,000	Wilkesville,	25

COUNTY OFFICERS.

Clerk Superior Court—A Edmund,

Commissioners—J H McNeill, chm'n; B Stansel, S J Cobb, John Leach, L R Hamer.

Register of Deeds—A S Thompson.

Sheriff—G B McLeod.

Solicitor Seventh District—S F Seawell.

Treasurer—E G Johnson.

County Examiner—W R Searls.

County Physician—Dr T A Norment, jr.

COURTS.

Fifth Monday before the first Monday in March; fifth Monday before the first Monday in September.

TOWN OFFICERS.

RED SPRINGS—*Mayor*, A B Pearsall; *Commissioners*, W F Williams, W J Council, W J McLeod, R F DeVane; *Town Clerk*, J M Pope; *Marshal*, Sidney Edens, W Rawland.

ROWLAND—*Mayor*, I T McLean; *Commissioners*, J C McCallum, W L Townsend, W S Ivey, S L Adams.

LUMBER BRIDGE—*Mayor*, A L Shaw; *Commissioners*, Thos Stamps, N Shaw, Edward Currie, A M Currie; *Marshal*, J E Clifton.

LUMBERTON—*Mayor*, E K Proctor, jr; *Commissioners*, O C Norment, T A McNeill, W J Linkhow, T N Higby; *Clerk*, C S Skipper; *Constable*, F J Floyd.

MAXTON—*Mayor*, A J McKinnon; *Commissioners*, J W Carter, T B Pace, M McNair, E McRae; *Town Clerk*, W F Steed; *Constable*, W O Burns.

NOTARIES PUBLIC.

D A Buie, Buie; J H McNeil, Lumberton; D N Oliver, Plainview; R McMillan, Lumber Bridge.

TOWNSHIPS AND MAGISTRATES.

Alfordsville—O C Folks, Charles McRae, Laurence McCallum, H M John, I T McLean, D H Smith, John D ars, John W McLean, James L Monroe (Alfordsville).

Black Swamp—Neill Townsend, A S Thompson, W F Howell, D C Buie, Abner Nash, J R Nance, B H McNeill, M C McIntyre, R X Bullard (Lumberton).

Blue Springs—John H Hodgin, Chas

ROBESON COUNTY.

A Purcell, D E McBryde, H McC Currie, M J McLeod, T B Russell, M J McPhail, J M Graham.

Britt's—J L Thompson, J F Ward, M D Edmunds, R O Pittman, J F Roberts, Reden Phillips, Alva Lawson, Willis Pitman, Nevit Cox, J F Roberts (Britt's).

Burnt Swamp—Jas Dees, Alex McIntyre, Jno A Humphrey, H B Ashley, H J McMillan, Alfred Britt, Thomas Tyner, O R Simpson (Lumberton).

Howellsville—W J Rogers, E J Kinlaw, J B Howell, N C Graham, N H Fisher, J C Smith, R E M White, M V Mercer, Dennis Kinlaw (Howellsville).

Lumberton—L S Townsend, J A McAllister, J T Prevatt, A W Fuller, T F Coon, Jos Prevatt, Simuel Phillips, R M Norment, J W Edmund, D P Allen (Lumberton).

Lumber Bridge—W C McPhail, J R Rackley, J W Cobb, J T Ansley, J A P Connoly, J S M White, C Connelly, S J McLeod, D S Klarpp (Lumber Bridge).

Maxton—E McRae, Jas McBryde, D R Caddell, W J Currie, J P Smith, J D Jowers, W L Byrnes (Maxton).

Raft Swamp—J E Carlyle, W C Townsend, R F Gregory, W C Powell, L E Tyner (Lumberton).

Red Springs—R T Covington, A D H Brown, D B McLean, C S Watson, H McNeill, A B Pearsall, W H Rowland, J G Brown, D A McLeod (Red Springs).

Saddletree—Warren Williams, E J Briggs, S A Humphrey (Saddletree).

Shoe Heel—W F Steed, G B Sellers, W B Harker, R T McElvea.

Smith's—D L Stewart, Daniel Wilkinson, Lucius McRae, J M McNair, Albert Buie, John A Campbell, Anderson Locklear, W G McLean, D J McKensie (Lumberton).

Sterling's Mills — Thompson Williams, J F Britt, E McQ Surles, W J Purvis, H H Barnes, W A Leggett, Kelly Johnson, Atlas Atkinson.

St Paul's—J D McGeachy, W S Johnson, Z T McMillan, N A McIntyre, Troy Fisher, A C Rozier, David McMillan, Alex McDonald (Lumberton).

Thompson's—Donald McLeod, L R Hamer, D P McKinnon, E C McNeill, C P Grantham, W H Graham, D McLeod, W J Smith, J P Thompson, A C Bridgers, W M Lowrie (Lumberton).

Wishart's—Wellington Wishart, R McK Rozier, Eli Wishart, Simeon McLean, J E Tyson, M D Edmund, G H Todd, R M Phillips (Lumberton).

White House—A E Floyd, A C Oliver, A J Floyd, W A Ford, J H Lewis, D H Nance, Gaston Floyd, J R Gaddy (Lumberton).

ROBESON COUNTY.

CHURCHES.

Names, Post Offices and Denominations.

BAPTIST.

Aaron Swamp — Alfordsville, A H Thompson.
Antioch—Allenton.
Ashpole—Leesville, J P Hedgepeth.
Back Swamp—Lumberton, J N Booth.
Big Branch—Barnesville.
Caurch—Red Springs, M L Kesler.
Church (col)—Red Springs.
Church—Lumberton, J N Booth.
Clayburn—Lumberton.
Green Springs — Roslin (Cumberland co).
Hickory Grove (col)—Fulmore, K McPhaul.
Hilly Branch(col)--Grady, A H Thompson.
Hog Swamp—Lumberton, K Barnes.
Holy Swamp—Moss Neck, E Thompson.
Marsh—St Paul's.
Mount Elam — Barnesville, Kinchen Barnes.
Mount Moriah—Alfordsville.
Mount Zion--Lumberton, Elias Thompson.
Pleasant Grove—St Paul's, Hector McDonald.
Pleasant Grove—Fulmore, J A Smith.
Pleasant Meadow—Lumberton, Wm Hammond.
Providence—Lumber Bridge, A R Pittman.
Raft Swamp—Lowe.
Saddle Tree—Lumberton, E D Johnson.
Sandy Grove—Lumberton, E Thompson.
Spring Hill—Brooklin.
Ten-Mile—Tolarsville, Dodridge Clark.

FREE-WILL BAPTIST.

Church (col)—Red Springs.

METHODIST.

Asberry--Fulmore, E Pope.
Barker's—Lumberton, J D Bundy.
Bethesda--Brooklin, E Pope.
Church—Queensdale.
Church—Red Banks, —— Smith.
Corinth—Leesville, E Pope.
Centenary--Alfordsville, E Pope.
Hopewell--Leesville, E Pope.
Horeb—Red Banks.
Lumberton—Lumberton, J D Bundy.
Macedonia (col)—Lumberton, S G Taylor.
Olivet—Fair Bluff, E Pope.
Pine Grove--Moss Neck, J D Bundy.
Providence (col)—Fulmore, S G Taylor.
Red Springs—Dora.
Regan's--Lumberton, J D Bundy.

ROBESON COUNTY.

Smith's--Lumberton, J D Bundy.
Zion Chapel (col)--Moss Neck.

A. M. E. ZION.

Church (col)--Red Springs.
Mt Olive--Lumberton, O Lutterloh.

PRESBYTERIAN.

Ashpole--Alfordsville, —— Craig.
Bethany (col)--Lumberton.
Bethel— —— Evander McNair, D D.
Centre--Maxton, H G Hill, D D.
Church--Antioch.
Church--Lumber Bridge, J P McPherson.
Church--Red Springs. S M Rankin.
Church (col)--Red Springs.
Church--St Paul's, J S Black.
Iona--Iona.
Lebanon--Red Banks.
Montpelier--Montpelier.
Mt Calvary (col)--Lumberton, Dr L A Rutherford.
Panther's Ford (col)--Red Springs.
Philadelphus--Moss Neck, Hector McMcLean.
Smyrna--Red Banks, A M Ferguson.

ZION METHODIST.

Antioch (col)--Red Banks. S G Taylor.
Argyle (col)--Alma, —— Williams.
Beauty spot (col)--Red Banks, O Lutterioh.
Chrysolite (col)--Lumberton, S G Taylor.
St Matthew (col)--Maxton, —— Williams.

MINISTERS RESIDENT.

Names, Post Offices and Denom.

BAPTIST.

Barnes, Kinchen, Barnesville.
Booth, J M, Lumberton.
Cobb, J H, Lumber Bridge.
Clark, J D, St Paul's.
Hammond, Wm (col), Lumberton.
Hedgepeth, J P, Lumberton.
McMillan, D C, Leesville.
McPhaul, K (col), Fulmore.
McDonald, Hector (col), St Paul's.
Mercer, Noah, Lumberton.
Mercer, Miles, Lumberton.
Prevatt, F A, Jr, Lumberton.
Prevatt, J T, Lumberton.
Sessoms, R M, Lumberton.
Thompson, A H (col), Lumberton.
Thompson, Elias (col), Lumberton.

METHODIST.

Bundy, J D, Lumberton.
Gaddy, J R, Gaddysville.
Lee, J W, Maxton.
Lutterloh, O (col), Lumberton.
Mercer, Miles, Lumberton.
Paul, Joseph, Lumberton.

Payne, W H (col), Lumberton.
Pope, E, Leesville.

PRESBYTERIAN.

Craig, Hugh, Rowland.
McLean, Hector, Melrose.

ZION METHODIST.

Simmons, C W (col), Lumberton.
Taylor, S G (col), Lumberton.

HOTELS AND BOARDING HOUSES.

Names, Post Offices and Proprietors.

Boarding house, Lumberton, Mrs Comfort Robeson.
Boarding house, Maxton, Mrs McRae.
Boarding house, Leesville, G P Floyd.
Boarding house, Gaddysville, J Auman.
Hotel, Red Springs, S R Townsend.
Hotel, Red Springs, Mrs Shooter.
Hotel, Maxton, Ed McRae.
McCaskell Hotel, Maxton, M Carter.
Maple Shoal Inn, Maxton, — Weatherly.
Merchants Hotel, Lumberton, N H Jones.
National Hotel, Lumberton, H B Pittman & Bro.
Restaurant, Maxton, H H Sampson.

LAWYERS.

Names and Post Offices.

French & Norment (W S), Lumberton.
McMillan, Hamilton, Red Springs.
McNeill & McLean, Lumberton.
McIntyre. —, Lumberton.
Proctor, E K, Jr, Lumberton.
Rowland, Alfred, Lumberton.
Townsend (C B), & McLean, (N A), Lumberton.

MANUFACTORIES.

Kinds, Post Offices and Proprietors.

Alma Lumber Co, Alma.
Blacksmithing and wheelwrighting, Red Banks, Blackman & Co.
Blacksmithing and wheelwrighting, Maxton, W M McNeill.
Blacksmithing and wheelwrighting, Lumberton, Harry McQueen.
Blacksmithing and wheelwrighting, Gaddysville, Jas Burnes.
Blacksmithing and wheelwrighting, Philadelphus, Alex Locklear.
Blacksmithing and wheelwrighting, Philadelphus, D McKay.
Blacksmithing and wheelwrighting, Philadelphus, F McKay.
Blacksmithing and wheelwrighting, Philadelphus, H J McMillan.

ROBESON COUNTY.

Blacksmithing and wheelwrighting, Philadelphus, Jno McNeill.

Blacksmithing and wheelwrighting, Gaddysville, A Taylor.

Blacksmithing and whe lwrighting, Plummersville, H H Reily.

Building and contracting, Philadelphus, W F Buie.

Building and contracting, Gaddysville, W B Hunt.

Building and contracting, Philadelphus, J Johnson.

Building and contracting, Lumberton, R R Nye.

Building and contracting, Alfordsville, A D McLean.

Building and contracting, Plummersville, J H Watson.

Cabinet making, Maxton, A A McLean.

Carding (wool), Antioch, Hodgin & McPhaul.

Carriages, buggies, e c., Maxton, Enoch Burnes.

Carriages, buggies, etc., Maxton, A J Burnes.

Carriages, Gaddysville. J R Burnes.

Chairs, trass, etc, Lumberton, G E Willoughby.

Coopering, Gaddysville, Jas Pittman.

Coopering, Philadelphus, Alex Brown.

Coopering, Philadelphus, A Locklan.

Coopering, Plummersville, Jno White.

Coopering, Plummersville, Alvin Cobb.

Distillery (turpentine), Moss Neck, J A Humphrey.

Distillery (turpentine) Alma. Patterson & McNair.

Distillery (turpentine), Red Banks, S R Townsend.

Distillery (turpentine), Moss Neck, McNair & Ausley.

Distillery (turpentine), Lumberton, S T Freeman.

Distill ry (turpentine), Moss Neck, T J Tolar.

Distillery (turpentine), Tolarsville, W H Fisher.

Distillery (turpentine), Brooklin, R R Barnes.

Distillery (turpentine), Tar Heel (Bladen co), L B Love.

Distillery (turpentine), Lumberton. J E Carlyle.

Distillery (turpentine), Lumber Bridge, H F Thames.

Distillery (turpentine), St Paul's, Lock Shaw.

Distillery (turpentine), Lee ville, A P Ashley.

Distillery (turpentine), Dora, W H McNeill.

Distillery (turpentine), Doro, Buie Bros.

Distillery (turpentine), Pates, R W Livermore.

ROBESON COUNTY.

Distillery (turpentine), Antioch, Thos McBryde.

Distillery (turpentine), Maxton, McRae Bros.

Harness, Rowland, W J Cooley.

Millwrighting, Philadelphus, H McNeill.

Millwrighting, Philadelphus, D B McNeill.

Red Springs Lumber Co, Red Springs.

Shoes, Lumberton, A T Baker.

Turpentine, McNatt's, J C D McNatt.

Turpentine, Lumberton, W C Townsend.

Turpentine, Lumberton, H D Williams.

Turpentine, Antioch, Hodgin & Son.

Turpentine, Kinlaw, Kinlaw & Bro.

Turpentine, Maxton, W S McNair.

Turpentine, Moss Neck, J W Culbreth.

Turpentine, Rowland, P K & D H McDonald.

Turpentine, Ryan, Thos McBryde.

MERCHANTS AND TRADESMEN.

Names, Post Offices, Lines of Business.

ALFORDSVILLE.

Bullock, A L & W F,	G S
McRae, Chas,	G S

ALFRED.

Tolar, T J,	G S

ALLENTON.

Stansell, Bunyan,	G S

ALMA.

McNair, H C,	G S

ANTIOCH.

Hodgen & Son (near),	G S

ASHPOLE.

Floyd, A J,	G S

BARNESVILLE.

Barnes, R R,	G S

BLANCHARD.

Ausley, J T,	G S
Gilmore, J F,	G S
McCraney, J D,	G S

BOWMORE.

Wilkes, J W,	G S

BRANCHVILLE.

Fowler, S W & Co,	G S
McLean, A D & Co,	G S

BUIE'S.

Buie, J N,	G S
Denny, J T & Co,	G S
Jones, A L,	G S
Williams, S B,	G S

ELROD.

Culbreth, W K,	G S
McCall, D A,	G S

ROBESON COUNTY.	ROBESON COUNTY.

ROBESON COUNTY.

FLORAL COLLEGE.

Alford, H C,	Fert
McBryde, Jas,	G S
McKinnon, Mrs M N,	G S

FULMORE.

| Hamer, L R, | G S |

IONA.

| Mitchell, H G, | G S |

KINLAW.

| Kinlaw & Bro, | G S |

LEESVILLE.

| Brown, J B & Son, | Drugs |

LUMBER BRIDGE.

Hall, J W,	G S
Shaw, A L,	G S
Shaw, N I,	G S

LUMBERTON.

Blake, P C,	G S
Caldwell, L H,	G S
Caldwell & Carlyle,	G S
Edmunds, D F, jr,	Gro
Freeman, Mrs A A,	G S
Fuller Bros,	Stock Dealers
Gough, Frank, Agt,	G S
Jones, N H,	G S
Linkhaw, Wm L,	Livery
McDiarmid, W W,	Job Printer
McLeod, A H,	G S
McMillan, Dr J D,	Drugs
McNeill, J H,	G S
Millsaps, D W,	G S
Morrison & Barker,	G S
Norment, O C & Co,	G S
Peterson, Mrs Fannie,	Millinery
Pittman, H B & Co,	G S
Pope, H T & Co,	Drugs
Prevat, A & W,	G S
Prevat, W J,	G S
Proctor, E K,	Jewelry
Proctor, E K, jr,	Furn and Hardw
Redmond, C B,	G S
Smith, J C,	G S
Stone, J,	Livery
Townsend, W C (near),	G S
Watson & Watson,	G S

MAXTON.

Burke, J M,	Gro
Carter & Alford,	G S
Carter, N A,	D G
Cash Racket Store, M M McNair, Prop	
Croom, Dr J D,	Drugs
Croom, W E & Co,	G S
Elwell, J W,	G S
Fine, Mrs S H,	D G and Clo
Freeland, J J,	Jeweler
Hargrave, D T,	Sewing Machines
Holland, C A,	Hdw
Leach, Jno,	G S
Lowe & Jones,	G S
McKenzie, M G,	Newspaper
McKinnon, A C,	G S

McKinnon, A J,	Livery
McLean & Sellers,	G S
McLean, M H & J D,	G S
McLean, M V,	G S
McNair, M,	Furn
McNair, W S,	G S
McRae, J S,	G S
McRae, M L (col),	Gro
Maxton Drug Co.	Drugs
Patterson & McKinnon, Misses,	Millinery
Pool, Mrs J T,	D G and Milliner
Robbins, J W,	G S
Sellers, J B & Co,	G S
Strickland, R H,	G S
Thompson, L,	G S

MELROSE.

| McCormick, Jas (col), | G S |

MILL PRONG.

| Gilbert, Dr W J, | Gro and Drugs |

MOSS NECK.

| Culbreth, J W, | G S |

PARKTON.

| McMillan & Hughes, | G S |

PATES.

| Livermore, R W, | G S |

PEMBROKE.

Bruce & McCormac,	G S
Downing & Thaggard,	G S
Speight, W E & Co,	G S

PHILADELPHUS.

| Humphrey, J A, | G S |

PLAINVIEW.

| McKinnon, D P, mgr, | G S |

PURCEPOLIS.

| Alderman & Buie, | G S |

PURVIS.

| Culbreth, W K, | G S |
| Pate, C T, | G S |

QUEENSDALE.

| McQueen, R M, | G S |

RED SPRINGS.

Carver, W H,	G S
Cope, E C,	G S
Council, W J,	G S
Covington, T A,	G S
Currie, B B,	Drugs
Hodgin, H H & Son,	G S
McKay, J A,	G S
McLeod, W J,	G S
McQueen, Peter,	G S
Pearsall, A B,	Lumber
Pope, J M,	Gro
Shooter, Mrs W J,	Millinery
Townsend, S R,	G S
Townsend & Garrett,	G S
Wharton, Dr L D,	Drugs

RENNERT.

| Tolar, S R, | G S |

34

| ROBESON COUNTY. | ROBESON COUNTY. |

ROCHESTER.

Rogers, D M,   G S

ROWLAND.

Adams, S L,   G S
Ivey, L L,   G10 and Fertilizers
Ivey & Jenkins,   G S
McCallum, J C,   G S
McCormack, H K,   G S
McDonald, P K & D H,   G S and Turp
McEachern & McCormack,   G S
McMillan & Pittman,   Drugs
Oliver, D N & Co,   G S
Smith, S C,   G S
Smith, J H & Co,   G S
Smith, S J,   G S
Ward, E B (near)   G S
Ward & Hedgepeth,   G S

ROZIER'S.

Rozier, Dr S B,   G S

RYAN.

McBryde, Thos,   G S and Turpentine

ST. PAUL.

McEachern, A R, .   G S
Shaw, L & Co,   G S
Willough, Sidney,   G S

SHANNON.

Hall, W H,   G S
Klarpp. D S,   —
McLeod, A & Son,   —
McPhail, W C,   G S

TOLARSVILLE.

Fisher, W H,   Turpentine
Whitted, Wm,   G S

VOLLERS.

Chisholm, Jno,   G S

MILLS.

Kinds, Post Offices and Proprietors.

Corn, Lumberton, John Warwick.
Corn, Lumberton, W Q Warwick.
Corn, St Paul's, Gideon Tyson and
   Lock Shaw.
Corn, Lumber Bridge, S P Klarpp.
Corn, Fulmore, L R Hamer.
Corn, Lumberton, Hector McE McMil-
   lan.
Corn and flour, Lumberton, J P Mercer
Corn and flour, Moss Neck, Alexander
   McIntyre.
Corn and flour, Moss Neck, W C Mc-
   Neill.
Corn and flour, Red Banks, S R Town-
   send.
Corn and flour, Lumber Bridge, J H
   McEachern.
Corn and flour, Howellsville, Robert A
   Rozier.
Corn and flour, Leesville, A P Ashley.
Corn and flour, Leesville, Hybert At-
   kinson.
Corn and flour, Lumberton, J W Ed-
   munds.

Corn and cotton-gin (steam), Lumber-
   ton, D Lewis.
Corn and gin, Lumber Bridge, Jas A
   McNeill,
Corn, flour and Tar Heel (Bladen co),
   Seth Smith.
Corn, flour and saw, Lumberton, Noah
   Mercer.
Corn, flour and gin, Barnesville, Lee
   Rhodes.
Corn, saw and gin (steam), St Paul's,
   Lock Shaw.
Corn and saw, Lumberton, S B Rozier.
Corn and saw, Lumberton, Warren
   Lewis.
Corn and saw, St Paul's, estate of Col.
   Nathaniel McLean.
Corn and saw, Gaddysville, E J Horn.
Corn and saw, Howellsville, S B Pow-
   ers.
Corn and saw, Antioch, W P McNeill.
Corn and saw, Antioch, Thomas Mc-
   Bryde.
Corn, saw and gin, Fulmore, Rev Wes-
   ley Thompson.
Corn, saw and gin (steam), Fulmore, L
   R Hamer.
Cotton-gin (steam), Maxton, T B Rus-
   sel.
Saw (steam), Lumberton, Warren Wil-
   liams.
Saw (steam), Maxton, A J Cottingham
   & Bro.
Saw, corn and flour (steam), Alfords-
   ville, Charles McRae.
Saw and gin (steam), Barnesville, R R
   Barnes.
Corn, flour and rice, Leesville, J P Pit-
   man.
Saw, gin and corn, St Paul's, Robert
   McGeachy.
Saw, gin and corn, Philadelphus, W J
   Brown.
Saw, flour and cotton-gin, Antioch,
   Allen McCormac.
Saw, Shannon, J H Singleton.
Saw, Red Springs, Rankin Bros.
Saw, Shannon, B F Barnard & Co.
Saw, Red Springs, S C Hall.
Saw, Red Springs, W J Love.
Saw, Purvis, N A McQueen.
Saw, Red Springs, R F Devane.
Saw, Maxton, S O Frostick.
Saw, Moss Neck, J W Culbreth.
Saw, Lumberton, H D Williams.
Saw, McNatt's, J C D McNatt.
Saw, Lumber Bridge, M L Marley.
Saw, Branchville, A D McLean & Co,
Saw, Alfordsville, W F & A L Bul-
   lock.
Saw and corn, Moss Neck, Archibald
   Buie's heirs.
Saw and corn, Maxton, N W Gaddy.
Saw and corn, Antioch, Daniel Biggs.
Saw and corn, Antioch, M J McPhaul.

ROBESON COUNTY.

Steam saw and planing mills, Red Springs, Fitzhugh Bros.

Steam saw, Red Springs, Vandegrift & Co.

Steam saw, Red Springs, Lester & Co.

Steam saw, Red Springs, A B Pearsal & Co.

Steam saw, Red Springs, Durant & Co.

Steam saw and gin, Lumber Bridge, N & A L Shaw.

Steam saw, Red Springs, D M McKay & Co.

Steam saw, Shannon, W P McHhail.

Steam saw and cotton gin, Antioch, H H Hodgin,

Steam saw, grist and gin, Grady, J A & G L Thompson.

Steam saw, grist and gin, Lumberton, McIntyre & Leggett,

Steam saw, grist and gin, Fulmore, J L Townsend & Co.

PHYSICIANS.

Names and Post Offices.

Bethune, Angus, Antioch.
Brown, J P, Leesville.
Byrnes, W L, Maxton.
Croom, J D, Maxton,
Currie, Angus, Lumber Bridge.
Dickson, A P, Antioch.
Horton, —— Red Springs.
Hughes, Daniel (dentist), Shannon.
Lewis, R F, Lumberton.
McBryde, David, Maxton.
McKinnon, —— Red Springs.
McMillan, J D, Lumberton.
McMillan, J L, Red Springs.
McMillan, B F, Plainview.
McNatt, W H, Maxton.
Norment, T A, Lumberton.
Norment, R M, Lumberton.
Norment, W B, Rowland.
Oliver, W A, Fair Bluff, (Columbus co).
Pope, H T, Lumberton.
Rozier, S B, Lumberton.
Sinclair, Duncan, Alfordsville.

SCHOOLS.

Names, Post Offices and Principals.

Ashpole Institute, Leesville, A T Rogers,

Clybronsville Academy, ——, D A Price.

Croatan Normal School, Pate's, (for Croatan Indians).

Female College, Red Springs.

Floral College (male), Shoe Heel.

High School, Gaddysville, Charles McCormick.

High School, Philadelphus, D A Buie.

Long Branch Academy, Charm, W R Surles.

ROBESON COUNTY.

Primary School, Maxton, Miss C B Miller (col).

Robeson Institute, Lumberton, Capt. John Duckett prin, and four assistants.

Whitin Normal School (col), Lumberton, D P Allen.

Public Schools—White, 96; colored, 23; Croatan Indian, 13.

LOCAL CORPORATIONS.

Ashpole Lodge, No. 825, A F and A M, Alfordsville. Time of meeting, second Saturday.

King Solomon Lodge, No 33, A F and A M, Lumber Bridge. Time of meeting, first Saturday evening and December 27th.

NEWSPAPERS.

Lumber Bridge News, P R Law, ed and prop.

Scottish Chief, Maxton (Dem. weekly); Kirkland Hill, ed and prop.

The Robesonian, Lumberton; W W McDiarmid, ed and prop.

The Maxton Blade, Red Springs (Rep. weekly); R B Russell, ed and prop.

The Citizen (Dem. weekly), Red Springs; McEachern & Branch, eds and props.

The Populist (Pop. weekly), Lumberton: S A Edmonds, ed and prop.

FARMERS.

Names and Post Offices.

Alfordsville—Evander J Alford, N T Alford, John W Baker, James L Baker, Stephen Bass, Charles Berry, Samel Bracy, Jas Bracy, D A Bracy, Othneal Bracy, Z Brigman, R A Brunson, R W Bullard, A E Bullard, Elias Bullard, L W Bullard, A L & W F Bullock, J B Bullock, John W Bullock, Alex Chisholm, C B Cox, James D Doares, E C Everett, Z Fullmore, A F Falks, O C Falks, C P Holcomb, D F Holcomb, H M John, Neill McCallum, J B McCallum, L McCallum, John A McKay, A D McLean, Archibald McLean, H R McLean, D L McLean, J R McLean, Spurgeon McLean, P B Meekins, A C Morrison, J H Morrison, N McNair, Malcolm Monroe, M A Monroe, James McQueen, Jas A McQueen, John A McRae, P P McRae, Chas McRae, J R McRimmon, N L Sinclair, Wm Stubbs, N B Watson, J W Willis, John Williams.

Allenton—Eli Hammond, David Israel, J B MbLean, F J Mears, A B

ROBESON COUNTY.

Moore, J T Phillips, W L Phillips, E R Phillips, John Phillips, J L Pittman, Henry Pittman, Council Pittman, Wright Pittman, Jordan Prevatt, W H Purnell, R McK Rozier, W W Singletary, Armstead Singletary, N R Smith, John W Smith, B Stansel, Jas A Taylor, J W Taylor, S J Taylor. Willis Taylor, G H Todd, B A Todd, H E Thompson, W Q Warwick, Lewis West, Elias West, S E Willoughby, J W Wishart.

Alma--A M Cobb, Edward Currie, R M McNair, J P Patterson. J F Payne.

Antioch--David Bethune, Daniel Biggs, D W Bsggs. John A Brown, N B Brown, James Campbell, D N Currie, J L Currie, J M Currie, J P Graham, Richard Graham, H H Hodgin, J W Hodgin. N D Johnson, Henry Jessup, N B McArthur, Jno A McBry, Joe A McBryde, D B McLauchlin. Joshua McMillan, M J McPhaul, M H McPhaul, jr, E G Yarboro.

Ashpole--Alex Andrews, N T Andrews, W A Bethea, Meredith Bullock, H C Bullock, Dr J B Brown. F L Floyd, Giles Floyd, A H Floyd, F F Floyd, H S Floyd, P M Floyd, G D Floyd, J H Floyd, G P Floyd, A E Floyd, C P Grantham, T L Grimsley, M K Griffin, Silas Griffin, J H Inman, C A Inman. H Johnson, J D Lewis, J P Lewis, P T Mitchell, J P Pitman, H P Ratley, E B Thompson.

Athens--Wm Burns, Jno McGeachy, Robt McGeachy, David McMilton, Alex Parham, N Sealey, Lock Shaw, Marcus Smith, C P Thames. C Thaggard.

Barnesville--James P Barnes, Wm Barnes, K Barnes, R R Barnes. Everett Bass, Isham Britt, E G Floyd, Bell Floyd, E T Floyd, F E Floyd, E K R R Flowers, Wm Haynes, I R Hedgepeth, Zaphaniah Ivy, W B Jenkins. Wingate Lawson, James A Lawson. J P Murray, K L Page, Everett Page, Melvin Sealey, Jackson Sealey, E McQ Surles. V S Walters. John Walters, sr, John Walters. jr, Haynes Walters, J P Walters, Daniel Walters. John B Walters, W P Walters, Thompson Williams, Oliver Williams, B P Williams.

Edenboro--Wyatt Adams, Jno Chisholm, Dr A P Dickson, Dr Wm Gilbert, James A McQueen.

Edgewood--Alex Brisson, Stephen Brisson, Wm Byrd, Wm Ivey, James Kinlaw, Byars Kinlaw, Thos Kinlaw, Oliver Kinlaw, E J Kinlaw. John G Smith, Jos Smith, J C Smith.

Fair Bluff--D Adams, J W Brewer. J Q Adams, P Arnett, Ed Arnett, Thos Evans, Mike Evans, J T Foard. W B Grantham, jr, W J Grimsley, C T Harrington, W W Hill, Norfleet Hayes, Jas A Hill. W B Hunt (Croatan), Silas Huggins, Jno Horne, Dan'l Jones, Jno B Lewis. J A McCormack, J W McKinley, J C Nye, A N Nance, D H Nance, R M Oliver, J S Oliver, A C Oliver, Jos Page, J D Rogers, W C Watson, J H Williams.

Floral College--H C Alford, Jas McBryde, Jno A Smith.

Fulmore--A C Bridgers, Jno Bridgers, W M Bridgers, A M Bullard, L R Hamer, Alex McKinzee, Wm B Oxendine, T B Thompson.

Gaddysville--J R Burns, J D Crawford, Jesse R Gaddy.

Howellsville--J R Barefoot. W I Barfield, Chas Barker, Henry Harker, A A Bethune, W J Blount, S E Britt, J O Byrd, J A Campbell. A McN Currie, Hugh Flowers, A B King, Jes King, A C McGeachy, Duncan NcNair, J P Mercer, Hiram Mercer, Rev M V Mercer, Hugh Musselwhite. D B Musselwhite, Duncan Musselwhite, Jacob Musselwhite, Wiley Musselwhite, J W Musselwhite, R M Patterson, Wm Pernell, H P Powers, L B Powers, H T Powers, J H Powers, S A Powers. Jos Regan, W J Regan, D C Regan, Robt A Rozier, sr, Reuben Rozier, Neill Russ, R M Sessoms, Seth Smith.

Ionia--Joel Byrd, A W Davis, John K Davis, Thos Davis, H B Easterling, J B Inman, Jas T Lee, P P Lee, Thos Lee. W A Lewis, A G Mitchell, H G Mitchell, Q B Mitchell. Henderson Oxendine (Croatan), J F Parker, R A Pitman, J E Price, Joel Stone. Arch Thompson, S A Thompson, Wesley Thompson, C O Williams, W J Wilkinson.

Leesville--R A Andrews, S W Ashley, E C Atkinson, Virgil Atkinson (col), Hybert Atkinson, J C Atkinson, Atlas Atkinson, Jas D Britt, James E Britt, J W Bullock, Michael Bullock, Henry Bullock, J H Byrd, Levi Hunt (Croatan), Willis Ivey, H P Jenkins, Lewis Jenkins. J W Leggett, W A Leggett, Robt Leggett, Wright Leggett. D B Lewis, Dwight Lewis, Norman Martin, S L Potter. E C Purvis, Henry Purvis, John Purvis, E W Willoughby.

Lumber Bridge--J W Adcock, E S Ausley, J T Ausley, C W Autrey, Thomas L Bass, William Baxter, Alex Black, John R Brown, Archibald Brown, Duncan Bethune, J H Chason, Jeff D Cobb, J A P Conoly, W S Conoly, A H Currie, William J Davis, W A Graham, E J Graham, Hugh Graham, Nathan Hall, M J Johnson, Henry Johnson, A G Johnson, R W

Kinlaw, J H Lancaster, D F Lewis, William Little, Cornelius Little, J D Malloy, D C Malloy, W H Maxwell, J H McEachern, Hector McEachern, A K McFaydan. D B McGugan, A C McGugan, Daniel McLeod, James A McNeill, R McMillan, A L Shaw, Neill Shaw, H F Thomas, J A Walder, Elijah Walker, M B Wilkes, R A Williams, C H Wright.

Lumberton—Clarida Allen, W P M Allen, Norman Allen, Simon Allen, J W Branch, A J Branch, Z V Britt, H P Britt, Kenneth Britt, Caswell Aritt, Amos Britt, Archie Britt, D H Britt, A G Britt, Timothy Britt, M C Britt, W R Bevan, W H Bullard. E P Bullard, M A Byrd, W J Byrd, Daniel Baker, J T Barker, W P Barker, Stephen Barnes, Benjamin Banes (col), M S Baxley, I J Belch. S W Bennette, R K Blake, Marshall Bodiford, George A Boon, Pink Campbell, J E Carlyle, E C Carlyle, Newett Cox, Giles Davis, Wm Davis, James P Davis, D F Edmund, sr, D F Edmund, jr, J A Edwards, Calvin Flowers, Henry Flowers, John Flowers, Calvin Freeman, Neill Freeman, Miles Godwin (Croatan), B Godwin, H W Harrell, J N Hayes, T N Higley, J R Hillard, William Hooper (col), H H Howell, H B Howell. W J Humphrey, Matthew Humphrey, Richard Humphrey, Alex Humphrey, E J Humphrey, J S Humphrey, W H Humphrey, A P Inman, Robert Inman, Jordan Jacobs (Croatan). N H Jones, Michael Lamb, W P Lewis, Robert Lewis, T W McHargue, J H McKay, A H McLeod, H McE McMillan, D T McNeill, D D McNeill, J S Neill, E D McNeill, Rev Noah Mercer, J P Mercer, J A Mercer, G B Moore, W P Moore, Orrin Moore, R A Moore, J J Nance, T A Norment, O C Normeut, Jerry Oldum, Allen Oliver, Redden Phillips, Killis Phillips, R M Phillips, Jesse Phillips, S S Phillips, Eli Phillips, E D Pitman, Willis Pitman, Lewis Pitman, Ira L Pope, H T Pope, Z R Prevatt, W W Prevatt, P P Prevatt, J P Prevatt, J T Prevatt, Rev F A Prevatt, W D Prevatt, Joseph Prevatt, H R Price, Henry Revels (Croatan), Redden Rice, William Rice, English Rice, J F Roberts, Alf Rowland, Dr S B Rozier, Jas Sealey, J K Singletary, W J Smith, T R Smith, C P Stephens, H G Stephens, J F Stephens, Giles Stephens, James R Stone, Alex Stone, W B Sutton, Henry Taylor, J A Thompson, A S Thompson, J S Thompson, J L Thompson, A D Thompson, J P Thompson, N A Thompson, C B Thompson, Mrs R C Toon, F F Townsend, D W Townsend, A R Townsend, Neill Townsend, Richardson Townsend, Haynes Townsend. J B Townsend. Richard Townsend, J F Ward, O M Watson, J G Watson, E C Watson, J W Watts, T D Watts, Stephen Wiggins, Isaiah Wilcox, Alex Wilkinson, Warren Williams, Alex Willoughby, Wellington Wishart, A S Wishart.

Maxton—W G Caddell, Mrs A E Cottingham, Taylor Douglas, J K Ferguson, James K Graham, J C Hamer, D H Hamer, W C Hamer, J C Hamer, Sr, D W Hasty, D A Johnson, Hugh Johnson, James H Jones, Hector Mc-Bryde, David McCall, J C McCaskill, Purcell McEachern, R T McElyea, Hector McKay, Murdock McKinzie, Archibald McLauchlin, D P McLauchlin, A Q McLaurin, A A McLean, J L McLean, W S McNair. M McNair, E E F McRae. Murdock McRae, M R McRae, D M McRae, Ed McRae, H W McRae, G A Ray, T B Russell, R T Sanday, Angus Shaw, Simon Shaw, A W Stewart, Joel Strickland, J L Sumner, Norman Stewart, King Wall (col), Drury Walters.

McNatt's—J C D McNatt, Jno G McNatt.

Melrose—James McCormack, John Nicholson.

Moss Neck—D C Buie, Wm R Carter (Croatan), Richard Carter (Croatan), Stephen Carter (Croatan, H Q Dial (Croatan), John N Graham, Joe Locklear, Leonard Locklear, Calvin Lowry (Croatan), Sinclair Lowry, D A McMillan, W R McNeill, Enoch McNeill, Hector McNeill, B F McNeill, Oakley McNeill. W B Odeum. F G Odeum, John J Oxendine, H T Oxendine, J P Oxendine (Croatans), Sol Oxendine (Croatan), Wm Perry, John Prevatt, J P Prevatt, W C Townsend, J H Tyner, L E Tyner, Carey Wilkins, W W Williamson, J T Willis, J A Woodell.

Pates—J C Bixley, Thomas Plue, Wm Brayboy (Croatan), M B Buie, Elias Bullard (Croatan), M O Butler, Angus Chavis (Croatan), Tnos Chavis (Croatan), Wm Jacobs (Croatan), Wash Lowry (Croatan), R W Livermore, A Locklear, Tom Locklear (Croatan), Shepherd Locklear, M L Lowry (Croatan), Evander Lowry (Croatan), Angus Mainor, Martin Ransom (Croatan), Tom Sanderson, D S Smith, J C Smith, Chas Baie, J I Lowry (Croatan), Zion Lowry (Croatan).

Philadelphus—J McI Brown, A T McCallum, H J McMillan, J N Regan.

Plainview—W H Adams, W C Alford, Arch Bracy, James A Bracy, R H Braswell, Aseneth Bullock, I R Butler, W J Edens, Allen Edens, Alexan-

ROBESON COUNTY.	ROBESON COUNTY.
der Edens, Johnson Graham, W H Graham, Chas F Hammond, Jno Hammond, S G Hubbard, Jno Hunt, Sr, Bias Hunt (Croatan), Allen Jackson, Norman Leitch, Jno A Leitch, Jno B Lewis, J McN Martin, D A McCall, D W McCall, M H McCall, W H McCallum, A B McCormack, Alex McCor-	mack, Daniel McCormack, H R McCormack, Neill McCormack, Neill C McCormack, Wesley McCormack, Peter McCormack, Angus McQuaig, J A McGirt, Joe T McGirt, D A McGirt, Jas McGirt, Alex McGirt, D P McKinnon, N T McLean, J B McLeod, Robert H Miller, Ellis Miller.

ROCKINGHAM COUNTY.

AREA 550 SQUARE MILES.

POPULATION 25,373; White 15,197, Colored 10,176.

ROCKINGHAM COUNTY was formed in 1785, from Guilford county, and was named in honor of Charles W. Wentworth, Marquis of Rockingham, who was a distinguished friend of America in the English Parliament.

WENTWORTH, the county seat, was named in honor of the family of the House of Rockingham, and is 110 miles northwest of Raleigh. Population (estimated) 500.

Surface—Moderately hilly; contains many beautiful farms and fine country seats, particularly along the banks of the Dan river, where the scenery is very fine and the lands rich.

Staples—Tobacco, corn, wheat, oats and fruits in great variety. This is one of the finest tobacco counties in the State.

Fruits–Apples, peaches, pears, cherries, plums, berries and other small fruits.

Timbers—Pine, oak and hickory.

Minerals—Coal, with a large number of iron springs.

Coroner—John F Jarrett.
Register of Deeds—Robt L Snead.
Sheriff—Wm B Wray.
Solicitor 9th District—Marshall Mott.
Standard Keeper— ——.
Surveyor—E P Ellington.
Treasurer— ——.
Superintendent Public Schools—N S Smith (Leaksville).
County Examiner—N S Smith.

COURTS.

Fifth Monday before the first Monday in March, and fifth Monday before the first Monday in September, and ninth Monday after the first Monday in September.

TOWN OFFICERS.

LEAKSVILLE—*Mayor*, T G Taylor.
REIDSVILLE—*Mayor*, E M Redd; *City Clerk*, ——; *Treasurer and Chief of Police*, John Lumbert; *Commissioners*, P H Williamson, Henry Motley, Robt Williams, Wm Lindsay.

TOWNS AND POST OFFICES.

	POP.		POP.
Adelaide,	15	McNeely,	10
Aspen Grove,	75	Madison,	700
Ailee,	—	Mayfield,	35
Bason,	20	Mayo,	35
Benaja,	10	Monroeton,	—
Berry,	25	Nance,	25
Boyd,	50	Oregon,	50
Case,	10	Pleasantville,	20
Douglas,	15	Price,	20
Ferndale,	10	Pritchett,	10
Gant's,	50	Reidsville,	5,000
Geneva,	15	Rock Level,	20
Gentry,	5	Rocky Springs,	40
Grogansville,	50	Ruffin,	300
Hogan,	25	Sharp,	25
Hopper,	—	Simpson's Store	25
Langdon,	--	Spray,	—
Lawsonville,	25	Stoneville,	200
Layton,	—	Thompsonville,	25
Leaksville,	250	Waddell's,	30
Lenox Castle,	25	Wentworth,	500

COUNTY OFFICERS.

Clerk Superior Court—Thos S Malloy.
Commissioners — John M Galloway, chm'n; A M Whitsett, A G Ferrell, D F King, W J Witty.

TOWNSHIPS AND MAGISTRATES.

Huntersville—R B Henderson (Hogan), A F Neal, J H Gentry, S G Gentry, J Simpson, C P Angel (Madison), J A Colly, WA Gourks (Rocky Springs).

Leaksville—B K Terry (Birdville, Va.), Jno W Edwards, S P Garrett, J W Flanegan, C J Land, Terrel Nance, A H Strong, C G Jones (Leaksville).

Madison—T McWoodburn, James Highfile, D W Busick, G W Mangum, R Satterfield, W H Suthern, G L Trogden, G C Johnson, Jno Yowing, E A McGhee, R G Lewellin (Madison), J A Vernon (Mayo).

Mayo—J E Roberts, N C Deshazo, N S Smith, W A Smith, J W Roberts, A W Combs, T B Lindsey (Mayo).

New Bethel—A H Garrett, J A Harlin, J E Purcell, John G Price, John Bailey, J P Wilson, Patrick S Williams (Aspen Grove).

Price—C W Smith, J M Stone, J M Currie, J M Barnes (Price).

Ruffin—J A Gibson, L L Bennett, W S Carter, J R Hopper, R A McDowell, T W Stokes, T R Williams, W T Lewis, sr, J W Foster, V Holderly (Ruffin), W L Gardner (Oregon), G W Neal (Mansfield).

ROCKINGHAM COUNTY.

Simpsonville —G R Shrives, J M Haines, J D Moon, W T King. Josiah Newman, W K Gibbs(Simpson's Store).

Reidsville—W C Staples, W D Hightower, G M Hazel, Geo J Meador, W G Terry, A J Davis, R L Saunders, R H Wray, J M Jones, D G Flack (Reidsville).

Wentworth—Jno R Moon, J C Lashley, W G Burten, T E Merphies, Jno Y McCollum, S O Green, P W Hudson, Jno G Mitchel, Levi Barnes (Wentworth).

Williamsburg—Jos Waywick, F L Simpson, G Pink Walker, W S McKinney, R H Saunders, G T Davis, W F Priddy (Reidsville).

CHURCHES.

Names, Pastors, Postoffices and Denom.

METHODIST.

Bethesda—Madison, C F Sherrill.
Bethlehem—Wentworth, F W Womble.
Church—Leaksville, W F Womble.
Cnurch—Madison, C F Sherrill.
Church—Reidsville, L W Crawford.
Church—Ruffin, J B Tabor.
Church—Wentworth, F W Womble.
Eden—Boyd, —— Gibson.
Hickory Grove—J B Tabor.
Lowes—Reidsville, F W Womble.
Mt Carmel—Reidsville, J B Tabor.
Mt Carmel—Stokesdale, —— Gibson.
Mt Pleasant—Stokesdale, —— Gibson.
Mt Zion—Rocky Springs, —— Gibson.
Pernell—Lawsonville, J B Tabor.
Salem—W F Womble.
Ward Chapel—Reidsville, J B Tabor.

METH. PROTESTANT.

Midway—Aspen Grove, Rev Raper.
Palestine— Rocky Springs, Rev Ogburn.
Sandy Cross—Ferndale, Rev Raper.

BAPTIST.

Church—Pleasantville, J A Bead.
Church—Reidsville, M A Adams.
Church—Madison, W H Wilson.
Church—Leaksville, J B Richardson.
Matrimony—Sanford Biggs.
Mt Hermon—Berry, W H Wilson.
Providence—Leaksville, W H Wilson.
Sharon—W H Wilson.
Shiloh—R W Dix.
Three Forks—M A Adams.

PRIMITIVE BAPTIST.

Lick Fork—Ruffin, James Dameron.
Sardis—Hogan, James Harris.
Wolf Island—Reidsville, James Dameron.

PRESBYTERIAN.

Church—Madison, Rev —— Rankin.

ROCKINGHAM COUNTY.

Church—Wentworth, D J Craig.
Church—Reidsville, D J Craig.
Church—Leaksville, Rev —— Doggett.
Speedwell—Reidsville, D J Craig.

CHRISTIAN.

Happy Home— ——, J Holt.
Howard Chapel — Wentworth, T B Dawson.
Kellums's Grove—Hogan, C B Dawson.
Mt Bethel—Swepson's Store, C B Dawson

EPISCOPAL.

Church—Reidsville, J W Baker.
Church—Madison, J W Baker.
Epiphany.-Leaksville, J W Baker.

FREE-WILL BAPTIST.

Church—Douglas.
Stoneville—Stoneville, C W Sherrill.
Troy—Price's Store, C W Sherrill.
Union—Mayfield.

DISCIPLES OF CHRIST.

Church—Stoneville, T I Stone.

MINISTERS RESIDENT.

Name, Post Office and Denomination.

METHODIST.

Anderson, J H, Nance.
Crawford, L W, Reidsville.
Field, Daniel, Leaksville.
Gibson, F F, Summerfield.
Strader, Thos I, Berry.
Tabor, J B. Reidsville.
Womble, W F, Wentworth.

BAPTIST.

Adams, M A, Reidsville.
Betts, I L, Madison.
Kerr, G S, Thompsonville.
McKinnery, Ren, Thompsonville.
Wilson, W H, Madison.

PRIM. BAPTIST.

Dameron, James, Nance.
Harris, James, Hogan.
Stone, F J, Stoneville.

EPISCOPAL.

Baker, J W. Leaksville.
Ellington, E P, Wentworth.

PRESBYTERIAN.

Craig, D I, Reidsville.

FREE-WILL BAPTIST.

Sherrill, G W, Madison.

HOTELS AND BOARDING HOUSES.

Names, Post Offices and Proprietors.

Boarding, Leaksville, Mrs A T Hopper.
Boarding, Leaksville, Mrs M Stamps.
Hotel, Ruffin, Rich Stokes.

ROCKINGHAM COUNTY.

Hotel, Leaksville, A T Hopper.
Hotel, Wentworth, M M Crafton.
Hotel, Madison, John Watkins.
Hotel, Reidsville, W R Vickers.
Hotel, Wentworth, Mesdames Wright and Johnston.
Reid House, Wentworth, Miss Nannie Wright.

LAWYERS.

Names and Post Offices.

Burton, R, Reidsville.
Fields, John E, Leaksville.
Johnson, P B, Wentworth.
Johnston & Johnston, Yanceyville
                (Caswell county).
McMichael, O, Madison.
Pannill, J T, Reidsville.
Reid & Reid, Reidsville.
Reid, Thomas S, Reidsville.
Reid, R D, Wentworth.
Scott, H R, Reidsville.

MANUFACTORIES.

Kinds, Post Offices and Proprietors.

Aluminum Works, Spray.
Berry Canning Co, Berry, Settle Bros.
Boyd Mfg Co, Reidsville, No. looms, 70.
Bricks, Madison, Jim Foust.
Buggies and wagons, Leaksville, Hampton & Co.
Building and contracting, Leaksville, Kemp & Hopper.
Cabinet, Leaksville, P H Stevens.
Carriages, Reidsville.
Carriages and buggies, Leaksville, J W Harper.
Carriages, Gentry, Fred Gant.
Carriages, Leaksville, J H Hampton & Company.
Coaches, Wentworth, S B Wray.
Cotton mill, Madison, S Mead, m'g'r.
Cotton mills, Leaksville, incorporation.
Cotton mills, Leaksville, B F Mebane, pres; looms, 174.
Distillery (brandy), Wentworth, J M Jones.
Edna Cotton Mills, Reidsville, J M Arrington, treas.
Furniture, Reidsville, J T Smith & Co.
Furniture, Madison, Jas W Moore.
Furniture, Leaksville, Jas R Stephens.
Harness and saddles, Madison.
Harness and saddles, Reidsville, J W Peas.
Harness and saddles, Case's, Jno Highfill.
Harness and saddles, Leaksville, P D Wade.

ROCKINGHAM COUNTY.

Iron and wood working, Ruffin, G Withers.
Iron and wood working, Madison, W Wall (col.).
Iron and wood working, Leaksuille, Kemp & Hopper.
Iron and wood working, Wentworth, T E Morphis.
Iron and wood working, Wentworth, S B Wray.
King Tobacco Mfg Co, Leaksville, D F King.
Millwrighting, Ruffin, F M Alcorn.
Millwrigh·ing, Adelaide, James Small.
Old North State Tobacco Works, Reidsville, R P Richardson, jr.
Paper boxes, Reidsville, W J Irvin.
Roller mills, Reidsville, J H Walker & Company.
Saddles and harness, Reidsville, J H Benson & Son.
Spray Mfg Co, Spray, manufacturers of acetyline gas.
Tannery, Cases, James Highfill.
Tobacco, Reidsville, D Barnes & Co.
Tobacco, Reidsville, Johnson & Bro.
Tobacco, Reidsville, Lindsay & Co.
Tobacco, Reidsville, Watt & Penn.
Tobacco, Reidsville, A H Motley & Co.
Tobacco Factory, Leaksville, B F Ivie.
Tobacco Factory, Leaksville, E V Gravely & Co.
Tobacco, Leaksville, Shultz Tobacco Co.
Tobacco, Leaksville T G Taylor.
Tobacco, Leaksville, Bateman & Turner.
Tobacco, Madison, I W Mangum.
Tobacco, Madison, Penn Bros & Co.
Tobacco, Madison, W H Planters.
Tobacco, Madison, R P Wall & Co.
Tobacco, Madison, Martin McGhee & Co.
Tobacco (plug and twist), Price's, W P & C Grogan.
Tobacco boxes, Madison, Jas W Moore.
Tobacco boxes, Reidsville, J M Walker & Co.
Tobacco (smoking), Reidsville, Robert Harris & Co.
Tobacco (smoking and cigarettes), Reidsville, Richardson, Denny & Co.
Tobacco, Reidsville, R P Richardson, sr.
Tobacco, Reidsville, Watt Bros.
Tobacco, Reidsville, Burton Bros.
Tobacco, Reidsville, Reid Wooten & Co
Tobacco, Leaksville, Dillard & Moir.
Tobacco, Leaksville, D F King.
Tobacco boxes, coffins and furniture, Boyd, J W Moore & Sons.
Tobacco, Reidsville, Robt Harris & Bro.
Tobacco, Reidsville, Johnson Bros.
Tobacco, Reidsville, Wm Lindsay & Co.
Tobacco, Reidsville, F R Penn & Co.

ROCKINGHAM COUNTY.

Tobacco, Leaksville, Samuel Williams.
Walfland Roller Mills, Pelham, Candler & Bethel.
Woolen mills, Leaksville, incorporation.
Wool-carding, Reidsville, S H Boyd.

MERCHANTS AND TRADESMEN.

Names, Post Offices and Lines of Business.

ADELAIDE.

Moseley, John,	G S
Shrives, J R,	G S

ASPEN GROVE.

Cummings, Mrs Eliz,	G S

ATLEE.

Setliffe, W H, jr,	G S

BASON.

Price, John S,	G S
Sharp, W P & Co,	G S
Smathers, W C,	G S

BENAJA.

Green, Wm,	G S

BERRY.

Mobley, C W & Co,	G S

BOYD.

Moore, J Wright,	G S

ELLISBORO.

Roberts, James,	G S

FERNDALE.

Small, James,	Millwright

GENEVA.

Price, J T,	G S

GENTRY.

Knight, William,	G S
Payne, J R,	G S

GROGANSVILLE.

Grogan, W P & Co,	G S

LANGDEN.

Wall, J T,	Poultry Farm

LAWSONVILLE.

Motley, Giles O,	G S

LAYTON.

Baker, W H & Co,	G S

LEAKSVILLE.

Carter & King,	Hdw and Fert
Carter & Moir,	Hdw and Fert
Dyer, Miss Mollie,	Millinery
Dyer, B H & G D,	Tob
Ellington, D R,	Gro
Fields, D E,	Dry Goods
Fields, J E,	Dry Goods
Gravely & Co,	Tob
Ivie Bros,	Gro and Livery
King, D F,	G S
King, Jos B,	Tob

Lane & Land,	Tob Warehouse
Martin, S L,	G S
Moir, H C,	Furniture
Ray, Mrs A M,	Millinery
Seay, E F,	Conf
Stephenson & Moir,	G S
Wade, P D,	Harness

LENOX CASTLE.

Citty, D B,	G S
McKinney & Stanfield,	G S

MADISON.

Adkins, J H,	Jeweler
Apple, J M,	G S
Busick, D W,	Gro
Carter, Jesse,	Drugs and G S
Cardwell, R M,	Miller
Carter, Jesse & Co,	Furniture
Cates, O J & Co,	G S
Coble, H L & Co,	G S
Gentry, W B,	G S
Hatch & Coble,	Gro
Lewis, Miss Mary,	Milliner
Lowe & Warren, Misses,	Milliners
Martin, G W,	Tob Warehouse
McGhee Bros,	G S
Moore, Jones & Co,	G S
Payne, Frank,	Confec
Pratt Bros,	Hdw
Price, Jno H.	Miller
Scales, Mrs P M,	Milliner
Simpson, H,	Confect
Smith & Wall,	G S
Swann, J W & Co,	G S
Wade, H H,	Harness
Wall, R P & Co,	Tob Warehouse
Webster, Rankin & Co,	G S
Wortham, T R,	G S

MAYFIELD.

Cook, G G,	G S
Neal, Geo W,	G S

MONROETON.

Huffines & Hopkins,	G S
Moore, R L,	Millwright

NANCE.

Gilley, T D,	G S
Gilley, W C,	G S

OREGON.

Adkins, J L,	G S
Foster, Jno W,	G S
Frinelle, W R & Co,	G S
French, W R,	G S
Lovelace, J A,	G S

PRICE'S.

Holland, Grogan & Co,	G S
Price, R P & Sons,	G S
Watkins, D W,	G S

REIDSVILLE.

Allen, W S,	Drugs
Allen, M A,	Tob
Beaman, L.	Clothing
Benson, J H & Son,	Confec

ROCKINGHAM COUNTY.		ROCKINGHAM COUNTY.	
Berman, L,	Second-hand Clo	Watts' Warehouse,	Tobacco
Blackburn, D L,	G S	Webster, Jno R,	Publisher
Blackwell, Pinnex & Co,	Com Tob	White, S N,	G S
Bradnax & Reavis,	Barbers	White, Mrs M A,	G S
Burton, A M,	Leaf Tob	Williams, Hopkins & Co,	Clothing
Burton, J H,	Leaf Tob	Williams, G D,	G S
Coverts, Dr W J & Sons,	—	Williamson, P H, & Co,	G S
Craig, J N,	Bookstore	Wood, G V,	Jeweler
Degrote, E H,	Shoemaker	Wooten Bros,	G S
Denny Bros,	Hdw and Crockery	Wooten, W T, & Bro,	G S
Fetzer & Overman,	Drugs	Wooten & Pool,	G S
Ford, H R,	Tinner	Young, William & Co,	Cig and Tob

ROCKY SPRINGS.

Giles & Co,	Hdw		
Gladstone, R G,	Tinner	Knight, Wm,	G S
Gosett, Geo T,	Marble Yard		

RUFFIN.

Graves, Walter,	Liquors		
Gwyn, Z V,	Leaf Tob	Allison, J C (near),	Carriages
Hall, E F,	Lumber and Brick	Blackwell, E B,	G S
Harris, Robt & Bro,	Tob	Cook, G T,	G S
Hendricks, D A,	Dry Goods	Fitzgerald, O L, & Co,	G S
Hester, J N,	Millinery	Griffith, Mrs A V,	G S
Hirston, Burton & Co,	Gro	Mitchell, R S,	G S
Huffines, J D,	Dry Goods	Neal, G W,	G S
Huffines, John,	Millinery	Rice & Ware,	G S
Hutchison, Will,	Clothing	Wariner, W H, & Co,	G S
Irwin, J W, Paper Box Mfr, Job Printer		Worsham Bros,	G S
Johnson, G W & Son,	Leaf Tob		

SHARP.

Johnson Bros,	Tob	Thomas, R,	G S
Jones, T B,	Gro		

SIMPSON'S STORE.

Keatts, W C,	Harness		
King, F M,	Livery Stables	Simpson, P H,	G S

STONEVILLE.

Koyer, J F col),	G S		
Lamberth & Huffnis,	G S	Boaz & Martin,	Drugs
Lindsay, Wm, & Co,	Tob	Garrett, W S, & Son,	G S
Loper, B E,	Liquors	Glenn, J H, & Co,	G S
Matthews, C J, & Co, Dry Goods & Gro		Joyce, Garrett & Stowe,	Tobacco
Mayo, R J, & Co,	Job Printers	Lewis, R H & Sons,	G S
Miller, J A,	G S	Ray, J B, agent,	Dry Goods
Motley, A H, & Co,	Tob	Smith, T L & Co,	G S
Parkinson, J N,	G S	Stone, R T & Co,	G S
Paylor & De Grote,	G S		

SPRAY.

Parrish, H G, Carriage & Repair Shops			
Pray, J W, & Co,	Hardware	Leaksville Mercantile Co,	
Penn, F R, & Co,	Tob		

THOMPSONVILLE.

Perkinson, R N,	Racket Store	Ware, N,	G S
Pinnix & Blackwell,	Tob		

WENTWORTH.

Purcell & Dudley,	Drugs	Johnson & Wright,	G S
Redd, E M, & Co,	Leaf Tob	Minor, J B,	Fertilizers
Reidsville Cotton Factory,	G S	Mitchell, J W,	G S
Review Pub. Co,	Job Printing	Whittmore, A J,	Livery
Richardson, R P, sr,	G S	Withers, D L,	G S
Richardson, R P, jr, & Co,	Tob		
Richardson, J T,	Confec		

MILLS.

Rosch, Mrs J A, & Son,	Millinery		
Sharp, J O,	Ice and Bottling	Kinds, Post Offices and Proprietors.	
Smith, J T, & Co,	Furniture		
Steer, ——,	Confec and Baker	Bag Factory, Reidsville, Geo Boyd,	
Storic, M P,	Photo	mgr	
Stokes, C H,	Fert	Corn, Wentworth, G S Whittmore.	
Terry, Lindsay & Co,	Racket Store	Cotton Mill, Reidsville.	
Tesh, J M, & Co,	Jewelers	Flour, corn and saw, Madison.	
Tullock, M A, & Co,	G S	Flour, corn and saw, Madison, L H	
Walker, J H, & Co,	Lumber	Anderson.	
Ware, J A, & Sons,	G S	Flour and corn, Berry, Mrs Lucy Moore	
Ware, W P, agt,	G S	& Sons.	

ROCKINGHAM COUNTY.

Flour and corn, Wentworth, Ed Wright.
Flour, corn and saw, Boyd, J Wright Moore.
Flour, corn and saw, Monroeton, William Cummings.
Flour, corn and saw, Monroeton, Shaw & Co.
Flour, corn and saw, Monroeton, J Cunningham.
Flour, corn and saw, Reidsville. T F Rankin.
Flour, corn and saw, Troublesome, Mrs E Wade.
Flour and saw, Madison, R M Cardwell.
Flour and corn, Reidsville, S H Boyd.
Flour and corn, Leaksville, T L Morehead & Co.
Flour and corn, Aspen Grove, Price Bors.
Flour and corn, Mayfield, T B Hagood.
Flour and corn, Madison, J Cardwell.
Flour and corn, Madison, Smith & Price.
Flour and corn, Aspen Grove, W M Cummings.
Flour and corn, Aspen Grove, Price Bros
Flour and corn, Matrimony, D L King.
Flour and corn, Rocky Springs, J Wright Moore.
Flour and corn. Ruffin, Rawley Bros.
Flour and corn, Boyd. J W Moore & Sons.
Flour and corn, Madison, John Price.
Flour and corn, Milling and Mfg Co, Reidsville, J H Walker.
Flour, Stoneville, T H Unna.
Flour, Ruffin, Bethel & Co.
Saw, Madison, H J Wall.
Saw, Madison, Geo Webster.
Saw, Reidsville, M Walker & Co.
Steam saw, Madison, A Webster.
Steam corn and saw, Berry, L B Suttle & Bro.

PHYSICIANS.

Names and Post Offices.

Balsley, T E, Reidsville.
Binford, J W. Oregon.
Carter, C G. Madison.
Courts, D W, Reidsville.
Courts, W J, Reidsville.
Ellington, Samuel, Wentworth.
Fields, B J (dentist), Leaksville,
Guarant, F W. Leaksville.
Hester, J H (dentist), Reidsville.
Johns & Martin, Leaksville.
Martin, Sidney, Leaksville.
Matthews, W R, Stoneville.
McAnally, Charles B, Madison.
Payne, W A, Hogan.
Powell, M A, Reidsville.
Rominger, C A (dentist), Reidsville.

ROCKINGHAM COUNTY.

Smith & Irie, Stoneville.
Smith, Marion, Price's Store.
Smith, J R, Stoneville.
Taylor, Thomas, Leaksville.
Walton & Mills, Reidsville.
Walton, J C, Reidsville.
Wharton, R G, Ruffin.
Whitsett, A M, Reidsville.

SCHOOLS.

Names, Post Offices and Principals.

Academy, Ruffin, James Dameron.
Academy, Madison, Miss Irene McGee.
Academy, Wentworth, Miss M M Mitchell.
Graded School, Reidsville, Professor Sheppe, Supt Darden.
Graded School (col.), Reidsville, Prof. Sheppe, Supt Darden.
High School, Stoneville, Prof. N S Smith.
School, Reidsville, Mrs Martha Wooten.
Seminary (female), Reidsville, Miss Anna Hughes. prin.
Public schools—white, 111; colored, 50.

TEACHERS.

Names and Post Offices.

WHITE.
Anderson, Emma. Leaksville.
Anderson, Bettie C. Ruffin.
Baker, Mrs Mary, Wentworth.
Barber. Josie, Reidsville.
Baughn, A S, Douglas.
Baughn, H W, Ayresville.
Baugh, Nannie, Stoneville.
Burnett, Mamie, Reidsville.
Carter, Lizzie, Leaksville.
Carter, Cornelia, Berry.
Case, Sallie E, Case's.
Clark, Minnie, Reidsville.
Dallas, A H, Berry.
Dallas, Winnie, Berry.
Dameron, Miss Wannie, Nance.
Dameron, S H, Nance.
Dameron, Mrs K E, Mayfield.
Dameron, James, Nance.
Dawson, T B, Bason.
Dawson, Geo W, Bason.
Deshazo, G W, Price's.
Dixon, A G, Monroeton.
Dodds, Daisy, Ruffin.
Dyer, Pattie, Leaksville.
Fagg, Cassie, Stoneville.
Farrish, Ella, Ruffin.
Gardner, Lula, Reidsville.
Grogan, Ella, Douglas.
Gwinn, Lena, Reidsville.
Henderson, R B, Hogan.
Harris, Emmett, Reidsville.
Hauser, J W, Leaksville.

ROCKINGHAM COUNTY.

Holderly, J H, Mayfield.
Hopper, Mary, Leaksville.
Humphreys, Mollie, Burne.
Humphrey, T F, Bason.
Hundly, Anna, Leaksville.
Irvin, Mary H. Reidsville.
Kallum, J R, Stoneville.
Kallum, Cornelia, Stoneville.
Kirness, Blanche, Leaksville.
Knight, W P, Simpson's Store.
Lewis, Annie, Madison.
Lewis, Pauline, Ruffin.
Malloy, Lelia, Ferndale.
Malloy, Mollie, Ferndale.
McGhee, Sallie F, Madison.
Mebane, Mattie R. Madison.
Millrue, Lucy P. Reidsville.
Mitchell, Maggie May, Wentworth.
Mitchell, Lizzie, Berry.
Moore, Florence, Berry.
Moore, Addie, Berry.
Moore, Alma, Reidsville.
Motley, Fannie S, Lawsonville.
Norman, Mattie, Reidsville.
Nunnally, Alice. Ruffin.
Nunnally, G, Reidsville.
Oliver, Mary, Madison.
Oliver, Anna L. Reidsville.
Osborne, Minnie B, Leaksville.
Paschal, Fannie S, Lenox Castle.
Pitts, Cora, Reidsville.
Pratt, D A, Leaksville.
Pratt, B A, Leaksville.
Price, Lottie, Reidsville.
Price, J R, Ayresville.
Price, Anna, Price.
Pritchett, Ella, Pritchett.
Purcell, Anna, Adelaide.
Radliffe, Berta H. Wentworth.
Ragland, Hattla, Leaksville.
Rakestraw, Mrs S M, Price's Store.
Reid, Anna D, Wentworth.
Robertson, Della, Reidsville.
Robertson, Fannie, Reidsville.
Roberts, Ida L, Wadell's.
Saunders, Lucy, Leaksville.
Saunders, Jennie, Leaksville.
Sheffield, Mrs Anna, Oregon.
Shell, Ora, Reidsville.
Shepperd, Mrs Rhoda, Brown's Summit.
Smith, Mrs S S, Madison.
Stewart, Isaiah, Oregon.
Suttle, Clara, Berry.
Taylor, Clara, Layton.
Taylor, Thomas, Ferndale.
Thomas, Delia, Berry.
Trogden, E F, Douglas.
Vernon, T L, Mayo.
Vernon, D M, Leaksville.
Vickers, Rena, Reidsville.
Walker, Sallie E, Reidsville.
Walker, Geo T, Reidsville.
Walkor, Jas M, Reidsville.
Wilson, J A, Leaksville.

ROCKINGHAM COUNTY.

Woltz, Anna, Reidsville.
Wommack, Mollie, Reidsville.
Wray, Attie, Reidsville.
Wray, Ida. Reidsville.

COLORED.

Aiken, Alex, Leaksville.
Anderson, Bepie, Wentworth.
Anderson, Mary E, Nance.
Bethell, Anna. Reidsville.
Bevel, Sallie, Reidsville.
Brodnax, Mary L, Reidsville.
Carter, Ibly, Reidsville.
Carter, Enoch, Reidsville.
Carter, Alma J, Reidsville.
Carter, Mary, Reidsville.
Cardwell, Geo W, Reidsville.
Craige, Moses, Madison.
Davis, Mattie, Reidsville.
Delany, Ennis, Ruffin.
Dersett, Anna, Leaksville.
Dillard, Charlotte, Leaksville.
Evans, J S, Madison.
Flood, John, Reidsville.
Forest, Belle, Reidsville.
Frazier, D J. Leaksville.
Galloway, Addie, Leaksville.
Garrett, J H, Lenox Castle.
Gibson, J F, Layton.
Graves, Caroline, Oregon.
Graves, Ollie, Reidsville.
Gunn, Mary, Reidsville.
Hairston, Maggie, Reidsville.
Hairston, P A, Leaksville.
Johnston, Victory, Reidsville.
Jones, Mattie, Reidsville.
Jones, F, Reidsville.
King, J H, Reidsville.
Lennox, W F, Pleasantville.
Lindsay, Sallie, Reidsville.
Lesure, Mamie, Reidsville.
Lowe, Prince, McKneely.
Lowe, Florence, Reidsville.
Martin, Clay, Leaksville.
Martin, H D, Madison.
Martin, J H, Reidsville.
McCallum, Nick, Bason.
Meador, Maggie, Reidsville.
Merguson, Anna, Reidsville.
Millner, Laura, Leaksville.
Miller, E D. Reidsville.
Morgan, J H, Reidsville.
Morgan, Sallie, Reidsville.
Morris, J B, Reidsville.
Neal, Salina B. Rudsville.
Owens, Sallie J. Reidsville.
Parham, E F, Wentworth.
Price, Fannie. Ruffin.
Price, Ruth E, Leaksville.
Price, Martha J, Wentworth.
Reed, Fannie, Leaksville.
Richardson, Jane, Madison.
Scales, Sallie, Reidsville.
Scales, Susan, Madison.
Scott, Cora, Liberty.

ROCKINGHAM COUNTY.

Seacy, Lizzie, Reidsville.
Settle, Lula, Bason.
Settle, Jacob, Reidsville.
Sharp, Morris, Leaksville.
Sharp, Eliz, Ayresville.
Smallwood, Charles, Leaksville.
Smallwood, Lorena, Leaksville.
Smith, Jackson, Ayresville.
Strong, Ella, Reidsville.
Summerville, Rev C C, Reidsville.
Summerville, A L, Reidsville.
Terry, Martha. Reidsville.
Walker, Thos J, Thompsonville.
Wall, Frances, Bason.
Wall, Martha. Madison.
Watt, Mary P, Reidsville.
Wendson, Ella, Reidsville.
Winchester, R W, Pleasantville.
Winchester, J W, Pleasantville.
Windsor, W B, Reidsville.
Withers, Warren, Rocky Springs.

LOCAL CORPORATIONS.

A O U W, Reidsville.
Bank, Reidsville, C N Evans, cash.
Citizens Bank, Reidsville, R L Watt, cash.
Reidsville Electric Light Co, J F Rison, pres; W N Ruffin, sec and treas.
Reidsville Cotton Mills.

NEWSPAPERS.

Gazette, Leaksville; (Democratic weekly); J T Darlington, editor and prop.
Review, Reidsville;(Democratic weekly); Edw Gilliam, editor.
Webster's Weekly, Reidsville; (Democratic); John R Webster, ed and pro.

FARMERS.

Names and Post Offices.

Adelaide—R L Apple, John Beril, Robt Brown, P J Carter, W T Carter, T T Carter, J A Coleman, G H Garrison, J W Hudson, J W Jones, J M Kallum, A M Loving, J T Loving, W P Sanders, Thos K Shrives, J N Shrives, Albert Wall, James P Wilson.
Aspen Grove—Bradshaw, L A Cummings, D J Cummings, Robert Cummings, Jas W Elinen, T G Elinen, T G Elmon, Jas W Elmon, J D Moore, W B Nance, Thos Oakley, Simon Simpson, W J Watts, P S Williams, F B Williams, A G Williams, S G Williams, G D Williams, R A Williams.
Ayresville—Jno Cardwell, J H Glenn, David Joyce, Thos Martin, Sam'l Martin, Robert Martin, P F Martin, Chas Martin, David Martin.
Bason—Jonathan Banes, Jas Banes,

ROCKINGHAM COUNTY.

Jr, T P Barham, A B Barham, J L C Bevil, A J Braim, F P Braim, W T Connor, A H Fields,Robt Fuqua, S G Fuqua, Garrett Fuqua, A R Griffin, W L Griffin, S A Harris, Bud Hays, V B Humphreys,R P Humphreys,D N Joiner, W S Joiner, James M Kallum, G T Lester, L C Paschal, J C Pearson, F F Sharp, H J Sharp, J M Sharp, J H Sharp, A M Simpson, R C Simpson, A J Smathers, T W Stewart, J C Strader, G W Suit, Levi Truett, L Truett. Jas H Turner, T D Nashburn, B G Wilson.
Benson—D F Wilson.
Benaja—J M Gerringer, Wm Green, R A Hopkins, D L Hopkins, T P Hopkins, T W Hopkins, M P Hopkins, W D Maxwell, William McCallum, Ben Moon.
Berry—J H Brindle, Jesse Brodnax, Nash Brodnax, J M Burton, Geo W Carver, Jas W Carver, Sam'l Carver, W W Dallas, G A Davis, J H Davis, Jacob Dixon, W H Duncan, Joe H Duncan, Robt J Duncan, M J Durham, Jno Gammon, Willie Gammon, W D Gammon, W M Harrison, Joe W King, Alex King, W J King, A M Lettliff, Jno R Miller, C W Mobley, J W Mobley, Jno W Moon, W F Moon, Geo Moon, J W Moore, Jno R Moore, Jas M Roberts, W H Shrives, Allen Strader, Charles Strader, R J Stone, Wm Summers, Wm Suttle.
Case's—Nathaniel Case, M L Case, Jas H Scales.
Douglas—S N Allen, A S Baughn, M D Baughn, R A Baughn, P W Carter, W J Carter, Robt L Carter, R P Henry, C J Lanten, R R Lewis, Wallace Lesure, T B Lindsay, J F Martin, J D Meader, Hyman Mills, T C Peay, Wm Pool, Poster Scales, Richmond Scales, Jas Trent, J B Ziglar, S B Ziglar.
Ferndale—J S Butler, T S Irby, Ellen M King, T S Malloy, D M Malloy, Jno W Miller, W P Miller, J W H Moore, Smith Moore, Jerry Morehead, Josiah Newman, Jas P Smathers, C W Woolen.
Hogan—N B Alley, D R Friddle, T F Gentry, J F Gooldsby, R B Henderson, Wm Knight, W M Knight, P B Neal, W F Neal, J H Neal, Jas M Neal, Thos D Neal, W A Payne, Mrs Minnie Price, Jas V Price, Jas Roberts, W T Wall, J P Wilson, T F Wilson, C G W Wilson, Fenner Wilson, J F Williams, R D Williams.
Lawsonville.—J W Burton, W S Butler, N Canada, W C Chambers, Thos Chambers, George W Cole, W B Motley, David Mullins, Mrs M T Neal, J H Nunn, R M Saunders, S Y Walker.

Leaksville.—Green Allen, E N Anderson, John Bateman, G W Brinn, Martin Carter, D L Carter, John Carter, J R Cox, J C Cox, J N Cox, W M Craddock, James P Dillard, Sam Dillard, Spott Dillane, J R Dunn, Geo Edwards, J W Edwards, Jas P Ellington, J M Ellington, sr, Jas E Estes, Geo W Estes, J W Fagg, D J Frazier, Aaron Galloway, Wm Gilly, Richard Gilly, Jas H Hampton, Peter Hamlin, C S Hamlin, Wm Holland, Nat Holbrook, F D Hopper, W C Jones, L H Jones, W C Kemp, J A Kemp, Thos W Kemp, J B King, C J Land, Wm Land, W J Land, J W Land, H C Martin, A J B Martin, W D Martin, Alex McDonald, Henry Meador, Geo W Miller, J H Newsom, A J Odell, C H Osborne, R V Osborne, J H Pratt, W F Pratt, A J Pratt, Josephus Pratt, P J Pratt, F P Pratt, John B Price, J H Price, Rufus Price, Henry Price, York Price, J T Pullen, E A Roberts, F A Roberts, Jas S Roberts, Robt P Saunders, J D Sledge, Davis Smallwood, Alex Smith, W D Stocks, Anderson Strong, W W Strong, A M Shultz, R K Terry, Elijah Thompson, Polk Thompson, N Thompson, Richard Thompson, J T Trent, W H Turner, J T Turner, D M Vernon, F P Walker, J B Webb, John S Wilson, Jos Willis, Peter Wilson, J F Wilson, Nat Wilkerson, J R Wyatt.

Lenox Castle—V S Boswell, B Y Bricefield, W H Brown, J P Brown, T H Burnsfield, T J Garrett, S W Garrett, G W Gwyn, Thomas Slade, M H Saunders.

Madison—W G Anderson, H W Baughn, T J Benton, D W Busick, J Ham Cardwell, J H Cardwell, J L Cardwell, W C Cardwell, George E Crews, Reuben Dalton, W P Dalton, J G Dalton, C H Dalton, W F Dalton, J W Garrett, R J Gentry, J H Gibson, Nathaniel Gunn, C A Hand, N J Highfill, L J Highfill, J M Hilton, G W Johnson, T B Knight, Robert Lewis, W R Lindsay, Abram Manns, A J Martin, J R Martin, W D Martin, C A McGhee, John D Meadows, Geo Mitchell, G W Moore, John J Phillips, J A Price, J H Price, George Richardson, T M Richardson, Joseph Richardson, Thos H Roberts, David Shrives, R C Smith, W C Truett, S M Tucker, E B Vaughn, M B Vaughn, Z L Wall, James T Wall, J M Wall, J C Young.

Matrimony—W L Garrett, W A Garrett, G A Smith, J R Turner, Hardin Turner.

Mayfield—T R Bass, J F Bishop, W R Combs, H Cooley, G T Cook, W T Cook, James Dameron, John Daniel,

Alvis Daniel, George W DeJarnette, E F Dix, W P Dix, J R Dix, Grean Dix, J F Dix, M G Dix, W H Ferguson, F A Ferrell, E B Gibson, J H Griffith, W L Hairston, V M Holdery, J W Lumkin, W B McKenny, N McKenny, R H Pruett, A T Walker, Jim Washington, J B Yates.

Mayo—J F Dixon, Jeff Burter, S T Gann, S N Gann, Thos J Glenn, Jas A Glenn, Nathaniel Glenn, L T Highfill, Jas Highfill, John Johnston, J J Joyce, H W Joyce, P H Joyce, Alex Joyce, G M Satterfield, A J Smith, Jas H Vernon, Jas A Vernon, V H Vernon, Alex Vernon.

Monroeton—J A Jones, G S Kernodle, J W Mehonry, W D Smith, V M Smith, H L Watson, D L Wright, J J Wayrick, G Westbrook, George R Wright.

Nance—J L Anderson, J H Anderson, P P Poster, W H Gilly, J T Hopper, J R Hopper, Richard Martin, J M Montgomery, R Montgomery, John Reese, John D Setliff.

Oregon—Geo W Anderson, Jackson Carmon, T C Chandler, Nick Cobb, W E Dix, G D Ellington, C F Ellington, W G Ellington, A J Ferguson, J W Foster, W S French, W R French, G D French, W F French, Taylor Hagood, Thos Hagood, John H Hagood, Thos Harrell, A A Hill, Henry Jeffreys, Wm Lander, G A Lillard, H C Lillard, J H Lovelace, J A Lovelace, G F Martin, Henry Martin, R E Scarlett, M Scott, Joe Setliff, J H Sheffield, M T Sparks, Jno Strader, S E Strader, Thos Strader, W H Wall, W D Wall.

Pleasant Hill—Thos J Carter, Geo W Carter, A C Conner, Asa Flinn, Cicero Knight, P D McCallum, J Y McCallum, Jesse McCallum, P D McCallum, Jr, W S McCallum, Thos McCallum, David McCallum, N D McCallum, Robt C Mills, J B Mitchell, B P Moore, R E Moore, D H Moseley, Robt Moseley, John Moseley, Turner Wall, T E Webb, W P Wells, Pleas Wright.

Price's Store—John Cox, —— Craddock, N C Deshazo, Henry Grogan, W T Grogan, L C Grogan, B Grogan, A G Grogan, C P Grogan, Reese Price, Joe H Price, D H Price, R P Price, J H Roberts, Dr D Smith, J C Smith.

Reidsville—F W Barber, W T Barler, W Z Barber, Jr, D Bateman, J H Bennett, Chas Boyd, S D Bran, Coleman Bran, T H Brincefield, T P Burton, E P Butler, Thos D Carroll, Geo W Carroll, J D Carroll, J L Carroll, Geo W Carter, Wm Clark, W J Clark, Geo T Davis, M L Delap, J G Duke, T I Duke,

T L Evans, G Fells, W Filman, D G Flack, Matt Galloway, T C Goodwin, Saml Hand, H W Harrell, J M Harris, J L Harrison, Geo Herlin, W D Hightower, John Hopkins. Craven Horseford, D G Horseford, G D Huffines, W A Irvin, Peter Jackson, J F Jarrett, W G Jenkins, D W Johnson, J Willie Jones, J A Jones, W S Laschal, Jos R Lindsay, T H Loftin, Jas Lucas, W C Madkins, Rufus Lynn, J T Madkins, J W Martin, G Z Martin, David McCallum, A B McKinny, B B McKinny, A W Meador, Geo F Meador, Samuel J Meador, J W Mims, Henry Neal, Philomon Neal, Mrs M T Neal, A L Palmer, W S Palmer, E D Paschal, D B Paschal, J T Paschal, W F Paschal, R T Paschal, Green Paschal, W A B Pearson, Ike Pearson, P A Pedegrew, Lem Pedegrew, J S Perkins, T H Pritchett, J L Pritchett, W N Pritchett, T F Rankin, J H Rich, R P Richardson, Simon Roach, W H Roberts, J W Roberts. J F Robertson, Mrs F J Robertson, Jos Rodgers, W H Schofield, T T Simpson, J J Smith, D L Smithey, N W Smothers, J W Stallings, A J Stallings, R W Stanfield, T A Stanfield, Samuel H Stone, G C Strader, P Summers, Jos Tucker, Q H Totten, J A Terry, B T Trent, I G Trent, J M Vaughn, J T Walker, P M Walker, Alfred Walker, Geo T Walker, W L Walker, U Ware, D F Ware, Nat Ware, Wm Were, Robert Watkins, Garland Watt, L L Waywick, C G Waywick, H J Wheeler, I M Whittimore, Hubbard Williams, W P Wommack, R J Young, H Young.

*Rocky Springs—*B H Angel, Rufus Angel, C B Angel, I W Angel, C D Angel, R W Baker, S E Caruthers, J F Caruthers, Jno Caruthers, H L Gant, J M Gant, W A Gourley, G M Knight, F M Knight, J W Landreth, J P Landreth, L D Landreth, W A Pegram, W C Pegram, B F Powers, R J Roberts, A L Self, Jas Sharon, P J Simmons, E N Sneed, J H Suthern, W P Suthern, Robt C Tucker, B F Turner, J R Turner, J W Webster, M H Webster.

*Ruffin—*L N Adams, Jas R Adkins, E Adkinson, F M Alcorn, C H Alverson, J H Alverson, Robt Blackwell, R C Blackwell, W P Blackwell, J A Burton, Thos Burton, Anthony Burton, Jos Burton, J F Burton, Cary Cameron Camson, G H Carter, W S Carter, J W Chandler, J C Chandler, J B Chelton, M L Cobb, N E Cobb, A G Dix, Thos Donaldson, Jas Dodd, Thomas A Ferguson, W B Ferguson, J H Ferguson, R T Fitzgerald, J P Flintoff, J D Gardner, W L Gardner, J A Gibson,

J L Gibson, jr, Wm Gilliam, G W Goodwin, N B Gwyn, L L Hamilson, J C Hannah, R D Harris. F A Hubbard, J P Johnston, J H Johnston, S Y Johnston, A L Jones, J L Jones, Robt M Jones, Jack Lawson, W T Lewis, Thos Lee, W A Lillard, R G Lindsay, R A McDowell, P A McKinny, J B McKinny, Fountain Nance, John H Nunnally, A R Poteat, A J Powell, W T Price, W H Price, S W Rainey, E H Rainey, R L Rawley, C M Robertson, T G Robertson, J T Robertson, J Saunders, R C Saunders, J C Sayers, A B Spalding, Jurson Stucy, H B Stevens, T W Stokes, Stephen Strader, J J Swan, W T Tally, Jas Tollock, T F Warf, Thos R Williams, J L Williams, J M Wilson, Wm Wright.

*Sharp—*Jas W Bethel, A S Bethel, John Buterman.

*Simpson's Store.—*E S Bailey, I W Bailey, J H Bailey, J Q Barham, A G Barham, A B Barham, J J Barham, J M Bennett, A R Bennett, W W Bennett, A H Garrett, Richard Gentry, Wm Herlin, Pinkney Knight, P H Simpson, S G Truit, R S Williams.

*Stokesdale.—*L Crawford, E Crawford, J N Gant, W B Gentry, Richard Gentry, J N Joyce, W L Joyce, Dodson, Nelson, Geo W Nelson, Q L Oliver, Joyce Thomas, P G W Walker.

*Stoneville.—*George L Baker, John Barnes, Jason Barnes, Jesse Barnes, W P Benton, W H Bowers, William Burns, S W Carter, A J Carter, Allen Charles, J S Claybrook, Jasper Claybrook, B F Clifton, Jas H Currie, Jas F Fagg, Samuel H Fagg, W S Fagg, Hardin Floyd, P F Galliker, Nash Galloway, Armstrong Galloway, George Griggs, Robt Grogan, Jas P Grogan, John Grogan, W P Grogan, Thomas Grogan, James H Hill, Tyler Hollingsworth, Patrick Hopper, A N Irvin, Henderson Joyce, R Joyce, R D Joyce, R F Joyce, J H Joyce, A T Kallum, Spencer Kallum, John F King, Thos Lemmon, W F Lemmon, Larkin Lemmon, Alex Lewellyn, R H Lewis, Jno McDonald, James Morgan, jr, James M Pratt, Granville Price, Whit Price, Thos Price, Daniel Roberts, Thos P Roberts, W A Roberts, Jas D Roberts, Geo W Roberts, James E Roberts, E S Roberts, W M Roberts, John S Roberts, R H Peter Roberts, Robert Simmons, R H Smith, W C Smith, C L Smith, Alford Smith, W Smith, Rufus Smith, J P Snead, W S Snead, Z T Snead, J W Vernon, J R Watkins, D M Watkins, J L Lawton.

*Thompsonville—*R S Boswell, W H Brannock, J H Combs, F M Combs, J

ROCKINGHAM COUNTY.

R Garrett, F L Herlin, W H Herlin, I H Simpson, P Q Haywick.

Troublesome—L R Dixon, James M Foster, Z W Griffin, J M Haynes, T W Huffines, T C Huffines, J W Hutcherson, T F Rankin.

Waddell's—Ruffin I Carter, E B Carter, A W Combs, J P Farrington, Hiram Gibson. W A Gibson, Robert Gwyn, George Irvin, W S Irvin, A R Irvin, Ed Jones, A D Ray, J P Roach, R H Robertson, G A Roberts, Allen Thomas, W F Thomas, Jos Trogden, Joel Walters.

Wentworth—A S Alcorn, W A Alcorn, Saul A Alcorn, Charles Allen, Creen Bailey, George W Baker, Levi Barnes, John Barker, Boyd Barker, Sawney Barker, James Bennett, Wm J Bennett, Isaac Bingham, John Bingham, George Booker, Zack Brim, Joe Brodnax, W G Burton, Geo C Cahall, John Cantrel, M H Cantrel, W A Carroll, J L Carroll, T E Carter, John T Carter, Anthony Carter, H A Clark, R R Cobb, W H Cobb, Richard Cobb, Thos J Cobb, W L Cole, R L Corum, Robert L Corum, jr, James T Combs, Jasper Cox, J R Cox, H Cox, John Craddock. Green Craddock, James Croften, P D Crowder, H C Crowder, John M Dallas, T S Dallas, J L Dearman, John W Delacey, F R Delgardo, John T Ellington. Jackson Ellington, Moses Ellington, Mrs Martha E Ellington, W S Ellington, John K Ellington, Jas M Fagg. Frank Flinn, J B Flinn,

ROCKINGHAM COUNTY.

Alex Flinn, G L Foard, Layton Foard, W S Fretwell, Samuel Galloway, Hubbard Galloway, Batt Galloway, James M Gunn, Samuel D Green, Wm Green, Dennis Gunn, J A Gunn. W W Gunn, W P Gunn, Willis Hamlin, Worris Hamlin, Robert Hancock, Jas A Hancock, J W Hancock, R J Harrison, A J Hudson. R D Hudson, A J Q Hudson, E T Hudson, W M Hudson, Jas W Hundley, John Huskin, W A Jarrell, R F Jarrell, W H Jarrell, R G Johnson, D W Johnson, Cicero Jones, C H Jones, Wash Jones, Rawley Jones, J D Jones, Robt M Jones, W H King, Wilson King, Samuel M King, Samuel Knight, J C Lashley, Jas R Lashley, Jas H Lillard, Bunn Lowe, W B Madison, Griff Martin, John Martin, Shadrach Martin, George McCain, J J McCargo, J W McDonald, E P Meador, W M Miller, Robert C Mills, James B Miner, Jas W Mitchell, Jno G Mitchell, T A Mitchell, Robt A Moir, Jno Moonfield, Zack S Moore, Alex Parks, Geo Parks, T W Perguson, T R Perguson, David Purcell, Wm G Rakestraw, Jno W Rakestraw, James J Ratliffe, T A Ratliffe, Jos Richardson, Sam Roberts, Jas M Roberts, John Robertson, Geo W Robertson, Jas Robertson, J J Scott, Anderson Settle, Alfred Settle, James Small. W C Smothers, T M Smothers, W C Stewart, Samuel Stire, J B Tally, Geo W Thonaston, Matt Thomas. Sam Walters, Will H Weeks, Thos Wedin, Geo S Whittimore, A J Whittimore, A M Wray.

ROWAN COUNTY.

AREA 450 SQUARE MILES.

POPULATION, 24,123; White 17,142, Colored 6,981.

ROWAN COUNTY was formed in 1753, from Anson county. Until Surry (in 1770) and Burke (in 1777) were taken off, this county comprised most of the western part of the State of North Carolina and Tennessee.

SALISBURY, the county seat, derives its name from a town in England. It is a word of Saxon origin, meaning a dry town. It is situated on the Piedmont Air-Line and Western North Carolina railroad, 118 miles from Raleigh. Population 7,000.

Surface—Rowan lies on the south side of the Yadkin river; moderately uneven, water-power plenty, soil very fine.

Staples—Corn, wheat, tobacco, oats, potatoes and live-stock. Rowan is a fine wheat county, and many of the farms are under a good state of cultivation. This is the largest hay-producing county in the State.

Fruits—Apples, peaches, pears, cherries, berries and other small fruits.

Timbers—Oak, hickory, ash, walnut, maple, poplar and pine.

Minerals—Gold, silver, copper, with sulphur springs.

TOWNS AND POST OFFICES.

	POP.		POP.
Alpha,	25	Mount Vernon,	48
Bear Poplar,	30	Omega,	25
Blackmer,	30	Organ Church,	20
China Grove,	500	Peeler,	—
Cleveland,	200	Phi,	25
Craven,	30	Pool,	55
Eli,	—	Rock,	76
Enochville,	150	Rockwell,	50
Faith,	—	Rowan,	—
Garfield,	20	Russell,	25
Gold Hill,	500	Salisbury	
Gold Knob,	—	(C H),	7,000
Harts,	25	Saw,	50
Heilig's,	60	South River,	36
Lentz,	25	Sunny Side,	25
Lipe,	30	Treadingford,	—
Lisk,	20	Verble,	30
Manning,	25	Watsonville,	35
Mill Bridge,	100	Woodleaf,	30
Millertown,	40	Woodside,	—
Miranda,	30	Yost,	20
Mitford,	—	Zeb,	50
Mount Ulla,	33		

COUNTY OFFICERS.

Clerk Superior Court—W G Watson.

Commissioners—W L Kluttz, chm'n; J H L Rice, J A Stewart, W A Houch.

Coroner—Dr E Rose Dorsett.

Register of Deeds—H N Woodson.

Sheriff—Jas M Monroe.

Solicitor 8th District—J Q Holton.

Surveyor—C M Miller.

Standard Keeper—C F Baker.

Treasurer—J S McCubbins, jr.

County Examiner—R G Kizer.

Supt of Health—Dr Jno Whitehead.

TOWN OFFICERS.

SALISBURY—*Mayor,* W C Coughenour: *Commissioners,* B N Marsh, D A Atwell, J T Shover, R W Price, J L Lowe, R L Wright, W H Overman; S F Lord; *Attorney,* K L Wright; *Clerk,* R W Price; *Chief of Police,* G H Shower.

CHINA GROVE—*Mayor,* J A Thorn; *Secretary and Treasurer,* W P Carpenter.

CLEVELAND—*Mayor,* R M Roseboro.

GOLD HILL—*Mayor,* Dr R A Slimpach.

TOWNSHIPS AND MAGISTRATES.

Atwell—J F McLean, Jacob S Lipe, W J Deal, J L Sloan, Alfred Goodman, W C Rose, C A Sloop, J A Shulenberger, Geo W Corrsber (Salisbury).

China Grove—M A Stirenait, C A Linn, J L Sifford, R A Smith, J A Thorne, A A Petre, H H Fink, Victor Correll (Salisbury).

Franklin—A L Hall, J L Cauble, J A Thomason, J N Froley, R J Halton, W A Hall, B F Shuping, M A Powlas (Salisbury).

Gold Hill—M J Earnhart, A W Kluttz, F H Maney, C L Brown, U E Miller, Calvin Lingle, A L Peeler (Gold Hill).

Litaker—J K P Heilig, P A Sloop, Isaac R Julian, P A Peeler, J C Bernhardt, H M L Agner (Salisbury).

Locke—J F Robinson, C H McKenzie, Paul A D Peeler, Jr, J A Fisher, D L Watson, L W Lingle, Miles Albright, John Zost (Salisbury).

Morgan—Isaac M Shaver, J W Miller, D A Lemley, John Trexler, P C Shaver, Allen Trexler, David Eagle (Salisbury).

Mt Ulla—Pni Alexander, A E Sherrill, J K Goodman, J A Bailey, Roland Miller, J K Graham, J L Miller, J O Houston (Salisbury).

Providence—H C Agner, J A Pool, T D Lynn, S A Earnhart, J S M Miller, H C Agner, W M Sapp, H C Peeler (Salisbury).

Salisbury — Wm Smithdeal, J W Brown, J M Horah, J P Gowan, J A Ramsey, S R Harrison, J B P Sowers, J M Trexler, M V Connor (Salisbury).

Scotch Irish—E P Hall, Haywood Harper, C A Guffey, J B Johnson, R C Current, W A Steele, W C Teague, H F Turner (Salisbury).

Steele—R L Blackwelder, D C White, Geo Hall, S F Baker, C M Varner, W L Kistler, J F Cowan, H N Goodnight (Salisbury).

Unity—M A Thomason, Caleb Penninger, J K Culbertson, J H L Rice, J F Gillin, W H Penninger, S J Brown, C McIntyre, Wm Skeen (Salisbury).

CHURCHES.

Names, Post Offices and Denominations.

METHODIST.

Bethel—Salisbury, —— Pusey.
Centenary—Woodleaf, P E Parker.
Chapel at County Home, Salisbury, A L Coburn.
Chestnut Hill—Salisbury, A L Coburn.
Church—Salisbury, T F Marr.
Church—Gold Hill.
Ebenezer—Salisbury, P E Parker.
Evergreen—Woodleaf.
Harris' Chapel—China Grove.
Lebanon—Salisbury.
Liberty—Gold Hill.
Mount Tabor—South River, — Pusey.
Oak Grove—Enochville.
Providence—Salisbury, —— Pusey.
Shiloh—Salisbury, —— Pusey.
South River—Woodleaf, —— Pusey.
Rehobeth—Spring Grove (Iredell co.).
Zion—Salisbury.

LUTHERAN.

Bethel—Salisbury, C A Rose.
Christ's Church—Salisbury, C A Rose.
Christianna—Rockwell, C A Brown.
Concordia—Saw, H W Jeffcoat.
Emanuel—China Grove.
Ebenezer—China Grove, H N Miller,
Grace Church—Salisbury, H N Miller.
Luther's Chapel—China Grove, J Q Wertz.
Luther's Church — Millertown, G H Cox.
Mt Moriah—China Grove.
Organ Church—Heilig's Mill.
Salem—Bear Poplar, H N Miller.

St Enoch's—Enochville, E R Stickley.
St John's—Salisbury, R S Patterson.
St Luke—Bear Poplar, H W Jeffcoat.
St Mark's—China Grove, J Q Wertz.
St Matthew's—Garfield, W R Huddle.
St Paul's—Salisbury, C A Rose.
St Peter's—Rockwell, C A Brown,
Union—Salisbury, C A Brown.

BAPTIST.

Church (col.)—Salisbury, John Washington.
Corinth—Lisk.
Dixonville (col.)—Salisbury, P A Lewis.
Mt Zion (col.)—Salisbury, John Washington.
Trading Ford—Salisbury.
Yadkin River—Salisbury.

PRESBYTERIAN.

Back Creek—Mill Bridge, J A Harris.
Chapel—Salisbury, J Rumple, D D.
Church (col.)—Salisbury, W H Bryant.
First Presbyterian—Salisbury, J Rumple, D D.
Franklin—Woodleaf, R S Arrowood.
Prospect—Mooresville (Iredell county), William W Pharr, D D.
Third Creek — Cleveland, R S Arrowood.
Thyatria—Mill Bridge.
Unity—Woodleaf, R S Arrowood.

EPISCOPAL.

Christ—Cleveland, S S Bost.
St Andrew's—Rowan Mills, S S Bost.
St Luke's—Salisbury, F J Murdoch, D D,
St Mary's Chapel—China Grove, F J Murdoch, D D.
St George's—Woodleaf, S S Bost.
St Jude—Blackmer, S S Bost.
St Matthew's—Zeb, S S Bost.
St John's—Salisbury, F J Murdoch, D D.
St Paul's—Salisbury, R B Owens.
St Peter's—Salisbury, F J Murdoch, D D.

GERMAN REFORM.

Grace—Heilig, Paul Barrieger.
Mt Hope—Salisbury, J M L Lylerly.
Mt Zion—China Grove.
Shiloh—Salisbury, P M Trexler.

CATHOLIC.

Sacred Heart-Salisbury, Father Joseph

A. M. E. ZION.

Arde's Chapel—Salisbury, H S McMillan.
Church—China Grove, H S McMillan.
Jerusalem—Salisbury, F B House.
Miller's Chapel—Salisbury, H S McMillan.
Soldier's Memorial — Salisbury, R C Collins.
Zion Wesley—Salisbury, G C Clement.

ROWAN COUNTY.

MINISTERS RESIDENT.

Names, Post Offices and Denom.

METHODIST.

Coburn, A L, Salisbury.
Marr, T F, Salisbury.
Parker, P E, Woodlief.
Pusey, ——, Salisbury.
Scroggs, J R (P E), Salisbury.

ZION METHODIST.

Goler, Wm H, Salisbury.
Harris, C R (Bishop), Salisbury.

PRESBYTERIAN

Arrowood, R S, Woodlief.
Bryan, W S M (col), Salisbury.
Harris, J A, Mill Bridge.
Rumple, J, D D, Salisbury.

EPISCOPAL.

Bost, S S, South River.
Murdock, F J, D D, Salisbury.
Owens, R B, Salisbury.

LUTHERAN.

Brown, R H, China Grove.
Brown, R L, Rockwell.
Cline, R H, China Grove.
Rose, C A, Zeb.

BAPTIST.

Crosby J O (col), Salisbury.
Denny, J C, Heilig.
Hodge, J F, Gold Hill,

A. M. E. ZION.

Ardes, C D (col), Salisbura.
Blackwell, G L, D D, Salisbury.
Clement, Geo C, Salisbury.
Collins, R C, Salisbury.
Harris, J R, D D (Bishop), Salisbury.
House, F B, Salisbury.
Huston, R L, Salisbury.
McMullen, H S, Salisbury.
Simmons, H L (P E), Salitbury.

HOTELS AND BOARDING HOUSES.

Names, Post Offices and Proprietors.

Boarding House, Salisbury, W H Kestler.
Boarding House, Gold Hill, Chas Montgomery.
Boarding House, Salisbury, Mrs J W Mauney.
Boarding House, Harts, Mrs E E Hart.
Boarding House, Enochville, H M Leezer.
Boarding House, Enochville, A Yost.
Central Hotel, Salisbury, O W Spencer and Mrs L B Cranck.
Kimball House, Salisbury, Mrs H A Kimball.
Mount Vernon House, Salisbury, P A Frericks.

ROWAN COUNTY.

Pearson House, Salisbury, B G Pearson.
Roman House, Salisbury, Mrs L M Walker.
Snuggs House, Gold Hill, J C Snuggs.

LAWYERS.

Names and Post Offices.

Craige & Clement, Salisbury.
Heilig, A S, Salisbury.
Henderson, J S, Salisbury.
Kluttz, T F, Salisbury.
Linn, T C, Salisbury.
Murphy, Walter, Salisbury.
Noble, F H (col), Salisbury.
Overman, Lee S & H J (Overman & Overman).
Price, A H, Salisbury.
Price, Chas, Salisbury.
Randleman, J L, Salisbury.
Stewart, J J, Jr, Salisbury.
Tyson, H G, Jr, Salisbury.
Wright, P L, Salisbury.
Wetmore, J B, Woodleaf.

MANUFACTORIES.

Kinds, Post Offices and Proprietors.

Blacksmithing and wheelwrighting, Salisbury, J P Weber.
Blacksmithing and wheelwrighting, Salisbury, Edmond Crowell (col).
Blacksmithing and wheelwrighting, Enochville, Wm Bradshaw.
Blacksmithing and wheelwrighting, Enochville, G R Rogers.
Blacksmithing and wheelwrighting, Garfield, Jos W Kesler.
Brick, Salisbury, Quinn & Co.
Brick, Salisbury, Cecil & Co.
Brick, Salisbury, J A Brady.
Brick, Salisbury, J W Hamilton.
Brooms, Harts, A Graham.
Building and contracting, Blackmer, Jno A Thompson.
Building and contracting, Enochville, Frank Rogers.
Building and contracting, Enochville, J N Plaster.
Building and contracting, Gold Hill, J C Casper & Son.
Building and contracting, Garfield, Jacob Reibling.
Building and contracting, Garfield, Pinkney Brady.
Building and contracting, Heilig's Mill, L A Fisher.
Cabinet, Gold Hill, D L Parker.
Coopering, Harts, J A Correll.
Cotton mill, Salisbury, F J Murdock, pres; O D Davis, vice-pres; ——, sec and treas; spindles, 16 000; looms, 503; capital stock, $250,000.

ROWAN COUNTY.

Foundry and machine shop, sash and blinds, Salisbury, P H Thompson & Co.

Kestler Mfg Co (cotton), Salisbury; H B McCanliss, pres; D R Julian, general manager; capital, $75,000.

Marble works, Salisbury, John Buis.

Millwrighting, Enochville, Jno A Lipe.

Millwrighting, Enochville, H M Leazer.

Millwrighting, Harts, J A Correll.

Patterson Mfg Company(cotton), China Grove; J W Cannon, pres; W J Swink, gen mgr.

Rope factory, Salisbury; J Littmann, owner and mgr; capital $30,000.

Rowan Knitting Co, Salisbury; T F Kluttz, pres; Theo Baerbaum, sec and treas; G F Seyffert, bus mgr; spindles, 512; capital, $20,000.

Saddles and harness, Salisbury, M V'B Capps.

Sash, doors and blinds, Salisbury, C A Price.

Sash, doors and blinds, Salisbury, P H Thompson.

Tannery, Gold Hill, J D Redwine.

Tannery, Salisbury, John H Verble.

Vance Cotton Mill, Salisbury; Dr F J Murdock, pres; N B McCanless, sec-treas and bus mgr; spindles, 10,000; capital, $100,000.

MERCHANTS AND TRADESMEN.

Name, Post Office, and Line of Business.

CHINA GROVE.

Bost, F W & Co,	G S
Bostain, Mrs G A,	Millinery
Carpenter, W P & Co,	G S
Eddleman, J M & Son,	G S
Gaeler, Henry,	G S
Graham & Randleman,	G S
Sechler, H S,	G S
Sechler, R S W,	Gro and Conf
Wilson, S N,	Miller
Wincoff, J M,	G S

CLEVELAND.

Creswell, W C,	Millwright
Lyerly Bros,	G S
Morris, B O & Co,	Hdw and Gro
Roseboro. R M,	G S
Thomas, W F & Co,	G S

ENOCHVILLE.

Deal, Calvin J,	G S
Lipe, J A & Co,	Millers
Plaster, H R,	G S
Yost, Aaron,	G S

FAITH.

Peeler Bros & Earnhardt,	G S

GOLD HILL.

Jenkins, J H,	G S
Mauney, E & Sons,	G S

ROWAN COUNTY.

Mauney, F H,	G S
Mesenheimer, Reid & Son,	G S
Morgan, C R,	G S
Nussman, C L,	Machinery
Ritchie, M M & Co,	G S
Russell, J S,	Gro
Shaver, R J,	G S
Shaver, W S,	G S

HART'S.

McLean, J C,	G S
Overcash (D E) & Carriker,	G S

MILL BRIDGE.

Burkhead & White,	G S
Harmony & Page,	G S
Sloan, J L,	Miller

MIRANDA.

Corriker, J L,	G S

MOUNT VERNON.

Fleming, D & Co,	G S

OMEGA.

Eaton, J D,	G S

POOL.

Reid, Wm F,	G S

ROCKWELL.

Beaver, J D,	G S
Holshouser & Co,	G S
McCombs, J B & Co,	G S
Miller, Holshouser & Co,	G S
Wagner Bros,	G S

ROWAN.

Sherrill, A E,	G S

RUSSELL.

Corriker, J L,	G S

SALISBURY.

Allen, J J,	G S
Atwell, D A,	Hardware
Baker, Chas F & Co,	Hardware
Baker, Mrs M R,	Millinery
Bernhardt, L C,	Agricultural Imp
Bingham & Co,	Gro
Brown, C M & H M,	Shoes
Brown, J Allen,	Fertilizers
Brown, J M,	Gro
Brown, M S & Co,	Clothing
Brown, R L,	Mdse Broker
Baurbaum, Thos,	Confec and Stationer
Buis, J H,	Marble
Burt, E W & Co,	G S
Capps, M V B,	Harness
Carter, N J,	Racket Store
Cauble, P A & Bro,	G S
Chesley & Frazier,	G S
Cornelison & Byrd,	G S
Cuthrell, E,	Drugs
Davis, R M,	Undertaker and Cabinetmaker
Eagle, Jno F,	Miller
Eagle, W A,	Gro
Ennis, J H, agent,	Drugs

ROWAN COUNTY.		ROWAN COUNTY.	
Fellman, Jacob, Cloth. and Dry Goods		Wallace, Victor,	G S
Frazier & Chesley,	Gro	Wheeler, R S & Co,	G S
Freriks, P A,	Hotel	Winecoff, J M,	G S
Frick, J W & Co, near,	G S	Winecoff, A W & Co,	Gro
Fry, Mrs W T,	G S	Woodson & Bernhardt,	G S
Gallimore, ——,	Gro	Wright, G W,	
Gaskill, D L,	Mfr Tobacco		G S, Furn and Undertaker
Goodman, D A,	Tanner	Wyatt, T B,	G S
Gordon, U,	Clothing	Young, T F,	G S
Gorman, J H, agent,	Jeweler		
Haden, J M,	G S	TRADING FORD.	
Hall & Long,	G S	Long, G W,	G S
Hammill, J W,	Gro		
Heilig, L E,	G S	WOODLEAF.	
Holmes, R J,	G S	Bailey Bros.	G S
Holmes & Miller,	Mfrs Tobacco	Lippard, J H A,	G S
Horah, J & H,	Jewelers	WOODSIDE.	
Huff, W H,	Gro	Brown, W S,	G S
Jacob, C P,	G S	Smith, A M,	G S
Julian, D R & Sons,	Dry Goods and		
	Groceries	YOST.	
Kestler, Mrs V A,	Restaurant	Yost Bros,	G S
Klutz & Randleman,	G S	ZEB.	
Lichtenstein, G,	G S	Lentz, H C,	G S
Littman & Lichtenstein,	G S	Thomason, W T,	G S
Ludwick, J E,	Livery		
McAllister & Shaver,	Gro	**MINES.**	
McCullough, T M,	G S		
McCubbins. J S,	Guano	Kinds, Post Offices and Proprietors.	
McIntire, M L,	Com	Alexander, iron, Salisbury, P Alexan-	
Marsh & Krider,	G S	der.	
Miller, D J,	G S	Bailey, gold, Salibury, M M Bailey.	
Miller, E C,	Gro	Barringer, gold, Sallsbury, D Barrin-	
Murphy, J A,	Gro	ger.	
Murphy, Mrs John A,	Millinery	Bean, gold, Gold Hill, L Graff.	
Murphy, N P,	Confec	Big Bonanza, gold, Salisbury, T F	
Nichols, A,	G S	Kluttz & Co.	
Outlaw, B C & Co,	G S	Boyden, gold, Salisbury, Mrs Margaret	
Overman, W H & Co,	Com	Smithers.	
Parker, Alex,	Confec and Notions	Brown, gold, Salisbury.	
Plummer, Jas,	Drugs	Bullion, gold, Salisbury. J D Haines.	
Plummer, W J,	Harnessmaker	Butler, gold, Salisbury, C E Mills.	
Price. R W,	Butcher	Crawford, gold, Salisbury, J R Craw-	
Quinn, M C,	Com	ford.	
Rake, T J,	Marble	Dunn's Mountain, gold, Salisbury, W	
Reid & Harry,	G S	F Buckley.	
Rogers Clothing Co,	Clothing	Dutch Creek, gold, Salisbury, J J New-	
Rouch & Sowers,	Millinery	man, sec.	
Rowan Knitting Co,	Hosiery	Dunn's Mountain, granite, Woodside	
Seyfert, G W,	Baker and Confec	near Salisbury, J C McCanless, pres	
Simmons, J C,	Drugs	and bus mgr; capital, $50,000.	
Small, J D,	Builder and Contractor	Gold Hill, gold, Salisbury, F Mauney.	
Smithdeal Hardware Co,	Hardw	Gold Knob, gold, Salisbury, F R Wil-	
Smoot & McCullough,	Gro	liams.	
Spencer, O W,	Hotel	Goodman, gold, Salisbury, C E Mills.	
Surratt Bros.	G S	Goodman, gold, Salisbury, S R Harri-	
Swicegood, S L,	G S	son.	
Swink, C H,	Gro	Hartman, gold, Salisbury.	
Swink, J L,	Gro	Hill, gold, Salisbury, Harrison & Lin-	
Swink & West,	Gro	ton.	
Taylor, J C.	G S	Hotshouser, gold, Salisbury, Stock Co;	
Thompson, P H,	Machinist	Francis Tiernon, supt.	
Tyson, H C,	Com	Howard, gold and copper, Salisbury,	
Verble, John H,	Tanner	Howard Gold and Copper Mining	
		Co.	

ROWAN COUNTY.

Kluttz, gold, Salisbury, W C Kluttz.
Little Barefoot, gold, Salisbury.
Marsh, gold, Salisbury.
Miller, gold, Salisbury.
Morgan gold placer, Salisbury, M Morgan.
Negus, gold, Salisbury, W S Negus.
Newsom's, gold and copper, Salisbury, A H Newsom.
New Discovery, gold, Salisbury, Duffield & Warber.
Peeler, gold, Salisbury, Moses Peeler.
Phillip's Mountain, granite, Faith, M G M Fisher, pres and bus mgr; capital $10,000.
Reimer, gold, Salisbury, C G Lanier, supt.
Roseman, gold, Salisbury, Mrs Margaret Smithers.
Rowan, gold, Salisbury, L Graff, Newark, New Jersey.
Salisbury Granite Co, Salisbury, W L Kluttz, pres; M E Quinn, sec-treas; capital, $25,000.
Southern Belle, gold, Salisbury, W J Dowd, supt.
Trexler, gold, Salisbury, Smith & Barringer.
Yadkin, gold, Salisbury, N C Gold Mining and Reduction Co; John Jacobs, supt.

MILLS.

Kinds, Post Offices and Proprietors.

Corn and flour, Mt. Vernon, Teague Bros & Current.
Corn and flour, Gold Hill, E Mauney.
Corn and flour, Mill Bridge, J W Page.
Corn and flour, Pool, C C Kesler.
Corn and flour, China Grove, S N Wilson.
Corn and flour, Salisbury, D W Cornelison.
Corn and flour, Salisbury, J P Trexler.
Corn and flour, Salisbury, R A Gobble.
Corn and flour, South River, Foard & Lindsay.
Corn and flour, Heilig's Mill, H A Bernhardt.
Corn and flour, Heilig's Mill, J D Heilig.
Corn, flour and saw, Enochville, Leazar, Lipe & Barnhardt.
Corn, flour and sow, Harts, Hart & West.
Corn, flour and saw, Salisbury, P A Phillips.
Northside roller flour mill, Salisbury, Julian, McCanless & Co.
Roller mill, Cleveland, P M Brown, manager.
Roller mill, China Grove, Patterson & Company.
Roller mill, Gold Hill, R J Shaver.

ROWAN COUNTY.

Roller mill, Faith, John W Frick & Co.
Roller mill, Faith, Peeler Bros.
Roller, flour and saw, —, H M Leazer.
Saw, Gold Hill, William Trexlar.
Saw, Enochville. H J Overcash.
Saw, Salisbury, J R Keen & Co.
Steam roller flouring, Salisbury, J S McCubbins, Sr, manager.
Steam saw, gin, hominy mill, etc, Zeb, Thomason Bros.
Steam saw, Salisbury, Kincaid & Mahaley.
Steam saw, Gold Hill, C R Morgan.
Steam saw, Salisbury, Philip Sowers.
Steam saw, Cleveland, Hillard Bros.

PHYSICIANS.

Names and Post Offices.

Brown, J S, Salisbury.
Burleyson, L M, Heilig's Mill.
Caldwell, Julius A, Salisbury.
Coleman, L W, Heilig's Mills.
Council, J B, Salisbury.
Cowan, Robert. Salisbury.
Crowell, A J, China Grove.
Crump, W L, South River.
Dorsett, E Rose, Salisbury.
Flippin, J M, Salisbury.
Gaither, John G, Mill Briege.
Griffith, J F (dentist). Salisbury.
Henderson, A J, Cleveland.
Jones, Isaac W, Salisbury.
Leazer, W A. Enochville.
Littleton, J W (dentist), Salisbury.
McCannaughey, J L, Salisbury.
McKenzie, W W, Salisbury.
McNairy, C B, Faith.
Pool, C M, Salisbury.
Ramseur, G A. China Grove.
Ramsey, J G, Cleveland.
Ramsey, R L (dentist). Salisbury.
Ramseur, G A, China Grove.
Reitzel. J R, Woodleaf.
Shimpoch, R A, Gold Hill.
Stevens, M L. Enochville.
Summerel, E M. Mill Bridge.
Tranthan, H T, Salisbury.
Treher, J H (dentist), Salisbury.
Whitehead, John, Salisbury.
Wood, D B, Elmwood.
Wright, J T, Salisbury.
Wright, S P (col.), Salisbury.

SCHOOLS.

Names, Post Offices and Principals.

Academy, Cleveland, Rev Jno Wilborn.
Academy, Zeb, Miss Azula R Willis.
Academy, South River. Miss A L Phillips.
Academy, Enochville, E H Miller.
Bethany Academy, Gold Hill, F B Brown.

ROWAN COUNTY.

Church High School, Salisbury, J M Hill.

Colored State Normal, Salisbury, Rev J O Crosby.

Colored graded, Salisbury, Rev W H Bryant (col).

Faith Academy, Faith, Luther Peeler.

Female academy, Salisbury, (Presby-terian), Misses Merle Dupey and Jo Coit.

Graded school, Salisbury, R G Kizer.

Livingstone College, Salisbury, Rev W H Goler, D D.

Music school, Salisbury, Prof W H Neave and wife.

Rowan Academy, Salisbury, Luther Dorr.

Union Academy, China Grove, P M Trexler, D D.

Public schools—white, 71; colored 60.

LOCAL CORPORATIONS.

Cordon Lodge, I O O F, Salisbury; R M Leonard, N G; C A McKethan, treas; D M Myers, V G; L M McInnis, sec.

Davis and Wiley Bank, Salisbury; T P Kluttz, pres; O D Davis. cash; capital, $60,000; surplus, $10 000.

Eureka Lodge, No 283, A F and A M, China Grove; time of meeting, first Saturday at 1 o'clock P M, and June 24th and December 27th.

First National Bank, Salisbury; R J Holmes, pres; W C Blackmer, cash; W H White, teller; E C Wheeler, bookkeeper; capital stock, $50,000.

Fulton Lodge. No 99, A F & A M, Salisbury; time of meeting. first and third —— evenings; W W Taylor, W M; R G Kizer, sec.

Gas Company, Salisbury; J A Brown, pres; O D Davis, sec and treas; O S Galliman, supt.

Home Circle, Salisbury; J P Lentz, Leader.

Knights of Honor, No 775, Salisbury; C T Bernhardt, Dic.

Knights of Pythias. No 24, Salisbury, C T Bernhardt, C C.

J O U A M, Salisbury; Jno Liedick, pres.

Meroney's Opera House, Salisbury; L J Meroney, prop.

Cordon Lodge. No 168, I O O F, Salisbury; Z N Epp, N G; time of meeting, Friday night.

Perpetual Building and Loan Association, Salisbury; Theo F Kluttz, pres; Rev F J Murdock, sec.

Rowan Council, No 173, Home Circle. Salisbury; J P Lentz, Leader.

Royal Arcanum, Salisbury; J P Lentz, Leader.

ROWAN COUNTY.

Salisbury Water Works; E B Neave, supt, sec and treas; capital stock, $85,000.

Scotch-Irish Lodge, No 154, A F and A M, Mt Vernon; time of meeting, Friday on or before full moon, and June 24th and December 27th.

Salisbury Council, No 272, Royal Arcanum; M Q Quinn, Regent; meets every second and fourth Monday nights.

Salisbury Lodge, No 775, K of H; C T Bernhardt, Dic.

Salisbury Chapter, No 20, R A M, R G Kizer, sec.

Salisbury Lodge, No 24, K of P; J R Whichard, C C; meets every Tuesday night.

Salisbury Commercial and Mfg Club; A H Boyden, pres; J J Newman, sec.

Western North Carolina Railroad, Salisbury; A B Andrews, pres.

Winona Lodge. No 18, J O U A M, Salisbury; J F Ludwick, C.

NEWSPAPERS.

Carolina Watchman (Pop. weekly); Samuel Arder, ed and prop.

The Herald, Salisbury (Dem, daily and weekly) J R Whichard, ed and prop.

The Truth, Salisbury (Dem. weekly); W H Stewart, ed.

World, Salisbury (Dem.daily and weekly); J M Julian, ed and prop.

FARMERS.

Names and Post Offices.

Alpha.—D M Campbell, C A Guffy, S Honley, J L Moore, T N Renshaw, H F Rudisill, Sol Teague.

Bear Poplar.—G H Brown, John K Goodman, J S Hall, John O Houston, B S Krider, J A Locke, Jesse W Miller, W W Miller, J F Stancill, C B White, D C White.

Blackmer.—F J Barrier, J M Barrier.

China Grove.—Martin Blackwelder, E Riley Blackwelder, D W Bostian, Jacob Correll, Chas Correll, J E Corriker, Joel Corriker, C W Corriker, Absalom Cress, J E Deaton, M L Efird, H A Fink, H H Fink. Rev Whitson Kimball, Atlas Kirk, A W Kluttz, Columbus Linn, George H Lipe, Cicero A Ludwick, Luther W Miller, Sam'l L Roberts, John Rogers, Jno C Rogers, Gen Andrew Jackson Sechler, Jeremiah L Sifferd, John Sloop, Harvey

ROWAN COUNTY.

C Sloop, Moses A Stirewalt, John C Wilhelm.

Cleveland.—John M Baker, John H Barringer, J M Cowan, J H Davis, D J Eaton, D J Goodman, J L Graham, R B Harris. C W Johnson, B A Knox, J S Knox, J W Knox, Wm Lverly, J A McConnaughe, M A Plyler, Eli Powlas, Jesse Powlas, J L Thompson, Dr D B Wood.

Edmiston.—Samuel M Furr.

Enochville.—L A Deal, C J Deal, J W Deal, W A Deal, J A Karriker, H M Leazer, Rufus Overcash, C A Smith, W A Weant, Aaron Yost.

Garfield.—D A Campbell, Jos Eagle, J W Kestler.

Gold Hill.—Calvin Brown, M V Fisher, M Halshower, F H Mauney, Eph Mauney, L H Rothrock, B J Shaver.

Gold Knob.—Andrew Barger, W T Morgan, J A Morgan, J M Trexler.

Hart's.—W R Belk, J F Brown, J A Gray, J S E Hart, S B Hart, S F Ludwick, J H McLaughlin, D E Overcash J L Richardson, R L Weddington, k L Wood.

Heileg's Mill.—Wm Beaver, A E Beaver, David Beaver, J H Foil, M A Fesperman, John V Fisher, George M Fisher, B W Freeze, J L Graham, E B C Hamley (stock farmer), L A Heilig, M M Ketner, Paul J Kluttz, Simeon Kluttz, W W Kluttz, W R Misenheimer.

Lisk.—J A Baringer, J A Lisk, P C Shaver, J M Shaver.

Manning.—Caleb Barger, M A Bost, Otho Cauble, S B Colly, J A Kluttz, J L Tingle, Geo W Rex, D A Sifferd, Edmond Sifferd.

Lipe—D A Fleming, W A Houck, Jacob Lipe, Caleb Lipe, S G Patterson, J L Shuping.

Mill Bridge—S F Baker, R L Blackwelder, J F Carrigan, J L Corriher, Geo Corriher, jr, Leroy Gillespie, J M Goodman, H N Goodnight, J M Harrison (stock farm), J W Neel, O T Rankin, H E Shoaf, J P Sillman, John L Sloan, C A Sloop, Dr E M Summerell, C M Varner.

Millertown—James A Lisk, John W Miller, Levi Miller, Emanuel Miller, C R Morgan, R A Morgan, Ivy C Morgan, Chas Morgan, M C Morgan.

Miranda—J A Bailey, Francis A Gaither, I A Gray, J E Jamison, Roe Miller, J A Stewart.

Mooresville—Richard Davis, J F McLean, R L Weddington.

Mt Vernon—S S Benson, John Carson, M L Carson, B C Cheshire, J C Cowan, R Z Cowan, J L Cowan, W W Daniels, R N Fleming, David Fleming,

ROWAN COUNTY.

N N Fleming, James Foster, W W Hall, J D Johnson, R F Johnson, W A Luckey, sr, T J McConnell, J A McCubbins, J W Morrow, Thomas Niblock, J W Phifer, M L Phifer, W A Poston, Dr J G Ramsey, Rev Joseph F Smoot, V L Steele, William L Steele, John M Steele, J S Wilkinson.

Mitford—J V Bradshaw, J S Brown, J F Carrigan, David Cooper, Martin Sloop.

Organ Church—A W Kluttz.

Pool—Noah Fiee, Eli C Fiee, John F Hodge, Richard Hodge, Leonard Hoffner, William A Huffman, D A Lemly, D C Reid, Levi Trexler, John Trexler, Eli Wyatt, J E Wyatt.

Rockwell—Moses J Barger, Dr L W Coleman, J A Eddleman, Crawford Holhouser, Lawson G Holhouser, John P Rymer, A A Trexler.

Rowan—J K Goodman, W W Miller, J F Miller, A E Sherrill.

Russell—J V Bradshaw, D C Bradshaw, T C Carriker, G W Carriker, H C Carriker, J H Carriker, J L Carriker, J W McLean, W S Shulenberger, David Sloop, S N Wilson.

Salisbury—Lewis Agner, H C Agner, D L Arey, M M Bailey, C F Baker, Andrew Barger, John V Barringer, Geo M Barringer, Paul M Barringer, A M Brown, Alexander Brown, D M Brown, S S Carter, John L Cauble, Mrs Caroline Chunn, James A Click, John C Coughenour, M V Conner, Jas A Craige, L W Crawford, Jas R Crawford, Reuben Cress, John N Cress, W E Dunham, Nehemiah Dunham, Wm Dunn, John Eagle, S A Earnhardt, I N Earnhardt, Julius Earnhardt, A W File, H A Fisher, J A Fisher, Wm T Gheen, R A Gobble, A L Hall, P A Hartman, John L Hedrick, John A Hedrick, R J Halton, W H Horah, David A Huffman, A L Johnson, Thos P Johnston, J T Julian, Geo W Julian, Thos M Kerns, John B Kerns, Tobias Kesler, S C Ketchey, D C Kenerly, Harris A Kimball, Jesse Kluttz, David S Knupp, John P Krider, John C Lingle, L W Lingle, P D Linn, George W Long, Peter Long, S F Lord, J A Ludwick, Benton Ludwick, Tobias Lyerly, Jacob Lyerly, Charles Lyerly, George Lyerly, G L Lyerly, Jesse Mahaley, J C McCanless, J S McCubbins, C H McKenzie, Jas C Miller, T B Monroe, Jas M Monroe, W F Murphy, J A Owens, Paul Peeler, Moses Peeler, Julius A Peeler, Andrew Peeler, Alex Peeler, David Peeler, Henry Peeler, Paul M Phillips, W T Pinkston, Dr C M Poole, Otho V Poole, Henry A Propst, Valentine Propst, Jas A Reid, John L Ran-

ROWAN COUNTY.	ROWAN COUNTY.

dleman, Peter A Richey, T D Roseman, R P Roseman, John L Rusher, John C Rusher, Walter M Sapp, R A Shoaf, Philip Sowers, W J Sumner, James M Trexler, James P Trexler, Jacob Trexler, sr, Jacob Trexler, jr, John H Verble, Fred Waller, Richard Walker, N R Windsor, Pleasant Wise.

Saw—C N Bostain, A A Bostain, A S Correll, W A Correll.

South River—S S Bost, Dr W L Crump, Jas A Hudson.

Sunnyside—S M Furr.

Woodleaf—John A Bailey, R B Bailey, Jonathan Barber, Richard Culbertson, J K Culbertson, M S Fraley, J H Gillean, W C Gillean, N M Graham, A J Gullett, A A Hart, Jesse Hellard, Thos S Lyerly, J P Martin, W H Nolly, J M C Penninger, Daniel Penninger, Levi Powlass, John W Powlass, Wm F Rice, J H Rice, S H Wetmore, H H Winecoff.

Zeb—J A Cauble, D J L Hoffman. B F Jacobs, H C Kenerly, H C Lentz, A W Lentz, H G Miller, Andrew Shuping, J A Thomason, Turner P Thomason. N A Thomason.

RUTHERFORD COUNTY.

AREA, 470 SQUARE MILES.

POPULATION, 18,770; White 15,073, Colored 3,697.

RUTHERFORD COUNTY was formed in 1779 from Tryon county (which was in this year abolished and divided between Rutherford and Lincoln), and was named in honor of Griffith Rutherford, who was a Brigadier General in the Revolutionary war.

RUTHERFORDTON, the county-seat, is situated 225 miles west from Raleigh. Population 800.

Surface — A beautiful, undulating country; soil good, scenery fine, and water-power excellent.

Staples — Wheat, cotton, corn, rice, oats, tobacco, butter, fruit and live-stock.

Fruits — Apples, pears, peaches, cherries, plums, berries and other small fruits.

Timbers — Oak, walnut, poplar, maple, hickory, ash, pine and wild cherry.

Minerals — Iron, gold, copper, mica, plumbago, corundum, and several mineral springs.

TOWNS AND POST OFFICES.

	POP.		POP.
Ayr,	80	Henrietta—	
Bostic,	125	No 2,	100
Brittain,	125	[In mile of Fac-	
Butler,	50	tory.]	
Chimney Rock,	20	Hicksville,	50
Cliffdale,	30	Hollis,	40
Clifford,	35	Island Ford,	25
Cuba,	75	Itom,	25
Darlington,	75	Line,	25
Duncan,	65	Logan's Store,	75
Ellenboro,	300	Mack,	—
Factory,	1,000	Memory,	25
Ferry,	45	Myrtle,	50
First Broad,	25	Oak Spring,	45
Forest City,	600	Otter Creek,	125
Gamble's Store,	65	Rutherford-	
Garnett,	45	ton,	800
Gilkey,	25	Sunshine,	200
Golden,	30	Thermal City,	50
Grassy Knob,	25	Tiger,	25
Green Hill,	65	Trio,	25
Hamric,	25	Twitty,	25
Henrietta—		Union Mills,	100
No 1,	200	Uree,	25
		Washburn,	35

COUNTY OFFICERS.

Clerk Superior Court—T C Smith.
Commissioners—J F Black, chm'n; M K Lynch, J B Blanton.

Coroner—Frank Moore.
Register of Deeds—W J Mode.
Sheriff—J V McFarland.
Solicitor 11th District—J L Webb.
Surveyor—John McAllen.
Treasurer—W O Baker.
County Examiner—H W Hoon.

COURTS.

Eighth Monday after the first Monday in March, and ninth Monday after the first Monday in September.

TOWN OFFICERS.

RUTHERFORDTON—*Mayor*, J A Allen.
FOREST CITY—*Mayor*, Thos Fortune; *Aldermen*, R E Biggerstaff, J C Green, G O Doggett; *Marshal*, A Bridges.
ELLENBORO — *Mayor*, J A Martin; *Marshal*, J L Wright; *Commissioners*, J F Flack, J C Cowan, M L Justice, M O Dickerson.

TOWNSHIPS AND MAGISTRATES.

Names and Post Offices.

Camp Creek—B M Edney, C C Goforth, jr, J D Fincannon, J C Keeter, L S Keeter (Union Mill), W L Walker (Rutherfordton), J C Walker (Thermal City), M J Sorrells (Millwood).

Chimney Rock—I M Frodey, W D Harris, J M Whiteside (Chimney Rock), J F Logon (Tiger), F Reynolds (Ayr).

Colfax—S M Beam, G B Pruitt, T L Harrell, A J Blanton, Elias Hamrick (Ellenboro), J C Gillespie (Henrietta), J M Gloan (Oak Spring).

Cool Spring — Frank Moore, Wm McDaniel, C L Tate, W E Toms (Forest City), J W Green (Bostic), P G Womack (Butler), Wm T Long (Forest City).

Duncan Creek—A B Martin, D D Martin, J B Palmer (Duncan's), C M Hunt, J M Mode M T Crow, (Gamble's Store), W P Smart (Golden).

Golden Valley—C M Hunt, M G Crow, J M Mode (Gamble's Store), W P Smart (Golden).

Green Hill—J W Elliott, H P Lynch, H E Edwards, D B Lynch (Green Hill).

High Shoal—J J Camp, L A Holland (Ferry), Jas O Simmons, J P Burgess,

RUTHERFORD COUNTY.

Sidney F Wall, T J Wilkins (Henrietta), G E McDaniell (Butler).

Logan's Store—M C Hardin (Myrtle), A R Yelton, C C DePriest (Sunshine), J D Weeks, O D Stody, M L Wilson, F L Freeman, Geo R Freeman (Logan's Store).

Morgan—C J Flack, S E Hardin, J D Morris, J A Nichols, M A Higgins, A B Haynes, L Allen (Otter Creek).

Rutherfordton—Geo H Mills, J F Arrowood, C W Watkins, Jas A Miller, C L Harris, A D K Wallace, P H Gross, J M Toms, N E Wallace (Rutherfordton).

Sulphur Springs—Berry Green (Forest City), L Fowler, T C Harris (Island Ford), Henry Blanton, V E McKinney (Poor's Ford), David McArthur, P H Holland (Hamrick).

Union—J A McClure, W L Twitty, N Scoggin (Rutherfordton), R W Abrams, C M Champion (Garnett).

CHURCHES.

Names, Post Offices, Pastors and Denom.

METHODIST.

Antioch—Otter Creek, E Myers.
Bethel—Grassy Knob, E Myers.
Cedar Grove—Sunshine, W L Gette.
Centennial—Brittain, G W Ivey.
Church—Rutherfordton, G W Ivey.
Gilboa—Rutherford, G W Ivey.
Gray's Chapel—Rutherfordton, J B Carpenter.
Henrietta—Henrietta, N R Richardson.
Henrietta No 2—Henrietta, N R Richardson.
Kistler's Chapel—Poor's Ford, J B Carpenter.
New Hope—Poor's Ford, J B Carpenter.
Oak Grove—Ellenboro, W L Gette.
Pisgah—Brittain, J W Ivey.
Pleasant Grove—Forest City, W L Gette.
Providence—Butler, W L Gette.
Robbins—Ellenboro, W L Gette.
Salem—Green Grove, W L Gette.
Tanner's Grove—Forest City, J B Carpenter.
Union—Rutherfordton, J B Carpenter.
Wesley's Chapel—Island Ford, J B Carpenter.

BAPTIST.

Beulah—Green Hill, C C Cash.
Bell's Creek—Otter Creek, Elbert Jackson.
Camp Creek—Trio, W H McClure.
Church—Rutherfordton, C B Justice.
Church—Stone Mountain, T K Bacon.
Church—Henrietta, —— Hambrick.
Church (col)—Rutherfordton.

RUTHERFORD COUNTY.

Concord—Bostic, G M Webb.
Cool Spring—Forest City, Z D Harrill.
Floyd's Creek—Hicksville.
Head First Broad—First Broad, Z D Harrill.
High Shoals—Henrietta.
Holly Spring—Poor's Ford, A McMahan.
Montford's Cove—Otter Creek, T J Moss.
Mountain Creek—Rutherfordton, C B Justice.
Mt Harmony—Logan's Store, I Hollifield.
Mt Pleasant—Forest City, A McMahan.
Mt Vernon—Logan's Store, G M Webb.
Mt Zion—Duncan's Creek, Z D Harrill.
Piney Knob—Valley Springs, Z D Harrill.
Pleasant Grove—Otter Creek, H D Harrill.
Pleasant Hill—Rutherfordton, A J Hensley.
Round Hill—Cuba, C B Justice.
Shiloh—Rutherfordton, J M Williams.
Whiteside Valley—Uree, Z T Whiteside.

FREE WILL BAPTIST.

Hillsdale—Cuba, I P Sorrels.

PRESBYTERIAN.

Church—Duncan's Creek, —— Boozer.
Church—Rutherfordton, G A Hough.
Little Brittain—Brittain, —— Boozer.

EPISCOPAL.

Church—Rutherfordton.
St John's—Rutherfordton.

A. M. E. ZION.

St John's—Rutherfordton, S D Watkins.

MINISTERS RESIDENT.

Names, Post Offices and Denominations.

METHODIST.

Belk, J A, Poor's Ford.
Carpenter, J B, Rutherfordton.
Gette, L W, Forest City.
Ivey, G W, Rutherfordton.
Lee, C, Henrietta.
Moore, P D, Duncan's Creek.
Richardson, N R, Henrietta.
Tate, D P, Forest City.
Washburn, R, Oak Spring.

BAPTIST.

Harris, Benjamin, Ayr.
Harrell, H D, Forest City.
Hensley, A J, Rutherfordton.
Hollifield, Isham, Bostic.
Justice, T B, Rutherfordton.
Justice, C B, Rutherfordton.
Logan, W H, Ayr.
McMahan, A, Forest City.

RUTHERFORD COUNTY.

Taylor, E L, Rutherfordton.
Whitesides, Z T, Uree.
Whitesides, W M, Uree.

PRESBYTERIAN.

Hennerson, M H, Rutherfordton.
Hough, G A, Rutherfordton.

A. M. E. ZION.

Watkins, S J, Rutherfordton.

HOTELS AND BOARDING HOUSES.

Names, Post Offices and Proprietors.

Boarding, Rutherford, Mrs Mary Carson.
Boarding, Rutherfordion, Mrs S E Wolf.
Boarding, Rutherfordton, Miss Julia DePriest.
Boarding, Rutherfordton, J M Toms.
Boarding, Henrietta, C M Robertson.
Boarding, Ellenboro, D R Harrill.
Boarding, Rutherfordton, Miss Matt Miller.
Guthrie House, Rutherfordton, W S Guthrie.
Hotel, Chimney Rock. Geo P Horion.
Hotel, Thermal City. Mrs Mary Surratt.
Hotel, Forest City, I N Biggerstaff.
Hotel, Chimney Rock, L W Logan.

LAWYERS.

Names and Post Offices.

Churchill, L F, Rutherfordton.
Eaves, R S, Rutherfordton.
Gallert, S. Rutherfordton.
Justice, M H, Rutherfordton.
Justice, E J, Rutherfordton.
McBrayer, Matt, Rutherfordton.

MANUFACTORIES.

Kinds, Post Offices and Proprietors.

Blacksmith and wheelwright, Butler. I Randal.
Blacksmith and wheelwright, First Broad, B Price.
Blacksmith and wheelwright, Golden, J R Melton.
Blacksmith and wheelwright, J K Harrison.
Blacksmith and wheelwright, Oak Spring, S D Green.
Blacksmith and wheelwright, Ellenboro, J H Goforth.
Blacksmith and wheelwright, Cuba, John Camp.
Blacksmith and wheelwright, Darlington, M L Blankenship.
Blacksmith and wheelwright, Green Hill, Henry White.

RUTHERFORD COUNTY.

Blacksmith and wheelwright, Green Rill, Samuel Payne (col).
Blacksmith and wheelwright, Green Hill, Anderson Bishop.
Blcksmith and wheelwright, Sunshine, J M Colton.
Brooms, Rutherfordton, Mrs W L Lynch.
Building and contracting, Darlington, C M Lewis.
Building and contracting, Green Hill, David Howser.
Coopering, Butler, William Sutton.
Coopering, First Broad, M O Mooney.
Coopering, First Broad, M S McCurry.
Coopering, Cuba, J Bradford.
Cotton mills, Rutherfordton, Dr E B Harris, pres
Cotton mills, Rutherfordton, D F Morrow.
Forest City Cotton Mills, Forest City, G O D ggett, sec and treas.
Fruit Canning Co, Rutherfordton, L P Erwin, pres.
Millwrighting, Cuba, A Nanny.
Millwrighting, Green Hill, D Howser.
Millwrighting, Ellenboro, J H Goforth.
Planing mill, Rutherfordton, J F Arrowood.
Rim Factory, Rutherfordton, J S Rowland.
Roller mill, Rutherfordton, J S Rowland.
Saddles and harness, Rutherfordton, Wm Keeter.
Saddles and harness, Rutherfordton, Frank Hicks.
Saddles and harness, Cuba, Wm Bland.
Sapdles and harness, Rutherfordton, J B Higans.
Sash and blinds, Rutherfordton, L E Powers & Co.
Shoes, Rutherfordton, A W Smith.
Tannery, Ayr, Frank Reynolds.
Tannery, Otter Creek, J W Morgan.
Tannery, Sunshine, Robert Lane.
Tannery, First Broad, J H Harrison.
The Florence Mills (cotton), Forest City, N C; R R Hanes, pres., S B Tanner. treas; capital stock, $40,000; raw material used daily, about five bales; daily production, 2,000 lbs yarns; number of hands, 50. (This mill will be enlarged this year to 6,000, and $100,000 capital).
The Henrietta Mills, No 1 (cotton) Henrietta, J S Spencer (Charlotte, N C), pres; S B Tanner, treas; capital stock, $700.000; raw material used daily, 35 bales cotton; produce, 40,000 yds cloth and 4,000 lbs yarn daily; average 600 hands; spindles, 21,000; looms, 646.
The Henrietta Mills (cotton), No 2, Henrietta, J S Spencer (Charlotte),

RUTHERFORD COUNTY.	RUTHERFORD COUNTY.

pres; S B Tanner, sec and treas;
capital, $700,000; raw material used
daily, 40 bales cotton; number hands,
650; number spindles, 40,000; number looms, 1,200. (Mills Nos 1 and 2
operated by the same company).

Wood Alcohol for mechanical purposes, Thermal City, Piedmont
Chemical Co, W S Clark, mgr.

Wool-carding, Forest City, Wm Martin.

MERCHANTS AND TRADESMEN.

Names, Post Offices, Lines of Business.

AYR.
Reynolds, F, — G S

BOSTIC.
Bostic & Smart, — G S
Freeman & Devinely, — G S
Grayson, J K & Co, — G S
Harrell, J C, — G S
Higgins, A P, — G S and Postmaster
Long, L L, — G S
Smart, A L, — Express Agent
Smart & Walker, — G S

BRITTAIN.
Goforth, C C, — Miller
Nabors, A H, — G S

BUTLER.
Webb, J L, — G S
Hollifield, W T, — G S

CHIMNEY ROCK.
Logan, J A, — G S

CLIFFDALE.
Thompson, A G, — G S

CLIFFORD'S.
Green, S D, — G S

CUBA.
Bird, M A, — G S
Hardin, Willie, — G S
Horn, W W, — G S
Nanny, P D, — G S

DARLINGTON.
Rucker, A P, — G S

DUNCAN.
Gettys, A D, — G S
Palmer, W B, — G S
Whisnant & Hunt, — G S

ELLENBORO.
Byers, B B, — G S
Green Bros, — G S
Harrell, A S, — G S
Martin Bros, — G S
Wall, Curtis, — Barber
Wright, A C & Co, — Contractors

FACTORY.
Webb, W F, — G S

FERRY.
Haynes, R R, — G S

FOREST CITY.
Bailey, G R, — G S
Bailey, J B, — G S
Beam, J H, — Gin and Mill
Biggerstaff, C M & Co, — G S
Biggerstaff, I N, — G S
Biggerstaff, J S, — Express Agent
Dickey, H L, — Barber
Green, J C, — G S
Hamrick, B M, — G S
Harrell, J B, — G S
Hyder, H L, — Gro
King & Moore, — Gro and Fert
Long, J B, — G S
Long, W T, — G S
McBrayer, Dr T C, — G S
McDaniel, A H, — G S
Martin, W, — Lumber
Mills, F, — G S
Moore, L A, — G S
Moore, J N, — G S
Padgett, M C, — Livery
Smith, R L & Son, — G S
Tate Bros, — G S
Young, G E & Co, — Drugs and Gro

GAMBLE'S STORE.
Deviney, A, — Jewelry
Fortune, F C & Co, — —

GARNETT.
Jones, A B, — G S

GOLDEN.
Early, J L & Co, — G S
Sinconley, P C, — G S
Smawley, P C, — G S
Smawley, W G & Co, — G S
Taylor, J T, — Gro

GRASSY KNOB.
Williams, W C, — G S

GREEN'S STORE.
Adams, J H, — G S
Washburn, Reuben, — G S

GREEN HILL.
Cook, John, — Carpenter
Coley, W C, — G S
McEntire, W H, — G S
McEntire, W B, — G S
McEntire, Willie, — G S
Ramsey, H A, — G S

GUILKEY.
Geer, R P, — G S

HENRIETTA.
Carpenter & Co, — G S
Davis, J R, — G S
Fullenwider & Co, — G S
Getty, M C, — G S
Harrell, P D & Co, — G S
Haynes, P H, — G S
Haynes, R R, — G S

RUTHERFORD COUNTY.

Kennedy & Matheny,	G S
Lovelace, Dr T B,	Drugs
Manly, J W,	G S
McDaniel, O R,	G S
Motler, J H & Bro,	G S
Robertson, C M,	Livery
Smith, J H,	Gro and Conf
Smith, J W,	G S
Smith & Hayes,	G S
Tanner, S B,	G S
Tanner, L B,	Post Master
Walker, J D,	G S

HICKSVILLE.

Camp, J J,	Ferry
Smith, J W,	G S

HOLLIS.

Withrow, J P D,	G S

HOLLY.

Champion, C M,	G S

ISLAND FORD.

Miller, J H.	G S
Simmons, J O,	G S

ITOM.

Fincannon, L J,	G S
Logan & Watson,	G S

LINE.

Rollins, L G,	G S
Westbrook, S W,	G S

LOGAN'S STORE.

Andrews, J S M,	G S
Deck, A W,	G S
Long, J A,	G S
Purgerson, L & Co,	G S
Thompson, A G,	G S

MILLWOOD.

Geer & Geer,	G S

MYRTLE.

Hardin, J J,	G S
Hardin, M C,	G S

OAK SPRINGS.

De Priest, W C & Son,	G S
Melton, B B,	G S

OTTER CREEK.

Ledbetter, J D,	—
Ledbetter, W P,	G S
Morgan, J W,	Tanner
Nicholson & Wilkerson,	G S
Wilkerson, J H,	G S

POOR'S FORD.

Page, T C,	G S

RUTHERFORDTON.

Allen, J L,	Tinner
Briscoe, G C,	G S
Carpenter, W H,	Butcher
Carpenter, H L,	Gent's Clothing
Carpenter, K L,	G S and Fertilizer
Carpenter & Morrow,	G S and Bankers
Cowan & Hicks,	G S
Dickerson, M O,	Postmaster

RUTHERFORD COUNTY.

Dixon, T W,	G S and Hardware
Eaves, A R,	Drugs
Ernest, Johnson (col),	Barber
Grayson, A L,	Stationery
Harrill Bros,	G S
Hardin, W J,	G S
Harris, J W & Son,	Drugs
Hester, W H,	G S
Hyder, J C,	Stoves and Tinware
Justice, M L,	Livery
Levi, M,	G S
Logan, G W,	Livery
Logan, B L,	Livery
McDaniel, M B,	G S
McDaniel, W J,	Gro
Manfredo, Carlo,	Furniture
Matthews, J,	Shoes
Mills, G H & Son,	G S
Morrow, D F,	G S
Nettles, A J,	G S
One Price Shoe Store.	
Reid & Carpenter,	G S
Shotwell, J H,	G S
Sims, J W,	Butcher
Simpson, J K,	G S
Smith, T C,	Mfr Boots and Shoes
Stevens, A B,	Depot Agent
Stonecypher & Co,	G S
Twitty & Thompson,	Drugs
Walker, McDonnell (col),	Barber
Walker, T B & Co,	G S
Washburn, J R,	G S
Whitesides, J B,	G S
Wilkinson, S M,	Gro
Wilkinson, T F,	Gro

SUNSHINE.

Biggerstaff, J W,	G S

THERMAL CITY.

Carpenter, K J,	G S

UNION MILLS.

Hester, W H,	G S

UREE.

Robertson, J A,	G S
Whitesides, Z T.	G S

WASHBURN.

Washburn, R,	G S

MINES.

Kinds, Post Offices and Proprietors.

Alta, gold, Itoma, Alta Mining Co.

Atkin, gold, Logan's Store, G W Long.

Biggerstaff, gold, Golden, S Gallert, agent.

Cathey's Creek, gold, Rutherfordton, Wm Elwood.

Collins, gold, Golden, L McCurry.

Gold, gold, Golden, Golden Valley Hydraulic Mining Co.

Jamestown, gold, Cuba, A Nanny.

Long, gold, Logan's Store, A B Long, Junior.

RUTHERFORD COUNTY.

Venzant, gold, Golden, K J McGrayson, G A Knox, supt.
Monazite is found in various places over the county, and has been successfully mined in large quantities; L A Gettys, state agent, Shelby.

MILLS.

Kinds, Post Offices and Proprietors.

Corn and flour, Garnett, S D Wilkins.
Corn and flour, Ayr, J H Bird.
Corn and flour, Brittain, Nathan Young
Corn and flour, Brittain, A H Nabors.
Corn and flour, Washburn, B F Andrews.
Corn and flour, Myrtle, L I Watson.
Corn and flour, Rutherfordton, W J Hardin's estate.
Corn and flour, Brittain, C C Goforth.
Corn and flour, Green Hill, A H Ramsey.
Corn and flour, Thermal City, L L Deck.
Corn and flour, Oak Spring, L B De Priest.
Corn and flour, Golden, Jacob Yelton.
Corn and flour, Sunshine, H Toney.
Corn, flour and saw, Forest City, W Martin.
Corn, flour and saw, Darlington, W H Rucker.
Corn, flour and saw, Cuba, W J Townsend.
Corn and gin (steam), Garnett, M W Logan.
Saw, Green Hill. W B McIntire.
Steam saw and gin, Ferry, L A Holland.
Steam saw, Millwood Store, Cypher & Norris.
Steam saw, Rutherfordton, W H Hector.
Steam saw, Rutherfordton, Matt McBrayer.
Steam saw, Rutherfordton, R W Hyder
Steam saw, Garnett, Allen & Taylor.

PHYSICIANS.

Names and Post Offices.

Bright, Frank, Ellenboro.
Carson, Thos (dentist), Bostic.
Chapman, G M, Logan's Store.
Edwards, A E, Millwood.
Gettys, R C, Duncan's.
Hamrick, T G, Henrietta No 2.
Harris, J W & E B, Rutherfordton.
Harril, Lawson, Oak Spring.
Hicks, Oliver, Rutherfordton.
Hicks, Romeo, Henrietta.
Howey, E W (dentist), Rutherfordton.
Keeter, Ed, Cuba.

RUTHERFORD COUNTY.

Lovelace, T B, Henrietta.
Lynch, W L (dentist), Rutherfordton.
Martin, J O, Oak Spring.
McBrayer, T C, Forest City.
Nabors, A H, Brittain.
Nelson, ——, Big Island.
Stacy, F M, Otter Creek.
Thompson, W A, Rutherfordton.
Twitty, T B, Rutherfordton.
Twitty, John, Mack.
Whisnant, J F (dentist), Henrietta.
Whisnant, J A (dentist), Henrietta.
Young, G E, Forest City.

SCHOOLS.

Names, Post Offices and Principals.

Academy, Cuba, Miss Meldona Livingstone.
Academy, Darlington,
Academy, Forest City, H W Hoon and Geo P Harrill.
High School, Otter Creek.
Preparatory School, Rutherfordton, Mrs J A Miller.
Select School, Ellenboro, John Blanton.
Sunshine Institute, Sunshine, Prof D M Stallings, prin; Mrs Buffalow, asst.
Public schools—white, 76; colored, 28.

TEACHERS.

Names and Post Offices.

Allhands, J M, Chimney Rock.
Andrews, Miss Lucy C. Cliffdale.
Andrews, Miss Clara, Cliffdale.
Bell, Capt W H, Butherfordton.
Blanton, J J (col), Butler.
Blanton, J C, Washburne.
Bland, John, Cuba.
Boozer, Rev T F, Brittain.
Bridges, T A, Boiling Springs.
Bridges, M (col), State Line, S C.
Brooks, Lucinda (col), Chimney Rock.
Calton, Spurgeon, Sunshine.
Cauble, Miss Ella, Brittain.
Carpenter, Roxie (col) Forest City.
Carson, Miss Florence, Forest City.
Carson, W O (col), Twitty.
Conley, Miss Nannie, Marion.
Cowan, G E. Brindletown
Crawford, Miss Mittie, Henrietta.
Davis, Miss Kate G, Forest City.
Davis, M C, Clifford.
Davis, Furman, Forest City.
Doggett, R L, Forest City.
Eaves, J K, Polkville.
Eaves, Everett, Forest City.
Edwards, Thomas, Darlington.
Edwards, Sarah, Rutherfordton.
Flack, J O F, Darlington.
Forney, Thos L (col), Gilkey.

RUTHERFORD COUNTY.

Forney, Cornelius (col), Gilkey.
Fox, Miss Susie L (col), Forest City.
Gettys, T A, Oak Springs.
Goforth, Miss M E, Brittain.
Green, J L, Repew.
Green, Miss Ida, Ellenboro.
Griggs, Miss Zora, Lawndale.
Griffin, J W, Forest City.
Gross, Miss Mattie (col), Forest City.
Hamrick, Mrs S H, Rutherfordton.
Hamilton, Miss Mary A (col), Rutherfordton.
Harris, E C, Otter Creek.
Harvill, G P, Forest City.
Haynes, Logan, Green Hill.
Head, A C, Grassy Knob.
Hemphill, J P, Otter Creek.
Hogue, Miss M E, Brittain.
Holland, E L, Sharon.
Hopper, Miss Alice, Henrietta.
Horton, Miss M L, Forest City.
Horton, Miss M T, Forest City.
Howser, D D, Cliffdale.
Hunt, C M, Gamble's Store.
Jenkins, Z O, Ferry.
Jones, J P, Golden.
Justice, G C, Gilkey.
Lee, Vashti (col), Logan's Store.
Lockey, J H, North Brook.
Logan, Matt C (col), Ayr.
Lynch, Miss Ella, Cuba.
McIntire, A L (col), Forest City.
McIntire, Miss Mamie (col), Rutherfordton.
McMurray, A L, Dimsdale.
Melton, W B, Sunshine.
Micholds, S H, Rutherfordton.
Miller, Jobe (col), Twitty.
Moon, C C, Forest City.
Morgan, T E, Rutherfordton.
Moseley, Miss Mary (col), Forest City.
Newton, W R, Sunshine.
Nichols, J L, Otter Creek.
Oates David (col), Waco.
Phillips, I I (col), Rutherfordton.
Roberts, Zula (col), Twitty.
Searcy, Miss U L, Grassy Knob.
Sharp, Miss Ora, Trio.
Stallinge, D M, Sunshine.
Staley, Miss Mary J (col), Green River.
Stewart, J B, Ellenboro.
Thompson, Fannie (col), Rutherfordton.

RUTHERFORD COUNTY.

Twitty, Miss Lilly (col), Rutherfordton.
Twitty, J W (col), Cuba.
Ware, Miss Argie, Kings Mountain.
Washburn, E N, Washburn.
Watkins, S D (col), Rutherfordton.
Wells, W D (col), Lawndale.
Whisnant, J C, Golden.
Whisnant, P M, Holly Bush.
Whitesides, J F, Wells.
Wilson, J E Myrtle.
Wings, Miss Alice L, Island Ford.
Woodside, Carrie, Thermal City.
Young, J W (col), Henrietta.
Young, Miss Belle, Forest City.

LOCAL CORPORATIONS.

Citizens Building and Loan Association, K J Carpenter, pres; A L Grayson, sec and treas.
Florence Cotton Mill, Forest City, R R Hayes, pres; G O Doggett, sec and treas.
Henrietta Mills, Henrietta, J S Spencer (Charlotte), pres; S B Tanner, sec and treas. Also, Henrietta Mill No 2, operated by the same company.
Henrietta Lodge, No —, A F and A M.
J O U A M, Rutherfordton; A H Justice, pres; O C Erwin, sec.
Private Bank, Rutherfordton; H J Carpenter & D F Murrow; capital stock, $8.000.
Rutherfordton Cotton Mill, Rutherfordton.
Western Star Lodge, No 91, A F and A M, Rutherfordton; time of meeting, first Monday night, and June 24th, and December 27th.

NEWSPAPERS.

Forest City Ledger, Forest City (Dem. weekly); Griffin & Tate, editors and proprietors.
Ellenboro Enterprise, Ellenboro (independent weekly), Frank Bright, editor and prop.
The Democrat, Rutherfordton, John C Tipton, editor and prop.

36

SAMPSON COUNTY.

AREA, 840 SQUARE MILES.

POPULATION, 25,096; White 15,960, Colored 9,136.

SAMPSON COUNTY was formed in 1784, from Duplin county, and was named in honor of Colonel John Sampson.

CLINTON, the county seat, is 65 miles south from Raleigh. Population 1,600.

Surface—Sampson is situated on the head branches of Black river; has a level, sandy soil, in places swampy. Much of the land is good. Timber is plentiful, and water-power sufficient for all ordinary purposes.

Staples—Cotton, corn, lumber and naval stores. This is a fine cotton county, and many of the farms are well cultivated. Naval stores are produced extensively and are often quite profitable.

Fruits—Apples, peaches, pears, berry grapes, melons and other small fruits

Timbers—Pine, oak, poplar, hickory, ash, walnut, cypress and juniper.

TOWNS AND POST OFFICES.

	POP.		POP.
Alpine,	25	Huntley,	65
Arcot,	30	Ingold,	30
Autryville,	250	Ivanhoe,	40
Bass,	30	Keener,	50
Beaman's Cross		Kerr,	25
Roads,	65	Lisbon,	25
Blackman's		Lissa,	50
Mills,	60	Lydia,	40
Bland,	50	McKoy,	60
Chance,	25	Maitland,	40
Clear Run,	65	Mingo,	60
Clement,	25	Mix,	25
Clinton (c h),	1,600	Newton Grove,	135
Coharie,	50	Ora,	30
Dalila,	25	Orange,	25
Delta,	70	Owenville,	65
Dismal,	110	Parkersburg,	150
Elliot,	50	Roseboro,	150
Garland,	45	Sixruns,	50
Giles Mills,	65	Taylor's Bridge.	75
Harrell's Store,	175	Timothy,	50
Hawley's Store	100	Tippecanoe,	30
Hayne,	50	Tomahawk,	35
Herring,	55	Turkey,	50
Hives,	30	Vega,	40
Hobton,	35	Waycross,	60

COUNTY OFFICERS.

Clerk Superior Court—W K Pigford.
Commissioners—A Hobbs, chm'n.
Register of Deeds—A F Herring.
Sheriff—J N Marshburn.

Solicitor 6th District—M C Richardson
Treasurer—J M Marshburn.
County Examiner—G E Butler.

COURTS.

Fourth Monday before the first Monday in March; eighth Monday after the first Monday in March; fifth Monday after the first Monday in September.

TOWNSHIPS AND MAGISTRATES.

Dismal Swamp—R O Autry, J R Maxwell. J L Autry, Randall Hall, S B Page, R W Howard, C H Williams, E R Hall, Rayford Autry, W E Williams (Dismal).

Franklin—W U Newkirk, R F Pigford, N F Highsmith, L D Highsmith, Jas A Moore, J B Leavey, Knox Taylor. W A Melvin, jr (Clinton).

Hall's—R K Herring, T A Hobbs, J H McCullen, I G West, T W Barbrey, J H Packer, R W Bass, G W Highsmith, E C Gore (Clinton).

Honeycutt's—A T Herring, M J Newman, W A Baggett, T S Underwood, R M Crumpler, Auma Royal, R N Butler, P B Lockerman (Clinton).

Lisbon—A M Blackburn, J D Johnson, D L Herring, C T Lamb, A F Robinson, J O Herring, J O Herring, S T Johnson, Rich Parker, A W Lamble, Cary Fennell (Lisbon).

Little Coharie—M M Hall, J L Warren, Thomas Owen, W F Sessoms, P M Bullard, Wm J Faircloth, H J Cooper, F J Cooper, Street Brewer, J F Owen, J W Underwood, Mark Sessoms (Clinton).

McDaniels—W J Watson, W W Hobbs, Sylvester Carter, Jas Gaylor, Robt Highsmith, R L Lewis, Jno Horn, G C Highsmith. J W Wright (Clinton.)

Mingo—J D Wiliams, N B Barefoot, Jos Baggett, Autrey Baggett, J C Draughan, W J Jernagin, W R Warren, J E Layton (Mingo).

Newton Grove—Uriah Hill, Wm Daughtry, R A Ingram, Jas A Warwick, B P Dameron, Isaac Williams, H C Giddens, Eleazar Rich (Newton Grove).

North Clinton—H J Duncan, W E Stevens, H B Giddens, W E Shipp, L S Bell, J R Draughan, W F Rockley, T W Britt, C Patrick (Clinton).

SAMPSON COUNTY.

Piney Grove—J S Hines, H E Brewer, M W Clifton, V A Royal, J E Boyett, G W Sutton, Daniel Karnegay, Dr J H Darden, B H Hatcher (Clinton).

South Clinton—Warren Johnson, J O Culbreth, I R Chestnut, J A Ferrell, A J Cooper, E M Peterson, Lewis Tew, O L Henning, J L Matthews, W J Powell (Clinton).

Taylor's Bridge—V J McArthur, A J Johnson, J O Matthis, E C Smith, A R Herring, C J Williams, J J Vann, A H Merritt, W J Friar (Taylor's Bridge).

Turkey—Wm Kirby, R M Middleton, F M Carroll, J T Kennedy, C L Cook, W F Hines, W J Moore, Leon Rogers, W H Colwell, Paul Armstrong (Turkey.)

Westbrook— Ransom West, Allen Daughtry, C H McLamb, Marshall Lee, B G E Daughtry, P G A Tart, D L Mc-Lean, J D Warren (Clinton).

CHURCHES.

Names, Post Offices and Denom.
METHODIST.
Andrews' Chapel—Clinton.
Bethel—Clinton.
Bethel—Blockers (Cumberland co).
Browning's Chapel—Clinton.
Church—Clinton.
Concord—Clinton.
Goshen—Clinton.
Halls—Clinton.
Hopewell—Beaman's Cross-Road.
Johnson's CTapel—Clinton.
Keener's Chapel—Clinton.
Nendall's—Clinton.
McGee's—Clinton.
Mt Zion—Clinton.
Newton Grove—Beaman's Cross-Roads.
Salem—Magnolia.
Wesley's Chapel—Beaman's X-Roads.
BAPTIST.
Bethel—Harrell's Store.
Beulah—Clinton.
Boykin's Chapel—Clinton.
Brown's—Clinton.
Brown's—Clinton.
Ebenezer—Clinton.
Lisbon—Clinton.
Mt Gilead—Clinton.
New Hope.
Piney Grove.
Rowan—Clinton.
PRESBYTERIAN.
Church—Clinton.
Oak Plain—Teachey's (Duplin co).
Spring Vale—Teachey's (Duplin co).
DISCIPLES OF CHRIST.
Pleasant Union.
Shady Grove.
Six Runs.
EPISCOPAL.
St Paul's—Clinton.

SAMPSON COUNTY.

LAWYERS.

Names and Post Offices.

Boykin, E T (Sup. Court Judge), Clinton.
Cooper & Fowler, T R, Clinton.
Faison, H E, Clinton.
Kerr, E W, Clinton.
Kerr, J D, Clinton.
Lee & Butler, T M L, Clinton.
Pigford, W K, Clinton.
Richardson, M C, Clinton.
Stewart, J L, Clinton.

MANUFACTORIES.

Names, Post Offices and Proprietors.

Carolina Veneer Works, Clinton, A F Johnson.
Carriages and buggies, Autryville, Lewis & Co.
Carriages, Clinton, E Turner & Bro.
Carriages, Clinton, W T Williamson.
Gin, Clinton, J H Royal.
Gin, Blackman's Mills, B G E Daugherty.
Lumber, Ivanhoe, W Z Atkinson.
Saddles and Harness, Clinton, W H Stetson.
Turpentine, Boykin's Bridge, H B Culbreth.
Turpentine, Clear Run, D L Herring.
Turpentine, Clinton, J A Beaman.
Turpentine, Clinton, H B Culbreth & Co.
Turpentine, Clinton, J O Culbreth.
Turpentine, Delta, J W S Robinson.
Turpentine, Parkersburg, W J Parker & Son.
Turpentine, Parkersburg, Simon Smith.
Turpentine, Roseboro, M McLamb & Son.
Warsaw Crate Works, Warsaw, T P Pierce.

MERCHANTS AND TRADESMEN.

Names, Post Offices, Lines of Business.

AUTRYVILLE.
Autry, J L,	G S
Bowen, H I,	G S
Faircloth & Williams,	G S
Lewis, E A,	G S
McKenzie & Cooper,	G S
Matthis, J B,	G S
Sessoms, W F,	G S
Strickland, L W,	G S
Williams, J T & Cooper,	G S

BASS.
McClamb, J D,	G S

BEAMAN'S CROSS ROADS.
McPhail, J R,	G S

SAMPSON COUNTY.	SAMPSON COUNTY.

BLACKMAN'S MILLS.

Daugherty, B G E,	Gin
Gregory, J W,	G S
Williams, M B,	G S

BLAND.

Faison, B F,	G S
Fennell & Fennell,	G S
Peterson, L H,	G S

BOYKIN'S BRIDGE.

Culbreth, H B,	G S
London & Edwards,	G S

CLEAR RUN.

Herring, D L,	G S
Johnson, O J,	G S
Robinson, B B,	G S

CLEMENT.

Autry, J L,	G S

CLINTON.

Bizzell & Beaman,	Undertakers
Butler, C T & Co,	G S
Carr, J H,	G S
Chestnut, H B,	G S
Culbreth, H B & Bro (near),	G S
Culbreth, J O,	G S
Faison & Faison,	G S
Ferrell, T M,	G S
Giddens, H B,	Jeweler
Gregory, J T,	Tailor
Hanstein, M,	D G and Clo
Holliday, Dr R H,	Drugs
Holliday, R W & Bro,	G S
Holmes, R C & Co,	Livery
Hubbard, R H,	Gro and Confec
Hunter, J W,	G S
Johnson, C P,	G S
Lee, A M,	Drugs
Lewis, Julian & Co,	G S
Moore & Stanford,	Millinery
Patrick, C,	Gro
Patrick, D M,	G S
Patrick, W S,	D G and Shoes
Peterson, J R (col),	G S
Powell, B F,	G S
Powell, O J,	G S
Rackley, W G,	G S
Rawles, G T,	Jeweler
Royal, J E,	G S
Royal, J H,	Gro
Sanders & Harper,	Drugs
Turner, Cicero,	Painter

DELILA.

Powell, O J,	G S

DELTA.

Robinson, J W S,	G S

DISMAL.

Autrey, D R,	G S

ELLIOTT'S.

Faison, E L,	G S

GARLAND.

Boykin, R L,	G S
Herring, E C,	G S

Johnson, A N & Son,	G S
Sloan, Wm,	G S

GIDDENSVILLE.

Hawley, W C,	G S
Thompson, C A,	G S

HAMPTON.

Sessoms, T & F,	G S

HARRELL'S STORE.

Bland, D W,	G S
Colwell, A J,	G S
Devane & Fennell,	G S
Jones, J L,	G S
Lewis, C T,	G S
Moore, W G,	G S

HAWLEY'S STORE.

Jackson, W S,	G S
Lee, S B,	G S
Peterson, S F A, Agt,	G S

HIVES.

Crumpler, E A,	G S

HOBTON.

Hobbs, C H,	G S
Hobbs, J C,	G S
Hobbs, Thos A,	G S
McCullen, W R,	G S
Sutton & Jackson,	G S

HUNTLEY.

Butler, Mrs Wiley,	G S
Honeycutt, J H,	G S
Matthews, J B,	G S
Underwood, A E,	G S

INGOLD.

Johnson, Amos N & Son,	G S
Parker, J P,	G S

IVANHOE.

Anders, E J W,	G S
Sessoms, T & F,	G S

KEENER.

EcMullen, J H,	G S
Cooper, J H,	G S

KERR'S DEPOT.

Corbett, W M, jr,	G S
Pridgen, T F,	G S
Weeks, J C,	G S

MINGO.

Layton, J G,	G S

NEWTON GROVE.

Benton, J H & Co,	Drugs
Gregory, J T,	G S
Rose & Bro,	G S
Underwood, T W,	G S
Warren, S,	G S

ORA.

Herring, E S,	G S
Sikes, J A,	G S

PARKERSBURG.

Landon & Edwards,	G S
Parker, W J & Son,	G S

SAMPSON COUNTY.

Peterson, G D (col), G S
Smith, Simon, G S

ROSEBORO.

Bullard, P M, G S
Butler, A M, G S
Butler, R B & Co, G S
Crumpler, W A, G S
Hall, A M, G S
Lucas, J H, G S
McLamb, M & Son, G S
Owens, J F, G S
Roberts, C M, G S
Underwood & Maultsby, G S
Williams, D P & Co, ——
White, J W, G S

STARLING'S BRIDGE.

Culbreth, Wm, G S

TAYLOR'S BRIDGE.

Fryar, W J, G S
Herring, J A, G S
Johnson, A J, G S
Merritt, W L, G S

TOMAHAWK.

Bannerman, E S, G S
Herring, J O, G S
Murphy, J T, G S
Murphy, W B, G S
Robinson, S L (col), G S

TURKEY.

Carroll, W W, G S
Mann, E, G S

WAYCROSS.

Balkcum, W J, G S
Robinson, T D, G S

MILLS.

Kinds, Post Offices and Proprietors.

Grist, Clinton, J H Royal.
Saw, Autreyville, E V Cooper.
Saw, Huntley, J H Honeycutt.

PHYSICIANS.

Names and Post Offices.

Benton, J H, Newton Grove.
Boyett, Frank (dentist), Clinton,
Cooper, A T, Clinton.
Darden, J H, Giddensville.
Faison, J H, Elliott.
Hall, Wright, Hawley's Store.
Holladay, R H, Clinton.
Holmes, A, Clinton.
Kerr, Charles, Delta.
Lee, A M, Clinton.
Lucas, Jesse, Harrell's Store.
McMillan, W D, Magnolia (Duplin co).
Marable, J R, Warsaw (Duplin co).
Matthis, Benedict, Taylor's Bridge.
Moseley, Geo W, Taylor's Bridge.

SAMPSON COUNTY.

Murphy, W B, Delta.
Sloan, Henry, Lisbon.
Stevens, J A, Clinton.
Thompson, W I, Faison's Depot (Duplin co).

SCHOOLS.

Names, Post Offices and Principals.

Female Institute, Clinton.
Male Academy, Clinton.
Mingo High School, Hawley's Store.
Private School, Clinton.
Public Schools—white, 75; colored, 51.

TEACHERS.

Names and Post Offices.

WHITE.

Alderman, L W, Giles' Mill.
Archer, Miss Carrie, Clinton.
Baggett, Freddie, Lydia.
Barbry, A M, Hobton.
Bland, Rev Wm, Hawley's Store.
Brewer, O A, Clinton.
Brewer, Street, Owensville.
Bryan, J W, Newton Grove.
Bullard, V C, Roseboro.
Butler, J E, Maitland,
Clute, Miss Annie, Clinton.
Cooper, Miss Hasie A, Huntley.
Cooper, Miss Lila J, Huntley.
Culbreth, Miss Willie, Owenville.
Damerson, E S W, Hobton.
Dameron, D P, Newton Grove.
Dudley, W B, jr, Bass.
Dudley, J J, Bass.
Duncan, N G, Ora.
Ezzell, J D, Hobton.
Faircloth, C M, Chance.
Ferrell, Miss Lizzie, Clinton.
Fisher, W J, Roseboro.
Fort, B I, Blackman's Mill.
Hargrove, Festus, Bass.
Hargrove, Miss Martha, Clinton.
Herring, Miss Anna V, Clear Run.
Herring, Miss Mamie, Clear Run.
Herring, Miss Mary, Clinton.
Highsmith, Geneva, Parkersburg.
Highsmith, Miss Mittie C, Coharie.
Highsmith, Charles, Parkersburg.
Highsmith, Seavey, Parkersburg.
Hobbs, Miss Cleone, Clinton.
Hobbs, L M, Clinton.
Hobbs, W A, Hobton.
Hobbs, E M, Clinton.
Howard, A F, Huntley.
Howard, C C, Clement.
Huggins, Miss S K, Mt Olive.
Ingram, Miss Stella, Newton Grove.
Jackson, W A, Timothy.
Jackson, N T, Bass.

SAMPSON COUNTY.

Kelly, W D, Lisbon.
Lamb, Miss Minnie, Six Runs.
Lawhorn, Willie, Coharie.
Lee, N B, Newton Grove.
Lee, T J, McKoy.
Lee, E F, Newton.
Lee, Miss Cora, Blackman's Mill.
Lee, Miss Lettie H, McKoy.
McArthur, Miss Ida, Lissa.
McArthur, Miss Lula, Lissa.
McCalop, J W, Clinton.
McCullen, Miss Minnie, Faison.
McCullen, Miss Sue, Faison's.
McIntire, T W H, Ivanhoe.
McLennon, Miss I L, Clinton.
Marshburn, Miss Berta, Taylor's Bridge.
Mangum, E P, Clinton.
Oliver, Miss Edna, Mt Olive.
Page, J M, Fish Creek.
McPhail, Jonah, Beaman's X-Roads.
Peterson, Miss Katie F, Clinton.
Peterson, Hyacinth, Clinton.
Pigford, J B, Turkey.
Reynolds, J R, Ora.
Rich, Miss Annie, Coharie.
Robinson, Miss Alberta, Clinton.
Robinson, Mrs J H, Clinton.
Robinson, Josiah, Taylor's Bridge.
Robinson, R B, Ingold.
Robinson, Billie, Taylor's Bridge.
Royal, Miss Minnie, Ingold.
Royal, Miss Cora M, Ora.
Sessoms, W F, Hayne.
Shipp, C E, Huntley.
Sloan, T, Ingold.
Sikes, Miss Berta, Ora.
Smith, Miss Lizzie C, Parkersburg.
Tew, O B, Cooper.

SAMPSON COUNTY.

Thompson, Miss Mary, Faison.
Thornton, Miss Sallie, Mingo.
Warren, G C, Newton Grove.
Warren, Miss Annie, Newton Grove.
Watson, Miss F J, Maitland.
Weeks, Mamie, Hobton.
West, Miss Novella, Timothy.
West, Miss Lillie O, Timothy.
Williams, Miss Ida J, Blackman's Mills.
Williford, Miss Lucy A, Autryville.
Williford, Miss L A, Giles' Mill.
Wilson, E R, Bass.

COLORED.

Ashford, W H, Clinton.
Bizzell, L H, Clinton.
Boykin, E W, Huntley.
Boykin, J E, Clinton.
Carlton, W C, Turkey.
Davis, Miss M B, Clinton.
Ferrell, J U, Harrell's Store.
Ferrell, J A, Harrell's Store.
Herring, George, Clinton.
Holmes, O D, Ora.
Holmes, W N, Clinton.
Hubbard, J C, Clinton.
Kerr, J T. Tomahawk.
Merritt, W E, Clinton.
Moore, W H, Kerr.
Peterson, S M, Maitland.
Robinson, O E, Taylor's Bridge.
Sampson, Miss Emma, Clinton.
Sampson, Miss Eliza J, Clinton.
Thornton, Josiah, Rome.
West, A D, Harrell's Store.

NEWSPAPERS.

Sampson Democrat (weekly), Clinton, L A Bethune, editor.

STANLY COUNTY.

AREA, 380 SQUARE MILES.
POPULATION, 12,136: White 10,629, Colored 1,507.

STANLY COUNTY was formed in 1841, from the western portion of Montgomery county, as divided by the Pee Dee river, and was named in honor of Hon. John Stanly, of Newbern.

ALBEMARLE, the county seat, is 100 miles west from Raleigh, and preserves the name of one of the Lords Proprietors. Population 500.

Surface—Broken, hilly and rocky, but well watered, and good lands on the margins of the streams. Stanly is located on the west bank of the Yadkin river and north of Rocky river, and has plenty of excellent water-power.

Staples—Corn, cotton, wheat and minerals. A great deal of gold has been taken from the mines in this county.

Fruits—Apples, peaches, pears, berries, plums, melons and other small fruits.

Timbers—Oak, hickory and pine.

Minerals—Gold and zinc, with a large number of mineral springs.

TOWNS AND POST OFFICES.

	POP.		POP.
Abi,	—	Mission,	60
Albemarle,	500	Millingport,	100
Big Lick,	150	Norwood,	500
Bloomington,	10	New London,	450
Bridgeport,	50	Palestine,	15
Capal Grove,	20	Palmerville,	20
Cottonville,	55	Pennington,	—
Dowd,	15	Plyler,	50
Efird's Mills,	50	Porter,	40
Finger,	30	Rest,	25
Ford,	40	Ritchie,	50
Gladstone,	20	Ritchfield,	75
Jackdaw,	—	Shankle,	50
Leo,	20	Silver,	100
Locust Level,	75	Whitley,	15
Lowder,	40	Yadkin Falls,	100
Mabry,	50		

TOWNS AND POST OFFICES.

Clerk Superior Court—S H Milton.
Commissoners—J P Efird, chm'n; J E Hertsell, J A Peck.
Coroner—W R McSwain.
Register of Deeds—W T Huckabee.
Sheriff—George R McCain.
Solicitor Eleventh District—J L Webb
Surveyor—D A Holt.

Standard Keeper—S Austin.
Treasurer—George D Palmer.
County Examiner—R A Crowell.
Cotton Weigher—C Spence.

COURTS.

Superior Court meets first Monday in March and September.

TOWNSHIPS AND MAGISTRATES.

Albemarle—J W Bastain, J D Ross, J M Redwine, J C Parker, C A Spankle, J S Misenheimer, G D Moose, A R Kirk (Albemarle).

Allmond—Wm E Furr, D A G Hatley, J H Southerly, J L Peck, Aaron Furr, C E Dick, J M Morton (Albemarle).

Big Lick—S D Bost, J D Tucker, M A Whitley, J W Efird, J A Little, C T Ledbetter, A T Honeycutt, J A Morton (Albemarle).

Centre—Jas W Smith, D J Allen, Julius Hathcock, F M Duke, T P Snuggs (Albemarle).

Furr—A A Harrell, E M Honeycutt, jr, E D Smith, R L Hartsell, Jas M M Lambert, Hiram Burres, J S Crayton, W R Hartsell, Jacob Hartsell, jr (Albemarle).

Harris—M S Parker, V Mauny, R J Ross, M J Peirce, E C Kirk, J W Hardister, T J Crowell, E T Eddins, H W Callaway (Albemarle).

Ridenhour—J C Ridenhour, W A Moody, R L Lipe, J S Ewing, M Rickie, W S Blackwilder, R A Hatley, E A Honeycutt (Albemarle).

Tyson—R W Thompson, M M Poplin, J M Reap, J T Crump, H L Green, J M Turner, W H Harwood (Albemarle).

CHURCHES.

Names, Post Offices, Pastors and Denom.

METHODIST.

Albemarle—Albemarle, R M Taylor.
Bethel—New London, R M Taylor.
Bethesda—Albemarle, R M Taylor.
Big Lick—Big Lick, E G Pusey.
Cedar Grove—Cottonville, T S Ellington.
Louis Chapel—Leo, E G Pusey.
New London—New London, R M Taylor.

STANLY COUNTY.

Norwood—Norwood, T S Ellington.
Oak Grove—Willingport, E G Pusey.
Palmerville—Palmerville, R M Taylor.
Pine Grove—Albemarle, E G Pusey.
Randall's—Norwood, T S Ellington.
Rehoboth—Cottonville, T S Ellington.
Salem—Willingpost, E G Pusey.
Stony Hill—Dowd, R M Taylor.
Zion—Norwood, T S Ellington.
Zoah—Norwood, T S Ellington.

METH. PROTESTANT.

Friendship—Plyler, J R Betts.
Love's Grove—Leo, J R Betts.
New London—New London, J R Betts.
Simpson's Grove — Albemarle, J R Betts.
Palestine—Palestine, —— Darnell.

BAPTIST.

Albemarle—Albemarle, J W Suttle.
Anderson's Grove — Albemarle, J W Suttle.
Barber's Grove — Bridgeport, Wm G Morton.
Big Lick—Big Lick, —— Davis.
Canton—Bloomington, E D Teeter.
Ebenezer—Palmerville, J W Suttle.
Holt's Grove—Albemarle, D S Morton.
Kendall's—New London, J W Suttle.
New Hope (col)—Pennington.
Norwood—Norwood, G O Wilhoit.
Palmerville—Palmerville, J W Suttle.
Prospect—Albemarle, —— Hodge.
Silver Spring—Jackdaw, D S Morton.

PRIMITIVE BAPTIST.

Bear Creek—Bloomington.
Liberty Hill—Big Lick, L M Clark.
Mountain Creek—Albemarle.

LUTHERAN.

Albemarle—Albemarle, B S Brown.
Bethel—Copa Grove, —— Lyerly.

GERMAN REFORM.

Bear Creek—Finger.

MINISTERS RESIDENT.

Name, Post Office and Denomination.

BAPTIST.

Carter, B H. Albemarle.
Eudy, I L, Bridgeport.
Hartsell, P G, Big Lick.
Littleton, J W, sr, Albemarle.
Morris, Haywood, Palmerville.
Morton, W G, Albemarle.
Morton, D S, Jackdaw.
Suttle, J W, Albemarle.
Teetin, E D, Locust.

PRIMITIVE BAPTIST.

Clark, L M, Big Lick.

METHODIST.

Crowell, G H, New London.
Ellington, T S, Norwood.
Pusey, E G, Millingport.

STANLY COUNTY.

Taylor, R M, Albemarle.

METH. PROTESTANT.

Betts, J R, Plyler.
Russell, W W, New London.

LUTHERAN.

Lyerly, ——, Copal Grove.

HOTELS AND BOARDING HOUSES.

Names, Post Offices and Proprietors.

Bastian Hotel, Albemarle, J W Bostian.
Boarding house, New London, J F Beatty.
Boarding house, New London, J L Culp.
Boarding house, Albemarle, C P Cox.
Hotel Hearne, Albemarle, S H Hearne.
Messenhein Springs Hotel, Gladstone, Mrs Messenhiem.
Rocky River Springs Hotel, Cottonville, S H Manor.
Turner's Hotel, Norwood, P H Turner.

LAWYERS.

Names and Post Offices.

Austin, R E, Albemarle.
Brown, J M, Albemarle.
Crowell, R A, Albemarle.
Jerome, T J, Albemarle.
Pemberton, S J, Albemarle.

MANUFACTORIES.

Kinds, Post Offices and Proprietors.

Big Lick Mills, Big Lick, D E Efird & Co.
Blacksmithing and wagon, Albemarle, R L Sibley & Co.
Blacksmithing and wagon, Albemarle, J A Hathcock.
Dressing, moulding, etc, Albemarle, L A Woody.
Eudy's Mills, Millingport, E Eudy.
Furniture, Albemarle, J M Bivens.
Long Creek Mills, Whitley, J S Efird.
McLean Roller Mills, Richfield, Richey Bros.
Roller Mills, Norwood, M E Blalock.
Stanly Mfg Co, sash, doors and blinds, New London, Jas Beatty.
Wagons, Albemarle, R S Sibley & Bro.

MERCHANTS AND TRADESMEN.

Names, Post Offices and Lines of Business.

ALBEMARLE.

Atkins, H F,	Groceries
Austin Bros,	Groceries
Burns, J M,	Furniture
Dry, Wadsworth & Co,	G S
Hearne, T C,	G S

STANLY COUNTY.

Johnson & Foreman,	Livery
Kluttz Bros,	G S
Kluttz, R B & Son,	Groceries
Little Bros,	G S
Moody, Forest & Co.	G S
Pennington & Bivens,	Furniture and Undertakers
Ross, J O,	Groceries
Sibley, B L & Co,	Hardware
Spence, Q,	Groceries
Swink, W J,	G S

BIG LICK.

Efird, D E & Co,	G S
Morgan, W G,	G S
Russell & Cagle,	G S

BLOOMINGTON.

Furr, Aaron & Co,	G S

BRIDGEPORT.

Hunneycutt, J S,	G S

COPAL GROVE.

Miller, John M,	G S

COTTONVILLE.

Hill, Allen,	G S
McSwain, W R & Bro,	G S
Simpson, C J,	G S

DOWD.

Kirk, S M,	G S

EFIRD'S MILLS.

Kinley & Bost,	G S
Tucker, L R,	G S

FINGER.

Shoe, D A,	G S

GLADSTONE.

Peeler, G W,	G S
Ritchie, Mrs Mary A E,	G S

KIRK'S MILLS.

Elliott, C B,	G S

LEO.

Furr, C N,	G S
Little, Jacob S,	G J
Morgan, Ezekiel,	G S

LOCUST LEVEL.

Hathcock, Lee,	G S
Honeycutt & Hartsell,	G S
Little, G F,	G S

MILLINGPORT.

Eudy, E & Co,	Millers
Robbins, C D,	G S

MISSION,

Almond, G F,	G S

NEW LONDON.

Beatty, J P,	G S
Culp, Bros & Co,	Livery
Hagler & Motley,	G S
Lefler, C & Sons,	G S
Russell, B,	G S
Swink, W J,	G S

STANLY COUNTY.

NORWOOD.

Barnhardt & Son,	Hdw
Blalock, W J,	G S
Blalock, M E,	Millinery
Johnson & Foreman,	Livery
Lanier & Moore,	Livery
Lilly, Fred,	Undertaker and Furn
Ronsaville Bros,	G S
Tyson, J A,	G S
Wagner, G B,	Racket Store
Watkins & Co,	G S
Whitley & Hathcock,	Drugs

PALMERVILLE.

Coggins, C L,	G S
Elliott, C P,	G S

PLYLER.

Southerly, Wm & Son,	G S

PORTER.

Fleming & Thompson,	G S
Missenheimer, W A & Son,	G S
Stedman, E W,	G S

RITCHFIELD.

Ritchie, D D,	Fert
Ritchie, G G,	G S

SILVER.

Coble & Carter,	G S
Green, R L,	G S
Hathcock, J S & Co,	G S
Simpson, C J,	G S

WHITLEY.

Efird, Jno S,	G S

MINES.

Kinds, Post Offices and Proprietors.

Barringer, Jol, Albemarle, Parker & Co.

Concord Mining Co (gold), New London.

Crawford (gold), Albemarle.

Fesperman (gold), Albemarle, T A Fesperman,

Layton (gold), Albemarle.

Shankle (gold); Albemarle, C A Shankle

Stanley, Freehold (Linn gold), New London.

Stone (grit), slate mine, Albemarle, N C Slate Co.

Thompson (gold), Albemarle.

Willson (gold), Albemarle.

MILLS.

Kinds, Post Offices and Proprietors.

Cotton gin and grist mill, Albemarle, Kluttz Bros.

Flour, saw and gin, Albemarle, W A Marks.

Grist, saw and gin, Norwood, W H Parker.

Grist, saw and gin, Palmerville, B F Cox & Co.
Grist and gin, Silver, Forman & Coble.
Grist and gin, Lowder,Thos A Lowder.
Grist, saw and gin, Bridgeport, Harwood & Co.
Grist and gin Efird's Mills, Kendley & Bost.
Grist, saw and gin, Pennington, Arnold Parker.
Grist, saw and gin, Big Lick, Efird, Hill & Co.
Grist, saw and gin, Locust, Smith, Tucker & Co.
Grist and gin, Plyler, Plyler Milling Co.
Grist, roller, saw and gin, Whitley, John Efird.
Roller and saw, Norwood, M E Blalock & Co.
Rollor and saw,Ritchfield,Richey Bros.
Roller and saw, Millingpost, E Eudy, Whitley & Co.
Saw and grist, Dowd, Miller & Son.

PHYSICIANS.

Names and Post Offices.

Anderson, A, Albemarle.
Anderson, J N, Albemarle.
Arie, Geo F, New London.
Cox, B F, Palmerville.
Douglass, J B, Big Lick.
Ivey, R W, New London (dentist).
King, O D, Albemarle.
Kluttz, S B, Albemarle (dentist).
Littleton, J W, Albemarle.
Tyson, J A, Norwood.
Whitley, D P, Millingport.
Whitley & Hathcock, Norwood.

SCHOOLS.

Names, Post Offices and Principals.

Academy, Silver, Miss F E Ufford.
Academy, New London, J D Barrier.
Academy, Millingport.
Academy, Big Lick, D J Harris.
Academy, Norwood, R L Smith.
Academy, Albemarle, Rev C M Gentry.
Palmerville Academy, Palmerville, E F Eddins.
Primary School, Albemarle, Miss F E Ufford.
Public Schools—white, 65; colored, 10.

TEACHERS.

Names and Post Offices.

Barrier, J D, New London.
Eddins, E T, Palmerville.
Harris, D J, Big Lick.
Smith, R L, Norwood.
Ufford, Miss F E, Albemarle.

LOCAL CORPORATIONS.

Anderson Council, No 913, R A, Albemarle; time of meeting, first and third Friday nights.
Millingport Lodge, No —, A F and A M, Millingport.
Pemberton Lodge, No 2074. K of H, Albemarle; time of meeting, first and third Saturday nights.
Stanly Lodge, No 348, A F and A M, Albemarle; time of meeting, Saturday of full moon at 3 o'clock.
Yadkin Falls, No 422, A F and A M, New London.

NEWSPAPERS.

Stanly News, Albemarle, T J Jerome, editor.
Stanly Enterprise, Albemarle (weekly). Rufus A Crowell, editor and prop.

FARMERS.

Names and Post Offices.

Abi—W S Duke, Eli Hamilton, Henry Hinson, Darmid Milton, J B Simpson, D G Thompson, A J Underwood.
Albemarle—Ebin Biles, Rufus Callaway, N A Clayton, W T Earnhardt, M M Efrid, J J Efrid, J D Forest, Q J Freeman, S H Hearne. John Hudson, W S Ingram, Dan'l Lowder, Jacob Lowder, Isaac Lowder, L Lowder, T A Lowder, Geo W Lowder, T S Parker, D F Parker, J C Parker, John Parker, J M Pickler, Nathan Poplin, N F Rimmage, Jas Rimmage, D F Rimmage, D R Seago,S E Sl⌐ck, J C Smith, J S Smith, G C Smith, D T Talbert, O H Whittby.
Big Lick—Jno W Austin, J L Blackwilder, Josh Brooks, W A Cayle, Jno T Dry, Michael Dry, S P Hill, Dan'l Hinson, Andrew Honeycutt, Eli Honeycutt, D S Murgar. M S Smith, A M Teeler, John A Vickers.
Bloomington—Jonah Almond, Marshall Furr, Aaron Furr, Wm E Furr, Green Hatty, Jas Louder.
Copal Grove-J S Ewing, Dan Lefler, Caleb Lefler, J M Miller, C Misenheimer, P W Misenheimer, C A Moose, G E Plyler, Geo H Plyler, C A Ridenhour, J C Ridenhour, L O Richie, John Underwood.
Cottonville-John Biles, W F Crump, John T Crump, W D Crump, H H Davis, A D Deese, J M Harwood, P A Harwood, Allen Hill, L D McSwain, D W Poplin, R W Thompson, C W West.

STANLY COUNTY.

Dowd—B F Bell, J C Bell, H L Bell, W J Blalock, R J Crowel, David Doley, J F Festerman, Noah Goodman, Daniel Kirk, T P Kirk, J A Melton, L D Melton, A W Miller, P W Miller, Travis Miller, Crawford Miller, J S Misenheimer, G K Shaver, Adolpus Shaver, S M Stokes.

Finger—Enesley Harwood, R Thos Hatley, Simeon Hatley, J E Hatley, Guilford Hatley, Rufus Lefler, J A Peck, J L Peck, D A Shoe, Isaac Shoe.

Kirk—R Harris.

Leo—J M Furr, R L Furr, L L Furr, A E Green, Jas M Green, Jo E Hartsell, J W Hartsell, Jas Hartsell, Wm Love, E Mergon.

Locust—Jack Barlee, Hiram Barlee, D M Dry, Hiram Eudy, J F Eudy, Israel Furr, Monroe Furr, J M Hathcock, J A Love, Thos Love, M P Love, H P Love, E M Ashurne.

Lowder—Julius Hathcock, Ephriam Hathcock, Frank Lilly, Thos A Lowder.

Millingport — H D Eudy, Ransom Eudy, Harrison Eudy, E Eudy, M F Furr, T A Harwood, James Hatly, D O G Hatley, W L Hatley, Andy Lipe, Daniel Lipe, Levi Lipe, J H Lowder, Crawford Lowder, J D Lowder, D H Lowder, H A Lowder, W H Perry, P C Sides.

Mission—J F Herrin, Eli R Herrin.

New London — Job Callaway, T J Crowell, John W Harris, C M Harris, D F Harris, John R Ivey, Wm M Ivey, D W F Kendall, John Kendall, R A Miller, J C Niceler, M S Parker, John Richey, R J Ross.

Norwood—D J Allen, A S Atkins, Martin Bird, M E Blalock, D B Burnett, D N Burnett, Thos Carilson, Geo T Dunlap, Eli Lentz, John Lisk, Eben

Lowder, John Mabry, W J Milton, Jno T Moore, John Morgan, Monroe Palmer, L F Shankle, W S Smith, James W Smith, T P Suggs, Geo I Swaringan, Eli Swaingen, Robt F Tyson.

Palmerville—H M Biles, J E Biles, John H Bost, J A Coggin, L C Coggin, W H Coggin, J W Davis, J M Jenkins, J L Kearns, Lafayette Kirk, J P Nash, Chas M Palmer, W P Palmer, Jno L Palmer, David Reeves, Wm H Russell.

Palestine.—Wm M Biles, J E Bussell, W A Calloway, D W Carter, B H Carter, Zeneri Coggin, Elam Coggin, A Crowell, M R Dry, Adam Dry, D D Green, D T F Hall, W K Little, W O Parker.

Pennington.—W B Biles, L A Biles, Wm Biles, C H Brooks, J C Bussell, Adolphus Crowell, F C Harris, Brady Morris, Jas Moss, F A Moss, Levison Taylor.

Plyler.—J S Burlayson, Adam Effrd, Dock Hatly, E D Lowder, Jas Mason, W C Pickly.

Rest.—B F Blalock, Z D Blalock, W M Kirk, E C Kirk, J I Kirk, A R Kirk, J M Parker.

Richfield.—Henry Arie, Frank Fraly, M I Pence, Julius Richie, D D Richie, Dan'l Richie, Solomon Sell, G L Wilhelm.

Shankle.—E J Lanier, A S Lentz, Jacob Shankle, Eli Shankle.

Silver—J D Austin, Thos H Brooks, T A Coble, P G Coggin, Wiley Crowell, C A Crowell, A J Crowell, J C Forman, B A Forman, Guilford Harris, Amos Van Hay, S H Mauer, A S Miller. Wesley Simpson, Wm Southerly, F M Withart.

Yadkin Falls.—W N Crowell, V V Mauney, J M Mauney.

STOKES COUNTY.

AREA 500 SQUARE MILES.

POPULATION 17,199; White 14,386, Colored 2,813.

STOKES COUNTY was formed in 1789, from Surry county, and was named in honor of Col. John Stokes, an officer of the Revolutionary war.

DANBURY, the county seat, is 125 miles northwest from Raleigh. Population, 265; including township, 2,659.

Surface—Moderately hilly; well watered and timbered; generally rich. Scenery fine, air salubrious.

Staples—Tobacco,corn,wheat,grasses, fruits in great abundance, and live-stock. This is a fine tobacco-producing country.

Fruits—Apples,peaches,pears,grapes, plums, cherries, berries and other small fruits.

Timbers—Pine, oak, chestnut, hickory, walnut and poplar.

Minerals—Coal, gold, zinc, with numerous iron, sulphur and limestone springs.

TOWNS AND POST OFFICES.

	POP.		POP.
Ayersville,	50	Kiger,	15
Big Creek,	20	Lime Rock,	15
Brown		Meadows,	20
Mountain,	50	Mizpah,	50
Campbell,	20	Neatman,	15
Clare,	20	Prestonville,	45
Culler,	20	Pine Hall,	15
Dalton,	87	Quaker,	15
Danbury,	265	Red Shoals,	20
Dan River,	50	Rella,	25
Delk,	25	Sandy Ridge,	60
Dillard,	15	Saxon,	75
Elko,	30	Slate.	—
Francisco,	20	Smith,	50
Fulp,	25	Tulip,	50
Germanton,	25	Walnut Cove,	200
Hilltop,	20	Watkinsville,	50
Hard Bank,	25	Wilson's Store,	30
Jewel,	20	Withers,	20
King's,	50		

COUNTY OFFICERS.

Clerk Superior Court—N O Petree.
Commissioners — Dr John W Neal, chm'n; J W Hylton, F L Moore.
Coroner—S F Slate.
Register of Deeds—D V Carroll.
Sheriff—Joel H Fulton.
Solicitor Seventh District—M L Mott.
Surveyor—G A Carroll.
Standard Keeper—N M Pepper.
Treasurer—Joel H Fulton.

COURTS.

Seventh Monday after the first Monday in March. and seventh Monday after the first Monday in September.

TOWNSHIPS AND MAGISTRATES.

Beaver Island—J W Davis, W S Wilsod, J P Dalton, R P McAnally, M T Mitchell (Danbury).

Danbury—T J Davis, J H Tuttle, S B Taylor (Danbury).

Meadow—G T Baker. J W Fowler, J D Lawson, I G Ross, J P Furguson, J E Crews (Meadow).

Peter's Creek—W F Campbell, M V Mabe, R F Shelton, J T Priddy, H Reid, Davis Fagg, J M Berge, W A Hylow (Danbury).

Quaker Gap—C T Christian, W M Beasley, W J Simmons, J C Flippier, G W Thore, J C Clark, P Pearce (Quaker).

Sauratown—J I Blackburn, S W Neal, T G Samuel, J L Hollow, Dr E Fulp, J F Fulton, S C Pierson (Danbury).

Snow Creek—P D Watkins, J T Wilson (Danbury).

Yadkin—E W Culler, James T Johnson, Wm Newson, A M Boyles, R F Fulk, S A Houser, J C Newsom (Danbury).

CHURCHES.

Names, Pastors, Postoffices and Denom.

METHODIST.

Antioch—Clara, M H Vestal.
Chestnut Grove—Dalton. M H Vestal.
Church—Germantown, M H Vestal.
Church—Danbury, J H Totten.
Davis' Chapel—Dillard, J H Totten.
Ebenezer—Culler, M H Vestal.
Little Yadkin—Culler.
Palmyra—Wilson's Store, J H Totten.
Stokesburg—(col), Walnut Cove. Will Martin.
Stokesburg—Walnut Cove,H M Vestal.
Trinity—Dalton's Chapel, H M Vestal.

METHODIST PROTESTANT.

Dalton's Chapel—Dalton, Isaac Hunt.

BAPTIST.

Mt Tabor—Walnut Cove, R M Loftes.
Bethel—Meadows, P Oliver.

STOKES COUNTY.

Church—Westfield, R M Loftes.
Friendship — Wilson's Store, Rufus Crews.
K-Fork—Dillard, C W Glidwell.
Mt Olive—Dalton, Rufus Crews.
Oak Ridge—Watkinsville, C W Glidwell.
Walnut Cove—Walnut Cove, R M Loftes.

PRIM. BAPTIST.

Buffalo—Aversville, P Hutchinson.
Church—Westfield, J A Ashburn.
Clear Spring—Walnut Cove, A Moran.
Flat Rock—Francisco, Alex Moran.
Swan Creek—Jewell, E Basserd.
Piney Grove—Hard Bank, J A Ashburn.
Rock House—Brown's Mountain, J A Ashburn.
Wilson—Dillard, J A Ashburn.

MORAVIAN

Church—Fulp, Jas T Lineback.

PRESBYTERIAN.

Asbury—Dan River, C M Miller.
Church—Danbury, C Miller.
Dan River—Francisco, C Miller.
Snow Hill—Jewell C Miller.

SOUTHERN CHRISTIAN.

Corinth—Germanton.

EPISCOPAL.

Houston's Chapel—Walnut Cove, Rev —— Fetter.

CHRISTIAN.

Haw Pond—Kiger, R T Williams.

LUTHERAN.

Bethel—Wilson's Store, Rev Trexler.

FRIENDS.

Church—Westfield, Henry Pell.

MINISTERS RESIDENT.

Names, Post Offices and Denom.

CHRISTIAN.

Allen, P W, Walnut Cove.

BAPTIST.

Caudle, J H. Hilltop.
Crews, R W, Germanton.
Gladwell, C W, Walnut Cove.
Oliver, P, Dalton.

PRIMITIVE BAPTIST.

Moran, Alex, Danbury.
Wright, J H. Westfield.

METHODIST.

Heslebach. S H, Rural Hall.
Johnson, Wesley, Francisco.
Long, A M, Culler.
Norman, Isaac, Westfield.

PRESBYTERIAN.

Miller, C, Danbury.

STOKES COUNTY.

HOTELS AND BOARDING HOUSES.

Names, Post Offices and Proprietors.

Dalton Hotel, Dalton, D N Dalton.
Hotel, Walnut Cove, J W Lewis.
Hotel, Germanton, C J Styers.
Hotel, Danbury, S B Taylor.
Laudreth Hotel, Walnut Cove, W P Landreth.
McCanless Hotel, Danbury, Drs W V & W L McCanless.
Moore Hotel, Culler, W J Moore.
Moore's Spring, Danbury, John Moore.
Piedmont Springs, Danbury, Piedmont Springs Co.
Webster Hotel, Walnut Cove, Mrs G W Webster.

LAWYERS.

Names and Post Offices.

Humphreys, J D, Danbury.
Joyce, A H, Danbury.
King, Walter W, Danbury.
Phillips, John Y. Dalton.
Stack, A M, Danbury.

MANUFACTORIES.

Kinds, Post Offices and Proprietors.

Blacksmith, Jewel, W R Shelton.
Blacksmith, Slate, Hip Tillston.
Blacksmith, Sandy Ridge, J W Hutcherson.
Blacksmith, Dillards, F M Davidson.
Blacksmith, Lime Rock, J E Sisk.
Blacksmith, Wilson's Store, L Chandler.
Blacksmith, Francisco, Alex Fulk.
Blacksmith, Danbury, Burrel Lemons.
Blacksmith, Danbury, C Moody & Son.
Blacksmith, Danbury, W T Simmons & Son.
Blacksmith, Danbury, J W Ashby.
Blacksmithing and wheelwrighting, Sandy Ridge, R P Tilly.
Blacksmithing and wheelwrighting, Jewel, S M Shelton.
Blacksmithing and wheelwrighting, Dalton, Alex Hargrave.
Blacksmithing and wheelwrighting, Neatman, James Overby.
Blacksmithing and wheelwrighting, Neatman, W H Tillston.
Blacksmithing and wheelwrighting, Walnut Cove, H Golding.
Blacksmithing and wheelwrighting, Walnut Cove, Luther Lash.
Blacksmithing and wheelwrighting, Walnut Cove, Stokes Covington.
Blacksmithing and wheelwrighting, Germanton, Thos Good.

STOKES COUNTY.

Blacksmithing and wheelwrighting, Germanton, Chas Covington.
Buggies, Walnut Cove, W W Landreth.
Building and contracting, Walnut Cove, D J B Cassel.
Building and contracting, Walnut Cove, D B Foucht.
Building and contracting, Danbury, Jno Burnett.
Building and contracting, Walnut Cove, John Gibson.
Building and contracting, Walnut Cove, D F Carter.
Building and contracting, Danbury, R H R Blair.
Cabinet and undertaker, Sandy Ridge, Hutcherson & Frazier.
Cabinet, Danbury, R H R Blair.
Cabinet, Germanton, W H Cumbia.
Foundry, Walnut Cove, Miller & Cook.
Iron, Pilot Mountain, Job & W A Hiatt.
Lime, Germanton, B J Bolejack.
Lime, Germanton, R J Petree.
Machine shop, Walnut Cove, W P Landreth.
Millwrighting, Colesville, G W Merritt.
Roller mills, Sandy Ridge, J E Shelton.
Saddles and harness, Danbury, J Hawkins (col.).
Saddles and harness, Danbury, J B Whitten.
Sash and blinds, Walnut Cove, Walnut Cove Cumber Co.
Tannery, Sandy Ridge, J C Andrews.
Tannery, Sandy Ridge, G W Andrews.
Tannery, Danbury, Pepper & Sons.
Tannery, Pilot Mountain, W D Turpin.
Tannery, Kiger, Gleon Fergerson.
Tobacco, Summerfield, H C Brittain.
Tobacco boxes, Dillard, R W Mitchell.
Tobacco boxes, Sandy Ridge, S Amos.
Tobacco, Pinnacle. Culler & Co
Tobacco, Culler, McD Boyd & Co.
Tobacco, Francisco, Dodd Bros.
Tobacco, King, D W Dodd.
Tobacco, Culler, E W Culler.
Tobacco, plug and twist, Walnut Cove, A J Fair.
Tobacco, Walnut Cove, A J Fair.
Tobacco, Pilot Mountain, Virgil Boyles
Tobacco, Dalton, D N Dalton.
Tobacco boxes, Dalton, D N Dalton.
Tobacco boxes, Sandy Ridge, J E Shelton.
Tobacco boxes, Jewell, J H Bright.
Wagons, Dalton, A H Hargrove.
Wagons, Sandy Ridge, John Hutcherson.
Wagons, Danbury, H M Joyce.

STOKES COUNTY.

MERCHANTS AND TRADESMEN.

Names, Post Offices, Lines of Business.

AYRESVILLE.

Martin, W F & Son,	G S

BIG CREEK.

Farris, G W,	G S
George, R W,	Miller
Smith & Francis,	Millers
Wright, J H,	G S

BROWN MOUNTAIN.

Boyles, V,	G S

CAMPBELL.

Hylton, W R,	Mill
Lackey, H C,	G S
Shepperd, C L,	G S

COLESVILLE.

Lackey, L J,	G S

CULLER.

Butner, C A & Co,	G S
Culler, E W & Son,	G S
Edwards & Edwards,	G S
Schaub, W H & Son,	G S
Spainhour & Co,	G S
Spainhour & Flynn,	G S
Spainhour, W E & Co,	G S
Stone & Co,	G S

DALTON.

Coe, H C,	G S
Coe, S F,	Canned Goods
Dalton, D N,	G S

DANBURY.

Hartman, R L,	G S
Joyce, H M,	G S
Martin, N A,	G S
McCanless, Dr W V & W L,	Drugs
Pepper, J F,	Tanyard
Pepper, N M,	G S
Taylor, J S,	Livery and G S

DAN RIVER.

Smith, W L,	G S

DELK.

Lawson, J P,	G S
Venable, H,	G S

DICO.

Sheppard, C L & Son,	G S

DILLARD'S.

Mitchell & Willis,	G S

FIVE FORKS.

Helsabeck, A J & J H,	Gro
Schaub, Samuel,	Miller
Stone, B,	G S

FRANCISCO.

Moir, Dr R P,	G S

GERMANTON.

Beck, R F & Co,	Drugs
Beaman, Fred,	Depot Agt

STOKES COUNTY.

Harris, R V,	G S
Moore, W T,	G S
Poindexter & Westmoreland,	G S
Rainey, Mrs A M,	G S
Stylers, E J & Co,	G S

JEWELL.

Bennett, W R,	Shoe Shop
Fagg, W J & Son,	G S
Jewell, Mrs A J.	G S

KING'S CABIN.

Grabbs, L E & Son,	G S
Spainhour, J W,	G S

LIME ROCK.

Sisk, Ed,	G S

MEADOWS.

Nelson, F E,	G S

MIZPAH.

McGee, H,	G S
Meadows, W G,	G S

NEATMAN.

Carroll, S L,	G S
Tuttle, R B,	G S

PINE HALL.

Anderson, L W,	Miller
Flinn, J C,	G S
Robertson & Preston,	G S

PINNACLE.

Butner, C A & Co,	G S
Stone, H L & Co,	G S

PRESTONVILLE.

Gann, T J,	G S
Hawkins & Wall,	Millers
Martin & Wall,	G S

QUAKER GAP.

Tuttle, A G & Co,	G S

RED SHOALS.

Davis, J W,	Miller
Hartman, R L,	G S

RELLA.

Lackey, L J,	G S

SANDY RIDGE.

Dobyns, F O (near),	G S
Joyce, J W & Co,	Alliance Store
Shelton, J E,	G S
Tillery, W L,	G S

SAXON.

McAnally, R P,	G S

SLATE.

Boyles, A (near),	G S

SMITH.

Collins, J T,	G S
Smith, C C,	G S

TULIP.

Simmons, M T,	G S

WALNUT COVE.

Bailey Mercantile House, Mrs B Bailey, prop,	—
Burton & Freeman,	G S

STOKES COUNTY.

Clodfelter, W C,	Wagon Shop
Freeman, Mrs T A,	Millinery
Fulp, Dr E,	Drugs
Fulton, Sons & Co,	G S
Fuller, Jacob.	G S
Gentry, W H.	Fert
Jones, Dr A G,	Drugs
Keller, L A,	Drugs
Lewis, J G.	Furn
Linville, A J,	Shoes
Landreth, W P,	Repair Shops
Martin, W J & Co,	G S
Murphy, R L,	G S
Rierson Bros,	Livery

WATKINSVILLE.

Shelton, H W,	G S

WENTWORTH.

Ellington & Bro.	Poultry Farmers
Johnson & Wright,	G S
Mitchell, John W,	G S
Whittemore, A J,	Livery
Withers, D L,	G S

WESTFIELD.

Christian. L P,	G S
Cook & Needham,	G S
Davis, B F,	G S
Dix, Mrs Ellen,	G S
Lowe, J H,	G S

WILSON'S STORE.

Ross, J G.	G S
Tillotson, W H,	Miller

MINES.

Kinds, Post Offices and Proprietors.

Asbestos, Danbury, Jeff Booz and others.

Beryl, Danbury, D C Pepper.

Chalcedony, Danbury, Walter W King.

Coal bed, Dan River.

Coal, Walnut Cove, C Hairston.

Flexible Sandstone, Danbury, Walter W King.

Iron (hematite). Pepper's heirs, and many others, own lands containing iron ores of different kinds, which is considered as being inexhaustible.

Iron, Danbury, R T Boleauman. R M Pearson and F S Taylor.

Iron, Jewell, J J Priddy.

Iron, magnetic (Morotock,) Danbury, Col J M Heck's heirs, Raleigh, N C.

Iron, Pilot Mountain.

Lime-kiln, Lime Rock, W A Estes.

Lime-kiln, Germanton, R J Petree.

Lime-kiln, Germanton, Wm Bolejack.

Limestone, Germanton, Philadelphia company.

Mica, Danbury, Smith Steel.

Mica, Jewell, G W Priddy.

Plumbago, Danbury, John Moore.

Soapstone (blue), Danbury, W V McCanless.

STOKES COUNTY.

Silver and lead, Danbury, Thos Ruffin, Hillsboro, N C.

Silver and lead ore, Danbury, A M Stack.

White fire-proof clay, Danbury, Dr W V McCanless and N M Pepper.

MINERAL WATERS.

Moore's Springs (alum and iron), six miles from Danbury, are noted for their cure of chronic diseases.

Pepper's Spring (alum), three miles from Danbury, is equally as good.

Piedmont Springs (chalybeate), within two and a half miles of Danbury, are known for their value by the thousands who have tried them.

There are many other mineral springs in this county, which have not been tested to the extent of the above.

MILLS.

Kinds, Post Offices and Proprietors.

Corn and flour, Francisco, R W George.

Corn and flour, Francisco, W M Moore.

Corn and flour, Pilot Mountain, Robert Hill.

Corn and saw, Sandy Ridge.

Corn, flour and saw, Lime Rock, Kelly Shepherd.

Corn and saw, Germanton, N G Westmoreland.

Corn, flour and saw, Mizpah, H W Kiser.

Corn, flour and saw, Lime Rock, J H Hawkins.

Corn and flour, Pine Hall, S S Wall.

Corn and saw, Sandy Ridge, J A Martin.

Corn, flour and saw, Red Shoals, J W Davis.

Corn, flour and saw, Walnut Cove, A J Fair.

Corn, flour and saw, Neatman, Tillotson & Son.

Corn, flour and saw, Dalton, D N Dalton.

Corn and flour, Brown Mountain, W K Thore.

Corn and flour, Neatman, W G Slate.

Corn and flour, Walnut Cove, J G Blackburn.

Corn and flour, Danbury, A D Dodd.

Corn and flour, Jewel, Moore & Jewel.

Corn and flour, Germanton, H A Morris.

Corn and flour, Germanton, N G Westmoreland & Son.

Corn and flour, roller, saw, etc, Sandy Ridge, J E Shelton.

Corn and flour, Francisco, Joe Francis.

Corn and flour, Francisco, Robert George.

STOKES COUNTY.

Corn and flour, Big Creek, Collins & Jessup.

Corn and flour, Pine Hall, L W Anderson.

Corn and flour, Slate, W G Steele.

Corn and flour, Germanton, N G Westmoreland.

Corn and flour, Francisco, Dodd Bros.

Flour and corn, Prestonville, Hawkins & Wall.

Flour and corn, Wilson's Store, W Tillton.

Flour and corn, Campbell, W M Moore.

Flour and corn, Campbell, W R Hylton.

Flour and corn, Francisco, Milton Smith.

Planing mills, Walnut Cove, Walnut Cove Lumber Co.

Saw and flour, Kiger, W H Tillotson.

Saw and planing, Slate, W G Slate.

Steam saw. Walnut Cove, J G Boyd.

Saw, Red Shoals, J G H Mitchell.

Saw, Germanton, G D Jackson.

Saw, Neatman, J G Southern.

Saw, Pine Hall, Cabrill & Binford.

Saw, Pilot Mountain, W A Hyatt.

Saw, Walnut Cove, A G Fair.

Saw, corn and flour, Campbell, H C Lackey.

Saw, Mizpath, J E Slate.

PHYSICIANS.

Names and Post Offices.

Banner, M R (dentist), Walnut Cove.

Ellington, J H. Sandy Ridge.

Flippin, S M, Westfield.

Fulp, Elias, Walnut Cove.

Hill, W L, Walnut Cove.

Hill, D J, Germanton.

Hill, L H. Germanton.

Jones, A G, Walnut Cove.

King, W S, Slate.

McCanless, W L, Danbury.

McCanless, W V, Danbury.

Moore, W J, Watkinsville.

Moir, R F, Francisco.

Neal, J W, Meadow's.

Worth, David, Pilot Mountain.

Phillips, M D, Dalton.

Pringle, Alonzo (dentist), Francisco.

Pringle, F, Elko.

Pierson, Nick, Pilot Mountain.

Shepherd, J M, Dico.

Watkins, Thos T, Culler.

Withers, W W, Withers.

SCHOOLS.

Names, Post Offices and Principals.

Academy, Danbury, S S Oliver.

Academy, Walnut Cove, Miss Wright.

STOKES COUNTY.

Academy, Westfield, ——.
Academy, Germanton, W B Harris.
Dalton Institute, Dalton, W A Flynn.
High School, Culler, Prof. Ball.
Institute, Germanton, J B Woodruff.
Institute, Mt'n View, W T Chilton.
Presbyterian Mission School, Elko.
Public schools—whitte, 66; colored, 22.

NEWSPAPERS.

Reporter, Danbury (Dem. weekly), N
M Pepper, editor and prop.
N C Voice, Culler (prohibition weekly),
W C Phillips, editor and prop.

FARMERS.

Names and Post Offices.

Big Creek—A J Collins, S H Durham, Joe France, J J France, W H H Nunn, Joe Nunn, P Pearce, Geo Pearce, J E Simmons, Jno Smith, J H Wright.
Brown Mountain—T J Boze, J A Covington, W R Covington, Burrel East, J B George, W R Hare, J F Hare, A H Martin, Jno Morefield, P R Nelson, W H Nunn, S P Simmons, W J Simmons, W A Smith.
Campbell—H C Lackey, Robt Lawson, Moses Lawson, J M Burge, R M Campbell, W L Campbell, J A Corn, Arch Fry, G R Fry, Powel Rhodes, A C Rhodes, J B Tucker.
Culler—Abel Edwards, J D Gordon, W M Gordon, J Mat Gordon, J G Gordon, J G Jones, T M Lawson, Levi Watson, V G Watson.
Danbury—J P Allen, J H Alley, Lenn Alley, F M Baker, J W Baker, A P Baker, J H Covington, H W Covington, T J Davis, W H Flinchman, Jas Flinchman, R L Hartman, J H Hart, J W Heathe, Mrs Sallie Hill, H M Joyce, A H Joyce, R P Joyce, W A King, Robt Mabre, J T Malre, W V McCauless, W L McCauless, J P Nelson, J A Pepper, A M Stack, J H Stewart, J S Taylor, Sam'l Westmoreland, A J White, L J Young.
Dan River—J C Clark, G W Farris, A J Flippin, J C Flippin, John Flippin, Geo Jessup, J E Jessup, W S Jessup, Jesse Owens, Thos Rogers, Geo Rogers, Gus Simmons, P E Slate, W L Smith, Garland Smith, Joshua Smith, J E Stuart, J A Tillery.
Dalton—H C Coe, D N Dalton, Wm Edwards, M A Edwards, D J Edwards, H C Gitson, M D Ham, J H Ham, J W Hauser, J T Meadows, S L Meadows, P Oliver, J Y Phillips, Matthew Phillips, J M Rutledge, J W Rutledge, W J Shultz, Chas Snider, W M Watts.

STOKES COUNTY.

Delk—Raleigh Brian, J P Covington, S P Gordon, Jas Lynch, J P Lynch, J H Mitchell, F W Owen, Jas Slaughter, J P Slaughter, W H Slaughter, Squire Venable, T M Venable, H Venable.
Dico—J F Foddrill, C C Foddrill, T J Mickolson, C L Sheppard, J T Sheppard, J A Sheppard, J M Sheppard, Kelly Sisk, J S Smith.
Dillard—P H Carter, C T Duggins, G T Dunlap, J M Fogg, J L Freeman, J W Johnson, J M Mitchell, W A Mitchell, M T Mitchell, J G H Mitchell, R W Simpson, W C Wilson.
Elko—G W Merritt, M L Merritt, J L Merritt, Jas Pierson, F Pringle, Thos Tillery, A J Tillery, H P Watkins, D S Watkins, W S Watkins.
Five Forks—G G Boles, T F Newsom, H T Newsom, J C Newsom, Wm Newsom.
Francisco—C W Blancett, S M Blancett, W H Collins, A D Dodd, J S Flippin, Wm France, Galean France, R W George, Thomas Hill, Nat Hill, A H Joyce, Henry Laurence, Wm Leake, P J Leake, Jos A Leake, Dr R F Moir, R H L Smith, Milton Smith, R E Smith, Dave Smith, Thos Smith.
Germanton—W D Browder, W A Chaffin, H B Golding, W W Hampton, M H Ligon, H A Morris, G W Newsom, R F Petree, R J Petree, W G Rutledge, J G Tuttle, W B Tuttle, Jas M Tuttle, W E Willis.
Hard Bank—W R Bennett, G H Fogg, Davis Fogg, J H Fogg, Julius Lawson, G B Lawson, M A Lawson, W P Nelson, W A Nelson, G W Smith.
Hilltop—T M Baker, W A Caudle, J W Caudle, R C Fowler, J W Fowler, W T Fowler, W T Johnson, a L Johnson, A Lewis, Geo D Turner, F L Tuttle, J F Webster, G M White.
Jewel—W T Bohannon, D K Marbe, M V Mabre, J M Mabre, Joe Martin, D B Mebe, T H Priddy, J J Priddy, G T Priddy, H H Reid, R L Rhodes, R W Shelton, W R Shelton, J H Stephens, J M Stevens, Lewis Taylor, Jas Young.
Kiger—J O Burnett, J H Carroll, H W Carroll, J T Carroll, W H Carroll, Gideon Ferguson, M W Holland, C W Holland, H R Holland, Joe A Neal, S L Rowell, R L Stuart, Irvin Tedder, J E Tedder, A G Tuttle.
King—Stephen Campbell, Sanders Fulk, R G Fulk, B Carringer, S M Goff, L S Grabbs, Sanders Green, J M Kiser, Ed Kiser, Samuel Kiser, Wm M Loyde, J S D Pulliam, S R Slate.
Meadows—S C Hicks, J D Hicks, J D Lawson, Thomas Martin, John Neal, J M Neal, W Neal, F E Nelson, W P

37

STOKES COUNTY.

Sands, Peter Smith, J C Thornburg, J H Tuttle.

Mizpah—J D Barr, J T Bates, Nat Bates, M M Bennett, G A Carroll, E H Cramer, Martin Fuller, V T Hartgrove, Wm H Kiser Daniel Kiser, H W Kiser, J W Kurfees, T E Petree, W A Petree, J E Slate, J F Slate, A J T Tuttle.

Neatman—A F Darnell, J H Darnell, H M Gibson, Jack Golding, W Y Gordan, H C O Hall, L J Kiser, P R Kiser, W G Meadows, W T Redman, M D Sizemore, J A Southern, H C Southern, J F Southern, J G Southern, Jas Tillotson.

Pine Hall—L W Anderson, A R Bennett, J R Blackwell, L W Blackwell, W M Chisman, J P Dalton, G F Daniel, C W Flinn, Jerry Martin, J S Tillotson, D H Tillotson, J C Tuttle, Z L Wall, A J Wall, E S Withers.

Prestonville—L J Duncan, W L Follin, T J Gunn, A J Gunn, Jno Gunn, B F Hawkins, L W Martin, T B Martin, Sam'l Martin, M F Martin, J M Perguson, John Ward, E L Wilkins.

Quaker Gap—R H Bennett, J A Benner, Sr, J A Bennett, Jr, R R Boyles, C J Carroll, J M Deaton, J H Ferguson, W L Hall, W J Johnson, J T Johnson, W W Johnson, Tip Johnson, G L Smith, D E Tuttle, W R Tuttle.

Red Shoals—W J Adkins, J W Davis, J N Losby, C W McAnally, Jno Pierson, J M Pitzer, A J Smith, J D Smith.

Sandy Ridge—A L Alley, J A Amos, G W Andrews, H H Brown, C W Ferguson, C H Ferguson, J Q S Hall, M L Hutcherson, Peter Hutcherson, J W Hylton, J L Joyce, J A Martin, B P Tillery, Lem Ziglar.

Slate—R A Bennett, P O Bennett, A M Boyles, W H Boyles, J O Boyles, R G Gentry, J B Gentry, J H Gibson, J H Grovill, C H Lunford, J W Marsh,

T B Smith, J E Smith, W L Smith, D F Tillotson, J W Wall.

Smith—John Aron, P F Hall, J F Hall, R B Hart, Wm Hart, R L Lockey, W M Moore, F L Moore, J M New, P F Overby, B A Overby, C W Sands, S U Shelton, Jr, C C Smith.

Walnut Cove—M R Banner, James Barker, Washington Barker, Jack Baver, J Blackburn, W N Blackburn, J M Early, G Flynt, D Fulp, S Fulp, J Fulton, W Fulton, P Fulton, Joel H Fulton, Jacob Fulton, W H Gentry, C W Glidewell, Gideon George, P W Hairston's heirs, C Hairston, B Heath, Jas Hicks, L Isom, S Isom, Dr A G Jones, Dr W A Lash, G W Lashley, G L Lewis, J M Linevllie, J E Marshall, Jerry Martin, John Martin, W C Matthews, S L Montgomery, Wm Morefield, Isaac Neal, Caleb Neal, S C Pierson, D Poindexter, F Redmond, Joe Redmond, J L Redmond, P Samuel, Jerry Smith, John Solomon, Rufus Southern, F J Tuttle, Caleb Tuttle, J G Tuttle, John Tuttle, W L Vaughan, W S Vaughan, E R Voss, P Young, John Young, H Young.

Watkinsville—A J Brown, John Corn, G W Corn, John Lester, B J Martin, W J Moore, Winston Newman, Stephen Poor, Joel Rhodes, John Shelton, H W Shelton, Hiram Smith, D P Watkins, D R Webster.

Westfield—Jerry Beasley, S P Christian, C T Christian, J M Dearman, Jno H Jessup, S M Jessup, J H Lowe, W W T Daniel, Ed Payne, Has Payne, C W Simmons, A Tillery.

Wilson's Store—R A Brown, G T Green, Wm Hall, Geo Lewis, Abram Lewis, M T Meadows, Chas H Meadows, B F Pullian, I G Ross, J M Smith, Sidney Smith, W H Smith, W H Slate, J C Southern, F G Southern, H M Southern, J D Tatum, Thos E Tillotson, M Vaughn, J G White, D E White.

SURRY COUNTY.

AREA, 500 SQUARE MILES.

POPULATION, 19,281; White 16,926, Colored 2,355.

SURRY COUNTY was formed in 1770, from Rowan county. It derives its name from Surry county in the south of England. Its name is Saxon and signifies "the South river."

DOBSON, the county seat, is 135 miles northwest of Raleigh. Population, 175

Surface— Hilly and mountainous; traversed by beautiful mountain streams, forming numerous water-powers and a scenery rarely, if ever, surpassed for beauty and grandeur. The Pilot Mountain and other places in this county are much resorted to in the summer by pleasure-seekers.

Staples—Wheat, corn, tobacco, oats, rye, fruits and live stock.

Fruits — Apples, peaches, pears, plums, cherries, berries, and other small fruits.

Timbers—Pine, oak, chestnut, poplar, hickory, walnut, locust and wild cherry.

Minerals—Lead, coal, mica, iron, manganese, asbestos, with one sulphur and three iron springs.

TOWNS AND POST OFFICES.

	POP.		POP.
Alberty,	—	Meigg's,	—
Ash Hill,	—	Moses,	—
Belo,	—	Mosley,	—
Bliss,	100	Mt Airy,	900
Brim,	—	Pirch,	—
Chatham,	—	Pilot Mountain,	85
Cody,	—	Pine Ridge,	30
Copeland,	30	Rockford,	80
Crutchfield,	—	Round Peak,	35
Dale,	—	Rush,	125
Deron,	—	Samuel,	—
Devotion,	—	Shelton,	—
Dobson (c h),	175	Shoals,	—
Edwardsville,	25	Siloam,	25
Elkin,	750	State Road,	30
Flat Shoal,	30	Stony Knoll,	—
Forge,	—	Stony Ridge,	70
Good Spring,	25	Turner's	
Harrellton,	—	Mountain,	—
Haystack,	25	Venable,	25
Kapp's Mill,	80	Wesley,	—
Ladonia,	—	Westfield,	—
Laurel Bluff,	—	White Plains,	85
Lowgap,	35		

COUNTY OFFICERS.

Clerk Superior Court—W W Hampton.

Commissioners—J A Farks, J J Burrus, A C Franklin.

Coroner— —— Hutchens.

Register of Deeds—C H Haynes.

Sheriff—J A Adams.

Solicitor 9th District—M L Mott.

Surveyor—Vestal Taylor.

Treasurer—J A Adams.

County Examiner—J B Sparger.

COURTS.

Second Monday after first Monday in March, and fifth Monday after first Monday in September.

TOWN OFFICERS.

DOBSON—*Mayor*, J A Stone. *Commissioners*—J C Dodson, G O Key, Job Hiatt. *Town Clerk and Treasurer*, J C Dodson.

ELKIN—*Mayor*, Dr J W Ring. *Commissioners*, J S Bell, A G Click, H G Chatham, G M Burcham, C M King. *Clerk and Treasurer*, W B Bell. *Constable*, Rev Braxton Woodruff.

TOWNSHIPS AND MAGISTRATES.

Bryan—C C Cockerbun, J H Thompson (Dobson).

Dobson—A N Freeman, G M Jervis (Dobson).

Eldora—W A Atkinson, D M Johnson (Dobson).

Franklin—W B Nixon, Riley Barker (Dobson).

Hotel—John C Hart, John S Bell (Dobson).

Marsh—J S Jones, J J Setliff.

Mt Airy—Sam L Gilmer, Albert L Banker, Alex J Thompson (Mt Airy).

Pilot—W E Stone, W S Redman (Pilot Mountain)

Rockford—D D McKeoghan, W F Sprinkle (Rockford),

Siloam—A P Whitaker, H W Stanford.

Stewart's Creek—G L Atkins, J F Miller.

Westfield—J H Inman, Jos White (Dobson).

CHURCHES.

Names, Post Offices, Pastors and Denom

BAPTIST.

Antioch—Mt Airy, J H Lewellyn

SURRY COUNTY.

Cadar Hill—Pilot Mountain, A M Denny.
Church—Pilot Mountain. S H Loftin.
Church—Dobson, J P Griffith.
Church—White Plains, J H Berner.
Church—Mt Airy, N L Young (col).
Church—Elkin, W R Bradshaw.
Church—Mt Airy, Joseph Lambeth.
Church—Ronda, W R Bradshaw.
Holly Springs—Pinnacle.
Stone Mountain—Pilot Mountain.
Sulphur Springs—Pilot Mountain.
Volunteer—Pilot Mountain.

PRIMITIVE BAPTIST.

Centre— ——, James Draughan.
Church—Round Peak.
Church—Pilot Mountain, G O Key.
Coddle Creek— ——. N Alberty.
Flat Top— ——, T J Lawson.
Fish River— ——, T J Lawson.
Mitchell's River— ——, T J Lawson.
Slate Road—.
Snow Creek—.
Stuart's Creek—Mt Airy, J Draughan.
White Oak—Mt Airy.

METHODIST.

Church—Rockford, E W Dixon.
Church—Siloam, E W Dixon.
Church—Ronda, S P Douglass.
Church—Mt Airy, —— Worth.
Church—Jonesville, W R Sherrill.
Church—Mt Airy.
Church—Elkin, W L Sherrill.
Church (col.)—Elkin, J W Jones.
Grassy Creek—Elkin, E W Dixon.
Hebron—Hay Stack, E W Dixon.
Hill's— Pilot Mountain, Will Needham.
Maple Springs—Elkin, E W Dixon.
New Hope—Pilot Mountain.

PRESBYTERIAN.

Church—Pilot Mountain, C B Ward (colored).
Church (col.)—Elkin. C B Ward.
Church—Elkin, C W Robinson.
Second—Mt Airy, A B Lawrence (col).

LUTHERAN.

Church—Elkin, W A Lutz.

MINISTERS RESIDENT.

Names, Post Offices and Denom.

BAPTIST

Berner, William, Mt Airy.
Haymore, C C, Mt Airy.
Key, G O, Pilot Mountain.
Key, Russell, Pilot Mountain.
Lewellyn, J H, Dobson.

PRIMITIVE BAPTIST.

Alberty, Nathan, Dobson.
Burcham, G M, Elkin.

SURRY COUNTY.

Denny, C B. Pilot Mountain.
Denny, G, Pilot Mountain.
Denny, A M, Pilot Mountain.
Harbor, Green, Dobson.
Lawson. T J. Edwardsville.
Laffoone, W J, Elkin.
Mathis, B, Elkin.
Rollins, B F, Elkin.
Woodruff, B, Elkin.

METHODIST.

Barnett. W R. Presiding Elder.
George, D S, Elkin.
Holcomb, Dr D F. Rockford.
Needham, James, Bliss.
Needham, Jesse, Bliss.

PRESBYTERIAN.

Laurence, A B (col.). Mt Airy.

CHRISTIAN.

Sanders, R T, Mt Airy.

HOTELS AND BOARDING HOUSES.

Names, Post Offices and Proprietors.

Bonner House, Mt Airy, Mrs Kate Bonner.
Boarding, Rockford, J G Burrus.
Boarding, Mt Airy, Dr W S Tayloe.
Boarding, Mt Airy, —— Stewart.
Boarding. Mt Airy, James Schaub.
Boarding, Mt Airy, W B Shelton.
Boarding, Mt Airy, C W Lewis.
Boarding, Elkin, C H Gwyn.
Boarding, Elkin, Mrs J Minish.
Boarding, Bliss, James Needham.
Boarding, Bliss, B F Davis.
Boarding, Pilot Mountain, John Flippin.
Hotel Lancaster. Pilot Mountain, Mrs Lancaster.
Hotel Central, Pilot Mt'n, J S Green.
Hotel, Stony Ridge, McD Boyd.
Hotel, Dobson, L J Norman.
Hotel, Pilot Mountain, Daniel Marion.
Hotel, Mt Airy, R A Tatten.
Hotel, Mt Airy, J K Reylonds.
Hotel, Dobson, H Snow and J C Cooper.
Mt Airy White Sulphur Springs, Mt Airy, Rufus Roberts.
Worth, D W, Pilot Mt, prop Mineral Springs.

LAWYERS.

Names and Post Offices.

Carter. W F, Mt Airy.
Dobson, J H. Rockford.
Folger, T W, Dobson.
Graves, S P. Mt Airy.
Haymore, R L, Mt Airy.
Hendren J F, Elkin.
Lewellyn. J R, Dobson.
Reece, Lewellyn, Dobson.

SURRY COUNTY.

MANUFACTORIES.

Kinds, Post Offices and Proprietors.

Blacksmithing and wheelwrighting, Pine Ridge, B B Ziglar.

Blacksmithing and wheelwrighting, Dobson, David Snow.

Blacksmithing and wheelwrighting, Bliss, Wm Jones.

Blacksmithing and wheelwrighting, State Road, Wm Carter.

Blacksmithing and wheelwrighting, Stony Ridge, J M Barber.

Blacksmithing and wheelwrighting, Elkin. Aquilla Bates.

Blacksmithing and wheelwrighting, State Road, L H Carter.

Brick, Pilot Mount, Wright & Valentine.

Brick, Pilot Mount, Joseph Bennett & Son.

Building and contracting, Elkin, L H Carter.

Building and contracting, Bliss, Noah Welch.

Building and contracting, Bliss, Wm. Jones.

Building and contracting, Bliss, Jesse James.

Building and contracting, Bliss, Henry James.

Building and contracting, Pine Ridge, S P Freeman.

Building and contracting, Rockford, E A Beele.

Building and contracting, Rockford, A Davenport.

Building and contracting, Rockford, N W Collins.

Building and contracting, Dobson, Sam Bethel.

Building and contracting, Mt Airy. L J Burge.

Building and contracting, Mt Airy, Rufus Roberts.

Building and contracting, Mt Airy, W H Belton.

Boxes, Mt Airy, Sparger Bros.

Cigars, Mt Airy, J F L Armfield.

Coopering, Rockford, Peter McCormick.

Coopering, Rockford, D N Crowder.

Cotton and woolen mills, Mount Airy (Alpine), Moore & Moore.

Cotton plaid mill, Mt Airy (Laurel Bluff), Alex Thompson.

Cotton mill, Elkin, Elkin Manufacturing Co.

Cotton mill, Mt Airy, Alex J Thompson & Co.

Elkin Mfg Co, Elkin; established 1848; Jas Gwyn, pres; R R Gwyn, treas; capital stock, $28,000; daily consumption, 700 pounds; daily produc-

SURRY COUNTY.

tion, 500 yards sheeting, 500 pounds yarn; number spindles, 1,200; number looms, 15; number hands employed, 35.

Elkin Valley Woolen Mills, Elkin Valley; Gwyn & Chatham, props; two sets mills; three self-operating spinning jacks, 240 spindles each; two sets 48-inch cards, etc.

Foundry, Mt Airy, John Spaugh.

Furniture, Elkin, Elkin Furniture Co.

Green Hill Mill, Mt Airy, H W Lilly.

Hamburg Cotton Mills, Mt Airy, Benbow & Gray.

Harness, Mt Airy, A C Dunagan.

Iron, Bliss, W A & Job Hiat.

Iron, Mt Airy, R D Harris & Bro.

Locust pins and brackets, Elkin, Bailey Mfg Co.

Locus pins and brackets, Elkin, R L Hubbard & Co.

Lumber, Elkin, J D Williams.

Lumber, Elkin, T L Gwyn. prop.

Saddles and harness, Bliss, F Gwyn.

Saddles and harness, Rockford, J G Barnes.

Sash, doors and blinds, Mt Airy, Galloway & Belton.

Sash and blinds, Mt Airy, A E Sides.

Surry Knitting Mills, Elkin Valley, G T Roth & Son.

Tannery, Mt Airy, H F Moore.

Tannery, Mt Airy, T F Prather.

Tannery, Mt Airy, Galloway & Co.

Tannery, Dobson, Ransom Wood.

Tannery, Rockford, B D McKaughan.

Tannery, Elkin Valley, J O Chatham.

Tinware and tobacco flues, Mt Airy, L W Seabote.

Tobacco, Stony Ridge, L S Marion.

Tobacco, Rockford, G M Burrns.

Tobacco manufactory, Pilot Mountain, Dodson Bros.

Tobacco manufactory, Pilot Mountain, E J Stone & Son.

Tobacco manufactory, Pilot Mountain, Key, Ginmans & Co.

Tobacco manufactory, Pilot Mountain, Dix, Flippin & Co.

Tobacco manufactory, Pilot Mountain, Daniel Marion.

Tobacco manufactory, Pilot Mountain, Boyles Tobacco Co.

Tobacco manufactory, Pilot Mountain, Redman Bros.

Tobacco manufactory, Pilot Mountain, Forkner, Redman & Son.

Tobacco manufactory, Pilot Mountain, Job Hiatt.

Tobacco, Rockford, H Holyfield.

Tobacco, Mt Airy, Fulton & Bro.

Tobacco, Mt Airy, R L Gwynn & Bro.

Tobacco, Mt Airy, McKinney, Winston & Bro.

Tobacco, Mt Airy, Patterson & Co.

Tobacco, Mt Airy, J D Satterfield.
Tobacco, Mt Airy, Sparger Bros.
Tobacco, Copeland, W R Doss & Co.
Tobacco (plug and twist), Mt Airy, L W Ashby's Sons.
Tobacco (plug and twist), Pilot Mountain, Dodson Bros.
Tobacco (plug and twist), Flat Shoal, G C & G S Welch.
Tobacco (plug and twist), Mt Airy, Fulton & Bro.
Tobacco (plug, twist and smoking), Mt Airy, Sparger Bros.
Tobacco (plug and twist), Pilot Mountain, Daniel Marion.
Tobacco (plug and twist), Mt Airy, G C Welch.
Tobacco (plug and twist), Mt Airy, W McKinney & Bro.
Tobacco (plug and twist), Mt Airy, R L Gwyn.
Tobacco (plug and twist), Mt Airy, Prather & Whitlock.
Tobacco (plug and twist), Mt Airy, J D Satterfield.
Wagons, Pilot Mountain, J L O'Neal.
Wagons and buggies, Pilot Mountain, J F Kirkman.
Wagons, Mt Airy, James Schoub.
Wagons, White Plains, J F & F E Marshall.
Wagons, White Plains, Marshall Bros.
Wagon shop, Mt Airy, James Deatherage.
Woolen factory, Mt Airy, W A Moore.
Woolen mill, Mt Airy, Albert Allred.

MERCHANTS AND TRADESMEN.

Names, Post Offices, Lines of Business.

ASH HILL.
Johnson, J M,   G S
BELO.
Key, L J,   G S
Perkins, W C,   G S
Watson, J M,   G S
BLISS.
Davis & Mitchell,   G S
COPELAND.
Doss, W R,   Mfr Tob and G S
DOBSON.
Folger, A R & R G,   G S
Norman & Norman,   G S
Reid, N J,   G S
Samuels, G W & Co,
                       G S and Mfrs Tob
EDWARDSVILLE.
McCann, J M,   G S
ELKIN.
Andrews & King,   G S
Bell, John S,   P M and G S
Bell, W B,   Real Estate

Butner, T M,   Watchmaker
Click & Co,   G S
Chatham, H G & R M,   Real Estate
Cockerham, D J & Son,   G S
Elkin Land Co,   Real Estate
Eidson, O O,   Tinner
Fowler, N W,   G S
Franklin, R G,   Tob Mfr
Galloway, A B,   G S
Hubbard & Roth, Hardw and Printers
King, Mrs C M,   Millinery
King & Greenwood,   ——
Morris, B,
Murray, Mrs B N,   G S
Poindexter, R L,   G S
Ring, Dr J W,   Druggist
Rounsaville, W H,   G S
Smitherman, O L,   G S
Thorp, F & Son,   Stoves and Tinners
Walsh, J F,   Jeweler
Wilmoth, S H,   G S
FLAT SHOAL.
Harrell, A B,   G S and Lumber
Haymore, B E,   G S
FORGE.
Fulp, S N,   Mfr Tob
GOLD SPRING.
Cockerham, C O,   G S
Young, W P & Co,   G S
HAYSTACK.
Hawkas (G W) & Snow,   G S
KAPP'S MILL.
Butner, Kapps & Co,   G S
LITTLE RICHMOND.
Burch, J E & Bro,   G S
LOW GAP.
Parker, A C.   G S
Woodruff, N, & W,   Mail Contractors
MT AIRY.
Allred, J F.   G S
Ashby, Jos W,   Fert and Tob
Belton, Robt,   D G and Gro
Booker, G M,   C S
Burke, W W,   G S
Clarke, W F,   G S
Durham & Poore,   G S
Foy, E C, & Co,   G S
Galloway, R J,   D G
Galloway & Belton,   Lumber
Graves & Co,   Tob Warehouse & Fert
Griffith, Wm M,   G S
Griffith & Smith,   G S
Hadley, L S,   Gro
Harrell, J E,   Gro
Harris, R D, & Bro,   Livery
Houston, D A,   Drugs
Inman & Dean,   G S
Jenkins. J D,   Gro and Notions
Jones, W E, & Son,   Produce
Kapp, E C, & Co,   Gro
McDuffie, N J,   Furniture
Martin, J A,   G S

SURRY COUNTY.

Merritt, W E,	H'd'ware
Moore, R L. & Co,	Jewelers
Mount Airy Jewelry Co.	
Nations, Jas,	Jeweler
Nutt, R G, & Co,	H'd'ware
Pace, S G,	Livery
Paddison, J R,	G S
Patterson. C D, & Co,	G S
Patterson & Johnson,	G S
Prather, J H,	Tannery
Prather, J W,	G S
Pulliam, J A,	Jeweler
Rawley, D A,	G S
Robins, M A,	G S
Satterfield, G A,	G S
Shafer, H,	Produce
Smith, J D,	G S
Spaugh, Jno E,	Foundry
Taylor & Banner,	Drugs
Thomas, H E,	B and S
Thompson, A J,	G S
Totten, R A,	Furniture
Walles & Co,	Clothing
Welch & Worth,	G S
West, Newbill & Co,	Drugs
Wilcox, C A,	B and S
Wrenn, E H,	G S

PILOT MOUNTAIN.

Boyles, V,	G S
Dean, B Y,	Gro
Flensheem, O B,	P M
Harrell, A B,	G S
Hiatt & Needham,	G S
Highfield & Willis,	G S
Hiatt, Job,	Livery
Hill, M L,	Livery
Key, Simmons & Co,	Tob Warehouse
Lewis, J P, & Co,	G S
Lowe, John H,	G S
Marion, Daniel,	G S
Patterson, Chas Z, Depot Agt & Tel Op
Peel, W A,	G S
Smith, Dr J B,	Drugs
Smith, F L,	H'd'ware
Swanson, J S, & Co;	G S
Stevens, Miss Eunice,	Millinery
Stone, E J, & Son,	Tob Warehouse
Venerable, S H,	Gro

ROCKFORD.

Burrus, T G,	Livery
Doss, W R.	
Hamlin & Dobson,	G S
Holcomb, D F, & Co,	G S
Reece, E S,	G S

ROUND PEAK.

Greenwood, J R,	G S

RUSK.

Burch, Wallace & Co,	G S
Kurfees, C F,	G S

SHOALS.

Carmichael, T C,	G S
Martin & Truelove,	G S

SURRY COUNTY.

SILOAM.

Atkinson, S J,	G S
Cundiff, W M,	G S
Flippen, J C,	G S
Marion Bros,	G S
Whitaker, A,	G S
Vestal, Dr W L,	Drugs

STATE ROAD.

Chipman & Wells,	G S
Hanes, J L,	G S
Johnson, Jno D,	G S
Mathis, B,	G S

STONY KNOLL.

McDowell, W M,	G S

STONY RIDGE.

Butner, F A & Co,	G S

WHITE PLAINS.

Jones, J W,	G S
Marshall, J & S E,	G S

TURNER'S MOUNTAIN.

Venerable, J M,	G S

VENABLE.

Dobbins, T A & Stanley,	G S
Snow, B W,	G S

MILLS.

Kinds, Post Offices and Proprietors.

Corn and wheat, Rusk, W V Burch & Co.
Corn and wheat, Rockford, W B Holyfield.
Corn and saw, Dobson, J Moser.
Corn, flour and saw, State Road, L H Carter.
Corn, flour and saw, Rockford, S S Bohannon
Corn, flour and saw, Dobson, Snow & Holton.
Corn and flour, Stony Ridge, W H Schaub.
Corn and flour, Stony Ridge, W A Ashburn.
Corn and flour, Bliss, James Armstrong.
Corn and flour, Bliss, J C Dodson.
Corn and flour, Pine Ridge, J C Beaman.
Corn and flour, Mount Airy, Dan Haymore.
Corn and flour, Elkin, Elkin Manufacturing Co.
Corn and flour, Mount Airy, Alex J Thompson & Co.
Corn and flour, Rockford, J H Holyfield.
Corn and flour, Round Peak, J R Greenwood.
Corn, Edwardsville, C C McMickle & Thompson.
Corn, Hay Stack, James Galyou.

SURRY COUNTY.

Corn, Dobson, J H Lewellyn & Jarvis.
Corn, Venable, C C Holyfield.
Corn, Dobson, Isham Edmonds.
Corn, Low Gap, Dan'l Barker.
Flour, corn and saw, Mt Airy, Moore & Moore.
Flour, corn and saw. Mt Airy, C W Barmer.
Flour, corn and saw, Dobson, R F Mc Guffin.
Flour, corn and saw, Rush, James Axom.
Flour, corn and saw, Mt Airy, A J Thompson & Co.
Flour, corn and saw, Hay Stack, C W Bunker.
Flour and grist, Elkin Valley, Gwyn & Chatham.
Flour and corn, Siloam, S J Atkinson.
Flour, Pilot Mountain, John C Dodson.
Grist and saw, Mt Airy, Alex Thompson.
Grist mill, Mt Airy, Moore & Moore.
Grist, Mt Airy, Benbow & Gray.
Grist, Mt Airy, Albert Allred.
Merchant flour, Elkin Valley, Gwynn & Chatham; products, jeans, cashmeres, blankets, knitting yarns, etc.
Roller mills, Elkin, A & H G Chatham.
Saw, Mt Airy, R L Gwyn & Bro.
Saw, Mt Airy, R R Marshall.
Saw, Mt Airy, L S Siceloff.
Saw, Elkin, John Hurt.
Steam saw, Pilot Mountain, Job Hiatt.
Steam saw, Pilot Mountain, Silas Hill.
Steam saw, Pilot Mountain, Gabriel Denny.
Steam saw, MtAiry, Galloway&Belton.
Steam saw, Pilot Mountain, Giles, Whitaker & Co.
Steam saw, Mt Airy, J A Forkner.

PHYSICIANS.

Names and Post Offices.

Allred, Edward, Mt Airy.
Ashby, Thomas B, Mt Airy.
Banner, C L, Mt Airy.
Flippin, R E L, Pilot Mountain.
Flippin, Samuel, Bliss.
Folger, W C, Dobson.
Holcomb, D F, Rockford.
Hollingsworth, Wm, Mt Airy.
Hollingsworth, John B, Mt Airy.
Hollingsworth, Jos, jr. Mt Airy.
Hollingsworth, Ed, Mt Airy.
Jenkins, W A, Rusk.
Mitchell, T J (dentist), Mt Airy.
Reece, J M, Elkin.

SURRY COUNTY.

Reece, R W (dentist), Elkin.
Ring, J W, Elkin.
Taylor, W S, Mt Airy.
Rierson, N E (dentist), Pilot Mountain.
Smith, J B, Pilot Mountain.
Thompson, K, Low Gap.
Waltz, John R, Dobson.
Wolff, W A, Stony Ridge.
Worth, D W, Bliss.

SCHOOLS.

Names, Post Offices and Principals.

Academy, Elkin, G D Brown.
Female Academy, Elkin, Mrs A B Galloway.
Female Academy, Mt Airy, Miss Lizzie Gilmer.
Male Academy, Mt Airy, R H Skeen.
Male and Female Academy, Mt Airy, L M Lyon.
Trinity Academy, Pilot Mountain, J B Sporger; Miss Lou Case, asst.
Public schools—white, 76; colored, 19.

TEACHERS.

Names and Post Offices.

Galloway, Mrs A B, Elkin.
Gilmer, Lizzie, Mt Airy.
Lyon, L M, Dobson.
Skeen, R H, Mt Airy.

LOCAL CORPORATIONS.

First National Bank, Mt Airy; Thomas Faucette, pres; M L Faucette, cash.
Granite Lodge, No 251, A F & A M, Rockford; time of meeting: Saturday evening on or before full moon.
Mt Airy Lodge, No 107, I O O F, Mt Airy; day of meeting: Thursday.
Pilot Bank and Trust Co: paid up capital, $10,000; W G Dodson, pres; J C Dodson, cash.
Rockford Lodge, No 251, A F & A M, Rockford; time of meeting: Saturday evening on or before full moon.

NEWSPAPERS.

Elkins Times, Elkin (Dem. weekly); W B Bell, editor; Hubbard & Roth, pubs.
Mt Airy News, Mt Airy; W J Boylin, ed and prop.
Yadkin Valley News, Mt Airy; P D Hamer, editor.

SWAIN COUNTY.

AREA 550 SQUARE MILES.

POPULATION, 7,877; White 5,652, Negroes 925, Indians 1,300.

SWAIN COUNTY was formed in 1871 from Mason and Jackson counties, and was named in honor of D. L. Swain, formerly Governor of North Carolina and President of the University.

The atmosphere is salubrious and the climate mild.

The Western North Carolina Railroad runs a distance of forty miles in, and very nearly through the centre, of the county.

Water-power is abundant and scenery fine. This county has 250,000 acres of the finest grazing land in the world.

BRYSON CITY, the county-seat, romantically situated on both sides of the Tuckaseegee river, about thirteen miles above its junction with the Tennessee, is 325 miles from Raleigh. Population, 450.

It was formerly called "Charleston;" was changed to Bryson City by an act of the Legislature, session 1889, in honor of Col. P. D. Bryson, a citizen of Swain county, and for a long time a member of the Legislature.

Surface—Mountainous, and watered by the Tennessee, Tuckaseegee, Nantahala and Ocona Lufty rivers.

Staples—Corn, wheat, oats, rye, buckwheat, tobacco, potatoes, and a variety of vegetables.

Fruits—Apples, peaches, grapes, pears.

Timbers—Walnut, cherry, oak, poplar, pine, birch, beech and ash.

Minerals—Gold, silver, lead, copper, marble, talc, kaolin, iron.

TOWNS AND POST OFFICES.

	POP.		POP.
Almond,	—	Jarrett's,	35
Birdtown,	—	Judson,	—
Bushnell,	—	Medlin,	—
Bryson City (c h),		Needmore,	—
	450	Ocona Lufty,	80
Cherokee,	50	Proctor,	—
Dorsey,	—	Ravens,	—
Forney's Creek,	50	Swain,	—
Governor's Isl'd	—	Wayside,	50
Hewitt's,	—	Whittier,	—

COUNTY OFFICERS.

Clerk Superior Court—I R Snow.
Commissioners—A H Hayes, chm'n.
Register of Deeds—N B Thompson.
Sheriff—J F Teague.

Solicitor 12th District—G A Jones.
Treasurer—D G Fisher.
County Examiner—L Lee Marr.

COURTS.

Fourteenth Monday after the first Monday in March, and eleventh Monday after the first Monday in September.

TOWNSHIPS AND MAGISTRATES.

Charleston—E Everett, M T Battle, A J Parris, P P McLean, G W McCracken, F G Case, Jno Parrish, A J Franklin, D P Ferguson, E Evert (Bryson City).

Forney's Creek—Jno Lester, Martin DeHart, R T Cunningham, A J Hall, J R Bradshaw, W B Cole, J E T Welch, Wm Cogdell (Forney's Creek).

Nantahala—C C Bryson, E C Monteith, N A Dorsey, Chas Calhoun, D M Slagle, R M Wright, W J Tetherow, E F Patterson, A L Clark (Bryson City).

Ocona Lufty—Jas Chambers, John Enloe, A H Haynes, N J Smith, J L Floyd, D H Keener, W H Queen, R P Hyde, S L Monteith, C W Parker, C G Logan (Ocona Lufty).

CHURCHES.

Names, Post Offices and Denom.

BAPTIST.

Birdtown—Quallatown (Jackson co).
Brush Creek—Nantahala.
Cold Springs—Quallatown (Jackson co).
Holly Springs—Forney's Creek.
Lufty—Ocona Lufty.

METHODIST.

Alarka—Ocona Lufty.
Deep Creek—Ocona Lufty.
Lufty—Ocona Lufty.

LAWYERS.

Names and Post Offices.

Bryson, T D, Bryson City.
Fisher, F C, Bryson City.
Fry, A M, Bryson City.
Leatherwood, R L, Bryson City.
Snow, J R, Bryson City.

SWAIN COUNTY.

MANUFACTORIES.

Kinds, Post Offices and Proprietors.

Excelsior Insulator Pin Factory, Bryson City, A B Allison & Co.
Insulator Pins, Bryson City, J W L Arthur.
Insulator Factory, Bryson City, E Everett.
Sash, Door and Blind, Bryson City, Coffin & McDonald.
Tannery, Bryson City, Jno Sutton.
Tannery, Swain, Wm McHan.

MERCHANTS AND TRADESMEN.

Names, Post Offices and Lines of Business.

BRYSON CITY.
Allison, A B, & Oo,   G S
Cline, J W R,   G S
Collins, D K,   G S
Davis, R L,   Drugs
DeHart, Dallas (near).   G S
Ditmore, J H,   H'd'w
Marr, L Lee, & Co,   G S
Simpson, T S,   G S
FAIRFAX.
Hoffman, ——,   G S
FORNEY'S CREEK.
Welch, S N,   G S
JUDSON.
Bryson, C C,   G S
MEDLIN.
Calhoun, A V,   G S
NANTAHALA.
Gibson, S B,   G S
NEEDMORE.
Breedlove & Burnett,   G S
OCONA LUFTY.
Beck, H J,   G S
SOPHIA.
Woodard, J S,   G S
WAYSIDE.
Calhoun, A V,   G S

WHITTIER.

Allison, A B, & Co,   G S
Cooper, S W,   G S
Montieth, G W, & Co,   G S

MINES.

Names, Post Offices and Proprietors.

Talc and Marble, Hewitt's, Richard & Hewitt.

TEACHERS.

Names and Post Offices.

Cooper, Miss Mary, Bushnell.
Cooper, Miss Addie, Whittier.
Davis, W H, Swain.
DeHart, Jas, Swain.
DeHart, Miss A J, Swain.
Hall, R C, Almond.
Humphrey, Prof Robt, Whittier.
Hughes, Prof W H H, Bryson City.
Keener, Miss Sallie, Whittier.
Keener, Miss Emma, Whittier.
Kerlee, Miss Bonnie, Whittier.
Kerlee, Miss Meck, Whittier.
Lowe, C C, Medlin.
McHan, Miss Laura, Whittier.
McHan, Miss Sarah, Whittier.
McHan, Miss Mary, Whittier.
McHan, H M, Needmore.
Raby, Miss Maggie, Whittier.
Seay, Geo W, Bryson City.
Smiley, J M, Needmore.
Smiley, J S, Swain.
Smiley, S B, Swain.
Thomason, R M, Bushnell.
Welch, J T, Needmore.
Woodard, L B, Needmore.

NEWSPAPERS.

Bryson City Times (weekly), Bryson City; R H Pender, ed.
Herald (weekly), Bryson City; Rev Jno S Smiley, ed.

TRANSYLVANIA COUNTY.

AREA, 330 SQUARE MILES.

POPULATION, 5,881; White 5,368, Colored 513.

TRANSYLVANIA COUNTY was formed in 1861, from Henderson and Jackson counties.

BREVARD, the county seat, is 310 miles west of Raleigh, and preserves a name that became distinguished in the Revolution. Population 500.

Surface- A beautiful mountain county, interspersed with beautiful streams, and displaying a scenery rarely surpassed; soil good; well adapted to grasses.

Staples—Corn, wheat, oats, rye, potatoes, cabbage, medicinal herbs and live stock.

Fruits — Apples, peaches, pears, plums, cherries, berries, and other small fruits.

Timbers—Oak, ash, hickory, chestnut, walnut, maple, pine, gum, poplar, locust.

Minerals—Mica, copper, iron, lime, gold, galina, corundum, asbestos, serpentine.

TOWNS AND POST OFFICES.

	POP.		POP.
Balsam Grove,	75	Ecusta,	125
Brevard		Galloway,	50
(C H),	500	Grange,	100
Buck Forest,	50	Hera,	—
Calhoun,	300	Hogback,	60
Carson's		Irvin.	25
Creek,	150	Jeptha,	150
Cedar Mt'n,	50	Loftis,	50
Cherryfield.	150	Montvale,	50
Clotho,	50	Penrose,	125
Davidson's		Tiptop,	40
River,	160	Toledo,	50
East Fork,	75		

COUNTY OFFICERS.

Clerk Superior Court—T H Hampton.
Commissioners—C L Osborn, chm'n; J M Southern, G W Wilson.
Coroner—Dr William Lyday.
Register of Deeds—E S English.
Sheriff—V B McGaha.
Solicitor Ninth District—J S Jones.
Surveyor—P P Orr.
Treasurer—Vance Galloway.
County Examiner—Judson Corn.

TOWN OFFICERS.

BREVARD—*Mayor*, T H Galloway; *Commissioners*, M I Cooper, D A Miller, C C Kilpatrick, R J Pickelsimer and T D England; *Marshal*, J A Marshall.

COURTS.

Fourth Monday after the first Monday in March, and first Monday in September.

TOWNSHIPS AND MAGISTRATES.

Boyd's—E B Clayton, P C Clayton, T R Duncan, J L Gash (Brevard).

Brevard—J J Shipman, M M Shipman, George C Neill, E T Henning, A F English, W L Hume, W C Hamilton (Brevard).

Cathey's Creek—G F Justus, J H Paxton, J M Southern, J H Parton, Geo Southern, G F Moore (Brevard).

Dunn's—T T Loftis, W S Lankford, Wm Maxwell, W H Aiken, Edward Batson (Brevard).

East Fork—J E Galloway, W E Galloway, W N Gillespie, M W Gearrin, E M Whitmore (East Fork).

Gloucester—W P Galloway, Thos Hays, Hansel McCall, T C McCall, M F Galloway (Brevard).

Hogback—S L Sanders, T B Reed, S W Reed, J E Revis, L E Reece, J L Fisher (Hogback Valley).

Little River—J E Merrell, A B Corn, J S Heath, L H Allison, A L Hardin, E W Blythe, Robt Kilpatrick (Brevard).

CHURCHES.

Names, Post Offices and Denominations.

METHODIST.

Church—Brevard, L A Falls.
Church—East Fork, L A Falls.
Conestee—Conestee, L A Falls.
Dividing Ridge—Conestee, L A Falls.
Greenwood—Jeptha, L A Falls.
Oak Grove—Brevard, L A Falls.
Pine Grove—Calhoun, L A Falls.

NORTH. METHODIST.

English Chapel—Ecusta, Wm Ballsow.
Mt Gaha's Chapel—Loftis, Wm Ballow.

BAPTIST.

Blue Ridge—Cedar Mountain, Calvin Hamilton.

TRANSYLVANIA COUNTY.

Carson's Creek—Cedar Mountain, F M Jordan.
Cathey's Creek—Cherry Field, J G Owen.
Church—Brevard, J T Newton.
Church—East Fork, T C Holtsclaw.
Aiken's Chapel—Carson's Creek, F M Jordan.
Little River—Grange, E Allison.
Laurel Creek—Grange, A W Beck.
Macedonia—Balsom Grove, E Allison.
Mt Moriah—Jeptha E Allison.
Rocky Hill—Cedar Mountain, Wm Anderson.
Zion—Jeptha, A J Manly.

PRESBYTERIAN.

Church—Brevard, J L Wicker.
Church—Davidson River, J L Wicker.

EPISCOPAL.

St Philip's—Brevard, A Rooney.

MINISTERS RESIDENT.

Names, Post Offices and Denom.

BAPTIST.

Allison, E, Brevard.
Beck, A W, Penrose.
Chambers, S A, Brevard.
Manly, A J, Cherryfield.
Owen, J C, Jeptha.
Galloway, J E, Galloway.
Hamlin, J M, Brevard.
Jordan, F M, East Fork.
Newton, I T, Brevard.

METHODIST.

Ballew, Wm, Ecusta.
Falls, L A, Brevard.

PRESBYTERIAN.

Wicker, J L, Brevard.

EPISCOPAL.

Rooney, A, Brevard.

HOTELS AND BOARDING HOUSES.

Names, Post Offices and Proprietors.

Boarding, Hogback Valley, H W Miller.
Boarding, Davidson River, Mrs Eli Patton.
Saphire Hotel, Saphire, Geo A Jacobs.
Boarding, Brevard, Mrs J J Shipman.
Boarding, Davidson River, Robt Patton.
Boarding, Balsam Grove, W H Robinson.
Boarding, Grange, W S Ashworth.
Calhoun House, Calhoun, Charles E Wilson.
Central Hotel, Brevard, N McMinn.
Red House, Brevard, Mrs W J De-Treville.
Henning Inn, Brevard, E T Henning.

TRANSYLVANIA COUNTY.

LAWYERS.

Names and Post Offices.

Duckworth, W B, Brevard.
DeTreville, W J, Brevard.
Faulkner, W H, Brevard.
Forsythe, J A, Brevard
Gash, W A, Brevard.
Pless, J W, Brevard.

MANUFACTORIES.

Kinds, Post Offices and Proprietors.

Blacksmithing and wheelwrighting, Cedar Mountain, J S Heath.
Blacksmithing and wheelwrighting, East Fork, C M Gillespie.
Wood-work, East Fork, Thos Galloway.
Blacksmithing and wheelwrighting, Grange, Benj Merrill.
Blacksmithing and wheelwrighting, Brevard, O C Morgan.
Blacksmithing and wheelwrighting, Cherryfield, J M Morgan.
Blacksmithing and wheelwrighting, Cherryfield, C R Dunn.
Brevard Lumber and Mfg Co, Brevard, J A Miller.
Building and contracting, Cedar Mountain, R W Lee.
Building and contracting, East Fork, S H Gillespie.
Building and contracting, Grange, M L Hamilton.
Building and contracting, Cedar Mountain, J S Heath.
Building and contracting, Brevard, J A Miller.
Gun and silversmithing, Brevard, J O Demrid.
Building, Brevard, Kilpatrick Bros.
Building, Brevard, P B Wilson.
Millwrighting, East Fork, B A Gillespie.
Saddles and harness, Brevard, A Aikin and I B Allison.
Tannery, Brevard, D B F Corn.
Wagons, Brevard, S J Tinsley.
Wagons, Grange, Perry Merrell.
Wool-carding, Brevard, P S King.
Wool-carding, Davidson's River, Robt Patton.

MERCHANTS AND TRADESMEN.

Names, Post Offices, Lines of Business.

BALSAM GROVE.
Galloway, Vance,   G S
BREVARD.
Aiken, James (col.),   Barber and Gro
Ashworth, W S,   G S

TRANSYLVANIA COUNTY.

Young, G W, G S
Cooper & Whitmire, Real Estate
Cooper. M D, Livery
Cox, M, Grocer and Barber
Duckworth, Mrs Ella F, G S
Duckworth, J E, Live Stock
England, T D. Gro
Fulkner, W H, Real Estate
Carmichael & Shipman, G S
Gash, Juanita, Millinery
Hamlin, B W, Paint r
Gillespie, M A, Painter
Jones & Aiken, Butchers
Pickl-simer. R J, G S
Orr, M J, Nurseryman
Osborne. W K, Live Stock
Symington, W N, Live Stock
Whitmire Bros, G S
Wood, Thomas, Live Stock
Watson, C E & Co, G S
Waters, T L, Livery
Bell & Blythe, Drugs

CALHOUN.

Beck, A W, Miller
Wilson, C E, G S

CARSON'S CREEK.

Duckworth, J E, G S

CEDAR MOUNTAIN.

McGaha, W, G S

CHERRYFIELD.

Batson & Batson, G S
Erwin, O L, G S

DAVIDSON RIVER.

Ledbetter, I B, G S

ECUSTA.

Deaver, Robert, G S

GALLOWAY'S.

Galloway, J E, G S
Hines, V M, G S

GRANGE.

Zachary & Rogers, G S

IRVIN.

Murrill, S N, G S

JEPTHA.

Gallaway, J D, G S
Zachary & Zachary, G S

PENROSE.

Wilson, W J, G S

TIP TOP.

Reece, L E, G S

MILLS.

Kinds, Post Offices and Proprietors.

Corn. flour and saw, Brevard, P S King.
Corn, flour and saw, Little River (Grange P O). M L Hamilton.

TRANSYLVANIA COUNTY.

Corn and flour, Brevard, G G Neill.
Corn and flour, Hogback, H W Miller.
Corn and flour, East Fork. T Galloway.
Corn and flour, Cherryfield, J M Morgan.
Corn and flour, Jeptha, G H Moore.
Corn and flour, Balsam Grove, W H Robinson.
Corn and flour, Balsom Grove, W R Galloway.
Corn and flour, Davidson's River, R E Patton.
Saw. East Fork, Garren & Holsclaw.
Saw and planing, Cedar Mountain, J S
Saw (steam). Brevard, P B Wilson.
Steam saw, ———, A F Paxton.
Saw, Cherryfield, J M Southern.
Saw, Cedar Mountain, B F Kilpatrick.
The Brevard Roller and Flour Mills, Brevard, F E B Jenkins, supt, owned by the heirs of Mary Hume Breese; capacity, 40 bbls per day.

PHYSICIANS.

Names and Post Offices.

Brooks, Whit, Jeptha.
Cannon, J A, Jeptha.
Fisher, W C, Hogback.
Grimshaw, C. Montvale.
Hunt, C W, Brevard.
King, M M, Brevard.
Lyday, W M. Penrose.
Lyday, Elliot, Penrose.
Morgan, J H, Cherryfield.
Young, G W, Ecusta.

SCHOOLS.

Kinds, Post Offices and Proprietors.

Academy, Brevard.
Academy, Davidson River, D E Ward.
Academy, Grange.
Academy, Zachary.
Public schools—white, 33; colored, 3.

TEACHERS.

Names and Post Offices.

Allison. Luther, Penrose.
Bell, Mrs J L, Brevard.
Brown, Velue, Ecusta.
Corn. Judson. Brevard.
English, D L. Ecusta
Gallamore C M. Brevard.
Galloway, T H, Brevard
Gillespie, Miss Jane. East Fork.
Glazener, Miss M, Brevard.
Glazener, Connie. Jeptha.
Hamlin. J M, Brevard.
Hardin, A L. Cedar Mountain.
Henderson, W B, Tiptop.

TRANSYLVANIA COUNTY.

Henderson, W P, Brevard.
Jenkins, Miss A J, Brevard.
Jordan, Miss Loula, Brevard.
Lyday, G T, Calhoun.
Robinson, Miss Sue, Balsam Grove.
Shipman, Ida, Brevard.
Shipman, Thomas, Brevard.
Waters, Cora, Brevard.
Wilson, Sutton, Penrose.

LOCAL CORPORATIONS.

Bank of Brevard, G H P Cole, pres;
  Zero Nichols, cash; capital, $10,000;
  individual responsibility, $100,000.
National Railway (Branch) Building
  and Loan Association; Thos Wood,
  pres; M L Shipman, sec and treas.
Transylvania Land and Improvement
  Co, Brevard; C W Hunt, pres; J S
  Forsythe, sec and treas; W B Duck-
  worth, atty.

TRANSYLVANIA COUNTY.

Young Men's Business League, Brevard; J A Forsythe, pres; M L Shipman, sec; W P Whitmore, treas.
Dunn's Rock Lodge, No 267, A F and
  A M, Brevard; time of meeting,
  Friday on or before full moon at 2
  o'clock P M.

NEWSPAPERS.

Brevard Hustler, Brevard, M L Ship-
  man, editor.
Sylvan Valley News (Pop. weekly), J
  J Miner, mgr.

FARMERS.

Names and Post Offices.

(Breece Farm), heirs of May Hume
Breese.

S. HUFFMAN,

DEALER IN

Dry Goods, Groceries,

AND

GENERAL MERCHANDISE,

MORGANTON, N. C.

JEROME & WILLIAMS,

Attorneys and Counsellors at Law,

MONROE, N. C.

Collections, Commercial and Corporation Law.

REFERENCES: People's Bank of Monroe; F. H. Wolfe, Clerk Superior
Court; J. W. Bivens, Register of Deeds; J. P. Horn, Sheriff; Heath Hardware
Co.; The English Drug Co.; J. H. Lee and Co.; Heath, Morrow & Co.

TYRRELL COUNTY.

AREA, 320 SQUARE MILES.

POPULATION, 4,225; White 3,000, Colored 1,225.

TYRRELL COUNTY is one of the oldest counties in the State, and one of the original precincts of the Lords Proprietors. It derives its name from Sir John Tyrrell, one of the original owners.

COLUMBIA, the county-seat, is 200 miles east from Raleigh, on the Scuppernong river. Population 250.

Surface—Low, level, and much of it swampy; soil generally good and very productive when well drained and cultivated.

Staples—Corn, cotton, shingles lumber, rice and fish.

Fruits—Apples, grapes, figs, pears, peaches, melons, etc.

Timbers—Pine, oak, juniper, gum, cypress, maple, poplar, etc.

TOWNS AND POST OFFICES.

	POP.		POP.
Bay,	—	Fort Landing,	130
Columbia		Gudger,	—
(C H),	250	Gum Neck,	160

COUNTY OFFICERS.

Clerk Superior Court—T D Holmes.
Commissioners—R I Hassell, chm'n.
Register of Deeds—D O Newburry.
Sheriff—A W Owens.
Solicitor 1st District—W J Leary.
Treasurer—J C Meekins, sr.
County Examiner—Arthur Spruill.

COURTS.

Eighth Monday after the first Monday in March, and eighth Monday after the first Monday in September.

TOWNSHIPS AND MAGISTRATES.

Names and Post Offices.

Alligator—J P Alexander, J W Horvett, E R Spruill, W B Alexander, J R Wright, J A Holmes, W H Bissnight, W W Belanga, B F Pritchett (Columbia).

Columbia—W S Davenport, Jos G Brickhouse, J E Swain, W W Norman, H W Liverman, D O Newberry, J C Wilkins, Wm Bodwell, Benj J West, E Spruill, J S Snell, Ellsburg Sexton (Columbia).

Gum Neck—W J Cahoon, J A Liverman, B S Midgett, Chas W Hussey, N C Spencer, T J Weatherly, J L Brickhouse, W E Cahoon, R J Armstrong, Arthur Leslie (Gum Neck).

Scuppernong—T S Downing, J B Walker, David Alexander, Charles Davenport, S A Belanga, S D Wynne, M D L Newberry, J K P Owens (Columbia).

South Fork—J B Spruill, D S Mann, Wm Woodley, S C Patrick (Columbia).

CHURCHES.

Names, Post Offices and Denominations.

BAPTIST.

Alligator—Fort Landing.
Church—Columbia.
Rider's Creek—Columbia.
Sound Side—Columbia.

METHODIST.

Ebenezer—Columbia.
Scuppernong—Bay.
Wesley Chapel—Fort Landing.

FREE.

Albemarle—Bay.
Gum Neck—Columbia.

DISCIPLES OF CHRIST.

Rider's Creek—Columbia.

EPISCOPAL.

St Andrew's—Columbia.

LAWYERS.

Names and Post Offices.

Leigh, J B, Columbia.
Majette, M, Columbia.
Spruill, Arthur, Columbia.

MANUFACTORIES.

Kinds, Post Offices and Proprietors.

Coachmaking, Columbia, D A Sample.
Wagon works, Columbia, D A Sample.

MERCHANTS AND TRADESMEN.

Name, Post Office, and Line of Business.

BAY.

Swain, T W.   Fert

TYRRELL COUNTY.

COLUMBIA.

Bateman, Chas,	G S
Brickhouse, Warren,	G S
Cooper, Mrs E C,	G S
Davenport, J S, & Co,	G S
Howell, J W,	G S
Liverman, W E,	G S
McClees, H W,	G S
McClees, J J,	G S
Marcus, A,	G S
Meekins, J C, sr,	G S
Norman, Mrs S J,	Millinery
Rhodes, Simeon,	G S
Spruill & Bro,	G S
Spruill, A E,	G S
Swan, Mrs S J,	Milliner
Swain & Spencer,	G S
Walker, A L & Co,	G S
Walker, Mrs R C,	G S

FORT LANDING.

Alexander, J P,	G S
Combs, J B,	G S
Leigh, J B & S,	G S
Spruill & Bro,	G S

GUDGER.

Basnight, C C,	G S
Howett, J W,	G S

GUM NECK.

Armstrong, R J,	G S
Cahoon, W A,	G S
Johnson, C R,	G S
Langley, W B,	G S
White & Liverman,	G S

MILLS.

Kinds, Post Offices and Proprietors.

Grist and saw, Columbia, R I Hassell.
Mill, Columbia, W E Liverman.
Saw and grist, Fort Landing, J B Combs.
Saw, Gum Neck, D B Armstrong.

UNION COUNTY.

AREA, 640 SQUARE MILES.

POPULATION, 21,259; White 15,712, Colored 5,547.

UNION COUNTY was formed in 1842, from Anson and Mecklenburg counties.

MONROE, the county seat, is 152 miles southwest from Raleigh, and was named in honor of James Monroe, the fifth President of the United States. Population 3,500.

Surface—Uneven, and in places mountainous; water power plenty, scenery fine, lands good.

Staples—Wheat, corn, cotton, rye, oats, fruits and live-stock.

Fruits — Apples, peaches, grapes, pears, melons and berries.

Timbers — Pine, oak, hickory, ash and poplar.

Minerals—Gold.

TOWNS AND POST OFFICES.

	POP.		POP.
Albans,	—	Oak Grove,	40
Altan,	—	Olive Branch,	200
Ames,	40	Peortith,	40
Baucom's,	—	Potter,	25
Brief,	—	Price's Mill,	40
Brown Creek,	40	Raywood,	45
Cleone,	25	Reuben,	—
Coburn's Store,	45	Richardson's	
Euto,	20	Creek,	65
Faulk,	—	Rock Rest,	50
Gibraltar,	50	Rushing,	50
Heath,	—	Sincerity,	—
Honey,	—	Stevens,	52
Hope,	25	Unionville,	250
Indian Trial,	100	Vann,	—
Judith,	—	Walkerville,	65
Lane's Creek,	65	Walkup,	500
Long's Store,	50	Wardlaw,	—
Love's Level,	25	Waterloo,	—
McCain's,	—	Waxhaw,	—
Monroe (c h),	3,500	Winchester,	20
Marshville,	525	Wolfsville,	70
Morgan's Mills,	50	Zoar,	40
Negrohead,	25		

COUNTY OFFICERS.

Clerk Superior Court—F H Wolfe.
Deputy Clerk—S S Wolfe.
Commissioners—R B Redwine, chm'n; A W Heath, W L Howie.
Coroner—H C Moore.
Register of Deeds—J W Bivens.
Sheriff—J P Horn.
Solicitor 11th District—J L Webb.
Standard Keeper—S S S McCauley.
Surveyor—M D L Biggers.

Treasurer—James McNeely.
County Examiner—J H Boyte.
County Physician—Dr J E Ashcraft.

COURTS.

Fifth Monday before the first Monday in March; second Monday before the first Monday in September.

TOWN OFFICERS.

MONROE—*Mayor*, Dr J W Stephenson; *Commissioners*, H A Shute, J M Blair, B A Morrow, S W Parham; *Clerk*, J M Stewart; *Treasurer*, J M Stewart; *Marshal*, N S Ogburn.

WAXHAW—*Mayor*, —— Hines; *Clerk and Treasurer*, J M Morrow.

TOWNSHIPS AND MAGISTRATES.

Bu'ord—J G Doster, S A Latham, D A Outen (Monroe), Jerre C Laney (Altan), Geo M Laney (Hope), P P W Plyler, H L Yarbrough (Mt Prospect).

Goose Creek—I A Clontz, C J Braswell (Sincerity), E J Griffin, W G Long (Unionville), A W McManus (Clear Creek, F F Duncan, H L Crowell, (Coburn Store, J C Benton (Monroe).

Jackson—J W Price, Henry McWhorter, S J Richardson, H M Williams (Waxhaw), R T Sisstare (Walkup), Wm McWhorter (Wilson's Store).

Lane's Creek—J G Trull (Beaver Dam), J T Lee, J S Little, H M Sherrin (Monroe), B F Parker (Lane's Cr'k), F P Huntley (Rushing). J J Cox (Brown's Creek).

Marshville—H F Davis, J C Morgan, A R Edwards (Marshville), A J Brooks (Richardson's Creek), J H Collins, A W Bass (Marshville).

Monroe—M B Simpson (Richardson's Creek), H C Moore. S S S McCauley, C N Simpson, W G McBride (Ames), A M Crowell, J D A Secrest, R L Helms, M L Floyd (Monroe).

New Salem — W H Austin, J S Smith, T C Braswell (Euto), H M Baucom, J F Bunn (Olive Branch), W A Austin (Gibraltar), P J C Efrid (Morgan's Mill).

Sandy Ridge—H L Price, J H Winchester, W W Reid, J N Price (Price's Mill), Jno L Porter (Waxhax), G W

38

UNION COUNTY.

Sutton, W M Parks, C C McIlwaine (Poortith).
Vance—J E Broom, W L Cuthbertson, F M Yandle, J M Harkey, J W Conder, P C Stinson (Indian Trail), R L Stewart (Unionville).

CHURCHES.

Names, Post Offices, Pastors and Denom.

METHODIST.

Bethel—Stout.
Bethlehem—Mt Prospect.
Centre—Monroe.
Church—Monroe.
Church—Waxhaw.
Gilboa—Marshville.
Mill Grove—Coburn's Store.
Oak Grove—Monroe.
Pleasant Grove—Winchester.
Prospect—Mt Prospect.
Rehobeth—Cureton's Store (South Carolina).
Sandy Ridge—Matthews (Mecklenburg co).
Shiloh—Monroe.
Smyrna—Wolf Pond.
Trinity—Hope.
Union—Wolfsville.
Wesley Chapel—Price's Mill.
Zion—Love's Level.

METHODIST PROTESTANT.

Antioch—Matthews.
Ebenezer—Raywood.
Tabernacle—Raywood.

BAPTIST.

Bethel—Marshville, J A Bivens.
Church—Monroe, H C Moore.
Church—Waxhaw, A B Caudle.
Church (col)—Monroe, T A Lomax.
Church—Marshville, J L Bennett.
Meadow Branch—Monroe, J B Richardson.
Olive Branch—D A Snider.
Shiloh—Monroe, R H Jones.

PRESBYTERIAN.

Bethlehem—Oak Grove, H M Dixon.
Church—Waxhax, W K Boggs.
Church—Monroe, H M Dixon.

EPISCOPAL.

St Paul's—Monroe, F H Hilliard.

LUTHERAN.

Emanuel—Oak Grove, S S Rahn.

A. M. E. ZION.

Church—Coburn's Store, J A Barber.
Church—Waxhaw, C W Simmons.
Mt Calvary—Monroe, W J Sides.
Union Springs—Monroe, C M Mason.

UNION COUNTY.

MINISTERS RESIDENT.

Names, Post Offices and Denominations.

METHODIST.

Ware, W R. Monroe.
West, —— Monroe.

BAPTIST.

Bennett, J L, Beaver Dam.
Bivens, J A, Beaver Dam.
Davis, A C, Love's Level.
Latta, A T, Monroe.
Moore, H C, Monroe.
Snyder, D A, Beaver Dam.

PRESBYTERIAN.

Dixon, H M, Monroe.
Hampton, S W, Monroe.

LUTHERAN.

Rahn, S S, Monroe.

EPISCOPAL.

Hilliard, F W, Monroe.

A. M. E. ZION.

Mason, C M, Monroe.
Sides, W J. Monroe.
Simmons, C W (col), Waxhaw.

HOTELS AND BOARDING HOUSES.

Names, Post Offices and Proprietors.

Boarding, Monroe, F Price.
Boarding, Monroe, H Shute.
Boarding, Monroe, Mrs Lingle.
Boarding, Monroe, N S Ogburn.
Boarding, Monroe, H Howie.
Boarding, Monroe, Mrs D J Harkey.
Boarding, Monroe, Jas Caldwell.
Hotel, Waxhaw, Mrs Nevens.
Ogburn House, Monroe, W C Ogburn.
Railroad Hotel, Monroe, Gresham & Jamison.
Stewart House, Monro, J C Fletcher.

LAWYERS.

Names and Post Offices.

Adams (H B), Covington (D A) & Redwire (R B). Monroe.
Armfield, Frank, Monroe.
Hilliard, Iredell, Monroe.
Jerome & Williams, Monroe.
Whitaker, F H, jr, Monroe.

MANUFACTORIES.

Kinds, Proprietors and Post Offices.

Blacksmithing and wheelwrighting, Stout, J T Haywood.
Blacksmithing and wheelwrighting, Raywood, A Griffin.

UNION COUNTY.

Blacksmithing and wheelwrighting, Monroe, E M Griffin.
Blacksmithing and wheelwrighting, Olive Branch, W A Gaddy.
Blacksmithing and wheelwrighting, Olive Branch, C M Reed.
Blacksmithing and wheelwrighting, Price's Mill, J D Davis.
Boots and shoes, Brown Creek, J S Little.
Boots and shoes, Brown Creek, J E Hinson.
Boots, shoes and harness, Monroe, Jas R Simpson.
Brick, Monroe, J Shute & Son.
Building and contracting, Stout. B F Fincher.
Canning, Monroe, J H Benton.
Canning, Love's Level, L L Love & Son.
Carriages, Monroe, E M Griffin.
Cotton-ginning (steam), Marshville, Marsh & Bailey.
Cotton-ginning (steam), Wolf Pond, Waters & Harris.
Cotton ginning (steam), Morgan's Mills, D R Pusser.
Cotton-ginning (steam), Gibralter, Brook & Baucom.
Cotton-ginning (steam), Coburn's St're, R J Howle.
Cotton-ginning (steam). Cureton's Store (South Carolina), J Carroll.
Cotton-ginning (steam), Brown Creek, Gullege Bros.
Cotton-ginning (steam), Monroe, B F Richardson.
Cotton-ginning (steam), Long's Store, W G Long.
Cotton-ginning (steam), Monroe, G W Flow.
Cotton-ginning, Ames, Perry & Stewart.
Cotton-ginning, Monroe, Lee & Williams.
Cotton-ginning, Monroe, T N Lee & Son.
Cotton-ginning (steam), Walkerville. J C Steele.
Cotton-ginning (steam), Olive Branch, A Fowler.
Cotton ginning (steam), Monroe, J Shute & Son.
Gunsmithing, Monroe, Brooks Myers.
Harness and shoes, Monroe, L F Price.
Monroe Iron Works, Monroe. J R English, pres; W C Heath, vice-pres; W F Morgan, sec-treas.
Tannery, Richard's Creek, J R Griffin.
Tannery, Stout, J F Haywood.
Tannery, Lane's Creek, J S Little.
The Monroe Cotton Mills, Monroe. O P Heath, pres; W C Heath, sec and treas; T A Davis, supt; capital $125,-

UNION COUNTY.

000; spindles, 8,500; 3,000 twist spindles—total 11,500; hands 280.
Wagons, etc, Monroe, J A Shepherd.
Wool-carding, Morgan's Mills, Mrs L Morgan.
Wool-carding, Monroe, J Shute & Sons.
Wool carding, Adam's Mills, Joseph Adams & Son.

MERCHANTS AND TRADESMEN.

Names and Post Offices.

AMES.
Stewart, Austin & Co,   G S
ALTAN.
Mangum, B F,   G S
ASHCRAFT'S MILLS.
Ashcraft, C J & T L,   G S
BRIEF.
McManus, W E,   G S
COBURN'S STORE.
Howie. Robinson & Co,   G S
Long, W S,   G S
Roberson & Stuart,   G S
EUTO.
Braswell, T C,   G S
GIBRALTAR.
Pusser, M D,   G S
Williams & Tarlton,   Millers
INDIAN TRAIL.
Hemby & Leonard,   G S
Williams, A J,   G S
LANE'S CREEK.
Belk, S E.   G S
Moore, J E & Co,   G S
LONG'S STORE.
Austin, Alford J & Son,   G S
Long & Little,   G S
LOVE'S LEVEL.
Helms, J T & Co,   G S
MARSHVILLE.
Bailey, J E,   G S
Collins, W E,   G S
Ashcraft, T J & Son,   G S
Lee, M K & Co,   G S
Little, L M & Co,   G S
Marsh, J W,   G S
MONROE.
Armfield, E A,   Stock Dealer
Belk, W H & Bro,   G S
Bishop, J S.   Tel Operator for S A L
Broom, H M,   G S
Browning. H D,   Southern Exp Agt
Bruner, C W,   Gro
Bivens, H F, Mgr Rodman, Heath & Bivens, Stock Dealers
Bundy, S B, Guano, Sew. Machines, etc

UNION COUNTY.	
Crow Bros,	G S
Crowell, J A,	G S
English Drug Co,	
English, J R & Co,	G S
Fairley, J M,	Cotton
Fletcher, J C,	Hotel
Flow, M L & Co,	Gro and Confec
Griffin, C W,	Livery
Griffin, E M,	Livery
Harkey, Mrs D J,	Hotel
Hart, S B,	Gro
Heflin, J D,	Postmaster
Hasky, J S,	Butcher
Heath Hardware Co,	Hardw
Heath, Morrow & Co,	G S
Helms, L R & Co,	G S
Houston, W B,	Dentist
Johnson, A C,	G S
Krauss, S,	Jeweler
Latta, A T,	Book Store
Lee, J H & Co,	Drugs
Lee, W S,	Gro and Hardw
Lee & Lee,	G S
Levy, Mrs M A,	Millinery
Lichtenstein & Levy,	D G
Liles, H,	Photographer
Long & Little,	G S
Marsh, G A,	Stock Dealer
McKenzie & Dillon,	Furn
McRae & Collins,	G S
Myers, Brooks,	Gunsmith
Norwood, Walton,	Jeweler
Ogburn, W C,	Hotel
Parker, J D,	Mdse Broker
Parham, S W,	Depot Agt S A L
Phifer & Whorley,	G S
Price, L F,	G S
Rochelle, C W,	Art Gallery
Rudge, J W,	Tin and Stoves
Shannon & Co,	G S
Shute, John & Sons,	G S
Simpson, J R & Co,	Gro
Starnes & Bigger,	G S
Stevenson, J W,	Dentist
Stewart, Jas,	Gro
Thomas, N G,	G S
Waller, Moses,	G S
Welsh, S J,	Drugs
Whitfield Bros,	G S

MORGAN'S MILLS.

Goodman, M A,	Tanner

MOUNT PROSPECT.

Plyler, W P,	G S

OAK GROVE.

Polk, J A & Son,	G S
Reid, C M,	Blacksmith
Russell, J B,	G S

OLIVE BRANCH.

Bost, J L,	D G and Gro

POORTITH.

Coan, J D,	G S
Durant & Son,	G S

UNION COUNTY.	

RUSHING.

Culledge, J A & Co,	G S

STOUT.

Gurley, M C,	G S

UNIONVILLE.

Long, M C,	G S

WAXHAW.

Bivens, H F & Co,	Drugs
Brown, C & Son,	G S
Hudson, T J,	G S
McCain Bros,	G S
McDonald. D C,	G S
McPherson, M E,	Millinery
Massey, C S & Bro,	G S
M rrow, Heath & Co,	G S and Cotton Buyers
Porter, W H & Bro,	G S
Rodman & Heath,	G S and Cotton Buyers

MINES.

Kinds, Post Offices and Proprietors.

Austin and Dismuke, gold, Monroe, Austin & Co.

Black, gold, Indian Trial, Thing & Co.

Brown Hill, gold, Indian Trail, Eli Henby.

Crump, gold, Stout, J C Bates, New York City.

Davis, gold, Price's Mill, A J Price & Bro.

Hotchkiss, gold, Monroe, W H Hotchkiss.

Henry Phifer, gold, Indian Trail, W H Phifer & Co.

Howie, gold, Monroe, J C Bates & Co.

Lewis, gold, Price's Mill; Mr —— Liles, New York City.

Moore, gold, Coburn's Store; C W Shurburne. Boston, Mass.

Nesbit, gold, Walkersville; Wadsworth & Rollins. Charlotte. N C.

Phifer, gold, Price's Mill, A J Price & Company.

Pyron, gold, Hope, A A Laney.

Pyron, gold, Hope, Mrs S A Covington.

Shannon, gold, Monroe, G C McClarty & Co

Smart, gold, Indian Trail; J C Bates, New York City.

Slate quarry, Monroe, Mrs M Medlin.

Stewart, gold, Coburn's Store, C W Alexander.

Truelight, Coburn's Store; owned by a Baltimore company.

Washington, gold, Winchester, J C Bates.

UNION COUNTY.	UNION COUNTY.

MILLS.

Kinds, Post Offices and Proprietors.

Corn, flour and saw, Ames, Perry & Stewart
Corn and flour, Gibratar, R P Tarlton.
Corn and flour, Marshville, W R Hasty.
Corn and flour, Morgan's Mills, Mrs L Morgan.
Corn and flour, Long's Store, J C Sikes & Sons.
Corn and flour, Coburn's Store, Stewart & Austin.
Corn and nour, Olive Branch, Parker & Brooks.
Born and flour, Olive Branch, J P Horn
Corn, flour and saw, Olive Branch, A H Nance & Co.
Corn, flour and saw, Olive Branch, Nance, Liles & Co.
Corn and saw, Oak Grove, Jas Clontz.
Gorn and flour, Moroe, Shute & Sons.
Corn, Monroe, Jas K Simpson.
Corn and flour, Monroe, T N Lee & Sons.
Corn, flour and saw, Monroe, J Shute & Sons.
Corn and flour, Walkersville, W W Norwood & McMurry.
Corn and flour, Adams' Mills, R G Blythe.
Coru, flour and saw, Marshville, C A Ashcroft & Co.
Corn, flour and saw, Marshville, J A Marsh.
Corn, flour and saw, Lane's Creek, S E Belk,
Corn, flour and saw, Raywood, J C Helms.
Corn, flour and saw, Wolfsville, E J Heath.
Corn, flour and saw, Unionville, W A Love.
Corn, flour and saw, Walkersville, J W McCain.
Saw, Adams' Mills, Joseph Adams.
Saw, Marshville, Marsh & Morgan.
Saw, Ames, Bennett & Nash.
Saw, Monroe, Jesse Griffin.
Saw, Monroe, J H Rogers,
Saw, Hope, Waters & Arant.

PHYSICIANS.

Names and Post Offices.

Armfield R, Marshville.
Ashcroft, J E, Monroe.
Ashcroft, J B, Monroe (Veterinary surgeon).
Austin, Jas A, Coburn's Store.
Blair, Matt. Olive Branch.
Blair, Jno M. Monroe.
Bost, J L, Olive Branch.

Brooks, H M, Olive Branch.
Dees, A, Marshville.
Eubanks, J B, Lane's Creek.
Fitzgerald, J Y, Monroe.
Green, J E, Marshville.
Gribble, W H, Hope.
Houston, W B (dentist), Monroe.
Massey, J S (col), Monroe.
McAlister, ——, Waxhaw.
Nance, J, Union.
Nisbet, ——, Waxhaw.
Pemberton, W D, Monroe.
Price, J H, Monroe.
Price, W H, Stout.
Redwine, T W, Wolfsville.
Sapp, ——, Wildcat.
Stephenson, J W (dentist), Monroe.
Welsh, S J, Monroe.

SCHOOLS.

Names, Post Offices and Principals.

Altan High School, Altan, Mrs Eva Belk.
Art School, Monroe, Miss Rochelle.
Academy, Marshville, Prof Plummer Stewart.
Colored Parochial School, Monroe, Rev R A Cottingham.
Cotton Mill Chapel, Monroe, Miss Carrie Stilt.
Colored school, Monroe, Prof S W Hampton.
High school, Monroe, Prof E E Britton.
Primary, Monroe, Miss Mamie Walsh.
Primary and Intermediate, Monroe, Miss Anna Blair.
Rock Rest High School, Monroe, Prof. H E Copple.
Union Institute, Unionville, Prof O C Hamilton.
Weddington Academy, Wardlaw, Prof Clegg.
Wingate Academy, Ames, Prof M B Dry.
Public schools—white, 76; colored, 29.

TEACHERS.

Names, Post Offices and Proprietors.

Baucom, J E, Long's Store.
Belk, Julia, Alton.
Blair, Mrs M P, Olive Branch.
Boyte, J H, Monroe.
Davis, M L, Waxhaw.
Fowler, R B, Reuben.
Funderburk, D H, Monroe.
Haglar, Ida, Love's Level.
Hasty, W D, Faulk.
Hunter, Minnie, Davenport.
James, G W, Faulk
Little, J C, Marshville.

UNION COUNTY.

Long, W Reese, Unionville.
Long, Thomas W, Unionville.
Love, Rena, Unionville.
McCay, Julia, Zoar.
McCain, E J, Walkup.
Meggs, H P, Olive Branch.
Nesbitt, R N, Jacksonham (S C).
Plyler, H W, Tradesville.
Pistole, Lillie, Unionville.
Presson, Florence, Unionville.
Presson, W H, Unionville.
Price, F L, Love's Level.
Richardson, L E, Waxhaw.
Rochelle, Miss (Art School), Monroe.
Scoggin, Miss Mollie (Music), Monroe.
Stewart, Plummer, Marshville.
Stewart, S A, Stevens.
Stewart, Sidney, Stevens.
Stewart, Annie, Stevens.
Sturdivant, Maggie, Monroe.
Thompson, F R, New Cut (S C).
Tucker, M M, Long's Store.
Winchester, Benj, Potter's.
Wolfe, Fleet, Vann.
Wolfe, Ed, Vann.

LOCAL CORPORATIONS.

Advance Council, No 589, Royal Arcanum; meets second and fourth Monday nights.
Beaver Dam Lodge, No 276, A. F. and A. M, Beaver Dam. Time of meeting, Saturday on or before full moon; June 24th and December 27th.
Graham Council, No. —, American Legion of Honor.
I. O. H., Monroe; R F, Beasley, Archon; F W Hilliard, sec; J W Bivens, treas.
Monroe Lodge, No. 2,095, Knights of Honor; meets first and third Monday nights.
Monroe Lodge, No. 244, A. F. and A-M., Monroe. Time of meeting, first and third Friday evenings; June 24th and December 27th. Rev. F. W. Hilliard, W M.
People's Bank of Monroe; capital stock paid in, $45,300; H. M. Houston, pres; W. C. Wolfe, cashier.

NEWSPAPERS.

Marshville News, E D Flake (col), ed.
Monroe Enquirer, Monroe (Dem. weekly); Ashcraft Bros, editors and props.
Monroe Journal, (Dem. weekly), Beasley Bros, eds.
Our Home (Pop. weekly), Marshville; Green & Flake, eds and props.

UNION COUNTY.

FARMERS.

Names and Post Offices.

Ames—Henry Bivens, J A Burnett, E W Griffin, Mac Helms, E L May, W G McBride, W M Perry, T J Perry, J M Perry, J N Perry.
Coburn's Store—W W Duncan, T T Duncan, I R Duncan, C T Helms, J T Helms, Russell Helms, W H Helms, W R Helms, R J Howie, William L Howie, jr.
Gibraltar—William A Austin, M C Austin, J M Austin, Josiah Austin, W H Austin, J C Baucom, J C Griffin, W D Liles, David Pusser, L D H Simpson, Allen Simpson, Richard Simpson, J E Simpson, G M Simpson, J R Stewart, L D H Willams.
Hope—P R Belk, H W Belk, A H A Belk, T C Eubanks, jr, W A Eubanks, J C Eubanks, T C Eubanks, sr, Thos Gay, W H Gribble, J P Laney, J C Laney, G M Laney, Louis Laney, J D Plyler, H W Pusser, J P Rogers, M A Walters.
Indian Trail—J E Broom, Eli Condor, J R Cuthbertson, W L Cuthbertson, S W Honeycutt, H B King, E J Krimminger, Garrison Medlin, J I Orr, W F Rea, D S Robinson, B I Simpson, J P Simpson, James Smith, D D Stinson, J T Starnes.
Long's Store—A J Austin, W T Baucom, Garrison Biggers, Henry Dry, J L Little, Mrs Serena Little, John I Long, Adam Long, J C Sikes, M L Tucker.
Love's Level—John A Clontz, J T Cuthbertson, J L Griffin, G A Long, W B Long, T L Love, A W H Price.
Marshville—C A Ashcraft, T J Ashcraft, G W Bailey, D B Barrino, A S Gaddy, J E Green, W S Hamilton, Jno C Hamilton, W R Hasty, K M Hasty, J C Hasty, B F Hasty, T C Hasty, L M Little, J A Marsh, W B Marsh, J D Marsh, A Marsh, J W Marsh, S D Moore, M A Moore, R W Stegall.
Monroe—E A Armfield, R T Barrett, Wm Bivens, E J Bivens, J T Bivens, N W Bivens, J W Bivens, T B Blakely, J W Chaney, J E Chaney, E M Griffin, J H Griffin, Jno Griffith, H C Griffin, C L Helms, S J Helms, L A Helms, J J Hill, Jerry Hinson, B F Houston, R V Houston, A A Laney, T N Lee, G C McLarty, J A McCallum, Jas McLarty, Ervin Medlin, J D Medlin, S R Moore, H C Moore, W H Phifer, S S Richardson, C Stewart, G M Stewart, J D A Secrest, L S Secrest, C N Simpson, Jas Small, G M Stewart, F M Sutton, W E Williams, H F Wil-

UNION COUNTY.

UNION COUNTY.

liams, S A Williams, Thos E Williams, Jno C Williams. E H Williams, T J Williams, D J Winchester.

Mt Prospect—L R Belk, W L Belk, A Cook, S A Fincher. W G Griffin. J C Harris, J R Lathan, S A Lathan, P P W Plyler, B F Richardson, H S Starnes

Oak Grove—Jas Clontz, W Clontz. W R Helms, James T Helms, J C Long, J H Long, A W McManus, N J Mc-Manus, John E Morgan, J A Polk, Reddick Pope, A J Pigg.

Olive Branch—M C Austin, J W Austin, H T Baucom, H M Bancom, J L Bost, Thomas Brewer. S R Brewer, G W Brewer, Jackson L Brewer, C Brooks, D Broom, G W Broom, T S Braswell, J C Carraway. Rev A C Davis, Henry Edwards, Wm Edwards, Thomas A Fowler, E G Gaddy. James W Godwin, Wm Godwin, J R Griffin, W L Griffin, Jacob Gurley, Archy Helms, Benjamin Liles, H P Meggs, Kenry Nance, Silas Nance, W L Parker, E C Phillips, H R Pritchard, C A Pritchard, J I Ross. G B Rushing, W B Smith, John W Smith, G W Simpson, John Simpson. J O Sinclair, Luke Sinclair, Jacob Thomas, Jos Thomas, J W Thomas, J J Thomas, M C Traywick.

Poortith—F S Crane, S P Durant, T J Ezzell, S M Ezzell. G W Howey, C C McIlwain, Jeff McIlwain, William M Parks, Will Parks, D C Ross, W J Stephenson, G W Sutton.

Unionville—T H Benton, G D Benton, E J Griffin. W T Hamilton, Jas T Helms. T D Helms, S A Helms, W G Long. M C Long, W A Love, J H McCallum. E E Presson, D Mac Price, T J Price, M D Pusser, L A Scott, G W Scott, W C Simpson.

Price's Mill—J A Biggers, W A Biggers, J D Davis, J A Deal. Robt Fowler, J I Harkey, J D Hemby, S G Howie. W T Kessiah, S W Matthews, T B Moore, Mrs R S Moore, A J Price, J Mac Price, H L Price. D W Reid, B F Sutton, I H Winchester.

Raywood—E W Belk. M H Benton, E L Benton, B F Benton, Wm Benton,

E Benton, J M Benton, John Dixon, A J Furr, J H Griffin, J J Hasty, J Q Helms, E J Helms, J D Helms, C C Lemmond, J E Rowell, S J Rowell, L Scott, C Simpson, W H Taylor, J H Trull.

Richardson's Creek—A Austin, H J Bivens, A J Brooks, J Q Griffin, M W Griffin, M A Griffin, W P Griffin, J R Helms, M B Simpson, T C Stewart, W J Stewart.

Stevens—J L Hooks, S D Stevens, R L Stewart, Harry Stewart.

Stout—B H Benton. J W Benton, J S Funderburk, Wm Griffin, M D Gurley. D M Gordon, C W Harkey, John F Haywood, J W Haywood, T A Honeycutt, A P House, Jas M Houston, W C Ritch, T C Ritch, G W Sherrin, P C Stinson, Wm Yandle, M M Yandle, C T Yandle, F M Yandle.

Walkerville—R A Davis, S H Huey, R T McCain, J J McCain. J W McCain, W R McNeely. H McWilliams, H A Norwood, W W Norwood, Mrs Isabella Robinson. O M Sanders, E Simpson, W H Sims, W D Starnes, J J C Steele, I P Walkup, S H Walkup, J L Walkup, W P Neely.

Winchester—T J Gordon, W H Howie, J H Rogers, J A Secrest, M Starnes, G R Winchester.

Wolfsville—A J Clark. R B Cuthbertson, G N Gordon. R F Howard, G W Honeycutt, J C Honeycutt, R A Hudson, Wm Jones, T W Redwine, W P Redwine.

Rock Rest—T C Bailey, M W Bivens, H E Copple, J H Griffin. H C Griffin, T B Liles, H C Moore. J H Williams, T E Williams, E H Williams.

Wardlaw—C O Howard, R A Hudson. Thos Hudson, R F Howard, N M S Matthews, H J McManus, R L Stevens, E W Thomas.

Waxhaw—Jos Adams, J D Adams, M N Austin, R J Belk, R G Blythe, Calvin Broom, H F Bivens, Wash Givens, J W Godfrey, D C Godfrey, A W Heath, Jas Houston, J W Price, J L Rodman, E G Yarbro.

VANCE COUNTY.

AREA 260 SQUARE MILES.

POPULATION, 17,581; White 6,434, Colored 11,147.

VANCE COUNTY was formed March 5th, 1881, from Granville, Franklin and Warren counties, and was named in honor of ex-Governor Z. B. Vance.

HENDERSON, the county-seat, is on the Raleigh and Gaston Railroad, at the junction of the Oxford and Henderson and Durham and Northern Railroads, 44 miles north from Raleigh. Population estimated at 5,256.

Surface—Undulating, with sandy loam and red clay soils.

Staples—Tobacco, corn, wheat, oats, rye, cotton, potatoes and a variety of vegetables.

Fruits—Apples, peaches, pears, grapes, melons, and other small fruits.

Timbers—Pine, oak, hickory, ash, walnut, poplar and maple.

Minerals—Iron, gold, silver, and several mineral springs.

TOWNS AND POST OFFICES.

	POP.		POP.
Bobbitt,	—	Henderson	
Brookston,	50	(c h)	5,256
Carlton,	25	Kittrell,	350
Cokes,	—	Middleburg,	300
Dabney,	50	Townesville,	250
Epsom,	25	Watkins,	—
Gillburg.	—	Williamsburg,	200
Greystone,	100	Woodworth,	75

COUNTY OFFICERS.

Clerk Superior Court—D H Gill.
Commissioners—J R Young, chm'n; Thos Taylor, J A Flemming, G W Kittrell, J E Burroughs.
Coroner—T T Hester.
Register of Deeds—T S Eaton.
Sheriff—Wm H Smith.
Solcitor Third District—C M Bernard.
County Attorney—W B Shaw.
Standard Keeper—W T Carter.
Surveyor—Geo Houghtaling.
Superintendent of Health—Dr J H Tucker.
Treasurer—H B Hicks.
County Examiner—C E Fuller.

COURTS.

Second Monday before the first Monday in March; eleventh Monday after the first Monday in March; fourth Monday after the 1st Monday in September.

CRIMINAL COURTS.

Fifth Monday before the first Monday in March; first Monday after the first Monday in September.

TOWN OFFICERS.

HENDERSON—*Mayor*, R J Southerland; *Commissioners*, J D Cooper, L W Barnes, W H Reavis (col), Wm Merrimon, Henry Perry, E A Powell, R Marston, Jas M Young; *Chief of Police*, A G Daniel.

TOWNSHIPS AND MAGISTRATES.

Dabney—G W Wright (Henderson), O H Parham, J L Capps, G N Fuller (Carlton), R A Wilson, W L Burroughs (Dabney).

Henderson—S H Allen, W E Gary, Simon P Kearney, M S Duke, J H Satterwhite, W H Hughes, E Powell, Z M Duke, W A Belvin (Henderson).

Kittrell—W W Ellis (Henderson), B A Capehart, J P Hunt, J M Person (Kittrell), H M Hight (Bobbitt), Thos Burwell, Jas P Hunt (Kittrell), Henry A Finch (Henderson), J D Davis (Kittrell).

Middleburg—Alfred E Jones (Middleburg). J P Satterwhite, Beter L D Hester (Henderson), C J Burton (Middleburg), Thos S Henderson (Henderson).

Nutbush—J W Caudle, Thos Hendricks, Jas Bullock, A A Harris, T A Riggan (Manson).

Sandy Creek—Jas H Ball (Henderson), J H Foster (Epsom), Eugene Thorne, Solon Southerland, Robert Southerland (Henderson), S W Duke, W B Daniel (Epsom), B F Grubbs (Henderson).

Townsville—M B Harris (Woodsworth), C H Davis, D R Brame, J H Taylor. D S Marrow, F M Marrow, N D Boyd (Townsville).

Williamsboro—A B Wyche, J L Kelly. A P Eaton (Henderson), P B Snead, J S Royster, W S Green (Williamsboro.

CHURCHES.

Names, Post Offices, Pastors and Denom.

METHODIST.

Church—Henderson, M D Hix.

VANCE COUNTY.

Church—Middleburg, K D Holmes.
Church—Kittrell.
Cokesbury— ——, —— Cokes.
Plank Chapel—Kittrell, K D Holmes.

METH. PROTESTANT.

Antioch—Kittrell, C L Whitaker.
Flat Rock—Henderson. Wm Porter.
Church—Henderson, T M Johnson.
Harris' Chapel—Dabney, Wm Porter.
Mt Carmel—Henderson, C L Whitaker.
New Hope—Manson, Wm Porter.
Union Chapel—Kittrell, —— Fishell.

BAPTIST.

Church—Henderson, J D Hufham, DD.
Church—Middleburg.
Carey—near Henderson, J A Stradley.
Church—near Kittrell.
Church—Williamsboro, J A Stradley.
First Church (col)—Henderson, R I
    Walden.
New Bethel—Epsom, T B Hill.
Poplar Creek—Dabney, T B Hill.
Second Church (col)—Henderson, Sandy Griggs.
Rock Spring—near Townsville.
Vaughn St (col)—Henderson, Buck Alston.

A. M. E. ZION.

Church (col)—Henderson, Rev Shaw.
Church (col)—Henderson, Rev Spruill.

CHRISTIAN

Church (col)—Henderson, Thos Bullock.

EPISCOPAL.

Holy Innocents—Henderson, J E Ingle.
St John's—Williamsburg, W S Pettigrew.
St James'—Kittrell, J B Averett.

PRESBYTERIAN.

Church — Henderson, W D Morton, D D.

MINISTERS RESIDENT.

Names, Post Offices and Denominations.

METHODIST.

Hicks, M D, Henderson.
Holmes, K D, Kittrell.

METH. PROTESTANT.

Johnson, T M, Henderson.
Porter, Wm. Dabney.
Whitaker, C L, Kittrell.

BAPTIST.

Allen, Lewis (col), Middleburg.
Bullock, O O (col), Middleburg.
Bullock, T H (col), Middleburg.
Burwell, Jeff (col), Middleburg.
Eaton, Allen (col), Henderson.
Henderson, S (col), Middleburg.
Hill, W C, Henderson.

VANCE COUNTY.

Horner, T J, Henderson.
Walden, R I (col), Henderson.

EPISCOPAL.

Averett, J B, Kittrell.
Ingle, J E Henderson.

A. M. E. ZION.

Bullock, Thos (col), Manson.
Spruill, —— (col), Henderson.

HOTELS AND BOARDING HOUSES.

Names, Post Offices and Proprietors.

Boarding, Middleburg, Jane Reavis.
Boarding, Henderson, T J Horner.
Boarding, Townesville, P J Overy.
Boarding, Brookston, Ned Baskerville (col).
Boarding, Henderson, Mrs W J Robards.
Boarding, Henderson, Mrs J H T Edwards.
Boarding Henderson, T R Manning.
Boarding, Henderson, Mrs Florence Davis.
Boarding, Henderson, Mrs M W Harris.
Henderson Hotel, Henderson, J W Beck.
Kittrell Hotel, Kittrell.
Masenburg Hotel, Henderson, J P Massenburg.

LAWYERS.

Names and Post Offices.

Bridgers, J H, Henderson.
Eaton, J Y (col), Henderson.
Harris, A J. Henderson.
Hicks, T T, Henderson.
Ingle, J E, jr, Henderson.
Pittman, Thos M, Henderson.
Shaw, W B, Henderson.
Wortham, A R, Henderson.
Zollicoffer, A C, Henderson.

MANUFACTORIES.

Kinds, Post Offices and Proprietors.

Building and contracting, and sash, doors and blinds, Henderson, R R Pinkston.
Coopering, Henderson, I B Gary & Co.
Greystone Granite Quarries, Henderson, Winder, Stagg & Worth.
Iron and wood-working, Williamsboro, H S Lemay.
Iron foundry, Henderson, Geo Crenshaw.
Iron and wood-working, Williamsburg, Jas Marrow, Jr.
Machine shops, Henderson, Crow & Marston.

VANCE COUNTY.	VANCE COUNTY.

Millwrighting, Henderson, John Falkner.

Millwrighting, Kittrell, J M Beckham.

Saddles and harness, Henderson, L T Howard.

Tannery, Williamsburg, S Petaford.

Tinware, Henderson, R B Hayes & Co.

Tobacco warehouse, Henderson, Harris, Gooch & Co, prop.

Tobacco warehouse, Henderson, D Y Cooper, prop.

Tobacco warehouse, Henderson, Owen Davis, prop.

Tobacco stemming, Henderson, Allen & Ginter Co, John D Cooper, manager.

MERCHANTS AND TRADESMEN.

Names, Post Offices, Lines of Business.

BOBBITT.

Bobbitt, P A,   G S

BROOKSTON.

Church, Mrs H D,   G S
Linehan, P & Son,   G S

CARLTON.

Parham, O H,   G S

DABNEY.

Borroughs, J E,   G S

EPSOM.

Dickie Bros,   G S

GILLBURG.

Satterwhite, S G,   G S

GREYSTONE.

Greystone Granite and Construction Co,   Quarry and G S
Linehan, P & Sons,   Quarry and G S

HENDERSON.

Alston, N F & W W,   G S
Austern, F.   Clo and Shoes
Aycock, D E,   Painter
Barnes Clo Store,   Clothing
Barnes, E G,   Tob
Beacon Bros,   G S
Beacon, C,   G S
Beck, J W,   Butcher
Boing, W T (near),   G S
Britt, W A (col),   G S
Burwell, W D,   Roots and Herbs
Clary, Paul,   Leaf Tob
Cooper & Mitchell,   G S
Cooper, D Y,   Leaf Tob
Cooper, J D,   Leaf Tob
Covington, W S.   G S
Crow & Marston,   Wagon Makers
Daniel & Co,   Hardw
Davis & Rose,   G S
Dorsey, Melvin,   Drugs
Field, Geo,   Mdse Broker
Gary, W E & Co,   Leaf Tob
Hardee, D W,   G S

Hardee & Marston,   Livery
Harris, Gooch & Co,   Tob Warehouse
Hart, W H,   Leaf Tob
Hight, E E,   Jeweler
Howard, L,   Harness
Kelly, J A,   G S and Lumber
Kittrell, E J & Bro (near),   G S
Lassiter-Parham Co,   G S
Lehman, N,   Clothier
Levin & Brown,   Clothiers
Lowery, P J,   Shoemaker
Lyman & Barnes,   Marbleyard
Mangum, D H,   Broker
Massenburg, J P,   Hotel
Moss. W E,   Confec
Parker, W S & Co,   Gro
Parker, W W,   Drugs
Ferry, G E,   Green Gro
Pinkston, R R,   Planing Mill
Powell, Silas,   Fert and Miller
Poythress, J S,   Lumber and Coal
Purcell, A O,   G S
Reavis, W W,   Gro and Livery
Roberts, J G,   Tob
Ross, W E,   Miller
Roland, J I (col.),   Produce
Stephens, Edwin,   Books
Strause, L L,   Leaf Tob
Southerland, R J,   Livery
Taylor & Co,   Gro
Taylor, J P & Co,   Tob
Teiser, S F,   G S
Thomas, P H,   Drugs
Thomason, Henry,   G S
Thorne, E,   G S
Townes & Bro,   G S
Watkins, John B,   Builder's Sup
Watkins, S,   G S
Wester, W H & Bro,   Gro
Wickoff, T,   Jeweler

KITTRELL.

Gill, R F (near),   Milling
Hedgepeth, M B,   G S
Hunt, J T,   G S
Moore & Crudup,   G S
Pleasant, J W,   Wheelwright
Raney, C W,   Guano and Cotton
Williams, C H & J T,   G S

MIDDLEBURG.

Fleming, J A (near),   Miller
Roland, T V,   G S
White Bros,   G S

STEEDSVILLE.

Finch, G H,   G S

TOWNESVILLE.

Deaves, C H & Co,   G S

WATKINS.

Parham, W A, jr,   G S

WILLIAMSBORO.

Field, R & F,   G S
Hardy, W T,   G S

WOODSWORTH.

Reade, R H, agt,   G S

VANCE COUNTY.

Leaf Tobacco Dealers in Henderson.

Allen & Ginter.
Barnes, E G.
Bobbitt, R L.
Barnard, J R.
Brodie, B T.
Burnett, J M.
Butler & Jenkins.
Clary, Paul.
Cooper, J D.
Cooper, D Y.
Currin. J L.
Davis, Owen.
Dean, S.
Gary, W E & Co.
Harris. Gooch & Co.
Hite, E W.
Hart, W H & Son.
Roberts, J G.
Satterwhite, R R.
Stark, W S.
Strauss & Raab.
Taylor, J P & Co.
Thomason, Henry.
Watkins, S & Co.
Watkins, J B.

MILLS.

Kinds, Post Offices and Proprietors.

Corn and flour, Brookston, G B Harris.
Corn and flour, Henderson. O O Young.
Corn and flour, Townesville, D S Marrow.
Corn and flour, Townesville, D W Hardee.
Corn and flour, Townesville, J T Starke.
Corn and flour, Epsom, Robt Southerland.
Corn and flour, Townesville, A Burwell.
Corn and flour, Henderson, W E Ross.
Corn and flour, Williamsboro, B T Hicks.
Corn and flour, Henderson, H Faulkner.
Corn and flour, Middleboro, J A Fleming.
Corn, flour and saw, Kittrell, W L Peace.
Corn, flour and saw, Kittrell.
Corn, flour and saw, Williamsboro, W T Hardy.
Corn, flour and saw, Townesville, Taylor Bros.
Corn and flour, Kittrell, Jos Beckham.

PHYSICIANS.

Names and Post Offices.

Alston, B B, Epsom.
Cheatham, W T, Henderson.

VANCE COUNTY.

Cheatham, Goode, Henderson.
Debnam, T C, Henderson,
Gill, R J. Henderson.
Harris, F S (dentist), Henderson.
Harris, F R. Henderson.
Judd, W J, Henderson.
Macon, F A (dentist). Henderson.
McAlister, ——. Middleburg.
Moss, J R, Henderson.
Royster, Thos S.
Rowland. D S, Kittrell.
Sugg, J P. Kittrell.
Tucker, J H, Henderson.
Wyche, C D, Dabney.

SCHOOLS.

Names. Post Offices and Principals.

Female College Henderson, W D Horner.
Male Academy. Henderson, Prof J A Gilmer.
Male School, Middleburg.
Primary, Henderson, Mrs Maria Harris.
Primary, Henderson, Mrs W H Amerson.
Primary, Henderson, Mrs. Gen Daniel.
Public Schools—white, 29; colored, 24.

TEACHERS.

Names and Post Offices.

Allen, Miss Jessie, Kittrell.
Ayscue, Miss Dora, Henderson.
Bowden, Miss I L, Henderson.
Bullock, A A (col), Williamsboro.
Bullock, Lucy A (col), Williamsdoro.
Bullock, James A (col), Middleburg.
Bullock, Miss Sallie H, Williamsboro.
Boyd, R B. Townesville.
Burwell, H J, Willamsburg.
Cheatham, Louisa (col), Henderson.
Crudup, E J (col), Kittrell.
Crudup, J T (col), Kittrell.
Eaton, Allen P (col). Henderson.
Eaton, Jas Y (col), Henderson.
Eaton, Clara J (col). Henderson.
Eaton, Abbie J (col), Kittrell.
Edwards, Ida, Henderson.
Foster, J H (col). Duke's Store.
Garden, Mrs N P W, Henderson.
Grissom, Ida G. Kittrell.
Horner, W D, Henderson.
Horner, Mrs W D. Henderson.
Jarman, M N, Middleburg.
Kearney, Simeon P (col), Henderson.
Kelly, Miss Susie A, Henderson.
Merriman. Laura J, Henderson.
Morrow, Emma J (col), Henderson.
Parham, Mrs Maria, Henderson.
Royster. R H (col), Williamsboro.
Riggin, Miss Martha A. Middleburg.
Rowland, Mrs Willis, Henderson.

VANCE COUNTY.

Sanders, Lillie J, Henderson.
Sutton, Rev Wm, Henderson.
Thorpe, J H (col), Kittrell.
Taylor, M L. Townesville.
White, Miss Nina, Middleburg.
Wyche, A J (col), Williamsboro.
Wyche, Nancy J (col), Williamsboro
Wyche, Mrs E B, Williamsboro.

LOCAL CORPORATIONS.

Citizens' Bank, Henderson; J B Owen, pres; W A Hunt, cashier; capital paid in $45,000.
Farmers' Alliance Warehouse, Henderson; Jenkins & Butler, props.
Henderson Lodge, No 229, A F and A M, Henderson; A J Harris, W M.
Henderson Electric Co, Henderson, J H Bridgers, mgr.
Henderson Storage Warehouse Co, Henderson; J P Taylor, pres.
Henderson Water Co, Henderson, J W Wood (Philipsburg, N J,) pres; J H Bridgers, supt.
Henderson Tobacco Board of Trade, Henderson, D T Cooper pres.
Knights of Honor, Henderson; E Stephens, sec.
I O O F (col), Henderson, Ed D Sanders, C C.
Ionic Lodge, No 337, A F and A M, Kittrell; J P Sugg, W M; time of meeting, Saturday evening on or before full moon.
Prince Hall Lodge, No 57, Masons (col), Henderson; G W Claiborne, W. M.
Royal Knights of King David (col), No 57, Henderson; N A Lewis, W M.
United Order True Reformers (col), No 361, Henderson; M M Pease, W M.
Vance County Medical Society.

NEWSPAPERS.

Gold Leaf, Henderson (dem; weekly); Thad R Manning, ed and prop.
The Hustler (ind. weekly), Henderson; D E Aycock.

FARMERS.

Names and Post Offices

Bobbitt—P A Bobbitt, J L Edwards, J L B Edwards, J A Edwards, W H Edwards, R F Gill, H M Hight
Brookston—B F Best, J P Bobbitt. C H Buchanan.
Carlton—J T Barnes, J L Capps. R R Collis, H B Hicks, J W Kittrell, J H Parham. B F Wade. G W Wright.
Dabney—J E Burroughs, J A Burroughs, Charles G Burroughs, G R Burroughs. E G Butler, S W Clark. H W Crews, E N Crews, N G Crews, S F

VANCE COUNTY.

Crews, J M Ellington. H H Ellington, J T Hart, W H Hester, Mrs S A Hicks, W C McCann.
Gilburg—R C Coghill, J A Gill, J M Green, R L Greenwood, W J Hoyle, S G Satterwhite.
Henderson—Jones Ames, J H Ball, H H Ball, A M Basket, Jos Basket, J T Blanks, Henry Blanks, Robert Beacom, W A Belvin, Wm Blanks, Thos J Blacknall, I C Bobbitt, Wm Booth, Peter Booth, D L Bowen, W T Bowen, P A Bobbitt, B F Brodie, B W Brame, J A Brame, Samuel Brame, Bennett Rreedlove, Wm Buchan, N H Chavasse, J D Clark, J F Coghill, D W Cooper, J H Dunn, M E Dorsey, J W Duke, W Durham, J T Edwards, W H Edwards, W W Ellis, C W Finch, H A Finch, T B Bloyd, J A Fuller, E A Fuller, Jas H Fuller, E F Fuller, Z T Garrett, D H Gill, R J Gill, L R Gooch, I P Grissom, Rufus Grissom, R L Green, W E Gary, G E Wortham, J F Harris, Sam Hammer, T J Horner, George Houghtalking, T C Hughes, G B Hughes, E Hughes, J H Lassiter, R Marston, Jno McMillan, J R Moss, J H Parham, W S Parker, S P Phipps, Silas Powell, M B Prince, R W Radcliff, W E Rose, G H Rowlands, W W Rowlands, Lewis Rowlands, A W Rowlands, J P Satterwhite, S H Satterwhite, Jos C Short, A Short, G M Stainback, Mrs M A Stewart, W Y Swine, E Thorn, P E Wilkerson, R H Wilson, G F Wortham, Frank Wortham, Thos M Young, Mrs Annie R Young, J R Young, A C Zollicoffer.
Kittrell—Alex Baker, E T Bobbitt, S Burwell, C R Cawthorne, E A Davis, G R Davis, Lon Lavis, W J Floyd, Stephen Floyd, Eppy Grissom, J M Harris, J P Hunt, J P Hargrove, John F Hedgepeth, H W Hunt, S W Hunt, C H Hunt, John W Kittrell. G W Kittrell, Thos G Kittrell, Thos Moss, Mrs E H Overton, Samuel O Pardue, J A Pace, Mrs Sarah Peace, Simon Perry, C W Raney, J L Rowland, Junius Rogers, Cecil Rogers, W C Rogers, Benjamin Smith, A A Smith, Thos G Smith, W H Smith, L H Stone, Thos Williams, J F White, Irvin Woodlief, Mary Woodlief, T C Woodlief, M W Woodlief, W A Woodlief, Patrick Woodlief, J E Woodlief, B H Woodlief. J P Woodlief, B S Woodlief, W H Woodlief, R K Young, J W Young.
Middlebarg—Gilbert Bullock, Sallie Bullock. Nathan Bullock. G R Burroughs, J R Carroll, J M Caudle, Robt Edwards, Chas J Fleming, John Fleming, J R Flming, John A Fleming, Thomas D Hester, West Henderson,

VANCE COUNTY.

Stephen Henderson, Richmond Henderson, John Jenkins, Robt W Jones, R W Kearney, Mrs M E Langford, Wiley D Mitchell, J H Paschall, Thos Plummer, J K Plummer, H F Plummer, Alfred Plummer, T W Reavis, Samuel J Reavis, Wm Reavis, T V Rowland, William Rowlands, W B G Sneed, Robt T Spain, Thos Stainback, Z T Turner, L H Twisdale, E W Watkins, T M Watkins, J T Wiggan, Richard Wilson.

Townesville—J R Alston, J P Blackwell, Grandison Boyd, J A Boyd, N D Boyd, W H Boyd, G L Burwell, A Burwell, Elizabeth Hargrove, J H Johnson, E A Lewis, J G Morgan, N D Morton, D S Morrow, W D Morrow, J Y Overby, J M Parish, J L Ridout, J J Riggin, R G Sneed, Jas P Stark, J A S Stegall, Herbert Taylor, E O Taylor, Thos Taylor, V D Wimbish.

Watkins—W L Burroughs, H E Crews, J T Floyd, W S Fuller, J A Parham, W A Parham.

Williamsboro—J T Evans, R A Evans, David Evans, W T Hardy, Jos W Hawkins, Nelson Hicks, Mrs E T Jenkins, Jesse L Kelly, J W Kelly, David W Knott, Wm M Moseley, T B Parham, W P Rice R H Royster, R M Satterwhite, Mrs J P Thomas, T R Wilkerson, Jno R Wilson, Albert Wyche.

Woodworth—W H Burwell, T A Epps, S L Graham, Col John Hargrove, Jas Rideout, T W Taylor.

J. H. BRIDGERS,

Attorney at Law,

HENDERSON, N. C.

WAKE COUNTY.

AREA, 950 SQUARE MILES.

POPULATION, 49,202; White 26,093, Colored 23,109.

WAKE COUNTY was formed in 1770 from Orange, Johnston and Cumberland counties, and was named in honor to the maiden name of Governor Tryon's wife.

RALEIGH, the county-seat, and also the Capital of the State, bears the name of the illustrious Sir Walter Raleigh, under whose auspices the first colony was planted on our soil. Population (estimated) 20,000, 5,000 being of the suburban villages. Raleigh was adopted as capital of the State in 1792.

Surface—Moderately uneven; soil varied, from light sandy in the eastern part to red clay in the western part; well watered by the Neuse river and branches; plenty of water-power. Good land along the streams.

Staples — Cotton, tobacco, c o r n, wheat, oats, sweet potatoes and fruits in great variety. Trucking is attracting attention and is profitable. Vineyards are already profitable, and are increasing in number and size.

Fruits—Apples, peaches, p e a r s, grapes, melons, apricots, berries and other small fruits.

Timbers—Pine, hickory, oak, poplar, maple and ash.

Minerals—Plumbago in great abundance.

TOWNS AND POST OFFICES.

	POP.		POP.
Apex,	500	Lull,	—
Auburn,	350	Massey,	50
Ballentine's		Millbrook,	300
Mills,	30	Morrisville,	450
Bangor,	20	Myatt's Mills,	50
Banks,	25	Neuse,	150
Beck,	30	New Hill,	200
Box,	30	New Light,	150
Cary,	450	Pace's,	—
Eagle Rock,	150	Pernell,	75
Enno,	50	Pitt,	—
Ewing,	—	Raleigh (c. h),	20,000
Falls,	200		
Flint,	25	Rand's Mills,	25
Forestville,	400	Rogers' Store,	—
Garner,	250	Rolesville,	179
Gulley's Mill	25	Rosinburg,	25
Hartsville,	35	Shotwell,	75
Hickory Grove,	65	Six Forks,	—
Holly Springs,	250	Temple,	25
Kadar,	—	Vanteen,	—
Kelvin Grove,	50	Varina,	50
Lemay,	25	Veto,	—

	POP.		POP.
Wakefield,	250	West Raleigh,	—
Wake Forest,	1,250	Wyatt's,	—

COUNTY OFFICERS.

Clerk Superior Court—Dan H Young.
Commissioners— Wm C Stronach, chm'n; W H Hood, D W Allen, —— Jones.
Coroner—Dr R B Ellis.
Register of Deeds—J J Rogers.
Sheriff—M W Page.
Solicitor 4th District—E W Pou, jr, Smithfield.
Treasurer—H H Knight.
County Examiner—J H Goodwin.
County Attorney—Armistead Jones.
County Physician—Dr P E Hines.
Crier of Court—A D Hill.
Jailer— —— Lowry.
Surveyor—Jos Blake.
Standard Keeper—J C Lumsden.
Superintendent Poor-house and Work-house—W G Allen.

COURTS.

SUPERIOR.

Eighth Monday before first Monday in March.
First Monday before first Monday in March.
Third Monday after first Monday in March.
Seventh Monday after first Monday in March.
Eighth Monday before first Monday in September.
Third Monday after first Monday in September.
Seventh Monday after first Monday in September.
Judge McIver, Spring Terms.
Judge Boykin, Fall Terms.

SUPREME COURT.

First Monday before first Monday in March.
Sixth Monday after first Monday in September.
For U. S. Courts, refer to pages 23, 25 and 27.
For State Officers, see page 5.
For Governor's Council, State Board of Education, Board of Medical Examiners and State Board of Pharmacy, and other State Institutions, see pages 32, 33, 34, 36 and 38.

WAKE COUNTY.

CITY OFFICERS.

RALEIGH—*Mayor*, William M Russ; *Aldermen*, 1st Ward, Frank Stronach, J C Drewry, J D Boushall; 2d Ward, F W Hunnicutt, L N White, C W Hoover; 3d Ward, James Baker, J A Mills, B J Robinson; 4th Ward, C E Johnson, H M Ivey, John R Ferrall; *Auditor*, W W Wilson; *City Attorney*, J N Holding; *Clerk*, H F Smith; *Chief of Fire Department*, L A Mahler; *Asst Chief Fire Department*, Walter Woollcott; *Chief of Police*, Chas D Heartt; *Commissioner of Sinking Fund*, B S Jerman; *City Treasurer*, J G Brown; *City Tax Collector*, W B Hutchings, *Janitor*, Tobe Marshall; *Keeper of Clocks*, Thos M Blake; *Supt of Health*, Dr Jas McKee; *Street Commissioner*, W Z Blake; *Sexton City Cemetery*, Seth Jones; *Sexton Oakwood Cemetery*, A B Forrest; *Sexton Mt. Hope Cemetery* (col.), S Anderson; *Weighmaster*, Jas H Harris; *Police Force*, J W Beasley, Martin Thompson, M Andrews, R J Conrad, J A Cates, Charles Crayton, L S Ellison, A H Haynes, Geo C Upchurch, J H Mullen, T B Alderson, P C Hardie, M Jonson, W A Woodall, G M Jones, F A Belvin; *Keeper of Market*, J A Nottingham; *Supt Fire Alarm Telegraph*, L A Mahler; *Sanitary Officer and Clerk Board of Health* T P Sale.

CARY—*Mayor*, John Nugeer.

WAKEFIELD—*Mayor*, John Kemp.

PUBLIC BUILDINGS IN RALEIGH.

Metropolitan Market House, Fayetteville street, between Exchange Place and E Market street; $50,000.

N C Agricultural Experiment Station, H B Battle, Ph D, director and state chemist.

North Carolina Insane Asylum, situated in the vicinity of Raleigh, will accommodate 250 patients; Dr E L Kirby, supt.

The North Carolina Institution for the Blind is located at Raleigh, and comprises two separate departments, one for the whites in the northwestern part of the city, the other for the colored in the southeastern part of the city.

The Capitol Building, Union Square in the centre of the city; cost about $600,000.

U S Weather Bureau, in Agricultural building, 3rd story; C F Von Herrmann, observer in charge; Roscoe

WAKE COUNTY.

Nunn, ass't; Bedford Brown, messenger; headquarters of the N C State Weather Service, having sixty-five sub-stations, from which Metrological Reports are received monthly, and issues monthly and annual weather reports and weekly climate and crop reports.

U S Post Office and Court House, cor. Fayetteville and Martin streets; C M Busbee, postmaster.

Wake County Jail, Salisbury street.

Wake County Court House, Fayetteville street; cost about $25,000.

PUBLIC HALLS.

Pythian Hall, 303 Fayetteville st.

Henry Hall, 307 Fayetteville st.

Masonic Hall, Holleman Building, 3d floor.

Metropolitan Hall, over Metropolitan Market, Fayetteville st.

Institution Hall, at Institution for Deaf and Dumb and the Blind.

Odd Fellows' Hall, Pullen Building.

Colored I O O F Hall, East Hargett st.

Pullen Hall, Pullen Building.

Academy of Music, cor Salisbury and Martin sts.

J O U A M Hall, Pullen Building.

State Hospital Hall, Insane Asylum.

CEMETERIES.

City Cemetery, East st, between Hargett st and Newbern ave; Seth A Jones, sexton.

Confederate Cemetery, Oakwood, east of Linden ave; in charge of Ladies' Memorial Association.

Oakwood Cemetery, Oakwood ave, foot of Linden ave; A B Forest, sexton.

Hebrew Cemetery, between Oakwood and Confederate Cemeteries.

National Cemetery, E Davie st on Smithfield road; Capt Elgy, supt.

Mt Hope Cemetery (col), foot of Fayetteville st; Sampson Anderson, sexton.

Catholic Cemetery—in northeast suburbs of city.

TOWNSHIPS AND MAGISTRATES.

Barton Creek—R L Thompson, R D Honeycut, W C Jones, O L Parham, Dudley Peed, J J Penny, A C Ray, G W Ray, John A Arnold (Rolesville).

Buckhorn—G W Olive, R C Patrick, H W Holleman, H C Barker, E A Holt, J F Mann, C W Lawrence (Holly Springs).

Cary—C H Clark, A W Moye, W G

WAKE COUNTY.

Crowder, W H Beckwith, Nat G Williams, J Q Williams, Thad Ivey, A W Thompson, J P H Adams (Cary).

Cedar Fork—B H Marcom, J K Gibson, A B Lynn, W C Surles, W M Arnold, W G Sears, T S Barbee, A L Nipper (Morrisville).

Holly Springs—J D Marcom, W H Burt, Alfred C Burt, C H Culin, F K Godwin, T A Council, J C Ballentine, A F Norris (Holly Springs).

House Creek—W H Peebles, Sion H Smith, C H Jackson, J R Medlin, Jet Carpenter, F G Sanders, O G Ellen, A H House (Raleigh).

Little River—W H Chamblee, R C Mitchel, A S Jones, W H Hester, J T Haywood, W K Brantley, W H Horton (Wakefield).

Marks Creek—A T Mial, jr, E F Scarborough, N P Jones, A B Marshburn, F M Ferrell, M G Todd, J M Ferrell, B D Marshburn (Raleigh).

Middle Creek—J D Ballentine, K H Utley, J P Bridges, S M Rowland, R R Sexton, Alfred Powell, C W Sugg, W S Adams (Morrisville).

Neuse River—J T Hunter, jr, Geo W Norwood, G Redick, L M Green, M V B Norwood, N G Sandford, W R Braswell, Paschal Redick (Neuse).

New Light—W D Ray, A L Lyman, A L Davis, Joseph Pearce, W T Suit, L Woodlief, J J Powell, I S Bailey (New Light).

Oak Grove—J H Lynn, W J Furgason, J W Jenkins, G D Hayes, J R Ray, I L B Penny, W R Lyon, R B Gully (Kelvin Grove).

Panther Branch — Jas Adams, J Wiley Jones, J M Turner, R N Wynne, L J Weathers, J L Banks, J J Jordan, G L Penny (Raleigh).

Raleigh—W M Russ, W M Graves, C N Hunter, W F Debnam, E S Cheek, J B Hill, J H Alford, W W Wynne, J Nichols, J D Newsom, E A Adams, H H Roberts, W B Roberts (Raleigh).

St Mary's— F A Whitaker, J D Johnson, C N Allen, D P Meacham, J P Goodwin, M T Wilder, S R Pool, G R Brygn (Auburn).

St Matthew's—C L Hinton, A R Hodge, N W Poole, J A Haywood, B B Buffaloe, M W Buffaloe, R A Baugh (Raleigh).

Swift Creek—B S Franklin, L D Stephenson, C E J Goodwin, Jno P Massey, T M Franks, Edwards Rea, W P Powell, J Z Bennett (Raleigh).

Wake Forest—W C Brewer, Geo E Gill, Marion Puretoy, J C Harris, C R Debnam, J A Stell, G D Wiggins, J W Lasiter, H T Jones, J M Jones, J W Jones (Wake Forest).

WAKE COUNTY.

White Oak—H B Holland, L D Baucom, G G Maynard, Nathan Holleman, Rufus Barbee, R E Webster, S S Rogers, Jno C Burns, W H Womble (Apex).

CHURCHES.

Names, Post Offices, Pastors and Denom

IN RALEIGH—WHITE.

METHODIST.

Brooklyn—N W suburbs, R H Whitaker, D D.

Central—Cor Morgan and Person sts, D H Tuttle.

Edenton Street—W Edenton and N Dawson sts, W C Norman.

Epworth Chapel—R H Whitaker.

BAPTIST.

First Baptist—Cor N Salisbury and W Edenton sts, J W Carter, D D.

Tabernacle—Cor Hargett and Person sts, A M Simms, D D

Fayetteville Street—John T Pullen, supply.

West End—West Raleigh, A L Betts. .

Swain Street Baptist Mission.

PRESBYTERIAN.

First Presbyterian—Cor Salisbury and Morgan sts, Eugene Daniel, D.D.

EPISCOPAL.

Christ Church—Wilmington st, between Newbern ave and Edenton st, M M Marshall, D D.

Church of the Good Shepherd—Hillsboro st, bet Salisbury and McDowell, I McK Pittinger, D D.

St. Mary's Chapel—At St. Mary's School, Bennett Smedes, B D.

St. Savior's—Johnson and West sts, Rev Mr Canfield.

CHRISTIAN.

Christian Church—Cor Hillsboro and Dawson sts, J L Foster.

CATHOLIC.

Church of the Sacred Heart—Corner Hillsboro and McDowell sts.

HEBREW.

Raleigh Hebrew Union.

PRIMITIVE BAPTIST.

Meeting House—Cor Dawson and Morgan sts.

Y. M. C. A.

Fayetteville st, W H Overton, general secretary.

COLORED.

METHODIST EPISCOPAL.

Cox Memorial—Newbern ave.

Wilson's Chapel—Oberlin, near Raleigh.

AFR. METH. EPISCOPAL.

Church—Mason Village, near Raleigh.

WAKE COUNTY.

St. Matthew—East Raleigh.
St. Paul's Church — Cor Harrington and W Edenton sts, R H W Leak.

BAPTIST.

First Baptist—N Salisbury, near Johnston st, J J Worlds,
Martin Street Baptist—East Raleigh.
Second Baptist—S Blount st, F R Howell.

PRESBYTERIAN.

First Presbyterian—Cor Davie and Person sts, A G Davis.

CHRISTIAN.

Christian Church—Manly street, near railroad, A A Bright.
Maple Temple—East Raleigh, J R Williams.

EPISCOPAL.

St, Augustine—Cor Dawson and Lane sts.

CONGREGATIONAL.

First Congregationalist—W South st, near Manly st, A W Curtis.

IN COUNTRY.

METHODIST.

Andrews' Chapel—Hayes' Store, J M Ashby.
Asbury—Cary, J M Ashby.
Church—Rolesville. J M Ashby.
Church—Cary, J W Jenkins.
Church—Apex, J W Jenkins.
Church—Garner, D H Tuttle.
Ebenezer—Raleigh, J W Jenkins.
Holland's—Banks, J W Jenkins.
Macedonia—Raleigh, R H Whitaker.
Oak Grove—Shotwell, J M Ashby.
Pleasant Grove—Hayes' Store, J M Ashby.
Sidney—Raleigh, J M Ashby.
Soapstone—Hayes' Store, J M Ashby.
Tucker's Grove—Raleigh, D H Tuttle.

BAPTIST.

Bay Leaf—Hutchinson's Store.
Church—Forestville.
Church—Morrisville, W S Olive.
Church—Wake Forest College, W R Gwaltney, D D.
Church—Rolesville, A C Cree.
Church—Cary, W R Cullom,
Church—Wakefield, A D Hunter.
Clyde's Chapel—Eagle Rock, G W Coppedge,
Ephesus—Cary, W Y Chappell.
Friendship—Bunn's Level (Harnett co), M A Stephens.
Green Level—Ewing, J M Hilliard.
Hepzibah—Eagle Rock, A A Pippin.
Holly Springs—Holly Springs, W S Olive.
Inwood—Near Raleigh, A D Hunter.

WAKE COUNTY.

Mt. Hermon—Morrisville, W H Edwards.
Mt. Moriah—Auburn, G N Cowan.
Mt. Vernon—Forestville, A D Hunter.
Mt. Zion—Raleigh, M W Sorrell,
New Bethel—Garner, H H Mashburn.
New Hope—Raleigh, A D Hunter.
Oberlin (col)—Raleigh.
Olive's Chapel—New Hill.
Piney Grove—Raleigh, J M Holleman.
Salem—Green Level.
Shady Grove—New Hill. W H Davis.
Swift Creek—Raleigh, J M White.
Wake Cross Roads—Rolesville.
Wake Union—Forestville, W B Royal.

CHRISTIAN.

Beulah—Hartsville, J D Wicker.
Catawba Springs—near Raleigh, J A Jones.
Church—Auburn, J O Atkinson.
Church—New Hill.
Church—Morrisville, J D Wicker.
Church—Morrisville, W D Howard.
Church—New Hill. W D Howard.
Church—Raleigh, J L Foster.
Ebenezer—Flynt, W G Clements.
Hayes' Chapel—Garner, W G Clements
Mt Herman—Auburn, J W Fuquay.
Piney Plains—Massey, W G Clements.
Plymouth—Banks, G R Underwood.
Six Forks—Raleigh, W G Clements.
Wake Chapel—Varina, W G Clements

A. M. E.

Lincolnville—Raleigh, P J Jordan,
Piney Grove—near Raleigh, P J Jordan,
S John's—Raleigh, W H Merrick.

MINISTERS RESIDENT.

Names, Post Offices and Denom.

METHODIST.

Bobbitt, J B, D D, Raleigh.
Branson, Levi, 101½ and 103½ Fayetteville st, Raleigh.
Burr, John, Holly Springs.
Norman, W C, Raleigh.
Sorrell, Johnson, Raleigh.
Tuttle, D H, Raleigh.
Whitaker, R H, D D, 509 N Person st, Raleigh.
White, I A, Raleigh.

A. M. E.

Buckner, J H, 213 E South st, Raleigh.
Farrabee, J R (col), East Raleigh.
Holt, K C (col.), Raleigh.
Jordan, P J, Raleigh.
Reynolds, S E, E Lenoir st, Raleigh.
Roberts, E L (col.), Raleigh.
O'Connell, P O (col.), Raleigh.

BAPTIST.

Atkinson, J W, Neuse.
Betts, A L, Raleigh.

39

Betts, Alvin, Raleigh.
Blake, P (col.), Auburn.
Blanchard, C W, Cary.
Brown, M W (col.), Apex.
Bynum, C H, (col.), Apex.
Carter, J W, D D, Raleigh.
Chappell, W Y, Raleigh.
Coppedge, G W, Wakefield.
Creech, Worley, Hare's Store.
Cree, A C, Wake Forest.
Edwards, D B, Morrisville.
Edwards, W H, Wake Forest.
Fisher, C J W (col.), Apex.
Hackney, Calvin (col.), Apex.
Hall, P T (col.), Raleigh.
Hall, Plummer (col.), Oberlin, West Raleigh.
Harris, G W (col.), Neuse.
Harris, J L (col.), Wake Forest.
Holden, L (col.), Raleigh.
Holleman, J M, Apex.
Howell, Jesse, Green Level.
Hunter, A D, Cary.
Jefferson, John (col.), Raleigh.
Jones, N S, Raleigh.
Jones, James (col.), Raleigh.
Johnson, Cæsar (col.), 540 E Edenton street, Raleigh.
Latta, M L (col.), West Raleigh.
Layton, J S, Rogers Store.
Maloy, H M (col.), Raleigh.
Mitchell, John, D D, Wake Forest.
Norris, H W, Ballentine's.
Olive, W S, Holly Springs.
Pair, H, Eagle Rock.
Perry, Jos. Raleigh.
Perry, G W (col.), Raleigh.
Purefoy, A F. Wake Forest.
Roberts, N F, D D (col.), 816 S Blount street, Raleigh.
Rogers, J W F, Apex.
Royall, W B, Wake Forest.
Sanders, Sam (col.), East Raleigh.
Shepherd, R (col.), Raleigh.
Shepherd, A (col.), Raleigh.
Simms, A M, Raleigh.
Skinner, T E, D D, Raleigh.
Sledge, J W, Cedar Rock.
Sorrell, M W, Cary.
Spilman, B W, Raleigh.
Stephenson, ——, Raleigh.
Stewart, H (col.), Apex.
Stringfield, O L. Raleigh.
Taylor, C E, D D, Wake Forest.
Tucker, D (col), Raleigh.
Weatherspoon, S H (col), Raleigh.
White, J E, Cor Sec Baptist State Convention, Cary.
White, J M, Apex.
Worlds, J J (col), Raleigh.
Wynne, R P (col), New Hill.

CHRISTIAN.

Bright, A A (col), Raleigh.
Clements, W G, Morrisville.

Dunn, Rufus (col), Raleigh.
Foster, J L, Raleigh.
Fuquay, J W, Varina.
Herndon, Dr W T, Morrisville.
Jones,. J A. Ballentine's.
Rowland, R C H, Varina.
Whitaker, R H (col) near Raleigh.

EPISCOPAL.

Marshall, M M, D D, Newbern Ave, Raleigh.
Pittinger, E McK, D D, Raleigh.
Smedes, Bennett, D D, St Mary's School, Raleigh.

PRESBYTERIAN.

Daniel, Eugene, D D, Raleigh.

CONGREGATIONAL.

Curtis, ——, D D, Raleigh.

HOTELS AND BOARDING HOUSES.

Names, Post Offices and Proprietors.

IN RALEIGH.

Boarding, 302 N Dawson st, Mrs M H Weddon.
Boarding, 421 S Blount st, Emma Boyd (col).
Boarding, 224 E Martin st, Mrs Blalock.
Boarding, 118 N Wilmington st, Mrs Celeste Smith.
Boarding, S Blount st, Mrs Myatt.
Boarding, Hillsboro st, Mrs A Johnson.
Boarding, 104 N McDowell st, Mrs Lucy B Evans.
Boarding, 404 Fayetteville st, Mrs Geo Williams.
Boarding, Raleigh, T N Richardson.
Boarding, Raleigh, Mrs C R Lee.
Boarding, 309 W Martin st, Capt R L Heflin.
Boarding, 508 Fayetteville st, Raleigh, Mrs M A Banks.
Boarding, Hargett st, Mrs S M Richardson.
Boarding, 310 W Cabarrus st, David Hare (col).
Branson House 101½ and 103½ Fayetteville st, Rev I A White.
Exchange Hotel, 213 Hillsboro st, Mrs Nannie W Smith.
Harrison House, Davie, cor Wilmington st, Mrs S D Harrison.
Park Hotel, Crawford & Brown.
Yarborough House, 319 Fayetteville st, Louis Brown.

LAWYERS.

Names and Post Offices.

RALEIGH.

Amis, Moses N, 135 Wilmington st.
Andrews, A B, jr.

WAKE COUNTY.	WAKE COUNTY.
Ashe, Capt S A, cor Fayetteville and Martin sts.	Blacksmithing and wheelwrighting, Thos Yates.
Batchelor, J B, Raleigh.	Blacksmithing and wheelwrighting,
Batchelor, W P, office of Secretary of State.	330 S Salisbury st, cor Davie st, S P Pennington.
Battle & Mordecai, W Martin st.	Blacksmithing and wheelwrighting,
Beckwith, B C, Com. and Farmer's Bank building.	101 S Blount st, Jno C Jordan.
Burton, R O, Fisher building.	Blacksmithing and wheelwrighting, 218 S Bloodworth st, John Day (col).
Clark, Col Walter (Supreme Court Judge), office in court-house.	Blacksmithing and wheelwrighting,
Creech, Joseph A, W Edenton st.	129 S Wilmington st, Hill & Haywood.
Devereux, Thos P, Adams building.	Blacksmithing and wheelwrighting,
Douglas, W C, Bagley building.	Hunter & Polk (col).
Fleming (J H) & Moffitt (Elijah).	Blank-books, 19 W Hargett st, Edwards & Broughton.
Gatling, John.	Blank-books, 239½ S Wilmington st,
Gray, R T, Martin st.	Ed M Uzzell.
Harris, J C L, cor Fayetteville and Davie sts.	Boots and shoes, Wilmington st, Edward Bryant.
Haywood, Ernest, 301 Fayetteville st.	Boots and shoes, 189 W Cabarrus st.
Holding, J N, cor Salisbury and Martin	

Smith, Weldon.	
Smith, E C, Com. and Farmers Bank building.	Boots and shoes, 129½ S Wilmington st, Jno Taylor.
Strong & Strong, cor. Salisbury and Martin sts.	Boots and shoes, 104 S Wilmington st, Moses Thompson.
Vass, W W, Jr.	Boots and shoes, S Salisbury st, L T Smith.
Watson, ——.	Boots and shoes, W Davie st, Coy & Hunter.
Whitaker, Spier, Pullen bldg.	Boots and shoes, 545 Newbern avenue, J M Jones.

MANUFACTORIES.

Kinds, Post Offices and Proprietors.

RALEIGH.

Anticephalalgine, 301 Fayetteville st and 2 and 3 Martin st, J I Johnson.	Boots and shoes, 165 S Wilmington st, D W Jones.
Blacksmithing, S Salisbury st, Andrews & Goodwin.	Boots and shoes, Hillsboro sreet, W C Haywood.
Blacksmithing and wheelwrighting, 316 W Morgan st, Austin Green (col).	Boots and shoes, 132 W Cabarrus st, Henry Green.
Blacksmithing and wheelwrighting, 124 S Blount st, Henry Hartsfield (col).	Boots and shoes, Fayetteville st, K Francis.
	Boots and shoes, 539 E Martin st, H W Earp.
Blacksmithing and wheelwrighting, Hargett st, W H Holloway.	Boots and shoes, 304 S Salisbury st, M H Dunston.
	Boots and shoes, 237 Fayetteville st, Robt Dobbin.

Boots and shoes, Fayetteville st, J P Weddon.
Bottling works, W Cabarrus st, Thos R Jones.
Brick-making, N C Penitentiary.
Bridge building, 538 N Person st, W V Clifton.
Brooms and mattresses, Raleigh, N C, Institution for Blind.
Cabinet, Wilmington st, J T Morris.
Cabinet, 110 E Martin st, J W Barber & Son.
Candy, Raleigh, Barbee & Pope.
Candy factory, Royster & Co.
Candy, Fayetteville st, Chas Bretch.
Car-building, north end Salisbury st, N C Car Co.
Car-building, Lane, bet Salisbury and McDowell sts, R & G R R Co.
Carriages and wagons, 135 E Morgan st, J W Evans.
Carriages and wagons, E Morgan st, T A Bowen.
Carriages and wagons, 130 E Morgan st, Yancey & Stronach.
Carriages and wagons, E Hargett st, W H Holloway.
Clothing, 14 E Martin st, William Woollcott & Son.
Contracting and building, 101 N West st, Elling, Royster & Hicks.
Contracting and building, N A McNeill.
Cotton-gins, Smithfield st, Artemus Honeycutt.
Cotton-gins, W R Rowland.
Cotton-mills, near R & G depot; capital, $100,000; C G Latta, pres; J S Wynne, sec and treas.
Crackers, cakes, etc, 103 Fayetteville st, Chas Bretch.
Caraleigh Cotton Mills, Raleigh, J J Thomas, pres; F O Moring, sec and treas.
Caraleigh Phosphate and Fertilizer Works, Raleigh, J R Chamberlain, pres; N L Chamberlain, sec and treas.
Carriages, etc, Raleigh, T B Yancey.
Carriage and buggy works, Raleigh, J W Evans.
Cigars, Raleigh, J M Norwood.
Falls of Neuse Mfg Co, Raleigh, J N Holding.
Farina Flouring Mills, Raleigh, J A Mills, pres.
Frame Works, Raleigh, F A Watson.
Foundry, Raleigh, J H Gill.
Foundry, Raleigh, Allen & Cram, machine Co.
Furniture, Raleigh, R Roles & Son.
Harness, Raleigh, B H Mitchell.
Harness and saddles, 117 S Wilmington st, L B Hinton.
Harness and saddles, 109 E Martin st, E F Wyatt & Son.

WAKE COUNTY.

Hosiery, 321 and 323 S Fayetteville st, W C Holman.
Ice factory, S West st, Jones & Powell.
Ice factory, foot of West Hargett st, Eberhardt & Baker.
Iron foundry and machine shops, Lane st, bet Salisbury and McDowell, R & G R R Co
Iron foundry and machine shops, 120 S West st, Allen & Cram.
Iron foundry and machine shops, 130 W Davie st, J H Gill.
Jewelry and fancy articles, 228 Fayetteville st, H Mahler's Sons.
Lobdell Car Wheel Works, Raleigh, W E Ashley, mgr.
Monuments and tombstones, Ed T Marks.
Machine Works, Raleigh, Allen & Cram Machine Co.
Marble and granite works, 421 Fayetteville st, Cooper Bros.
Millwrighting, 507 S West st, Thomas D Wray.
Mills Lumber Co, Raleigh, J A Mills, pres.
N C Wagon and Plow Co, Cary, J P H Adams.
N C Penitentiary Brick Co, Raleigh, A Leazer, supt.
N C Car Co, Raleigh, W E Ashley, sec.
N C Oil Mill and Fertilizer Co, Raleigh.
N C Cotton-Oil Co, Raleigh.
Pants Factory, Raleigh, W Woollcott & Son.
Paper boxes, 19 W Hargett st, Edwards & Broughton.
Paper Co, Raleigh, J N Holding, pres.
Paper boxes, 239½ S Wilmington st, Ed M Uzzell.
Pharmaceutical Preparations, Raleigh, Hicks & Rogers.
Picture frames, 112 Fayetteville st, Fred A Watson.
Pilot Cotton Mills, Raleigh, J N & W H Williamson.
Plate Ice Factory, Raleigh, Jones & Powell.
Plow works, Wake Forest, W R Dunn & Co.
Plow works, Raleigh, J H Gill.
Raleigh Oil and Fert Co, at N C depot.
Raleigh Cotton mills, Raleigh, Raleigh Cotton Mill Co.
Raleigh and Gaston Railroad works, Raleigh.
Saddles and harness, S Wilmington st, B F Mitchell.
Sash, doors and blinds, 101 N West st, Ellington, Hicks & Co.
Sash, doors, blinds and contracting, 531 W South st, M Upperman.
Sash, doors and blinds, 120 Saunders street, Ruffin Roles.

WAKE COUNTY.	WAKE COUNTY.

Sash, doors and blinds, north end Salisbury st, N C Car Co.

Sausage, Fayetteville st, W R Crawford.

Spokes, rims and plow-handles, near Raleigh, W D Williams.

Smoking tobacco, "Cupid," J G Ball, Raleigh.

Spring beds, Wake Forest, A F Purefoy.

Tannery, Raleigh, L R Wyatt.

Tanning Co, Raleigh, Louis Wilson.

Tinware, 224 Fayetteville street, Julius Lewis Hardware Co.

Tinware and sheet iron, 226 Fayetteville st, J C S Lumsden.

Tobacco (plug and twist), S Blount st, J E Pogue.

Tobacco, Raleigh, Alonzo Love.

Tobacco flues, Raleigh, Julius Lewis Hardware Co.

Tobacco flues, Raleigh, J C S Lumsden

Tobacco flues, Raleigh, Chas F Lumsden.

Undertaking, Salisbury street, Jno W Brown, manager.

Undertaking, E Davie st, Geo L Lane.

Undertaking, 113 S Salisbury st, Lockhart & Fields.

Undertaking and upholstering, G T Strickland.

Upholstering, 108 S Wilmington street, Thomas Palmer.

Wagons, S Fayetteville st, N C Wagon Co; J A Jones, pres; J A Mills, sec'y and treas; capital stock, $25,000.

Wagons, Raleigh, T A Bowen.

Wagons, Raleigh, W H Holloway.

Wagons and carts, Cary, Harrison Wagon Co.

MERCHANTS AND TRADESMEN.

Names, Post Offices, Lines of Business.

APEX.

Harward & Hunter,	G S
Hudson, S V,	G S
Matthews, C W,	G S
Mitchell, Hardison,	G S
Mitchell, J H,	G S
Mitchell, W J,	G S
Olive, H C,	G S
Proctor, W W H,	G S
Saunders, D A,	G S
Utley, W F,	G S
Wood, A J,	G S

AUBURN.

Pool, Troy,	G S
Watts, Samuel,	G S
Wilson, M T,	G S

BALLENTINE'S MILLS.

Powell, John G,	G S

BANGOR.

Ray, R I,	G S

BANKS.

Gulley, L J,	G S

BARTON'S CREEK.

Holloway, Joe,	G S
Jackson, Lee,	G S
Jones, Wm,	G S

BECK.

Beck, J P,	
O'Brien, J A,	G S

CARY.

Adams, J P H,	G S
Gray, F R & Bros,	G S
Guess, J R,	G S
Holleman & Stone,	G S
Pleasants, A J,	G S
Waldo, S P & Son,	G S
Warren, J W, jr,	G S

EAGLE ROCK.

Roberson, G E,	G S
Todd, V Z,	G S

ENNO.

Holleman, S P & Co,	G S

EWING.

Batchelor, V G & Co,	G S

FALLS.

Pace & Holding,	G S

FLINT.

Sorrell, R L,	G S
Sorrell & Holloway,	G S

FORESTVILLE.

Allen, David,	G S
Allen, Jas,	G S
Allen, J L & Co,	G S
Dunn, D O,	G S
Patterson, E S,	G S
Phillips, J L,	G S

GARNER.

Dupree, C H,	G S
Garner, J R,	G S
Hobby, J B,	G S
Montague, G B,	Drugs
Rand, H D,	G S
Williams, J R,	G S

GULLEY'S MILLS.

Jordan, J J,	G S

HARTSVILLE.

Brewer, R L,	G S

HICKORY GROVE.

Underhill, J W,	G S

HOLLY SPRINGS.

Alford, G B,	G S
Bledsoe, G C,	G S
Cartee, J R,	G S
Cross, W F,	G S
Jones, Wm,	G S

WAKE COUNTY.		WAKE COUNTY.	
Seagraves, J R,	G S	**OBERLIN.**	
Stephens, A J,	G S	Graves, Willis,	G S
Stevens, A T & Son,	G S	Pettyford, A B,	G S
KELVIN GROVE.		**PEACE.**	
Lynn, G H,	G S	Patrick, R C,	G S
Nichols, J K,	G S	**PURNELL.**	
LEMAY.		Davis, S C, agt,	G S
Johnson, E A,	G S	**PITT.**	
LITTLE RIVER.		Jones, T S,	G S
Stallings, W Bass,	G S	Powell, G T,	G S
LULL.		**RALEIGH.**	
Horton, C T,	G S	Adams, J G,	G S
MASSEY.		Adams, L H,	G S
Adams, Jno,	G S	Adams & Harris,	G S
Alexander, Jno,	G S	Adams, Jas,	G S
Patrick, J S,	G S	Adams, Alex,	G S
Rand, W M,	G S	Allen & Cram,	Foundry
Wood, J P,	G S	Alston, J S,	G S
METHOD.		Anderson, C H,	G S
Barber, P B,	G S	Andrews, Wm,	G S
Branch, Osborne,	G S	Arnold, T A,	G S
O'Kelly, Berry,	G S	Auburn, Louis,	Livery
Wiggins, Eliza,	G S	Austern, ——,	G S
Wilcox, C J,	G S	Baker, Isaac,	G S
MILBURNIE.		Baker, Jas,	G S
Baugh, J C,	G S	Ball, J G,	G S
Haywood, Jos,	G S	Ball, G F,	G S
Holloway, Junius,	G S	Banks, J M,	G S
MILLBROOK.		Baptist Sunday School Supply Store,	
Bland, H A,	G S	113 Fayetteville st, H R Watson,	
Harp, Robt,	G S	mgr,	Books and Sta
Holloway, F J,	G S	Barbour & Son,	Livery
Hunter, G W,	G S	Barber, J W & Son,	Furn
Rogers, Wm,	G S	Barbee & Pope,	Confec
Thompson, Sam,	G S	Beasley, J J,	G S
MORRISVILLE.		Beaman, Geo,	G S
Adams, J Q,	G S	Beine, C H & Co,	G S
Ellis, L F,	G S	Berwanger Bros,	Clo
Horne, S R,	G S	Besson, Mme E,	Millinery
Moring, J H,	G S	Betts Bros,	G S
Pollard, W T & J M,	G S	Blake, Nancy,	—
Sears, W G & Co,	G S	Blake, Jos,	Livery
MYATT'S MILL.		Blake, Thos W,	Jeweler
Matthews, W H,	G S	Bledsoe, D M,	G S
Temple, R G,	G S	Bobbitt, J H,	Drugs
NEUSE.		Braan, Jos,	G S
Hunter & Hatch,	G S	Bragassa, J A,	Confec
Reddish, J W,	G S	Branch, D M,	G S
NEW HILL.		Branch, W A,	G S
Barker, W R,	G S	Brestch, Charles,	Confec
Holleman, H W,	G S	Briggs, Thos H & Sons,	Hardw
Segraves, T B,	G S	Bright, C J,	G S
Stuart & Evans,	G S	Broadwell, D I,	G S
NEW LIGHT.		Brodie, Ed,	Livery
Bryant, Wm,	G S	Brooks, Frank,	Livery
Davis, W H,	G S	Broughton, J M & Co,	Real Estate
Jones & Woodlief,	G S	Brown, J W,	Undertaker
Woodlief, L,	G S	Brown, T H,	Livery
		Brown, Mrs Sally E,	Livery
		Brown, L T,	Hotel
		Brown, S W,	Drayman
		Bryan, P N,	G S
		Campbell, J A,	Furn
		Carroll, J D,	Drayman

WAKE COUNTY.		WAKE COUNTY.	
Caudle, W H T,	G S	Harp, J R,	G S
Chavis, Dan,	Livery	Harris, E L,	Com Mcht
Chavis & Thompson,	Livery	Hatch, C C,	G S
Chavis, Mark,	Livery	Hawkins, C M,	Livery
Cheeks, Mrs M F,	G S	Hawkins, Hand,	G S
Childress, T W,	G S	Hay, O P,	G S
Christmas, Potter,	Drayman	Haywood, Wright,	Dray
Cole, Reuben,	G S	Hayes, Jacob,	G S
Cole, J W.	Jeweler	Heller Bros,	Shoes
Conn, D G,	G S	Hicks & Rogers,	Drugs
Cooper Bros,	Marble and Granite	Higgs, Jas,	Drayman
Cooper, W W,	G S	Hinton, L B,	G B
Cooper, Ed,	Dray	Hinton, Reuben,	G S
Crenshaw, R E,	G S	Hodge, H C,	G S
Crocker, H H,	G S	Hodge, Clint,	G S
Cross & Linehan,	Clothiers	Hogan, Allen,	G S
Cross, J L,	G S	Holtzman & Page,	Restaurant
Crowder & Rand,	Com Merchants	Holloway, M M,	G S
Curtis, B J,	Livery	Holloway, A R,	G S
Darnell & Thomas,	Music House	Holloway, Wm,	G S
Davis, W T,	G S	Holtzman, R L,	G S
Davis, Sam,	G S	Honeycutt, J H,	G S
Davis, J R,	G S	Horton, F,	G S
Davis & Ligon,	G S	Horton, C E,	G S
Debnam, H D,	Drayman	Horton, G D,	Drayman
Dewar & Wilder.	G S	Hornbuckle, R T,	G S
Dughi, A.	Caterer and Fruits	House. T W & Co,	G S
Duke, J E,	G S	Hughes, W H,	Crockery
Dunn, J G,	G S	Hunter, J B,	Drayman
Duncan, J,	G S	Irwin, Mary C,	Drayman
Dupree, J J,	G S	Ivey, T,	—
Durham & Moseley,	G S	Jeffreys, P J,	G S
Eberhardt & Baker,	Wood and Coal	Johnson & Johnson,	Wood and Coal
Edwards & Broughton,	Job Printers	Johnson, D T, agt,	G S
Edwards, J T,	G S	Johnson, O H,	G S
Ellis, A J.	G S	Johnson, Jas I,	Drugs
Ellis & Hinton,	G S	Johnson, Lem & Nixon,	Livery
Elsworth, Chas,	G S	Johnson, J J,	G S
Emery, A V,	G S	Jolly, B R,	Jeweler
Fasnach, Ed,	Jeweler	Jones & Powell,	
Ferrall, J R,	Gro		Wood, Coal and Grain
Forsyth, W G,	G S	Jones, Alf,	G S
Forsyth, Ed,	G S	Jones, T R,	G S
Fort, D I & Co,	Real Estate	Jones, W C,	G S
Frances & Goodwin,	G S	Jones, E G,	G S
Franklin, A M & Bro,	G S	Jones, Wm,	Livery
Fuller, Mack,	Livery	Jones, Louis,	Livery
Fulcher, W A,	G S	Jones, Austin,	G S
Gattis, H O.	G S	Jonee, Jno,	Dray
Gibson & Moring,	G S	Jones, Jno S,	Gro
Gill, B T.	G S	Julius Lewis Hardware Co,	Hardw
Gilliam, Minerva,	G S	Karrer, E,	Fancy Goods
Goodwin, J T,	G S	Kennette Bros,	G S
Good, Jas,	G S	King, J W,	G S
Gorman, Maxwell J,	News Bureau	King, W H & Co,	Drugs
Gower, W A,	G S	King, Jas E,	Gen Ins Agt
Gower, G W,	G S	King, O G,	G S
Hailey, J S,	G S	Lamb, D P,	G S
Hailey. Thomas,	G S	Lanford, W L,	G S
Harris, W E,	Drayman	Lee & Horton,	Gro
Harrison, Mrs Rebecca,	—	Levine & Brown,	G S
Harp, J S,	G S	Lewis, Edmond,	G S
Harris, W N,	G S	Ligon, Washington,	G S
Harris, J J,	G S	Locklear, Emma,	G S

WAKE COUNTY.

Long, Wm,	Livery
Love, E H,	G S
Lumsden, J C S,	Hardw
Lyon, Mrs W H,	Millinery
Lyon, H,	G S
Mahler Bros,	Jewelry
Mann, W B & Co,	Gro
Martin, E M,	Livery
Maynard, J G,	G S
McDonald, C C, Real Estate	
Broker, Ins and Buildg and Loan	
McKimmon, Jas & Co,	Drugs
MacRae, Jno Y,	Drugs
Merritt, W H,	G S
Miller, Amanda,	Livery
Mitchell, Seawell,	G S
Mitchell, U S,	G S
Mitchell, B H,	G S
Mitchell, Jno,	G S
Mitchell, Young,	G S
Monie, J M,	G S
Morgan, R S,	G S
Moore, D M,	G S
Moore, J C,	G S
Moore, Thomas,	G S
Moore, John C,	Drayman
Moore, T E,	G S
Morris, Abram,	G S
Morris, J T,	G S
Morris, Robert,	G S
Moseley, W S,	G S
Myatt & Co,	Com Merchants
Neal, L C,	G S
Newsom, W R,	Gro
Nichols, John J,	—
Norris, C A,	G S
North Carolina Book Co,	
E G Harrell, manager	
Ogburn, Louisa,	Livery
O'Kelly, Isaac,	Livery
O'Kelly, J H, jr,	Livery
Olds, F A,	Cor
Pace, R A,	G S
Pace, John M,	G S
Pace, E R,	G S
Parker, C S,	Dray
Parker, J W,	G S
Parker, C S,	Teacher's Business
Paschal, E E,	G S
Patterson W H,	G S
Pearce, Mrs ——,	G S
Pearce, Britton,	G S
Peatroff, O V,	G S
Pescud, John S,	Drugs
Pescud, Thomas,	Gro
Petty, Robert,	G S
Phillips & Co,	G S
Pierce, Robert,	G S
Pool & Moring,	Com Mchts
Pool, E N,	G S
Pool, E J,	G S
Pool, J C,	G S
Pope, Mrs J T,	G S
Proctor, Ivan M,	G S
Raleigh Coffin Co, G T Strickland	

WAKE COUNTY.

Raleigh Stationery Co.	Sta
Rand & Pearson,	G S
Rayner, Simon,	G S
Ray, Sallie,	G S
Ray, W M,	G S
Ray, Wm,	G S
Reaves, W J,	G S
Reaves, Mrs Hannah,	G S
Reddish, J J,	G S
Reese, Miss Maggie,	Millinery
Renfrow, Berry,	G S
Richardson, Wallace,	G S
Riggan, J D, Toys and Confectionery	
Riggsbee, W M,	G S
Riles, J W & Co,	G S
Roberts, W S,	G S
Robinson, A D & Co,	G S
Rogers, W H,	Drayman
Rogers, W A,	Drayman
Rogers, J H,	G S
Rogers, W H,	G S
Rogers, J Rowan,	G S
Rogers, R W, Gen Agt and Mgr	
	Mutual Life
Rogers, R S,	G S
Rosengardner, ——,	G S
Rosenthal, M,	Gro
Rosenthal, I,	Clothing
Royster, A D & Bro,	Confectionery
Sanderford, W L,	G S
Sanderford, N G,	G S
Sanderford, S W,	G S
Saulter, J B,	G S
Scarboro, E F,	G S
Sheckler, R H,	G S
Sherwood, C A,	Dry Goods
Simpson, Robert,	Drugs
Simpson, Wm,	Drugs
Singer Machine Co.	
Smith, M,	G S
Smith, John U,	G S
Smith, S T,	G S
Smith, John,	G S
Smith, Ed,	Livery and G S
Smith, J C,	G S
Smith, M,	G S
Snelling, W N,	Gro
Snipes, Jane,	G S
Spence, M B,	G S
Spence, A A,	G S
Spence, J A,	G S
Standard Oil Co.	
Stevenson, Thos,	Plumber
Stewart, V M,	G S
Strickland, G A,	G S
Strickland, Hynes,	G S
Stronach, W C & Son,	Gro
Stronach, Frank,	Livery
Stronach, A B,	Dry Goods
Symes, Wm,	G S
Symes, W S,	G S
Taylor, Wash,	Livery
Taylor, Ella,	G S
Thomas & Herndon,	G S
Thomas, J J & Co,	Com Merchants

WAKE COUNTY.		WAKE COUNTY.	
Thomas, Sam'l A,	G S	Penny, Elijah,	G S
Tucker, W H & R S & Co,	Dry Goods	Perry, E M,	G S
Tucker, G S & Co,	Furniture	Ray, C B,	G S
Tucker, W A,	G S	**ROLESVILLE.**	
Turner, Jno,	G S	Arnold, W C,	G S
Turner, Junius,	Gro	Berwanger, S & D,	Clothiers
Tyson, Thos, Jr,	G S	Redford, Frank,	G S
Upchurch & Scarboro,	G S	Rogers, L,	G S
Upperman, M,	G S and Livery	Stell & Peebles,	G S
Upchurch, B W,	G S	Stell, H H,	G S
Upchurch, W A,	Livery	Terrell, S W,	G S
Utley, R H,	G S	Watkins & Watkins,	G S
Utzman, Rob' M,	Gro		
Waddell, G W,	G S	**SHOTWELL.**	
Waitt, S D,	Livery	Fowler, Mack,	G S
Walker, L J, agt,	—	McFarlan, Jas,	G S
Wallace, W W,	G S	Rhodes, B W,	G S
Warden, —,	G S	**SIX FORKS.**	
Warren, N,	G S		
Warren, J M,	G S	Bridges, Jackson,	G S
Wharton, T W,	G S	Justice, Rufus,	G S
Whitson, Mrs E F,	G S	Penny, E G,	G S
White, L N,	G S	Ray, W H & F J,	G S
Whiting Bros,	Clo	**SWIFT CREEK.**	
Whitaker, F A,	G S	Rowland, W R,	G S
Williams, J B,	G S		
Williams, G J,	G S	**TEMPLE.**	
Williams, A & Co,	Books and Sta	Young, G P,	G S
Williams, Thos,	G S	**VANTEEN.**	
Wimbush, Wm,	G S		
Womble, L D,	Gro	Penny, E O,	G S
Woodward, Miss J,	D G	**VARINA.**	
Woodward, M W,	G S	Ballentine, J D,	G S
Woollcott & Son,	D G	Johnson, A N,	G S
Woollcott, Fred,	G S	Rowland, Bennett,	G S
Worrell, Mrs Bettie,	G S	**VETO.**	
Worrell, J H,	G S		
Wright, J J,	G S	Adams, O S,	G S
Wyatt & Co,	G S	**WAKEFIELD.**	
Wyatt, F,	G S		
Wyatt, Job P & Bros.	G S	Chamblee, M C,	G S
Wynne & Birdsong,	Drugs	Honeycutt, T L,	G S
Wynne, Ellington & Co,	Real Est	Kemp, J A,	G S
Yates, A,	Livery	Pippin, C E,	G S
Young, J A,	G S	**WAKE FOREST.**	
Young, C W,	Gro	Alford, Simon,	G S
		Allen, D W,	G S

Stenographer and Typewriter, Chas D Wilde; r, 118 S Dawson st, Stenographer and Type-writer with Ernest Haywood.

Post-office—C M Busbee, Post Master; Phil H Andrews, Chief Clerk; Jas T Busbee, Reg and M O Clerk; W M Lambeth, Gen'l Delivery and Stamp Clerk; E R Ellis, Chief Mailing Clerk; Guy L Bunch, Ass't Mailing Clerk; T B Yancey, Jr, Clerk; Jno T Ross, Stamper; Enolia H Bland, Stamper.

RAND'S MILLS.		Allen, Ned,	G S
		Allen, E,	G S
		Brewer, W C,	G S
		Davis, A J & Co,	G S
		Dunn, N A,	G S
		Holding, Davis & Co,	G S
		Holding, Thos,	Drugs
		Holding, T & Co,	G S
		Lankford, W C,	G S
		Peed, Z V,	G S
		Purefoy & Reed,	G S
		Riggan, D H,	G S
		Rogers, R L,	G S
		Scarboro, E T,	G S
		Smith, Mrs W B,	G S
Jones, C B,	G S	Wingate, W J,	G S
ROGERS' STORE.		**WEST RALEIGH.**	
Gulley, Q B & J W,	G S	Sheppard, James,	G S

WAKE COUNTY.

WYATT.

Blalock, A J,	G S
Fort, J C & Co,	G S
Johnson, L B,	G S
Watkins, ——,	G S

MILLS.

Kinds, Post Offices and Proprietors.
[See Addenda.]

MINES.

Kinds, Post Offices and Proprietors.

Plumbago is found in large quantities near Raleigh, and has been worked at different times, with more or less advantage to the miners.

PHYSICIANS.

Names and Post Offices.

Ayer, J M (dentist), Raleigh.
Baker, William, Raleigh.
Bank, T L, Banks.
Banks, Braxton, Banks.
Battle, K P (throat specialist), Raleigh.
Bell, G M, Wakefield.
Bobbitt, W H, Raleigh.
Buffaloe, A J, Raleigh.
Burt, B W, Enno.
Carroll, Norwood G (dentist), Raleigh.
Chappell, Leroy, Forestville.
Crawford, J H (dentist), Raleigh.
Cotton, A T, Morrisville.
Dowd, C F, Banks.
Edwards, W H (dentist), Wake Forest
Ellis, R B. Raleigh.
Everett, D E (dentist), Raleigh.
Fleming, J M, jr (dentist), Raleigh.
Fowler, M L, Rolesville.
Fowler, J W, Wake Forest.
Gattis, M E, Garner.
Goodwin, A W, Raleigh.
Harris, Hal, Wake Forest.
Haywood, F J, Raleigh.
Haywood, Hubert, Raleigh.
Herndon, W T, Morrisville.
Hicks, M L, Rosenburg.
Hines, P E, Raleigh.
Jones, ——, Raleigh.
Knight, J B, Eagle Rock.
Knox, A W, Raleigh.
Lane,—— (col.), Raleigh.
Lankford, W C, Wake Forest.
Lewis, R H (specialist, eye and ear), Raleigh.
Lynn, G M, Flint.
Marshburn, H H, Raleigh.
McCullers, J J L, Raleigh.
McGee, J W, sr, Raleigh.
McGee, J W, jr, Raleigh.
McKee, James, Raleigh.
Patterson, R M, Cary.

WAKE COUNTY.

Penny, J A J, Hutchinson's Store.
Powers, J B, Wake Forest.
Renn. Geo A, Raleigh.
Rogers, J R, Raleigh.
Royster, W I, Raleigh.
Royster, Hubert, Raleigh.
Sorrell, L P, Flint.
Scruggs, L A (col), Raleigh.
Templeton, J Mc, Cary.
Thompson, S W, Wake Forest.
Turner, V E (dentist), Raleigh.
Utley, B S, Holly Springs.
Walters, H N (dentist)) Wake Forest.
Young, L B, Rolesville.

SCHOOLS.

Names, Post Offices and Principals.

Academy, Wakefield, Rev O L Stringfield.
Academy, Cary.
Acadmy, Rogers' Store.
Academy, Wake Forest.
Academy, Apex, Rev J M White.
Cary High School, —— prin.
Morrisville Collegiate Institute, Morrisville.
Peace Institute, Raleigh, J A Dinwiddie, pres.
Raleigh Public Schools, two for white children and three for colored children; L D Howell, supt.
Raleigh Male Academy, Bloodworth st, Hugh Morson and C B Denson, principals.
Shaw University, Raleigh, Prof Meserve, pres.
The N C Agricultural and Mechanical College, Raleigh, Alexander Q Holladay, pres.
St Augustine Normal School and Collegiate Institute (col). Raleigh.
St Mary's School, Raleigh, Rev Bennett Smedes, D D, pres.
Wake Forest College, Wake Forest, Rev C E Taylor, pres.

TEACHERS.

Names and Post Offices.

WHITE.

Adams, Mary, Raleigh.
Allred, J C, Oxford.
Allred, S H, Morrisville.
Baker, Grace T, Rosinburg.
Bagwell, E C, Method.
Baucom, J S, Ewing.
Bridges, Kate, Pett.
Bailey, Miss Eva, Veto.
Barbee, Miss Irene L, New Hill.
Barbee, M S, Morrisville.
Beasley, Miss Hester, Vanteen.
Betts, D S, Raleigh.

WAKE COUNTY.

Boling, Callie M, Ewing.
Booker, Miss E N, Plain.
Buffalo, J S, Rand's Mills.
Champion, J D, Chalk Level.
Crocker, W L, Cary.
Crowder, Miss M E, New Hill.
Conyers, Effie B, Youngsville.
Cowdon, Miss Idalia, Holly Springs.
Edwards, Helen, Apex.
Edwards, Jennie, Apex.
Franklin, Minnie L, Massey.
Ferguson, Miss Kate, Neuse.
Fowler, J H, Rolesville.
Garner, S E, Shotwell.
Harrison, Alice, Massey.
Harper, Myrtie, Eagle Rock.
Heartsfield, Susie, Matt.
Hodge, F M, Eagle Rock.
Holland, Pauline, Apex.
Holland, W H, Varina.
Holder, Miss Eva, Chalk Level.
Holland, J C, Varina.
House, L H, Raleigh.
Hunter, Miss Bessie, Neuse.
Johnson, Miss Maggie, Garner.
Johnson, Ella, Raleigh.
Jones, Geo W, Banks.
Jones, Nannie, Banks.
Jones, Carrie A, Massey.
Jones, Lucy, Franklinton.
Jones, Miss Loula, Cary.
Jones, Miss Lillie, Cary.
Joyner, R W, Raleigh.
Judd, J C, Enno.
Judd, J M, Enno.
Keith, Mrs V C, New Light.
Long, Prof Hugh, Wakefield.
Long, Miss Lula, Wakefield.
Lyon, Miss Jennie E, Flint.
Luther, J C, Enno.
Marcom, J D, Holly Springs.
Meacham, D P, Raleigh.
Penny, I L B, Dayton.
Penny, W H, Jr, Apex.
Pennington, S J, Flint.
Perry, W T, Roger's Store.
Pulley, Annie, Eagle Rock.
Ray, E H, New Light.
Robertson, Lizzie, Raleigh.
Roland, C H, Holly Springs.
Shellum, Kate, Raleigh.
Smith, Mildred H, Raleigh.
Smith, R P, Cary.
Stewart, R P, Varina.
Stephenson, J Q, Varina.
Stell, Pittman, Rogers' Store.
Stringfield, E C, Raleigh,
Thompson, S W, Falls.
Turner, J M, Garner.
Upchurch, Ellie M, Raleigh.
Utley, W W, Raleigh.
Utley, J C, Varina.
Waddill, E W, Fayetteville.
Waddill, A M, Raleigh.
Welch, J S, Apex.

WAKE COUNTY.

Whitted, W A, Durham.
Whitfield, Miss Kate, Forestville.
Whitley, Helen S, Wakefield.
Wilder, J N, Shotwell.
Wilder, J M, Shotwell.
Wilson, D G, Myatt's Mills.
Williams, Lela, Raleigh.
Williams, Joseph A, Barclayville.
Yates, Miss Annie C, Raleigh.
Yates, J E, Auburn.

TEACHERS OF RALEIGH CITY SCHOOLS.

Bailey, Miss Cornelia.
Barbee, Mrs J M.
Bates, Miss Grace.
Bellamy, Miss Lizzie.
Devereux, Miss ——.
Fleming, Miss Belle.
Hale, Miss Mabel.
Hicks, Miss Lillie.
Marsh, Miss Mary V.
Mills, Miss Mary.
Pattison, Mrs L M.
Pool, Miss E A.
Redford, Miss Minnie.
Riddle, Miss Lula.
Royster, Miss Edith.
Sherwood, Mrs Mamie.
Strong, Miss Carrie C.
Terrell, Mrs Mamie.
Williamson, Mrs James.
Williams, Mrs S S.
Womble, Miss Ada.

COLORED.

Anderson, J T, Raleigh.
Askew, W T, Raleigh.
Avera, D J, Franklinton.
Barnes, Hattie L, Wilson.
Betts, Mary A, Holly Springs.
Bethea, R D, Raleigh.
Blake, Rev R E, Raleigh.
Bookrum, Fannie P, Apex.
Bookrum, Bettie E, Apex.
Bright, Lucy R, Raleigh.
Brown, M T, New Hill.
Bruce, Emma J, Raleigh.
Bunch, Annie, Holly Springs.
Cannady, W P, Oxford.
Clayton, W J, Method.
Clayton, Mrs Henrietta, Method
Cooke, Bettie E, Raleigh.
Dixon, S C, Franklinton.
Dowd, Wm H, Raleigh.
Dunn, Martha, Huntsville.
Dunn, Jno G, Raleigh.
Dunn, S J, Raleigh
Dunn, Mary J, Rolesville.
Dunston, Maggie A, West Raleigh.
Dunston, Lizzie D, West Raleigh.
Freeman, F R, Rolesville.
Garner, A J, Raleigh.
Harris, W B S, Method.
Haywood, J F, Auburn.
Hinton, Claudia, Raleigh.
Holley, I N, Raleigh.

Holloway, W L, Raleigh.
Holland, Robt, Varina.
Holloway, M, Raleigh.
Howell, Tempie A. Holly Springs.
Hunter, Addie F, Apex.
Hunter, Isadore, Raleigh.
Ivey, Cora, Raleigh.
Johnson, J Q. Ascend.
Johnson, Hattie B, Raleigh.
Jones, Geneva, Cary.
Jones, Mis Melvina, Flint.
Jones, W A, West Raleigh.
Lacey, B J, Raleigh.
Levister, Johna, Raleigh.
Ligon, J W, Raleigh.
Linebarger, Cora H C, Charlotte.
McAlister, J W, Holly Springs.
Mitchell, Georgia, Raleigh.
Morrison, Thos, New Hill.
Morgan, Mary A, Raleigh.
Morris, Ida E, Raleigh.
Norman, Mrs Fannie B, Raleigh.
Norris, C C, Myatt's Kills.
Page, Esther A, Apex.
Page, G H, Apex.
Pair, Mary, Shotwell.
Patterson, Mrs Alice, Raleigh.
Phifer, Nannie, Charlotte.
Perry, Ella, Raleigh.
Price, Elsa L, Raleigh.
Ray, W H, Six Forks.
Ray, F J. Six Forks.
Saulter, D S, Wakefield.
Smith, L W, Pett.
Smith, Mary E, Pett.
Stroud, A, Cary.
Tanner, Sarah E, Wilson.
Terrell, Narcissa, Shotwell.
Thomas, Sarah A, Sutton.
Thorpe, F P, Six Forks.
Tucker, N Z, Raleigh.
Turner, A B, Raleigh.
Upperman, Sallie A, Raleigh.
Utley, Allie L, Holly Springs.
Watkins, Jas A, Neuse.
Watkins, N W, Rolesville.
Williams, Elizabeth, Chapel Hill.
Williams, Moses McM. Method.
Williamson, Jas A, Raleigh.
Whitaker, Addie, Raleigh.
Yates, Dillie B, New Hill.
Young, B W, Rolesville.

LOCAL CORPORATIONS.

American Legion of Honor, No 1118, over Citizens National Bank; D T Johnson, Commander.
Anchor Lodge, No 230, A F and A M, Auburn; time of meeting, Saturday before the 2d Sunday at 2 o'clock P M.
A O U W, Murphy, No 3. Pullen Building; W W Parish, W M; L W Smith, Recorder.
Capital Lodge, I O O F, Raleigh.

Capital Hose Co, No 3; J R Ferrall, foreman; Fred Woolcott, sec.
Carolina Lodge, No 779, Knights and Ladies of Honor; B F Faison, protector; W N Snellings, treas; Levi Branson, sec; W W Wilson, N G; J E Bridgers, V G; J J Bernard, sec.
Cary Lodge, No 198, A F and A M, Cary; time of meeting, Thursday evening before second Saturday.
Cedar Fork Lodge, No 342, A F and A M, Morrisville; time of meeting, Saturday before the first Sunday and December 27th.
Centre Lodge, No 3, Knights of Pythias, 301 Fayetteville st; meets every Monday night; R C Rivers, C C; W W Wilson, K of R and S.
Chamber of Commerce and Industry, J E Pogue, pres; Geo Allen, sec; regular meetings, second Tuesday night in each month.
Citizens National Bank, Raleigh; Jos G Brown, pres; W J Hawkins, vice-pres; H E Litchford, cashier; F P Haywood, bkpr; W W Robards, clk; I T Jones, collector.
Citizens Trust Co, 331 Fayetteville st; C M Hawkins, pres.
City Cemetery, East st, between Hargett st and Newbern ave; Seth A Jones, sexton.
Confederate Cemetery, Oakwood, east of Linden ave; in charge of Ladies' Memorial Association.
Cotton and Grocers Exchange, 315 S Wilmington st; Chas E Johnson, pres; J J Thomas, vice-pres; F O Moring, treas; A A Thompson, sec.
Eagle Rock Lodge, No 201, A F and A M, Eagle Rock; time of meeting, third Saturday.
Eastern Star, Ruth Chapel, No 2 (col), 133 Fayetteville st, up stairs; meets fourth Tuesday in every month; Julia Foy, W M.
Enno Lodge, No 354, A F and A M, New Hill; time of meeting, Thursday before third Sunday.
Enoch Council, No 5 (Royal and Select Masters), 212 Fayetteville st; meets first Monday in each month, J H Alford, recorder.
Excelsior Lodge, No 21 (col), Masonic, 133 Fayetteville st (up stairs); meets second and fourth Monday night in every month; A Johnson, W M.
Farmers and Commercial Nat Bank; J J Thomas, pres; B S Jerman, cashr.
Governor's Guards; Fred Woollcott, captain.
Grand Chapter of Royal Arch Masons; meets annually; time of meeting, Tuesday next preceding the first Monday in June.

WAKE COUNTY.

Grand Council of Royal and Select Masters, 212 Fayetteville st.

Grand Encampment, I O O F; H E Heartt, G P; Geo L Tonnoffski, G S.

Grand Lodge, I O O F; W T Dortch, Grand Master; B H Woodell, Grand Secretary.

Grand Lodge, A F and A M; meets in Raleigh second Tuesday in January annually; F M Moye, G M; J C Drewry, G S, Raleigh.

Grand United Order of Odd Fellows, No 1616 (col), 406 S McDowell st; meets third and fourth Tuesday night in each month; Charles Hunter, N G.

Hebrew Cemetery, bet Oakwood and Confederate cemeteries.

Hiram Lodge, No 40, A F and A M, 212 Fayetteville st; time of meeting, third Monday in each month; W W Willson, W M; E B Thomas, sec.

Holly Springs Lodge, No 115, A F and A M, Holly Springs; time of meeting, Saturday before the third Sunday, June 24th and December 27th.

Hook and Ladder Co (col), Raleigh; —, foreman; W N Fowler, second assistant foreman; J H Rhodes, sec.

Independent Order of Good Samaritans (col); Jesusalem, No 6; Lone Star, No 7; Golden Key, No 15; Mt Gerazim, No 16: Enoch, No 38; Star of Bethlehem; Queen of Honor.

Ladies' Memorial Association; Mrs L O'B Branch, sec.

Litchford Encampment, I O O F, Raleigh.

Legion of the White Stone, Raleigh, Levi Branson, Patriarch.

Local Board of Underwriters; J S Wynne, pres; B G Cowper, sec and treas.

Manteo Lodge, No 8, I O O F, Pullen building; meets every Tuesday night; J J Harris, N G; V C Glenn, V G; Geo L Tonnoffski, R S; C H Beine, fin sec; T W Blake, treas.

Mechanics Dime Savings Bank, C E Johnson, pres; B R Lacy, cash; W N Jones, attorney.

McKee Encampment, Pullen building; meets second and fourth Friday nights in each month; W R Blake, C P; Geo L Tonnoffski, Scribe.

Mission Rooms Baptist State Convention, 113 Fayetteville st, Rev J E White, sec.

Mt Hope Cemetery (col), foot of Fayetteville street; Sampson Anderson, sexton.

Mt Pleasant Lodge, No 157, A F and A M, Rogers Store; time of meeting, Saturday before first Sunday, at 2 o'clock P M.

Mutual Savings and Deposit Co; John

WAKE COUNTY.

C. Drewry, pres; H E Litchford, sec and treas.

National Cemetery, Davie st, on Smithfield road; Capt. Elzie, in charge.

North Carolina Car Co, north end Salisbury st; capital stock, $100,000; R F Hoke, pres; John Ward, sec and treas; W E Ashley, sup.

North Carolina Railroad, 317 Fayetteville st, A B Andrews, first vice-pres.

North Carolina Home Insurance Company, Fayetteville st; W S Primrose, pres; Charles Root, sec and treas; Pulaski Cowper, adjuster and supervisor.

Oak City Lodge, No 419, Knights of Honor; meets every Wednesday night over Citizens National Bank; A M Powell, Dec; R H Bradley, R; J A Jones, Treas; C C McDonald, F R.

Oakwood Cemetery, Oakwood ave, foot of Linden ave; R H Battle, pres; Wm C Stronach, vice-pres; A B Forrest, supt.

Olive Branch Lodge, No 378, A F and A M, Raleigh; time of meeting, Saturday before second Sunday.

Phalanx Lodge, No 34, Raleigh; A M McPheeters, jr, C C; J J Bernard, K of R and S; meets every Thursday night.

Postal Telegraph Cable Co, E Martin st, —— Crews, mgr.

Pullen Lodge, No 1916, K and L of H; Mrs A P Cheek, protector; L W Smith, sec.

Raleigh Academy of Medicine; W H Bobbitt, M D, pres; H J Buffaloe, M D, sec; P E Hines, M D, treas.

Raleigh Branch Southern Building and Loan Association, Knoxville, Tenn; Chas S Allen, pres; C C McDonald, sec and treas.

Raleigh Council, No 551, Royal Arcanum; W C McMackin, R; W H Dodd, sec.

Raleigh Gas Light Co, W Hargett st; capital stock, $50,000; B P Williamson, pres; Wm McGee, sec; M Bowes, supt.

Raleigh and Gaston Railroad, office, 313 Halifax st; Wm Smith, asst supt.

Raleigh Savings Bank, W C Stronach, pres.

Raleigh and Augusta Air-Line Railroad; office, 313 Halifax st. (Under same management and controlled by Seaboard Air Line.)

Raleigh Electric Company; Alfred Thompson, pres; F H Busbee, vice-pres and counsel; F H Briggs, treas; C C Johnson, sec and supt; capital stock, $25,000; length of track, five miles.

WAKE COUNTY.

Raleigh Typographical Union, No 54; meets first Wednesday evening in each month in Pullen building; J W Cheek, pres; C F Cooke, vice-pres; E C Owen, recording and financial sec; C D Christophers, treas; Simeon Smith, sergeant-at-arms.

Raleigh Water Co; Julius Lewis, pres; M M Moore, sec and engineer; W W Smith, treas; A M McPheeters, jr, supt; office at the tower, 115 W Morgan st.

Rescue Steam Fire-Engine and Reel Co, No 1; hall and engine-house in rear of court-house; meets first Monday evening in each month; R E Lumsden, foreman; C A Riddle, assistant foreman; W A Faucett, recording sec; T W Blake, treas; W Z Blake, engineer.

Rolesville Lode, No 156, A F and A M, Rolesville, time of meeting, first Saturday, and June 24th and December 27th.

Royal Arch Chapter, No 10, 212 Fayetteville st; meets Tuesday evening after third Monday in each month; M Bowes, H P.

Ruth Lodge, No 4, Degree of Rebekah, I O O F; Miss Mamie Edwards, N G; Mr J S Keith, R S; meets first and third Friday evenings in each month in Pullen bldg.

Seaton Gales Lodge, No 64, I O O F, Pullen building; meets every Thursday night; A M Powell, N G; H J Young, V G; Phil Thiem, R S; Wm Woollcott, treas; Phil Thiem, jr, F S; J F Smith, chaplain.

Southern Bell Telephone and Telegraph Co, Raleigh; J W Merrihew (New York), pres; D L Carson, sec and gen supt; Geo H Glass, local mgr and supt.

Southern Express Company, 108 Fayetteville st; A P C Bryan, mgr.

St John's Guild, guild room and rectory of Church of the Good Shepherd; Rev M M Marshall, pres; Rev Bennett Smedes, vice pres; A P C Bryan, treas; Hugh Morson, sec.

St John's Hospital, foot of Salisbury st, Miss McClester, matron.

St Augustine Tabernacle, No 28, G U O B and S of L and C (col); meets every Monday night; G G Jordan, W S.

Thelephone Exchange, 118 Fayetteville st; George H Glass, mgr.

The National Bank of Raleigh, Raleigh; C H Belvin, pres; F H Briggs, cash'r; F L Mahler, bookkeeper; J B Timberlake, teller; J W Hardin, clerk. Capital, $225,000.

The Raleigh Savings Bank, Raleigh; W C Stronach, pres; G Rosenthal,

WAKE COUNTY.

vice-pres; John T Pullen, cashier, directors, C S Allen, V E Turner, B R Harding, W C Stronach, J A Sexton, Julius Lewis, G Rosenthal; capital stock, $15,000; surplus, $2,000,

The Mechanics Dime Savings Bank, Fayetteville st, B R Lacy, cash'r.

Uniform Rank, Sir Walter Raleigh Division, K of P; ——, Sir Knight Captain: John Ward, S K R.

Wake Forest Lodge, No 97, A F and A M, Neuse; time of meeting: Saturday before second Sunday.

Western Union Telegraph Co., 309 Fayetteville st; J A Egerton, mgr.

White Stone Lodge, No 155, A F and A M, Wakefield; time of meeting: fourth Saturday at 11 o'clock A. M, and June 24th.

Widow's Son Lodge, No 4, Masonic (col.), meets first and third Monday nights in each month; J Davis W M.

William T Bain Lodge, No 231, A F and A M, Raleigh; time of meeting: Saturday before third Sunday, and June 24th and December 27th.

William G Hill Lodge, No 218, Raleigh; B R Lacy, W M; Z P Smith, sec.

NEWSPAPERS.

DAILIES.

News & Observer; Jos Daniels, editor, F B Arendell, business manager; News and Observer Co, publishers.

The Press-Visitor, G O Andrews, ed.

WEEKLIES.

Biblical Recorder (organ Baptist Convention N C); J W Bailey, editor; Edwards & Broughton, props.

Christian Sun (Christian), E E Moffitt, ed and prop.

The Progressive Farmer, Mrs L L Polk, prop; J L Ramsay, editor.

The North Carolinian, Jos Daniels, ed.

The Caucasian, Marion Butler and H W Ayer, eds.

The Lodge Weekly (Odd Fellows' organ)

Spirit of Age (Temperance), R H Whitaker.

The Gazette (col), Jas H Young, ed.

The Outlook (col), Rev R H W Leak, ed.

MONTHLIES.

Missionary Talk; Miss Fannie Heck, editor; Ladies' Mis. Soc'y, publishers.

Wake Forest Student; published by the Literary Societies of Wake Forest College.

Our Record (Baptist Tabernacle organ), N B Broughton and A M Sims, eds.

YEARLIES.

Christian Almanac; E A Moffitt, editor and proprietor.

WAKE COUNTY. | WAKE COUNTY.

Baptist Almanac; Rev N B Cobb, editor and proprietor.

Branson's N C Agricultural Almanac; calculated and published by Levi Branson, D D, 30th year.

Turner's N C Almanac; J H Ennis, editor and proprietor.

FARMERS.

Names and Post Offices.

Apex—L J Atkins, J L Atkins, A J Baker, John Baucom, J M Broadwell, Seth Broadwell, W W Burns, J E Council, S R Cuningham, J J Edwards, B B Freeman, A L Gardner, T T Holland, W S Holleman, R Honeycutt, H A Hunter, Hinton Jenks, Wm Jenks, K Johnson, A H Jones, H T Lawrence, John Lewis, T M Luther, W D Maynard, D W Maynard, J J Maynard, Thos Maynard, agt, L E McNeill, Britton Mills, J H Mills, sr, H E Norris, J A Norris, W J Olive. Miss J A Olive, Bennett Olive, J H Olive, W S Olive, W J Patrick, R C Patrick, J P Pearson, James Penny, W W Penny, C G Perry, W A Pierce, W J Ragan, M E Rogers, W J Rogers, J W F Rogers, P B Sears, W J Sears, James Segraves, Sewell Howell, J R Whitehead, W B Williams, Albert Williams, John Womble, L H Wood.

Auburn.—C W Allen, C N Allen, J M Baucom, G U Baucom, Thos Baucom, A M Bryan, C H Kelly, P H Johns, J S Johns, Thos Johns, Seth Jones, Gaston Jones, J E Langston, R R Pool, Peter Pool, Hardy Pool, sr, J C Pool, Hezekiah Pool, Calvin Pool, Troy Pool, A J Pool, J C Pool, J J Sanderford, M A Smith, Jefferson Smith, J A Stallings, Samuel Watts, Wm Watts.

Ballentine's Mills.—C J Burt, A G Jones, A J Mathews, C F Norris, J H Norris, D F Powell, M J Wood.

Bangor.—J W Atkinson, J A Bailey, A Y Bailey, J R Bledsoe, W C Bledsoe, J M Bledsoe, G C Bledsoe, Frank Brannan, A T Byrum, M D Byrum, J H Furgerson, R G Ray.

Banks.—J M Blalock, N M Blalock, Hugh Blalock, John W Blalock, W N Franks, L J Gulley, Ransom Gulley, W J Hobby, S C Hobby, J W Jones, W D Jones, J Wiley Jones, Paschal Parrish, L B Parrish, G P Partin, M A Partin, W D Partin, G W Partin, J H Partin, B K Partin, Marshall Partin, E M Partin, R Y Penny, J A Rhodes, N E Rowland, J W Rowland, John Rowland, Bennett Rowland, W I Rowland, S M Rowland, A A Sexton, R A

Smith, W T Smith, L H Smith, J A Smith, O H Stephenson, B T Stephenson, Lynn Stephenson, J H Stewart Rufus Sorrell, W P Turner, Mrs W D Turner, J W Turner, S S Turner, sr, S S Turner, jr, J M Turner, T T Young, J T Young, Rewlin Young, J E Young, W H Young, S D Williams.

Beck—F J Bailey, J P Beck, Junius Beck, Chas T Beck, Alex Byrd, Isaiah Cash, W H Jones, R P Jones, S H Keith, Albert Keith, B F Lawrence, Zack Mangum, J A J Robertson.

Cary—G E Boothe, J W Boothe, W H Cain, C H Clark, G A Cook, J T Crowder, W G Crowder, Sion Holleman, Mrs M A Holleman, Rufus Howell, R H Jones, Ransom Jones, Mrs N H Jones, J H Jones, A G Jones, Mrs H G Jordan, W A King, C L Lenzy, W C Lowe, G D Martin, J J Marcom, Alvis Maynard, —— Montague, Mrs H G Morris, A J Olive, R J Olive, P A Sorrell, J N Sorrell, P Y Spence, J B Steadman, M P Stone, J H Stone, G C Stone, Young Stone, S W Stone, J R Walker, agt, Mrs M E Whitaker, N G Williams, Jas Q Williams, agt, E W Yates, agt, A F Yates, adm of A B Yates, R A Young, J R Young.

Eagle Rock—S P Anderson, J L Anderson, Margaret Anderson, Dr T H Avera, Theo Broadwell, H Broadwell, Wm Bunn, T R Debnam, C F Debnam, Nat Debnam, W H Earp, Sidney Faison, agt, F M Ferrell, Dolphin Griffin, S D Griffin, A R Hodge, J A Hood, J C Hood, Joseph Horton, M H Horton, C T Horton, G R Horton, D T Lee, J E Liles, T H Massey, Ruffin Medlin, J R Nowell, J W Pair, R B Richardson, W M Rhodes, E P Robertson, G W Scarborough, M A Scarborough, W R Scarborough, J E Smith, H K Strickland, Josiah Strickland, sr, J W Smith, J E Todd, C H Watkins, H A Whitaker, Eppie Wiggs, C S Williams.

Dayton (Durham Co) — Martha E Colclough, L B Ferrell, J J Ferrell, Roland Gooch, C H Gooch, R H D Gooch, W A Holloway, C H Husketh, W D Husketh, E H Husketh, S H Nichols, W R Nichols, J Q Shaw.

Ellington—M F Batchelor, W A Ednard, J W Hilliard, A S Sears, W M Yates.

Enno—J F Avent, J W Avent, F H Avent, J E Baker, J L Boothe, J H Burns, C J Burt, J A Burt, J H Burt, J J Burt, A C Burt, J W Collins, C H Collins, S H Cross, A J D Cross, W F Cross, W T Davis, A C Davis, J M Dennis, H W Holleman, E A Holt, J T Judd, Alsey Murray, Gaston Rollins, T B Rollins, A T Stephens, Eldridge

WAKE COUNTY.

Weaver, D G Weaver, L J Weathers, H S Weathers, J B Welsh, R T Wilson, Mrs Margaret Wilson, T W Wilد ham, W S Wood.

Falls—J D Allen, E A Allen, W G L Allen, Augustus Carter, G H Mooneyham, H A Lowry, J C Pugh.

Forestville—W B Dunn, J R Dunn, R A Freeman, J C Freeman, B T Garner, J A Hartsfield, J W Jones, W B Smith.

Garner—J J Bagwell, G R Bagwell, H B Bagwell, W J Beasley, G H Broughton, J T Rroughton, W B Buffalo, Burton Dupree, J T Busbee, Samuel Crocker, R E Gattis, P H Gower, A R Holloway, J W Honeycutt, W D Johnson, S J Mitchener, Geo Mitchener, H N Parker, Weston Parker, E L Rand.

Hartsville—R S Baker, A L Baker, Chas Baker, John Baker, Wesley Baker; Jasper Barham, J R Barham, R J Barham, J P Eddins, W C Ferrell, J D Ferrell, J A Ferrell, M L Hicks, Jos Hicks, S Jones, C D Jones, A S Jones Bourton Liles. Henry Perry, W K Phillips, W H, Ray, B J Ray, L D Scarboro, G B Stallings, A J Stallings.

Hickory Grove.—W W Pace.

Holly Springs.—D T Adams, D C Adams, J T Adams, R L Adams, A J Alford, G B Alford, J A Atkins, S A Austin, J H Beaslay, W P Bobbitt, W A Branch, J A Brown, N G Burns, W H Burt, B C Campbell, J H Collins, W F Collins, B D Cotton, T A Council. Fielding Edwards, Quinton Edwards, Robt Fuquay (col), D H Fuquay, J M Hare, T B Holt, T A Holland, J P Holleman, Barney Johnson, A H Jones, W H Jones, Irvinton Jones, W M Jones, J M Jones, A D Liggon, J D Marcom, F M Norris, N M Norris, A F Norris, J W Oliver, Ellen Overby, Caswell Page, B J Pollard, A S Pope, Alfred Powell, Mrs Ruffin Prince, Matthew Sorrell, J W Turner, J M Weathers, W H Wheeler, A L Wood.

Hutchinson's Store.—J M Adams, Loftin Adams, Isham Adams, S F Bailey, J H Ferguson, E P Hester, Wm Holder, R D Honeycutt, Neverson Hunter, J H Hutchinson, R M Jones, A F King, J W King. L R King, J H Nipper, T H Pool, sr, T H Pool, jr, J H Pool, jr, R L Thompson, H P Thompson.

Kelvin Grove.—A M Adams, C Beavers, J C Beavers, W P Carlton, sr, W P Carlton, jr, A R Edwards, A Furgerson, J G Furgerson, J H Grady, G D Haynes, W M Jackson, sr, M C Jones, W C Jones, John King, Seawell King, Jemima King, W W King, J L King,

WAKE COUNTY.

J M Lynn (agt), J H Lynn (agt), T S Lynn, J H Lynn, Eliza Lynn, W G Marshal, C T Massey, C O May, W J May, C M McGee, A V O'Neal, Moses Page, W H Pennington, W M Perry, E M Ray, L P Sorrell, J J Sorrell R L Sorrell, A M Sorrell.

Massey—John Avent, N D Burns, William Edwards, T M Franks, W R Franks, R G Franks, J E Franks, G D Franks, B S Franklin, F R Franklin, J W Garner, K M Goodwin, Geo Green, Wm Gulley, T J Harrison, D M Johnson, M T Jones, B Jones, J M Jones, W R Jones, E B Jones, J G Langston, S R Lee, J P Massey, W Q Maynard, J H Murry, J W Penny, James Penny, R L Powell, Bryant Smith, J L Sorrell, Gray Stephens, R S Stephens, J L Stephens, W H Stephens, W H Utley, J H H Walton, J A Woodard.

Method—W D Bashford, Jas Bashford, Wiley Cooper, Jos Cozart, J M Davis, W J King, John Liggon (col.), Henry Machau, W H Martin, J R Medlin, Berry O'Kelly (col.), W H Pollard.

Millbrook—M Y Chappell, E K Chappell, J Y Chappell, L M Green, E H Harp, B F Harp, S D Harp, J S Harp, J R Harp. R W Jeffreys, G W Norwood, M V Norwood, Paschal Reddish.

Milburnie—J A Haywood, J A Askew.

Moore's Mills—B B Brantley, W R Brantley, H F Brinkley, J P Edwards, J F Hopkins, F R Horton, ex'r, R E Liles, J O Pearce, W R Perry, J H Robertson, Wm Underwood.

Morrisville—J Q Adams, jr, W M Arnold, V S Barbee, I S Barbee, Madison Barbee, Rufus Barbee, L D Baucom, G L Baucom, W H Beasley, C E Beavers, C F Beck, W D Butts. Saunders Burgess, W D Carlton, M L Carlton, Wm Carpenter, R J Carpenter, J H Dunston (col.), Martha Dupree, W W Edwards, J W Edwards, D D Edwards, W H Edwards, J J Edwards, W G Ford, N E Gattis, Rich d George, W W Haley, A Herndon, J H Hicks (col), S R Horne, S R Horne, agent, W B Howard, W J Johnson, J M King, W A King, W L King, Yancey King, W J Lewter, J F Lewter, Frances Lowe and sister. B H Marcom, G R Marcom, S C Marcom, H A Maynard, H M Maynard, Jas Maynard, P C Moring, W B Morgan, A L Nipper, M W Page, S F Page, A H Parker, J A Parker, J W Parker, Thos Pollard, W B Scott, W G Sears, W R Smith, A J Sorrell, J P Sorrell, Needham Stone, A W Thompson, T J Thompson, J R Upchurch, C F Upchurch, Burtus Upchurch, W P Warren.

Myatt's Mills—S A Adams, James

Adams, J Q Adams, D H Adams, L Q
Adams, Alex Blalock, A J Blalock, T
R Britt, W D Crowder, T A Crowder,
J W Fish, J E Fish, W T Huneycutt,
A J Huneycutt, J W Myatt, J D Page,
N E Page. J W Pegram, H F Smith,
A T Smith, G W Spivy, T J Stephens,
R P Stewart, C T Stewart, R B Strain,
W S Turner, J D Turner, S M Utley,
L J Weathers, J C Wilson, Anderson
Wood.

Nelson—P B Barbee, Zach Rich, sr,
Francis Ferrell, Marion Ferrell.

New Light—B R Barker, H C Bar-
ker, T B Barker, Brinkley Barker, R J
Bennett, W H Bennett, Wm Bright,
Orren Bright. J W Boling, G O Booth,
B H Booth, T H Booth, W S Chappell.
J B Davis, J H Dupree, Jas Enniss, D
H Gardner, Stewart Griffin, H H Har-
rison, P A Harrison, E F Holt, J L
Holland, J T Hunter, H T Johnson,
Jas Johnson, Isaac Keith, J E Keith,
A C Keith, Bryant Keith, Lemuel
Keith, C C Keith, H C Lashley, J T
Lawrence, J S Lowery, G W Lowery,
W T Lowery, A F Lynch, T M Luther,
H M Marcom. Jno Marcom, M F Ma-
son. T J Mims, W H Mims, W H H
O'Briant, W G Olive, L P Olive. Hen
derson Olive, W F Perry, E H Ray, A
C Ray, W P Ray. T W Richardson, J
D Richardson, C J Richardson, J M
Richardson, A D Richardson, J R R 1
lins, H K Sanderlin, Thos Segraves,
Calvin Segraves, J R Segraves, J R
Sloan, J J Stewart, W W Stroud, O J
Upchurch, J M Utley, J J Welch, J P
Welch. L A Wilson, J B Wilson, Mrs
Jane Womble, W B Womble. Eliza
beth Womble, A T Womble, Thomas
Womble, Mrs Martha Womble, Blair
Woodlief, Pattie Woodlief, Zachary
Barker.

Neuse—W M Bailey, C A Bailey,
Henry Davis, E S Dunn, J J Ferguson,
T S Fuller, F J H Iloway, J A Hun-
eycutt, D H Pugh, G F Reace. W G
Riddick, W H Richardson, Samuel
Walton, F E Weathers.

Purnell—W E Allen, Prisey A Bailey,
P D Bailey, L E Estes, R U Griffin,
H R Layton, J C Little, Terrell Lowery,
A L Lyram, J H Mangum, A H
O'Neal, H H O'Neal, A C O'Neal. Jas
Pearce, E G Penny, J A Perry, Robt
Pleasants, T C Powell, J A Powell, sr,
Willis Smith, J H Watkins.

Raleigh—C S Allen and wife, Phil
H Andrews, D S Avera, J H Aycock,
R V Bagwell, F L Bailey, Wm Barlow,
E B Barbee, J W Barbee, R H Battle,
C H Beire, C H Belvin, Anderson
Betts, H Bilyeu, Rev W S Black, Mrs

G W Blacknall, Rev J B Bobbitt, Mrs
Fanny Boylan (col), C M Bretsch, N B
Broughton, J M Broughton, W B Buffa-
loe, W C Buffaloe, M W Buffaloe, B B
Buffaloe, William C in, L D Castlebery,
D W Castleberry, J M Carlton, Chas
Cooper, C E Cope, S D Coley, W R Craw-
ford, T B Crowder, Jno Davis, sr, W F
Debnam (col), N D Boy, jr, Ed V Den-
ton, Jas Dowd, C B Edwards, C H Ed-
wards, J T Edwards, A J Ellis, R E
Emory, J L Emory, H M Farnsworth,
C G Fetts, agt. Mrs Julia Fisher. J M
Fleming, Thos Finch, Chas, Claiborne
Fletcher, W E Forrest, A B Forrest, D F
Fort. Mrs J E Gill, W H J Goodwin. E
McKee Goodwin, C E J Goodwin, C G
Goodin, J T Goodin, Fred Goodin, E F
Goodin, A G Green, A H Green, Miss M L
Green, P B Griffis, John Griffin, Mrs
Wm Grimes, J S Haley, J G Harward,
Dr A B Hawkins, J P Haywood, A G
Hill, C L Hinton, agt, Mrs Jane C Hin-
ton, N J Hodge. M C Hodge, S Hogan,
J N Holding, W J Holleman, J W
Holloway, Mrs W H Holleman, Mrs
W H Holleman, W H Hood, R H Hor-
ton. H W House, R P Howell, W T
Howle, C H Jackson, A M Jackson,
Daniel Jackson, G M Jackson, C C
Jewell, J A Jones, J J Johnson, Jno
Justice, Geo F Kenedy, H H Knight,
J L Johnson, K Jones, M T Leach,
J W Lee, C R Lee, R H Lewis, Julius
Lewis, T L Love, J J Lynn, sr, J C S
Lumsden, Mrs H Mahler, J J L Mc-
Cullers, W R McDade, Dr Jas McKee,
E P Maynard, A T Mial, Millard Mial,
B F Montague, Van B Moore, Ben M
and V B Moore, Jas Moore, T H Mur-
ray, W A Myatt, M T Norris, J T Olive,
H D Olive, W H Overby, Mrs W H
Pace, R E Parham, Sidney Partin, Geo
W Partin, R S Perry, J S Pescud, S C
Pool, I M Proctor, Thos J Rand, L C
Reggin, Allen Rogers, N F Roberts
(col), J Rowan Rogers, J R Rogers,
V C Royster, Vitruvius Royster, R H
Sanders, Robt Snelling, W N Snelling
(for Crocker children), H T Smith,
J R Smith, W F Smith, S H Smith,
Mrs L W Sorrell, W C Stronach,
H Steinmetz, Alex Stephens, W R
Stephenson, Chas H Stephenson, L D
Stephenson, J Y Stinson, A D Taylor,
Jesse F Taylor, W H Terry, H B
Thomas, J C Thompson, J J Thomas,
A M Thompson, N T Thompson, Mrs R S
Tucker, Henry Turner, Nath Warren,
B J Upchurch, W D Upchurch, C M
Walters, F A Watson, Mrs Lena F Whit-
field, F A Whitaker, T M Whitaker,
W H Whitaker, W J Whitaker, S W
Whiting, B T Wilson, W B Wilder,
W D Williams, B P Williamson, J P

40

WAKE COUNTY.

Wyatt, L R Wyatt, Job P Wyatt, W W Wynne, J S Wynne, O G Womble, M W Woodward, R E L Yates, P Yates, T B Yancey, E M Yarborough, Riley Yearby.

Rand's Mills—D B Buffaloe, C E McCullers, S J Mitchener, H D Rand, C P Rand.

Rogers' Store—J D R Allen, J A Arnold, J P Ball, W L Bledsoe, W A Brogdon, Wiley Clayton, Mary W Cooley, J B Davis, Wm Dozier, Sam'l Edgerton, J B Ferrell, A G Ferrell, sr. J T Glenn, Willie Glenn, M H Gullie, A P Holloway, F H Holloway, N M Honeycutt, W M Honeycutt, agt, M J Jackson, W L Jackson, J M Lynn, D K Moore, G B Norwood, J R O'Briant. J W Patterson, J A J Penny, W D Perry, E M Perry, J L Pugh, J R Ray, G W Ray, C B Ray, W H Ray, Dudley Reed, W C Rogers, J C Ross, A D Ross, R T Saintsing, Elihu Sater, Brinkley Simeon, J P Snipes, M S Thompson, W A Whitted.

Rolesville—Clem Alford, W B Alford, J R Broughton, W S Broughton, L W Dent, M L Fowler, E C Fowler, T L Honeycutt, C H Horton, T H Massey, Wm Mitchell, C G O'Neal, W P O'Neal, J T Pearce, R P Pearce, John Pearce, W E Redford, J B Redford, B R Riggan, W W Rogers, J H Scarborough, S H Scarborough, J S Stell, J A Stell, Pittman Stell, J H Walker, N R Watkins.

Shotwell—B a r h a m Bridges, L L Doub, Lank Faison, J W Faison, J S Ferrell, Isaiah Hall, Sr. D B Harrison, B T Honeycutt, Sid Honeycutt, N P Jones, W B Medlin, A T Mial, Sr, Millard Mial, G T Powell, R E Talton, C

WAKE COUNTY.

Z Todd, R B Todd, A H Tucker, Gary Wall, Ashley Wilder.

Temples—Josiah Broadwell, Henry Kelley, A B Marshburn, W P O'Neal, N W Pool, H H Stell, J A Temple, B J Temple, R F Temple, J L Watkins, Sr.

Varina—G B Adams, J A Adams, D L Adams, C A Alford, Almon Austin, J E Ballentine, W M Ballentine, J D Ballentine, S J Betts, Allen Betts, S N Betts. J J Betts, A J Blanchard, R A Blalock, J A Dudley, B G Ennis, Jos Fish, J W Fuquay, B H Fuquay, S S Fuquay, B F Gardner, J A Gilbert, J M Griffis, Isaac Guy, A L Harris, D C Holland, J L Holland, W H Holland, W W Johnson, A N Johnson, B A Jones, J A Jones, A D Jones, W H H Jones, A M Jones, Washington Laws, J H Matthews, W J Mills, J A Mills, H D Olve, D H Smith, G T Spence, J G Stephens, T G Stephens, M H Stephens, A J Stephens, C W Suggs, A F Taylor, Norris Utley, R N Utley, M O Utley, J L Vaughn, S G Wilborn.

Wakefield—G M Bell, J R Bolton, C D Bunn, W W Bunn, W H Chamblee, M C Chamblee, Robt Chamblee, W H Chamblee, jr, W B Chamblee, J M Crenshaw, J C Ferrell, W B Ferrell, H H Foster, A P Hopkins, A R Horton, R B Horton, S S Horton, S L Horton, E M Hunt, Ed Moseley, S W Pearce, W R Privett, Riley Privett, Robert Privett, S A Richardson, J A Richardson, C J Rhodes, B T Strickland, G W Temple, R J Whitley, Mrs F T Whitley.

Wake Forest—J C Caddell, G W Davis, P A Dunn, Geo E Gill, Dr H H Harris, J T Holding, W S Holding, Willis Holding, J R Holland, P W Johnson, P H Mangum, W J Mitchell, W H Sherron, C E Taylor, G H Wall.

WARREN COUNTY.

AREA, 450 SQUARE MILES.

POPULATION, 19,360; White 5,880, Colored 13,480.

WARREN COUNTY was formed in 1779 from a portion of Bute county (which was that year divided into Warren and Franklin counties), and was named in honor of Dr. Joseph Warren, of Massachusetts.

WARRENTON, the county-seat, is 60 miles northeast from Raleigh. Population (estimated), 1,500.

Surface—Pleasantly undulating; a beautiful rolling country, mostly watered by small streams: climate pleasant, soil kind and susceptible of a high state of cultivation.

Staples—Tobacco, wheat, corn, cotton, oats, potatoes and fruits. The lands along the railroad are very desirable for trucking.

Fruits—Apples, peaches, pears, grapes, melons, berries and other small fruits.

Timbers—Oak, pine, poplar, walnut, hickory, ash and maple.

Minerals—Gold, with several mineral springs.

TOWNS AND POST OFFICES.

	POP.		POP.
Afton,	25	Merry Mount,	50
Arcola,	125	Mountainview,	40
Axtell,	—	Newman,	—
Brodie,	50	Oakville,	100
Churchill,	45	Odell,	—
Creek,	50	Oine,	—
Elam's	50	Poplar Mount,	—
Embro,	—	Ridgeway,	275
Fitts,	—	Shocco,	25
Greenback,	25	Vaughan,	90
Grove Hill,	56	Vicksboro,	—
Inez,	—	Warren Plains,	100
Macon,	150	Warrenton (c h),	
Manson,	50		1,500
Marmaduke,	—	Wise,	—

COUNTY OFFICERS.

Clerk Superior Court and Criminal Court—W A White.

Commissioners—M J Hawkins, chm'n; Peter H Allen, M E Newsom, J D Elam, R W Alston.

Register of Deeds—M F Thornton.

Sheriff—W E Davis.

Surveyor—Grant Beardsley.

Treasurer—N W Palmer.

County Examiner—J R Rodwell.

COURTS.

SUPERIOR.

Second Monday after first Monday in March, and second Monday after first Monday in September.

CRIMINAL.

Sixth Monday before the first Monday in March, and eighth Monday before first Monday in September.

TOWN OFFICERS.

MACON—*Mayor*, R B Thornton. *Commissioners*, W G Egerton, J E Rodwell, J L Coleman, M P Ferry, B I Edgerton.

WARRENTON—*Mayor*, J L Henderson. *Commissioners*, C A Thomas, F P Hunter, W A Burwell, H J Burwell, J W Harris, J M Ransom (col), J S Plummer (col).

TOWNSHIPS AND MAGISTRATES.

Fishing Creek—M T Duke (Creek), R L Harrington (Arcola), George W Booker, Irvin P Powell, W T Robertson (Grove Hill).

Fork—J A Dameron, P B Williams, P G Alston, jr, Jonas C Williams (Inez), Robt W Alston Thos J Pitchford (Creek), Thos Cornell (Warrenton), Jesse Alston (Centreville).

Hawtree—John M Brame (Macon), Pete M Stallings (Fitts), Peter F King, Armistead King, R H M Paschall. W Otis Harris (Wise), W P Rodwell (Oakville), Jno Cawthorn (Warren Plains).

Judkins—Samuel W Dowtin, Budley Plummer (Macon), A D Stallings, S E Loyd (Embro), G N Pittard, J A Pitchford, Henry Wollet (Odell) J G Newsom (Littleton), John W Riggan (Mt View).

Nut Bush—B M Collins, O Y Herekoft, R D Paschall (Ridgeway), W D Newman, John W Evans (Newman), Jas H Bullock (Manson), Thos H Jones (Poplar Mount).

River—M E Newsom, J H Harris, jr, J P Johnston, C J Devine, J R Boyd (Littleton), W T Carter, T B Fleming, E J Carter (Vaughan).

Roanoke—Thomas W Walker, J M Ford, Jas D Elam, J H Wall, A M Harrison (Elam).

WARREN COUNTY.

Sandy Creek—Jno W Allen, B. S Field (Warrenton), Jos S Jones (Steedsville), Grant Beardsley (Axtel), J T Northcott (Vicksboro), Sidney Davis (Afton), S S Reeks, J B Jones (Brodie).

Shocco—J B Ellis (Shocco), John H Burrough (Afton), W B Williams, Richard G Parker, J J Egerton (Warrenton), Lucius Boyd (Creek), J B W Jones (Brodie).

Sixpound—Horace Palmer, sr (Greenback), Jno A Nicholson Robt B Thornton, J H Nicholson (Macon), W C Drake, W G Coleman, J W Stewart, J H Wright (Churchill), Geo R Scoggin (Oakville).

Smith's Creek—Robt B Cole, Jno W Pattillo, J H Mayfield, G H Fleming, C D Curtis, Jno H White (Oine), Dr T B Williams, R F Rose (Ridgeway).

Warrenton (c h)—H B Hunter, sr, S L Crowder (Ridgeway), W G Powell, Alex Katzenstin, Thomas R Walker (Warren Plains), Peter H Allen, John Turnbull, Jno O Drake, Robt H Ford, Jos B Sumerville (Warrenton).

CHURCHES.

Names, Post Offices, Pastors and Denom.

METHODIST.

Bethlehem—Fork. W T Daily.
Church—Macon, P L Hermon.
Church—Warrenton, P L Hermon.
Church—Ridgeway, J A Hornaday.
Cokesbury—Ridgeway, J T Daily.
Hebron—Oaksville, P L Herman.
Jerusalem—Merry Mount, J A Hornaday.
Prospect—Warrenton, J T Daily.
Providence—Afton, J T Daily.
Shady Grove—Warrenton, J T Daily.
Shocco—Brodie, J T Daily.
Church—Warren Plains, P L Hermon.
Zion—Ridgeway, J A Hornaday.

BAPTIST.

Brown's—Warrenton, T J Taylor.
Church—Macon, —— Faut.
Church—Warrenton, T J Taylor.
Church—Warren Plains, —— Faut.
Church (col)—Warrenton, J A Whitted.
Gardner's—Macon, —— Harmon.
Jones' Springs—Afton, —— Sledge.
Pine Grove (col)—Church Hill, M E Hall.
Reedy Creek—Warrenton, A G Wilcox.
Sharon—Wise, —— Harmon.

PRESBYTERIAN.

Church—Warrenton, C Wharton.
Church—Littleton, C Wharton.

WARREN COUNTY.

EPISCOPAL.

Emmanuel—Warrenton, B S Bronson.
Good Shepherd—Ridgeway, C W Pettigrew.

REFORM.

Church—Ridgeway, Rev Wolf.

CHRISTIAN

Mount Auburn—Manson, Wm Long.

MINISTERS RESIDENT.

Names, Post Offices and Denominations.

METHODIST.

Daily, T J, Warrenton.
Davis, E H, Littleton.
Hermon, P L, Warrenton.
Hornaday, J A, Ridgeway.
Rhodes, J M, Littleton.

METH. PROTESTANT.

Fishell, D A, Vaughan.

BAPTIST.

Perkinson, L C, Oakville.
Taylor, T J, Warrenton.

EPISCOPAL.

Brown, B S, Warrenton.
Pettigrew, C W, Ridgeway.

PRESBYTERIAN.

Wharton, C, Warrenton.

REFORM.

Wolf, ——, Ridgeway.

HOTELS AND BOARDING HOUSES.

Names, Post Offices and Proprietors.

Hotel Macon, Edgerton Bros.
Norwood House, Warrenton, W J Norwood.
Palmer House, Warrenton, H W Palmer.
Phoenix Hotel, Warrenton, Mrs B F Long.

LAWYERS.

Names and Post Offices.

Boyd, H A, Warrenton (refers to Gardner & Jeffreys, Bankers).
Cook, C A, Warrenton.
Foote, C A, Warrenton.
Ferguson, M M, Littleton.
Greene, Benj (Cooke & Green), Warrenton.
Hawkins, M J, Ridgeway.
Hawkins, R A, Warrenton.
Kerr, J H, Jr (Pittman & Green), Warrenton.
Milam, Henry, Warrenton.
Polk, Tasker, Warrenton.

WARREN COUNTY.

MANUFACTORIES.

Kinds, Post Offices and Proprietors.

Blacksmithing, Warrenton, Cyrus Green.
Blacksmithing and wheelwrighting, Vaughn, P W Harris.
Blacksmithing and wheelwrighting, Ridgeway, Adam Williams.
Blacksmithing and wheelwrighting, Warrenton, J N Ransom.
Blacksmithing, Warrenton, J W Harris (col).
Blacksmithing, Warrenton, Allen Falkner.
Bright Belt Tobacco Co, Warrenton, H J White, sec and treas.
Building and contracting, Warren Plains, J N Weldon.
Building and contracting, Warrenton, John Branch.
Building and contracting, Warrenton, Peter Collins.
Carts, wagons, etc, Warrenton, E G Gupton.
Coaches, Warrenton, J M Ransom.
Coaches, Warrenton, W E Davis.
Coopering, Warrenton, W J Norwood.
Lumber and shingles, Arcola, G W Davis.
Millwrighting, Warrenton, H M Williams.
Millwrighting, Churchill, W A Shaw.
Saddles and harness, Warrenton, Jno Pender.
Spokes and handles, Warrenton, A & W B Crinkley.
Tinware, Warrenton, A M Miles.
Tinware, Warrenton, T M Casserly & Co.
Tobacco, Warrenton, Hugh White
Wagons and carriages, Warrenton, J M Ransom.
Wagons and Carriages, Warrenton, W E Davis.

MERCHANTS AND TRADESMEN.

Names, Post Offices, Lines of Business.

AFTON.

Hunter, E P,	G S
Munter, H B,	G S

ARCOLA.

Davis, G W,	G S

AXTELL.

Watson, J P & W A,	G S

CHURCH HILL.

Bell, R L,	G S
Coleman, J M,	G S
McCallum, John,	G S
Pennington, Henry.	G S

WARREN COUNTY.

CREEK.

Davis, B P,	G S

ELAM'S.

Elam, J D,	G S
Mosely, H C,	G S

EMBRO.

Harriss, J B,	G S

GROVE HILL.

Davis, R P,	G S
Vaughn, C B,	G S

LITTLETON.

Bobbitt, J H,	G S
Bond & Harriss,	G S
Moore, C G,	G S
Myuck, J J,	G S

MACON.

Bobbitt, A E.	G S
Coleman & Rodwell,	G S
Edgerton, Walter,	G S
Edgerton, Wm G,	G S
Nowell, J S,	Drugs
Shearin, Z R,	Miller and G S
Williams, O B (near),	G S

MANSON.

Abbett, B L,	G S
Bullock, J H (near),	G S
Duill, J K,	G S
Fleming, M V,	G S
Henderson, W B,	G S

MARMADUKE.

Clark, S K,	G S
Williams, O B,	G S

MERRY MOUNT.

Robinson, R E,	G S

OAKVILLE.

Rodwell, W P, agent,	G S

ODELL

Perkinson, L C, jr,	G S
Stallings, A D,	G S

OINE.

Hayes, A G,	G S

POPLAR MOUNT.

Duke, W T,	G S

RIDGEWAY.

Baxter, W L,	Nursery
Crowder, G F,	G S
Faulkner, S F & Co,	G S
Goodwin, J A (near),	G S
Mabry & Read,	G S
Meader, J A,	G S
Montgomery, James & Co,	G S
Petar, Charles, sr,	Nursery
Ridgeway Drug Co,	Drugs
Scott, J W,	G S

VAUGHAN.

Morris, Mrs Don F,	G S
Vucker, R H,	G S
Vaughan, C B,	G S

WARREN COUNTY.	WARREN COUNTY.

VINESBORO.

Finch Bros,   G S

WARREN PLAINS.

Booker, P W,   Livery
Davis, J B,   G S
Felts, P,   ——
Fites, J M,   Mill
Johnson & Co,   ——
Reavis, J T,   Mill
Sherrin, T W, agent,   G S
Terrell, W R,   So Ex and Depot Agt
Walker, T R,   G S

WARRENTON.

Aycock & Co,   G S
Batchelor, Jack,   G S
Boyd, J E & Co,   Leaf Dealer
Boyd, G V,   Leaf Dealer
Boyd, W B,   Leaf Dealer
Boyd, R B,   Leaf Dealer
Boyd & Rogers,   Tob Warehouse
Burwell, H J,   Leaf Dealer
Burwell Bros,   Leaf Tob
Burwell & Boyd,   Leaf Tob Brokers
Casserley, T M & Co,   Hdw
Casserley, Mrs T M & Co,   Millinery
Cawthorn, Wm (col),   Shoemaker
Cayce, H H,   Leaf Dealer
Draper, Jerry,   Furn and Undertkr
Edgerton & Co,   Barbers
Fleming, R D & Co,   G S
Gardner & Jeffries,   Fert and Gro
Garner & White,   Fire Ins
Green, Cyrus,   Blacksmith
Green, R T,   Shoemaker
Hardwick, Aaron,   Livery
Harris, Julius,   Blacksmith
Harris, A D,   G S
Harris, C N,   Conf
Heflin, R A,   Life Ins
Hendrick, Aaron (col),   Livery
Henderon & Cole,   Leaf Dealers
Hunter, F P,   Drugs
Jackson, C E,   G S
Johnson, J A,   G S
Johnson, W T,   Livery
Johnson, Mrs N E,   G S
Katzenstein, E, agt,   G S
Laughlin, J J,   Gro
Macon, H T,   Life, Fire and Acdt Ins
Macon, Jesse A,   Com Trav
Miles, Miss M J,   Gro
Miles, S T,   Gro
Miles, W A,   Tinner
Nicholas, A,   Conf
Palmer, H W,   Hdw
Pender, John,   Harness
Plummer, J S,   Livery
Powell, J C,   G S
Powell, W,   Jeweler
Richardson & Haithcock,   Shoemkrs
Riggan, D H,   G S
Shaw, N L & Co,   G S
Shaw, J H,   Leaf Dealer
Shell, O P,   Depot Agt W R R

Taylor, Mrs M G,   Millinery
Thomas, Dr C A,   Drugs
Tucker, G W S,   Auctioneer
Watkins, R K,   Auctioneer
Watson, W R,   Leaf Dealer
White, W J,   G S
Williams, S B,   Mdse Broker

WISE.

Johnson & Co,   G S

MINES.

Kinds, Post Offices and Proprietors.

Asbestos, Axtell, J W Allen.
Gold, Arcola, G H Macon's estate.
Gold, Arcola, Dr C S Boyd's estate.
Gold, Warrenton, Edward Alston.
Mica, Inez, Thos Connell.
Portis, gold, Ransom Ridge, —— Sturgis, of N Y.

MILLS.

Kinds, Post Offices and Proprietors.

Corn (steam), Warrenton, Thos Connell.
Corn (steam), Warrenton, T A Williams.
Corn, Wise, Zack Shearing.
Flour and corn (roller), Warrenton R D Fleming.
Flour and corn, Warrenton, J C Powell.
Flour and corn, Warrenton, Mrs Laura Taylor.
Flour and corn, Brodie, Dr R D Fleming.
Flour and corn, Littleton, J P Leach.
Flour and corn, Mountain View, J W Riggan.
Flour and corn, Metalie, Rodwell, Gardner & Milan.
Flour and corn, Vaughn, Thos B Fleming.
Flour and corn, Manson, G Beardsley.
Flour and corn, Ridgeway, H B Hunter.
Roller Mill, Warrenton. R D Fleming.
Steam saw and gin, Wise, Perkinson, Hicks & Co.
Steam saw, Warrenton, A & J Crinkley.

PHYSICIANS.

Names and Post Offices.

Alston, Willis, Littleton.
Browning, B R, Littleton.
Dugger, J R (dentist), Warrenton.
Foote, G A, Warrenton.
Green, S T, Warrenton.
Jerman, T P, Ridgeway.
King, J G, Warrenton.
Landis, G W, Shocco.

WARREN COUNTY.

Macon, P J, Warrenton.
Palmer, J R, Oakville.
Perry, Mark P, Macon.
Picot, L J, Littleton.
Taylor, A Z (dentist), Warrenton.
Thomas, C A, Warrenton.
Whitaker, M W, Littleton.
Williams, R E, Fork.
Williams, T B, Ridgeway.

SCHOOLS.

Names, Post Offices and Principals.

Academy, Arcola, Miss Mary Davis.
Female College, Warrenton, Miss Lucy W Hawkins.
High School, Ridgeway, John Graham.
Littleton Female College, Littleton, Rev J M Rhodes.
Male Academy, Warrenton, Prof Dargan.
Primary School (col), Miss Fitzgerald.
Primary School, Warrenton, Miss Mattie Brown.
Select Boarding School, Warrenton, Rev B S Branson.
Shiloh Institute (col), Rev M E Hall, prin, with two assistants.
Public Schools—white, 35; colored, 33.

WARREN COUNTY.

LOCAL CORPORATIONS.

Collection Exchange and Brokerage, Warrenton, Gardner & Jeffreys.
Grand Lodge of Honor for N E, N L Shaw, Grand Dictator, Warrenton, N C; P C Carlton, Grand Reporter, Statesville, N C.
Johnston-Caswell Lodge, No 10, A F & A M, Warrenton.
Knights of Honor, Warrenton Lodge, No 1898; N L Shaw, dictator; Rev T J Taylor, rep'r; H Tallarson, fin rep.
Mystic Circle, A D Harris, sec'y.
Warrenton Lodge, No 131, I O O F, W H Aycock, N G.
Warrenton Railroad; W J White, pres; J M Gardner, sec'y and treas; O P Shell, supt and gen'l manager; road three miles long. Directors—Dr J G King, Jerry Draper, W B Boyd, T M Carseby. Road connects Warrenton with Warren Plains. Capital stock, $15,000.

NEWSPAPERS.

The Record (Dem. weekly), Warrenton; J R Rodwell, editor and prop.
The Youth, Littleton, J M Rhodes, ed.
The Gazette, H A Foote, ed, Warrent'n.
The Monitor, W F Osborn, Littleton.

WASHINGTON COUNTY.

AREA 350 SQUARE MILES.

POPULATION, 10,200; White 4,961, Colored 5,239.

WASHINGTON COUNTY was formed in 1799, from Tyrrell county, and was named in honor of the Father of his Country, General George Washington.

PLYMOUTH, the county seat, is 162 miles east from Raleigh, and is located on the Roanoke river. Population, 1,500.

Surface—Low and level; much of it swampy, but quite rich, and very productive when well drained.

Staples—Cotton, corn, rice, shingles, lumber, peanuts and fish.

Fruits—Apples, peaches, pears, berries, plums, grapes, melons, and a variety of small fruits.

Timbers — Cypress, juniper, pine, oak, ash and poplar.

TOWNS AND POST OFFICES.

	POP.		POP.
Creswell,	300	Roper,	150
Mackey's Ferry,	75	Scuppernong,	200
Monticello,	25	Skinnersville,	25
Plymouth (c. h.),	1,500		

COUNTY OFFICERS.

Clerk Superior Court—T J Merrimer.
Commissioners—Joseph Skittlethorpe, chm'n; B D Latham, W C Merrimer, H M Snell, H A Litchfield.
Register of Deeds—Wm H Stubbs.
Sheriff—Levi Blount.
Solicitor 1st District—Wm J Leary, sr.
Standard Keeper—J P Hilliard, jr.
Treasurer—T J Basnight.
Superintendent of Health—Dr W H Ward.
County Examiner—H S Ward.

COURTS.

Superior Court meets seventh Monday after the first Monday in March and September and second Monday in June.

TOWN OFFICERS.

PLYMOUTH — *Mayor*, J W Bryan; *Commissioners*, J P Hilliard, L P Hornthal, D O Brinkley, C J Norman, C D Loane, Sampson Tone, Jos Mitchell; *Chief of Police*, Joseph Tucker.

TOWNSHIPS AND MAGISTRATES.

Scuppernong—C J Spear, A L Cahoon, H W Tarkenton, L M Barnes, J P Ambrose, D D Barnes, J F Davenport, C T Spruill, J H Snell (Creswell).

Skinnersville—Abram Newberry (Skinnersville), H C Spruill, J F McCabe, T S Swain (Scuppernong).

Lee's Mill—Jas A Chesson, J T Silkerson, Wm M Bateman, A C Wentz (Roper), W S Spruill (Mackey's Ferry), G T Hassell (Roper).

Plymouth—W W S Walters, Thos S Armistead, J F Norman, J P Hilliard, J W Bryan, H W Sawyer, N B Yearger, Thos N Pearce, Benj D Bateman (Plymouth), C B Latham (Monticello).

CHURCHES.

Names, Post Offices, Pastors and Denom.

BAPTIST.

Church—Creswell.
Church—Roper, A W Burfast.
Lilly of the Valley (col)—Plymouth, J H Johnson.
McDelane (col)—Plymouth, R W Norman.
Mt Spree (col)-Roper, W H Hockaday.
New Chapel (col)—Plymouth, S P Knight.
Second Bap.,Zion Hill (col)-Plymouth, John F Foulk.
White Marsh (col)— ——, J K Lamb.
Zion Grove (col)—Plymouth, C M Bullups.

PRIMITIVE BAPTIST.

Piney Groat (col)—Plymouth, George Rollins.
Concord—Scuppernong.
Morratock—Plymouth, N J Harrison.

FREE-WILL BAPTIST.

White Chapel—Scuppernong.

DISCIPLES OF CHRIST.

Christian Hope—Long Ridge, H W Gurganous.
Church (col)—Plymouth, — Pettiford.
Long Acre—Monticello.
Phillippi—Scuppernong.
Spring Glen (col)—Plymouth, Isham Darden.
Sound Side—Skinnersville.
Spring Green (col)—Plymouth, J T Pettiford.

WASHINGTON COUNTY.

EPISCOPAL.

Church of the Advent-Roper, L Eborn.
Grace—Plymouth, E P Green.
St David's—Creswell, Luther Eborn.

METHODIST.

Church—Plymouth, Jesse Lee Cunninggim.
Hebron—Roper, J J Barber.

METHODIST PROTESTANT.

Rehobeth—Scuppernong.
Salem—Plymouth.
White Marsh—Plymouth.

A. M. E. ZION.

Alligator (col)—Creswell, A Prindle.
Church (col)—Plymouth.
Church (col)—Roper, A Prindle.
Church (col)—Creswell, A Prindle.
Maccedonia (col)—Plymouth, W L Clayton.
Mt Hebron (col)-Plymouth, W L Clayton.

MINISTERS RESIDENT.

Names, Post Offices and Denominations.

BAPTIST.

Burfast, A W, Roper.
Cherry, W D (col), Plymouth.
Crosby, H C (col), Plymouth.
Lynax, B J (col), Plymouth.
Norman, R W (col), Roper.

PRIM. BAPTIST.

Harrison, H N, Plymouth.

DISCIPLES OF CHRIST.

Gurganus, H H, Plymouth.
Gurganus, J W, Plymouth.
Jackson, G W, jr, Plymouth.
Pettiford, J Thos (col), Plymouth.
Swain, C H, Roper.

METHODIST.

Barker, J J, Roper.
Cunninggim, J L, Plymouth.

EPISCOPAL.

Eborn, Luther, Creswell.
Green, E P, Plymouth.

A. M. E. ZION.

Hicks, H S, Plymouth.

LAWYERS.

Names and Post Offices.

Gaylord, A O. Plymouth.
Spruill, S B, Plymouth.
Ward, H S, Plymouth.

HOTELS AND BOARDING HOUSES.

Names, Post Offices and Proprietors.

Boarding, Plymouth, Jos J Chesson.

WASHINGTON COUNTY.

Boarding, Roper, J W Woodard.
Boarding, Plymouth, Martha Fanshaw.
Hotel, Creswell, A G Walker.
Hotel Robertson, Roper, Geo G Robertson.
Latham House, Plymouth, Mrs Laura M Latham.
River View, Plymouth, Miss F O Nelson.
Restaurant, Plymouth, E D Maecole.

MANUFACTORIES.

Kinds, Post Offices and Proprietors.

Building and contracting, Plymouth, A J Leggett & Co.
Building and contracting, Plymouth, Jackson & Marriner.
Boots and shoes, Plymouth, C W Askew.
Boots and shoes, Plymouth, Sampson Fawe (col).
Cabinet and undertaker, Plymouth, Marriner & Jackson.
Carriages and buggies, Plymouth, Hosea Teal.
Carriages and buggies, Plymouth, Geo R Bateman.
Saddles and harness, Plymouth, Joseph Tucker.

MERCHANTS AND TRADESMEN.

Names, Post Offices, Lines of Business.

CRESWELL.

Alexander, M M,	G S
Barnes, L M,	G S
Belanga, W E,	G S
Cahoon, A C & Co,	G S
Craddock, W A & Co,	G S
Hicks, Mrs Jennie,	Millinery
Howell, Mrs M E,	Millinery
Newbold, E S & Co,	Millinery
Spear & Ambrose,	G S
Spruill, C T & Co,	G S
Walker, A G,	G S
Williams, Wiley,	G S
Woodley & Swain,	G S

MACKEY'S FERRY.

Baxter, S B,	Groceries
Chesson, Mrs A L & Co,	G S
Davenport, W S,	G S
Holder, A D,	G S
Marriner, W C & L C,	G S
Snell, C W,	G S
Wiley, Geo,	G S

PLYMOUTH.

Ayres, W C,	G S
Blount, Mrs S A,	Millinery
Brinkley & Gurganus,	Livery
Bryan, S W,	Druggist
Bunch, M J & Co,	G S

Dailey, W H,   G S
Everett, Addison & Co (col), Green Gro
Fagan, F F,   Stationery
Goldstein, J,   Clothing
Hallsey, Dr B F,   Druggist
Hampton, W H,   G S
Harrison, A H,   Gro
Headen & Son,   G S
Hornthal & Alexander,   G S
Jacob, E,   G S
Landing, L S,   G S
Leggett & Bro,   G S
Lee, D (col),   Gro
Marriner & Jackson,   Undertakers
Mizell, H W,   Jeweler
Moore, J D,   Gro
Nearney, B,   Undertaker
Norman, J F & Co,   G S
Norman, M J & Co,   G S
Owens, B F,   Livery
Owens, Mrs A L,   Livery
Owens, M & Co,   G S
Owens, B F & Co,   Brokers
Peal, Mrs S D & Co,   Milliners
Plymouth Bargain House,   Clothing
Plymouth Drug Co,   Druggist
Skittlethorpe & Cooper,   G S
Smith, J H & Co,   Gro
Spruill & Bro,   G S
Wiggins, J H (col),   Gro
Yearger, N B,   Jeweler

ROPER.

Ausborn, Mrs M E,   Milliner
Blount, Alfred,   G S
Blount, Thos W,   G S
Blount's Opera House,   T W Blount
Carstarphen & Blount,   Milliners
Carstarphen, A C,   Millinery
Clark, B S,   Depot Agt, Tel Op and
                            Ex Co Agt
Cooper & Bell,   G S and Livery
Cooper & Thompson,   Livery and
                      Exchange Stables
Dailey, W H,   G S
Gaston & Pool (col),   Grocers
Gould, W E,   G S
Haulsey, Dr Ben,   Drugs
Herrington, J T,   G S
Herrington, E L,   G S
Jarrell, Frank,   Gro
Jones, D R,   G S
Jordan & Gould,   G S
Leary, D B,   Gro
Lewis & Johnston,   G S
Mizell, N B,   G L
Moore, J D (col),   Gro
Marriner, W C,   Livery, Feed and
                      Exchange Stables
Marriner & Cooper,   Livery
Munders, R B,   G S
Newby, John (col),   Gro
Roper, Geo W, Vice Pres and Gen Sup
               of Roper Lumber Co

Roper, Jno L, Lumber Co,   Lumber
Roper, L G,   Local Sup Roper Lum-
                             ber Co
Smith, R W,   Drugs
Trafton & Williams,   Gro
Williams, H S,   G S

SKINNERSVILLE.

Newberry, J T,   G S
Patrick, H H P,   G S

SCUPPERNONG.

Norman, I & Co,   Gro
Norman, J E,   G S
Basnight, T J,   G S
Davenport, ——,   G S
Hopkin, W T,   G S

MILLS.

Kinds, Post Offices and Proprietors.

Flour and corn, Plymouth, Norman & Harrison.
Flour and corn, Plymouth, A A Harrison.
Flour and corn, Lee's Mills.
Grist and gin, Roper, C F Blount & Son.
Roanoke R R and Lumber Co, Lumber
Saw, Mackey's Ferry, Alfred Blount.
Steam saw, Creswell, Alfred Alexander.
Steam saw, Plymouth, Walker & Myers.
Steam saw, Roper, John Roper Lumber Co.
Steam gin, Plymouth, T O Vail.
Steam gin, Plymouth, J M Reid.
Steam gin, Plymouth, L H Hornthal.
Steam saw, Plymouth, Hassell Lumber Co.
Steam saw, Plymouth, Loon & Co.
Steam gin, Plymouth, B F Owens.
Steam corn and gin, Plymouth, Rufus Swain.
Steam corn, Scuppernong, T J Basnight & Son.

PHYSICIANS.

Names and Post Offices.

Halsey, B F, Roper.
Hardison, W H, Creswell.
Hassel, James L, Creswell.
Hassell, S P, Plymouth.
Norman, H H, Roper.
Smith, R W, Roper.
Ward, W H, Plymouth.
Wolfe, H E, sr (dentist), Plymouth.
Wolfe, H E, jr (dentist), Plymouth.
Wolfe, T B (dentist), Plymouth.

WASHINGTON COUNTY.

SCHOOLS.

Names, Post Offices and Principals.

Academ, Mackey's Ferry.
Academy, Plymouth, Nathan Toms.
Academy, Roper, L R Christie.
State Normal School (col). Plymouth,
Rev H C Crosby, prin; J W McDon-
ald and E J Davis, assts.
Public shcools—white, 30; colored, 18.

TEACHERS.

Names and Post Offices.

Arnold, D W, Creswell.
Bardin, Miss Blanche, Plymouth.
Bateman, Daniel R, Creswell.
Bateman, Herbert, Plymouth.
Bennett. Miss Myrtle, Plymouth,
Bracket, Geo W, Creswell.
Everett, J O, Plymouth.
Gaylord, C A R, Roper.
Harrison, Mrs Mary, Plymouth.
Knight, Miss Ella, Creswell.
Norman, Miss Sallie, Creswell.
Spruill, Wm H. Crewell.
Spruill, Miss Matilda, Creswell.
Swain, Miss Ella, Roper.
Tucker, Miss Lula, Plymouth.
Walker, S W, Creswell.
Woodley, Miss Ornee, Creswell.

LOCAL CORPORATIONS.

Colored Odd Fellows' Lodge,Plymouth.
K and L of Honor, Plymouth.
Masonic Lodge (col), Roper; Jno Down-
ing, W M.
Norfolk and Southern R R.
Perseverance Lodge, A P and A M,
Plymouth; Thos T Armstead, W M.
Plymouth Lodge K of H, Plymouth;
L H Hornthal, dictator.
Roanoke R R and Lumber Co, Plym-
outh; F M Whaley, gen supt; runs
from Plymouth south, 25 miles com-
pleted.
Roper Electric Light Plant, Roper; T
W Blount, owner.
Roper Lodge, A F and A M, No 443,
Roper; Thos W Blount, W M; J L
Savage, sec.
Telephone Company, line from Cres-
well to Plymouth; W J Mercer, mgr,
Creswell.

NEWSPAPERS.

Boanoke Beacon, Plymouth, W F Aus-
bon, editor.

FARMERS.

Names and Post Offices.

Plymouth—A S Allen, Jos S Allen, O

M Allen, L L Allen, E R Allen, Geo
Allen, R A Ayers, E W Ayers, W H
Ange, J E Askew, Warren Ambrose,
H H Bateman, Jno B Bateman, John-
son B Bateman, G R Bateman, Jno M
Bateman, G L Bowen, Jno I Bowen,
W H Bowen, H A Bowen, W C Bowen,
L R Bowen. G W Bowen, Jr, G H
Bowen, J Z Bowen, B F Bowen, J L M
Bowen, Arthur Borden, Jos Bosten, D
O Brinkley, O M Chesson, J M Cutler,
F M Davenport, E H Davenport, D G
Dardin, A B Etheridge, Kenneth Gar-
rett, A T Gaylord, R H Gurganus, H S
Gurganus, C W Gurganus, E B Gur-
ganus, J W Gurganus, W H Hamp-
ton, Asa A Harrison, N H Harrison, A
L Harrison, W H Harrison, Jas S Har-
rison, J W W Harrison, J P Hilliard,
Sr, J P Hilliard, Jr, J H Hoff, Horn-
thal & Bro, Isaac Jackson, I H Jack-
son, A M Johnston, F R Johnston,
Cicero Kelly, C B Latham, B D Lath-
am, W W Long, W F Lucas, Rufus
McNair, J F McNair, W R Mizell, Peter
Moore, Stuart Moore, B J Norcum, B
F Owens, W N Pate, T N Pierce, Jno
R Respass, L F Respass, L S Respass,
M M Respass, J E Reid, Willis Robert-
son, C E Robertson, Jas Skittlethorpe,
Jas A Spruill, M J Stillman, J M Still-
man, Geo Tettertur, A T Tettertur, B
F Tettertur, T L Satterthwaite, H W
Sawyer, Mrs Martha Vail, A W Wal-
ker, Sam'l Waters, E B Waters, W C
Weede, J S Woodard.

Roper—A B Alexander, G W Allen,
W S Ambrose, Joseph Ansley, A L
Ansley, Levi Arnold, Sam'l Baxter, J
W Blount, Alfred Blount, C W Blount,
E F Blount, Thos W Blount, John M
Bowen, T W Chesson, H G Chesson,
W R Chesson, W H Chesson, E F
Ches on, J A Chesson, R B Cheeson, F
F Chesson, Jno B Ches-on, T L Ches-
son, W M Chesson, O M Chesson, War-
ren Cahorn, S M Clugon, W H Cherry,
N T Craft, T C Craddock, M C Crad
dock, R J Cooper, W D Cooper, H H
Davis, M S Davis, W H Davenport,
Jehu Everett, W T Freeman, Jas H
Gaylord, B S Harrison, E F Hassell, I
T Hassell, Jas Hassell, N T Harring-
ton. S R Johnston, D W Johnston, J
R Knowles, C R Knowles, E B Leary,
A D Leary, W W Leary, G W Lewis,
Jno Lewis. B S Lucas, Geo Manns L C
Marriner, W C Marriner, J T McAllis-
ter, J B Miller, J D Mizell, W J Mizell,
J H Oliver. E S Patrick, Romulus Pea-
cock, R M Peacock, J J Rea, J M Reid,
W L Robertson, L G Roper, W L Sher-
rod, J H Sitterman, J T Sitterman, T
J Sitterman, J E Singleton, Nathan
Spencer, L N C Spruill, W S Spruill,

W M Spruill, A G Spruill, Jesse Spruill, H C Spruill, W T Spruill, Edward Swain, John Swain, C W Swain, Rufus Swain, R S Swain, A H Swain, W J Swanner, H L Swanner, J F Tarkenton, T L Tarkenton. S R Turner. Josephus Vail, A V Vail, Riddick Ward, Thos J Walker, A C Wentz, H J Williams, Levi Woodley.

Scuppernong—Alfred Alexander, M M Alexander, W A Alexander, W D Ambrose, A W Ambrose. L D Ambrose, J H Ambrose, N W Ambrose, D D Barnes. L M Barnes, Thos B Bateman, Jos I Bateman, J F Belanga, Wm Chaplin, Stephen Clifton, C W Clifton, J L Combs, L B Comstock, Roberson Davenport. Doctrine Davenport, David Furlangle, P N Gray, G W Holmes, L E Holton, Sam'l Jarvis. H A Litchfield, Norman & Litchfield, Chas McGowan, Wilson Oliver, W F Owens, H W Phelps, J B Phelps, H Walter Phelps, R W Phelps, G W Phelps, Jas Phelps, J J Powers, J H Snell, C J Spear, Johnson W Spruill.

Dempsey Spruell. Magzie Spruell, J H Spruell, Jose Spruell. G W Spruell, W J Starr, T A Swain, A G Walker, J W White, D A Williams. J J Woodley, G F Woodley, T S Woodley. S W Woodley.

Skinnersville—J P Alexander, H S Basnight, T J Basnight. N D Bateman. B F Bateman, D F Bateman, Wm M Biggs, Willis Boyd, J R Cahoon, W J Cahoon, E S Cahoon, Henderson Clifton, E E Davenport, M L Davenport, George Davenport. J A S Davenport. Richard Elliott, C H Freeman, J W Hallsey, W T Hatfield. W T Hopkins, W L Hopkins, E H Leary, J H Lucas, Joshua Lucas, J F McCabe, Abram Newberry, T L Norman, J W Patrick, M R Patrick, G C Patrick, Hattie Phelps, W D Phelps, J B Phelps. E R Spruell. A W Spruell, D W Snell, E W Snell, H M Snell. Eli Snell, J F Snell. Abram Swain, C W Swain, T S Swain, H J Starr, J D Stillman. J A Stillman. J S Tarkenton, J A Twidder, C V White. W B Whitt, Geo Wiley.

WATAUGA COUNTY.

AREA, 460 SQUARE MILES.

POPULATION, 8,160; White 7,751, Colored 409

WATAUGA COUNTY was formed in 1849, from Ashe, Calwell and Yancey counties, and derives its name from the river that runs through it, which is an Indian name, and signifies "the River of Islands."

BOONE, the county seat, is 200 mile northwest of Raleigh, and was called in honor of the celebrated Daniel Boone, who once lived near Holeman's Ford on the Yadkin river. Population estimated at 425.

Surface—Mountainous; interspersed with beautiful streams; splendid water-power; soil rich; scenery rarely surpassed for beauty and grandeur.

Staples — Wheat, corn, rye, oats, Irish potatoes, fruits in great abundance, and medicinal herbs.

Fruits—Apples, peaches, pears, berries, cherries and a variety of small fruits.

Timbers—Oak, chesnut, poplar, white and yellow pine, sugar-maple, wild cherry and walnut.

Minerals—Iron, gold, mica, plumbago, silver, copper, with several mineral springs.

TOWNS AND POST OFFICES.

	POP.		POP.
Abo,	—	Mortez,	50
Amantha,	—	Norris,	60
Bamboo,	—	Penley,	—
Banner Elk,	50	Reese,	—
Beech Creek,	50	Rutherwood,	50
Blowing Rock,	100	Saint Jude,	50
Boone (C H),	425	Sands,	25
Brookside,	—	Shull's Mills,	50
Dark Ridge,	25	Silverstone,	—
Deckhill,	—	Sida Hill,	60
Deerfield,	—	Stony Fork,	—
Foscoe,	—	Sugar Grove,	150
Grandfather,	—	Sweet Water,	110
Green Park,	—	Tracy,	—
Grier,	—	Triplett,	50
Harman,	—	Valle Cruces,	90
Hattie,	—	Vilas,	30
Kelly,	—	Virgil,	—
Leander,	—	Watauga Falls,	—
Mabel,	—	Yerger,	—
Mast,	—	Yuma,	—
Meat Camp,	25	Zionville,	—
Middle Cane,	50		

COUNTY OFFICERS.

Clerk Superior Court — M B Blackburn.

Commissioners — W C Coffey, H H Farthing, Thos Bingham.
Register of Deeds—J W Hodges.
Sheriff—W H Calloway.
Solicitor 10th District—J F Spainhour.
Standard Keeper—John Culler.
Surveyor—L Trivett.
Treasurer—L A Greene.
County Examiner—W M Francrom.

COURTS.

Eighth Monday after the first Monday in March, and fifth Monday after the first Monday in September.

TOWNSHIPS AND MAGISTRATES.

Names and Post Offices.

Beaver Dam—H H Farthing, J B Green, Leonard Wilson, J K Perry, Wm Eller, Jas C Shell, Thos Farthing, H H Green, John Green (Boone).

Bald Mountain—John Tatum, C P Todd, H A Doblin, jr, W H McGuire, J I Wilson, Spencer Tucker, J W Phillips, Thos Ray, jr (Boone).

Blowing Rock—R K Hartly, G W Sherrill, H C Martin, H W Wheedon, J B Johnson, J P Fry, Sidney Bolinger, Job Backburn (Blowing Rock).

Blue Ridge—J B Robins, W B Rogers, A W Penley, J B Robbins, G H Hairston, Thos L Day, Smith Ford, Milton Stone, Jerry Harrison, Jesse Stone, J B Robbins (Boone).

Boone—J C Horton, Wm E Dugger, D F Horton, L N Perkins, F M Cook, W P Hodges, L M Trivett, Lafayette Critcher (Boone).

Cove Creek—M L Mast, T P Adams, Newton Combs, N L Mast, J M Morelz, Abram Reton, Bennett Smith, Thos Bingham, George Bingham, Rev Sol Younce, Ash Wilson (Boone).

Yadkin Elk—Sam J Hendricks, A E Welborne, Esau Hodges, Samuel Hendrix, P L Hamby, Joel Hayes, R H Parker, Henry Brown.

Laurel Creek—Erwin Green, W H Tester, Jno A Herman, T J Ward, Noah Mast, Lewis Glenn, M P Edmonston.

Meat Camp—J H Brown, A J Morelz, T J Tugman, Manly Green, Caleb Wirebarger, C Roy Norris, Jos Brown, David Regan, Amos Stanberry, Richard Gregg (Meat Camp).

WATAUGA COUNTY.

North Fork—Andrew J Wilson, Jas South, W N Thomas, W M Thomas, J M South, J H South, Wm Michael, W N Thomas, H T Bannon, jr, J J L Church (Boone).

Stony Fork—C A Grubb. L G Maxwell, J E Luther, J L Welborn, J A Norris, Thos Cook, Granville Norris, M A Norris (Stony Fork).

Shawneehaw—Geo W McGuire, jr, W M Michael, Wm Voncannon, Sam Banner, J C Chapel, Wesley Norman, James Gwynn (Shawneehaw).

Watauga—Alexander Townsend, S W Coffey, G W Caudill, Jos Phipps, M G Church, Filmore Presnell, G W Robbins, J T Church (Watauga Falls).

CHURCHES.

Names, Post Offices and Denom.

METHODIST.

Banner's Elk—Banner's Elk, Hunt.
Blackburn's Chapel—Elk Cross Roads (Ashe county), Hunt.
Boone Chapel—Boone,
Center—Valle Cruces.
Henson's Chapel—Mast.
Hopewell—Soda Hill.
Morris Chapel—Blowing Rock.

BAPTIST.

Antioch—Watauga Falls.
Beaver Dam—Boone.
Bethel—Sugar Grove.
Bushy Fork—Boone.
Church—Boone.
Cove Creek—Sugar Grove.
Ebenezer—Trade (Tennessee).
Flat Top—Blowing Rock.
Meat Camp—Moretz Mills.
Mt Ephraim—Boone.
Mt Vernon—Boone.
Mt Zion—Boone.
Poplar Grove—Boone.
Three Forks—Boone.
South Fork—Boone.
Stony Fork—Stony Fork.

EPISCOPAL.

Church—Boone.

LUTHERAN.

Church—Valle Cruces.
Mt Pleasant—Moretz Mills.

ASSO. REFORMED.

Mt Bethel—Blowing Rock, Joseph L Murphy, Hickory.

MINISTERS RESIDENT.

Names, Post Offices and Denom.

METHODIST.

Blackburn, H B, Boone.

WATAUGA COUNTY.

Combs, W C. Boone.
Osborn, G W, McBride's Mill.

N. METHODIST.

Matney, Jas, Aho.

BAPTIST.

Farthing, A C, Sweet Water.
Farthing, R P, Sweet Water.
Farthing, J H, Sweet Water.
Jones, Frank, Zionsville.
Monroe, Gragg, Foscoe.
Sherwood, J J L, Vilas.

EPISCOPAL.

Jones, M, Valle Cruces.

HOTELS AND BOARDING HOUSES.

Names, Post Offices and Proprietors.

Boarding, Boone, Dr W B Council.
Fairview Hotel, Blowing Rock, Wm Clark.
Grandfather Hotel, Foscue, S M Dugger.
Hotel, Blowing Rock, Mrs M J Brady.
Hotel, Blowing Rock, King & Gray.
Hotel, Blowing Rock, W W Stringfellow.
Hotel, Boone, W L Bryan.
Hotel, Boone, T J Coffey & Bro.
Hotel, Elk Cross Roads (Ashe co), W C L Hulcher.
Morris House, Blowing Rock, W M Morris.
Silver Lake Hotel, Blowing Rock, L W Estes.

LAWYERS.

Names and Post Offices.

Coffey, W S, Boone,
Council, W B, Jr, Boone.
Fletcher, J C, Boone.
Green, L L, Boone.
Lovell, E F, Boone.

MANUFACTORIES.

Kinds, Post Offices and Proprietors.

Blacksmithing and wheelweighting, Boone, J Council.
Blacksmithing and wheelwrighting, Boone, H L Huggins.
Blacksmithing and wheelwrighting, Watauga Falls, Benj. Baird.
Blacksmithing and wheelwrighting, Dark Ridge, L H Cook.
Blacksmithing and wheelwrighting, Stony Fork, L W Greene.
Blacksmithing and wheelwrighting, Stony Fork, Lee Greene.
Blacksmithing and wheelwrighting, Bamboo, John Hartley.

WATAUGA COUNTY.	WATAUGA COUNTY.

Building and contracting, Bamboo, G A Critcher.

Building and contracting, Bamboo, W P Critcher.

Building and contracting, Stony Fork. J E Luther.

Building and contracting, Boone, Council Bros.

Building and contracting, Stony Fork, J C Winkler.

Building and contracting, Dark Ridge, B T McGuire.

Building and contracting, Rutherwood. C A Grubbs.

Building and contracting, Boone, J L Kincaid.

Coopering, Watauga Falls, A J Baird.

Coopering, Stony Fork, Henry Church.

Coopering, Stony Fork, J Church, jr.

Distillery (brandy), Watauga Falls, Wm Baird.

Millwrighting, Blowing Rock, J E Greene.

Millwrighting, Valle Cruces, A Townsend & Son.

Millwrighting, Stony Fork, J C Winkler.

Saddles and harness, Boone, T J Coffey & Co.

Spokes, shingles, etc, Boone, J A Critcher & Co.

Tannery, Boone, T J Coffey & Bro.

Tannery, Boone, J H Cook.

Tannery, Boone, H W Hardin.

Tannery, Watauga Falls, E M Greene.

Tannery, Watauga Falls, Marshall Greer.

Tannery, Watauga Falls, Jno Walker.

Wagons, Boone, J D Council.

Wagons, furniture, etc, Beaver Dam, Geo Sherrill.

MERCHANTS AND TRADESMEN.

Names, Post Offices and Lines of Business.

AHO.

Wagener, W E & Co,	G S
AMANTHA.	
Sherwood, W F & Co,	G S
BAMBOO.	
Critcher, T A,	G S
BANNER'S ELK.	
Lowe & Stinson,	G S
Proffitt & Vuncannon,	G S
BEECH CREEK.	
Reese, I V,	G S
BLOWING ROCK.	
Blowing Rock Hotel Co.	
Edmiston & Palmer,	G S
Green Park Monument Co.	
Martin, H C & Co,	G S

Stringfellow, W W,	Mill
Watauga Hotel Co.	
BOONE.	
Blackburn, Cottrell & Miller,	G S
Bryan, W L.	G S
Coffey, T J & Bro,	G S
Reeves, Dr L C,	G S
DECK HILL.	
Winkler, J S,	G S
FOSCOE.	
Calloway & Johnson,	G S
MABEL.	
Moretz, McKoy,	G S
MAST.	
Mast, N L,	G S
MEAT CAMP.	
Moretz, J M & Co,	G S
MORETZ MILLS.	
Tatum & Goodman,	G S
NORRIS.	
Coffey & Green,	G S
Green, Allen,	G S
RUTHERWOOD.	
Hodges & Bros,	G S
SHULL'S MILLS.	
Shull, J C,	G S
SILVERSTONE.	
Holsclaw, A A,	G S
STONEY FORK.	
Hendricks, W L,	G S
SUGAR GROVE.	
Phillips, J B & J W,	G S
SWEET WATER.	
Farthing, L W,	G S
VALLE CRUCES.	
Baird, W B,	G S
Taylor, C D,	G S
VILAS.	
Holsclaw, W W,	G S
VIRGIL.	
Walker, R W,	G S
WATAUGA FALLS.	
Harmon, J E,	Mill
Miller, Benton,	G S
YERGER.	
Dougherty, E H,	G S
ZIONVILLE.	
Church, E M,	G S
Eggers, J S,	G S

MINES.

Kinds, Post Offices and Proprietors.

Copper. Elk Cross-Roads (Ashe county), R C Rhea & Co.

WATAUGA COUNTY.

Copper, Elk Cross-Roads (Ashe county), J B Miller.
Council, gold, Boone, I P Connell.
Council, gold, Elk Knob, Wagner & Co.
Flexible sandstone, Stony Fork, J R Hodges & Co.
Grandfather Silver Mine, Foscoe, W A Davis
Gragg, gold, Boone, John Gragg.
Hardin, gold, Boone, H W Hardin.
Iron, Boone, D B Dougherty & Co.
Iron, Boone, James McGhee.
Mica, Elk Cross Roads (Ashe county), L Ray & Co.
Mica, Valle Cruces, W Vuncannon.
Poga, silver, Beech Creek, Dr Stewart.
Silver, Watauga Falls, ———·
Silver, Taylorsville (Tennessee), Wagner & Co.
Silver, Boone, Leventhorpe & Douglass.
Silver, Middle Cane, J R Hodges.

MILLS.

Kinds, Post Offices and Proprietors.

Corn and flour, Penley, A W Penley.
Corn and flour, Triplett, Eli Woff.
Corn and flour, Boone, S Winkler.
Corn and flour, Stony Fork, D B Wagner.
Corn and flour, Valle Cruces, H Taylor.
Corn and flour, Dark Ridge, Joel Trivett.
Corn and flour, Boone, W T Hayes.
Corn and flour, Boone, W J Crutcher & Son.
Corn and flour, D B Dougherty.
Corn and flour, Banner's Elk, Samuel Banner.
Corn and flour, Blowing Rock, W W Stringfellow.
Corn and flour, Mast, John McGuire.
Corn and flour, Mast, William Miller & Son.
Corn and flour, Soda Hill, A J Moretz.
Corn and flour, Meat Camp, Hosea Wineberger.
Corn and flour, Watauga Falls, Elijah Mast.
Corn and flour, Watauga Falls, Jackson Baird.
Corn and flour, Watauga Falls, Calvin Ward.
Corn, flour and saw, Stony Fork, A J Moretz.
Corn, flour and saw, Shull's Mills, A C Calloway.
Corn, flour and saw, Shull's Mills, W W Lenoir's heirs.

WATAUGA COUNTY.

Corn, flour and saw, Shull's Mills, W C Coffey.
Saw, Boone, W Critcher.
Saw, Watauga Falls, William Mast & Co.
Saw, Bamboo, Rogers & Co.
Saw and grist, Foscoe, M T Preswell.
Saw and grist mill, Vilas, J P Council.
Saw, Watauga Falls, J E Harmon.
Saw, Zionville, J R Reece.

PHYSICIANS.

Names and Post Offices.

Blackburn, T C, Zionsville.
Bingham, F M, Amantha.
Council, W B, sr, Boone.
Perlear, ———, Boone.
Phipps, C W, Foscoe.
Phillips, J B, Sugar Grove.
Reeves, ———, Boone.

SCHOOLS.

Names, Post Offices and Principals.

Cove Creek, ———, E J Blackburn.
High school, Boone, J W Thomas.
High school, Valle Cruces.
New River Academy, Boone, W M Francrom.
Skyland Academy, Blowing Rock, Miss Pruden.
Valle Cruces, Valle Cruces.
Public schools—white, 53; colored, 3.

TEACHERS.

Names and Post Offices.

Blackburn, E J, ———.
Frankum, W M, Valle Cruces.
Rivers, Nannie J, Boone.
Spainhour, W, Horton.

LOCAL CORPORATIONS.

Elk Lodge, No 373, A F and A M, Elk Cross Roads (Ashe county). Time of meeting, Friday evening after each full moon.
Snow Lodge, No 363, A F and A M, Sugar Grove. Time of meeting, Friday evening after full moon, and June 24th and December 27th.
Watauga Lodge, No 273, A F and A M, Boone. Time of meeting, first Friday evening on or before full moon, and June 24th and December 27th.

WAYNE COUNTY.

AREA, 500 SQUARE MILES.
POPULATION, 26,100; White 15,715, Colored 10,385.

WAYNE COUNTY was formed in 1779 from Dobbs county (subsequently divided into Greene and Lenoir), and was named in honor of Anthony Wayne, of Pennsylvania, distinguished in the Revolution.

GOLDSBORO, the county seat, is 49 miles east from Raleigh, and is located at the junction of the North Carolina, Atlantic and North Carolina and Wilmington and Weldon Railroads. Population (estimated), 6,500.

Surface—Level and sandy; soil generally good and very productive when well-drained. Soil and climate well suited for trucking.

Staples—Cotton, corn, rice, wheat, sweet potatoes and naval stores. This is a fine cotton county, and many of the farms are under a high state of cultivation.

Fruits—Apples, peaches, pears, melons, grapes, berries and a variety of small fruits.

Timbers—Oak, ash, hickory, pine, maple, juniper, poplar, walnut and cypress.

TOWNS AND POST OFFICES.

	POP.		POP.
Aaron,	—	Goldsboro	
Angle,	25	(C H),	6,500
Beston,	50	Grantham,	50
Bizzell,	20	Greenleaf,	75
Cogdell,	25	McClammy,	25
Dobbersville,	60	Mount Olive,	800
Dudley,	150	Pikeville,	150
Elroy,	—	Pinkney,	25
Eureka,	100	Saulston,	50
Faro,	—	Seven Springs,	150
Freemont,	525	Starlight,	30
Genoa,	—	Walter,	25

COUNTY OFFICERS.

Clerk Superior Court—C F Herring.
Commissioners—J E Peterson, chm'n; Wm Holmes, J M Wood, John Loftin, M T Johnson.
Coroner—Dr Thomas Hill.
Register of Deeds—G C Kornegay.
Sheriff—B F Scott.
Solicitor 4th District—E W Pou.
Standard Keeper—S Pittman.
Surveyor—J J Herring.
Tax-collector—One for each township.
Treasurer—A T Uzzell.

County Attorneys—Allen & Dortch.
Supt of Health—Dr W J Jones, jr.
County Examiner—E T Atkinson.
Keeper of Home of the Indigent—J Edmondson.

COURTS.

Sixth Monday before the first Monday in March; sixth Monday after the first Monday in March; first Monday after the first Monday in September; sixth Monday after the first Monday in September.

TOWN OFFICERS.

FREMONT — *Mayor*, B F Aycock; *Commissioners*, J P Aycock, C C Aycock, J W Sasser, J F Hook, W H Barn; *Policeman*, J H Hinnant.

GOLDSBORO—*Mayor*, J H Hill; *Aldermen*, J A Washington, W G Britt, F R Borden, F W Hilker, J W Nash, W D Creech, Burke Artes, B S Stevens, J L Payton; *Clerk*, T H Bain; *Treasurer*, Frank Miller; *Constable*, Thos Head; *Chief of Police*, A B Freeman; *City Physician*, W M Cobb, jr.

MOUNT OLIVE—*Mayor*, J R Hatch; *Commissioners*, William Holmes, Y H Knowles, W T Horn, W E Wilkerson, J W Kornegay.

SAULS' CROSS-ROADS — *Mayor*, S S Strather.

SEVEN SPRINGS—*Mayor*, W R Simmons.

TOWNSHIPS AND MAGISTRATES.

Brogden—D E Stevens, J T Hollowell, Wiley Thompson, L W Winne, J C Rhodes, H C Williamson, W C O'Berry, G F Parker, M B Farmer (Goldsboro).

Fork—W H Brogden, G W Pipkin, B D Hooks, J L Pearson, A L Swinton, J H Caldwell, E L Reid (Goldsboro).

Grantham—G M Bridgers, C J McCullen, J B Kennedy, Julius Jordan, D A Cogdell, J F Grantham, Erastus Goodwin (Goldsboro).

Goldsboro — W T Hollowell, J M Swearinger, D J Broadhurst, Hugh Humphrey, W A Deans, J F Dobson, Siover Bryant, W P Lane, A T Grady (Goldsboro).

Great Swamp—E S Dees, Green

41

WAYNE COUNTY.

Copeland, Barnes Aycock, N G Holland, C L Rose, B R Edgerton, J L Barden, H W Godwin (Goldsboro).

Indian Springs—S B Smith, S C Casey, W B Whitfield, B S Barwick, J H Grady, G O Griffin, S A Casey, S O Holmes (Goldsboro).

Nahunta—L D Misshew, R F Aycock, J D Mayho, J F Ormond, J W Smith, Z P Davis, Jason Coley, H S Reed, T C Blalock (Goldboro).

Newhope—Thos Sutton, J W Isler, N McBuie. J M Wood, C Tripp, J W Daily; B W Daniels, W Garris, T W Uzzle, (Goldsboro).

Pikeville—Albert Aycock,T N Wiggs, J F Hosea, E A Pearson, W E Ham. Calhoun Sherrard, W L Ezzell, J E Person, Benj Deans (Pikeville).

Sauston—J B Parks, B A Parks, J J Roberts. W P Exum, F Thompson, Jos Parks. J W Gardner (Saulston).

Stony Creek—M J Ham. N J Smith, N A Howell. Jackson Pate, Curtis Howell, E F Hodge, H D Ham (Goldsboro).

CHURCHES.

Names, Pastors, Postoffices and Denom.

METHODIST.

Bethel—Newsom, A L Ormond.
Church—Mt Olive, N M Jurney.
Church—Fremont.
Church (col)—Dudley.
Dennis' Chapel—Goldsboro.
Ebenezer—Walter.
Falling Creek—Grantham's Store, N M Jurney.
Indian Spring—Dudley, N M Jurney.
Mt Carmel—Pikeville, A L Ormond.
Piny Grove—Seven Springs, G T Simmonds.
Providence—Dudley, A L Ormond.
Salem—Goldsboro, A L Ormond.
Smith's Chapel—Mt Olive—N M Jurney.
St John's—Goldsboro, J E Bristowe.
St Paul's—Goldsboro, R C Beaman.
Thompson Chapel—Goldsboro, A L Ormond.
Yelverton—Pikeville.

ZION METHODIST.

Church (col)—Goldsboro.

BAPTIST.

Church—Goldsboro, J S Long.
Church—Mt Olive.
Church (col)—Goldsboro.
Church (col)—Fremont.
Church (col)—Mount Olive.
Falling Creek—Grantham's Store.
Mount Calvary—Goldsboro.
Stony Creek—Pikeville.

WAYNE COUNTY.

PRIM. BAPTIST.

Aycock's—Fremont, Wm Woodard.
Friendship—Walter.
Memorial—Fremont, J T Edgerton.
Nahunta—Fremont, R H Holland.
New Chapel—Goldsboro, Wm Woodard.
Pleasant Plains—Seven Springs.

FREE-WILL BAPTIST.

Church (col)—Fremont.
Church (col)—Dudley.
Church—Fremont—R H Holland.
Daly's Chapel—Seven Springs, Alfred Rouse.
Hood Swamp—Goldsboro.
Indian Spring—Dudley, Alfred Rouse.
Mt Olive—Mt Olive.
North Creek—Mt Olive.
Pleasant Grove — Pikeville, Daniel Davis.
Spring Hill—Goldsboro, —— Mitchell.
Stony Creek—Greenleaf, Elias Heart.
Union Grove—Fremont, Joy Phillips.
Watery Branch—Fremont, Geo Davis.

UNION BAPTIST.

New Hope—Goldsboro.

PRESBYTERIAN.

Church—Mt Olive, Peter McIntyre.
Church—Goldsboro, F W Farriss.
Church—Seven Springs, J D Stanford.
Church (col)—Goldsboro, C Dillard.

EPISCOPAL.

St Stephen's—Goldsboro, Stewart McQueen.

FRIENDS.

Bethel—Goldsboro.
Mineral Springs—Dudley.
Nahunta—Fremont.
Neuse—Goldsboro.
Newhope—Goldsboro.
Oakland—Goldsboro.
Quaker Neck—Goldsboro.

CONGREGATIONAL.

Church (col)—Dudley.

HEBREW.

Oheb Sholom. Goldsboro, J L Mayerburg.

MINISTERS RESIDENT.

Names, Post Offices and Denom.

METHODIST.

Bristowe. J E, Goldsboro.
Brogden, John T, Goldsboro.
Beaman, R C, Goldsboro.
Jurney, N M, Mt Olive.
Swindell, F D, D D, Goldsboro.

BAPTIST.

Albritton, J T, Mt Olive.
Long, J S, Goldsboro.
Nelson, C J, Goldsboro.

FREE WILL BAPTIST.

Davis, Daniel, Pikeville.
Johnson, L E, Fremont.
Hill, Jacob, Saulston.

WAYNE COUNTY.

PRIMITIVE BAPTIST.

Clark, Thomas, Fremont.
Edgerton, John T, Pikeville.

UNION BAPTIST.

Nash, B W, Goldsboro.

PRESBYTERIAN.

Farris, F W, Goldsboro.
Isler, Simeon H, Goldsboro.

EPISCOPAL.

Stewart, McQueen, Goldsboro.

HEBREW.

Mayerberg, J L, Goldsboro.

HOTELS AND BOARDING HOUSES.

Post Offices and Proprietors.

Boarding, Goldsboro, D H Bridgers.
Boarding, Goldsboro, S S Hardison.
Boarding. Goldsboro, Mrs Alex Privett.
Borden House, Fremont, J J Borden.
Hotel, Mount Olive, R J Southerland.
Hotel, Seven Springs, J H Fonville.
Kennon. Goldsboro, B H Griffin.
Village Inn, Fremont, J K Smith.

LAWYERS.

Names and Post Offices.

Allen, W R (Allen & Dortch), Goldsboro.
Aycock (C B) & Daniels (F A), Goldsboro.
Best, E J. Goldsboro.
Dortch, W T (Allen & Dortch), Goldsboro.
Dortch, I F, Goldsboro.
Faircloth, W T, Chief Justice, Goldsboro.
Hardy, Dal M (Hardy & Mayerberg), Goldsboro.
Humphrey, E H (Robinson & Humphrey), Goldsboro.
Isler, S W, Goldsboro.
Mayerberg. J L, Goldsboro.
Monroe, W C (Monroe & Parker), Goldsboro.
Parker, H B, jr, Goldsboro.
Robinson, Jos E (Robinson & Humphrey), Goldsboro.
Robinson, W S O'B, Judge Superior Court, Goldsboro.

MANUFACTORIES.

Kinds, Post Offices and Proprietors.

Agricultural implements, Goldsboro, Wayne Agricultural Works; W H Smith, pres.
Artificial ice, Goldsboro, N C Ice Co, Worth & Co, agents.
Barrels, crates, etc, Mt Olive, G W Bridges.

WAYNE COUNTY.

Barrels, hoops, etc, Goldsboro, F C Overman.
Blacksmithing and wheelwrighting, Pikeville, T A Jackson.
Blacksmithing and wheelwrighting, Seven Springs, Ira D Hines.
Brick, Goldsboro, H Weil & Bros.
Brick and tile, Goldsboro, H L Grant.
Building and contracting, Goldsboro, R B Bassett.
Building and contracting, Seven Sp'gs, A T Davis.
Chairs, Goldsboro, Royall & Borden.
Coaches and carriages, Goldsboro, Moore & Robinson.
Contractors and builders, Goldsboro, Porter & Godwin.
Cotton-seed oil, Goldsboro, Goldsboro Oil Co.
Cotton-seed oil and fertilizers, Goldsboro, E B Borden, pres.
Engines and saw-mills, etc, Goldsboro, Dewey Bros.
Enterprise Lumber Co, Goldsboro, N O Berry, pres; Thos Edmondson, Sec'y and treas.
Foundry and machine shop, Goldsboro, Dewey Bros.
Furniture, Goldsboro, Goldsboro Furniture Co; W H Borden, pres; John L Borden, sec and treas.
Goldsboro Rice Co; Stock Co.
Handles, Goldsboro, Dean, Pearson & Company.
Harness, Goldsboro, J W Lamb.
Standard Mfg Co. Goldsboro, J F Sutherland, pres.
Tin, sheet-iron, etc, Goldsboro, J J Slaughter.
Wagons and buggies, Goldsboro, Moore & Robinson.
Wayne Cotton Mills, Goldsboro, Sol Weil, pres; E B Borden, jr, sec and treas.

MERCHANTS AND TRADESMEN.

Names, Post Offices, Lines of Business.

AARON.

Daniel, J R,	Confec
Hinson, Ed,	G S
Walker, Dr W S,	Drugs

BESTON.

Hadley, G E,	G S

BIZZLE.

Whitfield, R A,	Confec

DOBBERSVILLE.

Johnson, J H,	G S
Jordan, R H,	G S
Sutton, G W,	G S

DUDLEY.

Borden, W B,	G S
Grady, S,	G S

WAYNE COUNTY.	WAYNE COUNTY.

WAYNE COUNTY.

Hatch. G W,   G S
Holloman, John,   G S

ELROY.

Adams, W D,   G S

EUREKA.

Bailey, N H,   G S
Bailey, W L,   G S
Minskew, N D,   G S
Outland. R,   G S
Sauls & Ormond,   G S
Seabury, Aaron,   G S
Strother, S S,   G S

FARO.

Scott, W L,   G S
West, C D,   G S
West, Jos,   G S

FREMONT.

Aycock Bros & Co,   G S
Aycock & Hooks,   G S
Barden, J J,   G S
Barnes & Flower,   G S
Bogue. A G,   G S
Cook, S E & Co,   G S
Hales, M C,   G S
Johnson & Overby,   G S
Overman. Bros,   G S
Peacock, Davis & Co,   G S
Roland & Short,   G S
Smith & Co,   G S
Stone, J M,   G S
Yelverton Bros,   G S

GOLDSBORO.

Abram, J,   Second-hand Clo
Aldridge, M W (col),   Gro
Argus Pub Co,
Alphin, L L,   Confec
Barnes, W H,   Bakery and Confec
Bass, L B,   Gro
Bass, L D,   Gro
Bennett, Geo D,   Livery
Best, M B,   Gro
Best & Thompson,   G S
Bizzell, J W & Co,   G S
Bizzell Bros & Co,   G S
Borden, Arnold,   Cotton Buyer
Boston Store, Hall &Lancaster, props
Brown, J H & Co,   Mdse Brokers
Brown & Gardner.   Gro
Bryan, J E,   Gro
Bryant. S L (col),   Gro
Carr, Mrs L H,   Gro
Castex, M E & Co,   Millinery
Cohen, B & Co,   D G
Cohencius, Samuel,   Clo
Cox, E W,   Real Estate
Crawford. W W,   Confec
Clayton, Dixie,   Ins Agt
Creech, R A,   Jeweler
Creech, W D,   G S
Croom & Nixon,   Confec
Crow, J E,   Gro
Daniels, J D,   Gro
Davis, Col A C,   Ins Agt

Deans, Pate & Co,   Com and Jobbers
Denning & Summerlin,   Confec
Dewey Bros, Foundry and Machine
          [Supplies and Gen Fire Ins
Draper. S W,   Gro
Earp, J E,   Gro
Edgerton, M,   Tanner
Edmundson. E L & Bro.   G S
Edwards, Asher,   G S and Livery
Edwards, Erastus & Son,   G S
Edwards, Jos.   G S, Fert and Livery
Edwards, Samuel,   D G and Clo
Edwards. W L,   Rest
Einstein Clo Co,   Clo
Everitt, Green (col),   Blacksmith
Farwell, W B,   Ins Agt
Finklestein, F,   Second-hand Clo
Finlayson, Dr W H,   Drugs
Fonviele, I B,   Gro
Foust, L A,   Confec
Giddens, L D,   G S and Jewelry
Ginn, Hiram,   G S
Ginn. J T,   Gro
Goldsboro Book Store, J F Miller, pro
Goldsboro Furniture Co,
Goldsboro Oil Co,   Oil and Fert
Goldsboro Storage & Warehouse Co
Grady, B F,   Gro
Grady, H G & Co,   Gro
Grainger. Wm P,   Jeweler
Grantham. D A,   Marble
Griffin & Worth,   Ice
Griffin, C F,   Confec
Griffin, B H,   Hotel
Griffin, J R,   Confec
Guess, H,   Gro
Gulley, L D,   Cotton Broker
Hall & Lancaster,   G S
Ham, H J,   Horse Trader
Ham, Rufus,   Gro
Harrell, A J & Son,   G S
Hill, Jno H, Jr,   Drugs
Hinson, Giles,   Gro
Hinson, J G,   Gro
Hogan & Odem,   Gro
Hollingsworth, J B,   Gro
Hood & Britt,   G S
Howell, J V,   Confec
Huggins, W H,   Hdw
Hurtt, D W,   Tailor
Isaacs, Jos.   Crockery, Gro, Cigars
Jeffries, Z M L,   Com
Johnson, G K,   Gro
Johnson, Richard,   Gry
Jones, W M,   Gro
Joyner. E,   Gro
King, W R,   Gro
Lamb. J W,   Livery
Lee, H & M L,   Gro
Lumley. J M,   Insurance
Maxwell & McGee,   Gro
Merritt, Dr J H,   Drugs
Miller, A A,   Photog
Miller, J F.   Stationery
Miller, J F & Son,   Drugs

WAYNE COUNTY.

Moore, Wm,   Gro
Nash Bros,   Printers
Parker, S B,   Tinner
Pate, A M,   Gro
Payton, L J,   G S
Perkins, Mrs P A,   G S
Pettaway, Mrs S D,   G S
Pipkin, R E,   Gro
Pitman Bros,   Gro
Powell, Dr J H,   Drugs
Rivenbark & Son,   Mdse B o
Robinson, J J,   Gro
Robinson, M E & Bro,   Drugs
Roscower, A,   Ed Newspaper
Royal & Borden,   Furn
Royal, J A,   Confec
Saul Bros,   Clo
Shannon, H C,   Drugs
Shiago, A M & Co,   Clo
Slaughter, J,   Roofing
Smith, A B (col),   Gro
Smith, D ck,   Gro
Smith & Yeverton,   Hdw
Southerland, B W,   Livery
Southerland, J F,   G S
Southerland, Brinkley & Co,   G S
Speight, G R,   G S
Spair, S S,   Insurance
Spicer, J D,   Drugs
Strickland, J D,   Gro
Thompson, W R,   Gro
Underhill, W H,   Gro
Waters, A L,   Confec
Waters, T N,   Gro
Watts & Watts,   Jewelry
Weil, H & Bro,   G S
Williams, H G,   G S
Winslow & Kornegay,   G S
Winslow Bros,   Livery Stables
Witherington, M S,   Livery

GRANTHAM'S STORE.

Byrd, Zack,   G S
Worrell, J D,   G S

GREENLEAF.

Deans, W A & Co,   Fert
Howell, Langston & Co,   G S
Pike, Jno,   G S
Pate & Lancaster,   G S
Worrell, J S,   G S

MOUNT OLIVE.

Alphin, G E,   G S
Culbreth, B L,   G S
Davis, W G & Co,   G S
Ham, H T,   G S
Harrell, H C,   Gro
Hatch, B H,   G S
Hatch, C B,   G S
Hatch, J R,   G S
Hollingsworth, N N,   G S
Kornegay, Robt,   G S
Knowles, Y H,   G S
Lambert, F J,   G S

WAYNE COUNTY.

Lee, R E,   Cotton Buyer and Fert
Martin, E J & Son,   G S
Price, C B,   G S
Smith, J R,   Drugs
Southerland, R J,   G S
Williams, G W,   G S

PIKEVILLE.

Albritton, W B,   Gro
Edgerton & Hooks,   G S
Pike, W L,   G S
Rouse, J W,   Confec
Smith, Scott & Co,   G S
Worrell, S F,   G S

PINKNEY.

Borden, J L,   G S
Dees, E S,   G S
Pike, Phillips,   G S

SAULSTON.

Etheridge, W B,   G S
May & Malpass,   G S
Lancaster, T B,   G S
Seymore, Duffy,   G S

SEVEN SPRINGS.

Allen, Jos,   G S
Davis, S H,   G S
Herring, J I,   G S
Quinn, G G,   G S
Simmons, F P,   G S
Simmons, W R,   G S
Spence, Mrs Maggie,   G S

WALTER.

Yelverton, G J,   G S

MILLS.

Kinds, Post Offices and Proprietors.

Carolina Rice Mill Co, Goldsboro, J Pembroke Jones & Co.
Corn and flour, Fremont, E T Sasser.
Corn and flour, Sleepy Creek, W T Smith.
Corn and flour, Beston, J A Hadley.
Corn and flour, LaGrange (Lenoir co), J W Isler.
Corn and flour, Brogden's Hill, Ira Hatch.
Corn and flour, Goldsboro, J M Wood.
Corn and flour, Angle, Henry Bizzell.
Corn and flour, Grantham's Store, S B Stevens.
Corn, flour and saw, Sleepy Creek, N Walker.
Corn, flour and saw, Grantham's Store, W K Grantham & Bro.
Cotton-seed oil, Goldsboro, E B Borden, pres; F K Borden, sec.
Grist saw and gin, Fremont, Ely Sasser.
Saw, Eureka, H J Sauls.

PHYSICIANS.

Names and Post Offices.

Cobb, W H H, jr, Goldsboro.

Exum, W P, Goldsboro.
Faison, W W, Goldsboro.
Finlayson, W H, Goldsboro.
Hill, John H, Goldsboro.
Hill, Thomas, Goldsboro.
Jones, Mrs ——, Goldsboro.
Jones, W J, Goldsboro.
Kennedy, J B, Grantham's Store.
Kirby, George L, Goldsboro (Supt Insane Asylum Raleigh).
Miller, J F, Goldsboro (Supt Colored Asylum).
Kornegay, J W, Mt Olive.
Parks, M W, Seven Springs.
Peacock, John J, Fremont.
Person, J T, Fremont.
Person, J B, Fremont.
Person, A G, Fremont.
Robinson, M E, Goldsboro.
Smith, R A, Goldsboro.
Spicer, J D, Goldsboro.
Steele, W C, Mt Olive.
Tatum, M McJ, Mt Olive.
Thompson, J R, Walter.
Turlington, J L, Fremont.
Walker, W S, Goldsboro.

SCHOOLS.

Names, Post Offices and Principals.

Academy, Fremont, Mrs W H Speight.
Collegiate Institute, Dudley.
Graded school, Golsboro, J I Foust, supt.
Graded school (col), Goldsboro, C Dillard.
High school, Mt Olive.
Nahunta Academy, Pinkney.
Public schools—white, 68; colored, 42.

TEACHERS.

Names and Post Offices.

Adams, Miss Mattie, Saulston.
Atkinson, Miss C C, Goldsboro.
Atkinson, Miss C E, Goldsboro.
Atkinson, Miss Dora, Goldsboro.
Barnes, Mrs T, Eureka.
Becton, E L, Eureka.
Best, G P, Fremont.
Bizzell, Miss Ora, Angle.
Blackman, M, Grantham.
Boyette, J D, Lucama.
Broadhurst, J C, Seven Springs.
Caldwell, Miss Mollie, Walter.
Carr, Miss Susie, Mt Olive.
Cox, Miss Julia, Fremont.
Copeland, W A, Fremont.
Crawford, Mrs J O, Walter.
Daniel, T J, Moyeton.
Darden, Miss Mattie, Fremont.
Doly, Miss Lizzie, Seven Springs.
Edgerton, A R, Fremont.
Edgerton, Miss Libbie, Pinkney.

Edmundson, Mrs L W, Goldsboro.
Elmore, J G, Mt Olive.
English, Miss Roberta, Mt Olive.
Fields, Miss Ida C, Goldsboro.
Flowers, Miss Alice, Mt Olive.
Frantham, Murray, Goldsboro.
Frazier, Mrs J M, Greenleaf.
Grady, Miss Lilly, Serecta.
Grantham, Mrs G H, Princeton.
Grantham, G H, Goldsboro.
Hadley, Miss Florence, Beston.
Ham, E D, Pikeville.
Ivey, Miss Alice, Seven Springs.
Ivey, Miss Ina, Seven Springs.
Ivey, Wilson, Bizzell.
Jennett, Miss Sarah, Goldsboro.
Kornegay, ——, Branch's Store.
Lee, E F, Newton Grove.
Lowe, J B, Faro.
May, Miss Dora, Beston.
Moore, Miss L O, Goldsboro.
Moore, Miss M E, Goldsboro.
Oats, Mrs L F, Mt Olive.
O'Berry, W C, Dudley.
Outlaw, Miss Hadie, Goldsboro.
Parker, Miss Kittie, Goldsboro.
Parker, S F, Mt Olive.
Parker, Miss Fannie, Goldsboro.
Parks, J S, LaGrange.
Parks, Miss Bettie, Saulston.
Pearsall, Miss Susetta, Goldsboro.
Peele, W M, Black Creek.
Pennington, Miss Ina, Aaron.
Pike, N R, Kenly.
Quinn, G G, Seven Springs.
Reaves, L H, Goldsboro.
Rosebury, Miss Addie, Goldsboro.
Sasser, B T, Mt Olive.
Scarborough, Miss Nonie, Greenleaf.
Smith, Mrs Debbie, Pikeville.
Smith, Chas A, Mt Olive.
Speight, Mrs W H, Fremont.
Speight, Miss Daisy, Fremont.
Starling, G B, Pikeville.
Stevens, Miss Lillie, Goldsboro.
Stevens, L H, Starlight.
Summerlin, Miss Annie, Mt Olive.
Thompson, Miss Carrie, Goldsboro.
Thornton, G W, Bentonville.
Uzzell, Miss E W, Beston.
Waters, Miss Lucy, LaGrange.

LOCAL CORPORATIONS.

Antioch Lodge, No 69, I O O F, Fremont; day of meeting, Thursday.
Bank of Wayne, Goldsboro; established 1890; capital stock, $125,000; E B Borden, pres; W E Borden, cash; T W Dewey, asst. cash.
Eastern Insane Asylum (col), Goldsboro; Dr J F Miller, supt; Dr W W Faison, asst; Dan'l Reid, steward.
Electric Light Co, Goldsboro; I J Plaisted, manager.

WAYNE COUNTY.

Goldsboro National Bank; G A Norwood, Jr, pres; L C Southern, cash; capital, $50,000.

Goldsboro Oil Co; E B Borden, pres; F K Borden, sec and treas; Chas Taylor, supt.

Goldsboro Water Works, Goldsboro; H P Dortch, mgr.

Harmony Lodge, No 340, A F and A M, Pikeville; time of meeting, first Thursday, at 10 o'clock A M.

Messenger Opera House, Goldsboro; B H Griffin, prop.

Neuse Lodge, No 6, I O O F, Goldsboro; day of meeting, Tuesday evening; C B Aycock.

Ruffin Lodge, No 6, Knights of Pythias, Goldsboro; A B Freeman.

Stonewall Lodge, No 426, Knights of Honor, Goldsboro.

Washington Lodge, No 578, Knights and Ladies of Honor, Goldsboro; I Fuchtler, protector: J F Thompson, sec.

Wayne Lodge, No 112, A F and A M, Goldsboro; time of meeting, first and third Monday evenings; J F Dobson, W M; J J Robinson, S W; W H Parker, J W.

NEWSPAPERS.

The Argus (daily and weekly), Goldsboro; Jos E Robinson, editor.

The Headlight, Goldsboro (Democratic weekly); A Roscower, editor and prop.

FARMERS.

Names and Post Offices.

Beston—G W Best, R Garris, J A Hadley, B F Herring, Ed Herring, J W Isler, B V May, R Mozingo, R A Newsom, R L Rollins, James Rollins, Theo Tripp, M W Uzzell, John Uzzell, M Uzzell, James Uzzell, J M Wood.

Brogden's Mills—G H Grantham, Wm Hollomon, Henry Jennett, Wm King, L Lancaster, G W Parker, Rich Parker.

Dudley—W B Baker, W B Dowden, I Cox, L Cox, P Dunbar, W R Farmer, Simeon Grady, John Grady, G H Grantham, B J Griswold, John Hollomon, Josiah Hollomon, W H Hood, R Kornegay, Giles Kornegay, Jas Lewis, John Lewis, John Moore, G C Moore, J R O'Berry, W C O'Berry, John R Overman, Urban Potts, W L Wiggins, J M Wiggins, P Wynne.

Eureka.—Jefferson Bradshaw, E L Becton, B O Coley, Calvin Edmundson, R P Edmundson, G H Lane, J J

WAYNE COUNTY.

Overman, Mrs Cecelia Sauls, B West, I F Ormond, W J Outland, H J Sauls, R S Yelverton.

Fremont—John T Aycock, J W Aycock, J F Aycock, H B Ballance, A J Barnes, J C Barnes, J A Barnes, G D Best, Henry Blalock, Thos Clarke, D Copeland, G Copeland, P C Coley, Wiley Daniels, Isaac Daniels, T F Daniels, Wm Daniels, Z P Davis, J E Davis, J B Eavis, E H Davis, L Dickerson, Calvin Edmundson, Elijah Egerton, J R Floars, J G Floars, W B T Fort, Napoleon Hagan, Bennett Hooks, P H Hooks, Wm Hooks, Jas Hooks, N G Holland, J N Jenkins, M T Johnson, B H Bane, G H Lane, E Overman, Mrs N Outland, B Peacock, Z M L Peacock, Robert Peel, E W Peel, E G Pippin, A A G Bogue. B F Scott, R L Scott, J F Smith, Jas Wellington, J B Yelverton, Sohn Yelverton, R S Yelverton, R W Yelverton, J E Yelverton, T H Davis.

Goldsboro—J W Borden, E B Borden, J W Best, H J Best, W T Best, F K Borden, C H Brogden, J H Caldwell, S Cohen, M Crawford, D Creech, P Dortch, J E Earp, L E Edgerton, R W Edgerton, E L Edmunson, A Edwards, J J Elmore, W P Exum, W T Faircloth, A T Grady, Wm Grantham, W H Griffin, J M Hadley, M J Ham, R H Ham, H J Ham, J B Ham, B J Herring, J Z Hinnant, E Hinnant, T E Hodgins, D H Hooks, S T Hooks, L B Holt, T H Howell, C D Howell, J A Howell, Stephen Howell, J H Johnson, G L Kirby, W P Lane, B J Langston, A Leggett, J F Miller, E Mitchell, G W Murphy, B F Murphy, M W Parks, B Parks. John Parks, J H Parks, Charles Pate, G W Peel, R D Perry, J W Perry, A M Prince, B H Shadding, R Smith, J R Smith, W H Speight, J D Spicer, G W Southerland, L Strickland, D Sutton, Thos Sutton, T W Swann, W Thompson, J W Thomas, W B Thompson, J Tolar, H S Weil, C A Whitley, B F Whitfield.

Grantham's Store—S J Barfield, D H Bridgers, H Bridgers, K Britt, J M Cogdell, J A Cogdell, J E Cox, W K Grantham, R A Grantham, Fred Grantham, J R Hood, jr, W H Hood, W B Hood, J R Hood, sr, L P Hood, D C Hood, N P Hood, D J Kennedy, J H McCullen, C J McCullen, Geo McCullen, James Warrick, J B Warrick, L L Warrick.

Greenleaf—W F Atkinson, N W Best, W Bizzell, H L Bizzell, J W Borden, W H Brogden, J W Bryan, J J Casey, I H Cox, W T Cox, G W Crumpler, J W Dailey, George Dailey, Wm Daniel, B Daniel, W A Deans, W T

WAYNE COUNTY.	WAYNE COUNTY.

Dortch, H Dortch. R Garris, H Garris, H L Grant, W H Ham, H D Ham, Dr George L Kirby, W P Lane, G W Langston, Henry Lee, Alf Leggett, W A J Peacock, J Person, J E Raspberry, John R Smith, Dr J D Spicer.

Mt Olive—S Barfield, W Barfield, A Barfield, D A Cogdell, J W Cox, J J Cox, W R Davis, N B Farmer, J F Fields, R B Flowers, A Flowers, S B Flowers, F F Flowers, G P C Hall, W J Hall, I W Hatch, C F R Kornegay, Robert Kornegay, J H Loftin, J Parker, Hay Parker, L W Parker, W Price, B Smith, D E Smith, E Smith, C A Smith, R J Southerland, Robert Williams.

Pikeville—Albert Aycock, W D Barden, W H Best, S T Blow, J W Bunn, Samuel Colyer, J A Crawford, Daniel Davis, T Eatman, N T Edgerton, E D Edgerton, E H Edgerton, J T Edgerton, W B Fort, J Garris, W T Hales, W H Ham, T S Hollowell, J D Hooks, J W Pate, B E Perkins, S T Perkins, Dr J E Person, M Pike, Silas Pike, H

C Sherrod, J P Smith, W H Smith, H J Vail, H Yelverton,

Seven Springs—W H Barrick, A W Barrick, sr, W G Broadhurst, J W Casey, Wm Cober, S M Croom, C J Dail, J E Dale, Thomas Fields, Henry Graddy, sr, George O Griffin, J M Hardy, Wm Holmes, John Holmes, R N Ivey, John J Ivey, J M Kornegay, A Kornegay, N W Outlaw, John Parks, J C Price, Wm Price, L H Price, George Price, W P Price, H E Spence, D B Singleton, John Smith, R B Southerland, Thomas Sutton, D M Sutton, Alfred Sutton, Berry Sutton, Daniel Sutton, T W Uzzell, O K Uzzell, N Walker, Sydney Ward, H Ward, Lewis Whitfield, A W Whitfield, N B Whitfield, W B Whitfield, James Wiggins, John Williams.

Sleepy Creek—Daniel Cobb, Willis Cobb, Peter Faison, E J Flanagan, E Holmes. Henry Odom, L B Price, J Munro Rich, E W Shiver, W T Smith, Wm Tilghman, A Tillman, E L Vernon, C Walker.

WILKES COUNTY.

AREA, 700 SQUARE MILES.

POPULATION, 22,675; White 20,633, Colored 2,042.

WILKES COUNTY was formed in 1777, from Surry county, and was named in honor of John Wilkes, an English statesman and a member of Parliament.

WILKESBORO, the county seat, is 175 miles northwest from Raleigh. Population (estimated) 1,500.

Surface—A beautiful and rich valley, watered by the Yadkin river and its tributaries; on the north and south are mountains. The lands are generally rich, finely watered, and abounding in romantic scenery.

Staples—Wheat, corn, tobacco, rye, oats, butter, live-stock and medicinal herbs.

Fruits—Apples, peaches, pears, berries, grapes and cherries

Timbers—Oak, pine, chestnut, hickory, walnut, poplar, cherry and dogwood.

Minerals—Gold, copper, mica, manganese, with several mineral springs.

TOWNS AND POST OFFICES.

	POP.		POP.
Abshers,	50	Lovelace,	50
Adley,	25	Lucile,	—
Austin,	30	Maple Springs,	40
Benham,	20	Miller's Creek,	75
Boomer,	50	Moravian Falls,	100
Bowles,	60	Mount Zion,	25
Brier Creek,	50	Mulberry,	129
Brushy Moun-		New Castle,	25
tain,	30	North Wilkes-	
Burcham,	25	boro.	—
Byrd,	40	Oakwood,	—
Clingman,	38	Osbornville,	40
Cricket,	60	Ozark,	50
Darby,	50	Parks,	60
Dehart,	20	Parsonville,	25
Dellaplane,	30	Poor's Knob,	50
Dockery,	75	Purlear,	100
Elkville,	40	Ready Branch,	50
Fairplane,	—	Reddie's River,	50
Felts,	—	Roaring Gap,	75
Gilreath,	40	Roaring River,	75
Goshen,	50	Ronda,	100
Hall's Mills,	40	Round M'tain,	50
Harley,	—	Springfield,	40
Hay Meadow,	50	Straw,	25
Hendrix,	40	Summit,	75
Hunting Creek,	50	Trap Hill,	300
Ink,	50	Vannoy,	100
Ira,	—	Viands,	50
Joynes,	60	Whittington,	25
Kendall,	—	Wilbar,	50
Knottville,	75	Wiles,	100
Lewis Fork,	25	Wilkesboro	
Lomax,	25	(c h),	1,500

COUNTY OFFICERS.

Clerk Superior Court—A M Vannoy.
Commissioners—W M Absher, chm'n.
Coroner—S J Caudell,
Register of Deeds—D R Edwards,
Sheriff—Clarence Call,
Solicitor Ninth District—M L Mott,
Standard Keeper—J C Hubbard,
Surveyor—B R Transeau,
Treasurer—Clarence Call,
County Examiner—Rev. R W Barker.

COURTS.

First Monday in March and first Monday in September.

TOWNSHIPS AND MAGISTRATES.

Antioch—T C Inseen, N W Gray, C C Parks, Isaac Mathas, S E Chapel, J M Jones, H C Douthit, James H Foote (Wilkesboro).

Beaver Creek—Nathan Horton, J E Phillips, T L Gibbs, Z T Ferguson, J S Ferguson, Sidney Swason, W P Ferguson, Isaac Grayhill, William Andrews (Wilkesboro).

Brushy Mountain—W O Hendren, Purvis Penix, D A Reece, B F Tedder, J E Hays, A Carson, J H Estiss, Loyd Hays (Brushy Mountain).

Edwards—W H Carter, F A Harris, J I Parks, P A Lomax, Henry Simmons, Hiram Settle, T M Byrd, Jacob Hoots, T M Billings, S Jolly (Wilkesboro).

Elk—W T Land, David Land, Fritz Newland, J M Jones, G W Bradley, H Kendall, T H West, W F Hendrix (Elkville).

Goslin—A L Foster, J H Ferguson, J F Barlow, W E Triplett, L E Davis, (Wilksboro).

Job Cabin—W S Hall, Charles Walker, C C Blackburn, Wm Beshears, Wm M Lee, F M Baker, L Thomason, W A Blackburn (Wilksboro).

Lewis' Fork—Wesley Fletcher, B F Eller, L L Church, David Hall, W C Fletcher, E Dyer, R C Billings, A M Foster (Lewis' Fork).

Lovelace—B R Transou, Rufus Transou, York Hayes, W E Anderson, R A Somers, H Williams, T P Combs, J R Hubbard (Lovelace).

Moravian Falls—Elisha Parker, W H Hubbard, T J Gilreath, L C Jennings, W G Meadows, R D Laws, J S Jennings, W M Duncan, A T Laws (Moravian Falls).

WILKES COUNTY.

Mulberry—W P Absher, J O Owen, D M Hall, L W Sebastian, J P Elledge, W Walker, C E Warren, J M Harold (Mulberry).

New Castle—R W Wooten, A L Hendrix, G W Sale, A Mathers, Oly Bagley, R C Triplett, W D Adams, Perry Wooten (New Castle).

North Wilkesboro—T C James, Leonard Vyne, Frank Mayberry (North Wilkesboro).

Reddie's River—J A Crysel, R P Yates, J H McNeill, James Bullis, R P Yeates, W A Bishop, W J Hays, T F Bumgarner, J W Gaither (Reddie's River).

Rock Creek—J W Felts, Spencer Blackburn, B F Foster, W N Alexander, Hiram Wiles, J F Shepherd, Dan'l Wood (Wilkesboro).

Somer's—D C Jarvis, E M Felts, A Warran, N M Pruett, W A Souther, V E Staley, N N Fitts, S J Henderson, Samuel Harrris, W E Mayberry (Wilkesboro).

Trap Hill—J S Hollbrook, J A McCann, S L Spicer, A A Parks, A C Bryan, C L Hamby, Richland Brown, J H Johnson, Jas McCann (Trap Hill).

Union—T C B Whitington, Obediah Dancy, Joshua Shepherd, A F Brown, Charles Colvard, Jas Pitkinton, J C Vannoy, Joshua Stephen (Wilkesboro).

Walnut Cove—H E Spicer, Daniel Shumate, F Miles, J T Alexander, W B Gambill, S L Myers, Wilson Walker, Oliver Blevins (Wilkesboro).

Wilkesboro—J T Somers, J P Gilreath, T B James, A M Church, D E Smoak, E O Matsen, T C Foster, T J Williams, J A Glap (Wilkesboro).

CHURCHES.

Names, Post Offices and Denominations.

BAPTIST.

Antioch—Dellaplane.
Church—Beaver Creek.
Brier Creek—Dellaplane.
Chapel—Boomer.
Church—Wilkesboro.
Covenant—Hay Meadow.
Cub Creek—Moravian Falls.
Church—Double Creek.
Church—Fishing Creek.
Church—Lewis Forks.
Church—Liberty.
Mulberry—Mulberry.
Oak Forest—Dellaplane.
Rachael—Round Mountain.
Roaring River—Trap Hill.
Church—Walnut Grove.
White Oak—Roaring Gap.
Yellow Hill—Yellow Hill.

WILKES COUNTY.

METHODIST.

Bethel—Wilkesboro.
Chapel—Wilkesboro.
Dunkirk—Wilkesboro.
Eschol—Wilkesboro.
Sharon—Wilkesboro.

EPISCOPAL.

Gwyn's Chapel—Wilkesboro.
St Paul's—Wilkesboro.

PRESBYTERIAN.

Wilkesboro—Wilkesboro.

MANUFACTORIES.

Kinds, Proprietors and Post Offices.

Hackney Bros Buggy Co, Wilkesboro, Hall & Davidson.
N C Pine and Bracket Works, Wilkesboro, R A Spainhour.
Tobacco, Moravian Falls, Spainhour & Holman.
Tobacco, Wilkesboro, R N Hackett.
Wagons and plows, Moravian Falls, J W Leach.

MERCHANTS AND TRADESMEN.

Names, Post Offices and Lines of Business.

ABSHERS.	
Joines, J H,	G S
Wlker, F,	G S
BENHAM.	
Cockerham, F,	G S
BOOMER.	
Carlton, J A,	G S
Phillips, Jno,	G S
BOWLES.	
Church, R L,	G S
BRUSHY MOUNTAIN.	
Hendren, W O,	G S
CLINGMAN.	
Cole, J A,	G S
Gilliam & Co,	G S
Green, J C,	G S
Green, T M,	G S
CRICKETT.	
Gaither, J M,	G S
McLean, J A.	G S
DELLAPLANE.	
Brown, W H,	G S
Staley, E,	G S
DOCKERY.	
Billings, A C & Co,	G S
Hanks, T P & Son,	G S
ELKVILLE.	
Newiand, H T,	G S
GLASS.	
Glass, J G,	G S

WILKES COUNTY.

GOSHEN.
Forester, W L,   G S

HALL'S MILLS.
Hall, D M,   G S
Owens, J O,   G S
Walker Bros,   G S

HARDY.
Morris & Hanby,   G S

HAY MEADOW.
Absher, W P   G S
Hayes, P L,   G S

HUNTING CREEK.
Combs, Jas,   G S
Combs, N C,   G S
Reid & Fulbert,   G S

JOINES.
Joines, H M & M,   G S

KNOTTSVILLE.
Henderson, J C,   G S

LEWIS' FORK.
Eller, J M,   G S
Jones, Robt,   G S

LOMAX.
Lomax, P A,   G S

LOVELACE.
Lunsford, L W,   G S

MILLER'S CREEK.
Faw, T H,   G S
Wyatt, R F,   G S

MORAVIAN FALLS.
Brayhill, T J,   Miller
Bullis, J E,   Miller
Holman, F G & Co,   G S
Hubbard, J T,   G S
Leach, J B,   G S
Lowe, J A,   G S
Meadows, W C,   Miller
Meadows. W G,   G S
Parlier, T P,   G S

MT. ZION.
Jones, Jno M,   G S

MULBERRY.
Adams, M V & Sons,   G S

NORTH WILKESBORO.
Absher Hardware Co,   Hardware
Absher & Wallace,   Grocers
Absher, W M.   G S
Church, A M,   G S
Church, A M.   G S
Coffey & Pritchett,   G S
Doughton, Dr Geo,   Drugs
Finley Bros,   Livery and G S
Forrister. F D,   G S
Horton & Absher,   G S
Isley, Coffey & Pritchard,   G S
Jarvis, L A,   G S
McGee, A M,   G S
Marlow, J L.   G S
Smith & Andrews Bros,   G S

WILKES COUNTY.

Turner, J L,   Furn and Undertaker
Vannoy, W W,   G S

OSBORNVILLE.
Myers, J E,   G S
Myers, W C,   G S
Norman, J R,   G S

PARKS.
Johnson, J H,   G S
McCann, J M,   G S

PARSONVILLE.
Hall, W S,   G S
Wilcox, W M,   G S

POOR'S KNOB.
Bobbitt, Fletcher,   G S

PURLEAR.
Eller, J M,   Tanner
Jones, R M,   G S
Marlow, J L,   G S

READY BRANCH.
Church, L L,   G S

REDDIES' RIVER.
Whittington, A A,   G S
Whittington & Boland,   G S

ROARING GAP.
Sisk, J A,   G S

ROARING RIVER.
Combs, J R,   G S
Dimmitte, J T & J W,   Millwrights
Reeves, R A,   G S
Reeves, Wm H & Son,   Tob Mfrs

RONDA.
Bailey, R D & Co,   G S
Crouch, J B,   G S
Dimmitte Bros,   G S

ROUND MOUNTAIN.
Myers, J W,   G S

STONY FORK.
Hendrix, W L,   G S
McGee & Lindeman,   G S
McGlamery, L M,   G S and Tannery

SUMMIT.
Lee & Carmichael,   G S
Tucker & Wilcox,   G S

TRAP HILL.
Kilby, J S,   G S
McCann & Spicer (near),   G S

WHITTINGTON.
McNeill, W G,   G S
Whittington, A G,   G S
Whittington, J L,   G S

WILBUR.
Pilkenton, J M & Bro,   G S

WILES.
Dimmitte, J F,   G S

WILKES COUNTY.		WILKES COUNTY.	
WILKESBORO.		Spainhour, R A,	G S
Berry Bros,	Drugs	Staley & Co,	Drugs
Call, B S,	Gro	Starr, W H & Co,	Tinners
Deal, R A,	Ed. Chronicle	Vannoy, W W,	G S
Gilreath, Andy,	Blacksmith	Webster, J L,	Blacksmith
Ginnings, S J.	G S	Wellborn, A C,	Livery
Hall & Davidson,	Tob	Wellborn, J T & Co,	Tob
Hix, Mrs Robt,	Clo	Wynne, G,	Lumber
McNeill, Milton.	G S		
Mayberry, D W,	G S	**ZIMMERMAN.**	
Morrison, C F,	G S	Combs & Hubbard,	G S
Somers, C H & Co,	G S	Reid & Tulbert.	G S

WILSON COUNTY.

AREA 350 SQUARE MILES.

POPULATION, 18,644; White 10,884, Colored 7,760,

WILSON COUNTY was formed in 1855, from Edgecombe, Nash, Wayne and Johnston counties, and was named in honor of Louis D. Wilson, who died in Mexico serving his country.

WILSON, the county-seat, is 50 miles east from Raleigh, and located on the Wilmington and Weldon railroad, which extends through the county from north to south. Population (estimated) about 5,000.

Surface—Level, sandy and generally rich; very productive when well cultivated; well adapted to trucking.

Staples—Tobacco,cotton,corn, sweet potatoes, wheat and oats.

Fruits — Apples, peaches, pears, grapes, cherries, melons, berries and a variety of small fruits.

Timbers—Pine, oak, hickory, ash, cypress, gum, dogwood and persimmon.

Minerals — Iron, and one sulphur, with fourteen iron and magnesia springs.

TOWNS AND POST OFFICES.

	POP.		POP.
Barnes' Store,	50	Meeksville,	—
Black Creek,	500	Moyton,	50
Boyett,	75	Saratoga,	300
Cliftonville,	—	Stantonsburg,	150
Connor,	25	Talbot,	25
Elm City,	800	Taylor,	50
Filmore,	—	Wilbanks,	100
Lamm,	—	Wilson (C H),5,000
Lucama,	200		

COUNTY OFFICERS.

Clerk Superior Court—J D Barden.
Commissioners—W W Farmer, chm'n; J J Bynum, Wm Woodward, jr, Perry Renfrow, W D P Sharp.
Coroner—Dr C E Moore.
Register of Deeds—Wm Wells.
Sheriff—Jonas W Crowell.
Solicitor Third District—C M Bernard.
Standard Keeper—F W Taylor.
Surveyor—J W Taylor.
Treasurer—W F Farmer.
Supt of Health—Nathan Anderson.
County Examiner—J W Hays.

COURTS.

Fourth Monday before the first Monday in March; thirteenth Monday after the first Monday in March; eighth Monday after the first Monday in September.

TOWN OFFICERS.

WILSON—*Mayor*, J F Bruton; *Commissioners*, Geo Hackney, P B Deans, U H Cozart, J D Lee, J T Ellis; *Treasurer*, J R Moore; *Chief of Police*, D P Christman; *Clerk*, John R Moore.

BLACK CREEK—*Mayor*, Lee Woodward; *Constable*, Henry Mattox.

ELM CITY—*Mayor*, J T Sharp; *Commissioners*, W H Pridgen, J D Daws, E R Brinkley, W B Barnes, J F Winstead; *Constable*, E C Winstead; *Town Clerk*, E R Brinkley.

TOWNSHIPS AND MAGISTRATES.

Black Creek—T J Rowe, Wiley Barnes, O W Spivey, Nathan Bass, Buryan Barefoot, M L Aycock, Perry Bass, W E Yelverton, Henry Menshaw (Black Creek).

Cross Creek—A T Barnes, L F Lucas, L O Hayes, W R Davis, T E Newsom, J G Barnes, J H Lamm, William Barnes, C B Capps (Wilson).

Gardner's—Ed Thorne, W S Robbins, Coffield Barnes, W D P Sharp, J T Lewis, J E Pittman, Calvin Woodard, A T Parker, W T Holden, Eli Robbins (Wilson).

Old Fields—W H Williamson, J T Eatman, E B Deans, Seba High, R A Boyette, H N Boykin, B D Stott, T M Bunn (Wilson).

Saratoga—S H Tyson, T R Eagles, J J Bynum, Thos Felton, J L Gay. S J Ellis, P M Owens, B E Gardner (Saratoga).

Spring Hill—E G Barnes, Wm Hinnant, Simon Barnes, J T Revel, Lewin Watson, Josiah Stancil, Ira Raper, C E Braim (Wilson).

Stantonsburg—J H Applewhite, J A Lane, J T Graves, Jesse Moore, B J Thompson, W J Batts, Daniel Whitley, John C Stanton (Stantonburg).

Taylor's—J J Hales, M M Matthews, Jesse Taylor, W B Thompson, A M Thompson, J J Farmer, C W O'Neal, A W Parker (Taylor's).

Toisnot—W L Dew, L A Pender, J H Barkley, J L Bailey, B H Barnes,

WILSON COUNTY.

W H Langley, Calley Brasswell, J D Mears, Z T Sharp, J R Gardner, W W Batts (Toisnot).

Wilson—F W Barnes, Calvin Barnes, Warren Woodard, sr, K H Watson, J B Farmer, J W Lancaster, J J Batts, S J Watson, L D Tomlinson, J P Clark, Spencer Daniel (Wilson).

CHURCHES.

Names, Post Offices and Denominations.

METHODIST.

Barefoot's—Wilson, B B Culbreth.
Barnes' Cross Roads—Black Creek, B B Culbreth.
Buckhorn—Barnes' Store, B B Culbreth.
Church—Elm City, —— Jackson.
Church—Black Creek.
Church—Stantonsburg.
Church—Wilson, T N Ivey.
Church—Elm City.
Horn's Chapel—Barnes' Store.
Mt Zion—Elm City, B B Culbreth.
Pleasant Grove—Stanhope (Nash co), —— Taylor.

AFRICAN METHODIST.

Church (col)—Wilson, L J Moore.

BAPTIST.

Church—Wilson, J A Rood.
Church—Elm City, W C Nowell.
Church (col)—Wilson, —— Smith.
New Hope—Wilson, W C Nowell.

PRIM. BAPTIST.

Black Creek—Black Creek, A J Moore.
Church—Elm City, A J Moore.
Contentnea—Wilson, W Woodard, sr.
Healthy Plains—Wilson, Wm Woodard, sr.
London's (col)—Wilson, Peter Coley.
Moore's Chapel—Wilson, A J Moore.
Scott's—Wilson, Wm Woodard, sr.
Upper Black Creek—Black Creek, Jas S Woodard.
Upper Town Creek—Elm City, B C Pitt.
White Oak—Saratoga, Sylvester Hassell.
Wilson—Wilson, P D Gold,

FREE WILL BAPTIST.

Aspen Grove—Saratoga, A A Tyson.
Barnes' Cross Roads—Lucama, P T Lucas.
Church—Saratoga, Geo Davis.
Red Oak Grove—Talbot, P T Lucas.
St Mary's—Boyette, D Davis.
Wilson's Grove—Talbot, Hardy Boykin.

PRESBYTERIAN.

Church—Wilson, C R Thomas.
Church (col)—Wilson, M L Melton.

WILSON COUNTY.

EPISCOPAL.

Church (col)—Wilson.
St. Timothy's—Wilson, J C Wingate.

DISCIPLES OF CHRIST.

Church—Wilson, D W Davis.

MINISTERS RESIDENT.

Name, Post Office and Denomination.

METHODIST.

Gay, W J, Wilson.
Hoover, J T B, Wilson.
Ivey, T N, Wilson.

PRIM. BAPTIST.

Farmer, J T, Wilson.
Gold, D P, Wilson.
Williams, W B, Elm City.
Woodard, Wm, sr, Wilson.

BAPTIST.

Barnes, Isaac (col), Elm City.
Williams, Lem (col), Elm City.

DISCIPLES OF CHRIST.

Moye, M T, Wilson.
Taylor, R T, Wilson.

PRESBYTERIAN.

Thomas, James, Wilson.

HOTELS AND BOARDING HOUSSE.

Names, Post Offices and Proprietors.

Boarding, Wilson, Mrs Wm Woodward.
Boarding, Wilson, Mrs Wiley Edwards
Boarding, Wilson, Mrs Dr King.
Boarding, Wilson, Mrs Celestia Smith.
Boarding, Wilson, Mrs G Fulghum.
Boarding, Wilson, Mrs A N Daniel.
Boarding, Wilson, Mrs J E Woodard.
Boarding, Wilson, P T Sutzer.
Boarding, Wilson, Lewis Harrell.
Briggs Hotel, Wilson, B F Briggs.
Central Hotel, Wilson, Mrs J T Manning.
Hotel, Elm City, Harris Winstead.
Ward House, Wilson, J T Ward.

LAWYERS.

Names and Post Offices.

Bardin, Jeff D, Wilson.
Bruton, Jno F, Wilson.
Conner, H G, Wilson.
Deans, A B, Wilson.
Finch, Atlas, Wilson.
Harris, C T, Wilson.
Lancaster, J W, Wilson.
Mewborne, M G, Wilson.
Smith, S A (col), Wilson.
Taylor, B F, Wilson.
Uzzell, J R, Wilson.

WILSON COUNTY.

Woodard, J E, Wilson.
Woodard, F A & S A, Wilson.

MANUFACTORIES.

Kinds, Post Offices and Proprietors.

Blacksmithing and wheelwrighting, Wilson, Hackney Bros.
Blacksmithing and wheelwrighting, Saratoga, S Dilde.
Building and contracting, Elm City, Alex Winstead.
Building and contracting, Wilson, J B Deans.
Building and contracting, Wilson, Jas Wilkins.
Cabinet, Wilson, Wooten & Stephens
Canning, Wilson, W T Farmer.
Carriages and wagons, Wilson, Hackney Bros.
Coach and wagons, Wilson, J J Farmer.
Contractors, Wilson, D J Ross & Bro.
Contractor, Elm City, R Braswell.
Coaches, Elm City, J F Winstead.
Coaches, Elm City, W C Williams.
Foundry and plow shop, Wilson, Geo H Wainwright.
Iron foundry, machine shops and agricultural implements, Wilson, Geo H Wainwright.
Iron working, Wilson, Chas Battle.
Iron working, Wilson, John Williamson.
Iron working, Wilson, Paschall Bros.
Millwrighting, Wilbanks, Wilson Todd.
Millwrighting, Saratoga, S Dilde.
Millwrighting, Peel's Store, Wm Gardner.
Millwrighting, Wilson, Charles Darden (col).
Millwrighting, Wilson, Arthur Young (col).
Moravian Falls Tob Co, Wilson, B W Kincaid.
Planing mill, Elm City, O J Winstead & Bro.
Sash, doors and blinds, Wilson, W W Simms & Co.
Star Tob Co, Wilson, Hackney Bros.
Tobacco Flues, Elm City, C Parker & Bro.
Wilson Cotton Mills, Wilson, G D Green.

MERCHANTS AND TRADESMEN.

Names, Post Offices and Line of Business.

BARNES.
Knight, C W,   G S
BLACK CREEK.
Aycock Bros,   G S
Bass, E B,   G S

WILSON COUNTY.

Gardner. B E,   G S
Hoover & Woodward,   G S
Paschal, J B,   G S
Peacock, J W,   G S
Privett, H W,   G S
Privett, R G,   G S
Woodward, S,   G S

BOYETTE.
Hawley & Raper,   G S
Hinnant & Son,   G S
Kirby, Henry,   G S
Walton, J,   G S
Watson, Dempsey,   G S

ELM CITY.
Bailey, J L,   G S
Barnes, G A,   G S
Barnes, W B,   G S
Botts & Williams,   G S
Carter, W D, agent,   P M and G S
Dawes & Williams,   G S
Dixon, A C & Co,   G S
Doles, Mrs S W,   Millinery
Farmer, J L,   G S
Griffin, G H,   G S
Jordan, J T,   Jeweler
Lamb, C L & S R,   G S
Moore, E G,   Drugs
Perry, C L,   Depot Agt and Tel Op
Pridgen, W H & M C,   G S
Simmons & Beland,   G S
Vick, E H,   G S
Wells, R S,   Cotton Buyers and G S
Whitehead, G W (near),   G S
Williams & Langley,   G S
Williams. Iredell,   Drugs
Winstead, J H,   Gro

LUCAMA.
Boyette, M,   G S
Boyette, S A,   G S
Davis, W R & Bro,   G S
Davis & Boyette,   G S
Hooks, J (col),   Clo
John, J H,   D G
Lucas, Jesse,   Gro
Lucas, L F,   Gra
Matthews, E,   Gro
Newsom, W J & Bro,   G S
Tomlinson, R W,   G S
Tyson, C R,   G S
Williamson & Boykin,   G S

MOYTON.
Applewhite, G S,   G S
Hill, D B & Son,   G S

SARATOGA.
Ellis, Gray,   ——
Ellis Bros,   G S
Gay, J L,   G S
Owens, B M & Co (near),   G S
Owens, N B & Co,   G S
Walston, H,   G S
Yelverton, D A,   G S

STANTONSBURG.
Exum, E C (near),   G S

WILSON COUNTY.

WILBANKS,

Bridges. J F,	G S
Sharp, W D,	G S

WILSON.

Advance Pub Co, W L Cantwell, m'g'r
Aiken & Holderby, Leaf Tob Dealers
Anderson, W S, Drugs
American Tob Co, Leaf Tob Dealers
Anderson & Jones, Tob Warehouse
Anderson, W P & Bro, Leaf Tob
Baker Bros, G S
Beard, A R (near), G S
Blount, G W, Mirror
Best, Robert, Livery
Boykin & Co, Gro
Boykin, W J, Broker and Leaf Tob
Branch, A P, G S
Briggs & Flemming, Brokers and Leaf Tob Dealers
Chatham, J H, Confec
Christman, S, Leaf Tob Dealer
Churchwell, W J & Co, Jewelry
Clark, J A, Ice and Guano
Clark, S P, Hardware
Cooper, Watson & Gibbons, Tobacco, (The New Watson Warehouse)
Cozart & Washington, Tobacco, Centre Warehouse
Corbett, J A, Mdse Broker
Corbett, W, (agent), G S
Davis, J W & Son, Machinery
Deans, P B, Mdse Broker
Erskins & Deans, Misses, Millinery
Edwards Bros, Horse Dealers
Farmer, G E, G S
Farmer, J F, Livery
Farmer, I O, G S
Farmer, W H, G S
Farrior, J D, Livery
Finch, C F & Sons, G S
Friedman, M H & Co, G S
Fulcher. L H, G S
Gay, E R, G S
Gay & Griffin, G S
Godwin & Williams, G S
Gold, P D, Ed. "Zion Landmark"
Gorham, W C, Lightning Rods
Green, G D & Co, Hardware
Hadley, J C, G S
Hadley, J J & Son, G S
Hargrave, B W, Drugs
Harris, I, G S
Harris, Max, Jeweler
Hardy, D L, Agl So Ex Co
Herring Doane, Drugs
Hines, Mrs E A & Co, Millinery
Holloman, L O, Leaf Tobacco Dealer
Howard & Co, G S
Hutchinson, H H, Butcher
Jackson. D G, Gro
Jordan, Ed Tel Op W U Tel
Jordan & Bro, Grocers
Joyner, R W, Dentist
Lachman, Mrs M, ——

Lamond & Finch, G S
Leath, J M (agent), Racket Store
Lee, Bettie H, Millinery
Littman, Mrs A, ——
Leeper, M J & Co, G S
McCraw & Co, G S
McKay, C W, Tinner
Mercer, E N, G S
Moore & Selby, Livery
Moseley, C F, G S
Nurney, C N, Coal
Oettinger, J & D, G S
Paschal Bros, Machinists
Planters' Tobacco Warehouse Co.
Privett, J J, Music
Richmond, Mowry & Co, Leaf Tobacco Dealers and Exporters
Qualls & Manning, Millinery
Qualls, Alex, Tinner
Rawles, J G, Jeweler
Rentfrew, J T, Butcher
Riley & Tomlinson, G S
Rose, R G, Gro
Rountree, Emma (col) G S
Ruffin, C B, G S
Selby & Moore, Horse Dealers
Summerfield, Rose, G S
Townsend & Kirby, G S
Tyson, C R, Photographer
Venable, S W, jr & Co, Leaf Tobacco
Wainwright, G H, Foundry
Walls, S J & Bro, Tailors
Walston, G D, G S
Warren, W E (near) G S
Watson, R P, Tobacco Dealer and Deaf Broker
Wells, S C, G S
Wiggins, J T, Leaf Tobacco
Williams, Mrs O E & Co, Millinery
Wilson Tobacco Works.
Winstead & Boswell, G S
Woodard Warehouse Co.
Woodard, Leep (near). G S
Wooten & Stevens. Furn and Undertaker
Wyatt, R L, jr, Tin and Copper
Young, M T, G S
Young, W B, Shoes

MILLS.

Kinds, Post Offices and Proprietors.

Corn and flour, Wilson, Wm Woodard, Sr.
Corn and flour, Wilson, Noah Strickland.
Corn and flour, Wilson, W W Farmer.
Corn and flour, Wilson, C F Finch.
Corn and flour, Wilson, Harris Winstead.
Corn and flour, Wilson, Thos Bridges, Jr.

WILSON COUNTY.

Corn and flour, Wilson, J J Wilson.
Corn and flour, Wilson, J T Wiggins.
Flour and corn, Stantonsburg, William Applewhite.
Flour and corn, Saratoga, Howard & Owens.
Flour and corn, Elm City, Harris Winstead.
Flour and corn, Meeksville, A T Ward.
Flour, corn and saw, Wilson, K K Eatman.
Flour, corn and saw, Wilson, T R Lamm.
Flour, corn and saw, Wilson, W H Ward.
Flour, corn and saw, Lucama, Sarah Barnes.
Flour, corn and saw, Taylor's, First Nat Bank.
Flour, corn and saw, Wilson, Arnold Nichols.
Flour, corn and saw, Taylor's, Dicey Boykin.
Steam saw, Elm City, O J Winstead & Bro.
Steam grist and saw, Elm City, J H Weaver.
Steam saw, Elm City, R W & J H Bone.
Steam saw, Wilson, Jas Gay.
Steam saw, Paschal & Winstead.

PHYSICIANS.

Names and Post Offices.

Anderson, W S, Wilson.
Anderson, Albert, Wilson.
Anderson, Nathan, Wilson.
Crocker, S H, Stantonsburg.
Crocker, W D, Lucama.
Drake, W T, Wilson
Freeman, H F, Taylor.
Graves, J T, ——.
Herring, N B, Wilson,
Hoover, Rhodes, Black Creek.
Joyner, R W (dentist), Wilson.
Mercer, W P, Elm City.
Moore, Chas E, Wilson.
Moore, E G, Elm City.
Moye, F M, Wilson.
Person, D T, Wilson.
Ruffin, Jno K, Wilson.
Walton, C B, Saratoga.
Whitley, R B, Elm City.
Wright, E K (dentist), Wilson.
Woodard, Ben (col), Black Creek.

SCHOOLS.

Names, Post Offices and Principals.

Academy, Rock Ridge, Rev E T Phillips.
Elm City Academy, J W Hayes.

WILSON COUNTY.

Graded schools (white and colored), Wilson, Geo Conner. sup.
Graded school (col), Wilson, S A Smith, principal.
Public schools—white, 47; colored, 31.

TEACHERS.

Names and Post Offices.

Adams, Mrs E W, Wilson.
Bass, Joseph, col, Black Creek.
Battle, Ella, col., Wilson.
Battle, Ada, col, Wilson.
Clark, John H, col, Black Creek.
Cooper, Carrie, col, Wilson.
Cotton, James A, col, Wilson.
Dawson, A D, col, Wilson.
Parker, Hattie, Elm City.
Jones, A W, col, Wilson.
Jordan, Charlotte, col, Wilson.
Joyner, Maggie, col, Wilson.
Lucas, Lanie A, Lucama.
Moore, A M, Saratoga.
Moore, A J C, col, Wilson.
Parker, Silas, col, Elm City.
Snakenburg, Miss Alice, Wilson.
Vick, Henry, col, Wilson.
Wilder, Hinton, col, Meeksville.
Winstead, B R, col, Wilson.

LOCAL CORPORATIONS.

Black Creek Lodge, No 330, A F and A M, Black Creek; time of meeting, third Saturday.
Branch & Co, Bankers, Wilson; H G Cannon, pres; J C Hales, cash'r; capital, $50,000.
Centennial Lodge, No 96, I O O F, Elm City; day of meeting, Thursday; W H Adams, N G.
Edgecombe Lodge, No 298, A F and A M, Elm City; time of meeting, fourth Thursday.
Enterprise Lodge, No 44, I O O F, Wilson; day of meeting, Friday; E B Taylor, N G.
First National Bank, Wilson; capital stock, $51,000; F W Barnes, pres; J F Bruton, vice pres; W E Warren, cash'r; surplus, $5,000.
Hatcher Lodge, No 310, A F and A M, Wilson; time of meeting, third Saturday, and June 24th and December 27th.
Joseph Warren Lodge, No 92, A F and A M, Stantonsburg; time of meeting, first Thursday and June 24th.
Mt Lebanon Lodge, No 117, A F and A M, Wilson; time of meeting, every Monday evening and second Thursday.
Wilson Cotton Mills, Wilson; G D Green, pres; Jones Lipscombe, sec and treas; authorized capital, $100,

42

WILSON COUNTY.

000; daily consumption, 35,000 lbs; daily production, 3,000 lbs yarns; number spindles, 6,500; number hands employed, 85.

Wilson Telephone Co; G D Green, pres; Dr E K Wright, sec and treas; Howard F Jones, supt.

NEWSPAPERS.

Wilson Advance, Wilson (Democratic weekly), W L Cantwell, editor and prop.

Wilson Times (Democratic weekly), Chas Gold, editor and prop.

Z on's Landmark, Wilson (Primitive Baptist semi-monthly); Elder P D Gold, editor and prop; $2 per annum.

FARMERS.

Names and Post Offices.

Black Creek—J W Aycock, J J Aycock, J S Barnes. G W Barnes. Augustus Barnes, W B Barnes, Wiley Barnes, J J Barnes, W T Barnes, L G Barefoot. A Bass, Isaac Bass, E G Bass, J Bass, sr, J Bass, jr. E J Bass, Perry Bass, David Bass, Nathan Bass, J H Bell, J T Blaniford, F Bardin, John P Bardin. A L Bardin, J B Bardin, Simon Braswell, Alfred Braswell, Thomas A Boyette, Mrs Alice Brooks, R E Copeland, Jas L Daniel, David Daniel, Josiah Daniel, John A Davis, J B Davis, G J Evans, J W Ferrell, J B Ferrell, O Ferrell, David Godwin, B F Goff, James Grice, Reuben Hays, Jesse Hinnant, L B Jones, Turner Joyner, Edwin Lamm, N W Lamm, Isham Lamm, Thomas Lamm, Calvin Lancaster, Redden Lancaster, H D Lucus, W D Lucus, E T Lucus, W H Marlow, William Matthews, Noel Matthews, Hervy Minshaw, Nathaniel Moore, W T Moore, W L Moore Larry Newsome, C T Newsome, G P Pool, R G Privett, J C Rice, Harvey A Raper. Robinson Raper, Ruffin Rose, W T Rose, Thomas J Rowe. Jesse Sauls, L Scott, M L Smith, J T Smith, O W Spivey, W P Stallings, Warren Tomlinson, Lewis Tomlinson, John Valentine, Thomas Vick, T W Watson, John Watson, F G Wiggs, F J Woodard, Dr Stephen Woodard, F A Woodard, Elisha Woodard, W E Yelverton, Wiley Yelverton, J C Yelverton.

Boyett—Ashley Atkinson, James D Atkinson, Josiah Atkinson, Chesterfield Atkinson, Daniel Aycock.

Elm City—Jas H Adams, W H Adams, J L Bailey, Rodman Barnes, Josh L Barnes, Dempsey Barefoot, J

WILSON COUNTY.

H Barkley, B R Barkley, J R Batts, E B Batts, Wm Batts. H B Batts, A R Batts, J L Batts, W J T Beland, J T Braswell, J R Braswell, R B Braswell, H C Braswell, B R Brinkley, J W Cherry, Ben Cobb, J H Cobb, Elisha Cobb, M Cobb, Aug Cobb, T B Collins, Wm Crumpler, W L Crumpler, Henry Crumpler, J D Dawes, Wells Dawes, W L Dew, W G Dixon, T J Dixon, Jerry Dixon, L O Dixon, A C Dixon, W H Dixon, Jos P Dixon, K Edwards, J B Farmer, Wiley Farmer, Grady Farmer, W D Farmer. J A Farmer, Augustus Farmer, W W Flowers, Jos Gardner, Frank Gardner, W L Green, W F Green, D T Hawkins, Jerry Jackson, Robt Jackson. E J Jordan, J B Jordan, Drew Joyner, Bud Lancaster, Geo Lassiter, R R Lewis, W H Langtrey, J E Moore, Dr E G Moore, N C Nichols. Jesse Norris, W H Page, Bennett Page, M M Page, Cad Page, Isaac Page, Fred Page, D W Parker, L P Parker, Jerry Parker, C G Peele, T W Pender, L A Pender, Thos Petteway, W H Pridgen, J J Sessoms, W G Sharp, R H Sharp, J T Sharp, J M Stevenson, J W Taylor, W M Thorne, E P Thornell, M L Trantham, W H Turner, D W Weaver, J B Weeks, Jno L Wells, H H Wells, R S Wells, Thos Wiggins, Elisha Williams, H H Williams, Gray L Williams, H A Williams, M T Williams, Jno B Williams, Josh Wilson, A W Wilkins, G W Winstead, N B Winstead, Redmond Winstead, J H Winstead, Jordan Winstead, H H Winstead, Harris Winstead, W E Winstead, J R Whitehead, W H Whitehead, J W Whitehead, W J Whitehead, Jerry Whitehead, B R Whitley.

Lucama—Jno D Adams, Calvin Atkinson, Amos Atkinson, Hervey Atkinson, T R Atkinson, John Atkinson, J T Aycock, Claud Aycock, Jesse Aycock, C C Barnes, Reddin Barnes, E J Barnes, Stephen Barnes, jr, Bennett Barnes, jr, J B Barnes, Simon Barnes, Amos Barnes, P S Barnes, L D H Barnes, V Barnes, Henly Barnes, Thos Bass, W H Bass, Ephraim Bass, S D Braswell, W S Braswell, S A Boyett, C B Capps, J T Capps, B C Campbell, Geo Creech, Jacob Daniel, Josiah Davis, J & C Davis, Ezekiel Davis, J B Davis, L P Duncan, A J Ellis, Hilbert Evans, Irvin Ferrell, Noel Ferrell, B Ferrell, Enos Ferrell, Wiley Ferrell, N T Hayes, J T Hayes, D R Holland, Perry Hooks, Wiley Howell, Freeman Howell, W H W Johnson, Jonas Lamm, Thos J Lamm, Isaiah Lamm, Jno H Lamm, Elias W Lamm, Enos Lamm, Jonathan T Lamm, J W Lamm,

WILSON COUNTY.

S M Lamm, J H Lamm. Josiah Lamm, B A Lamm, Solomon Lamm, Abraham Lamm, H H Love, W T Lucas, L F Lucas, Larry Lucas, P T Lucas, J A Lucas, E H Lucas, Noel Matthews, Benjamin Moore, Jethro Moore. Alfred Moore, Jos Moore, jr, J M Newsom, Wm Newsom, Richard Pate, Wilson Pedder, R S Peel, M V Peel, Perry Rentfrow, Ruffin Rentfrow, Rufus Rentfrow, W G Raper. Matthew Rose. Matthew Riper, B A Scott, John D Scott, R L Scott. David A Scott, Blaney Scott, J T Smith, T T Thomas, W H Tomlinson, Amos Watson, Jas Wilkinson, Ashley Wilkinson, Thos Woodard.

Meeksville—James Barnes, John M Barnes, W H Barnes, John W Barnes, Josiah Barnes, G W Barnes, Jos Barnes M S Barnes, John Q Barnes, Simon Barnes, jr, Edwin Barnes, Jesse D Barnes, Simon Barnes, Robert Bass, John S Boykin, Samuel Collins, Asa B Collins, John M Creech, Joseph Davis, Harris Davis, Jno D Ellis, Isaac Evans, Jos H Evans, Benajah Ferrel, Jethro Ferrel, A B Ferrel, Thos Ferrel, Perry Ferrel, W H Grice, Perry Hale, James Hawley, L S Hinnant, Jos Hinnant, D H Hinnant, Gray Hinnant, James H Hinnant, B R Hinnant, Rinal Hinnant, Jesse Hinnant, Ira G Hinnant. Jos T. H nnant, Van orne Hinnant, V S Hinnant, Ransom Hinnant, Needham Holland, Uriah Holland, James M Howell, Wm M Johnson, J A Johnson, Henry Keen, Council Keen, Isaac Kirby, Henry Kirby, C W Knight, Bryant Lamm, Jessie Lamm, Elias Lamm. Edward Lamm, V Q Mason, W A Overman, J W Peacock, Stephen Peel, Jesse Peel, Wm Pender, A J Pierce, Hay wood Pitman, Riley Rentfrow, Hinnant Rentfrow, John H Rentfrow, J R Rentfrow, John Rentfrow, Jas H Rentfrow, C A Rentfrow, W R R entfrow, Benajah Rentfrow, John T Rovell, R H Raper, Rob't Raper, Ruffin Roper, J E Roper, James Raper, D A Scott, J A Stancil, Jacob Stancil, Julius Talton, W J Thorn, Thos Thorn, Wm Ward, W G Watkins, Barnes Watson, Eli Watson, John Watson, Thos Watson, Burkett Watson, J K Watson, G Watson, Gaston Watson, Columbus Watson, Lewis Watson, T R Watson, W T Williams, J B Williams.

WILSON COUNTY.

Stantonsburg—W H Applewhite, J H Applewhite, Alvin Bagley, William Barnes, jr, Wiley Barnes, Larry Bass, W J Betts, Chas Corden, B R Daniel, R Dunn, W L Dunn, Wiley Ellis, B F Ellis, WJ Farmer, Jonathan Farmer, J L Farmer, Birney Flowers, Will Graves, Dr J L Graves, Eli Harrell, David Hill, H R Jones, Chesley Jordan, Henry Lane, Matthew Lamm, James Lamm, H B Lane, John M Morton, John H Morgan, J W Peacock, W J Petteway, John Stanton.

Wilson—Dr W S Anderson, K A Anderson, Hinnant Barnes, H Barnes, Calvin Barnes, Martin Barnes, John Barnes, L D Barnes, McArthur Barnes, F W Barnes, Edwin Barnes, J J Batts, H M Boykin, S D Boykin, A B Boykin. W M Boykin, L B Boyett, A B Boykin, J A Brown, Bennett Bullock, W J Bullock, B J Bunn, J M Burnett, S R Coleman, Wiley Corbett, W J Daniel, Josiah Daniel, Barnes Daniel, Spencer B Daniel, Ephriam Davis, S J Deans, O J Deans, Wiley Deans, Daniel Deans, Wesley Deans, A B Deans, Jonathan Dew, John Dew. Moses Dew, Larry Dew, G W Dew, Raymond Eatman, D B Eatman, J F Eatman, H D Ellis, Joe R Etheridge, Thos Etheridge, Jack Etheridge, Jas E Farmer, Kirk Farmer, J F Farmer, Joshua L Farmer, Ceborn Farmer, W T Farmer, J J D Farrier, Jos Farmer, J E Finch, W A Gill, John W Gardner, Jas Gay, Thos J Hadley, W H Harrison, Capt A J Hines, David Horn, H H Hutchinson, O G Jones, Thos Jordan, Sr, Thos Jordan, Jr, B W Kincaid, L D Killett, B F Lane, J T Lewis, Liles Lucas. Jr, Wm Meecham, John T Moore, J C Morris, Stephen Morris, Jos Marlow, J R Marlow, W H Morris, V F M ss. A Nadal, John G Owens, Stephen J Peele, J C Person, Thos Perry, D G Peteway, C V Petteway, Herbert Rountree, C C Rountree, Calvin Rountree, W D Ruffin, Jno Selby, W W Simm, Will Singletary, T B Sugg, Lemuel Sullivan, Wm Taylor, J W Thorn, J B Tomlinson, W Woodard, S J Watson, K Watson, W B Weaver, R B Whitehead, Howell Whitehead, Jas T Wiggins, Frank Winstead. Jas Woodard, Wm Woodard, W F Woodard, Jim B Woodard, D W Woodard, F A Woodard, Jas E Wood ard, J Ed Woodard, C A Young, M T Young, Taylor Young.

YADKIN COUNTY.

AREA, 320 SQUARE MILES.

POPULATION, 13,790; White 12,421, Colored 1,369.

YADKIN COUNTY was formed in 1851, from Surry, and derives its name from the river which runs through it.

YADKINVILLE, the county seat, is 175 miles west of Raleigh. Population (estimated) 400.

Surface—Moderately uneven; lies on the south and west of the Yadkin river; a pleasant country; well watered; land productive. Scenery fine.

Staples—Corn, wheat, tobacco, rye, oats, medicinal herbs, and fruits in great variety.

Fruits—Apples, peaches, pears, cherries, grapes, melons, berries, and a variety of small fruits.

Timbers—Pine, oak, hickory, ash, poplar and gum.

Minerals—Iron, with several mineral springs.

TOWNS AND POST OFFICES.

	POP.		POP.
Algood,	50	Marler.	—
Boonville,	150	Martin,	—
Bean Shoals,	100	Mount Nebo,	100
Buck Shoals,	50	Otis.	50
Charity,	40	Panther Creek,	50
Chestnut Ridge,	90	Poindexter,	25
Cockrum,	—	Republic,	50
Conrads,	100	Richmond Hill,	40
Cross Roads		Shore,	100
Church,	59	Spillman,	—
East Bend,	180	Swan Creek,	60
Footville,	50	Tilden,	40
Forbush,	75	Tracadia,	—
Hamptonville,	95	Williams,	—
Huntsville,	90	Wyo,	—
Jonesville,	275	Yankinville	
Longtown,	100	(C H),	400
Mara,	50		

COUNTY OFFICERS.

Clerk Superior Court—R E Holton.
Commissioners—J M Jones, chmn.
Register of Deeds—W A Hall.
Sheriff—W L Kelly.
Solicitor 8th District—J Q Holton.
Treasurer—A P Woodruff.
County Examiner—J C Pinnix.

COURTS.

Ninth Monday after first Monday in March, and seventh Monday after first Monday in September.

TOWN OFFICERS.

YADKINVILLE—*Mayor*, R C Puryear; *Commissioners*, A E Holton, J D Hamlin, T L Tulburt, E D Farmington, M W Mackie; *Constable*, C C Howell.

TOWNSHIPS AND MAGISTRATES.

Boonville—J H Flemming, W R Cram, J W Shore, A R Poindexter. John Hinshaw. Aaron G Speer, M A Casterins, Hiram Wagenor. M L Shugart (Boonville).

Buck Shoals—J S Wallace, J M Bell, D L Talton, Wm M Cheek, A D Gentry, C T Tucker, J E Pinnix, F F Holcombe (Buck Shoals).

Deep Creek—W H Brown, jr, J A Lindley, P H Underwood, C S Reavis, C C Royall, C B Reavis, J H Mackin, W S Arnold (Yadkinville).

East Bend—T F Mathis. P A Apperson, J H Martin, J M Whittington, S D Davis, J M Davis. S F Shore, J I F Norman, E J Williams (East Bend).

Falls Creek—H A Swain, J V Mathis, Joshua Holson, Frank Warden, C H Adams. H R Williams, R E Mathews, E B Vestal (Yadkinville).

Forbush—A E Cornelius, Jno Long, E T Davis, Geo Brown, M F Lakey, Thos North, Thomas Brewbaker, A R Lakey (Yadkinville).

Knobs—D C Rose, E D Swain, J E Johnson, Wm Evans, W R Martin, J F George (Yadkinville).

Liberty—Thos Williams, D J Reavis, T C Myers, N S May, J H James, W A A Royall. Ben Shore, T A Royall, J J Taylor (Yadkinville).

Little Yadkin—Philip Brann, J A Litlington, B F James, B D Hauser, S H Nading. Thos Poindexter (Yadkinville).

CHURCHES.

Names, Post Offices, Pastors and Denom.

METHODIST.

Center—Yadkinville.
Church—Jonesville. J F Craven.
Church—Yadkinville, J F Craven.
Macedonia—East Bend, J F Craven.
Prospect—East Bend, J F Craven.
Providence—Boonville. J F Craven.
Wesley's Chapel—Huntsville, J F Craven.

YADKIN COUNTY.

Zion's Chapel—Huntsville. J F Craven.

NORTH. METHODIST.

Church—Jonesville.
Hickory Grove—Jonesville.

ZION METHODIST.

Cedar Hill—Mana.
Church—Boonville.
Double Springs—Panther Creek.
Green Grove—East Bend.
Patterson (col)—Forbush.
Tabernacle—Huntsville.

BAPTIST.

Chinquapin—Cross Roads.
Church—Yadkinville, W B Carstevens.
Cross Roads—Yadkinville.
Enon-- —
Flat Rock—Hamptonville.
Forbush Union—Huntsville.
Island Ford—Jonesville.
Mt Zion—Panther Creek.
Pleasant Grove—Yadkinville.
Rece's—Boonville.
Union Grove—Mt Nebo.
Church—Boonville.

LAWYERS.

Names and Post Offices.

Phillips, Thos C, Yadkinville.
Puryear, R C, Yadkinville.
Stanford, E D, Yadkinville.

MANUFACTORIES.

Kinds, Post Offices and Proprietors.

Buggy Works, Boonville, M L Woodhouse.
Cabinet and lumber, Jonesville, J F Cook.
Cabinet, East Bend, W K Kelly.
Cabinet-making, Boonville, C D Dedricks.
Cabinet-making, Chestnut Ridge, J V Sheek.
Canning, East Bend, R Patterson.
Carriages, Boonville, M L Woodhouse & Bro.
Enon Wagon and Buggy Works, Mana, Geo Kiger.
Furniture, Yadkinville, Jno James.
Hall & Davidson Tobacco Factory, East Bend, Morse & Wade.
Harness, Yadkinville, S C Mackee.
Lumber, Shore. H E Shore.
Shoes, Hamptonville, P H Underwood.
Tanning, Hamptonville, Luther Miller.
Tanning, Hamptonville, S H Mackey.
Tanning, Hamptonville, G W Miller.
Tanning, Footville, G W M Miller & Son.
Tanning, Hamptonville, A M Haines.
Tanning, Boonville, J H Williams.

YADKIN COUNTY.

Tobacco, Yadkinville, S R Yackery.
Tobacco, Jonesville, E C Kerkinon.
Tobacco, Boonville, Jas Spear.
Tobacco, Yadkinville, J D Hamlin.
Tobacco, Yadkinville, W L Kelly.
Tobacco, East Bend Jno A Martin.
Tobacco, Yadkinville, E L Jarvis.
Tobacco, East Bend, R G Patterson.
Tobacco, Yadkinville, J D Hamlin.
Tobacco, Poindexter, J G Nicholson.
Tobacco, Boonville, J M Spear.
Wagons, East Bend, S A Smitherman.
Wagons, East Bend, J G Huff.
Wagons. East Bend, J S Patterson.
Yadkin Valley Roller Mills, East Bend, J G Huff.

MERCHANTS AND TRADESMEN.

Name, Post-office and Line of Business.

BOONVILLE.

Crummel & Day,	G S
Spear, A S,	Fert
Wilmoth & Fleming.	G S

BUCK SHOALS.

Crater, R P,	G S

CHESTNUT RIDGE.

Speer & Shugart,	G S

CONRADS.

Davis, E T,	G S

CROSS-ROADS CHURCH.

Bagley, C L,	G S
Cranfield, A J,	G S
Reaves, D I,	G S

EAST BEND.

Martin, J A,	G S
Morse & Wade,	G S
Patterson, R G,	G S
Vogler, W F & Co,	G S

FOOTVILLE.

Reavis, C B,	G S
Vestal, Jno H,	G S

FORBUSH.

Freeman, W G,	G S

HAMPTONVILLE.

Gough, Jno E & Son,	G S
Green, I L & Co,	G S

JONESVILLE.

Adams, J T & Son,	G S
Barker, L J,	G S
Claywell, J S,	G S
Greenwood, J H & Son,	G S
Kirkman, E C,	G S

LONG TOWN.

Holcomb, C E & Co,	G S
Reeves, Mrs S N,	G S

MANA.

Wade, C B,	G S

YADKIN COUNTY.

MARLER.
Pinnix, J C,   G S
MARTIN.
Stallings & Co,   G S
MOUNT NEBO.
Millinder, Mrs M P,   G S
PANTHER CREEK.
Jones, J S,   G S
POINDEXTER.
Allen & Stimpson,   G S
Chaplin, J S,   G S
Nicholson, J G,   Tobacconist
REPUBLIC.
Hobson, Joshua,   G S
SHOALS.
Carmichael, T C,   G S
Martin & Truelove,   G S
SHORE.
Craft, N W,   Nursery
Sprinkle, W C,   G S
SPILLMAN.
Williams & Warren,   G S
SWAN CREEK.
Adams, J T & Son.   G S
TRACADIA.
Benbow & Doub,   G S
YADKINVILLE.
Hamlin, J D,   G S
Logan, J A,   G S
Sheek, J A,   G S
Shores & Shores (near),   Millers
Shugart, J A (near),   Miller
Shugart, N (near),   G S
Sprinkle, J H,   G S
Warden Bros (near),   G S
ZION.
Cooper, T A,   G S
Windsor, E A, near.   G S
Windsor, J W,   G S

MILLS.

Kinds, Post Offices and Proprietors.

Mill, Buck Shoals, Slade Bell.
Mill, East Bend, Benbow & Doub.
Saw, Footville, Foot & Miller.
Saw, Hamptonville, J L Johnson.
Shoes, Hamptonville, P H Underwood.
Mill, Long Town, Bull & Long.
Saw, Long Town, N Long.
Mill, Republic, W E Bovender.
Tobacco, Yadkinville. J D Hamlin.
Mill, Yadkinville, N H Vestel.

PHYSICIANS.

Names and Post Offices.

Benbow, W E, East Bend.
Harding, J R. M D, Yadkinville.
Phillips, Jno M (dentist). Yadkinville.
Royall, M A, Yadkinville.

YADKIN COUNTY.

TEACHERS.

Names and Post Offices.

Adams. L C, Longtown.
Bell, C A, Hamptonville.
Boughton, W D C, Cockrum.
Burgess, Thos, Buck Shoal.
Casey, Miss M J, Buck Shoal.
Cook, G W. Buck Shoal.
Crater, J M, Cockrum.
Davis, J M, East Bend.
Davis, R H, East Bend.
Davis, Miss Alice, East Bend.
Denny, W L, Buck Shoal.
Dobbins, J C, Marler.
Doub, S L, Tracadia.
Gentree, L D, Hamptonville.
Gentree, Houston, Hamptonville.
George, J F. Longtown.
George, A W, Longtown.
Gross, W S. Marler.
Hampton, J E. Boonville.
Hampton, Miles, Yadkinville.
Haynes, F W, Hamptonville.
Hinshaw, S T, Chestnut Ridge.
Holloman, W A, Jonesville.
Holcomb, P M, Longtown.
Hools, J A, Tileler.
Johnson, J D, Jonesville.
Johnson. A L, Buck Shoal.
Kirkman, Leon, Longtown.
Long, Walter. Chestnut Ridge.
Mackie, D W, Yadkinville.
Madison, C L, Buck Shoal.
Martin, A J, Hamptonville.
Mathis, J H, Marler.
Mathis, M L, East Bend.
Meed, L S, Allgood.
Mowen, J D, Marler.
Myers, E G, Buck Shoal.
Poindexter, J T Kisk, Mt Nebo.
Poindexter, Miss Lula, Mana.
Reavis, C M, Allgood.
Skinner, J W S, Yadkinville.
Smith, Calona, Hamptonville.
Swain, V M, Hamptonville.
Turner, J H, Boonville.
Vanhoy, W H, Hamptonville.
Waggoner, D G, Longtown.
Williams, S P, Boonville.
Williams, H D, Spillman.
Williams. Lodishia, Mt Nebo.
Willard, W H, Spillman.

LOCAL CORPORATIONS.

Yadkinville Lodge. No 118, I O O F.
  Meets Saturday night before the full
  moon and second Saturday after the
  full moon in each month.

NEWSPAPERS.

The Yadkin Ripple, Yadkinville.

YANCEY COUNTY.

AREA, 400 SQUARE MILES.

POPULATION 9,490; White 9,197, Colored 293.

YANCEY COUNTY was formed in 1833, from Burke and Buncombe counties, and was named in honor of Hon Bartlett Yancey, of Caswell county.

BURNSVILLE, the county seat, is 245 west miles of Raleigh, and was named in honor of Captain Otway Burns, of Carteret county. Population 450.

Surface—Yancey county is bounded almost entirely by mountain ranges, and the Black mountains run through the centre. The Toe river and branches give abundant water-power. The climate is enchanting in summer; the soil is rich, and the scenery enrapturing.

Staples—Corn, wheat, butter, live stock, medicinal herbs, and fruits in great variety and richness.

Fruits—Apples, peaches, pears and berries.

Timbers — Poplar, ash, chestnut, hickory, sugar-maple and buckeye.

Minerals—Iron and mica, with several mineral springs.

TOWNS AND POST OFFICES.

	POP.		POP.
Athlone,	25	Hensley,	75
Bald Creek,	300	Higgins,	25
Bee Log,	100	Micaville,	60
Burnsville		Paint Gap,	50
(C H),	450	Pensacola,	175
Cane River,	200	Price's Creek,	25
Celo,	25	Ramsaytown,	75
Day Book,	200	South Toe,	75
Dobag,	35	Sioux,	25
Elmer,	30	Three Forks,	50
Flinty,	50	Wilhite,	25
Green Moun-			
tain,	80		

COUNTY OFFICERS.

Clerk Superior Ceurt—W Bauks.
Commissioners—A J Bennett, chmn; J E R Robertson, E M Honeycutt.
Coroner—Dr J L Ray.
Register of Deeds—A B Silver.
Sheriff—J S Huskins.
Solicitor 10th District—J F Spainhour.
Surveyor—J O Griffith.
Treasurer—C H Byrd.
County Examiner—J L Hyatt, jr.
Supt of Health—Dr J L Ray.

COURTS.

Superior Court meets 11th Monday after the 1st Monday in March, and 8th Monday after the 1st Monday in September.

TOWN OFFICERS.

BURNSVILLE—*Mayor*, J S Boon; *Aldermen*, Sol Ivens, J R Ray, T F Rowland; *Treasurer*, J P McInturff; *Marshal*, Jeff Davis Collis.

TOWNSHIPS AND MAGISTRATES.

Brush Creek—J C Sparks, Samuel Jarrett, Malone Randolph, N H Deyter, Wm Preswell, Jas J Smith (Burnsville).

Burnsville—M W Ray, M B Robinson, B E Riddle, W N Tipton, D A Angle, L H Smith, L H Hutchinson (Burnsville).

Crabtree—J A Bowditch, M D Hunton, Wm Presnell, Jas J Smith (Burnsville).

Cane River—Sam'l Higgins, Rupert Ray, C W Burton, W R Holcomb, Chas Hensley (Cane River).

Egypt—D W Duncan, Theodore Higgins, F Howell, G W Higgins, W M Phillips (Burnsville).

Green Mountain—P B Horton, Sam'l Peterson, R Peterson, U Bennett, O Peterson (Burnsville).

Jack's Creek—Lycurgus Piercy, M P Honeycutt, J W Hunter, W J Edney, A J Burton.

Pensacola—R N Boone, Sam'l Riddle, Jas Riddle, Jas Silver, Rich. Wilson (Pensacola).

Price's Creek—C T Davis, Pender Robinson, J W Shephard, N Gibbs, W R Rowland (Price's Creek).

Ramseytown—Geo McIntosh, S F Howell, Swinfield Howell, N B Atkins, J G Cooper (Ramseytown).

South Toe—Whit Ballew, Wm Gragg Robt Gibbs, Geo Autry, Chas Gibbs (South Toe).

CHURCHES.

Names, Post Offices and Denominations.

METHODIST.

Church—Price's Creek.
Church—South Toe.
Church—Micaville.

Church—Elmer.
Church—Jack's Creek.
Church—Green Mountain.
Church—Bee Log.
Chnrch—Cane River.
Church—Burnsville.

NORTH. METHODIST.

Church—Micaville.
Church—South Toe.
Church—Pensacola.
Church—Price's Creek.

BAPTIST.

Church—Price's Creek.
Church—Pensacola.
Church—South Toe.
Chuech—Elmer.
Church—Micaville.
Church—Jacks Creek.
Church—Green Mountain.
Church—Ramseytown.
Cnuch—Bee Log.
Church—Cane River.
Church—Burnsville.

FREE-WILL BAPTIST.

Church—Bee Log.
Church—Ramseytown.
Church—Jack's Creek.
Cnurch—Micaville.
Church—Pensacola.

DUNKARDS.

Church—Bee Log.
Church—Ramseytown.
Church—Elmer.

DISCIPLES OF CHRIST.

Church—Green Mountain.

MINISTERS RESIDENT.

Names, Post Offices and Denom.

BAPTIST.

King, R, Wampler.
Miller, D, Ramseytown.
Riddle, B B, Pensacola.
Robinson, W A, Burnsville.
Tipton, Samuel, Burnsville.
Wilson, S, Bee Log.

FREE-WILL BAPTIST.

Atkins, D W, Ramseytown.
Bennett, Uriah, Green Mountain.
Howell, D L, Day Book.
Hunter, John, Day Book.

METHODIST.

Campbell, Jas M, Burnsville.
Gibbs, W, Celo.
Glaspee, Dr D L, Micaville.

DUNKARD.

Bradshaw, John, Green Mountain.
Langner, W J, Green Mountain.

HOTELS AND BOARDING HOUSES.

Names, Post Offices and Proprietors.

Hotel, Burnsville, J S Boone.
Hotel, Burnsville. Bev W A Roberson.
Hotel, Burnsville, J C Byrd.
Hotel, Burnsville, G D Ray & Son.

LAWYERS.

Names and Post Offices.

Moore, W M, Burnsville.
Watson, E F, Burnsville.
Whittington. H A, Cane River.

MANUFACTORIES.

Kinds, Post Offices and Proprietors.

Blacksmithing, Burnsville, J S & K Boon.
Blacksmithing, Burnsville, J H Roland.
Blacksmithing, Burnsville, Ed Boon.
Blacksmithing, Burnsville, M B Roberson.
Blacksmithing, Cane River, R B Anglin.
Blacksmithing, Cane River, J W Wilson.
Blacksmithing, Cane River, Jesse Radford.
Blacksmithing, Dobag, J G Thomas.
Blacksmithing, Dobag, E t Robinson.
Boots and shoes, Burnsvllle. W B Ledford.
Boots and shoes, Burnsville, J Ledford.
Boots and shoes, Burnsville, G Parkin.
Cabinet work, Burnsville, James McCampbell.
Cabinet work, Burnsville, M B Robinson.
Cabinet work, Burnsville, D M Bryant.
Carpentering, Ramseytown, E H Howell.
Carpentering, Ramseytown, D W Adkins.
Carpentering, South Toe, C F Gibbs.
Carpentering, Burnsville, M B Robinson.
Carpentering, Burnsville, Jas M Campbell.
Carpentering, Burnsville, W A McLelland.
Carpentering, Burnsville, Geo Rowland.
Carpentering, Burnsville, D A Cassidar.
Carpentering, Burnsville, J P McInturff.
Carriages, Day Book, —— Briggs.

MERCHANTS AND TRADESMEN.

Names, Post Offices, Lines of Business.

BALD CREEK.

Foster, B C,	G S
Hensley & Neill,	G S
Wilson, W M,	G S

BURNSVILLE.

Abernethy, J A, agt,	G S
Burnsville Drug C ,,	Drugs
Elliott, W A, mgr Burnsville Drug Co,	Drugs
Harris, J Moore,	Jeweler
Higgins & Evans,	G S
Horton, Capt J P,	Post Master
McInturff, J P,	Jeweler
McInturff & Rowland,	G S
Moore, W W,	Real Est Dealer
Ray, G D & Son,	G S and Mica
Riddle, S C,	Photograher

CANE CREEK.

Carpenter, H P & Son,	G S
Horton, Jesse,	G S

GREEN MOUNTAIN.

Bennett, U S & Son,	G S and Mill
Haskins, J S,	G S
Peterson, R & Son,	G S

HENSLEY.

Hensley, B S.	G S

MICAVILLE.

Clontz, W E,	G S

RAMSEYTOWN.

Byrd, C R,	G S

SOUTH TOE RIVER.

Robinson, Geo,	G S
Westall, A H,	G S

WILHITE.

Anglin, Moses,	G S

MILLS.

Kinds, Post Offices and Proprietors.

Corn, Micaville, W S Young.
Corn, Micaville, B Young.
Corn, South Toe, Thos Gill.
Corn, Green Mountain, J S Laws.
Corn, Elmer, W Robinson.
Corn, Ramsaytown, W Adkins
Corn, Ramsaytown, Rix Adkins.
Corn and saw, Bee Log, Robt Lewis.
Corn and saw, Bee Log, B S Hensly.
Corn, Micaville, J G Marsh.
Flour, Elmer, W H Deyton.
Flour and corn, Burnsville, V Ray.
Flour and corn (Ray's mill), Burnsville, W A Harris.
Flour and corn, Micaville, D E Young.
Flour and corn, South Toe, M W Young's heirs.

Flour and corn, Pensacola, B S Ray.
Flour and corn, Cane River, B B Whittington.
Flour and corn, Cane River, Edwards & Hensley.
Flour and corn, Cane River, Hurst & Byrd.
Flour and corn, Cane River, J W Burton.
Flour, corn and saw, Day Book, W A Peterson.
Flour, corn and saw, Day Book, O Peterson.
Flour and corn, Elmer, H Deyton.
Flour and corn, Ramsaytown, James Hughes.
Roller flour and corn, Burnsville, W M Moore.
Steam saw, Cane River, W H Gardner.
Steam saw, Cane River, C Lesenbee.

MINES.

Kinds, Post Offices and Proprietors.

Iron, Cane River.
Mica, Burnsville, Hide & Co.
Mica, Burnsville, G D Ray.
Mica, Burnsville, Smith & Geer.
Mica, Burnsville, Young & Proffett.
Mica, Burnsville, Young & Carters.
Mica, Burnsville, J L Hyatt.
Mica, Micaville, Jas W Gibbs.
Mica, Micaville, P Robeson.
Mica, Micaville, P McD Young.
Mica, Micaville, Z Young.

PHYSICIANS.

Names and Post Offices.

Austin, W M, Burnsville.
Boone, J S (specialist, cancer), Burnsville.
Fairchild, J M, Cane River.
Hall, Mathew. Micaville.
Howell, S F, Ramseytown,
Lewis, O M, Burnsville.
Penland, W L, Paint Gap.
Towe, W C, Paint Gap.
Whittenton B B, Cane River.
Whittenton, W W, Cane River.

SCHOOLS.

Names, Post Offices and Principals.

Academy, Burnsville, Prof Hawkins.
Public Schools—White, 38; colored, 4.

TEACHERS.

Names and Post Offices.

Hawkins, Prof E E, Burnsville.

YANCEY COUNTY.

LOCAL CORPORATIONS.

Burnsville Lodge, No 192, A F and A M, Burnsville.

NEWSPAPERS.

Black Mountain Eagle, (Dem. weekly), Burnsville, J M Lyon, editor.
The Courier (Rep. weekly), Burnsville, Rayburn & Ray.

FARMERS.

Names and Post Offices.

Burnsville—N H Allison, W B Banks, S M Bennett, Robert McCracken, J H McPeters, B E Riddle, L H Smith, Mrs D E Young.
Cane River—J W Burton, Wash Burton, Jerry Ferguson, N Gibbs, W Hensley, S T Proffitt, J T Sams, E S Wilson, B B Whitington.
Crabtree—Nat Bowditch, J O Grif-

YANCEY COUNTY.

fith, Dr L D Glaspie, M D Hunter, W J Thomas, W S Young.
Doush Creek — N H Deyton, C P Deyton, P H Fittz, Alf Masters, J C Sparks, G B Woody.
Egypt—C R Bradford, Thos Duncan, John Higgins, Charles Higgins, H H Howard, Samuel Peek.
Green Mountain—Jacob Bailey, Wm Bailey, U Bennett, D M Horton, R Peterson, D Renfro.
Jack's Creek—A J Burton, Mack McCoury, C C Renfro, L Percy, E Presnell, W S Parsons.
Pensacola—J R Penland, "**Big Tom**" Wilson.
Price's Creek—M C Byrd, N H Gardener, W C Hunt, A J Phiff, D M Ray, J G Wilson.
Ramseytown—D W Adkins, C R Byrd, J C Cooper, Wm Howell, Wm Tipton, C R Whitson.
South Toe—R A Ballew, J Ballew, Wm Brockham, Josh Gibbs, J D Patton, Jas Burleson, H C Rathbone, D J Ray.

ADDENDA.

MACON COUNTY.

LAWYERS.

Names and Post Offices.

Crawford, Lee. Franklin.
Elias, Kope, Franklin.
Jones & Johnson, (G, A J), Franklin.
Ray, J F. Franklin.
Stuart, Henry, jr, Franklin.

MADISON COUNTY.

LAWYERS.

Names and Post Offices.

Gudger, J M. Marshall.
Hendwill, J A. Mar-hall.
McElroy, P A. Marshall.
Morfoni, C B. Marshall.
Pritchard, J C. Marshall.
Zachery, W, Marshall.

DUPLIN COUNTY.

MINISTERS RESIDENT.

Names, Post Offices and Denominations.

BAPTIST.

Albritton, Jno T, Mt Olive.
Bilber, W L, Warsaw.
Brown, S, Rose Hill.
Butler, A A, Warsaw.
Carr, Henry (col), Wallace.
Carroll, L R, Warsaw.
Cowans, Jas, Wallace.
Cowan, W C. Wallace.
Fennell, Jno (col), Rose Hill.
Parker, Thos, Warsaw.
Taylor, A J, Kenansville.
Walker, R J, Mt Olive.
Wells, G G, Warsaw.

FREE-WILL-BAPTIST.

Cavenaugh, Jas, Wallace.
Dunn, G W, Branch's Store.
Henderson, J Q, Wallace.
Jones, Haskill, Branch's Store.
Puckett, Frank, Branch's Store.
Wallace, T F, Branch's Store.

METHODIST.

Geddie, D C, Magnolia.
Kendall, J T, Kenansville.

PRESBYTERIAN.

McIntire, Peter, Faison.
Stanford, J D, Kenansville.

HOTELS AND BOARDING HOUSES.

Names, Post Offices and Proprietors.

Boarding house, Kenansville, B Bowden
Carlton House, Warsaw, H J Carlton.
Hotel, Magnolia, Mrs J W Stokes.
Hotel, Faison, Mrs Kedar Bryan.
Johnson Hotel, Warsaw, Mrs S A Johnson.

LAWYERS.

Names and Post Offices.

Allen & Ward (O H A).
Beasley, L A, Kenansville.
Grady, L V, Kenansville.
Hill, W L, Warsaw.
Kornegay, H R, Kenansville.
Lee, T M, Kenansville.
Stevens, H L, Warsaw.

PHYSICIANS.

Names and Post Offices.

Blount, J W, Kenansville.
Faison, J M, Faison.
Fearington, J P, Faison.
Graham, D McL, Wallace.
Graham, G A, Warsaw.
Grady, J C, Magnolia.
Hatcher, T R. Rose Hill.
Hussey, La Fayette, Warsaw.
Jones, Amos, Kenansville.
Kennedy, W P, Warsaw.
Kenan, Owen, Kenansville.
Maxwell, J F & A W (dentists), Albertson.
Moore, Matthew, Warsaw.
Robinson, L W, Wallace.
Ward, E G, Kenansville.

TEACHERS.

Names and Post Offices.

Andrews, Callie, Lyman.
Andrews, Glennie, Lyman.
Beasley, Ella, Magnolia.
Bowey, Myrtie. Rosehill.
Bowey, Lula, Wallace.
Bryant, Mary, Kenansville.
Carr, E McN, Joford.
Carr, Effie, Wallace.
Carr, Valeria, Safe.
Carr, Mattie, Pearsall.
Carr, Fannie, Xenia.
Chambers, Emma, Pearsall.
Cavenaugh, Betty, Postey.
Chestnut, Pollie, Warsaw.
Clement, S W, Wallace.

DUPLIN COUNTY.

Darden, J G. Faison.
Davis, Freeman. Outlaw's Bridge.
Dobson, Hood, Kenansville.
Dobson, Cyrus, Kenansville.
Euhawk, W A, Beulaville.
Faison, Edw, Faison.
Frederick, Minnie C, Kenansville.
Frederick, Cora C, Warsaw.
Frederick, Eleanor, Warsaw.
Frederick, Maud, Warsaw.
Grady, Lula, Kenansville.
Grady, Wm. Albertson.
Hall, Ella, Magnolia.
Hines, Eugenia, Faison.
James, Beulah, Magnolia.
Johnson, Alberta, Kenansville.
Johnson, Effie, Kenansville.
Johnson, R J, Warsaw.
Jones, Julia, Warsaw.
Kerr, Winnie, Faison
Koonce, Geo, Bowden.
Kornegar, Idella, Branch's Store.
Laden, J A, Chinquapin.
Landen, Jeff, Chinquapin.
Loftin, Elaine, Kenansville.
Mark, Katie, Magnolia.
Maxwell, R G, Outlaw's Bridge.
Middleton, Martha E Kenansville.
Middleton, Carrie, Kenansville.
Millard, R W, Kenansville.
Moore, Mrs D, Kenansville.
Moore, Fannie, Kenansville.
Moore, Lizzie, Warsaw.
Moore, W A, Natural Wells.
Murray, Abbie, Warsaw.
Murphy, Laura, Kenansville.
Murphy, Laura, Magnolia.
Murray, Ida, Warsaw.
Noble, Maubie, Leon.
Pierce, Maggie, Warsaw.
Pickett, Alice, Magnolia.
Powell, Carrie, Warsaw.
Register, Laura, Rose Hill.
Rouse, Mrs E, Rose Hill.
Sandlin, Susie, Beulaville.
Swinson, Pollie, Warsaw.
Southerland, Sallie, Rose Hill.
Sprunt, Nellie, Kenansville.
Stanford, Leonidas, Wallace.
Stokes, Julia, Kenansville.
Taylor, C F, Magnolia.
Thompson, Carrie, Branch's Store.
Thornton, R Faison.
Thornton, Sila, Faison.
Ward, Cassie, Joford.
Weeks, Katie, Warsaw.
Wells, C G, Warsaw.
Whitehurt, Adella, Faison.
White, J C, Warsaw.
Wilkins, Melissa, Beulaville.
Williams, Martha E, Warsaw.
Williams, Lucy, Magnolia.
Williams, Holly, Magnolia.
Williams, Estelle, Kenansville.
Vernon, Judson, Branch's Store.

DUPLIN COUNTY.

FARMERS.

Names and Post Offices.

Albertson—J Grady, W H Grady, J M R Grady, B F Grady, jr. Z D Grady, S H Kornegay, Hugh Maxwell, J C Maxwell, S H Phillips, D H Simmons, A W Simmons, Lafayette Smith, Owen Stroud, R Stroud.

Beulaville—J W Andrews, M W Brown, J Fountain, J W Gresham, O W Quinn, R Sandlin, Jerry Sandlin, J G Thigpen.

Bowden's—Albert Kornegay, J F Watkins, Arthur Weeks.

Branch's Store—J D Davis, J H Grady, W B Herring, Paul Jones, J W Kornegay, J R Outlaw. Geo Outlaw, L L Sullivan, J H Westbrook, B Witherington.

Buena Vista—John Mercer, L B Mercer, J R Miller, J Smith, jr, D Williams, B Williams.

Chinquapin—G W Lamb, J N Lamb, G B D Parker

Faison—B B Carr, I R Faison, E J Faison, W P Faison, A D Hicks, Col W E Hill, Mrs B W Hill, J S Martin, Mrs M E Pass, C C Rich, J F Shine, J A Shine.

Hallsville—Thos Botts, W P Dobson, T G Dobson, E W Houston, S O Middleton, Jas O'Daniel, S C Register, G C Rhodes, Jas Rhodes, Robt Sandlin, G L Swinson, H N Wilkin.

Humphrey—Jacob James, M James.

Joford—Dallas Herring, W R Hufham, Jno Hufham, Jacob Hufham, Chas Vann, Boney Williams, David Williams.

Kenansville—Samuel Albertson, S D Bostick, Jno A Bryan, J H Carr, J B Carr, G W Carroll, D F Chambers, T G Dobson, Stephen Graham, James G Kenan, A D McGowan, J W Murray, S B Newton, Jos Pearsall, J W Pearsall, S C Register, A F Williams.

Leon—Jno Mercer, L D Mercer, J R Miller, J Smith, jr, D Williams, B Williams.

Lyman—W J Andrews, W H Pickett.

Magnolia—M A Beasley, Steven Boon, John Boon, N W Bowen, Joseph Carr, A W Carlton, J T Croom & Bro, Marshall Drew, A Hall, Willie Hall, J C Hollingsworth, Jethro Johnson, G S Murray, J A Newbrick, Abner Pickett, Isaah Robinson, J W Stokes.

Mount Olive—J H Bennett, G T Bennett, D F Brock, D B Brown, B B Carr, J M Cox, D H Garner, M B Jones, Albert Jones, Thad Jones, Sr, M B Jones, J L Kornegay, J O Loftin, J A Loftin, J B Oliver, Adam Reaves, O W Sutton, L Swinson, J W Taylor, D A

DUPLIN COUNTY.

Thompson, R J Walker, G W Williams, G W Wilson.

Nalo—Jas Boon, Wm Brice, G B Carr, J A Fennell, Randal Powell, N F Register, J E Ward, J T Ward, Jas Wells, David S Williams, D H William, Daniel Williams, H J Williams, S A Williams.

Outlaw's Bridge—W D Chambers, J W Davis, A Jones, J Jones, W M Kornegay, F M Keathley, J W Outlaw, Lewis Outlaw, H K Outlaw, S D Outlaw, N B Whitfield.

Resuca—Sherwood Grady, Ahaz Grady, James Hardy, W J Harper, D C Lee, J H Maxwell, Alex Rouse, David Simmons, Stephen Simmons, J R Taylor.

Rose Hill—I J Johnson.

Surecta — P H Albertson, D W, Boney, Priestly Huston.

Teachey's—D T Boney, D W Boney, W A Boney, David Brock, W B Bryan, G R Carr, G S Carr, J O Carr, James Dixon, Robt Dixon, A J Furlaw, B Fussell, H Fussell, G J McMillan, J C McMillan, Geo Rivenbark, Jno Savage, W A Southerland, Wiley Teachy, D Teachy, D T Teachy, W B Teachy, Wm Teachy, E W Teachy, D W Turner, Jas Wells, D H Williams.

Wallace — D W Alderman, E M Batchelor, Z Blanchard, J W Boney, John Botts, J L Bradham, A G Bryan, S H Cavenaugh, Jos Cole, Monroe English, H Fountain, J G Halso, Owen Hanchey, G W Lamb, S Lanier, R Lanier, D Moready, J Murray, J J Poyner, D Sholar.

Warsaw—A W Bell, R S Best, Geo Blackburn, R T Blackburn, H S Boyette, J A Boyette, S M Carlton, L C Carlton, W C Carlton, R D Costin, B L Ezzell, F L Faison, J F Faison, W A Faison, J R Gavin, J W Herring, W L Hill, Thos Kinniear, W S Loftin, D J Middleton, O P Middleton, L Middleton, F G Middleton, W H Middleton, R S Moore, Dr M Moore, T M Moore, A G Moseley, T B Pierce, R F Pollock, J A Powell, L C Powell, A W Pollock, Geo Pridgen, J W Swinson, D J West, W H Williams Jr, J R Wilson, J W Winders, J B Winders, R J Williams, D I Woodward, J F Woodward.

ROBESON COUNTY.

FARMERS—Continued.

Plainview—Mary Roberison, J Ed Smith, M P Smith, A Stewart, Charles Stubbs, Sr, J W Ward, C W Wiggins, L C Williams, Colon Williams, Trim-

ROBESON COUNTY.

migan Williams, E A Williams, W D Williams, J A Williams, R C Williams, Geo L Williams.

Purcepolis—Thos Percell, Charles A Percell, J E Percell, T M Watson, A A Watson.

Queensdale—W H Adams, Melton, Baxter, Daniel Cameron, J W Chesholm, J H Coholy, T J Covington, Adam Currie, David Currie, J A Currie, G A Leach, A D Leach, Robert A Love, A E McEachern, D P McEachern, J A McGugon, A E McNeill, Lauchlin McNeill, F P McNeill.

Red Banks—Malcolm Buie, Jno Bullard (col.), Archibald Bullard, John A Campbell, E W Campbell, T F Carlisle, Columbus Chambers, S W Cobb, Jas Dial (Croatan), Jacob Duncan, Peter Duncan, Preston Locklear (Croatan), Winslow Locklear (Croatan), Malachi Locklear (Croatan), Daniel Locklear (Croatan), Neill McArthur, A T McCallum, Hugh McGregor, W N D McMillan, J M McNair, S R Townsend, A M Watson, Arch Watson, Daniel Watson, Harry Watson, J H Watson.

Red Springs—Dennis Baxley, J D Brown, J G Brown, Albert Buie, D McP Buie, Mrs C E Buie, Mary Ann Buie, W W Gilbert, J C Graham, Sampson Haywood, Jas A McCallum, A D McCallum, Alan McCormack, N N McHuen (col.), J Frank McKay, D M McKay, A D McLeod, D H McMillan, Archie McMillan, Hector McMillan, Archibald McNeill, W P McNeill, J S McNeill, D W McNeill, D W McNeill, H B McNeill, M C McNeill, M H McPhaul, Wm McPhaul, G G McPherson, C S Ray, S L Smith, A C Smith, J W Smith, B W Townsend, J C Watson.

Shannon—M L Bell, S J Cobb, J W Coob, Hiram Conoly, G B Conoly, D S Klarpp, Thos McBryde, A A McInnis, H A McKinzie, R G McNair, W C McPhaul, Neill Smith, Paisley Smith.

Sterlings—John F Britt, J T Hedgpeth, Arthur Hedgpeth, R C Rhodes, Hezekiah Rhodes, B W Rhodes, J L Rhodes.

St Paul's—R R Baxley, Alex Baxley, A D Biggs, W J Birch, Benj Blount, R Brisson, John S Brown, W B Burns, John Caldwell, Daniel Campbell, J C Carlyle, D D Carlyle, E A Carlyle, A J Carlyle, Rev J D Clark, Wm Councill, Alfred Crawford, Edward Currie, Jno C Evans, J S Fisher, Troy Fisher, Archibald Graham, John Harrell, G M D Howard, J P Inman, E D Johnson, W S Johnson, E J Johnson, James A Little, N A McCormick, Robert McGeachy, John McGeachy, J D McGeachy, N A McIntyre, Z T McMillan,

DUPLIN COUNTY.

D A McMillan, Sandy McMillan, Wm McNeill, Neill McNeill, R D Melvin, J P Paul, T J Riddle, John H Smith, T J Tolar, Wm Townsend, A J Watson, Archie Willis, A Willoughby.

Tolarsville—H L Brisson, W H Fisher, D C Humphrey, T M Sinclair, Chas Townsend.

Wakulla—J D McLean, N Wm McLean, W G McLean, W D McLean, D H McNeill, John McNeill, Milton Mc Neill, A S McNeill, H A McNeill, Neill McNeill, Lucius McRae, Charles Oxendine (Croatan), Mrs M J Smith, Wm Stewart, S W Thames, Mrs S E Walker, Neill Watson, J T Webb, Christian Wilkinson, W C Wilks, Mary L Wilks, Milton Wright.

HALIFAX COUNTY.

FARMERS.

Aurelian Springs—Abram Brinkley, L E Blackwell, W E Bowers, Dr W M Perkins, J B Phelps, J E Bowers, A Brinkley, B R Browing, W W Butts, A E Carter, Henry N Clark, J W Crowley, C W Dickens, J K Dickens, R A Dickens, J O Heptinstall, J N Harris, W F Jenkins, Matthew Lucus, L D Morris, B B Nicholson, Dr R A Patterson, J H Pittard, W H Hix, W I Clark, D T Cook, J F Cullum, L R Dickens, W L Dickens, W P Harris, E A Harris, G E Hix, W H Hix, S A Hix, Wm Hudson, W S Johnson, J W Hale, J P Lewis, R V Moore, J E Morecock, A P Mingo, W R Nevelle, W G Powell, W M Perkins, T E Pender, T J Pepper, W M Pepper, J R Parker, J F Shaw, W J B Smith, F H Taylor, Y L Williams, W T Warren.

Brinkleyville—J C Arrington, Piston Arrington, B L Arrington, B F Arrington, Lawrence Arrington, J H Arrington, J L Adcock, Adcock & Tibbetts, Jerry Brinkley (col), Napoleon Brinkley (col), W V Bobbitt, F H Battle, Jesse McW Boone, J D Boone, Jesse A Boone, Mrs E M Boone, J H Connell, Mary E Crowley, Mrs M T Cousins, Mrs L C Capehart, J B Dickens, Geo W Davis, J F Davis, W B Drewry, Mrs S W Duke, Joe Evans (col), R D Flemming, N M Harrison & Co, S B Hunter, Mrs L H Hunter, S A Harvey, W R Marvey, B F Higgs, Mrs S N Harper, W C Harper, R A Hardy, F C Hardy, J H Hardy, Whit Hardy (col), Mrs M W Ivey, D D Johnson, A C Johnson, Leach & Bros, R A Laughter, P B Laughter, Dudley Lynch (col), E L Lee, J G Lee, Jones Lee, Gid H

HALIFAX COUNTY.

Lee, Altimar Lee, sr (col), Washington Lee (col), J I Marshall, J C Marks, W C Montague, W H Mabrey, W E Mabrey, H C Matthews, Dr G E Matthews, Mrs M M Matthews, B F Moore, Sallie A Moore, D P Moon, W T Motley, Robt H Mills (col), H T Macon, R P Mitchell, James W Nicholson, Mrs Annie P Norman, J H Norman, S S Norman, J W Old, J H Parks, Mrs S P Parks, H P Pitts, W L Powell, J W Powell, Rev. W M Pike, B F Pittman, E E Pain, A F Shearn, J H Shearn, J R Shearn, Mrs M M Shearn, W N Shearn, W L Shearn, Jno H Shearn, J A Shwez, E W Spruell, W P Sledge, R H Spate, Wm Sykes, I H Taylor, J P Taylor, Nelson Thorne (col), W P Threewitts, G W Threewitts, L Vincent, J H Vincent, W G Vincent, C C Viverette, J H Whitley.

Crowell's Cross-Roads—J L Barkley, W H Cook, Nick Fitzpatrick, Geo E Lewis, Fletcher Merritt, L E Pope.

Dawson's Cross-Roads—L E DeBerry, L E DeBrule.

Enfield—J N Boseman, J R Boseman, Ed Wills, C A Williams, Mrs J C Alford, S S Alsop, R L Allsbrook, Louis Allsbrook, H C Alston, Jno Anderson, J C Anderson, —— Applewhite, Mose Arrington, J W Avent, M V Barnhill, John Bivens, Walter Bivens, D Bell, John T Bellamy, W T Bellamy, R B Benton, John Benton, Jas Billups, jr, J G Bradley, J H Branch, N Braswell; C Braswell, R B Britt, S G Britt, J L Britt, H D Browning, D B Bryant, G W Buffalow (col), C H Buffalow (col), E C Bullock, G W Bumpass, J J Burt, W D Bustin, Mills Butts, N J Carr, S J Clark, J D Clark, Dr John A Collins, R Cook, Geo B Curtis, I C Dickens, D Dunn, Balford Dunn, C A Fitt, Thos A Foster, I H Gaskins, F C Glass, J W Hardie, Junius Hardie, W C Harper, W B Harris, Wm Ingram (col), S F Johnson, Peyton Keel, S M Lewis, Alex Lewis, L Leggett, L S Lock, H L Merritt, R C Millikin, D P Moore, G W Morris, R F Neville, A Neville, S W Neville, J W Neville, J H Overstreet, W F Parker, R B Parker, Thomas Partin, Sam Pearson, A D Pender, Geo W Pettitt, J W Pittman, R J Pope, Sam Pope, M D Reid, J B Ricks, C P Simmons, W T Smith, O C Stallings, M W Sykes, J F Turner, C L Whitaker, T L Whitaker, S G Whitffeld, J W Whitley, R Wilkins, T L Willes, A R Williams, J B Wood.

Essex—N L Keen, W W Rosser, Wm Stokes, J Wesley Shearn.

HALIFAX COUNTY.

Halifax—L D Browning, B V Butts, J M Butts, J C Butts, J H Burt, John W Dickens, W C Daniel, J T Goodwin, S L Gibson, J D Johnson, Devereaux Keter, K E Kilpatrick, J D Whitehead, King White, L M Alston, J H Batchelor, J J Cobb, M H Clark, J J Daniel, W T Eure, W E Fenner, R L Fenner, Dr H B Ferguson, J T Gregory, D Hilliard, C H B Howerton, L H Hale, F J Keter, Henry Neville, J L Owsley, W T Purnell, Eli Stephenson, Geo W Shearn, T L Vick, W A Willcox.

Heathsville—R D Dannie.

Hobgood—C C Allsbrook, C V Andrews, L J Baker, J B Bell, L C Bell, J J Burgess, J H Curry, Wm Drew, J T Davis, I H Edmondson, G W Fisher, B T Harrell, Brinkley Allsbrook, Benj Ballard, J N Butts, B M Bradley, J B Burgess, Ben F Bryant, L B Bradley, Levi Cherry, Wiley Cherry, Amos Cherry, Jesse DeBrule, Fred Edmonds, L E Griffin, Calvin Gray, Wm Hodges, W F Hackney, W R House, Thos H Hicks, W H Johnson, W T Joyner, R F Lewis, John H Medford, Calvin Medford, Samuel Moore, C G Minchew, S O Purvis, R H Pennington, M B Pitt, Berry Price, M A Quincy, Dr M T Sagage, M T Strickland, W E Staton, W T Vaughn, Asa Wommock, Samuel Whitehead, W T Whitehead.

Littleton—Len H Allen, Eugene Alston, R L Anderson, W E Spencer, S C Arrington, James Shearn, C J Smith, W J Smith, W H Thorn, S T Thorn, jr, G P Williams, Presley Williams, S C Alston, Leo Alston, R L Alston, A E Bobbitt, J W Bobbitt, W E Bowers, J D Brown, T R Cooly, Henry S Clark, E W Ferguson, J L Freeman, T E Glasgow, B D Hammell, W W Hawkins, B W Hawkins, C B Harris, Osborn Harris, Jr, Harvey L, Hines, G L Harper, Jas H House, J A House, C D House, T W Hawkins, A W Ivey, D E Iles, S Johnson, Whit Johnson, J E Johnson, W D Johnson, E D Jenkins, Jesse Jarrell, G S King, W T Little, V W Land, T L Myrick, W H Myrick, M J Morris, M L Morris, B F Moss, W M Martin, I J Miles, J J Northington, W H Pepper, E L Perkins, M V Perry, W E Pearson, H P Roberson, A H Ramsey, S W Rigan, W H Shaw, W E Spencer, J L Sledge, Wm Standsberry, J H Tucker, Ransom Vaughn, R H Walker, J S Wilson, F D Wilson, R A White.

Medoc—C W Garrett & Co, Mrs Wm A Hales, E G Hales.

Palmyra—R W Hyman, Lawrence House, J F Hopkins, H L James, W T

HALIFAX COUNTY.

Jones, G W Johnson, Dr K Leggett, L M Lawrence, W L Mizell, T L Pender, R E L Pitt, R E Roberson, J D Ray, R J Shields, Louis Savage, E W Staton, R Taylor, J A White, W P White, J T Weathersbee, W R Weathersbee, L E Whitehead.

Ringwood—J H Harrison, N M Harrison, Mrs L C Hunter.

Roanoke Rapids—R W Brown, P E Lynn, W B Whitehead.

Scotland Neck—B H Allsbrook, J H Allsbrook, W T Askew, J H Baker, C C Baker, J J Barnes, J L Barnes, W H Bell, Noah Biggs, Dr R M Johnson, W R Bond, J S Barnes, J Frank Brinkley, G W Bryan, W F Butterworth, J E Coudrey, C H Cock, James Cotton, —— Coughenour, J H Darden, J S Darden, W P Darden, W E Davenport, Henry Dixon, A S Dixon, C W Dunn, W A Dunn, J B Edwards, J B Edmondson, R N Evans, T W Fenner, M C Flemming, J P Futrell, G W Gray, R Gardner, J B Hall, S D Hancock, R E Hancock, J E Hancock, Louis Harris, R L Hardy, E K Hassell, E H Height, W R Highsmith, J H Hopkins, H S Hyman, E W Hyman, J R Herring, K Jenkins, W H Johnson, W W Jones, H G Jones, G W Jones, R C Josey, N B Josey, W H Josey, J L Josey, Jack Kell, Claude Kitchen, W H Kitchen, J A Kitchen, G Lamb, C T Lawrence, J W Leggett, J E Lewis, J H Lewis, D J Maddrey, J G Moore, J B Neal, E N Nelson, J S Paul, C H Pender, E E Powell, C E Pope, A L Purrington, J D Ray, Ed Shields, F P Shields, Isaac H Smith, W J Smith, A L Smith, J B Stephenson, Joseph Stern, J B Vaughn, Ed Watson, W R Walston, B D Webb, G C Weeks, G S White, W H White, W T White, J T Woodard.

Spring Hill—J F Lawrence, D I McKeathan, C C Minchen, J R Weeks, J D Weeks.

Tillery—W S Biggs, Wm Barnhill, E D B shop, W M Crump, Stewart Davis (col), J P Ellen, Futrell & Carter, W E Gray, J I Howell, C F Hancock, J C Mullen, C F Mason (col), J A Norfleet, A E Pope, J F Pope, N D Parks, A J Parks, John G Powell, W H Randolph, P G Riddick, J I Riddick, W D Shield, P V Tillery, J L Tillery, J R Tillery, B F Tillery, H L Tillery & Bros, W D Tillery.

Weldon—W H Allsbrook, C E Bishop, R G Branch, W B Boseman, W H Brown, E Clark, J D Cox, C L Clark, Thos H Christie, W E Demsey, W B Dickens, M Freelander, Sedan Goode, Paul Garrett, A H Green, A A Grace, Dr T E Green, W S Hockaday, J A

HALIFAX COUNTY.	HALIFAX COUNTY.
Holdford, W H Holdford, J E Hockaday, Geo W Harrison, R D Harris, Hiram Holt, R B Ivey, A M Inge, W W Jenkins, J A Johnson, J A King, J W Love, Geo W Lewis, A E Lynch, E I Medlin, W R Miles, M F Medlin, Geo W Mayo, Geo W Mosley, C S Northington, W G Purnell, E A Pearson, G P Phillips, Willis Price, W T Parker,	W M Powell, J W Pierce, Lafayette Powell, C M Pearson, B F Powell, W A Pierce, B A Pope, T N Powell, C P Rodwell, W A Richards, Lafayette Shaw, Sterling Shaw, Ridley Shearin, J H Summerell, J A Smith, J B Tillman, Sam Trueblood, V J Vincent, John Williams, John H Wood, Dr A R Zollicoffer.

www.ingramcontent.com/pod-product-compliance
Lightning Source LLC
Chambersburg PA
CBHW050447270326
41927CB00009B/1635